ADOLESCENCE

Eighteenth Edition

JOHN W. SANTROCK

University of Texas at Dallas

ADOLESCENCE, EIGHTEENTH EDITION

Published by McGraw Hill LLC, 1325 Avenue of the Americas, New York, NY 10019. Copyright © 2023 by McGraw Hill LLC. All rights reserved. Printed in the United States of America. Previous editions © 2019, 2016, and 2014. No part of this publication may be reproduced or distributed in any form or by any means, or stored in a database or retrieval system, without the prior written consent of McGraw Hill LLC, including, but not limited to, in any network or other electronic storage or transmission, or broadcast for distance learning.

Some ancillaries, including electronic and print components, may not be available to customers outside the United States.

This book is printed on acid-free paper.

1 2 3 4 5 6 7 8 9 LWI 27 26 25 24 23 22

ISBN 978-1-260-24583-7 (bound edition)
MHID 1-260-24583-7 (bound edition)
ISBN 978-1-260-44920-4 (loose-leaf edition)
MHID 1-260-44920-3 (loose-leaf edition)

Senior Portfolio Manager: *Ryan Treat*
Product Development Manager: *Dawn Groundwater*
Marketing Manager: *Olivia Kaiser*
Content Project Managers: *Mary E. Powers* (Core), *Jodi Banowetz* (Assessment)
Buyer: *Laura Fuller*
Designer: *Beth Blech*
Content Licensing Specialist: *Carrie Burger*
Cover Image: *leaf/123RF*
Compositor: *Aptara®, Inc*

All credits appearing on page or at the end of the book are considered to be an extension of the copyright page.

Library of Congress Cataloging-in-Publication Data

Names: Santrock, John W., author.
Title: Adolescence / John W. Santrock, University of Texas at Dallas.
Description: Eighteenth edition. | New York, NY : McGraw Hill Education,
  [2023] | Includes bibliographical references and index.
Identifiers: LCCN 2021030227 (print) | LCCN 2021030228 (ebook) | ISBN
  9781260245837 (hardback ; alk. paper) | ISBN 9781260449204 (spiral bound;
  alk. paper) | ISBN 9781260449198 (ebook) | ISBN 9781260449235 (ebook other)
Subjects: LCSH: Adolescence. | Adolescent psychology.
Classification: LCC HQ796 .S26 2023 (print) | LCC HQ796 (ebook) | DDC
  305.235—dc23
LC record available at https://lccn.loc.gov/2021030227
LC ebook record available at https://lccn.loc.gov/2021030228

The Internet addresses listed in the text were accurate at the time of publication. The inclusion of a website does not indicate an endorsement by the authors or McGraw Hill LLC, and McGraw Hill LLC does not guarantee the accuracy of the information presented at these sites.

mheducation.com/highered

brief contents

contents

CHAPTER 9   PEERS, ROMANTIC RELATIONSHIPS, AND LIFESTYLES   298

SpeedKingz/Shutterstock

CHAPTER 10   SCHOOLS   336

FatCamera/E+/Getty Images

CHAPTER 13　PROBLEMS IN ADOLESCENCE AND EMERGING ADULTHOOD　436

LightField Studios Inc./Alamy Stock Photo

connect　**McGraw Hill's Psychology APA Documentation Style Guide**

guide to diversity, equity, and inclusion

Special attention is given to diversity, equity, and inclusion (DEI) in this new edition, including updating preferred pronouns and terminology and ensuring that the citations of studies and researchers represent diverse and global populations and topics. Following is a chapter-by-chapter list of the related topics along with new content and revisions involving DEI issues and research.

Chapter 1: Introduction

- Edits made based on comments by leading diversity expert James Graham
- Replacement of the label "Latino" with the gender-neutral and more inclusive "Latinx"
- Significant reorganization, expansion, and updating of main section, "Social Contexts," to include more content on culture, socioeconomic status, ethnicity, and gender
- Updated data on the percentage of U.S. children and adolescents 17 years of age and younger from different ethnic groups in 2017 and projected to 2050, with dramatic increases in Latinx and Asian American children (ChildStats.gov, 2018)
- Coverage of a recent research review of 3- to 19-year-old U.S. children and adolescents in which variations in socio-economic status (SES) were linked to different levels of psychopathology (Peverill & others, 2021)
- New commentary on the racism and discrimination many children and adults continue to experience in the United States and around the world and a new Developmental Connection on "Culture"
- New coverage of transgender adolescents
- Updated poverty rates showing a considerable drop in poverty from 2018 to 2019 for African American, Latinx, and Asian American children and adolescents, including a much larger drop than for non-Latinx white children and adolescents (Semega & others, 2020). Also, the lowest poverty rate in 2019 occurred for Asian American children and adolescents (Semega & others, 2020).
- New commentary on the importance of considering the intersection of culture, socioeconomic status, ethnicity, and gender, especially because when combined they can create systems of power and privilege as well as oppression and discrimination
- Section on minimizing bias in gender research and culture/diversity research
- Image comparing a group of all non-Latinx adolescent boys and a group of diverse adolescents from different ethnic groups to illustrate the importance of obtaining diverse samples in research on adolescents

Chapter 2: Puberty, Health, and Biological Foundations

- Cross-cultural comparisons indicating earlier pubertal onset in recent years
- Gender differences in adolescents' body images, with body image being more problematic for girls due to media portrayals that idealize slenderness
- Description of recent research with adolescents indicating associations of cognitive control with SES (Brieant & others, 2021)
- New coverage of the roles of poverty and ethnicity in health disparities in adolescents, including evidence that a number of factors are involved (Perrin & others, 2020)
- New discussion of health disparities that characterize Latinx and African American adolescent hospitalizations due to COVID-19 (Kim & others, 2020)
- Inclusion of new data on persistent health disparities in health coverage and health conditions that involve ethnicity (Carratala & Maxwell, 2020; U.S. Health and Human Services Office of Minority Health, 2020)
- *Connecting with Careers* box on Bonnie Halpern Felsher, a university professor of pediatrics who also serves as a mentor for underrepresented adolescents
- Inclusion of recent research indicating ethnic disparities in exercise during adolescence (Underwood & others, 2020)
- Discussion of a recent World Health Organization study of 11- to 17-year-olds' physical activity in 146 countries that concluded 81 percent of the adolescents were engaging in insufficient physical activity (Guthold & others, 2020)
- Inclusion of a recent comparison of the roles of gender and SES in adolescents' exercise levels in 52 countries (Bann & others, 2020)
- Coverage of the female athlete triad
- Inclusion of a recent large-scale study of adolescents in the United States, the United Kingdom, and the Netherlands in which 51.5 percent reported getting less than 8 hours of sleep per night and 18 percent indicated that they experienced daytime sleepiness (Kocevska & others, 2021)

Chapter 3: The Brain and Cognitive Development

- Coverage of how depressed brain activity has been found in children and adolescents who grow up in a deprived environment (Turesky & others, 2020)
- Inclusion of recent research showing that children in a Romanian orphanage experienced significant brain damage but that those who were subsequently placed in stable foster

- care showed improved brain development at 16 years of age (Debnath & others, 2020)
- Discussion of a recent longitudinal study in which 11- to 18-year-olds who lived in poverty had diminished brain activity at 25 years of age (Brody & others, 2017). However, the adolescents whose families participated in a supportive parenting intervention did not show this diminished brain activity at 25 years of age.
- New photograph and caption describing how in 2020, across the United States and many countries around the world, the Black Lives Matter protests attracted many adolescents from diverse backgrounds, then asking whether this involvement might be linked to adolescents' ability to reason hypothetically and to evaluate what is ideal and what is real, thereby increasing their likelihood of participating in such protests
- Content on how culture and education exert stronger influences on development than Piaget envisioned (Kirmayer & others, 2021; Riccio & Castro, 2021)
- Description of Vygotsky's social constructivist cognitive theory that emphasizes the importance of developing the skills that are needed for success and adaptation within one's own culture
- Inclusion of a recent study in which mindfulness training reduced the anxiety, stress, and depression of Latinx adolescents (Clarke & others, 2021)
- *Connecting with Adolescents* box featuring Rochelle Ballantyne, who became one of the top African American female chess stars as an adolescent, including an update on her subsequent enrollment in law school at New York University
- Discussion of a recent survey of 102 experts on intelligence around the world that found most supported the concept of general intelligence (G) (Rindermann, Becker, & Coyle, 2020)
- New commentary about the ethnic intelligence gap that has existed—and continues to exist—and how it is influenced by racism and discrimination (such as lower levels of family wealth, increased segregation of schools, limited access to healthcare, and lower teacher expectations for minority group children and adolescents)
- Coverage of stereotype threat, which refers to anxiety that one's behavior might confirm a negative stereotype about one's group, such as a particular ethnic group (Chin & others, 2020)
- Expanded and updated content on the Flynn effect, with decreases in intelligence recently emerging in Scandinavian countries
- New content on how IQ gains continue to occur in the United States and developing countries such as Romania (Gunnesch-Luca & Iliescu, 2020)
- New main section on bilingualism, including content on cultural variations in students' likelihood of learning a second language
- Discussion of a recent research analysis across a number of countries that found bilingual children consistently had better executive function than monolingual children (Schirmbeck, Rao, & Maehler, 2020)

- New description of bilingualism in adolescence, with research indicating that bilingualism is linked to superior information processing in a number of areas (Antovich & Graf Estes, 2020)

Chapter 4: The Self, Identity, Emotion, and Personality

- Inclusion of recent research on Mexican-origin adolescents living in the United States that found the dimension of exploitativeness at 14 years of age predicted a number of problems at age 16 (drug use, delinquency, conduct disorder, and sexual intercourse) (Wetzel, Atherton, & Robins, 2021). Also, in this study, there was little association of the superiority dimension of narcissism to problem behaviors.
- Coverage of a recent study of Mexican-origin youth living in the United States that found a reciprocal relation between self-esteem and academic achievement at ages 10, 12, 14, and 16 (Zheng & others, 2020)
- Description of a recent study conducted in Brazil, Portugal, and Spain that found parental warmth was a key factor in adolescent self-esteem in all three countries (Isabel Martinez & others, 2020)
- Inclusion of research indicating that regardless of neighborhood context and economic advantage or disadvantage, self-regulation predicted adolescents' academic achievement (Davisson, Hoyle, and Andrade, 2021)
- Inclusion of a recent study of Mexican-origin adolescents exploring the factors in their lives that were linked to different levels of effortful control (Atherton, Lawson, & Robins, 2020)
- Greatly expanded and updated coverage of ethnic and racial identity based on feedback from leading expert Kevin Cokley
- Discussion of a recent study of Latinx emerging adults that revealed the bicultural harmony component of bicultural identity development was associated with lower levels of psychological stress (Cano & others, 2021)
- New coverage of racial identity
- Inclusion of recent research on 13- to 17-year-old African American girls' racial socialization indicating that pride was linked to positive feelings about being Black while depression was linked to oppressive messages about Black women (Stokes & others, 2020)
- Description of a recent study of 11- to 12-year-olds that found more frequent discrimination from peers was linked to lower ethnic-racial commitment (Del Toro, Hughes, & Way, 2021)
- Coverage of a recent study of adolescents that revealed on days when adolescents reported more negative peer ethnic/racial interaction, they had lower school engagement (Wang, 2021). Also in this study, on days when adolescents reported more positive peer ethnic/racial interaction, they engaged in more prosocial behavior.
- Inclusion of a recent research review of Latinxs that concluded perceived discrimination was linked to poorer mental health but that having a greater sense of ethnic pride attenuated this link (Andrade, Ford, & Alvarez, 2021)

- New discussion of the singular concept of ethnic-racial identity (ERI) (Atkin & others, 2021)
- Description of a recent study of young Cherokee adolescents' ERI that revealed both girls and boys reported strong positive attitudes about being a Cherokee (Hoffman, Kurtz-Coates, & Shaheed, 2021). However, youths' perceptions that others hold Cherokees in high regard decreased across the years.
- Coverage of a recent study that revealed enhanced resilience against discrimination in Latinx youth who had experienced greater ethnic family socialization and had engaged in ethnic identity exploration and resolution (Martinez-Fuentes, Jager, & Umaña-Taylor, 2021)
- Discussion of a recent study of adolescent girls in low-income families that found lower levels of negative emotion in girls who had experienced higher levels of emotional support from their mothers and peers (Cui & others, 2020)

Chapter 5: Gender

- Extensive revisions and updates based on leading expert Sabra Katz-Wise's feedback and comments
- Description of recent research that revealed adolescents' motivational beliefs at the start of high school were associated with STEM achievement and course-taking throughout high school and their college major choices seven years later (Jiang, Simpkins, & Eccles, 2020)
- New commentary noting that categories such as gender and ethnicity intersect and can reinforce systems of power, privilege, and discrimination
- Coverage of a recent study of the inequities experienced in relation to ethnicity/race and gender in the graduate programs of chemistry departments in the 100 top-ranked STEM programs in U.S. universities (Stockard, Rohlfing, & Richmond, 2021)
- Discussion of a recent study of seventh-graders that found girls' perception that teachers had gendered expectations favoring boys over girls was linked to girls having lower math expectations and lower math achievement (McKellar & others, 2019)
- New discussion of the term *two-spirit* that is used by some indigenous North Americans to refer to individuals who are perceived as having both male and female spirits within them
- Extensively edited, expanded, and updated coverage of transgender individuals
- Description of recent research that confirmed victimization and discrimination predicted increased suicidal ideation while community connection reduced suicidal ideation in transgender individuals (Rabasco & Andover, 2021)
- Coverage of a recent study of transgender individuals in which gender affirmation was associated with a lower rate of suicide ideation and psychological distress while gender discrimination was linked to a higher rate of suicide ideation and psychological distress (Lelutiu-Weinberger, English, & Sandanpitchai, 2020)
- Inclusion of a recent study that found a majority of transgendered individuals experienced discrimination in the last

year and those who encountered greater discrimination were more likely to develop depression and anxiety symptoms (Puckett & others, 2020)
- New commentary acknowledging that because trans individuals experience considerable discrimination, it is important that society provide a more welcoming and accepting attitude toward them (Vargas, Huey, & Miranda, 2020)
- Coverage of a recent study that found psychotherapy targeting internalized stigma and non-affirmation experiences can be effective in reducing gender-related stress and increasing resilience (Budge, Sinnard, & Hoyt, 2021)
- New *Connecting with Careers* feature on psychotherapist Dr. Stephanie Budge, a leading expert on transgender research and issues (Budge, 2021)

Chapter 6: Sexuality

- Discussion of a recent study of young adolescents conducted at 14 sites across four continents that found consistent evidence for a sexual script of boys' social gains for having girlfriends and girls' risk for having boyfriends (Moreau & others, 2018)
- Updated national data (2019) from the Youth Risk Behavior Surveillance study on the timing of sexual intercourse in U.S. adolescents, including ethnic variations and the percentage of adolescents who have had sexual intercourse prior to 13 years of age (Underwood & others, 2020)
- Description of a recent study of urban, predominately Latinx and African American adolescents that found talk with extended family members about sexual protection was linked to adolescents having fewer sexual partners, while talk about risks involved in sex was associated with having more sexual partners (Grossman & others, 2020)
- Discussion of a recent study indicating ethnic disparities in adolescent girls' level of developmental assets (internal and external) and attitudes and behaviors conducive to delaying sexual activity (Messer & others, 2021)
- Coverage of a recent study of 18- to 25-year-old sexual minority women in which alcohol use was associated with a greater likelihood of engaging in future hookups and those who reported having more minority stress subsequently hooked up with more partners (Jaffe & others, 2021)
- Inclusion of recent research involving prevalence of suicidal thoughts in sexual minority adolescents (including gender variations) (Feigelman & others, 2020).
- Coverage of recent research on the percentage of adolescents who use condoms when they have sex, including ethnic variations (Szucs & others, 2020)
- Updated data on ethnic variations in rates of adolescent pregnancy, which continue to drop among ethnic minority adolescents (Martin & others, 2021)
- Inclusion of a recent Canadian study that found SES variations in adolescent mothers involving rates of mental health issues and substance use (Wong & others, 2020)
- New description of the effectiveness of pre-exposure prophylaxis (PrEP), including its recent approval for adolescents (Whitfield & others, 2020)

- Update on rates of chlamydia infection in the United States, with the highest rates continuing to occur in the 15- to 24-year-old age group, including new data on ethnic differences in chlamydia rates (Centers for Disease Control and Prevention 2021)
- New *Connecting with Careers* box on Dr. Maria Eva Trent, one of the world's leading adolescent reproductive health specialists, whose research especially focuses on underserved urban adolescent girls
- New coverage of a recent study of sexual assault in sexual minority college students (Eisenberg & others, 2021)
- New content on the "Me Too" (or "#MeToo") movement and the importance of providing safe contexts for women to openly discuss their experiences of sexual harassment (Yecies & others, 2020)
- Update as of October 2020 on the number of states that require sex education and/or HIV education (Guttmacher Institute, 2020)
- New entry in *Improving the Lives of Adolescents and Emerging Adults* on Dr. Maria Trent and her colleagues' insightful analysis of the influence of race on various aspects of child and adolescent health and recommended interventions for reducing racism. This article was requested by the American Academy of Pediatrics and states their position on addressing racism.

Chapter 7: Moral Development, Values, and Religion

- Opening vignette on Jewel Cash, an African American adolescent who grew up in a Boston housing project and was strongly motivated to promote changes that would improve her community
- Inclusion of content on the importance of considering the failure of Kohlberg's cognitive theory to describe cultural variations in moral development
- New main section, "Culture," in the coverage of contextual influences on adolescents' moral development
- Description of differences in behavior between WEIRD (Western, Educated, Industrialized, Rich, and Democratic) cultures that emphasize individual rights and independent behavior and non-WEIRD cultures that are characterized by duty-based communal obligations and collective, interdependent behavior
- Inclusion of research indicating that familism is especially important in Mexican American and Latinx families. In one study, young adolescents in Mexican American families who strongly endorsed familism values had higher scores on measures of prosocial tendencies (Knight & others, 2014).
- Discussion of differences in morality within a culture, such as comparisons of people in lower- and higher-SES contexts
- Increased emphasis on the importance of cultural variations in adolescent religion and the view that a "one-size-fits-all" approach fails to take this variation into account (Jensen, 2021)
- Coverage of recent research with Thai adolescents indicating that they report an increasing boredom with the country's

dominant religion, Buddhism, mainly because there is nothing new in it (McKenzie, 2019)
- Description of a study of religious participation among adolescents in different ethnic groups (Lopez, Huynh, & Fuligni, 2011)

Chapter 8: Families

- New main section, "Sociocultural and Historical Influences," that highlights major cultural and historical changes that have affected and are affecting adolescents and their families, including decreases in neighborhood and family support systems, increased mobility of families from one location to another, increased numbers of Latinx and Asian American immigrant adolescents and their families, dramatic increases in media use by adolescents and their family members, and increased restlessness and uneasiness among adults
- New content on China's one-child policy that was instituted in 1980 to limit population growth, then revised in 2016 to a two-child policy and in 2021 to a three-child policy
- Updated statistics on divorce rates in the United States and comparisons with other countries (U.S. Census Bureau, 2019; OECD, 2019)
- Inclusion of recent research indicating gender variations in same-gender and heterosexual parenting competence with adolescents (Farr & Vazquez, 2020a)
- Coverage of a UK longitudinal study of gay father, lesbian mother, and heterosexual parent families when their children reached early adolescence that found little difference between the three family styles but indicated that better parenting quality and parental mental health were linked to fewer adolescent problems (McConnachie & others, 2021)
- Deletion of section, "Culture and Ethnicity," in this chapter because of significant overlap with coverage of families in the "Culture" chapter

Chapter 9: Peers, Romantic Relationships, and Lifestyles

- Inclusion of a study in which increasing and chronic loneliness of Latinx high school students was associated with academic difficulties (Benner, 2011). In this study, support from friends buffered the negative relation of loneliness to academic difficulties.
- Content indicating that there are more than 400 national youth organizations in the United States, including ethnic groups such as Indian Youth of America
- Discussion of youth organizations that provide intensive educational enrichment programs for at-risk minority students
- Inclusion of main section on peer relations: "Socioeconomic Status and Ethnicity"
- New description of a recent study of young adolescents that revealed for non-Latinx whites and Asian Americans, higher academic achievement was associated with having same-ethnic friends, while for African Americans and Latinxs, higher academic achievement was linked with having cross-ethnic friends (Chen, Saafir, & Graham, 2020)

- Coverage of main section on peer relations: "Culture"
- Content indicating that in some countries, adults restrict adolescents' access to peers (Chen, Lee, & Chen, 2018). For example, in many areas of rural India and in Arab countries, opportunities for peer relations in adolescence are severely restricted, especially for girls. If girls attend school in these regions of the world, they are usually educated in sex-segregated schools.
- Discussion of a recent study of Latina emerging adults in which lower friend support was linked to their loneliness (Lee & others, 2020)
- Inclusion of main section, "Romantic Relationships in Sexual Minority Youth" (Diamond & Alley, 2018; Savin-Williams, 2018)
- Coverage of the roles of ethnicity and culture in romantic relationships
- New data indicating ethnic variations in single adults (Brown, 2020)
- Inclusion of a recent national poll indicating that in 2020 there was an increase of almost 25 percent in young people who said they were open to dating someone of a different ethnic group, and over a 10-year period this proportion increased by 58 percent (Match.com, 2020). Also, 74 percent of Generation Z adults and 66 percent of millennials said they wanted to know if their date supports Black Lives Matter.
- New comparison of the number of single adults in the United States compared with other countries, with the fastest growth in the number of single adults occurring in developing countries such as India and Brazil
- New content on cohabitation increasing in China and Taiwan but remaining rare in Japan and South Korea
- New content and data on the recent increases in percentages of newlyweds and all married people who are married to someone from a different ethnic group (Livingston & Brown, 2017)
- New comparison of age at first marriage in a number of developed countries, with individuals in Sweden getting married latest and those in Israel and Turkey earliest (OECD, 2019)
- Coverage of a recent study that found men had a higher level of marital satisfaction than women across a number of countries (Sorokowski, Kowal, & Sorokowska, 2019). In this study, marital satisfaction was similar among Muslims, Christians, and atheists.
- Inclusion of main section, "Gay and Lesbian Adults"
- Coverage of misconceptions about gay and lesbian couples
- Discussion of a recent study in which adults in same-sex relationships experienced levels of commitment, satisfaction, and emotional intimacy that were similar to those of adults in different-sex relationships (Joyner, Manning, & Prince, 2019)

Chapter 10: Schools

- Chapter-opening vignette focusing on a former at-risk student who is now a math teacher and a recent Florida Teacher of the Year, African American Henry Brown. Brown engages his students by teaching real-world math skills.
- Updated data on school dropout rates, including those of ethnic minority groups, which continue to drop considerably (National Center for Education Statistics, 2020)
- Photograph and description of students spending time in the computer room at the Ahfachkee School on the Big Cypress Reservation of the Seminole Tribe in Florida. This school has reduced its dropout rate by providing a challenging and caring environment for students, as well as emphasizing strong connections with families.
- Content indicating that the average U.S. high school dropout rates mask some very high dropout rates in low-income areas of inner cities. For example, in high-poverty areas of some cities such as Detroit, Cleveland, and Chicago, dropout rates can reach 50 percent or higher.
- Discussion of the successful dropout prevention program Talent Search, which provides low-income high school students with mentoring, academic tutoring, and training on test-taking and study skills, as well as career development coaching, assistance in applying for financial aid for college, and visits to college campuses
- Coverage of the impressive results of "I Have a Dream" (IHAD), an innovative, comprehensive, long-term dropout prevention program
- Inclusion of a study focusing on African American families that examined links between mothers' reports of family management practices, including routine and achievement expectations, and adolescents' school-related behavior (Taylor & Lopez, 2005)
- Description of research by Eva Pomerantz and her colleagues (Pomerantz, Cheung, & Qin, 2012; Pomerantz & Grolnick, 2017; Wei & others, 2020) indicating that the more involved parents are in their children's learning, the higher the level of achievement their children will attain. East Asian parents are far more involved in their children's and adolescents' learning than are U.S. parents.
- Description of a recent study of more than 15,000 U.S. high school students that documented bullying experiences of sexual minority and heterosexual adolescents (Webb & others, 2021)
- Inclusion of a recent study of more than 150,000 12- to 15-year-olds in low- and middle-income countries that found victims of bullies were characterized by obesity-related factors such as anxiety-induced sleep problems, no physical exercise, sedentary behavior, and fast food consumption (Smith & others, 2021)
- Coverage of a recent study conducted in 48 countries worldwide in which being the victim of a bully was a risk factor for suicidal behavior in 47 countries (Koyanagi & others, 2019)
- Inclusion of major section, "Culture," that focuses on culture and schooling
- Main section, "Socioeconomic Status," discussing SES variations in adolescents' schooling
- *Connecting with Adolescents* interlude featuring African American teacher Tommie Lindsey, who teaches competitive

forensics (public speaking and debate) at Logan High School in Union City, California. In U.S. schools, forensics classes are mainly offered in affluent areas, but most of Lindsey's students come from impoverished or at-risk backgrounds. His students have won many public speaking honors.

- Inclusion of content on poverty interventions with very low-income students (Albert & others, 2020). In a recent intervention with first-generation immigrant children attending high-poverty schools, the City Connects program was successful in improving children's math and reading achievement at the end of elementary school (Dearing & others, 2016).
- Content on an important effort to improve the education of children growing up in low-income conditions, Teach for America (2021), a nonprofit organization that recruits and selects college graduates from universities to serve as teachers. The selected members commit to teaching for two years in a public school in a low-income community.
- *Connecting with Careers* feature on Ahou Vaziri, Teach for America Instructor
- Main section, "Ethnicity," focusing on numerous aspects of ethnic minority students' experiences in schools
- Coverage of Jonathan Kozol's classic book, *The Shame of the Nation*, that focuses on the inequities ethnic minority students experience in schools
- Description of a number of strategies for improving the school experiences of ethnic minority students
- Inclusion of James Comer's community-based team approach as the best way to educate students
- Discussion of multicultural education
- Main section, "Cross-Cultural Comparisons," focusing on how U.S. secondary schools differ from those in many other countries
- Update on the Global Student Laboratory Project in which students around the world collaborate on various projects (Globallab, 2021)
- Coverage of cross-cultural comparisons of the percentage of students who obtain post-secondary degrees
- Description of a study conducted before and after schools closed in March 2020 because of the COVID-19 pandemic that indicated student achievement in math decreased by approximately 50 percent after schools closed, with the decrease greatest in low-income zip code areas (Chetty & others, 2020)
- Content on how students with sensory and learning difficulties, such as those who are deaf or blind, as well as those who have a learning disability or ADHD, do not learn as effectively online as they do in a classroom (Centers for Disease Control and Prevention, 2020)
- Updated data on the percentage of children with a disability who are receiving special education services in different disability categories (National Center for Education Statistics, 2020)
- Description of recent research conducted in 2018 by the Centers for Disease Control indicating that among 3- to 17-year-olds, ethnic variations occurred in ever having a learning disability or having attention deficit hyperactivity disorder (ADHD) (Zablotsky & Alford, 2020)
- Inclusion of recent research indicating that African American children and adolescents with ADHD are often underdiagnosed, while those engaging in disruptive behavior are often overdiagnosed (Fadus & others, 2020)
- Coverage of recent research indicating SES variations in development of ADHD and other aspects of brain functioning (Machlin, McLaughlin, & Sheridan, 2020)
- Discussion of the concern that ethnic minority children and adolescents are underrepresented in gifted programs (Ford, 2016)

Chapter 11: Achievement, Work, and Careers

- Changes made in response to feedback from leading expert Sandra Graham
- Chapter-opening vignette of immigrant adolescents indicating that not all Asian American immigrants come from well-to-do families and that some are not academically successful and need more support
- Coverage of research indicating that believing that math ability can be learned helped to protect females from negative gender stereotyping about math (Good, Rattan, & Dweck, 2012)
- Description of recent research that revealed having a growth mindset helped to protect women's and minorities' outlook when they chose to confront expressions of bias toward them (Rattan & Dweck, 2018)
- Content on special concerns being voiced about the lower academic expectations parents and teachers have for many ethnic minority adolescents (Rowley & others, 2014)
- Inclusion of a recent study of Mexican-origin parents and their adolescents in which parents' educational expectations when their children were in seventh grade were linked to their adolescents' educational expectations in ninth and eleventh grades (Aceves & others, 2020). Also in this study, seventh-grade students' educational expectations predicted their perceived academic competence in the ninth and eleventh grades.
- *Connecting with Careers* profile of Jaime Escalante, a Latinx immigrant who became an outstanding math teacher and took on the specific challenge of improving the math skills of Latinx adolescents
- New content on how teacher expectations need to provide students with wise feedback—written evaluations that communicate high expectations rather than phony praise or benign neglect. Students who are at increased risk for academic underperformance or failure, such as low-SES students and students of color, may misinterpret teacher feedback as a lack of confidence in their academic ability and thus need reassurance that the teacher has high expectations for their achievement and confidence that they can improve their learning.
- Description of recent research with ninth- and tenth-grade Latinx students in which natural mentoring quality was linked to the Latinx adolescents' development of a more

- positive ethnic identity, which in turn was associated with a stronger belief in the economic value of education (Sanchez & others, 2020)
- Discussion of one of the largest mentoring programs in the United States, Big Brothers/Big Sisters (BBBS), which pairs caring volunteer mentors with at-risk youth (Larose & others, 2018). Research indicates that this mentoring program has been successful in improving adolescents' academic achievement.
- Content on how mentoring may be especially important for immigrant adolescents who live in neighborhoods with few college graduates (Flye, 2017). In some mentoring programs, such as AVID (Advancement Via Individual Determination), immigrant adolescents are taken to local colleges where they meet immigrant mentors and guest speakers who are college students or graduates (Watt, Huerta, & Martinez, 2017).
- Coverage of a study in which African American male high school students who participated in an AVID program were more likely to enroll in rigorous courses such as advanced placement and honors classes (Taylor, 2016)
- Main section, "Ethnicity and Socioeconomic Status," that describes how too often research on ethnicity has not investigated or controlled for socioeconomic status and that when deficits occur in research with ethnic minority adolescents, the results often are due to socioeconomic status rather than ethnicity
- Content on how regardless of their ethnic background, students from middle- and upper-income families fare better than their counterparts from low-income backgrounds on a host of achievement factors, including expectations for success, achievement aspirations, and recognition of the importance of effort, for example (Zhang & others, 2020)
- Description of how an especially important factor in the lower achievement of students from low-income families is lack of adequate resources at home, such as an up-to-date computer or even any computer at all, to support students' learning (Schunk, Meece, & Pintrich, 2014)
- Coverage of a longitudinal study that revealed African American children or children from low-income families benefited more than children from higher-income families when they did homework more frequently, had Internet access at home, and had a community library card (Xia, 2010)
- Description of a research review that concluded increases in family income for children in poverty were associated with higher achievement in middle school, as well as greater educational attainment in adolescence and emerging adulthood (Duncan, Magnuson, & Votruba-Drzal, 2017)
- Discussion of how for too many ethnic minority adolescents, the presence of stereotype threat (anxiety that one's behavior might confirm a negative stereotype about one's group) can harm their motivation. For example, in a recent study, African American and Latinx 13- to 17-year-olds experienced higher stereotype threat in high school mathematics classrooms than their non-Latinx white peers did (Seo & Lee, 2021).
- Inclusion of findings from the 2019 Trends in International Mathematics and Science Study (TIMSS), a comparison of math and science achievement in a number of countries, in which East Asian countries took 19 of the top five spots in fourth- and eighth-grade science and fourth- and eighth-grade math. Singapore was number one in three of the four comparisons.
- Description of research conducted by Harold Stevenson and his colleagues on factors that help to explain why U.S. adolescent do much worse than Asian adolescents on achievement tests
- Discussion of Asian American "tiger mothers" who maintain tight control of their adolescents' achievement and recent research indicating a more positive influence when Asian American mothers show more warmth toward their adolescents
- Coverage of a recent longitudinal study in which adolescents' gender stereotypes became much more traditional from the ninth to eleventh grades (Starr & Simpkins, 2021). Also, parents were three times more likely to say that boys are better at math/science than girls are. And adolescents' math/science gender stereotypes were related to their math/science identity, which in turn was linked to their STEM outcomes in high school.
- Discussion of a recent study of tenth graders indicating that, in line with math stereotypes about male and female students, believing an "innate" math ability was associated with lower ability self-concept and intrinsic motivation in girls but not in boys (Heyder, Weidinger, & Steinmayr, 2021)
- Inclusion of a recent research review that found STEM secondary school interventions were more successful when they involved repeated or sustained engagement activities and when they combined an inclusive curriculum with teaching strategies that emphasized female role models (Prieto-Rodriguez, Sincock, & Blackmore, 2020)
- Description of recent research in which college students who perceived that their STEM professors endorsed a stronger fixed rather than growth mindset reported reduced feelings of belonging in class, more negative affect, and greater imposter feelings, which in turn predicted more dropout intentions, less end-of-semester interest in STEM careers, and lower grades (Muenks & others, 2020)
- Content mentioning the challenges that youth in high-poverty neighborhoods often face when looking for work. Joblessness is a common feature of such neighborhoods, as are poor-quality schooling and high crime rates.
- Inclusion of section, "Profiles of Adolescent Work Around the World"
- Sections that focus on how culture and socioeconomic status influence adolescents' career interests
- *Connecting with Careers* profile on Armando Ronquillo, a Latinx high school counselor/college advisor

Chapter 12: Culture

- Revisions made based on feedback from leading experts Margaret Beale Spencer, Deborah Vietze, Sandra Graham, Elizabeth Trejos-Castillo, and Melinda Gonzalez-Bracken

- New chapter-opening vignette about two Latinx undocumented adolescents, their struggle with school when they came to the United States, and how a Latina counselor at the school helped them become better adjusted academically and socially
- Expanded coverage of what the term *culture* means, including content on how everyone has a culture, with multiple examples provided
- Description of a recent study that indicated mask use during the COVID-19 pandemic was higher in collectivist countries than in individualist countries (Lu, Jin, & English, 2021)
- Inclusion of a recent study of African American and non-Latinx white children and adolescents that found African American children and adolescents had higher levels of individualism (Smith & others, 2020). Also in this study, adolescents with collectivist values were less likely to engage in delinquent behavior, while those with individualist values were less likely to behave in prosocial ways.
- Coverage of a recent study in which lower SES was linked to less cortical surface area in the brains of adolescents as well as less effective working memory (Judd & others, 2020). The SES factor most responsible for the lower level of brain functioning was less parental education.
- Inclusion of a recent Chinese study that found low family SES was linked to children's low academic achievement, especially in conjunction with low parental academic involvement in children's lives (Zhang & others, 2020)
- Description of a recent Australian study that revealed SES variations in adolescents' ability to achieve a healthy physical fitness level (Peralta & others, 2019)
- Discussion of a longitudinal study that found lower SES in childhood was linked to lower cognitive function and more cognitive decline in middle and late adulthood (Liu & Lachman, 2020)
- Inclusion of a recent Swedish study in which high-SES individuals were more likely to have completed 12 or more years of school by 20 years of age than low-SES individuals (Lindberg & others, 2021)
- Coverage of a recent meta-analysis that concluded low SES is a meaningful contributor to the development of lower cognitive ability and achievement (Korous & others, 2021)
- Description of a recent Japanese study that indicated adolescents in low-SES families had more health-related problems than adolescents in middle- or high-SES families (Okamoto, 2021)
- New coverage of excessive pressure to excel, especially in affluent contexts, being recently listed as one of the four main risk factors for adolescent mental health problems, with the other three risk factors being poverty, trauma, and discrimination (Luthar, Kumar, & Zilmer, 2020)
- New content on recent research by Suniya Luthar and her colleagues (Luthar, Ebert, & Kumar, 2020) focusing on risk factors and outcomes for adolescents attending high-achieving schools
- Description of recent research on adolescents in high-achieving schools that revealed a link between students'

- engagement in social comparison and increased levels of internalizing symptoms (Luthar & others, 2020)
- Updated data on the percentage of children and adolescents under the age of 18 living in poverty, which decreased to 16.2 percent in 2018 (Children's Defense Fund, 2020)
- Updated data on variations in ethnic minority adolescents living in poverty, figures that reflect a decrease in 2018 (Children's Defense Fund, 2020)
- Inclusion of a recent study that indicated higher poverty levels from 0 to 9 years of age were associated with reduced inhibitory control in emerging adulthood (23 to 25 years of age) (Evans, Farah, & Hackman, 2021). Also contributing to this link was a lower level of maternal responsiveness during adolescence.
- Coverage of a recent study in which higher poverty levels from 0 to 9 years of age were linked to the following developmental trajectories from 9 to 24 years of age: (1) higher levels of internalizing problems that diminished more slowly with maturation; (2) higher levels of externalizing problems that increased more rapidly over time; (3) reduced task persistence; and (4) higher levels of chronic stress that increased more rapidly over time (Evans & De France, 2021)
- Updated data on the percentage of single-mother families living in poverty (34 percent), which was nearly 5 times the poverty rate of two-parent families (6 percent) (U.S. Census Bureau, 2019)
- New commentary noting that despite the extensive challenges and difficulties that low-income families face, many low-income parents guide their children and adolescents to become resilient and flourish (Masten, 2021b; Masten & others, 2021). They rear children and adolescents who have positive friendships; maintain good relationships with parents, teachers, and other adults; earn good grades in school; attend college; and pursue positive career paths (Wilson-Simmons, Jiang, & Aratani, 2017).
- New opening commentary in the section on ethnicity focusing on the importance of not using a deficit model in studying ethnic minority adolescents and recognizing not just stressors in their lives but also positive aspects of their lives (Perrin & others, 2020)
- New content on the immigrant paradox and recent research supporting this concept (Zhang, Bo, & Lu, 2021)
- Coverage of a recent study in which immigrant children who were separated from their parents had lower levels of literacy and higher levels of psychological problems than those who had migrated with their parents (Lu, He, & Brooks-Gunn, 2020). Also in this study, a protracted period of separation and prior undocumented status of parents further increased the children's disadvantages.
- New discussion of research by Yoonsun Choi and her colleagues (Choi & Hahn, 2017; Choi & others, 2020a, b, c) on generational differences in Filipino Americans and Korean Americans, as well as younger-generation Asians' belief that older-generation Asians place too much emphasis on education

- New content on multi-ethnic individuals and the discrimination they often encounter (Tan & others, 2019; Woo & others, 2020)
- New content acknowledging that ethnic minority adolescents who have a positive ethnic identity are more likely to experience positive outcomes (Umaña-Taylor & others, 2020)
- New discussion of a recent study of Latinx families that revealed parents' educational expectations for their seventh-graders were linked to their perceived academic competence as ninth-graders (Aceves & others, 2020)
- Updated statistics indicating that Latinx immigrants are increasingly graduating from college, reaching the highest level in 2018 (28 percent for those in the United States for 5 years or less, compared with only 11 percent in 2000 and 14 percent in 2014) (Noe-Bustamante, 2020)
- Inclusion of recent research linking familism to Latinx youths' academic motivation (Stein & others, 2020)
- New discussion of a recent study in which Latinx adolescents showed enhanced resilience against discrimination encounters when they had more family ethnic socialization experiences and engaged in greater identity exploration and resolution (Martinez-Fuentes, Jager, & Umaña-Taylor, 2021)
- New main section, "Racism and Discrimination"
- New coverage of the Black Lives Matter movement and the George Floyd killing in Minneapolis as well discussion of past and current racism and discrimination in the United States
- New content noting that in 2021, a number of hate crimes involving physical attacks on Asian Americans occurred
- Inclusion of recent research with African American, Latinx, and Asian American college students that revealed stable peer discrimination across three years and increased discrimination by professors over the three years (Toro & Hughes, 2020). Also in this study, discrimination by peers and professors was linked to lower grades, less likelihood of graduating on time, and less school satisfaction.
- New content on the Native American ethnic group population's long history of experiencing discrimination and racism, along with commentary that this history often has received inadequate attention (NETWORK, 2021)
- Coverage of recent efforts by an increasing number of Native American activists at colleges and universities who are pushing their schools to do more to atone for past wrongs (Marcelo, 2021). The call for college and universities to increase their support of Native American students comes at a challenging time because the COVID-19 pandemic has especially made education difficult for Native American students, who already had the lowest college graduation rates of any ethnic group (Burki, 2021; Tsethlikai & others, 2020).
- New discussion of how to talk with children and adolescents about racism, based on the Intentional Parenting for Equity and Justice program proposed by Diane Hughes and her colleagues (Hughes, Fisher, and Cabrera, 2020)

- Recommendation of a recent book that helps BIPOC parents talk with their children and youth about race: *The ABCs of Survival* (National Black Child Family Institute, 2021)
- Inclusion of new end-of-chapter entry recommending *Social Science-Based Pathways to Reduce Social Inequality in Youth Outcomes and Opportunities at Scale* (2021) by Andrew Nalani, Hirokazu Yoshikawa, and Prudence Carter, which draws on initiatives from the social sciences to discuss six pathways that may create solutions for reducing youth inequality

Chapter 13: Problems in Adolescence and Emerging Adulthood

- Coverage of acculturative stress, which refers to the negative consequences that result from contact between two different cultural groups. Many individuals who have immigrated to the United States have experienced acculturative stress.
- New discussion of a recent research review of refugee children and adolescents that concluded their mental health problems were related to pre-migration individual risk factors, such as exposure to war-related trauma, as well as post-migration family factors, such as parental mental health issues and impaired parenting (Scharpf & others, 2020)
- Inclusion of a recent study in which Latinx adolescents experienced more depressive symptoms when both the adolescents and their parents were experiencing high levels of acculturative stress (Wu & others, 2020)
- Description of a recent study in which neighborhood poverty was linked to adolescent delinquency, especially through maternal stress and adverse childhood experiences (Wang, Choi, & Shin, 2020)
- Updated data on the percentage of U.S. adolescents who seriously consider suicide or attempt suicide each year, including gender and ethnicity variations (Underwood & others, 2020)
- Discussion of a recent study that found in 32 of 38 countries assessed, early sexual intercourse (at 12 to 15 years of age) and having sexual intercourse with multiple partners were linked to increased suicide attempts (Smith & others, 2020)
- Content indicating that adolescent problems are linked to the social contexts of family, peers, schools, socioeconomic status, poverty, and neighborhoods (Suter, Beycan, & Ravazzini, 2021)
- Discussion noting that although delinquency is less exclusively a phenomenon of lower socioeconomic status than it was in the past, some characteristics of the low-SES culture might promote delinquency (Gold, 2020)
- Description of a recent study in which neighborhood poverty was linked to delinquency in adolescence, especially through maternal stress and adverse childhood experiences (Wang, Choi, & Shin, 2020)
- Content mentioning that getting into and staying out of trouble are prominent features of life for some adolescents in low-income neighborhoods. These adolescents may sense that they can gain attention and status by performing

antisocial actions, and they may observe many adults who engage in criminal activities. Quality schooling, educational funding, and organized neighborhood activities may be lacking in these communities (Nishina & Bellmore, 2018).

- *Connecting with Careers* feature on Rodney Hammond, health psychologist, who worked extensively with adolescents living in poverty and those from low-income ethnic minority backgrounds to help them improve their lives
- Content on the role of cultural contexts in adolescent suicide attempts
- Inclusion of recent cross-cultural comparisons of 15- to 19-year-olds that indicated the highest suicide rates occurred in New Zealand, followed by Iceland, and that the lowest rates occurred in Greece and Israel (OECD, 2017a)
- Coverage of a recent cross-cultural study of more than 130,000 12- to 15-year-olds that revealed in 47 of 48 countries surveyed, being a victim of bullying was associated with a higher probability of attempting suicide (Kovanagi & others, 2019)
- Description of the National Youth Risk Behavior Surveillance Survey that revealed ethnic and gender variations in being overweight or obese (Kann & others, 2016)

- Coverage of a recent survey of 35 countries that indicated U.S. 15-year-olds had the highest obesity rate (31 percent), while 15-year-olds in Denmark had the lowest obesity rate (10 percent) (OECD, 2017b)
- Inclusion of a longitudinal study on an intervention with young children from low-income families in Head Start that involved a social-emotional learning program and an interactive reading program. The intervention resulted in significant reductions in conduct problems, emotional symptoms, and peer problems compared with a control group of children who did not receive the intervention (Bierman & others, 2021).
- Description of the Perry Preschool program, operated by the High Scope Foundation in Ypsilanti, Michigan, that serves as an excellent model for the prevention of delinquency, pregnancy, substance abuse, and dropping out of school and has had a long-term positive impact on its students (Schweinhart & others, 2005; Weikert, 1993)
- Discussion of the Fast Track program that attempts to reduce the risk of juvenile delinquency and other problems (Conduct Problems Prevention Research Group, 2007, 2015, 2019)

about the author

John W. Santrock

John Santrock received his Ph.D. from the University of Minnesota in 1973. He taught at the University of Charleston and the University of Georgia before joining the program in Psychology in the School of Behavioral and Brain Sciences at the University of Texas at Dallas, where he currently teaches a number of undergraduate courses. He has taught the undergraduate

John Santrock (back row middle) with recipients of the Santrock Travel Scholarship Award in developmental psychology. Created by Dr. Santrock, this annual award provides undergraduate students with the opportunity to attend a professional meeting. A number of the students shown here attended the Society for Research in Child Development meeting.
Courtesy of Jessica Serna

course in adolescence once or twice a year for more than three decades and has received the University's Teaching Award. In 2010, Dr. Santrock created the UT-Dallas Santrock undergraduate travel scholarship, an annual award that is given to outstanding undergraduate students majoring in developmental psychology to enable them to attend research conventions. In 2019, he created an endowment that will permanently provide the travel awards for students at UT-Dallas in future decades.

Also in 2019, Dr. Santrock and his wife, Mary Jo, created a permanent endowment that will provide academic scholarships for 6 to 10 undergraduate psychology students a year, with preference given to those majoring in developmental psychology.

John has been a member of the editorial boards of *Child Development* and *Developmental Psychology*. His research has focused on children and adolescents in divorced families, and his father custody research is widely cited and used in expert witness testimony to promote flexibility and alternative considerations in custody disputes. He also has conducted research on social cognition, especially the influence of affectively-toned cognition on self-regulation. John also has authored these exceptional McGraw Hill texts: *Psychology* (7th edition), *Child Development* (15th edition), *Children* (15th edition), *Life-Span Development* (18th edition), *A Topical Approach to Life-Span Development* (11th edition), and *Educational Psychology* (7th edition).

For many years, John was involved in tennis as a player, teaching professional, and coach of professional tennis players. At the University of Miami (FL), the tennis team on which he played still holds the NCAA Division I record for most consecutive wins (137) in any sport. His wife, Mary Jo, has a master's degree in special education and has worked as a teacher and a Realtor. She created the first middle school behavioral disorders special education program in Clarke County, Georgia. He has two daughters—Tracy and Jennifer—both of whom are Realtors. Jennifer was inducted into the SMU Athletic Hall of Fame and the Southwest Conference Athletic Hall of Fame. He has one granddaughter, Jordan, age 30, who completed the MBA program at Southern Methodist University and works for Ernst & Young in Dallas. He also has two grandsons, Alex, age 16, and Luke, age 15. In the last decade, John also has spent time painting expressionist art.

Dedication:

To my daughters, Tracy and Jennifer, and to my grandchildren, Jordan, Alex, and Luke, who, as they have matured, have helped me to appreciate the marvels of adolescent development.

expert consultants

Adolescent development has become an enormous, complex field, and no single author, or even several authors, can possibly keep up with all of the rapidly changing content in the many periods and different areas in this field. To solve this problem, author John Santrock has sought the input of leading experts about content in a number of areas of adolescent development. These experts have provided detailed evaluations and recommendations in their area(s) of expertise.

The following individuals were among those who served as expert consultants for one or more of the previous editions of this text:

Susan Harter	Gerald Patterson	Daniel Lapsley
Valerie Reyna	Nancy Galambos	Luc Goosens
John Schulenberg	Peter Benson	Seth Schwartz
Charles Irwin	Catherine Cooper	Brad Brown
Ruth Chao	L. Monique Ward	Candice Feiring
Wyndol Furman	Bonnie Leadbetter	Daniel Offer
Elizabeth Susman	Reed Larson	Harold Grotevant
Ritch Savin-Williams	Lisa Crockett	James Byrnes
Shirley Feldman	Allan Wigfield	Duane Buhrmester
Lisa Diamond	Lawrence Walker	Lorah Dorn
James Marcia	Pamela King	Jerome Dusek
Kathryn Wentzel	Daniel Keating	Elizabeth Trejos-Castillo
Moin Syed	Diane Halpern	Robert Roeser
Bonnie Halpern-Felsher	Jane Kroger	Darcia Narváez
Joseph Allen	John Gibbs	
Nancy Guerra	James Rest	

Following are the expert consultants for the eighteenth edition, who (like those of previous editions) literally represent a *Who's Who* in the field of adolescent development.

 Margaret Beale Spencer Dr. Margaret Beale Spencer is one of the world's leading experts on the development of individuals from ethnic minority backgrounds, including aspects such as ethnic identity and sociocultural contexts that influence inequality, discrimination, vulnerability, and resilience. She currently is the Charles L. Grey Distinguished Service Professor in Comparative Human Development, the Marshall Field IV Professor of Urban Education in the Department of Comparative Human Development, and Professor of Life Course Human Development at the University of Chicago.

A developmental psychologist, Dr. Spencer is also an alumna of the Committee on Human Development at the University of Chicago. Before returning to the University of Chicago, she was the endowed Board of Overseers Professor and Director of the Interdisciplinary Studies of Human Development (ISHD) Program and faculty member in the Graduate School of Education at the University of Pennsylvania (Psychology in Education Division). Additionally, Dr. Spencer was director of the University of Pennsylvania's Center for Health Achievement Neighborhood Growth and Ethnic Studies (CHANGES), and also was the inaugural director of the W. E. B. Du Bois Collective Research Institute.

Dr. Spencer's Phenomenological Variant of Ecological Systems Theory (P-VEST) provides an identity-focused cultural ecological perspective that frames the roles of gender, race, culture, and context in influencing human development. Recognizing the universality of human vulnerability, the theory addresses resiliency, identity, and competence in diverse humans situated both in the United States and around the world.

"I continue to value and enjoy John Santrock's textbooks; thus, I value the invitation and appreciate the opportunity to provide input. . . . Like prior editions, the entire volume continues to be incredibly important, particularly given the current historical moment. . . . Your text continues to
afford students the resources needed for tolerating the uncomfortableness expected." —**Margaret Beale Spencer** *University of Chicago*
(photo): Courtesy of Ven Sherrod

 Daniel Lapsley Dr. Daniel Lapsley is one of the world's leading experts on adolescents' cognitive and moral development. Professor Lapsley is the ACE Collegiate Professor and former chair of the Department of Psychology at the University of Notre Dame.

Dr. Lapsley's research focuses on various topics in adolescent social cognitive and personality development, including adolescent invulnerability and risk behavior, narcissism, separation-individuation, self, ego and identity development, and college adjustment. Dr. Lapsley also studies the moral dimensions of personality and other topics in moral psychology and has written on moral identity and moral and character education. He teaches courses on Adolescent Development, Lifespan Development, Educational Psychology, and Research Methods.

Professor Lapsley is the author or editor of seven books, including *Personality, Identity and Character: Explorations in Moral Psychology* (co-edited with Darcia Narváez; 2009); *Character Psychology and Character Education* (co-edited with F. Clark Power; 2005); *Moral Development, Self, and Identity* (co-edited with Darcia Narváez; 2004); and *Moral Psychology* (1996; translated into Korean and Mandarin Chinese). He has published over 120 articles and chapters on various topics in adolescent development and educational psychology, and he currently serves on the editorial boards of the periodicals *Applied Developmental Science, Educational Psychologist*, and the *Journal of Early Adolescence*.

". . . I am in awe of John's ability to pull together vast literatures to tell a lucid, straightforward story about adolescent cognitive development. The chapter (The Brain and Cognitive Development) seems updated and fresh,

nothing seems amiss, everything is accurate. This chapter is an amazing, lucid summary of some of the foundational themes in adolescent cognitive development. It ranges appropriately, horizontally as it were, over traditional (Piaget-Vygotsky, information-processing) and newer topics (the brain, neuroscience). It also ranges vertically from very basic things (neurons, schemas, assimilation-accommodation, ZPD, for example) to some more recent research (Grossman on wisdom, for example). Putting myself into the mindset of a student, I found the narrative easy to follow, easy to track the main points. There are numerous pedagogical supports along the way. Returning to my usual mindset as an instructor, I found the narrative does a lot of the work for me in the sense that it takes care of business in an informative but meaty way, well-anchored to the literatures."
—Daniel Lapsley *University of Notre Dame*

Elizabeth Trejos-Castillo
Dr. Elizabeth Trejos-Castillo is a leading expert on the influence of culture and ethnicity on adolescent development. She is the C.R Hutcheson Professor in Human Development and Family Sciences at Texas Tech University. Dr. Trejos-Castillo serves as Fulbright Liaison at the Office of International Affairs and Faculty Fellow at the Office of the Provost at Texas Tech University.

Dr. Trejos-Castillo's research focuses on the development of risk-taking behaviors, toxic stress, trauma, and resilience in vulnerable youth, with an emphasis on ethnic minorities and underserved populations in cross-cultural and cross-national populations. She has edited two books: *Handbook of Foster* (2018) and *Youth: Practices, Perspectives, Challenges* (2013) and has published over 45 research papers and book chapters.

Dr. Trejos-Castillo is also an International Adjunct Professor in Applied Social Sciences at the State University of Ponta Grossa, Paraná-Brazil and in Medicine, Biostatistics & Epidemiology and Psychology at CES University, Medellín-Colombia (South America). She has more than 25 years of experience working within the local community, with statewide partners, and with international collaborators supporting the resilience and well-being of vulnerable youth.

"For all chapters, the narrative and perspective reflect the latest research. I particularly appreciate the incorporation and discussion of recent international studies that allow the audience to get a global perspective on adolescent development in context. The chapters are well balanced. Across the chapters reviewed, diversity is properly addressed. I appreciate the inclusive language and tone of the narrative used throughout the chapters. I feel those invite students to have an open dialogue and would help facilitate having important and difficult discussions in the classroom (in-campus/virtual). The cases and story inserts, the overview, the description of concepts and scholarship, and the review/connect/reflect guide separating the main sections of each chapter makes the content easy to digest, follow, and understand. Youths' descriptions of experiences, thoughts, emotions, and so on are a great addition to the book by elevating the voices of youth and highlighting their unique world views, challenges, and more importantly, their strengths. The chapters cover a great breadth of knowledge across different fields related to adolescent development as well as provide a global perspective of youth and emerging adults' development in context." **—Elizabeth Trejos-Castillo** *Texas Tech University*

Deborah Vietze
Dr. Deborah Vietze is a Professor of Psychology and Urban Education at the City University of New York, the largest urban university system in the United States comprising 25 campuses offering undergraduate, graduate, and post-graduate degrees. It houses 17 Ph.D. specializations in psychology with over 200 psychology faculty. Dr. Vietze earned a Ph.D. in psychology from Columbia University, specializing in psychometrics and evaluation, in 1979. For the past forty years, her research has focused on the developmental significance of social identity for health and social development in underserved populations. Research with graduate students has explored the nature of power dynamics in social relations, the influence of perceived discrimination and optimal life experience on social identity, and the self-concept's influence on environmental conservation. She is currently working with students on the coming-out process among gay men, and African American English use effects on identity formation. Dr. Vietze served on the American Psychological Association's team representing the APA at the United Nations, working to bring the science and applications of psychology to the permanent missions at the UN and nongovernmental organizations (NGOs) working on problems of global concern. Dr. Vietze received the APA Achievement Award for Excellence in Integrating Research and Service for Ethnic Minority Populations and the C. Everett Koop Public Health Award for health-related services research. She was one of ten original National Institute of Mental Health Graduate Research Fellows and an APA Minority Research Fellow (1975 to 1978). She was also a member of the 2000 National Academy of Sciences committee that reviewed the science of early development for the public. She has served on many professional advisory committees and community boards and written extensively for journals and edited books. She is the co-author of *The Psychology of Diversity: Beyond Racism and Prejudice.*

"Ideas are well developed, and the organization of the Culture chapter is logical. The text is well-developed, researched, and organized. As an admirer of previous editions of Adolescence, I see that this one is substantially updated. In terms of diversity, the chapter did a great job looking at other cultures and comparing cultures related to adolescents' development. In addition, the chapter also discussed different significant minority ethnic groups and how adolescents are raised differently in each of them." **—Deborah Vietze** *The City College of New York*

Valerie Reyna
Dr. Reyna is one of the world's leading experts on adolescent brain development and cognitive development. She obtained her Ph.D. from Rockefeller University. Currently, she is the Lois and Melvin Tukman Professor of Human Development at Cornell University, as well as director of the Cornell University Human Neuroscience Institute and co-director of the Center for Behavioral Economics and Decision Making.

Dr. Reyna created fuzzy-trace theory, a model of memory and decision-making that is widely applied in law, medicine, and public health. Her recent work has focused on the neuroscience of risky decision making and its implications for health and well-being, especially in adolescents; applications of cognitive models and artificial intelligence to improving understanding of genetics (in breast cancer, for example); and medical and legal decision making (about jury awards, medication decisions, and adolescent culpability).

President-elect of the Society for Experimental Psychology and Cognitive Science and past president of the Society for Judgment and Decision Making, she is a Fellow in numerous scientific societies and has served on scientific panels of the National Science Foundation, National Institutes of Health, and National Academy of Sciences. Dr. Reyna is editor of *Developmental Review*, former editor of *Psychological Science in the Public Interest*, and has been an associate editor for *Psychological Science*. She has received many years of research support from private foundations and U.S. government agencies and currently serves as principal investigator of several grants and awards from organizations such as the National Science Foundation. Her service has included leadership positions in organizations dedicated to equal opportunity for minorities and women, and membership in national executive and advisory boards of centers and grants with similar goals, such as the Arizona Hispanic Center of Excellence, National Center of Excellence in Women's Health, and Women in Cognitive Science (supported by a National Science Foundation ADVANCE leadership award).

"It is remarkable how up-to-date this textbook remains (due to regular updating of references). I always learn something new when I read it, even in my areas of specialization. The new references are well-integrated into the flow of the prose, too. The material on exercise and cognition is quite topical and is presented in a deeper way than typically conveyed in textbooks, but it is still very accessible. Including the material on neuroscience, the adolescent brain, decision making, and recent theories of adolescent development (such as fuzzy trace theory) really sets this textbook apart with respect to its currency and excellence. The emphasis on empirical research is appropriate, especially well-controlled experiments, but the text also includes socially relevant survey research. The 'connections' sections are excellent." —**Valerie Reyna** *Cornell University*
(photo): Courtesy Cornell University

Dale Schunk Dr. Schunk is one of the world's leading experts on adolescent schooling, achievement, and motivation. He is Professor of Education in the School of Education at the University of North Carolina at Greensboro. His research specializations are learning, motivation, and self-regulation. Dr. Schunk's current topics of interest include developing self-regulation in college undergraduates and changes in self-efficacy in response to instructional and social influences.

Dr. Schunk is a Fellow in Division 15 (Educational Psychology) of the American Psychological Association and past president of that division. Dr. Schunk is also a Fellow in the American Educational Research Association and is listed in *Who's Who in America*. His text *Learning Theories: An Educational Perspective* is in its eighth edition, and his text *Motivation in Education* is in its fourth edition. He has published articles in leading research journals, including the *Journal of Educational Psychology*, *Educational Psychologist*, *Educational Psychology Review,* and *Contemporary Educational Psychology*. Dr. Schunk recently was honored with the Barry Zimmerman Award for Career Achievement by the AERA Studying and Self-Regulated Learning Special Interest Group.

"The narrative for the 'Schools' chapter reflects the current and important research in the field. There are many references published in the last 5 to 10 years. The chapter is well-framed and written. Diversity is addressed very well. I'm impressed that several research studies cited were conducted outside the U.S. The many suggestions for teachers are excellent, and I like the Review-Reflect-and Connect sections. The vignettes with teachers are a strength. This is an excellent chapter. . . . The 'Achievement, Work, and Careers' chapter definitely reflects the latest and most important research. The chapter has a clear framework and is well written and clear." —**Dale Schunk** *University of North Carolina-Greensboro*
(photo): Courtesy of Maria K. DiBenedetto

Melinda Gonzales-Backen Dr. Gonzales-Backen is an expert in the formation of ethnic-racial identity and other cultural processes among Latinx adolescents and families. She obtained her Ph.D. in Family and Human Development from Arizona State University. She is currently an Associate Professor in the Department of Family and Child Sciences at Florida State University.

Dr. Gonzales-Backen's research focuses on the psychosocial well-being of Latinx youth and families. Specifically, Dr. Gonzales-Backen is interested in how cultural stressors (such as discrimination and acculturative stress), cultural strengths (ethnic identity and familial ethnic socialization, for example), adolescent development, and family processes intersect to predict adolescent adjustment. She is currently a member of the editorial boards of the *Journal of Youth and Adolescence* and *Cultural Minority and Ethnic Diversity Psychology*. Her research has been published in leading research journals such as *Child Development*, *Developmental Psychology*, and *Family Process*.

"The narrative and perspective reflect the latest and most important research in the field. Both chapters ('Families' and 'Culture') provide a nice breadth of literature from leading scholars in the field. The research is nicely summarized. My students greatly benefit from the examples throughout the textbook. These include described scenarios and direct quotes from adolescents. The integration of diversity throughout the text has improved over the past few editions." —**Melinda Gonzales-Backen** *Florida State University*
(photo): Courtesy of Sarah Graves

Sandra Graham Dr. Graham is one of the world's leading experts on children's and adolescents' achievement and motivation with special attention to ethnicity. She currently holds the position of Distinguished Professor in the Department of Education at UCLA and the University of California Presidential Chair in Education and Diversity. She obtained a BA from Barnard College, an MA in History from Columbia University, and a PhD in Education from UCLA. Her major research interests include the study of academic motivation and socioemotional development in children and adolescents of color, especially African American youth, with a particular emphasis on development in school contexts that vary in racial/ethnic diversity.

Professor Graham has published widely in developmental, social, and educational psychology journals. Among her awards, she is a recipient of the Distinguished Scientific Contributions to Child Development Award from the Society for Research on Child Development and the E. L. Thorndike Career Award for Distinguished Contributions to Educational Psychology, Division 15 of the American Psychological Association. Recently, Dr. Graham was elected to the National Academy of Education. She also is a Fellow in the American Psychological Association, Association of Psychological Science, and the American Educational Research Association.

—**Sandra Graham** *University of California-Los Angeles*
(photo): Courtesy of Sandra Graham

Germine Awad Dr. Germine Awad is an Associate Professor in the Department of Educational Psychology at the University of Texas at Austin. Dr. Awad's scholarship is characterized by three interrelated areas of inquiry: prejudice and discrimination, identity and acculturation, and more recently, body image among women of color. She has also written in the area of multicultural research methodology.

The majority of Dr. Awad's research is guided by the questions *"What factors lead to discrimination against ethnic minorities?"* and *"What impacts perceptions of experienced discrimination?"* The two populations that she has primarily focused on are Arab/Middle Eastern Americans and African Americans. Although overt discrimination toward ethnic minorities has decreased over the years, the practice of more covert, subtle forms of prejudice remains. The events of September 11, 2001, however, reintroduced more explicit forms of prejudice towards Arab/

Middle Eastern Americans, and those perceived to be Muslim, complicating the dialogue on discrimination in the United States.

Dr. Awad is concerned with how prejudicial attitudes and ideology impact attitudes towards ethnic minorities generally and within specific domains such as the workplace and higher education. In addition, she examines how racial/ethnic identity and acculturation impact ethnic minorities' perception of discrimination. Most recently, she has expanded her identity and acculturation research to the study of body image concerns among women of color.

–Germine Awad *University of Texas–Austin*
(photo): Courtesy of Germine Awad

 Kevin Cokley Dr. Kevin Cokley holds the Oscar and Anne Mauzy Regents Professorship for Educational Research and Development in the College of Education at the University of Texas at Austin. He is a Fellow of the University of Texas system and University of Texas Academy of Distinguished Teachers, Director of the Institute for Urban Policy Research & Analysis, and Professor of Educational Psychology and African and African Diaspora Studies.

Dr. Cokley's research and teaching can be broadly categorized in the area of African American psychology, with a focus on racial identity and understanding the psychological and environmental factors that impact African American students' academic achievement. Dr. Cokley studies the psychosocial experiences of African American students and students of color and is currently exploring the impostor phenomenon and its relationship to mental health and academic outcomes.

Elected to Fellow status in the American Psychological Association for his contributions to ethnic minority psychology and counseling psychology, Dr. Cokley is the recipient of the Charles and Shirley Thomas Award for mentoring ethnic minority students. He holds the title of Distinguished Psychologist and received the Scholarship Award from the Association of Black Psychologists.

–Kevin Cokley *University of Texas–Austin*
(photo): Courtesy of Kevin Cokley

 Sabra L. Katz-Wise Dr. Sabra L. Katz-Wise is an Assistant Professor in Adolescent/Young Adult Medicine at Boston Children's Hospital (BCH), in Pediatrics at Harvard Medical School (HMS), and in Social and Behavioral Sciences at the Harvard T. H. Chan School of Public Health. She also co-directs the Harvard SOGIE (Sexual Orientation Gender Identity and Expression) Health Equity Research Collaborative and is a Senior Faculty Advisor for the BCH Office of Health Equity and Inclusion.

Dr. Katz-Wise's research investigates sexual orientation and gender identity development, sexual fluidity, health inequities related to sexual orientation and gender identity in adolescents and young adults, and psychosocial functioning in families with transgender youth. She is currently working on an NIH-funded community-based study to develop an intervention to support families with transgender youth.

In addition to research, Dr. Katz-Wise is involved with advocacy efforts at BCH to improve the workplace climate and patient care for LGBTQ individuals, including her leadership role on the Queer Council for the BCH Rainbow Alliance Diversity and member of the BCH Equity, Diversity, and Inclusion Council. She also serves on the HMS LGBT Advisory Committee and is a Faculty Fellow in the HMS Sexual and Gender Minority Health Equity Initiative.

–Sabra Katz-Wise *Boston Children's Hospital*
(photo): Courtesy of Sabra Katz-Wise

Connecting *Research* and *Results*

As a master teacher, John Santrock connects current research and real-world applications, helping students see how adolescent psychology plays a role in their own lives and future careers. Through an integrated, personalized digital learning program, students gain the insight they need to study smarter, and improve performance.

McGraw Hill **Connect**® is a digital assignment and assessment platform that strengthens the link between faculty, students, and coursework, helping everyone accomplish more in less time.

Apply Concepts and Theory in an Experiential Learning Environment

An engaging and innovative learning game, **Quest: Journey Through the Lifespan**® provides students with opportunities to apply content from their human development curriculum to real-life scenarios. Students play unique characters who range in age and make decisions that apply key concepts and theories for each age as they negotiate events in an array of authentic environments. Additionally, as students analyze real-world behaviors and contexts, they are exposed to different cultures and intersecting biological, cognitive, and socioemotional processes. Each quest has layered replayability, allowing students to make new choices each time they play—or offering different students in the same class different experiences. Fresh possibilities and outcomes shine light on the complexity of and variations in real human development. This experiential learning game includes follow-up questions, assignable in Connect and auto-graded, to reach a higher level of critical thinking.

Prepare Students for Higher-Level Thinking

At the higher end of Bloom's taxonomy, **Power of Process** for Psychology helps students improve critical thinking skills and allows instructors to assess these skills efficiently and effectively in an online environment. Available through Connect, pre-loaded journal articles are available for instructors to assign. Using a scaffolded framework such as understanding, synthesizing, and analyzing, Power of Process moves students toward higher-level thinking and analysis.

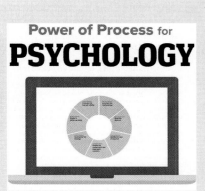

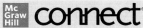

Real People, Real World, Real Life

Also at the higher end of Bloom's taxonomy (analyze, evaluate, create), the McGraw Hill **Milestones** video series is an observational tool that allows students to experience life as it unfolds, from infancy to adolescence. This ground-breaking, longitudinal video series tracks the development of real children as they progress through the early stages of physical, social, and emotional development in their first few weeks, months, and years of life. Assignable and assessable within Connect Psychology, Milestones also includes interviews with adolescents to reflect developmental changes. New to this edition, Milestones are available in a more engaging, WCAG-compliant format. Ask your McGraw Hill representative about this new upgrade!

Connect Media Sources to Content

At the lower end of Bloom's and located in Connect, **NewsFlash** is a multi-media assignment tool that ties current news stories, TedTalks, blogs, and podcasts to key psychological principles and learning objectives. Students interact with relevant news stories and are assessed on their ability to connect the content to the research findings and course material. NewsFlash is updated twice a year and uses expert sources to cover a wide range of topics, such as emotion, personality, stress, drugs, COVID-19, abilities and disabilities, social justice, stigma, bias, inclusion, gender, LGBTQA+, and many more.

Develop Effective Responses

McGraw Hill's new **Writing Assignment Plus** tool delivers a learning experience that improves students' written communication skills and conceptual understanding with every assignment. Assign, monitor, and provide feedback on writing more efficiently and grade assignments within McGraw Hill Connect. Writing Assignment Plus gives you time-saving tools with a just-in-time basic writing and originality checker.

Personalized Learning

McGraw Hill | SMARTBOOK®

McGraw Hill's **SmartBook** helps students distinguish the concepts they know from the concepts they don't, while pinpointing the concepts they are about to forget. SmartBook's real-time reports help both students and instructors identify the concepts that require more attention, making study sessions more efficient.

SmartBook is optimized for mobile and tablet use and is accessible for students with disabilities. Content-wise, measurable and observable learning objectives help improve student outcomes.

SmartBook personalizes learning to individual student needs, continually adapting to pinpoint knowledge gaps and focus learning on topics that need the most attention. Study time is more productive, and, as a result, students are better prepared for class and coursework. For instructors, SmartBook tracks student progress and provides insights that can help guide teaching strategies.

Current Research, Guided by Experts

With more than 1,400 research citations and reviewed by experts in the field, *Adolescence* provides the most thorough and up-to-date information on issues related to today's adolescents and emerging adults.

connecting with adolescents

Are Social Media an Amplification Tool for Adolescent Egocentrism?

Are teens drawn to social media to express their imaginary audience and personal fable's sense of uniqueness? One analysis concluded that amassing a large number of friends (audience) on social media may help to validate adolescents' perception that everyone is watching them (Psychster Inc., 2010). Also, one study found that Facebook use does indeed increase self-interest (Chiou, Chen, & Liao, 2014). And a recent meta-analysis concluded that a greater use of social networking sites was linked to a higher level of narcissism (Gnambs & Appel, 2018).

A look at a teen's comments on Instagram or Snapchat may suggest to many adults that what teens are reporting is often rather mundane and uninteresting. Typical comments might include updates like the following: "Studying heavy. Not happy tonight." or "At Starbucks with Jesse. Lattes are great." Possibly for adolescents, though, such comments are not trivial but rather an expression of the personal fable's sense of uniqueness.

Might social media, such as Facebook, increase adolescent egocentrism?
Andrey_Popov/Shutterstock

What do you think? Are social media, such as Facebook, Instagram, and Snapchat, amplifying the expression of adolescents' imaginary audience and their personal fable's sense of uniqueness? (Source: Psychster Inc., 2010)

Online Instructor Resources

The resources listed here accompany *Adolescence,* Eighteenth Edition. Please contact your McGraw Hill representative for details concerning the availability of these and other valuable materials that can help you design and enhance your course.

Instructor's Manual   Broken down by chapter, this resource provides chapter outlines, suggested lecture topics, classroom activities and demonstrations, suggested student research projects, essay questions, and critical thinking questions.

Test Bank and Test Builder   This comprehensive Test Bank includes more than 1,500 multiple-choice, short answer, and essay questions. Organized by chapter, the questions are designed to test factual, applied, and conceptual knowledge. New to this edition and available within Connect, Test Builder is a cloud-based tool that enables instructors to format tests that can be printed and administered within a Learning Management System. Test Builder offers a modern, streamlined interface for easy content configuration that matches course needs without requiring a download. Test Builder enables instructors to:

- Access all test bank content from a particular title
- Easily pinpoint the most relevant content through robust filtering options
- Manipulate the order of questions or scramble questions and/or answers
- Pin questions to a specific location within a test
- Determine your preferred treatment of algorithmic questions
- Choose the layout and spacing
- Add instructions and configure default settings

PowerPoint Slides   The PowerPoint presentations, now WCAG compliant, highlight the key points of the chapter and include supporting visuals. All of the slides can be modified to meet individual needs.

Remote Proctoring   New remote proctoring and browser-locking capabilities are seamlessly integrated within Connect to offer more control over the integrity of online assessments. Instructors can enable security options that restrict browser activity, monitor student behavior, and verify the identity of each student. Instant and detailed reporting gives instructors an at-a-glance view of potential concerns, thereby avoiding personal bias and supporting evidence-based claims.

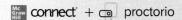

preface

Making Connections . . . From My Classroom to *Adolescence* to You

When I wrote the Preface for the first edition of *Adolescence* in 1980, I never envisioned I would be sitting here today writing the Preface for the eighteenth edition. It is extremely gratifying that more undergraduate students in the world continue to learn from this text than any other.

As with adolescent and emerging adult development, there have been major changes and transitions across the 18 editions. Over the course of these many editions, the field has become transformed from one in which there were only a handful of scholars (mainly in the United States) studying adolescent and emerging adult development to the thousands of researchers around the world today who are making enormous strides in our understanding of adolescence and emerging adulthood. When I wrote early editions of *Adolescence*, there were no discussions of such topics as adolescents' brain development, decision making, self-regulation, attachment, self-efficacy, religious and spiritual development, ethnic pride, immigration, and technology because research on those topics in the adolescent years had not yet been conducted. And the term *emerging adulthood* had not even been coined yet.

Across the last four decades, I have seen not only a dramatic increase in the quantity of research studies on adolescence and emerging adulthood but also an equally impressive increase in the quality of research. For example, today there are far more high-quality longitudinal studies that provide important information about developmental changes from childhood through emerging adulthood than there were several editions ago. In addition, there is increasing concern about improving the quality of life for adolescents and emerging adults, resulting in more applied research and intervention efforts.

Having taught an undergraduate class on adolescent development one to four times every year across four decades, I'm always looking for ways to improve my course and text. Just as McGraw Hill looks to those who teach the adolescence and emerging adult course for input, each year I ask the 50 to 100 students in my adolescent and emerging adult development course to tell me what they like about the course and the text, and what they think could be improved. What have my students told me lately about my course, this text, and themselves?

More than ever before, one word highlights what students have been talking about in the last several years when I ask them about their lives and observe them: **Connecting.** Connecting and communicating have always been important themes of adolescents' and emerging adults' lives, but the more I've talked with students recently, the more the word *connecting* comes up in conversations with them.

In further conversations with my students, I explored how they thought I could improve the course and the text by using *connecting* as a theme. Following is an outgrowth of those conversations focused on a *connections* theme and how I have incorporated it into the main goals of the eighteenth edition:

1. **Connecting with today's students** To help students learn about adolescent and emerging adult development more effectively.

2. **Connecting research to what we know about development** To provide students with the best and most recent *theory and research* in the world today about adolescence and emerging adulthood.

3. **Connecting topical processes in development** To guide students in making *topical connections* across different aspects of adolescent and emerging adult development.

4. **Connecting development to the real world** To help students understand ways to *apply* content about adolescence and emerging adulthood to the real world and improve the lives of youth; and to motivate them to think deeply about *their own personal journeys of youth* and better understand who they were, are, and will be.

Connecting with Today's Students

In *Adolescence*, I recognize that today's students are as different in some ways from the learners of the last generation as today's discipline of life-span development is different from the field 30 to 40 years ago. Students now learn in multiple modalities; rather than sitting down and reading traditional printed chapters in linear fashion from beginning to end, their work preferences tend to be more visual and more interactive, and their reading and study often occur in short bursts. For many students, a traditionally formatted printed textbook is no longer enough when they have instant, 24/7 access to news and information from around the globe. Features that specifically support today's students are the adaptive ebook, Smartbook, and the learning goals system.

The Learning Goals System

My students often report that the adolescent and emerging adult development course is challenging because of the amount of material covered. To help today's students focus on the key ideas, the Learning Goals System I developed for *Adolescence* provides extensive learning connections throughout the chapters. The learning system connects the chapter opening outline, learning goals for the chapter, mini-chapter maps that open each main section of the chapter, *Review, Connect, Reflect* questions at the end of each main section, and the chapter summary at the end of each chapter.

The learning system keeps the key ideas in front of the student from the beginning to the end of the chapter. The main headings of each chapter correspond to the learning goals that are presented in the chapter-opening spread. Mini-chapter maps that link up with the learning goals are presented at the beginning of each major section in the chapter.

Then, at the end of each main section of a chapter, the learning goal is repeated in *Review, Connect, Reflect,* which prompts students to review the key topics in the section, connect to existing knowledge, and relate what they learned to their own personal journey through life. *Reach Your Learning Goals,* at the end of the chapter, guides students through the bulleted chapter review, connecting with the chapter outline/learning goals at the beginning of the chapter and the *Review, Connect, Reflect* questions at the end of major chapter sections.

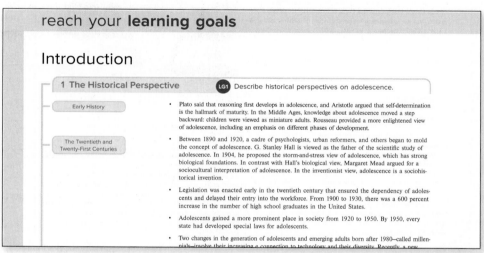

Connecting Research to What We Know about Development

Over the years, it has been important for me to include the most up-to-date research available. The tradition of obtaining detailed, extensive input from a number of leading experts in different areas of adolescent and emerging adult development continues in this edition. Biographies and photographs of the leading experts in the field of adolescent and emerging adult development appear on pages xxi–xxiv, and the extensive list of chapter-by-chapter highlights of new research content are listed on pages xxxii–liv. Finally, the research discussions have been updated in every area and topic. I expended every effort to make this edition of *Adolescence* as contemporary and up-to-date as possible. To that end, there are more than 1,400 citations from 2019, 2020, 2021, and 2022.

Connecting Developmental Processes

Too often we forget or fail to notice the many connections from one point or topic in development to another.

developmental **connection**

Brain Development

Although the prefrontal cortex shows considerable development in childhood, it is still not fully mature in adolescence. Connect to "The Brain and Cognitive Development."

Developmental Connections, which appear multiple times in each chapter, point readers to where the topic is discussed in a previous or subsequent chapter. *Developmental Connections* highlight links across topics and age periods of development *and* connections between biological, cognitive, and socioemotional processes. These key developmental processes are typically discussed in isolation from each other, and students often fail to see their connections. Included in the *Developmental Connections* is a brief description of the backward or forward connection.

Also, a *Connect* question appears in the section self-reviews—*Review, Connect, Reflect*—so students can practice making connections between topics. For example, students are asked to connect the discussion of autonomy and attachment to what they have already read about emotional development.

Connecting Development to the Real World

In addition to helping students make research and developmental connections, *Adolescence* shows the important connections between the concepts discussed and the real world. In recent years, students in my adolescence and emerging adulthood course have increasingly told me that they want more of this type of information. In this edition, real-life connections are explicitly made through the chapter opening vignette, *Connecting with Health and Well-Being,* *Connecting with Adolescents, Connecting with Emerging Adults,* and *Connecting with Careers.*

Each chapter begins with a story designed to increase students' interest and motivation to read the chapter. For example, the chapter on moral development introduces you to Jewel Cash, an emerging adult who was raised by a single mother in a Boston housing project and has become a vocal and active participant in improving her community.

Connecting with Health and Well-Being describes the influence of development in a real-world context on topics including increasing health and well-being in emerging adulthood, helping adolescents cope with pubertal changes, strategies for engaging in regular exercise, strategies for developing better sleep habits, guiding adolescents to improve their decision making skills, adolescents' self-esteem, effective sex education, parenting moral children and adolescents, strategies for emerging adults and their parents, effective and ineffective strategies for making friends, and coping strategies in adolescence and emerging adulthood.

Connecting with Adolescents and *Connecting with Emerging Adults* share personal experiences from real adolescents and emerging adults. *Improving the Lives of Adolescents and Emerging Adults* at the end of each chapter describes numerous resources such as books, websites, and organizations that provide valuable information for improving the lives of adolescents in many different areas. As with every edition, our goal in this edition is to reflect diverse voices, issues, and research. A complete list of related topics can be found in the "Guide to Diversity, Equity, and Inclusion" on pages x–xix.

Connecting with Careers profiles careers including a clinical psychologist who especially works with Latinx adolescents and emerging

connecting with health and well-being

How Can We Raise Moral Children and Adolescents?

Parental discipline contributes to children's moral development, but other aspects of parenting also play important roles, including providing opportunities for perspective taking and modeling moral behavior and thinking. Nancy Eisenberg and her colleagues (Eisenberg, Spinrad, & Knafo, 2015; Eisenberg & Valiente, 2002; Spinrad & Eisenberg, 2020) suggest that parents who adopt the following strategies are more likely to have children and adolescents who behave morally:

- Be warm and supportive, use inductive reasoning, and engage in authoritative parenting.
- Avoid being punitive, and do not use love withdrawal as a disciplinary strategy.
- Use inductive discipline.
- Provide opportunities for children and youth to learn about others' perspectives and feelings.
- Involve children and youth in family decision making and in the process of thinking about moral decisions.
- Model moral behaviors and thinking, and provide opportunities for children and youth to do so.
- Provide information about what behaviors are expected and why.
- Foster an internal rather than an external sense of morality.
- Help children and youth to understand and regulate negative emotion rather than becoming overaroused.

Parents who show this configuration of behaviors are likely to foster concern and caring about others in their children and youth, and to create a positive parent-child relationship. In terms of relationship quality, secure attachment may play an important role in children's and

What are some parenting characteristics and practices that are linked with children's and adolescents' moral development?
Digital Vision/Getty Images

adolescents' moral development (Goffin, Boldt, & Kochanska, 2018). A secure attachment can place children on a positive path for internalizing parents' socializing goals and adhering to family values. In one study, early secure attachment defused a maladaptive trajectory toward antisocial outcomes (Kochanska & others, 2010a). In another study, securely attached children's willing, cooperative stance was linked to positive future socialization outcomes such as a lower incidence of externalizing problems (aggression, for example) (Kochanska & others, 2010b).

connecting with adolescents

Rochelle Ballantyne, Chess Star

Rochelle Ballantyne, a Stanford University student who grew up in Brooklyn, New York, is close to becoming the first female African American to reach the level of chess master (Kastenbaum, 2012). Born in 1995, she grew up in a single-parent family in a lower-income context. Her grandmother taught her to play chess because she didn't want Rochelle's impoverished background to prevent her from reaching her full potential. Rochelle was fortunate to attend IS 318, an inner-city public middle school whose chess team is one of the best in the United States. Rochelle has won several national chess championships, and she is a rising star in the world of chess. Rochelle's motivation and confidence are reflected in her comment: "When I push myself, then nothing can stop me." After getting her undergraduate degree at Stanford and then her master's degree from Columbia University, she currently is a law school student at New York University.

Rochelle Ballantyne, shown here at age 17, is a rising star in the world of chess. *How might her ability to process information about chess be different than for a novice chess player?*
First Run Features/Courtesy Everett Collection

adults, an educational psychologist, a teacher with Teach for America, a family and consumer science educator, a marriage and family therapist, and a career counselor.

The careers highlighted extend from the Careers Appendix that provides a comprehensive overview of careers in adolescent and emerging adult development to show students where knowledge of adolescent development could lead them.

Part of applying development to the real world is understanding its impact on oneself. An important goal I have established for my adolescence and emerging adulthood course and *Adolescence* is to motivate students to think deeply about their own journey through life. To further encourage students to make personal connections to content in this edition, *Reflect: Your Own Personal Journey of Life* appears in the end-of-section reviews in each chapter. This feature involves a question that asks students to reflect on some aspect of the discussion in the section they have just read and connect it to their own life. For example, students are asked:

connecting with careers

Grace Leaf, College/Career Counselor and College Administrator

Grace Leaf is a counselor at Spokane Community College in Washington. She has a master's degree in educational leadership and is working toward a doctoral degree in educational leadership at Gonzaga University in Washington. Her college counseling job has involved teaching, providing orientation for international students, conducting individual and group advisory sessions, and doing individual and group career planning. Leaf has focused on connecting students with their own goals and values and helping them design an educational program that fits their needs and visions. Following a long career as a college counselor, she is now vice-president of instruction at Lower Columbia College in Washington.

Grace Leaf counsels college students at Spokane Community College about careers.
Courtesy of Grace Leaf

For more information about what career counselors do, see the Careers in Adolescent Development appendix.

- *What are some examples of circumstances in which you think you were stereotyped as an adolescent?*

- *How was your adolescence likely similar to, or different from, the adolescence of your parents and grandparents?*

In addition, students are asked a number of personal connections questions in the photograph captions.

Content Revisions

A significant reason why *Adolescence* has been successfully used by instructors for edition after edition is the painstaking effort and review that goes into making sure the text provides the latest research on all topic areas discussed in the classroom. This new eighteenth edition is no exception, with more than 1,400 citations from 2019, 2020, 2021, and 2022.

This new edition is publishing as the world is well over a year into the COVID-19 pandemic health crisis, as more and more people are being vaccinated and parts of the world are slowly returning to pre-pandemic status while other areas are still battling the raging virus. We are already seeing a great deal of research in many related topics, which are mentioned throughout this edition. Additionally, a new main section, "Schools and the Coronavirus Pandemic," has been added on how K-12 and college education had to be quickly reconfigured to address this challenge and some of the immediate outcomes.

Also since the last edition was published, a number of events have occurred that have exposed the results of discrimination, systemic racism, and social injustice in the United States and throughout the world. *Adolescence* has been significantly updated to more extensively cover these important issues and related research, which can be easily found by using the "Guide to Diversity, Equity, and Inclusion" on pages x–xix.

Additional areas of targeted revision include the positive aspects of adolescents' lives, including health and well-being; identity issues, including gender and transgender; social contexts involving families, peers, and schools; technology, including social media; neuroscience and the brain; and genetics and epigenetics.

Following is a sample of the many chapter-by-chapter changes that were made in this new edition of *Adolescence*.

Chapter 1: Introduction

- Revisions based on comments by leading diversity expert James Graham
- Updated coverage of generations, with individuals born in 1997 or later now labeled generation Z, a generation even more entrenched in technology than millennials, especially in terms of social media (Dimock, 2019)
- Replacement of the label "Latino" with the gender neutral and more inclusive "Latinx"
- Inclusion of recent research indicating that positive youth development (PYD) characteristics predicted a lower level of Internet addiction in adolescents (Dou & Shek, 2021; Yu & Shek, 2021)
- Coverage of recent research that found PYD attributes were linked to fewer internalizing problems in adolescents (Wang, Peng, & Chi, 2021)
- Description of a recent study in which PYD characteristics helped to protect adolescents from developing mental health problems in traumatic situations such as the COVID-19 pandemic (Shek & others, 2021)
- Significant reorganization, expansion, and updating of main section, "Social Contexts," to include more content on culture, socioeconomic status, ethnicity, and gender
- Updated data on the percentage of U.S. children and adolescents 17 years of age and younger from different ethnic groups in 2017 and projected to 2050, with dramatic increases in Latinx and Asian American children (ChildStats.gov, 2018)
- Coverage of a recent research review of 3- to 19-year-old U.S. children and adolescents that concluded variations in socioeconomic status were linked to different levels of psychopathology (Peverill & others, 2021)
- New commentary on the racism and discrimination many children and adults continue to experience in the United States and around the world and a new Developmental Connection on "Culture"

- New coverage of transgender adolescents
- Updated statistics indicating that poverty rates dropped considerably from 2018 to 2019 for African American, Latinx, and Asian American children and adolescents, including a much larger drop than for non-Latinx white children and adolescents (Semega & others, 2020). Also, the lowest poverty rate in 2019 occurred for Asian American children and adolescents (Semega & others, 2020).
- New commentary on the importance of considering the intersection of culture, socioeconomic status, ethnicity, and gender, especially because, when combined, they can create systems of power and privilege as well as oppression and discrimination
- Expanded coverage of emerging adulthood and the possibility that its upper boundary might be changed from 25 to 29
- New content on how establishing a stable work pattern is being delayed until the late twenties or even early thirties for increasing numbers of young adults (Arnett, Robinson, & Lachman, 2020)
- Inclusion of a new proposal that an age period of 30 to 45 might be called "established adulthood" (Mehta & others, 2020)
- Image comparing a group of all non-Latinx adolescent boys and a group of diverse adolescents from different ethnic groups to illustrate the importance of obtaining diverse samples in research on adolescents

Chapter 2: Puberty, Health, and Biological Foundations

- Description of a recent study of adolescent boys that indicated a high level of testosterone was linked to greater impatience and less delay of gratification (Laube, Lorenz, & van den Bos, 2020)
- Inclusion of a recent study of early adolescent boys in Japan that found a lower level of testosterone was associated with social withdrawal (Hayashi & others, 2020)

- Coverage of recent research in Denmark that found obesity was associated with earlier pubertal onset in boys (Busch & others, 2020)

- New research content indicating that higher levels of DHEA during puberty were linked to lower conscientiousness and openness to experience (Van den Akker & others, 2021)

- Discussion of recent research on physical fitness in early-maturing boys and girls (Albadaldejo-Saura & others, 2021; Nevill & others, 2021)

- Inclusion of recent research in which early-maturing boys engaged in more externalizing behaviors and more violent behavior throughout adolescence but not in early adulthood (Dimler & Natsuaki, 2021). Also in this study, early-maturing girls engaged in more externalizing behaviors throughout adolescence but not in early adulthood.

- Description of a recent study of girls in rural China that found earlier pubertal onset was linked to greater weight for their height and rapid weight gain from birth to 2 years of age (Wei & others, 2021)

- Coverage of a recent study in which early life stress was linked to earlier onset of menarche (Holdsworth & Appleton, 2020)

- Inclusion of a recent Italian study that revealed earlier pubertal onset occurred after the onset of the COVID-19 pandemic rather than prior to its occurrence (Verzani & others, 2021)

- Discussion of a recent study that revealed age at menarche has dropping in recent years in Portugal (Queiroga & others, 2020)

- Description of recent research with adolescents indicating that lower SES was associated with lower cognitive control, which in turn was linked to increased risk-taking (Brieant & others, 2021)

- Inclusion of a recent meta-analysis that concluded pubertal onset of breast development decreased 3 months per decade from 1977 to 2013 (Eckert-Lind & others, 2020)

- Coverage of a Taiwanese study that found the age of menarche onset had dropped by 0.43 years per decade in the last 30 years (Chow & others, 2020)

- Description of a recent study of Chinese adolescents that revealed girls were more dissatisfied with their appearance than boys were, but boys were more dissatisfied with their sexual organs (Zhang & others, 2020)

- Discussion of a recent Japanese study of 10-year-olds in which greater exposure to social media networking sites was associated with a stronger desire to be thin for girls but not for boys (Sugimoto & others, 2020)

- Coverage of recent research in which higher social media use was linked to more negative body images for adolescents, more so for girls than for boys (Kelly & others, 2019)

- Inclusion of a recent study of young adolescents in which girls had a more negative body image when they identified with an idealized social media portrayal (Rodgers & others, 2020)

- Description of a recent study in which early-maturing boys and girls tended to affiliate with delinquent peers, which increased their engagement in externalizing problems (Stepanyan & others, 2020)

- Inclusion of recent research with 11- to 14-year-old girls that found those who felt negatively about their body because of social media had higher rates of depressive symptoms, had more online social anxiety, found it harder to make new friends, and were more socially isolated (Charmaraman & others, 2021)

- New content on the effects of the COVID-19 pandemic on various aspects of adolescents' physical and mental health (Magson & others, 2021)

- Discussion of a recent study in which 70 percent of children and adolescents were less likely to visit a general hospital emergency room after the COVID-19 pandemic emerged than before it appeared (Goldman & others, 2021)

- New coverage of the roles of poverty and ethnicity in creating health disparities in adolescents, including indications that a number of factors are involved (Perrin & others, 2020)

- New discussion of health disparities that characterize Latinx and African American adolescent hospitalizations due to the COVID-19 pandemic (Kim & others, 2020)

- Inclusion of new data on persistent health disparities in health coverage and health conditions that involve ethnicity (Carratala & Maxwell, 2020; U.S. Health and Human Services Office of Minority Health, 2020)

- New discussion of peer presence and adolescent risk-taking, including a recent study in which peer presence increased risk-taking for adolescent boys more than for girls (Defoe & others, 2020)

- New description of recent research indicating that peer presence in adolescence increased risk-taking behavior for adolescents with low self-esteem but not for those with high self-esteem (Tian & others, 2020)

- New coverage of suicide, indicating that it is now the second leading cause of death in adolescence after being the third leading cause of adolescent deaths for several decades (National Center for Health Statistics, 2020)

- Inclusion of a longitudinal study that found binge drinking in the twelfth grade was linked to driving while impaired (DWI), riding with an impaired driver (RWI), blackouts, and riskier driving up to 4 years later (Vaca & others, 2020)

- Update on the continuing decline in the number of adolescents who eat vegetables (Underwood & others, 2020)

- Discussion of a recent study in which a higher level of parental monitoring was linked to adolescents having a healthier diet and reduced likelihood of being overweight (Kim & others, 2019)

- Inclusion of recent research that found energy drink use by adolescents was linked to increased numbers of emergency room visits, increased risk of adverse cardiovascular effects, increased alcohol use, reduced sleep duration, and increased fast food consumption (Almulla & Faris, 2020; Galimov & others, 2020; Moussa & others, 2021)

- Description of a recent study of college students in which regularly eating breakfast was associated with having a higher grade point average (GPA), while regularly eating fast food was linked to having a lower GPA (Reuter, Forster, & Brister, 2021)

- Description of recent research exploring ethnic disparities in exercise during adolescence (Underwood & others, 2020)

- Inclusion of a recent comparison of adolescents' exercise levels in 52 countries indicating that boys exercised more than girls and adolescents in higher-income families exercised more than those in lower-income families (Bann & others, 2020)

- Coverage of a recent experimental study that found a 12-week jump rope exercise program was effective in improving obese adolescent girls' body composition, blood pressure, insulin levels, and self-regulation (Kim & others, 2020)

- Inclusion of a recent research review of 27 studies in which children's and adolescents' aerobic exercise was associated with a reduction in body fat, lower fasting insulin, decreased inflammatory markers, and improved physical fitness (Lee, 2021)

- New description of a Chinese study indicating that adolescents showed more depressive symptoms after the appearance of COVID-19, but engaging in more physical activity during the quarantine helped to buffer the association between the pandemic and depressive symptoms (Ren & others, 2021)

- Discussion of a recent World Health Organization study of 11- to 17-year-olds' physical activity in 146 countries that concluded 81 percent of the adolescents were engaging in insufficient levels of physical activity (Guthold & others, 2020)

- New coverage of a recent study of adolescents that linked increased involvement in exercise to better processing speed, selective attention, and concentration (Reigal & others, 2020)

- Description of a recent research review that concluded physical activity interventions improve cognitive performance (especially executive function) in overweight or obese adolescents (Sun & others, 2020)

- Discussion of recent research with 10- to 14-year-olds that revealed being physically inactive was associated with being female, not having sports facilities in the neighborhood, and perceiving that the neighborhood is not safe (Judice & others, 2021)

- Inclusion of a recent study in which adolescents who engaged in less physical activity and more screen time than their peers were more likely to be overweight/obese (Crowe & others, 2019)

- Inclusion of a recent research review that concluded participation in sports during adolescence predicted greater engagement in physical activity in adulthood (Batista & others, 2020)

- New coverage of a recent study in which participation in team sports during adolescence had long-term positive

mental outcomes for those who had been exposed to adverse childhood experiences (Easterlin & others, 2020)

- Updated data on the continuing decrease in the number of hours adolescents sleep per night (Kann & others, 2018)

- Inclusion of a recent large-scale study of adolescents in the United States, United Kingdom, and the Netherlands in which 51.5 percent reported getting less than 8 hours of sleep per night and 18 percent said they experienced daytime sleepiness (Kocevska & others, 2021)

- Coverage of a recent study of adolescents in which insufficient sleep (less than 8 hours) was linked to increased alcohol and marijuana use (Kwon & others, 2021)

- Description of a recent study of 13- to 15-year-olds that found heavy use of screen media was linked to multiple dimensions of sleep impairment, especially if the screen time involved social media or the Internet (Hisler, Twenge, & Krizan, 2020)

- Discussion of research indicating that frequency of cordless phone calls, mobile phone dependency, and tablet use were linked to sleep problems in adolescence (Cabre-Riera & others, 2019)

- Coverage of a recent study linking consumption of energy drinks to shorter sleep duration (Almulla & Faris, 2020)

- Inclusion of a recent study of college students in which sleep deprivation was linked to a lower grade point average and delayed college graduation (Chen & Chen, 2019)

- Description of a recent study that found poorer sleep quality was associated with smartphone dependence and less effective stress management (Wang & others, 2019)

- Discussion of a recent research review of 112 studies of college students concluding that more physical activity and positive social relationships improved their sleep quality while greater caffeine intake, higher stress levels, and irregular sleep-wake patterns decreased their sleep quality (Wang & Biro, 2021)

- Coverage of the National Sleep Foundation's (2020) recommendation that emerging adults should get 7 to 9 hours of sleep per night

- New content on the National Sleep Foundation's (2020) explanation of why pulling an all-nighter to cram for an exam is not likely to be a good idea

- Expanded criticism of evolutionary psychology to indicate that it is very difficult to offer direct proof to support this view

- New criticism of the modularity of the human mind concept offered by evolutionary psychologists, pointing out that the human brain has extensive connections across different domains and does not function in nearly as compartmentalized a way as the modularity view proposes

- Updated estimate of the number of genes humans have— 20,000 to 25,000 (National Institutes of Health, 2021)

- Expansion of gene expression discussion to include loneliness (Brown & others, 2020)

- Expanded coverage of DNA methylation to include its influence on a wide range of outcomes, including sleep

(Koopman & Verhoeff, 2020), stress (Gatta & others, 2021), depression (Lapato & others, 2021), attention deficit hyperactivity disorder (Kim & others, 2017), and obesity (Nishida & others, 2020)

- Coverage of a recent research review that concluded variations in the 5-HTTPLR gene may contribute to the tendency to ruminate when individuals face life stress (Scaini & others, 2021)

Chapter 3: The Brain and Cognitive Development

- Revisions based on feedback from leading experts Daniel Lapsley and Valerie Reyna
- New coverage of a recent study in which an increase in the brain's white matter was attributed to greater myelination and an increase in the diameter of axons (Lynch & others, 2020)
- New description of how myelination not only improves processing speed but also provides an energy source and increased communication for neurons (Shen & others, 2020)
- Inclusion of recent research indicating that the thickening of the corpus callosum continues into the third decade of life (Danielson & others, 2020)
- Discussion of recent research indicating that connectivity between the frontal cortex and hippocampus increased from adolescence to emerging and early adulthood, with this connectivity linked to improvement in higher-level cognition, especially in problem solving and planning (Calabro & others, 2020)
- Expanded and updated coverage of adolescent risk-taking, with a special emphasis on the effects of decreasing parental monitoring too early, which allows increased peer/friend influence on risk-taking (DeFoe, Dubas, & Romer, 2019)
- Expanded and increased coverage of research on how environmental experiences can influence adolescent brain development (Ismail, Ljubisavljec, & Johnson, 2020)
- Inclusion of recent research indicating that children in a Romanian orphanage who had significant brain damage but were subsequently placed in stable foster care showed improved brain development at 16 years of age (Debnath & others, 2020)
- Discussion of a recent longitudinal study in which 11- to 18-year-olds who lived in poverty had diminished brain activity at 25 years of age (Brody & others, 2020). However, the adolescents whose families participated in a supportive parenting intervention did not show this diminished activity at 25 years of age.
- Description of a recent study that revealed aerobic activity increased the brain's white matter and thickened the corpus callosum, resulting in improved working memory (Ruotsalainen & others 2020)
- Updated and expanded discussion of Sternberg's (2019) balance theory of wisdom
- New description of the views of Igor Grossman and his colleagues (2020) and Judith Gluck (2020) suggesting that wisdom involves balancing your perspectives with those of

others and being motivated to attain some common good in a larger group, such as one's family, an institution, or even a country. These experts believe that metacognitive thinking with a moral grounding is a critical factor in attaining this wisdom.

- Coverage of research with 8- to 12-year-olds that found faster processing speed predicted higher language abilities, such as expressive vocabulary (Park & others, 2020)
- Discussion of recent research indicating that slower processing speed was linked to children having ADHD or a learning disability (Kramer & others, 2020)
- Inclusion of a recent study of young adolescents in which executive attention was a good predictor of self-regulation (Tiego & others, 2020)
- Discussion of recent research confirming that working memory is a foundational cognitive ability, with the frontoparietal network playing a key role in its development (Rosenberg & others, 2020)
- Coverage of research indicating that children and adolescents with ADHD have working memory deficits (Kofler & others, 2020; Valladares & others, 2020)
- New content on autobiographical memory and how it develops during adolescence (Nelson & Fivush, 2020)
- New description of mind-wandering and how it can interfere with adolescents' attention control on learning tasks (Gyurkovics, Stafford, & Levita, 2020)
- Coverage of a recent study of college students in which those with ADHD had less cognitive flexibility than their counterparts without ADHD (Roshani & others, 2020)
- Inclusion of a recent study of 7- to 13-year-olds that found inhibition and working memory were key aspects of mindfulness (Geronimi & others, 2020)
- Discussion of a recent research review that concluded mindfulness training was effective in improving adolescents' physical and mental health in a number of areas (Lin, Chadi, & Shrier, 2019)
- Description of recent research that revealed mindfulness training increased the resilience of adolescents during the COVID-19 pandemic (Yuan, 2021)
- Coverage of a recent research review that concluded mindfulness training reduced adolescents' depressive symptoms (Reangsing, Punsuwun, & Kraezle Schneider, 2021)
- Discussion of a recent study in which mindfulness training reduced the anxiety, stress, and depression of Latinx adolescents (Clarke & others, 2021)
- Inclusion of a recent study that found a college course on meditation improved the students' happiness and well-being (Crowley, Kapitula, & Munk, 2021)
- New quotation to go with the discussion of intellectual risk-taking in creativity.
- Inclusion of a recent study with 11- to 15-year-olds that revealed metacognitive skills increased students' math engagement (Wang & others, 2021)
- New discussion of a recent study that found in contrast to children, adolescents are less likely to rely on misleading

advice (Moses-Payne & others, 2021). Also in this study, adolescents' reduced reliance on others was predicted by their meta-cognitive skills, suggesting that these skills likely enhance their independent decision-making.

- New description of Sternberg's (2020a, b, 2021a, b) view of successful intelligence that emphasizes the importance of setting and accomplishing personally meaningful goals. His view also stresses that a person can do this by exploring and figuring out his or her strengths and weaknesses and capitalizing on the strengths while correcting or improving on the weaknesses.
- New coverage of a recent meta-analysis in which emotional intelligence was the third best predictor of academic performance, following general intelligence and the personality trait of conscientiousness (MacCann & others, 2020)
- Discussion of a recent survey of 102 experts on intelligence around the world that found most supported the concept of general intelligence (G) (Rindermann, Becker, & Coyle, 2020)
- Inclusion of a recent study that found genes were a better predictor of scientific achievement than artistic achievement (de Manzano & Ullen, 2018)
- Inclusion of a recent Danish study in which IQ test scores were positively associated with education in early and middle adulthood (Hegelund & others, 2020). Also in this study, individuals with low intelligence in childhood benefitted the most from education.
- New commentary about the ethnic intelligence gap and how it is influenced by racism and discrimination (such as reduced family wealth, segregation of schools, less access to healthcare, and lower teacher expectations for minority-group children and adolescents)
- Expanded and updated content on the Flynn effect, with decreases in intelligence recently found in Scandinavian countries
- New coverage of content on how IQ gains continue to occur in the United States and developing countries such as Romania (Gunnesch-Luca & Iliescu, 2020)
- Updated estimate of the percentage of children classified as gifted in the United States (National Association for Gifted Children, 2020)
- Inclusion of Sternberg's (2018) recent view of giftedness, which he believes should include not only assessment of successful intelligence but also wisdom
- Inclusion of a major new section, "Language Development"
- New overview of some changes in language development, including greater sophistication in use of words, better abstract thinking skills that provide analysis of the role a word plays in a sentence, and metacognitive monitoring
- Discussion of a recent analysis across a number of countries that found bilingual children consistently had better executive function than monolingual children (Schirmbeck, Rao, & Maehler, 2020)
- New description of bilingualism in adolescence with research indicating that bilingualism is linked to superior information processing in a number of areas (Antovich & Graf Estes, 2020)

- New commentary that some recent research studies have not found a cognitive advantage for bilingual children (Dick & others, 2019; Donnelly & others, 2019)
- New description of writing skills in adolescence with most adolescents being better writers than children. Metacognitive monitoring and strategies are key aspects of becoming a better writer in adolescence (Graham & Harris, 2021).
- New coverage of the considerable concern being expressed about U.S. adolescents' lack of writing competence (Graham & Rui, 2022)
- New entry for *Improving the Lives of Adolescents:* Sternberg, R.J. (2021). *The Nature of Intelligence and Its Development in Childhood.* New York: Cambridge University Press.

Chapter 4: The Self, Identity, Emotion, and Personality

- Coverage of a recent study that found adolescents who perceived their family functioning in more positive terms had more positive possible selves (Molina & Schmidt, 2020)
- Inclusion of a recent study of adolescents in which their perspective-taking skills influenced their willingness to give to others, especially strangers (van de Groep, Zanolie, & Corone, 2020)
- New discussion of different types of narcissism, including vulnerable narcissism and grandiose narcissism (Donnellan, Ackerman, & Wright, 2021; Ponti, Ghinnasi, & Tani, 2020)
- Coverage of a recent study that found grandiose narcissists actually were characterized by greater life satisfaction than vulnerable narcissists but also were characterized as inauthentic (Kaufman & others, 2020)
- Discussion of a recent study of Chinese adolescents in which mental health outcomes of narcissists depended on their self-esteem. Narcissism and high self-esteem were associated with positive mental health outcomes, while narcissism and low self-esteem were linked to problematic mental health outcomes (Xu, Huebner, & Tian, 2020).
- Inclusion of recent research on Mexican-origin adolescents living in the United States that found the exploitativeness dimension of narcissism at 14 years of age predicted a number of problems at age 16 (drug use, delinquency, conduct disorder, and sexual intercourse) (Wetzel, Atherton, & Robins, 2021). This study found little association between the superiority dimension of narcissism and problem behaviors.
- Coverage of a recent study of Mexican-origin youth living in the United States that found a reciprocal relation between self-esteem and academic achievement at ages 10, 12, 14, and 16 (Zheng & others, 2020)
- Description of a recent study in three countries—Brazil, Portugal, and Spain—that found parental warmth was a key factor in adolescent self-esteem in all three countries (Martinez & others, 2020)
- Inclusion of a recent study in which parental warmth, monitoring, low maternal depression, economic well-being, and father presence (versus father absence) were linked to higher

- self-esteem in children and adolescents (Krauss, Orth, & Robins, 2020)
- Discussion of a 10-year longitudinal study following individuals from early adolescence to emerging adulthood that revealed high self-esteem in adolescence predicted more long-term personal goals, better self-rated physical health, and fewer depressive symptoms in emerging adulthood; high self-esteem in emerging adulthood was linked to higher life satisfaction, more positive self-rated mental health, and fewer anxiety and depression symptoms (Arsandaux, Galera, & Salamon, 2021)
- Updated and expanded outcomes of self-esteem levels in a number of areas, including sexual health (Sahlan & others, 2021; Sakaluk & others, 2020)
- Description of a meta-analysis that found lack of support for the notion that self-evaluations reach a critical low point in many domains in early adolescence (Orth & others, 2021)
- Discussion of a recent study of 13- to 16-year-olds in which females reported having a higher level of self-control and self-monitoring than their male counterparts (Tetering & others, 2020)
- Coverage of a recent research review that indicated self-regulation decreases from 10 to 14 years of age and increases from 14 to 19 years of age (Atherton, 2020)
- Inclusion of research in which regardless of neighborhood context and economic advantage or disadvantage, self-regulation predicted adolescents' academic achievement (Davisson, Hoyle, and Andrade, 2021)
- Description of a recent meta-analytic review concluding that low self-regulation at 8 years of age was linked to externalizing problems, depressive symptoms, obesity, cigarette smoking, and illicit drug use at 13 years of age (Robson, Allen, & Howard, 2020)
- Inclusion of a recent study of Mexican-origin adolescents identifying factors associated with different levels of effortful control (Atherton, Lawson, & Robins, 2020)
- New coverage of a distinction between the dual-cycle and narrative identity approaches: The dual-cycle approach emphasizes the formation of an identity commitment, while the narrative approach focuses on the construction of an autobiographical life story (van Doeselaar & others, 2020)
- New discussion of a study of identity development from 25 to 33 years of age (Eriksson & others, 2020). In this study, fewer individuals were characterized by a moratorium status and more by an identity achievement status as they became older during this time frame.
- Description of a recent study of Flemish 17- to 26-year-olds in northern Belgium in which commitment and responsibility characterized older and employed participants more than younger and unemployed participants (Mattys & others, 2020)
- New discussion of a longitudinal study following individuals from early adolescence (age 13) into emerging adulthood (age 24) that confirmed the existence of a dual-cycle identity formation process (Becht & others, 2021)

- Inclusion of a recent study that revealed emerging adults who were identity confused were more likely to present an ideal self and a false self on Facebook, focusing on appearing socially desirable in their online self-presentation (Michikyan, 2020)
- Much expanded and updated coverage of ethnic and racial identity based on feedback from leading expert Kevin Cokley
- Discussion of a recent study of Latinx emerging adults that revealed the bicultural harmony component of bicultural identity development was associated with lower levels of psychological stress (Cano & others, 2021)
- New coverage of racial identity
- Inclusion of recent research on 13- to 17-year-old African American girls' racial socialization that linked pride to positive feelings about being Black and depressed feelings to oppressive messages about Black women (Stokes & others, 2020)
- Description of a recent study of 11- to 12-year-olds that found more frequent discrimination from peers was linked to lower ethnic-racial commitment (Del Toro, Hughes, & Way, 2021)
- Coverage of a recent study of adolescents that revealed on days when adolescents reported more negative peer ethnic/racial interaction, they had lower school engagement (Wang, 2021). Also in this study, on days when adolescents reported more positive peer ethnic/racial interaction, they engaged in more prosocial behavior.
- Inclusion of a recent research review of Latinxs that concluded perceived discrimination was linked to poorer mental health but that having a greater sense of ethnic pride attenuated this link (Andrade, Ford, & Alvarez, 2021)
- New discussion of the singular concept of ethnic-racial identity (ERI) (Atkin & others, 2021)
- Description of a recent study of Cherokee young adolescents' ERI in which girls and boys reported strong positive attitudes about being a Cherokee (Hoffman, Kurtz-Coates, & Shaheed, 2021). However, youths' perceptions that others hold Cherokees in high regard decreased across the years.
- Coverage of a recent study that found enhanced resilience against discrimination in Latinx youth who had experienced more ethnic family socialization and had engaged in ethnic identity exploration and resolution (Martinez-Fuentes, Jager, & Umaña-Taylor, 2021)
- Inclusion of a recent study that found 9- to 12 year-olds had less effective emotion regulation strategies than 13- to 16-year-olds (Sanchis Sanchis & others, 2020)
- Description of a recent study in which emotion regulation expressed in being able to manage feelings of sadness and worry served as a buffer against internalized symptoms associated with peer victimization (Cooley & others, 2021)
- Discussion of a recent study of adolescent girls in low-income families that found higher levels of emotionally supportive strategies from mothers and peers were linked to lower levels of negative emotion (Cui & others, 2020)

- Expansion and updating of the Big Five factors of personality, including links to aspects of mental health (Widiger & McCabe, 2021) and achievement (Szalma, 2021)
- Description of a recent study that indicated adolescents high in conscientiousness are less likely to engage in excessive screen time, including time spent on social networking sites (Yanez & others, 2020)
- Coverage of a recent study that revealed adolescents high in conscientiousness have higher life-satisfaction (Heilmann & others, 2021)
- Inclusion of a recent study of adolescents in which high levels of neuroticism were linked to increased anxiety, depressive, and obsessive-compulsive symptoms (Tonarely & others, 2020)
- Discussion of a recent study of adolescents that found effortful control predicted a lower probability of engaging in suicidal ideation and behavior (Lawson & others, 2021)

Chapter 5: Gender

- Extensive revisions and updates based on feedback and comments from leading expert Sabra Katz-Wise
- Coverage of a recent meta-analysis that found higher testosterone levels were linked to increased aggression, although the link was not very strong (Geniole & others, 2020)
- Inclusion of recent research that found young adolescent boys were more likely to feel pressure from parents to engage in gender-conforming behavior and to feel pressure from peers to avoid engaging in gender-nonconforming behavior (Jackson, Bussey, & Myers, 2021)
- Description of a recent study that found adolescents who watched more music television than their same-aged peers were more likely to have a stronger acceptance of rape myths five years later in emerging adulthood (Vangeel, Eggermont, & Vandenbosch, 2020)
- Discussion of a recent study of adolescents that revealed social media use was linked to negative body images, more so for girls than for boys (Kelly & others, 2019)
- Inclusion of a recent study of 13- to 15-year-olds in which social media and Internet use were more strongly linked to compromised mental health (depressive symptoms, for example) for girls than for boys (Twenge & Farley, 2021)
- Coverage of recent conclusions that indicate male brains have more intrahemispheric connections while female brains have more interhemispheric connections (Grabowska, 2020)
- Inclusion of recent research with 14- to 18-year-olds that found believing in innate math ability was associated with lower ability self-concept and intrinsic motivation in girls but not in boys (Heyder, Weidinger, & Steinmayr, 2021)
- Description of recent research that revealed adolescents' motivational beliefs at the start of high school were associated with STEM achievement and courses taken throughout high school and their college major courses seven years later (Jiang, Simpkins, & Eccles, 2020)

- New commentary noting that categories such as gender and ethnicity intersect and can create systems of power, privilege, and discrimination
- Coverage of a recent study of the inequities experienced in relation to ethnicity/race and gender in the graduate programs in the chemistry departments in the 100 top-ranked STEM programs in U.S. universities (Stockard, Rohlfing, & Richmond, 2021)
- Updating of national scores in eighth-grade reading (Nation's Report Card, 2019), with girls still scoring higher than boys in reading
- Discussion of a recent study of seventh-graders that found girls' perception that teachers had gendered expectations favoring boys over girls was linked to girls having lower math expectations and lower math achievement (McKellar & others, 2019)
- Inclusion of a recent study that found adolescents who observed relational aggression on television were more likely to engage in relational aggression when texting one year later (Coyne & others, 2019)
- Discussion of a longitudinal study following individuals from 14 to 20 years of age that found a large portion of the participants had a low level of relational aggression that decreased over time, while a small portion (12 percent) had a high level of relational aggression that increased over time (Coyne & others, 2020). High maternal psychological control, sibling hostility, and exposure to relational aggression in the media in early adolescence predicted which individuals would be in the high and increasing group.
- New coverage of recent research that revealed girls show more emotional concern for others than boys do (Trentini & others, 2021)
- Description of a recent study of Spanish adolescents that found girls showed higher levels of positive and negative emotion but also had a lower sense of purpose in life (Esteban-Gonzalo & others, 2020)
- Coverage of a recent study in which females were better than males at facial recognition of emotion across the lifespan (Olderbak & others, 2019)
- New description of a recent study that found girls had much better self-regulation than boys at 13 to 16 years of age (van Tetering & others, 2020)
- New discussion of the term *two-spirit* that is used by some indigenous North Americans to refer to individuals who are perceived as having both male and female spirits within them
- Extensively edited, expanded, and updated coverage of transgender individuals
- Description of recent research that confirmed victimization and discrimination predicted increased suicidal ideation, while community connection reduced suicidal ideation (Rabasco & Andover, 2021)
- Coverage of a recent study of transgender individuals in which gender affirmation was associated with reduced risk of

suicidal ideation and psychological distress, while gender discrimination was linked to higher risk of suicidal ideation and psychological distress (Lelutiu-Weinberger, English, & Sandanpitchai, 2020)

- Inclusion of a recent study that found a majority of transgender individuals had experienced discrimination in the past year and those who had encountered greater discrimination were more likely to develop symptoms of depression and anxiety (Puckett & others, 2020)

- New commentary noting that because trans individuals experience considerable discrimination, it is important that society provide a more welcoming and accepting attitude toward them (Vargas, Huey, & Miranda, 2020)

- Coverage of a recent study that found psychotherapy targeting internalized stigma and non-affirmation experiences can be effective in reducing gender-related stress and increasing resilience (Budge, Sinnard, & Hoyt, 2021)

- New *Connecting with Careers* feature on psychotherapist Dr. Stephanie Budge, a leading expert on transgender research and issues (Budge, 2021)

- New main section, "Going Beyond Gender as Binary" (Hyde & others, 2020)

- Coverage of a recent study of children, adolescents, and emerging adults that found middle adolescents (mean age = 14.8 years) were the most likely age group to adopt stereotypically masculine and feminine traits (Klaczynski, Felmban, & Kole, 2020)

Chapter 6: Sexuality

- Discussion of a recent study of young adolescents at 14 sites across 4 continents that found consistent evidence for a sexual script of boys' social gains from having girlfriends and girls' risk from having boyfriends (Moreau & others, 2018)

- Coverage of a recent Taiwanese study that found early exposure (eighth grade) to sexually explicit media was linked to early sexual debut, unsafe sex, and multiple sexual partners (Lin, Liu, & Yi, 2020)

- Inclusion of a recent national study that focused on the percentage of U.S. middle and high school students who engage in sexting (Patchin & Hinduja, 2019)

- Coverage of a recent study of emerging adults that found receiving unwanted sexts and sexting under coercion were linked to higher rates of anxiety, stress, and depression, as well as lower self-esteem (Klettke & others, 2019)

- Description of a recent meta-analysis of emerging adults that found 38.3 percent were sending sexts, 41.5 percent were receiving sexts, and 47.7 percent were engaging in reciprocal sexting (Mori & others, 2020)

- Discussion of recent research with adolescents and young adults in which various aspects of sexting were linked to the dark triad of personality traits (Machiavellianism, narcissism, and psychopathy) (Morelli & others, 2021)

- Updated national data (2019) from the Youth Risk Behavior Surveillance study on the timing of sexual intercourse in U.S. adolescents, including ethnic variations and the percentage of adolescents who have had sexual intercourse prior to 13 years of age (Underwood & others, 2020)

- New projections from the National Survey of Family Growth indicating that the probability of having sexual intercourse by age 20 in the United States is 77 percent for males and 79 percent for females (Martinez & Abma, 2020)

- Coverage of a recent Australian study indicating that having sexual intercourse at age 15 or younger predicted a higher risk of emerging adult (age 21) lifetime sexual partners and having sex without a condom (Prendergast & others, 2019). Also in this study, early sexual intercourse was linked to higher rates substance use and delinquency in emerging adulthood.

- Description of a recent study revealing that the likelihood of initiating sexual intercourse prior to age 13 was higher in adolescents with substance use and mental health problems (Okumu & others, 2019)

- Discussion of a recent study of adolescents in which spending more quality time with parents was linked to a lower incidence of engaging in vaginal sex, anal sex, oral sex, pornography access, and masturbation (Astle, Leonhardt, & Willoughby, 2020)

- Description of a recent study of urban, predominately Latinx and African American adolescents indicating that talk with extended family members about sexual protection was linked to adolescents having fewer sexual partners, while talk about risks involved in sex was associated with having more sexual partners (Grossman & others, 2020)

- New coverage of a recent study in which associating with antisocial peers predicted early engagement in sexual intercourse (Clark & others, 2021)

- Inclusion of a recent study that indicated low self-control is linked to engaging in risky sexual behavior in adolescence (Magnusson, Crandall, & Evans, 2019)

- Discussion of a recent study indicating ethnic disparities in adolescent girls' level of developmental assets (internal and external) and attitudes and behaviors conducive to delaying sexual activity (Messer & others, 2021)

- Coverage of recent research in which across the college years, rates of kissing, touching, performing and receiving oral sex, and penetrative sex increased (Lefkowitz & others, 2019). Also in this study, contraceptive use decreased across the college years, especially for males and for students in a serious romantic relationship.

- Discussion of a recent study of first-year college students in six focus groups that found a common theme was "Sex is easier to get and love is harder to find" (Anders & others, 2020)

- Description of a recent study of emerging adults in which a higher percentage of women than men reported having sex, hooking up with an acquaintance, using partner characteristics as a reason to hook up, and having negative reactions to their most recent hookup (Olmstead, Noroan, & Anders, 2019). Also in this study, a higher percentage of men

- reported hooking up with a stranger, meeting at a bar/club, and hooking up at a party.
- Coverage of a recent study of 18- to 25-year-old sexual minority women that revealed alcohol use was associated with a greater likelihood of engaging in future hookups and those who reported having more sexual minority stress subsequently hooked up with more partners (Jaffe & others, 2021)
- Inclusion of recent research indicating levels of suicidal thoughts in sexual minority adolescents (including gender variations) (Feigelman & others, 2020)
- Coverage of recent research on the percentage of adolescents who use condoms when they have sex, including ethnic variations (Szucs & others, 2020)
- Coverage of a recent national study that indicated adolescent use of long-acting reversible contraception (LARC) increased from 1.8 percent in 2013 to 5.3 percent in 2017 (Aligne & others, 2020)
- Updated data on the incidence of adolescent pregnancy, which continues to decline dramatically, reaching its lowest point ever in 2019—16.7 births per 1,000 15- to 19-year-olds, less than half the percentage (41.5 percent) in 2008 (Martin & others, 2021)
- Updated data on ethnic variations in rates of adolescent pregnancy, which continue to drop for ethnic minority adolescents (Martin & others, 2021)
- Discussion of a recent Canadian study that found SES variations in adolescent mothers involving mental health and substance use (Wong & others, 2020)
- Coverage of a recent Jamaican study that revealed adolescent mothers younger than 16 years of age were more likely to deliver preterm and low birth weight infants than those 16 to 19 years of age (Harrison & others, 2021)
- Updated content on the Girls Inc (2021) program for girls at risk for adolescent sexual problems, including recent research documenting the effectiveness of the program in reducing rates of adolescent pregnancy
- Update on the continuing government funding of pregnancy prevention programs through the Office of Adolescent Health (2021) and a description of the focus of several of the programs
- Description of a recent research review and analysis that concluded research over the last three decades strongly supports comprehensive sex education across a range of topics and grade levels (Goldfarb & Lieberman, 2021)
- Significant updating of data on HIV and AIDS in U.S. adolescents, including recent HIV infection rates (Centers for Disease Control and Prevention, 2020)
- Substantial updating of HIV and AIDS rates worldwide (UNICEF, 2020)
- New description of the effectiveness of pre-exposure prophylaxis (PrEP), including its recent approval for adolescents (Whitfield & others, 2020)
- Update on the dosage and age at which adolescents should be given the HPV vaccine to prevent HPV infections and

- cervical precancers (Centers for Disease Control and Prevention, 2020)
- Update on the dramatic increase in gonorrhea infections in the United States since an historic low in 2009, including a 5.7 percent increase from 2018 to 2019 (Centers for Disease Control and Prevention, 2021)
- Update on the number of new syphilis cases (nearly 130,000) in the United States in 2019, an increase of 70 percent since 2015 (Centers for Disease Control and Prevention, 2021)
- Update on chlamydia rates in the United States, with the highest rates continuing to be found in the 15- to 24-year-old age group, including new data on ethnic differences in chlamydia rates (Centers for Disease Control and Prevention 2021)
- New *Connecting with Careers* box on Dr. Maria Eva Trent, one of the world's leading adolescent reproductive health specialists, whose research focuses on underserved urban adolescent girls
- New coverage of a recent study of sexual assault in sexual minority college students (Eisenberg & others, 2021)
- Description of a recent study of college students that indicated alcohol dependence was a risk factor for both perpetrators and victims of sexual and physical assault (Caamano-Isorna & others, 2021)
- Update on the percentage of ninth- to twelfth-grade students who reported having been forced to have sex against their will, including data indicating that this is more than three times as likely for female as male adolescents (Kann & others, 2018)
- Coverage of a recent study that found more than 87 percent of alcohol-involved sexual assaults on college campuses were committed by serial perpetrators (Foubert & others, 2020). Also in this study, fraternity men and student athletes were more likely to commit alcohol-involved assault than other men on campus.
- Coverage of a recent study that indicated women who had experienced sexual assault were more likely to subsequently have more academic problems and engage in fewer serious romantic relationships while in college and nine years later to have more symptoms of depression, anxiety, and posttraumatic stress (Rothman & others, 2021b)
- Inclusion of recent research on acquaintance rape of college women that revealed 84 percent of the women knew their perpetrator and 65.5 percent encountered the perpetrator after the attack (Bell, Wolff, & Skolnick, 2021). Women who encountered their perpetrator after the attack reported more lifestyle changes and more severe symptoms of posttraumatic stress syndrome.
- New content on how affirmative consent for sexual activity is being encouraged on many college campuses (Goodcase, Spencer, & Toews, 2020)
- Discussion of a recent study of sexual harassment of college students by faculty/staff and peers, with female students at much greater risk of harassment than male students (Wood & others, 2021)

- New content on the "Me Too" (or "#MeToo") movement and the importance of providing safe contexts for women to openly discuss their experiences of sexual harassment (Yecies & McNeil, 2021)
- Update as of October 2021 on the number of states that require sex education and/or HIV education in public schools (Guttmacher Institute, 2020)
- New entry in *Improving the Lives of Adolescents* on Dr. Maria Trent and her colleagues' insightful analysis of the influence of race on various aspects of child and adolescent health and strategies to optimize interventions for reducing this racism. This article was requested by the American Academy of Pediatrics and states their position on addressing this racism.

Chapter 7: Moral Development, Values, and Religion

- Important changes made based on the recommendations of leading experts Daniel Lapsley and Gustavo Carlo
- Significantly revised discussion of Kohlberg's three levels of moral reasoning for greater clarification and accuracy
- New content on the role of peer relations in adolescent prosocial behavior (Cui & others, 2020)
- Coverage of a longitudinal study that found being around prosocial peers predicted an increase in prosocial behavior (Clark & others, 2020)
- Discussion of a recent study that indicated associating with prosocial peers at 12 years of age was linked to lower rates of drug use and property-offending delinquency a year later (Walters, 2020)
- Coverage of a recent study in which the collective prosocial nature of a school classroom when students were 14 years of age predicted a higher level of prosocial behavior two years later (Busching & Krahe, 2020)
- New content on the association of prosocial behavior with other positive aspects of development in adolescence (Donahue, Tillman, & Luby, 2020)
- Inclusion of a recent meta-analysis of 55 studies following individuals from childhood through emerging adulthood that revealed higher levels of prosocial behavior were related to lower levels of internalizing and externalizing problems (Memmott-Elison & others, 2020)
- Coverage of a recent study in which harsh parenting was linked to adolescents engaging in less prosocial behavior (Bevilacqua & others, 2021)
- Discussion of recent research that revealed maternal warmth was associated with a higher level of adolescent prosocial behavior (Kanacri & others, 2021)
- Description of a recent study of Chinese adolescents in which empathy played an important role in increasing forgiveness of an offender's transgression (Ma & Jiang, 2020)
- Discussion of a recent study of adolescents that revealed both gratitude and forgiveness were linked to a lower level of reactive and proactive aggression through their connection to self-control (Garcia-Vazquez & others, 2020)

- Inclusion of recent research indicating that other-praising gratitude expressions improve social relationships (Ling & others, 2021)
- Description of recent research that found adolescents having the character strength of gratitude engaged in more prosocial behavior and received greater peer acceptance (Lavy & Benish-Weisman, 2021)
- Coverage of a recent study in which adolescents with lower levels of empathy were more likely to engage in dating violence (Glowacz & Courtain, 2021)
- Expanded and updated discussion of moral disengagement (Lapsley, LaPorte, & Kelley, 2022)
- Inclusion of recent research documenting the role of moral disengagement in bullying and increases in the bully's aggression (Bijared & others, 2021; Mascia & others, 2021)
- New Figure 1 that provides students an opportunity to determine whether they have a moral identity by evaluating themselves on a number of moral traits
- Discussion of a recent study in which children and adolescents said that changes in moral beliefs are more disruptive to one's identity than changes in social conventional beliefs (Lefebvre & Krettenaur, 2020). Also in this study, the children and adolescents reported that changes in negative moral beliefs are more disruptive to one's identity than changes in positive moral beliefs.
- Inclusion of a recent survey in which 86 percent of college students said they had cheated in school (Kessler International, 2017)
- New main section, "Culture"
- Description of differences in behavior between WEIRD (Western, Educated, Industrialized, Rich, and Democratic) cultures that emphasize individual rights and independent behavior and non-WEIRD cultures that are characterized by duty-based communal obligations and collective, interdependent behavior
- Discussion of differences in morality within a culture, such as differences between people in lower- and higher-SES contexts
- New Figure 2 ("What Are My Values?") that allows students to determine the values that are most important to them
- Updated content on American college freshmen's views on the importance of being well-off financially versus developing a meaningful philosophy of life (Stolzenberg & others, 2020)
- New content indicating that a number of studies have found that adolescents who are more religious are more likely to engage in service learning activities (Hart, 2020)
- Updated data on the percentage of adolescents who adopt the same religion as their parents (48 percent) (Diamant & Sciupac, 2020)
- Inclusion of recent research indicating a bidirectional link between self-control and religiousness in 11- to 22-year-olds (Hardy & others, 2020)
- Coverage of a recent study in which religiosity was linked to a delayed initiation of alcohol use, more so for girls than for boys (Barry, Valdez, & Russell, 2020)

- Coverage of a recent study of 11- to 34-year-olds that revealed attendance at religious services declined with age but the importance of religion increased and the importance of prayer remained stable over time (Dew, Fuemmeler, & Koenig, 2020)
- Updated content from a national study on the continuing decline of attending religious services by high school seniors (Stolzenberg & others, 2020)
- Description of a study of levels of religious participation by adolescents in different ethnic groups (Lopez, Huynh, & Fuligni, 2011)
- Increased emphasis on the importance of recognizing cultural variations in adolescents' religiosity rather than taking a "one-size-fits-all" approach to research in this area (Jensen, 2021)
- Coverage of recent research with Thai adolescents indicating that they report an increasing boredom with the country's dominant religion, Buddhism, mainly because there is nothing new in it (McKenzie, 2019)
- Description of a recent study of 11- to 22-year-olds that found a positive bidirectional link between religiousness and self-control (Hardy & others, 2020)
- Discussion of a recent Danish study in which participating in a religious organization and praying were associated with fewer risk factors for engaging in an unhealthy lifestyle (Herold & others, 2021)

Chapter 8: Families

- New main section, "Sociocultural and Historical Influences," that highlights major cultural and historical changes that have affected and are affecting adolescents and their families, including decreased availability of neighborhood and family support systems, increased mobility of families from one location to another, greater numbers of Latinx and Asian American immigrant adolescents and their families, a dramatic increase in media use by adolescents and other family members, and a general restlessness and uneasiness among adults
- Inclusion of recent research indicating that a higher level of general parental monitoring of adolescents' spending habits, friends, and whereabouts was linked to adolescents' healthier weight status, better dietary habits, greater engagement in physical exercise, and less screen time (Kim & others, 2019)
- Discussion of a recent study that revealed when parents had little awareness of their adolescents' whereabouts, adolescents were more likely to smoke cigarettes and to initiate smoking at an earlier age (Sartor & others, 2020)
- Coverage of a recent study in which parental use of active tracking measures during adolescence and college were associated with better health in both time frames (Abar & others, 2021)
- Description of a recent study in which high-monitoring, high-autonomy-supportive parenting was linked to better outcomes for adolescents than other conditions (Rodriguez-Meirinhos

& others, 2020). In this study, the worst outcomes for adolescents occurred when their parents engaged in low monitoring and high psychological control.
- Discussion of a recent study that revealed authoritarian parenting was associated with being a bully perpetrator in adolescence (Krisnana & others, 2021)
- Inclusion of a recent study that revealed authoritative parenting was associated with a higher self-concept and lower level of externalizing behavior in adolescents, while authoritarian parenting was related to a lower self-concept and a higher level of externalizing behavior (Calders & others, 2020)
- Description of recent research in which authoritative parenting served as a protective factor against adolescents engaging in delinquency and later in criminal behavior (Xiong, De Li, & Xia, 2020)
- Discussion of a recent study that indicated authoritative parenting in grades 7 and 12 predicted greater internalizing of values in emerging adulthood (Williams & Ciarrochi, 2020)
- Coverage of a recent Chinese study that found authoritative parenting increased children's favorable trajectories of math achievement (Wang, Chen, & Gong, 2021)
- Description of recent research indicating that authoritative parenting reduced adolescent screen time (Xu, 2021)
- Discussion of a recent Lebanese study in which authoritative parenting was associated with better adolescent health outcomes (Hayek & others, 2021)
- Coverage of a recent study of adolescents in which neglectful parenting was linked to early initiation of sex and engagement in unsafe sex (Reiss & others, 2020)
- Inclusion of recent research with 7- to 9-year-olds that revealed indulgent parenting was associated with increased body mass index (BMI) (Hughes & others, 2021)
- Discussion of a recent study that found adolescents' emotion regulation benefitted from mother-adolescent relationships that were supportive and father-adolescent relationships that involved a loosening of behavioral control (Van Lissa & others, 2019)
- Coverage of a recent study in which destructive marital conflict was linked to less effective coparenting (Kopystynska, Barnett, & Curran, 2020)
- Inclusion of a recent study of low-income, unmarried couples that revealed cooperative coparenting at earlier points in time resulted in fewer child behavior problems later on (Choi, Parra, & Jiang, 2019)
- Description of a recent study of Chinese adolescents in which a lower level of parent-adolescent conflict was linked to lower adolescent risk-taking (Liu, Wang, & Tian, 2020). Also in this study, if parent-adolescent conflict was high, adolescents with higher self-control showed diminished risk-taking.
- Coverage of recent research indicating that 13-year-olds engaged in fewer problem behaviors when both of their parents engaged in autonomy-supportive behavior (Vrolijk & others, 2020)

- Inclusion of a longitudinal study that revealed insecure attachment in infancy was linked to having less effective emotion-regulation strategies 20 to 35 years later (Girme & others, 2021)

- Description of a recent study of Lebanese adolescents that found those who were securely attached had lower rates of addiction to alcohol and cigarettes than their insecurely attached counterparts (Nakhoul & others, 2020)

- Coverage of a recent study that indicated maltreated and delinquent adolescents had higher levels of insecure attachment (Protic & others, 2020)

- Discussion of a research review that revealed having an insecure attachment style increased the risk of engaging in suicidal thoughts (Zortea, Gray, & O'Connor, 2021)

- Description of a recent study that indicated college students with an anxious attachment style were more likely to be addicted to social networking sites (Liu & Ma, 2019)

- Coverage of a recent meta-analysis that revealed adults with insecure attachment styles were more likely to engage in risky sexual behaviors (Kim & Miller, 2020)

- Inclusion of recent research that found insecure anxious and insecure avoidant adults were more likely to engage in risky health behaviors, were more susceptible to physical illnesses, and had poorer disease outcomes (Pietromonaco & Beck, 2018)

- Inclusion of a recent study indicating that college students whose parents were classified as autonomy-supportive reported better life satisfaction, self-efficacy, and relationships with their parents than college students whose parents were classified as helicopter or uninvolved (Hwang & Jung, 2021)

- Discussion of a recent study in which helicopter parenting was associated with detrimental outcomes (lower school engagement and higher depression, for example) in emerging adult children (age 19), but only when parents also were high in control. However, helicopter parenting did not have negative effects on emerging adult children whose parenting style was characterized by warmth (Padilla-Walker, Lehman, & Neppl, 2021).

- Description of a longitudinal study in which helicopter parenting declined when emerging adults matured from 19 to 21 years of age (Nelson, Padilla-Walker, & McLean, 2021)

- Inclusion of a new term that characterizes a number of parents today—"lawn mower parent"—a mother or father who goes to great lengths to prevent their child from experiencing adversity, stress, or failure. By "mowing down" all obstacles and potential negative experiences for their children, these parents are not allowing their children to learn how to cope with such experiences on their own.

- Coverage of a recent study of 22- to 31-year-old "boomerang kids" who reported that the main communication dilemma they encountered with their parents was figuring out how to best communicate the idea that living with their parents represented investing in their future rather than creating a stigma (Abetz & Romo, 2021). Also in this study, the "boomerang kids" said that the best strategies they could adopt were to state their expectations clearly, contribute to the household, behave like an adult, and propose clear timelines.

- New content about China's one-child policy that was instituted in 1980 to limit population growth, then revised to a two-child policy in 2016 and a three-child policy in 2021

- Update on the significant number of grandparents alive today in the United States (70 million) (AARP, 2019)

- Coverage of a recent study that found when children live with their grandparents, the arrangement especially benefits low-income and single parents by allowing them to spend more of their income on their children's education and activities rather than on child-care costs (Amorin, 2019)

- Discussion of a recent study that revealed middle-aged adults were happiest when they had harmonious relationships with their parents and their adult children (Kim & others, 2020)

- Update on the divorce rate in the United States and comparisons with divorce rates in other countries (U.S. Census Bureau, 2019; OECD, 2019)

- Discussion of a recent meta-analysis of 54 studies that concluded children who experience parental divorce are at higher risk for depression, anxiety, suicide attempts, distress, alcohol abuse, drugs, and smoking (Auersperg & others, 2019)

- Description of a recent meta-analysis of divorced families that found links between high levels of interparental conflict, less effective parenting, and children's and adolescents' psychological problems (van Dijk & others, 2020)

- Coverage of a recent study that found adolescents' emotional and behavioral problems increased after their parents divorced, not before (Tullius & others, 2021)

- Inclusion of a recent study of custodial arrangements in 37 North American and European countries that indicated adolescents reported better life satisfaction in joint custody arrangements (50 percent of their time spent with each parent) than in asymmetric custody arrangements (Steinbach, Augustijn, & Corkadi, 2021). However, further analysis indicated that it was not joint custody that was responsible for the higher life satisfaction of adolescents but rather adolescent and family characteristics such as family affluence and communication effectiveness.

- Discussion of a 15-year longitudinal study of divorced families that involved an 11-session parenting improvement program that improved child, adolescent, and adult outcomes (Wolchik & others, 2021)

- Description of a recent study that indicated birth fathers, who are often less likely to be included in open adoption, would like to be part of the open adoption triad (adoptee, birth parents, and adoptive parents) (Clutter, 2020)

- Inclusion of recent research indicating gender variations in same-gender and heterosexual parenting competence with adolescents (Farr & Vazquez, 2020a)

- Coverage of a U.K. longitudinal study of gay father, lesbian mother, and heterosexual parent families indicating that when their children reached early adolescence, there was little difference between the three family styles, but better parenting quality and parental mental health was linked to fewer adolescent problems (McConnachie & others, 2021)

- Deletion of the section "Culture and Ethnicity" because of its significant overlap with the coverage of families in the "Culture" chapter

Chapter 9: Peers, Romantic Relationships, and Lifestyles

- Inclusion of content indicating that adolescents often rely on peers for emotional support, which became especially difficult because of the social isolation created by the COVID-19 pandemic (Magson, 2021)
- Coverage of a recent Chinese study in which peer drug use increased adolescent drug use frequency, regardless of gender (Zhang & Dement, 2021)
- Description of a longitudinal study that found shyness in childhood predicted lower emotional stability and lower extraversion in adolescence, with these links mainly due to negative peer experiences (Baardstu & others, 2020)
- Discussion of recent research with third- and fourth-graders in which feeling related to peers at school was associated with the children's positive emotions both at school and at home (Schmidt, Dirk, & Schmiedek, 2019)
- Inclusion of a recent study that revealed peers' influence on adolescents' eating behavior is often negative and characterized by increased consumption of energy-dense foods that are low in nutritional value (Rageliene & Gronhoj, 2020)
- Coverage of a recent study in the United States and China that found parents' increased peer restriction predicted a decrease in children's adjustment over time (Xiong & others, 2020)
- Inclusion of a recent study of eighth-graders that revealed peer pressure was associated with substance use (Jelsma & Varner, 2020)
- Discussion of a recent study in which perceived peer rejection was frequently preceded by either aggression or depression in adolescence (Beeson, Brittain, & Vaillancourt, 2020)
- New content on how peer rejection is consistently linked to a greater incidence of conduct disorder and delinquency (Kornienko, Ha, & Dishion, 2020)
- Inclusion of a recent study that found being a fun person to be around was a key component of adolescents' popularity with their peers (Laursen & others, 2020)
- Coverage of a recent study that revealed friends' social support was linked to engaging in more physical activity during adolescence (Lisboa & others, 2021)
- Discussion of a recent study in which adolescent girls with few friends had more depressive symptoms than girls with more than two very close friends (Rodrigues & others, 2020)
- Coverage of a recent study of Saudi Arabian youth that found they had a higher rate of suicidal thoughts and behavior when

their friends disclosed depression and self-harm (Copeland & others, 2021)

- Coverage of a recent study of Latina emerging adults in which lower friend support was linked to their loneliness (Lee & others, 2020)
- Inclusion of a recent large-scale study in which younger and older adolescents who had no friends were much more likely to engage in suicidal ideation (Campisi & others, 2020)
- Description of a recent meta-analytic review that concluded friendship experiences may be more closely related to loneliness than to depressive symptoms (Schwartz-Mette & others, 2020)
- Discussion of a recent study in which associating with the Hip Hop crowd and the alternative crowd were linked to increased risk for a number of negative behaviors (Jordan & others, 2019)
- New coverage of the effects of social distancing requirements on adolescents during the coronavirus pandemic in 2020
- Inclusion of a recent study in which girl-girl friendships were less likely to dissolve than boy-boy friendships from the beginning to the end of the sixth grade (Nielson & others, 2020)
- Description of research indicating that higher-intensity friendships are likely to amplify an adolescent's preexisting tendencies toward depression or aggression (Costello & others, 2020)
- Inclusion of recent research involving adolescent girls who engaged in high levels of co-rumination that found poor emotional awareness was related to depressive symptoms in their friends (Miller, Borowski, & Zeman, 2020). Also in this study, in high co-rumination contexts, when girls engaged in strong emotion regulation they had fewer depressive symptoms.
- New description of a recent study of young adolescents indicating that for non-Latinx white and Asian Americans, higher academic achievement was associated with having more same-ethnic friends, while for African American and Latinxs, higher academic achievement was linked with having more cross-ethnic friends (Chen, Saafir, & Graham, 2020)
- Discussion of youth organizations that provide intensive educational enrichment programs for at-risk minority students
- Coverage of a longitudinal study that revealed continuous singles (individuals who never dated from 10 to 20 years of age) reported lower life satisfaction in adolescence and early adulthood than moderate daters (Gonzales Aviles, Finn, & Neyer, 2021). The never-daters also were less satisfied with their lives than the later starters.
- Inclusion of a recent meta-analysis that found adolescents reported more negative aspects of their romantic relationships than their friendships (Kochendorfer & Kerns, 2020)
- New discussion of a recent study that found adolescents with an authoritative parent-adolescent relationship were

more likely to have positive emerging adult romantic relationships, while those with a distant parent-adolescent relationship were more likely to have problematic emerging adult romantic relationships (Hadiwijaya & others, 2020)

- Description of recent data indicating that in July 2020, for the first time since the Great Depression, a majority (52 percent) of 18- to 29-year-olds were living with their parents (U.S. Census Bureau, 2020). This abrupt increase (compared with 47 percent pre-pandemic) was clearly due to the onset of the COVID-19 pandemic.

- Updated data on the increasing percentage of U.S. adults who live in a single-person household—36 million in 2019 compared with 7 million in 1960 (U.S. Census Bureau, 2019)

- New data indicating ethnic variations in single adults (Brown, 2020)

- New comparison of the number of single adults in the United States and other countries, with the fastest growth in the number of single adults occurring in developing countries such as India and Brazil

- Expanded content on the reasons that more adults are remaining single than in past decades

- Coverage of a recent nationally representative survey of more than 35,000 U.S. single adults that found they are increasingly having uncommitted sexual encounters and taking far longer to make a formal commitment to a partner, a circumstance described as "fast sex and slow love" (Fisher & Garcia, 2019). Nonetheless, in this survey, today's singles show a strong interest in finding romantic love and a partner they can live with for the rest of their lives.

- Inclusion of a recent survey that found more young people were seeking love and romance through video chats during the COVID-19 pandemic (Fisher, 2020)

- New coverage of a number of trends in seeking love and romance based on the 10th annual match.com survey of 6,000 singles (Match.com, 2020). Among the trends are increasing percentages of young people who are waiting longer to get married so they can get to know a potential partner much better, being more selective about the people they go out with on a date, wanting to know a partner's political viewpoints, and being open to dating someone from a different ethnic group.

- Updated data on the increasing percentage of emerging and young adults who are cohabiting (U.S. Census Bureau, 2019)

- New content indicating that at lower SES levels, couples are more likely to cohabit and give birth prior to marriage and less likely to marry (Karney, 2021)

- New description of the recent trend of more U.S. adults engaging in serial cohabitation during the last decade (Eickmeyer & Manning, 2018)

- New content on cohabitation increasing in China and Taiwan while remaining rare in Japan and South Korea

- Discussion of a recent study that indicated early transitioning into a stepfamily home, especially for females, was

linked to earlier entry into cohabitation (Johnston, Cavanagh, & Crosnoe, 2020)

- New content on cohabitation being more often perceived as a stepping stone to marriage in the United States but more frequently perceived as an alternative to marriage in Europe, especially in the Scandinavian countries (Sassler & Lichter, 2020)

- Inclusion of a recent national survey that found married couples reported higher relationship satisfaction than those living with an unmarried partner (Horowitz, Graf, & Livingston, 2019)

- Updated data on the age of first marriage in the United States, which in 2019 was 30 for men and 28 for women, older than at any point in history (U.S. Census Bureau, 2019)

- New content and data on the dramatically increased percentages of newlyweds and all married people who are married to someone from a different ethnic group (Livingston & Brown, 2017)

- New comparison of age at first marriage in a number of developed countries, with individuals in Sweden getting married latest and those in Israel and Turkey earliest (OECD, 2019)

- Inclusion of a recent study that explored reasons that individuals get married, with love (88 percent of the respondents) at the top of their list (Geiger & Livingston, 2019)

- Coverage of a recent study that found men had a higher level of marital satisfaction than women across a number of countries (Sorokowski, Kowal, & Sorokowska, 2019). In this study, marital satisfaction was similar among Muslims, Christians, and atheists.

- Description of recent data on the percentage of U.S. adults who have been married at least once. In 2019, 65 percent of men and 70 percent of women had been married at least once (U.S. Census Bureau, 2019). However, this rate is declining—in 1990, 70 percent of men and 77 percent of women had been married at least once.

- Discussion of a recent study in which adults in same-sex relationships experienced similar levels of commitment, satisfaction, and emotional intimacy compared with their counterparts in different-sex relationships (Joyner, Manning, & Prince, 2019)

Chapter 10: Schools

- Inclusion of a recent experimental study of almost 1,900 middle school students in which enhancements to peer relations created by structured small group learning (cooperative learning, for example) improved peer relations, reduced stress, and in turn, decreased emotional problems and promoted academic achievement (Van Ryzin & Roseth, 2021)

- New commentary that in 2020, the federal government suspended standardized testing in schools because of the coronavirus pandemic and that ESSA was scheduled for reauthorization after the 2020–2021 school year

- Inclusion of recent study in which students in the first year of middle school had lower levels of adaptive coping and higher levels of maladaptive coping than elementary school students (Skinner & others, 2020)

- New coverage of a recent Chinese study in which students transitioning into middle school had worse health and lower academic achievement than students who were not transitioning (Anderson & others, 2020)

- Description of recent research in which first-year middle school students whose teachers received training to improve students' classroom behavior, academic skills, and engagement had lower anxiety, fewer emotional problems, and better adjustment than students whose teachers did not receive the training (Dawes & others, 2020)

- Coverage of a recent experimental study indicating that students transitioning to middle school who participated in a social and emotional learning mentoring program showed better decision making, problem solving, emotion regulation, and resilience than their counterparts who did not experience the mentoring program (Green & others, 2021)

- Discussion of a recent study in which teacher-student conflict during the transition to middle school or high school was linked to increased externalizing symptoms during students' first year at the new school (Longobardi & others, 2019)

- Updated data on school dropout rates, including those of ethnic minority groups, which continue to drop considerably (National Center for Education Statistics, 2020)

- Inclusion of recent research that revealed a social contagion effect in which non-trivial time spent with same-age friends, romantic partners, or siblings who had recently quit school increased the likelihood that adolescents would drop out of school themselves (Dupere & others, 2021). In the same study, when students' same-age social networks included more than one of these types of individuals (a friend and a sibling, for example) the adolescents were increasingly at risk for dropping out.

- Updated data on the transition to college, with a much higher percentage of first-year college students today than in the past saying they feel overwhelmed with all they have to do (Stolzenberg & others, 2020)

- Updated data on the value of a college degree, which in 2018 had increased to more than $30,000 additional income per year for college graduates compared with individuals who had only a high school diploma (Federal Reserve Bank of New York, 2018). In the 1980s, this income gap was approximately $20,000 a year.

- Discussion of a longitudinal study that found high school students benefitted from engaging in extracurricular activities characterized by both breadth and intensity (Haghighat & Knifsend, 2019)

- Inclusion of a recent study in which adolescents who participated in extracurricular activities were less likely to engage in screen time after school, reported greater life satisfaction, were more optimistic, and had lower levels of anxiety and depression (Oberle & others, 2020)

- New coverage of a recent study that revealed greater participation in high school extracurricular activities predicted an increased likelihood of completing a college degree in 4 years (Gardner & others, 2020)

- Inclusion of a recent study in the United States that found cyberbullying increased from 1998 to 2017 (Kennedy, 2021). Also in this study, face-to-face bullying in females increased across this time frame.

- Description of a recent study of more than 15,000 U.S. high school students that found greater amounts of bullying were experienced by sexual minority than by heterosexual adolescents (Webb & others, 2021)

- Inclusion of a recent Chinese study in which adults 60 years of age and older who had experienced bullying victimization as children had more severe depressive symptoms than their counterparts who had not been victimized by bullies as children (Hu, 2021)

- Discussion of a longitudinal study in which after being bullied, bullying victims' self-esteem decreased and this lower self-esteem was linked with an increase in further bullying victimization (Choi & Park, 2021)

- Inclusion of a recent study of more than 150,000 12- to 15-year-olds in low- and middle-income countries that found victims of bullies were characterized by these obesity-related factors: anxiety-induced sleep problems, lack of physical exercise, sedentary behavior, and fast food consumption (Smith & others, 2021)

- Description of a recent large-scale Norwegian study that concluded bullies, victims, and bully-victims are at risk for developing sleep problems, including shorter duration of sleep and higher prevalence of insomnia, as well as a lower grade point average (Hysing & others, 2021)

- Coverage of a recent study that revealed in 47 of 48 countries worldwide, being the victim of a bully was a risk factor for suicidal behavior (Koyanagi & others, 2019)

- Discussion of a recent study of university students in which being a cybervictim increased the risk of suicidal ideation and led to higher levels of anxiety, stress, and depression (Martinez-Monteagudo & others, 2020)

- Update on the Global Student Laboratory Project, in which students around the world collaborate on various projects (Globallab, 2020)

- Updated data on the percentage of 25- to 34-year-olds who have a post-secondary degree in the 30 member countries of the Organisation for Economic Co-operation and Development (OECD, 2020)

- New main section, "Schools and the COVID-19 Pandemic," with separate subsections on K-12 education and college education

- New description of recent research indicating that too often schools did not closely monitor the learning of students following the change to online instruction after the coronavirus virus abruptly shut down in-person classes in 2020 (Gross, 2020)

- Inclusion of a recent study documenting a significant drop in math achievement scores after instruction went online during the coronavirus pandemic (Chetty & others, 2020)

- Updated data on the percentage of children with a disability receiving special education services in different disability categories (National Center for Education Statistics, 2020)

- Description of research conducted by the Centers for Disease Control in 2018 that found ethnic variations in rates of learning disabilities and attention deficit hyperactivity disorder (ADHD) among students from 3 to 17 years of age (Zablotsky & Alford, 2020)

- Inclusion of recent research indicating that African American children and adolescents with ADHD are often underdiagnosed, while those who engage in disruptive behavior are often overdiagnosed (Fadus & others, 2020)

- Description of recent research that found preterm birth was linked to ADHD (Walczak-Kozlowska & others, 2020)

- Coverage of recent research indicating SES variations in development of ADHD and other problems with brain functioning (Machlin, McLaughlin, & Sheridan, 2020)

- Inclusion of content indicating that the neurotransmitter GABA is linked to the development of ADHD (Puts & others, 2020)

- Description of a research review of meta-analyses and randomized experiments that concluded neurofeedback has medium to large effects on ADHD, with 32 to 47 percent remission rates lasting from 6 to 12 months (Arns & others, 2020)

- Inclusion of an extensive set of meta-analyses that concluded neurofeedback is effective in reducing inattention symptoms in children with ADHD but that stimulant medication is more effective than neurofeedback in reducing inattention (Riesco-Matias & others, 2021)

- Coverage of a recent meta-analysis that found regular exercise was more effective than neurofeedback, cognitive training, and cognitive therapy in treating ADHD (Lambez & others, 2020)

- Description of a recent study that revealed children with ADHD were 21 percent less likely to engage in regular exercise than children not diagnosed with ADHD (Mercurio & others, 2021)

- Updated and revision of autism spectrum disorders (ASD) discussion

- New content on the dramatic increase in the percentage of children who are autistic (Centers for Disease Control and Prevention, 2020) and the percentage of autistic children who are receiving special education services (National Center for Education Statistics, 2020)

- Discussion of a recent research summary that concluded key early warning signs for ASD are lack of social gestures at 12 months, using no meaningful words at 18 months, and having no interest in other children or no spontaneous two-word phrases at 24 months (Tsang & others, 2019)

- Update on the increasing percentage of students with a disability who are being educated in the regular classroom (National Center for Education Statistics, 2017)

- Update on the estimated percentage of children who are classified as gifted in the United States (National Association for Gifted Children, 2020)

- Inclusion of Sternberg's (2018b) recent view of giftedness, which he believes should include not only assessment of successful intelligence but also wisdom

- New entry in *Improving the Lives of Adolescents and Emerging Adults:* ERIC (Education Resources Information Center), an extensive online library of education research and information that is sponsored by the Institute of Education Sciences (IES) of the U.S. Department of Education.

Chapter 11: Achievement, Work, and Careers

- Revisions made based on feedback from leading experts Sandra Graham and Dale Schunk

- Coverage of a recent study of tenth-grade Chinese students in which extrinsic motivation was detrimental to the performance of students with high intrinsic motivation but beneficial to the academic achievement of students with low intrinsic motivation (Liu & others, 2020)

- Description of a recent meta-analysis that revealed peer social acceptance was linked to higher academic achievement (Wentzel, Jablansky, & Scalise, 2021)

- New discussion on the potential influence of peer mindsets (Sheffler & Chenug, 2020), including a description of a recent study that found students who were around peers with a growth mindset for 7 months increased their growth mindset across that time frame (King, 2020)

- Inclusion of recent research indicating that engaging in a strategic mindset was critical in achieving goals (Chen & others, 2020). College students with a strategic mindset used more metacognitive strategies, had higher grade point averages, and made greater progress toward their professional, educational, and health goals.

- New content on a national experimental study conducted by David Yeager and his colleagues (Yeager, Dahl, & Dweck, 2018) in which a brief, online, direct-to-student growth mindset intervention increased the grade point averages of underachieving students and improved the challenge-seeking mental activity of higher-achieving students. In other recent research, the positive outcomes of the U.S. online growth mindset intervention were replicated with students in Norway (Bettinger & others, 2018; Rege & others, 2021).

- New content on how having a growth mindset has positive outcomes for many adolescents, but additional skills may be needed by some students. For example, research with 11- to 15-year-olds revealed that believing intelligence is malleable and capable of growth over time only predicted higher math engagement among students who also had metacognitive skills to reflect on and be aware of the learning process (Wang & others, 2021).

- New content on the importance of teachers giving wise feedback to students and communicating high expectations for student outcomes

- Inclusion of a recent study of high school students that found a program emphasizing the importance of self-monitoring and self-reward was effective in reducing procrastination (Efendi & Wagid, 2021)

- Coverage of a recent Chilean study that revealed adolescents' mathematics achievement was linked to parental expectations (Marine, Giaconi, & Ludivine, 2021)

- New description of a recent meta-analysis of 169 research studies that concluded changes in parental expectations predict changes in children's and adolescents' achievement (Pinquart & Ebeling, 2020). Also in this meta-analysis, transmitting positive expectations to children and adolescents and encouraging their academic engagement were more effective than active involvement in students' academic work, such as checking homework and staying in contact with teachers.

- New discussion of a recent study of 13- to 16-year-olds that found their positive appraisal of their academic goals and receiving support from peers were linked to their belief that their academic goals were achievable (Brumley & others, 2021)

- New main section, "Grit"

- Description of a recent study of adolescents in which a reciprocal relation of grit and growth mindset across two academic years was found, with each predicting increases in the other (Park & others, 2020)

- Inclusion of recent research that revealed a higher level of grit predicted better outcomes in postsecondary education that provided better student support, especially in achieving on-time graduation (Goyer, Walton, & Yeager, 2021)

- New list of self-assessment questions to determine the presence of grit (Clark & Malecki, 2019)

- Inclusion of a recent study of Mexican-origin parents and their adolescents in which parental expectations for academic achievement in seventh grade were linked to adolescents' ninth- and eleventh-grade educational expectations (Aceves & others, 2020). In the same study, seventh-grade students' educational expectations predicted their perceived academic competence in the ninth and eleventh grades.

- Discussion of a recent study with high school students in which a higher level of grit was linked to receiving greater support from parents and classmates (Clark & others, 2020). Also in this study, the association of grit and achievement was related to social support from teachers but not from parents and classmates.

- Description of recent research with ninth- and tenth-grade Latinx students in which natural mentoring quality was linked to the Latinx adolescents' development of a more positive ethnic identity, which in turn was associated with a stronger belief in the economic value of education (Sanchez & others, 2020)

- Inclusion of recent research involving the Big Sisters and Big Brothers mentoring program in which minimal difficulties in pairing mentors and youth, perceptions of youths' shared attributes with their mentors, mentor emotional engagement and support, and a longer mentoring relationship predicted higher-quality mentoring relationships (De Wit & others, 2020)

- Description of a recent meta-analysis that found higher math anxiety was linked to lower math achievement in adolescents (Barroso & others, 2021), with a stronger link for adolescents than for emerging adults

- Discussion of a recent study of college students in which self-handicapping was negatively related to academic achievement and flow was positively related to academic achievement (Adil, Ameer, & Ghayas, 2020)

- Inclusion of the recent 2019 Trends in International Mathematics and Science Study (TIMSS), a comparison of math and science achievement in a number of countries, with East Asian countries taking 19 of the top five spots in fourth- and eighth-grade science and fourth- and eighth-grade math. Singapore was number one in three of the four comparisons.

- New content on how stereotype threat can harm the motivation of ethnic minority students, including discussion of a recent study in which African American and Latinx 13- to 17-year-olds experienced higher stereotype threat in high school mathematics classrooms than their non-Latinx white peers (Seo & Lee, 2021)

- Update on the percentage of full-time and part-time students who are working while going to college (National Center for Education Statistics, 2020)

- New content on the major change in the context of work that was mandated by the onset of the coronavirus pandemic, in which huge numbers of employees abruptly moved from working in an office, school, or other context to working at home

- New data on the abrupt increase in the unemployment rate of recent U.S. college graduates following the onset of the COVID-19 pandemic (U.S. Department of Labor, 2020)

- New coverage of the highly positive job outlook for college graduates at the beginning of 2020, followed by a steep downward trend in March and April of 2020 with the onset of the coronavirus pandemic (NACE, 2020) and subsequently by an improved job outlook for college graduates in 2021

- New data on the decrease in average salaries for recent entry-level college graduates following the onset of the COVID-19 pandemic

- New discussion of the increased stress and health problems caused by unemployment (Puterman & others, 2020)

- Discussion of research indicating that alcohol-related death was elevated 0 to 5 and 11 to 20 years after the onset of unemployment (Junna, Moustgaard, & Martikainen, 2021)

- Updated information about the fastest-growing jobs anticipated through 2028 in the 2020–2021 *Occupational Outlook Handbook*

- Inclusion of a survey of 1,500 first-year college students that found 34 percent of students said their interest in a particular career had been influenced by their friends (GTI Media, 2020)

- Coverage of a recent national survey indicating that the student-to-counselor ratio in U.S. schools was 440 to 1 during the 2018–2019 school year, well above the recommended ratio of 250 to 1 (American School Counselor Association, 2020)
- Discussion of recent research indicating that a student-counselor ratio of 250 to 1 was linked to fewer student absences from school, lower school suspension rates, higher SAT scores, and higher graduation rates (Parzych & others, 2020)
- Coverage of a recent longitudinal study in which adolescents' gender stereotypes became much more traditional from between the ninth and eleventh grades (Starr & Simpkins, 2021). Also, parents became three times more likely to say that males are better at math/science than girls are. Adolescents' math/science gender stereotypes were related to their math/science identity, which in turn was linked to their STEM outcomes in high school.
- Discussion of a recent study of tenth-graders indicating that, in line with male math stereotypes, believing in "innate" math ability was associated with lower ability, self-concept, and intrinsic motivation in girls but not in boys (Heyder, Weidinger, & Steinmayr, 2021)
- Inclusion of a recent research review that concluded STEM secondary school interventions were more successful when they involved repeated or sustained engagement activities and when they combined an inclusive curriculum with teaching strategies that emphasized female role models (Prieto-Rodriguez, Sincock, & Blackmore, 2020)
- Description of recent research in which college students' perceptions of their STEM professors' mindset beliefs found that students who perceived their professors as endorsing a stronger fixed than growth mindset reported lower feelings of belonging in class, more negative affect, and greater imposter feelings, which in turn predicted more dropout intentions, less end-of-semester interest in STEM, and lower grades (Muenks & others, 2020)

Chapter 12: Culture

- Changes made based on feedback from leading experts Margaret Beale Spencer, Deborah Vietze, Sandra Graham, Elizabeth Trejos-Castillo, and Melinda Gonzalez-Bracken
- New chapter-opening vignette about two Latinx undocumented adolescents, their struggle with school when they came to the United States, and how a Latina counselor at their school helped them become better adjusted academically and socially
- Expanded coverage of what the term *culture* means, including content on how everyone has a culture, with multiple examples provided
- Description of a recent study that indicated mask use during the COVID-19 pandemic was higher in collectivist countries than in individualist countries (Lu, Jin, & English, 2021)
- Inclusion of a recent study of African American and non-Latinx white children and adolescents that found African American children and adolescents had higher levels of

individualism (Smith & others, 2020). Also in this study, adolescents with collectivist values were less likely to engage in delinquent behavior, while those with individualist values were less likely to behave in prosocial ways.
- Coverage of a recent study in which lower SES was linked to less cortical surface area in the brains of adolescents as well as less effective working memory (Judd & others, 2020). The SES factor most responsible for the lower level of brain functioning was less parental education.
- Inclusion of a recent Chinese study that found low family SES was linked to children's low academic achievement, with the most influential factor being lower parental academic involvement in children's schooling (Zhang & others, 2020)
- Description of a recent Australian study that revealed children and adolescents from lower-SES backgrounds were less likely to achieve a healthy physical fitness level than their higher-SES counterparts (Peralta & others, 2019)
- Discussion of a longitudinal study that found lower SES in childhood was linked to lower cognitive function and more cognitive decline in middle and late adulthood (Liu & Lachman, 2020)
- Inclusion of a recent Swedish study in which high-SES individuals were more likely than low-SES individuals to complete at least 12 years of schooling by 20 years of age (Lindberg & others, 2021)
- Coverage of a recent meta-analysis that concluded low SES is a meaningful contributor to the lower cognitive ability and achievement (Korous & others, 2021)
- Description of a recent Japanese study that indicated adolescents from low-SES families had more health-related problems than their counterparts in middle- or high-SES families (Okamoto, 2021)
- New discussion of excessive pressure to excel, especially in affluent contexts, being recently listed as one of the four main risk factors for adolescent mental health problems, with the other three being poverty, trauma, and discrimination (Luthar, Kumar, & Zilmer, 2020)
- New content on Suniya Luthar and her colleagues' (Luthar, Ebert, & Kumar, 2020) recent research emphasis on risk factors and outcomes for adolescents attending high-achieving schools
- Description of recent research on adolescents in high-achieving schools that revealed a link between students' engagement in social comparison and increased internalizing symptoms (Luthar & others, 2020)
- Updated data on the percentage of U.S. children and adolescents under the age of 18 living in poverty, which decreased to 16.2 percent in 2018 (Children's Defense Fund, 2020)
- Updated data on variations in ethnic minority adolescents living in poverty, figures that reflect a decrease in 2018 (Children's Defense Fund, 2020)
- Inclusion of a recent study that indicated higher poverty levels from 0 to 9 years of age were associated with reduced

inhibitory control in emerging adulthood (23 to 25 years of age) (Evans, Farah, & Hackman, 2021). Also contributing to this link was a lower level of maternal responsiveness during adolescence.

- Coverage of a recent study in which higher poverty levels from 0 to 9 years of age were linked to the following developmental trajectories from 9 to 24 years of age: (1) higher levels of internalizing problems that diminished more slowly with maturation; (2) higher levels of externalizing problems that increased more rapidly over time; (3) less task persistence; and (4) higher levels of chronic stress that increased more rapidly over time (Evans & De France, 2021)

- Updated data on the percentage of single-mother families living in poverty (34 percent), which was nearly six times the poverty rate of their married counterparts (6 percent) (U.S. Census Bureau, 2019)

- New commentary noting that despite the extensive challenges and difficulties that low-income families face, many low-income parents guide their children and adolescents to become resilient and flourish (Masten, 2021b; Masten & others, 2021). They rear children and adolescents who establish positive friendships; maintain good relationships with their parents, teachers, and other adults; make good grades in school; go to college; and pursue a positive career path (Wilson-Simmons, Jiang, & Aratani, 2017).

- New opening commentary in the section on ethnicity that emphasizes the importance of not using a deficit model in studying ethnic minority adolescents and recognizing not just stressors in their lives but also the positive aspects of their lives (Perrin & others, 2020)

- New content on the immigrant paradox and recent research supporting this concept (Zhang, Bo, & Lu, 2021)

- Coverage of a recent study in which immigrant children who were separated from their parents had a lower level of literacy and a higher level of psychological problems than those who migrated with their parents (Lu, He, & Brooks-Gunn, 2020). Also in this study, a protracted period of separation and prior undocumented status of parents further increased the children's disadvantages.

- New discussion of research conducted by Yoonsun Choi and her colleagues (Choi & Hahn, 2017; Choi & others, 2020a, b, c) on generational difference in Filipino Americans and Korean Americans, as well as younger-generation Asians' belief that older-generation Asians place too much emphasis on education

- New content on multi-ethnic/racial individuals and the discrimination they often encounter (Tan & others, 2019; Woo & others, 2020)

- New content on ethnic minority adolescents whose positive ethnic identity is related to positive outcomes (Umaña-Taylor & others, 2020)

- New description of a recent study in which Latinx adolescents showed enhanced resilience against discrimination encounters when they had more family ethnic socialization experiences and engaged in greater identity exploration and resolution (Martinez-Fuentes, Jager, & Umaña-Taylor, 2020)

- New discussion of a recent study of Latinx families that revealed parents' educational expectations for their seventh-graders was linked to their perceived academic competence as ninth-graders (Aceves & others, 2020)

- New description indicating that Latinx immigrants are increasingly graduating from college, reaching the highest level ever in 2018 (28 percent for those in the United States for 5 years or less, compared with only 11 percent in 2000 and 14 percent in 2014) (Noe-Bustamante, 2020)

- Inclusion of recent research that indicated familism was linked to Latinx youths' academic motivation (Stein & others, 2020)

- New discussion of a recent study in which Latinx adolescents showed enhanced resilience against discrimination encounters when they had more family ethnic socialization experiences and engaged in greater identity exploration and resolution (Martinez-Fuentes, Jager, & Umaña-Taylor, 2021)

- New main section, "Racism and Discrimination"

- New coverage of the Black Lives Matter movement and the George Floyd killing in Minneapolis as well as discussion of past and current racism and discrimination in the United States

- New content mentioning that a number of hate crimes involving physical attacks on Asian Americans occurred in 2021

- Inclusion of recent research with African American, Latinx, and Asian American college students that revealed stable discrimination by peers across three years and increased discrimination by professors during the same period (Toro & Hughes, 2020). Also in this study, discrimination by peers and professors was linked to lower grades, less likelihood of graduating on time, and less school satisfaction.

- New content acknowledging Native Americans' long exposure to discrimination and racism and noting that often this discrimination and racism has received inadequate attention (NETWORK, 2021)

- Inclusion of recent efforts by an increasing number of Native American activists at colleges and universities who are pushing their schools to do more to atone for past wrongs (Marcelo, 2021). The call for college and universities to increase their support for Native American students comes at a challenging time because the COVID-19 pandemic has made education difficult for Native American students, who already had the lowest college graduation rates of any U.S. ethnic group (Burki, 2021; Tsethlikai & others, 2020).

- New discussion of how to talk with children and adolescents about racism based on the Intentional Parenting for Equity and Justice program proposed by Diane Hughes and her colleagues (Hughes, Fisher, and Cabrera, 2020)

- Recommendation of a recent book that helps BIPOC parents talk with their children and youth about race: *The ABCs of Survival* (National Black Family Institute, 2021)

- Coverage of a recent study of 11,000 children in which screen time was linked to lower sleep duration, later sleep onset, and more sleep disturbances (Hisler & others, 2020)
- New commentary mentioning that the COVID-19 pandemic has led to excessive screen time among children and adolescents and that excessive screen time is associated with less exercise and more sedentary time (Nagata & others, 2020)
- Inclusion of recent research on 13- to 18-year-olds in the United States and the United Kingdom that revealed significant gender differences in the types of digital media they used (Twenge & Martin, 2020)
- Coverage of a recent research review that revealed engaging in video games involving physical activity (also called exergames) was effective in increasing adolescents' physical activity levels (Williams & Ayres, 2020)
- Description of a recent meta-analysis that found exposure to sexual media influenced sexual attitudes and behavior, with the effects greater for adolescents than emerging adults (Coyne & others, 2019). Also in this review, exposure to sexual media was linked to having more permissive sexual attitudes, engaging in riskier sexual behavior, and earlier sexual initiation. Further, the effects of exposure to sexual media were stronger for males than for females.
- Discussion of recent research with adolescents that found greater use of screen time was related to lower academic achievement in English and math (Hunter, Leatherdale, and Carson, 2018)
- Update on the percentage of adolescents who own a smartphone, which increased from 66 percent in 2009 to 95 percent in 2018 (Anderson & Jiang, 2018), with 96 percent of U.S. individuals 18 to 29 years of age owning a smartphone in 2021 (Pew Research Center, 2021)
- Inclusion of the results of a 2019 survey indicating the percentage of 18- to 24-year-olds using various social media platforms: YouTube (90 percent), Facebook (76 percent), Instagram (75 percent), and Snapchat (73 percent) (Perrin & Anderson, 2019)
- Discussion of a recent large-scale study of more than 32,000 15-year-olds in 37 countries that found problematic social media use and low social support were the best predictors of low life-satisfaction (Walsh & others, 2020)
- Description of a recent study of university students that concluded approximately 23 percent of the students can be classified as "smartphone addicted" (Randjelovic & others, 2021)
- Inclusion of recent research with 13- to 15- year-olds that revealed higher parental monitoring, authoritative parenting, and higher socioeconomic status were linked to reduced likelihood of excessive Internet use (Faltynkova & others, 2020)
- Coverage of recent research indicating that social media can be used as a positive coping strategy in dealing with anxious feelings during the COVID-19 pandemic (Cauberghe & others, 2021)

- Description of a recent study in which a higher level of social media use was associated with heavier drinking in adolescence (Vannucci & others, 2020)
- Inclusion of recent research with 13- and 15- year-olds that revealed heavy social media users had more sleep problems including later sleep onset and more difficulty in getting back to sleep after nighttime awakening (Scott & others, 2020)
- Coverage of a recent study that found spending more time daily on Instagram and Snapchat was linked to disordered eating behavior in adolescent girls (Wilksch & others, 2020)
- Discussion of recent research with 10-year-olds in which greater social media use was related to a greater desire for thinness (Sugimoto & others, 2020)
- Coverage of a recent study that indicated more time spent on social media was linked to depressed mood and anxiety (Thorisdottir & others, 2020)
- New commentary about the need to exercise caution when interpreting conclusions about links between social media and adolescent health because most research in this area is cross-sectional rather than longitudinal or experimental
- Inclusion of a new article in *Improving the Lives of Adolescents and Emerging Adults:* "Social Science-Based Pathways to Reduce Social Inequality in Youth Outcomes and Opportunities at Scale" (2021) by Andrew Nalani, Hirokazu Yoshikawa, and Prudence Carter that draws on initiatives from the social sciences to discuss six pathways that may create solutions for reducing youth inequality

Chapter 13: Problems in Adolescence and Emerging Adulthood

- Coverage of a recent study that found low self-regulation at 10 to 12 years of age predicted worse decision making in risky situations in adolescence, while higher self-regulation throughout childhood predicted better decision making in risky situations in adolescence (Weller & others, 2020)
- Updates based on more extensive research organizing the 40 key developmental assets originally proposed by the Search Institute into four main internal asset categories (academic engagement, positive identity, positive values, and social competencies) and four main external asset categories (support, mattering and belonging, boundaries, and extracurricular activities) that include a number of individual assets (Syvertsen, Scales, & Toomey, 2019)
- New description of the acute stress adolescents experience when negative life events such as disasters occur in their lives (Masten, Motti-Stefanidi, & Rahl, 2020)
- New content on how the COVID-19 pandemic has disrupted medical care for children and adolescents
- Inclusion of a recent study in which children and adolescents were 70 percent less likely to visit a general hospital emergency department after the COVID-19 pandemic emerged than before it appeared (Goldman & others, 2021)
- Inclusion of recent research in which negative life events were associated with increased adolescent depression, with

- social support and family cohesion serving as protective factors to reduce the association (Askeland & others, 2020)
- Coverage of a recent study that revealed higher-quality parent and peer relationships reduced the negative effects of stressful life events on adolescents (McMahon, Creaven, & Gallagher, 2020)
- New description of research with college students that found a high level of rumination increased the likelihood that negative life events were linked to suicidal ideation, while a low level of rumination deceased that link (Wang & others, 2020)
- New discussion of a recent research review of refugee children and adolescents that concluded their mental health problems were related to pre-migration individual risk factors (such as exposure to war-related trauma) and post-migration family factors (such as parental mental health and impaired parenting) (Scharpf & others, 2020)
- Inclusion of a recent study in which Latinx adolescents experienced more depressive symptoms when both the adolescents and their parents had a higher level of acculturative stress (Wu & others, 2020)
- Coverage of recent research on coping with academic challenges in which fathers' problem-focused suggestions (strategizing and help seeking, for example) were associated with adolescents' more effective coping (Tu, Cai, & Li, 2020)
- New discussion of a longitudinal study that revealed adolescents' avoidant coping preceded an increase in anxiety symptoms and disordered eating, while adolescents' depressive symptoms predicted later increases in maladaptive coping (Richardson & others, 2021)
- New description of recent research in which adolescents at high risk for depression experienced more stressors and used more disengagement coping strategies (Ozkul & Gunusen 2021)
- Inclusion of a recent study that focused on college students' coping during the COVID-19 pandemic and found the most frequently used coping strategies were maintaining positivity and staying connected (Waselewski, Waselewski, & Chang, 2020)
- New coverage of recent research that found when parents used effective coping strategies, so did their adolescents, suggesting a parent modeling effect (Liga & others, 2020)
- New discussion of a recent study of how adolescents coped with the death of a parent that revealed the following were helpful: family support, friend support, religion, exercising, and journal writing (Ludik & Greeff, 2021)
- Updated national data on the extent of illicit drug use by U.S. eighth-, tenth-, and twelfth-graders, which is now leveling off (Johnston & others, 2021; Miech & others, 2020)
- Updated national data documenting decreased alcohol use by U.S. adolescents (Johnston & others, 2021)
- Coverage of a longitudinal study that found binge drinking in the twelfth grade was linked to driving while impaired (DWI), riding with an impaired driver (RWI), blackouts, and riskier driving up to 4 years later (Vaca & others, 2020)
- Updated national data on the dramatic increase in U.S. adolescents who are vaping nicotine, which now far surpasses their rates of cigarette smoking (Johnston & others, 2021)
- Description of recent research indicating that not only is e-cigarette smoking a gateway to subsequent combustible cigarette smoking, but it is also a gateway to marijuana use (Fadus, Smith, & Squeglia, 2019)
- Updated coverage of marijuana use among U.S. adolescents, which has been increasing considerably in recent years (Johnston & others, 2021)
- New description of a recent study of 15- to 25-year-olds that indicated online peer group affiliation and belonging were linked to stimulant and opioid use (Miller & others, 2021)
- Updated data on binge drinking and extreme binge drinking in emerging adults (Schulenberg & others, 2020)
- Discussion of a recent study in which associating less often with prosocial peers predicted a rise in future adolescent drug use, while associating more often with prosocial peers led to a reduction in future adolescent drug use (Walters, 2020)
- Inclusion of recent research that linked higher-quality parenting to reduced rates if marijuana use by adolescents and associating with deviant peers to higher risk of alcohol, cigarette, and marijuana use (Greenwood & others, 2021)
- Description of a recent study in which a reduction in parental supervision in early adolescence was associated with increased marijuana use as well as increased frequency and quantity of alcohol use, with the link strongest at 14 to 15 years of age (Prins & others, 2021)
- Updated data on the percentage of children and youth who have conduct disorder (up to 10 percent) and new data indicating that approximately 25 percent of these individuals subsequently develop antisocial personality disorder (Rubin, 2020)
- Updated data on the percentage of adolescents who are classified as juvenile delinquents (Hockenberry & Puzzanchera, 2019)
- Coverage of a British longitudinal study of males from 8 to 61 years of age in which the childhood factors that best predicted which individuals would have criminal careers lasting at least 20 years were harsh discipline, poor parental supervision, parental conflict, and a father who had been convicted of crimes (Farrington, 2020)
- Description of the longitudinal Pittsburgh Youth Study that revealed the adolescent factors that best predicted which boys were most likely to be in the worst category of criminal offenders through their thirties were frequency of sexual activity, school problems, and having friends who were a bad influence (Ahonen & others, 2020)
- Discussion of a recent study that found neighborhood poverty was linked to delinquency in adolescence, especially through maternal stress and adverse childhood experiences (Wang, Choi, & Shin, 2020)
- Description of a recent study that revealed parental monitoring was a protective factor against delinquency for both boys

- and girls but had a stronger effect for girls than boys (Liu & Miller, 2020)
- Coverage of a recent study in which having a best friend who was a delinquent was linked to a higher probability of adolescents becoming delinquents themselves (Levey & others, 2019)
- Inclusion of a recent research review that linked juvenile delinquency to a lack of academic success and having a learning disability (Grigorenko & others, 2019)
- Discussion of a recent study in which students who had been suspended from school for the first time, compared with their peers who had not been suspended, were less likely to have earned a high school diploma or a bachelor's degree 12 years after the suspension and were more likely to have been arrested and to have been on probation (Rosenbaum, 2020)
- Description of a recent study in rural China that found low self-control was linked to delinquent behavior in adolescents (Jiang, Chen, & Zhuo, 2020)
- New discussion of a Chinese study in which adolescents showed more depressive symptoms after the appearance of COVID-19, but engaging in more physical activity during the quarantine helped to buffer the association between the pandemic and depressive symptoms (Ren & others, 2021)
- Description of recent research in which interpersonal stress was linked to increased depression in adolescent girls (Slavich & others, 2020)
- Coverage of a recent meta-analysis that concluded experiencing early life stress predicted an increased risk for major depressive disorder prior to 18 years of age (LeMoult & others, 2020)
- Coverage of a research analysis that found women were twice as likely as men to develop depression, with this difference linked to a sharp increase in girls' depression in mid-adolescence (Bone, Lewis, & Lewis, 2020)
- Inclusion of a recent research review that concluded adolescents are very poor at recognizing depression, more likely to seek help from informal rather than professional sources, and tend to attach stigma to depression (Singh, Zaki, & Farid, 2019)
- Discussion of a longitudinal study that found a majority of adolescents who had a major depressive episode were likely to experience a recurrence of depression 15 years later (Alaie & others, 2019). In addition, adolescent depression was associated with other mental health problems, low educational attainment, and problems in intimate relationships 15 years later.
- Coverage of recent research that found adolescents whose parents had experienced depression were more likely to experience depression themselves (Chang & Fu, 2020). Also in this study, a higher level of adolescent self-esteem weakened the link between parental depression and adolescent depression.
- Description of a recent study in which parental emotional support was linked to a lower incidence of depressive symptoms in adolescents (Rasing & others, 2020)

- Discussion of recent research that revealed adolescent girls with few friends were more likely to experience depression than adolescent girls with two or more very close friends (Rodrigues & others, 2020)
- Inclusion of a recent research review by the U.S. Agency for Healthcare Research and Quality (Viswanathan & others, 2020) assessing the effectiveness of various treatments for adolescent depression, including cognitive behavior therapy, family therapy, and drug therapy
- New content based on a national study of 10- to 19-year-olds indicating that suicide rates for males and females have increased since 2007, with a disproportionate, steeper increase for 10- to 14-year-old females (Ruch & others, 2019)
- New content noting that suicide has replaced homicide as the second leading cause of death in adolescence (National Center for Health Statistics, 2020)
- Updated data on the percentage of U.S. adolescents who seriously consider suicide each year and attempt suicide each year, including gender and ethnicity figures (Underwood & others, 2020)
- Description of a recent national study indicating the rate at which girls 12 to 17 years of age visited an emergency department for suspected suicide attempts increased 51 percent in February and March of 2021 compared with the same time period in 2019, prior to the COVID-19 pandemic. Among adolescent boys in this time frame, suspected suicide attempts resulting in emergency room visits increased by 4 percent (Yard & others, 2021).
- Discussion of a recent study of adolescents in Hong Kong that found suicide attempts were linked to having experienced child abuse (Wong & others, 2020)
- Inclusion of a recent study of 9- to 10-year-olds in which family conflict was linked to increased suicidal ideation and low parental monitoring was linked to suicidal ideation and attempts (DeVille & others, 2020)
- Discussion of a recent study that revealed harsh parental disciplinary practices were associated with increased suicidal ideation in adolescents (Kingsbury & others, 2020)
- Description of recent research with more than 290,000 adolescents across a four-year period that revealed the highest stressor leading to suicidal ideation was peer conflict, followed by family circumstances such as conflict with parents (Kim, 2021)
- Inclusion of a recent research review that described the most significant risk factors for adolescent suicide and bullying (Cuesta & others, 2021)
- Coverage of a recent study in which combined school difficulties (academic failure and inappropriate behavior) were associated with higher risk of suicide (Ligier & others, 2020)
- Discussion of a recent study that found in 32 of 38 countries assessed, early sexual intercourse (at 12 to 15 years of

age) was linked to increased suicide attempts, and having sexual intercourse with multiple partners increased the risk further (Smith & others, 2020)

- Description of a recent research analysis that revealed the main factor in adolescent suicidal deaths was the occurrence of recent stressful life events (Werbart Tomblom & others, 2020)
- Discussion of a recent study in which a higher level of parental monitoring was linked to adolescents having a healthier diet and reduced likelihood of being overweight (Kim & others, 2019)
- Coverage of a recent research meta-analysis that concluded being overweight was associated with low self-esteem and body dissatisfaction (Moradi & others, 2021)
- Description of recent research with 10- to 17-year-olds in which obesity was linked to poor academic and coping skills (Gill & others, 2021)
- Inclusion of recent research indicating that overweight adolescents were less likely than normal-weight adolescents to be nominated as a romantic interest, as popular, and as admired (Jacobs & others, 2020)

- Description of a recent study in which an after-school exercise program reduced the obesity risk of adolescent one year after the intervention (Glabska & others, 2019)
- Coverage of a recent meta-analysis that concluded anorexics and bulimics engage in maladaptive perfectionism (Norris, Gleaves, & Hutchinson, 2020)
- Inclusion of a longitudinal study on an intervention with young children from low-income families in Head Start that involved a social-emotional learning program and an interactive reading program, resulting in significant reductions in conduct problems, emotional symptoms, and peer problems compared with a control group of children who did not receive the intervention (Bierman & others, 2021)
- Coverage of recent research that found the Fast Track intervention decreased the probability of suicidal ideation and hazardous drinking in adolescence and emerging adulthood as well as opioid use in emerging adulthood (Godwin & the Conduct Problems Prevention Research Group, 2020)
- Update on the National Longitudinal Study of Adolescent to Adult Health (2021) that recently completed its fifth wave of data collection in 2016 to 2018

Acknowledgments

I very much appreciate the support and guidance provided to me by many people at McGraw Hill. Ryan Treat, Senior Portfolio Manager for Psychology, has provided excellent guidance, vision, and direction for this book. Vicki Malinee has contributed considerable expertise in coordinating many aspects of the editorial process. Janet Tilden again did an outstanding job as the book's copy editor. Mary Powers did a terrific job in coordinating the book's production. Jennifer Blankenship provided me with excellent choices of new photographs for this edition. Dawn Groundwater, Product Development Manager, did excellent work on various aspects of the book's development, technology, and learning systems. Special thanks also go to Olivia Kaiser for her outstanding work in marketing *Adolescence*.

I also want to thank my wife, Mary Jo, our children, Tracy and Jennifer, and our grandchildren, Jordan, Alex, and Luke, for their wonderful contributions to my life and for helping me to better understand the marvels, challenges, and adaptations that adolescents and emerging adults experience.

QUEST: JOURNEY THROUGH THE LIFESPAN BOARD OF ADVISORS AND SUBJECT MATTER EXPERTS

Admiration and appreciation to the following experts who have devoted a significant portion of their time and expertise to creating the first of its kind learning game for Developmental Psychology: Cheri Kittrell, *State College of Florida*; Brandy Young, *Cypress College*; Becky Howell, *Forsyth Technical College*; Gabby Principe, *College of Charleston*; Karen Schrier Shaenfield, *Marist College*; Steven Prunier, *Ivy Tech*; Amy Kolak, *College of Charleston*; Kathleen Hughes Stellmach, *Pasco-Hernando State College*; Lisa Fozio-Thielk, *Waubonsee Community College*; Tricia Wessel-Blaski, *University of Wisconsin-Milwaukee, Washington County*; Margot Underwood, *Joliet Junior College*; Claire Rubman, *Suffolk County Community College*; Alissa Knowles, *University of California-Irvine*; Cortney Simmons, *University of California-Irvine*; Kelli Dunlap; Level Access-WCAG Accessibility Partners.

EXPERT CONSULTANTS

As I develop a new edition, I consult with leading experts in their respective areas of adolescent development. Their invaluable feedback ensures that the latest research, knowledge, and perspectives are presented throughout the text. Their willingness to devote their time and expertise to this endeavor is greatly appreciated. The Expert Consultants who contributed to this edition, along with their biographies and commentary, can be found on pages xxi–xxiv.

Special thanks also go to Germine Awad, *University of Texas-Austin*; Kevin Cokley, *University of Texas-Austin*; and Sabra Katz-Wise, *Harvard University*.

REVIEWERS

With my appreciation, thank you to those reviewers who provided valuable guidance on issues of inclusion and diversity: Diane Byrd, *Fort Valley State University*; Russ Berger, *Rowan University*; Nancy Blum, *California State University-Northridge*; Melinda Gonzales-Backen, *Florida State University*; Sandra Jemison, *Stillman College*; Theresa Kearns-Cooper, *Jackson State University*; Bob Luckett, *South Texas College*; Natasha Otto, *Morgan State University*; Debra Roberts, *Howard University*; and Mary Shelton, *Tennessee State University*.

I owe a special debt of gratitude to the reviewers who have provided detailed feedback on *Adolescence* over the years.

Alice Alexander, *Old Dominion University*; **Sandy Arntz,** *Northern Illinois University*; **Frank Ascione,** *Utah State University*; **Carole Beale,** *University of Massachusetts*; **Luciane A. Berg,** *Southern Utah University*; **David K. Bernhardt,** *Carleton University*; **Fredda Blanchard-Fields,** *Louisiana State University*; **Kristi Blankenship,** *University of Tennessee*; **Belinda Blevins-Knabe,** *University of Arkansas*; **Robert Bornstein,** *Miami University*; **Ioakim Boutakidis,** *Fullerton State University*; **Geraldine Brookins,** *University of Minnesota*; **Jane Brower,** *University of Tennessee–Chattanooga*; **Deborah Brown,** *Friends University*; **Janine Buckner,** *Seton Hall University*; **Nancy Busch-Rossnagel,** *Fordham University*; **James I. Byrd,** *University of Wisconsin–Stout*; **Cheryl A. Camenzuli,** *Hofstra University*; **Elaine Cassel,** *Marymount University*; **Mark Chapell,** *Rowan University*; **Stephanie M. Clancy,** *Southern Illinois University–Carbondale*; **Ronald K. Craig,** *Cincinnati State College*; **Gary Creasey,** *Illinois State University*; **Laura Crosetti,** *Monroe Community College*; **Rita Curl,** *Minot State University*; **Peggy A. DeCooke,** *Northern Illinois University*; **Nancy Defates-Densch,** *Northern Illinois University*; **Gypsy Denzine,** *Northern Arizona University*; **Imma Destefanis,** *Boston College*; **R. Daniel DiSalvi,** *Kean College*; **James A. Doyle,** *Roane State Community College*; **Mark W. Durm,** *Athens State University*; **Laura Duvall,** *Heartland Community College*; **Kimberly DuVall-Early,** *James Madison University*; **Celina Echols,** *Southern Louisiana State University*; **Richard M. Ehlenz,** *Lakewood Community College*; **Gene Elliot,** *Glassboro State University*; **Steve Ellyson,** *Youngstown State University*; **Robert Enright,** *University of Wisconsin–Madison*; **Jennifer Fager,** *Western Michigan University*; **Lisa Farkas,** *Rowan University*; **Douglas Fife,** *Plymouth State College*; **Urminda Firlan,** *Michigan State University*; **Leslie Fisher,** *Cleveland State University*; **Martin E. Ford,** *Stanford University*; **Gregory T. Fouts,** *University of Calgary*; **Mary Fraser,** *San Jose State University*; **Rick Froman,** *John Brown University*; **Charles Fry,** *University of Virginia*; **Anne R. Gayles-Felton,** *Florida A&M University*; **Margaret J. Gill,** *Kutztown University*; **Sam Givham,** *Mississippi State University*; **William Gnagey,** *Illinois State University*; **Page Goodwin,** *Western Illinois University*; **Nicole Graves,** *South Dakota State University*; **B. Jo Hailey,** *University of Southern Mississippi*; **Dick E. Hammond,** *Southwest Texas State University*; **Sam Hardy,** *Brigham Young University*; **Frances Harnick,** *University of New Mexico, Indian Children's Program, and Lovelace-Bataan Pediatric Clinic*; **Dan Houlihan,** *Minnesota State University*; **Kim Hyatt,** *Weber State University*; **June V. Irving,** *Ball State University*; **Beverly Jennings,** *University of Colorado at Denver*; **Joline Jones,** *Worcester State College*; **Linda Juang,** *San Francisco State University*; **Alfred L. Karlson,** *University of Massachusetts–Amherst*; **Lynn F. Katz,** *University of Pittsburgh*; **Carolyn Kaufman,** *Columbus State Community College*; **Michelle Kelley,** *Old Dominion University*; **Marguerite D. Kermis,** *Canisius College*; **Roger Kobak,** *University of Delaware*; **Tara Kuther,** *Western Connecticut State University*; **Emmett C. Lampkin,** *Scott Community College*; **Royal Louis Lange,** *Ellsworth Community Center*;

Philip Langer, *University of Colorado;* Heidi Legg-Burross, *University of Arizona;* Tanya Letourneau, *Delaware County College;* Neal E. Lipsitz, *Boston College;* Nancy Lobb, *Alvin Community College;* Daniel Lynch, *University of Wisconsin–Oshkosh;* Joseph G. Marrone, *Siena College;* Ann McCabe, *University of Windsor;* Susan McCammon, *East Carolina University;* Sherri McCarthy-Tucker, *Northern Arizona University;* E. L. McGarry, *California State University–Fullerton;* D. Rush McQueen, *Auburn University;* Sean Meegan, *Western Illinois University;* Jessica Miller, *Mesa State College;* John J. Mirich, *Metropolitan State College;* John J. Mitchell, *University of Alberta;* Suzanne F. Morrow, *Old Dominion University;* Lloyd D. Noppe, *University of Wisconsin–Green Bay;* Delores Vantrice Oates, *Texas Southern University;* Daniel Offer, *University of Michigan;* Shana Pack, *Western Kentucky University;* Michelle Paludi, *Michelle Paludi & Associates;* Joycelyn G. Parish, *Kansas State University;* Ian Payton, *Bethune-Cookman College;* Andrew Peiser, *Mercy College;* Peggy G. Perkins, *University of Nevada;* Richard Pisacreta, *Ferris State University;* Gayle Reed, *University of Wisconsin–Madison;* James D. Reid, *Washington University;* Vicki Ritts, *St. Louis Community College;* Anne Robertson, *University of Wisconsin–Milwaukee;* Melinda Russell-Stamp, *Weber State University;* Traci Sachteleben, *Southwestern Illinois College;* Tonie E. Santmire, *University of Nebraska;* Douglas Sawin, *University of Texas;* Mary Schumann, *George Mason University;* Paul Schwartz, *Mount St. Mary College;* Jane Sheldon, *University of Michigan–Dearborn;* Kim Shifren, *Towson University;* Susan Shonk, *State University of New York;* Ken Springer, *Southern Methodist University;* Ruby Takanishi, *Foundation for Child Development;* Patti Tolar, *University of Houston;* Vern Tyler, *Western Washington University;* Rhoda Unger, *Montclair State College;* Angela Vaughn, *Wesley College;* Elizabeth Vozzola, *Saint Joseph's College;* Barry Wagner, *Catholic University of America;* Rob Weisskrich, *California State University–Fullerton;* Deborah Welsh, *University of Tennessee;* Andrea Wesley, *University of Southern Mississippi;* Wanda Willard, *State University of New York–Oswego;* Carolyn L. Williams, *University of Minnesota;* Shelli Wynants, *California State University.*

chapter 1

INTRODUCTION

chapter **outline**

1 The Historical Perspective

Learning Goal 1 Describe historical perspectives on adolescence.

Early History

The Twentieth and Twenty-First Centuries

Stereotyping of Adolescents

A Positive View of Adolescence

2 Today's Adolescents in the United States and Around the World

Learning Goal 2 Discuss the experiences of adolescents in the United States and around the world.

Adolescents in the United States

The Global Perspective

3 The Nature of Development

Learning Goal 3 Summarize the developmental processes, periods, transitions, and issues related to adolescence.

Processes and Periods

Developmental Transitions

Developmental Issues

4 The Science of Adolescent Development

Learning Goal 4 Characterize the science of adolescent development.

Science and the Scientific Method

Theories of Adolescent Development

Research in Adolescent Development

kali9/Getty Images

Jeffrey Dahmer's senior portrait in high school.
AP Images

Alice Walker.
Monica Morgan/WireImage/Getty Images

Dr. Michael Maddaus counsels a troubled youth.
Courtesy of Dr. Michael Maddaus

Jeffrey Dahmer had a troubled childhood and adolescence. His parents constantly bickered before they divorced. His mother had emotional problems and doted on his younger brother, and Jeffrey felt that his father neglected him. In addition, he was sexually abused by another boy when he was 8 years old. But the vast majority of people who suffer through a painful childhood and adolescence do not become serial killers as Dahmer did. Dahmer murdered his first victim in 1978 with a barbell and went on to kill 16 other individuals before being caught and sentenced to 15 life terms in prison.

A decade before Dahmer's first murder, Alice Walker, who would later win a Pulitzer Prize for her book *The Color Purple,* spent her days battling racism in Mississippi. Born the eighth child of Georgia sharecroppers, Walker knew the brutal effects of poverty. Despite the challenges facing her, she went on to become an award-winning novelist. Walker writes about people who, as she puts it, "make it, who come out of nothing. People who triumph."

Consider also the transformative life of Michael Maddaus (Broderick, 2003; Masten, Obradovic, & Burt, 2006). During his childhood and adolescence in Minneapolis, his mother drank heavily and his stepfather abused him. He coped by spending most of his time on the streets. Michael was arrested more than 20 times for delinquency, frequently placed in detention centers, and rarely attended school. At 17 he joined the Navy, and the experience helped him to gain self-discipline and hope. After his brief stint in the Navy, he completed a GED and began taking community college classes. However, in emerging adulthood he continued to have setbacks with drugs and alcohol. A defining moment came when he delivered furniture to a surgeon's home. The surgeon became interested in helping Michael, and his mentorship led Michael to volunteer at a rehabilitation center and then to get a job with a neurosurgeon. Eventually he obtained his undergraduate degree, went to medical school, got married, and started a family. Today, Michael Maddaus is a successful surgeon. One of his most gratifying volunteer activities is telling his story to troubled youth.

What leads an adolescent like Jeffrey Dahmer to commit brutal acts of violence and another adolescent, like Alice Walker, to turn poverty and trauma into a rich literary harvest? How can we attempt to explain how someone like Michael Maddaus can turn a childhood and adolescence shattered by abuse and delinquency into a career as a successful surgeon while another person seems to come unhinged by life's minor hassles? Why is it that some adolescents are whirlwinds—successful in school, surrounded by a network of friends, and full of energy—whereas others hang out on the sidelines, mere spectators of life? If you have ever wondered what makes adolescents tick, you have asked yourself the central question we will explore here.

preview

This edition of *Adolescence* is a window into the nature of adolescent development—your own and that of every other human being who experiences this stage of life's journey. In this first chapter, you will read about the history of the field of adolescent development, the characteristics of today's adolescents in the United States and the rest of the world, and the ways in which adolescents develop.

1 The Historical Perspective

LG1 Describe historical perspectives on adolescence.

| Early History | The Twentieth and Twenty-First Centuries | Stereotyping of Adolescents | A Positive View of Adolescence |

What have the portraits of adolescence been like at different points in history? When did the scientific study of adolescence begin?

EARLY HISTORY

In early Greece, the philosophers Plato and Aristotle both commented about the nature of youth. According to Plato (fourth century BC), reasoning first appears in adolescence. Plato thought that children should spend their time in sports and music, whereas adolescents should study science and mathematics.

Aristotle (fourth century BC) argued that the most important aspect of adolescence is the ability to choose, and that self-determination is a hallmark of maturity. Aristotle's emphasis on the development of self-determination is not unlike some contemporary views that see independence, identity, and career choice as the key themes of adolescence. Aristotle also recognized adolescents' egocentrism, commenting once that adolescents think they know everything and are quite sure about it.

In the Middle Ages, children and adolescents were viewed as miniature adults and were subjected to harsh discipline. In the eighteenth century, French philosopher Jean-Jacques Rousseau offered a more enlightened view of adolescence, restoring the belief that being a child or an adolescent is not the same as being an adult. Like Plato, Rousseau thought that reasoning develops in adolescence. He said that curiosity should especially be encouraged in the education of 12- to 15-year-olds. Rousseau argued that from 15 to 20 years of age individuals mature emotionally and their selfishness is replaced by an interest in others. Thus, Rousseau concluded that development has distinct phases. But his ideas were speculative; not until the beginning of the twentieth century did the scientific exploration of adolescence begin.

THE TWENTIETH AND TWENTY-FIRST CENTURIES

The end of the nineteenth century and the early part of the twentieth century saw the invention of the concept we now call adolescence. Between 1890 and 1920, a number of psychologists, urban reformers, educators, youth workers, and counselors began to develop the concept. At this time, young people, especially boys, were increasingly viewed as passive and vulnerable—qualities previously associated only with adolescent females. G. Stanley Hall's book on adolescence would play a major role in restructuring thinking about adolescence.

G. Stanley Hall's Storm-and-Stress View   G. Stanley Hall (1844–1924) pioneered the scientific study of adolescence. In 1904, Hall published his ideas in a two-volume set: *Adolescence.* Hall was strongly influenced by Charles Darwin, the famous evolutionary theorist. Applying Darwin's view to the study of adolescent development, Hall proposed that development is controlled primarily by biological factors.

G. Stanley Hall, father of the scientific study of adolescence.
Bettmann/Getty Images

Anthropologist Margaret Mead in the Samoan Islands. *How does Mead's view of adolescence differ from G. Stanley Hall's?*
ASSOCIATED PRESS/AP Images

The **storm-and-stress view** is Hall's concept that adolescence is a turbulent time charged with conflict and mood swings. In his view, adolescents' thoughts, feelings, and actions oscillate between conceit and humility, good intentions and temptation, happiness and sadness. An adolescent might be nasty to a peer one moment and kind the next moment; in need of privacy one moment but seconds later want companionship.

Hall was a giant in the field of adolescent development. His theorizing, systematizing, and questioning went beyond mere speculation and philosophizing. Indeed, we owe the beginnings of the scientific study of adolescence to Hall.

Margaret Mead's Sociocultural View of Adolescence

Anthropologist Margaret Mead (1928) studied adolescents on the South Sea island of Samoa. She concluded that the basic nature of adolescence is not biological, as Hall envisioned, but rather sociocultural. In cultures that provide a smooth, gradual transition from childhood to adulthood, which is the way adolescence is handled in Samoa, she found little storm and stress associated with the period. Mead's observations of Samoan adolescents revealed instead that their lives were relatively free of turmoil. Mead concluded that a relatively stress-free adolescence is the norm in cultures that allow adolescents to observe sexual relations, see babies born, regard death as natural, do important work, engage in sex play, and know clearly what their adult roles will be. However, in cultures like the United States, in which children are considered very different from adults and adolescents are restricted from full participation in society, the period is more likely to be stressful.

More than half a century after Mead's Samoan findings were published, her work was criticized as biased and error-prone (Freeman, 1983). Current criticism states that Samoan adolescence is more stressful than Mead suggested and that delinquency appears among Samoan adolescents just as it does among Western adolescents. Despite the controversy over Mead's findings, some researchers and analysts have defended Mead's work (Coffman, 2021; Holmes, 1987).

The Inventionist View

Although adolescence has a biological base, as G. Stanley Hall argued, it also has a sociocultural base, as Margaret Mead maintained. Indeed, sociohistorical conditions contributed to the emergence of the concept of adolescence. According to the **inventionist view,** adolescence is a sociohistorical creation. Especially important in this view of adolescence are the sociohistorical circumstances at the beginning of the twentieth century, a time when legislation was enacted that ensured the dependency of youth and made their move into the economic sphere more manageable. These sociohistorical circumstances included a decline in apprenticeship; increased mechanization during the Industrial Revolution, which raised the level of skill required of laborers and necessitated a specialized division of labor; the separation of work and home; age-graded schools; urbanization; the appearance of youth groups such as the YMCA and the Boy Scouts; and the writings of G. Stanley Hall.

Schools, work, and economics are important dimensions of the inventionist view of adolescence. Some scholars argue that the concept of adolescence was invented mainly as a by-product of the movement to create a system of compulsory public education. In this view, the function of secondary schools is to transmit intellectual skills to youth. However, other scholars argue that the primary purpose of secondary schools is to deploy youth within the economic sphere. In this view, American society conferred the status of adolescence on youth through child-saving legislation (Lapsley, Enright, & Serlin, 1985).

Historians now call the period between 1890 and 1920 the "age of adolescence." In this period, lawmakers enacted a great deal of compulsory legislation aimed at youth. In virtually every state, they passed laws that excluded youth from most employment and required them to attend secondary school. Much of this legislation included extensive enforcement provisions. Two clear changes resulted from this legislation: decreased employment and increased school attendance among youth. From 1910 to 1930, the number of 10- to 15-year-olds who were gainfully employed dropped about 75 percent. In addition, between 1900 and 1930 the number of high school graduates increased substantially. Approximately 600 percent more individuals graduated from high school in 1930 than in 1900. Let's take a closer look at how conceptions of adolescence and experiences of adolescents changed with the changing times of the twentieth century and beyond.

storm-and-stress view G. Stanley Hall's concept that adolescence is a turbulent time charged with conflict and mood swings.

inventionist view The view that adolescence is a sociohistorical creation. Especially important in this view are the sociohistorical circumstances at the beginning of the twentieth century, a time when legislation was enacted that ensured the dependency of youth and made their move into the economic sphere more manageable.

Further Changes in the Twentieth Century and the Twenty-First Century

Discussing historical changes in the way individuals have experienced adolescence involves focusing on changes in generations. A *cohort* is a group of people who are born at a similar point in history and share similar experiences as a result. For example, individuals who experienced the Great Depression as teenagers are likely to differ from their counterparts who were teenagers in the 1950s during the optimistic aftermath of World War II. In discussing and conducting research on such historical variations, the term **cohort effects** is used, which refers to influences attributed to a person's year of birth, era, or generation, but not to actual chronological age (Orri & others, 2021; Salway & others, 2021; Schaie, 2016). Let's now explore potential cohort effects on the development of adolescents and emerging adults in the last half of the twentieth century and the early part of the twenty-first century.

1950s to 1970s By 1950, the developmental period referred to as adolescence had come of age. It encompassed not only physical and social identities but a legal identity as well, for every state had developed special laws for youth between the ages of 16 and 20. Getting a college degree—the key to a good job—was on the minds of many adolescents during the 1950s, as was getting married, starting a family, and settling down to the life of luxury depicted in television commercials.

Although adolescents' pursuit of higher education continued into the 1960s, many African American adolescents not only were denied a college education but received an inferior secondary education as well. Ethnic conflicts in the form of riots and sit-ins became pervasive, and college-age adolescents were among the most vocal participants.

Political protests reached a peak in the late 1960s and early 1970s when millions of adolescents reacted violently to what they saw as the United States' immoral participation in the Vietnam War. By the mid-1970s, the radical protests of adolescents began to abate along with U.S. involvement in Vietnam. Political activism was largely replaced by increased concern for upward mobility through achievement in high school, college, or vocational training. Material interests began to dominate adolescents' motives again, while ideological challenges to social institutions began to recede.

During the 1970s the feminist movement changed both the description and the study of adolescence. In earlier years, descriptions of adolescence had pertained more to males than to females. The dual family and career objectives that female adolescents have today were largely unknown to female adolescents of the 1890s and early 1900s.

Millennials In recent years, generations have been given labels by the popular culture. One label is **millennials,** which applies to the generation born after 1980—the first to come of age and enter emerging adulthood in the new millennium. Two characteristics of millennials stand out: (1) their connection to technology, and (2) their ethnicity.

The dramatic increase in the use of media and information/communication devices has led to the use of the term *screen time*, which encompasses the total amount of time individuals spend watching television or DVDs, playing video games, and using computers or mobile media such as smartphones.

Because their ethnic diversity is greater than that of prior generations, many millennial adolescents and emerging adults are more tolerant and open-minded than their counterparts in previous generations. One survey indicated that 60 percent of millennial adolescents say their friends include people from diverse ethnic groups (Teenage Research Unlimited, 2004). Another survey found that 60 percent of U.S. 18- to 29-year-olds had dated someone from a different ethnic group (Jones, 2005).

Until recently, the youngest generation was labeled *millennials.* However, the Pew Research Center, which has periodically assessed generational trends in recent decades, now describes millennials as anyone born between 1981 and 1996, with anyone born in 1997 or later as part of a new generation dubbed *generation Z* (Dimock, 2019). The oldest members of this new generation turned 23 in 2020, while the oldest millennials turned 40 in 2020. What characterizes this new generation? They are even more technologically sophisticated and ethnically diverse than millennials. These young people have technological devices that are always available and always on; they are immersed in social media; and they tend to communicate with others online and through mobile devices far more than in person (Flores Vizcaya-Moreno & Perez-Canaveras, 2021). Also, generation Z is the best-educated

developmental **connection**
Technology
When media multitasking is taken into account, 11- to 14-year-olds spend an average of almost 12 hours exposed to media per day. Connect to "Culture."

cohort effects Characteristics related to a person's year of birth, era, or generation rather than to his or her actual chronological age.

millennials The generation born after 1980, the first to come of age and enter emerging adulthood in the new millennium. Two characteristics of millennials stand out: (1) their connection to technology, and (2) their ethnic diversity.

How is technology changing the lives of adolescents?
Monkey Business Images/Shutterstock

generation yet: they are more likely to go to college and to have a college-educated parent than millennials are.

Although the majority of adolescents are navigating the passage from childhood to adulthood in a competent manner, far too many are not (Mazza & Miller, 2021). Laurence Steinberg (2014), in a book titled *Age of Opportunity*, called attention to some of the problems today's American adolescents are experiencing: U.S. adolescents' achievement in a number of academic areas, such as math and science, is far lower than that of their counterparts in many other countries, especially those in Asia; the United States no longer has the highest college graduation rate and recently was not even in the top ten; approximately 20 percent of U.S. high school seniors engage in alcohol abuse; almost one-third of U.S. adolescent girls become pregnant by the age of 20; and adolescent obesity has increased threefold in recent decades. As we discuss adolescent development in other chapters, we will address problems such as these in much greater detail.

So far in this chapter we have considered the important sociohistorical circumstances surrounding the development of the concept of adolescence, evaluated how society has viewed adolescents at different points in history, and examined several major changes that characterize the current generation of adolescents. Next, we will explore why it is important to exercise caution in generalizing about the adolescents of any era.

STEREOTYPING OF ADOLESCENTS

A **stereotype** is a generalization that reflects our impressions and beliefs about a broad category of people. All stereotypes carry an image of what the typical member of a specific group is like. Once we assign a stereotype, it is difficult to abandon it, even in the face of contradictory evidence.

Stereotypes of adolescents are plentiful: "They say they want a job, but when they get one, they don't want to work." "They are all lazy." "All they think about is sex." "They are all into drugs, every last one of them." "Kids today don't have the moral fiber of my generation." "The problem with adolescents today is that they all have it too easy." "They are so self-centered." Indeed, during most of the twentieth century and the first few decades of the twenty-first century, adolescents have been portrayed as abnormal and deviant rather than normal and nondeviant. Consider Hall's image of storm and stress. Consider, too, media portrayals of adolescents as rebellious, conflicted, faddish, delinquent, and self-centered. Especially distressing is that, when given evidence of youths' positive accomplishments—that a majority of adolescents participate in community service, for example—many adults either deny the facts or say that these adolescents must be exceptions.

Stereotyping of adolescents is so widespread that adolescence researcher Joseph Adelson (1979) coined the term **adolescent generalization gap,** which refers to generalizations that are based on information about a limited, often highly visible group of adolescents. Some adolescents develop confidence in their abilities despite negative stereotypes about them. And some individuals (like Alice Walker and Michael Maddaus, discussed at the beginning of this chapter), triumph over poverty, abuse, and other adversities.

A POSITIVE VIEW OF ADOLESCENCE

The negative stereotyping of adolescents is overdrawn (Paricio & others, 2020). In a cross-cultural study, Daniel Offer and his colleagues (1988) found no support for such a negative view. The researchers assessed the self-images of adolescents around the world—in the United States, Australia, Bangladesh, Hungary, Israel, Italy, Japan, Taiwan, Turkey, and West Germany—and discovered that at least 73 percent of the adolescents had a positive self-image. The adolescents were self-confident and optimistic about their future. Although there were some exceptions, as a group the adolescents were happy most of the time, enjoyed life, perceived themselves as capable of exercising self-control, valued work and school, expressed confidence in their sexuality, showed positive feelings toward their families, and felt they had the capacity to cope with life's stresses—not exactly a storm-and-stress portrayal of adolescence.

stereotype A generalization that reflects our impressions and beliefs about a broad group of people. All stereotypes refer to an image of what the typical member of a specific group is like.

adolescent generalization gap Adelson's concept of generalizations being made about adolescents based on information regarding a limited, often highly visible group of adolescents.

Further, a recent study of non-Latinx white and African American 12- to 20-year-olds in the United States found that they were characterized much more by positive than problematic development, even in their most vulnerable times (Gutman & others, 2017). Their engagement in healthy behaviors, supportive relationships with parents and friends, and positive self-perceptions were much stronger than their angry and depressed feelings.

Old Centuries and New Centuries

For much of the last century in the United States and other Western cultures, adolescence was perceived as a problematic period of the human life span, in line with G. Stanley Hall's (1904) storm-and-stress portrayal. But as the research study just described indicates, a large majority of adolescents are not nearly as disturbed and troubled as the popular stereotype suggests.

Have adolescents been stereotyped too negatively? Explain.
Tom Grill/Getty Images

The end of an old century and the beginning of the next has a way of stimulating reflection on what was, as well as visions of what could and should be. In the field of psychology in general, as in its subfield of adolescent development, psychologists have looked back at a century in which the discipline became too negative (Seligman & Csikszentmihalyi, 2000). Psychology had become an overly grim science in which people were too often characterized as being passive victims. Psychologists are now calling for a focus on the positive side of human experience and greater emphasis on hope, optimism, positive individual traits, creativity, and positive group and civic values, such as responsibility, nurturance, civility, and tolerance (Snyder & others, 2021).

Generational Perceptions and Misperceptions Adults' perceptions of adolescents emerge from a combination of personal experience and media portrayals, neither of which produces an objective picture of how adolescents typically develop (Feldman & Elliott, 1990). Some of the readiness to assume the worst about adolescents likely involves the short memories of adults. Adults often portray today's adolescents as more troubled, less respectful, more self-centered, more assertive, and more adventurous than they were.

However, in matters of taste and manners, the youth of every generation have seemed radical, unnerving, and different from adults—different in how they look, how they behave, the music they enjoy, their hairstyles, and the clothing they choose. It is an enormous error to confuse adolescents' enthusiasm for trying on new identities and indulging in occasional episodes of outrageous behavior with hostility toward parental and societal standards. Acting out and boundary testing are time-honored ways in which adolescents move toward accepting, rather than rejecting, parental values.

In no order of things is adolescence the simple time of life.

—Jean Erskine Stewart
American Writer, 20th Century

Positive Youth Development What has been called positive youth development (PYD) in adolescence reflects the positive psychology approach. Positive youth development emphasizes the strengths of youth and the positive qualities and developmental trajectories that are desired for youth. Positive youth development has especially been promoted by Jacqueline Lerner, Richard Lerner, and their colleagues (Lerner, 2017; Lerner & others, 2015, 2018), who have recently described the "Five Cs" of PYD:

- *Competence*, which involves having a positive perception of one's actions in domain-specific areas—social, academic, physical, career, and so on

What characterizes the positive youth development approach?
Hero Images/Getty Images

Wanting to Be Treated as an Asset

"Many times teenagers are thought of as a problem that no one really wants to deal with. People are sometimes intimidated and become hostile when teenagers are willing to challenge their authority. It is looked at as being disrespectful. Teenagers are, many times, not treated like an asset and as innovative thinkers who will be the leaders of tomorrow. Adults have the power to teach the younger generation about the world and allow them to feel they have a voice in it."

—Zula, age 16
Brooklyn, New York

- *Confidence*, which consists of an overall positive sense of self-worth and self-efficacy (a sense that one can master a situation and produce positive outcomes)
- *Connection*, which is characterized by positive relationships with others, including family, peers, teachers, and individuals in the community
- *Character*, which comprises respect for societal rules, an understanding of right and wrong, and integrity
- *Caring/compassion*, which encompasses showing emotional concern for others, especially those in distress

Lerner and her colleagues (2015) conclude that to develop these five positive characteristics, youth need access to positive social contexts—such as youth development programs and organized youth activities—and competent adults—such as caring teachers, community leaders, and mentors. We will further explore youth development programs in the chapter on "Peers, Romantic Relationships, and Lifestyles." In the chapter on "Problems in Adolescence and Emerging Adulthood," we will examine Peter Benson's emphasis on the importance of developmental assets in improving youth development, which reflects the positive youth development approach.

Recent research has confirmed the importance of PYD characteristics in competent adolescent development. For example, research indicated that PYD characteristics predicted a lower level of adolescent Internet addiction (Dou & Shek, 2021; Yu & Shek, 2021). Other research studies have linked PYD attributes to fewer internalizing problems in adolescents (Wang, Peng, & Chi, 2021). And another study revealed that PYD characteristics were protective in reducing the likelihood that adolescents would develop mental health problems from undergoing traumatic situations such as the COVID-19 pandemic (Shek & others, 2021).

Review *Connect* Reflect

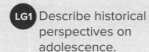 Describe historical perspectives on adolescence.

Review
- What was the early history of interest in adolescence?
- What characterized adolescence in the twentieth century, and how are adolescents changing in the twenty-first century?
- How extensively are adolescents stereotyped?
- What are the benefits of a positive view of adolescence?

Connect
- How have the social changes of the twentieth century, as described in this section, influenced society's views of adolescence?

Reflect *Your Own Personal Journey of Life*
- You likely experienced some instances of stereotyping as an adolescent. What are some examples of circumstances in which you think you were stereotyped as an adolescent?

2 Today's Adolescents in the United States and Around the World

 LG2 Discuss the experiences of adolescents in the United States and around the world.

Adolescents in the
United States

The Global
Perspective

You should now have a good sense of the historical aspects of adolescence, the stereotyping of adolescents, and the importance of considering the positive aspects of many adolescents' development. Now let's further explore the current status of adolescents.

ADOLESCENTS IN THE UNITED STATES

Growing up has never been easy. In many ways, the developmental tasks today's adolescents face are no different from those of adolescents 50 years ago. For a large majority of youth, adolescence is not a time of rebellion, crisis, pathology, and deviance. Rather, it is a time of evaluation, decision making, commitment, and finding a place in the world.

However, adolescents are not a homogeneous group. Most adolescents successfully negotiate the lengthy path to adult maturity, but a substantial minority do not (McNamara, 2021). Socioeconomic, ethnic, cultural, gender, age, and lifestyle differences influence the developmental trajectory of each adolescent.

Social Contexts   Of special interest to researchers is how social contexts influence adolescent development (Bornstein, 2021). **Contexts** are the settings in which development occurs; they are influenced by historical, economic, social, and cultural factors (Makarova, 2021). To understand the influence of contexts on adolescent development, consider the task of a researcher who wants to discover whether today's adolescents are more racially tolerant than those of a decade or two ago. Without reference to the historical, economic, social, and cultural aspects of race relations, adolescents' racial tolerance cannot be fully evaluated. Each adolescent's development occurs against a cultural backdrop of contexts that includes family, peers, school, religion, neighborhood, community, region, and nation, each with its cultural legacies (Dore & McMurtrie, 2021). Let's now further examine the social contexts of culture, socioeconomic status and poverty, ethnicity, gender, and technology.

Culture encompasses the behavior patterns, beliefs, and all other products of a particular group of people that are passed on from generation to generation. Culture results from the interaction of people over many years (Kulich & others, 2021). A cultural group can be as large as the United States or as small as an isolated Appalachian town. Whatever its size, the group's culture influences the behavior of its members. **Cross-cultural research** compares aspects of two or more cultures. The comparison provides information about the degree to which development is similar, or universal, across cultures, or instead is culture-specific (Bhawuk & Landis, 2021; Mahon & Cushner, 2021).

Ethnicity (the word *ethnic* comes from the Greek word for "nation") is rooted in cultural heritage, nationality, race, religion, and language. African Americans, Latinxs, Asian Americans, Native Americans, European Americans, and Arab Americans are examples of broad ethnic groups in the United States. Diversity exists within each ethnic group (Gollnick & Chinn, 2021). A special concern is the racism, discrimination, and prejudice experienced by ethnic minority children and youth (Clauss-Ehler, Roysircar, & Hunter, 2021). Recent research by Adriana Umaña-Taylor and her colleagues (Sladek, Umaña-Taylor, & others, 2020; Umaña-Taylor & Hill, 2020) indicates that pride in one's ethnic identity group and exploration of ethnic identity have positive developmental outcomes.

The sociocultural context of the United States has become increasingly diverse in recent years. Its population includes a greater variety of cultures and ethnic groups than ever before. Relatively high rates of minority immigration have contributed significantly to the growing proportions of some ethnic minorities within the U.S. population (Schwartz & others, 2020).

contexts The settings in which development occurs. These settings are influenced by historical, economic, social, and cultural factors.

culture The behavior, patterns, beliefs, and all other products of a group of people that are passed on from generation to generation.

cross-cultural research Comparisons of one culture with one or more other cultures. These provide information about the degree to which development is similar, or universal, across cultures, and the degree to which it is culture-specific.

ethnicity Categorization of an individual based on cultural heritage, nationality characteristics, race, religion, and language.

Latinx adolescents have become the largest percentage of ethnic group adolescents in the United States.
(left) Richard Green/Alamy Stock Photo; (right) areetham/Shutterstock

Asian American adolescents are the fastest-growing ethnic group of adolescents in the United States.

In 2017, 50.5 percent of children 17 years and younger were non-Latinx white; by 2050, this figure is projected to decrease to 38.8 percent (ChildStats.gov, 2018). In 2017 in the United States, 25.2 percent of children were Latinx, but in 2050 that figure is projected to increase to 31.9 percent. Asian Americans are expected to be the fastest-growing ethnic group of children percentage-wise: In 2017, 5.1 percent were Asian American, and that figure is expected to grow to 7.4 percent in 2050. The percentage of African American children is anticipated to decrease from 2017 to 2050 (13.6 to 13.1 percent).

This changing demographic tapestry promises not only the richness that diversity produces but also difficult challenges in extending the American dream to all individuals (Banks, 2020; Zeiders & others, 2021). In 2020, the latter point became front and central in the United States as not only African Americans but members of other groups protested the killing of African Americans such as George Floyd by police officers.

Socioeconomic status (SES) refers to a person's position within society based on occupational, educational, and economic characteristics. Socioeconomic status implies certain inequalities. Differences in the ability to control resources and to participate in society's rewards produce unequal opportunities (Brieant & others, 2021; Mayo & Wadsworth, 2020). A recent research review of studies involving 3- to 19-year-old U.S. children and adolescents concluded that individuals growing up in low-SES settings are more likely to have higher levels of psychopathology (Peverill & others, 2021).

Gender refers to the characteristics of people as males and females. Few aspects of our development are more central to our identity and social relationships than gender (Cheung & Halpern, 2020; Erickson-Schroth & Davis, 2021; Heyder, Weidinger, & Steinmayr, 2021). *Transgender* is a broad term that refers to individuals who adopt a gender identity that differs from the one assigned to them at birth (Ellis, Riggs, & Peel, 2020; Geist & others, 2021). For example, individuals may have a female body but identify more strongly with being masculine than feminine, or have a male body but identify more strongly with being feminine than masculine (Erickson-Schroth, 2021). A transgender identity of being born male but identifying with being a female is much more common than the reverse (Zucker, Lawrence, & Kreukels, 2016). We will have much more to say about gender and transgender later in the text.

In this section, you have read about such important aspects of individuals as their cultural and socioeconomic backgrounds, ethnicity, and gender. As adolescents develop, these categories intersect and can create systems of power and privilege as well as oppression and discrimination. For example, non-Latinx white adolescents of high socioeconomic status (SES) have experienced considerably greater privilege and less discrimination than African American adolescents. At various points in this text, we will further explore these category connections.

Clinical psychologists are among the health professionals who help adolescents and emerging adults improve their well-being. Read about one clinical psychologist who works with those

socioeconomic status (SES) Classification of a person's position in society based on occupational, educational, and economic characteristics.

gender Characteristics of people as males and females.

who have problems to improve their developmental outcomes, especially those from a Latinx background, in *Connecting with Careers*.

Changing social contexts receive special attention in this edition, with separate chapters on families, peers, schools, work, and culture. A dramatic change in the culture that adolescents and emerging adults are experiencing today is the proliferation of technology in their lives (Maloy & others, 2021). From the mid-'50s when television was introduced, through the replacement of typewriters with computers that could do far more than just print words, and later to the remarkable invention of the Internet and then smartphones, followed by the pervasiveness of social media, the lives of adolescents and emerging adults have been changed forever by technological advances (Tahmud & Mesch, 2021). We will explore these and many other aspects of technology in various chapters.

Social Policy and Adolescents' Development

Social policy is the course of action designed by the national government to influence the welfare of its citizens. Currently, many researchers in adolescent development are attempting to design studies that will facilitate wise and effective social policy decision making (Ganson, Murray, & Nagata, 2020).

Peter Benson and his colleagues (Benson & others, 2004; Benson & Scales, 2011) have argued that the United States has a fragmented social policy for youth that too often has focused only on the negative developmental deficits of adolescents, especially health-compromising behaviors such as drug use and delinquency, and not enough on positive, strength-based approaches. According to Benson and his colleagues (2004, p. 783), a strength-based approach to social policy for youth adopts more of a wellness perspective, places particular emphasis on the existence of healthy conditions, and expands the concept of health to include the skills and competencies needed to succeed in employment, education, and life. It moves beyond the eradication of risk and deliberately argues for the promotion of well-being.

In the view of these researchers, what the United States needs is a *developmentally attentive* youth policy that emphasizes "the family, neighborhood, school, youth organization, places of work, and congregations as policy intervention points. Transforming schools into more developmentally rich settings, building linkages across multiple socializing institutions, launching community-wide initiatives organized around a shared vision of strength building, and expanding funding for quality out-of-school programs" would reflect this policy (Benson & others, 2004, p. 798). The need for such an approach is

---

developmental connection

Culture

Many children and adults still face racism and discrimination in the United States and around the world. Connect to "Culture"

---

social policy A national government's course of action designed to influence the welfare of its citizens.

Doly Akter, Improving the Lives of Adolescent Girls in the Slums of Bangladesh

Doly Akter grew up in a slum in Dhaka, Bangladesh, where sewers overflow, garbage rots in the streets, and children are undernourished. Nearly two-thirds of young women in Bangladesh got married before age 18. Doly organized a club supported by **UNICEF** in which girls went door-to-door to monitor the hygiene habits of households in their neighborhoods. The monitoring led to improved hygiene and health in the families. Doly's group also managed to stop several child marriages by meeting with parents and convincing them that the marriages were not in their daughters' best interests. When talking with parents in their neighborhoods, the girls in the club emphasized that keeping girls in school would improve their future. Doly said the girls in her **UNICEF** group had become far more aware of their rights than their mothers ever were **(UNICEF, 2007)**.

What insights might U.S. adolescents draw from Doly's very different experience of growing up?

Doly Akter, shown here at age 17, organized other adolescents to help improve the lives of youth in Bangladesh.
Naser Siddique/UNICEF Bangladesh

---

developmental connection

Environment

An increasing number of studies are showing that positive outcomes can be achieved through intervention in the lives of children and adolescents living in poverty. Connect to "Culture"

illustrated by a survey in which only 20 percent of U.S. 15-year-olds reported having meaningful relationships outside of their family that were helping them to succeed in life (Search Institute, 2010).

Research indicates that youth benefit enormously when they have caring adults in their lives in addition to parents or guardians (Davis & McQuillin, 2021; Kuperminc & others, 2020). Caring adults—such as coaches, neighbors, teachers, mentors, and after-school leaders—can serve as role models, confidantes, advocates, and resources. Caring-adult relationships are powerful when youth know they are respected, that they matter to the adult, and that the adult wants to be a resource in their lives (Search Institute, 2022).

Children and adolescents who grow up in poverty represent a special concern. In 2019, 14.3 percent of U.S. children under 18 years of age were living in families with incomes below the poverty line, an increase from 2001 (16 percent) but a decrease from a peak of 23 percent in 1993 and also down from 19.7 percent in 2015 (Children's Defense Fund, 2020; Semega & others, 2020). In 2019, African American (26.4 percent, down from 36 percent in 2015) and Latinx (20.9 percent, down from 30 percent in 2015) families with children had especially high rates of poverty (Semega & others, 2020). In 2019, 8.3 percent of non-Latinx white U.S. children and adolescents were living below the poverty line. In 2019, 7.3 percent of Asian American children and adolescents (down from 11.3 percent in 2018) were living below the poverty line. The U.S. figure of 14.3 percent of children and adolescents living in poverty is much higher than the rates in other developed countries. For example, Canada has a child and adolescent poverty rate of 9 percent and Sweden has a rate of 2 percent.

The well-being of adolescents should be one of America's foremost concerns (Yung, McGorry, & Cotter, 2021). The future of our youth is the future of our society. Adolescents who do not reach their full potential, who make fewer contributions to society than it needs, and who do not take their place in society as productive adults diminish our society's future.

THE GLOBAL PERSPECTIVE

The way adolescence is presented in this text is based largely on the writing and research of scholars in the Western world, especially Europe and North America. At the beginning of the twenty-first century, some experts argued that adolescence was typically thought of in a "Eurocentric" way (Nsamenang, 2002). Others noted that advances in transportation and telecommunication were spawning a global youth culture in which adolescents everywhere wore the same type of clothing, had similar hairstyles, listened to the same music, and used similar slang expressions (Larson, Wilson, & Rickman, 2009). Several years later, a study of more than 11,000 adolescents from 18 countries living mainly in middle- and upper-income families found that in all of these countries adolescents were experiencing considerable stress regarding their future (Seiffge-Krenke, 2012). Most adolescents gave a high stress rating (1 or 2) to their fear of not being able to pursue the vocational training or academic studies they desired; the majority of adolescents assigned a medium stress rating (3 or 4) to their fear of becoming unemployed; and the majority of adolescents gave a low stress rating (7 or 8) to the potential difficulty they might have in combining their education or employment with marriage and family.

In today's world, however, cultural differences among adolescents have by no means disappeared (Jeon, Dimitriou, & Halstead, 2021; Kapetanovic & others, 2020). Consider some of the following variations of adolescence around the world (Brown & Larson, 2002):

developmental **connection**

Culture

Cross-cultural studies compare a culture with one or more other cultures. Connect to "Culture."

- Two-thirds of Asian Indian adolescents accept their parents' choice of a marital partner for them.

- In the Philippines, many female adolescents sacrifice their own futures by migrating to the city to earn money that they can send home to their families.

- Street youth in Kenya and other parts of the world learn to survive under highly stressful circumstances. In some cases abandoned by their parents, they may engage in delinquency or prostitution to provide for their economic needs.

- In the Middle East, many adolescents are not allowed to interact with the other sex, even in school.

- Youth in Russia are marrying earlier to legitimize sexual activity.

Thus, depending on the culture being observed, adolescence may involve many different experiences.

Rapid global change is altering the experience of adolescence, presenting new opportunities and challenges to young people's health and well-being. Around the world, adolescents' experiences may differ depending on their gender, families, schools, peers, and religion (Qu & others, 2020; Vazsonyi & others, 2021). However, some adolescent traditions remain the same in various cultures. Brad Brown and Reed Larson (2002) summarized some of these changes and traditions in the lives of the world's youth:

- *Health and well-being.* Adolescent health and well-being have improved in some areas but not in others (Sawyer & Patton, 2018). Overall, fewer adolescents around the world die from infectious diseases and malnutrition now than in the past (UNICEF, 2021). However, a number of adolescent health-compromising behaviors (especially illicit drug use and unprotected sex) continue to place adolescents at risk for serious developmental problems. Extensive increases in the rates of HIV in adolescents have occurred in many sub-Saharan countries (UNICEF, 2021). Almost two-thirds of adolescent deaths in the world occur in just two regions, sub-Saharan Africa and southeast Asia, yet only 42 percent of the world's adolescents live in those regions (Fatusi & Hindin, 2010).

- *Gender.* Around the world, the experiences of male and female adolescents continue to be quite different (Qu & others, 2020). Except in a few areas, such as Japan and Western countries, males have far greater access to educational opportunities than females do. In many countries, adolescent females have less freedom to pursue a variety of careers and to engage in various leisure activities than males do. Gender differences in sexual expression are widespread, especially in India, Southeast Asia, Latin America,

Asian Indian adolescents in a marriage ceremony.
Dinodia Photos/Alamy Stock Photo

Boys-only Muslim school in the Middle East.
Lens Hitam/Shutterstock

and Arab countries, where there are far more restrictions on the sexual activity of adolescent females than on that of males. These gender differences do appear to be narrowing over time. In some countries, educational and career opportunities for women are expanding, and in some parts of the world control over adolescent girls' romantic and sexual relationships is decreasing.

- *Family*. In a study conducted in 12 countries around the world (located in Africa, Asia, Australia, Europe, the Middle East, and the Americas), adolescents validated the importance of parental support in their lives (McNeely & Barber, 2010). However, variations in families across countries also characterize adolescent development (Bornstein & Putnick, 2018). In some countries, adolescents grow up in closely knit families with extended kin networks that provide a web of connections and reflect a traditional way of life. For example, in Arab countries, "adolescents are taught strict codes of conduct and loyalty" (Brown & Larson, 2002, p. 6). However, in Western countries such as the United States, many adolescents grow up in divorced families and stepfamilies. Parenting in many families in Western countries is less authoritarian than in the past. Other trends that are occurring in many countries around the world "include greater family mobility, migration to urban areas, family members working in distant cities or countries, smaller families, fewer extended-family households, and increases in mothers' employment" (Brown & Larson, 2002, p. 7). Unfortunately, many of these changes tend to reduce the ability of families to provide time and resources for adolescents.

- *School*. In general, the number of adolescents enrolled in school in developing countries is increasing. However, schools in many parts of the world—especially Africa, South Asia, and Latin America—still do not provide education to all adolescents (UNICEF, 2018). Indeed, there has been a decline in recent years in the percentage of Latin American adolescents who have access to secondary and higher education (Welti, 2002). Further, many schools do not provide students with the skills that will be required for success in adult work.

- *Peers*. Some cultures give peers a stronger role in adolescence than other cultures do (French & Cheung, 2018). In most Western nations, peers figure prominently in adolescents' lives, in some cases taking on responsibilities that would otherwise be assumed by parents. Among street youth in South America, the peer network serves as a surrogate family that supports survival in dangerous and stressful settings. In other regions of the world, such as in Arab countries, peers have a very limited role, especially for girls.

Street youth in Rio de Janeiro.
Ricardo Mazalan/AP Images

In sum, adolescents' lives are characterized by a combination of change and tradition (Bornstein, 2021). Researchers have found both similarities and differences in the experiences of adolescents in different countries (Koenig & others, 2020); this topic will be discussed in more detail in other chapters.

Review *Connect* Reflect

 LG2 Discuss the experiences of adolescents in the United States and around the world.

Review

- What is the current status of today's adolescents? What is social policy? What are some important social policy issues concerning today's adolescents?
- How is adolescence changing for youth around the globe?

Connect

- Do you think adolescents in other countries experience stereotyping, as described earlier in the chapter? If so, why or how?

Reflect *Your Own Personal Journey of Life*

- How was your adolescence likely similar to, or different from, the adolescence of your parents and grandparents?

Processes and Periods

Developmental Transitions

Developmental Issues

In certain ways, each of us develops like all other individuals; in other ways, each of us is unique. Most of the time, our attention focuses on our individual uniqueness, but researchers who study development are drawn to our shared as well as our unique characteristics. As humans, we travel some common paths. Each of us—Leonardo da Vinci, Joan of Arc, George Washington, Martin Luther King, Jr., you, and I—walked at about the age of 1, talked at about the age of 2, engaged in fantasy play as a young child, and became more independent as a youth.

What do we mean when we speak of an individual's development? **Development** is the pattern of change that begins at conception and continues throughout the life span. Most development involves growth, although it also includes decay (as in death and dying). The pattern is complex because it is the product of several processes.

developmental **connection**

Brain Development

Might there be a link between changes in the adolescent's brain and increases in risk taking and sensation seeking? Connect to "The Brain and Cognitive Development."

PROCESSES AND PERIODS

Human development is determined by biological, cognitive, and socioemotional processes. It is often described in terms of periods.

Biological, Cognitive, and Socioemotional Processes   **Biological processes** involve physical changes in an individual's body. Genes inherited from parents, the development of the brain, height and weight gains, advances in motor skills, and the hormonal changes of puberty all reflect biological processes. We discuss these biological processes extensively in the chapter on "Puberty, Health, and Biological Foundations."

Cognitive processes involve changes in an individual's thinking and intelligence. Memorizing a poem, solving a math problem, and envisioning what it would feel like to be famous all reflect cognitive processes. The chapter on "The Brain and Cognitive Development" discusses cognitive processes in detail.

Socioemotional processes involve changes in an individual's emotions, personality, relationships with others, and social contexts. Talking back to parents, aggression toward peers, assertiveness, enjoyment of social events such as a senior prom, and gender-role orientation all reflect the role of socioemotional processes. Nine chapters in this edition focus on socioemotional processes in adolescent development.

Biological, cognitive, and socioemotional processes are intricately interwoven. Socioemotional processes shape cognitive processes, cognitive processes advance or restrict socioemotional processes, and biological processes influence cognitive processes. Although you will read about these processes in separate chapters of this edition, keep in mind that you are learning about the development of an integrated human being whose mind and body are interdependent (see Figure 1).

Nowhere is the connection across biological, cognitive, and socioemotional processes more obvious than in two rapidly emerging fields:

- *Developmental cognitive neuroscience*, which explores links between development, cognitive processes, and the brain (Baum & others, 2020; Overbye & others, 2021)
- *Developmental social neuroscience*, which examines connections between socioemotional processes, development, and the brain (Andrews, Ahmed, & Blakemore, 2021; Qu, Jorgensen, & Telzer, 2021)

Periods of Development   Human development is commonly described in terms of periods. We consider developmental periods that occur in childhood, adolescence, and adulthood. Approximate age ranges are given for the periods to provide a general idea of when they begin and end.

development The pattern of change that begins at conception and continues through the life span. Most development involves growth, although it also includes decay (as in death and dying).

biological processes Physical changes in an individual's body.

cognitive processes Changes in an individual's thinking and intelligence.

socioemotional processes Changes in an individual's personality, emotions, relationships with other people, and social contexts.

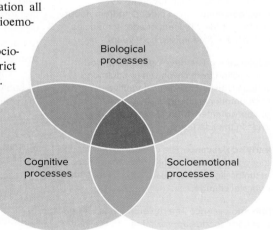

FIGURE 1

DEVELOPMENTAL CHANGES ARE THE RESULT OF BIOLOGICAL, COGNITIVE, AND SOCIOEMOTIONAL PROCESSES. These processes interact as individuals develop.

Childhood   Childhood includes the prenatal period, infancy, early childhood, and middle and late childhood.

The **prenatal period** is the time from conception to birth, which lasts approximately 9 months. It is a time of tremendous growth—from a single cell to an organism complete with a brain and behavioral capabilities.

Infancy, the period from birth to about 24 months of age, is a time of extreme dependency on adults. Many psychological activities—for example, language, symbolic thought, sensorimotor coordination, social learning, and parent-child relationships—begin in this period.

Early childhood extends from about 2 to 5 years of age, sometimes called the preschool years. During this time, young children learn to become more self-sufficient and to care for themselves. They develop school readiness (learning how to follow instructions, identify letters, and so on) and spend many hours in play, both alone and with peers. First grade typically marks the end of early childhood.

Middle and late childhood lasts from about 6 to 11 years of age. During this period, sometimes called the elementary school years, children master the fundamental skills of reading, writing, and arithmetic, and they are formally exposed to the larger world and its culture. Achievement becomes a central theme of the child's development, and self-control increases.

Adolescence   As our developmental timetable suggests, considerable development and experience have occurred before an individual reaches adolescence. No girl or boy enters adolescence as a blank slate, with only a genetic code to determine thoughts, feelings, and behaviors. Rather, the combination of heredity, childhood experiences, and adolescent experiences determines the course of adolescent development. As you read this chapter and others, keep in mind the continuity of development between childhood and adolescence.

Defining adolescence requires a consideration not only of age but also of sociohistorical influences: recall our discussion of the inventionist view of adolescence. With the sociohistorical context in mind, we define **adolescence** as the period of transition between childhood and adulthood that involves biological, cognitive, and socioemotional changes. A key task of adolescence is preparation for adulthood. Indeed, the future of any culture hinges on how effective this preparation is.

Although the age range of adolescence can vary with cultural and historical circumstances, in the United States and most other cultures today adolescence begins at approximately 10 to 13 years of age and ends in the late teens. The biological, cognitive, and socioemotional changes of adolescence range from the development of sexual functions to abstract thinking processes to independence.

Increasingly, developmentalists describe adolescence in terms of early and late periods. **Early adolescence** corresponds roughly to the middle school or junior high school years and includes most pubertal change. **Late adolescence** refers approximately to the latter half of the second decade of life. Career interests, dating, and identity exploration are often more pronounced in late adolescence than in early adolescence. Researchers often specify whether their results generalize to all of adolescence or are specific to early or late adolescence.

The old view of adolescence was that it is a singular, uniform period of transition resulting in entry to the adult world. Current approaches emphasize a variety of transitions and events that define the period, as well as their timing and sequence. For instance, puberty and school events are key transitions that signal entry into adolescence; completing school and taking one's first full-time job are key transitional events that signal an exit from adolescence and entry into adulthood.

Today, developmentalists do not believe that change ends with adolescence. Remember that development is defined as a lifelong process. Adolescence is part of the life course and as such is not an isolated period of development. Though it has many unique characteristics, what takes place during adolescence is connected with development and experiences in both childhood and adulthood (Choe, 2021; Wickersham & others, 2021).

Adulthood   Like childhood and adolescence, adulthood is not a homogeneous period of development. Developmentalists often describe three periods of adult development: early adulthood, middle adulthood, and late adulthood.

Early adulthood usually begins in the late teens or early twenties and lasts through the thirties. It is a time of establishing personal and economic independence and engaging in career development.

prenatal period The time from conception to birth.

infancy The developmental period that extends from birth to 18 or 24 months of age.

early childhood The developmental period extending from the end of infancy to about 5 or 6 years of age; sometimes called the preschool years.

middle and late childhood The developmental period extending from about 6 to about 10 or 11 years of age; sometimes called the elementary school years.

adolescence The developmental period of transition from childhood to adulthood, which involves biological, cognitive, and socioemotional changes. Adolescence begins at approximately 10 to 13 years of age and ends in the late teens.

early adolescence The developmental period that corresponds roughly to the middle school or junior high school years and includes most pubertal change.

late adolescence The developmental period that corresponds approximately to the latter half of the second decade of life. Career interests, dating, and identity exploration are often more pronounced in late adolescence than in early adolescence.

early adulthood The developmental period beginning in the late teens or early twenties and lasting through the thirties.

Periods of Development

| Prenatal period (conception to birth) | Infancy (birth to 18–24 months) | Early childhood (2–5 years) | Middle and late childhood (6–11 years) | Adolescence (10–13 to late teens) | Early adulthood (20s to 30s) | Middle adulthood (35–45 to 55–65) | Late adulthood (60s–70s to death) |

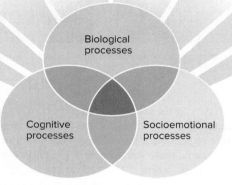

Biological processes

Cognitive processes

Socioemotional processes

Processes of Development

FIGURE 2

PROCESSES AND PERIODS OF DEVELOPMENT. The unfolding of life's periods of development is influenced by the interaction of biological, cognitive, and socioemotional processes.
(left to right) Steve Allen/Brand X Pictures/Getty Images; Dr. John Santrock; Digital Vision/Alamy; Digital Vision/Photodisc/Getty Images; Comstock/Getty Images; Blue Moon Stock/Alamy Stock Photo; Sam Edwards/Caiaimage/Glow Images; Ronnie Kaufman/Blend Images LLC.

Middle adulthood begins at approximately 35 to 45 years of age and ends at some point between approximately 55 and 65 years of age. For most adolescents, their parents are either in this period or about to enter it. Middle adulthood is a time of increasing interest in transmitting values to the next generation, deeper reflection about the meaning of life, and enhanced concern about a decline in physical functioning and health. In the "Families" chapter, we see how the maturation of both adolescents and parents contributes to the parent-adolescent relationship.

Eventually, the rhythm and meaning of the human life span wend their way to **late adulthood,** the developmental period that lasts from approximately 60 or 70 years of age until death. This is a time of adjustment to decreasing strength and health and to retirement and reduced income. Reviewing one's life and adapting to changing social roles also characterize late adulthood, as do lessened responsibility and increased freedom. Figure 2 summarizes the developmental periods in the human life span and their approximate age ranges.

DEVELOPMENTAL TRANSITIONS

Developmental transitions are often important junctures in people's lives. Such transitions include moving from the prenatal period to birth and infancy, from infancy to early childhood, and from early childhood to middle and late childhood. For our purposes, two important transitions are from childhood to adolescence and from adolescence to adulthood. Let's explore these transitions.

Childhood to Adolescence   The transition from childhood to adolescence involves a number of biological, cognitive, and socioemotional changes. Among the biological changes are the growth spurt, hormonal changes, and sexual maturation that come with puberty. In early adolescence, changes take place in the brain that allow for more advanced thinking. Also at this time, adolescents begin to stay up later at night and sleep later in the morning.

One's children's children's children. Look back to us as we look to you; we are related by our imaginations. If we are able to touch, it is because we have imagined each other's existence, our dreams running back and forth along a cable from age to age.

—ROGER ROSENBLATT
Contemporary American Writer

middle adulthood The developmental period that is entered at about 35 to 45 years of age and exited at about 55 to 65 years of age.

late adulthood The developmental period that lasts from about 60 to 70 years of age until death.

Developmental transitions from childhood to adolescence involve biological, cognitive, and socioemotional changes. *What are some of these changes?*
(both): Ariel Skelley/Blend Images LLC/Getty Images

---- ---- ---- ---->
developmental **connection**

Schools

The transition to middle or junior high school can be difficult and stressful for many students. Connect to "Schools."

<---- ---- ---- ----

Among the cognitive changes that occur during the transition from childhood to adolescence are thinking more abstractly, idealistically, and logically. In response to these changes, parents place more responsibility for decision making on the young adolescent's shoulders, although too often adolescents make decisions that are filled with risk, especially when they are with their peers (Osmont & others, 2021; Tian & others, 2020). Compared with children, adolescents process information more rapidly, can sustain their attention longer, and engage in more effective executive function, which includes monitoring and managing their cognitive resources, exercising cognitive control, and delaying gratification (Baum & others, 2020; Ferguson, Brunsdon, & Bradford, 2021).

Among the socioemotional changes adolescents undergo are a quest for independence, increased conflict with parents, and a desire to spend more time with peers (Mastrotheodoros & others, 2020). Conversations with friends become more intimate and include more self-disclosure. As children enter adolescence, they attend schools that are larger and more impersonal than their neighborhood elementary schools. Achievement becomes more serious business, and academic challenges increase. Also at this time, increased sexual maturation produces a much greater interest in romantic relationships (Aviles, Finn, & Neyer, 2021; Espinosa-Hernandez & others, 2020). Young adolescents also experience more dramatic mood swings than they did when they were children (Alsaad, Azhari, & Al Nasser, 2021).

In sum, the transition from childhood to adolescence is complex and multidimensional, involving change in many different aspects of an individual's life. Success in handling this transition requires considerable adaptation and thoughtful, sensitive support from caring adults.

Adolescence to Adulthood   Another important transition occurs from adolescence to adulthood (Arnett, 2012, 2015). It has been said that adolescence begins in biology and ends in culture. That is, the transition from childhood to adolescence begins with the onset of pubertal maturation, whereas the transition from adolescence to adulthood is determined by cultural standards and experiences.

Emerging Adulthood   Recently, the transition from adolescence to adulthood has been referred to as **emerging adulthood,** a developmental period from approximately 18 to 25 years of age. Experimentation and exploration characterize the emerging adult. At this point in their development, many individuals are still exploring which career path they want to follow, what they want their identity to be, and which lifestyle they want to adopt (for example, single, cohabiting, or married) (Becht & others, 2021; Henneberger, Witzen, & Preston, 2021; Nelson, 2021).

Jeffrey Arnett (2006, 2015, 2016a, b) described five key characteristics of emerging adulthood:

- *Identity exploration*, especially in love and work. Emerging adulthood is a time when key changes in identity take place for many individuals.
- *Instability*. Residential changes peak during emerging adulthood, a time during which there also is often instability in love, work, and education.

emerging adulthood The developmental period occurring from approximately 18 to 25 years of age; this transitional period between adolescence and adulthood is characterized by experimentation and exploration.

Chris Barnard

Emerging adult Chris Barnard is a single 24-year-old. Two years ago he moved back into his parents' home, worked as a temp, and thought about his next step in life. One of the temp jobs became permanent. Chris now works with a trade association in Washington, D.C. With the exception of technological advances, he says that his life is similar to what his parents' lives must have been like as they made the transition to adulthood.

Chris' living arrangements reflect the "instability" characteristic of emerging adulthood. While in college, he changed dorms each year; then as a senior he moved to an off-campus apartment. Following college, Chris moved back home, then moved to another apartment, and now is in yet another apartment. In Chris' words, "This is going to be the longest stay I've had since I went to college. . . . I've sort of settled in" (Jayson, 2006, p. 2D).

Would you characterize Chris' life experiences since college as continuous or discontinuous?

- *Self-focused.* According to Arnett (2006, p. 10), emerging adults "are self-focused in the sense that they have little in the way of social obligations, little in the way of duties and commitments to others, which leaves them with a great deal of autonomy in running their own lives."

- *Feeling in-between.* Many emerging adults don't consider themselves adolescents or full-fledged adults. In a national survey, 45 percent of U.S. 18- to 29-year-olds reported that they considered themselves in-between, but during their twenties they steadily increased their self-perception of being a full-fledged adult (Arnett, 2012).

- *The age of possibilities, a time when individuals have an opportunity to transform their lives.* Arnett (2006) describes two ways in which emerging adulthood is the age of possibilities: (1) many emerging adults are optimistic about their future; and (2) for individuals who have experienced difficult times while growing up, emerging adulthood presents an opportunity to reorient their lives in a more positive direction.

Research indicates that these five characteristics apply not only to individuals in the United States as they make the transition from adolescence to early adulthood, but also to their counterparts in European countries and Australia (Sirsch & others, 2009). Although emerging adulthood is not represented in all cultures, it does appear to occur in those in which assuming adult roles and responsibilities is postponed (Kins & Beyers, 2010).

Does life get better for individuals when they enter emerging adulthood? To explore this question, see the *Connecting with Health and Well-Being* interlude.

Becoming an Adult Determining just when an individual becomes an adult is difficult. In the United States, the most widely recognized marker of entry into adulthood is holding a more or less permanent, full-time job, which usually happens when an individual finishes school—high school for some, college for others, graduate or professional school for still others. However, other criteria are far from clear. Economic independence is one marker of adult status, but achieving it is often a long process. College graduates are increasingly returning to live with their parents as they attempt to establish themselves economically. A longitudinal study found that at age 25 only slightly more than half of the participants were fully financially independent of their family of origin (Cohen & others, 2003). The most dramatic findings in this study, though, involved the extensive variability in the individual trajectories of adult roles across ten years from 17 to 27 years of age; many of the participants moved back and forth between increasing and decreasing economic dependency.

What characterizes emerging adulthood? Even when emerging adults have experienced a troubled childhood and adolescence, what are some factors that can help them become competent?
Juice Images/Getty Images

Do Health and Well-Being Change in Emerging Adulthood?

In a recent analysis, Seth Schwartz (2016) described the two-sided coin of emerging adulthood. As indicated by Arnett, for emerging adults who have experienced troubled times while growing up, emerging adulthood represents a time when they can redirect their lives and move into a more positive developmental trajectory. Indeed, for many individuals, emerging adulthood brings more positive well-being than adolescence. But for others, emerging adulthood is a time of increasing anxiety, depression, and problems, as well as considerable worry about one's future. Emerging adulthood is a time when many individuals engage in unhealthy behaviors; for example, during this period binge drinking peaks (Schulenberg & others, 2017), eating disorders are common (Lipson & Sonneville, 2017), risky sexual behavior is more frequent than in the late twenties (Savage, Menegatos, & Roberto, 2017), and poor sleep habits are common among college students (Schlarb, Friedrich, & Clausen, 2017). However, as with any period of development, there are clusters of emerging adults who engage in health-enhancing behaviors while others display health-compromising behaviors. Much more information about health and well-being in emerging adulthood appears in the chapters on "Puberty, Health, and Biological Foundations" and "Problems in Adolescence and Emerging Adulthood."

What factors can emerging adults control that might influence their health and well-being?

One study revealed that continued co-residence with parents during emerging adulthood slowed the process of becoming a self-sufficient and independent adult (Kins & Beyers, 2010).

Several studies show that taking responsibility for oneself may be viewed as an important marker of adult status by many individuals (Arnett, 2016a, b; Smith & others, 2017). In one study, more than 70 percent of college students said that being an adult means accepting responsibility for the consequences of one's actions, deciding on one's own beliefs and values, and establishing a relationship with parents as an equal adult (Arnett, 1995). In another study, both parents and college students agreed that taking responsibility for one's actions and developing emotional control are important aspects of becoming an adult (Nelson & others, 2007). A more recent U.S. study of community college students found that they believed adulthood would mean being able to care for themselves and others (Katsiaficas, 2017). However, parents and college students didn't always agree on other aspects of what it takes to become an adult. For example, parents were more likely than college students to emphasize that driving safely and not getting drunk are important aspects of becoming an adult.

At some point in the late teens through the early twenties, then, individuals reach adulthood. In becoming an adult, they accept responsibility for themselves, become capable of making independent decisions, and gain financial independence from their parents (Arnett, 2016a, b). The new freedoms and responsibilities of emerging adulthood represent major changes in individuals' lives. Keep in mind, though, that considerable continuity still glues adolescence and adulthood together. For example, a longitudinal study found that religious views and behaviors of emerging adults were especially stable and that their attitudes toward drugs were stable to a lesser degree (Bachman & others, 2002).

What we have said so far about the determinants of adult status mainly addresses individuals in industrialized societies, especially the United States. In developing countries, marriage is often a more significant marker for entry into adulthood than in the United States, and it usually occurs much earlier than in the United States (Arnett, 2016a, b; Eccles, Brown, & Templeton, 2008). Thus, some developmentalists argue that the term "emerging adulthood" applies more to Western countries such as the United States and European countries, and to some Asian countries such as Japan, than to developing countries (Arnett, 2007). In one study, the majority of 18- to 26-year-olds in India felt that they had achieved adulthood (Seiter & Nelson, 2011).

Contextual variations in emerging adulthood also may occur in cultures and subpopulations within a country (Arnett & Brody, 2008). For example, in the United States,

"Mormons marry early and begin having children . . . so they have a briefer period of emerging adulthood before taking on adult roles" (Arnett, 2004, p. 22). Also, one study revealed that at-risk youth entered emerging adulthood slightly earlier than the general population of youth (Lisha & others, 2012). Further, in some countries, such as China and India, emerging adulthood is more likely to occur in urban areas than in rural areas because young people in the urban areas of these countries "marry later, have children later, obtain more education, and have a greater range of occupational and recreational opportunities" (Arnett, 2004, p. 23).

What determines an individual's well-being in the transition to adulthood? In the view of Jacquelynne Eccles and her colleagues (Eccles, Brown, & Templeton, 2008), three types of assets are especially important in making a competent transition through adolescence and emerging adulthood: intellectual development, psychological/emotional development, and social development. Figure 3 provides examples of these three types of assets.

Resilience   At the beginning of the chapter, you read the captivating story of Michael Maddaus, who got his life together as an emerging adult following a troubled childhood and adolescence. Michael Maddaus was resilient. What do we mean by the term *resilience*? **Resilience** refers to adapting positively and achieving successful outcomes in the face of significant risks and adverse circumstances.

In Project Competence, Ann Masten and her colleagues (Masten, 2014, 2017, 2019, 2021a, b; Masten & others, 2021) examined the resilience of individuals from childhood through adulthood. They found that adults who had experienced considerable adversity while growing up but became competent young adults were characterized by certain individual and contextual factors. Competence was assessed in areas such as achievement, conduct, and social relationships. In emerging adulthood (assessed at 17 to 23 years of age), individuals who became competent after experiencing difficulties while growing up were more intelligent, experienced higher parenting quality, and were less likely to have grown up in poverty or low-income circumstances than their counterparts who did not become competent as emerging adults.

A further analysis focused on individuals who were still showing maladaptive patterns in emerging adulthood but had gotten their lives together by the time they were in the late twenties and early thirties. The three characteristics shared by these "late-bloomers" were receiving support from adults, being planful, and showing positive aspects of autonomy. In other longitudinal research, "military service, marriage and romantic relationships, higher education, religious affiliations, and work opportunities may provide turning-point opportunities for changing the life course during emerging adulthood" (Masten, Obradovic, & Burt, 2006, p. 179).

The Changing Landscape of Emerging and Early Adulthood
In earlier generations, by their mid-twenties at the latest, individuals were expected to have finished college, obtained a full-time job, and established their own household, most often with a spouse and a child. However, individuals are now taking much longer to reach these developmental milestones, many of which they are not experiencing until their late twenties or even thirties (Vespa, 2017). It is not surprising that their parents recall having had a much earlier timetable of reaching these developmental milestones.

Consider that for the first time in the modern era, in 2014 living with parents was the most frequent living arrangement for 18- to 34-year-olds (Fry, 2016). Dating all the way back to 1880, living with a romantic partner, whether a spouse or a significant other, was the most common living arrangement for emerging and young adults. In 2014, 32.1 percent of 18- to 34-year-olds lived with their parents, followed by 31.6 percent who lived with a spouse or partner in their own home, while 14 percent headed the household in which they lived alone. The remaining 22 percent lived in another family member's home, with a non-relative, or in group quarters (a college dorm, for example).

Intellectual development

Knowledge of essential life and vocational skills

Rational habits of mind—critical thinking and reasoning skills

Good decision-making skills

In-depth knowledge of more than one culture

Knowledge of skills necessary to navigate through multiple cultures

School success

Psychological and emotional development

Good mental health including positive self-regard

Good emotional self-regulation and coping skills

Good conflict resolution skills

Mastery motivation and positive achievement motivation

Confidence in one's personal efficacy

Planfulness

Sense of personal autonomy/responsibility for self

Optimism coupled with realism

Coherent and positive personal and social identity

Prosocial and culturally sensitive values

Spirituality and/or a sense of purpose in life

Strong moral character

Social development

Connectedness—perceived good relationships and trust with parents, peers, and some other adults

Sense of social place/integration—being connected and valued by larger social networks

Attachment to prosocial/conventional institutions such as school, church, out-of-school youth development centers

Ability to navigate in multiple cultural contexts

Commitment to civic engagement

FIGURE 3

PERSONAL ASSETS THAT FACILITATE POSITIVE YOUTH DEVELOPMENT

resilience Adapting positively and achieving successful outcomes in the face of significant risks and adverse circumstances.

In terms of education, today's emerging and young adults are better educated than their counterparts in the 1970s (Vespa, 2017). For example, they are much more likely to have a college degree today. The biggest reason for this improved educational attainment since the 1970s, though, is a gender difference reversal. In 1975, more young men than young women had college degrees, but today young women are more likely than young men to earn a college degree.

In terms of work, more young adults are working today than in 1975 (Vespa, 2017). The main reason for this increase also involves a gender change—the significant rise in the percentage of young women in the workforce, which has increased from slightly below 50 percent to more than two-thirds of young women being in the workforce today. In 1975, almost all of the young women who were not in the workforce indicated that they were taking care of their home and family. However, in 2016, less than 50 percent of the young women who were not in the workforce were homemakers.

As we see next, though, parents can play an important role in guiding and preparing adolescents for the changing landscape of emerging adulthood.

Is Adolescence Taking Too Long? Joseph and Claudia Allen (2009) wrote a book titled *Escaping the Endless Adolescence: How We Can Help Our Teenagers Grow Up Before They Grow Old*, and opened the book with a chapter titled, "Is Twenty-five the New Fifteen?" They argue that in recent decades adolescents have experienced a world that has made it more difficult to become competent adults. In their words (p. 17):

> Generations ago, fourteen-year-olds used to drive, seventeen-year-olds led armies, and even average teens contributed labor and income that helped keep their families afloat. While facing other problems, those teens displayed adult-like maturity far more quickly than today's, who are remarkably well kept, but cut off from most of the responsibility, challenge, and growth-producing feedback of the adult world. Parents of twenty-somethings used to lament, "They grow up so fast." But that seems to be replaced with, "Well, . . . Mary's living at home a bit while she sorts things out."

The Allens conclude that what is happening to the current generation of young adults is that after adolescence, they are experiencing "more adolescence" instead of adequately being launched into the adult years. Even many adolescents who have gotten good grades and then as emerging adults continued to achieve academic success in college later find themselves in their mid-twenties not having a clue about how to find a meaningful job, manage their finances, or live independently. In a recent study, maturity fears among undergraduate students were assessed from 1982 to 2012 (Smith & others, 2017). Both male and female undergraduates' maturity fears increased across time. Thus, recent cohorts of emerging adults seem more reluctant to mature than earlier cohorts were.

The Allens offer the following suggestions for helping adolescents become more mature on their way to adulthood:

- *Provide them with opportunities to be contributors.* Help them move away from being consumers by creating more effective work experiences (quality work apprenticeships, for example), or service learning opportunities that allow adolescents to make meaningful contributions.

- *Give candid, quality feedback to adolescents.* Don't just shower praise and material things on them, but let them see how the real world works. Don't protect them from criticism, constructive or negative. Protecting them in this way only leaves them ill-equipped to deal with the ups and downs of the real world of adulthood.

- *Create positive adult connections with adolescents.* Many adolescents deny that they need parental support or attachment to parents, but to help them develop maturity on the way to adulthood, they do. Exploring a wider social world than in childhood, adolescents need to be connected to parents and other adults in positive ways to be able to handle autonomy maturely.

- *Challenge adolescents to become more competent.* Adults need to do fewer things for adolescents that they can accomplish for themselves. Providing adolescents with opportunities to engage in tasks that are just beyond their current level of ability stretches their minds and helps them to make progress along the road to maturity.

What are some strategies parents can use to help their adolescents become more competent and mature as they move toward adulthood?
kali9/Getty Images

developmental **connection**

Community

Service learning is linked to many positive outcomes for adolescents. Connect to "Moral Development, Values, and Religion."

A Longer Emerging Adulthood and Established Adulthood   Increasingly, instead of describing emerging adulthood as occurring from 18 to 25 years of age, proposals advocate that the age range be expanded to 18 to 29 (Arnett, 2014). However, in a recent study of individuals 18 to 60, the five characteristics of emerging adulthood mentioned above (identity exploration, self-focus, feeling in-between, instability, and possibilities/optimism) were more likely to be endorsed by 18- to 25-year-olds than by older individuals (Arnett & Mitra, 2020).

Another consideration is that individuals are entering a stable work trajectory later than ever before (Arnett, Robinson, & Lachman, 2020). The best-paying jobs today increasingly require the ability to use information and technology, and thus emerging adults must pursue more education and training to prepare for these occupations.

Today there are proposals for *early adulthood* (or a new term, *established adulthood*) to extend from approximately 30 to 45 years of age (Mehta & others, 2020). The key characteristics of this period would be the delay of stable work and family patterns (getting married and having children, for example) until this time frame.

DEVELOPMENTAL ISSUES

Is development due more to nature (heredity) or to nurture (environment)? Is it continuous and smooth or discontinuous and stage-like? Is it due more to early experience or to later experience? These three important questions motivate research on adolescent development.

Nature and Nurture   The **nature-nurture issue** involves the debate about whether development is primarily influenced by nature or nurture. Nature refers to an organism's biological inheritance, nurture to its environmental experiences. "Nature" proponents claim that the most important influence on development is biological inheritance. "Nurture" proponents claim that environmental experiences are the most important influence.

According to the nature advocates, just as a sunflower grows in an orderly way—unless flattened by an unfriendly environment—so does the human grow in an orderly way. The range of environments can be vast, but the nature approach argues that evolutionary and genetic processes produce commonalities in growth and development (Mason, Duncan, & Losos, 2021). We walk before we talk, speak one word before two words, grow rapidly in infancy and less so in early childhood, experience a rush of sexual hormones in puberty, reach the peak of our physical strength in late adolescence and early adulthood, and then physically decline. The nature proponents acknowledge that extreme environments—those that are psychologically barren or hostile—can depress development. However, they believe that basic growth tendencies are genetically wired into humans (Hoefnagels, 2021).

By contrast, other psychologists emphasize the influence of nurture, or environmental experiences, on development (Bembenutty, 2021). Experiences run the gamut from the individual's biological environment—nutrition, medical care, exposure to drugs, and physical accidents—to the social environment—family, peers, schools, community, media, and culture.

Some adolescent development researchers maintain that, historically, too much emphasis has been placed on the biological changes of puberty as determinants of adolescent psychological development. They recognize that biological change is an important dimension of the transition from childhood to adolescence, one that is found in all primate species and in all cultures throughout the world. However, they argue that social contexts (nurture) play important roles in adolescent psychological development as well, roles that until recently have not received adequate attention (Kuo, 2021).

There has been a dramatic increase in the number of studies that reflect the *epigenetic view,* which states that development involves an ongoing, bidirectional interchange between genes and the environment. These studies explore specific DNA sequences (Franzago & others, 2020). The epigenetic mechanisms involve the actual molecular modification of the DNA strand as a result of environmental inputs in ways that alter gene functioning (Champagne, 2021). In "Puberty, Health, and Biological Foundations," we will explore the epigenetic approach in greater depth.

developmental **connection**

Nature and Nurture

The epigenetic view emphasizes the ongoing, bidirectional interchange between heredity and environment. Connect to "Puberty, Health, and Biological Foundations."

nature-nurture issue Debate about whether development is primarily influenced by an organism's biological inheritance (nature) or by its environmental experiences (nurture).

Continuity

Discontinuity

FIGURE 4

CONTINUITY AND DISCONTINUITY IN DEVELOPMENT. *Is human development like a seedling gradually growing into a giant oak? Or is it more like a caterpillar suddenly becoming a butterfly?*

developmental **connection**

Families

Secure attachment to parents increases the likelihood that adolescents will be socially competent. Connect to "Families."

continuity-discontinuity issue Controversy regarding whether development involves gradual, cumulative change (continuity) or distinct stages (discontinuity).

early-later experience issue Controversy regarding the degree to which early experiences (especially early in childhood) or later experiences are the key determinants of development.

Continuity and Discontinuity   Think for a moment about your development. Was your growth into the person you are today gradual, like the slow, cumulative growth of a seedling into a giant oak? Or did you experience sudden, distinct changes during your growth, like the remarkable transformation from a caterpillar into a butterfly (see Figure 4)? The **continuity-discontinuity issue** focuses on the extent to which development involves gradual, cumulative change (continuity) or distinct stages (discontinuity). For the most part, developmentalists who emphasize experience have described development as a gradual, continuous process; those who emphasize nature have described development as a series of distinct stages.

In terms of continuity, a child's first word, while seemingly an abrupt, discontinuous event, is actually the result of weeks and months of growth and practice. Similarly, puberty, while also appearing to be abrupt and discontinuous, is actually a gradual process that occurs over several years.

In terms of discontinuity, each person is described as passing through a sequence of stages in which change is qualitatively, rather than quantitatively, different. As the oak moves from seedling to giant tree, it becomes more oak—its development is continuous. As a caterpillar changes into a butterfly, it does not become more caterpillar; it becomes a different kind of organism—its development is discontinuous. For example, at some point a child moves from not being able to think abstractly about the world to being able to do so. This is a qualitative, discontinuous change in development, not a quantitative, continuous change.

Early and Later Experience   Another important debate is the **early-later experience issue,** which focuses on the degree to which early experiences (especially those that take place early in childhood) or later experiences are the key determinants of development (Dagan & Sagi-Schwartz, 2021). That is, if infants or young children experience negative, stressful circumstances in their lives, can the impact of those experiences be outweighed by later, more positive experiences in adolescence? Or are the early experiences so critical, possibly because they are the infant's first, prototypical experiences, that they cannot be overridden by a later, more enriched environment in childhood or adolescence?

The early-later experience issue has a long history, and developmentalists continue to debate it. Some emphasize that unless infants experience warm, nurturant caregiving in the first year or so of life, their development will never be optimal (Woodhouse & others, 2020). Plato was sure that infants who were rocked frequently became better athletes. Nineteenth-century New England ministers told parents in Sunday sermons that the way they handled their infants would determine their children's future character. The emphasis on the importance of early experience rests on the belief that each life is an unbroken trail on which a psychological quality can be traced back to its origin.

The early-experience doctrine contrasts with the later-experience view that, rather than achieving statue-like permanence after change in infancy, our development resembles the ebb and flow of a river. The later-experience advocates argue that children and adolescents are malleable throughout development and that later sensitive caregiving is just as important as earlier sensitive caregiving (Mikulincer & Shaver, 2021). A number of life-span developmentalists, who focus on the entire life span rather than only on child development, stress that too little attention has been given to the influence of later experiences on development. They accept that early experiences are important contributors to development but assert that they are no more important than later experiences. Jerome Kagan (2013) points out that even children who show the qualities of an inhibited temperament, which is linked to heredity, have the capacity to change their behavior.

Evaluating the Developmental Issues   As we consider further these three salient developmental issues—nature and nurture, continuity and discontinuity, and early and later experience—it is important to realize that most developmentalists consider it unwise to take an extreme position on these issues. Development is not all nature or all nurture, not all continuity or all discontinuity, and not all early experience or all later experience. Nature and nurture, continuity and discontinuity, and early and later experience all affect our development throughout the life span. For example, in considering the nature-nurture issue, the key to development is the interaction of nature and nurture rather than the influence of either factor

To what extent is an adolescent's development due to earlier or later experiences?
(left) Shutterstock; (right) Photodisc/Getty Images

alone (Greenberg, 2021; Lewis, Al-Shawaf, & Buss, 2021). An individual's cognitive development, for instance, reflects heredity-environment interaction, not heredity or environment alone. Much more about the role of heredity-environment interaction appears in the chapter on "Puberty, Health, and Biological Foundations."

Although most developmentalists do not take extreme positions on the developmental issues we have discussed, this consensus has not meant the absence of spirited debate about how strongly development is determined by these factors (Cowan & Smith, 2021; Landis & Bhawuk, 2021). Consider adolescents who, as children, experienced poverty, parental neglect, and poor schooling. Could enriched experiences in adolescence overcome the "deficits" they encountered earlier in development? The answers developmentalists give to such questions reflect their stance on the issues of nature and nurture, continuity and discontinuity, and early and later experiences. The answers also influence public policy about adolescents and how each of us navigates the human life span.

Review Connect Reflect

LG3 Summarize the developmental processes, periods, transitions, and issues related to adolescence.

Review
- What are the key processes involved in adolescent development? What are the main childhood, adolescent, and adult periods of development?
- What is the transition from childhood to adolescence like? What is the transition from adolescence to adulthood like?
- What are three important developmental issues?

Connect
- Describe how nature and nurture might each contribute to an individual's degree of resilience.

Reflect *Your Own Personal Journey of Life*
- As you go through this course, reflect on how you experienced various aspects of adolescence. Be curious. Ask your friends and classmates about their experiences in adolescence and compare them with yours. For example, ask them how they experienced the transition from childhood to adolescence. Also ask them how they experienced, or are experiencing, the transition from adolescence to adulthood.

LG4 Characterize the science of adolescent development.

Science and the Scientific Method

Theories of Adolescent Development

Research in Adolescent Development

How can we answer questions about the roles of nature and nurture, stability and change, and continuity and discontinuity in development? How can we determine, for example, whether an adolescent's achievement in school changes or stays the same from childhood through adolescence, and how can we find out whether positive experiences in adolescence can repair the harm done by neglectful or abusive parenting in childhood? To effectively answer such questions, we need to turn to science.

SCIENCE AND THE SCIENTIFIC METHOD

There is nothing quite so practical as a good theory.

—Kurt Lewin
American Social Psychologist, 20th Century

theory An interrelated, coherent set of ideas that helps explain phenomena and make predictions.

hypotheses Specific assertions and predictions that can be tested.

psychoanalytic theories Theories that describe development as primarily unconscious and heavily colored by emotion. Behavior is merely a surface characteristic, and the symbolic workings of the mind must be analyzed to understand behavior. Early experiences with parents are emphasized.

Some individuals have difficulty thinking of adolescent development as being a science in the same way that physics, chemistry, and biology are sciences. Can a discipline that studies pubertal change, parent-adolescent relationships, or adolescent thinking be equated with disciplines that investigate how gravity works and the molecular structure of compounds? The answer is *yes*, because science is not defined by what it investigates but by how it investigates. Whether you are studying photosynthesis, Saturn's moons, or adolescent development, it is the way you study the subject that matters.

In taking a scientific path to study adolescent development, it is important to follow the *scientific method* (Smith & Davis, 2016). This method is essentially a four-step process: (1) conceptualize a process or problem to be studied, (2) collect research information (data), (3) analyze data, and (4) draw conclusions.

In step 1, when researchers are formulating a problem to study, they often draw on theories and develop hypotheses. A **theory** is an interrelated, coherent set of ideas that helps to explain phenomena and make predictions. It may suggest **hypotheses,** which are specific assertions and predictions that can be tested. For example, a theory on mentoring might state that sustained support and guidance from an adult can enhance the lives of children from impoverished backgrounds because the mentor gives the children opportunities to observe and imitate the behavior and strategies of the mentor.

THEORIES OF ADOLESCENT DEVELOPMENT

This section discusses key aspects of four theoretical orientations to development: psychoanalytic, cognitive, behavioral and social cognitive, and ecological. Each contributes an important piece to the adolescent development puzzle. Although the theories disagree about certain aspects of development, many of their ideas are complementary rather than contradictory. Together they let us see the total landscape of adolescent development in all its richness.

Psychoanalytic Theories **Psychoanalytic theories** describe development as primarily unconscious (beyond awareness) and heavily colored by emotion. Psychoanalytic theorists emphasize that behavior is merely a surface characteristic and that a true understanding of development requires analyzing the symbolic meanings of behavior and the deep inner workings of the mind. Psychoanalytic theorists also stress that early experiences with parents extensively shape development. These characteristics are highlighted in the main psychoanalytic theory, that of Sigmund Freud (1856–1939).

Freud's Theory   As Freud listened to, probed, and analyzed his patients, he became convinced that their problems were the result of experiences early in life. He thought that as children grow up, their focus of pleasure and sexual impulses shifts from the mouth to the anus and eventually to the genitals. As a result, according to Freud's theory, we go through five stages of psychosexual development: oral, anal, phallic, latency, and genital (see Figure 5). Our adult personality, Freud (1917) claimed, is determined by the way we resolve conflicts between sources of pleasure at each stage and the demands of reality.

Sigmund Freud, the pioneering architect of psychoanalytic theory. *What are some characteristics of Freud's theory?*
Bettmann/Getty Images

Oral stage	Anal stage	Phallic stage	Latency stage	Genital stage
Infant's pleasure centers on the mouth.	Child's pleasure focuses on the anus.	Child's pleasure focuses on the genitals.	Child represses sexual interest and develops social and intellectual skills.	A time of sexual reawakening; source of sexual pleasure becomes someone outside the family.
Birth to 1½ Years	**1½ to 3 Years**	**3 to 6 Years**	**6 Years to Puberty**	**Puberty Onward**

FIGURE 5
FREUDIAN STAGES

Freud stressed that adolescents' lives are filled with tension and conflict. To reduce the tension, he thought adolescents bury their conflicts in their unconscious mind. Freud said that even trivial behaviors can become significant when the unconscious forces behind them are revealed. A twitch, a doodle, a joke, a smile—each might betray unconscious conflict. For example, 17-year-old Barbara, while kissing and hugging Tom, exclaims, "Oh, *Jeff*, I love you so much." Repelled, Tom explodes: "Why did you call me Jeff? I thought you didn't think about him anymore. We need to have a talk!" You probably can remember times when such a "Freudian slip" revealed your own unconscious motives.

Freud (1917) divided personality into three structures: the id, the ego, and the superego. The id consists of instincts, which are an individual's reservoir of psychic energy. In Freud's view, the id is totally unconscious; it has no contact with reality. As children experience the demands and constraints of reality, a new structure of personality emerges—the ego, which deals with the demands of reality. The ego is called the "executive branch" of personality because it makes rational decisions.

The id and the ego have no morality—they do not take into account whether something is right or wrong. The superego is the moral branch of personality. The superego takes into account whether something is right or wrong. Think of the superego as what we often refer to as our "conscience." You probably are beginning to sense that both the id and the superego make life rough for the ego. Your ego might say, "I will have sex only occasionally and be sure to take the proper precautions because I don't want a child to interfere with the development of my career." However, your id is saying, "I want to be satisfied; sex is pleasurable." Your superego is at work, too: "I feel guilty about having sex outside of marriage."

Freud considered personality to be like an iceberg. Most of personality exists below our level of awareness, just as the massive part of an iceberg is beneath the water's surface. The ego resolves conflict between its reality demands, the id's wishes, and the superego's constraints through *defense mechanisms*. These are unconscious methods of distorting reality that the ego uses to protect itself from the anxiety produced by the conflicting demands of the three personality structures. When the ego senses that the id's demands may cause harm, anxiety develops, alerting the ego to resolve the conflict by means of defense mechanisms.

According to Freud, *repression* is the most powerful and pervasive defense mechanism. It pushes unacceptable id impulses out of awareness and back into the unconscious mind. Repression is the foundation on which all other defense mechanisms rest, since the goal of every defense mechanism is to repress, or to push threatening impulses out of awareness. Freud thought that early childhood experiences, many of which he believed are sexually laden, are too threatening and stressful for people to deal with consciously, so they repress them.

Erikson's Psychosocial Theory   Erik Erikson recognized Freud's contributions but argued that Freud misjudged some important dimensions of human development. For one thing, Erikson (1950, 1968) said we develop in *psychosocial* stages, rather than in *psychosexual* stages, as Freud maintained. According to Freud, the primary motivation for human behavior is sexual in nature; according to Erikson, it is social and reflects a desire to affiliate with other people. According to Freud, our basic personality is shaped in the first five years of life; according to Erikson, developmental change occurs throughout the life span. Thus, in terms of the early- versus later-experience issue we discussed earlier in the chapter, Freud argued that early experience is far more important than later experiences, whereas Erikson emphasized the importance of both early and later experiences.

developmental **connection**

Identity

Adolescents and emerging adults can be classified as having one of four identity statuses: diffusion, foreclosure, moratorium, or achievement. Connect to "The Self, Identity, Emotion, and Personality."

Erikson's Stages	Developmental Period
Integrity versus despair	Late adulthood (60s onward)
Generativity versus stagnation	Middle adulthood (40s, 50s)
Intimacy versus isolation	Early adulthood (20s, 30s)
Identity versus identity confusion	Adolescence (10 to 20 years)
Industry versus inferiority	Middle and late childhood (elementary school years, 6 years to puberty)
Initiative versus guilt	Early childhood (preschool years, 3 to 5 years)
Autonomy versus shame and doubt	Infancy (1 to 3 years)
Trust versus mistrust	Infancy (first year)

FIGURE 6

ERIKSON'S EIGHT LIFE-SPAN STAGES

Erikson's theory Theory that includes eight stages of human development. Each stage consists of a unique developmental task that confronts individuals with a crisis that must be faced.

Piaget's theory A theory stating that children actively construct their understanding of the world and go through four stages of cognitive development.

In **Erikson's theory,** eight stages of development unfold as we go through life (see Figure 6). At each stage, a unique developmental task confronts individuals with a crisis that must be resolved. According to Erikson, this crisis is not a catastrophe but a turning point marked by both increased vulnerability and enhanced potential. The more successfully an individual resolves the crises, the healthier development will be.

Trust versus mistrust is Erikson's first psychosocial stage, which is experienced in the first year of life. Trust in infancy sets the stage for a lifelong expectation that the world will be a good and pleasant place to live.

Autonomy versus shame and doubt is Erikson's second stage, occurring in late infancy and toddlerhood. After gaining trust, infants begin to discover that their behavior is their own, and they start to assert their independence.

Initiative versus guilt, Erikson's third stage of development, occurs during the preschool years. As preschool children encounter a widening social world, they face new challenges that require active, purposeful, responsible behavior. Feelings of guilt may arise, though, if the child is irresponsible and is made to feel too anxious.

Industry versus inferiority is Erikson's fourth developmental stage, occurring approximately in the elementary school years. Children now need to direct their energy toward mastering knowledge and intellectual skills. The negative outcome is that the child can develop a sense of inferiority—feeling incompetent and unproductive.

During the adolescent years, individuals explore who they are, what they are all about, and where they are going in life. This is Erikson's fifth developmental stage, *identity versus identity confusion*. If adolescents explore roles in a healthy manner and arrive at a positive path to follow in life, they achieve a positive identity; if not, identity confusion reigns.

Intimacy versus isolation is Erikson's sixth developmental stage, which individuals experience during early adulthood. At this time, individuals face the developmental task of forming intimate relationships. If young adults form healthy friendships and create an intimate relationship with another individual, intimacy will be achieved; if not, isolation will result.

Generativity versus stagnation, Erikson's seventh developmental stage, occurs during middle adulthood. By generativity Erikson means primarily a concern for helping the younger generation to develop and lead useful lives. The feeling of having done nothing to help the next generation is stagnation.

Integrity versus despair is Erikson's eighth and final stage of development, which individuals experience in late adulthood. During this stage, a person reflects on the past. If the person's life review reveals a life well spent, integrity will be achieved; if not, the retrospective glances likely will yield doubt or gloom—the despair Erikson described.

Evaluating Psychoanalytic Theories
Contributions of psychoanalytic theories include their emphasis on a developmental framework, family relationships, and unconscious aspects of the mind. Criticisms include a lack of scientific support, too much emphasis on sexual underpinnings, and an image of people that is too negative.

Cognitive Theories   Whereas psychoanalytic theories stress the importance of the unconscious, cognitive theories emphasize conscious thoughts. Three important cognitive theories are Piaget's cognitive developmental theory, Vygotsky's sociocultural cognitive theory, and information-processing theory.

Piaget's Cognitive Developmental Theory   **Piaget's theory** states that individuals actively construct their understanding of the world and go through four stages of cognitive development. Two processes underlie this

Erik Erikson with his wife, Joan, an artist. Erikson generated one of the most important developmental theories of the twentieth century. *Which stage of Erikson's theory are you in? Does Erikson's description of this stage characterize you?*
Jon Erikson/Science Source

Sensorimotor stage	Preoperational stage	Concrete operational stage	Formal operational stage
The infant constructs an understanding of the world by coordinating sensory experiences with physical actions. An infant progresses from reflexive, instinctual action at birth to the beginning of symbolic thought toward the end of the stage.	The child begins to represent the world with words and images. These words and images reflect increased symbolic thinking and go beyond the connection of sensory information and physical action.	The child can now reason logically about concrete events and classify objects into different sets.	The adolescent reasons in more abstract, idealistic, and logical ways.
Birth to 2 Years of Age	**2 to 7 Years of Age**	**7 to 11 Years of Age**	**11 Years of Age Through Adulthood**

FIGURE 7
PIAGET'S FOUR STAGES OF COGNITIVE DEVELOPMENT

cognitive construction of the world: organization and adaptation. To make sense of their world, adolescents organize their experiences. For example, they separate important ideas from less important ideas and connect one idea to another. In addition to organizing their observations and experiences, they adapt, adjusting to new environmental demands.

Piaget (1954) also maintained that people go through four stages in understanding the world (see Figure 7). Each stage is age-related and consists of a distinct way of thinking, a different way of understanding the world. Thus, according to Piaget, cognition is qualitatively different in one stage compared with another. What are Piaget's four stages of cognitive development like?

The *sensorimotor stage*, which lasts from birth to about 2 years of age, is the first Piagetian stage. In this stage, infants construct an understanding of the world by coordinating sensory experiences (such as seeing and hearing) with physical, motoric actions—hence the term *sensorimotor*.

The *preoperational stage*, which lasts from approximately 2 to 7 years of age, is Piaget's second stage. In this stage, children begin to go beyond simply connecting sensory information with physical action and represent the world with words, images, and drawings. However, according to Piaget, preschool children still lack the ability to perform what he calls *operations*, which are internalized mental actions that allow children to do mentally what they previously could only do physically. For example, if you imagine putting two sticks together to see whether they would be as long as another stick without actually moving the sticks, you are performing a concrete operation.

The *concrete operational stage*, which lasts from approximately 7 to 11 years of age, is the third Piagetian stage. In this stage, children can perform operations that involve objects, and they can reason logically as long as they can apply reasoning to specific or concrete examples. For instance, concrete operational thinkers cannot imagine the steps necessary to complete an algebraic equation, which is too abstract for thinking at this stage of development.

The *formal operational stage*, which appears between the ages of 11 and 15 and continues through adulthood, is Piaget's fourth and final stage. In this stage, individuals move beyond concrete experiences and think in abstract and more logical terms. As part of thinking more abstractly, adolescents develop images of ideal circumstances. They might think about what an ideal parent is like and compare their parents to this ideal standard. They begin to entertain possibilities for the future and are fascinated with what they can be. In solving problems, they become more systematic, developing hypotheses about why something is happening the way it is and then testing these hypotheses. We examine Piaget's cognitive developmental theory further in the chapter on "The Brain and Cognitive Development."

Vygotsky's Sociocultural Cognitive Theory Like Piaget, the Russian developmentalist Lev Vygotsky (1896–1934) emphasized that individuals actively construct their knowledge. However, Vygotsky (1962) gave social interaction and culture far more

Jean Piaget, the famous Swiss developmental psychologist, changed the way we think about the development of children's minds. *What are some key ideas in Piaget's theory?*
Yves de Braine/Black Star/Stock Photo

There is considerable interest today in Lev Vygotsky's sociocultural cognitive theory of child development. *What were Vygotsky's basic claims about children's development?*
A.R. Lauria/Dr. Michael Cole, Laboratory of Human Cognition, University of California, San Diego

bfk/Shutterstock

- - - - - - - ➤

developmental **connection**

Social Cognitive Theory

Bandura emphasizes that self-efficacy is a key person/cognitive factor in adolescents' achievement. Connect to "Achievement, Work, and Careers."

◄ - - - - - - -

Vygotsky's theory A sociocultural cognitive theory that emphasizes how culture and social interaction guide cognitive development.

information-processing theory A theory emphasizing that individuals manipulate information, monitor it, and strategize about it. Central to this approach are the processes of memory and thinking.

social cognitive theory The view that behavior, environment, and person/cognition are the key factors in development.

important roles in cognitive development than Piaget did. **Vygotsky's theory** is a sociocultural cognitive theory that emphasizes how culture and social interaction guide cognitive development.

Vygotsky portrayed development as inseparable from social and cultural activities (Baggs & Chemero, 2020). He stressed that cognitive development involves learning to use the inventions of society, such as language, mathematical systems, and memory strategies. Thus, in one culture, individuals might learn to count with the help of a computer; in another, they might learn by using beads. According to Vygotsky, children's and adolescents' social interaction with more-skilled adults and peers is indispensable to their cognitive development (Holzman, 2017). Through this interaction, they learn to use the tools that will help them adapt and be successful in their culture. Later we will examine ideas about learning and teaching that are based on Vygotsky's theory.

Information-Processing Theory   **Information-processing theory** emphasizes that individuals manipulate information, monitor it, and strategize about it. Unlike Piaget's theory, but like Vygotsky's theory, information-processing theory does not describe development as stage-like. Instead, according to this theory, individuals develop a gradually increasing capacity for processing information, which allows them to acquire increasingly complex knowledge and skills (Gordon & others, 2020).

Robert Siegler (2006, 2017), a leading expert on children's information processing, states that thinking is information processing. In other words, when adolescents perceive, encode, represent, store, and retrieve information, they are thinking. Siegler and his colleagues (Siegler & Alibali, 2020; Siegler & Lortie-Forgues, 2017) emphasize that an important aspect of development is learning good strategies for processing information. For example, becoming a better reader might involve learning to monitor the key themes of the material being read.

Evaluating Cognitive Theories   Contributions of cognitive theories include their positive view of development and their emphasis on the active construction of understanding. Criticisms include skepticism about the pureness of Piaget's stages and too little attention paid to individual variations.

Behavioral and Social Cognitive Theories   *Behaviorism* essentially holds that we can study scientifically only what we can directly observe and measure. Out of the behavioral tradition grew the belief that development is observable behavior that can be learned through experience with the environment (Schunk, 2020). In terms of the continuity-discontinuity issue we discussed earlier in this chapter, the behavioral and social cognitive theories emphasize continuity in development and argue that development does not occur in stage-like fashion. Let's explore two versions of behaviorism: Skinner's operant conditioning and Bandura's social cognitive theory.

Skinner's Operant Conditioning   According to B. F. Skinner (1904–1990), through *operant conditioning* the consequences of a behavior produce changes in the probability of the behavior's occurrence. A behavior followed by a rewarding stimulus is more likely to recur, whereas a behavior followed by a punishing stimulus is less likely to recur. For example, when an adult smiles at an adolescent after the adolescent has done something, the adolescent is more likely to engage in the activity again than if the adult gives the adolescent a nasty look.

In Skinner's (1938) view, such rewards and punishments shape development. For example, Skinner's approach argues that shy people learn to be shy as a result of experiences they have while growing up. It follows that modifications in an environment can help a shy adolescent become more socially oriented. Also, for Skinner the key aspect of development is behavior, not thoughts and feelings. He emphasized that development consists of the pattern of behavioral changes that are brought about by rewards and punishments.

Bandura's Social Cognitive Theory   Some psychologists agree with the behaviorists' notion that development is learned and is influenced strongly by environmental interactions. However, unlike Skinner, they argue that cognition is also important in understanding development. **Social cognitive theory** holds that behavior, environment, and person/cognition are the key factors in development.

American psychologist Albert Bandura (1925–) is the leading architect of social cognitive theory. Bandura (2001, 2015. 2018) emphasizes that cognitive processes have important links with the environment and behavior. His early research program focused heavily on *observational learning* (also called *imitation*, or *modeling*), which is learning that occurs through observing what others do. For example, a young boy might observe his father yelling in anger and treating other people with hostility; with his peers, the young boy later acts very aggressively, showing the same characteristics as his father's behavior. Social cognitive theorists stress that people acquire a wide range of behaviors, thoughts, and feelings through observing others' behavior and that these observations play an important part in adolescent development.

What is *cognitive* about observational learning, in Bandura's view? He proposes that people cognitively represent the behavior of others and then sometimes adopt this behavior themselves.

Bandura's (2015, 2018) most recent model of learning and development includes three elements: behavior, the person/cognition, and the environment. An individual's confidence in being able to control his or her success is an example of a person factor; strategies are an example of a cognitive factor. As shown in Figure 8, behavioral, person/cognitive, and environmental factors operate interactively.

Evaluating Behavioral and Social Cognitive Theories   Contributions of the behavioral and social cognitive theories include their emphasis on scientific research and environmental determinants of behavior. Criticisms include too little emphasis on cognition in Skinner's views and inadequate attention given to developmental changes.

Ecological Theory   One ecological theory that has important implications for understanding adolescent development was created by Urie Bronfenbrenner (1917–2005). **Bronfenbrenner's ecological theory** (1986, 2004; Bronfenbrenner & Morris, 1998, 2006) holds that development reflects the influence of five environmental systems: microsystem, mesosystem, exosystem, macrosystem, and chronosystem (see Figure 9).

The *microsystem* is the setting in which the adolescent lives. These contexts include the adolescent's family, peers, school, and neighborhood. It is in the microsystem that the most direct interactions with social agents take place—with parents, peers, and teachers, for example.

Albert Bandura developed social cognitive theory.
Courtesy of Dr. Albert Bandura

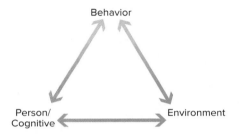

FIGURE 8

BANDURA'S SOCIAL COGNITIVE THEORY.
Bandura's social cognitive theory emphasizes reciprocal influences of behavioral, environmental, and person/cognitive factors.

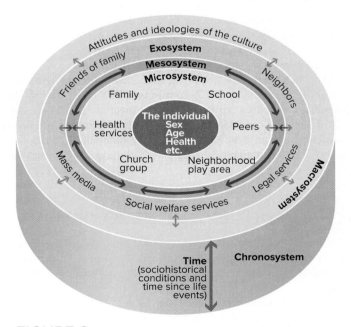

FIGURE 9

BRONFENBRENNER'S ECOLOGICAL THEORY OF DEVELOPMENT. Bronfenbrenner's ecological theory consists of five environmental systems: microsystem, mesosystem, exosystem, macrosystem, and chronosystem.

Bronfenbrenner's ecological theory A theory focusing on the influence of five environmental systems: microsystem, mesosystem, exosystem, macrosystem, and chronosystem.

Urie Bronfenbrenner developed ecological theory, a perspective that is receiving increased attention. *What is the nature of ecological theory?*
Cornell University Photography

The adolescent is not a passive recipient of experiences in these settings but someone who helps to construct the settings.

The *mesosystem* involves relations between microsystems or connections between contexts. Examples are the relation of family experiences to school experiences, school experiences to religious experiences, and family experiences to peer experiences. For example, adolescents whose parents have rejected them may have difficulty developing positive relationships with teachers.

The *exosystem* consists of links between a social setting in which the adolescent does not have an active role and the individual's immediate context. For example, a husband's or an adolescent's experience at home may be influenced by a mother's experiences at work. The mother might receive a promotion that requires more travel, which might increase conflict with the husband and change patterns of interaction with the adolescent.

The *macrosystem* involves the culture in which adolescents live. *Culture* refers to the behavior patterns, beliefs, and all other products of a group of people that are passed on from generation to generation.

The *chronosystem* consists of the patterning of environmental events and transitions over the life course, as well as sociohistorical circumstances. For example, divorce is one transition. Researchers have found that the negative effects of divorce on children often peak in the first year after the divorce (Hetherington, 2006). By two years after the divorce, family interaction is less chaotic and more stable. As an example of sociohistorical circumstances, consider how the opportunities for adolescent girls to pursue a career have increased during the last fifty years.

Bronfenbrenner (2004; Bronfenbrenner & Morris, 2006) has added biological influences to his theory and describes the newer version as a bioecological theory. Nonetheless, ecological, environmental contexts still predominate in Bronfenbrenner's theory.

Contributions of ecological theory include its systematic examination of macro and micro dimensions of environmental systems and its attention to connections between environmental systems. Criticisms include inadequate attention to biological factors, as well as too little emphasis on cognitive factors.

An Eclectic Theoretical Orientation   No single theory described in this chapter can explain entirely the rich complexity of adolescent development, but each has contributed to our understanding of it. Psychoanalytic theory best explains the unconscious mind. Erikson's theory best describes the changes that occur in adult development. Piaget's, Vygotsky's, and the information-processing views provide the most complete description of cognitive development. The behavioral and social cognitive and ecological theories have been the most adept at examining the environmental determinants of development.

In short, although theories are helpful guides, relying on a single theory to explain adolescent development probably would be a mistake. This book instead takes an **eclectic theoretical orientation,** which does not follow any one theoretical approach but rather selects from each theory whatever is considered its best features. In this way, you can view the study of adolescent development as it actually exists—with different theorists making different assumptions, stressing different empirical problems, and using different strategies to discover information.

RESEARCH IN ADOLESCENT DEVELOPMENT

If scholars and researchers follow an eclectic orientation, how do they determine that one feature of a theory is somehow better than another? The scientific method discussed earlier provides the guide. Through scientific research, the features of theories can be tested and refined.

Generally, research in adolescent development is designed to test hypotheses, which in some cases are derived from the theories just described. Through research, theories are modified to reflect new data and occasionally new theories arise.

In the twenty-first century, research on adolescent and emerging adult development has expanded a great deal (Arnett & Mitra, 2020; Nelson, 2021). Also, research on adolescent development has increasingly examined applications to the real worlds of adolescents (Koenig & others, 2020). This research trend involves a search for ways to improve the health and

Truth is arrived at by the painstaking process of eliminating the untrue.

—SIR ARTHUR CONAN DOYLE
British Physician and Detective-story Writer, 20th Century

eclectic theoretical orientation An orientation that does not follow any one theoretical approach but rather selects from each theory whatever is considered the best aspects of it.

well-being of adolescents. The increased application emphasis in research on adolescent development is described in all of the chapters in this text. Let's now turn our attention to the collection of data on adolescent development and the creation of research designs for studying adolescent development.

Methods for Collecting Data   Whether we are interested in studying pubertal change, cognitive skills, parent-adolescent conflict, or juvenile delinquency, we can choose from several ways of collecting data. Here we consider the measures most often used, beginning with observation.

Observation   Scientific observation requires an important set of skills (Stanovich, 2019). For observations to be effective, they have to be systematic. We need to have some idea of what we are looking for. We have to know whom we are observing, when and where we will observe, how we will make the observations, and how we will record them.

Where should we make our observations? We have two choices: the laboratory and the everyday world.

When we observe scientifically, we often need to control certain factors that determine behavior but are not the focus of our inquiry (Gravetter & others, 2021). For this reason, some adolescent development research is conducted in a **laboratory,** a controlled setting with many of the complex factors of the "real world" removed. Laboratory research does have some drawbacks, however. First, it is almost impossible to conduct laboratory research without letting the participants know they are being studied. Second, the laboratory setting is unnatural and therefore can cause the participants to behave unnaturally. Third, people who are willing to come to a university laboratory may not fairly represent groups from diverse cultural backgrounds. In addition, people who are unfamiliar with university settings and with the idea of "helping science" may be intimidated by the laboratory setting.

Naturalistic observation provides insights that sometimes cannot be achieved in the laboratory (Neuman, 2020). **Naturalistic observation** means observing behavior in real-world settings, making no effort to manipulate or control the situation. Life-span researchers conduct naturalistic observations in neighborhoods, at schools, sporting events, work settings, and malls, and in other places adolescents frequent.

Survey and Interview   Sometimes the best and quickest way to get information about adolescents is to ask them for it. One technique is to interview them directly. A related method is the survey (sometimes referred to as a questionnaire), which is especially useful when information from many people is needed. A standard set of questions is used to obtain people's self-reported attitudes or beliefs about a specific topic. In a good survey, the questions are clear and unbiased, allowing respondents to answer unambiguously.

Surveys and interviews can be used to study a wide range of topics, from religious beliefs to sexual habits to attitudes about gun control to beliefs about how to improve schools. Surveys and interviews today are conducted in person, over the telephone, and on the Internet.

One problem with surveys and interviews is the tendency of participants to answer questions in a way that they think is socially acceptable or desirable rather than telling what they truly think or feel. For example, on a survey or in an interview, some adolescents might say that they do not use drugs even though they do.

Standardized Test   A **standardized test** has uniform procedures for administration and scoring. Many standardized tests allow a person's performance to be compared with the performance of other individuals; thus, they provide information about individual differences among people (Cohen, Schneider, & Tobin, 2022). One example is the Stanford-Binet intelligence test. Your score on the Stanford-Binet test tells you how your performance compares with that of thousands of other people who have taken the test.

One criticism of standardized tests is that they assume a person's behavior is consistent and stable, yet personality and intelligence—two primary targets of standardized testing—can vary with the situation. For example, adolescents may perform poorly on a standardized intelligence test in an office setting but score much higher at home, where they are less anxious.

laboratory A controlled setting in which many of the complex factors of the "real world" are removed.

naturalistic observation Observation of behavior in real-world settings.

standardized test A test with uniform procedures for administration and scoring. Many standardized tests allow a person's performance to be compared with the performance of other individuals.

When conducting surveys or interviews with adolescents, what are some strategies that researchers need to exercise?
Monkey Business Images/Shutterstock

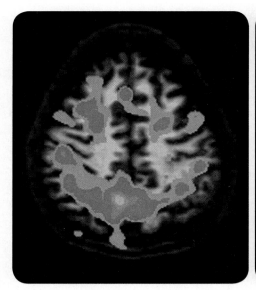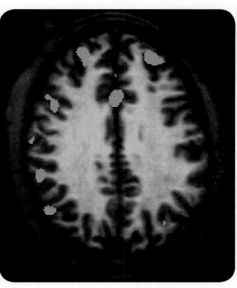

FIGURE 10

BRAIN IMAGING OF 15-YEAR-OLD ADOLESCENTS. The two brain images indicate how alcohol can influence the functioning of an adolescent's brain. Notice the pink and red coloring (which indicates effective brain functioning involving memory) in the brain of the 15-year-old non-drinker while engaging in a memory task, and the lack of those colors in the brain of the 15-year-old under the influence of alcohol.
(both): Dr. Susan F. Tapert, University of California, San Diego

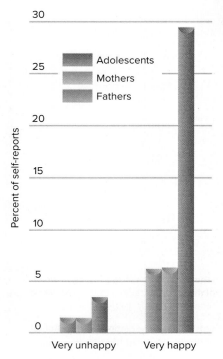

FIGURE 11

SELF-REPORTED EXTREMES OF EMOTION BY ADOLESCENTS, MOTHERS, AND FATHERS USING THE EXPERIENCE SAMPLING METHOD. In the study by Reed Larson and Maryse Richards (1994), adolescents and their mothers and fathers were beeped at random times by researchers using the experience sampling method. The researchers found that adolescents were more likely to report emotional extremes than their parents were.

experience sampling method (ESM) Research method that involves providing participants with electronic pagers and then beeping them at random times, at which point they are asked to report on various aspects of their lives.

case study An in-depth look at a single individual.

Physiological Measures   Researchers are increasingly using physiological measures when they study development at different points in the life span. Hormone levels are increasingly used in developmental research. Cortisol is a hormone produced by the adrenal gland that is linked to the body's stress level and has been used in studies of temperament, emotional reactivity, mood, and peer relations (Peckins & others, 2020). Also, as puberty unfolds, the blood levels of certain hormones increase. To determine the nature of these hormonal changes, researchers analyze blood samples from adolescent volunteers (Bae & others, 2019). The body composition of adolescents also is a focus of physiological assessment. There is a special interest in the increase in fat content in the body during pubertal development.

Until recently, little research had focused on the brain activity of adolescents. However, the development of neuroimaging techniques has led to a flurry of research studies. One technique that is being used in a number of studies is *magnetic resonance imaging (MRI)*, in which radio waves are used to construct images of a person's brain tissue and biochemical activity (Kirmayer & others, 2021). Figure 10 compares the brain images of two adolescents—one a non-drinker, the other a heavy drinker who was intoxicated at the time that the image was collected—while they were engaging in a memory task.

Yet another dramatic change in physiological measures is the advancement in methods to assess the actual units of hereditary information—genes—in studies of biological influences on development (Brooker, 2021). For example, recent advances in assessing genes have revealed several specific genes that are linked to child and adolescent obesity (Saeed & others, 2020; Seral-Cortes & others, 2021). We will have much more to say about genetic influences on adolescent development in "Puberty, Health, and Biological Foundations."

Experience Sampling   In the **experience sampling method (ESM),** participants in a study are given electronic pagers. Then, researchers "beep" them at random times. When they are beeped, the participants report on various aspects of their immediate situation, including where they are, what they are doing, whom they are with, and how they are feeling.

The ESM has been used in a number of studies to determine the settings in which adolescents are most likely to spend their time, the extent to which they spend time with parents and peers, and the nature of their emotions. Using this method, Reed Larson and Maryse Richards (1994) found that across the thousands of times they reported their feelings, adolescents experienced emotions that were more extreme and more fleeting than those of their parents. For example, adolescents were five times more likely than their parents to report being "very happy" when they were beeped, and three times more likely to feel "very unhappy" (see Figure 11).

Case Study   A **case study** is an in-depth look at a single individual. Case studies are performed mainly by mental health professionals, when for practical or ethical reasons the unique

FIGURE 12

(a)

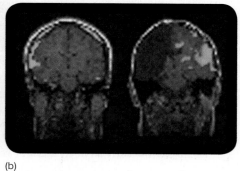

(b)

PLASTICITY IN THE BRAIN'S HEMISPHERES.
(*a*) Michael Rehbein at 14 years of age.
(*b*) Michael's right hemisphere (*right*) has reorganized to take over the language functions normally carried out by corresponding areas in the left hemisphere of an intact brain (*left*). However, the right hemisphere is not as efficient in processing speech as the left, and more areas of the brain are recruited to process speech.
(both): Courtesy of The Rehbein Family

aspects of an individual's life cannot be duplicated and tested in other individuals. A case study provides information about one person's fears, hopes, fantasies, traumatic experiences, upbringing, family relationships, health, or anything else that helps the psychologist to understand the person's mind and behavior.

Consider the case study of Michael Rehbein, which illustrates the flexibility and resilience of the developing brain. At age 7, Michael began to experience uncontrollable seizures—as many as 400 a day. Doctors said that the only solution was to remove the left hemisphere of his brain where the seizures were occurring. Though Michael's recovery was slow, eventually his right hemisphere began to reorganize and take over functions that normally reside in the brain's left hemisphere, such as speech. The neuroimage in Figure 12 shows this reorganization of Michael's brain vividly.

Although case histories provide dramatic, in-depth portrayals of people's lives, we must be cautious in generalizing from them. The subject of a case study is unique, with a genetic makeup and personal history that no one else shares. In addition, case studies involve judgments of unknown reliability. Psychologists who conduct case studies rarely check to see whether other psychologists agree with their observations.

In conducting research on adolescent development, in addition to selecting a method for collecting data you will also need to choose a research design. There are three main types of research designs: descriptive, correlational, and experimental.

Descriptive Research   All of the data-collection methods that we have discussed can be used in **descriptive research,** which aims to observe and record behavior (Neuman, 2020). For example, a researcher might observe the extent to which adolescents are altruistic or aggressive toward each other. By itself, descriptive research cannot prove what causes specific phenomena, but it can reveal important information about people's behavior.

Correlational Research   In contrast with descriptive research, correlational research goes beyond describing phenomena to provide information that will help us to predict how people will behave (Gravetter & others, 2021). In **correlational research,** the goal is to describe the strength of the relationship between two or more events or characteristics. The more strongly the two events are correlated (or related or associated), the more effectively we can predict one event from the other.

For example, to study whether adolescents of permissive parents have less self-control than other adolescents, you would need to carefully record observations of parents' permissiveness and their children's self-control. You could then analyze the data statistically to yield a numerical measure, called a **correlation coefficient,** a number based on a statistical analysis that is

descriptive research Research that aims to observe and record behavior.

correlational research Research whose goal is to describe the strength of the relationship between two or more events or characteristics.

correlation coefficient A number based on a statistical analysis that is used to describe the degree of association between two variables.

Observed Correlation: As permissive parenting increases, adolescents' self-control decreases.

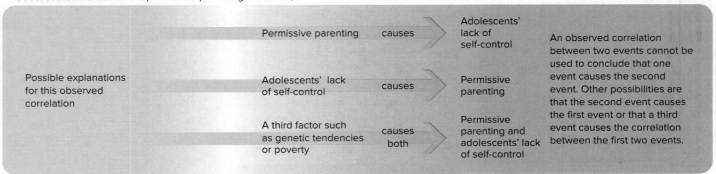

FIGURE **13**
POSSIBLE EXPLANATIONS OF CORRELATIONAL DATA

used to describe the degree of association between two variables. The correlation coefficient ranges from −1.00 to +1.00. A negative number means an inverse relation. For example, researchers often find a negative correlation between permissive parenting and adolescents' self-control. By contrast, they often find a positive correlation between parental monitoring of children and adolescents' self-control.

The higher the correlation coefficient (whether positive or negative), the stronger the association between the two variables. A correlation of 0 means that there is no association between the variables. A correlation of −.40 is stronger than a correlation of +.20 because we disregard whether the correlation is positive or negative in determining the strength of the correlation.

A caution is in order, however (Christensen, Johnson, & Turner, 2020). Correlation does not equal causation. The correlational finding just mentioned does not mean that permissive parenting necessarily causes low self-control in adolescents. It could have that meaning, but it also could mean that an adolescent's lack of self-control caused the parents to give up trying to control the adolescent. It also could mean that other factors, such as heredity or poverty, caused the correlation between permissive parenting and low self-control in adolescents. Figure 13 illustrates these possible interpretations of correlational data.

Experimental Research　To study causality, researchers turn to **experimental research.** An experiment is a carefully regulated procedure in which one or more factors believed to influence a specific behavior are manipulated while all other factors are held constant. If the behavior under study changes when a factor is manipulated, researchers say that the manipulated factor has caused the behavior to change (Graziano & Raulin, 2020). In other words, the experiment has demonstrated cause and effect. The cause is the factor that was manipulated. The effect is the behavior that changed because of the manipulation. Nonexperimental research methods (descriptive and correlational research) cannot establish cause and effect because they do not involve manipulating factors in a controlled way.

All experiments involve at least one independent variable and one dependent variable. The **independent variable** is the factor that is manipulated. The term *independent* indicates that this variable can be manipulated independently of all other factors. For example, suppose we want to design an experiment to establish the effects of peer tutoring on adolescents' academic achievement. In this example, the amount and type of peer tutoring could be the independent variable.

The **dependent variable** is the factor that is measured; it can change as the independent variable is manipulated. The term *dependent* indicates that this variable depends on what happens as the independent variable is manipulated. In the peer tutoring study, adolescents' academic achievement would be the dependent variable. It might be assessed in a number of ways, perhaps by grade point averages or scores on a nationally standardized achievement test.

In an experiment, researchers manipulate the independent variable by giving different experiences to one or more experimental groups and one or more control groups. An *experimental group* is a group whose experience is manipulated. A *control group* is a group that is treated like the experimental group in every way except for the manipulated factor. The control group serves as a baseline against which the effects on the manipulated group can be compared. In the peer tutoring study, we would need to have one group of adolescents who received peer tutoring (experimental group) and one who did not (control group).

experimental research Research that involves an experiment, a carefully regulated procedure in which one or more of the factors believed to influence the behavior being studied are manipulated while all other factors are held constant.

independent variable The factor that is manipulated in experimental research.

dependent variable The factor that is measured in experimental research.

An important principle of experimental research is *random assignment*—assigning participants to experimental and control groups by chance. This practice reduces the likelihood that the results of the experiment will be affected by preexisting differences between the groups. In our study of peer tutoring, random assignment would greatly reduce the probability that the two groups differed in age, family background, initial achievement, intelligence, personality, or health.

To summarize, in our study of peer tutoring and adolescent achievement, we would assign participants randomly to two groups. One (the experimental group) would receive peer tutoring and the other (the control group) would not. The different experiences that the experimental and control groups receive would be the independent variable. After the peer tutoring had been completed, the adolescents would be given a nationally standardized achievement test (the dependent variable). Figure 14 applies the experimental research method to a different problem: whether a time management program can improve adolescents' grades.

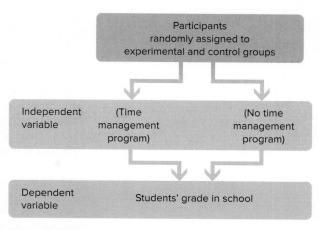

FIGURE **14**

RANDOM ASSIGNMENT AND EXPERIMENTAL DESIGN

Time Span of Research   A special concern of developmentalists is the time span of a research investigation. Studies that focus on the relation of age to some other variable are common. Researchers have two options: They can study different individuals of varying ages and compare them, or they can study the same individuals as they age over time.

Cross-Sectional Research   **Cross-sectional research** involves studying a group of people at the same time. For example, a researcher might study the self-esteem of 10-, 15-, and 20-year-olds. In a cross-sectional study, all participants' self-esteem would be assessed at one time.

The main advantage of a cross-sectional study is that researchers do not have to wait for the individuals to grow older. Despite its time efficiency, however, the cross-sectional approach has drawbacks. It gives no information about how individuals change or about the stability of their characteristics. The increases and decreases of development—the hills and valleys of growth and development—can become obscured in the cross-sectional approach. For example, in a cross-sectional study of self-esteem, average increases and decreases might be revealed. But the study would not show how the life satisfaction of individual children waxed and waned over the years. It also would not tell us whether younger children who had high or low self-esteem as young adults continued to have high or low self-esteem, respectively, when they became older.

Longitudinal Research   **Longitudinal research** involves studying the same individuals over a period of time, usually several years or more. In a longitudinal study of self-esteem, the researcher might examine the self-esteem of a group of 10-year-olds, then assess their self-esteem again when they are 15, and then again when they are 20.

Longitudinal studies provide a wealth of information about such important issues as stability and change in development and the importance of early experience for later development (Kramer & Rodgers, 2020). However, they are not without their problems. They are expensive and time-consuming. The longer the study lasts, the greater the number of participants who drop out—they move, get sick, lose interest, and so forth. Changes in the participant group can bias the outcome of a study, because those who remain may be dissimilar to those who drop out. Those individuals who remain in a longitudinal study over a number of years may be more compulsive and conformity-oriented, for example, or they might lead more stable lives.

Conducting Ethical Research   Ethics in research may affect you personally if you ever serve as a participant in a study. In that event, you need to know your rights as a participant and the responsibilities of researchers to assure that these rights are safeguarded.

If you ever become a researcher in life-span development yourself, you will need an even deeper understanding of ethics. Even if you carry out experimental projects only in psychology courses, you must consider the rights of the participants in those projects. A student might think, "I volunteer in a home for individuals with an intellectual disability several hours per week. I can use the residents of the home in my study to see if a specific treatment helps improve their memory for everyday tasks." Howevewr, without proper permissions, the most well-meaning, kind, and considerate studies still violate the rights of the participants.

Today, proposed research at colleges and universities must pass the scrutiny of a research ethics committee before the research can be initiated. In addition, the American Psychological Association (APA) has developed ethics guidelines for its members. The APA code of ethics

cross-sectional research A research strategy that involves studying different people of varying ages all at one time.

longitudinal research A research strategy in which the same individuals are studied over a period of time, usually several years or more.

instructs psychologists to protect their participants from mental and physical harm. The participants' best interests need to be kept foremost in the researcher's mind (Neuman, 2020). APA's guidelines address four important issues. First, *informed consent*—all participants must know what their research participation will involve and what risks might develop. Even after informed consent is given, participants must retain the right to withdraw from the study at any time and for any reason. Second, *confidentiality*—researchers are responsible for keeping all of the data they gather on individuals completely confidential and, when possible, completely anonymous. Third, *debriefing*—after the study has been completed, participants should be informed of its purpose and the methods that were used. In most cases, the experimenter also can inform participants in a general manner beforehand about the purpose of the research without leading participants to behave in a way they think that the experimenter is expecting. Fourth, *deception*—in some circumstances, telling the participants beforehand what the research study is about substantially alters the participants' behavior and invalidates the researcher's data. In all cases of deception, however, the psychologist must ensure that the deception will not harm the participants and that the participants will be told the complete nature of the study (will be debriefed) as soon as possible after the study is completed.

Minimizing Bias   Studies of adolescent development are most useful when they are conducted without bias or prejudice toward any particular group of people. Of special concern is bias based on gender and bias based on culture or ethnicity.

Gender Bias   Society continues to have a **gender bias,** a preconceived notion about the abilities of females and males that prevents individuals from pursuing their own interests and achieving their potential. But gender bias also has had a less obvious effect within the field of adolescent development. For example, too often researchers have drawn conclusions about females' attitudes and behaviors from research conducted with males as the only participants (Helgeson, 2021).

When gender differences are found, they sometimes are unduly magnified (Dettori & Gupta, 2018). For example, a researcher might report in a study that 74 percent of the boys had high achievement expectations versus only 67 percent of the girls and go on to talk about the differences in some detail. In reality, this might be a rather small difference. It also might disappear if the study were repeated, or the study might have methodological problems that don't allow such strong interpretations.

Cultural and Ethnic Bias   At the same time that researchers have been struggling with gender bias, there is an increasing awareness that research needs to include more people from diverse ethnic groups (Gollnick & Chinn, 2021). Historically, members of ethnic minority groups (African American, Latinx, Asian American, and Native American) have been discounted from most research in the United States and simply thought of as variations from the norm or average. Because their scores don't always fit neatly into measures of central tendency (such as a mean score to reflect the average performance of a group of participants), minority individuals have been viewed as confounds or "noise" in data. Consequently, researchers have deliberately excluded them from the samples they have selected. Given the fact that individuals from diverse ethnic groups were excluded from research on adolescent development for so long, we might reasonably conclude that adolescents' real lives are perhaps more varied than research data have indicated in the past.

Researchers also have tended to overgeneralize about ethnic groups. **Ethnic gloss** is using an ethnic label such as African American or Latinx in a superficial way that portrays an ethnic group as being more homogeneous than it really is (Trimble, 2021). For example, a researcher might describe a research sample like this: "The participants were 20 Latinxs and 20 Anglo-Americans." A more complete description of the Latinx group might be something like this: "The 20 Latinx participants were Mexican Americans from low-income neighborhoods in the southwestern area of Los Angeles. Twelve were from homes in which Spanish is the dominant language spoken, 8 from homes in which English is the main language spoken. Ten were born in the United States, 10 in Mexico. Ten described themselves as Mexican American, 4 as Mexican, 3 as American, 2 as Chicano, and 1 as Latinx." Ethnic gloss can cause researchers to obtain samples of ethnic groups that are not representative of the group's diversity, which can lead to overgeneralization and stereotyping.

Research on ethnic minority children and their families has not been given adequate attention, especially in light of their significant rate of growth within the overall population

developmental **connection**

Gender

Research continues to find that gender stereotyping is pervasive. Connect to "Gender."

developmental **connection**

Diversity

Too often differences between ethnic minority groups and the non-Latinx white majority group have been characterized as deficits on the part of ethnic minority groups. Connect to "Culture."

gender bias A preconceived notion about the abilities of females and males that prevents individuals from pursuing their own interests and achieving their potential.

ethnic gloss Use of an ethnic label such as *African American* or *Latinx* in a superficial way that portrays an ethnic group as being more homogeneous than it really is.

Look at the two photographs, one of all non-Latinx white males (*left*) and one of a diverse group of females and males from different ethnic groups, including some non-Latinx white individuals (*right*). Consider a topic in adolescent development, such as parenting, identity, or cultural values. *If you were conducting research on this topic, might the results be different depending on whether the participants in your study were the individuals in the photograph on the left or the individuals in the photograph on the right?*
(left) PA Images/Alamy Stock Photo; (right) FatCamera/Getty Images

(Romero & others, 2020). Until recently, ethnic minority families were combined in the category "minority," which masks important differences among ethnic groups as well as diversity within an ethnic group. At present and in the foreseeable future, the growth of minority families in the United States will be mainly due to the immigration of Latinx and Asian families (Clauss-Ehlers, Roysircar, & Hunter, 2021). Researchers need to take into account the acculturation level and generational status of both parents and adolescents. More attention also needs to be given to biculturalism because many immigrant children and adolescents identify with two or more ethnic groups (Woo & others, 2020).

Pam Reid is a leading researcher who studies the influences of gender and ethnic bias on development. To read about her interests, see the *Connecting with Careers* profile.

connecting with careers

Pam Reid, Educational and Developmental Psychologist

When she was a child, Pam Reid liked to play with chemistry sets. Reid majored in chemistry during college and wanted to become a doctor. However, when some of her friends signed up for a psychology class as an elective, she also decided to take the course. She was intrigued by learning about how people think, behave, and develop—so much so that she changed her major to psychology. Reid went on to obtain her Ph.D. in psychology (American Psychological Association, 2003, p. 16).

For a number of years, Reid was a professor of education and psychology at the University of Michigan, where she also was a research scientist at the Institute for Research on Women and Gender. Her main focus has been on how children and adolescents develop social skills, with a special interest in the development of African American girls (Reid & Zalk, 2001). In 2004, Reid became provost and executive vice-president at Roosevelt University in Chicago, and from 2008 to 2015 she was president of the University of Saint Joseph in Hartford, Connecticut, before retiring to pursue other interests.

Pam Reid (*center*) with some of the graduate students she mentored at the University of Michigan.
Courtesy of Dr. Pam Reid

For more information about the work that educational psychologists do, see the "Careers in Adolescent and Emerging Adult Development" appendix.

Review
- What is the nature of the scientific study of adolescent development? What is meant by the concept of theory?
- What are four main theories of adolescent development?
- What are the main methods used to collect data on adolescent development? What are the main research designs? What are some concerns about potential bias in research on adolescents?

Connect
- Which research method do you think would best address the question of whether adolescents around the world experience stereotyping?

Reflect *Your Own Personal Journey of Life*
- Which of the theories of adolescent development do you think best explains your own adolescent development?

reach your **learning goals**

Introduction

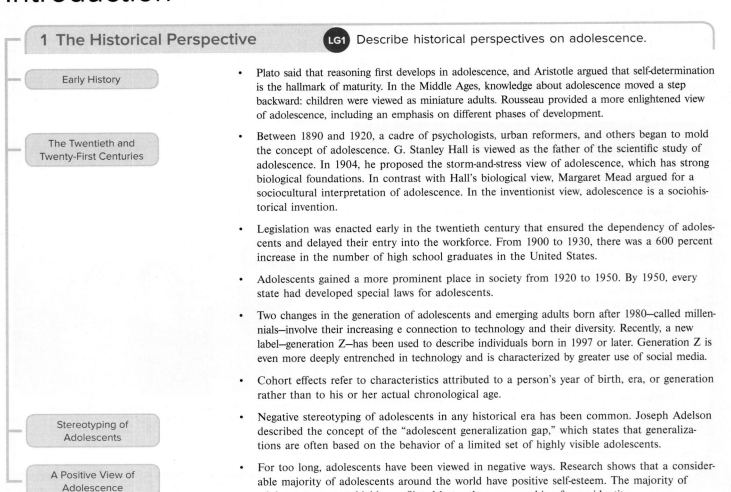

1 The Historical Perspective
LG1 Describe historical perspectives on adolescence.

Early History

The Twentieth and Twenty-First Centuries

- Plato said that reasoning first develops in adolescence, and Aristotle argued that self-determination is the hallmark of maturity. In the Middle Ages, knowledge about adolescence moved a step backward: children were viewed as miniature adults. Rousseau provided a more enlightened view of adolescence, including an emphasis on different phases of development.

- Between 1890 and 1920, a cadre of psychologists, urban reformers, and others began to mold the concept of adolescence. G. Stanley Hall is viewed as the father of the scientific study of adolescence. In 1904, he proposed the storm-and-stress view of adolescence, which has strong biological foundations. In contrast with Hall's biological view, Margaret Mead argued for a sociocultural interpretation of adolescence. In the inventionist view, adolescence is a sociohistorical invention.

- Legislation was enacted early in the twentieth century that ensured the dependency of adolescents and delayed their entry into the workforce. From 1900 to 1930, there was a 600 percent increase in the number of high school graduates in the United States.

- Adolescents gained a more prominent place in society from 1920 to 1950. By 1950, every state had developed special laws for adolescents.

- Two changes in the generation of adolescents and emerging adults born after 1980—called millennials—involve their increasing e connection to technology and their diversity. Recently, a new label—generation Z—has been used to describe individuals born in 1997 or later. Generation Z is even more deeply entrenched in technology and is characterized by greater use of social media.

- Cohort effects refer to characteristics attributed to a person's year of birth, era, or generation rather than to his or her actual chronological age.

Stereotyping of Adolescents

- Negative stereotyping of adolescents in any historical era has been common. Joseph Adelson described the concept of the "adolescent generalization gap," which states that generalizations are often based on the behavior of a limited set of highly visible adolescents.

A Positive View of Adolescence

- For too long, adolescents have been viewed in negative ways. Research shows that a considerable majority of adolescents around the world have positive self-esteem. The majority of adolescents are not highly conflicted but rather are searching for an identity.

2 Today's Adolescents in the United States and Around the World

 Discuss the experiences of adolescents in the United States and around the world.

Adolescents in the United States

- Adolescents are heterogeneous. Although a majority of adolescents successfully make the transition from childhood to adulthood, too large a percentage do not and are not provided with adequate opportunities and support. Different portraits of adolescents emerge depending on the particular set of adolescents being described.

- Contexts, the settings in which development occurs, play important roles in adolescent development. These contexts include families, peers, schools, culture, ethnicity, socioeconomic status, and gender. In recent decades, the United States has experienced a dramatic increase in immigration, especially from Latinx and Asian countries. A special concern is racism and discrimination against ethnic minority adolescents.

- Social policy is a national government's course of action designed to influence the welfare of its citizens. The U.S. social policy on adolescents needs revision to provide more services for youth. Benson and his colleagues argue that social policy regarding U.S. youth has focused too much on deficits and not enough on strengths.

The Global Perspective

- There are similarities and differences in adolescents across different countries. Much of what has been written and researched about adolescence comes from American and European scholars.

- With technological advances, a global youth culture with similar characteristics may be emerging. However, there still are many variations in adolescents across cultures. In some countries, traditions are being continued in the socialization of adolescents, whereas in others, substantial changes in the experiences of adolescents are taking place. These traditions and changes involve health and well-being, gender, families, schools, peers, and culture.

- Considering culture and the global perspective reflects the importance of social contexts in the lives of adolescents and emerging adults. Recently, the culture that adolescents and emerging adults experience has included a dramatic infusion of technology.

3 The Nature of Development

 Summarize the developmental processes, periods, transitions, and issues related to adolescence.

Processes and Periods

- Development is the pattern of movement or change that occurs throughout the life span. Biological processes involve physical changes in the individual's body. Cognitive processes consist of changes in thinking and intelligence. Socioemotional processes focus on changes in relationships with people, in emotion, in personality, and in social contexts.

- Development is commonly divided into the following periods: prenatal, infancy, early childhood, middle and late childhood, adolescence, early adulthood, middle adulthood, and late adulthood. Adolescence is the developmental period of transition between childhood and adulthood that involves biological, cognitive, and socioemotional changes. In most cultures, adolescence begins at approximately 10 to 13 years of age and ends in the late teens. Developmentalists increasingly distinguish between early adolescence and late adolescence.

Developmental Transitions

- Two important transitions in development are from childhood to adolescence and from adolescence to adulthood. In the transition from childhood to adolescence, pubertal change is prominent, although cognitive and socioemotional changes occur as well. It sometimes has been said that adolescence begins in biology and ends in culture.

- The concept of emerging adulthood has been proposed to describe the transition from adolescence to adulthood. Five key characteristics of emerging adulthood are identity exploration (especially in love and work), instability, being self-focused, feeling in-between, and experiencing possibilities to transform one's life. Competent individuals in emerging adulthood who experienced difficulties while growing up have often turned their lives in a positive direction through relationships with supportive adults, intelligence, and planfulness. Today's emerging and young adults are experiencing life quite differently from their counterparts in earlier generations. Among the criteria for determining adulthood are self-responsibility, independent decision making, and economic independence. A recent proposal argues that adolescence is taking too long and that adolescents are not being provided with adequate opportunities to mature. Also, recent proposals have been made to extend emerging adulthood until 29 years of age for many individuals, followed by a period of established adulthood.

- Three important issues in development are (1) the nature-nurture issue (Is development mainly due to heredity [nature] or environment [nurture]?), (2) the continuity-discontinuity issue (Is development more gradual and cumulative [continuity] or more abrupt and sequential [discontinuity]?), and (3) the early-later experience issue (Is development shaped more by early experiences, especially in infancy and early childhood, or by later experiences?). Most developmentalists do not take extreme positions on these issues, although these topics are debated extensively.

4 The Science of Adolescent Development

 Characterize the science of adolescent development.

Science and the
Scientific Method

- To answer questions about adolescent development, researchers often turn to science. They usually follow the scientific method, which involves four main steps: (1) conceptualize a problem, (2) collect data, (3) analyze data, and (4) draw conclusions. Theory is often involved in conceptualizing a problem. A theory is a coherent set of interrelated ideas that can be used to explain phenomena and to make predictions. Hypotheses are specific assertions and predictions, often derived from theory, that can be tested.

Theories of Adolescent
Development

- According to psychoanalytic theories, development primarily depends on the unconscious mind and is heavily couched in emotion. Two main psychoanalytic theories were proposed by Freud and Erikson. Freud theorized that individuals go through five psychosexual stages. Erikson's theory emphasizes eight psychosocial stages of development.

- Cognitive theories emphasize thinking, reasoning, language, and other cognitive processes. Three main cognitive theories are Piaget's, Vygotsky's, and information processing. Piaget's cognitive developmental theory proposes four stages of cognitive development with entry into the formal operational stage taking place between 11 and 15 years of age. Vygotsky's sociocultural cognitive theory emphasizes how culture and social interaction guide human development.

- The information-processing approach stresses that individuals manipulate information, monitor it, and strategize about it.

- Two main behavioral and social cognitive theories are Skinner's operant conditioning and social cognitive theory. In Skinner's operant conditioning, the consequences of a behavior produce changes in the probability of the behavior's occurrence. In social cognitive theory, observational learning is a key aspect of life-span development.

- Bandura emphasizes reciprocal interactions among person/cognitive, behavioral, and environmental factors.

- Ecological theory is Bronfenbrenner's environmental systems view of development. It proposes five environmental systems.

- An eclectic orientation does not follow any one theoretical approach but rather selects from each theory whatever is considered the best aspects of it.

Research in Adolescent
Development

- The main methods for collecting data about life-span development are observation (in a laboratory or a naturalistic setting), survey (questionnaire) or interview, standardized test, physiological measures, experience sampling method, and case study.

- Three main research designs are descriptive, correlational, and experimental. Descriptive research aims to observe and record behavior. In correlational research, the goal is to describe the strength of the relationship between two or more events or characteristics. Experimental research involves conducting an experiment, which can determine cause and effect.

- To examine the effects of time and age, researchers can conduct cross-sectional or longitudinal studies.

- Researchers' ethical responsibilities include obtaining participants' informed consent, ensuring confidentiality, debriefing them about the purpose of the study and potential personal consequences of participating, and avoiding unnecessary deception of participants. Researchers need to guard against gender, cultural, and ethnic bias in research.

key terms

adolescence	dependent variable	gender	nature-nurture issue
adolescent generalization gap	descriptive research	gender bias	Piaget's theory
biological processes	development	hypotheses	prenatal period
Bronfenbrenner's ecological theory	early adolescence	independent variable	psychoanalytic theories
case study	early adulthood	infancy	resilience
cognitive processes	early childhood	information-processing theory	social cognitive theory
cohort effects	early-later experience issue	inventionist view	social policy
contexts	eclectic theoretical orientation	laboratory	socioeconomic status (SES)
continuity-discontinuity issue	emerging adulthood	late adolescence	socioemotional processes
correlation coefficient	Erikson's theory	late adulthood	standardized test
correlational research	ethnic gloss	longitudinal research	stereotype
cross-cultural research	ethnicity	middle adulthood	storm-and-stress view
cross-sectional research	experience sampling method (ESM)	middle and late childhood	theory
culture	experimental research	millennials	Vygotsky's theory
		naturalistic observation	

key people

Joseph Adelson	Brad Brown	Richard Lerner	Robert Siegler
Claudia Allen	Jacquelynne Eccles	Ann Masten	B. F. Skinner
Joseph Allen	Erik Erikson	Margaret Mead	Laurence Steinberg
Jeffrey Arnett	Sigmund Freud	Daniel Offer	Adriana Umaña-Taylor
Albert Bandura	G. Stanley Hall	Jean Piaget	Lev Vygotsky
Peter Benson	Reed Larson	Maryse Richards	
Urie Bronfenbrenner	Jacqueline Lerner	Seth Schwartz	

improving the lives of adolescents and emerging adults

Age of Opportunity: Lessons from the New Science of Adolescence (2014)
Laurence Steinberg
Boston: Houghton Mifflin

> Leading researcher Laurence Steinberg writes about recent discoveries in the field of adolescent development that can help parents and educators better understand teens. Steinberg especially highlights recent research on the development of the adolescent's brain.

Cambridge Handbook of International Prevention Science (2017)
Edited by Moshe Israelashvili and John Romano
New York: Cambridge University Press

> Provides up-to-date coverage of social policy and intervention in children's lives to improve their well-being and development in the United States and countries around the world.

Emerging Adulthood (2nd ed.) (2014)
Jeffrey Arnett
New York: Oxford University Press

> Jeffrey Arnett, who coined the term "emerging adulthood," provides updated research on emerging adulthood that includes recent polls he has taken of 18- to 29-year-olds.

Encyclopedia of Adolescence (2011)
Edited by B. Bradford Brown and Mitch Prinstein
New York: Elsevier

> A three-volume set with more than 140 articles written by leading experts in the field of adolescent development. Topics covered include various biological, cognitive, and socioemotional processes.

Encyclopedia of Lifespan Development **(2018)**

Edited by Marc Bornstein

Thousand Oaks, CA: SAGE

> Leading experts provide up-to-date discussions of many topics in child and adolescent development.

Escaping the Endless Adolescence **(2009)**

Joe Allen and Claudia Allen

New York: Ballantine

> A superb, well-written book on the lives of emerging adults, including extensive recommendations for parents on how to effectively guide their children through the transition from adolescence to adulthood.

Flourishing in Emerging Adulthood **(2017)**

Laura Padilla-Walker and Larry Nelson (Eds.)

New York: Oxford University Press

> This book focuses on the diverse opportunities emerging adults have for experiencing positive development. Topics cover many aspects of emerging adulthood, including identity, purpose, family formation, and making contributions to society, as well as positive development in emerging adults in many different countries.

The Search Institute (www.search-institute.org)

> The Search Institute conducts large, comprehensive research projects to help define the pathways to healthy development for 12- to 25-year-olds. The Institute develops practical resources based on this research to foster reform, parent education, effective after-school programs, and community mobilization. Many resources are available for downloading from the Institute's website.

appendix

Careers in Adolescent and Emerging Adult Development

Some of you may be quite sure about what you plan to make your life's work. Others may not have decided on a major yet and are uncertain about which career path you want to follow. Each of us wants to find a rewarding career and enjoy the work we do. The field of adolescent development offers an amazing breadth of career options that can provide extremely satisfying work.

If you decide to pursue a career involving adolescent or emerging adult development, what career options are available to you? There are many. College and university professors teach courses in adolescent and emerging adult development, education, family development, and medicine. Middle school and high school teachers impart knowledge, understanding, and skills to adolescents. Counselors, clinical psychologists, and physicians help adolescents to cope more effectively with the unique challenges of adolescence. And various professionals work with families of adolescents to improve the adolescent's development.

By choosing one of these career options, you can guide adolescents and emerging adults in improving their lives, help others to understand them better, or even advance the state of knowledge in the field. You can have an enjoyable time while you are doing these things. Although an advanced degree is not absolutely necessary in some areas of adolescent and emerging adult development, you usually can expand your opportunities (and income) considerably by obtaining a graduate degree. Many careers in adolescent and emerging development pay reasonably well. For example, psychologists earn well above the median salary in the United States.

If you are considering a career in adolescent and emerging adult development, as you go through this term, try to spend some time with adolescents and emerging adults of different ages. Observe their behavior; talk with them about their lives. Think about whether you would like to work with people in these age periods in your life's work.

Another worthwhile activity is to talk with people who work with adolescents and emerging adults. For example, if you have some interest in becoming a school counselor, call a school, ask to speak with a counselor, and set up an appointment to discuss the counselor's career path and work. Be prepared with a list of questions to ask, and take notes if you wish.

Working in one or more jobs related to your career interests while you are in college can also benefit you. Many colleges and universities offer internships or work experiences for students who major in fields such as development. In some instances, these opportunities are for course credit or pay; in others, they are strictly on a volunteer basis. Take advantage of these opportunities. They can provide you with valuable experiences to help you decide whether this is the right career area for you, and they can help you get into graduate school, if you decide you want to go.

In the following sections, we profile careers in four areas: education/research; clinical/counseling/medical; families/relationships; and juvenile delinquency. These are not the only career options in the field of adolescent and emerging adult development, but they should provide you with an idea of the range of opportunities available and information about some of the main career avenues you might pursue. In profiling these careers, we address the amount of education required, the nature of the training, and a description of the work.

Education/Research

Education and research offer a wide range of career opportunities to work with adolescents and emerging adults. These range from being a college professor to a secondary school teacher or school psychologist.

College/University Professor

Courses in adolescent and emerging adult development are taught in different programs and schools in colleges and universities, including psychology, education, child and family studies, sociology, social work, and medicine. They are taught at research universities that offer one or more master's or Ph.D. programs in development; at four-year colleges with no graduate programs; or at community colleges. The work done by college professors includes teaching courses either at the undergraduate or graduate level (or both); conducting research in a specific area; advising students and/or directing their research; and serving on college or university committees. Some college instructors do not conduct research but instead focus mainly on teaching. Research is most likely to be part of the job description at universities with master's and Ph.D. programs.

A Ph.D. or master's degree almost always is required to teach in some area of adolescent and emerging adult development in a college or university. Obtaining a doctoral degree usually takes four to six years of graduate work. A master's degree requires approximately two years of graduate work. The training involves taking graduate courses, learning to conduct research, and attending and presenting papers at professional meetings. Many graduate students work as teaching or research assistants to professors, an apprenticeship relationship that helps them to develop their teaching and research skills.

If you are interested in becoming a college or university professor, you might want to make an appointment with your instructor to learn more about the profession and what his or her career/work is like. **You can also read a profile of a counseling psychologist and university professor in the "Gender" chapter.**

Researcher

In most instances, individuals who work in research positions will have either a master's degree or Ph.D. in some area of adolescent and emerging adult development. They might work at a university, perhaps in a research program; in government at agencies such as the National Institute of Mental Health; or in private industry. Those who have full-time research positions generate innovative research ideas, plan studies, and carry out research by collecting data, analyzing the data, and then interpreting it. Some spend much of their time in a laboratory; others work outside the lab in schools, hospitals, and other settings. Researchers usually attempt to publish their research in a scientific journal. They often work in collaboration with other researchers and may present their work at scientific meetings, where they learn about other research.

Secondary School Teacher

Secondary school teachers teach one or more subjects, prepare the curriculum, give tests, assign grades, monitor students' progress, conduct parent-teacher conferences, and attend in-service workshops. At minimum, becoming a secondary school teacher requires an undergraduate degree. The training involves taking a wide range of courses, with a major or concentration in education, as well as completion of a supervised practice-teaching internship. **Read profiles of secondary school teachers in the chapters on "The Brain and Cognitive Development" and "Achievement, Work, and Careers."**

Exceptional Children (Special Education) Teacher

Teachers of exceptional children concentrate their efforts on individual children who either have a disability or are gifted. Among the children they might work with are children with learning disabilities, ADHD (attention deficit hyperactivity disorder), intellectual disability, or a physical disability such as cerebral palsy. Some of their work is done outside of the regular classroom, some of it in the regular classroom. A teacher of exceptional children works closely with both the regular classroom teacher and parents to create the best educational program for each student. Becoming a teacher of exceptional children requires a minimum of an undergraduate degree. The training consists of taking a wide range of courses in education with a concentration of courses in educating children with disabilities or children who are gifted. Teachers of exceptional children often continue their education after obtaining their undergraduate degree, and many attain a master's degree in special education.

Family and Consumer Science Educator

Family and consumer science educators may specialize in early childhood education or instruct middle and high school students about matters such as nutrition, interpersonal relationships, human sexuality, parenting, and human development. Hundreds of colleges and universities throughout the United States offer two- and four-year degree programs in family and consumer science. These programs usually include an internship requirement. Additional education courses may be needed to obtain a teaching certificate. Some family and consumer science educators go on to graduate school for further training, which provides preparation for jobs in college teaching or research. **Read a profile of a family and consumer science educator in the "Sexuality" chapter.**

Educational Psychologist

Most educational psychologists teach in a college or university setting and conduct research on learning, motivation, classroom management, or assessment. These professors help to train students to enter the fields of educational psychology, school psychology, and teaching. Many educational psychologists have a doctorate in education, which requires four to six years of graduate work. **Read a profile of an educational psychologist in the "Introduction" chapter.**

School Psychologist

School psychologists focus on improving the psychological and intellectual well-being of elementary and secondary school students. They may work in a school district's centralized office or in one or more schools where they give psychological tests, interview students and their parents, consult with teachers, and provide counseling to students and their families. School psychologists usually have a master's or doctoral degree in school psychology. In graduate school, they take courses in counseling, assessment, learning, and other areas of education and psychology.

Clinical/Counseling/Medical

A wide variety of clinical, counseling, and medical professionals work with adolescents and emerging adults, from clinical psychologists to adolescent drug counselors and adolescent medicine specialists.

Clinical Psychologist

Clinical psychologists seek to help people who have psychological problems. They work in a variety of settings, including colleges and universities, clinics, medical schools, and private practice. Most clinical psychologists conduct psychotherapy; some perform psychological assessment as well; and some do research.

Clinical psychologists must obtain either a Ph.D. that involves clinical and research training or a Psy.D. degree, which involves only clinical training. This graduate training, which usually takes five to seven years, includes courses in clinical psychology and a one-year supervised internship in an accredited setting. In most cases, candidates for these degrees must pass a test to become licensed to practice and to call themselves clinical psychologists. **Read a profile of a clinical psychologist in the "Problems in Adolescence and Emerging Adulthood" chapter.**

Psychiatrist

Like clinical psychologists, psychiatrists might specialize in working with adolescents and emerging adults. They might work in medical schools, both as teachers and researchers, in medical clinics, and in private practice. Unlike psychologists, however, psychiatrists can administer psychiatric drugs to clients. Psychiatrists must first obtain a medical degree and then do a residency in psychiatry. Medical school takes approximately four years to complete and the psychiatric residency another three to four years.

Psychiatric Nurse

Psychiatric nurses work closely with psychiatrists to improve adolescents' and emerging adults' mental health. This career path requires two to five years of education in a certified nursing program. Psychiatric nursing students take courses in the biological sciences, nursing care, and psychology and receive supervised clinical training in a psychiatric setting. Designation as a clinical specialist in adolescent nursing requires a master's degree or higher in nursing.

Counseling Psychologist

Counseling psychologists go through much the same training as clinical psychologists and work in the same settings. They may do psychotherapy, teach, or conduct research, but they normally do not treat individuals with severe mental disorders such as schizophrenia. Counseling psychologists must have either a master's degree or a doctoral degree, as well as a license to practice their profession. One type of master's degree in counseling leads to the designation of licensed professional counselor. **Read a profile of a counseling psychologist in the "Gender" chapter.**

School Counselor

School counselors help students to identify their abilities and interests, and then guide them in developing academic plans and exploring career options. High school counselors advise students on choosing a major, meeting the admissions requirements for college, taking entrance exams, applying for financial aid, and obtaining vocational and technical training. School counselors may also help students to cope with adjustment problems, working with them individually, in small groups, or even in the classroom. They often consult with parents, teachers, and school administrators when trying to help students with their problems. School counselors usually have a master's degree in counseling. **Read a profile of a high school counselor in the "Achievement, Work, and Careers" chapter.**

Career Counselor

Career counselors help individuals to identify their career options and guide them in applying for jobs. They may work in private industry or at a college or university, where they usually interview individuals to identify careers that fit their interests and abilities. Sometimes career counselors help individuals to create professional résumés, or they conduct mock interviews to help them prepare for a job interview. They may also create and promote job fairs or other recruiting events to help individuals obtain jobs. **Read a profile of a career counselor in the "Achievement, Work, and Careers" chapter.**

Social Worker

Social workers are often involved in helping people who have social or economic problems. They may investigate, evaluate, and attempt to rectify reported cases of abuse, neglect, endangerment, or domestic disputes. They can intervene in families if necessary and provide counseling and referral services to individuals and families. They often work for publicly funded agencies at the city, state, or national level, although increasingly they work in the private sector in areas such as drug rehabilitation and family counseling. In some cases, social workers specialize in certain types of work. For example, family-care social workers often work with families in which a child, adolescent, or older adult needs support services. Social workers must have at least an undergraduate degree from a school of social work, including course work in various areas of sociology and psychology. Some social workers also have a master's or doctoral degree.

Drug Counselor

Drug counselors provide counseling to individuals with drug-abuse problems, either on an individual basis or in group therapy sessions. They may work in private practice, with a state or federal agency, for a company, or in a hospital setting. Some specialize in working with adolescents. At a minimum, drug counselors must have an associate degree or certificate. Many have an undergraduate degree in substance-abuse counseling, and some have master's and doctoral degrees. In most states, drug counselors must fulfill a certification procedure to obtain a license to practice.

Health Psychologist

Health psychologists work with many different health-care professionals, including physicians, nurses, clinical psychologists, psychiatrists, and social workers, in an effort to improve the health of adolescents. They may conduct research, perform clinical assessments, or provide treatment. Many health psychologists focus on prevention through research and clinical interventions designed to foster health and reduce the risk of disease. More than half of all health psychologists provide clinical services. Among the settings in which health psychologists work are primary care programs, inpatient medical units, and specialized care programs in areas such as women's health, drug treatment, and smoking cessation.

Health psychologists typically have a doctoral degree (Ph.D. or Psy.D.) in psychology. Some receive training in clinical psychology as part of their graduate work. Others have obtained their doctoral degree in some area other than health psychology and then pursue a postdoctoral degree in health psychology. A postdoctoral degree usually takes about two additional years of graduate study. Many doctoral programs in clinical, counseling, social, and experimental psychology have specialized tracks in health psychology.

Adolescent Medicine Specialist

Adolescent medicine specialists evaluate medical and behavioral problems that are common among adolescents, including growth disorders (such as delayed puberty), acne, eating disorders, substance abuse, depression, anxiety, sexually transmitted infections, contraception and pregnancy, and sexual identity concerns. They may work in private practice, in a medical clinic, in a hospital, or in a medical school. Their medical degree allows them to administer drugs, and they may counsel parents and adolescents on ways to improve the adolescent's health. Many adolescent medicine specialists on the faculty of medical schools also teach and conduct research on adolescents' health and diseases.

Adolescent medicine specialists must complete medical school and then obtain further training in their specialty, which usually involves at least three more years of schooling. They must become board certified in either pediatrics or internal medicine.

Adolescent Nursing Specialist

Earlier we described careers in psychiatric nursing. Here we explore careers in a wider range of nursing areas and settings. Individuals who get an undergraduate and/or graduate degree in pediatric nursing can specialize in working with adolescents. Adolescent nursing specialists may get a general degree in pediatric nursing or specialize in some area of medicine, such as psychiatric nursing, that qualifies them to work with adolescents who have psychological problems and disorders. Adolescent nursing specialists can work in a variety of settings, including hospitals, clinics, physicians' offices, and secondary schools. They also may teach adolescent nursing in colleges and universities. Thus, their work can involve treating adolescents who have medical conditions or psychiatric problems, and/or training college students to become adolescent nursing specialists.

Families/Relationships

Adolescents sometimes benefit from help that is provided to the entire family. One career that involves working with adolescents and their families is marriage and family therapy.

Marriage and Family Therapist

Many individuals who have psychological problems benefit when psychotherapy is provided within the context of a marital or family relationship. Marriage and family therapists may provide marital therapy, couple therapy to individuals who are not married, and family therapy to two or more members of a family.

Marriage and family therapists must have a master's or doctoral degree. Their training is similar to that of a clinical psychologist but with a focus on marital and family relationships. In most states, professionals must go through a licensing procedure to practice marital and family therapy. **Read a profile of a marriage and family therapist in the "Families" chapter.**

Juvenile Delinquency

A variety of careers involve working with juvenile delinquents. Individuals who want to work with juvenile delinquents can become a probation or juvenile detention officer with a juvenile court, a re-entry case manager or re-engagement specialist, an administrator in the juvenile justice system or a youth justice institute, a social worker, a mentor or life coach, or a counselor. Also, many of the career possibilities described in other categories, such as education/research, clinical/counseling/medical, and families/relationships, can be tailored for work with juvenile delinquents.

chapter 2

PUBERTY, HEALTH, AND BIOLOGICAL FOUNDATIONS

chapter outline

1 Puberty

Learning Goal 1 Discuss the determinants, characteristics, and psychological dimensions of puberty.

Determinants of Puberty

Growth Spurt

Sexual Maturation

Secular Trends in Puberty

Psychological Dimensions of Puberty

2 Health

Learning Goal 2 Summarize the nature of adolescents' and emerging adults' health.

Adolescence: A Critical Juncture in Health

Emerging Adults' Health

Nutrition

Exercise and Sports

Sleep

3 Evolution, Heredity, and Environment

Learning Goal 3 Explain the contributions of evolution, heredity, and environment to adolescent development.

The Evolutionary Perspective

The Genetic Process

Heredity-Environment Interaction

monkeybusinessimages/Getty Images

I am pretty confused. I wonder whether I am weird or normal.

My body is starting to change, but I sure don't look like a lot of my friends. I still look like a kid for the most part. My best friend is only 13, but he looks like he is 16 or 17. I get nervous in the locker room during PE class because when I go to take a shower, I'm afraid somebody is going to make fun of me since I'm not as physically developed as some of the others.

—Robert, age 12

I don't like my breasts. They are too small, and they look funny. I'm afraid guys won't like me if they don't get bigger.

—Angie, age 13

I can't stand the way I look. I have zits all over my face. My hair is dull and stringy. It never stays in place. My nose is too big. My lips are too small. My legs are too short. I have four warts on my left hand, and people get grossed out by them. So do I. My body is a disaster!

—Ann, age 14

I'm short and I can't stand it. My father is six feet tall, and here I am only five foot four. I'm 14 already. I look like a kid, and I get teased a lot, especially by other guys. I'm always the last one picked for sides in basketball because I'm so short. Girls don't seem to be interested in me either because most of them are taller than I am.

—Jim, age 14

The comments of these four adolescents in the midst of pubertal change underscore the dramatic upheaval in their bodies following the calm, consistent growth of middle and late childhood. Young adolescents develop an acute concern about their bodies.

preview

Puberty's changes are perplexing to adolescents. Although these changes bring forth doubts, fears, and anxieties, most adolescents move through adolescence in a healthy manner. We will explore many aspects of pubertal change in this chapter, ranging from growth spurts and sexual maturation to the psychological aspects of puberty. We will also examine other topics related to adolescent physical development, including health and the roles of evolution, heredity, and environment in adolescent development.

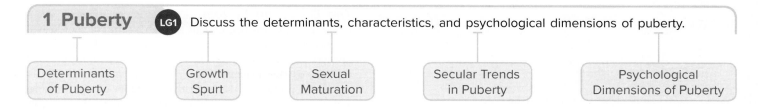

1 Puberty **LG1** Discuss the determinants, characteristics, and psychological dimensions of puberty.

| Determinants of Puberty | Growth Spurt | Sexual Maturation | Secular Trends in Puberty | Psychological Dimensions of Puberty |

Puberty can be distinguished from adolescence (Dorn & others, 2019). For virtually everyone, puberty ends long before adolescence is exited. Puberty is often thought of as the most important marker for the beginning of adolescence. **Puberty** is a brain-neuroendocrine process occurring primarily in early adolescence that provides stimulation for the rapid physical changes that take place during this period of development (Pfeifer & Allen, 2021; Sanfilippo & others, 2020).

puberty A brain-neuroendocrine process occurring primarily in early adolescence that provides stimulation for the rapid physical changes that accompany this period of development.

DETERMINANTS OF PUBERTY

Although we do not know precisely what initiates puberty, a number of complex factors are involved. Puberty is accompanied by changes in the endocrine system, weight, and body fat, but we don't know if these are causes or consequences of puberty (Dorn & Biro, 2011). Researchers are also exploring the roles that birth weight, rapid weight gain in infancy, obesity, and sociocultural factors might play in pubertal onset and characteristics (Calcaterra & others, 2021). As discussed next, heredity is an important factor in puberty.

Heredity   Puberty is not an environmental accident. Programmed into the genes of every human being is the timing for the emergence of puberty (Lardone & others, 2020). Puberty does not take place at 2 or 3 years of age, nor does it occur in the twenties. For most individuals, puberty takes place between about 9 and 16 years of age. Recently, scientists have begun to conduct molecular genetic studies in an attempt to identify specific genes that are linked to the onset and progression of puberty (Omariba & Xiao, 2020; Wright & others, 2021). Environmental factors can also influence puberty's onset and duration, as we will examine shortly.

Hormones   Behind the first whisker in boys and the widening of hips in girls is a flood of **hormones,** powerful chemical substances secreted by the endocrine glands and carried throughout the body by the bloodstream (Rey, 2021). Two classes of hormones have significantly different concentrations in males and females: **androgens,** the main class of male sex hormones, and **estrogens,** the main class of female hormones. Note that although these hormones function more strongly in one sex or the other, they are produced by both males and females (Guercio & others, 2020).

Testosterone is an androgen that plays an important role in male pubertal development (Madsen & others, 2020). Testosterone is primarily secreted by the testes in boys. Throughout puberty, rising testosterone levels are associated with a number of physical changes in boys, including growth and development of external genitals, increases in height, and deepening of the voice (Guo & others, 2020). Testosterone levels in adolescent boys are also linked to sexual desire and activity (Cameron, 2004).

Estradiol is an estrogen that plays an important role in female pubertal development (Whittle & others, 2020). Estradiol is primarily secreted by the ovaries in girls. As estradiol levels rise, breast development, uterine development, and skeletal changes occur. The contributions of hormones to sexual desire and activity in adolescents girls is less clear than it is for boys (Cameron, 2004).

Both boys and girls experience increases in testosterone and estradiol during puberty. However, in one study, testosterone levels increased 18-fold in boys but only 2-fold in girls during puberty; estradiol levels increased 8-fold in girls but only 2-fold in boys during puberty (Nottelmann & others, 1987) (see Figure 1). Also, a study of 9- to 17-year-old boys found that testosterone levels peaked at 17 years of age (Khairullah & others, 2014).

The Endocrine System   Puberty is not a specific event but rather a process that unfolds through a series of coordinated neuroendocrine changes (Garg & Berga, 2020). Puberty onset involves the activation of the hypothalamic-pituitary-gonadal (HPG) axis (see Figure 2). The *hypothalamus* is a structure in the higher portion of the brain that monitors eating, drinking, and sex. The *pituitary gland* is the endocrine gland that controls growth and regulates other glands. The *gonads* are the sex glands—the testes in males, the ovaries in females. How does the endocrine system work? The pituitary gland sends a signal via gonadotropins (hormones that stimulate sex glands) directing the testes or ovaries to manufacture the hormone (Naule, Malone, & Kaiser, 2021). Then, through interaction with the

hormones Powerful chemicals secreted by the endocrine glands and carried through the body by the bloodstream.

androgens The main class of male sex hormones.

estrogens The main class of female sex hormones.

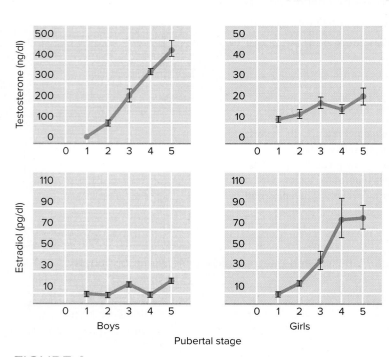

FIGURE 1

HORMONE LEVELS BY SEX AND PUBERTAL STAGE FOR TESTOSTERONE AND ESTRADIOL. The five stages range from the early beginning of puberty (stage 1) to the most advanced stage of puberty (stage 5). Notice the significant increase in testosterone in boys and the significant increase in estradiol in girls.

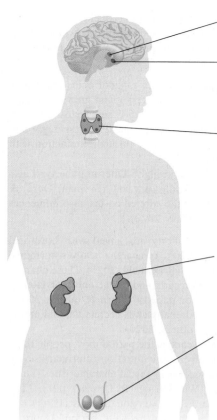

Hypothalamus: A structure in the brain that interacts with the pituitary gland to monitor the bodily regulation of hormones.

Pituitary: This master gland produces hormones that stimulate other glands. It also influences growth by producing growth hormones; it sends gonadotropins to the testes and ovaries and a thyroid-stimulating hormone to the thyroid gland. It sends a hormone to the adrenal gland as well.

Thyroid gland: It interacts with the pituitary gland to influence growth.

Adrenal gland: It interacts with the pituitary gland and likely plays a role in pubertal development, but less is known about its function than about sex glands. Recent research, however, suggests it may be involved in adolescent behavior, particularly for boys.

The gonads, or sex glands: These consist of the testes in males and the ovaries in females. The sex glands are strongly involved in the appearance of secondary sex characteristics, such as facial hair in males and breast development in females. The general class of hormones called estrogens is dominant in females, while androgens are dominant in males. More specifically, testosterone in males and estradiol in females are key hormones in pubertal development.

FIGURE 2

THE MAJOR ENDOCRINE GLANDS INVOLVED IN PUBERTAL CHANGE

hypothalamus, the pituitary gland detects when the optimal level of the hormone has been reached and maintains it with additional gonadotropin secretions (Spaziani & others, 2021).

Levels of sex hormones are regulated by two hormones secreted by the pituitary gland: *FSH* (*follicle-stimulating hormone*) and *LH* (*luteinizing hormone*) (Emmanuel & Bokor, 2020). FSH stimulates follicle development in females and sperm production in males. LH regulates estrogen secretion and ovum development in females and testosterone production in males (Holesh, Bass, & Lord, 2021). In addition, the hypothalamus secretes a substance called *GnRH* (*gonadotropin-releasing hormone*), which is linked to pubertal timing (Casteel & Singh, 2021).

These hormones are regulated by a *negative feedback system*. If the level of sex hormones rises too high, the hypothalamus and pituitary gland reduce their stimulation of the gonads, decreasing the production of sex hormones. If the level of sex hormones falls too low, the hypothalamus and pituitary gland increase their production of the sex hormones.

Figure 3 shows how the feedback system works. In males, the pituitary gland's production of LH stimulates the testes to produce testosterone. When testosterone levels rise too high, the hypothalamus decreases its production of GnRH, and this decrease reduces the pituitary's production of LH. When the level of testosterone falls as a result, the hypothalamus produces more GnRH and the cycle starts again. The negative feedback system operates in a similar way in females, except that LH and GnRH regulate the ovaries and the production of estrogen.

This negative feedback mechanism in the endocrine system can be compared to a thermostat and furnace. If a room becomes cold, the thermostat signals the furnace to turn on. The action of the furnace warms the air in the room, which eventually triggers the thermostat to turn off the furnace. The room temperature gradually begins to fall again until the thermostat once again signals the furnace to turn on, and the cycle is repeated. This type of system is called a *negative* feedback loop because a *rise* in temperature turns *off* the furnace, while a *decrease* in temperature turns *on* the furnace.

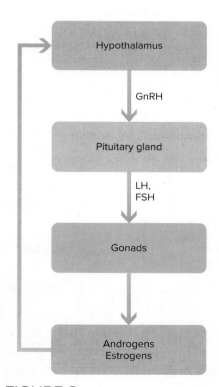

FIGURE 3

THE FEEDBACK SYSTEM OF SEX HORMONES

The level of sex hormones is low in childhood but increases in puberty (Breehl & Caban, 2020). It is as if the thermostat is set at 50 degrees F in childhood and then becomes set at 80 degrees F in puberty. At the higher setting, the gonads have to produce more sex hormones, and they do so during puberty.

Growth Hormones   We know that the pituitary gland releases gonadotropins that stimulate the testes and ovaries (Holesh, Bass, & Lord, 2020). The pituitary gland grows in adolescence, and its volume is linked to circulating blood levels of estradiol and testosterone. In addition, through interaction with the hypothalamus, the pituitary gland also secretes hormones that lead to growth and skeletal maturation either directly or through interaction with the *thyroid gland*, located in the neck region (see Figure 2).

At the beginning of puberty, growth hormone is secreted at night. Later in puberty, it also is secreted during the day, although daytime levels are usually very low (Susman, Dorn, & Schiefelbein, 2003). Cortisol, a hormone that is secreted by the adrenal cortex, also influences growth, as do testosterone and estrogen (van Keulen & others, 2020).

Adrenarche and Gonadarche   Two phases of puberty are linked with hormonal changes: adrenarche and gonadarche (Whittle & others, 2020). **Adrenarche** involves hormonal changes in the adrenal glands, located just above the kidneys (Rosenfield, 2021). These changes occur surprisingly early, from about 6 to 9 years of age in girls and about one year later in boys, before what is generally considered the beginning of puberty (Dorn & others, 2006). During adrenarche and continuing through puberty, the adrenal glands secrete adrenal androgens, such as dehydroepiandrosterone (DHEA) (King & others, 2020).

Gonadarche, which follows adrenarche by about two years, is the period most people think of as puberty (Casteel & Singh, 2021). Gonadarche involves the maturation of primary sexual characteristics (ovaries in females, testes in males) and secondary sexual characteristics (pubic hair, breast development, and genital development) (Wu, Chang, & Leung, 2021). "The hallmark of gonadarche is reactivation of the hypothalamic-pituitary-gonadal axis (HPG). . . . The initial activation of the HPG axis was during the fetal and neonatal period" (Dorn & others, 2006, p. 35).

In the United States, the gonadarche period begins at approximately 9 to 10 years of age in non-Latinx white girls and 8 to 9 years in African American girls (Herman-Giddens, Kaplowitz, & Wasserman, 2004). In boys, gonadarche begins at about 10 to 11 years of age. **Menarche,** the first menstrual period, occurs in mid- to late gonadarche in girls. In boys, **spermarche,** a boy's first ejaculation of semen, occurs in early to mid-gonadarche. Robert, Angie, Ann, and Jim, the adolescents who were quoted at the beginning of this chapter, are in various phases of adrenarche and gonadarche.

Weight and Body Fat   Some researchers argue that a child must reach a critical body mass before puberty, especially menarche, emerges (Ackerman & others, 2006). A number of studies have found that higher weight, especially obesity, is linked to earlier pubertal development (Pereira & others, 2021). For example, a recent study in Denmark revealed that obesity was associated with earlier pubertal onset in boys (Busch & others, 2020).

Other scientists have hypothesized that the onset of menarche is influenced by the percentage of body fat in relation to total body weight, although a precise percentage has not been consistently verified. However, both anorexic adolescents whose weight drops dramatically and females who participate in certain sports (such as gymnastics and swimming) may not menstruate. In boys, undernutrition may delay puberty (Susman, Dorn, & Schiefelbein, 2003).

Leptin and Kisspeptins   Reproduction is an energy-demanding function and thus puberty is said to be "metabolically gated" as a way to prevent fertility when energy conditions are very low (Larabee, Neely, & Domingos, 2020). Also, as we just indicated, obesity is linked to earlier menarche. The metabolic control of puberty, ranging from energy deficit to extreme overweight, is carried out by hormones that send information to the GnRH neurons (Kelsey & others, 2020).

The hormone *leptin*, which is secreted by fat cells and in abundance stimulates the brain to increase metabolism and reduce hunger, has been

adrenarche Puberty phase involving hormonal changes in the adrenal glands, which are located just above the kidneys. These changes occur from about 6 to 9 years of age in girls and about one year later in boys, before what is generally considered the beginning of puberty.

gonadarche Puberty phase involving the maturation of primary sexual characteristics (ovaries in females, testes in males) and secondary sexual characteristics (pubic hair, breast and genital development). This period follows adrenarche by about two years and is what most people think of as puberty.

menarche A girl's first menstrual period.

spermarche A boy's first ejaculation of semen.

What are some of the factors that likely determine the onset of puberty?
Fuse/Corbis/Getty Images

proposed to play an important role in regulating puberty, especially in females (Nieuwenhuis & others, 2020; Wright & others, 2021). Some researchers argue that leptin deficiency inhibits food intake and reduces body fat, thus delaying pubertal onset or interrupting pubertal advances, and that leptin treatment can restore puberty (Kang & others, 2018). The increased leptin levels seen in obese children have been linked to earlier pubertal onset in some studies (Shalitin & Kiess, 2017). Further, recently *kisspeptins*, which are products of the Kiss 1 gene, have been reported to regulate GnRH neurons and thus play a role in pubertal onset and change (Ruohonen, Poutanen, & Tena-Sempere, 2020). Interestingly, the Kiss 1 gene was discovered by researchers in Hershey, Pennsylvania, and named in recognition of Hershey chocolate kisses!

Weight at Birth and in Infancy   Might puberty's onset and characteristics be influenced by birth weight and weight gain during infancy? There is increasing research evidence supporting this link (Calcaterra & others, 2021). Low-birth-weight girls experience menarche approximately 5 to 10 months earlier than normal-birth-weight girls, and low-birth-weight boys are at risk for small testicular volume during adolescence (Ibanez & de Zegher, 2006). Also, a recent study in rural China found that pubertal onset occurred earlier in girls who had been heavier than average for their height in infancy and who had experienced rapid weight gain from birth to 2 years of age (Wei & others, 2021).

How might birth weight and weight gain in infancy be linked to pubertal onset?
Science Photo Library/Getty Images

Sociocultural and Environmental Factors   Might sociocultural and environmental factors be linked to pubertal timing? Recent research indicates that cultural variations and early experiences may be related to earlier pubertal onset (Bleil & others, 2021). Adolescents in developed countries and large urban areas reach puberty earlier than their counterparts in less-developed countries and rural areas (Graham, 2005). Children who have been adopted from developing countries to developed countries often enter puberty earlier than their counterparts who continue to live in developing countries (Teilmann & others, 2002). African American females enter puberty earlier than Latinx and non-Latinx white females, and African American males enter puberty earlier than non-Latinx white males (Talpade, 2008).

Early experiences that are linked to earlier pubertal onset include adoption, father absence, low socioeconomic status, family conflict, maternal harshness, child maltreatment, and early substance use (Ellis & others, 2011; Novello & Speiser, 2018). For example, a recent study found that child sexual abuse was linked to earlier pubertal onset (Noll & others, 2017). And in a recent study, early life stress was linked to earlier age at menarche (Holdsworth & Appleton, 2020). And a recent Italian study revealed that rates of early puberty in girls were higher after the onset of the COVID-19 pandemic than prior to its occurrence (Verzani & others, 2021). The earlier onset of puberty is likely explained by high rates of conflict and stress in these social contexts (Dorn & others, 2019).

GROWTH SPURT

Growth slows throughout childhood, and then puberty brings forth the most rapid increases in growth since infancy. Figure 4 shows that the growth spurt associated with puberty occurs approximately two years earlier for girls than for boys. For girls, the mean beginning of the growth spurt is 9 years of age; for boys, it is 11 years of age. The peak of pubertal change occurs at 11½ years for girls and 13½ years for boys. During their growth spurt, girls increase in height about 3½ inches per year; boys, about 4 inches.

An individual's ultimate height is often a midpoint between the biological mother's and the biological father's height, adjusted a few inches down for a female and a few inches up for a male. The growth spurt typically begins before menarche and ends earlier for girls. The growth spurt for boys, as indicated earlier, begins later and ends later than it does for girls.

Boys and girls who are shorter or taller than their peers before adolescence are likely to remain so during adolescence. At the beginning of adolescence, girls tend to be as tall as or taller than boys of their age, but by the end of the middle school years most boys have caught up with them, or in many cases even surpassed them in height. Though height in elementary school is a good predictor of height later in adolescence, as much as 30 percent of an individual's height in late adolescence is unexplained by the child's height in elementary school.

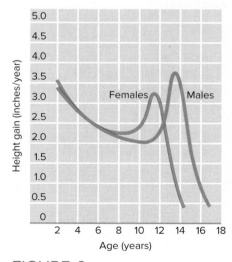

FIGURE 4

PUBERTAL GROWTH SPURT. On average, the peak of the growth spurt that characterizes pubertal changes occurs two years earlier for girls (11½) than for boys (13½).

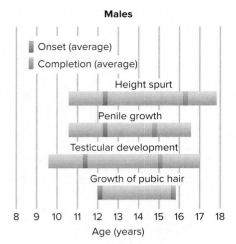

Males

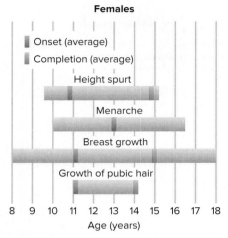

Females

FIGURE 5

NORMAL RANGE AND AVERAGE DEVELOPMENT OF SEXUAL CHARACTERISTICS IN MALES AND FEMALES

precocious puberty The very early onset and rapid progression of puberty.

The rate at which adolescents gain weight follows approximately the same developmental timetable as the rate at which they gain height. Marked weight gains coincide with the onset of puberty (Bratke & others, 2017). Fifty percent of adult body weight is gained during adolescence (Rogol, Roemmich, & Clark, 1998). At the peak of this weight gain, girls gain an average of 18 pounds in one year at roughly 12 years of age (approximately six months after their peak height increase). Boys' peak weight gain per year (20 pounds) occurs about the same time as their peak increase in height, about 13 to 14 years of age. During early adolescence, girls tend to outweigh boys, but—just as with height—by about 14 years of age, boys begin to surpass girls in weight.

In addition to increases in height and weight, puberty brings changes in hip and shoulder width. Girls experience a spurt in hip width, whereas boys undergo an increase in shoulder width. In girls, increased hip width is linked with an increase in estrogen. In boys, increased shoulder width is associated with an increase in testosterone (Susman & Dorn, 2009).

Finally, the later growth spurt of boys produces a greater leg length in boys than in girls. In many cases, boys' facial structure becomes more angular during puberty, whereas girls' facial structure becomes rounder and softer.

SEXUAL MATURATION

Think back to the onset of your puberty. Of the striking changes that were taking place in your body, what was the first that occurred? Researchers have found that male pubertal characteristics develop in this order: increased penis and testicle size; appearance of straight pubic hair; minor voice change; first ejaculation (spermarche—this usually occurs through masturbation or a wet dream); appearance of kinky pubic hair; onset of maximum growth; growth of hair in armpits; more detectable voice changes; and growth of facial hair. Three of the most noticeable signs of sexual maturation in boys are penis elongation, testes development, and growth of facial hair. The normal range and average age of development for these sexual characteristics, along with height spurt, are shown in Figure 5.

Figure 6 illustrates the typical course of male and female sexual development during puberty. The five numbers in Figure 6 reflect the five stages of secondary sexual characteristics known as the Tanner stages (Tanner, 1962). A longitudinal study revealed that on average, boys' genital development preceded their pubic hair development by about 4 months (Susman & others, 2010). In this study, African American boys and girls began puberty almost one year earlier than non-Latinx white boys and girls.

What is the order of appearance of physical changes in females? On average, breast development occurs first, followed by the appearance of pubic hair. Later, hair appears in the armpits. As these changes occur, the female grows in height, and her hips become wider than her shoulders. Her first menstruation (menarche) occurs rather late in the pubertal cycle. Initially, her menstrual cycles may be highly irregular, and for the first several years she might not ovulate in every cycle. In some instances, a female does not become fertile until two years after her period begins. No voice changes occur that are comparable to those in pubertal males. By the end of puberty, the female's breasts have become more fully rounded. Two of the most noticeable aspects of female pubertal change are pubic hair and breast development. Figure 5 shows the normal range and average development for two of these female sexual characteristics and provides information about menarche and height spurt. Figure 6 illustrates the typical course of female sexual development during puberty. A longitudinal study revealed that on average, girls' breast development preceded their pubic hair development by about two months (Susman & others, 2010).

Note that there may be wide individual variations in the onset and progression of puberty. For boys, the pubertal sequence may begin as early as 10 years of age or as late as 13. It may end as early as 13 years or as late as 17. The normal range is wide enough that given two boys of the same chronological age, one might complete the pubertal sequence before the other one has begun it. For girls, the normal age range for menarche is even wider, between 9 and 15 years of age.

Precocious puberty is the term used to describe the very early onset and rapid progression of puberty (Kota & Ejaz, 2020). Precocious puberty is usually diagnosed when pubertal onset occurs before 8 years of age in girls and before 9 years of age in boys (Chen & Liu, 2021). Precocious puberty occurs approximately 10 times more often in girls than in boys. Girls who are overweight or obese are more likely to have precocious puberty (Wei & others, 2020).

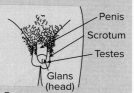

Penis
Scrotum
Testes
Glans (head)

1.
No pubic hair. The testes, scrotum, and penis are about the same size and shape as those of a child.

2.
A little soft, long, lightly colored hair, mostly at the base of the penis. This hair may be straight or a little curly. The testes and scrotum have enlarged, and the skin of the scrotum has changed. The scrotum, the sack holding the testes, has lowered a bit. The penis has grown only a little.

3.
The hair is darker, coarser, and more curled. It has spread to thinly cover a somewhat larger area. The penis has grown mainly in length. The testes and scrotum have grown and dropped lower than in stage 2.

4.
The hair is now as dark, curly, and coarse as that of an adult male. However, the area that the hair covers is not as large as that of an adult male; it has not spread to the thighs. The penis has grown even larger and wider. The glans (the head of the penis) is bigger. The scrotum is darker and bigger because the testes have gotten bigger.

5.
The hair has spread to the thighs and is now like that of an adult male. The penis, scrotum, and testes are the size and shape of those of an adult male.

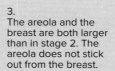
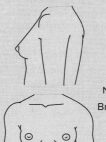
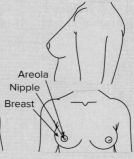

Areola
Nipple
Breast

1.
The nipple is raised just a little. The rest of the breast is still flat.

2.
The breast bud stage. The nipple is raised more than in stage 1. The breast is a small mound, and the areola is larger than in stage 1.

3.
The areola and the breast are both larger than in stage 2. The areola does not stick out from the breast.

4.
The areola and the nipple make up a mound that sticks up above the shape of the breast. (Note: This may not happen at all for some girls; some develop from stage 3 to stage 5, with no stage 4.)

5.
The mature adult stage. The breasts are fully developed. Only the nipple sticks out. The areola has moved back to the general shape of the breast.

FIGURE 6

THE FIVE PUBERTAL STAGES OF MALE AND FEMALE SEXUAL DEVELOPMENT

When precocious puberty occurs, it usually is treated by medically suppressing gonadotropic secretions, which temporarily stops pubertal change (Gangat & Radovick, 2020). The reason for this treatment is that children who experience precocious puberty are ultimately likely to have short stature, early sexual capability, and the potential for engaging in age-inappropriate behavior (Choi & Kim, 2016).

SECULAR TRENDS IN PUBERTY

Imagine a toddler displaying all the features of puberty—a 3-year-old girl with fully developed breasts, or a slightly older boy with a deep male voice. One proposal was that this was what we would likely see by the year 2250 if the age at which puberty arrived continued to drop at

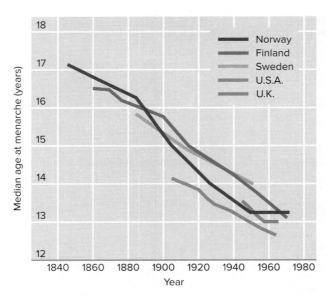

FIGURE **7**

MEDIAN AGES AT MENARCHE IN SELECTED NORTHERN EUROPEAN COUNTRIES AND THE UNITED STATES FROM 1845 TO 1969. Notice the steep decline in the age at which girls experienced menarche in five different countries. Recently the rate of decrease in the age at which girls experience menarche has been slowing.

secular trends Patterns of the onset of puberty over historical time, especially across generations.

Adolescents show a strong preoccupation with their changing bodies and develop mental images of what their bodies are like. *Why might adolescent males have more positive body images than adolescent females?*
Corbis/VCG/Getty Images

the rate at which it was falling for much of the twentieth century (Petersen, 1987). However, we are unlikely to ever see pubescent toddlers because of genetic limits on how early puberty can occur (Omariba & Xiao, 2020). The earlier arrival of pubertal onset historically is believed to be due to improved health and nutrition.

The term **secular trends** refers to patterns of pubertal onset over historical time, especially across generations. For example, in Norway, menarche now occurs at just over 13 years of age, compared with 17 years of age in the 1840s (Ong, Ahmed, & Dunger, 2006). In the United States, where children mature physically up to a year earlier than in European countries, menarche now occurs at about 12½ years of age, compared with over 14 years of age a century ago (see Figure 7). An increasing number of U.S. girls are beginning puberty at 8 and 9 years of age, with African American girls developing earlier than non-Latinx white girls (Herman-Giddens, 2007).

Puberty also is occurring earlier in a number of other countries in recent years (Sultan & others, 2018). For example, from 1965 to 2005 in Korea and from 1950 to 2010 in Japan, pubertal growth occurred earlier but shrank in its duration (Cole & Mori, 2018). In another study, spermarche (onset of sperm production in testicles) occurred earlier in Chinese boys in 2010 than it had in 1995, with the earlier onset of sperm production linked to an increase in body mass index across the time frame (Song & others, 2016). Also, in one study, menarche appeared earlier in girls in Saudi Arabia than it had for their mothers (Al Alwan & others, 2017). In addition, a recent study found that puberty has been occurring earlier in Portugal (Queiroga & others, 2020). Further, a recent meta-analysis concluded that the age of pubertal onset of breast development in girls decreased 3 months per decade from 1977 to 2013 (Eckert-Lind & others, 2020). And a recent study in Taiwan revealed that the average age at menarche had declined 0.43 years per decade in the past 30 years (Chow & others, 2020).

So far, we have been concerned mainly with the physical dimensions of puberty. As we see next, the psychological dimensions of puberty are also important.

PSYCHOLOGICAL DIMENSIONS OF PUBERTY

A host of psychological changes accompanies an adolescent's pubertal development (Pfeifer & Allen, 2021). Try to remember when you were entering puberty. Not only did you think of yourself differently, but your parents and peers also began treating you differently. Maybe you were proud of your changing body, even though it perplexed you. Perhaps you or your parents felt they could no longer sit in bed and watch television with you or even kiss you good night.

Far less research has been conducted on the psychosocial aspects of male pubertal transitions than on female pubertal transitions, possibly because of the difficulty of detecting when the male transitions occur. Wet dreams are one marker, yet there has been little research on the topic. Not only are the effects of puberty easier to study in girls, they also are more likely to have a strong effect on girls because they are more obvious than the pubertal changes in boys. For example, female breast enlargement is much easier to see in most societies than male genital growth.

Body Image One psychological aspect of puberty is certain for both boys and girls: Adolescents are preoccupied with their bodies (Milene-Moehlecke & others, 2020; Miranda & others, 2021). Perhaps you looked in the mirror on a daily, or sometimes even hourly, basis as a young teenager to see whether you could detect anything different about your changing body. Preoccupation with one's body image is strong throughout adolescence, but it is especially acute during pubertal change, a time when adolescents are more dissatisfied with their bodies than in late adolescence.

Gender Differences Gender differences characterize adolescents' perceptions of their bodies (Cabaco & others, 2021; Hosseini & Padhy, 2021).

In general, throughout puberty girls are less happy with their bodies and have more negative body images than do boys, which to some extent may be due to media portrayals of the attractiveness of being thin and the increase in body fat in girls during puberty (Hartman-Munick, Gordon, & Guss, 2020). In a recent U.S. study of young adolescents, boys had a more positive body image than girls did (Morin & others, 2017). Also, a study of undergraduate students in the United Kingdom found that 35 percent of females but only 8 percent of males reported being moderately or markedly concerned with their body image (El Ansari, Dibba, & Stock, 2014).

As pubertal change proceeds, girls often become more dissatisfied with their bodies, probably because their body fat increases (Yuan, 2010). In contrast, boys become more satisfied as they move through puberty, probably because their muscle mass increases. Also, in a recent Chinese study of adolescents, girls were more dissatisfied with their appearance than boys were, but boys were more dissatisfied with their sexual organs (Zhang & others, 2020). And another study found that both boys' and girls' body images became more positive as they moved from the beginning to the end of adolescence (Holsen, Carlson Jones, & Skogbrott Birkeland, 2012).

With recent dramatic increase in Internet and social media use have come concerns about adolescents' body images (Hosseini & Padhy, 2021; Scully, Swords, & Nixon, 2021). A recent Japanese study of 10-year-olds indicated that greater exposure to social networking sites was associated with a stronger desire to be thin for girls but not for boys (Sugimoto & others, 2020). Also, in a recent study, higher social media use was linked to more negative body images among adolescents, more so for girls than boys (Kelly & others, 2019). In addition, a recent study of young adolescents indicated that girls had a more negative body image when they identified with an ideal social media portrayal (for example, stating that they want their body to look like the models they see on social media) (Rodgers & others, 2020). Further, a recent study of 11- to 14-year-olds indicated that those who felt negatively about their body image because of social media had higher rates of depressive symptoms, online social anxiety, difficulty in making new friends, and social isolation (Charmaraman & others, 2021). In the same study, those who followed celebrities checked social media more often and were more likely to have depressive symptoms and online social anxiety. In another recent study, U.S. college women who spent more time on Facebook engaged in more frequent body and weight comparisons with other women, paid more attention to the physical appearance of others, and experienced more negative feelings about their own bodies (Eckler, Kalyango, & Paasch, 2017). And research indicated that exposure to attractive female celebrity and peer images on Instagram was detrimental to female college students' body image (Brown & Tiggemann, 2016). In sum, various aspects of exposure to the Internet and social media are increasing the body dissatisfaction of adolescents and emerging adults, especially females.

Body Art   An increasing number of adolescents and college students are engaging in body modifications that include obtaining tattoos, body piercings, or engaging in scarification (scratching, etching, burning, or branding designs, pictures, or words into their skin) (Breuner & others, 2018). In one survey, 38 percent of 18- to 29-year-olds had at least one tattoo and 23 percent had piercings in places other than an earlobe (Pew Research Center, 2010). Many of these youth engage in such body modifications to be different, to stamp their identity as unique. Some studies indicate that tattoos and body piercings are markers for risk taking in

What are some links between social media and adolescents' body image?
William Perugini/Image Source/Getty Images

Use of body art, such as tattoos and body piercing, is increasing in adolescence and emerging adulthood. *Why do youth engage in such body modification?*
Corbis/VCG/Getty Images

adolescence (Deschesnes, Fines, & Demers, 2006). However, other researchers argue that body art is increasingly used to express individuality and self-expression rather than rebellion (Van Hoover, Rademayer, & Farley, 2017).

Hormones and Behavior   Are concentrations of hormones linked to adolescent behavior? Hormonal factors are thought to account for at least part of the increase in negative and variable emotions that characterize adolescents (Vosberg & others, 2021). In a recent study, higher concentrations of DHEA during puberty were linked to lower conscientiousness and openness to experience in boys and girls (Van den Akker & others, 2021). Further, in boys, higher levels of androgens are associated with violence and acting-out problems (Van Goozen & others, 1998). In addition, a recent study of adolescent boys revealed that higher testosterone levels were linked to greater impatience and lower delay of gratification (Laube, Lorenz, & van den Bos, 2020). And in a recent study of early adolescent boys in Japan, a lower level of testosterone was associated with social withdrawal (Hayashi & others, 2020).

There is also some indication that increased estrogen levels are linked to depression in adolescent girls (Blakemore, Berenbaum, & Liben, 2009). Further, high levels of adrenal androgens are associated with negative emotions in girls (Susman & Dorn, 2009). One study found that early-maturing girls with high levels of adrenal androgens had higher emotional arousal and depression than did other girls (Graber, Brooks-Gunn, & Warren, 2006).

However, hormonal factors alone are not responsible for adolescent behavior (Perry & others, 2021). For example, one study found that social factors accounted for two to four times as much variance as hormonal factors in young adolescent girls' depression and anger (Brooks-Gunn & Warren, 1989). Another study found little direct connection between adolescent males' and females' testosterone levels and risk-taking behavior or depression (Booth & others, 2003). In contrast, a link with risk-taking behavior depended on the quality of parent-adolescent relations. When relationship quality was lower, rates of testosterone-linked risk-taking behavior and symptoms of depression were higher. And, in one study, negative life events mediated links between hormones (estradiol and an adrenal hormone) and aggression in 10- to 14-year-old girls (Graber, Brooks-Gunn, & Warren, 2006). Thus, hormones do not function independently; instead, hormonal activity is influenced by many environmental factors, including parent-adolescent relationships. Stress, eating patterns, sexual activity, and depression can also activate or suppress various aspects of the hormone system (Phan & others, 2021).

Early and Late Maturation   Did you enter puberty early, late, or on time? When adolescents mature earlier or later than their peers, they often perceive themselves differently and behave differently (Hoyt & others, 2020). A recent meta-analysis concluded that early-maturing boys and girls are more physically fit than average (Albaladejo-Saura & others, 2021). In another recent study, early-maturing boys also were more physically fit but girls who matured on time were more physically fit (Nevill & others, 2021). Also, in other recent research, early-maturing boys had higher than average rates of externalizing and violent behaviors throughout adolescence but not in early adulthood (Dimler & Natsuaki, 2021). In the same study, early-maturing girls had higher than average rates of externalizing behaviors during adolescence but not in early adulthood.

In the Berkeley Longitudinal Study conducted many years ago, early-maturing boys perceived themselves more positively and had more successful peer relations than did late-maturing boys (Jones, 1965). The findings for early-maturing girls were similar but not as strong as for boys. Also, one study found that in the early high school years, late-maturing boys had a more negative body image than early-maturing boys (de Guzman & Nishina, 2014).

In the Berkeley Longitudinal Study, when the late-maturing boys were in their thirties, however, they had developed a more positive identity than the early-maturing boys had (Peskin, 1967). Perhaps the late-maturing boys benefited from having more time to explore life's options, or perhaps the early-maturing boys continued to focus on their physical status instead of paying attention to career development and achievement.

An increasing number of researchers have found that early maturation increases girls' vulnerability to a number of problems (Black & Rofey, 2018). Early-maturing girls are more likely to smoke, drink, be depressed, have an eating disorder, engage in delinquency, struggle for earlier independence from their parents, and have older friends; and their bodies are likely to elicit responses from males that lead to earlier dating and earlier sexual experiences (Ibitoye & others, 2017; Pomerantz & others, 2017; Wang & others, 2016). In a recent study, onset of menarche before 11 years of age was linked to a higher incidence of distress disorders, fear disorders, and externalizing disorders in females (Platt & others, 2017). Also, researchers recently found that early-maturing girls had higher rates of depression and antisocial behavior as middle-aged adults mainly because their difficulties began in adolescence and did not lessen over time (Mendle, Ryan, & McKone, 2018). Further, researchers have found that early-maturing girls tend to have sexual intercourse earlier and have more unstable sexual relationships (Moore, Harden, & Mendle, 2014), as well as being at higher risk for physical and verbal abuse in dating (Chen, Rothman, & Jaffee, 2017). And early-maturing girls are less likely to graduate from high school and more likely to cohabit and marry earlier (Cavanagh, 2009). Further, in a recent study, heterosexual girls who experienced menarche before 12 years of age had a lower level of relationship quality in early adulthood compared with on-time maturers (Reese, Trinh, & Halpern, 2017). In this study, sexual minority girls who experienced early pubertal onset reported having a lower relationship quality in early adulthood. Apparently, the combination of their social and cognitive immaturity and early physical development result in early-maturing girls being more easily lured into problem behaviors, not recognizing the possible long-term negative effects of these behaviors on their development.

What are some risk factors associated with early maturation in girls?
Britt Erlanson/Getty Images

Are there sex differences in the effects of pubertal timing on various aspects of problem behavior? A recent meta-analysis of more than 100 studies found few sex differences but did conclude that early maturation had negative outcomes for both girls and boys in a number of areas, including internalized problems (depression, for example) and externalized problems (juvenile delinquency, for example) (Ullsperger & Nikolas, 2017). For example, in a recent study, early-maturing boys and girls tended to affiliate with delinquent peers, which increased their engagement in externalizing problems (Stepanyan & others, 2020).

In sum, early maturation may have favorable outcomes in adolescence for boys, especially in early adolescence. However, late maturation may ultimately be more favorable for boys, especially in terms of identity and career development. Research increasingly has found that early-maturing girls are vulnerable to a number of problems.

We have explored many aspects of puberty in this part of the chapter. To read about some effective strategies for guiding adolescents through puberty, see the *Connecting with Health and Well-Being* interlude.

Anne Petersen has made numerous contributions to our understanding of puberty and adolescent development. To read about her work and career, see the *Connecting with Careers* profile.

connecting with health and well-being

Strategies for Effectively Guiding Adolescents Through Puberty

Following are some effective ways to help adolescents cope with pubertal changes (McNeely & Blanchard, 2009):

- Become familiar with accurate information about pubertal changes. Experts recommend communicating with children about puberty as early as 8 or 9 years of age to prepare them for the changes that are coming.
- Take young adolescents' comments about puberty seriously and listen carefully to what they are saying so that you can help them understand it better.
- Allow adolescents to talk freely about their feelings and fears, especially what they don't understand about their changing bodies and the stress it is causing them.

- When adolescents are willing to talk about puberty, show an interest in what they have to say and listen to them. Don't jump in too fast with advice, or even worse, tell them that their feelings are unfounded or irrational.
- Encourage early-maturing adolescents to not spend time with older peer groups of adolescents but instead to connect with peers their own age.
- Recognize that although adolescents may seem to be physically mature, they can't be expected to have the same levels of cognitive and socioemotional maturity as adults do.

Anne Petersen, Researcher and Administrator

Anne Petersen has had a distinguished career as a researcher and administrator whose main focus is adolescent development. Petersen obtained three degrees (B.A., M.A., and Ph.D.) from the University of Chicago in math and statistics. Her first job after she obtained her Ph.D. was as a research associate/professor involved in statistical consultation, and it was on this job that she was introduced to the field of adolescent development, which became the focus of her subsequent work.

Petersen moved from the University of Chicago to Pennsylvania State University, where she became a leading researcher in adolescent development. Her research included a focus on puberty and gender. Petersen also has held numerous administrative positions. In the mid-1990s Petersen became deputy director of the National Science Foundation, and from 1996 to 2005 she was senior vice-president for programs at the W. K. Kellogg Foundation. In 2006, she became the deputy director of the Center for Advanced Study in the Behavioral Sciences at Stanford University and also assumed the position of professor of psychology at Stanford. Subsequently, Petersen started her own foundation—Global Philanthropy Alliance—that develops young social entrepreneurs in Africa by providing training in skills that will help them contribute to the social health of their families and communities. She also is a member of the faculty at the Center for Growth and Human Development at the University of Michigan.

Anne Petersen interacts with adolescents.
Courtesy of Anne Petersen, W.K. Kellogg Foundation

Petersen says that what inspired her to enter the field of adolescent development and take positions at various universities and foundations was her desire to make a difference for people, especially youth. Her goal is to make a difference for youth in the United States and around the world. She believes that too often adolescents have been neglected.

Review Connect Reflect

 LG1 Discuss the determinants, characteristics, and psychological dimensions of puberty.

Review
- What are puberty's main determinants?
- What characterizes the growth spurt in puberty?
- How does sexual maturation develop in puberty?
- What are some secular trends in puberty?
- What are some important psychological dimensions of puberty?

Connect
- How do nature and nurture affect pubertal timing?

Reflect *Your Own Personal Journey of Life*
- Think back to when you entered puberty. How strong was your curiosity about the pubertal changes that were taking place? What misconceptions did you have about those changes?

2 Health   **LG2** Summarize the nature of adolescents' and emerging adults' health.

| Adolescence: A Critical Juncture in Health | Emerging Adults' Health | Nutrition | Exercise and Sports | Sleep |

Why might adolescence be a critical juncture in health? What characterizes emerging adults' health? What are some concerns about adolescents' eating habits? How much do adolescents exercise, and what role does sports play in their lives? Do adolescents get enough sleep? These are among the questions we explore in this section.

ADOLESCENCE: A CRITICAL JUNCTURE IN HEALTH

Adolescence is a critical juncture in the adoption of behaviors that are relevant to health (Bem & Small, 2020; Insel & Roth, 2022). Many of the behaviors that are linked to poor health habits and early death in adults begin during adolescence (Alsaad, Azhar, & Nasser, 2021). Conversely, the early formation of healthy behavior patterns, such as regular exercise and a preference for foods low in fat and cholesterol, not only has immediate health benefits but helps in adulthood to delay or prevent disability and mortality from heart disease, stroke, diabetes, and cancer (Taylor, 2021).

A special recent concern is the impact of the COVID-19 pandemic on adolescent health care, since parents avoided taking their children and adolescents to their primary care physicians for routine health evaluations or treatment of new health issues because of the fear of contracting the COVID-19 virus. In addition, a recent study found that children and adolescents were 70 percent less likely to visit a general hospital emergency department after the pandemic began than before it appeared (Goldman & others, 2021). Further, the pandemic was associated with increased mental health issues in youth, including stress, depression, and suicidal ideation (Magson & others, 2021; Saggioro de Figueiredo & others, 2021).

Unfortunately, even though the United States has become a health-conscious nation, many adolescents (and adults) still smoke, have poor nutritional habits, and spend too much of their lives as "couch potatoes" (Belcher & others, 2021). Why might many adolescents develop poor health habits? In adolescence, many individuals reach a level of health, strength, and energy that they will never match during the remainder of their lives. Given this high level of physical strength, good health, and energy, it is not surprising that many adolescents take their well-being for granted and develop poor health habits.

Adolescence is a critical time or the development of health-enhancing and health-compromising behaviors.
Albert Shakirov/Alamy Stock Photo

Many health experts conclude that improving adolescents' health involves far more than taking them to the doctor's office when they are sick. Increasingly, experts recognize that whether or not adolescents develop health problems depends primarily on their behavior (Agostinis-Sobrinho & others, 2021; Andrews, Ahmed, & Blakemore, 2021). These experts' goals are (1) to reduce adolescents' *health-compromising behaviors*, such as drug abuse, violence, unprotected sexual intercourse, and dangerous driving; and (2) to increase adolescents' *health-enhancing behaviors*, such as exercising, eating nutritious foods, wearing seat belts, and getting adequate sleep.

In most educational interventions that are designed to improve various aspects of adolescents' health, the strategy is to increase their awareness of health risks and teach skills that will lead to more health-enhancing behavior. In a recent analysis, it was concluded that this strategy doesn't always work with adolescents, especially those from about 13 to 17 years of age (Yeager, Dahl, & Dweck, 2018). Rather, David Yeager and his colleagues (2018) propose that effective intervention to improve adolescent health should focus more on treating adolescents with respect and according them higher status. These interventions would treat adolescents as having valuable knowledge, being able to competently make good choices, and having the potential to contribute positively to the lives of others. These types of interventions don't tell adolescents what to do or what not to do but rather encourage them to discover on their own what is best for their health, honoring their desire not to be treated as children.

In one intervention taking this innovative approach, the adolescents' initial assumption was that healthy eating is for nerds who just do what their parents tell them to do (Bryan & others, 2016). The researchers then modified their definition of healthy eating to demonstrate more social-status respect by describing healthy eaters as independent thinkers who make the world a better place to live in. To reflect this intent, eighth-grade students were given a news article and told that the food industry didn't want them to read it. Then the students read quotations from angry high-status older adolescents (football stars, for example) who said they had previously read the article and pledged not to eat junk food in protest of the food industry's manipulations. Next, the adolescents were asked to write a letter to a future student about why she or he was rebelling against the food companies by eating healthy rather than unhealthy food. The next day the students were given the option of eating healthy foods (nuts, fruits, water) or unhealthy foods (Cheetos, Oreos, Coca-Cola). The students who experienced the intervention were less likely to choose the unhealthy foods. While this intervention lasted only one day, it illustrates how treating adolescents with respect can lead to healthier behavior.

Special concerns about adolescent health also focus on the roles of adverse experiences and events linked to poverty and ethnicity (Marchetti & others, 2021; Weil, 2020). Disparities

developmental connection

Social Contexts

Social contexts play an important role in adolescent decision making. Connect to "The Brain and Cognitive Development."

How might poverty and ethnicity be linked to adolescents' health?
ericsphotography/Getty Images

in adolescent health related to poverty and ethnicity include homelessness, neighborhood crime and violence, housing insecurity, hunger, malnutrition, lack of health insurance coverage, compromised health and well-being of parents, racism, and discrimination (Perrin & others, 2020). Adolescents growing up in poverty and ethnic minority groups, such as African American and Latinx families, are more likely to experience these inequities. Further, the COVID-19 pandemic adversely affected adolescents and their families, with rates of the disease higher in families living in poverty and families of African American or Latinx ethnicity. From March through July of 2020, Latinx children and adolescents were eight times more likely and African American children and adolescents five times more likely than their non-Latinx white counterparts to be hospitalized with the virus (Kim & others, 2020). The most common underlying condition linked to adverse outcomes was obesity.

There also are persistent ethnic disparities in health coverage and chronic health conditions in U.S. children and adolescents (Carratala & Maxwell, 2020). For example, in 2017, 7.7 percent of Latinx children and adolescents were uninsured, compared with 4.1 percent of non-Latinx white children (National Center for Health Statistics, 2018). Also in 2017, 12.6 percent of African American children and adolescents had asthma, compared with 7.7 percent of non-Latinx white children (National Center for Health Statistics, 2018). In addition, Native American and Alaska Native adolescents were 30 percent more likely to be obese than non-Latinx white adolescents (U.S. Department of Health and Human Services Office of Minority Health, 2020).

Risk-Taking Behavior   One type of health-compromising behavior that increases in adolescence is risk taking (Korucuoglu & others, 2020). In a recent study of more than 5,000 individuals from 10 to 30 years of age in 11 countries in Africa, Asia, Europe, and the Americas, sensation seeking increased steadily from 11 years of age through late adolescence, peaking at 19 years of age and declining through the twenties (Steinberg & others, 2018). However, in this study, self-regulation increased steadily from 11 years of age into emerging adulthood, reaching a plateau at 23 to 26 years of age.

Ron Dahl (2004, p. 6) provided the following vivid description of adolescent risk taking:

> Beginning in early adolescence, many individuals seek experiences that create high-intensity feelings . . . Adolescents like intensity, excitement, and arousal. They are drawn to music videos that shock and bombard the senses. Teenagers flock to horror and slasher movies. They dominate queues waiting to ride the high-adrenaline rides at amusement parks. Adolescence is a time when sex, drugs, very loud music, and other high-stimulation experiences take on great appeal. It is a developmental period when an appetite for adventure, a predilection for risks, and a desire for novelty and thrills seem to reach naturally high levels. While these patterns of emotional changes are evident to some degree in most adolescents, it is important to acknowledge the wide range of individual differences during this period of development.

Researchers also have found that the more resources there are in the community, such as youth activities and adults as role models, the less likely adolescents are to engage in risky behavior (Yancey & others, 2011). One study found that a higher level of what was labeled *social capital* (in this study, number of schools, number of churches/temples/synagogues, and number of high school diplomas) was linked with lower rates of outcomes associated with adolescent risky behavior (in this study, gunshot wounds, pregnancy, alcohol and drug treatment, and sexually transmitted infections) (Youngblade & Curry, 2006). Another study revealed that "hanging out" with peers in unstructured contexts was linked with an increase in adolescents' risk-taking behavior (Youngblade & Curry, 2006). Further, adolescents who had better grades were less likely to engage in risk taking than their counterparts with lower grades. And parental monitoring and communication skills are linked to a lower level of adolescent risk taking (Chen & others, 2008).

Researchers also have found that peer presence increases adolescent risk-taking (Kwon & others, 2021). In a recent study, adolescent boys increased their risk-taking behavior more than girls when they were in the presence of a same-sex peer (Defoe & others, 2020). Further, another recent study found that peer presence increased risk-taking behavior for adolescents with low self-esteem but not those with high self-esteem (Tian & others, 2020). And other research with adolescents indicated that lower SES was associated with lower cognitive control, which in turn was linked to increased risk-taking (Brieant & others, 2021).

Recently, neurobiological explanations of adolescent risk taking have been proposed (Reyna, 2020; Telzer & others, 2021). The *prefrontal cortex*, the brain's highest level that is

What are some characteristics of adolescents' risk-taking behavior?
Thomas Barwick/Getty Images

developmental **connection**

Brain Development

Although the prefrontal cortex shows considerable development in childhood, it is still not fully mature in adolescence. Connect to "The Brain and Cognitive Development."

involved in reasoning, decision making, and self-control, matures much later (continuing to develop in late adolescence and emerging adulthood) than the *amygdala*, which is the main structure involved in emotion in the brain. The later development of the prefrontal cortex combined with the earlier maturity of the amygdala may explain the difficulty younger adolescents have in putting the brakes on their risk-taking adventures. These developmental changes in the brain provide one explanation of why risk taking declines as adolescents get older. We will consider much more about these developmental changes in the adolescent brain in the chapter on "The Brain and Cognitive Development."

What can be done to help adolescents satisfy their craving for risk taking without compromising their health? It is important for parents, teachers, mentors, and other responsible adults to effectively monitor adolescents' behavior (Pollak & others, 2020). In many cases, adults decrease their monitoring of adolescents too early, leaving them to cope with tempting situations alone or with friends and peers. When adolescents are in tempting and dangerous situations with minimal adult supervision, their inclination to engage in risk-taking behavior combined with their lack of self-regulatory skills can make them vulnerable to a host of negative outcomes.

To read about an individual who has made a number of contributions to a better understanding of adolescent risk-taking and ways to reduce such risk-taking, see the *Connecting with Careers* profile.

Health Services Adolescents underutilize health-care systems. Health services are especially unlikely to meet the needs of younger adolescents, ethnic minority adolescents, sexual minority adolescents, and adolescents living in poverty (Desai & Romano, 2017). There is a need for specialized training of providers of adolescent health care that takes into account the numerous emotional and social changes adolescents experience and the implications of those changes for their behavior and health. However, not all of the blame should be placed on

RubberBall Productions/Getty Images

connecting with careers

Bonnie Halpern-Felsher, University Professor in Pediatrics, Director of Community Efforts to Improve Adolescents' Health, and Mentor for Underrepresented Adolescents

Dr. Halpern-Felsher recently became a professor in the Department of Pediatrics at Stanford University after holding this position for a number of years at the University of California–San Francisco. Her work exemplifies how some professors not only teach and conduct research in a single discipline such as psychology, but also participate in multiple academic disciplines while contributing to community projects in an effort to improve the lives of youth. Dr. Halpern-Felsher is a developmental psychologist with additional training in adolescent health. She is especially interested in understanding why adolescents engage in risk-taking behaviors and using this research to develop intervention programs that will improve adolescents' lives.

In particular, Dr. Halpern-Felsher has studied adolescent sexual decision-making and reproductive health, including cognitive and socioemotional predictors of sexual behavior. Her research also has examined how parenting and peer relationships influence adolescent sexual behavior. She has served as a consultant for a number of community-based adolescent health promotion campaigns, and she has been involved in community-based efforts to reduce substance abuse in adolescence. For example, recently Dr. Halpern-Felsher worked with the state of California to implement new school-based tobacco prevention and education materials. As a further indication of her strong commitment to improving adolescents'

Dr. Bonnie Halpern-Felsher (*second from left*) with some of the students she is mentoring in the STEP-UP program.
Courtesy of Dr. Bonnie Halpern-Felsher

lives, Dr. Halpern-Felsher coordinates the state's STEP-UP program (Short-Term Research Experience for Underrepresented Persons), in which she has personally mentored and supervised 22 to 25 middle and high school students every year since 2007.

What is the pattern of adolescents' use of health services?
Ariel Skelley/Getty Images

health-care providers. Many adolescents don't believe that health-care providers can help them. And some health-care providers may want to provide better health care for adolescents but lack adequate training and/or time during their visit.

Professional guidelines for adolescent health care recommend annual preventive visits with screening and guidance for health-related behaviors. However, a large-scale survey revealed that only 38 percent of adolescents had experienced a preventive visit in the previous 12 months, and few were given guidance for health-related behaviors (Irwin & others, 2009). Of special concern is the low use of health services by high school males, who use health services less than younger adolescent males. However, high school and college females are more likely to use health services than young adolescents (Marcell & others, 2002). And adolescents are much more likely to seek health care for problems related to disease than problems related to mental health, tobacco use, or sexual behavior (Marcell & Halpern-Felsher, 2007).

Among the chief barriers to better health care for adolescents are cost, poor organization and availability of health services, lack of confidentiality, and reluctance on the part of health-care providers to communicate with adolescents about sensitive health issues (Desai & Romano, 2017). Few health-care providers receive any special training in working with adolescents. Many say they feel unprepared to provide services such as contraceptive counseling or to evaluate what constitutes abnormal behavior in adolescents. Health-care providers may transmit to patients their discomfort in discussing topics such as sexuality and drugs, causing adolescents to avoid discussing sensitive issues with them.

developmental **connection**

Problems and Disorders

Both early and later experiences may be involved in suicide attempts. Connect to "Problems in Adolescence and Emerging Adulthood."

Leading Causes of Death   Medical improvements have increased the life expectancy of today's adolescents and emerging adults compared with their counterparts in the early twentieth century. Still, life-threatening factors do exist for adolescents and emerging adults (Gijzen & others, 2021; Hawton & others, 2020).

The three leading causes of death in adolescence are unintentional injuries, suicide, and homicide (National Center for Health Statistics, 2020). Almost half of all deaths among individuals from 15 to 24 years of age are attributed to unintentional injuries, the majority of them involving motor vehicle accidents. Risky driving habits, such as speeding, tailgating, and driving under the influence of alcohol or other drugs, may be more important contributors to these accidents than lack of driving experience (White & others, 2018). In a recent study, twelfth-grade binge drinking was linked to driving while impaired (DWI), riding with an impaired driver (RWI), blackouts, and riskier driving in emerging adults up to four years later (Vaca & others, 2020).

In about 50 percent of motor vehicle fatalities involving adolescents, the driver has a blood alcohol level of 0.10 percent or higher—twice the level at which a driver is designated as "under the influence" in some states. Of growing concern is the increasingly common practice of mixing alcohol and energy drinks, which is linked to a higher rate of driving while intoxicated (Wilson & others, 2018). A high rate of intoxication is also found in adolescents who die as pedestrians or while using vehicles other than automobiles.

Suicide was the third-leading cause of death among adolescents for a number of years but recently replaced homicide as the second-leading cause of death for adolescents, with accidents still being the number one cause of adolescent deaths in the United States (National Center for Health Statistics, 2020).

EMERGING ADULTS' HEALTH

Emerging adults have more than twice the mortality rate of adolescents (Park & others, 2008). As indicated in Figure 8, males are mainly responsible for the higher mortality rate of emerging adults.

Also, compared with adolescents, emerging adults engage in more health-compromising behaviors, have more chronic health problems, are more likely to be obese, and are more likely to have a mental health disorder (Andraka-Christou & others, 2020). In a research analysis, most health and health care indicators had changed little across the last decade for adolescents and young adults (Park & others, 2014). In this analysis, improvements for adolescents and young adults occurred in the form of reduced rates of unintentional injury, assault, and tobacco

What are the leading causes of death in adolescence?
(Left) jabejon/Getty Images (Right) Ranta Images/Shutterstock

use. Adolescents improved in sexual/reproductive health, but young adults engaged in greater health risks and had worse health outcomes than adolescents.

Although emerging adults may know what it takes to be healthy, they often don't apply this information to their own behavior. In many cases, emerging adults are not as healthy as they seem. Few emerging adults stop to think about how their personal lifestyles will affect their health later in their adult lives. As emerging adults, many of us develop a pattern of not eating breakfast, not eating regular meals, and relying on snacks as our main food source during the day; eating excessively to the point where we exceed the normal weight for our height; smoking moderately or excessively; drinking moderately or excessively; failing to exercise; and getting by with only a few hours of sleep at night (Fahey, Insel, & Roth, 2021; Schiff, 2021). These lifestyles are associated with poor health. A recent study of college students revealed that regularly eating breakfast was positively linked to their grade point average (GPA) while regularly eating fast food was negatively associated with their GPA (Reuter, Forster, & Brister, 2021). In the Berkeley Longitudinal Study—in which individuals were evaluated over a period of 40 years—physical health at age 30 predicted life satisfaction at age 70, more so for men than for women (Mussen, Honzik, & Eichorn, 1982).

There are some hidden dangers in the peaks of performance and health in early adulthood. Young adults can draw on physical resources for a great deal of pleasure, often bouncing back easily from physical stress and abuse. However, this behavior can lead them to push their bodies too far. The negative effects of abusing one's body might not show up in emerging adulthood, but they are likely to surface during early adulthood or middle adulthood.

Emerging adults often ignore symptoms that require immediate medical attention, such as the following: breast lumps, unexplained weight loss, a fever that lasts more than a week, coughing up blood, persistent or severe headaches, fainting spells, and unexplained shortness of breath. If you experience any of these health problems, seek medical attention without delay.

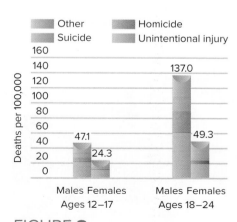

FIGURE **8**

MORTALITY RATES OF U.S. ADOLESCENTS AND EMERGING ADULTS

Thirteen/Shutterstock

NUTRITION

Nutrition is an important aspect of health-compromising and health-enhancing behaviors (Schiff, 2021). The eating habits of many adolescents are health-compromising, and an increasing number of adolescents have an eating disorder (Teague, Mackenzie, & Rosenthal, 2022; Verschueren & others, 2020). A comparison of adolescents in 28 countries found that U.S. and British adolescents were more likely to eat fried food and less likely to eat fruits and vegetables than adolescents in most other countries that were studied (World Health Organization, 2000). Also, a recent national survey found that 14.1 percent of U.S. adolescents had not eaten breakfast in the 7 days before they took the survey (Kann & others, 2018).

Concern is often expressed over adolescents' tendency to eat between meals. However, their choice of foods is much more important than the time or place of eating. Fresh vegetables and fruits as well as whole-grain products are needed to complement the foods adolescents commonly choose, which tend to be high in protein and calories. One analysis found that family dinners in France were more likely to emphasize fruits and vegetables than were family dinners in the United States (Kremer-Sadlik & others, 2015). In recent decades U.S. adolescents have been decreasing their intake of fruits and vegetables. The National Youth Risk Survey found that U.S. high school students showed a linear decrease in their intake of fruits and vegetables since 1999, with 59.2 percent of high school students not eating vegetables one or more times in the last 7 days in 2019 (Underwood & others, 2020). In recent research, a higher level of parental monitoring was linked to adolescents having a healthier diet and reduced likelihood of being overweight (Kim & others, 2019). And one study revealed that eating regular family meals during early adolescence was linked to healthy eating habits five years later (Burgess-Champoux & others, 2009). Thus, parents can play an important role in adolescents' nutrition by making healthy food choices available to adolescents, by serving as models for healthy nutrition, and by including adolescents in regular family meals. Also, one study found that increased screen time (TV, electronic games, DVDs) was linked to increased consumption of foods and beverages with low nutritional quality and decreased consumption of fruits and vegetables (Falbe & others, 2014).

More frequent family meals are linked to a number of positive outcomes for adolescents, including better dietary intake, lower substance use, and greater academic success (Winter, Jones, & O'Neill, 2019). A 10-year longitudinal study revealed that the more often adolescents ate family meals, the less likely they were to be overweight or obese in early adulthood (Berge & others, 2015).

Schools also can play an important role in adolescents' eating patterns. One study revealed that a comprehensive school intervention in the fourth and fifth grades resulted in increased vegetable consumption two years later (Wang & others, 2010). Another study found that promoting positive nutritional practices in a low-income middle school increased students' intake of fruit and fiber while decreasing their cholesterol levels (Alaimo & others, 2015).

A special concern in American culture is the amount of fat in our diets. Many of today's adolescents virtually live on fast-food meals, which contribute to the high fat levels in their diets (Schiff, 2021). A longitudinal study revealed that frequent intake of fast food (three or more times per week) was reported by 24 percent of 15-year-old males and 21 percent of 15-year-old females (Larson & others, 2008). At 20 years of age, the percent increased to 33 percent for males but remained at 21 percent for females.

Another special concern in adolescents' diets is the recent increase in consumption of energy drinks that tend to have high caffeine levels (Ozde & others, 2020). Researchers recently have found that consumption of energy drinks in adolescence is linked to more emergency room visits, adverse cardiovascular effects such as atrial fibrillation, alcohol use, reduced sleep duration, and fast food consumption (Almulla & Faris, 2020; Galimov & others, 2020; Moussa & others, 2021).

We will have much more to discuss about nutrition in the chapter on "Problems in Adolescence and Emerging Adulthood." There we also examine three eating disorders: obesity, anorexia nervosa, and bulimia nervosa.

developmental connection

Problems and Disorders

The percentage of overweight and obese adolescents has increased dramatically in recent years. Connect to "Problems in Adolescence and Emerging Adulthood."

What family factors are linked to better nutrition in adolescents?
monkeybusinessimages/Getty Images

EXERCISE AND SPORTS

Do American adolescents get enough exercise? How extensive is the role of sports in adolescent development? The answers to these questions influence adolescents' health and well-being.

Exercise In the fourth century BC, Aristotle commented that the quality of life is determined by its activities. Today, we know that exercise is one of the principal activities that improve the quality of life, both in adolescence and adulthood (Lumpkin, 2021).

Developmental Changes Researchers have found that individuals become less active as they enter and progress through adolescence (Chong & others, 2020). Also, a recent national survey found that in 2019, 23 percent of ninth- through twelfth-graders had engaged in physical activity for 60 minutes or more in each of the last seven days, compared to 28.7 percent in 2011 (Underwood & others, 2020). Adolescent girls were much less likely to engage in physical activity for 60 minutes or more per day in each of the last seven days (15.4 percent) than were boys (30.9 percent) (Underwood & others, 2020). Ethnic differences in exercise participation rates of U.S. adolescents also occur, and these rates vary by gender. In the National Youth Risk Survey, non-Latinx white boys exercised the most, African American girls the least (Underwood & others, 2020).

In a recent World Health Organization study of 11- to 17-year-olds' physical activity in 146 countries, it was concluded that 81 percent of the adolescents were insufficiently physically active (78 percent boys, 85 percent girls) (Guthold & others, 2020). Also, in a recent study of exercise in 52 countries, a consistent gender difference occurred across the countries, with girls exercising less than boys (Bann & others, 2019). Also in this study, adolescents in higher-income families exercised more than those in lower-income families.

Further, a comparison of adolescents in 28 countries found that U.S. adolescents exercised less and ate more junk food than did adolescents in most of the other countries (World Health Organization, 2000). Just two-thirds of U.S. adolescents exercised at least twice a week, compared with 80 percent or more of adolescents in Ireland, Austria, Germany, and the Slovak Republic. U.S. adolescents were more likely to eat fried food and less likely to eat fruits and vegetables than were adolescents in most other countries studied. U.S. adolescents' eating choices were similar to those of adolescents in England.

Positive Benefits of Exercise in Adolescence Exercise is linked with a number of positive outcomes in adolescence (Powers & Howley, 2021). Engaging in regular exercise in adolescence is linked to being more physically fit in adulthood (Mikkelsson & others, 2006). Also, engaging in regular exercise in adolescence is associated with lower rates of being overweight or obese (Saidi & others, 2020). For example, a recent experimental study of obese adolescent girls found that a 12-week jump rope exercise program was effective in improving their body composition, blood pressure, insulin level, and self-regulation (Kim & others, 2020). In addition, a recent research review of 27 studies concluded that aerobic exercise was associated with children's and adolescents' reduction of body fat, lower fasting insulin, decreased inflammatory markers, and increased physical fitness (Lee, 2021). Other positive outcomes of exercise in adolescence are reduced triglyceride levels, lower blood pressure, and a lower incidence of type 2 diabetes (Huang & others, 2020). Research also indicates that adolescents who engage in higher levels of exercise have lower levels of alcohol, cigarette, and marijuana use (Terry-McElrath, O'Malley, & Johnston, 2011). And in a recent large-scale study of Dutch adolescents, physically active adolescents had fewer emotional and peer problems (Kuiper, Broer, & van der Wouden, 2018).

What are developmental and gender differences in exercise during adolescence?
Hero Images/Getty Images

connecting with adolescents

In Pitiful Shape

A lot of kids in my class are in pitiful physical shape. They never exercise, except in gym class, and even then they hardly break a sweat. During lunch hour, I see some of the same loafers hanging out and smoking a bunch of cigarettes. Don't they know what they are doing to their bodies? All I can say is that I'm glad I'm not like them. I'm on the basketball team, and during the season, the coach runs us until we are exhausted. In the summer, I still play basketball and swim often. I don't know what I would do without exercise. I couldn't stand to be out of shape.

—Brian, age 14

What are some of the lifelong benefits of the positive health habits cited in this passage?

What are some of the positive benefits of exercise for adolescents?
FatCamera/E+/Getty Images

Research studies also underscore other positive benefits of exercise for adolescents (Wuest & Walton-Fisette, 2021). For example, adolescents with high levels of physical fitness have better connectivity between brain regions than adolescents who are less fit (Herting & others, 2014). Regular physical exercise also can help adolescents reduce their stress and depression. For example, a recent study of adolescents with major depressive disorder (MDD) revealed that engaging in aerobic exercise for 12 weeks lowered their depressive symptoms (Jaworska & others, 2019). Further, in a recent Chinese study, adolescents showed more depressive symptoms after COVID-19 appeared although engaging in more physical exercise during the quarantine helped to buffer the link between the pandemic and depressive symptoms (Ren & others, 2021). And a longitudinal study of more than 1 million Swedish males found that 18-year-olds who had lower cardiovascular fitness had an increased risk of early-onset dementia and mild cognitive impairment 42 years later (Nyberg & others, 2014).

Aerobic exercise also increasingly is linked to children's and adolescents' cognitive skills. A recent research review concluded that school and community-based physical activity interventions improve overweight and obese adolescents' executive function (higher-level thinking) (Martin & others, 2018). Also, a recent study found that adolescents who exercised more per week had better processing speed, selective attention, and concentration (Reigal & others, 2020). Other research studies have revealed that aerobic exercise in adolescence is associated with better memory, executive function, and creativity (Best, 2011; Davis & others, 2011; Ludyga & others, 2018). And a recent research review concluded that physical activity interventions improved the cognitive performance (especially executive function) of overweight or obese adolescents (Sun & others, 2021). Further, researchers recently have found that exercise reduces the symptoms of attention deficit hyperactivity disorder (ADHD) (Villa-Gonzalez & others, 2020).

Overall, what types of interventions and activities have been successful in helping overweight adolescents and emerging adults reach their weight loss goals? Research indicates that dietary changes and regular exercise are key components of weight reduction in adolescence and emerging adulthood (Powers & Howley, 2021; Schiff, 2021). For example, a recent study found that a combination of regular exercise and a diet plan results in weight loss and enhanced executive function in adolescents (Xie & others, 2017). Next, we will explore further interventions for improving adolescents' exercise patterns.

Roles of Families, Peers, Schools, and Screen-Based Activity in Adolescent Exercise What contextual factors influence whether adolescents engage in regular exercise? Four important influences are families, peers, schools, and screen-based activity.

Parents have an important influence on adolescents' exercise patterns (Judice & others, 2021). Children and adolescents benefit when parents engage in regular exercise and are physically fit. Children whose parents got them involved in regular exercise and sports during their elementary school years are likely to continue engaging in exercise on a regular basis as adolescents. One study revealed that 9- to 13-year-olds were more likely to engage in physical activity during their free time if they felt safe, had a number of places to be active, and had parents who participated in physical activities with them (Heitzler & others, 2006). And in a recent study, among 10- to 14-year-olds, being physically inactive was associated with being a girl, not having sports facilities in the neighborhood, and not perceiving the neighborhood as a safe place (Judice & others, 2021).

Peers often influence adolescents' physical activity (Chung, Ersig, & McCarthy, 2017). In a research

In 2007, Texas became the first state to test students' physical fitness. The student shown here is performing the trunk lift. Other assessments include aerobic exercise, muscle strength, and body fat. Assessments will be done annually.
Dallas Morning News, Vernon Bryant Photographer

review, peer/friend support of exercise, presence of peers and friends, friendship quality and acceptance, and peer crowds were linked to adolescents' physical activity (Fitzgerald, Fitzgerald, & Aherne, 2012).

Some of the blame for the poor physical condition of U.S. children and adolescents falls on U.S. schools, many of which fail to provide physical education classes on a regular basis (Wang & Chen, 2020). In a recent national survey, only 51 percent of U.S. ninth- to twelfth-grade students participated in one more physical education classes per week (Kann & others, 2018). In this survey, 72 percent of ninth-graders had one or more PE classes, compared with 39 percent of twelfth-graders. A recent research review concluded that school-based interventions for promoting physical activity can be effective if they focus on the content, quality, duration, and priority of the physical activity (Yuksel & others, 2020).

Screen-based activity (watching television, using computers, talking on the phone, texting, and instant messaging for long hours) is associated with a number of adolescent health problems, including lower levels of physical fitness and higher rates of sedentary behavior in adolescence (Rodriguez-Ayllon & others, 2020). In a recent study of adolescents, of four combinations of physical activity and screen time, those with lower physical activity and higher screen time were more likely to be overweight/obese than those in the other three categories (Crowe & others, 2020).

How might screen time be linked to adolescents' lower exercise levels?
Hero Images/Corbis

Sports Sports play an important role in the lives of many adolescents (Williams & Krane, 2021). A national study revealed that in 2013, 57.6 percent of ninth- through twelfth-grade U.S. students played on at least one sports team at school or in the community (Kann & others, 2016a). In the 2015 assessment, boys (62 percent) were more likely to play on a sports team than girls (53 percent). African American boys had the highest participation rate (66.5 percent) and Latinx girls the lowest participation rate (40.7 percent) (Kann & others, 2016a). From 2013 to 2015, girls increased their sports participation overall by 4.5 percent but Latinx girls decreased their sports participation by 4.3 percent.

Sports can have both positive and negative influences on adolescent development (Prentice, 2021). Many sports activities can improve adolescents' physical health and well-being, mental health, self-confidence, motivation to excel, and ability to work with others (Jackson & others, 2020; Snedden & others, 2020). In a recent study of adolescents' use of out-of-school time, time spent in organized sports was associated with increased positive self-identity (Lee & others, 2018). Adolescents who spend considerable time in sports are less likely than others to engage in risk-taking behaviors such as using drugs, are less likely to be overweight or obese (Stricker & others, 2020), show a lower cardiovascular risk profile, and have higher self-esteem and self-confidence (O'Connor & others, 2020). Further, a research review concluded that participation in sports in adolescence predicted a greater likelihood of engaging in physical activity in adulthood (Batista & others, 2019). And a recent study found that team sports participation in adolescence had long-term positive mental outcomes for those who were exposed to adverse childhood experiences (Easterlin & others, 2020).

Sports also can have negative outcomes for adolescents, including pressure to achieve and win, physical injuries, distraction from academic work, and unrealistic expectations for success as an athlete (De Matteo & others, 2020). One downside of the extensive participation in sports by American adolescents is pressure by parents and coaches to win at all costs. Adolescents' participation in competitive sports is linked with competition anxiety and self-centeredness (Smith & Smoll, 1997). Furthermore, some adolescents spend so much time in sports that their academic performance suffers.

Injuries are common when adolescents play sports (Chun & others, 2021; Maat & others, 2020). A national study of ninth- through twelfth-graders revealed that of the 80 percent of adolescents who exercised or played sports during the 30 previous days, 22 percent had seen a doctor or nurse for an exercise- or sports-related injury (Eaton & others, 2008). Ninth-graders were most likely to incur exercise- or sports-related injuries, twelfth-graders the least likely.

Increasingly, adolescents are pushing their bodies beyond their capabilities, stretching the duration, intensity, and frequency of their training to the point that they cause overuse injuries (Trentacosta, 2020). Another problem that has surfaced is the use of performance-enhancing drugs, such as steroids, by adolescent athletes (Parent & others, 2016).

developmental **connection**

Schools

Adolescents who participate in extracurricular activities such as sports have higher grades, are more engaged in school, and are less likely to drop out of school. Connect to "Schools."

developmental **connection**

Technology

When media multitasking is taken into account, U.S. 11- to 14-year-olds use media an average of nearly 12 hours a day. Connect to "Culture."

Sylvain Sonnet/Photographer's Choice RF/Getty Images

Effective College Student Strategies for Exercising

Following are some good strategies for increasing your exercise in healthy ways:

- **Manage your time effectively and schedule a regular time for exercise.** College students commonly say they just don't have enough time for exercise. If you feel that way, put together a weekly schedule and fit exercise into it.
- **Find an exercise partner or two.** Seek out exercise partners who are conscientious, have a strong commitment to exercise, and view physical fitness as a high priority in their lives.
- **Get involved in sports.** If you are not on a college sports team, get involved in club sports.
- **Talk with an exercise trainer/counselor.** Many colleges have a staff of exercise trainers/counselors you can confer with to improve your exercise profile.

- **Consider how regular exercise will increase your energy level.** When you engage in a regular exercise routine, you will have more energy, which can help you remain alert longer while studying and likely sleep better, which in turn will give you more energy and keep you from feeling tired all the time.
- **Think about how regular exercise will improve the efficiency of your information processing.** As the research we discussed indicates, regular exercise can improve your attention, executive function, and many aspects of your information processing, which should have positive outcomes for your academic achievement.

---

developmental connection

Achievement

Carol Dweck argues that a mastery orientation (focusing on the task and process of learning) produces more positive achievement outcomes than a performance orientation in which the outcome—winning—is the most important aspect of achieving. Connect to "Achievement, Work, and Careers."

female athlete triad A combination of disordered eating, amenorrhea, and osteoporosis that may develop in female adolescents and college students.

Coaches play an important role in youth sports (Eather & others, 2020; Prentice, 2021). Too often youth coaches create a performance-oriented motivational climate that is focused on winning above all else, receiving public recognition, and performing better than other participants. But other coaches place more emphasis on mastery motivation that focuses adolescents' attention on developing their skills and meeting self-determined standards of success. Researchers have found that athletes who have a mastery focus are more likely than others to see the benefits of practice, to persist in the face of difficulty, and to show significant skill development over the course of a season (Roberts, Treasure, & Kavussanu, 1997).

A final topic involving sports that needs to be examined is the **female athlete triad** (also known as relative energy deficiency in sports), which involves a combination of disordered eating (weight loss), amenorrhea (absent or irregular menstrual periods), and osteoporosis (thinning and weakening of bones) (Raj, Creech, & Rogol, 2020). Once menstrual periods have become somewhat regular in adolescent girls, not having a menstrual period for more than three or four months can reduce bone strength. Fatigue and stress fractures may develop. The female athlete triad often goes unnoticed by parents and coaches of female secondary school and college athletes (Dipla & others, 2021). Treatment of the female athlete triad includes (1) maintaining adequate calorie consumption to restore a positive energy balance, (2) determining the cause of menstrual dysfunction and resuming regular menses, and (3) ensuring adequate intake of calcium and vitamin D for optimal bone development (Thein-Nissenbaum & Hammer, 2017).

Now that we have discussed many aspects of the positive influence of exercise on development, see the *Connecting with Health and Well-Being* interlude for some effective strategies for engaging in exercise as a college student.

SLEEP

Might changes in sleep patterns between childhood and adolescence contribute to adolescents' health-compromising behaviors? Recently there has been a surge of research interest in adolescent sleep patterns (Galvan, 2020; Simon & others, 2021).

What are some positive and negative aspects of sports participation in adolescence?
HRAUN/Getty Images

In a national survey of youth, only 25 percent of U.S. adolescents got eight or more hours of sleep on an average school night, 7 percent less than only 4 years earlier (Kann & others, 2018). In this study, the percentage of adolescents getting eight or more hours of sleep on an average school night decreased as they got older (see Figure 9). Also, in a recent large-scale study in the United States, the United Kingdom, and the Netherlands, 51.5 percent of adolescents reported getting less than 8 hours of total sleep time and 18 percent indicated they experienced daytime sleepiness (Kocevska & others, 2021).

How might insufficient sleep harm adolescents' development? Research indicates that getting too little sleep is linked to academic deficiencies, less efficient information processing, a greater incidence of emotional, mood, and substance abuse problems, as well as poorer relationships with peers (Verkooijen & others, 2018). In a longitudinal study in which adolescents completed an activity diary every 14 days in ninth, tenth, and twelfth grades, regardless of how much time students spent studying each day, when the students sacrificed sleep time to study more than usual they had difficulty understanding what was taught in class and were more likely to struggle with class assignments the next day (Gillen-O'Neel, Huynh, & Fuligni, 2013). In a study of 13- to 19-year-olds in Singapore, short sleep duration (less than 7 hours) on school nights was associated with an increased risk of being overweight, having depressive symptoms, being less motivated, not being able to concentrate adequately, having a high level of anxiety, and engaging in self-harm/suicidal thoughts (Yeo & others, 2019). Further, a recent study of adolescents indicated that insufficient sleep was associated with alcohol and marijuana use (Kwon & others, 2021).

Why are adolescents getting too little sleep? Explanations include overuse of electronic media, high intake of caffeine, and changes in the brain coupled with early school start times (Agostini & Centofanti, 2021; Kokka & others, 2021). A recent study of 13- to 15-year-olds found that spending too much time on screen media was linked to multiple dimensions of sleep impairment, especially if screen use involves social media or the Internet (Hisler, Twenge, & Krizan, 2020). Recent research also indicated that frequency of cordless telephone calls, mobile phone dependency, and tablet use were linked to sleep problems in adolescence (Cabre-Riera & others, 2019). Further, in a recent national study of high school students, using electronic devices other than television 5 or more hours a day was linked to getting inadequate sleep (Kenney & Gortmaker, 2017).

Caffeine intake also likely is related to adolescent sleep problems, including later sleep onset, shorter sleep duration, and increased daytime sleepiness (Galland & others, 2020). The association of caffeine consumption and daytime sleepiness is also related to lower academic achievement (James, Kristjansson, & Sigfusdottir, 2011). Also, a recent study found that high consumption of energy drinks by adolescents was linked to shorter sleep duration (Almulla & Faris, 2020).

Many adolescents, especially older adolescents, stay up later at night and sleep longer in the morning than they did when they were children. These findings have implications for the hours during which adolescents learn most effectively in school (Touitou, Touitou, & Reinberg, 2017).

Mary Carskadon (2002, 2004, 2006, 2011, 2020; Carskadon & Barker, 2020) and her colleagues have conducted a number of research studies on adolescent sleep patterns. They found that when given the opportunity, adolescents will sleep an average of 9 hours and 25 minutes a night. Most get considerably less than 9 hours of sleep, especially during the week. This shortfall creates a sleep deficit, which adolescents often attempt to make up on the weekend. The researchers also found that older adolescents tend to be sleepier during the day than younger adolescents. They theorized that this sleepiness was not due to academic work or social pressures. Rather, their research

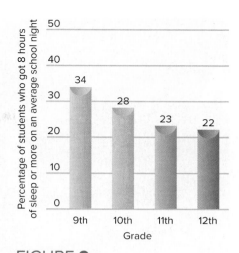

FIGURE 9

DEVELOPMENTAL CHANGES IN U.S. ADOLESCENTS' SLEEP PATTERNS ON AN AVERAGE SCHOOL NIGHT

How might caffeine intake be associated with inadequate sleep during adolescence?
Phanie/Alamy Stock Photo

What are some developmental changes in sleep patterns during adolescence?
Tomwang112/Getty Images

In Mary Carskadon's sleep laboratory at Brown University, an adolescent girl's brain activity is being monitored. Carskadon (2005) says that in the morning, sleep-deprived adolescents' "brains are telling them it's nighttime . . . and the rest of the world is saying it's time to go to school" (p. 19).

Courtesy of Jim LoScalzo

suggests that adolescents' biological clocks undergo a shift as they get older, extending their period of wakefulness by about one hour. A delay in the nightly release of the sleep-inducing hormone melatonin, which is produced in the brain's pineal gland, seems to underlie this shift (Eckerberg & others, 2012). Melatonin is secreted at about 9:30 p.m. in younger adolescents and approximately an hour later in older adolescents.

Carskadon has suggested that early school starting times may cause grogginess, inattention in class, and poor performance on tests. Based on her research, some schools began starting classes later (Cassoff & others, 2013). For example, school officials in Edina, Minnesota, decided to start classes at 8:30 a.m. rather than the usual 7:25 a.m. With the new starting time there were fewer referrals for discipline problems and fewer students who reported being ill or depressed. Test scores improved for high school students but not for middle school students. This finding supports Carskadon's suspicion that early start times are likely to be more stressful for older than for younger adolescents. Also, in a recent study, when the Seattle School District delayed the school start time for secondary school students, it resulted in a 34-minute average increase in sleep duration, a 4.5 percent increase in grades, and an improvement in school attendance (Dunster & others, 2018). Based on such research, the American Academy of Pediatrics recently advocated that schools shift their start times from 8:30 to 9:30 a.m. to improve students' academic performance and quality of life (Adolescent Sleep Working Group, AAP, 2014).

Do sleep patterns change in emerging adulthood? Research indicates that they do (Kloss & others, 2016). In one study that revealed more than 60 percent of college students were categorized as poor-quality sleepers, the weekday bedtimes and rise times of first-year college students were approximately 1 hour and 15 minutes later than those of seniors in high school (Lund & others, 2010). However, the first-year college students had later bedtimes and rise times than third- and fourth-year college students, indicating that at about 20 to 22 years of age, a reverse in the timing of bedtimes and rise times occurs. In this study, poor-quality sleep was linked to worse physical and mental health, and the students reported that emotional and academic stress negatively affected their sleep. In addition, a recent study of college students indicated that shorter sleep duration was associated with increased suicide risk (Becker & others, 2018a). Also, in another recent study of college students, 27 percent described their sleep as poor and 36 percent reported getting 7 hours or less of sleep per night (Becker & others, 2018b). A recent recommendation from the National Sleep Foundation (2020) is that emerging adults should get 7 to 9 hours of sleep a night, although clearly many emerging adults do not get this much sleep (Mamun & others, 2020). In addition, a recent study of college students found that sleep deprivation was linked to having a lower grade point average and delayed college graduation (Chen & Chen, 2019). Also, in another recent study of female college students, poorer sleep quality was associated with smartphone dependence and less effective stress management (Wang & others, 2019). And research indicated that higher consumption of energy drinks was linked to more sleep problems in college students (Faris & others, 2017). And a recent research review of 112 studies concluded that engaging in more physical activity and maintaining positive social relationships improved college students' sleep patterns, while greater caffeine intake, higher stress levels, and irregular sleep-wake patterns impaired their sleep quality (Wang & Biro, 2021).

Many college students occasionally or often pull an all-nighter to cram for an exam. Recently, the National Sleep Foundation (2020) described why this might not be a good idea and could harm exam performance: Sleep deprivation can distort your memory, cause thinking to be less clear, and impair concentration. Thus, exam performance will likely be much better if you engage in effective planning, effective time management, and spread your studying sessions over a number of days and weeks.

What are some strategies that can help college students improve their sleep habits? For some effective strategies, see the *Connecting with Health and Well-Being* interlude.

Effective College Student Strategies for Improving Sleep

The following strategies can improve sleep habits of college students (Halonen & Santrock, 2013):

- **Make your sleeping area a good context for sleeping.** It should have minimum light, minimum sound, a comfortable mattress and temperature, and good ventilation.
- **Get in a calm mood before you go to bed.** Listen to soft music, tone down your arousal level, and don't engage in stressful conversations with others.
- **Exercise regularly, but do so earlier in the day.** Exercising in the late evening or night before you go to bed increases your energy and alertness too much for you to easily fall asleep.

- **Reduce your use of electronic devices and screen time, especially near bedtime.** As the research studies described in this section documented, these activities tend to increase the likelihood of sleep problems.
- **Keep your caffeine intake low.** The research described in this section also indicated that higher levels of caffeine interfere with getting enough sleep.
- **Be a good time manager.** If you effectively manage your time during the day, you are more likely to have completed the tasks you set out to do and will be less stressed about them when you go to bed.

Review *Connect* Reflect

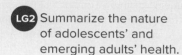 **LG2** Summarize the nature of adolescents' and emerging adults' health.

Review

- Why is adolescence a critical juncture in health? How extensive is risk taking in adolescence? How good are adolescents at using health services? What are the leading causes of death in adolescence?
- What characterizes emerging adults' health?
- What are some concerns about adolescents' eating habits?
- What roles do exercise and sports play in adolescents' lives?
- What are some concerns about adolescent sleep patterns?

Connect

- Compare the health issues of adolescents with those of emerging adults.

Reflect *Your Own Personal Journey of Life*

- What were your health habits like from the time you entered puberty to the time you completed high school? Describe your health-compromising and health-enhancing behaviors during this time. After graduating from high school, did you reduce your health-compromising behaviors? Explain.

3 Evolution, Heredity, and Environment

 LG3 Explain the contributions of evolution, heredity, and environment to adolescent development.

The Evolutionary Perspective · The Genetic Process · Heredity-Environment Interaction

The size and complexity of the adolescent's brain emerged over the long course of evolution. Let's explore the evolutionary perspective on adolescent development and then examine how heredity and environment interact to influence adolescent development.

THE EVOLUTIONARY PERSPECTIVE

In terms of evolutionary time, humans are relative newcomers to Earth. If we think of the broad expanse of time as a calendar year, then humans arrived on Earth in the last moments of December (Sagan, 1977). As our earliest ancestors left the forest to feed on the savannahs and finally to form hunting societies on the open plains, their minds and behaviors changed. How did this evolution come about?

Natural Selection and Adaptive Behavior   *Natural selection* is the evolutionary process that favors those individuals of a species who are best adapted to survive and reproduce. To understand natural selection, let's return to the middle of the nineteenth century, when the British naturalist Charles Darwin (1809–1882) was traveling the world, observing many different species of animals in their natural habitats. In his groundbreaking book, *On the Origin of Species* (1859), Darwin noted that most species reproduce at rates that would cause enormous increases in their population and yet populations remained nearly constant. He reasoned that an intense struggle for food, water, and resources must occur among the many young born in each generation, because many of them do not survive. Darwin believed that those who do survive to reproduce and pass on their genes to the next generation are probably superior to others in a number of ways. In other words, the survivors are better adapted to their world than the non-survivors are (Cowan & Smith, 2021). Over the course of many generations, Darwin reasoned, organisms with the characteristics needed for survival would compose a larger and larger percentage of the population, producing a gradual modification of the species. If environmental conditions changed, however, other characteristics might be favored by natural selection, moving the evolutionary process in a different direction.

To understand the role of evolution in behavior, we need to understand the concept of adaptive behavior (Hoefnagels, 2021). In evolutionary conceptions of psychology, **adaptive behavior** is a modification of behavior that promotes an organism's survival in its natural habitat. All organisms must adapt to specific places, climates, food sources, and ways of life in order to survive (Johnson, 2020). In humans, attachment ensures an infant's closeness to the caregiver for feeding and protection from danger. This behavioral characteristic promotes survival just as an eagle's claw, which facilitates predation, ensures the eagle's survival.

Evolutionary Psychology   Although Darwin introduced the theory of evolution by natural selection in 1859, his ideas only recently have been used to explain behavior (Lewis, Al-Shawaf, & Buss, 2021). The field of **evolutionary psychology** emphasizes the importance of adaptation, reproduction, and "survival of the fittest" in explaining behavior. Because evolution favors organisms that are best adapted to survive and reproduce in a specific environment, evolutionary psychology focuses on the conditions that cause individuals to survive or perish (Crespi, 2020). In this view, the process of natural selection favors those behaviors that increase organisms' reproductive success and their ability to transmit their genes to the next generation (Zagaria, Ando, & Zennaro, 2020).

David Buss' (2012, 2015, 2019) ideas on evolutionary psychology have sparked interest in how evolution might explain human behavior. Buss argues that just as evolution shapes our physical features such as our body shape and height, it also influences our decision making, our aggressive behavior, our fears, and our mating patterns.

Evolutionary Developmental Psychology   There is growing interest in using the concepts of evolutionary psychology to understand human development (Henrich & Muthukrishna, 2021; Ko & others, 2020). Following are some ideas proposed by evolutionary developmental psychologists (Bjorklund & Pellegrini, 2002).

One important concept is that an extended childhood period evolved because humans require time to develop a large brain and learn the complexity of human societies. Humans take longer to become reproductively mature than any other mammal (see Figure 10). During this extended childhood period, they develop a large brain and acquire the experiences needed to become competent adults in a complex society.

Another key idea is that many evolved psychological mechanisms are *domain-specific*. That is, the mechanisms apply only to a specific aspect of a person's makeup. Information processing is one example. From the perspective of evolutionary psychology, the mind is not a general-purpose device that can be applied equally to a vast array of problems. Instead, as our ancestors dealt with certain recurring problems such as hunting and finding shelter, specialized modules evolved to process information related to those problems, such as a module for physical knowledge for tracking animals, a module for mathematical knowledge for trading, and a module for language.

Mike Price/Shutterstock

adaptive behavior A modification of behavior that promotes an organism's survival in the natural habitat.

evolutionary psychology An approach that emphasizes the importance of adaptation, reproduction, and "survival of the fittest" in explaining behavior.

This view of the modularity of the mind has sometimes been referred to as the *Swiss army knife theory* because much like a Swiss army knife, the human mind includes a number of independent domains or tools. This view has been increasingly criticized because it suggests that the brain is extensively fragmented. Indeed, as you will see in our discussion of the brain at various points in this text, there is considerable connection between many areas of the brain and it is not exclusively compartmentalized as proposed by the modularity of mind view.

Evolved mechanisms are not always adaptive in contemporary society. Some behaviors that were adaptive for our prehistoric ancestors may not serve us well today. For example, the food-scarce environment of our ancestors likely led to humans' propensity to gorge when food is available and to crave high-caloric foods, a trait that might lead to an epidemic of obesity when food is plentiful.

Evaluating Evolutionary Psychology   Albert Bandura (1998), the author of social cognitive theory, has criticized the "biologizing" of psychology. Bandura acknowledges the influence of evolution on human adaptation and change. However, he rejects what he calls "one-sided evolutionism," in which social behavior is seen as the product of evolved biology. Bandura stresses that evolutionary pressures favored biological adaptations that encouraged the use of tools, allowing humans to manipulate, alter, and construct new environmental conditions. In time, humans' increasingly complex environmental innovations produced new pressures that favored the evolution of specialized brain systems to support consciousness, thought, and language.

In other words, evolution gave humans body structures and biological potentialities, not behavioral dictates. Having evolved our advanced biological capacities, we can use them to produce diverse cultures—aggressive or pacific, egalitarian or autocratic. As American scientist Stephen Jay Gould (1981) concluded, in most domains, human biology allows a broad range of cultural possibilities. The sheer pace of social change, Bandura (1998) notes, underscores the range of possibilities biology permits.

The "big picture" idea of natural selection leading to the development of human traits and behaviors is difficult to refute or test because it is on a time scale that does not lend itself to empirical study. Indeed, as with evolution, it is very difficult to offer direct proof of an argument to support evolutionary psychology. Thus, studying specific genes in humans and other species—and their links to traits and behaviors—may be the best approach for testing ideas coming out of the evolutionary psychology perspective.

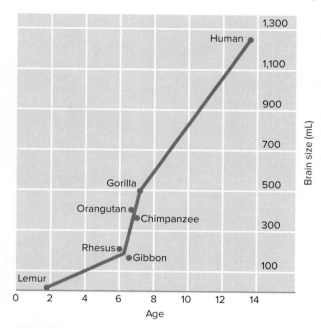

FIGURE **10**

THE BRAIN SIZES OF VARIOUS PRIMATES AND HUMANS IN RELATION TO THE LENGTH OF THE JUVENILE PERIOD

THE GENETIC PROCESS

Genetic influences on behavior evolved over time and across many species (Lewis, 2021). The many traits and characteristics that are genetically influenced have a long evolutionary history that is retained in our DNA. In other words, our DNA is not just inherited from our parents; it's also what we've inherited as a species from the species that came before us (Chess, 2021). Let's take a closer look at DNA and its role in human development.

How are characteristics that suit a species for survival transmitted from one generation to the next? Darwin could not answer this question because genes and the principles of genetics had not yet been discovered. Each of us carries a "genetic code" that we inherited from our parents. Because a fertilized egg carries this human code, a fertilized human egg cannot grow into an egret, eagle, or elephant.

DNA and the Collaborative Gene   Each of us began life as a single cell weighing about one twenty-millionth of an ounce! This tiny piece of matter housed our entire genetic code—instructions that orchestrated growth from that single cell to a person made of trillions of cells, each containing a perfect replica of the original genetic code. That code is carried by our genes. What are they and what do they do?

The nucleus of each human cell contains **chromosomes,** which are thread-like structures that contain the remarkable substance deoxyribonucleic acid, or DNA. **DNA** is a complex molecule that contains genetic information. It has a double helix shape, like a spiral staircase.

> What is inherited is DNA. Everything else is developed.
>
> **—JAMES TANNER**
> *British Pediatrician, 20th Century*

chromosomes Threadlike structures that contain deoxyribonucleic acid, or DNA.

DNA A complex molecule that contains genetic information.

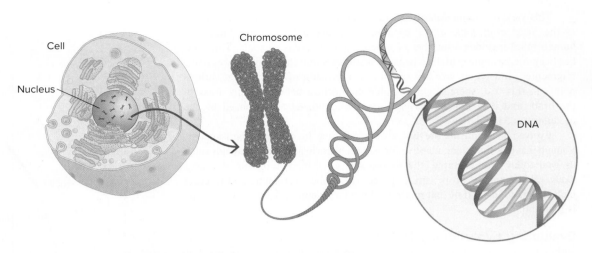

Cell

Nucleus

Chromosome

DNA

FIGURE **11**

CELLS, CHROMOSOMES, GENES, AND DNA. (*Left*) The body contains trillions of cells, which are the basic structural units of life. Each cell contains a central structure, the nucleus. (*Middle*) Chromosomes and genes are located in the nucleus of the cell. Chromosomes are made up of threadlike structures composed of DNA molecules. (*Right*) A gene, a segment of DNA that contains the hereditary code. The structure of DNA is a spiraled double chain.

Genes, the units of hereditary information, are short segments composed of DNA, as you can see in Figure 11. They direct cells to reproduce themselves and to assemble proteins. Proteins, in turn, serve as the building blocks of cells as well as the regulators that direct the body's processes (Mason, Duncan, & Losos 2021).

Each gene has its own function, and each gene has its own location, its own designated place on a specific chromosome. Today, there is a great deal of enthusiasm about efforts to discover the specific locations of genes that are linked to certain functions (Goldberg & others, 2021). An important step in this direction was accomplished when the Human Genome Project and the Celera Corporation completed a preliminary map of the human *genome*—the complete set of instructions for making a human organism.

One of the big surprises of the Human Genome Project was a report indicating that humans have only about 30,000 genes (U.S. Department of Energy, 2001). More recently, the number of human genes has been revised downward further to approximately 20,000 to 25,000 (National Institutes of Health, 2021). Scientists had thought that humans had as many as 100,000 or more genes. They had also believed that each gene programmed just one protein. In fact, humans appear to have far more proteins than they have genes, so there cannot be a one-to-one correspondence between them (Moore, 2015, 2017). Each segment of DNA is not translated, in automaton-like fashion, into one and only one protein. It does not act independently, as developmental psychologist David Moore (2001) emphasized by titling a book *The Dependent Gene*.

Rather than being an independent source of developmental information, DNA collaborates with other sources of information to specify our characteristics (Moore, 2017). The collaboration operates at many points. Small pieces of DNA are mixed, matched, and linked by the cellular machinery. That machinery is sensitive to its context—that is, it is influenced by what is going on around it. Whether a gene is turned "on," working to assemble proteins, is also a matter of collaboration. The activity of genes (genetic expression) is affected by their environment (Brooker, 2021). For example, hormones that circulate in the blood make their way into the cell, where they can turn genes "on" and "off." And the flow of hormones can be affected by environmental conditions such as light, day length, nutrition, and behavior. Numerous studies have shown that external events outside the cell and the person, and internal events inside the cell, can support or inhibit gene expression (Moore, 2017).

Recent research has documented that factors such as stress, exercise, nutrition, respiration, radiation, temperature, sleep, and loneliness can influence gene expression (Brown & others, 2020; McGhee & Hargreaves, 2020; Shu, Swanda, & Qian, 2020). For example, one study revealed that an increased concentration of stress hormones such as cortisol produced a fivefold increase in DNA damage (Flint & others, 2007). Another study found that exposure to

genes Units of hereditary information, which are short segments composed of DNA.

radiation changed the rate of DNA synthesis in cells (Lee & others, 2011). And research indicates that sleep deprivation can affect gene expression in negative ways such as increased inflammation, expression of stress-related genes, and impairment of protein functioning (da Costa Souza & Ribeiro, 2015).

Scientists have found that certain genes are turned on or off as a result of exercise, mainly through a process called *methylation* in which tiny atoms attach themselves to the outside of a gene (Galvao & Kelsey, 2021). This process makes the gene more or less capable of receiving and responding to biochemical signals from the body (Brooker & others, 2020). In this way the behavior of the gene, but not its structure, is changed. Researchers have found that diet (Ramos-Lopez & others, 2021), stress (Gatta & others, 2021), tobacco use (Maeda & others, 2020), and sleep (Koopman-Verhoeff & others, 2020) can affect gene behavior through the process of methylation. Also, recent research indicates that methylation is involved in hypertension (Amenyah & others, 2021), breast cancer (Xu & others, 2021), colorectal cancer (Jamialahmadi & others, 2021), leukemia (Kingsley & others, 2020), obesity (Gomez-Alonso & others, 2021), depression (Lapato & others, 2021), and attention deficit hyperactivity disorder (Kim & others, 2017).

In short, a single gene is rarely the source of a protein's genetic information, much less of an inherited trait (Moore, 2017). Rather than being a group of independent genes, the human genome consists of many genes that collaborate with each other.

The term *gene-gene interaction* is increasingly used to describe studies that focus on the interdependence of two or more genes in influencing physical characteristics, behavior, diseases, and development. For example, recent studies have documented the roles of gene-gene interaction in immune system functioning (Kostel Bal & others, 2020), asthma (Hua & others, 2016), obesity (Wang & others, 2019), type 2 diabetes (Dominguez-Cruz & others, 2020), alcoholism (Chen & others, 2017), cancer (Wu & others, 2021), and cardiovascular disease (Deng & others, 2020).

Genotype and Phenotype   No one possesses all the characteristics that his or her genetic structure makes possible. A person's genetic heritage—the actual genetic material—is called a **genotype.** Not all of this genetic material is apparent in our observed and measurable characteristics. The way an individual's genotype is expressed in observed and measurable characteristics is called a **phenotype.** Phenotypes include physical traits, such as height, weight, eye color, and skin pigmentation, as well as psychological characteristics, such as intelligence, creativity, personality, and social tendencies.

For each genotype, a range of phenotypes can be expressed (Brooker, 2021). Imagine that we could identify all the genes that would make an adolescent introverted or extraverted. Could we predict introversion or extraversion in a specific person from our knowledge of those genes? The answer is no, because even if our genetic model was adequate, introversion and extraversion are characteristics that are shaped by our experiences throughout life. For example, a parent might push an introverted child into social situations, encouraging the child to become more gregarious. Or the parent might support the child's preference for solitary play.

HEREDITY-ENVIRONMENT INTERACTION

So far, we have discussed genes and how they work, and one theme is apparent: Heredity and environment interact to produce development. Whether we are studying how genes produce proteins or how they influence a person's height, we end up discussing heredity-environment interactions. Is it possible, though, to untangle the influence of heredity from that of environment and discover the role of each in producing individual differences in development? When heredity and environment interact, how does heredity influence the environment and vice versa?

Behavior Genetics   **Behavior genetics** is the field that seeks to discover the influence of heredity and environment on individual differences in human traits and development (Herle & others, 2021). If you think about all of the people you know, for example, you have probably realized that they differ in terms of their levels of introversion/extraversion. Behavior geneticists try to figure out what is responsible for such differences—that is, to what extent do people differ because of differences in genes, environment, or a combination of these?

genotype A person's genetic heritage; the actual genetic material.

phenotype The way an individual's genotype is expressed in observed and measurable characteristics.

behavior genetics The field that seeks to discover the influence of heredity and environment on individual differences in human traits and development.

Am I an "I" or "We"?

College freshman Colin Kunzweiler (2007) wrote about his thoughts and experiences related to being an identical twin:

> As a monozygotic individual, I am used to certain things. "Which one are you?" happens to be the most popular question I'm asked, which is almost always followed by "You're Colin. No, wait, you're Andy!" I have two names: one was given to me at birth, the other thrust on me in random, haphazard way. . . . My twin brother and I are as different from each other as caramel sauce is from gravy. We have different personalities, we enjoy different kinds of music, and I am even taller than he is (by a quarter of an inch). We are different; separate; individual. I have always been taught that I should maintain my own individuality; that I should be my own person. But if people keep constantly mistaking me for my twin, how can I be my own person with my own identity?

"Am I an 'I' or 'We'?" was the title of an article written by Lynn Perlman (2008) about the struggle twins have in developing a sense of being an individual. Of course, triplets have the same issue, possibly even more strongly so. One set of triplets entered a beauty contest as one person and won the contest!

Perlman, an identical twin herself, is a psychologist who works with twins (her identical twin also is a psychologist). She says that how twins move from a sense of "we" to "I" is a critical task for them as children and sometimes even as adults. For nontwins, separating oneself from a primary caregiver—mother and/or father—is an important developmental task in childhood, adolescence, and emerging adulthood. When a child has a twin, the separation process is likely to be more difficult because of the constant comparison with a twin. Since they are virtually identical in their physical appearance, identical twins are likely to have more problems in distinguishing themselves from their twin than are fraternal twins.

The twin separation process often accelerates in adolescence when one twin is likely to mature earlier than the other (Pearlman, 2013). However, for some twins it may not occur until emerging adulthood when they may go to different colleges and/or live apart for the first time. And for some twins, even as adults their separation can be emotionally painful. One 28-year-old identical twin female got a new boyfriend but found that the relationship caused a great deal of stress and conflict with her twin sister (Friedman, 2013).

In Lynn Perlman's (2008) view, helping twins develop their own identities needs to be done on a child-by-child basis, taking into account their preferences and what is in their best interests. She commented that most of the twins she has counseled consider having a twin a positive experience, and while they also are usually strongly attached to each other they are intensely motivated to be considered unique persons.

To study the influence of heredity on behavior, behavior geneticists often use either twin or adoption situations (Jiang & others, 2021). In the most common **twin study,** the behavioral similarity of identical twins is compared with the behavioral similarity of fraternal twins. *Identical twins* (called monozygotic twins) develop from a single fertilized egg that splits into two genetically identical replicas, each of which becomes a person. *Fraternal twins* (called dizygotic twins) develop from separate eggs and separate sperm. Although fraternal twins share the same womb, they are no more alike genetically than are non-twin brothers and sisters, and they may be of different sexes.

twin study A study in which the behavioral similarity of identical twins is compared with the behavioral similarity of fraternal twins.

By comparing groups of identical and fraternal twins, behavior geneticists capitalize on the basic knowledge that identical twins are more similar genetically than are fraternal twins (O'Reilly & others, 2021; Rappaport & others, 2020). For example, one study found that conduct problems were more prevalent in identical twins than fraternal twins; the researchers concluded that the study demonstrated an important role for heredity in conduct problems (Scourfield & others, 2004).

Several issues complicate interpretation of twin studies (Grigorenko & others, 2016). For example, perhaps the environments of identical twins are more similar than the environments of fraternal twins. Adults might stress the similarities of identical twins more than those of fraternal twins, and identical twins might perceive themselves as a "set" and play together more than fraternal twins do. If so, observed similarities in identical twins could be more strongly influenced by the environment than the results suggested.

In an **adoption study,** investigators seek to discover whether the behavior and psychological characteristics of adopted children are more like those of their adoptive parents, who have provided a home environment, or more like those of their biological parents, who have contributed their heredity (Leve & others, 2019). Another form of the adoption study involves comparing adopted and biological siblings (Kendler & others, 2016).

Twin studies compare identical twins with fraternal twins. Identical twins develop from a single fertilized egg that splits into two genetically identical organisms. Fraternal twins develop from separate eggs, making them genetically no more similar than non-twin siblings. *What is the nature of the twin study method?*
Jack Hollingsworth/Getty Images

Heredity-Environment Correlation	Description	Examples
Passive	Children inherit genetic tendencies from their parents, and parents also provide an environment that matches their own genetic tendencies.	Musically inclined parents usually have musically inclined children and they are likely to provide an environment rich in music for their children.
Evocative	The child's genetic tendencies elicit stimulation from the environment that supports a particular trait. Thus genes evoke environmental support.	A happy, outgoing child elicits smiles and friendly responses from others.
Active (niche-picking)	Children actively seek out "niches" in their environment that reflect their own interests and talents and are thus in accord with their genotype.	Libraries, sports fields, and a store with musical instruments are examples of environmental niches children might seek out if they have intellectual interests in books, talent in sports, or musical talents, respectively.

FIGURE 12
EXPLORING HEREDITY-ENVIRONMENT CORRELATIONS

Heredity-Environment Correlations The difficulties that researchers encounter when they interpret the results of twin studies and adoption studies reflect the complexities of heredity-environment interaction. Some of these interactions are heredity-environment correlations—that is, there is a potential for individuals' genes to influence the types of environments to which they are exposed. In a sense, individuals "inherit" environments that are related or linked to genetic propensities. Behavior geneticist Sandra Scarr (1993) described three ways that heredity and environment are correlated (see Figure 12):

- **Passive genotype-environment correlations** occur because biological parents, who are genetically related to their child, provide a rearing environment for the child. For example, the parents might have a genetic predisposition to be intelligent and read skillfully. Because they read well and enjoy reading, they provide their sons and daughters with books to read. The likely outcome is that in adolescence, given their own inherited predispositions from their parents, these individuals will be skilled readers.

- **Evocative genotype-environment correlations** occur because an adolescent's genetically shaped characteristics elicit certain types of physical and social environments. For example, an active, smiling adolescent receives more social stimulation than a passive, quiet adolescent does. Cooperative, attentive adolescents evoke more pleasant and instructional responses from the people around them than uncooperative, distractible adolescents do. Athletically inclined youth tend to elicit encouragement to engage in school sports. As a consequence, these adolescents tend to be the ones who try out for sports teams and go on to participate in athletically oriented activities.

- **Active (niche-picking) genotype-environment correlations** occur when individuals seek out environments that they find compatible and stimulating. *Niche-picking* refers to finding a setting that is suited to one's abilities. Adolescents select from their surrounding environment some aspect that they respond to, learn about, or ignore. Their active selections of environments are related to their specific genotype. For example, attractive adolescents tend to seek out attractive peers. Adolescents who are musically inclined are likely to select musical environments in which they can successfully perform their skills.

Scarr concludes that the relative importance of the three genotype-environment correlations changes as children develop from infancy through adolescence. In infancy, much of the environment that children experience is provided by adults. Thus, passive genotype-environment correlations are more common in the lives of infants and young children than they are for older children and adolescents, who can extend their experiences beyond the family's influence and create their environments to a greater degree.

Critics argue that the concept of heredity-environment correlation gives heredity too much influence in determining development (Moore, 2017). Heredity-environment correlation stresses that heredity determines the types of environments children experience.

adoption study A study in which investigators seek to discover whether the behavior and psychological characteristics of adopted children are more like those of their adoptive parents, who have provided a home environment, or more like those of their biological parents, who have contributed their heredity. Another form of adoption study involves comparing adopted and biological siblings.

passive genotype-environment correlations Correlations that occur because biological parents, who are genetically related to the child, provide a rearing environment for the child.

evocative genotype-environment correlations Correlations that occur because an adolescent's genetically shaped characteristics elicit certain types of physical and social environments.

active (niche-picking) genotype-environment correlations Correlations that occur when children seek out environments that they find compatible and stimulating.

**Heredity-Environment
Correlation View**

Heredity ⟶ Environment

Epigenetic View

Heredity ⟷ Environment

FIGURE 13

**COMPARISON OF THE HEREDITY-
ENVIRONMENT CORRELATION AND
EPIGENETIC VIEWS**

developmental **connection**

Nature and Nurture

The nature and nurture debate is one of
the main issues in the study of adolescent
development. Connect to "Introduction."

*What conclusions can we make about
the roles of heredity and environment in
influencing this adolescent girl's musical
talent?*
Inti St Clair/Getty Images

epigenetic view Belief that development
is the result of an ongoing bidirectional
interchange between heredity and
environment.

gene × environment (G × E) interaction The
interaction of a specific measured variation in
DNA and a specific measured aspect of the
environment.

The Epigenetic View The heredity-environment correlation view emphasizes how
heredity directs the kind of environmental experiences individuals have. However, earlier we
discussed how DNA is collaborative, not determining an individual's traits in an independent
manner but rather in an interactive manner with the environment (Champagne, 2021). In line
with the concept of a collaborative gene, the **epigenetic view** emphasizes that development is
the result of an ongoing, bidirectional interchange between heredity and the environment (Hoye
& others, 2020). Figure 13 compares the heredity-environment correlation and epigenetic views
of development.

An increasing number of studies are exploring how the interaction between heredity and
environment influences development, including interactions that involve specific DNA
sequences (Topart, Werner, & Arimondo, 2020; Yang & others, 2021). The epigenetic mechanisms involve the actual molecular modification of the DNA strand as a result of environmental inputs in ways that alter gene functioning (Majumdar & others, 2021).

One study found that individuals who have a short version of a gene labeled 5-HTTLPR
(a gene involving the neurotransmitter serotonin) have an elevated risk of developing depression only if they *also* lead stressful lives (Caspi & others, 2003). Thus, the specific gene did
not directly cause the development of depression; rather, the gene interacted with a stressful
environment in a way that allowed the researchers to predict whether individuals would develop
depression (Thorne, Ellenbroek, & Day, 2021). Also, a recent research review concluded that
variations in the 5-HTTLPR gene may contribute to the tendency to ruminate when individuals experience life stress (Scaini & others, 2021). In other research, adolescents who experienced negative life events drank heavily only when they had a particular variation of the
CRHR1 gene (Blomeyer & others, 2008). The type of research just described is referred to as
gene × environment (G × E) interaction—the interaction of a specific measured variation in
DNA and a specific measured aspect of the environment (Champagne, 2021).

Conclusions About Heredity-Environment Interaction Heredity and environment operate together—or cooperate—to produce a person's intelligence, temperament, height,
weight, ability to pitch a baseball, ability to read, and so on. If an attractive, popular, intelligent
girl is elected president of her senior class in high school, is her success due to heredity or to
environment? Of course, the answer is both.

The relative contributions of heredity and environment are not quantifiable. That is, we can't
say that such-and-such a percentage of nature and such-and-such a percentage of experience make
us who we are. Nor is it accurate to say that full genetic expression happens once, around conception or birth, after which we carry our genetic legacy into the world to see how far it takes us.
Genes produce proteins throughout the life span, in many different environments. Or they don't
produce these proteins, depending in part on how harsh or nourishing those environments are.

The emerging view is that many complex behaviors likely have some genetic loading that
gives people a propensity for a specific developmental trajectory (Sallis, Smith, & Munato,
2021). However, the actual development requires more—an environment. And that environment
is complex, just like the mixture of genes we inherit (Bornstein & Esposito, 2021). Environmental influences range from the things we lump together under "nurture" (such as parenting,
family dynamics, schooling, and neighborhood quality) to biological encounters (such as
viruses, birth complications, and even biological events in cells).

In developmental psychologist David Moore's (2017) view, the biological systems that
generate behaviors are extremely complex, but too often these systems have been described in
overly simplified ways that can be misleading. Thus, although genetic factors clearly contribute
to behavior and psychological processes, they do not determine these phenotypes independently from the contexts in which they develop. From Moore's (2017) perspective, it is misleading to talk about "genes for" eye color, intelligence, personality, or other characteristics. Moore
commented that in retrospect we should not have expected to be able to make the giant leap
from DNA's molecules to a complete understanding of human behavior any more than we
should anticipate being able to easily link the movement of air molecules in a concert hall
with a full-blown appreciation of a symphony's wondrous experience.

Imagine for a moment that a cluster of genes is somehow associated with youth violence
(this example is hypothetical because we don't know of any such combination). The adolescent
who carries this genetic mixture might experience a world of loving parents, regular nutritious
meals, lots of books, and a series of masterful teachers. Or the adolescent's world might include
parental neglect, a neighborhood in which gunshots and crime are everyday occurrences, and

inadequate schooling. In which of these environments are the adolescent's genes likely to manufacture the biological underpinnings of criminality?

If heredity and environment interact to determine the course of development, is that all there is to answering the question of what causes development? Are adolescents completely at the mercy of their genes and environment as they develop? Genetic heritage and environmental experiences are pervasive influences on adolescents' development (Kuo, 2021; Lewis, 2021). But in thinking about what causes development, adolescents not only are the outcomes of their heredity and the environment they experience, but they also can author a unique developmental path by changing their environment. As one psychologist concluded:

> In reality, we are both the creatures and creators of our worlds. We are . . . the products of our genes and environments. Nevertheless, . . . the stream of causation that shapes the future runs through our present choices. . . . Mind matters. . . . Our hopes, goals, and expectations influence our future (Myers, 2010, p. 168).

Review *Connect* Reflect

LG3 Explain the contributions of evolution, heredity, and environment to adolescent development.

Review

- What role has evolution played in adolescent development? How do the fields of evolutionary psychology and evolutionary developmental psychology describe evolution's contribution to understanding adolescence?
- What is the genetic process?
- What is the nature of heredity-environment interaction?

Connect

- Which side of the nature and nurture issue does evolutionary developmental psychology take? Explain.

Reflect *Your Own Personal Journey of Life*

- A friend tells you that she has analyzed your genetic background and environmental experiences and reached the conclusion that the environment definitely has had little influence on your intelligence. What would you say to this person about her ability to reach this conclusion?

reach your **learning goals**

Puberty, Health, and Biological Foundations

1 Puberty

LG1 Discuss the determinants, characteristics, and psychological dimensions of puberty.

Determinants of Puberty

- Puberty is a brain-neuroendocrine process occurring primarily in early adolescence that provides stimulation for the rapid physical change involved in this period of development. Puberty's determinants include heredity, hormones, weight, and percentage of body fat. Two classes of hormones—androgens and estrogens—are involved in pubertal change and have significantly different concentrations in males and females.

- The endocrine system's role in puberty involves the interaction of the hypothalamus, pituitary gland, and gonads. FSH and LH, which are secreted by the pituitary gland, are important aspects of this system. So is GnRH, which is produced by the hypothalamus. The sex hormone system is a negative feedback system. Leptin and kisspeptins have been proposed as pubertal initiators, but research has not consistently supported this role. Growth hormone also contributes to pubertal change.

- Low birth weight and rapid weight gain in infancy are linked to earlier pubertal onset. Puberty has two phases: adrenarche and gonadarche. The culmination of gonadarche in boys is spermarche; in girls, it is menarche.

Growth Spurt

Sexual Maturation

Secular Trends in Puberty

Psychological Dimensions
of Puberty

- The onset of pubertal growth occurs on average at 9 years of age for girls and 11 years for boys. The peak of pubertal change is 11½ years for girls and 13½ years for boys. Girls grow an average of 3½ inches per year during puberty, while boys grow an average of 4 inches per year.

- Sexual maturation is a key feature of pubertal change. Individual variation in puberty is extensive and is considered to be normal within a wide age range.

- Secular trends in puberty took place in the twentieth century, with puberty coming earlier. Recently, there are indications that earlier puberty is occurring only for overweight girls.

- Adolescents show heightened interest in their bodies and body images. Younger adolescents are more preoccupied with body image than are older adolescents. Adolescent girls often have a more negative body image than adolescent boys do.

- Adolescents and emerging adults increasingly obtain tattoos and body piercings (body art). Some scholars conclude that body art is a sign of rebellion and is linked to risk taking, whereas others argue that body art is increasingly being used to express uniqueness and self-expression rather than rebellion.

- Researchers have found connections between hormonal change during puberty and behavior, but environmental influences need to be taken into account. Early maturation often favors boys, at least during early adolescence, but as adults late-maturing boys have a more positive identity than early-maturing boys do. Early-maturing girls are at heightened risk for a number of developmental problems. Most early- and late-maturing adolescents weather the challenges of puberty successfully. For those who do not adapt well to pubertal changes, discussions with knowledgeable health-care providers and parents can improve the coping abilities of early- or late-maturing adolescents.

2 Health

LG2 Summarize the nature of adolescents' and emerging adults' health.

Adolescence: A Critical Juncture in Health

- Many of the behaviors that are linked to poor health habits and early death in adulthood begin during adolescence. Engaging in healthy behavior patterns in adolescence, such as regular exercise, helps to delay the onset of disease in adulthood. Important goals are to reduce adolescents' health-compromising behaviors and to increase their health-enhancing behaviors.

- Risk-taking behavior increases during adolescence and, combined with a delay in developing self-regulation, makes adolescents vulnerable to a number of problems. Developmental changes in the brain have recently been proposed as an explanation for adolescent risk-taking behavior. Among the strategies for preventing engagement in unhealthy risk are to limit adolescents' opportunities for harm and to monitor their behavior. Adolescents tend to underutilize health services. The three leading causes of death in adolescence are accidents, homicide, and suicide.

Emerging Adults' Health

- Although emerging adults have a higher death rate than adolescents, emerging adults have few chronic health problems. However, many emerging adults are not inclined to consider how their personal lifestyles will affect their health later in life.

Nutrition

- Special nutrition concerns in adolescence are eating between meals, high levels of fat in adolescents' diets, and increased reliance on fast-food meals.

Exercise and Sports

- A majority of adolescents are not getting adequate exercise. At approximately 13 years of age, their rate of exercise often begins to decline. American girls especially have a low rate of exercise. Regular exercise has many positive outcomes for adolescents, including a lower risk of being overweight and higher self-esteem. Family, peers, schools, and screen-based activity influence adolescents' exercise patterns.

- Sports play an important role in the lives of many adolescents. Sports can have positive outcomes (improved physical health and well-being, confidence, ability to work with others) or negative outcomes (intense pressure by parents and coaches to win at all costs, injuries). Recently, the female athlete triad has become a concern.

Sleep

- Adolescents tend to go to bed later and get up later than children do. This pattern may be linked to developmental changes in the brain. A special concern is the extent to which these changes in sleep patterns in adolescents affect academic behavior and achievement. Developmental changes in sleep continue to occur in emerging adulthood.

3 Evolution, Heredity, and Environment

 LG3 Explain the contributions of evolution, heredity, and environment to adolescent development.

> **The Evolutionary Perspective**

- Natural selection—the process that favors the individuals of a species that are best adapted to survive and reproduce—is a key aspect of the evolutionary perspective. Evolutionary psychology is the view that adaptation, reproduction, and "survival of the fittest" are important influences on behavior. Evolutionary developmental psychology has promoted a number of ideas, including the view that an extended "juvenile" period is needed to develop a large brain and learn the complexity of human social communities. Critics argue that the evolutionary perspective does not give adequate attention to experience or the role of humans as a culture-making species.

> **The Genetic Process**

- The nucleus of each human cell contains chromosomes, which contain DNA. Genes are short segments of DNA that direct cells to reproduce and manufacture proteins that maintain life. DNA does not act independently to produce a trait or behavior. Rather, it acts collaboratively. Genotype refers to the unique configuration of genes, whereas phenotype involves observed and measurable characteristics.

> **Heredity-Environment Interaction**

- Behavior genetics is the field concerned with the degree and nature of behavior's hereditary basis. Research methods used by behavior geneticists include twin studies and adoption studies. In Scarr's view of heredity-environment correlations, heredity directs the types of environments that children experience. Scarr describes three categories of genotype-environment correlations: passive, evocative, and active (niche-picking). Scarr argues that the relative importance of these three genotype-environment correlations changes as children develop.

- The epigenetic view emphasizes that development is the result of an ongoing, bidirectional interchange between heredity and environment. Many complex behaviors have some genetic loading that gives people a propensity for a specific developmental trajectory. However, actual development also requires an environment, and that environment is complex. The interaction of heredity and environment is extensive. Much remains to be discovered about the specific ways that heredity and environment interact to influence development.

key **terms**

active (niche-picking) genotype-environment correlations
adaptive behavior
adoption study
adrenarche
androgens
behavior genetics
chromosomes

DNA
epigenetic view
estrogens
evocative genotype-environment correlations
evolutionary psychology
female athlete triad
gene × environment (G × E) interaction

genes
genotype
gonadarche
hormones
menarche
passive genotype-environment correlations
phenotype
precocious puberty

puberty
secular trends
spermarche
twin study

key **people**

Albert Bandura
David Buss

Mary Carskadon
David Moore

Sandra Scarr
David Yeager

improving **the lives of adolescents and emerging adults**

The Developing Genome (2015)
David Moore
New York: Oxford University Press
> David Moore provides valuable information about the epigenetic view of development and describes how genetic explanations often have been overblown.

Journal of School Health (www.blackwellpublishing.com)
> This journal publishes articles that pertain to the school-related aspects of children's and adolescents' health, including a number of health education programs.

National Adolescent Health Information Center (NAHIC)
(http://nahic. ucsf.edu/)
> This organization, associated with the University of California–San Francisco, has an excellent website that includes adolescent health data; recommendations for research, policy, and programs; health-care resources; and information about a national initiative to improve adolescent health.

The Society for Adolescent Health and Medicine
(www.adolescenthealth.com)
> This organization is a valuable source of information about competent physicians who specialize in treating adolescents. It maintains a list of recommended adolescent specialists across the United States. The society also publishes the *Journal of Adolescent Health*, which contains articles on a wide range of health-related and medical issues involving adolescents.

chapter 3

THE BRAIN AND COGNITIVE DEVELOPMENT

chapter **outline**

1 The Brain

Learning Goal 1 Describe the developmental changes in the brain during adolescence.

The Neuroconstructivist View

Neurons

Brain Structure, Cognition, and Emotion

Experience and Plasticity

2 The Cognitive Developmental View

Learning Goal 2 Discuss the cognitive developmental view of adolescence.

Piaget's Theory

Vygotsky's Theory

3 The Information-Processing View

Learning Goal 3 Characterize the information-processing view of adolescence.

Cognitive Resources

Attention and Memory

Executive Function

4 The Psychometric/ Intelligence View

Learning Goal 4 Summarize the psychometric/ intelligence view of adolescence.

Intelligence Tests

Multiple Intelligences

The Neuroscience of Intelligence

Heredity and Environment

5 Social Cognition

Learning Goal 5 Explain how social cognition is involved in adolescent development.

Adolescent Egocentrism

Social Cognition in the Remainder of This Edition

6 Language Development

Learning Goal 6 Discuss key aspects of language development in adolescence.

Overview

Bilingualism

Writing

©monkeybusinessimages/Getty Images

One of my most vivid memories of my oldest daughter, Tracy, involves something that happened when she was 12 years of age. I had accompanied her and her younger sister, Jennifer (10 at the time), to a tennis tournament. As we walked into a restaurant to have lunch, Tracy bolted for the restroom. Jennifer and I looked at each other, wondering what was wrong. Five minutes later Tracy emerged, looking calmer. I asked her what had happened. Her response: "This one hair was out of place and every person in here was looking at me!"

Consider another adolescent—Megan. During a conversation with her girlfriend, 16-year-old Megan said, "Did you hear about Caitlyn? She's pregnant. Do you think I would ever let that happen to me? No way."

Also think about 13-year-old Adam's predicament: "No one understands me, especially my parents. They have no idea of what I am feeling. They have never experienced the pain I'm going through."

Comments like Tracy's, Megan's, and Adam's reflect the emergence of egocentric thought during adolescence. When we think about thinking, we usually consider it in terms of school subjects like math and English, or solutions to intellectual problems. But people's thoughts about social circumstances also are important. Later in the chapter we will further explore adolescents' social thoughts.

preview

When we think about adolescence, we often focus on the biological changes of puberty or socioemotional changes, such as the motivation for independence, relationships with parents and peers, and problems such as drug abuse and delinquency. Further, when developmentalists have studied cognitive processes, their main focus has been on infants and young children, not on adolescents. However, you will see in this chapter that adolescents also display some impressive cognitive changes and that increasingly researchers are finding that these changes are linked to the development of the brain. Indeed, to begin this chapter, you will read about the explosion of interest in the changing adolescent brain, and then you will study three different views of cognitive development: cognitive developmental, information processing, and psychometric. At the chapter's close you will study social cognition, including the emergence of adolescent egocentrism.

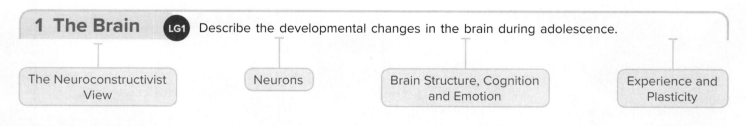

1 The Brain **LG1** Describe the developmental changes in the brain during adolescence.

| The Neuroconstructivist View | Neurons | Brain Structure, Cognition and Emotion | Experience and Plasticity |

Until recently, little research had been conducted on developmental changes in the brain during adolescence. Although research in this area is still in its infancy, an increasing number of studies are under way (Modabbernia & others, 2021; Vasa & others, 2020). Scientists now note that the adolescent's brain differs from the child's brain and that the brain continues to develop during adolescence (Luna, Tervo-Clemmens, & Calabro, 2021; Volkow & others, 2020).

The dogma of the unchanging brain has been discarded, and researchers are focusing primarily on context-induced plasticity of the brain over time (Biagianti & others, 2020; Pozzi & others, 2021). The development of the brain mainly changes in a bottom-up, top-down sequence, with sensory, appetitive (eating, drinking), sexual, sensation-seeking, and risk-taking brain linkages maturing first and higher-level brain linkages such as self-control, planning, and reasoning maturing later (Zelazo, 2013). This extensive plasticity is further explored in the next section, which describes the neuroconstructivist view of brain development.

THE NEUROCONSTRUCTIVIST VIEW

Not long ago, scientists thought that our genes primarily determine how our brains are "wired" and that the brain cells that are responsible for processing information just develop on their own with little input from environmental experiences. According to that view, whatever brain your genes have provided to you, you are essentially stuck with it. That view of the brain, however, turned out to be wrong. Instead, it is clear that the brain has plasticity and its development is shaped by context (Horvitz & Jacobs, 2022; Ismail, Ljubisavljevic, & Johnston, 2020).

The brain depends on experiences to determine how connections are made (Herzberg & Gunnar, 2020; Modabbernia & others, 2021). Before birth, it appears that genes mainly direct basic wiring patterns in the formation of the brain. Neurons grow and travel to distant places where they await further instructions. After birth, the inflowing stream of sights, sounds, smells, touches, language, and eye contact helps to shape the brain's neural connections. Throughout the human life span, experiences continue to influence the functioning of the brain (Minhas & others, 2021; Pliatsikas & others, 2020).

In the increasingly popular **neuroconstructivist view,** (a) biological processes (genes, for example) and environmental experiences (enriched or impoverished, for example) influence the brain's development; (b) the brain has plasticity and is context dependent; and (c) development of the brain is linked closely with cognitive development. These factors constrain or advance the construction of cognitive skills (Andrews, Ahmed, & Blakemore, 2021; Mento & Granziol, 2020). The neuroconstructivist view emphasizes the importance of interactions between experiences and gene expression in the brain's development, much as the epigenetic view proposes (Hoare & others, 2020).

NEURONS

Neurons, or nerve cells, are the nervous system's basic units. A neuron has three basic parts: the cell body, dendrites, and axon (see Figure 1). The dendrite is the receiving part of the neuron, and the axon carries information away from the cell body to other cells. Through a process called **myelination,** the axon portion of a neuron becomes covered and insulated with a layer of fat cells (called the myelin sheath), increasing the speed and efficiency of information processing in the nervous system (Muzio & Cascella, 2020). Myelination also is involved in providing energy to neurons and in facilitating communication (Shen & others, 2020). Myelination continues during adolescence and emerging adulthood (Vanes & others, 2020).

In the language of neuroscience, the term *white matter* is used to describe the whitish color of myelinated axons, and the term *gray matter* refers primarily to dendrites and the cell body of the neuron (Beck & others, 2021; Budday & others, 2021). A significant developmental change in adolescence is the increase in white matter and the decrease in gray matter in the prefrontal cortex (Lebel & Deoni, 2018; Ruotsalainen & others, 2021). In a recent study, an increase in white matter in adolescence was due to greater myelination and an increase in the diameter of axons (Lynch & others, 2020).

In addition to the encasement of axons through myelination, another important aspect of the brain's development is the dramatic increase in connections between neurons, a process that is called *synaptogenesis* (Tran & Silver, 2020). **Synapses** are gaps between neurons, where connections between the axon and dendrites take place. Synaptogenesis begins in infancy and continues through adolescence.

Researchers have discovered that nearly twice as many synaptic connections are made as will ever be used (Huttenlocher & Dabholkar, 1997). The connections that are used are strengthened and survive, while the unused ones are replaced by other pathways or disappear altogether (Bettio & others, 2020). In the language of neuroscience, these connections are

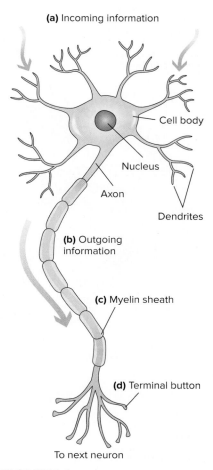

(a) Incoming information

Cell body

Nucleus

Axon

Dendrites

(b) Outgoing information

(c) Myelin sheath

(d) Terminal button

To next neuron

FIGURE 1

THE NEURON. (a) The dendrites of the cell body receive information from other neurons, muscles, or glands. (b) An axon transmits information away from the cell body. (c) A myelin sheath covers most axons and speeds information transmission. (d) As the axon ends, it branches out into terminal buttons.

neuroconstructivist view Developmental perspective in which biological processes and environmental conditions influence the brain's development; the brain has plasticity and is context dependent; and cognitive development is closely linked with brain development.

neurons Nerve cells, which are the nervous system's basic units.

myelination The process by which the axon portion of the neuron becomes covered and insulated with a layer of fat cells, which increases the speed and efficiency of information processing in the nervous system.

synapses Gaps between neurons, where connections between the axon and dendrites occur.

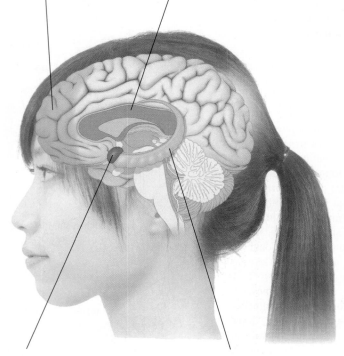

Prefrontal cortex
This "judgment" region reins in intense emotions but doesn't finish developing until at least emerging adulthood.

Corpus callosum
These nerve fibers connect the brain's two hemispheres; they thicken in adolescence to process information more effectively.

Amygdala
Limbic system structure especially involved in emotion.

Limbic system
A lower, subcortical system in the brain that is the seat of emotions and experience of rewards. This system is almost completely developed in early adolescence.

FIGURE 2

THE PREFRONTAL CORTEX, LIMBIC SYSTEM, AMYGDALA, AND CORPUS CALLOSUM
(photo): Takayuki/Shutterstock

corpus callosum A large bundle of axon fibers that connect the brain's left and right hemispheres.

prefrontal cortex The highest level of the brain's frontal lobes that is involved in reasoning, decision making, and self-control.

limbic system A lower, subcortical system in the brain that is the seat of emotions and experience of rewards.

amygdala A portion of the brain's limbic system that is the seat of emotions such as anger.

"pruned." As a result of this pruning, by the end of adolescence individuals have "fewer, more selective, more effective neuronal connections than they did as children" (Kuhn, 2009, p. 153). And this pruning indicates that the activities adolescents choose to engage in and not to engage in influence which neural connections will be strengthened and which will disappear.

With the onset of puberty, the levels of *neurotransmitters*—chemicals that carry information across the synaptic gap between one neuron and the next—change (Larsen & others, 2020). For example, an increase in the neurotransmitter dopamine occurs in both the prefrontal cortex and the limbic system during adolescence (Dahl & others, 2018). Increases in dopamine have been linked to increased risk taking and the use of addictive drugs (Hamidullah & others, 2020). Researchers have found that dopamine plays an important role in reward seeking (Everett & others, 2021).

BRAIN STRUCTURE, COGNITION, AND EMOTION

Neurons do not simply float in the brain. Connected in precise ways, they form the various structures in the brain. The brain is hierarchically organized and mainly develops from the bottom up, with sensory areas reaching full maturity before the higher-level association areas of the prefrontal cortex.

Using functional magnetic resonance imaging (fMRI) to scan the brain, scientists have recently discovered that adolescents' brains undergo significant structural changes (Baker & Galvan, 2020). An fMRI creates a magnetic field around a person's body and bombards the brain with radio waves. The result is a computerized image of the brain's tissues and biochemical activities.

Among the most important structural changes in the brain during adolescence are those involving the corpus callosum, the prefrontal cortex, the limbic system, and the amygdala. The **corpus callosum,** a large bundle of axon fibers that connects the brain's left and right hemispheres, thickens in adolescence, and this thickening improves adolescents' ability to process information (Giedd, 2008). Recent research indicates that the corpus callosum continues to thicken well into the third decade of life (Danielsen & others, 2020). Advances in the development of the **prefrontal cortex**—the highest level of the frontal lobes that is involved in reasoning, decision making, and self-control—continue through emerging adulthood, which lasts from approximately 18 to 25 years of age (Cohen & Casey, 2017). However, at a lower, subcortical level, the **limbic system,** which is the seat of emotions and where rewards are experienced, matures much earlier than the prefrontal cortex and is almost completely developed by early adolescence (Andrews, Ahmed, & Blakemore, 2021). The limbic system structure that is especially involved in emotion is the **amygdala.** Figure 2 shows the locations of the corpus callosum, prefrontal cortex, limbic system, and amygdala.

Leading researcher Charles Nelson (2003) points out that although adolescents are capable of very strong emotions, their prefrontal cortex hasn't adequately developed to the point at which they can control these passions. It is as if the prefrontal cortex doesn't yet have the brakes to slow down the limbic system's emotional intensity and moderate its reward focus. Another researcher describes adolescence as a period that combines "early activation of strong 'turbo-charged' feelings with a relatively un-skilled set of 'driving skills' or cognitive abilities to modulate strong emotions and motivations" (Dahl, 2004, p. 18).

Recall from the earlier discussion of neurotransmitters that increased dopamine production in early adolescence is linked to increased reward seeking and risk taking. Dopamine activity is greater in the limbic system pathways during early adolescence than at any other point in development (Steinberg, 2015). In research conducted by Laurence Steinberg (Albert & Steinberg, 2011a, b; Steinberg, 2015), preference for immediate rewards (assessed in such contexts as a gambling task and a video driving game) increased from 14 to 16 years of age and then declined.

The self-regulatory skills necessary to inhibit risk taking often don't develop fully until later in adolescence or emerging adulthood (LaSpada & others, 2020). And, as we just saw, this gap between the increase in risk-taking behavior and the delay in self-regulation is linked to brain development in the limbic system (involved in pleasure seeking and emotion) taking place earlier than development of the frontal lobes (involved in self-regulation) (Andrews, Ahmed, & Blakemore, 2021).

It is important for parents, teachers, mentors, and other responsible adults to effectively monitor adolescents' behavior. In many cases, adults decrease their monitoring of adolescents too early, leaving them to cope with tempting situations alone or with friends and peers (Defoe, Dubas, & Romer, 2019). When adolescents are in tempting and dangerous situations with minimal adult supervision, their inclination to engage in risk-taking behavior combined with their immature self-regulatory skills can make them vulnerable to a host of negative outcomes (Smout & others, 2020).

The increase in risk taking in adolescence is usually thought to produce negative outcomes. However, there are some aspects of risk taking that benefit adolescents (Duell & Steinberg, 2019). Being open to new experiences and challenges, even risky ones, can help adolescents stretch themselves to learn about aspects of the world they would not have encountered if they had shied away from such exploration (Allen & Allen, 2009).

In middle and late childhood, there is increased focal activation within a specific brain region, such as the prefrontal cortex, but limited connections across distant brain regions. By the time individuals reach emerging adulthood, there is an increase in connections across brain areas (Gratton, Smith, & Dorn, 2020). The increased connectedness (referred to as brain networks) is especially prevalent across more distant brain regions. In a recent study, reduced connectivity between the brain's frontal lobes and amygdala during adolescence was linked to increased depression (Scheuer & others, 2017).

Developmental neuroscientist Mark Johnson and his colleagues (Johnson, Jones, & Gliga, 2015) have proposed that the prefrontal cortex likely orchestrates the functions of many other brain regions during development. As part of this neural leadership and organizational role, the prefrontal cortex may provide an advantage to neural connections and networks that include the prefrontal cortex. In their view, the prefrontal cortex likely coordinates the best neural connections for solving a problem.

In late adolescence and emerging adulthood, the increase in myelination allows greater connectivity and integration of brain regions (Cui & others, 2020). For example, the important connections between the prefrontal cortex and limbic system strengthen in late adolescence and emerging adulthood (Cohen & Casey, 2017). This strengthening is especially important for emotional control (Goddings & Mills, 2017).

By the time individuals reach emerging adulthood, there are increased connections across brain areas (Bellantuono & others, 2021; Leibenluft & Barch, 2021). In a recent study, connectivity between the prefrontal cortex and hippocampus increased from adolescence to emerging and early adulthood, with this connectivity linked to improvement in higher-level cognition, especially in problem solving and planning (Calabro & others, 2020).

A topic of some controversy involves which comes first—biological changes in the brain or experiences that stimulate these changes (Tooley & others, 2020). Scientists have yet to determine whether the brain changes come first because of biological factors, such as the genes adolescents inherit, or whether the brain changes are caused mainly by experiences with peers, parents, and others. Once again, we encounter the nature-nurture issue that is so prominent in examining development through the life span.

Clearly, biological/genetic factors are important determinants of brain development. In the words of leading expert Jay Giedd (2007, pp. 1–2D), "Biology doesn't make teens rebellious or have purple hair or take drugs. It does not mean you are going to do drugs, but it gives you more of a chance to do that."

However, an increasing number of research studies are documenting how environmental experiences make important contributions to the brain's development (Ismail, Ljubisavljevic, & Johnston, 2020; Modabbernia & others, 2021). Let's examine several of those studies.

- Depressed brain activity has been found in children and adolescents who grow up in a deprived environment (Turesky & others, 2020). For example, in a recent study, children who grew up in the unresponsive and unstimulating environment of a

developmental **connection**

Brain Development

Developmental social neuroscience is a recently developed field that focuses on connections between development, socioemotional factors, and neuroscience. Connect to "Introduction."

Romanian orphanage showed considerably depressed brain activity compared with children who grew up in a normal environment (Nelson, Fox, & Zeanah, 2014). However, in a recent follow-up assessment at 16 years of age, the orphanage children who subsequently were placed in stable foster care showed improved brain functioning (Debnath & others, 2020).

• In a longitudinal study, 11- to 18-year-olds who lived in poverty conditions had diminished brain functioning at 25 years of age (Brody & others, 2017). However, the adolescents from poverty backgrounds whose families participated in a supportive parenting intervention did not show this diminished brain functioning in adulthood.

• In a recent study of adolescents, aerobic activity increased the brain's white matter and thickened the corpus callosum, a region that is linked to working memory (Ruotsalainen & others, 2021).

Does our increased understanding of changes in the adolescent brain have implications for the legal system? For example, can the recent brain research we have just discussed be used to argue that because the adolescent's brain, especially the higher-level prefrontal cortex, is still developing, adolescents are less mature than adults and therefore should not receive the death penalty for acts of violence? Leading expert Elizabeth Sowell (2004) points out that scientists can't do brain scans on adolescents to determine whether they should be tried as adults. In 2005, giving the death penalty to adolescents (individuals younger than 18) was prohibited by the U.S. Supreme Court, but the topic continues to be debated (Casey & others, 2020).

EXPERIENCE AND PLASTICITY

Scientists are especially interested in the extent to which environmental experiences influence the brain's development. They also want to know how much plasticity the brain retains as individuals progress through childhood, adolescence, and adulthood (Baum & others, 2020; Garriz-Luis & others, 2021). Let's examine three questions involving the roles of experience and plasticity in the development of the brain in adolescence:

• *Can new brain cells be generated in adolescence?* Until close to the end of the twentieth century, scientists argued that the brain generated no new cells (neurons) past early childhood. However, it is now accepted that neurogenesis can occur in humans (Berdugo-Vega & others, 2020), although researchers have documented neurogenesis only in two brain regions: the hippocampus (Moreno-Jimenez & others, 2021), which is involved in memory, and the olfactory bulb (Kouremenou, Piper, & Zalucki, 2020), which is involved in smell. Researchers are studying factors that might inhibit and promote neurogenesis, including various drugs, stress, and exercise (Kempermann, 2019; Liang & others, 2021). They also are examining how grafting neural stem cells to various regions of the brain, such as the hippocampus, might increase neurogenesis (Tsutsui, 2020).

What do we know about applying information about brain development to adolescents' education?
Fuse/Getty Images

• *Can the adolescent's brain recover from injury?* In childhood and adolescence, the brain has a remarkable ability to repair itself (Caliendo & others, 2021; Chohan, 2020). In the "Introduction" chapter we discussed Michael Rehbein, whose left hemisphere was removed because of brain seizures. The plasticity of the human brain was apparent as his right hemisphere reorganized itself to take over functions that normally take place in the left hemisphere, such as speech. The brain retains considerable plasticity in adolescence, and the earlier a brain injury occurs, the higher the likelihood of a successful recovery.

• *What do we know about applying information on brain development to adolescents' education?* Unfortunately, too often statements about the implications of brain science for secondary education are speculative and far removed from what neuroscientists know about the brain (Blakemore & Mills, 2014). We don't have to look any further than the hype about "left-brained" individuals being more logical and "right-brained" individuals being more creative to see that popular ideas about brain function are often inaccurate.

Another commonly promoted link between neuroscience and brain education is the assertion that most of the key changes in the brain occur prior to adolescence. However, recent research on the plasticity of the adolescent's brain and the continuing development of the prefrontal cortex through adolescence support the view that education can benefit adolescents considerably (Volkow & others, 2020). In this regard, higher-level cognitive functioning, especially in managing one's thoughts, engaging in goal-directed behavior, and controlling emotions (as discussed later in this chapter) are especially important potential areas of change in adolescence (Delalande & others, 2020).

In closing this section on the development of the brain in adolescence, a caution is in order. Much of the research on neuroscience and the development of the brain in adolescence is correlational in nature, and thus causal statements need to be scrutinized carefully.

Review *Connect* Reflect

 LG1 Describe the developmental changes in the brain during adolescence.

Review

- What characterizes the neuroconstructivist view?
- What are neurons? How do the brain's neurons change in adolescence?
- What changes involving brain structure, cognition, and emotion occur in adolescence?
- How much plasticity does the brain have in adolescence?

Connect

- Relate the structural changes in the brain that occur during adolescence to psychological dimensions of puberty.

Reflect *Your Own Personal Journey of Life*

- Evaluate your lifestyle in terms of factors such as your exercise patterns, eating habits, whether you get adequate sleep, and how much you challenge yourself to learn and achieve. Considering what you have learned about the brain's plasticity, what are some implications for your lifestyle's influence on the development of your brain in adolescence and emerging adulthood?

2 The Cognitive Developmental View

LG2 Discuss the cognitive developmental view of adolescence.

Piaget's Theory

Vygotsky's Theory

The process of brain development that we have just discussed provides a biological foundation for the cognitive changes that characterize adolescence. Reflect for a moment about your thinking skills as a young adolescent. Were your thinking skills as good then as they are now? Could you solve difficult abstract problems and reason logically about complex topics? Or did those skills improve during your high school years? Can you describe any ways in which your thinking skills are better now than they were in high school?

We have briefly examined Jean Piaget's theory of cognitive development in the "Introduction" chapter. Piaget was intrigued by the changes in thinking that take place during childhood and adolescence. In this section, we further explore his ideas about adolescent cognition, as well as the increasingly popular sociocultural cognitive theory of Lev Vygotsky that also was briefly summarized in the "Introduction" chapter,

PIAGET'S THEORY

We begin our coverage of Piaget's theory by describing the main processes he viewed as responsible for cognitive changes throughout the life span. Then we examine each of his cognitive stages, giving special attention to concrete operational and formal operational thought.

Jean Piaget, the main architect of the field of cognitive development.
Bettmann/Getty Images

schema A mental concept or framework that is useful in organizing and interpreting information.

assimilation The incorporation of new information into existing knowledge.

accommodation An adjustment of a schema in response to new information.

equilibration A mechanism in Piaget's theory that explains how individuals shift from one state of thought to the next. The shift occurs as individuals experience cognitive conflict or a disequilibrium in trying to understand the world. Eventually the individual resolves the conflict and reaches a balance, or equilibrium, of thought.

sensorimotor stage Piaget's first stage of development, lasting from birth to about 2 years of age. In this stage, infants construct an understanding of the world by coordinating sensory experiences with physical, motoric actions.

preoperational stage Piaget's second stage, which lasts approximately from 2 to 7 years of age. In this stage, children begin to represent their world with words, images, and drawings.

concrete operational stage Piaget's third stage, which lasts approximately from 7 to 11 years of age. In this stage, children can perform operations. Logical reasoning replaces intuitive thought as long as the reasoning can be applied to specific or concrete examples.

Cognitive Processes Piaget's theory is the best-known, most widely discussed theory of adolescent cognitive development. According to his theory, adolescents are motivated to understand their world because doing so is biologically adaptive. Adolescents actively construct their own cognitive worlds; information doesn't just pour into their minds from the environment. To make sense of the world, adolescents organize their experiences, separating important ideas from less important ones and connecting one idea to another. They also adapt their thinking to include new ideas because the additional information furthers their understanding.

In actively constructing their world, adolescents use schemas. A **schema** is a mental concept or framework that is useful in organizing and interpreting information. Piaget was especially interested in how children and adolescents use schemas to organize and make sense out of their current experiences.

Piaget (1952) found that children and adolescents use and adapt their schemas through two processes: assimilation and accommodation. **Assimilation** is the incorporation of new information into existing knowledge. In assimilation, the schema does not change. **Accommodation** is the adjustment of a schema in response to new information. In accommodation, the schema changes.

Suppose, for example, that a 13-year-old girl wants to learn how to use a new smartphone her parents have given her for her birthday. Although she has never had the opportunity to use one, from her experience and observation she realizes that she needs to press a button to turn on the phone. This behavior fit into an existing conceptual framework (assimilation). Once the phone is activated, she presses an icon on the screen, but it doesn't take her to the screen she wants. She also wants to add an application but can't figure out how to do that. Soon she realizes that she needs help in learning how to use the smartphone—either by studying the instructions further or by getting help from a friend who has experience using this type of phone. This adjustment in her approach shows her awareness of the need to alter her conceptual framework (accommodation).

Equilibration, another process Piaget identified, is a shift in thought from one state to another. At times adolescents experience cognitive conflict or a sense of disequilibrium in their attempts to understand the world. Eventually they resolve the conflict and reach a balance, or equilibrium, of thought. Piaget maintained that individuals move back and forth between states of cognitive equilibrium and disequilibrium.

Stages of Cognitive Development Piaget theorized that individuals develop through four cognitive stages: sensorimotor, preoperational, concrete operational, and formal operational (see Figure 3). Each of these age-related stages consists of distinct ways of thinking. This *different* way of understanding the world is what makes one stage more advanced than another; simply knowing more information does not make an adolescent's thinking more advanced. Thus, in Piaget's theory, a person's cognition is *qualitatively* different in one stage compared with another.

Sensorimotor and Preoperational Thought The **sensorimotor stage,** which lasts from birth to about 2 years of age, is the first Piagetian stage. In this stage, infants construct an understanding of the world by coordinating sensory experiences (such as seeing and hearing) with physical, motoric actions—hence the term *sensorimotor.*

The **preoperational stage,** which lasts approximately from 2 to 7 years of age, is the second Piagetian stage. In this stage, children begin to represent the world with words, images, and drawings. Symbolic thought goes beyond simple connections of information and action.

Concrete Operational Thought The **concrete operational stage,** which lasts approximately from 7 to 11 years of age, is the third Piagetian stage. Logical reasoning replaces intuitive thought as long as the reasoning can be applied to specific or concrete examples. According to Piaget, concrete operational thought involves operations—mental actions that allow individuals to do mentally what earlier they did physically.

Piaget used the term *conservation* to refer to an individual's ability to recognize that the length, number, mass, quantity, area, weight, and volume of objects and substances does not change through transformations that alter their appearance. Concrete operational thinkers have conservation skills; preoperational thinkers don't.

Another characteristic of concrete operational thought is *classification*, or class inclusion reasoning. Children who engage in classification can systematically organize objects into hierarchies of classes and subclasses.

Sensorimotor Stage

Infants gain knowledge of the world from the physical actions they perform on it. Infants coordinate sensory experiences with these physical actions. An infant progresses from reflexive, instinctual action at birth to the beginning of symbolic thought toward the end of the stage.

Birth to 2 Years of Age

Preoperational Stage

The child begins to use mental representations to understand the world. Symbolic thinking, reflected in the use of words and images, is used in this mental representation, which goes beyond the connection of sensory information with physical action. However, there are some constraints on the child's thinking at this stage, such as egocentrism and centration.

2 to 7 Years of Age

Concrete Operational Stage

The child can now reason logically about concrete events, understands the concept of conservation, organizes objects into hierarchical classes (classification), and places objects in ordered series (seriation).

7 to 11 Years of Age

Formal Operational Stage

The adolescent reasons in more abstract, idealistic, and logical (hypothetical-deductive) ways.

11 Years of Age Through Adulthood

FIGURE 3

PIAGET'S FOUR STAGES OF COGNITIVE DEVELOPMENT
(Left to right): Stockbyte/Getty Images; Jacobs Stock Photography/BananaStock/Getty Images; Fuse/image100/Corbis; Purestock/Getty Images

Although concrete operational thought is more advanced than preoperational thought, it has limitations. Logical reasoning replaces intuitive thought if the principles can be applied to specific, *concrete* examples. For example, the concrete operational child cannot imagine the steps necessary to complete an algebraic equation—an abstract statement with no connection to the concrete world.

Formal Operational Thought   The **formal operational stage** is Piaget's fourth and final stage of cognitive development. Piaget argued that this stage emerges at 11 to 15 years of age. Adolescents' developing power of thought opens up new cognitive and social horizons. What are the characteristics of formal operational thought? Most significantly, formal operational thought is more abstract than concrete operational thought. Adolescents are no longer limited to actual, concrete experiences as anchors for thought. They can conjure up make-believe situations—events that are purely hypothetical possibilities or strictly abstract propositions—and try to reason logically about them.

The abstract quality of the adolescent's thought at the formal operational level is evident in the adolescent's verbal problem-solving ability. Whereas the concrete operational thinker would need to see the concrete elements A, B, and C to be able to make the logical inference that if A = B and B = C, then A = C, the formal operational thinker can solve this problem merely through verbal representation.

Another indication of the abstract quality of adolescents' thought is their increased tendency to think about thought itself. As one adolescent commented, "I began thinking about why I was thinking what I was. Then I began thinking about why I was thinking about why I was thinking about what I was." If this statement sounds abstract, it is, and it characterizes the adolescent's enhanced focus on thought and its abstract qualities. Later in this chapter, we return to the topic of thinking about thinking, which is called *metacognition*.

Besides being abstract, formal operational thought is full of idealism and possibilities. Whereas children frequently think in concrete ways about what is real and limited, adolescents

formal operational stage Piaget's fourth and final stage of cognitive development, which he argued emerges at 11 to 15 years of age. It is characterized by abstract, idealistic, and logical thought.

In 2020, across the United States and many countries around the world, the Black Lives Matter protests attracted many adolescents from diverse backgrounds. *Might adolescents' ability to reason hypothetically and to evaluate what is ideal and what is real increase their likelihood of participating in such protests?*
Tom Williams/CQ-Roll Call, Inc/Getty Images

begin to engage in extended speculation about ideal characteristics—qualities they desire in themselves and others. Such thoughts often lead adolescents to evaluate themselves and others in regard to such ideal standards. And, during adolescence, the thoughts of individuals are often fantasy flights into future possibilities. It is not unusual for adolescents to become impatient with these newfound ideal standards and perplexed over which of many ideals to adopt.

At the same time that adolescents think more abstractly and idealistically, they also think more logically. Adolescents begin to reason more as a scientist does, devising ways to solve problems and test solutions systematically. Piaget gave this type of problem solving an imposing name, **hypothetical-deductive reasoning,** referring to the ability to develop hypotheses, or best guesses, about how to solve problems, such as algebraic equations. Having developed a hypothesis, the formal operational thinker then systematically deduces, or reaches conclusions, regarding the best path to follow in solving the problem. In contrast, children are more likely to solve problems by trial and error.

Piaget maintained that formal operational thought is the best description of how adolescents think. Formal operational thought is not a homogeneous stage of development, however. Not all adolescents are full-fledged formal operational thinkers. Instead, some developmentalists argue that the stage of formal operational thought consists of two subperiods (Broughton, 1983):

- *Early formal operational thought.* Adolescents' newfound ability to think in hypothetical ways produces unconstrained thoughts with unlimited possibilities. In this early period, flights of fantasy may submerge reality and the world is perceived subjectively and idealistically. Assimilation is the dominant process in this subperiod.

- *Late formal operational thought.* As adolescents test their reasoning against experience, intellectual balance is restored. Through accommodation, adolescents begin to adjust to the upheaval they have experienced. Late formal thought may appear in the middle adolescent years.

In this two-subperiod view, assimilation characterizes early formal operational thought, while accommodation characterizes late formal operational thought (Lapsley, 1990).

In his early writings, Piaget (1952) indicated that both the onset and consolidation of formal operational thought are completed during early adolescence, from about 11 to 15 years of age. Later, Piaget (1972) revised his view and concluded that formal operational thought is not completely achieved until later in adolescence, between approximately 15 and 20 years of age.

Still, his theory does not adequately account for the individual differences that characterize the cognitive development of adolescents, which have been documented in a number of investigations (Kuhn, 2009). Some young adolescents are formal operational thinkers; others are not. For instance, a review of investigations about formal operational thought revealed that only about one of every three eighth-grade students is a formal operational thinker (Strahan, 1983). Some investigators have found that formal operational thought increased with age in adolescence, but others have not attained this result. In fact, many college students and adults do not think in formal operational ways. Investigators have found that from 17 to 67 percent of college students think on the formal operational level (Elkind, 1961; Tomlinson-Keasey, 1972).

At the same time that many young adolescents are just beginning to think in a formal operational manner, others are at the point of consolidating their concrete operational thought, using it more consistently than they did in childhood. By late adolescence, many youth are beginning to consolidate their formal operational thought, using it more consistently. And there often is variation across the content areas of formal operational thought, just as there is in concrete operational thought in childhood. A 14-year-old adolescent might reason at the formal operational level when analyzing algebraic equations but not when solving verbal problems or when reasoning about interpersonal relations.

hypothetical-deductive reasoning Piaget's term for adolescents' ability, in the formal operational stage, to develop hypotheses, or best guesses, about ways to solve problems; they then systematically deduce, or conclude, the best path to follow in solving the problem.

Evaluating Piaget's Theory What were Piaget's main contributions? Has his theory withstood the test of time? In this section, we examine Piaget's contributions and consider criticisms of his work.

Contributions   Piaget has been a giant in the field of developmental psychology. We owe to him the present field of cognitive development as well as a long list of masterful concepts of enduring power and fascination, including assimilation, accommodation, conservation, and hypothetical-deductive reasoning, among others. We also owe to Piaget the current vision of children as active, constructive thinkers (Miller, 2016).

Piaget was a genius when it came to observing children. His careful observations documented inventive new ways to discover how children act on and adapt to their world. Piaget showed us some important things to look for in cognitive development, such as the shift from preoperational to concrete operational thinking. He also pointed out that children need to make their experiences fit their schemas, or cognitive frameworks, yet they can simultaneously adapt their schemas based on information gained through experience. He revealed that cognitive change is likely to occur if the context is structured to allow gradual movement to the next higher level. We owe to Piaget the current belief that a concept does not emerge suddenly, full blown, but develops gradually through a series of partial accomplishments that lead to an increasingly comprehensive understanding.

Criticisms   Piaget's theory has not gone unchallenged (Miller, 2016). Questions have been raised about the timing and nature of his stage view of cognitive development, whether he failed to adequately study in detail key cognitive processes, and the effects of culture on cognitive development. Let's consider each of these criticisms in turn.

In terms of timing and stages, some cognitive abilities have been found to emerge earlier than Piaget had thought (Oakes, 2021). For example, conservation of number (which Piaget said emerged at approximately 7 years of age during the concrete operational stage) has been demonstrated as early as age 3 (which instead is early in Piaget's preoperational stage). Other cognitive abilities often emerge later than Piaget indicated (Cui & others, 2020). Many adolescents still think in concrete operational ways or are just beginning to master formal operations. Even as adults, many individuals are not formal operational thinkers. The evidence does not support Piaget's view that prior to age 11 children don't engage in abstract thinking and that from 11 years onward they do (Kuhn, 2009). Thus, adolescents' cognitive development is not as stage-like as Piaget envisioned (Siegler & Alibali, 2020).

One group of cognitive developmentalists, the **neo-Piagetians,** conclude that Piaget's theory does not adequately focus on attention, memory, and cognitive strategies that adolescents use to process information, and that Piaget's explanations of cognitive changes are too general. They especially maintain that a more accurate vision of children's and adolescents' thinking requires more knowledge of the strategies they use, how rapidly and automatically they process information, the particular cognitive tasks involved in processing information, and the division of cognitive problems into smaller, more precise steps.

The leading proponent of the neo-Piagetian view has been Canadian developmental psychologist Robbie Case (1992, 2000). Case accepts Piaget's four stages of cognitive development but emphasizes that a more precise description of changes within each stage is needed. He notes that children's and adolescents' growing ability to process information efficiently is linked to their brain growth and memory development. In particular, Case cites the increasing ability to hold information in working memory (a mental workbench similar to short-term memory) and to manipulate it more effectively as critical components of cognitive development.

neo-Piagetians Theorists who argue that Piaget got some things right but that his theory needs considerable revision. They give more emphasis to information processing that involves attention, memory, and strategies, and they also seek to provide more precise explanations of cognitive changes.

An outstanding teacher and education in the logic of science and mathematics are important cultural experiences that promote the development of operational thought. *Might Piaget have underestimated the roles of culture and schooling in children's cognitive development?*
Wendy Stone/Corbis/Getty Images

Finally, culture and education exert stronger influences on development than Piaget envisioned (Kirmayer & others, 2021; Riccio & Castro, 2021). For example, the age at which individuals acquire conservation skills is associated to some extent with the degree to which their culture provides relevant educational practice (Cole, 2006). In many developing countries, educational opportunities are limited and formal operational thought is rare. You will read shortly about Lev Vygotsky's theory of cognitive development, in which culture is given a more prominent role than in Piaget's theory.

developmental **connection**

Emotion

Emotional fluctuations in early adolescence may be linked to hormone levels. As adolescents move into adulthood, their emotions become less extreme. Connect to "Puberty, Health, and Biological Foundations" and "The Self, Identity, Emotion, and Personality."

Cognitive Changes in Adulthood   As we discussed earlier, according to Piaget adults and adolescents use the same type of reasoning. Adolescents and adults think in qualitatively the same way. Piaget did acknowledge that adults can be quantitatively more advanced in their knowledge. What are some ways that adults might be more advanced in their thinking than adolescents?

Realistic and Pragmatic Thinking   Some developmentalists have proposed that as young adults move into the world of work, their way of thinking changes. One idea is that as they face the constraints of reality, which work promotes, their idealism decreases (Labouvie-Vief, 1986).

Reflective and Relativistic Thinking   William Perry (1999) also described changes in cognition that take place in early adulthood. He said that adolescents often view the world in terms of polarities—right/wrong, we/they, or good/bad. As youth age into adulthood, they gradually move away from this type of absolutist thinking as they become aware of the diverse opinions and multiple perspectives of others. Thus, in Perry's view, the absolutist, dualistic thinking of adolescence gives way to the reflective, relativistic thinking of adulthood.

Expanding on Perry's view, Gisela Labouvie-Vief (2006) proposed that the increasing complexity of cultures in the past century has generated a greater need for more reflective, complex thinking that takes into account the changing nature of knowledge and challenges. She also emphasizes that the key aspects of cognitive development in emerging adulthood include deciding on a specific worldview, recognizing that the worldview is subjective, and understanding that diverse worldviews should be acknowledged. From her perspective, considerable individual variation characterizes the thinking of emerging adults, with the highest level of thinking attained only by some. She argues that the level of education emerging adults achieve especially influences how likely they are to maximize their cognitive potential.

Cognition and Emotion   Labouvie-Vief and her colleagues (Labouvie-Vief, 2009; Labouvie-Vief, Gruhn, & Studer, 2010) also argue that to understand cognitive changes in adulthood it is necessary to consider how emotional maturation might affect cognitive development. They conclude that although emerging and young adults become more aware that emotions influence their thinking, at this point thinking is often swayed too strongly by negative emotions that can produce distorted and self-serving perspectives. In this research, a subset of emerging adults who are high in empathy, flexibility, and autonomy are more likely to engage in complex, integrated cognitive-emotional thinking. Labouvie-Vief and her colleagues have found that the ability to think in this cognitively and emotionally balanced, advanced manner increases in middle adulthood. Further, they emphasize that in middle age, individuals become more inwardly reflective and less context-dependent in their thinking than they were as young adults. In the work of Labouvie-Vief and her colleagues, we see the effort to discover connections between cognitive and socioemotional development, which is an increasing trend in the field of life-span development.

What are some characteristics that have been proposed for a fifth stage of cognitive development called postformal thought?
Yuri Arcurs/Alamy Stock Photo

Is There a Fifth, Postformal Stage?   Some theorists have pieced together these descriptions of adult thinking and have proposed that young adults move into a new qualitative stage of cognitive development: postformal thought (Sinnott, 2003).

Postformal thought has the following characteristics:

- *Reflective, relativistic, and contextual.* As young adults engage in solving problems, they might think deeply about many aspects of work, politics, relationships, and other areas of life (Labouvie-Vief, 1986). They find that what might be the best solution to a problem at work (with a boss or co-worker) might not be the best solution at home (with a romantic partner). Thus, postformal thought holds that the correct answer to a problem requires reflective thinking and may vary from one situation to another. Some psychologists argue that reflective thinking continues to increase and becomes more internal and less contextual in middle age (Labouvie-Vief, Gruhn, & Studer, 2010; Mascalo & Fischer, 2010).

- *Provisional.* Many young adults also become more skeptical about the truth and seem unwilling to accept an answer as final. Thus, they come to see the search for truth as an ongoing and perhaps never-ending process.

- *Realistic.* Young adults understand that thinking can't always be abstract. In many instances, it must be realistic and pragmatic.

- *Recognized as being influenced by emotion.* Emerging and young adults are more likely than adolescents to understand that their thinking is influenced by emotions. However, too often negative emotions produce thinking that is distorted and self-serving at this point in development.

What are some characteristics of wisdom?
Westend61/Getty Images

How strong is the evidence for a fifth, postformal stage of cognitive development? Researchers have found that young adults are more likely to engage in postformal thinking than adolescents are (Commons & Richards, 2003). But critics argue that research has yet to document that postformal thought is a qualitatively more advanced stage than formal operational thought.

Wisdom   Paul Baltes and his colleagues (2006) define **wisdom** as expert knowledge about the practical aspects of life that permits excellent judgment about important matters. This practical knowledge involves exceptional insight about human development and life matters, good judgment, and an understanding of how to cope with difficult life problems. Thus, wisdom, more than standard conceptions of intelligence, focuses on life's pragmatic concerns and the human condition (Wang & others, 2021).

In regard to wisdom, research by Baltes and his colleagues (Baltes & Kunzmann, 2007; Baltes, Lindenberger, & Staudinger, 2006; Baltes & Smith, 2008) has led to the following conclusions:

- *High levels of wisdom are rare.* Few people, including older adults, attain a high level of wisdom. That only a small percentage of adults show wisdom supports the contention that it requires experience, practice, or complex skills.

- *The time frame of late adolescence, emerging adulthood, and early adulthood is the main age window for wisdom to emerge.* No further advances in wisdom have been found for middle-aged and older adults beyond the level they attained as young adults, but this may have been because the problems studied were not sufficiently relevant to older adults' lives.

- *Factors other than age are critical for wisdom to develop to a high level.* For example, certain life experiences, such as being trained and working in a field concerned with difficult life problems and having wisdom-enhancing mentors, contribute to higher levels of wisdom. Also, people higher in wisdom have values that are more likely to consider the welfare of others rather than their own happiness.

- *Personality-related factors, such as openness to experience and creativity, are better predictors of wisdom than cognitive factors such as intelligence.*

Robert J. Sternberg (1998, 2019) has proposed the **balance theory of wisdom,** which states that wisdom consists of using one's intelligence, creativity, common sense, and knowledge in a balanced, ethical manner. Individuals should apply their wisdom in a balanced way across intrapersonal (one's identity, for example), interpersonal (being caring and kind to others, for example), and extrapersonal (contributing in positive ways to one's community, for example)

postformal thought Thought that is reflective, relativistic, and contextual; provisional; realistic; open to emotions and subjective.

wisdom Expert knowledge about the practical aspects of life that permits excellent judgment about important matters.

balance theory of wisdom Sternberg's theory that wisdom consists of using one's intelligence, creativity, common sense, and knowledge in a balanced, ethical manner. Individuals should apply their wisdom in a balanced way across intrapersonal, interpersonal, and extrapersonal contexts especially for the common good.

Upper limit

Level of additional responsibility
child can accept with assistance
of an able instructor

**Zone of proximal
development (ZPD)**

Lower limit

Level of problem solving
reached on these tasks by
child working alone

FIGURE **4**

**VYGOTSKY'S ZONE OF PROXIMAL
DEVELOPMENT (ZPD).** Vygotsky's zone of
proximal development has a lower limit and
an upper limit. Tasks in the ZPD are too
difficult for the child or adolescent to perform
alone. They require assistance from an adult
or a more-skilled youth. As children and
adolescents experience the verbal instruction
or demonstration, they organize the
information in their existing mental structures
so they can eventually perform the skill or
task alone.
Ariel Skelley/Blend Images LLC

zone of proximal development (ZPD)
Vygotsky's concept that refers to the range
of tasks that are too difficult for an individual
to master alone, but that can be mastered
with the guidance or assistance of adults
or more-skilled peers.

social constructivist approach Approach that
emphasizes the social contexts of learning
and the construction of knowledge through
social interaction.

contexts. To become wise, he believes individuals need to apply practical knowledge in dealing with problems. For Sternberg, wisdom is about doing the right thing, especially when confronted with difficult decisions. In his view, if you look at people like Martin Luther King and Mother Teresa and compare them with Adolf Hitler and Joseph Stalin, they likely did not differ much in IQ but differed a great deal in their wisdom.

Other researchers, such as Igor Grossman and his colleagues (2020) and Judith Gluck (2020), have proposed a view that is close to Sternberg's view. In their perspective, wisdom involves being aware of your perspectives and beliefs in relation to others' and being motivated to attain some common good for a larger group, such as one's family, an institution, or even an entire nation. They believe that metacognitive thinking with a moral grounding is a critical factor in achieving this wisdom.

VYGOTSKY'S THEORY

Lev Vygotsky's (1962) theory has stimulated considerable interest in the view that knowledge is *situated* and *collaborative* (Esteban-Guitart, 2018). That is, knowledge is distributed among people and their environments, which include objects, artifacts, tools, books, and the communities in which people live. This distribution suggests that knowing can best be advanced through interaction with others in cooperative activities.

One of Vygotsky's most important concepts is the **zone of proximal development (ZPD),** which refers to the range of tasks that are too difficult for an individual to master alone, but that can be mastered with the guidance and assistance of adults or more-skilled peers (Kantar, Ezzeddine, & Rizk, 2020). Thus, the lower level of the ZPD is the level of problem solving reached by an adolescent working independently. The upper limit is the level of thinking the adolescent can attain with the assistance of an able instructor (see Figure 4). Vygotsky's emphasis on the ZPD underscored his belief in the importance of social influences on cognitive development.

In Vygotsky's approach, formal schooling is but one of the cultural agents that determine an adolescent's growth. Parents, peers, the community, and the culture's technological orientation also influence adolescents' thinking (Clara, 2017). For example, parents' and peers' attitudes toward intellectual competence affect adolescents' motivation to acquire knowledge. So do the attitudes of teachers and other adults in the community.

Even though their theories were proposed at about the same time, most of the world learned about Vygotsky's theory later than they learned about Piaget's theory, so Vygotsky's theory has not yet been evaluated as thoroughly as Piaget's. Vygotsky's view of the importance of sociocultural influences on children's development fits with the current belief that it is important to evaluate the contextual factors in learning (Baggs & Chemero, 2020).

Although both theories are constructivist, Vygotsky's is a **social constructivist approach,** which emphasizes the social contexts of learning and the construction of knowledge through social interaction (Baggs & Chemero, 2020). In moving from Piaget to Vygotsky, the conceptual shift is from the individual to collaboration, social interaction, and sociocultural activity (Gauvain, 2016). The end point of cognitive development for Piaget is formal operational thought. For Vygotsky, the end point can differ, depending on which skills are considered to be the most important in a particular culture. For Piaget, children construct knowledge by transforming, organizing, and reorganizing previous knowledge. For Vygotsky, children and adolescents construct knowledge through social interaction (Daniels, 2017). The implication of Piaget's theory for teaching is that children need support to explore their world and discover knowledge. The main implication of Vygotsky's theory for teaching is that students need many opportunities to learn with the teacher and more-skilled peers. In both Piaget's and Vygotsky's theories, teachers serve as facilitators and guides, rather than as directors and molders of learning. Figure 5 compares Vygotsky's and Piaget's theories.

Criticisms of Vygotsky's theory also have surfaced. Some critics point out that Vygotsky was not specific enough about age-related changes (Gauvain & Perez, 2015). Another criticism focuses on Vygotsky not adequately describing how changes in socioemotional capabilities contribute to cognitive development. Yet another criticism is that he overemphasized the role of language in thinking. Also, his emphasis on collaboration and guidance has potential pitfalls. Might facilitators be too helpful in some cases, as when a parent becomes overbearing and controlling? Further, some adolescents might become lazy and expect help when they could have done something on their own.

	Vygotsky		Piaget	
Sociocultural Context	Strong emphasis		Little emphasis	
Constructivism	Social constructivist		Cognitive constructivist	
Stages	No general stages of development proposed		Strong emphasis on stages (sensorimotor, preoperational, concrete operational, and formal operational)	
Key Processes	Zone of proximal development, language, dialogue, tools of the culture		Schema, assimilation, accommodation, operations, conservation, classification	
Role of Language	A major role; language plays a powerful role in shaping thought		Language has a minimal role; cognition primarily directs language	
View on Education	Education plays a central role, helping children learn the tools of the culture		Education merely refines the child's cognitive skills that have already emerged	
Teaching Implications	Teacher is a facilitator and guide, not a director; establish many opportunities for children to learn with the teacher and more-skilled peers		Also views teacher as a facilitator and guide, not a director; provide support for children to explore their world and discover knowledge	

FIGURE 5

COMPARISON OF VYGOTSKY'S AND PIAGET'S THEORIES

(Vygotsky): A.R. Lauria / Dr. Michael Cole, Laboratory of Human Cognition, University of California, San Diego; (Piaget): Bettmann/Getty Images

Review *Connect* Reflect

LG2 Discuss the cognitive developmental view of adolescence.

Review

- What is Piaget's view of adolescence? What are some contributions and criticisms of Piaget's theory? What are some possible cognitive changes in adulthood?
- What is Vygotsky's view of adolescence?

Connect

- Compare the concepts of postformal thought and wisdom.

Reflect *Your Own Personal Journey of Life*

- Think back to when you were 8 years old and 16 years old. Imagine that you are watching a political convention on television at these two different ages. In terms of Piaget's stages of cognitive development, how would your perceptions of the proceedings likely have differed when you were at these two different ages? What would you have "seen" and comprehended as an 8-year-old? What would you have "seen" and comprehended as a 16-year-old? What Piagetian concepts would these differences in your cognition reflect?

3 The Information-Processing View

LG3 Characterize the information-processing view of adolescence.

Cognitive Resources

Attention and Memory

Executive Function

We briefly discussed the information-processing view in the "Introduction" chapter. We saw that information processing includes how information gets into adolescents' minds, how it is stored, and how adolescents retrieve information to think about and solve problems.

The mind is an enchanting thing.

—MARIANNE MOORE
American Poet, 20th Century

Information processing is both a framework for thinking about adolescent development and a facet of that development. As a framework, the information-processing view includes certain ideas about how adolescents' minds work and how best to study those workings (Siegler & Alibali, 2020). As a facet of development, information processing changes as children make the transition from adolescence to adulthood. Changes in attention and memory, for example, are essentially changes in the way individuals process information.

Deanna Kuhn (2009) has discussed some important characteristics of adolescents' information processing and thinking. In her view, in the later years of childhood and continuing through adolescence, individuals approach cognitive levels that may or may not be achieved, in contrast with the largely universal cognitive levels that young children attain. During adolescence, considerable variation in cognitive functioning is present across individuals. This variability supports the argument that adolescents are producers of their own development to a greater extent than are children.

In our exploration of information processing, we will discuss developmental changes in attention, memory, and a number of higher-order cognitive processes involved in executive function. But first let's examine the importance of cognitive resources in processing information.

COGNITIVE RESOURCES

Information processing is influenced by both the capacity and the speed of processing. These two characteristics are often referred to as *cognitive resources*, and adolescents—especially older adolescents—are better than children at managing and deploying these resources in controlled and purposeful ways (Kuhn & Franklin, 2006).

Most information-processing psychologists argue that an increase in capacity improves processing of information (Halford & Andrews, 2011). For example, as adolescents' information-processing capacity increases, they likely can hold in mind several dimensions of a topic or problem simultaneously, whereas younger children are more prone to focus on only one dimension.

What is the role of processing speed? Generally, fast processing is linked with good performance on cognitive tasks (Tam & others, 2015). However, some compensation for slower processing speed can be achieved through the use of effective strategies.

There is abundant evidence that the speed at which cognitive tasks are completed improves dramatically across childhood and adolescence (Motes & others, 2018). In one study, 10-year-olds were approximately 1.8 times slower in processing information than young adults on tasks involving reaction time and abstract matching (Hale, 1990). Twelve-year-olds were approximately 1.5 times slower than young adults, but 15-year-olds processed information on the tasks as fast as the young adults. Also, a study of 8- to 13-year-old children revealed that processing speed increased

What are some changes in attention during childhood and adolescence?
Hero Images/Getty Images

with age and the developmental change in processing speed preceded an increase in working memory capacity (Kail, 2007). In addition, in a recent research study involving 8- to 12-year-olds, faster processing speed predicted better language abilities, such as expressive vocabulary (Park & others, 2020). And in recent research, slower processing speed was related to children having ADHD or a learning disability (Kramer & others, 2020).

ATTENTION AND MEMORY

When adolescents and emerging adults process information quickly, they have to focus their attention on the information. And, if they need to use the information later, they will have to remember it. Attention and memory are key aspects of adolescents' information processing.

Attention **Attention** is the concentration and focusing of mental effort. Individuals can allocate their attention in different ways (Bell & Broomell, 2021). Psychologists have labeled these types of allocation as selective attention, divided attention, sustained attention, and executive attention.

- **Selective attention** is focusing on a specific aspect of experience that is relevant while ignoring others that are irrelevant. Focusing on one voice among many in a crowded room is an example of selective attention.
- **Divided attention** involves concentrating on more than one activity at the same time. An example of divided attention is text messaging while listening to an instructor's lecture.
- **Sustained attention** is the ability to maintain attention to a selected stimulus for a prolonged period of time. Staying focused on reading this chapter from start to finish without interruption is an example of sustained attention.
- **Executive attention** involves planning actions, allocating attention to goals, detecting and compensating for errors, monitoring progress on tasks, and dealing with novel or difficult circumstances. An example of executive attention is effectively deploying attention to engage in the aforementioned cognitive tasks while writing a 10-page paper for a history course.

Let's further explore divided, sustained, and executive attention. In one investigation, 12-year-olds were markedly better than 8-year-olds, and slightly worse than 20-year-olds, at dividing their attention between two tasks (Manis, Keating, & Morrison, 1980). Adolescents may have more resources available to them than children (through increased processing speed, capacity, and automaticity), or they may be more skilled at directing the resources.

One trend involving divided attention is adolescents' and emerging adults' multitasking, which in some cases involves dividing attention not just between two activities but between three or even more (Poplawska, Szumowska, & Kus, 2021). A major influence on the increase in multitasking is the availability of multiple electronic media. If a key task is complex and challenging, such as trying to figure out how to solve a homework problem, multitasking considerably reduces attention to the key task (Myers, 2008). A recent analysis of research studies concluded that heavy media multitasking in adolescence is linked to poorer memory, increased impulsivity, and reduced volume in the cerebral cortex (Uncapher & others, 2017). Thus, in many contexts multitasking harms performance (Lopez, Heatherton, & Wagner, 2020).

Sustained and executive attention also are very important aspects of adolescent and emerging adult cognitive development (O'Halloran & others, 2018). As adolescents and emerging adults are required to engage in larger, increasingly complex tasks that require longer time frames to complete, their ability to sustain attention is critical for succeeding on the tasks. One study found that sustained attention continues to improve during adolescence due to maturation of the brain's frontal lobes (Thillay & others, 2015). An increase in executive attention supports the rapid increase in effortful control required to effectively engage in complex academic tasks (Rothbart, 2011). And in a recent study, young adolescents' executive attention was a good predictor of their self-regulation (Tiego & others, 2020).

As with any cognitive process, there are wide individual differences in how effectively adolescents and emerging adults use these different types of attention in their everyday lives. For example, individuals with attention deficit hyperactivity disorder (ADHD) have severe problems in effectively allocating attention (Posner, Polanczyk, & Sonuga-Barke, 2020; Rodriguez-Martinez & others, 2021).

developmental connection

Media

One study revealed that when media multitasking is taken into account, 11- to 14-year-olds use media nearly 12 hours a day (Rideout, Foehr, & Roberts, 2010). Connect to "Culture."

Is multitasking beneficial or distracting for adolescents?
Image Source/Getty Images

attention Concentration and focusing of mental resources.

selective attention Focusing on a specific aspect of experience that is relevant while ignoring others that are irrelevant.

divided attention Concentrating on more than one activity at the same time.

sustained attention The ability to maintain attention to a selected stimulus for a prolonged period of time.

executive attention Type of attention that involves planning actions, allocating attention to goals, detecting and compensating for errors, monitoring progress on tasks, and dealing with novel or difficult circumstances.

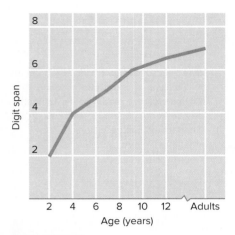

FIGURE 6

DEVELOPMENTAL CHANGES IN MEMORY SPAN. In one study, memory span increased about three digits from 2 years of age to five digits at 7 years of age (Dempster, 1981). By 12 years of age, memory span had increased on average another 1½ digits.

Working Memory

Visuospatial working memory

Central executive

Long-term memory

Input via sensory memory

Rehearsal

Phonological loop

FIGURE 7

WORKING MEMORY. In Baddeley's working memory model, working memory is like a mental workbench where a great deal of information processing is carried out. Working memory consists of three main components. The phonological loop and visuospatial working memory serve as assistants, helping the central executive do its work. Input from sensory memory goes to the phonological loop, where information about speech is stored and rehearsal takes place, and to visuospatial working memory, where visual and spatial information, including imagery, is stored. Working memory is a limited-capacity system, and information is stored there for only a brief time. Working memory interacts with long-term memory, using information from long-term memory in its work and transmitting information to long-term memory for longer storage.

Memory   There are few moments when adolescents' and emerging adults' lives are not steeped in memory. Memory is at work with each step they take, each thought they think, and each word they utter. **Memory** is the retention of information over time. It is central to mental life and to information processing (van Kesteren & Meeter, 2020). To successfully learn and reason, adolescents and emerging adults need to hold on to information and retrieve it when necessary. It is important to understand that memory in human beings does not function like a tape recorder, camera, or flash drive. Instead, adolescents construct and reconstruct their memories (Rubinova & others, 2021). Let's now examine three important memory systems—short-term memory, working memory, and long-term memory—that are involved in adolescents' learning.

Short-Term Memory   *Short-term memory* is a limited-capacity memory system in which information is retained for up to 30 seconds, unless the information is rehearsed (repeated), in which case it can be retained longer. A common way to assess short-term memory is to present a list of items to remember, which is often referred to as a memory span task. If you have taken an IQ test, you probably were asked to remember a string of numbers or words. You simply hear a short list of stimuli—usually digits—presented at a rapid pace (one per second, for example). Then you are asked to repeat the digits back. Using the memory span task, researchers have found that short-term memory increases extensively in early childhood and continues to increase in older children and adolescents, but at a slower pace. For example, in one investigation, memory span increased by 1½ digits between the ages of 7 and 12 (Dempster, 1981) (see Figure 6). Keep in mind, though, that individuals have widely varying memory spans, as reflected in their scores on IQ assessments and various aptitude tests.

Working Memory   Short-term memory is like a passive storehouse with shelves to store information until it is moved to long-term memory. In recent years, the more active, dynamic term *working memory* has been used to provide a more accurate depiction of memory storage. Working memory is a kind of mental "workbench" where individuals manipulate and assemble information when they make decisions, solve problems, and comprehend written and spoken language (Baddeley, 2015, 2017, 2018, 2019) (see Figure 7). Use of working memory involves bringing information to mind and mentally working with or updating it, as when you link one idea to another and relate what you are reading now to something you read earlier. Recent research confirms that working memory is a foundational cognitive activity, with the frontoparietal (frontal and parietal lobes) brain network playing a key role in its development (Rosenberg & others, 2020).

In one study, the performances of individuals from 6 to 57 years of age were examined on both verbal and visuospatial working memory tasks (Swanson, 1999). As shown in Figure 8, working memory increased substantially from 8 through 24 years of age, no matter what the task. Thus, the adolescent and emerging adult years are likely to be an important developmental period for improvement in working memory. Note that working memory continues to improve through the transition to adulthood and beyond.

Working memory is linked to many aspects of children's, adolescents' and emerging adults' development (Baddeley, 2019; Vernucci & others, 2020). One study revealed that working memory capacity at 9 to 10 years of age predicted foreign language comprehension at 11 to 12 years of age (Andersson, 2010). Another study found that the prefrontal cortex plays a more important role in working memory in late adolescence than in early adolescence (Finn & others, 2010). Further, one study found that working memory deficits at age 15 were associated with risk-taking behavior at age 18 (Thomas & others, 2015). And recent research indicates that children and adolescents with ADHD have working memory deficits (Kofler & others, 2020; Valladares & others, 2020).

Working memory serves as a cognitive filter that allows individuals to hold information in their minds so they can consider the

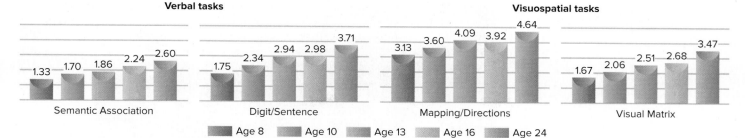

Verbal tasks

Semantic Association · Digit/Sentence

Visuospatial tasks

Mapping/Directions · Visual Matrix

Age 8 · Age 10 · Age 13 · Age 16 · Age 24

FIGURE 8

DEVELOPMENTAL CHANGES IN WORKING MEMORY. Note: The scores shown here are the means for each age group, and the age also represents a mean age. Higher scores reflect superior working memory performance.

potential consequences of their actions. Thus, when adolescents have working memory deficits, this may contribute to risky decision making (Thomas & others, 2015). A recent study found that working memory training in adolescents decreased their rates of risk taking in the presence of peers (Rosenbaum & others, 2017).

Long-Term Memory *Long-term memory* is a relatively permanent memory system that holds huge amounts of information for a long period of time. The capacity for long-term memory increases substantially in middle and late childhood and likely continues to improve during adolescence, although this has not been well documented by researchers. One thing is clear about long-term memory, however: it depends on the learning activities engaged in when an individual is acquiring and remembering information (Graham & others, 2021). Most learning activities fit under the category of *strategies*—activities that are under the learner's conscious control. There are many such activities, but one of the most important is organization, the tendency to group or arrange items into categories. We will have more to say about strategies shortly.

Memory of significant events and experiences in one's life is called *autobiographical memory* (Nelson & Fivush, 2020). You are engaging in autobiographical memory when you answer questions such as the following: What is the earliest event you can remember about your childhood? Who was your first date, and where did you go?

As we go through adolescence and emerging adulthood, our autobiographical narratives broaden and become more elaborated (Fivush, 2011). In one study, 8- to 20-year-olds were asked to narrate seven personally significant events and place them on a personal timeline (Habermas & de Silveira, 2008). It wasn't until 12 years of age that the participants could link single events together causally, and their autobiographical reasoning and causal connections continued to improve as they went through adolescence. Thus, one's life narrative increases in complexity and coherence during adolescence. This life narrative is at the heart of autobiographical memory.

EXECUTIVE FUNCTION

Attention and memory are important dimensions of information processing, but other dimensions also are significant. Especially fundamental to adolescent and emerging adult cognition are higher-order, complex cognitive processes that involve an umbrella-like concept called **executive function.** These cognitive processes are linked to the development of the brain's prefrontal cortex and involve managing one's thoughts to engage in goal-directed behavior and exercise self-control (Baum & others, 2020; Finders & others, 2021). Executive function is hard at work when adolescents and emerging adults are making decisions, thinking critically, and engaged in thinking about thinking.

Two categories of executive function are *cool executive function,* psychological processes involving conscious control driven by logical thinking and critical analysis, and *hot executive function,* psychological processes driven by emotion, with emotion regulation an especially important process (Zelazo, 2020). In a recent study of 12- to 17-year-olds, cool executive function increased with age while hot executive function peaked at 14 to 15 years of age and then declined (Poon, 2018).

developmental **connection**

Cognitive Development

Researchers recently have found that sleep deficits during adolescence are related to lower working memory. Connect to "Puberty, Health, and Biological Foundations."

developmental **connection**

Self and Identity

The narrative approach to understanding identity development provides an in-depth account of one's life story. Connect to "The Self, Identity, Personality, and Emotion"

developmental **connection**

Exercise

Recent research indicates that physically fit adolescents have better thinking skills, including those involving executive function, than adolescents who are less physically fit. Connect to "Puberty, Health, and Biological Foundations."

memory The retention of information over time.

executive function An umbrella-like concept that involves higher-order, complex cognitive processes that include exercising cognitive control, making decisions, reasoning, thinking critically, thinking creatively, and engaging in metacognition.

What characterizes executive function?
Derek Trask/Alamy Stock Photo

Executive function becomes increasingly strong during adolescence (Kuhn, 2009; Kuhn & Franklin, 2006). This dimension of information processing

"assumes a role of monitoring and managing the deployment of cognitive resources as a function of task demands. As a result, cognitive development and learning itself become more effective. . . . Emergence and strengthening of this executive (function) is arguably the single most important and consequential intellectual development to occur in the second decade of life" (Kuhn & Franklin, 2006, p. 987).

Cognitive Control　**Cognitive control** involves effective control and flexible thinking in a number of areas, including directing attention, reducing interfering thoughts, and being cognitively flexible. Cognitive control also has been referred to as *inhibitory control* or *effortful control* to emphasize the ability to resist a strong inclination to do one thing but instead to do what is most effective.

Across childhood, adolescence, and emerging adulthood, cognitive control increases with age (Calabro & others, 2020). The increase in cognitive control is thought to be due to the maturation of brain pathways and circuitry we considered earlier in the chapter. For example, one study found less diffusion and more focal activation in the prefrontal cortex from 7 to 30 years of age (Durston & others, 2006). The activation change was accompanied by increased efficiency in cognitive performance, especially in *cognitive control*. Thus, while cognitive control increases in adolescence, its development continues into emerging and early adulthood (Crone & Konijn, 2018).

Think about all the times adolescents and emerging adults need to engage in cognitive control, such as the following activities (Galinsky, 2010):

- Making a real effort to stick with a task, avoiding interfering thoughts or environmental events, and instead doing what is most effective;
- Stopping and thinking before acting to avoid blurting out something that they might later wish they hadn't said;
- Continuing to work on something that is important but boring when there is something a lot more fun to do, but inhibiting their behavior and doing the boring but important task, saying to themselves, "I have to show the self-discipline to finish this."

A longitudinal study of an important dimension of executive function—inhibitory control—found that 3- to 11-year-old children who early in development showed better inhibitory control

cognitive control The capacity to control attention, reduce interfering thoughts, and be cognitively flexible.

(they were able to wait their turn, not easily distracted, more persistent, and less impulsive) were more likely to still be in school, less likely to engage in risk-taking behavior, and less likely to use drugs in adolescence (Moffitt & others, 2011). Thirty years after they were initially assessed, the children with better inhibitory control had better physical and mental health (they were less likely to be overweight, for example), earned more money in their careers, were more law-abiding, and were happier (Moffitt, 2012; Moffitt & others, 2011).

Control Attention and Reduce Interfering Thoughts   Controlling attention is a key aspect of learning and thinking in adolescence and emerging adulthood (Brooker & others, 2020). Distractions that can interfere with attention in adolescence and emerging adulthood come from the external environment (other students talking while the student is trying to listen to a lecture, or the student turning on a laptop during a lecture and looking at a new friend request on Facebook, for example) or intrusive distractions from competing thoughts in the individual's mind. Self-oriented thoughts, such as worrying, self-doubt, and intense, emotionally laden thoughts (Walsh, 2011) as well as mind-wandering (Gyurkovics, Stafford, & Levita, 2020) may especially interfere with focusing attention on thinking tasks (Walsh, 2011).

Be Cognitively Flexible   *Cognitive flexibility* involves being aware that options and alternatives are available and adapting to the situation (Stepanyan & others, 2020). Before adolescents and emerging adults adapt their behavior in a situation, they need to become aware that they ought to change their way of thinking and be motivated to do so (Gopnik & others, 2019). Having confidence in their ability to adapt their thinking to a particular situation, an aspect of *self-efficacy,* also is important in being cognitively flexible (Bandura, 2012). In a recent study of college students, those with attention deficit hyperactivity disorder had less cognitive flexibility than their counterparts without ADHD (Roshani & others, 2020).

Decision Making   Adolescents and emerging adults face increasing numbers of decisions—which friends to choose; whom to date; whether to have sex, buy a car, go to college; which career to pursue; and so on (Reyna, 2020; Reyna & Broniatowski, 2020; Reyna & Panagiotopoulos, 2020). How competent are adolescents at making decisions? In some reviews, older adolescents are described as more competent than younger adolescents, who in turn are more competent than children (Keating, 1990). Compared with children, young adolescents are more likely to generate different options, examine a situation from a variety of perspectives, anticipate the consequences of decisions, and consider the credibility of sources.

One study documents that older adolescents are better at decision making than younger adolescents are (Lewis, 1981). Eighth-, tenth-, and twelfth-grade students were presented with dilemmas involving the choice of a medical procedure. The oldest students were most likely to spontaneously mention a variety of risks, to recommend consultation with an outside specialist, and to anticipate future consequences. For example, when asked a question about whether to have cosmetic surgery, a twelfth-grader said that different aspects of the situation need to be examined along with its effects on the individual's future, especially relationships with other people. In contrast, an eighth-grader presented a more limited view, commenting on the surgery's effects on getting turned down for a date, the money involved, and being teased by peers.

In sum, older adolescents often make better decisions than do younger adolescents, who in turn make better decisions than do children. The ability to regulate one's emotions during decision making, to remember prior decisions and their consequences, and to adapt subsequent decision making on the basis of those consequences appears to improve with age at least through early adulthood (Klaczynski, Byrnes, & Jacobs, 2001). Older adolescents' decision-making skills are far from perfect, but adults also are imperfect in making decisions (Kuhn, 2009). Adolescents and adults who are impulsive and seek sensation are often not very effective decision makers, for example (Korucuoglu & others, 2020).

Being able to make competent decisions does not guarantee that individuals will make them in everyday life, where

What are some of the decisions adolescents have to make? What characterizes their decision making?
Big Cheese Photo/SuperStock

How do emotions and social contexts influence adolescents' decision making?
Jodi Jacobson/E+/Getty Images

breadth of experience often comes into play. As an example, driver-training courses improve adolescents' cognitive and motor skills to levels equal to, or sometimes superior to, those of adults. However, driver training has not been effective in reducing adolescents' high rate of traffic accidents, although researchers have found that implementing a graduated driver licensing (GDL) program can reduce crash and fatality rates for adolescent drivers (Keating, 2007). GDL components include a learner's holding period, practice-driving certification, night-driving restriction, and passenger restriction. In addition to GDL, parental monitoring can reduce adolescents' driving accidents (Simons-Morton & others, 2020). For example, parents can restrict and monitor the presence of adolescents' peers in the vehicle.

Most people make better decisions when they are calm rather than emotionally aroused, which may especially be true for adolescents (Crone & Konijn, 2018). Recall from our discussion of brain development earlier in the chapter that adolescents have a tendency to be emotionally intense. Thus, the same adolescent who makes a wise decision when calm may make an unwise decision when emotionally aroused. In the heat of the moment, then, adolescents' emotions are especially likely to overwhelm their decision-making ability.

The social context plays a key role in adolescent decision making (Smith, Chein, & Steinberg, 2014). For example, adolescents' willingness to make risky decisions is more likely to increase in contexts where intoxicating substances and other temptations are readily available (Reyna & Rivers, 2008). Research reveals that the presence of peers in risk-taking situations increases the likelihood that adolescents will make risky decisions (Defoe & others, 2020). In one study of risk taking involving a simulated driving task, the presence of peers increased an adolescent's decision to engage in risky driving by 50 percent but had no effect on adults (Gardner & Steinberg, 2005). One view is that the presence of peers activates the brain's reward system, especially dopamine pathways (Dow-Edwards & others, 2020).

Adolescents need more opportunities to practice and discuss realistic decision making. Many real-world decisions on matters such as sex, drugs, and daredevil driving occur in an atmosphere of stress that includes time constraints and emotional involvement. One strategy for improving adolescent decision making in such circumstances is to provide more opportunities for them to engage in role-playing and group problem solving. Another strategy is for parents to involve adolescents in appropriate decision-making activities.

To better understand adolescent decision making, Valerie Reyna and her colleagues (Reyna, 2018, 2020; Reyna & Brainerd, 2011; Reyna & Broniatowski & others, 2020; Reyna & Panagiotopoulos, 2020) have proposed the **fuzzy-trace theory dual-process model,** which states that decision making is influenced by two cognitive systems—"verbatim" analytical thinking (literal and precise) and gist-based intuition (simple, bottom-line meaning)—which operate in parallel. According to this theory, it is gist-based intuition that benefits adolescents' decision making most. In this view, adolescents don't benefit from engaging in reflective, detailed, higher-level cognitive analysis about a decision, especially in high-risk, real-world contexts where analysis would cause them to get bogged down in trivial detail. In such contexts, adolescents need to rely on the simple, bottom-line reality that some circumstances are so dangerous that they must be avoided at all costs.

In risky situations it is important for an adolescent to quickly get the *gist,* or meaning, of what is happening and glean that the situation is a dangerous context, which can cue personal values that will protect the adolescent from making a risky decision (Reyna, 2020). One experiment showed that encouraging gist-based thinking about risks (in addition to providing factual information) reduced self-reported risk-taking up to one year after exposure to the curriculum (Reyna & Mills, 2014). Further, adolescents who have a higher level of trait inhibition (self-control that helps them to manage their impulses effectively) and find themselves in risky contexts are less likely to engage in risk-taking behavior than their adolescent counterparts who have a lower level of trait inhibition (Chick & Reyna, 2012).

In the *Connecting with Health and Well-Being* interlude, you can read about strategies that parents, teachers, and other adults who work with adolescents can use to improve their decision making and reduce their risk taking.

fuzzy-trace theory dual-process model
States that decision making is influenced by two systems—"verbatim" analytical thinking (literal and precise) and gist-based intuition (simple, bottom-line meaning), which operate in parallel; in this model, it is the gist-based system that benefits adolescents' decision making most.

critical thinking Thinking reflectively and productively and evaluating the evidence.

Critical Thinking Critical thinking is thinking reflectively and productively and evaluating evidence (Baron, 2020; Sternberg & Halpern, 2020). In this book, the third part of the Review *Connect* Reflect sections challenges you to think critically about a topic or an issue related to the

Guiding Adolescents to Engage in Better Decision Making

Here are some effective strategies for helping adolescents to make better and safer choices (Wargo, 2007):

- ***Don't assume that adolescents think they are immortal.*** Later in the chapter, you will read about research indicating that adolescents actually say that they are more likely to have dangerous experiences and even die than actually is the case.
- ***Talk with adolescents about benefits of a positive course of action rather than only about risks.*** Get adolescents to reflect on how they will benefit from safer courses of actions.
- ***Explore positive images or models of healthy behavior and negative images or models of unhealthy behaviors and show these to adolescents.*** Such images or models can increase adolescents' gist-based decision making and remind them of the benefits of safe behavior.
- ***Give adolescents practice at recognizing signs of danger.*** Talk with adolescents about red flags for high-risk behavior such as being home alone after school with a boyfriend or a girlfriend with no adults around.
- ***Limit adolescents' exposure to risky situations.*** For instance, limit the number of peers in a vehicle and try to reduce their exposure to and temptation to take drugs. Monitor who their friends are and the individuals they are spending time with after school and in the summer.

discussion. Thinking critically includes asking not only what happened, but how and why; examining supposed "facts" to determine whether there is evidence to support them; evaluating what other people say rather than immediately accepting it as the truth; and asking questions and speculating beyond what is known so you can create new ideas and gather additional information.

Mindfulness   According to Ellen Langer (2005), *mindfulness*—being alert, mentally present, and cognitively flexible while going through life's everyday activities and tasks—is an important aspect of thinking critically. Mindful children, adolescents. and emerging adults maintain an active awareness of the circumstances in their life and are motivated to find the best solutions to tasks (Lux, Decker, & Nease, 2020). They create new ideas, are open to new information, and operate from multiple perspectives. By contrast, children, adolescents, and emerging adults who are not mindful are entrapped in old ideas, engage in automatic behavior, and operate from a single perspective. In a recent study that examined different components of executive function in 7- to 13-year-olds, inhibition and working memory were key aspects of children's and adolescents' mindfulness (Geronimi, Arellano, & Woodruff-Borden, 2020).

A recent research review concluded that mindfulness-based interventions have positive effects on a number of physical and mental health outcomes in adolescence. Mindfulness training has been effective in reducing symptoms of anxiety and depression, preventing and treating eating disorders, reducing sleep problems, and decreasing ADHD symptoms (Lin, Chadi, & Shrier, 2019).

Some experts also have proposed implementing mindfulness training in schools and colleges through practices such as using age-appropriate activities that increase individuals' reflection on moment-to-moment experiences and result in improved self-regulation (Amundsen & others, 2020). In one study, mindfulness training improved young adolescents' attention self-regulation (Felver & others, 2017). In addition, recent research indicated that mindfulness training increased the resilience of adolescents during the COVID-19 pandemic (Yuan, 2021). Also, a recent research review concluded that mindfulness training reduced adolescents' depressive symptoms (Reangsing, Punsuwun, & Schneider, 2021). And a recent study revealed that mindfulness training reduced the anxiety, stress, and depression of Latinx adolescents (Clarke & others, 2021).

In addition to mindfulness training, interventions involving yoga, meditation, and tai chi have been recently proposed as candidates for enhancing children's, adolescents', and emerging adults' cognitive and socioemotional development (Flett & others, 2020). For example, recently a college course in meditation improved the happiness and well-being of students (Crowley, Kapitula, & Munk, 2021).

Together these activities and mindfulness are being grouped under the topic of *contemplative science*, a cross-disciplinary term that involves the study of how various types of mental and physical training might enhance children's and adolescents' development (Garcia-Campayo, Lopez Del Hoyo, & Navarro-Gil, 2021; Roeser & Zelazo, 2012).

How might mindfulness training improve adolescents' development?
mheim3011/Getty Images

Developmental Changes   Adolescence is an important transitional period in the development of critical thinking (Sternberg & Halpern, 2020). In one study of fifth-, eighth-, and eleventh-graders, critical thinking increased with age but still occurred in only 43 percent of eleventh-graders (Klaczynski & Narasimham, 1998). Many adolescents showed self-serving biases in their thinking.

Among the cognitive changes that facilitate improvement of critical thinking skills during adolescence are the following:

- Increased speed, automaticity, and capacity of information processing, which free cognitive resources for other purposes
- Greater breadth of content knowledge in a variety of domains
- Increased ability to construct new combinations of knowledge
- A greater range and more spontaneous use of strategies and procedures for obtaining and applying knowledge, such as planning, considering the alternatives, and cognitive monitoring

Although adolescence is an important period in the development of critical-thinking skills, if a solid base of fundamental skills (such as literacy and math skills) has not been developed during childhood, critical-thinking skills are unlikely to develop adequately in adolescence.

Schools   Considerable interest has been directed to teaching critical thinking in schools (Sternberg & Halpern, 2020). Cognitive psychologist Robert J. Sternberg (1985) concludes that most school programs that teach critical thinking are flawed. He thinks that schools focus too much on formal reasoning tasks and not enough on the critical-thinking skills needed in everyday life. Among the critical-thinking skills that Sternberg notes that adolescents need in everyday life are these: recognizing that problems exist, defining problems clearly, handling problems that have no single right answer or any clear criteria for determining the point at which the problem will be solved (such as selecting a rewarding career), making decisions on issues of personal relevance (such as deciding to undergo a risky operation), obtaining information, thinking in groups, and developing long-term approaches for addressing long-term problems.

Getting students to think critically is not always an easy task. Many students come into a class with a history of passive learning, having been encouraged to recite the correct answer to a question rather than put forth the intellectual effort to think in more complex ways. By using more assignments that require students to focus on an issue, a question, or a problem, rather than just to recite facts, teachers stimulate students' ability to think critically. To read

connecting with careers

Laura Bickford, Secondary School Teacher

Laura Bickford teaches English and journalism in grades 9 to 12 and serves as chair of the English Department at Nordhoff High School in Ojai, California.

Bickford believes it is especially important to encourage students to think. Indeed, she says that "the call to teach is the call to teach students how to think." She believes that teachers need to show students the value of asking their own questions, having discussions, and engaging in stimulating intellectual conversations. Bickford says that she also encourages students to engage in metacognitive strategies (knowing about knowing). For example, she asks students to comment on their learning after particular pieces of projects have been completed. She requires students to maintain reading logs so they can observe their own thinking as it happens.

Laura Bickford, working with students who are writing papers.
Courtesy of Laura Johnson Bickford.

For more information about the work that secondary school teachers do, see the Careers in Adolescent Development appendix.

about the work of one secondary school teacher who encourages students to think critically, see the *Connecting with Careers* profile.

Creative Thinking **Creativity** is the ability to think in novel ways and discover unique solutions to problems. Thus, intelligence, which we discuss shortly, is not the same thing as creativity (Glaveanu & others, 2020; Sternberg, 2021c). J. P. Guilford (1967) first made this distinction by contrasting **convergent thinking,** which produces one correct answer and is characteristic of the kind of thinking required on a conventional intelligence test, and **divergent thinking,** which produces many answers to the same question and is more characteristic of creativity. For example, a typical item on a conventional intelligence test is "How many quarters will you get in return for 60 dimes?" This question has only one correct answer. In contrast, the following questions have many possible answers: "What image comes to mind when you hear the phrase *sitting alone in a dark room*?" or "Can you think of some unique uses for a paper clip?"

Are intelligence and creativity related? Although most creative adolescents are quite intelligent, the reverse is not necessarily true (Lubart, 2003). Not all highly intelligent adolescents are highly creative.

A special concern is that adolescents' creative thinking appears to be declining. A study of approximately 300,000 U.S. children, adolescents, and adults found that creativity scores rose until 1990 but since then have been steadily declining (Kim, 2010). Among the likely causes of the creativity decline are the number of hours U.S. children and adolescents spend watching TV, playing video games, connecting on social media platforms, and text messaging instead of engaging in creative activities, as well as the lack of emphasis on creative-thinking skills in schools (Kaufman & Sternberg, 2021). Some countries, though, are placing increased emphasis on encouraging creative thinking in students. For example, historically, creative thinking was discouraged in Chinese schools. However, Chinese educational administrators are now encouraging teachers to spend more classroom time on creative activities (Plucker, 2010).

An important teaching goal is to help students become more creative (Sternberg, 2020c, 2021c). Teachers need to recognize that students will show more creativity in some domains than in others (Plucker, Karwowski, & Kaufman, 2020). A student who shows creative-thinking skills in mathematics may not exhibit creativity in art, for example.

Here are some good strategies for increasing adolescents' creative-thinking skills:

- *Have adolescents engage in brainstorming to come up with as many ideas as possible.* Brainstorming is a technique in which individuals are encouraged to come up with creative ideas in a group, play off each other's ideas, and say practically anything that comes to mind. However, it is important to recognize that some adolescents are more creative when they work alone. Indeed, one review of research on brainstorming concluded that for many individuals, working alone can generate more ideas and better ideas than working in groups (Rickards & deCock, 2003). One reason for this is that in groups, some individuals contribute only a few ideas while others do most of the creative thinking. Nonetheless, there may be benefits to brainstorming, such as team building, that support its use.

- *Introduce adolescents to environments that stimulate creativity.* Some settings nourish creativity while others stifle it (Kaufman & Sternberg, 2021). People who encourage creativity often rely on adolescents' natural curiosity. They provide exercises and activities that stimulate adolescents to find insightful solutions to problems, rather than asking a lot of questions that require rote answers (Beghetto, 2021; Reis & Renzulli, 2020). Adults also encourage creativity by taking adolescents to locations where creativity is valued.

- *Don't overcontrol.* Teresa Amabile (2018) says that telling individuals exactly how to do things leaves them feeling that any originality is a mistake and exploration would be a waste of time. Encouraging adolescents to discover and follow their own inclinations is less likely to destroy their natural curiosity than dictating which activities they should engage in.

An adolescent boy painting in the streets of the African nation of Zanzibar. *If you were going to work with adolescents to encourage their creativity, what strategies would you adopt?*
Gideon Mendel/Corbis/Getty Images

developmental **connection**
Achievement
Intrinsic motivation comes from a combination of factors, such as self-determination and personal choice, optimal experiences, interest, and cognitive engagement. Connect to "Achievement, Work, and Careers."

creativity The ability to think in novel and unusual ways and discover unique solutions to problems.

convergent thinking A pattern of thinking in which individuals produce one correct answer; characteristic of the items on conventional intelligence tests.

divergent thinking A pattern of thinking in which individuals produce many answers to the same question; more characteristic of creativity than convergent thinking.

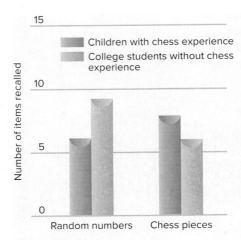

FIGURE **9**

MEMORY FOR NUMBERS AND CHESS PIECES

I want to stand as close to the edge as I can without going over. Out on the edge you see all kinds of things you can't see from the center.

—Kurt Vonnegut
American Novelist, 20th Century

How are talent and deliberate practice involved in expertise?
Rayman/Getty Images

- *Build adolescents' confidence.* To expand adolescents' creativity, encourage them to believe in their own ability to create something innovative and worthwhile. Building adolescents' confidence in their creative skills aligns with Bandura's (2012) concept of self-efficacy, the belief that one can master a situation and produce positive outcomes.
- *Encourage internal motivation.* Excessive use of rewards such as recognition or money can stifle creativity by undermining the intrinsic pleasure adolescents derive from creative activities. Creative adolescents' motivation is the satisfaction generated by the work itself. Competing for prizes and striving for high performance on formal evaluations often undermine intrinsic motivation and creativity (Hennessey, 2021).
- *Guide adolescents to be persistent and to delay gratification.* Most highly successful creative products take years to develop. Creative individuals often work on ideas and projects for months and years without being rewarded for their efforts (Sternberg, 2020c, 2021c). Adolescents don't become experts at sports, music, or art overnight. It usually takes many years of working at something to become an expert at it; the same is true for a creative thinker who produces a unique, worthwhile product.
- *Encourage adolescents to take intellectual risks.* Creative individuals take intellectual risks and seek to discover or invent something never before discovered or invented (Sternberg & Williams, 1996). They risk spending extensive time on an idea or project that may not work. Adolescents' creativity benefits when they are not afraid of failing or getting something wrong (Kaufman & Sternberg, 2021; Sternberg, 2021c).
- *Introduce adolescents to creative people.* Think about some of the most creative people in your community. Teachers can invite these people to their classrooms and ask them to describe what strengthens their creativity or to demonstrate their creative skills. A writer, poet, musician, scientist, and many others can bring their props and productions to the class, turning it into a theater for stimulating students' creativity.

Expertise Recently psychologists have shown increased interest in exploring the differences between experts and novices in a specific knowledge domain (Kua & others, 2021; Zimmer & Fischer, 2020). An expert is the opposite of a novice (someone who is just beginning to learn a content area). What is it, exactly, that experts do so well? They are better than novices at the following activities (National Research Council, 1999):

- Detecting features and meaningful patterns of information
- Accumulating more content knowledge and organizing it in a manner that shows an understanding of the topic
- Retrieving important aspects of knowledge with little effort

In areas where children and adolescents are experts, their memory is often extremely good. In fact, it often exceeds that of adults who are novices in that content area. This superiority was documented in a study of 10-year-old chess experts (Chi, 1978). These children were excellent chess players but not especially brilliant in other ways. As with most 10-year-olds, their memory spans for digits were shorter than those of adults. However, when they were presented with chessboards, they remembered the configurations far better than did adults who were novices at chess (see Figure 9).

Experts' knowledge is organized around important ideas or concepts more than novices' knowledge is (National Research Council, 1999). This ability provides experts with a much deeper understanding of knowledge than novices possess. Experts in a specific area usually have far more elaborate networks of information about that area than novices do. The information they represent in memory has more nodes, more interconnections, and better hierarchical organization.

What determines whether someone becomes an expert? Can motivation and practice elevate someone to expert status? Or does expertise also require a great deal of talent?

One perspective asserts that a specific kind of practice—deliberate practice—is required to become an expert. Deliberate practice involves practice that is at an appropriate level of difficulty for the individual, provides corrective feedback, and offers opportunities for repetition (Ericsson & others, 2018). In one study of violinists at a music academy, the extent to which

Rochelle Ballantyne, Chess Star

Rochelle Ballantyne, a Stanford University student who grew up in Brooklyn, New York, is close to becoming the first female African American to reach the level of chess master (Kastenbaum, 2012). Born in 1995, she grew up in a single-parent family in a lower-income context. Her grandmother taught her to play chess because she didn't want Rochelle's impoverished background to prevent her from reaching her full potential. Rochelle was fortunate to attend IS 318, an inner-city public middle school whose chess team is one of the best in the United States. Rochelle has won several national chess championships, and she is a rising star in the world of chess. Rochelle's motivation and confidence are reflected in her comment: "When I push myself, then nothing can stop me." After getting her undergraduate degree at Stanford and then her master's degree from Columbia University, she currently is a law school student at New York University.

Rochelle Ballantyne, shown here at age 17, is a rising star in the world of chess. *How might her ability to process information about chess be different than for a novice chess player?*
First Run Features/Courtesy Everett Collection

children and adolescents engaged in deliberate practice differed for novices and experts (Ericsson, Krampe, & Tesch-Romer, 1993). The top violinists averaged 7,500 hours of deliberate practice by age 18, the good violinists only 5,300 hours. Many individuals give up on becoming an expert because they are unwilling to put forth the effort required to engage in extensive deliberate practice over a number of years.

Such extensive practice requires considerable motivation. Students who are not motivated to practice long hours are unlikely to become experts in a specific area. Thus, a student who complains about all of the work involved, doesn't persevere, and is unwilling to practice solving math problems extensively over a number of years is not going to become an expert in math. However, talent is also usually required to become an expert (Plomin & others, 2014). Many individuals have attempted to become great musicians and athletes but have stopped trying after achieving only mediocre results. Nonetheless, musicians such as Beethoven and athletes such as LeBron James would not have developed expertise in their fields without being highly motivated and engaging in extensive deliberate practice. Talent alone does not make someone an expert.

Metacognition   So far you have studied some important ways in which adolescents and emerging adults process information. In this section, you will read about how they can effectively monitor their information processing and think about thinking.

What Is Metacognition?   Earlier in this chapter, in discussing Piaget's theory, you learned that adolescents increase their thinking about thinking. Cognitive psychologists call this kind of thought **metacognition**—that is, cognition about cognition, or "knowing about knowing" (Flavell, 2004). Metacognition can take many forms. It includes thinking about and knowing when and where to use particular strategies for learning or for solving problems (Doherty & others, 2021; Pennequin & others, 2020). Conceptualization of metacognition includes several dimensions of executive function, such as planning (deciding how long to focus on a task, for example), evaluation (monitoring progress toward task completion, for example), and self-regulation (modifying strategies while working on the task, for example) (Bellon, Fias, & Smedt, 2020).

Metacognition is increasingly recognized as an important cognitive skill not only in adolescence but also in emerging adulthood. In comparison with children, adolescents have an increased capacity to monitor and manage cognitive resources to effectively meet the demands of a learning task (Kuhn, 2009, 2013). This increased metacognitive ability results in improved cognitive functioning and learning. A longitudinal study revealed that from 12 to 14 years of age, adolescents increasingly used metacognitive skills and applied them more effectively in

metacognition Cognition about cognition, or "knowing about knowing."

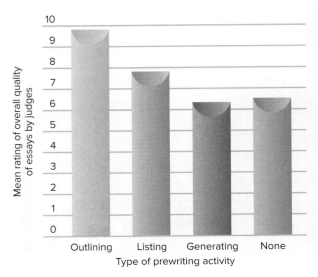

FIGURE 10

THE RELATION OF PREWRITING ACTIVITIES TO ESSAY QUALITY. The most effective prewriting activity for college students was outlining, which involved creating an outline with relevant ideas under multilevel headings. Judges rated the quality of each essay from 1 (lowest) to 10 (highest).

math and history classes (van der Stel & Veenman, 2010). For example, 14-year-olds monitored their own text comprehension more frequently and did so more effectively than did their younger counterparts. Further, a recent study of 11- to 15-year-olds revealed that metacognitive skills improved students' math engagement (Wang & others, 2021). In addition, another study documented the importance of metacognitive skills, such as planning, strategizing, and monitoring, in college students' ability to think critically (Magno, 2010). And a recent study found that in contrast with children, adolescents are more likely to question others' advice if the advice seems misleading (Moses-Payne & others, 2021). Also in this study, adolescents' reduced reliance on others was predicted by their metacognitive skills, suggesting that these skills likely enhance their independent decision making.

Theory of Mind **Theory of mind** refers to awareness of one's own mental processes and the mental processes of others (Grosse Wiesmann & others, 2020). Studies of theory of mind view adolescents as thinkers who are trying to explain, predict, and understand people's thoughts, feelings, and utterances.

In early adolescence, children begin to understand that people can have ambivalent feelings (Flavell & Miller, 1998). They start to recognize that the same person can feel both happy and sad about the same event. They also engage in more recursive thinking: thinking about what other people are thinking about. Also, adolescents who perform better at such executive function tasks show a better understanding of theory of mind (Muller & Kerns, 2015).

Strategies Metacognition especially emphasizes knowledge about strategies (Graham & Rui, 2022). In the view of Michael Pressley (2003), the key to education is helping students learn a rich repertoire of strategies that produce solutions to problems. Good thinkers routinely use strategies and effective planning to solve problems (Graham & others, 2021). Good thinkers also know when and where to use strategies. Understanding when and where to use strategies often results from monitoring the learning situation.

Pressley and his colleagues (Pressley & others, 2001, 2003, 2004, 2007) spent considerable time in observing strategy instruction by teachers and strategy use by students in elementary and secondary school classrooms. They conclude that strategy instruction is far less complete and intense than what students need in order to learn how to use strategies effectively. They argue that education ought to be restructured so that students are provided with more opportunities to become competent strategic learners.

As an example of how important strategies are for adolescents, a meta-analysis revealed that strategy instruction was the most successful intervention for improving the writing quality of fourth- through twelfth-grade students (Graham & Perin, 2007).

Domain-Specific Thinking Skills Our coverage of metacognition has mainly emphasized the importance of some general cognitive skills, such as strategies and self-regulation, in becoming a better thinker. Indeed, researchers have found that metacognitive skills can be taught (Macoun & others, 2021). For example, adolescents have been effectively taught how to become aware of their thinking processes and engage in self-regulation of their learning (Schunk, 2020).

However, it also is very important to teach domain-specific thinking skills to adolescents (Schoevers, Kroesbergen, & Kattou, 2020). In this regard, a research review concluded that one of educational psychology's greatest accomplishments is the teaching of domain-specific thinking skills (Mayer & Wittrock, 2006). Thus, a rich tradition in quality education programs has been the teaching of thinking skills within specific subjects, such as writing, mathematics, science, and history (Graham & Harris, 2021). Researchers have found that "it is possible to analyze and teach the underlying cognitive processes required in tasks such as comprehending a passage, writing an essay, solving an arithmetic word problem, answering a scientific question, or explaining an historical event . . ." (Mayer & Wittrock, 2006).

Planning is an important general cognitive skill for adolescents and emerging adults to use, but they also benefit when they apply this and other cognitive skills to specific subjects (Halonen & Santrock, 2013). For example, one study examined how prewriting activities can affect the quality of college students' writing (Kellogg, 1994). As indicated in Figure 10, the planning activity of outlining was the prewriting activity that helped writers the most.

theory of mind Awareness of one's own mental processes and the mental processes of others.

Review *Connect* Reflect

LG3 Characterize the information-processing view of adolescence.

Review

- What characterizes the development of cognitive resources?
- What developmental changes characterize attention and memory in adolescence?
- What is executive function?
- How can adolescent decision making be described?
- What characterizes critical thinking in adolescence?
- What distinguishes experts from novices, and how do individuals become experts?
- What is metacognition, and how does it change developmentally?
- What is self-regulatory learning?
- How important is domain-specific thinking?

Connect

- How does research on cognitive control shed light on adolescents' risk-taking behavior?

Reflect *Your Own Personal Journey of Life*

- What were your study skills like during adolescence? How have your study skills changed since adolescence? Has metacognition played a role in improving your study skills?

4 The Psychometric/Intelligence View

LG4 Summarize the psychometric/intelligence view of adolescence.

- Intelligence Tests
- Multiple Intelligences
- The Neuroscience of Intelligence
- Heredity and Environment

The two views of adolescent cognition that we have discussed so far—cognitive developmental and information processing—do not emphasize individual variations in intelligence. The **psychometric/intelligence view** does emphasize the importance of individual differences in intelligence; many advocates of this view favor the use of intelligence tests (Coyle, 2021). Individual differences in intelligence generally have been measured by intelligence tests designed to tell us whether a person can reason better than others who have taken the test (Elkana & others, 2020).

An increasing focus of interest in the field of intelligence involves pinning down what the components of intelligence really are. How can intelligence be defined? **Intelligence** is the ability to solve problems and to adapt and learn from experiences. But even this broad definition doesn't satisfy everyone. As you will see shortly, Robert J. Sternberg (2020a, b, 2021a, b) proposes that practical know-how should be considered part of intelligence. In his view, intelligence involves weighing options carefully and acting judiciously, as well as developing strategies to improve shortcomings. Sternberg (2020a, b, 2021a, b) also recently described intelligence as the ability to adapt to, shape, and select environments. In adapting to the environment, if individuals find the environment suboptimal, they can change it to make it more suitable for their skills and desires.

psychometric/intelligence view A view that emphasizes the importance of individual differences in intelligence; many advocates of this view also argue that intelligence should be assessed with intelligence tests.

intelligence The ability to solve problems and to adapt to and learn from everyday experiences; not everyone agrees on what constitutes intelligence.

INTELLIGENCE TESTS

Robert Sternberg recalls being terrified of taking IQ tests as a child. He literally froze, he says, when the time came to take such tests. Even as an adult, Sternberg is stung by humiliation when he recalls in the sixth grade being asked to take an IQ test with fifth-graders. Sternberg eventually overcame his anxieties about IQ tests. Not only did he begin to perform better on them, but at age 13 he devised his own IQ test and began using it to assess his classmates—that

Alfred Binet constructed the first intelligence test after being asked to create a measure to determine which children would benefit from instruction in France's schools.
Bettmann/Getty Images

is, until the chief school-system psychologist found out and scolded him. Sternberg became so fascinated by intelligence that he made its study one of his lifelong pursuits. Later in this chapter we will discuss his theory of intelligence. To begin, though, let's step back in time to examine the first valid intelligence test.

The Binet Tests   In 1904, the French Ministry of Education asked psychologist Alfred Binet to devise a method of identifying children who were unable to learn in school. School officials wanted to reduce crowding by placing students who did not benefit from regular classroom teaching in special schools. Binet and his student Theophile Simon developed an intelligence test to meet this request. The test is called the 1905 Scale. It consisted of 30 questions on topics ranging from the ability to touch one's ear to the ability to draw designs from memory and to define abstract concepts.

Binet developed the concept of **mental age (MA),** an individual's level of mental development relative to others. Not much later, in 1912, William Stern created the concept of **intelligence quotient (IQ),** a person's mental age divided by chronological age (CA), multiplied by 100—that is, IQ = MA/CA × 100. If mental age is the same as chronological age, then the person's IQ is 100. If mental age is above chronological age, then IQ is greater than 100. If mental age is below chronological age, then IQ is less than 100.

The Binet test has been revised many times to incorporate advances in the understanding of intelligence and intelligence tests. These revisions are called the *Stanford-Binet tests* (the revisions were done at Stanford University). By administering the test to large numbers of people of different ages from different backgrounds, researchers have found that scores on the Stanford-Binet approximate a normal distribution (see Figure 11). A **normal distribution** is symmetrical, with a majority of the scores falling in the middle of the possible range of scores, and few scores appearing toward the extremes of the range.

In 2004, the test—now called the Stanford-Binet 5—was revised to analyze an individual's responses in five content areas: fluid reasoning, knowledge, quantitative reasoning, visual-spatial reasoning, and working memory. A general composite score is still obtained.

mental age (MA) An individual's level of mental development relative to others; a concept developed by Binet.

intelligent quotient (IQ) A person's tested mental age divided by chronological age, multiplied by 100.

normal distribution A symmetrical distribution of values or scores, with a majority of scores falling in the middle of the possible range of scores and few scores appearing toward the extremes of the range.

The Wechsler Scales   Besides the Stanford-Binet, the other most widely used intelligence tests are the Wechsler scales. In 1939, David Wechsler introduced the first of his scales, designed for use with adults (Wechsler, 1939); the current edition is the Wechsler Adult Intelligence Scale–Fourth Edition (WAIS-IV). The Wechsler Intelligence Scale for Children–Fourth Edition (WISC-IV) is designed for children and adolescents between the ages of 6 and 16. The Wechsler Preschool and Primary Scale of Intelligence–Fourth Edition (WPPSI-IV) was published in 2012 and is appropriate for children from age 2 years 6 months to 7 years 7 months (Syeda & Climie, 2014).

Not only do the Wechsler scales provide an overall IQ, but they also yield a number of additional composite scores (for example, the Verbal Comprehension Index, the Working Memory Index, and the Processing Speed Index), allowing the examiner to quickly see patterns

FIGURE **11**

THE NORMAL CURVE AND STANFORD-BIENT IQ SCORES. The distribution of IQ scores approximates a normal curve. Most of the population falls in the middle range of scores, between 84 and 116. Notice that extremely high and extremely low scores are rare. Only about 1 in 50 individuals has an IQ higher than 132 or lower than 68.

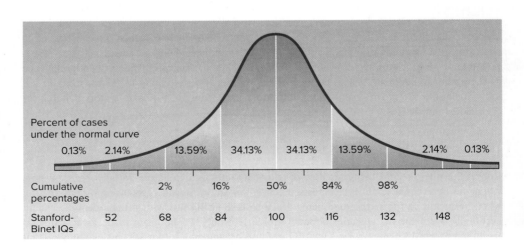

Percent of cases under the normal curve								
0.13%	2.14%		13.59%	34.13%	34.13%	13.59%	2.14%	0.13%

Cumulative percentages			2%	16%	50%	84%	98%	

Stanford-Binet IQs	52	68	84	100	116	132	148

Types of Items on WAIS-IV

Name	Goal of Item	Example
Information	Assess general information	Who wrote *Tom Sawyer*?
Comprehension	Assess understanding and evaluation of social norms and past experience	Why is copper often used for electrical wires?
Arithmetic	Assess math reasoning through verbal problems	Three women divided 18 golf balls equally among themselves. How many golf balls did each person receive?
Similarities	Test understanding of how objects or concepts are alike, tapping abstract reasoning	In what way are a circle and a triangle alike?
Figure weights	Test perceptual reasoning	Problems require test-taker to determine which possibility balances the final scale. 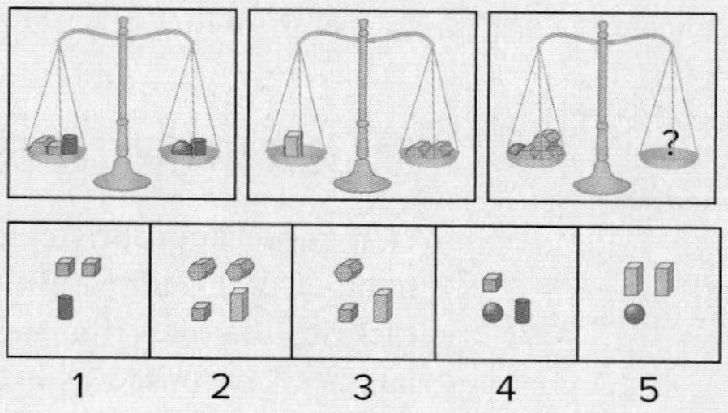
Matrix reasoning	Test spatial reasoning	Test-taker must decide which of the five possibilities replaces the question mark and completes the sequence. 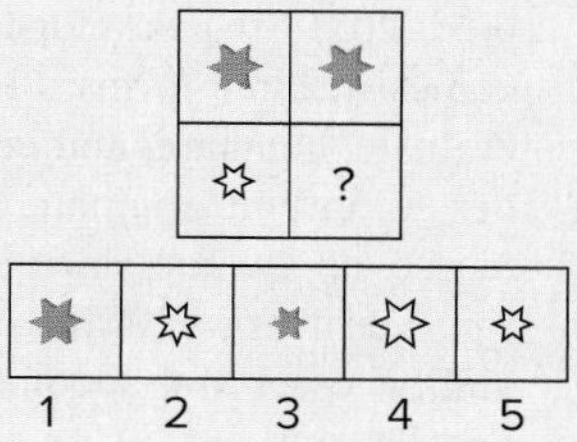
Block design item	Test understanding of relationship of parts to whole	Problems require test-takers to reproduce a design in fixed amount of time. 

FIGURE 12

SAMPLE SUBSCALES OF THE WECHSLER ADULT INTELLIGENCE SCALE–FOURTH EDITION (WAIS-IV). The Wechsler includes 11 subscales: 6 verbal and 5 nonverbal. Six of the subscales are shown here.

Source: Pearson Education, Inc., "Wechsler Adult Intelligence Scale-Fourth Edition (WAIS-IV)."

of strengths and weaknesses in different areas of the student's intelligence. The WISC-V now not only provides an overall IQ score but also yields five composite scores (Verbal Comprehension, Working Memory, Processing Speed, Fluid Reasoning, and Visual Spatial) (Canivez, Watkins, & Dombowski, 2017). These scores allow the examiner to quickly see whether the individual is strong or weak in different areas of intelligence. The Wechsler also includes 16 verbal and nonverbal subscales. Three of the Wechsler subscales are shown in Figure 12.

Using Intelligence Tests Psychological tests are tools. Like all tools, their effectiveness depends on the knowledge, skill, and integrity of the user. A hammer can be used to build a beautiful kitchen cabinet, or it can be used as a weapon of assault. Like a hammer, psychological tests can be used for positive purposes or they can be badly abused. Here are some cautions about IQ that can help you avoid the pitfalls of using information about an adolescent's intelligence in negative ways:

- *Avoid stereotyping and expectations.* A special concern is that the scores on an IQ test easily can lead to stereotypes and expectations about adolescents. Sweeping generalizations are too often made on the basis of an IQ score. An IQ test should always be considered a measure of current performance. It is not a measure of fixed potential. Maturational changes and enriched environmental experiences can advance an adolescent's intelligence.
- *Know that IQ is not a sole indicator of competence.* Another concern about IQ tests occurs when they are used as the main or sole assessment of competence. A high IQ is not the ultimate human value. It is important to consider not only students' competence in such areas as verbal skills but also their practical skills, their relationship skills, and their moral values.

MULTIPLE INTELLIGENCES

Is it more appropriate to think of an adolescent's intelligence as a general ability or as a number of specific abilities? Robert Sternberg and Howard Gardner have proposed influential theories that describe specific types of intelligence. The concept of emotional intelligence also has been proposed as a type of intelligence that differs from what is measured by traditional intelligence tests.

Sternberg's Triarchic Theory Robert J. Sternberg (1986, 2004, 2010, 2015, 2020a, b, c, 2021a, b) developed the **triarchic theory of intelligence,** which states that intelligence comes in three forms: (1) *analytical intelligence*, which refers to the ability to analyze, judge, evaluate, compare, and contrast; (2) *creative intelligence*, which consists of the ability to create, design, invent, originate, and imagine; and (3) *practical intelligence*, which involves the ability to use, apply, implement, and put ideas into practice.

Sternberg (2021a, b) emphasizes that successful intelligence involves an individual's ability to set and accomplish personally meaningful goals. A person does this by exploring and figuring out his or her strengths and weaknesses, then capitalizing on the strengths and correcting or improving on the weaknesses. An individual needs to analyze these strengths and weaknesses in the three domains of intelligence just discussed—analytical, creative, and practical. In addition, recently Sternberg has argued that a fourth domain—wisdom—should be considered, especially in terms of doing the right thing and making ethical decisions that take into account the common good. Recall our discussion of his view of wisdom earlier in this chapter.

Sternberg (2021a, b) says that students with different triarchic patterns perform differently in school. Students with high analytic ability tend to be favored in conventional schools. They usually do well in classes where the teacher lectures and gives objective tests. They often are considered smart students, typically get good grades, do well on traditional IQ tests and the SAT, and later gain admission to competitive colleges.

Students who are high in creative intelligence often are not in the top rung of their class. Creatively intelligent students might not conform to the expectations that teachers have about how assignments should be done. They give unique answers, for which they might get reprimanded or marked down.

Like students high in creative intelligence, students who are high in practical intelligence often do not relate well to the demands of school. However, these students frequently do well outside the classroom's walls. Their social skills and common sense may allow them to become successful managers, entrepreneurs, or politicians, despite undistinguished school records.

Robert J. Sternberg, who developed the triarchic theory of intelligence.
Courtesy of Dr. Robert Sternberg

triarchic theory of intelligence Sternberg's view that intelligence comes in three main forms: analytical, creative, and practical.

Gardner's Eight Frames of Mind Howard Gardner (1983, 1993, 2002, 2016) has proposed eight types of intelligence, or "frames of mind." These are described here, with examples of the types of vocations in which they are regarded as strengths (Campbell, Campbell, & Dickinson, 2004):

- *Verbal.* The ability to think in words and use language to express meaning (occupations: authors, journalists, speakers)
- *Mathematical.* The ability to carry out mathematical operations (occupations: scientists, engineers, accountants)
- *Spatial.* The ability to think three-dimensionally (occupations: architects, artists, sailors)
- *Bodily-kinesthetic.* The ability to manipulate objects and be physically adept (occupations: surgeons, craftspeople, dancers, athletes)
- *Musical.* A sensitivity to pitch, melody, rhythm, and tone (occupations: composers, musicians)
- *Interpersonal.* The ability to understand and effectively interact with others (occupations: successful teachers, mental health professionals)
- *Intrapersonal.* The ability to understand oneself (occupations: theologians, psychologists)
- *Naturalist:* The ability to observe patterns in nature and understand natural and human-made systems (occupations: farmers, botanists, ecologists, landscapers)

Which of Gardner's eight intelligences are adolescent boys using in this situation?
John Kelly/Stone/Getty Images

According to Gardner, everyone has all of these intelligences but to varying degrees. As a result, we prefer to learn and process information in different ways. People learn best when they can apply their strong intelligences to the task at hand.

Both Gardner's and Sternberg's theories include one or more categories related to social intelligence. In Gardner's theory, the categories are interpersonal intelligence and intrapersonal intelligence, while Sternberg's theory includes the category of practical intelligence. Another theory that emphasizes interpersonal, intrapersonal, and practical aspects of intelligence is called **emotional intelligence,** an idea popularized by Daniel Goleman (1995) in his book *Emotional Intelligence.* The concept of emotional intelligence was initially developed by Peter Salovey and John Mayer (1990), who defined it as the ability to perceive and express emotion accurately and adaptively (such as taking the perspective of others), to understand emotion and emotional knowledge (such as understanding the roles that emotions play in friendship and marriage), to use feelings to facilitate thought (such as being in a positive mood, which is linked to creative thinking), and to manage emotions in oneself and others (such as being able to control one's anger). In one study, assessment of emotional intelligence predicted high school students' final grades in their courses (Gil-Olarte Marquez, Palomera Martin, & Brackett, 2006).

There continues to be considerable interest in the concept of emotional intelligence (Dave & others 2021; Di Fabio & Saklofske, 2021; Romera-Mesa, Pelaez-Fernandez, & Extremera, 2021). A study of college students revealed that scores on both a general mental abilities test and an emotional intelligence assessment were linked to academic performance, although the general mental abilities test was a better predictor of success (Song & others, 2010). And in a recent meta-analysis, emotional intelligence was the third best predictor of academic performance, following general intelligence and the personality trait of conscientiousness (MacCann & others, 2020). However, critics argue that too often emotional intelligence broadens the concept of intelligence too far and that its accuracy has not been adequately assessed and researched (Matthews, Zeidner, & Roberts, 2011).

emotional intelligence The ability to perceive and express emotion accurately and adaptively, to understand emotion and emotional knowledge, to use feelings to facilitate thought, and to manage emotions in oneself and others.

Do People Have One or Many Intelligences?

Figure 13 provides a comparison of Sternberg's, Gardner's, and Mayer/Salovey/Goleman's views of intelligence. Notice that Sternberg's view is unique in emphasizing creative intelligence and that Gardner's includes a number of types of intelligence that are not addressed by the other views. These theories of multiple intelligences have much to offer. They have stimulated us to think more broadly about what makes up people's intelligence and competence (Gardner, 2016; Sternberg, 2021a, b). And they have motivated educators to develop programs that instruct students in different domains (Kornhaber, 2020).

Theories of multiple intelligences have their critics (Bouchard, 2018). Some critics argue that the research base to support these theories has not yet developed. In particular, critics say that Gardner's classification seems arbitrary. For example, if musical skills represent a type of intelligence, why don't we also refer to chess intelligence, prize-fighter intelligence, and so on?

Sternberg	Gardner	Mayer/ Salovey/Goleman
Analytical	Verbal Mathematical	
Creative	Spatial Movement Musical	
Practical	Interpersonal Intrapersonal	Emotional
	Naturalistic	

FIGURE 13

COMPARISON OF STERNBERG'S, GARDNER'S, AND MAYER/SALOVEY/GOLEMAN'S VIEWS

A number of psychologists still support the concept of *g* (general intelligence) (Bouchard, 2018). For example, in a recent survey of 102 experts on intelligence around the world, most supported the concept of *g* (Rindermann, Becker, & Coyle, 2020). One expert on intelligence, Nathan Brody (2007) argues that people who excel at one type of intellectual task are likely to excel in other intellectual tasks. Thus, individuals who do well at memorizing lists of digits are also likely to be good at solving verbal problems and spatial layout problems. This general intelligence includes abstract reasoning or thinking, the capacity to acquire knowledge, and problem-solving ability (Brody, 2007).

Advocates of the concept of general intelligence point to its accuracy in predicting school and job success. For example, scores on tests of general intelligence are substantially correlated with school grades and achievement test performance, both at the time of the test and years later (Sackett, Shewach, & Dahlke, 2020). In addition, a recent meta-analysis of 240 independent samples and more than 100,000 individuals found a correlation of +.54 between intelligence and school grades (Roth & others, 2015).

Some experts who argue for the existence of general intelligence conclude that individuals also have specific intellectual abilities (Hunt, 2011). In one study, John Carroll (1993) conducted an extensive examination of intellectual abilities and concluded that all intellectual abilities are related to each other, a view that supports the concept of general intelligence, but he also pointed out that there are many specialized abilities as well. Some of these specialized abilities, such as spatial abilities and mechanical abilities, are not adequately reflected in the curricula of most schools. In sum, controversy still surrounds the question of whether it is more accurate to conceptualize intelligence as a general ability, as specific abilities, or as both. Sternberg (2021a, b) actually accepts that there is a *g* in the kinds of analytical tasks that traditional IQ tests assess but thinks that the range of intellectual tasks those tests measure is too narrow.

THE NEUROSCIENCE OF INTELLIGENCE

In the current era of extensive research on the brain, interest in the neurological underpinnings of intelligence has increased (Barbey, Karama, & Haier, 2021; Haier, 2020; Martinez & Colom, 2021). Among the questions about the brain's role in intelligence that are being explored are these: Is having a bigger brain linked to higher intelligence? Is intelligence located in certain brain regions? Is the speed at which the brain processes information linked to intelligence? We will examine each of these questions next.

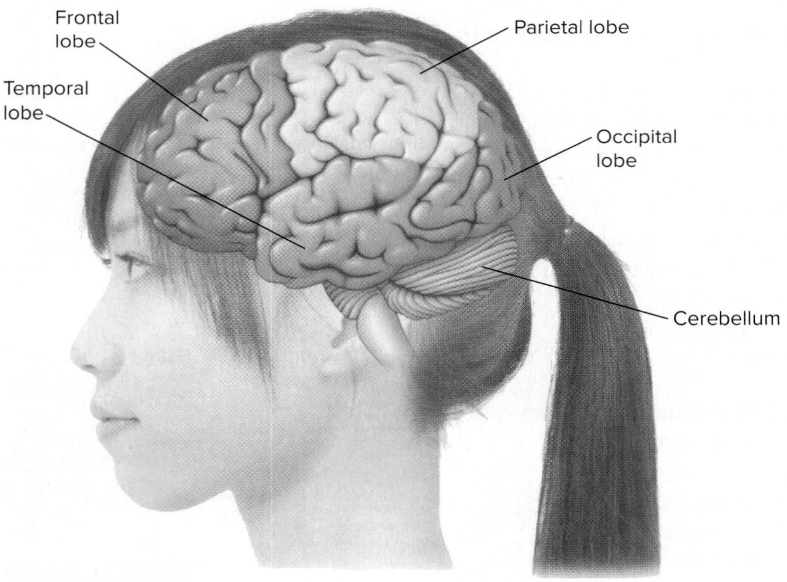

Are individuals with bigger brains more intelligent than those with smaller brains? Studies using MRI scans to assess total brain volume indicate a moderate correlation (about .3 to .4) between brain size and intelligence (Carey, 2007; Luders & others, 2009).

Might intelligence be linked to specific regions of the brain? Early consensus was that the frontal lobes are the likely location of intelligence. However, subsequent researchers have found that intelligence is distributed across brain regions (Cohen & D'Esposito, 2021; Kundu & Risk, 2021). The most prominent finding from brain-imaging studies is that a distributed neural network involving the frontal and parietal lobes is related to higher intelligence (Haier, 2020) (see Figure 14). An autopsy revealed that Albert Einstein's total brain size was average, but a region of his brain's parietal lobe that is very active in processing math and spatial information was 15 percent larger than average (Witelson, Kigar, & Harvey, 1999). Other brain regions that have been linked to higher intelligence (although at a lower level of significance than the frontal/parietal lobe network) include the temporal and occipital lobes as well as the cerebellum (Luders & others, 2009).

FIGURE **14**

INTELLIGENCE AND THE BRAIN. Researchers have found that a higher level of intelligence is linked to a distributed neural network in the frontal and parietal lobes. To a lesser extent than the frontal/parietal network, the temporal and occipital lobes, as well as the cerebellum, also are linked to intelligence. The current consensus is that intelligence is likely to be distributed across brain regions rather than being localized in a specific region such as the frontal lobes.
(photo): Takayuki/Shutterstock

Examining the neuroscience of intelligence has also led to study of the role that neurological speed might play in intelligence (Waiter & others, 2009). Research results have not been consistent for this possible link, although one study found that children who are gifted showed faster processing speed and more accurate processing of information than children who are not gifted (Duan, Dan, & Shi, 2014).

As technological advances allow closer study of the brain's functioning in coming decades, we are likely to see more specific conclusions about the brain's role in intelligence. As this research proceeds, keep in mind that both heredity and environment likely contribute to links between the brain and intelligence, including the connections we discussed between brain size and intelligence (Barbey, Karama, & Haier, 2021).

HEREDITY AND ENVIRONMENT

An ongoing issue involving intelligence is the extent to which it is due to heredity or to environment. It is difficult to tease apart these influences, but that has not kept psychologists from trying to untangle them (Kamatani, 2021).

Heredity   Some psychologists argue that the effect of heredity on intelligence is strong (Kamatani, 2021). However, most research on heredity and environment does not include environments that differ radically. Thus, it is not surprising that many studies of heredity, environment, and intelligence show environment to be a fairly weak influence on intelligence.

One strategy for examining the role of heredity in intelligence is to compare the IQs of identical and fraternal twins. Identical twins have exactly the same genetic makeup, but fraternal twins do not. If intelligence is genetically determined, say some investigators, identical twins' IQs should be more similar than the intelligence of fraternal twins. Researchers have found that the IQs of identical twins are more similar than those of fraternal twins, but in some studies the difference is not very large (Grigorenko, 2000) (see Figure 15). And genetic influences may be more influential in some aspects of life than others. For example, researchers have found that genes are much more strongly linked to scientific achievement than to artistic achievement (de Manzano & Ullen, 2018).

Environment   Although genetic endowment influences a child's intellectual ability, the environmental experiences of children do make a difference (Mayer, 2020). One of the ways researchers have studied environmental influences on intelligence is to examine changes in IQ when certain groups of individuals experience improved conditions in their lives. For example, a research analysis found a 12- to 18-point increase in IQ scores when children are adopted from low-income families into middle- and upper-income families (Nisbett & others, 2012). Further, as African Americans have gained social, economic, and educational opportunities, the gap between African Americans and non-Latinx whites on standardized intelligence tests has begun to narrow (Daley & Onwuegbuzie, 2020). An earlier research review concluded that the IQ gap between African Americans and non-Latinx whites has diminished considerably in recent years (Nisbett & others, 2012). Further, it still is important to emphasize that the ethnic intelligence gap that has existed, and continues to exist, is influenced by racism and discrimination (such as reduced family wealth, segregation of schools, less access to healthcare, and lower teacher expectations for minority group children and adolescents).

Another potential influence on intelligence test performance is **stereotype threat,** which refers to anxiety that one's behavior might confirm a negative stereotype about one's group (Chin & others, 2020). For example, when African Americans take an intelligence test, they may experience anxiety about confirming an old stereotype that Blacks are "intellectually inferior." Some studies have confirmed the existence of stereotype threat (Wasserberg, 2014). Also, African American students do more poorly on standardized tests if they perceive that they are being evaluated. If they think the test doesn't count, they perform as well as white students (Aronson, 2002). However, some critics argue that the extent to which stereotype threat explains the testing gap has been exaggerated (Sackett, Borneman, & Connelly, 2009).

Another way to study the environment's influence on intelligence is to compare adolescents who have experienced different amounts of schooling (Mayer, 2020). The biggest effects have been found when large groups of children received no formal education for an extended

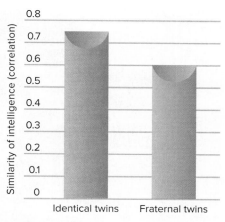

FIGURE 15

CORRELATION BETWEEN INTELLIGENCE TEST SCORES AND TWIN STATUS. The graph represents a summary of research findings that have compared the intelligence test scores of identical and fraternal twins. An approximate 0.15 difference has been found, with a higher correlation for identical twins (0.75) and a lower correlation for fraternal twins (0.60).

stereotype threat Anxiety that one's behavior might conform to a negative stereotype about one's group.

How does education influence intelligence?
Christopher Robbins/Image Source

period, resulting in lower intelligence. In a recent Danish study, IQ test scores were positively associated with educational attainment in early and middle adulthood (Hegelund & others, 2020). Also in this study, individuals with low intelligence in childhood benefited the most from education.

Another possible effect of education can be seen in rapidly increasing IQ test scores around the world (Flynn, 2013, 2018, 2020). IQ scores have been increasing so rapidly that a high percentage of people regarded as having average intelligence at the turn of the century would be considered below average in intelligence today (see Figure 16). If a representative sample of people today took the Stanford-Binet test used in 1932, about one-fourth would be defined as having very superior intelligence, a label usually accorded to fewer than 3 percent of the population. Because the increase has taken place in a relatively short time, it can't be due to heredity, but rather may be due to increasing levels of education attained by a much greater percentage of the world's population or to other environmental factors such as the explosion of information to which people are exposed (Flynn, 2020). The worldwide increase in intelligence test scores that has occurred over a short time frame has been called the *Flynn effect* after the researcher who discovered it, James Flynn (2018, 2020).

Although rising intelligence test scores have been found in most countries in which cohort effects on intelligence have been assessed, a decrease in intelligence test scores has been found in Scandinavian countries (Finland, Norway, Denmark, and Norway) beginning in about 1995 (Dutton & Lynn, 2013; Ronnlund & others, 2013). Explanations of the IQ decline focus on technological advances, such as television, smartphones, and social media, as well as weakening education systems. However, IQ gains continue to occur in the United States and most developing countries (Flynn, 2020). For example, in a recent study in the Sudanese capital of Khartoum, IQ scores increased by 10 points from 2004 to 2016 (Dutton & others, 2018). And in another study, IQ scores increased slightly more than 5 points from 2003 to 2018 in Romania (Gunnesch-Luca & Iliescu, 2020).

Heredity and Environment Interaction   Today, most researchers agree that genetics and environment interact to influence intelligence (Grigorenko & Burenkova, 2020). For many adolescents, this means that positive modifications in environment can change their IQ scores considerably. Although genetic endowment may always influence adolescents' intellectual ability, the environmental influences and opportunities provided to children and adolescents do make a difference (Schiariti, Simeonsson, & Hall, 2021).

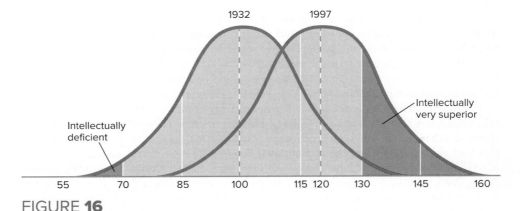

FIGURE **16**

THE INCREASE IN IQ SCORES FROM 1932 TO 1997. As measured by the Stanford-Binet intelligence test, American children and adolescents seem to be getting smarter. Scores of a group tested in 1932 fell along a bell-shaped curve, with half below 100 and half above. Studies show that if children and adolescents took that same test today, half would score above 120 on the 1932 scale. Very few of them would score in the "intellectually deficient" end, on the left side, and about one-fourth would rank in the "very superior" range.

Review *Connect* Reflect

LG4 Summarize the psychometric/intelligence view of adolescence.

Review
- What is intelligence? What are the main individual tests of intelligence? What are some strategies for interpreting intelligence test scores?
- What theories of multiple intelligences have been developed? Do people have one intelligence or many intelligences?
- What are some links between the brain and intelligence?
- What roles do heredity and environment play in intelligence?

Connect
- Compare creative and critical thinking.

Reflect *Your Own Personal Journey of Life*
- Apply Gardner's, Sternberg's, and Mayer/Salovey/Goleman's categories of intelligence to yourself as an adolescent and emerging adult. Write a description of yourself based on each of these views.

5 Social Cognition   **LG5** Explain how social cognition is involved in adolescent development.

| Adolescent Egocentrism | Social Cognition in the Remainder of This Edition |

Social cognition refers to the way individuals conceptualize and reason about their social worlds—the people they watch and interact with, their relationships with those people, the groups they participate in, and the way they reason about themselves and others. Our discussion will focus on adolescent egocentrism and on our coverage of social cognition in the remainder of this edition.

ADOLESCENT EGOCENTRISM

Adolescent egocentrism is the heightened self-consciousness of adolescents, which is reflected in their belief that others are as interested in them as they are in themselves, and in their sense of personal uniqueness and invulnerability. David Elkind (1976) argues that adolescent egocentrism can be dissected into two types of social thinking—imaginary audience and personal fable.

The *imaginary audience* refers to the aspect of adolescent egocentrism that involves attention-getting behavior—the attempt to be noticed, visible, and "onstage." An adolescent boy might think that others are as aware of a few hairs that are out of place as he is. An adolescent girl walks into her classroom and thinks that all eyes are riveted on her complexion. Adolescents especially sense that they are onstage in early adolescence, believing they are the main actors and all others are the audience. You may recall the story about Tracy at the beginning of this chapter. Tracy was exhibiting adolescent egocentrism when she perceived that every person in the restaurant was looking at her single out-of-place hair.

According to Elkind, the *personal fable* is the part of adolescent egocentrism that involves an adolescent's sense of personal uniqueness and invulnerability. Adolescents' sense of personal uniqueness makes them feel that no one can understand how they really feel. For example, an adolescent girl may think that her mother cannot possibly sense the hurt she feels because her boyfriend has broken up with her. As part of their effort to retain a sense of personal uniqueness, adolescents might craft stories about themselves that are filled with fantasy, immersing themselves in a world that is far removed from reality. Personal fables frequently show up in adolescent diaries.

Elkind (1985) argued that the imaginary audience and personal fable reflect the cognitive egocentrism involved in the transition to formal operational thought. However, Daniel Lapsley and his colleagues (Hill, Duggan, & Lapsley, 2012; Lapsley & Stey, 2012) conclude that the distortions in the imaginary audience and personal fable involve the adolescent's ego. As adolescents increasingly develop their own self and identity apart from their parents, their personal fable ideation likely reflects an adaptive narcissism that supports their ego.

social cognition The way individuals conceptualize and reason about their social worlds—the people they watch and interact with, their relationships with those people, the groups they participate in, and the way they reason about themselves and others.

adolescent egocentrism The heightened self-consciousness of adolescents, which is reflected in their belief that others are as interested in them as they themselves are, and in their sense of personal uniqueness and invulnerability.

Are Social Media an Amplification Tool for Adolescent Egocentrism?

Are teens drawn to social media to express their imaginary audience and personal fable's sense of uniqueness? One analysis concluded that amassing a large number of friends (audience) on social media may help to validate adolescents' perception that everyone is watching them (Psychster Inc., 2010). Also, one study found that Facebook use does indeed increase self-interest (Chiou, Chen, & Liao, 2014). And a recent meta-analysis concluded that a greater use of social networking sites was linked to a higher level of narcissism (Gnambs & Appel, 2018).

A look at a teen's comments on Instagram or Snapchat may suggest to many adults that what teens are reporting is often rather mundane and uninteresting. Typical comments might include updates like the following: "Studying heavy. Not happy tonight." or "At Starbucks with Jesse. Lattes are great." Possibly for adolescents, though, such comments are not trivial but rather an expression of the personal fable's sense of uniqueness.

Might social media, such as Facebook, increase adolescent egocentrism?
Andrey_Popov/Shutterstock

What do you think? Are social media, such as Facebook, Instagram, and Snapchat, amplifying the expression of adolescents' imaginary audience and their personal fable's sense of uniqueness? (Source: Psychster Inc., 2010)

Some developmentalists conclude that the sense of uniqueness and invincibility that egocentrism generates is responsible for some of the seemingly reckless behavior of adolescents, including drag racing, drug use, failure to use contraceptives during intercourse, and suicide (Dolcini & others, 1989). For example, one study found that eleventh- and twelfth-grade females who were high in adolescent egocentrism were more likely to say they would not get pregnant from engaging in sex without contraception than were their counterparts who were low in adolescent egocentrism (Arnett, 1990).

A study of sixth- through twelfth-graders examined whether aspects of the personal fable were linked to various aspects of adolescent adjustment (Aalsma, Lapsley, & Flannery, 2006). A sense of invulnerability was linked to engaging in risky behaviors such as smoking cigarettes, drinking alcohol, and engaging in acts of delinquency, whereas a sense of personal uniqueness was related to depression and suicidal thoughts. A subsequent study confirmed the findings of the first study in regard to the correlation between personal uniqueness, depression, and suicidal thoughts (Goossens & others, 2002).

These findings indicate that personal uniqueness fables should be treated as a risk factor for psychological problems, especially depression and suicidal tendencies in girls (Aalsma, Lapsley, & Flannery, 2006). Treating invulnerability as a risk factor for adjustment problems is less certain because in the earlier study just described (Aalsma, Lapsley, & Flannery, 2006), a sense of invulnerability was associated not only with risky behavior but also with some positive aspects of adjustment, such as coping and self-worth.

What characterizes adolescent egocentrism?
Image Source/Getty Images

An increasing number of research studies suggest that, rather than perceiving themselves to be invulnerable, adolescents tend to portray themselves as vulnerable to experiencing a premature death (Jamieson & Romer, 2008; Reyna & Rivers, 2008). For example, in one study, 12- to 18-year-olds were asked about their likelihood of dying in the next year and prior to age 20 (Fischhoff & others, 2010). The adolescents greatly overestimated their likelihood of dying.

In early research, Elkind found that adolescent egocentrism peaked in early adolescence and then declined (Elkind & Bowen, 1979). However, a study of more than 2,300 adolescents and emerging adults from 11 to 21 years of age revealed that adolescent egocentrism was still prominent in the 18- to 21-year-olds (emerging adults) and the results varied by gender (Schwartz, Maynard, & Uzelac, 2008). For example, emerging adult males scored higher on

How are personal uniqueness and invulnerability linked to adolescent adjustment and problems?
Jack Affleck/Getty Images

the imaginary audience scale than did males in late adolescence (15- to 18-year-olds), but no age differences on this scale occurred for females.

SOCIAL COGNITION IN THE REMAINDER OF THIS EDITION

Interest in social cognition has blossomed, and the approach has infiltrated many aspects of the study of adolescent development. In our overview of the self and identity in this book, we explore social cognition's role in the development of self-understanding and identity. In our evaluation of moral development, considerable time is devoted to discussing various social cognitive dimensions of morality. Further, in our discussion of families, the emerging cognitive abilities of the adolescent are evaluated in concert with parent-adolescent conflict and parenting strategies. Also, our description of peer relations highlights the importance of social knowledge and social information processing in peer relations.

In the chapter on "The Self, Identity, Emotion, and Personality," you will read extensively about the changes that occur in self-understanding during adolescence. As described in this chapter, the development of the brain coupled with advances in information processing provide a foundation for adolescent self-understanding, which gradually becomes more conscious and reflective.

developmental **connection**

Identity

Major changes in self-understanding take place in the adolescent years. Connect to "The Self, Identity, Emotion, and Personality."

Review *Connect* Reflect

LG5 Explain how social cognition is involved in adolescent development.

Review
- What characterizes adolescent egocentrism?
- How is social cognition related to other topics discussed in this text?

Connect
- Compare and contrast the concepts of the imaginary audience and the personal fable.

Reflect *Your Own Personal Journey of Life*
- Think about your friends in early adolescence, late adolescence, and emerging adulthood. Did adolescent egocentrism decline for all of them as they moved through late adolescence and emerging adulthood? Explain how it might especially be maladaptive if adolescent egocentrism continues to strongly characterize the outlook of individuals in emerging adulthood.

6 Language Development

LG6 Discuss key aspects of language development in adolescence.

Overview   Bilingualism   Writing

During adolescence, advances in cognitive development are linked to improvements in language development. Also, bilingualism is linked to improvement in many aspects of cognitive development in adolescence. And adolescence is a period of development when key aspects of writing skills develop.

OVERVIEW

Language development during adolescence includes greater sophistication in the use of words. With increasing ability to engage in abstract thinking, adolescents are much better than children at analyzing the role a word plays in a sentence. Adolescents also develop more subtle abilities with words. They make strides in understanding **metaphor,** which is an implied comparison between unlike things. For example, individuals "draw a line in the sand" to indicate a nonnegotiable position; a political campaign is said to be a marathon, not a sprint; a person's faith is shattered. And adolescents become better able to understand and apply **satire,** which is the use of irony, derision, or wit to expose folly or wickedness. Caricatures are an example of satire. More advanced logical thinking also allows individuals from about 15 to 20 years of age to begin understanding complex literary works.

Everyday speech changes during adolescence, and part of being a successful teenager is being able to talk like one. Young adolescents often speak a **dialect** with their peers that is characterized by jargon and slang. A dialect is a variety of language that is distinguished by its vocabulary, grammar, or pronunciation. For example, when meeting a friend, instead of saying hello, a young adolescent might say, "Sup?" ("What's up?"). Nicknames that are satirical and derisive ("Stilt," "Refrigerator," "Spaz") also characterize the dialect of young adolescents. Such labels might be used to show that one belongs to the group and to reduce the seriousness of a situation.

BILINGUALISM

Are there sensitive periods in learning a second language? That is, if individuals want to learn a second language, how important is the age at which they begin to learn it? For many years, it was claimed that if individuals did not learn a second language prior to puberty they would never reach native-language speakers' proficiency in the second language (Johnson & Newport, 1991). However, research suggests a more complex conclusion: Sensitive periods likely vary across different language systems (Thomas & Johnson, 2008). Thus, for late language learners, such as adolescents and adults, new vocabulary is easier to learn than new sounds or new grammar (Neville, 2006). For example, children's ability to pronounce words with a native-like accent in a second language typically decreases with age, with an especially sharp drop occurring after the age of about 10 to 12. Also, adolescents and adults tend to learn a second language faster than children do, but their final level of second-language attainment is not as high as children's.

Students in the United States lag far behind their counterparts in many developed countries in learning a second language. For example, in Russia, schools have 10 grades, called *forms,* which roughly correspond to the 12 grades in American schools. Russian children begin school at age 7 and begin learning English in the third form. Because of this emphasis on teaching English, most Russian adolescents and adults today are able to speak at least some English. The United States is the only technologically advanced Western nation that does not have a national foreign-language requirement at the high school level, even for students in rigorous academic programs.

Some aspects of children's and adolescents' ability to learn a second language are transferred more easily to the second language than others (Hernandez, Fernandez, & Aznar-Bese, 2019). Children and adolescents who are fluent in two languages perform better than their

metaphor An implied comparison between two unlike things.

satire The use of irony, derision, or wit to expose folly or wickedness.

dialect A variety of language that is distinguished by its vocabulary, grammar, or pronunciation.

single-language counterparts in control of attention, concept formation, analytical reasoning, inhibition, cognitive flexibility, cognitive complexity, and cognitive monitoring (Bialystok, 2011, 2015, 2017). Also, in a recent analysis across a number of countries, bilingual children and adolescents consistently demonstrated better executive function (Schirmbeck, Rao, & Maehler, 2020). In addition, bilingual children and adolescents are more conscious of the structure of spoken and written language and better at noticing errors of grammar and meaning, skills that benefit their reading ability (Kuo & Anderson, 2012).

Thus, it appears that bilingualism is linked to positive outcomes for children's and adolescents' cognitive development (Antovich & Graf Estes, 2020; Tao & others, 2021). However, some recent studies have not found cognitive advantages for bilingual children (Dick & others, 2019; Donnelly, Brooks, & Homer, 2019). Thus, a firm conclusion about cognitive outcomes of bilingualism awaits further research.

What are some of the outcomes for adolescents who speak two languages fluently?
Eye Ubiquitous/Alamy Stock Photo

WRITING

Most adolescents are much better writers than children are. They are better at organizing ideas before they write, at distinguishing between general and specific points as they write, at stringing together sentences that make sense, and at organizing their writing into an introduction, body, and concluding remarks. Adolescents also are better than children at persuasive writing in which they have to take a position and try to convince the reader of the accuracy and strength of their position (Nippold, 2016).

The metacognitive monitoring and strategies involved in being a competent writer are linked with those required to be a competent reader because the writing process involves competent reading and rereading during composition and revision (Longa & Graham, 2020). Further, researchers have found that strategy instruction involving planning, drafting, revising, and editing improves metacognitive awareness and writing competence (Graham & Harris, 2021).

There are increasing concerns about students' lack of writing competence (Graham & Rui, 2022; Vukelich & others, 2020). One study revealed that 70 to 75 percent of U.S. students in grades 4 through 12 are low-achieving writers (Persky, Dane, & Jin, 2003). Two studies—one of elementary school teachers, the other of high school teachers—raise concerns about the quality of writing instruction provided in U.S. schools (Gilbert & Graham, 2010; Kiuhara, Graham, & Hawken, 2009). The teachers in both studies reported that their college courses had inadequately prepared them to teach writing. The fourth- through sixth-grade teachers reported that they taught writing only 15 minutes a day. The high school teachers said that their writing assignments infrequently involved analysis and interpretation, and almost 50 percent of them had not assigned any multi-paragraph writing assignments in the past month.

Review Connect Reflect

LG6 Discuss key aspects of language development in adolescence.

Review
- Provide an overview of some key changes in language development during adolescence.
- What are outcomes of bilingualism in adolescence?
- Characterize some key aspects of writing in adolescence.

Connect
- What are some key aspects of cognitive development and information processing in adolescence discussed earlier in this chapter that are connected to the development of language competence?

Reflect *Your Own Personal Journey of Life*
- Think back to your own development through adolescence. How did your language development change in middle school and high school? How good was the quality of your teachers' writing instruction? Based on what you read here about language development in adolescence, are there aspects of writing skills, such as metacognitive strategies, that you think would have helped you become a better writer during your adolescent years?

The Brain and Cognitive Development

1 The Brain

 Describe the developmental changes in the brain during adolescence.

- The Neuroconstructivist View
- Neurons
- Brain Structure, Cognition, and Emotion
- Experience and Plasticity

- This increasingly popular view states that biological processes and environmental conditions influence the brain's development; the brain has plasticity; and cognitive development is closely linked with brain development.

- Neurons, the basic units of the nervous system, are made up of a cell body, dendrites, and an axon. Myelination is the process by which the axon portion of the neuron becomes covered and insulated with a layer of fat cells, which increases the speed and efficiency of information processing in the nervous system. Myelination continues to take place during adolescence. Synaptogenesis in the prefrontal cortex, where reasoning and self-regulation occur, also continues through adolescence.

- The corpus callosum, a large bundle of axon fibers that connects the brain's left and right hemispheres, thickens in adolescence, and this thickening improves the adolescent's ability to process information.

- The prefrontal cortex, the highest level of the frontal lobes that is involved in reasoning, decision making, and self-control, matures much later (continuing to develop in emerging adulthood) than the amygdala, the part of the limbic system that is the seat of emotions such as anger. The later development of the prefrontal cortex combined with the earlier maturity of the amygdala may explain the difficulty adolescents have in putting the brakes on their emotional intensity.

- Experience plays an important role in development of the brain in childhood and adolescence. Although early experiences are important influences on brain development, the brain retains considerable plasticity in adolescence. New brain cells may be generated during adolescence. The earlier brain injury occurs, the more successful recovery is likely to be.

2 The Cognitive Developmental View

 Discuss the cognitive developmental view of adolescence.

- Piaget's Theory

- Piaget's widely acclaimed theory stresses the concepts of adaptation, schemas, assimilation, accommodation, and equilibration. Piaget said that individuals develop through four cognitive stages: sensorimotor, preoperational, concrete operational, and formal operational. Formal operational thought, which Piaget expected to appear between 11 and 15 years of age, is characterized by abstract, idealistic, and hypothetical-deductive thinking. Some experts argue that formal operational thought has two phases: early and late. Individual variation in adolescent cognition is extensive. Many young adolescents are still consolidating their concrete operational thought or are early formal operational thinkers rather than full-fledged ones.

- Piaget's ideas have been applied to education. In terms of Piaget's contributions, we owe to him the entire field of cognitive development and a masterful list of concepts. He also was a genius at observing children. Criticisms of Piaget's theory focus on estimates of competence, stages, training to reason at higher stages, and the role of culture and education. Neo-Piagetians have proposed some substantial changes in Piaget's theory. Some experts argue that the idealism of Piaget's formal operational stage declines in young adults, being replaced by more realistic, pragmatic thinking. Perry said that adolescents often engage in dualistic, absolutist thinking, whereas young adults are more likely to think reflectively and relativistically. Postformal thought is reflective, relativistic, and contextual; provisional; realistic; open to emotions and subjective.

- Wisdom is expert knowledge about the practical aspects of life that permits excellent judgment about important matters. Baltes and his colleagues have found that high levels of wisdom are rare, the time frame of late adolescence and early adulthood is the main age window for wisdom to emerge, factors other than age are critical for a high level of wisdom to develop, and personality-related factors are better predictors of wisdom than cognitive factors such as intelligence. Sternberg argues that wisdom involves both academic and practical aspects of intelligence. His balance theory of wisdom emphasizes making competent decisions that take into account self-interest, the interests of others, and contexts to produce a common good. Sternberg argues that wisdom should be taught in schools.

Vygotsky's Theory

- Vygotsky's view stimulated considerable interest in the idea that knowledge is situated and collaborative. One of his important concepts is the zone of proximal development, which involves guidance by more skilled peers and adults. Vygotsky argued that learning the skills of the culture is a key aspect of development. Piaget's and Vygotsky's views are both constructivist, although Vygotsky developed a stronger social constructivist view than Piaget did. In both views, teachers should be facilitators, not directors, of learning. Criticisms of Vygotsky's view focus on facilitators possibly being too helpful and adolescents expecting others to do things for them.

3 The Information-Processing View Characterize the information-processing view of adolescence.

Cognitive Resources

- Capacity and speed of processing, often referred to as cognitive resources, increase across childhood and adolescence. Changes in the brain serve as biological foundations for developmental changes in cognitive resources. In terms of capacity, the increase is reflected in older children and adolescents being able to hold in mind simultaneously several dimensions of a topic. A reaction-time task has often been used to assess speed of processing. Processing speed continues to improve during adolescence.

Attention and Memory

- Attention is the focusing of mental resources. Adolescents typically have better attentional skills than children do, although there are wide individual differences in how effectively adolescents deploy their attention. Four ways that adolescents can allocate their attention are selective attention, divided attention, sustained attention, and executive attention. Multitasking is an example of divided attention, and it can harm adolescents' attention when they are engaging in a challenging task. Adolescents have better short-term memory, working memory, and long-term memory than children do.

Executive Function

- Higher-order cognitive processes such as exercising cognitive control, making decisions, reasoning, thinking critically, thinking creatively, and metacognition are often called executive function. Adolescence is characterized by a number of advances in executive function.

- Cognitive control involves aspects such as focusing attention, reducing interfering thoughts, and being cognitively flexible. Across childhood and adolescence, cognitive control (inhibition) increases with age, and this increase is likely due to maturation of the prefrontal cortex.

- Older adolescents make better decisions than younger adolescents, who in turn are better at this than children are. Being able to make competent decisions, however, does not mean adolescents will make such decisions in everyday life, where breadth of experience comes into play. Adolescents often make better decisions when they are calm than when they are emotionally aroused. Social contexts, especially the presence of peers, influence adolescent decision making.

- Critical thinking involves thinking reflectively and productively and evaluating the evidence. Mindfulness is an important aspect of thinking critically. Cognitive and physical training, such as mindfulness and yoga, are increasingly being recommended to improve adolescents' functioning. Adolescence is an important transitional period in critical thinking because it includes cognitive changes such as increased speed, automaticity, and capacity of information processing; more breadth of content knowledge; increased ability to construct new combinations of knowledge; and a greater range and spontaneous use of strategies.

- Thinking creatively is the ability to think in novel and unusual ways and discover unique solutions to problems. Guilford distinguished between convergent and divergent thinking. A number of strategies, including brainstorming, not overcontrolling, encouraging internal control, and introducing adolescents to creative people, can be used to stimulate creative thinking.

- An expert is the opposite of a novice (someone who is just beginning to learn a content area). Experts are better than novices at detecting features and meaningful patterns of information, accumulating more content knowledge and organizing it effectively, and retrieving important aspects of knowledge with little effort. Becoming an expert usually involves talent, deliberate practice, and motivation.

- Metacognition is cognition about cognition, or knowing about knowing. In Pressley's view, the key to education is helping students learn a rich repertoire of strategies that can be applied in solving problems. Adolescents' thinking skills benefit when they are taught general metacognitive skills and domain-specific thinking skills.

4 The Psychometric/Intelligence View

 LG4 Summarize the psychometric/intelligence view of adolescence.

Intelligence Tests

- Intelligence is the ability to solve problems and to adapt and learn from everyday experiences. A key aspect of intelligence focuses on its individual variations. Traditionally, intelligence has been measured by tests designed to compare people's performance on cognitive tasks. Alfred Binet developed the first intelligence test and created the concept of mental age. William Stern developed the concept of IQ for use with the Binet test. Revisions of the Binet test are called the Stanford-Binet. The test scores on the Stanford-Binet approximate a normal distribution. The Wechsler scales, created by David Wechsler, are the other main intelligence assessment tool. These tests provide an overall IQ and other composite scores, including the Working Memory Index and the Information Processing Speed Index. The single number provided by many IQ tests can lead to false expectations, and IQ test scores should be only one type of information used to evaluate an adolescent's capabilities.

Multiple Intelligences

- Sternberg's triarchic theory states that there are three main types of intelligence: analytical, creative, and practical. Gardner has proposed that there are eight types of intelligence: verbal, mathematical, spatial, bodily-kinesthetic, musical, interpersonal, intrapersonal, and naturalist. Emotional intelligence is the ability to perceive and express emotion accurately and adaptively, to understand emotion and emotional knowledge, to use feelings to facilitate thought, and to manage emotions in oneself and others.

- The multiple intelligences approaches have broadened the definition of intelligence and motivated educators to develop programs that instruct students in different domains. Critics maintain that the multiple intelligence theories have classifications that seem arbitrary and factors that are not aspects of intelligence, such as musical skills and creativity.

The Neuroscience of Intelligence

- Interest in discovering links between the brain and intelligence has been stimulated by advances in brain imaging. A moderate correlation has been found between brain size and intelligence. Some experts emphasize that the highest level of intelligence that involves reasoning is linked to the prefrontal cortex. However, other researchers recently have found a link between high intelligence and a distributed neural network in the frontal and parietal lobes. The search for a connection between neural processing speed and intelligence has produced mixed results.

Heredity and Environment

- Many studies show that by late adolescence intelligence is strongly influenced by heredity, but many of these studies do not reflect environments that are radically different. A well-documented environmental influence on intelligence is schooling. Also, probably because of increased education, intelligence test scores have risen considerably around the world in recent decades—a phenomenon called the Flynn effect—and this supports the role of environment in intelligence. In sum, intelligence is influenced by both heredity and environment.

5 Social Cognition

 LG5 Explain how social cognition is involved in adolescent development.

Adolescent Egocentrism

- Social cognition refers to how people conceptualize and reason about their social world, including the relation of the self to others. Adolescent egocentrism is adolescents' heightened self-consciousness, mirrored in their belief that others are as interested in them as they are. According to Elkind, adolescent egocentrism consists of an imaginary audience and a personal fable.

- Researchers have recently found that adolescents actually overestimate their chance of experiencing a premature death, indicating that they perceive themselves to be far less invulnerable than Elkind's personal fable indicates. An alternative to Elkind's cognitive egocentrism concept is the view that the imaginary audience and personal fable are mainly the result of changes in perspective taking and the adolescent's ego. Also, recently invulnerability has been described as having two dimensions—danger invulnerability and psychological invulnerability—which have different outcomes for adolescents.

Social Cognition in the Remainder of This Edition

- We study social cognition throughout this text, especially in chapters on the self and identity, moral development, peers, and families.

6 Language Development

 LG6 Discuss key aspects of language development in adolescence.

Overview

Bilingualism

Writing

- In adolescence, language changes include more effective use of words as well as improvements in the ability to understand metaphor, satire, and adult literary works.

- Recent research indicates a complex conclusion about whether there are sensitive periods in learning a second language. Children and adolescents who are fluent in two languages have more advanced information-processing skills than those who are not.

- Most adolescents are better writers than children. Development of metacognitive strategies is an important aspect of becoming a better writer in adolescence. Planning, drafting, editing, and revising are key metacognitive strategies for improving writing. There is considerable concern about deficits in the writing competence of adolescents today.

key **terms**

accommodation
adolescent egocentrism
amygdala
assimilation
attention
balance theory of wisdom
cognitive control
concrete operational stage
convergent thinking
corpus callosum
creativity
critical thinking
dialect
divergent thinking

divided attention
emotional intelligence
equilibration
executive attention
executive function
formal operational stage
fuzzy-trace theory dual-process
   model
hypothetical-deductive
   reasoning
intelligence
intelligence quotient (IQ)
limbic system
memory

mental age (MA)
metacognition
metaphor
myelination
neo-Piagetians
neuroconstructivist view
neurons
normal distribution
postformal thought
prefrontal cortex
preoperational stage
psychometric/intelligence
   view
satire

schema
selective attention
sensorimotor stage
social cognition
social constructivist
   approach
stereotype threat
sustained attention
synapses
theory of mind
triarchic theory of intelligence
wisdom
zone of proximal development
   (ZPD)

key **people**

Paul Baltes
Alfred Binet
Nathan Brody
Robbie Case
David Elkind
Jay Giedd

Daniel Goleman
J. P. Guilford
Mark Johnson
Deanna Kuhn
Gisela Labouvie-Vief
Ellen Langer
Daniel Lapsley

John Mayer
Charles Nelson
William Perry
Jean Piaget
Michael Pressley
Valerie Reyna
Peter Salovey

Elizabeth Sowell
Laurence Steinberg
William Stern
Robert Sternberg
Lev Vygotsky
David Wechsler

improving **the lives of adolescents and emerging adults**

The Adolescent Brain **(2017)**
Eveline Crone
New York: Routledge.
> Provides up-to-date coverage of the many changes that occur in the adolescent's brain, with extensive examples, applications, and connections to physical, cognitive, and socioemotional development.

Building Executive Function: The Missing Link to Student Achievement **(2018)**
Sandra Wiebe and Julia Karbach
New York: Routledge.
> An excellent application of the importance of executive function in educating children and adolescents. Includes recommendations for getting students to engage in a number of activities aimed at improving their executive function skills.

The Nature of Intelligence and Its Development in Childhood **(2021)**
Robert J. Sternberg
New York: Cambridge University Press.
> Leading intelligence expert Robert Sternberg provides a very up-to-date view of many aspects of children's and adolescents' intelligence.

The Neuroscience of Decision Making **(2014)**
Edited by Valerie Reyna and Vivian Zayas
Washington, DC: American Psychological Association
> Leading experts in such diverse areas as neuroscience, psychology, and behavioral economics explore research and social implications of risky decisions, with many applications to adolescent development.

ACT for Youth (www.actforyouth.net)
> ACT (Assets Coming Together) for Youth Center of Excellence connects research with practice to promote positive youth development. The center's website presents a number of videos and webinars on various aspects of adolescent development that provide excellent strategies for parents, teachers, and youth practitioners to improve adolescents' lives and help them make health-enhancing decisions.

chapter 4

THE SELF, IDENTITY, EMOTION, AND PERSONALITY

chapter **outline**

1 The Self

Learning Goal 1 Describe the development of the self in adolescence.

Self-Understanding and Understanding Others
Self-Esteem and Self-Concept
Self-Regulation

2 Identity

Learning Goal 2 Explain the many facets of identity development.

Erikson's Ideas on Identity
The Four Statuses of Identity
Developmental Changes in Identity
Identity and Social Contexts
Identity and Intimacy

3 Emotional Development

Learning Goal 3 Discuss the emotional development of adolescents.

The Emotions of Adolescence
Hormones, Experience, and Emotions
Emotion Regulation
Emotional Competence
Social-Emotional Education Programs

4 Personality Development

Learning Goal 4 Characterize the personality development of adolescents.

Personality
Temperament

Image Source

How do adolescents describe themselves? How would you have described yourself when you were 15 years old? What features of yourself would you have emphasized? Compared to when they were children, adolescents become much more self-reflective, asking themselves questions like "Who am I?" "What am I good at?" "What am I bad at?" and "What will my future be like?"

As they explore who they are, what they are all about, and what they might turn out to be, following are some adolescents' self-reflections:

"I'm not always sure who I am. One day I might say that I'm attractive, friendly, successful, and get along good with my friends, then another day I might say I'm ugly, shy, not doing well in life, and am having problems with my friends."

"A lot of people don't know what I'm really like, what my true self is. And I'm not always the same with different people. I might be shy on a date but outgoing with my friends. My parents really don't know me very well. My best friend and my sister know me a lot better than they do."

"I'm very self-conscious and get embarrassed easily. I'm afraid if I say the wrong thing, people won't like me and will make fun of me."

"I know I need to get good grades and want to get into a good college, but studying enough to do that keeps me from having a good time with my friends. It all seems so complicated, especially how to use my time."

"I've been spending too much time on Facebook lately. Last week, somebody said something that wasn't so nice on my Facebook page, so I keep looking at it in case I need to delete what someone says about me."

"I have started thinking more about what I want to be when I grow up, but I still really don't know for sure. I would like to do something that helps others, like a doctor or a nurse. And I love animals, so being a veterinarian might be in my future."

preview

These teenagers' self-portraits illustrate the increased self-reflection, identity exploration, and emotional changes that are among the hallmarks of adolescent development. Far more than children, adolescents seek to know who they are, what they are all about, and where they are going in life. In the first sections of this chapter, you will read about the self and identity, which are often considered to be central aspects of personality development in adolescence. Next, you will study emotional development in adolescence. Finally, you will explore the personality traits and temperaments of adolescents.

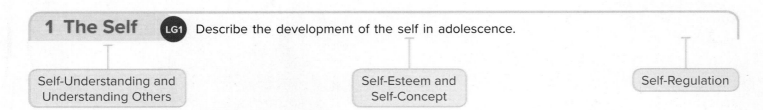

1 The Self **LG1** Describe the development of the self in adolescence.

Self-Understanding and Understanding Others

Self-Esteem and Self-Concept

Self-Regulation

The **self** consists of all the characteristics of a person. Theorists and researchers who focus on the self usually argue that the self is the central aspect of the individual's personality and that the self lends an integrative dimension to our understanding of different personality

self All of the characteristics of a person.

characteristics (Robinson & Sedikides, 2021). Several aspects of the self have been studied more than others. These include self-understanding and understanding others, self-esteem and self-concept, and self-regulation.

More so than children, adolescents carry with them a sense of who they are and what makes them different from everyone else. Consider one adolescent boy's self-description: "I am male, bright, an athlete, a political liberal, an extravert, and a compassionate individual." He takes comfort in his uniqueness: "No one else is quite like me. I am 5 feet 11 inches tall and weigh 160 pounds. I live in a suburb and plan to attend the state university. I want to be a sports journalist. I am an expert at building canoes. When I am not going to school and studying, I write short stories about sports figures, which I hope to publish someday." Real or imagined, an adolescent's developing sense of self and uniqueness is a motivating force in life. Our exploration of the self begins with information about adolescents' self-understanding and understanding others, then turns to their self-esteem and self-concept.

SELF-UNDERSTANDING AND UNDERSTANDING OTHERS

Although individuals become more introspective in adolescence and even more so in emerging adulthood, this self-understanding is not completely internal; rather, self-understanding is a social cognitive construction (Harter, 2006, 2012, 2013, 2016). That is, adolescents' and emerging adults' developing cognitive capacities interact with their sociocultural experiences to influence their self-understanding. These are among the questions you will explore in this section: What is self-understanding? What are some important dimensions of adolescents' and emerging adults' self-understanding? What developmental changes characterize understanding others?

What Is Self-Understanding? **Self-understanding** is the individual's cognitive representation of the self—the substance and content of self-conceptions. For example, a 12-year-old boy understands that he is a student, a football player, a family member, and a video game lover. A 14-year-old girl understands that she is a soccer player, a student council member, a movie lover, and a rock music fan. An adolescent's self-understanding is based, in part, on the various roles and membership categories that define who adolescents are (Harter, 2012). Although self-understanding provides the rational underpinnings, it is not the whole of personal identity.

Self-Understanding in Adolescence The development of self-understanding in adolescence is complex and involves a number of aspects of the self (Harter, 2006). Let's examine how the adolescent's self-understanding differs from the child's, then describe how self-understanding changes during emerging adulthood.

Abstraction and Idealism Remember from our discussion of Piaget's theory of cognitive development that many adolescents begin to think in more abstract and idealistic ways. When asked to describe themselves, adolescents are more likely than children to use abstract and idealistic terms. Consider 14-year-old Laurie's abstract description of herself: "I am a human being. I am indecisive. I don't know who I am." Also consider her idealistic description of herself: "I am a naturally sensitive person who really cares about people's feelings. I think I'm pretty good-looking." Not all adolescents describe themselves in idealistic ways, but most adolescents distinguish between the real self and the ideal self.

Differentiation Over time, an adolescent's self-understanding becomes increasingly *differentiated* (Harter, 2006, 2012, 2013, 2016). Adolescents are more likely than children to note contextual or situational variations when describing themselves (Harter, Waters, & Whitesell, 1996). For example, a 15-year-old girl might describe herself by using one set of characteristics in connection with her family and another set of characteristics in connection with her peers and friends. Yet another set of characteristics might appear in her self-description of her romantic relationship. In sum, adolescents are more likely than children to understand that they possess several different selves, each one to some degree reflecting a specific role or context.

Know thyself, for once we know ourselves, we may learn how to care for ourselves, but otherwise we never shall.

—SOCRATES
Greek Philosopher, 5th Century BC

developmental **connection**

Cognitive Theory

In Piaget's fourth stage of cognitive development, thought becomes more abstract, idealistic, and logical. Connect to "The Brain and Cognitive Development."

self-understanding The individual's cognitive representation of the self; the substance and content of self-conceptions.

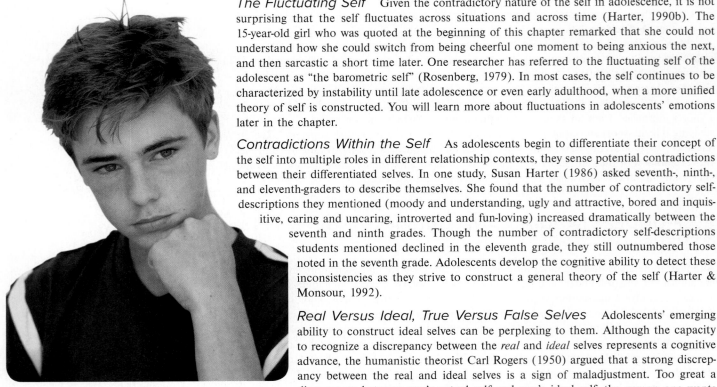

The Fluctuating Self   Given the contradictory nature of the self in adolescence, it is not surprising that the self fluctuates across situations and across time (Harter, 1990b). The 15-year-old girl who was quoted at the beginning of this chapter remarked that she could not understand how she could switch from being cheerful one moment to being anxious the next, and then sarcastic a short time later. One researcher has referred to the fluctuating self of the adolescent as "the barometric self" (Rosenberg, 1979). In most cases, the self continues to be characterized by instability until late adolescence or even early adulthood, when a more unified theory of self is constructed. You will learn more about fluctuations in adolescents' emotions later in the chapter.

Contradictions Within the Self   As adolescents begin to differentiate their concept of the self into multiple roles in different relationship contexts, they sense potential contradictions between their differentiated selves. In one study, Susan Harter (1986) asked seventh-, ninth-, and eleventh-graders to describe themselves. She found that the number of contradictory self-descriptions they mentioned (moody and understanding, ugly and attractive, bored and inquisitive, caring and uncaring, introverted and fun-loving) increased dramatically between the seventh and ninth grades. Though the number of contradictory self-descriptions students mentioned declined in the eleventh grade, they still outnumbered those noted in the seventh grade. Adolescents develop the cognitive ability to detect these inconsistencies as they strive to construct a general theory of the self (Harter & Monsour, 1992).

What are some characteristics of self-understanding in adolescence?
Jupiterimages/Getty Images

Real Versus Ideal, True Versus False Selves   Adolescents' emerging ability to construct ideal selves can be perplexing to them. Although the capacity to recognize a discrepancy between the *real* and *ideal* selves represents a cognitive advance, the humanistic theorist Carl Rogers (1950) argued that a strong discrepancy between the real and ideal selves is a sign of maladjustment. Too great a discrepancy between one's actual self and one's ideal self—the person one wants to be—can produce a sense of failure and self-criticism and can even trigger depression.

Although some theorists consider a strong discrepancy between the ideal and real selves maladaptive, others argue that it need not always be so, especially in adolescence. In one view, an important aspect of the ideal or imagined self is the **possible self:** what individuals might become, what they would like to become, and what they are afraid of becoming (Markus & Nurius, 1986). Thus, adolescents' possible selves include both what they hope to be as well as what they fear they could become (Wainwright, Nee, & Vrij, 2018). In this view, the presence of both hoped-for and feared ideal selves is psychologically healthy, lending balance to an adolescent's perspective and motivation. That is, the attributes of the future positive self—getting into a good college, being admired, having a successful career—can direct an adolescent's positive actions, whereas the attributes of the future negative self—being unemployed, feeling lonely, not getting into a good college—can identify behaviors to be avoided. One study of Hong Kong secondary school students found that the main content of hoped-for possible selves focused on school and career (Zhu & others, 2014). In this study, girls had more strategies to attain their positive selves than did boys. And a recent study found that adolescents who perceived their family functioning in positive terms had more positive possible selves (Molina & Schmidt, 2020).

possible self What individuals might become, what they would like to become, and what they are afraid of becoming.

Can adolescents distinguish between their *true* and *false* selves? In one research study, they could (Harter & Lee, 1989). Adolescents are most likely to show their false selves with classmates and in romantic or dating situations; they are least likely to show their false selves with close friends. Adolescents may display a false self to impress others or to try out new behaviors or roles. They may feel that others do not understand their true selves or that others force them to behave in false ways. Some adolescents report that they do not like their false-self behavior, but others say that it does not bother them. One study found that experienced authenticity of the self is highest among adolescents who say they receive support from their parents (Harter, Stocker, & Robinson, 1996).

What characterizes adolescents' possible selves?
Elisabeth Schmitt/Getty Images

Social Comparison   Young adolescents are more likely than children to compare themselves with others and to understand that others are comparing themselves with them (Sebastian, Burnett, & Blakemore, 2010). An individual's beliefs about how he or she is viewed by others are referred to as the *looking glass* self. However, most adolescents are unwilling to

How does self-consciousness change as individuals go through adolescence?
(left): Alys Tomlinson/Image Source; (right): Randy Faris/Getty Images

admit that they engage in social comparison because they view social comparison as socially undesirable. That is, they think that acknowledging their social comparison motives will endanger their popularity. Relying on social comparison information can be confusing to adolescents because of the large number of reference groups available to them. Should adolescents compare themselves to classmates in general? To friends of their own gender? To popular adolescents, good-looking adolescents, athletic adolescents? Considering all of these social comparison groups simultaneously can be perplexing for adolescents.

Self-Consciousness   Adolescents are more likely than children to be *self-conscious* about, and preoccupied with, their self-understanding (Harter, 2006). Although adolescents become more introspective, they do not always develop their self-understanding in social isolation. Adolescents turn to their friends for support and self-clarification, seeking out their friends' opinions in shaping their emerging self-definitions. As one researcher on self-development commented, adolescents' friends are often the main source of reflected self-appraisals, the social mirror into which adolescents anxiously stare (Rosenberg, 1979).

Self-Protection   In adolescence, the sense of confusion and conflict that is stimulated by efforts to understand oneself is accompanied by a need to *protect the self*. In an attempt to protect the self, adolescents are prone to deny their negative characteristics. For example, in Harter's investigation of self-understanding, adolescents were more likely than not to see positive self-descriptions such as *attractive, fun-loving, sensitive, affectionate*, and *inquisitive* as central, important aspects of the self, and to see negative self-descriptions such as *ugly, mediocre, depressed, selfish,* and *nervous* as peripheral, less important aspects of the self (Harter, 1986). This tendency is consistent with adolescents' tendency to describe themselves in idealistic ways.

The Unconscious Self   In adolescence, self-understanding involves greater recognition that the self includes unconscious as well as conscious components. This recognition is not likely to occur until late adolescence, however. That is, older adolescents are more likely than younger adolescents to believe that certain aspects of their mental experience are beyond their awareness or control.

Not Quite Yet a Coherent, Integrated Self   Because of the proliferation of selves and unrealistic self-portraits during adolescence, the task of integrating these varying self-conceptions becomes problematic (Harter, 2006, 2012, 2016). Only later, usually in emerging adulthood, do individuals successfully integrate the many aspects of the self.

When I say "I," I mean something absolutely unique, not to be confused with any other.

—Ugo Betti
Italian Playwright, 20th Century

How does self-understanding change in emerging adulthood?
Peter Cade/Photodisc/Getty Images

Self-Understanding in Emerging Adult-hood and Early Adulthood In emerging adulthood, self-understanding becomes more integrative, with the disparate parts of the self pieced together more systematically. Emerging adults may detect inconsistencies in their earlier self-descriptions as they attempt to construct a general theory of self, an integrated sense of identity.

Gisela Labouvie-Vief (2006) concludes that considerable restructuring of the self can take place in emerging adulthood. She emphasizes that key aspects of self-development in emerging adulthood involve an increase in self-reflection and a decision about a specific worldview.

However, Labouvie-Vief (2006) argues that although emerging adults engage in more complex and critical thinking than they did when they were adolescents, many still have difficulty integrating their complex view of the world. She says this difficulty occurs because emerging adults are still easily influenced by their emotions, which can distort their thinking and cause them to be too self-serving and self-protective. In her research, it is not until 30 to 39 years of age that adults effectively develop a coherent, integrated worldview.

Self-Awareness An aspect of self-understanding that becomes especially important in emerging and early adulthood is *self-awareness*—that is, the extent to which an emerging adult is aware of his or her psychological makeup, including strengths and weaknesses. Many individuals do not have very good awareness of their psychological makeup and skills, as well as the causes of their weaknesses (Hull, 2012). For example, how aware are individuals that they are a good or bad listener, use the best strategies to solve personal problems, and are assertive rather than aggressive or passive in resolving conflicts? Awareness of strengths and weaknesses in these and many other aspects of life is an important dimension of self-understanding throughout the adult years, and emerging adulthood is a time when individuals can benefit considerably from addressing some of their weaknesses.

Possible Selves Another important aspect of self-understanding in emerging adulthood involves *possible selves* (Beck & Jackson, 2020). Possible selves are what individuals might become, what they would like to become, and what they are afraid of becoming (Tausen, Csordas, & Macrae, 2020). Emerging adults mention many possible selves that they would like to become and might become. Some of these are unrealistic, such as being happy all of the time and being very rich. As individuals get older, they often describe fewer possible selves and portray them in more concrete and realistic ways. By middle age, individuals frequently describe their possible selves in terms of areas of their life in which they already have performed well, such as "being good at my work" or "having a good marriage" (Cross & Markus, 1991).

Self-Understanding and Social Contexts You have learned that the adolescent's self-understanding can vary across relationships and social roles. Researchers have found that adolescents' portraits of themselves can differ depending on whether they are describing themselves when they are with their mother, father, close friend, romantic partner, or peer. They also can differ depending on whether they describe themselves in the role of student, athlete, or employee. Similarly, adolescents might create different selves depending on their ethnic and cultural background and experiences (Umana-Taylor & others, 2020).

The multiple selves of ethnically diverse youth reflect their experiences in navigating their multiple worlds of family, peers, school, and community (McKenzie, 2020). As U.S. youth from different ethnic backgrounds move from one culture to another, they can encounter barriers related to language, racism, gender, immigration, and poverty. In each of their different worlds, however, they also can find resources—in institutions, in other people, and in themselves. Youth who have difficulty moving between worlds can experience alienation from their

> The contemporary perspective on the self emphasizes the construction of multiple self-representations across different relational contexts.
>
> —SUSAN HARTER
>
> *Contemporary Developmental Psychologist, University of Denver*

school, family, or peers. This in turn can lead to other problems. However, youth who can navigate effectively between different worlds can develop bicultural or multicultural selves and become "culture brokers" for others.

Of course, becoming a competent adolescent involves not only understanding oneself but also understanding others (Bosacki & others, 2020; Crone & Fuligni, 2020). Among the aspects of understanding others that are important in adolescent development are perceiving others' traits and understanding multiple perspectives.

Perceiving Others' Traits   One way to study how adolescents perceive others' traits is to ask them to assess the extent to which others' self-reports are accurate. In one comparison of 6- and 10-year-olds, the 10-year-olds were much more skeptical about others' self-reports of their intelligence and social skills than the 6-year-olds were (Heyman & Legare, 2005). In this study, the 10-year-olds understood that other people at times may distort the truth about their own traits to make a better impression on others.

As adolescence proceeds, teenagers develop a more sophisticated understanding of others (Ojanen & Findley-Van Nostrand, 2020). They come to understand that other people are complex and have public and private faces (Harter, 2012).

What are some important aspects of social understanding in adolescence?
Thinkstock/Getty Images

Perspective Taking   **Perspective taking** is the ability to assume another person's perspective and understand his or her thoughts and feelings. Robert Selman (1980) proposed a developmental theory of changes in perspective taking that occur between 3 years and 15 years of age. These developmental changes begin with the egocentric viewpoint in early childhood and end with in-depth perspective taking in adolescence.

Only recently has research on perspective taking in adolescence taken hold (Lougheed, Main, & Helm, 2020). Following are the results of several research investigations on this topic. In a recent study of adolescents, their perspective taking skills were linked to how much they were willing to give to others, especially strangers (van de Groep, Zanolie, & Crone, 2020). In another study, young adolescent girls engaged in more social perspective taking than did boys, but they also experienced more empathic distress by taking on their friend's distress as their own than did boys (Smith & Rose, 2011). Further, research indicated that a lower level of perspective taking was linked to increased relational aggression (intentionally harming someone through strategies such as spreading vicious rumors) one year later in middle school students (Batanova & Loukas, 2011). And research found that adolescents who do not have good perspective taking skills were more likely to have difficulty in peer relations and engage in more aggressive behavior (Nilsen & Bacso, 2017).

Social Cognitive Monitoring   An important aspect of metacognition is cognitive monitoring, which can also be very helpful in social situations. As part of their increased awareness of themselves and others, adolescents monitor their social world more extensively than they did when they were children. Adolescents engage in a number of social cognitive monitoring activities on virtually a daily basis. An adolescent might think, "I would like to get to know this guy better, but he is not very open. Maybe I can talk to some other students about what he is like." Another adolescent might check incoming information about a club or a clique to determine if it is consistent with her impressions of the club or clique. Yet another adolescent might question someone or paraphrase what the person has just said about her feelings to make sure that he has accurately understood what was said. Adolescents' ability to monitor their social cognition may be an important aspect of their social maturity (Flavell, 1979).

At this point, we have discussed many aspects of self-understanding and social understanding. Recall, however, that the self involves not only self-understanding but also self-esteem and self-concept. That is, not only do adolescents try to define and describe attributes of the self (self-understanding), but they also evaluate those attributes (self-concept and self-esteem).

SELF-ESTEEM AND SELF-CONCEPT

What are self-esteem and self-concept? How are they measured? Are some domains more salient to the adolescent's self-esteem than others? How do relationships with parents and peers influence adolescents' self-esteem? What are the consequences of low self-esteem in adolescents and emerging adults, and how can their self-esteem be raised?

The living self has one purpose only: to come into its own fullness, as a tree comes into full blossom, or a bird into spring beauty, or a tiger into luster.

—D. H. Lawrence
English Author, 20th Century

perspective taking The ability to assume another person's perspective and understand his or her thoughts and feelings.

Positive indicators

1. Gives others directives or commands
2. Uses voice quality appropriate for situation
3. Expresses opinions
4. Sits with others during social activities
5. Works cooperatively in a group
6. Faces others when speaking or being spoken to
7. Maintains eye contact during conversation
8. Initiates friendly contact with others
9. Maintains comfortable space between self and others
10. Has little hesitation in speech, speaks fluently

Negative indicators

1. Puts down others by teasing, name-calling, or gossiping
2. Uses gestures that are dramatic or out of context
3. Engages in inappropriate touching or avoids physical contact
4. Gives excuses for failures
5. Brags excessively about achievements, skills, appearance
6. Verbally puts self down; self-deprecation
7. Speaks too loudly, abruptly, or in a dogmatic tone

FIGURE 1
BEHAVIORAL INDICATORS OF SELF-ESTEEM

self-esteem The global evaluative dimension of the self; also referred to as self-worth or self-image.

self-concept Domain-specific evaluations of the self.

What Are Self-Esteem and Self-Concept? In the field of developmental psychology, leading expert Susan Harter (2006, 2012, 2016) distinguishes between self-esteem and self-concept. In her view, **self-esteem**, also referred to as *self-worth* or *self-image*, is the global evaluative dimension of the self. For example, an adolescent or emerging adult might perceive that she is not merely a person but a good person. Of course, not all adolescents and emerging adults have an overall positive image of themselves. An adolescent with low self-esteem may describe himself as a bad person.

In Harter's view, **self-concept** refers to domain-specific evaluations of the self. Adolescents and emerging adults make self-evaluations in many domains—academic, athletic, physical appearance, and so on. For example, an adolescent may have a negative academic self-concept because he is getting poor grades but have a positive athletic self-concept because he is a star swimmer. In sum, self-esteem refers to global self-evaluations, self-concept to domain-specific evaluations.

Investigators have not always made a clear distinction between self-esteem and self-concept, sometimes using the terms interchangeably or not defining them precisely (Easterbrook, Kuppens, & Manstead, 2020). As you read the remaining discussion of self-esteem and self-concept, recalling the distinction between self-esteem as global self-evaluation and self-concept as domain-specific self-evaluation can help you to keep the terms straight.

Measuring Self-Esteem and Self-Concept Measuring self-esteem and self-concept hasn't always been easy, especially in assessing adolescents. For many years, such measures were designed primarily for children or for adults, with little attention paid to adolescents. Then Susan Harter (1989) developed a separate measure for adolescents: the Self-Perception Profile for Adolescents. It assesses eight domains—scholastic competence, athletic competence, social acceptance, physical appearance, behavioral conduct, close friendship, romantic appeal, and job competence—plus global self-worth. The adolescent measure has three skill domains not present in the measure she developed for children: job competence, romantic appeal, and close friendship.

Some assessment experts argue that a combination of several methods should be used in measuring self-esteem. In addition to self-reporting, rating of an adolescent's self-esteem by others and observations of the adolescent's behavior in various settings could provide a more complete and accurate self-esteem picture. Peers, teachers, parents, and even others who do not know the adolescent could be asked to rate the adolescent's self-esteem.

Adolescents' facial expressions and the extent to which they congratulate or condemn themselves are also good indicators of how they view themselves. For example, adolescents who rarely smile or rarely act happy are revealing something about their self-esteem.

One investigation that used behavioral observations in assessing self-esteem shows some of the positive as well as the negative behaviors that can provide clues to the adolescent's self-esteem (see Figure 1) (Savin-Williams & Demo, 1983). By using a variety of methods (such as self-report and behavioral observations) and obtaining information from various sources (such as the adolescent, parents, friends, and teachers), investigators are likely to construct a more accurate picture of the adolescent's self-esteem than they could get by relying on only one assessment method.

Self-Esteem: Perception and Reality Self-esteem reflects perceptions that do not always match reality (Derry, Ohan, & Baylis, 2020). An adolescent's or emerging adult's self-esteem might indicate a perception about whether he or she is intelligent and attractive, for example, but that perception may not be accurate. Thus, high self-esteem may refer to accurate, justified perceptions of one's worth as a person and one's successes and accomplishments, but it can also indicate an arrogant, grandiose, unwarranted sense of superiority over others. In the same manner, low self-esteem may suggest either an accurate perception of one's shortcomings or a distorted, even pathological sense of insecurity and inferiority.

Narcissism refers to a self-centered and self-concerned approach toward others. Typically, narcissists are unaware of their actual self and how others perceive them. This lack of awareness contributes to their adjustment problems (Kaufman & others, 2020). Narcissists are excessively self-centered and self-congratulatory, viewing their own needs and desires as paramount. As a result, narcissists rarely show any empathy toward others. In fact, narcissists often devalue people around them to protect their own precarious self-esteem, yet they often respond with rage and shame when others do not admire them or treat them in accordance with their grandiose fantasies about themselves. Narcissists are at their most grandiose when their self-esteem is threatened. Narcissists may fly into a frenzy if they have given an unsatisfactory performance.

What characterizes narcissistic individuals?
CSP_karelnoppe/Fotosearch LBRF/age fotostock

One study revealed that narcissistic adolescents were more aggressive than other adolescents but only when they were shamed (Thomaes & others, 2008). Low self-esteem was not linked to aggression, but narcissism combined with high self-esteem was related to exceptionally high aggression. And a longitudinal study found that narcissistic adolescents and emerging adults were more impulsive, histrionic (behaving dramatically), active, and self-focused as young children than were others (Carlson & Gjerde, 2010). In this study, narcissism increased from 14 to 18 years of age, then declined slightly from 18 to 23.

So far, narcissism has been portrayed as a general trait. However, there have been an increasing number of efforts to describe different types of narcissism (Donnellan, Ackerman, & Wright, 2021; Ponti, Ghinassi, & Tani, 2020). One of the most common distinctions that has been made is the difference between vulnerable and grandiose narcissism. *Vulnerable narcissism* is characterized by excessive self-absorption, introversion, and insecurity. *Grandiose narcissism* is characterized by an exaggerated sense of superiority, extraversion, and domineering behavior. In a recent study, grandiose narcissism was related to having higher life satisfaction as well as being inauthentic (Kaufman & others, 2020). Also, in a recent study of Chinese adolescents, whether or not narcissism was linked to mental health problems depended on self-esteem—adolescents with high narcissism and high self-esteem had positive mental health outcomes, while those with high narcissism and low self-esteem had problematic mental health outcomes (Xu, Huebner, & Tian, 2020). And recent research investigated two dimensions of narcissism—exploitativeness and superiority—and found that Mexican-origin adolescents living in the United States with higher exploitativeness (taking advantage of others for one's own benefit or benefiting from others' vulnerabilities) at age 14 predicted increased rates of a number of problem behaviors (drug use, delinquency, conduct disorder, and sexual intercourse) at age 16 (Wetzel, Atherton, & Robins, 2021). Also in this study, superiority had little association with problem behaviors.

Are today's adolescents and emerging adults more self-centered and narcissistic than their counterparts in earlier generations? Research by Jean Twenge and her colleagues (2008a, b) indicated that compared with baby boomers who were surveyed in 1975, twelfth-graders surveyed in 2006 were more self-satisfied overall and far more confident that they would be very good employees, mates, and parents. Today's adolescents are sometimes labeled "Generation Me." However, other large-scale analyses have revealed no increase in high school and college students' narcissism from 1976 through 2006 (Trzesniewski & Donnellan, 2010; Trzesniewski, Donnellan, & Robins, 2008a, b). In sum, the extent to which recent generations of adolescents have higher self-esteem and are more narcissistic than earlier generations is controversial (Donnellan & Trzesniewski, 2010; Twenge, Carter, & Campbell, 2017).

Does Self-Esteem Change During Adolescence and Emerging Adulthood?

Researchers have found that self-esteem often decreases when children make the transition from elementary school to middle or junior high school (Twenge & Campbell, 2001). Indeed, during and just after many life transitions, individuals' self-esteem often decreases.

One study found that preexisting gender differences in self-esteem (higher in males) narrowed between the ninth and twelfth grades (Falci, 2012). In this study, adolescents from higher-SES backgrounds had higher self-esteem than did their lower-SES counterparts.

Self-esteem fluctuates across the life span (Miller & Cho, 2018; Trzesniewski, Donnellan, & Robins, 2013; von Soest & others, 2018). One cross-sectional study assessed the self-esteem of a very large, diverse sample of 326,641 individuals from 9 to 90 years of age (Robins &

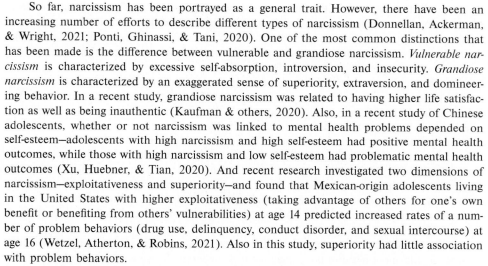

developmental **connection**

Social Cognition

Adolescent egocentrism increases in early adolescence, especially the imaginary audience dimension. Connect to "The Brain and Cognitive Development."

narcissism A self-centered and self-concerned approach toward others.

FIGURE 2

SELF-ESTEEM ACROSS THE LIFE SPAN.
One large-scale study asked more than 300,000 individuals to rate the extent to which they have high self-esteem on a 5-point scale, with 5 being "strongly agree" and 1 being "strongly disagree." Self-esteem dropped in adolescence and late adulthood. Self-esteem of females was lower than self-esteem of males through most of the life span.
(Robins & others, 2002)

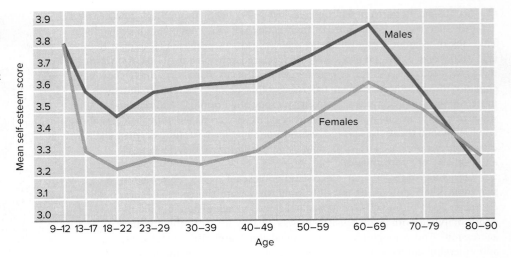

others, 2002). About two-thirds of the participants were from the United States. The individuals were asked to respond to the statement, "I have high self-esteem" on a 5-point scale in which 5 stood for "strongly agree" and 1 stood for "strongly disagree." Self-esteem decreased in adolescence, increased in the twenties, leveled off in the thirties, rose in the forties through the mid-sixties, and then dropped in the seventies and eighties (see Figure 2). At most ages, males reported higher self-esteem than females did.

Another study also found that the gender gap (lower for females) in self-esteem decreased as individuals went through emerging adulthood from 18 to 25 years of age (Galambos, Barker, & Krahn, 2006). In this study, social support and marriage were linked to increased self-esteem, whereas unemployment was related to decreased self-esteem.

Some researchers argue that although there may be a decrease in self-esteem during adolescence, the drop is actually very slight and not nearly as pronounced as it is presented in the media (Harter, 2013). Also note in Figure 2 that, despite the drop in self-esteem among adolescent girls, their average score (3.3) was still slightly higher than the neutral point on the scale (3.0). Also, a recent meta-analysis concluded that the findings do not support the notion that self-evaluations reach a critical low point in many domains in early adolescence (Orth & others, 2021).

One explanation for the decline in self-esteem among females during early adolescence focuses on girls' more negative body images during pubertal change compared with boys (Harter, 2006). Another explanation involves the greater interest young adolescent girls take in social relationships and society's failure to reward that interest.

A current concern is that too many of today's college students grew up receiving empty praise and as a consequence have inflated self-esteem (Graham, 2005; Stipek, 2005). Too often they were given praise for performance that was mediocre or even poor. Now that they are in college, they may have difficulty handling competition and criticism. The title of a book, *Dumbing Down Our Kids: Why American Children Feel Good about Themselves but Can't Read, Write, or Add* (Sykes, 1995), vividly captures the theme that many U.S. students' academic problems may stem at least in part from unmerited praise that was provided in an effort to prop up their self-esteem. A similar theme—the promise of high self-esteem for students in education, especially those who are impoverished or marginalized—characterized a more recent book, *Challenging the Cult of Self-Esteem in Education* (Bergeron, 2018). In a series of studies, researchers found that inflated praise, although well intended, may cause students with low self-esteem to avoid important learning experiences such as tackling challenging tasks (Brummelman & others, 2014).

Is Self-Esteem Linked to Academic Success or Initiative?   School performance and self-esteem are only moderately correlated, and these correlations do not suggest that high self-esteem produces better school performance (Baumeister & others, 2003). Efforts to increase students' self-esteem have not always led to improved school performance (Davies & Brember, 1999). A recent study found a reciprocal relation between self-esteem and academic

developmental **connection**

Gender

Gender differences characterize adolescents' body images, with adolescent girls having a more negative body image than boys do, especially in early adolescence. Connect to "Puberty, Health, and Biological Foundations."

achievement (Zheng & others, 2020). In this study of Mexican-origin youth living in the United States, students were assessed at ages 10, 12, 14, and 16. Those who had high global and academic self-esteem showed improvement in their grades but not their test scores, and those who received higher grades and test scores showed increases in global and academic self-esteem.

Adolescents with high self-esteem have greater initiative, but this can produce positive or negative outcomes (Baumeister & others, 2003). Adolescents with high self-esteem are prone to take both prosocial and antisocial actions.

Are Some Domains More Closely Linked to Self-Esteem Than Others?   Many adolescents are preoccupied with their body image (Markey, 2010). Physical appearance is an especially powerful contributor to self-esteem in adolescence (Harter, 2013). In Harter's (1999) research, for example, global self-esteem was correlated most strongly with physical appearance, a link that has been found in both the United States and other countries (see Figure 3). In another study, adolescents' concept of their physical attractiveness was the strongest predictor of their overall self-esteem (Lord & Eccles, 1994). This strong association between perceived appearance and general self-worth is not confined to adolescence but holds across most of the life span, from early childhood through middle age (Harter, 1999).

Domain	Harter's U.S. samples	Other countries
Physical Appearance	.65	.62
Scholastic Competence	.48	.41
Social Acceptance	.46	.40
Behavioral Conduct	.45	.45
Athletic Competence	.33	.30

FIGURE 3

CORRELATIONS BETWEEN GLOBAL SELF-ESTEEM AND DOMAINS OF COMPETENCE. Note: The correlations shown are the average correlations computed across a number of studies. The other countries in this evaluation were England, Ireland, Australia, Canada, Germany, Italy, Greece, the Netherlands, and Japan. Recall that correlation coefficients can range from –1.00 to +1.00. The correlations between physical appearance and global self-esteem in the United States and in other countries (.65 and .62, respectively) are moderately high.

Social Contexts and Self-Esteem   Social contexts such as the family, peers, and schools contribute to the development of an adolescent's self-esteem (Robinson & Sedikides, 2021). One study found that as family cohesiveness increased, adolescents' self-esteem increased over time (Baldwin & Hoffman, 2002). In this study, family cohesion was based on the amount of time the family spent together, the quality of their communication, and the extent to which the adolescent was involved in family decision making. Also, a recent study in three countries—Brazil, Portugal, and Spain—found that parental warmth was a key factor in adolescent self-esteem in all three countries (Martinez & others, 2020). Further, in another recent study, maternal warmth, monitoring, low maternal depression, economic well-being, and father presence were linked to higher self-esteem in children and adolescents (Krauss, Orth, & Robins, 2020). And in a longitudinal study, the quality of children's home environment (which involved assessment of parenting quality, cognitive stimulation, and the physical home environment) was linked to their self-esteem in early adulthood (Orth, 2018). This study explored one of the main issues in adolescent development described in the "Introduction" chapter: the relative importance of early versus later experiences.

Consequences of Low Self-Esteem   For most adolescents and emerging adults, the emotional discomfort of low self-esteem is only temporary, but for some, low self-esteem can develop into other problems. Low self-esteem has been implicated in overweight and obesity (Gow & others, 2020); anxiety and depression (Sahlan & others, 2021); suicide (Reid-Russell & others, 2021); delinquency (Gauthier-Duchesne, Hebert, & Blais, 2021); and better sexual health (Sakaluk & others, 2020). One study revealed that youth with low self-esteem had lower life satisfaction at 30 years of age (Birkeland & others, 2012). Another study found that low and decreasing self-esteem in adolescence was linked to adult depression two decades later (Steiger & others, 2014). In addition, a longitudinal study indicated that low self-esteem in early adolescence was linked to lower levels of mental and physical health, worse economic prospects, and a higher level of criminal behavior at 26 years of age (Trzesniewski & others, 2006). And in another longitudinal investigation from early adolescence through emerging adulthood, high self-esteem in adolescence was linked to more long-term personal goals, better self-rated physical health, and fewer depressive symptoms in emerging adulthood; high self-esteem in emerging adulthood was linked to higher life-satisfaction, better self-rated mental health, fewer symptoms of anxiety and depression, less alcohol use, and more positive health outcomes (Arsandaux, Galera, & Salamon, 2021).

Also keep in mind that the seriousness of the problem of low self-esteem depends not only on the nature of the adolescent's or emerging adult's low self-esteem but on other conditions as well. When low self-esteem is compounded by difficult school transitions, a troubled family life, or other stressful events, an individual's problems can intensify.

An important point needs to be made about much of the research on self-esteem: It is correlational rather than experimental. Remember that correlation does not equal causation. Thus, if a correlational study finds an association between self-esteem and depression, it could be equally likely that depression causes low self-esteem or that low self-esteem causes depression. A longitudinal study explored whether self-esteem is a cause or consequence of social support in youth (Marshall & others, 2014). In this study, self-esteem predicted subsequent changes in social support, but social support did not predict subsequent changes in self-esteem. However, a longitudinal study with Mexican-origin youth found a reciprocal relation between self-esteem and achievement (Zheng & others, 2020). In this study, adolescents with high global and academic self-esteem subsequently received higher grades, and adolescents with higher grades subsequently had higher global and academic self-esteem.

Given the potential consequences of low self-esteem, how can the self-esteem of adolescents and emerging adults be increased? To explore possible answers to this question, see the *Connecting with Health and Well-Being* interlude.

connecting with health and well-being

How Can Adolescents' Self-Esteem Be Increased?

Four ways to improve adolescents' and emerging adults' self-esteem are to (1) identify the causes of low self-esteem and the domains of competence important to the self; (2) provide emotional support and social approval; (3) foster achievement; and (4) help adolescents to cope with challenges.

Identifying an adolescent's or emerging adult's sources of self-esteem—that is, the domains that are important to the self—is critical to improving self-esteem. Self-esteem theorist and researcher Susan Harter (1990b) points out that the self-esteem enhancement programs of the 1960s, in which self-esteem itself was the target and individuals were encouraged to simply feel good about themselves, were ineffective. Rather, Harter (1998) concludes that in-

What are some strategies for increasing self-esteem?
Mixmike/E+/Getty Images

tervention must occur at the level of the causes of self-esteem if self-esteem is to improve significantly. Adolescents and emerging adults have the highest self-esteem when they perform competently in domains important to the self. Therefore, adolescents and emerging adults should be encouraged to identify and value their domains of competence. For example, some adolescents and emerging adults might have artistic talent, others might have strong academic skills, and yet others might excel in sports.

Emotional support and social approval in the form of confirmation from others can also powerfully influence self-esteem (Harter, 1990a, b). Some youth with low self-esteem come from conflictual families or conditions in which they experienced abuse or neglect—situations in which support is unavailable. In some cases, alternative sources of support can be implemented, either informally through the encouragement of a

teacher, a coach, or another significant adult, or more formally through programs such as Big Brothers and Big Sisters. Although peer approval becomes increasingly important during adolescence, both adult and peer support are important influences on the adolescent's self-esteem. In one study, both parental and peer support were related to the adolescent's general self-worth (Robinson, 1995).

Achievement can also improve adolescents' and emerging adults' self-esteem (Ferradás Canedo & others, 2018). For example, the straightforward teaching of real skills to adolescents and emerging adults often results in increased achievement and thus in enhanced self-esteem. Adolescents and emerging adults develop higher self-esteem when they know what tasks are important for achieving goals and they have experienced success in performing them or similar behaviors. This emphasis on the importance of achievement in improving self-esteem has much in common with Albert Bandura's (2010) social cognitive concept of self-efficacy, which refers to individuals' beliefs that they can master a situation and produce positive outcomes.

Self-esteem often increases when adolescents face a problem and try to cope with it rather than avoid it (Dyson & Renk, 2006). Facing problems realistically, honestly, and nondefensively produces favorable self-evaluative thoughts, which lead to the self-generated approval that raises self-esteem.

Can individuals have too much self-esteem? How can research address this question?

SELF-REGULATION

Self-regulation involves the ability to control one's behavior without having to rely on others' help (Clarkson, 2021). Self-regulation includes the self-generation and cognitive monitoring of thoughts, feelings, and behaviors in order to reach a goal (Carver & Scheier, 2021; Inzlicht & others, 2021). Throughout most of the life span, individuals who engage in self-regulation are higher achievers, enjoy better health, and are more satisfied with their lives than their counterparts who let external factors dominate their lives (Schunk, 2020). For example, researchers have found that, compared with low-achieving students, high-achieving students engage in greater self-regulation (Schmidt & others, 2020). They do this by setting more specific learning goals, using more strategies to learn and adapt, self-monitoring more, and more systematically evaluating their progress toward a goal (Schunk, 2020). A recent study found that regardless of neighborhood context and socioeconomic advantage or disadvantage, adolescents' self-regulation predicted academic achievement (Davisson, Hoyle, and Andrade, 2021). And in a recent meta-analytic review, low self-regulation at 8 years of age was linked to externalizing problems, depressive symptoms, obesity, cigarette smoking, and illicit drug use at 13 years of age (Robson, Allen, & Howard, 2020).

What characterizes self-regulation in adolescence?
martiapunts/Shutterstock

Researchers have recently found that adolescents often struggle with self-regulation, especially in early adolescence. In a recent review, it was concluded that self-regulation decreases from 10 to 14 years of age, then improves from 14 to 19 years of age (Atherton, 2020).

A key component of self-regulation is engaging in *effortful control*, which involves inhibiting impulses and not engaging in destructive behavior, focusing and maintaining attention despite distractions, and initiating and completing tasks that have long-term value, even if they may seem unpleasant. In a recent study, effortful control at 2 to 3 years of age predicted higher academic achievement at 14 to 15 years of age (Dindo & others, 2017). Another study found that effortful control at 17 years of age predicted academic persistence and educational attainment at 23 to 25 years of age (Veronneau & others, 2014). In this study, effortful control was just as strong a predictor of educational attainment as were parents' education and past grade point average. In addition, a recent study indicated that among 13- to 16-year-olds, females reported having a higher level of self-control and self-monitoring than did their male counterparts (Tetering & others, 2020). And in a study of Mexican-origin families, adolescents who experienced more hostility from their parents, associated more with deviant peers, lived in more violent neighborhoods, and encountered more ethnic discrimination were characterized by steeper declines in effortful control between 10 and 14 years old (Atherton, Lawson, & Robins, 2020). Also in this study, adolescents whose parents closely monitored their behavior and whereabouts showed smaller declines in effortful control between 10 and 14 years of age.

> **developmental connection**
> **Achievement**
> Self-regulation and delay of gratification are key processes in the development of achievement and academic success in adolescence. Connect to "The Brain and Cognitive Development" and "Achievement, Work, and Careers."

> **developmental connection**
> **School**
> The transition to middle or junior high school is stressful for many individuals because it coincides with a number of physical, cognitive, and socioemotional changes. Connect to "Schools."

self-regulation The ability to control one's behavior without having to rely on others for help.

Review *Connect* Reflect

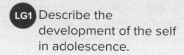 Describe the development of the self in adolescence.

Review
- What is self-understanding? What are the key dimensions of self-understanding in adolescence? What are some important aspects of understanding others in adolescence?
- What are self-esteem and self-concept? How can they be measured? Are some domains more salient than others to adolescents' self-esteem? How are social contexts linked with adolescents' self-esteem? What are the consequences of low self-esteem? How can adolescents' self-esteem be increased?
- What characterizes self-regulation in adolescence?

Connect
- Contrast self-esteem, self-concept, and narcissism.

Reflect *Your Own Personal Journey of Life*
- Think about what your future selves might be. What do you envision will make you the happiest about the future selves you aspire to become? What prospective selves hold negative possibilities?

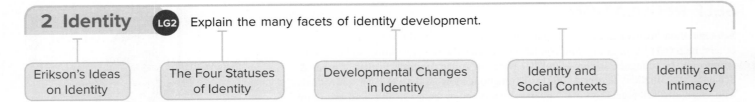

2 Identity   **LG2**   Explain the many facets of identity development.

| Erikson's Ideas on Identity | The Four Statuses of Identity | Developmental Changes in Identity | Identity and Social Contexts | Identity and Intimacy |

"Who are you?" said the Caterpillar. Alice replied, rather shyly, "I—I hardly know, Sir, just at present—at least I know who I was when I got up this morning, but I must have changed several times since then."

—LEWIS CARROLL
English Writer, 19th Century

Erik Erikson.
Bettmann/Getty Images

- - - - - - - ▷

developmental **connection**

Theories

Erikson theorized that individuals go through eight stages in the course of human development. Connect to "Introduction."

◁ - - - - - - -

identity Who a person believes he or she is, representing a synthesis and integration of self-understanding.

identity versus identity confusion Erikson's fifth developmental stage, which occurs during adolescence. At this time, individuals are faced with deciding who they are, what they are all about, and where they are going in life.

psychosocial moratorium Erikson's term for the gap between childhood security and adult autonomy that adolescents experience as part of their identity exploration.

Identity is who a person believes she or he is, representing a synthesis and integration of self-understanding. By far the most comprehensive and provocative theory of identity development is that of Erik Erikson. In fact, some experts on adolescence consider Erikson's ideas to be the single most influential theory of adolescent development. Let's look further at his theory, beginning with an analysis of his ideas on identity.

ERIKSON'S IDEAS ON IDENTITY

Who am I? What am I all about? What am I going to do with my life? What is different about me? How can I make it on my own? These questions, not usually considered in childhood, surface as a common, virtually universal concern during adolescence. Adolescents clamor for solutions to questions of identity. Erik Erikson (1950, 1968) was the first to realize how central such questions are to understanding adolescent development. Today's emphasis on identity as a key concept in adolescent development results directly from Erikson's masterful thinking and analysis.

Identity Versus Identity Confusion In Erikson's theory, **identity versus identity confusion** is the fifth developmental stage (or crisis) in the human life span and it occurs during the adolescent years. Adolescents are in the process of deciding who they are, what they are all about, and where they are going in life. They confront many new roles, from vocational to romantic. As part of their identity exploration, adolescents experience a **psychosocial moratorium**, Erikson's term for the gap between childhood security and adult autonomy. In the course of exploring and searching their culture's identity files, they often experiment with different roles. Youth who cope successfully with these conflicting roles and identities emerge with a new sense of self that is both refreshing and acceptable. But adolescents who do not successfully resolve the identity crisis suffer what Erikson calls *identity confusion*. Either they withdraw, isolating themselves from peers and family, or they immerse themselves in the world of peers and lose their identity in the crowd.

Role Experimentation A core ingredient of Erikson's theory of identity development is role experimentation. As we have seen, Erikson stressed that adolescents face an overwhelming number of choices and at some point during their youth enter a period of psychosocial moratorium. During this moratorium and before they reach a stable sense of self, they try out different roles and behaviors. They might be argumentative one moment, cooperative the next. They might dress neatly one day and sloppily the next day. One week they might like a particular friend, and the next week they might despise the same person. This identity experimentation is a deliberate effort on the part of adolescents to find their place in the world.

As adolescents gradually come to realize that they will soon be responsible for themselves and their lives, they try to determine what those lives are going to be like. Many parents and other adults, accustomed to having children go along with what they say, may be bewildered or incensed by the wisecracks, rebelliousness, and rapid mood changes that accompany adolescence. But it is important for adults to give adolescents the time and opportunity to explore different roles and personalities. In turn, most adolescents eventually discard undesirable roles.

There are literally hundreds of roles for adolescents to try out and probably just as many ways to pursue each role. Erikson argued that by late adolescence, vocational roles become central to identity development, especially in a highly technological society like that of the United States. Youth who have been well trained to enter a workforce that offers the potential of reasonably high self-esteem will experience the least stress during this phase of identity development. Some youth may reject jobs offering good pay and traditionally high social status, choosing instead work that allows them to be more genuinely helpful to others—perhaps in a mental health clinic or at an elementary school in a low-income neighborhood. Some youth may prefer unemployment to the prospect of work that they feel they could not perform well or that would make them feel useless. To Erikson, such choices reflect the desire to achieve a meaningful identity by being true to oneself rather than by burying one's identity within the larger society.

When identity has been conceptualized and researched, it typically is explored in a broad sense. However, identity is a self-portrait that is composed of many pieces and domains:

- The career and work path a person wants to follow (vocational/career identity)
- Whether a person is politically conservative, liberal, or middle of the road (political identity)
- A person's spiritual beliefs (religious identity)
- Whether a person is single, married, divorced, or cohabiting (relationship identity)
- The extent to which a person is motivated to achieve and is intellectually oriented (achievement, intellectual identity)
- Whether a person is heterosexual, homosexual, or bisexual (sexual identity)
- Which part of the world or country a person is from and how intensely the person identifies with his or her cultural heritage (cultural/ethnic identity)
- The things a person likes to do, including sports, music, and hobbies (interests)
- An individual's personality characteristics—being introverted or extraverted, anxious or calm, friendly or hostile, and so on (personality)
- A person's body image (physical identity)

Currently, too little research attention has been given to examining specific domains of identity such as those described here.

One of Erik Erikson's strategies for explaining the nature of identity development was to analyze the lives of famous individuals. One such individual was Mahatma Gandhi (*center*), the spiritual leader of India in the mid-twentieth century, about whom Erikson (1969) wrote in *Gandhi's Truth*.
Bettmann/Getty Images

Some Contemporary Thoughts on Identity
Contemporary views of identity development suggest that it is a lengthy process, in many instances more gradual and less cataclysmic than Erikson's term *crisis* implies (Eriksson & others, 2020). Today's theorists note that this extraordinarily complex process neither begins nor ends with adolescence. It begins in infancy with the appearance of attachment, the development of a sense of self, and the emergence of independence. It ends with a life review and integration in old age. What is important about identity development in adolescence and emerging adulthood is that this is the first time when physical, cognitive, and socioemotional development advance to the point at which the individual can sort through and synthesize childhood identities and identifications to construct a viable path toward adult maturity (Marcia & Carpendale, 2004). Resolution of the identity issue during adolescence and emerging adulthood does not mean that identity will be stable through the remainder of one's life (Kroger & Marcia, 2021). An individual who develops a healthy identity is flexible and adaptive, open to changes in society, in relationships, and in careers. This openness assures numerous reorganizations of identity throughout the individual's life.

Just as researchers increasingly describe adolescents' and emerging adults' self-understanding in terms of multiple selves, there also is a trend toward characterizing adolescents' and emerging adults' identity in terms of multiple identities, such as ethnicity, spirituality, sexuality, and so on (Umana-Taylor & others, 2020). Although adolescent and emerging adult identities are preceded by childhood identities, central questions such as "Who am I?" come up more frequently during the adolescent and emerging adult years. During adolescence and emerging adulthood, identities are characterized more strongly by the search for balance between the needs for autonomy and for connectedness.

Identity formation seldom happens neatly, nor is it usually cataclysmic (McLean & others, 2021). At a bare minimum, it involves commitment to a vocational direction, an ideological stance, and a sexual orientation. Synthesizing the components of identity can be a long, drawn-out process, with many negations and affirmations of various roles. Identity

As long as one keeps searching, the answers come.

—Joan Baez
American Folk Singer, 20th Century

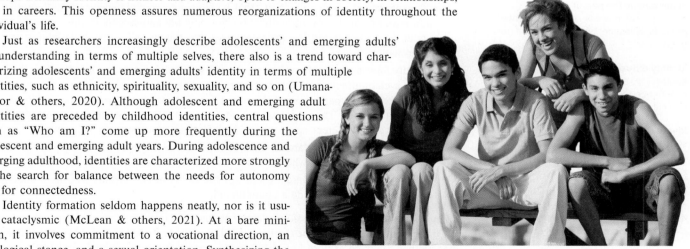

What are some contemporary thoughts about identity formation and development?
Somos/Veer/Caroline Mowry/Getty Images

development takes place in bits and pieces. Decisions are not made once and for all but must be made again and again. Although the decisions might seem trivial at the time—whom to date, whether or not to have sex, whether to break up, whether to take drugs; whether to go to college or get a job, whether to study or play, whether to be politically active or not—over the years, they form the core of what an individual is all about.

A current concern about the development of identity in adolescence and emerging adulthood was voiced in William Damon's (2008) book, *The Path to Purpose*. In this book, Damon acknowledged that successful identity development is a long-term process of extended exploration and reflection, and in some instances it can involve postponing decisions for a number of years. However, what concerned Damon was that too many youth were not moving toward any identity resolution. In Damon's (2008, pp. 5, 7) words,

> Their delay is characterized more by indecision than by motivated reflection, more by confusion than by pursuit of clear goals, more by ambivalence than by determination. Directionless shift is not a constructive moratorium in either a developmental or a societal sense. Without a sense of direction, opportunities are lost, and doubt and self-absorption can set in. Maladaptive habits are established and adaptive ones not built. . . . What is too often missing is . . . the kind of wholehearted dedication to an activity or interest that stems from serious purpose, a purpose that can give meaning and direction to life.

developmental **connection**

Achievement

In interviews with 12- to 22-year-olds, Damon found that only about 20 percent had a clear vision of where they wanted to go in life, what they wanted to achieve, and why. Connect to "Achievement, Work, and Careers."

In Damon's (2008, p. 47) view, too many youth are left to their own devices in dealing with some of life's biggest questions: "What is my calling?" "What do I have to contribute to the world?" "What am I here for?" Damon acknowledges that adults can't make youths' decisions for them, but he emphasizes that it is very important for parents, teachers, mentors, and other adults to provide guidance, feedback, and contexts that will increase the likelihood that youth will develop a positive identity. In other words, youth need a cultural climate that inspires them and supports their chances of reaching their aspirations.

THE FOUR STATUSES OF IDENTITY

James Marcia (1980, 1994, 2002) analyzed Erikson's theory of identity development and concluded that it involves four identity statuses, or ways of resolving the identity crisis: identity diffusion, identity foreclosure, identity moratorium, and identity achievement. That is, Marcia uses the extent of an adolescent's crisis and commitment to classify individuals according to these four identity statuses. He defines the term **crisis** as a period of identity development during which the adolescent is choosing among meaningful alternatives. (Most researchers use the term *exploration*.) By **commitment,** he means a personal investment in what an individual is going to do.

crisis A period of identity development during which the adolescent is choosing among meaningful alternatives.

commitment The part of identity development in which adolescents show a personal investment in what they are going to do.

identity diffusion Marcia's term for the state adolescents are in when they have not yet experienced an identity crisis or made any commitments.

identity foreclosure Marcia's term for the state adolescents are in when they have made a commitment but have not experienced an identity crisis.

identity moratorium Marcia's term for the state of adolescents who are in the midst of an identity crisis but who have not made a clear commitment to an identity.

identity achievement Marcia's term for an adolescent who has undergone an identity crisis and made a commitment.

Let's examine each of Marcia's four identity statuses:

- **Identity diffusion** is Marcia's term for the state adolescents are in when they have not yet experienced an identity crisis (that is, have not yet explored meaningful alternatives) and have not made any commitments. Not only are adolescents in this status undecided about occupational and ideological choices, but they usually show little interest in such matters.
- **Identity foreclosure** is Marcia's term for the state adolescents are in when they have made a commitment but have not experienced an identity crisis. This status occurs most often when parents hand down commitments to their adolescents, usually in an authoritarian way. Thus, adolescents with this status have not had adequate opportunities to explore different approaches, ideologies, and vocations on their own.
- **Identity moratorium** is Marcia's term for the state of adolescents who are in the midst of an identity crisis but who have not made a clear commitment to an identity.
- **Identity achievement** is Marcia's term for the status of adolescents who have undergone an identity crisis and made a commitment.

Figure 4 summarizes Marcia's four identity statuses.

Let's explore some specific examples of Marcia's identity statuses. A 13-year-old adolescent has neither begun to explore her identity in a meaningful way nor made an identity commitment; she is *identity diffused*. An 18-year-old boy's parents want him to be a doctor, so he is planning on majoring in premedicine in college and has not adequately explored any other

Identity Status

Position on Occupation and Ideology	Identity Diffusion	Identity Foreclosure	Identity Moratorium	Identity Achievement
Crisis	Absent	Absent	Present	Present
Commitment	Absent	Present	Absent	Present

FIGURE **4**

MARCIA'S FOUR STATUSES OF IDENTITY

options; he is *identity foreclosed*. Nineteen-year-old Sasha is not quite sure what life path she wants to follow, but she recently went to the counseling center at her college to learn about different careers; she is in an *identity moratorium*. Twenty-one-year-old Marcelo extensively explored a number of different career options in college, eventually got his degree in science education, and is looking forward to his first year of teaching high school; he is *identity achieved*. Although these examples of identity statuses focus on careers, remember that the whole of identity has multiple dimensions.

Earlier in this chapter we described various dimensions of identity and indicated that too little research has been done in these domains (McLean & others, 2021). To explore your identity status on a number of identity's dimensions, see Figure 5.

Marcia's approach has been sharply criticized by some researchers who conclude that it distorts and overly simplifies Erikson's concepts of crisis and commitment (Coté, 2015; Klimstra & others, 2017). Erikson emphasized that youth question the perceptions and expectations of their culture and explore the development of an autonomous position with regard to their society. In Marcia's approach, these complex questions are reduced to whether a youth has thought about certain issues and considered the alternatives. Similarly, in Marcia's approach, Erikson's idea of commitment loses its meaning of investing oneself in certain lifelong projects and is interpreted simply as having made a firm decision. Other researchers still maintain that Marcia's approach is a valuable contribution to understanding identity (Kroger, 2015; Kroger & Marcia, 2021).

Think deeply about your exploration and commitment in the areas listed here. For each area, check whether your identity status is diffused, foreclosed, moratorium, or achieved.

Identity Component	Identity Status			
	Diffused	Foreclosed	Moratorium	Achieved
Vocational (career)				
Political				
Religious				
Relationships				
Achievement				
Sexual				
Gender				
Ethnic/Cultural				
Interests				
Personality				
Physical				

FIGURE **5**

EXPLORING YOUR IDENTITY. If you checked diffused or foreclosed for any areas, take some time to think about what you need to do to move into a moratorium identity status in those areas.

Belgian psychologists Luc Goossens, Koen Luyckx, and their colleagues (Goossens & Luyckx, 2007; Hatano, Sugimura, & Luyckx, 2020; Luyckx & others, 2010) have proposed an extension of Marcia's concepts of exploration and commitment. Their revisionist theorizing stresses that effective identity development involves evaluating identity commitments on a continuing basis. These theorists have developed a *dual-cycle identity model* that separates identity development into two different processes: (1) a formation cycle that relies on exploration in breadth and identification with commitment, and (2) a maintenance cycle that involves exploration in depth as well as reconsideration of commitments (Luyckz & others, 2014). A 10-year longitudinal study of individuals from early adolescence (age 13) to emerging adulthood (age 24) confirmed the existence of a dual-cycle identity formation process (Becht & others, 2021).

For example, consider a first-year college student who makes a commitment to become a lawyer. Exploring this commitment in depth might include finding out as much as possible about what is involved in being a lawyer, such as educational requirements, the work conducted by lawyers in different areas, what types of college classes might be beneficial for this career, and so on. It might also include talking with several lawyers about their profession. As a result of this in-depth exploration, the college student may become more confident that being a lawyer is the career that best suits her. As she goes through the remainder of her college years, she will continue to evaluate the commitment she has made to becoming a lawyer and may change her commitment as she continues to gather new information and reflect on the life path she wants to take. In one study, planfulness was a consistent predictor of engagement in identity exploration and commitment (Luyckx & Robitschek, 2014).

One way that researchers are examining identity changes in depth is to use a *narrative approach* (Glaxoglau & Georgakopoulou, 2021). This involves asking individuals to tell their life stories and evaluate the extent to which their stories are meaningful and integrated (McAdams, 2021; McLean & others, 2021). The term *narrative identity* refers to the stories individuals construct and tell about themselves. Beginning in adolescence and young adulthood, our narrative identities are the stories we live by (McAdams, 2021). While the narrative approach focuses on the construction of an autobiographical life story, the dual-cycle approach emphasizes the formation of an identity commitment (van Doeselaar & others, 2020).

DEVELOPMENTAL CHANGES IN IDENTITY

During early adolescence, most youth are primarily in the identity statuses of *diffusion, foreclosure*, or *moratorium*. According to Marcia (1987, 1996), at least three aspects of the young adolescent's development are important to identity formation. Young adolescents must be confident that they have parental support, must have an established sense of industry (positive orientation toward work), and must be able to take a self-reflective stance toward the future.

Researchers have developed a consensus that many of the key changes in identity are most likely to take place in emerging adulthood, the period from about 18 to 25 years of age, not in adolescence (Mattys & others, 2020). For example, Alan Waterman (1985, 1992) has found that from the years preceding high school through the last few years of college, the number of individuals who are identity achieved increases, whereas the number of individuals who are identity diffused decreases. Many young adolescents are identity diffused. College upperclassmen are more likely than high school students or college freshmen to be identity achieved.

Why might college produce some key changes in identity? Increased complexity in the reasoning skills of college students combined with a wide range of new experiences that highlight contrasts between home and college and between themselves and others stimulate them to reach a higher level of integrating various dimensions of their identity (Phinney, 2008). College contexts serve as a virtual "laboratory" for identity development through such experiences as diverse coursework and exposure to peers from diverse backgrounds. Also, one of emerging adulthood's key themes is not having many social commitments, which gives individuals considerable independence in developing a life path (Arnett & Mitra, 2020).

How does identity change in emerging adulthood?
lev dolgachov/age fotostock

James Coté (2015) argues that, because of this freedom, developing a positive identity in emerging adulthood requires considerable self-discipline and planning. Without this self-discipline and planning, emerging adults are likely to drift and not follow any particular direction. Coté also stresses that emerging adults who obtain a higher education are more likely to be on a positive identity path. Those who don't obtain a higher education, he says, tend to experience frequent job changes, not because they are searching for an identity but rather because they are just trying to eke out a living in a society that rewards higher education.

A meta-analysis of 124 studies by Jane Kroger and her colleagues (2010) revealed that during adolescence and emerging adulthood, identity moratorium status rose steadily to age 19 and then declined; identity achievement rose across late adolescence and emerging adulthood; and foreclosure and diffusion statuses declined across the high school years but fluctuated during the late teens and emerging adulthood. The studies also found that a large portion of individuals were not identity achieved by the time they reached their twenties. This important finding—that so few older adolescents and emerging adults had reached an identity achieved status—suggests that mastering identity development by the end of adolescence is more elusive for most individuals than Erikson (1968) envisioned. For example, consider the identity variations in emerging adults in the following two studies. In a recent study of Flemish 17- to 26-year-olds in northern Belgium, commitment and responsibility characterized the identity of older participants and employed participants more than that of younger participants and unemployed participants (Mattys & others, 2020). And in another recent study, emerging adults who were identity confused were more likely to present an ideal self and a false self on Facebook, indicating they were less realistic and more oriented toward appearing socially desirable in their online self-presentation (Michikyan, 2020).

Despite such fluctuations in emerging adulthood, many young adults have a stable identity. A recent study examined identity development between ages 25 and 33 (Eriksson & others, 2020). In this study, fewer individuals were characterized by a moratorium status and more by an identity achievement status as they became older during this time frame. Also, stable identity statuses with established commitments (identity achievement and foreclosure) were by far the most common patterns across this time period.

However, resolution of identity during adolescence and early adulthood does not mean that identity will remain stable until the end of life (Ferrer-Wreder & Kroger, 2020). Many individuals with positive identities undergo what are called "MAMA" cycles; that is, their identity status changes from *m*oratorium to *a*chievement to *m*oratorium to *a*chievement (Marcia, 1994). These cycles may be repeated throughout life (Francis, Fraser, & Marcia, 1989). Marcia (2002) points out that the first identity is just that—it is not, and should not be expected to be, the final product.

Researchers have shown that identity consolidation—the process of refining and enhancing the identity choices that are made in emerging adulthood—continues well into early adulthood and possibly into the early part of middle adulthood (Ferrer-Wreder & Kroger, 2020). One study found that women and men continued to show identity development from 27 through 36 years of age, with the main changes in the direction of greater commitment (Pulkkinen & Kokko, 2000). In this study, adults more often moved into achieved and foreclosed identities than into moratorium or diffused identities. Further, from early to middle adulthood, individuals become more certain about their identity. For example, a longitudinal study of Smith College women found that identity certainty increased from the thirties through the fifties (Stewart, Ostrove, & Helson, 2001).

IDENTITY AND SOCIAL CONTEXTS

Social contexts influence an adolescent's identity development (Moffitt, Juang, & Syed, 2020). Questions we will explore in this regard are: Do family relationships influence identity development? What roles do peers, romantic relationships, and the digital world play in identity formation? How are culture and ethnicity linked to identity development? Is the identity development of females and males different?

Family Influences on Identity   Parents are important figures in the adolescent's development of identity (Constante & others, 2020). Catherine Cooper and her colleagues (Cooper, 2011;

developmental **connection**
Emerging Adulthood
Emerging adults have few social obligations, which allows them considerable autonomy in running their lives (Arnett, 2010, 2014). Connect to "Introduction."

developmental **connection**

Attachment

Even while adolescents seek autonomy, attachment to parents is important; secure attachment in adolescence is linked to a number of positive outcomes. Connect to "Families."

Cooper, Behrens, & Trinh, 2009) have found that a family atmosphere that promotes both individuality and connectedness is important in the adolescent's identity development:

- **Individuality** consists of two dimensions: self-assertion, which is the ability to have and communicate a point of view; and separateness, which is the use of communication patterns to express how one is different from others.
- **Connectedness** also consists of two dimensions: mutuality, which involves sensitivity to and respect for others' views; and permeability, which involves openness to others' views.

Increasing research interest also has focused on the role that attachment to parents might play in identity development. In a meta-analysis, securely attached adolescents were far more likely to be identity achieved than were insecurely attached adolescents (Arseth & others, 2009).

How might parents influence the adolescent's identity development?
Mike Watson Images/Getty Images

Identity and Peer/Romantic Relationships Researchers have found that the capacity to explore one's identity during adolescence and emerging adulthood is linked to the quality of peer, friendship, and romantic relationships (Umana-Taylor & others, 2020). For example, one study found that an open, active exploration of identity when adolescents are comfortable with close friends contributes to the positive quality of the friendship (Doumen & others, 2012). In another study, friends were often a safe context for exploring identity-related experiences, providing a testing ground for how self-disclosing comments are viewed by others (McLean & Jennings, 2012). Recent longitudinal studies also documented that the ethnic identity of adolescents is influenced by positive and diverse friendships (Santos, Komienko, & Rivas-Drake, 2017).

In terms of links between identity and romantic relationships in adolescence and emerging adulthood, individuals in a romantic relationship are in the process of constructing their own identity while providing their partner with a context for identity exploration (Pittman & others, 2011). The extent of their secure attachment to each other can influence how each partner constructs his or her own identity.

What role might romantic relationships play in identity development?
Mike Kemp/Rubberball/Corbis

Identity Development and the Digital Environment For today's adolescents and emerging adults, contexts involving the digital world, especially social media platforms such as Instagram, Snapchat, and Facebook, have introduced new ways for youth to express and explore their identity (Davis, 2021; Davis & others, 2020). Adolescents and emerging adults often cast themselves in as positive a light as possible on their digital devices—posting their most attractive photos and describing themselves in idealistic ways, continually editing and reworking their online self-portraits to enhance them. Adolescents' and emerging adults' online world provides extensive opportunities for both expressing their identity and getting feedback about it (Davis, 2021). Of course, such feedback is not always positive, just as in their offline world. We will have much more to say about the roles of social media in adolescence and emerging adulthood in the chapter on "Culture."

individuality An important element in adolescent identity development. It consists of two dimensions: self-assertion, the ability to have and communicate a point of view; and separateness, the use of communication patterns to express how one is different from others.

connectedness An important element in adolescent identity development. It consists of two dimensions: mutuality, which is sensitivity to and respect for others' views; and permeability, which is openness to others' views.

Cultural and Ethnic Identity Most research on identity development has historically been based on data obtained from adolescents and emerging adults in the United States and Canada, especially those who are non-Latinx whites (Schwartz & others, 2020). Many of these individuals have grown up in cultural contexts that value individual autonomy. However, in many countries around the world, adolescents and emerging adults have grown up influenced by a collectivist emphasis on fitting in with the group and connecting with others (Kulich & others, 2021). The collectivist emphasis is especially prevalent in East Asian countries such as China. Researchers have found that self-oriented identity exploration may not be the main process through which identity achievement is attained in East Asian countries (Schwartz & others, 2012). Rather, East Asian adolescents and emerging adults may develop their identity through identification with and imitation of others in their cultural group (Bosma & Kunnen, 2001). The interdependence in East Asian cultures includes an emphasis on adolescents and

What are some cross-cultural variations in identity in countries such as China and Italy?
(left): IMAGEMORE Co, Ltd. /Getty Images; (right): Zero Creatives/Getty Images

emerging adults accepting and embracing social and family roles (Berman & others, 2011). Thus, some patterns of identity development, such as the foreclosed status, may be more adaptive in East Asian countries than in North American countries (Chen & Berman, 2012).

Seth Schwartz and his colleagues (2012, 2020) have pointed out that while everyone identifies with a particular "culture," many individuals in cultural majority groups take their cultural identity for granted. Thus, many adolescents and emerging adults in the cultural majority of non-Latinx whites in the United States likely don't spend much time thinking of themselves as "white Americans." However, for many adolescents and emerging adults who have grown up as a member of an ethnic minority group in the United States or emigrated from another country, cultural dimensions likely are an important aspect of their identity. Researchers have found that at both the high school and college level, Latinx students were more likely than non-Latinx white students to indicate that their cultural identity was an important dimension of their overall self-concept (Urdan, 2012).

Throughout the world, ethnic minority groups have struggled to maintain their ethnic identities while blending in with the dominant culture (Wang & Yip, 2020). **Ethnic identity** is an enduring aspect of the self that includes a sense of membership in an ethnic group, along with the attitudes and feelings related to that membership (Constante & others, 2020). Thus, for adolescents and emerging adults from ethnic minority groups, the process of identity formation has an added dimension: the choice between two or more sources of identification—their own ethnic group and the mainstream, or dominant, culture (Cano & others, 2020). Many adolescents resolve this choice by developing a **bicultural identity.** That is, they identify in some ways with their ethnic group and in other ways with the majority culture (Sharma, Shaligram, & Yoon, 2020). A study of Mexican American and Asian American college students found that they identified both with the American mainstream culture and with their culture of origin (Devos, 2006). Also, in a recent study of Latinx emerging adults, the bicultural harmony component of bicultural identity development was linked to lower levels of psychological stress (Cano & others, 2021).

With their advancing cognitive skills of abstract thinking and self-reflection, adolescents (especially older adolescents) increasingly consider the meaning of their ethnicity and also have more ethnic-related experiences (Syed & McLean, 2016). Because adolescents are more mobile and independent from their parents, they are more likely to experience ethnic stereotyping and discrimination as they interact with diverse individuals in school contexts and other public settings (Potochnick, Perreira, & Fuligni, 2012). Many ethnic minority groups experience stereotyping and discrimination, including African American, Latinx, and Asian American adolescents (Gonzalez Barrera & Lopez, 2020). Further, African American and Latinx adolescents living in impoverished conditions may not go to college even if they have the academic skills to succeed in college, which may preclude identity pursuits that are stimulated by a college education and experiences (Oyserman & Destin, 2010). In some cases, ethnic minority adolescents may need to go to work to help their parents meet their family's expenses, which also may make their pursuit of a college education more difficult (Schwartz & others, 2012).

developmental **connection**

Culture and Ethnicity

Historical, economic, and social experiences produce differences between various ethnic groups and the majority non-Latinx white group in the United States. Connect to "Culture."

Many ethnic minority youth must bridge "multiple worlds" in constructing their identities.

—**Catherine Cooper**
Contemporary Developmental Psychologist, University of California–Santa Cruz

ethnic identity An enduring, basic aspect of the self that includes a sense of membership in an ethnic group and the attitudes and feelings related to that membership.

bicultural identity Identity formation that occurs when adolescents identify in some ways with their ethnic group and in other ways with the majority culture.

One adolescent girl, 16-year-old Michelle Chinn, made these comments about ethnic identity development: "My parents do not understand that teenagers need to find out who they are, which means a lot of experimenting, a lot of mood swings, a lot of emotions and awkwardness. Like any teenager, I am facing an identity crisis. I am still trying to figure out whether I am a Chinese American or an American with Asian eyes." *What are some other aspects of developing an ethnic identity in adolescence?*
Red Chopsticks/Getty Images

How do social contexts influence adolescents' ethnic identity?
ericsphotography/Getty Images

racial identity The collective identity of any group of people socialized to think of themselves as a racial group.

Time spent in the dominant culture is another factor that influences ethnic identity. The indicators of identity often differ for each succeeding generation of immigrants (Phinney, 2006; Phinney & Baldelomar, 2011; Phinney & Vedder, 2013). The degree to which first-generation immigrants begin to feel "American" appears to be related to whether or not they learn English, develop social networks beyond their ethnic group, and become culturally competent in their new country. For second-generation immigrants, ethnic identity is likely to be linked to retention of their ethnic language and social networks. In the third and later generations, the issues become more complex. Broad social factors may affect the extent to which members of this generation retain their ethnic identities. For example, media images may either discourage or encourage members of an ethnic group to identify with their group or retain parts of its culture. Discrimination may force people to see themselves as cut off from the majority group and encourage them to seek the support of their own ethnic culture (Marks & others, 2015). In a recent study, Latinx youth showed enhanced resilience against discrimination encounters when they had more family ethnic socialization experiences and engaged in greater ethnic identity exploration and resolution (Martinez-Fuentes, Jager, & Umana-Taylor, 2021).

Adriana Umana-Taylor and her colleagues (2020) are also increasingly finding that a positive ethnic identity is related to favorable outcomes for ethnic minority adolescents. For example, in a recent study, strong ethnic group affiliation and connection served a protective function in reducing risk for psychiatric problems (Anglin & others, 2018). In another study, Asian American adolescents' ethnic identity was associated with high self-esteem, positive relationships, academic motivation, and lower levels of depression over time (Kiang, Witkow, & Champagne, 2013).

The Contexts of Ethnic Identity Development The contexts in which ethnic minority youth live influence their identity development (Cano & others, 2020). In the United States, many ethnic minority youth live in low-SES urban settings where there is little support for developing a positive identity. Many of these youth live in pockets of poverty; are exposed to drugs, gangs, and criminal activities; and interact with youth and adults who have dropped out of school or are unemployed. In such settings, supportive organizations and programs for youth can make an important contribution to their identity development.

Might there be aspects of the social contexts in which adolescents live that increase the likelihood they will develop a positive ethnic identity? One study analyzed 60 youth organizations that served 24,000 adolescents over a period of five years and found that these organizations were especially good at building a sense of ethnic pride in inner-city youth (Heath & McLaughlin, 1993). Many inner-city youth have too much time on their hands, too little to do, and too few places to go. Organizations that nurture youth and respond positively to their needs and interests can enhance their identity development. And organizations that perceive youth as capable, worthy, and eager to have a healthy and productive life contribute in positive ways to the identity development of ethnic minority youth.

Given the history of race and discrimination in the United States, the identities of adolescents and emerging adults are also influenced by their social status in a racial hierarchy that privileges individuals who are non-Latinx white (Hope, Cryer-Coupet, & Stokes, 2020). While race is understood to be a social concept, the lived experience of being a racial minority and treated differently can greatly impact identity formation. **Racial identity** is the collective identity of any group of people socialized to think of themselves as a racial group (Helms & Cook, 1999). Researchers have found that racial identity is positively associated with self-esteem (Rowley & others, 1998) and academic attitudes (Chavous & others, 2003) among African American students. In a recent study of African American 13- to 17-year-old girls, general and gendered racial socialization about pride were linked to positive feelings about being African American, while oppressive messages about African American women were associated with depressive symptoms (Stokes & others, 2020). Also, another recent study of 11- to 12-year-olds found that more frequent discrimination by peers was linked to lower ethnic-racial commitment (Del Toro, Hughes, & Way, 2021). Further, a recent study of adolescents revealed that on days when adolescents reported more negative peer ethnic/racial interaction (ethnic/racial discrimination and teasing, for example), they had lower school engagement (Wang, 2021). On days when they reported more positive peer ethnic/racial interaction (support against discrimination, for example), they engaged in more prosocial behavior. In addition, a research review of Latinxs concluded that perceived discrimination was linked to poorer mental health but that having a greater sense of ethnic pride attenuated this link (Andrade, Ford, & Alvarez, 2021).

There is also emerging research suggesting that ethnic identity and racial identity are best conceptualized as a singular concept of ethnic-racial identity (ERI), where the focus is on ERI development (Atkin & Yoo, 2021; Sladek & others, 2021). In a recent study of Cherokee young adolescents' ERI, both girls and boys reported strong positive attitudes about being a Cherokee (Hoffman, Kurtz-Coates, & Shaheed, 2021). However, the adolescents' perceptions that others hold Cherokees in high regard decreased across grade levels. Overall, high levels of ERI have been found to be a source of protection from discrimination while also being associated with increased vulnerability (Yip, 2018).

Ethnic Identity in Emerging Adulthood   For many individuals from ethnic minority backgrounds, emerging adulthood is an important juncture in their identity development. Jean Phinney (2006) described how ethnic identity may change in emerging adulthood, especially highlighting how certain experiences may shorten or lengthen the duration of emerging adulthood among ethnic minority individuals. For ethnic minority individuals who have to take on family responsibilities and do not go to college, identity commitments may occur earlier. By contrast, especially for ethnic minority individuals who go to college, identity formation may take longer because of the complexity of exploring and understanding a bicultural identity. The cognitive challenges of higher education likely stimulate ethnic minority individuals to reflect on their identity and examine changes in the way they want to identify themselves. This increased reflection may focus on integrating parts of one's ethnic minority culture with the mainstream non-Latinx white culture. For example, some emerging adults face a conflict between the values of family loyalty and interdependence emphasized in their ethnic minority culture and the values of independence and self-assertion emphasized by the mainstream non-Latinx white culture (Arnett, 2014).

Moin Syed and Margarita Azmitia (Azmitia, 2015; Syed, 2013; Syed & Azmitia, 2008, 2009) have examined ethnic identity in emerging adulthood. In one study, they found that ethnic identity exploration and commitment increased from the beginning to the end of college (Syed & Azmitia, 2009). Exploration especially began to increase in the second year of college and continued to increase into the senior year.

What characterizes ethnic identity development in emerging adulthood?
Mark Edward Atkinson/Blend Images/Getty Images

Gender and Identity   Girls and women are more likely to report having a more advanced level of identity formation (moratorium or achievement statuses) than are boys and men (Galliher & Kerpelman, 2012). Further, girls and women tend to have more elaborate self-representations in their identity narratives (Fivush & others, 2003; Fivush & Zaman, 2015). And one study revealed that female adolescents were more likely to engage in identity exploration related to dating (Pittman & others, 2012).

Erikson's (1968) classic presentation of identity development reflected the traditional division of labor between the sexes that was common at the time. Erikson wrote that males were mainly oriented toward career and ideological commitments, whereas females were mainly oriented toward marriage and childbearing. In the 1960s and 1970s, researchers found support for this assertion of gender differences in identity. For example, they found that vocational concerns were more central to male identity, whereas affiliative concerns were more central to female identity (LaVoie, 1976). In the last several decades, however, as females have developed stronger vocational interests, these gender differences have begun to disappear (Hyde & Else-Quest, 2013; Sharp & others, 2007).

What are some gender differences in identity development?
Aldo Murillo/Getty Images

IDENTITY AND INTIMACY

Erikson (1968) argued that intimacy should develop after individuals are well on their way to establishing a stable and successful identity. **Intimacy versus isolation** is Erikson's sixth developmental stage, which individuals experience during early adulthood. At this time, individuals face the task of forming intimate relationships with others. Erikson describes intimacy as finding oneself, yet merging oneself with another. If young adults form healthy friendships and

intimacy versus isolation Erikson's sixth developmental stage, which individuals experience during early adulthood. At this time, individuals face the developmental task of forming intimate relationships with others.

developmental **connection**

Gender

Debate continues about gender similarities and differences in adolescents and possible reasons for the differences. Connect to "Gender."

an intimate relationship with another individual, intimacy will be achieved; if not, isolation will result.

Research has consistently shown that successful identity achievement is an important precursor to positive intimate relationships. One study supported Erikson's theory that development of a positive identity during adolescence predicts better intimacy in romantic relationships during emerging adulthood (Beyers & Seiffge-Krenke, 2011). Another study also found that a higher level of intimacy was linked to a stronger identity for both male and female college students, although the intimacy scores were higher for the females than for the males (Montgomery, 2005).

Review *Connect* Reflect

LG2 Explain the many facets of identity development.

Review
- What is Erikson's view of identity development?
- What are the four statuses of identity development?
- What developmental changes characterize identity?
- How do social contexts influence identity development?
- What is Erikson's view on identity and intimacy?

Connect
- Compare the influences of family and of ethnicity/culture on identity development.

Reflect *Your Own Personal Journey of Life*
- How would you describe your identity in adolescence? How has your identity changed since adolescence?

3 Emotional Development

LG3 Discuss the emotional development of adolescents.

| The Emotions of Adolescence | Hormones, Experience, and Emotions | Emotion Regulation | Emotional Competence | Social-Emotional Education Programs |

Defining emotion is difficult because it is not easy to tell when an adolescent is in an emotional state. For our purposes, we will define **emotion** as feeling, or affect, that occurs when a person is in a state or an interaction that is important to the individual, especially to his or her well-being. Emotion is characterized by behavior that reflects (expresses) the pleasantness or unpleasantness of the state the individual is in, or the transactions he or she is experiencing.

How are emotions linked to the two main concepts we have discussed so far in this chapter—the self and identity? Emotion is closely connected to self-esteem. Negative emotions, such as sadness, are associated with low self-esteem, whereas positive emotions, such as joy, are linked to high self-esteem. The emotions involved in events such as emerging sexual experiences, dating and romantic encounters, and driving a car contribute to the adolescent's developing identity.

THE EMOTIONS OF ADOLESCENCE

Adolescence has long been described as a time of emotional turmoil (Hall, 1904). In its extreme form, this view is too stereotypical because adolescents are not constantly in a state of "storm and stress." Nonetheless, early adolescence is a time when emotional highs and lows occur more frequently (Cheung, Chan, & Chung, 2020). Young adolescents can be on top of the world one moment and down in the dumps the next. In many instances, the intensity of their emotions seems out of proportion to the events that elicit them (Hosseini & Padhy, 2020). Young adolescents may sulk a lot, not knowing how to express their feelings adequately. With little or no provocation, they may blow up at their parents or siblings, projecting their unpleasant feelings onto others.

In research conducted with families, adolescents reported more extreme emotions and more fleeting emotions than did their parents (Larson & Richards, 1994). For example, adolescents were five times more likely than their parents to report being "very happy" at any given moment and three times more likely to report being "very sad." These findings lend

emotion Feeling, or affect, that occurs when a person is in a state or an interaction that is important to the individual, especially to his or her well-being.

support to the perception that adolescents are moody and changeable (Rosenblum & Lewis, 2003). Researchers have also found that from the fifth through the ninth grades, both boys and girls experience a 50 percent decrease in the state of being "very happy" (Larson & Lampman-Petraitis, 1989). In this study, adolescents were more likely than preadolescents to report mildly negative mood states.

It is important for adults to recognize that moodiness is a *normal* aspect of early adolescence and that most adolescents eventually emerge from these moody times and become competent adults. Nonetheless, for some adolescents, intensely negative emotions can reflect serious problems (Ford & others, 2021). For example, rates of depressed moods become more frequent in girls during adolescence (Mash & Wolfe, 2019). We will have much more to say about adolescent depression in "Problems in Adolescence and Emerging Adulthood."

Parents and peers influence adolescents' emotional development. For example, in a recent study of adolescent girls in low-income families, higher levels of emotionally supportive socialization practices by mothers and peers were linked to lower levels of daily negative affect (Cui & others, 2020). Also in this study, both maternal and peer emotionally unsupportive practices predicted increased rates of internalizing problems (depression, for example).

What characterizes adolescents' emotions?
Robert Daly/Age Fotostock

HORMONES, EXPERIENCE, AND EMOTIONS

Significant hormonal changes occur during puberty, and the emotional fluctuations of early adolescence may be related to variability in hormone levels during this period. As adolescents move into adulthood, their moods become less extreme, perhaps because of their adaptation to hormone levels over time or to maturation of the prefrontal cortex (Gratton, Smith, & Dorn, 2020).

Pubertal change is associated with an increase in negative emotions (Zimmerman & Iwanski, 2018). However, the hormonal influences involved in pubertal change can be associated with other factors, such as stress, eating patterns, sexual activity, and social relationships (Whittle & others, 2020). Indeed, environmental experiences may contribute more to the emotions of adolescence than do hormonal changes (Hartman-Munic, Gordon, & Guss, 2020). In one study, social factors accounted for two to four times as much variance as hormonal factors in young adolescent girls' depression and anger (Brooks-Gunn & Warren, 1989).

Among the stressful experiences that might contribute to changes in emotion during adolescence are the transition to middle or junior high school and the onset of sexual experiences and romantic relationships (Shulman & others, 2020). In one study, real and fantasized sexual/romantic relationships were responsible for more than one-third of ninth- to twelfth-graders' strong emotions (Wilson-Shockley, 1995).

In sum, both hormonal changes and environmental experiences are involved in the changing emotions of adolescence. So is the ability to manage emotions, as we explore next.

EMOTION REGULATION

The ability to effectively manage and control one's emotions is a key dimension of positive outcomes in adolescent development (Cole, Ram, & English, 2019). Emotion regulation consists of effectively managing arousal in order to adapt and reach a goal (English, Eldesouky, & Gross, 2021). Arousal involves a state of alertness or activation, which can reach levels that are too high for effective functioning in adolescence. Anger, for example, often requires regulation.

Emotion regulation is involved in many aspects of adolescents' development, and there are wide variations in adolescents' ability to modulate their emotions (Larsson & others, 2020). Indeed, a prominent feature of adolescents with problems is that they often have difficulty managing their emotions (Reinelt & others, 2020). Ineffective emotion regulation is linked with a lower level of executive function, difficulty succeeding in school, a lower level of moral development (weak conscience and lack of internalization of rules, for example), failure to adequately cope with stress, and difficulty in peer relations (Hoffman & others, 2020). In a recent study, emotion regulation expressed in

What characterizes emotion regulation in adolescence?
funstock/iStockphoto/Getty Images

What are some characteristics of emotional competence in adolescence and emerging adulthood?
izusek/Getty Images

being able to manage feelings of sadness and worry served as a buffer against the internalized symptoms associated with peer victimization (Cooley & others, 2021). Many researchers consider the growth of emotion regulation in children and adolescents as a fundamental component of the development of social competence (Schweizer, Gotlib, & Blakemore, 2020).

Young adolescents often have difficulty controlling their emotion. A recent study found that 9- to 12-year-olds had less effective emotion regulation strategies than 13- to 16-year-olds (Sanchis-Sanchis & others, 2020). Toward the end of adolescence and in emerging adulthood, the use of cognitive strategies for regulating emotion, modulating emotional arousal, becoming more adept at managing situations to minimize negative emotion, and choosing effective ways to cope with stress often increase. Of course, though, as mentioned above, there are wide variations in individuals' ability to modulate their emotions.

- - - - - - - - ➤

developmental **connection**

Problems

In many circumstances, a problem-focused coping strategy is better than an emotion-focused strategy. Connect to "Problems in Adolescence and Emerging Adulthood."

developmental **connection**

Intelligence

Emotional intelligence includes managing one's emotions effectively. Connect to "The Brain and Cognitive Development."

◄ - - - - - - - -

EMOTIONAL COMPETENCE

In adolescence, individuals are more likely to become aware of their emotional cycles, such as feeling guilty about being angry. This new awareness may improve their ability to cope with their emotions. Adolescents also become more skillful at presenting their emotions to others. For example, they become aware of the importance of covering up their anger in social relationships. And they are more likely to understand the importance of being able to communicate their emotions constructively to improve the quality of a relationship (Saarni & others, 2006).

Although the increased cognitive abilities and awareness of adolescents prepare them to cope more effectively with stress and emotional fluctuations, as we indicated earlier in our discussion of emotion regulation, many adolescents do not effectively manage their emotions. As a result, they may become prone to depression, anger, and poor emotion regulation, which in turn can trigger problems such as academic difficulties, drug abuse, juvenile delinquency, or eating disorders. For example, one study illustrated the importance of emotion regulation and mood in academic success (Gumora & Arsenio, 2002). In this study, young adolescents who reported experiencing more negative emotion about academic routines had lower grade-point averages.

The emotional competencies that are important for adolescents to develop include the following (Saarni, 1999):

Emotional Competence	Example
• Being aware that the expression of emotions plays a major role in relationships.	• Knowing that expressing anger toward a friend on a regular basis can harm the friendship.
• Adaptively coping with negative emotions by using self-regulatory strategies that reduce the intensity and duration of such emotional states.	• Reducing anger by walking away from a negative situation and engaging in an activity that takes one's mind off it.
• Understanding that inner emotional states do not have to correspond to outer expressions. (As adolescents become more mature, they begin to understand how their emotionally expressive behavior may impact others and to take that understanding into account in the way they present themselves.)	• Recognizing that one can feel anger yet manage one's emotional expression so that it appears neutral.
• Being aware of one's emotional states without becoming overwhelmed by them.	• Differentiating between sadness and anxiety, and focusing on coping rather than being overwhelmed by these feelings.
• Being able to discern others' emotions.	• Perceiving that another person is sad rather than afraid.

SOCIAL-EMOTIONAL EDUCATION PROGRAMS

Adolescents' education has mainly focused on their academic and cognitive development. However, as we discuss in the "Schools" chapter, it is important to educate adolescents more broadly by focusing not only on academic and cognitive development but also on physical and socioemotional development.

An increasing number of programs have been developed to improve many aspects of children's socioemotional development. Two such programs are the Second Step program created by the Committee for Children (2021) and the social and emotional learning (SEL) programs developed by the Collaborative for Academic, Social, and Emotional Learning (CASEL) (2021):

- *Second Step* focuses on the following aspects of social and emotional learning from pre-K through the eighth grade: (1) self-regulation and executive function skills that improve students' attention and help them control their behavior; (2) skills for making friends and solving social and emotional problems; and (3) skills for communicating effectively, coping with stress, and making decisions that help them avoid problem behaviors.

- *CASEL* targets five core social and emotional learning domains in elementary, middle, and high schools: (1) self-awareness (recognizing one's emotions and how they affect behavior, for example); (2) self-management (self-control, coping with stress, and impulse control, for example); (3) social awareness (perspective taking and empathy, for example); (4) relationship skills (developing positive relationships and communicating effectively with individuals from diverse backgrounds, for example); and (5) responsible decision making (engaging in ethical behavior and understanding the consequences of one's actions, for example).

Students participating in the Second Step program. *What characterizes this program?*
Education Images/UIG/Getty Images

Review Connect Reflect

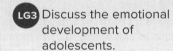
LG3 Discuss the emotional development of adolescents.

Review
- How would you characterize adolescents' emotions?
- How extensively are adolescents' emotions linked to their hormones and experiences?
- What characterizes emotion regulation in adolescence?
- What does it take to be emotionally competent in adolescence?
- What are social-emotional education programs like, and what are the two main programs in this area?

Connect
- Connect the development of emotional competence to the development of self-esteem, as described in the preceding section of this chapter.

Reflect *Your Own Personal Journey of Life*
- How would you describe your emotions in early adolescence? Did you experience more extremes of emotion when you were in middle or junior high school than you do today? Have you learned how to control your emotions better now than you did in early adolescence? Explain.

Personality

Temperament

So far in this chapter, we have discussed the development of the self, identity, and emotion in adolescence and emerging adulthood. In this section, we explore the nature of personality and temperament in adolescence and emerging adulthood.

PERSONALITY

How can personality be defined? **Personality** refers to the enduring personal characteristics of individuals. How is personality linked to the self, identity, and emotion? Personality is usually viewed as encompassing the self and identity (McLean & others, 2021). The description of an individual's personality traits sometimes involves emotions (Reisenzein, Hildebrandt, & Weber, 2021). For example, an adolescent may be described in terms of emotional stability/instability and positive/negative affectivity. How are such traits manifested in adolescence? Which traits are most important?

Big Five Factors of Personality One trait theory that has received considerable attention involves the **Big Five factors of personality**—the view that personality is made up of *o*penness to experience, *c*onscientiousness, *e*xtraversion, *a*greeableness, and *n*euroticism (emotional instability) (see Figure 6). (Notice that if you create an acronym from these trait names, you will get the word *OCEAN*.) A number of research studies point toward these five factors as important dimensions of personality (Atherton, Donnellan, & Robins, 2021; Hakulinen & others, 2021; McCrae, 2021).

The Big Five factors have been linked to important aspects of a person's life, including physical health (Heilmayr & Friedman, 2021); mental health (Widiger & McCabe, 2021); intelligence (Schermer & Saklofske, 2021); cognitive functioning (Matthews, 2021); achievement (Szalma, 2021); work (Salgado, Anderson, & Moscoso, 2021); and relationships (Austin & others, 2021). The following research supports these links:

- *Openness to experience.* Individuals high in openness to experience are more likely to engage in identity exploration (Luyckx & others, 2014); to be tolerant (McCrae & Sutin, 2009); to have superior cognitive functioning, achievement, and IQ across the life span (Briley, Domiteaux, & Tucker-Drob, 2014); to have better health and well-being (Strickhouser, Zell, & Krizan, 2017); to eat fruits and vegetables (Conner & others, 2017); and to cope more effectively with stress (Leger & others, 2016).
- *Conscientiousness.* The major finding in the study of the Big Five factors in adolescence is the emergence of conscientiousness as a key predictor of adjustment and competence (Roberts & Nickel, 2021). Individuals high in conscientiousness often do well in a variety of life domains. For example, they achieve higher grade point averages in college

personality The enduring personal characteristics of individuals.

Big Five factors of personality Five core traits of personality: openness to experience, conscientiousness, extraversion, agreeableness, and neuroticism (emotional instability).

Openness	**C**onscientiousness	**E**xtraversion	**A**greeableness	**N**euroticism (emotional stability)
• Imaginative or practical	• Organized or disorganized	• Sociable or retiring	• Softhearted or ruthless	• Calm or anxious
• Interested in variety or routine	• Careful or careless	• Fun-loving or somber	• Trusting or suspicious	• Secure or insecure
• Independent or conforming	• Disciplined or impulsive	• Affectionate or reserved	• Helpful or uncooperative	• Self-satisfied or self-pitying

FIGURE 6

THE BIG FIVE FACTORS OF PERSONALITY. Each of the broad super traits encompasses more narrow traits and characteristics. Use the acronym OCEAN to remember the Big Five personality factors (openness, conscientiousness, extraversion, agreeableness, neuroticism).

(Roberts & Damian, 2018); have better study habits (Klimstra & others, 2012); are more likely to set and accomplish goals (McCabe & Fleeson, 2016); have better peer and friend relationships (Jenson-Campbell & Malcolm, 2007); have a higher level of marital satisfaction (Sayehmiri & others, 2020); have a lower risk for alcohol problems (Raketic & others, 2017); are less likely to engage in suicidal ideation and behavior (Lawson & others, 2021); have better health and less stress (Strickhouser, Zell, & Krizan, 2017); display superior problem-focused coping skills (Sesker & others, 2016); are less likely to engage excessively in screen time and use of social networking sites (Yanez & others, 2020); have greater life-satisfaction (Heilmann & others, 2021); and live longer (Chapman & others, 2020).

- *Extraversion.* Individuals high in *extraversion* are more likely to live longer (Graham & others, 2017); to be satisfied in their relationships (Toy, Nai, & Lee, 2016); to engage in social activities (Emmons & Diener, 1986); to cope more effectively with stress (Soto, 2015); to have fewer sleep problems (Hintsanen & others, 2014); and to have a positive view of their well-being in the future (Soto, 2015).

An adolescent with a high level of conscientiousness organizes her daily schedule and plans how to use her time effectively. *What are some characteristics of conscientiousness? How is it linked to adolescents' competence?*
Alejandro Rivera/Getty Images

- *Agreeableness.* People who are high in agreeableness are more likely to be generous and altruistic (Caprara & others, 2010); to have more satisfying romantic relationships (Donnellan, Larsen-Rife, & Conger, 2005); to view other people more positively (Wood, Harms, & Vazire, 2010); to cope more effectively with stress (Leger & others, 2016); to lie less about themselves in online dating profiles (Hall & others, 2010); and to have a positive view of their well-being in the future (Soto, 2015).

- *Neuroticism.* People high in neuroticism are more likely to die at a younger age (Graham & others, 2017); to have worse health and report having more health complaints (Strickhouser, Zell, & Krizan, 2017); to feel negative emotion more than positive emotion in daily life and to experience more lingering negative states (Widiger, 2009); to have symptoms of anxiety, depression, and obsessive-compulsive disorder (Tonarely & others, 2020); to become drug dependent (Valero & others, 2014); to have a greater probability of engaging in suicidal ideation and behavior (Lawson & others, 2021); and to have a lower sense of well-being 40 years later (Gale & others, 2013).

How do the Big Five factors change during adolescence? A large-scale cross-sectional study found that several of the Big Five factors show negative trends in early adolescence (Soto & others, 2011). In this study, young adolescents experienced declining levels of conscientiousness, extraversion, and agreeableness. However, conscientiousness and agreeableness increased in late adolescence and the beginning of emerging adulthood.

Optimism   Another important personality characteristic is **optimism**, which involves having a positive outlook on the future and a tendency to minimize problems (Baranski & others, 2021). Optimism is often referred to as a style of thinking.

Somewhat surprisingly, little research has been conducted recently on optimism in children, adolescents, and emerging adults. In *The Optimistic Child,* Martin Seligman (2007) described how parents, teachers, and coaches can instill optimism in children and adolescents, which he argues will help to make them more resilient and less likely to develop depression. One study found that having an optimistic style of thinking in adolescence predicted a reduction in suicidal ideation for individuals who had experienced negative and potentially traumatic life events (Hirsch & others, 2009). Another study revealed that adolescents with an optimistic thinking style had a lower risk of developing depressive symptoms than their pessimistic counterparts (Patton & others, 2011b). Also, a recent study indicated that higher levels of optimism are linked to lower levels of emotional distress in adolescents (Jimenez, Montorio, & Izal, 2017). And, in a recent study, college students who were more pessimistic had more anxious mood and stress symptoms (Lau & others, 2017). Further, one recent study indicated that being optimistic was associated with having higher health-related quality of life in adolescence (Haggstrom Westberg & others, 2019) and another study found that being more optimistic was linked to better academic achievement five months later in seventh grade (Tetzner & Becker, 2018). In addition, a recent study of Latinx young adoles-

optimism Involves having a positive outlook on the future and minimizing problems.

cents revealed that higher resilience and school attachment predicted higher levels of optimism (Taylor & others, 2020).

Traits and Situations   Many psychologists argue that it is better to view personality not only in terms of traits but also in terms of contexts and situations (Furr & Funder, 2021). They conclude that the trait approach ignores environmental factors and places too much emphasis on stability and lack of change. This criticism was first leveled by social cognitive theorist Walter Mischel (1968), who argued that personality varies according to the situation. Thus, adolescents who are in a library might behave quite differently from the way they would act at a party.

Today, most psychologists are interactionists, arguing that both traits and situations need to be taken into account in understanding personality (Asendorpf & Rauthmann, 2021). Let's again consider the situations of being in a library or at a party and consider the preferences of two adolescents—Jenna, who is an introvert, and Stacey, who is an extravert. Jenna, the introvert, is more likely to enjoy being in the library, whereas Stacey, the extravert, is more likely to have a good time at the party.

TEMPERAMENT

Although the study of personality has focused mainly on adults, the study of temperament has been limited primarily to infants and children (Ertekin, Gunnar, & Berument, 2021). However, both personality and temperament are important influences on adolescent development.

Temperament can be defined as an individual's behavioral style and characteristic way of responding. Many psychologists emphasize that temperament forms the foundation of personality. Through increasing capacities and interactions with the environment, temperament evolves or becomes elaborated across childhood and adolescence into a set of personality traits.

The close link between temperament and personality is supported by research that connects some of the Big Five personality factors to temperament categories (Shiner & DeYoung, 2013). For example, the temperament category of positive emotionality is related to the personality trait of extraversion, negative emotionality maps onto neuroticism (emotional instability), and effortful control is linked to conscientiousness (Putnam, Sanson, & Rothbart, 2002).

What temperament categories have been used to describe adolescents?
Ollyy/Shutterstock

temperament An individual's behavioral style and characteristic way of responding.

easy child A child who generally is in a positive mood, quickly establishes regular routines, and adapts easily to new experiences.

difficult child A child who reacts negatively to many situations and is slow to accept new experiences.

slow-to-warm-up child A child who has a low activity level, is somewhat negative, and displays a low intensity of mood.

Temperament Categories   Just as with personality, researchers are interested in discovering the key dimensions of temperament (Rothbart, Posner, & Sheese, 2021). Psychiatrists Alexander Chess and Stella Thomas (Chess & Thomas, 1977; Thomas & Chess, 1991) followed a group of infants into adulthood and concluded that there are three basic types, or clusters, of temperament:

- An **easy child** is generally in a positive mood, quickly establishes regular routines, and adapts readily to new experiences.
- A **difficult child** reacts negatively to many situations and is slow to accept new experiences.
- A **slow-to-warm-up child** has a low activity level, is somewhat negative, and displays a low intensity of mood.

New classifications of temperament continue to be forged (Bates, McQuillan, & Hoyniak, 2019; Rothbart, 2011). In a review of temperament research, Mary Rothbart and John Bates (1998) concluded that the best framework for classifying temperament involves a revision of Chess and Thomas' categories of easy, difficult, and slow to warm up. The general classification of temperament now focuses more on the following aspects:

- *Positive affect and approach.* This category is much like the personality trait of extraversion/introversion.
- *Negative affectivity.* This involves being easily distressed. Children with a temperament that involves negative affectivity may fret and cry often. Negative affectivity is closely related to the personality traits of introversion and neuroticism (emotional instability).
- *Effortful control (self-regulation).* This involves the ability to control one's emotions. Thus, adolescents who are high in effortful control show an ability to keep their arousal from getting too high and have strategies for soothing themselves. By

contrast, adolescents who are low on effortful control often show an inability to control their arousal, and they become easily agitated and intensely emotional (Eisenberg & others, 2002). Earlier in the chapter, we described the influence of effortful control in academic persistence and educational attainment (Veronneau & others, 2014). Also, in a recent study, children with a lower level of effort control at 3 years of age were more likely to have ADHD symptoms at 13 years of age (Einziger & others, 2018). Further, one study revealed that adolescents characterized by high positive affectivity, low negative affectivity, and high effortful control had lower levels of depressive symptoms (Verstraeten & others, 2009). And a recent study of adolescents found that effortful control was linked to a lower probability of suicidal ideation and behavior (Lawson & others, 2021).

Developmental Connections and Contexts   How stable is temperament from childhood to adulthood? Do young adults show the same behavioral style and characteristic emotional responses that they did when they were infants or young children? For instance, activity level is an important dimension of temperament. Are children's activity levels linked to their personality in emerging and early adulthood? In one longitudinal study, children who were highly active at age 4 were likely to be very outgoing at age 23, a finding that reflects continuity (Franz, 1996, p. 337). Yet, in other ways, temperament may change. From adolescence into early adulthood, most individuals show fewer mood swings, greater responsibility, and less risk-taking behavior—changes that suggest discontinuity of temperament (Caspi, 1998).

Is temperament in childhood linked to adjustment in adolescence and adulthood? Here is what is known based on the few longitudinal studies that have been conducted on this topic (Caspi, 1998). A longitudinal study using Chess and Thomas' categories found a link between temperament assessed at 1 year of age and adjustment at 17 years of age (Guerin & others, 2003). Individuals who had easier temperaments as infants showed more optimal development across behavioral and intellectual domains in late adolescence. These individuals also experienced a family environment that was more stimulating and cohesive and had more positive relationships with their parents during adolescence than did their counterparts with more difficult temperaments. When the participants were characterized by a difficult temperament in combination with a family environment that was high in conflict, rates of externalizing behavior problems (conduct problems, delinquency) increased.

In regard to a link between temperament in childhood and adjustment in adulthood, one longitudinal study found that children who had an easy temperament at 3 to 5 years of age were likely to be well adjusted as young adults (Chess & Thomas, 1977). In contrast, many children who had a difficult temperament at 3 to 5 years of age were not well adjusted as young adults. Other researchers have found that boys who have a difficult temperament in childhood are less likely than others to continue their formal education as adults; girls with a difficult temperament in childhood are more likely to experience marital conflict as adults (Wachs, 2000).

In sum, across a number of longitudinal studies, having an easy temperament in childhood is linked with more optimal development and adjustment in adolescence and adulthood. When the contexts in which individuals live are problematic, such as a family environment high in conflict, the long-term outcomes of having a difficult temperament are exacerbated.

Inhibition is another temperament characteristic that has been studied extensively (Kagan, 2013). Researchers have found that individuals with an inhibited temperament in childhood are less likely to be assertive or to experience social support as adolescents and emerging adults, and more likely to delay entering a stable job track (Wachs, 2000). And in a longitudinal study, an increasing trajectory of shyness in adolescence and emerging adulthood was linked to social anxiety, mood, and substance use disorders in adulthood (Tang & others, 2017).

Yet another aspect of temperament is emotionality and the ability to control one's emotions (Rothbart, 2011). In one longitudinal study, individuals who as 3-year-old children showed good control of their emotions and were resilient in the face of stress were likely to continue to handle their emotions effectively as adults (Block, 1993). In contrast, individuals who as 3-year-olds had low emotional control and were not very resilient were likely to show those same problems as young adults. Also, in a recent study, a high level of emotionality was related to depression in emerging adulthood (Bould & others, 2015).

	Child A	Child B
Intervening Context		
Caregivers	Caregivers (parents) who are sensitive and accepting, and let child set his or her own pace.	Caregivers who use inappropriate "low-level control" and attempt to force the child into new situations.
Physical Environment	Presence of "stimulus shelters" or "defensible spaces" that the children can retreat to when there is too much stimulation.	Child continually encounters noisy, chaotic environments that allow no escape from stimulation.
Peers	Peer groups with other inhibited children with common interests, so the child feels accepted.	Peer groups consist of athletic extraverts, so the child feels rejected.
Schools	School is "undermanned," so inhibited children are more likely to be tolerated and feel they can make a contribution.	School is "overmanned," so inhibited children are less likely to be tolerated and more likely to feel undervalued.
Personality Outcomes		
	As an adult, individual is closer to extraversion (outgoing, sociable) and is emotionally stable.	As an adult, individual is closer to introversion and has more emotional problems.

FIGURE 7

TEMPERAMENT IN CHILDHOOD, PERSONALITY IN ADULTHOOD, AND INTERVENING CONTEXTS. Varying experiences with caregivers, the physical environment, peers, and schools may modify links between temperament in childhood and personality in adulthood. The example given here is for inhibition.

In sum, these studies reveal some continuity between certain aspects of temperament in childhood and adjustment in early adulthood (Shiner & DeYoung, 2013; Wachs & Kohnstamm, 2013). Keep in mind, however, that these connections between childhood temperament and adult adjustment are based on only a small number of studies; more research is needed to verify the links. Indeed, Theodore Wachs (1994, 2000) has proposed ways that the links between childhood temperament and adult personality might vary, depending on the intervening contexts and individual experiences (see Figure 7).

The match between an individual's temperament and the environmental demands the individual must cope with, called **goodness of fit,** can be important to an adolescent's adjustment (Bates, McQuillan, & Hoyniak, 2019). In general, the temperament characteristics of effortful control, manageability, and agreeableness reduce the effects of adverse environments, whereas negative emotionality increases their effects (Rothbart, 2011).

In this chapter, we examined many aspects of the self, identity, emotions, and personality. In our discussion of identity and emotion, we evaluated the role of gender, a topic that is discussed in more detail in the chapter "Gender."

goodness of fit The match between an individual's temperament style and the environmental demands faced by the individual.

Review Connect Reflect

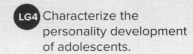 Characterize the personality development of adolescents.

Review

- What are some key personality traits in adolescence? Is personality influenced by situations?
- What is temperament, and how is it linked to personality? What are some key temperament categories? What developmental connections and contexts characterize temperament?

Connect

- How might the Big Five factors of personality be linked to the concept of risk taking?

Reflect *Your Own Personal Journey of Life*

- Consider your own temperament. We described a number of different temperament categories. Which one best describes your temperament? Has your temperament changed as you have grown older, or is it about the same as it was when you were a child or an adolescent? If your temperament has changed, what factors contributed to the changes?

reach your **learning goals**

The Self, Identity, Emotion, and Personality

1 The Self

LG1 Describe the development of the self in adolescence.

Self-Understanding and Understanding Others

- Self-understanding is the adolescent's cognitive representation of the self, the substance and content of the adolescent's self-conceptions. Dimensions of the adolescent's self-understanding include abstraction and idealism; differentiation; contradictions within the self; real and ideal selves; true and false selves; social comparison; self-consciousness; the unconscious self; and not yet being self-integrative.

- The increasing number of selves in adolescence can vary across relationships with people, social roles, and sociocultural contexts. In emerging adulthood, self-understanding becomes more integrative, reflective, and complex, and is characterized by decisions about a worldview. However, it is not until the thirties that a coherent and integrative worldview develops for many individuals.

- Three important aspects of understanding others in adolescence are perceiving others' traits, perspective taking, and social cognitive monitoring.

Self-Esteem and Self-Concept

- Self-esteem is the global, evaluative dimension of the self, and also is referred to as self-worth or self-image. Self-concept involves domain-specific self-evaluations. For too long, little attention was given to developing measures of self-esteem and self-concept specifically tailored to adolescents. Harter's Self-Perception Profile is one adolescent measure. Self-esteem reflects perceptions that do not always match reality. Thus, high self-esteem may be justified or it might reflect an arrogant, grandiose view of oneself that is not warranted. An increasing number of studies document the problems of adolescents who are narcissistic.

- Controversy characterizes the extent to which self-esteem changes during adolescence and whether there are gender differences in self-esteem. Researchers have found that self-esteem often drops during and just after developmental transitions, such as going from elementary school to middle or junior high school. Some researchers have found that the self-esteem of girls declines in adolescence, especially during early adolescence, although other researchers argue that this decline has been exaggerated and actually is only modest in nature.

- Self-esteem is only moderately linked to school success. Adolescents with high self-esteem have greater initiative, but this can produce positive or negative outcomes. Perceived physical appearance is an especially strong contributor to global self-esteem. Peer acceptance also is linked to global self-esteem in adolescence. In Coopersmith's study, children's self-esteem was associated with such parenting practices as showing affection and allowing children freedom within well-defined limits. Peer and friendship relations also are linked with self-esteem. Self-esteem is higher in elementary school than in middle or junior high school.

- For most adolescents, low self-esteem results in only temporary emotional discomfort. However, for others, especially when low self-esteem persists, it is linked with depression, delinquency, and even suicide. Four ways to increase adolescents' self-esteem are to (1) identify the causes of low self-esteem and determine which domains of competence are important to the adolescent, (2) provide emotional support and social approval, (3) help the adolescent to achieve success, and (4) improve the adolescent's coping skills.

Self-Regulation

- Self-regulation involves the ability to control one's behavior without having to rely on others' help. Self-regulation includes the self-generation and cognitive monitoring of thoughts, feelings, and behavior in order to reach a goal. Self-regulation plays a key role in many aspects of adolescent development, especially achievement and academic success. Various factors might enhance or inhibit an adolescent's ability to engage in self-regulation.

2 Identity

LG2 Explain the many facets of identity development.

Erikson's Ideas on Identity

- Identity versus identity confusion is Erikson's fifth developmental stage, which individuals experience during adolescence. As adolescents are confronted with new roles, they enter a psychosocial moratorium. Role experimentation is a key ingredient of Erikson's view of identity development. In technological societies like that of the United States, the vocational role is especially important. Identity development is extraordinarily complex and takes place in bits and pieces. A current concern voiced by William Damon is the difficulty too many youth today encounter in developing a purposeful identity.

The Four Statuses of Identity

- Marcia proposed four identity statuses: diffused, foreclosed, moratorium, and achieved. A combination of crisis (exploration) and commitment yields each of the statuses. Some critics argue that Marcia's four identity statuses oversimplify identity development. Recently, emphasis has been given to expanding Marcia's concepts of exploration and commitment to focus more on in-depth exploration and ongoing evaluation of one's commitment.

Developmental Changes in Identity

- Some experts argue that the main identity changes take place in late adolescence rather than in early adolescence. College upperclassmen are more likely to be identity achieved than are freshmen or high school students, although many college students are still wrestling with ideological commitments. Individuals often follow MAMA ("moratorium-achievement-moratorium-achievement") cycles.

Identity and Social Contexts

- Parents are important figures in adolescents' identity development. Researchers have found that democratic parenting, individuality, connectedness, and enabling behaviors are linked with positive aspects of identity. Erikson was especially sensitive to the role of culture in identity development, underscoring the fact that throughout the world ethnic minority groups have struggled to maintain their cultural identities while blending into majority culture. Identity development also is influenced by the types of peers, friends, and romantic partners adolescents and emerging adults interact with. In recent years, the digital world has provided a broader platform for adolescents and emerging adults to express their identity and get feedback about it. Adolescence is often a special juncture in the identity development of ethnic minority individuals because for the first time they consciously confront their ethnic identity. Many ethnic minority adolescents have a bicultural identity. Ethnic identity increases with age during adolescence and emerging adulthood, and higher levels of ethnic identity are linked to more positive attitudes. The contexts in which ethnic minority youth live influence their identity development. There also has been increasing interest in the concept of racial identity as well as a unified concept of ethnic-racial identity.

- Erikson noted that adolescent males have a stronger vocational identity, female adolescents a stronger social identity. However, researchers are finding that these gender differences are disappearing.

Identity and Intimacy

- Intimacy versus isolation is Erikson's sixth stage of development, which individuals experience during early adulthood. Erikson argued that an optimal sequence is to develop a positive identity before negotiating the intimacy versus isolation stage.

3 Emotional Development

LG3 Discuss the emotional development of adolescents.

The Emotions of Adolescence

- Emotion is feeling, or affect, that occurs when a person is in a state or an interaction that is important to the individual, especially to his or her well-being. Adolescents report more extreme and fleeting emotions than do their parents, and as individuals go through early adolescence they are less likely to report being very happy. However, it is important to view moodiness as a normal aspect of early adolescence.

Hormones, Experience, and Emotions

- Although pubertal change is associated with an increase in negative emotions, hormonal influences are often small, and environmental experiences may contribute more to the emotions of adolescence than do hormonal changes.

Emotion Regulation

- The ability to manage and control one's emotions is a key dimension of positive outcomes in adolescence. With increasing age, adolescents are more likely to use cognitive strategies for regulating emotion, although there are wide individual variations in this aspect of adolescence. A prominent feature of adolescents with problems is their inability to effectively manage their emotions. Cognitive reappraisal is often a more effective emotion regulation strategy than suppression.

Emotional Competence

- Adolescents' increased cognitive abilities and awareness provide them with the opportunity to cope more effectively with stress and emotional fluctuations. However, the emotional burdens of adolescence can be overwhelming for some adolescents. Among the emotional competencies that are important for adolescents to develop are being aware that the expression of emotions plays a major role in relationships, adaptively coping with negative emotions by using self-regulatory strategies, understanding how emotionally expressive behavior influences others, being aware of one's emotional states without being overwhelmed by them, and being able to discern others' emotions.

Social-Emotional Education Programs

- An increasing number of programs are being used in schools to improve the socioemotional development of children. Two such programs are (1) Second Step and (2) CASEL.

4 Personality Development Characterize the personality development of adolescents.

Personality

- There has been a long history of interest in discovering the core traits of personality, and recently that search has focused on the Big Five factors of personality: openness to experience, conscientiousness, extraversion, agreeableness, and neuroticism (emotional instability). Much of the research on the Big Five factors has focused on adults, but an increasing number of studies focus on adolescents. Having an optimistic thinking style is linked to positive adjustment in adolescents.

- Researchers continue to debate what the core characteristics of personality are. Critics of the trait approach argue that it places too much emphasis on stability and not enough on change and situational influences. Today, many psychologists stress that personality is best described in terms of both traits and situational influences.

Temperament

- Many psychologists emphasize that temperament is the foundation of personality. Chess and Thomas described three basic types of temperament: easy child, difficult child, and slow-to-warm-up child. New classifications of temperament focus on positive affect and approach, negative affectivity, and effortful control (self-regulation). Connections between the temperament of individuals from childhood to adulthood have been found, although these links may vary according to the contexts of people's lives. Goodness of fit refers to the match between an individual's temperament and the environmental demands he or she encounters.

key **terms**

bicultural identity	ethnic identity	individuality	racial identity
Big Five factors of personality	goodness of fit	intimacy versus isolation	self
commitment	identity	narcissism	self-concept
connectedness	identity achievement	optimism	self-esteem
crisis	identity diffusion	personality	self-regulation
difficult child	identity foreclosure	perspective taking	self-understanding
easy child	identity moratorium	possible self	slow-to-warm-up child
emotion	identity versus identity confusion	psychosocial moratorium	temperament

key **people**

Margarita Azmitia	Erik Erikson	Koen Luyckx	Moin Syed
Alexander Chess	Luc Goossens	James Marcia	Stella Thomas
Catherine Cooper	Susan Harter	Walter Mischel	Adriana Umana-Taylor
James Coté	Jane Kroger	Jean Phinney	Alan Waterman
William Damon	Gisela Labouvie-Vief	Seth Schwartz	

improving **the lives of adolescents and emerging adults**

The Construction of the Self (**2nd ed.**) (**2012**)
Susan Harter
New York: Guilford Press
> Leading self theorist and researcher Susan Harter provides an in-depth analysis of how the self develops in childhood and adolescence.

Emotion Regulation (**2018**)
Edited by Pamela Cole and Tom Hollenstein
New York: Routledge
> This book includes four chapters on emotion regulation in adolescence by leading experts, including developmental changes in emotion regulation and how emotion regulation is best attained in various contexts.

Gandhi's Truth (**1969**)
Erik Erikson
New York: Norton
> This Pulitzer Prize–winning book by Erik Erikson, who developed the concept of identity as a central aspect of adolescent development, analyzes the life of Mahatma Gandhi, the spiritual leader of India in the middle of the twentieth century.

Identity Development Process and Content: Toward an Integrated and Contextualized Science of Identity (**2017**)
Developmental Psychology, *53,* 2009–2217
> Leading experts provide an up-to-date, in-depth exploration of many aspects of identity development in adolescence and emerging adulthood, with papers on topics such as models of identity development, ethnic and cultural identity, and links between identity and various areas of psychosocial functioning.

Oxford Handbook of Identity Development (**2015**)
Edited by Kate McLean and Moin Syed
New York: Oxford University Press
> Leading experts provide contemporary and important reviews of research and theory on identity development in adolescence and emerging adulthood.

The Structure of Temperament and Personality Traits (**2013**)
Rebecca Shiner and Colin DeYoung
In P. D. Zelazo (Ed.), *Oxford Handbook of Developmental Psychology.*
New York: Oxford University Press
> Leading experts describe recent research on how temperament and personality are structured and how they develop.

GENDER

chapter outline

"You know, it seems like girls are more emotionally sensitive than guys, especially teenage guys.** We don't know all the reasons, but we have some ideas about why this might be true. Once a girl reaches 12 or so and begins to mature physically, it seems as though nature is preparing her to be sensitive to others the way a mother might be to her baby, to feel what others feel so she can provide love and support to her children. Our culture tells boys different things. They are expected to be 'tough' and not get carried away with their feelings. . . . In spite of this, don't think that girls cannot be assertive and boys cannot be sensitive. In fact, boys do feel emotions but many of them simply don't know how to express their feelings or fear that they will be teased."

—ZOE, AGE 13

(ZAGER & RUBENSTEIN, 2002, PP. 21–22)

"With all the feminist ideas in the country and the equality, I think guys sometimes get put on the spot. Guys might do something that I think or they think might not be wrong at all, but they still get shot down for it. If you're not nice to a girl, she thinks you don't care. But if you are nice, she thinks you are treating her too much like a lady. Girls don't understand guys, and guys don't understand girls very well."

—TOBY, AGE 17

(POLLACK, 1999, P. 164)

The comments of these two adolescents—one girl, one boy—reflect the confusion that many adolescents feel about how to act as a girl or a boy. Nowhere in adolescents' socioemotional development have more sweeping changes occurred in recent years than in the area of gender, and these changes have led to confusion about gender behavior.

preview

What exactly is meant by gender? **Gender** refers to characteristics related to femininity and masculinity based on social and cultural norms. **Gender identity** involves a sense of one's own gender, including knowledge, understanding, and acceptance of being a boy/man, a girl/woman, or another gender. **Gender roles** are expectations that prescribe how girls/women or boys/men should think, act, and feel. For example, should boys/men be more assertive than girls/women, and should girls/women be more sensitive than boys/men to others' feelings? Though individuals become aware of gender early in childhood, a new dimension is added to gender with the onset of puberty and the sexual maturation it brings. This chapter begins with a discussion of the biological as well as the social and cognitive influences on gender. We will distinguish gender stereotypes from actual differences between the sexes and examine the range of gender roles that adolescents can adopt. The chapter closes by exploring the developmental changes in gender that characterize adolescence.

gender Characteristics related to femininity and masculinity based on social and cultural norms.

gender identity Involves a sense of one's own gender, including knowledge, understanding, and acceptance of being a boy/man, a girl/woman, or another gender.

gender roles Expectations that prescribe how girls/women and boys/men should think, act, and feel.

| Biological Influences on Gender | Social Influences on Gender | Cognitive Influences on Gender |

Gender development is influenced by biological, social, and cognitive factors (Erickson-Schroth & Davis, 2021). Our discussion of these influences focuses on questions like these: How strong is biology's influence on gender? How extensively does experience shape children's and adolescents' gender development? To what extent do cognitive factors influence gender development?

BIOLOGICAL INFLUENCES ON GENDER

Pubertal change is a biological influence on gendered behavior in adolescence (Hines, 2013, 2015). Both Freud and Erikson argued that the physical characteristics of boys/men and girls/women influence their behavior. And evolutionary psychologists emphasize the role of gender in the survival of the fittest.

Pubertal Change and Sexuality Puberty intensifies the sexual aspects of adolescents' gender attitudes and behavior (Hines, 2020a, b). As their bodies flood with hormones, young adolescents incorporate sexuality into their gender attitudes and behaviors, especially when they interact with an individual to whom they are sexually attracted. Thus, an adolescent girl might behave in a sensitive, charming, and soft-spoken manner with a boy to whom she is sexually attracted, whereas a boy might behave in an assertive, cocky, and forceful way when he is around an attractive girl, perceiving that such behaviors enhance his sexual and romantic status.

Few attempts have been made to relate puberty's sexual changes to gender behavior. Researchers have found, however, that sexual behavior is related to hormonal changes during puberty (Hines, 2020a, b). Levels of testosterone are correlated with sexual behavior in boys during puberty (Nguyen, 2018). However, a recent meta-analysis concluded that while higher testosterone levels are linked to increased aggression, the link is not very strong (Geniole & others, 2020).

Freud and Erikson—Anatomy Is Destiny Both Sigmund Freud and Erik Erikson argued that an individual's genitals influence his or her gender behavior and, therefore, that anatomy is destiny. One of Freud's basic assumptions was that human behavior is directly related to reproductive processes. From this assumption arose his belief that gender and sexual behavior are essentially unlearned and instinctual. Erikson (1968) extended Freud's argument, claiming that the psychological differences between males and females stem from their anatomical differences. Erikson argued that, because of genital structure, males are more intrusive and aggressive, females more inclusive and passive. Critics of the anatomy-is-destiny view stress that experience is not given enough credit. The critics say that females and males have more freedom to choose their gender roles than Freud and Erikson envisioned. In response to the critics, Erikson modified his view, saying that females in today's world are transcending their biological heritage and correcting society's overemphasis on male intrusiveness.

Evolutionary Psychology and Gender Evolutionary psychology emphasizes that adaptation during the evolution of humans produced psychological differences between males and females (Lewis, Al-Shawaf, & Buss, 2021). Evolutionary psychologists argue that primarily because of their differing roles in reproduction, males and females faced different pressures in primeval environments when the human species was evolving (Thoni, Volk, & Cortina, 2021). In particular, because having multiple sexual liaisons improves the likelihood that males will

developmental **connection**

Biological Processes

Hormones are powerful chemical substances secreted by the endocrine glands and carried through the body by the bloodstream. Connect to "Puberty, Health, and Biological Foundations."

developmental **connection**

Theories

Evolutionary psychology emphasizes the importance of adaptation, reproduction, and "survival of the fittest" in shaping behavior. Connect to "Puberty, Health, and Biological Foundations."

pass on their genes, natural selection favored males who adopted short-term mating strategies. These males competed with other males to acquire more resources in order to access females. Therefore, say evolutionary psychologists, males evolved dispositions that favor violence, competition, and risk taking (Hoefnagels, 2021).

In contrast, according to evolutionary psychologists, females' contributions to the gene pool were improved by securing resources for their offspring, which was promoted by obtaining long-term mates who could support a family. As a consequence, natural selection favored females who devoted effort to parenting and chose mates who could provide their offspring with resources and protection (Marzoli, Havlicek, & Roberts, 2018). Females developed preferences for successful, ambitious men who could provide these resources (Jonason, 2017).

This evolutionary unfolding, according to some evolutionary psychologists, explains key gender differences in sexual attitudes and sexual behavior (Anholt & others, 2020). For example, in one study, men said that ideally they would like to have more than 18 sexual partners in their lifetime, whereas women stated that ideally they would like to have only 4 or 5 (Buss & Schmitt, 1993). In another study, 75 percent of the men but none of the women approached by an attractive stranger of the opposite sex consented to a request for sex (Clark & Hatfield, 1989).

Such gender differences, says David Buss (2019), are exactly the type predicted by evolutionary psychology. Buss argues that men and women differ psychologically in those domains in which they have faced different adaptive problems during evolutionary history. In all other domains, predicts Buss, the sexes will be psychologically similar.

Critics of evolutionary psychology argue that its hypotheses are backed by speculations about prehistory, not evidence, and that in any event people are not locked into behavior that was adaptive in the evolutionary past. Critics also claim that the evolutionary view pays too much attention to biology and too little attention to environmental experiences in explaining gender differences (Hyde & DeLamater, 2020).

SOCIAL INFLUENCES ON GENDER

Many social scientists do not locate the cause of psychological gender differences in biological dispositions (Helgeson, 2020). Rather, they argue that these differences are due mainly to social experiences (Pang & Baumann, 2020). Alice Eagly (2001, 2010, 2018) proposed **social role theory,** which states that gender differences mainly result from the contrasting roles of females and males. In most cultures around the world, females have less power and status than males have, and they control fewer resources (UNICEF, 2021). Compared with men, women perform more domestic work, spend fewer hours in paid employment, receive lower pay, and are more thinly represented in the highest levels of organizations. In Eagly's view, as women adapted to roles with less power and less status in society, they showed more cooperative, less dominant profiles than men. Thus, the social hierarchy and division of labor are important causes of gender differences in power, assertiveness, and nurturing behavior (Eagly, 2018).

developmental **connection**

Achievement

Parents' and teachers' expectations are important influences on adolescents' achievement. Connect to "Achievement, Work, and Careers."

Parental Influences Parents, by action and example, influence their children's and adolescents' gender development (MacMullin & others, 2021; Mousavi & others, 2020). During the transition from childhood to adolescence, parents give more independence to their sons than to their daughters, and concern about girls' sexual vulnerability may cause parents to monitor their behavior more closely and ensure that they are chaperoned. Families with young adolescent daughters indicate that they experience more intense conflict about sex, choice of friends, and curfews than do families with young adolescent sons (Papini & Sebby, 1988).

Parents may also have different achievement expectations for their adolescent sons and daughters, especially in academic areas such as math and science (Wigfield & others, 2015). For example, many parents believe that math is more important to their sons' futures than to their daughters'. These beliefs influence the value that adolescents place on math achievement. We will discuss gender and achievement in more detail later in this chapter.

Mothers and fathers often interact differently with their adolescents (Itahashi & others, 2020). Mothers are more involved with their children and adolescents than are fathers, although fathers increase the time they spend in parenting when they have sons and are less likely to become divorced when they have sons (Diekmann & Schmidheiny, 2004). Mothers' interactions

social role theory Theory stating that gender differences mainly result from the contrasting roles of women and men, with women having less power and status and controlling fewer resources than men.

How do mothers and fathers interact differently with their daughters and sons?
(left): Ariel Skelley/Getty Images; (right): Fuse/Getty Images

with their adolescents often center on caregiving and teaching activities, whereas fathers' interactions often involve leisure activities (Galambos, Berenbaum, & McHale, 2009).

Mothers and fathers also often interact differently with their sons and daughters (Morawska, 2020). In a research review, the following conclusions were reached (Bronstein, 2006):

- *Mothers' socialization strategies.* In many cultures, mothers socialize their daughters to be more obedient and responsible than their sons. They also place more restrictions on daughters' autonomy.

- *Fathers' socialization strategies.* Fathers show more attention to sons than daughters, engage in more activities with sons, and put forth more effort to promote sons' intellectual development.

Thus, despite a trend toward more egalitarian gender roles in many aspects of society, many mothers and fathers showed marked differences in the way they interacted with their sons and daughters, and these differences persisted through adolescence (Bronstein, 2006; Galambos, Berenbaum, & McHale, 2009).

Recent research has provided further support for the belief that some aspects of gender roles are still not egalitarian (Eagly, 2018; Lord & others, 2017). In one study, college students were interviewed about their future selves in the near future (1 year) and the distant future (10–15 years) (Brown & Diekman, 2010). Stronger gender patterns were found for distant than near selves. For distant selves, women were more likely to list "family" while men were more likely to list "career." In terms of "family" selves in the future, men were more likely to list their role as "economic provider" while women were more likely to list their role as "caregiver."

Social cognitive theory has been especially important in understanding social influences on gender (Bussey & Bandura, 1999). The **social cognitive theory of gender** emphasizes that children's and adolescents' gender development is influenced by their observation and imitation of others' gender behavior, as well as by the rewards and punishments they experience for gender-appropriate and gender-inappropriate behavior. By observing parents and other adults, as well as peers, at home, at school, in the neighborhood, and in the media, adolescents are exposed to a myriad of models that display masculine and feminine behavior (Twenge & Martin, 2020). And parents often use verbal reinforcement to teach their daughters to be feminine ("Karen, that dress you are wearing makes you look so beautiful") and their sons to be masculine ("Bobby, you were so aggressive in that game. Way to go!").

Siblings Siblings also play a role in gender socialization (Galambos, Berenbaum, & McHale, 2009). One study revealed that over a two-year time frame in early adolescence, younger siblings became more similar to their older siblings in terms of gender-role and leisure activity (McHale & others, 2001). For example, if a younger sibling had an older sibling who was masculine and engaged in masculine leisure activities, over the two years the younger sibling became more masculine and participated in more masculine leisure activities. In contrast, older siblings became less like their younger siblings over the two-year period.

developmental **connection**

Social Cognitive Theory

Social cognitive theory holds that behavior, environment, and person/cognitive factors are the key aspects of development. Connect to "Introduction."

social cognitive theory of gender Theory emphasizing that children's and adolescents' gender development occurs through observation and imitation of gender behavior, and through rewards and punishments they experience for gender-appropriate and gender-inappropriate behavior.

What role does gender play in adolescent peer relations?
Fuse/Getty Images

Peers   Parents provide the first models of gender behavior, but before long peers also are responding to and modeling masculine and feminine behavior (McGuire, Jefferys, & Rutland, 2020). In middle and late childhood, children show a clear preference for being with and liking same-sex peers (Maccoby, 1998, 2002). After extensive observations of elementary school playgrounds, two researchers characterized the play settings as "gender school," pointing out that boys teach one another the required masculine behavior and reinforce it, and that girls also teach one another the required feminine behavior and reinforce it (Luria & Herzog, 1985).

Adolescents spend increasing amounts of time with peers (Orben, Tomova, & Blakemore, 2020). In adolescence, peer approval or disapproval is a powerful influence on gender attitudes and behavior. Peer groups in adolescence are more likely to be a mix of boys and girls than they were in childhood. However, one study of 15- to 17-year-olds indicated that gender segregation characterizes some aspects of adolescents' social life (Mehta & Strough, 2010). In this study, 72 percent of peers said they were most likely to "hang out" with adolescents of the same gender as themselves.

Peers can socialize gender behavior partly by accepting or rejecting others on the basis of their gender-related attributes (Bagwell & Bukowski, 2018; Rose & Smith, 2018). From adolescence through late adulthood, friendships mainly involve same-sex peers (Mehta & Strough, 2009, 2010).

Peers extensively reward and punish gender behavior (Kwan & others, 2020). For example, when children and adolescents behave in ways that the culture says are sex-appropriate, they tend to be rewarded by their peers (Nabbijohn & others, 2020). Those who engage in activities that are considered sex-inappropriate tend to be criticized or abandoned by their peers. It is generally more accepted for girls to act like boys than it is for boys to act like girls; thus, use of the term *tomboy* to describe masculine girls is often thought of as less derogatory than the term *sissy* to describe feminine boys (Pasterski, Golombok, & Hines, 2011). In a recent British study, gender-nonconforming boys were most at risk for peer rejection (Braun & Davidson, 2017). In this study, gender-nonconforming girls were preferred over gender-conforming girls, with children most often citing masculine activities as the reason for this choice. Also in recent research, young male adolescents felt more pressure from parents to engage in gender-conforming behavior and felt more pressure from peers to avoid engaging in gender-nonconforming behavior (Jackson, Bussey, & Myers, 2021). And in a cross-cultural study of 11- to 13-year-olds in Shanghai (China), New Delhi (India), Ghent (Belgium), and Baltimore (United States), there was a growing acceptance of girls who wore boyish clothes and engaged in stereotypical masculine activities such as playing soccer or football, but no comparable acceptance of boys who engaged in traditionally feminine behaviors (Yu & others, 2017).

Schools and Teachers   Some observers have expressed concern that schools and teachers have biases against both boys and girls (Berkowitz & others, 2020; Sadker, Zittleman, & Koch, 2022). What evidence exists that the classroom setting is biased against boys? Here are some factors to consider (DeZolt & Hull, 2001):

- Compliance, following rules, and being neat and orderly are valued and reinforced in many classrooms. These behaviors usually characterize girls more than boys.

- A large majority of teachers are female, especially at the elementary school level. This trend may make it more difficult for boys than for girls to identify with their teachers and model their teachers' behavior. One study revealed that male teachers perceived boys more positively and viewed them as more educationally competent than did female teachers (Mullola & others, 2012).

- Boys are more likely than girls to have a learning disability or ADHD and to drop out of school.

- Boys are more likely than girls to be criticized by their teachers.

- School personnel tend to ignore clear evidence that many boys are having academic problems, especially in the language arts.

- School personnel tend to stereotype boys' behavior as problematic.

What evidence is there that the classroom setting is biased against girls? Consider these differences (Sadker, Zittleman, & Koch, 2022):

- In a typical classroom, girls are more compliant and boys are more rambunctious. Boys demand more attention, and girls are more likely to quietly wait their turn. Teachers are more likely to scold and reprimand boys, as well as send boys to school authorities for disciplinary action. Educators worry that girls' tendency to be compliant and quiet comes at a cost: diminished assertiveness.

- In many classrooms, teachers spend more time watching and interacting with boys, whereas girls work and play quietly on their own. Most teachers don't intentionally favor boys by spending more time with them, yet somehow the classroom frequently ends up with this type of gendered profile.

- Boys get more instruction than girls and more help when they have trouble with a question. Teachers often give boys more time to answer a question, more hints at the correct answer, and further tries if they give the wrong answer.

- Boys are more likely than girls to get lower grades and to be grade repeaters, yet girls are less likely to believe that they will be successful in college work.

- Girls and boys enter first grade with roughly equal levels of self-esteem. Yet by the middle school years, girls' self-esteem is lower than boys'.

- When elementary school children are asked to list what they want to do when they grow up, boys describe more career options than girls do.

How does gender affect school experiences during adolescence?
FatCamera/Getty Images

Thus, there is evidence of gender bias against both males and females in schools. Many school personnel are not aware of their gender-biased attitudes. These attitudes are deeply entrenched in and supported by the general culture. Increasing awareness of gender bias in schools is clearly a prerequisite for reducing such bias.

Might single-sex education be better for adolescents than coed schools? The argument for single-sex education is that it eliminates distraction from the other sex and reduces sexual harassment. Single-sex public education has increased dramatically in recent years. In 2002, only 12 public schools in the United States provided single-sex education; during the 2011–2012 school year, 116 public schools were single-sex and an additional 390 provided such experiences (NASSPE, 2012).

The increase in single-sex education has especially been fueled by its inclusion in the No Child Left Behind legislation as a means of improving the educational experiences and academic achievement of low-income students of color. It appears that many of the public schools offering single-sex education have a high percentage of such youth (Klein, 2012). However, multiple research reviews conclude that there are no documented benefits of single-sex education, especially in the highest-quality studies (Goodkind, 2013; Halpern & others, 2011; Pahlke, Hyde, & Allison, 2014). One review, titled "The Pseudoscience of Single-Sex Schooling," by Diane Halpern and her colleagues (2011) concluded that single-sex education is misguided, misconstrued, and unsupported by any valid scientific evidence. They emphasize that among the many arguments against single-sex education, the strongest is its reduction in the opportunities for boys and girls to work together in a supervised, purposeful environment. Other leading experts on gender also have argued that the factors that benefit students' education and development are more likely to be found in coeducational rather than single-sex schools (Bigler, Hayes, & Liben, 2014).

There has been a special call for single-sex public education for one group of adolescents—African American boys—because of their historically poor academic achievement and high dropout rate from school (Mitchell & Stewart, 2013). In 2010, Urban Prep Academy for Young Men became the first all-male, all African American public charter school. One hundred percent of its first graduates enrolled in college, despite the school's location in a section of Chicago where poverty, gangs, and crime predominate. Few public schools focus solely on educating African American boys, however, and it is not yet clear whether single-sex education might be more effective than coeducational schooling across a wider range of participants (Barbarin, Chinn, & Wright, 2014).

What are some recent changes in single-sex education in the United States? What does research say about whether same-sex education is beneficial?
Jim Weber/The Commercial Appeal/Landov

Girls/women are often portrayed in sexually provocative ways in entertainment and music videos.
David Bro/ZUMA Press, Inc./Alamy Stock Photo

developmental **connection**

Identity

Girls have more negative body images than do boys during adolescence. Connect to "Puberty, Health, and Biological Foundations."

How might social media influence adolescents' body images?
monkeybusinessimages/Getty Images

Mass Media Influences   As already described, adolescents encounter gender roles in their everyday interactions with parents, peers, and teachers. The messages about gender roles carried by the mass media also are important influences on adolescents' gender development (Sampasa-Kanyinga & others, 2020). Television shows directed at adolescents are highly stereotyped in their portrayal of the sexes, especially teenage girls (Starr, 2015). One study found that teenage girls were portrayed as being concerned primarily with dating, shopping, and their appearance (Campbell, 1988). They rarely were shown as being interested in school or career plans. Attractive girls were often stereotyped as "airheads" and intelligent girls as unattractive.

Another highly stereotyped form of programming that specifically targets teenage viewers is music videos. The behavior that adolescents see on MTV and some other TV networks is highly stereotyped and slanted toward a male audience. MTV has been described as a teenage boy's "dream world," filled with beautiful, aroused women who outnumber men, seek out and even assault them to have sex, and always mean yes, even when they say no (Jhally, 1990). One study found that MTV videos reinforced stereotypical notions of women as sexual objects and women as subordinate to men (Wallis, 2011). And in a recent study, adolescents who watched more music television than their same-aged peers had a stronger acceptance of rape myths (stereotyped and false beliefs about rape that are especially used to deny or justify male sexual aggression against females) five years later in emerging adulthood (Vangeel, Eggermont, & Vandenbosch, 2020).

Early adolescence may be a period of heightened sensitivity to televised messages about gender roles. Increasingly, young adolescents view programs designed for adults that include messages about gender-appropriate behavior, especially in heterosexual relationships. Cognitively, adolescents engage in more idealistic thoughts than children do, and media programs are filled with idealized images that adolescents may identify with and imitate—highly appealing actors and models who are young, thin, and glamorous, for example.

The world of television is highly gender-stereotyped and conveys clear messages about the relative power and importance of girs/women and boys/men (Wille & others, 2018). Men are portrayed as more powerful than women on many TV shows. On music videos, boys/men are portrayed more often than girls/women as aggressive, dominant, competent, autonomous, and active, whereas girls/women are more often portrayed as passive. In one study of prime-time commercials, women were underrepresented as primary characters except in commercials for health and beauty products (Ganahl, Prinsen, & Netzley, 2003).

The media influence adolescents' body images, and some studies reveal gender differences in this area (Hartman-Munick & others, 2020). For example, one study of 10- to 17-year-olds found that girls were more likely than boys to perceive that the media influenced their body images (Polce-Lynch & others, 2001). Also, in a recent study, higher social media use was linked to more negative body images among adolescents, more so for girls than boys (Kelly & others, 2019). Another study revealed that the more time adolescent girls and boys spent watching television for entertainment, the more negative their body images were (Anderson & others, 2001). Adolescent boys are exposed to a highly muscular body ideal for males in media outlets, especially in advertisements that include professional athletes and in video games (Near, 2013). An analysis of men's magazines found that more than half of their advertisements reflected hyper-masculine beliefs (toughness as emotional control, violence as manly, danger as exciting, and callous attitudes toward women and sex) (Vokey, Tefft, & Tysiaczny, 2013). Some of the magazines included at least one hyper-masculine belief in more than 90 percent of their ads.

In the last decade, adolescents have spent huge amounts of time on social media (Walsh & others, 2020). Are social media influencing the body images of adolescents, especially girls? In a recent study of U.S. college women, more time on Facebook was related to more negative feelings about their own bodies (Eckler, Kalyango, & Paasch, 2017), Further, recent research found that exposure to attractive celebrity and peer images of women on Instagram were detrimental to the body images of college women (Brown & Tiggemann, 2016). And in a recent study involving 13- to 15-year-olds, social media and Internet use were more strongly linked to compromised mental health for girls than for boys (Twenge & Farley, 2021). For example, girls who were heavy Internet users were 166 percent more likely than low users to have clinical levels of depressive symptoms, compared with 75 percent for boys.

COGNITIVE INFLUENCES ON GENDER

Observation, imitation, rewards and punishment—these are the mechanisms by which gender develops, according to social cognitive theory. From this perspective, interactions between the child/adolescent and the social environment are the most influential mechanisms for gender development. However, some critics who adopt a cognitive approach argue that social cognitive explanations pay too little attention to the adolescent's own mind and understanding, portraying adolescents as passively accepting gender roles (Martin, Ruble, & Szkrybalo, 2002).

One influential cognitive theory is **gender schema theory,** which states that gender-typing emerges as children and adolescents gradually develop gender schemas of what is gender-appropriate and gender-inappropriate in their culture (Martin & others, 2017). A schema is a cognitive structure: a network of associations that guide an individual's perceptions. A gender schema organizes the world in terms of female and male. Children and adolescents are internally motivated to perceive the world and to act in accordance with their developing schemas. Bit by bit, children and adolescents pick up what is gender-appropriate and gender-inappropriate in their culture, developing gender schemas that shape how they perceive the world and what they remember. Children and adolescents are motivated to act in ways that conform to these gender schemas.

In sum, cognitive factors contribute to the way adolescents think and act as males and females (Martin & others, 2017). Through biological, social, and cognitive processes, children and adolescents develop their gender attitudes and behaviors (Rose & Smith, 2018).

Regardless of the factors that influence gender behavior, the consequences of gender have become the subject of intense focus and research over the last several decades (Erickson-Schroth & Davis, 2021). In the next section, we explore the myths and realities of how girls/women and boys/men do or do not differ from each other.

Review *Connect* Reflect

LG1 Describe the biological, social, and cognitive influences on gender.

Review

- How can gender and gender roles be defined? What are some important biological influences on gender?
- What are some important social influences on gender?
- What are some important cognitive influences on gender?

Connect

- How might the characteristics of Piaget's stage of formal operational thought be linked to the way adolescents think about gender?

Reflect *Your Own Personal Journey of Life*

- Which theory do you think best explains your gender development through adolescence? What might an eclectic view of gender development be like?

2 Gender Stereotypes, Similarities, and Differences

LG2 Discuss gender stereotypes, similarities, and differences.

| Gender Stereotyping | Gender Similarities and Differences | Gender Controversy | Gender in Context |

How pervasive is gender stereotyping? What are the real differences between boys/men and girls/women, and why is this issue such a controversial one? In this section, our goal is not just to answer these questions but also to discuss controversy regarding gender and to place gender behavior in context.

GENDER STEREOTYPING

Gender stereotypes are general impressions and beliefs about girls/women and boys/men. For example, boys/men are powerful; girls/women are weak. Boys/men will make good mechanics; girls/women will make good nurses. Boys/men are good with numbers; girls/women are good

gender schema theory Theory stating that an individual's attention and behavior are guided by an internal motivation to conform to gender-based sociocultural standards and stereotypes.

gender stereotypes Broad categories that reflect our impressions and beliefs about girls/women and boys/men.

with words. Girls/women are emotional; boys/men are not. All of these are stereotypes. They are generalizations about a group that reflect widely held beliefs. Researchers have found that gender stereotypes are, to a great extent, still present in today's world, in the lives of both children and adults (Zarzeczna & others, 2020). Researchers also have found that boys' gender stereotypes are more rigid than girls' (Blakemore, Berenbaum, & Liben, 2009).

A classic study in the early 1970s assessed which traits and behaviors college students believed were characteristic of girls/women and which they believed were characteristic of boys/men (Broverman & others, 1972). The traits associated with boys/men were labeled *instrumental:* They included characteristics such as being independent, aggressive, and power-oriented. The traits associated with girls/women were labeled *expressive:* They included characteristics such as being warm and sensitive.

Thus, the instrumental traits associated with boys/men suited them for the traditional masculine role of going out into the world as the breadwinner. The expressive traits associated with girls/women paralleled the traditional feminine role of being the sensitive, nurturing caregiver in the home. These roles and traits, however, are not just different—they also are unequal in terms of social status and power. The traditional feminine characteristics are child-like, suitable for someone who is dependent on others and subordinate to them. The traditional masculine characteristics suit one to deal competently with the wider world and to wield authority.

GENDER SIMILARITIES AND DIFFERENCES

What is the reality behind gender stereotypes? Let's now examine some of the differences between the sexes, keeping the following in mind:

- The differences are based on averages and do not apply to all girls/women or all boys/men.
- Even when gender differences occur, there often is considerable overlap between boys/men and girls/women, especially in aspects of cognitive and socioemotional development.
- The differences may be due primarily to biological factors, to sociocultural factors, or to both.

Physical Similarities and Differences   We could devote many pages to describing physical differences between the average boy/man and girl/woman. For example, girls/women have about twice the body fat of men, most of it concentrated around breasts and hips. In boys/men, fat is more likely to go to the abdomen. On average, boys/men grow to be 10 percent taller than girls/women. Boys/men have greater physical strength than girls/women.

Many physical differences between boys/men and girls/women are tied to health. From conception on, girls/women have a longer life expectancy than boys/men do, and girls/women are less likely than boys/men to develop physical or mental disorders. Girls/women also are more resistant to infection, and their blood vessels are more elastic than boys'/men's.

Much of the research on gender similarities and differences in the brain has been conducted with adults rather than children or adolescents. Among the differences that have been discovered in studies with adults are the following:

- One part of the hypothalamus involved in sexual behavior tends to be larger in men than in women (Swaab & others, 2001).
- An area of the parietal lobe that functions in visuospatial skills tends to be larger in boys/men than in girls/women (Frederikse & others, 2000).
- The brains of girls/women are approximately 10 percent smaller than the brains of girls/women (Giedd, 2012).
- The brains of girls/women have more folds, and the larger folds (called convolutions) allow more surface brain tissue within the skulls of girls/women than of boys/men (Luders & others, 2004).
- The brains of boys/men have more intrahemisphere connectivity, while the brains of girls/women have more interhemisphere connectivity (Grabowska, 2020)

Although some gender differences in brain structure and function have been found, many of these differences are either small or research is inconsistent regarding the differences (Hyde & others, 2019). Also, when gender differences in the brain have been revealed, in many cases they have not been directly linked to behavioral and psychological differences (Grabowska, 2020). Similarities and differences in the brains of boys/men and girls/women could be due to evolution and heredity, as well as to experiences (Hyde & others, 2019).

Cognitive Similarities and Differences   No gender differences occur in overall intellectual ability—but in some cognitive areas, gender differences do appear (Berkowitz & others, 2020; Halpern, Flores-Mendoza, & Rindermann, 2020).

Are there gender differences in mathematical abilities? A very large-scale study of more than 7 million U.S. students in grades 2 through 11 revealed no differences in math scores for boys and girls (Hyde & others, 2008). In the most recent National Assessment of Educational Progress (2016) reports, boys scored slightly higher in math achievement than girls in the twelfth grade.

One area of math that has been examined for possible gender differences is visuospatial skills, which include being able to rotate objects mentally and determine what they would look like when rotated. These types of skills are important in courses such as plane and solid geometry and geography. Research reviews have revealed that boys have better visuospatial skills than girls do (Halpern, Flores-Mendoza, & Rindermann, 2020). For example, despite equal participation in the National Geography Bee, in most years all 10 finalists have been boys (Liben, 1995). A research review found that having a stronger masculine gender role was linked to better spatial ability in boys and girls (Reilly & Neumann, 2013).

However, some experts in gender, such as Janet Shibley Hyde (2014, 2016), conclude that the cognitive differences between girls/women and boys/men have been exaggerated. For example, Hyde points out that there is considerable overlap in the distributions of scores on math and visuospatial tasks for girls/women and boys/men (see Figure 1).

Are there gender differences in reading and writing skills? There is strong evidence that girls/women outperform boys/men in reading and writing. In the 2019 Nation's Report Card, girls had higher reading achievement than boys in both fourth- and eighth-grade assessments, with girls 11 points higher (269) than boys (258) in the eighth grade. Girls also have consistently outperformed boys in writing skills in the National Assessment of Educational Progress in fourth-, eighth-, and twelfth-grade assessments.

Keep in mind that measures of achievement in school or scores on standardized tests may reflect many factors besides cognitive ability. For example, performance in school may in part reflect attempts to conform to gender roles or differences in motivation, self-regulation, or other socioemotional characteristics (Pang & Baumann, 2020).

Let's further explore gender differences related to schooling and achievement. Gender differences characterize U.S. dropout rates, with boys more likely to drop out than girls (6.2 versus 4.4 percent) (data for 2017) (National Center for Education Statistics, 2020). Boys predominate in the academic bottom half of high school classes. That is, although many boys perform at the average or advanced level, the bottom 50 percent academically is made up mainly of boys. Half a century ago, in 1961, less than 40 percent of girls who graduated from high school went on to attend college. Beginning in 1996, girls were more likely to enroll in college than boys were. In 2012, 76 percent of girls attended college after high school, compared with 62 percent of boys (Pew Research Center, 2014; Women in Academia, 2011). In 1994, 63 percent of girls and 61 percent of boys enrolled in college; thus, girls' college enrollment gains have left boys behind. Also, in 2012, the gender gap in college attendance was significant for African Americans (69 percent of girls/women versus 57 percent of boys/men) and Latinxs (76 percent of girls/women versus 62 percent of boys/men), but college attendance was similar for Asian Americans (86 percent of girls/women, 83 percent of boys/men) (Pew Research Center, 2014). Further, recent data indicate that women are more likely to earn a college degree than are men. In 2015, women were 33 percent more likely to have earned a college degree by 27 years of age than were men (U.S. Bureau of Labor Statistics, 2015).

Piecing together the information about school dropout rates, the percentage of boys in the bottom half of high school classes, the percentage of boys/men enrolled in college classes, and the percentage of boys/men obtaining college degrees, we can conclude that currently girls/women show greater overall academic interest and achievement than do boys/men in the United States (Berkowitz & others, 2020). Girls/women are more likely than boys/men to be engaged with academic material, to pay close attention in class, to put forth academic effort, and to participate in class (DeZolt & Hull, 2001). A large-scale study revealed that girls had

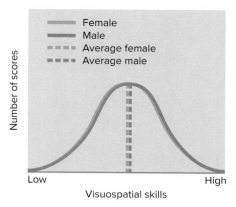

FIGURE 1

VISUOSPATIAL SKILLS OF BOYS/MEN AND GIRLS/WOMEN. Notice that although an average boy's/man's visuospatial skills are higher than an average girl's/woman's, scores for the two sexes almost entirely overlap. Not all boys/men have better visuospatial skills than all girls/women do—the overlap indicates that, although the average score of boys/men is higher, many girls/women outperform most boys/men on such tasks.

more positive attitudes about school than boys did (Orr, 2011). Also in this study, girls' positive attitudes about school were linked to their higher grades; boys' negative attitudes about school were related to their lower grades.

Despite the positive academic characteristics of girls, increasing evidence of similarity in the math and science skills of girls and boys, and legislative efforts to attain gender equality in recent years, gender differences in STEM (science, technology, engineering, and math) careers continue to favor boys/men (Eccles, 2014). In the most recent national assessment of educational performance, boys scored higher on science achievement than girls did in both the eighth and twelfth grades (National Assessment of Educational Progress, 2016). And in a recent study of 14- to 18-year-olds, believing in innate math ability was associated with lower ability self-concept and intrinsic motivation in girls but not boys (Heyder, Weidinger, & Steinmayr, 2021).

Toward the end of high school, girls are less likely to be enrolled in high-level math courses and less likely to plan to enter the so-called "STEM" career fields of science, technology, engineering, and math (Eccles, 2014; Liben & Coyle, 2014; Wigfield & others, 2015). A recent large-scale study of seventh-graders' attitudes toward math found that girls' perception that teachers had gendered expectations favoring boys over girls was linked to girls having more negative math beliefs and lower math achievement (McKellar & others, 2019). Also, in this study, when girls perceived that the math curriculum was personally meaningful and relevant for them, they had more positive math beliefs and higher math achievement. And a recent study revealed that adolescents' motivational beliefs at the start of high school were positively associated with STEM achievement and course taking throughout high school and their college majors seven years later (Jiang, Simpkins, & Eccles, 2020).

As people go through the human lifespan, categories such as gender and ethnicity intersect and can create systems of power, privilege, and discrimination. For example, higher-socioeconomic-status non-Latinx white boys/men have experienced considerably greater power, privilege, and less discrimination than African American girls/women. A recent study examined the inequities experienced in relation to ethnicity/race and gender in the graduate programs of the chemistry departments in the top 100 STEM programs in U.S. universities (Stockard, Rohlfing, & Richmond, 2021). In this study, graduate students who identified as a member of an underrepresented racial/ethnic minority group (URM) were less likely than other students to report that their financial support was insufficient to meet their needs (Stockard, Rohlfing, & Richmond, 2021). Also, when there was at least one URM faculty member in their department, URM students expressed greater commitment to completing their degree and staying in the chemistry field. Women, and especially underrepresented minority (URM) women, were less likely to report having supportive relationships with their advisor.

We will have more to say about gender disparity in career development in the chapter on "Achievement, Work, and Careers."

Socioemotional Similarities and Differences   Are "men from Mars" and "women from Venus," as John Gray (1992) suggested in the title of his highly popular book attributing relationship problems to gender differences? The answer to the question is no. Boys/men and girls/women are not so different that they should be thought of as being from different planets (Hyde & others, 2019). For just about every imaginable socioemotional characteristic, researchers have examined whether there are differences between boys/men and girls/women. Here we examine four of these characteristics: aggression, communication in relationships, prosocial behavior (behavior that is intended to benefit other people), and emotion.

Aggression   One of the most consistent gender differences is that boys/men are more physically aggressive than girls/women. The difference occurs in all cultures and appears very early in children's development (Hyde, 2017). The difference in physical aggression is especially pronounced when individuals are provoked. Although boys/men are consistently more physically aggressive than girls/women, might girls/women show as much verbal aggression, such as yelling, as boys/men do? When verbal aggression is examined, gender differences typically either disappear or the behavior is more pronounced in girls/women than in boys/men (Eagly & Steffen, 1986).

What have researchers found about gender similarities and differences in relational aggression in children and adolescents?
SW Productions/Getty Images

Recently, increased interest has been shown in *relational aggression,* which involves harming someone by manipulating a relationship (Brandes & others, 2021). Relational aggression includes such behaviors as trying to make others dislike a certain individual by spreading malicious rumors about the person or ostracizing him or her (Chen & Cheng, 2020). Relational aggression increases in middle and late childhood (Dishion & Piehler, 2009). Mixed findings have characterized research on whether girls show more relational aggression than boys, but one consistent finding is that relational aggression comprises a greater percentage of girls' overall aggression than it does for boys (Putallaz & others, 2007). Also, a research review revealed that girls engage in more relational aggression than boys in adolescence but not in childhood (Smith, Rose, & Schwartz-Mette, 2010). In addition, in a recent study of adolescents, those who observed relational aggression on television were more likely to engage in relational aggression when they were texting one year later (Coyne & others, 2019). And a longitudinal study tracking individuals from 14 to 20 years of age found that 88 percent

What have researchers found about gender similarities and differences in communication in relationships?
Ariel Skelley/Blend Images/Corbis

of the youth showed low levels of relational aggression that decreased over time, while a small portion (12 percent) had high, increasing levels of relational aggression (Coyne & others, 2020). In this study, high maternal psychological control, sibling hostility, and relational aggression in the media in early adolescence predicted which adolescents would be in the high and increasing group.

Communication in Relationships   In comparing communication styles of boys/men and girls/women, sociolinguist Deborah Tannen (1990) distinguishes between rapport talk and report talk:

- **Rapport talk** is the language of conversation and a way of establishing connections and negotiating relationships. Girls/women enjoy rapport talk and conversation that is relationship-oriented more than boys/men do.
- **Report talk** is talk that gives information. Public speaking is an example of report talk. Boys/men hold center stage through report talk with such verbal performances as storytelling, joking, and lecturing with information.

Tannen says that boys and girls grow up in different worlds of talk—parents, siblings, peers, teachers, and others talk differently to boys and girls. The play of boys and girls is also different. Boys tend to play in large groups that are hierarchically structured, and their groups usually have a leader who tells the others what to do and how to do it. Boys' games have winners and losers and often are the source of arguments. And boys often boast of their skills and argue about who is best at what. In contrast, girls are more likely to play in small groups or pairs, and at the center of a girl's world is often a best friend. In girls' friendships and peer groups, intimacy is pervasive. Turn-taking is more characteristic of girls' games than of boys' games. And much of the time, girls simply like to sit and talk with each other, focusing more on being liked by others than jockeying for status in some obvious way.

Researchers have found that adolescent girls are more "people oriented" and adolescent boys are more "things oriented" (Galambos, Berenbaum, & McHale, 2009; Su, Rounds, & Armstrong, 2009). In a research review, this conclusion was supported by findings that girls spend more time in relationships while boys spend more time playing video games and participating in sports; that girls work at part-time jobs that are people-oriented such as waitressing and baby-sitting, while boys are more likely to take part-time jobs that involve manual labor and using tools; and that girls are interested in careers that are more people-oriented, such as teaching and social work, while boys are more likely to be interested in object-oriented careers such as mechanics and engineering (Perry & Pauletti, 2011). Also, in support of Tannen's view, researchers have found that adolescent girls engage in more self-disclosure (communication of intimate details about themselves) in close relationships, are better at actively listening in a conversation than are boys, and emphasize affiliation or collaboration (Leaper, 2015). Adolescent girls, in particular, are more likely to engage in self-disclosure and to provide emotional support in friendship than are boys (Leaper, 2015). By contrast, boys are more likely to value self-assertion and dominance than are girls in their interactions with friends and peers (Rose & Rudolph, 2006).

developmental **connection**

Moral Development

Prosocial behavior is behavior intended to benefit other people. Connect to "Moral Development, Values, and Religion."

rapport talk The language of conversation, establishing connections and negotiating relationships.

report talk Talk that gives information, such as public speaking.

However, Tannen's view has been criticized on the grounds that it is overly simplistic and that communication between boys/men and girls/women is more complex than Tannen suggests (Edwards & Hamilton, 2004). Further, some researchers have found similarities in the relationship communication strategies of girls/women and boys/men (Hyde, 2014). In one study, men and women talked about and responded to relationship problems in ways that were more similar than different (MacGeorge, 2004).

Prosocial Behavior   Are there gender differences in prosocial behavior? Not only do girls view themselves as more prosocial and empathic than boys across childhood and adolescence (Eisenberg, Spinrad, & Knafo, 2015), but girls also engage in more prosocial behavior and show more empathy than boys do (Christov-Moore & others, 2014). A research meta-analysis concluded that girls/women are better than boys/men at being kind, considerate, and generous (Thompson & Voyer, 2014).

Emotion and Its Regulation   Gender differences occur in some aspects of emotion (Dollar & Calkins, 2020). Girls/women express emotion more readily than do girls/women, are better than boys/men at decoding emotions, smile more, cry more, and are happier (Gross, Fredrickson, & Levenson, 1994; LaFrance, Hecht, & Paluck, 2003). Further, a recent study of Spanish adolescents found that girls showed more positive affect and negative affect but also showed a lower level of purpose in life (Esteban-Gonzalo & others, 2020). In addition, a recent study of adolescents found that girls express more emotional concern for others than boys (Trentini & others, 2021). Also, a recent study revealed that girls/women are better than boys/men at facial emotion perception across the life span (Olderbak & others, 2019).

An important skill is the capacity to regulate and control one's emotions and behavior (Dollar & Calkins, 2020). A recent study found that girls had much better self-regulation than boys at 13 to 16 years of age (van Tetering & others, 2020). The lower self-control of boys can translate into behavior problems (Beckes & Edwards, 2020; Schunk, 2020).

GENDER CONTROVERSY

> There is more difference within the sexes than between them.
>
> –IVY COMPTON-BURNETT
> *English Novelist, 20th Century*

Controversy surrounds the topic of gender differences and what might cause them (Gangestad & Chang, 2021). As we saw earlier, evolutionary psychologists such as David Buss (2019) argue that gender differences are extensive and caused by the adaptive problems the genders have faced across evolutionary history. Alice Eagly (2018) also concludes that gender differences are substantial but reaches a very different conclusion about their cause. She emphasizes that gender differences are due to social conditions that have resulted in women having less power and controlling fewer resources than men do.

By contrast, Janet Shibley Hyde (Hyde & others, 2019) concludes that gender differences have been greatly exaggerated, especially after the publication of popular books such as John Gray's (1992) *Men Are from Mars, Women Are from Venus* and Deborah Tannen's (1990) *You Just Don't Understand*. She argues that the research shows that girls/women and boys/men are similar on most psychological factors. In one research review, Hyde (2005) summarized the results of 44 meta-analyses of gender differences and similarities. Gender differences either were nonexistent or small in most areas, including math ability and communication. The largest difference occurred on motor skills (favoring males), followed by sexuality (boys/men masturbate more and are more likely to endorse sex in a casual, uncommitted relationship), and physical aggression (boys/men are more physically aggressive than girls/women). A research review also concluded that gender differences in adolescence are quite small (Perry & Pauletti, 2011).

Hyde's summary of meta-analyses and the research review by Perry and Pauletti are not likely to resolve the controversy about gender differences and similarities anytime soon, but further research should continue to provide a basis for more accurate conclusions about this topic (Eliot, 2020).

GENDER IN CONTEXT

In thinking about gender, it is important to consider the context of behavior, as gender behavior often varies across contexts (Qu & others, 2020). Consider helping behavior. Boys/men are more likely to help in contexts in which a

How might gender-role socialization for these adolescent girls in Iran compare with that in the United States?
Andres Hernandez/Getty Images

perceived danger is present and they feel competent to help (Eagly & Crowley, 1986). For example, boys/men are more likely than girls/women to help a person who is stranded by the roadside with a flat tire; automobile problems are an area in which many boys/men feel competent. In contrast, when the context involves volunteering time to help a child with a personal problem, girls/women are more likely to help than boys/men are because there is little danger present and girls/women feel more competent at nurturing. In many cultures, girls/women show more caregiving behavior than boys/men do. However, in the few cultures where adolescents of both genders care for younger siblings on a regular basis, girls and boys are similar in their tendencies to nurture (Whiting, 1989).

Context is also relevant to gender differences in the display of emotions (Pang & Baumann, 2020). Consider anger. Boys/men are more likely to show anger toward strangers, especially other boys/men, when they think they have been challenged. Boys/men also are more likely than girls/women to turn their anger into aggressive action, especially when their culture endorses such action (Tavris & Wade, 1984).

Contextual variations regarding gender in specific situations occur not only within a particular culture but also across cultures (Kim-Prieto, Heye, & Mangino, 2020). Although in recent decades roles assumed by boys/men and girls/women in the United States have become increasingly similar, in many countries gender roles have remained more gender-specific. For example, in a number of Middle Eastern countries, the division of labor between men and women is dramatic: males are socialized to work in the public sphere, females in the private world of home and child rearing; a man's duty is to provide for his family, while a woman's duty is to care for her family and household. Any deviations from this traditional division of gender roles encounter severe disapproval. In a study of eighth-grade students in 36 countries, girls consistently held more egalitarian attitudes about gender roles than boys did (Dotti Sani & Quaranta, 2017). In this study, girls had more egalitarian gender attitudes in countries with higher levels of societal gender equality. In a study of 15- to 19-year-olds in Qatar, boys expressed more negative views of gender equality than girls did (Al-Ghanim & Badahdah, 2017).

developmental connection

Theories

Bronfenbrenner's ecological theory emphasizes the importance of contexts; in his theory, the macrosystem includes cross-cultural comparisons. Connect to "Introduction."

Review Connect Reflect

 LG2 Discuss gender stereotypes, similarities, and differences.

Review

- How extensive is gender stereotyping?
- How similar or different are adolescent boys and girls in their physical, cognitive, and socioemotional development?
- What is the controversy about the cause of gender differences?
- How extensively is gender development influenced by contexts?

Connect

- How do socioemotional similarities and differences between girls and boys relate to the development of self-esteem?

Reflect *Your Own Personal Journey of Life*

- Some decades ago, the word *dependency* was used to describe the relational orientation of femininity. Dependency took on a negative connotation for girls/women—for instance, the perception that girls/women can't take care of themselves whereas boys/men can. Today, the term *dependency* is being replaced by the term *relational abilities,* which has more positive connotations (Caplan & Caplan, 1999). Rather than being thought of as dependent, girls/women are now more often described as skilled in forming and maintaining relationships. Make up a list of words that you associate with masculinity and femininity. Do these words have any negative connotations for boys/men and girls/women? For the words that do have negative connotations, can you think of words with positive connotations that could be used instead?

3 Gender-Role Classification

LG3 Characterize the variations in gender-role classification.

Masculinity, Femininity, and Androgyny | Transgender | Going Beyond Gender as Binary

Examples of masculine items

- Defends own beliefs
- Forceful
- Willing to take risks
- Dominant
- Aggressive

Examples of feminine items

- Does not use harsh language
- Affectionate
- Loves children
- Understanding
- Gentle

FIGURE **2**

THE BEM SEX-ROLE INVENTORY (BSRI). These items are from the Bem Sex-Role Inventory. When taking the BSRI, a person is asked to indicate on a 7-point scale how well each of the 60 characteristics describes herself or himself. The scale ranges from 1 (never or almost never true) to 7 (always or almost always true). The items are scored on independent dimensions of masculinity and femininity as well as androgyny and undifferentiated classifications.

Source: Bem, Sandra, Bem Sex Role Inventory. Consulting Psychologists Press, 1978, 1981.

Gender can be classified in multiple ways. Not long ago, it was accepted that boys should grow up to be masculine and girls to be feminine, that boys are made of "frogs and snails" and girls are made of "sugar and spice and all that's nice." In recent years, increasing emphasis has been placed on flexibility and equality in gender roles (Halpern & Cheung, 2020).

MASCULINITY, FEMININITY, AND ANDROGYNY

In the past, a well-adjusted boy/man was supposed to be independent, aggressive, and powerful. A well-adjusted girl/woman was supposed to be dependent, nurturing, and uninterested in power. The masculine characteristics were considered to be healthy and good by society; the feminine characteristics were considered weak.

In the 1970s, as both males and females became dissatisfied with the burdens imposed by their stereotyped roles, alternatives to "masculinity" and "femininity" were explored. Instead of thinking of masculinity and femininity as mutually exclusive, with more of one characteristic meaning less of the other, it was proposed that individuals could show both expressive and instrumental traits. This thinking led to the development of the concept of **androgyny,** the presence of a high degree of masculine and feminine characteristics in the same individual (Bem, 1977; Spence & Helmreich, 1978). The androgynous individual might be a boy/man who is both assertive (masculine) and sensitive to others' feelings (feminine), or a girl/woman who is both dominant (masculine) and caring (feminine).

Measures have been developed to assess androgyny. One of the most widely used gender measures, the *Bem Sex-Role Inventory*, was constructed by a leading early proponent of androgyny, Sandra Bem (1977). Figure 2 shows examples of masculine and feminine items on the Bem Sex-Role Inventory. Based on their responses to the items in this inventory, individuals are classified as having one of four gender-role orientations–masculine, feminine, androgynous, or undifferentiated (see Figure 3):

- The androgynous individual is simply a girl/woman or a boy/man who has a high degree of both feminine and masculine traits. No new characteristics are used to describe the androgynous individual.
- A feminine individual is high on expressive traits and low on instrumental traits.
- A masculine individual is high on instrumental traits and low on expressive traits.
- An undifferentiated person is low on both feminine and masculine traits.

androgyny The presence of a high degree of desirable feminine and masculine characteristics in the same individual.

Androgynous girls/women and boys/men, according to Bem, are more flexible and more mentally healthy than either masculine or feminine individuals; undifferentiated individuals are the least competent. One study found that androgyny was linked to well-being and lower levels of stress (Stake, 2000). Another study conducted with emerging adults revealed that androgynous individuals reported better health practices (such as consistently using safety belts and not smoking) than masculine, feminine, or undifferentiated individuals (Shifren, Furnham, & Bauserman, 2003). And a recent study found that androgynous boys and girls had higher self-esteem and fewer internalizing problems than masculine or feminine individuals did (Pauletti & others, 2017).

		Masculine: High	Masculine: Low
Feminine	High	Androgynous	Feminine
Feminine	Low	Masculine	Undifferentiated

FIGURE **3**

GENDER-ROLE CLASSIFICATION

Context, Culture, and Gender Roles

The concept of gender-role classification involves a personality-trait-like categorization of a person. However, it is important to think of personality in terms of both traits and contexts rather than traits alone (Asendorpf & Rauthmann, 2021). In close relationships, a feminine or androgynous gender role may be more desirable because of the expressive nature of close relationships. However, a masculine or androgynous gender role may be more desirable in academic and work settings that require action and assertiveness. For example, one study found that masculine and androgynous individuals had higher expectations for being able to control the outcomes of their academic efforts

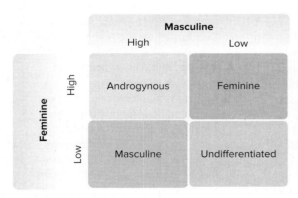

Cynthia de las Fuentes, College Professor and Counseling Psychologist

Cynthia de las Fuentes is a professor at Our Lady of the Lake University in San Antonio. She obtained her undergraduate degree in psychology and her doctoral degree in counseling psychology at the University of Texas in Austin. Among the courses she teaches are the psychology of women, Latinx psychology, and counseling theories.

Dr. de las Fuentes is president of the Division of the Psychology of Women in the American Psychological Association. "Many young women," she says, "take for granted that the women's movement has accomplished its goals—like equal pay for women, or reproductive rights—and don't realize that there is still work to be done." She is interested in "learning about people's intersecting identities, like female and Latina, and how the two work together." (Winerman, 2005, pp. 66–67)

Cynthia de las Fuentes.
Courtesy of Dr. Cynthia de las Fuentes

For more information about the work that college professors and counseling psychologists do, see the Careers in Adolescent Development appendix.

---

than did feminine or undifferentiated individuals (Choi, 2004). In a recent analysis, this emphasis on considering contexts in understanding gender identity was described in terms of *functional flexibility*, in which one's gender identity is positively linked to adjustment and competence involves flexibility in adapting to specific situations (Martin & others, 2017).

The importance of considering gender in context is nowhere more apparent than when examining what is culturally prescribed behavior for girls/women and boys/men in different countries around the world (Sotiriou & Awad, 2020). However, it may be helpful to think of gender in terms of person-situation interaction instead of gender-associated traits alone (Twenge & Campbell, 2017). Thus, in our discussion of gender-role classification, we have described how specific gender roles might be more appropriate for some cultural contexts than others.

Increasing numbers of children and adolescents in the United States and other developed countries such as Sweden are being raised to behave in androgynous ways. In the last 30 to 40 years in the United States, a decline in the adoption of traditional gender roles has occurred. For example, in recent years U.S. college women have shown a propensity for pursuing careers outside the home. In 1967, more than 40 percent of college women and more than 60 percent of college men agreed with the statement, "The activities of married women are best confined to home and family." In 2005, those percentages had dropped to 15 percent for college women and 26 percent for college men (Pryor & others, 2005). As shown in Figure 4, the greatest change in these attitudes occurred in the late 1960s and early 1970s.

But traditional gender roles continue to dominate the cultures of many countries around the world today (Reichard & others, 2020). As indicated earlier in this chapter, in such cultures the man's duty is to provide for his family and the woman's duty is to care for her family and household. Any deviations from this traditional gender-role orientation meet with severe disapproval. In the United States, the cultural backgrounds of adolescents influence how boys and girls will be socialized. In one study, Latino and Latina adolescents were socialized differently as they were growing up (Raffaelli & Ontai, 2004). Latinas experienced far greater restrictions than Latinos in curfews, interaction with members of the other sex, acquisition of a driver's license, exploration of job possibilities, and involvement in after-school activities. To read about the work of one individual who is interested in expanding the horizons of Latinas, see the *Connecting with Careers* profile.

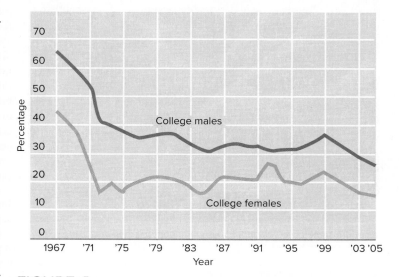

FIGURE 4

CHANGING ATTITUDES ABOUT GENDER ROLES. Note: Data show the percentage of first-year U.S. college students agreeing with the statement, "The activities of married women are best confined to home and family" from 1967 through 2005.

Access to education for girls has improved somewhat around the world, but girls' educational opportunities continue to lag behind those available to boys (UNICEF, 2021). For example, according to a UNICEF (2003) analysis of education around the world, by age 18, girls have received an average of 4.4 years less education than boys. This deficit reduces their chances of reaching their full potential. Exceptions to lower participation and completion rates in education for girls occur in Western nations, Japan, and the Philippines (Brown & Larson, 2002). Opportunities to receive advanced training or advanced degrees are higher in most countries for menthan for women (Fussell & Greene, 2002).

Despite these gender gaps, evidence of increasing gender equality is appearing. For example, "among upper income families in India and Japan, fathers are assuming more child-rearing responsibilities. Rates of employment and career opportunities for women are expanding in many parts of the globe. Control over adolescent girls' social relationships, especially romantic and sexual relationships, is easing in some nations" (Brown & Larson, 2002, p. 16).

Traditional Masculinity and Problem Behaviors in Adolescent Males   In our discussion of masculinity so far, we have considered how the masculine role has been accorded a prominent status in the United States and in most other cultures. However, might there be a negative side to traditional masculinity, especially in adolescence? An increasing number of gender theorists and researchers conclude that there is (Levant, 2001).

Concern about the effects of bringing up boys in traditional ways has brought attention to what has been called a "national crisis of boyhood" by William Pollack (1999) in his book *Real Boys*. He says that although there has been considerable talk about the "sensitive male," little has been done to change what he calls the "boy code."

Pollack argues that this code tells boys they should show little if any emotion as they are growing up. Too often boys are socialized to mask their feelings and to act tough, says Pollack. Boys learn the boy code in many different contexts—sandboxes, playgrounds, schoolrooms, camps, hangouts—and are taught the code by parents, peers, coaches, teachers, and other adults. Pollack, as well as many others, notes that boys would benefit from being socialized to express their anxieties and concerns rather than keeping them bottled up, as well as being taught how to better regulate their aggression.

There also is a special concern about boys who adopt a strong masculine role in adolescence, because this is increasingly being found to be associated with problem behaviors. Joseph Pleck (1983, 1995) concludes that the model of traditional masculinity in many Western cultures includes behaviors that lack social approval but nonetheless validate the adolescent boy's masculinity. That is, in the male adolescent culture, male adolescents perceive that they will be thought of as more masculine if they engage in premarital sex, drink alcohol and take drugs, and participate in illegal delinquent activities. And one study revealed that both boys and girls who engaged in extreme gender-typed (hyper-gender) behaviors had lower levels of school engagement and school attachment (Ueno & McWilliams, 2010).

Gender-Role Transcendence   Some critics of androgyny say that there is too much talk about gender. They stress that androgyny is less of a panacea than was originally envisioned (Paludi, 2002). An alternative is **gender-role transcendence,** the view that when an individual's competence is at issue, it should be conceptualized on a person-by-person basis rather than on the basis of masculinity, femininity, or androgyny (Pleck, 1983). That is, we should think of ourselves as people first, not as masculine, feminine, or androgynous. Parents should rear their children to be competent persons, not masculine, feminine, or androgynous, say the gender-role critics. They argue that such gender-role classification encourages stereotyping.

What are some concerns about boys who adopt a strong masculine role?
Blue Jean Images/Alamy Stock Photo

gender-role transcendence The belief that, when an individual's competence is at issue, it should be conceptualized not in regard to masculinity, femininity, or androgyny but on an individual basis.

TRANSGENDER

Transgender is a broad term that refers to individuals who have a gender identity that differs from the gender typically associated with their sex assigned at birth (Lelutiu-Weinberger, English & Sandanapitchai, 2020). For example, an individual may be assigned female at birth and identify as a boy or man, or be assigned male at birth and identify as a girl or woman. An individual may also be assigned female or male and identify as another gender outside of the girl/woman versus boy/man gender binary. A transgender identity of being assigned male but identifying as a girl or woman is much more common than the reverse (Zucker, Lawrence, & Kreukels, 2016). Transgender persons with a nonbinary identity (see below) also may not want to be called "he" or "she" but prefer a gender-neutral pronoun such as "they" or "ze."

What are some characteristics of transgender adolescents?
Jonathan Kirn/Getty Images

Because of the nuances and complexities involved in such gender categorizations, some experts have recently argued that a better overarching umbrella term might be *trans* or *gender diverse* to identify a variety of gender identities and expressions different from the gender typically associated with the sex that was assigned at birth (Nieder, Eyssel, & Kohler, 2020). The variety of gender identities include binary transgender identities (for example, transgender girl/woman, transgender boy/man) and nonbinary gender identities (individuals who have a gender identity that is outside the girl/woman and boy/man binary, such as gender queer individuals who are not exclusively masculine or exclusively feminine and gender-nonconforming individuals whose behavior/appearance does not conform to social expectations for what is appropriate for their gender).

In addition, the term *two-spirit* is used by some indigenous North Americans to describe gender-diverse individuals who are perceived to have spirits from both women and men. *Cisgender* can be used to describe individuals whose gender identity and expression conform to their sex assigned at birth (Hyde & others, 2019; Platt, 2020). Although the term "transsexual" has been used historically to refer to transgender people, it is now regarded as outdated and may be perceived as offensive by some transgender individuals.

As with cisgender individuals, transgender individuals can have any sexual orientation. A research review concluded that transgender youth have higher rates of depression, suicide attempts, and eating disorders than their cisgender peers (Connolly & others, 2016). Among the explanations for higher rates of mental health concerns are the distress of living in the wrong body and the discrimination and misunderstanding encountered by gender-minority individuals (Bretherton & others, 2021; Yockey, King, & Vidourek, 2021). In a recent study of transgender individuals, gender affirmation—being recognized as one' gender identity, gender expression, or gender role—was associated with a lower probability of suicidal ideation and psychological distress, while discrimination was linked to a higher probability of suicidal ideation and psychological distress (Lelutiu-Weinberger, English, & Sandanapitchai, 2020). And another recent study confirmed that victimization and discrimination predicted increased suicidal ideation, while community connectedness reduced suicidal ideation (Rabasco & Andover, 2021).

Among youth who identify themselves as transgender persons, the majority eventually adopt a gender identity in line with the body into which they were born (Byne & others, 2012; King, 2020, 2022). Some transgender individuals seek gender-affirming surgery to change their physical body to more closely match their gender identity, but many do not. Some choose to receive hormonal treatments, such as assigned females who use testosterone to enhance their masculine physical characteristics or assigned males who use estrogen to increase their feminine physical characteristics. Yet other transgender individuals opt for another, broader strategy that involves choosing a lifestyle that challenges the traditional view of having a gender identity that fits within one of two opposing categories (Waryold & Kornahrens, 2020).

A special concern is the discrimination directed at trans individuals (Sherman & others, 2020). A recent study found that a majority of transgender individuals had experienced discrimination in the last year and those with greater exposure to discrimination were more likely to develop depression and anxiety symptoms (Puckett & others, 2020). Estimates indicate that 40 percent or more of transgender individuals have attempted suicide at least once in their lives (Dickey & Budge, 2020). Because transgender individuals experience considerable discrimination, it is important that society provide a more welcoming and accepting attitude toward them (Vargas, Huey, & Miranda, 2020). Also, recent research indicates that psychotherapy targeting internalized stigma and non-affirmation experiences can be effective in reducing gender-related stress and improving resilience (Budge, Sinnard, & Hoyt, 2021). To read about one individual who conducts research and psychotherapy with transgender individuals, see the *Connecting with Careers* interlude.

transgender A broad term that refers to individuals who adopt a gender identity that differs from the one assigned to them at birth.

Stephanie Budge, Transgender Researcher and Psychotherapist

Dr. Stephanie Budge is a leading expert on transgender research, issues, and psychotherapy. She is a professor in the Department of Counseling at the University of Wisconsin–Madison, where she obtained her Ph.D. in counseling psychology. Her research examines emotional development and coping in transgender youth and adults, as well as psychotherapy with transgender clients (Budge, 2021). Dr. Budge also works nationally and internationally in training individuals to provide help related to LBGTQ issues, with a focus on increasing practitioners' self-efficacy, knowledge, and skills.

At the University of Wisconsin–Madison, Dr. Budge has given pro-bono therapy to transgender youth and adults. Dr. Budge has received the LGBTQ Outstanding Community Contributions award from the American Psychological Association and the LGBT Early Career Award from the Society for Counseling Psychology. She is currently associate editor of two journals: *Psychotherapy* and *Psychology of Sexual Orientation and Gender Diversity*. Dr. Budge also serves on the editorial board of the *International Journal of Transgender Health*.

Courtesy of Dr. Stephanie Budge

GOING BEYOND GENDER AS BINARY

In a number of places in our coverage of gender, we have indicated that the long-existing (for more than a century) concept of gender as having just two categories—boys/men and girls/women—is being challenged. In a recent analysis, leading expert Janet Shibley Hyde and her colleagues (2019) described a number of aspects of gender where this challenge is occurring. These include the following developments: (1) neuroscience research indicates the presence of a gender mosaic rather than "his or her" brains that are highly different; (2) endocrinology research reveals more hormonal similarities in males and females than had been previously envisioned; (3) recent conceptual changes in gender role classification go far beyond characterizing individuals as masculine or feminine and add a number of new gender identity categories such as transgender and nonbinary; (4) developmental research indicates that the tendency to view gender as a binary category is not due only to biological factors but also culturally determined and malleable. Further, gender categories are not mutually exclusive—an individual can identify with more than one category. Also, gender categories are fluid because an individual's gender identity can change over time. Each of the ideas described here reflects a substantial change in how gender is conceptualized and reflected in individuals' daily lives, but as we indicated earlier in the chapter there is still controversy about the extent of gender similarities and differences.

Review Connect Reflect

LG3 Characterize the variations in gender-role classification.

Review
- How can traditional gender roles be described? What is androgyny? How is androgyny related to social competence? What are some contextual variations in gender roles?
- What characterizes transgender adolescents?
- How is the conceptualization of gender going beyond gender as binary?

Connect
- Compare and contrast the concepts of androgyny, gender-role transcendence, and transgender.

Reflect *Your Own Personal Journey of Life*
- How would you describe your gender-role classification today? How satisfied are you with your gender-role classification? What factors contributed to your classification?

Early Adolescence and Gender Intensification

Is Early Adolescence a Critical Juncture for Females?

What changes take place during early adolescence that might affect gender roles? Is early adolescence a critical juncture in girls' development?

EARLY ADOLESCENCE AND GENDER INTENSIFICATION

Near the beginning of this chapter, we considered how pubertal changes might be linked to gendered behavior. Now we will expand on the earlier discussion. As girls and boys experience the physical and social changes of early adolescence, they must come to terms with new definitions of their gender roles (Qu & others, 2020). During early adolescence, individuals develop the adult, physical attributes of their sex. Some theorists and researchers have proposed that with the onset of puberty, girls and boys experience an intensification in gender-related expectations. The **gender intensification hypothesis** states that psychological and behavioral differences between boys and girls become greater during early adolescence because of increased socialization pressures to conform to traditional masculine and feminine gender roles (Hill & Lynch, 1983; Lynch, 1991). Puberty may signal to socializing others—parents, peers, and teachers—that an adolescent is approaching adulthood and should begin to act in stereotypical male or female ways. Some researchers have reported evidence of gender intensification in early adolescence (Hill & Lynch, 1983). In a recent study of children, adolescents, and emerging adults, middle adolescents (average age = 14.8 years) were the most likely age group to adopt stereotypically masculine and feminine traits (Klaczynski, Felmban, & Kole, 2020). However, a longitudinal study of individuals from 7 to 19 years of age revealed stable gender differences in activity interests but a decline in both boy- and girl-typed activity interests across the age range (McHale & others, 2009). And another study found no evidence for intensification in masculinity or femininity in young adolescents (Priess, Lindberg, & Hyde, 2009). Thus, the jury is still out on the validity of the gender intensification hypothesis.

What is the gender intensification hypothesis? How strong is the evidence for this hypothesis?
Laurence Mouton/PhotoAlto/Getty Images

gender intensification hypothesis
Hypothesis stating that psychological and behavioral differences between boys and girls become greater during early adolescence because of increased socialization pressure to conform to masculine or feminine gender roles.

IS EARLY ADOLESCENCE A CRITICAL JUNCTURE FOR FEMALES?

Carol Gilligan has conducted extensive interviews with girls from 6 to 18 years of age (Gilligan, 1982, 1996; Gilligan, Brown, & Rogers, 1990). She and her colleagues have reported that girls consistently reveal detailed knowledge of human relationships that is based on their experiences with others. According to Gilligan, girls are sensitive to different rhythms and emotions in relationships. Gilligan argues that girls experience life differently from boys; in her words, girls have a "different voice."

Gilligan also stresses that adolescence is a critical juncture in girls' development. In early adolescence (usually around 11 to 12 years of age), she says, girls become aware that the male-dominated culture does not value their intense interest in intimacy, even though society values women's caring and altruism. The dilemma, says Gilligan, is that girls are presented with a choice that makes them appear either selfish (if they become independent and self-sufficient) or selfless (if they remain responsive to others). As young adolescent girls struggle with this dilemma, Gilligan states, they begin to "silence" their "different voice," becoming less confident and more tentative in offering their opinions. This reticence often persists into adulthood. Some researchers note that the self-doubt and ambivalence girls experience in early adolescence translate into depression and eating disorders.

Contextual variations influence the degree to which adolescent girls silence their "voice" (Ryan, 2003). In one study, Susan Harter and her colleagues (Harter, Waters, & Whitesell, 1996) found that feminine girls reported lower levels of voice in public contexts (at school

Why does Carol Gilligan think that adolescence is a critical juncture in the lives of girls?
Courtesy of Dr. Carol Gilligan

----------→

developmental connection

Moral Development

Gilligan argues that the care perspective, which emphasizes the importance of connectedness to others, is especially important in adolescent girls' moral development. Connect to "Moral Development, Values, and Religion."

developmental connection

Identity

Self-esteem, also referred to as self-worth or self-image, is the global evaluative dimension of the self. Connect to "The Self, Identity, Emotion, and Personality."

←----------

with teachers and classmates) but not in more private interpersonal relationships (with close friends and parents). However, androgynous girls reported a strong voice in all contexts. Harter and her colleagues found that adolescent girls who buy into societal messages that females should be seen and not heard are at the greatest risk in their development. The greatest liabilities occurred for girls who not only lacked a "voice" but who emphasized the importance of appearance. In focusing on their outer selves, these girls faced formidable challenges in meeting the punishing cultural standards of attractiveness.

Some critics argue that Gilligan and her colleagues overemphasize differences in gender (Dindia, 2006; Hyde, 2014). One of those critics is developmentalist Eleanor Maccoby (2007), who says that Gilligan exaggerates the differences in intimacy and connectedness between girls and boys. Other critics fault Gilligan's research strategy, which rarely includes a comparison group of boys or statistical analysis. Instead, Gilligan conducts extensive interviews with girls and then provides excerpts from the girls' narratives to buttress her ideas. Other critics fear that Gilligan's findings reinforce stereotypes—females as nurturing and self-sacrificing, for example—that might undermine females' struggle for equality. These critics say that Gilligan's "different voice" perhaps should be called "the voice of the victim." What we should be stressing, say these critics, is the need to provide more opportunities for females to reach higher levels of achievement and self-determination.

Whether you accept the connectionist arguments of Gilligan or the achievement/self-determination arguments of her critics, there is increasing evidence that early adolescence is a critical juncture in the psychological development of girls (Basow, 2006). A large-scale national study revealed a decrease in the self-esteem of boys and girls during adolescence, but a more substantial decrease for adolescent girls than boys (Robins & others, 2002). In another national survey that was conducted by the American Association of University Women (1992), girls experienced a significantly greater drop in self-esteem during adolescence than boys did. In yet another study, the self-esteem of girls declined during adolescence (Rosner & Rierdan, 1994). At ages 8 and 9, 60 percent of the girls were confident and assertive and felt positive about themselves, compared with 67 percent of the boys. However, over the next eight years, the girls' self-esteem fell 31 percentage points—only 29 percent of high school girls felt positive about themselves. Across the same age range, boys' self-esteem dropped 21 points—leaving 46 percent of the high school boys with high self-esteem, which makes for a gender gap of 17 percentage points. Another study found that the self-esteem of high school girls was lower than the self-esteem of elementary school girls and college women (Frost & McKelvie, 2004). Keep in mind, though, that some psychologists conclude that gender differences in self-esteem during adolescence are quite small (Hyde, 2007).

We should also recognize that many experts emphasize the need for adolescent girls and emerging adult women to maintain their competency in relationships and also to be self-motivated (Brabeck & Brabeck, 2006). In Phyllis Bronstein's (2006, p. 269) view, "It is beneficial neither to individuals nor to society as a whole to assign one set of values and behaviors to one sex and a different set to the other." How might we put this view into practice? The *Connecting with Health and Well-Being* interlude provides some recommendations for improving the gendered lives of adolescents.

In this chapter, you have read about many aspects of gender. You learned that sexuality influences gender in adolescence more than in childhood. We'll discuss adolescent sexuality more extensively later in this edition.

Review Connect Reflect

 LG4 Summarize developmental changes in gender.

Review

- How might early adolescence influence gender development?
- Is early adolescence a critical juncture for females?

Connect

- How might gender intensification be linked to media influences?

Reflect *Your Own Personal Journey of Life*

- Did your gender behavior change as you went through early adolescence? Explain.

connecting with health and well-being

How Can We Best Guide Adolescents' Gender Development?

Boys

- *Encourage boys to be more sensitive in relationships and to engage in more prosocial behavior*. An important socialization task is to help boys become more interested in having positive close relationships and become more caring. Fathers can play an especially important role for boys in this regard by being a model of a male who is sensitive and caring.

- *Encourage boys to be less physically aggressive*. Too often, boys are encouraged to be tough, virile, and aggressive. A positive strategy is to encourage them to be self-assertive but not overly physically aggressive.

- *Encourage boys to handle their emotions more effectively*. This guideline involves not only helping boys to regulate their emotions, as in controlling their anger, but also helping them learn to express their anxieties and concerns rather than to keep them bottled up.

- *Work with boys to improve their school performance*. Girls get better grades, put forth more academic effort, and are less likely than boys to be assigned to special/remedial classes. Parents and teachers can help boys by emphasizing the importance of school and expecting better academic effort from them.

Girls

- *Encourage girls to be proud of their relationship skills and caring*. The strong interest that girls show in relationships and caring should be rewarded by parents and teachers.

- *Encourage girls to develop their self-competencies*. While guiding girls to retain their relationship strengths, adults can help girls to develop their ambition and achievement.

- *Encourage girls to be more self-assertive*. Girls tend to be more passive than boys and can benefit from being encouraged to be more self-assertive.

- *Encourage girls' achievement*. Girls should be encouraged to have higher academic expectations, and they should be introduced to a wide range of career options.

Boys and Girls

- *Help adolescents to reduce gender stereotyping and discrimination*. Don't engage in gender stereotyping and discrimination yourself, because in doing so, you would be providing a model of gender stereotyping and discrimination for adolescents.

How can adopting one set of suggestions for girls and another for boys ensure that we do not "assign one set of values and behaviors to one sex and a different set to the other"?

reach your learning goals

Gender

1 Biological, Social, and Cognitive Influences on Gender

 LG1 Describe the biological, social, and cognitive influences on gender.

Biological Influences on Gender

- Gender refers to the characteristics of people as girls/women and boys/men. Gender identity involves a sense of one's own gender, including knowledge, understanding, and acceptance of being a boy/man, a girl/woman, or another gender.

- Gender roles are expectations that prescribe how girls/women and boys/men should think, act, and feel. Because of pubertal change, sexuality plays a more important role in gender development for adolescents than for children.

- Freud's and Erikson's theories promote the idea that anatomy is destiny. Today's developmentalists are interactionists when biological and environmental influences on gender are at issue.

- In the evolutionary psychology view, evolutionary adaptations produced psychological sex differences, especially in the area of mate selection. However, criticisms of the evolutionary psychology view have been made, such as gender differences being influenced more strongly by environmental experiences than by evolution.

- Gender differences have been found in the developmental trajectories of the brain in adolescence, but overall there are more similarities than differences in the brains of males and females.

Social Influences on Gender

- In the social role view, women have less power and status than men do and control fewer resources. In this view, gender hierarchy and sexual division of labor are important causes of sex-differentiated behavior.

- The social cognitive theory of gender emphasizes that adolescents' gender development is influenced by their observation and imitation of others' gender behavior, as well as by rewards and punishments for gender-appropriate and gender-inappropriate behavior.

- Parents and siblings influence adolescents' gender roles. Mothers and fathers often interact with their adolescents differently and also interact differently with sons and daughters. Peers are especially adept at rewarding gender-appropriate behavior. There is still concern about gender inequity in education. Despite improvements, TV continues to portray males as more competent than females.

Cognitive Influences on Gender

- Gender schema theory states that gender-typing emerges as individuals develop schemas for what is gender-appropriate and gender-inappropriate in their culture.

2 Gender Stereotypes, Similarities, and Differences Discuss gender stereotypes, similarities, and differences.

Gender Stereotyping

- Gender stereotypes are general impressions and beliefs about males and females. Gender stereotypes are widespread.

Gender Similarities and Differences

- There are a number of physical differences in boys/men and girls/women. In the cognitive domain, gender differences in math ability are either small or nonexistent. However, girls significantly outperform boys in reading and writing skills, get better grades in school, and are less likely to drop out of school. Socioemotional differences include the following: boys are more physically aggressive and active; girls show a stronger interest in relationships, are better at self-regulation of behavior and emotion, and engage in more prosocial behavior.

Gender Controversy

- There continues to be controversy about the extent of gender differences and what causes them. Buss argues that gender differences are extensive and attributable to evolutionary history. Eagly also concludes that gender differences are extensive but believes that they are caused by social conditions. Hyde states that gender differences have been exaggerated and that girls/women and boys/men are similar on most psychological factors.

Gender in Context

- Gender in context is an important concept. Gender roles can vary according to the culture in which adolescents develop and the immediate contexts in which they behave.

3 Gender-Role Classification Characterize the variations in gender-role classification.

Masculinity, Femininity, and Androgyny

- In the past, the well-adjusted boy/man was supposed to show instrumental traits, the well-adjusted girl/woman expressive traits. In the 1970s, alternatives to traditional gender roles were introduced. It was proposed that competent individuals could show both masculine and feminine traits. This thinking led to the development of the concept of androgyny, the presence of masculine and feminine traits in one individual.

- Gender-role measures often categorize individuals as masculine, feminine, androgynous, or undifferentiated. Most androgynous individuals are flexible and mentally healthy, although the specific context and the individual's culture also determine how adaptive a gender-role orientation is.

- In thinking about gender, keep in mind the context in which gendered behavior is displayed. In many countries around the world, traditional gender roles are still dominant. A special concern is boys who act in hypermasculine ways. One alternative to androgyny is gender role transcendence.

Transgender

- Transgender is a broad term that refers to individuals who adopt a gender identity that differs from the one assigned to them at birth. Increasingly, the term *trans* is being used to describe transgender individuals.

- The traditional conceptualization of gender as being binary and having only two categories—male and female—is being challenged. These challenges occur in neuroscience, where human brains are increasingly described more as a mosaic than as "his or her" brains; in endocrinology research that reveals more hormonal similarities in males and females than used to be thought; in the use of an increasing number of gender identity categories, including gender-nonconforming, transgender, cisgender, and many more; and in developmental research that reveals the gender worlds of males and females are not only due to biological factors but are culturally influenced and malleable. Also, gender categories are not mutually exclusive and can change over time.

4 Developmental Changes and Junctures

 LG4 Summarize developmental changes in gender.

- The gender intensification hypothesis states that psychological and behavioral differences between boys and girls become greater during adolescence because of increased socialization pressures to conform to traditional gender roles. The jury is still out on the validity of the gender intensification hypothesis, although an increasing number of studies do not support this hypothesis.

- Gilligan argues that girls reach a critical juncture in their development during early adolescence. Girls become aware that their intense interest in intimacy is not prized by the men-dominate society. Some critics say that Gilligan exaggerates gender differences in intimacy.

key **terms**

androgyny	gender roles	gender stereotypes	social cognitive theory of gender
gender	gender-role transcendence	rapport talk	social role theory
gender identity	gender schema theory	report talk	transgender
gender intensification hypothesis			

key **people**

Sandra Bem	Alice Eagly	Carol Gilligan	Eleanor Maccoby
Stephanie Budge	Erik Erikson	Diane Halpern	Joseph Pleck
David Buss	Sigmund Freud	Janet Shibley Hyde	Deborah Tannen

improving **the lives of adolescents and emerging adults**

***Analysis and Evaluation of the Rationales of Single-Sex Schooling* (2014)**
Rebecca Bigler, Amy Hayes, and Lynn Liben
Advances in Child Development and Behavior, 47, 225–260.
> Leading experts provide a number of arguments supporting their assertion that coeducational schools are better for adolescents than are single-sex schools.

***A Content Analysis of Literature on Trans People and Issues: 2002–2012* (2016)**
Bonnie Moradi and others
The Counseling Psychologist, 44, 960–965.
> An excellent overview of the lives of transgender individuals by leading experts in this field.

Gender Development in Adolescence (2009)
Nancy Galambos, Sheri Berenbaum, and Susan McHale
In R. Lerner and L. Steinberg (Eds.), *Handbook of Adolescence* (3rd ed.)
New York: Wiley
 Discusses many different research areas exploring gender development in adolescence.

Gender Similarities and Differences (2014)
Janet Shibley Hyde
Annual Review of Psychology (Vol. 65). Palo Alto, CA: Annual Reviews
 An up-to-date overview of research findings on many topics related to gender similarities and differences.

The Inside Story on Teen Girls (2002)
Karen Zager and Alice Rubenstein
Washington, DC: American Psychological Association
 Provides insight into the lives of adolescent girls and offers many excellent recommendations in areas such as identity, puberty, sex, dating, school, peers, and relationships with parents.

Real Boys (1999)
William Pollack
New York: Owl Books
 Pollack examines the ways boys have been reared and concludes that major changes are needed.

YMCA (www.ymca.net)
The YMCA provides a number of activities for teenage boys, including personal health and sports programs. The organization's website provides information about the YMCA closest to your location.

YWCA (www.ywca.org)
The YWCA promotes health, sports participation, and fitness for women and girls. Its programs include instruction in health, teen pregnancy prevention, family life education, self-esteem enhancement, parenting, and nutrition. The organization's website provides information about the YWCA closest to your location.

SEXUALITY

chapter outline

Jacob Lund/Shutterstock

" I guess when you give a girl a sexy kiss you're supposed to open your lips and put your tongue in her mouth.** That doesn't seem very sexy to me. I can't imagine how a girl would like that. What if she has braces on her teeth and your tongue gets scratched? And how are you supposed to breathe? Sometimes I wish I had an older brother I could ask stuff like this."

—FRANK, AGE 12

"I can't believe I'm so much in love! I just met him last week but I know this is the real thing. He is much more mature than the boys who have liked me before. He's a senior and has his own car. When he brought me home last night, we got so hot I thought we were going to have sex. I'm sure it will happen the next time we go out. It goes against everything I've been taught—but I can't see how it can be wrong when I'm so much in love and he makes me feel so fantastic!"

—AMY, AGE 15

"Ken and I went on a camping trip last weekend and now I'm sure that I'm gay. For a long time I've known I've been attracted to other guys, like in the locker room at school it would sometimes be embarrassing. Ken and I are great friends and lots of times we would mess around wrestling or whatever. I guessed that he felt the way I did. Now I know. Sooner or later, I'll have to come out, as they say, but I know that is going to cause a lot of tension with my parents and for me."

—TOM, AGE 15

"I'm lucky because I have a good figure and I'm popular. I've had boyfriends since middle school and I know how to take care of myself. It's fun when you're out with a guy and you can be intimate. The only thing is, Dan and I had sex a few weeks ago and I'm wondering if I'm pregnant. He used a contraceptive, but maybe it didn't work. Or maybe I'm just late. Anyway, if I have a baby, I could deal with it. My aunt wasn't married when she got pregnant with my cousin, and it turned out okay."

—CLAIRE, AGE 16

"About a month ago my mom's friend's daughter tested positive for HIV. Until then my mom and stepfather never talked about sex with me, but now they're taking turns lecturing me on the theme of 'don't have sex until you're married.' Give me a break! Nicole and I have been together for a year and a half. What do they think we do when we go out, just talk? Besides, my real father never remarried and has girlfriends all the time. All my life I've been seeing movies and TV shows where unmarried people sleep together and the worst that happens is maybe a broken heart. I don't know that woman's daughter, but she must have been mixed up with some pretty bad characters. Me, I always use a condom."

—SEAN, AGE 17

preview

During adolescence and emerging adulthood, the lives of adolescents are wrapped in sexuality. Adolescence and emerging adulthood are time frames when individuals engage in sexual exploration and incorporate sexuality into their identity. We have studied the biological basis of sexual maturation, including the timing of these changes and the hormones that are involved. This chapter focuses on the sexual experiences, attitudes, feelings, and behaviors of adolescents and emerging adults, including the sexual culture and developing a sexual identity. We begin with an overview of sexuality in adolescence and emerging adulthood and then examine problems involving sexual activity, such as adolescent pregnancy, sexually transmitted infections, and forcible sex. Finally, we explore the ways in which adolescents learn about sex.

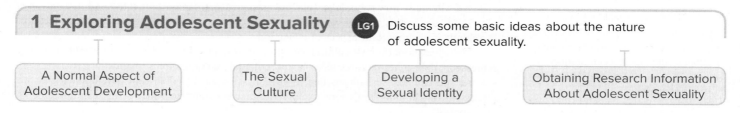

1 Exploring Adolescent Sexuality

LG1 Discuss some basic ideas about the nature of adolescent sexuality.

| A Normal Aspect of Adolescent Development | The Sexual Culture | Developing a Sexual Identity | Obtaining Research Information About Adolescent Sexuality |

Adolescents have an almost insatiable curiosity about the mysteries of sex. They wonder whether they are sexually attractive, how to behave sexually, and what the future holds for their sexual lives. Most adolescents eventually manage to develop a mature sexual identity, even though, as adults can attest, there are always times of vulnerability and confusion along life's sexual journey.

> Sexual arousal emerges as a new phenomenon in adolescence, and it is important to view sexuality as a normal aspect of adolescent development.
>
> —SHIRLEY FELDMAN
> *Contemporary Psychologist, Stanford University*

A NORMAL ASPECT OF ADOLESCENT DEVELOPMENT

Much of what we hear about adolescent sexuality involves problems, such as adolescent pregnancy and sexually transmitted infections. Although these are significant concerns, it is important not to lose sight of the fact that sexuality is a normal part of adolescence.

An important theme of adolescence that is underscored in this book is that too often adolescents are negatively stereotyped (Beckmeyer & Weybright, 2020). The themes of negative stereotyping and adolescent problems also apply to the topic of adolescent sexuality (Diamond & Alley, 2018). Although we will discuss a number of problems that can occur in the area of adolescent sexuality, it is important to keep in mind that the majority of adolescents have healthy sexual attitudes, experience positive emotions related to sexuality, and engage in sexual behaviors that will not compromise their journey to adulthood.

Every society pays some attention to adolescent sexuality. In some societies, adults chaperone adolescent females to protect them from males; others promote very early marriage. Still other societies, such as the United States, allow some sexual experimentation, although there is a wide range of opinions about just how far this experimentation should be allowed to go.

In previous chapters we introduced topics that provide a backdrop for understanding sexual attitudes and behavior in adolescence. We saw that an important aspect of pubertal change involves sexual maturation and a dramatic increase in androgens in males and estrogens in females. We also discussed how puberty is coming earlier today than in previous generations, which can lead to early dating and early sexual activity.

We noted that the prefrontal cortex (where the highest level of cognitive functioning occurs in processes such as self-control, reasoning, and decision making) develops later than the limbic system (a lower, subcortical system that is the seat of emotions and experience of rewards). Thus, the prefrontal cortex may not have developed to the point at which it can adequately control the adolescent's sexual feelings and passions.

We considered sexual identity as one of the dimensions of personal identity. Intimacy with another is an important aspect of the dyadic nature of adolescent sexuality.

We examined the physical and biological differences between females and males. We also saw that, according to the gender intensification hypothesis, pubertal changes can lead boys and

---

developmental connection

Biological Processes

Early maturation in girls is linked with earlier sexual experiences. Connect to "Puberty, Health, and Biological Foundations."

---

girls to conform to traditional masculine and feminine behavior, respectively. Further, when college students are asked to rate the strength of their sex drive, men report higher levels of sexual desire than women. The adolescent developmental transition, then, may be seen as a bridge between the asexuality of childhood and the fully developed sexual identity of adulthood.

Subsequent chapters also include discussions that are important for understanding adolescent sexuality. We will learn that intense, prolonged conflict with parents is associated with adolescent sexual problems, as is a lack of parental monitoring. Better relationships with parents are correlated with the postponement of sexual intercourse, less frequent intercourse, and fewer partners in adolescence. Later in this chapter, we see that adolescents tend to receive very little sex education from parents and that parents and adolescents rarely discuss sex.

We will read about how same-sex siblings, peers, and friends often discuss sexuality. We will also learn that early dating is associated with a number of adolescent problems and that romantic love is important (especially for girls) in adolescence.

We will study how schools are playing an increasingly important role in adolescent sexuality. And later in this chapter, we will see that most parents now recognize that sex education in schools is an important aspect of education.

We will explore the vast cultural variations in sexuality. In some cultures sexuality is highly repressed, while other cultures have far more liberal standards for sexuality.

As you can see, sexuality is tied to virtually all areas of adolescent development that we discuss in this edition. Let's now explore the sexual culture to which American adolescents are exposed.

- - - - - - - - →

developmental **connection**

Peers

Early dating and "going with" someone are linked with adolescent pregnancy. Connect to "Peers, Romantic Relationships, and Lifestyles."

←- - - - - - - -

THE SEXUAL CULTURE

It is important to put adolescent sexuality into the broader context of sexuality in the American culture (Herdt & Polen-Petit, 2021). Whereas in the mid-twentieth century sex was perceived to be more appropriate for married couples, today adult sex is openly acknowledged as appropriate for both married and single adults. Sex among unmarried teenagers is an extension of this general trend toward greater sexual permissiveness in the adult culture. In the United States, society sends mixed messages about sex to youth—on the one hand, adolescents (especially girls) are told not to have sex, and on the other hand, they see sex portrayed in the media as positive (especially for boys). Thus, it is no wonder that adolescents find sexual development and choices so confusing. Consider the portrayal of sex in the media:

> The messages conveyed about sexuality (in the media) are not always ideal . . . and they are often limited, unrealistic, and stereotypical. Dominating is a recreational orientation to sexuality in which courtship is treated as a competition, a battle of the sexes, characterized by dishonesty, game playing, and manipulation. . . . Also prominent are stereotypical sexual roles featuring women as sexual objects, whose value is based solely on their physical appearance, and men as sex-driven players looking to "score" at all costs. . . . (Ward, Day, & Epstein, 2006, p. 57)

Sex is explicitly portrayed in movies, TV shows, videos, lyrics of popular music, MTV, and websites. A recent study of prime-time television shows viewed by U.S. adolescents and emerging adults found that sexual violence and abuse, casual sex, lack of contraception, and no coverage of the consequences of risky sexual behavior were common (Kinsler & others, 2018). Another recent study of television shows revealed that sexual behavior with casual acquaintances was shown almost as frequently as sexual behavior in committed relationships (Timmermans & Van den Bulck, 2018). Further, a study of 12- to 17-year-olds found that those who watched

Adolescents are exposed to sex virtually everywhere in the American culture, and sex is used to sell just about everything.
John Flournoy/McGraw Hill

more sexually explicit TV shows were more likely than their counterparts who watched fewer of these shows to initiate sexual intercourse within the next 12 months (Collins & others, 2004). Adolescents in the highest 10 percent of time spent viewing sexually explicit TV shows were twice as likely to engage in sexual intercourse as those in the lowest 10 percent. In addition, a study of adolescents across a three-year period revealed a link between watching sex on TV and subsequent higher risk of pregnancy (Chandra & others, 2009). And in a recent study of Latina and non-Latinx white girls' preferred TV programs, female characters were more likely to be portrayed in a sexualized manner (clothing, sexual comments, and so on) than were male characters (McDade-Montez, Wallander, & Cameron, 2017). Adolescents increasingly have had access to sexually explicit websites. One study revealed that adolescents who reported ever visiting a sexually explicit website were more sexually permissive and were more likely to have multiple lifetime sexual partners, to have had more than one sexual partner in the last three months, to have used alcohol or other substances at their last sexual encounter, and to engage in anal sex more than their counterparts who reported that they had never visited a sexually explicit website (Braun-Courville & Rojas, 2009). Also, a recent Taiwanese study found that exposure to sexually explicit media in the eighth grade was linked to risky sexual behavior that included early sexual debut, unsafe sex, and multiple sexual partners (Lin, Liu, & Yi, 2020). Adolescent engagement in *sexting,* which involves sending sexually explicit images, videos, or text messages via electronic communication, has become increasingly common (Bianchi & others, 2021; Lee & Darcy, 2021). For example, in a recent national study of U.S. middle and high school students, 13 percent reported they had sent a sext and 18.5 percent indicated they had received a text (Patchin & Hinduja, 2019). Also, a recent study of adolescents and young adults in 11 countries revealed that the dark triad of personality traits (narcissism, Machiavellianism, and psychopathy) were linked to sexting (Morelli & others, 2021). In this study, sharing one's own sexts was positively predicted by Machiavellianism (manipulating others) and narcissism (inflated view of self and self-love, for example), while both risky and aggravated sexting were associated with Machiavellianism and psychopathy (lack of empathy and emotional shallowness).

Also, in a meta-analysis of emerging adults, 38.3 percent were sending sexts, 41.5 were receiving sexts, and 47.7 percent were engaged in reciprocal sexting (Mori & others, 2020). Further, a recent study of emerging adults found that receiving unwanted sexts and sexting under coercion were linked to higher levels of anxiety, stress, and depression, as well as lower self-esteem (Klettke & others, 2019).

Adolescents are exposed to sex in many contexts, including TV and the Internet. *Is it surprising, then, that adolescents are so curious about sex and tempted to experiment with sex?*
The CW/Courtesy Everett Collection

DEVELOPING A SEXUAL IDENTITY

Dealing with emerging sexual feelings and forming a sense of sexual identity is a multifaceted process (Sokkary, Awad, & Paulo, 2021). This lengthy process involves learning to manage sexual feelings such as sexual arousal and attraction, developing new forms of intimacy, and learning the skills required to regulate sexual behavior so as to avoid undesirable consequences (Goldberg & Halpern, 2017). Developing a sexual identity also involves more than just sexual behavior. Sexual identities emerge in the context of physical factors such as puberty's hormones, social factors, and cultural factors, with most societies placing constraints on the sexual behavior of adolescents. An adolescent's sexual identity is strongly influenced by social norms related to sex—the extent to which adolescents perceive that their peers are having sex, using protection, and so on. These social norms have important influences on adolescents' sexual behavior. For example, one study revealed that when adolescents perceived that their peers were sexually permissive, the adolescents had a higher rate of initiating sexual intercourse and engaging in risky sexual practices (Potard, Courtois, & Rusch, 2008).

An adolescent's sexual identity involves an indication of sexual orientation (whether an individual has same-sex or other-sex attractions), and it also involves activities, interests, and styles of behavior. A study of 470 tenth- to twelfth-grade Australian youth found considerable variation in their sexual attitudes and practices (Buzwell & Rosenthal, 1996). Some were virgins and sexually naive. Some had high anxiety about sex and perceived their bodies as underdeveloped and unappealing, whereas others had low anxiety about sex and an interest in exploring sexual options. Yet others felt sexually attractive, were sexually experienced, and had confidence in their ability to manage sexual situations.

OBTAINING RESEARCH INFORMATION ABOUT ADOLESCENT SEXUALITY

developmental **connection**

Research Methods

One drawback of surveys and interviews is the tendency of some participants to answer questions in a socially desirable way. Connect to "Introduction."

Assessing sexual attitudes and behavior is not always a straightforward matter (Pfeffer & others, 2017). Consider how you would respond if someone asked you, "How often do you have intercourse?" or "How many different sexual partners have you had?" The individuals most likely to respond to sexual surveys are those who have liberal sexual attitudes and engage in liberal sexual behaviors. Thus, research is limited by the reluctance of some individuals to provide candid answers to questions about extremely personal matters, and by researchers' inability to get any answer, candid or otherwise, from individuals who simply refuse to talk to strangers about sex. In addition, when asked about their sexual activity, individuals may respond truthfully or they may give socially desirable answers. For example, a ninth-grade boy might report that he has had sexual intercourse even if he has not, because he is afraid someone will find out that he is sexually inexperienced. One study of high school students revealed that 8 percent of the girls understated their sexual experience, while 14 percent of the boys overstated their sexual experience (Siegel, Aten, & Roghmann, 1998). Thus, boys tend to exaggerate their sexual experiences to increase perceptions of their sexual prowess, while girls tend to downplay their sexual experiences so they won't be perceived as irresponsible or promiscuous.

Review Connect Reflect

LG1 Discuss some basic ideas about the nature of adolescent sexuality.

Review

- How can sexuality be explained as a normal aspect of adolescent development?
- What kind of sexual culture are adolescents exposed to in the United States?
- What is involved in developing a sexual identity in adolescence?
- What are some difficulties involved in obtaining research information about adolescent sexuality?

Connect

- How does the sexual culture you learned about in this section contribute to gender stereotypes?

Reflect *Your Own Personal Journey of Life*

- How would you describe your sexual identity as an adolescent and emerging adult? What contributed to this identity? How did your sexual identity evolve, and when did you become aware of it?

2 Sexual Attitudes and Behavior

LG2 Summarize sexual attitudes and behavior in adolescence.

| Heterosexual Attitudes and Behavior | Sexual Minority Youths' Attitudes and Behavior | Self-Stimulation | Contraceptive Use |

Let's now explore adolescents' sexual attitudes and behavior. First, we study heterosexual attitudes and behavior, and then we examine sexual minority attitudes and behavior.

HETEROSEXUAL ATTITUDES AND BEHAVIOR

How early do adolescents engage in various sexual activities? What sexual scripts do adolescents follow? Are some adolescents more vulnerable than others to irresponsible sexual behavior? We will examine each of these questions in this section.

Development of Sexual Activities in Adolescents   What is the current profile of sexual activity of adolescents? In a U.S. national survey, in 2019, 38.4 percent of ninth- to twelfth-graders reported ever having had sexual intercourse (Underwood & others, 2020).

Compared with earlier national figures, sexual intercourse in adolescence has been declining recently—in 1991, the national figure was 54.1 percent, and in 2011 it was 47.4 percent. Nationally, in 2019, 56.7 percent of twelfth-graders, 46.5 percent of eleventh-graders, 33.6 percent of tenth-graders, and 19.2 percent of ninth-graders reported having engaged in sexual intercourse. A recent estimate by the National Survey of Family Growth for the probability of having sexual intercourse in the United States by age 20 was 77 percent for males and 79 percent for females (Martinez & Abma, 2020).

Age at sexual initiation varies by ethnic group in the United States (Underwood & others, 2020). In the 2019 U.S. survey of ninth- to twelfth-graders, 42.3 percent of African Americans, 42.3 percent of Latinxs, 38 percent of non-Latinx whites, and 15.6 percent of Asian Americans said they had experienced sexual intercourse (Underwood & others, 2020). The African American percentage has especially been dropping in recent years—it was 49 percent in 2015. Also, in this study, 3 percent of U.S. adolescents reported that their first sexual experience had taken place before 13 years of age—down from 6.2 percent in 2011 and 10.2 percent in 1991 (Underwood & others, 2020). Further in this study, 6.9 percent of African American high school students (compared with 3.8 percent of Latinxs, 1.9 percent of non-Latinx whites, and 0.8 percent of Asian Americans) said they had their first sexual experience before 13 years of age. In sum, these figures represent a significant decrease in recent years of having sexual intercourse in adolescence and having sexual intercourse prior to age 13.

Oral Sex   Research indicates that oral sex is now a common occurrence among U.S. adolescents (Fava & Bay-Cheng, 2012). In a recent national survey of more than 7,000 15- to 24-year-olds, 58.6 percent of the females reported ever having performed oral sex and 60.4 percent said they had ever received oral sex (Holway & Hernandez, 2018). Also, in another national survey, 51 percent of U.S. 15- to 19-year-old boys and 47 percent of girls in the same age group said they had engaged in oral sex (Child Trends, 2015). Thus, more youth engage in oral sex than vaginal sex, likely because they perceive oral sex to be more acceptable and to present fewer health risks.

In an editorial in the *Journal of Adolescent Health*, Bonnie Halpern-Felsher (2008) discussed the pluses and minuses of oral versus vaginal sex. Oral sex negates the risk of pregnancy and is linked to fewer negative outcomes than is vaginal sex. However, oral sex is not risk-free, being related to such negative health outcomes as sexually transmitted infections (herpes, chlamydia, and gonorrhea, for example). Thus, it is recommended that if adolescents have oral sex they use condoms. However, in the recent national study mentioned above, only 7.6 percent of females and 9.3 percent of males used a condom the most recent time they had oral sex (Holway & Hernandez, 2018).

Halpern-Felsher and her colleagues have further examined the merits of engaging in oral versus vaginal sex (Brady & Halpern-Felsher, 2007; Goldstein & Halpern-Felsher, 2018; Song & Halpern-Felsher, 2010). In one study, the temporal order between oral and vaginal sex in sexually active adolescents was examined (Song & Halpern-Felsher, 2010). In this study, most of the adolescents had initiated vaginal sex after or within the same 6-month period of starting to have oral sex. Those who initiated oral sex at the end of the ninth grade had a 50 percent chance of having vaginal sex by the end of the eleventh grade, but those who delayed having oral sex until the end of the eleventh grade had less than a 20 percent chance of initiating vaginal sex by the end of the eleventh grade.

In another study, the consequences of having oral sex versus vaginal sex were explored (Brady & Halpern-Felsher, 2007). Compared with adolescents who engaged in vaginal sex with or without oral sex, adolescents who engaged only in oral sex were less likely to become pregnant or incur a sexually transmitted infection, feel guilty or used, have their relationship deteriorate, and get into trouble with their parents about sex. Adolescents who engaged only in oral sex also were more likely to report experiencing pleasure, feeling good about themselves, and having their relationship improve as a result of the sexual experience than did their counterparts who engaged only in vaginal sex or in both oral and vaginal sex.

In one study, among female adolescents who reported having vaginal sex first, 31 percent reported having a teen pregnancy, whereas among those who initiated oral-genital sex first, only 8 percent reported having a teen pregnancy (Reese & others, 2013). Thus, how adolescents initiate their sex lives may have positive or negative consequences for their sexual health.

How might adolescent sexual patterns be different in cross-country comparisons?
FangXiaNuo/Getty Images

Cross-Cultural Comparisons   The timing of teenage sexual initiation in different countries varies widely by culture and gender, and in most instances is linked to the culture's values and customs. In one study, the proportion of females having first intercourse by age 17 ranged from 72 percent in Mali to 47 percent in the United States and 45 percent in Tanzania (Singh & others, 2000). The proportion of males who had their first intercourse by age 17 ranged from 76 percent in Jamaica to 64 percent in the United States and 63 percent in Brazil. Not all countries were represented in this study, and it is generally agreed that in some Asian countries, such as China and Japan, first intercourse occurs much later than in the United States. Also, since this cross-cultural comparison in 2000, as indicated earlier, the percentage of high school students who have had sexual intercourse has declined in recent years.

Sexual activity patterns for 15- to 19-year-olds differ greatly for males and females in almost every geographic region of the world (Singh & others, 2000). In developing countries, the vast majority of sexually experienced males in this age group are unmarried, whereas two-thirds or more of the sexually experienced females in this group are married. However, in the United States and in other developed nations such as the Netherlands, Sweden, and Australia, the overwhelming majority of 15- to 19-year-old females are unmarried.

What are some trends in the sexual behavior of adolescents? What characterizes adolescents' sexual scripts?
Hill Street Studios/Getty Images

Sexual Scripts   As adolescents and emerging adults explore their sexual identities, they are guided by sexual scripts (Schuster, Tomaszewska, & Krahe, 2021). A **sexual script** is a stereotyped pattern of role prescriptions for how individuals should behave sexually (Thompson & others, 2020). By the time individuals reach adolescence, girls and boys have been socialized to follow different sexual scripts. Differences in female and male sexual scripting can cause problems and confusion for adolescents as they work out their sexual identities. In a recent research review, it was concluded that a sexual double standard continues to exist, with females being subjected to stricter social norms for sexual behavior and males being granted more sexual freedom and not being criticized for having multiple sexual partners (Bousuard, van de Bongardt, & Blais, 2016). A recent international study of young adolescents in 14 sites across four continents found consistent evidence for a sexual script of boy's social gains for having girlfriends and girls' risk for having boyfriends (Moreau & others, 2018). Another sexual script is that female adolescents learn to link sexual intercourse with love (Tolman & Chmielewski, 2019). They often rationalize their sexual behavior by telling themselves that they were swept away by the passion of the moment. A number of studies have found that adolescent girls are more likely than their male counterparts to report being in love as the main reason they are sexually active (Hyde & DeLamater, 2020). Other reasons that girls give for being sexually active include giving in to male pressure, gambling that sex is a way to get a boyfriend, curiosity, and sexual desire unrelated to loving and caring.

The majority of adolescent sexual experiences involve the male making sexual advances and the female setting limits on the male's sexual overtures. Adolescent boys experience considerable peer pressure to have sexual intercourse. As one adolescent remarked, "I feel a lot of pressure from my buddies to go for the score."

sexual script A stereotyped pattern of role prescriptions for how individuals should behave in sexual contexts. Females and males have been socialized to follow different sexual scripts.

One study explored heterosexual sexual scripts in focus groups with 18- to 26-year-old males and females (Sakaluk & others, 2014). The following sexual scripts were supported:

- *Sex Drive.* Men are always ready for sex; women inhibit their sexual expression.
- *Physical and Emotional Sex.* Men have a physical approach to sex; women have an emotional/relational approach to sex.
- *Sexual Performance.* Men and women should both be sexually skilled and knowledgeable. One new aspect of this sexual script for women was agreement that women should especially have oral sex skills.
- *Initiation and Gateway Scripts.* Men initiate sex (most men and some women agreed with this script); women are gatekeepers (most men and women agreed that women set the sexual limits).
- *Sexual Evaluation.* Single women who appear sexual are judged negatively; men are rewarded for being sexual. However, there was negative judgment of men who come across as too sexual and too often engage in casual sex, especially with different women.

Risk Factors in Adolescent Sexuality   Many adolescents are not emotionally prepared to handle sexual experiences, especially in early adolescence (Bozzini & others, 2021). Early sexual activity is linked with risky behaviors such as drug use, delinquency, mental health problems, and school-related problems (Rivera & others, 2018). A study of more than 3,000 Swedish adolescents revealed that sexual intercourse before age 14 was linked to risky behaviors such as an increased number of sexual partners, experience of oral and anal sex, negative health behaviors (smoking, drug, and alcohol use), and antisocial behavior (being violent, stealing, running away from home) at 18 years of age (Kastbom & others, 2015). Further, a recent South African study found that early sexual debut predicted a lower probability of graduating from high school (Bengesai, Khan, & Dube, 2018). And in an Australian study, having sexual intercourse at age 15 or younger predicted higher numbers of sexual partners and lower use of condoms during emerging adulthood (average age 21) (Prendergast & others, 2019). Also in this study, early sexual intercourse also was associated with higher rates of emerging adult substance use and antisocial behavior.

In addition to having sex in early adolescence, other risk factors for sexual problems in adolescence include contextual factors such as socioeconomic status (SES) and poverty, immigration/ethnic minority status, substance use, family/parenting and peer factors, school-related influences, and sports activities (Warner, 2018). The percentage of sexually active young adolescents is higher in low-income areas of inner cities (Morrison-Beedy & others, 2013). Substance abuse, especially in early adolescence, is linked to risky sexual behaviors. For example, in a recent study, the likelihood of initiating sexual intercourse before age 13 was higher among individuals who engaged in substance abuse and had mental health problems (Okumu & others, 2019).

A number of family factors are associated with sexual risk taking. In a recent study of adolescents, spending higher amounts of quality time with parents was linked to lower rates of engaging in vaginal sex, anal sex, oral sex and masturbation or viewing pornographic pictures and videos (Astle, Leonhardt, & Willoughby, 2020). And a recent study revealed that of a number of parenting practices the factor that best predicted a lower level of risky sexual behavior by adolescents was supportive parenting (Simons & others, 2016). Also, having older sexually active siblings or pregnant/parenting teenage sisters placed adolescent girls at increased risk for pregnancy (Miller, Benson, & Galbraith, 2001). Further, in a recent study of urban, predominantly Latinx and African American adolescents, talk with extended family members about sexual protection was linked to adolescents having fewer sexual partners, while talk about risks involved in sex was associated with adolescents having more sexual partners (Grossman & others, 2019).

Peer, school, sports, religious, and development asset contexts provide further information about sexual risk taking among adolescents (Widman & others, 2016). One study found that adolescents who associated with more deviant peers in early adolescence were likely to have had more sexual partners by age 16 (Lansford & others, 2010). Further, a recent study revealed that associating with antisocial peers predicted early engagement in sexual intercourse (Clark & others, 2021). And a research review found that school connectedness was linked to positive sexuality outcomes (Markham & others, 2010). Also, a study of middle school students revealed that higher academic achievement reduced the risk of early initiation of sexual intercourse (Laflin, Wang, & Barry, 2008). In addition, researchers found

What are some risks for early initiation of sexual intercourse?
Stockbyte/Punchstock/Getty Images

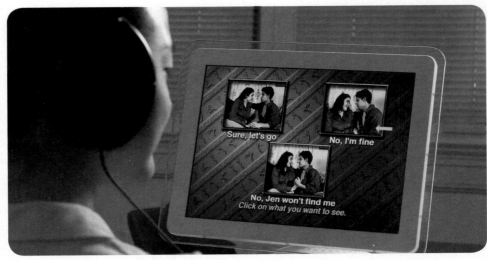

An adolescent participates in an interactive video session developed by Julie Downs and her colleagues at the department of Social and Decision Sciences at Carnegie Mellon University. The videos help adolescents evaluate their responses and decisions in high-risk sexual contexts.
Michael Ray

developmental **connection**

Religious Development

Certain aspects of being religious are linked to lower sexual risk taking. Connect to "Moral Development, Values, and Religion."

that adolescent females who skipped school or failed a test were more likely to engage in frequent sexual intercourse and less likely to use contraceptives (Hensel & Sorge, 2014). Also, a recent study found that adolescent males who play sports engage in a higher level of sexual risk taking, while adolescent females who play sports engage in a lower level of sexual risk taking (Lipowski & others, 2016). Further, a recent study of African American adolescent girls indicated that those who reported that religion was of low or moderate importance to them had a much earlier sexual debut than their counterparts who said that religion was very or extremely important to them (George Dalmida & others, 2018). And a recent study found that non-Latinx white adolescent girls showed the most consistent link between a higher level of developmental assets (internal and external) and attitudes and behaviors indicative of delaying sexual activity, while African American youth had the fewest associations (Messer & others, 2021).

Cognitive and personality factors also are increasingly implicated in sexual risk taking in adolescence. Two such factors are self-control and impulsiveness. A recent study confirmed that low self-control is linked to risky sexual behavior in adolescence (Magnusson, Crandall, & Evans, 2019).

Further Exploration of Sexuality in Emerging Adults   We already have covered some aspects of heterosexual attitudes and behavior in emerging adults. For example, recall in our discussion of sexual scripts that a number of sexual scripts continue to characterize emerging adult females and males (Lefkowitz & others, 2014; Sakaluk & others, 2014). Here we consider further analysis and integration of information about patterns of heterosexual behavior in emerging adults.

Surveys indicate that at the beginning of emerging adulthood (age 18), a little more than half of individuals have experienced sexual intercourse—but by the end of emerging adulthood (age 25), most individuals have had sexual intercourse (Wesche & Lefkowitz, 2020). Also, the average age of marriage in the United States is currently 30 for males and 28 for females (U.S. Census Bureau, 2019). Thus, emerging adulthood is a time frame during which most individuals are both sexually active and unmarried (Wesche & Lefkowitz, 2020). In a recent study, across the college years, rates of kissing, touching, performing and receiving oral sex, and engaging in penetrative sex increased (Lefkowitz & others, 2019). Also in this study, contraceptive use decreased during the college years, especially for men and for students in serious romantic relationships.

Uncertainty characterizes many emerging adults' sexual relationships (Wesche & Lefkowitz, 2020). Consider a study of emerging adult daters and cohabitors that found nearly half reported a reconciliation (a breakup followed by a reunion) (Halpern-Meekin & others, 2013). Also, emerging adults report that on days when they have vaginal sex they have more positive affect; however, they report higher levels of negative affect or other negative consequences if they have sex with someone they are not dating (Vasilenko & Lefkowitz, 2018).

Christine's Thoughts About Sexual Relationships

As a college freshman, Christine tried to suppress the sexual feelings she had in her romantic relationship and later decided it was better to lose her virginity to a friend than to a boyfriend:

> I think the first time you have sex should be with a friend, not necessarily with a boyfriend, because there's too many emotions involved. And with a friend, there's that closeness there but there's not those deep-running feelings that could really (mess) you up if the relationship doesn't work out.

Christine also commented:

> I won't really enjoy (sex) until after college . . . because in college, everything's so helter-skelter. You don't know what you're going to

do the next day or the day after that. And after college, you're probably going to get into a routine of going to work, coming back home, feeding your dog, feeding your boyfriend, you know? It's going to feel like you have more of a stable life with this person, and think that they're going to be more intimate. And with that, you're probably going to have better sex.

_____

(Source: Gilmartin, 2006, pp. 444, 447)

Do Christine's efforts to be selective about her sexual partners mirror an observed pattern of behavior among people her age?

Casual sex is more common in emerging adulthood than it is during the late twenties (Wesche & Lefkowitz, 2020). A recent trend has involved "hooking up" to have non-relationship sex (from kissing to intercourse) (Sutton, Simons, & Tyler, 2021). In a recent analysis of first-year college students in six focus groups, a common theme they expressed was: "Sex is easier to get and love is harder to find" (Anders & others, 2020). Along the same lines, 40 percent of 22-year-olds in an earlier study reported having had a recent casual sexual partner (Lyons & others, 2015). Another study found that 20 percent of first-year college women on one large university campus had engaged in at least one hookup over the course of the school year (Fielder & others, 2013). In this study, impulsivity, sensation seeking, and alcohol use were among the predictors of a higher likelihood of hooking up. Further, in a recent study, a greater percentage of emerging adult women than men reported having sex, hooking up with an acquaintance, using partner characteristics as a reason to hook up, and having negative reactions to their most recent hookup (Olmstead, Norona, & Anders, 2019). In this study, a greater percentage of emerging adult men than women reported hooking up with a stranger, meeting at a bar/club, and hooking up at a party. And a recent study of sexual minority women between the ages of 18 and 25 revealed that alcohol use was associated with a greater likelihood of engaging in any future hookups and those who reported more minority stress subsequently hooked up with more partners (Jaffe & others, 2021).

What are some characteristics of sexual patterns in emerging adulthood?
Sam Edwards/OJO Images/AGE Fotostock

In addition to hooking up, another type of casual sex that has recently increased in emerging adults is "friends with benefits (FWB)," which involves a relationship formed by the integration of friendship and sexual intimacy without an explicit commitment characteristic of an exclusive romantic relationship (Weger, Cole, & Akbulut, 2019). A recent study found that suicidal ideation was associated with entrance into a friends-with-benefits relationship as well as continuation of the FWB relationship (Dube & others, 2017).

What are some predictors of risky heterosexual behavior in emerging adults, such as engaging in casual and unprotected sexual intercourse? Some research findings indicate that individuals who become sexually active in adolescence engage in more risky sexual behaviors in emerging adulthood than do their counterparts who delay their sexual debuts until emerging adulthood (Shulman, Seiffge-Krenke, & Walsh, 2017). One study revealed that emerging adults who were enrolled in college or who had graduated from college reported having had fewer casual sex partners than those without a high school diploma (Lyons & others, 2013). Also, more religious emerging adults have had fewer sexual partners and engage in less risky sexual behaviors than their less religious counterparts (Lefkowitz, Boone, & Shearer, 2004). Further, when emerging adults drink alcohol, they are more likely to have casual sex and less likely to discuss possible risks (Simons & others, 2018). Another, a recent study found that pregaming (getting drunk or generally intoxicated before an event or a night out) occurred more frequently in college women when they drank alcohol mixed with energy drinks (Linden-Carmichael & Lau-Barraco, 2017). And one study found that more frequent viewing of pornography by college students was associated with a higher incidence of hooking up and a larger number of different hookup partners (Braithwaite & others, 2015).

How extensive are gender differences in sexuality? A meta-analysis revealed that men said they engaged more often in masturbation, pornography viewing, and casual sex, and they expressed more permissive attitudes about casual sex than did their female counterparts (Petersen & Hyde, 2010).

SEXUAL MINORITY YOUTHS' ATTITUDES AND BEHAVIOR

The majority of sexual minority individuals experience their first same-sex attraction, sexual behavior, and self-labeling as a gay or lesbian just before or during adolescence (Diamond, 2019). However, some sexual minority individuals have these experiences for the first time during emerging adulthood. Also, while most gays and lesbians have their first same-sex experience just prior to or during adolescence, they often have their first extended same-sex relationship in emerging adulthood. In the timing and sequence of sexual developmental milestones, there are few individual differences between heterosexual and sexual minority adolescents except that sexual minority adolescents have to cope with their sexual identity in more stressful ways and also in disclosing this identity to others (Savin-Williams, 2019).

Preference for a sexual partner of the same or other sex is not always a fixed decision, made once in a lifetime and then adhered to forever. For example, it is not unusual for an individual, especially a male, to engage in same-sex experimentation in adolescence but not to engage in same-sex behavior as an adult. For others, the opposite progression applies.

Until the middle of the twentieth century, it was generally thought that people were either heterosexual or homosexual. However, there has been a move away from using the term "homosexual" because the term has negative historical connotations (Herdt & Polen-Petit, 2021). Also, the use of the term "homosexual" as a clear-cut sexual type is often oversimplified. For example, many more individuals report having same-sex attractions and behavior than the number who identify themselves as members of a **sexual minority**—individuals who self-identify as lesbian, gay, or bisexual. The term **bisexual** refers to someone who is attracted to people of both sexes. Researchers have gravitated toward more descriptive and limited terms than "homosexual," preferring such terms as "individuals with same-sex attractions," or "individuals who have engaged in same-sex behavior." Another approach is to consider

sexual minority Someone who self-identifies as lesbian, gay, bisexual, or transgender.

bisexual A person who is attracted to people of both sexes.

What are some characteristics of sexual minority adolescents?
Nati Harnik/AP Images

adolescent sexuality not in terms of categories but on a continuum in sexual and romantic dimensions from exclusive attraction to the opposite sex to exclusive attraction to the same sex (Savin-Williams, 2019).

In the most recent national survey of sexual orientation that included men and women from 18 to 44 years of age, almost three times as many women (17.4 percent) as men (6.2 percent) reported having had any same-sex contact in their lifetime (Copen, Chandra, & Febo-Vazquez, 2016). Feelings of attraction only to the opposite sex were more frequent for men (92.1 percent) than for women (81 percent). Also in this study, 92.3 percent of the women and 95.1 percent of the men said they were heterosexual or straight. Further, 1.3 percent of the women and 1.9 percent of the men said they were homosexual, gay, or lesbian, and 5.5 percent of women and 2 percent of men reported that they were bisexual.

Factors Associated with Sexual Minority Behavior   Researchers have explored the possible biological basis of sexual minority behavior (LeVay, 2016). In this regard, we next evaluate hormone, brain, and twin studies regarding same-sex attraction. The results of hormone studies have been inconsistent. Indeed, if sexual minority males are given male sexual hormones (androgens), their sexual orientation does not change; their sexual desire merely increases.

A very early critical period might influence sexual orientation (Hines, 2020a, b). In the second to fifth months after conception, exposure of the fetus to hormone levels characteristic of females might cause the individual (female or male) to become attracted to males (Ellis & Ames, 1987). If this critical-period hypothesis turns out to be correct, it would explain why clinicians have found that sexual orientation is difficult, if not virtually impossible, to modify (Meyer-Bahlburg & others, 1995).

Researchers have also examined genetic influences on sexual orientation by studying twins (Sanders & others, 2017). A Swedish study of almost 4,000 twins found that only about 35 percent of the variation in homosexual behavior in men and 19 percent in women were explained by genetic differences (Langstrom & others, 2010). This result suggests that although genes play a role in sexual orientation, they are not the only influence (King, 2020). That said, it has become clear that whether a person is heterosexual, gay, lesbian, or bisexual, that individual cannot be talked out of his or her sexual orientation (King, 2020).

Researchers have also explored childhood behavior patterns of sexual minority adolescents. A recent study of more than 4,500 boys and girls explored whether early childhood sex-typed behavior might be linked to adolescent sexual orientation (Li, Kung, & Hines, 2017). In this study, gender-typed behavior (rough-and-tumble play was a male sex-typed item and playing house was a female sex-typed item, for example) at 3.5 and 4.75 years (but less so at 2.5 years) predicted sexual orientation at 15 years of age, with the results stronger for boy than for girls.

An individual's sexual orientation—same-sex, heterosexual, or bisexual—is most likely determined by a combination of genetic, hormonal, cognitive, and environmental factors (King, 2020, 2022). Most experts on same-sex relations believe that no one factor alone causes sexual orientation, and that the relative weight of each factor can vary from one individual to the next (Savin-Williams, 2019).

Developmental Pathways   It is commonly perceived that most sexual minority adolescents quietly struggle with same-sex attractions in childhood, do not engage in heterosexual dating, and gradually recognize that they are gay or lesbian in mid- to late adolescence (Diamond, 2019). However, there is much more fluidity in sexual orientation than this developmental milestone approach suggests (Savin-Williams, 2019). Many youth do follow this developmental pathway, but others do not. For example, many youth have no recollection of same-sex attractions and experience a more abrupt sense of their same-sex attraction in late adolescence (Savin-Williams, 2019). Researchers also have found that the majority of adolescents with same-sex attractions also experience some degree of other-sex attractions at some point in their lives; this is particularly true of females (Diamond, 2019). And, although some adolescents who are attracted to same-sex individuals fall in love with these individuals, others claim that their same-sex attractions are purely physical (Savin-Williams, 2017).

In sum, sexual minority youth have diverse developmental trajectories, encompassing their patterns of initial attraction, the presence or absence of sexual and romantic attractions to both sexes, and the possibility of a disjuncture in their physical and emotional attraction to one sex or the other (Savin-Williams, 2019).

developmental **connection**

Research Methods

A twin study compares the behavioral similarities of identical twins with those of fraternal twins. Connect to "Puberty, Health, and Biological Foundations."

Gay or Lesbian Identity and Disclosure Establishing a gay or lesbian identity and disclosing that information to others is often a long process, frequently beginning just before adolescence or in early adolescence and concluding in emerging adulthood (Diamond, 2019). In one study of gay adolescents, the majority said that as children they felt different from other boys (Newman & Muzzonigro, 1993). The average age at which they had their first crush on another boy was 12.7 years, and the average age when they realized they were gay was 12.5 years. Most of the boys said they felt confused when they first became aware that they were gay. About half the boys said they initially tried to deny their identity as a gay male.

Similarities and Differences with Heterosexual Youth Many gender differences that appear in heterosexual relationships also occur in same-sex relationships (Diamond, 2019). A large-scale study found similarities and differences in the lives of adolescents who are heterosexual, those who have same-sex attractions, and those who are bisexual (Bosséri & others, 2006). Similarities across sexual orientations occurred for friendship quality, academic orientation, and perception of school climate. Bisexual adolescents reported the most negative results, including areas of their lives such as relationships with parents, psychological functioning, and victimization. Adolescents with same-sex attractions reported less positive experiences than did exclusively heterosexual adolescents in relationships with parents, psychological functioning, and victimization. These results confirm findings in other studies that suggest that non-heterosexual adolescents face additional risks and challenges in their lives. However, the findings also indicate that adolescents with same-sex attractions have a number of positive aspects to their lives, including intrapersonal strengths (academic orientation) and interpersonal resources (friendship quality) (Bosséri & others, 2006).

Discrimination, Bias, and Violence Having irrational negative feelings against individuals who have same-sex attractions is called **homophobia.** In its more extreme forms, homophobia can lead individuals to ridicule, physically assault, or even murder people they believe to have same-sex attractions. More typically, homophobia is associated with avoidance of individuals who have same-sex attractions, faulty beliefs about sexual minority lifestyles (such as falsely thinking that most child molesters have same-sex attractions), and subtle or overt discrimination in housing, employment, and other areas of life (Meyer, 2003).

One of the harmful aspects of the stigmatization of same-sex attraction is the self-devaluation engaged in by sexual minority individuals (Diamond, 2019). One common form of self-devaluation is called passing, the process of hiding one's real social identity. Without adequate support, and with fear of stigmatization, many sexual minority youth retreat to the closet during high school and then emerge at a safer time later, often in college.

Sexual minority youth are more likely to be targeted for violence than heterosexual youth in a number of contexts, including forced sex and dating violence, and verbal and physical harassment at school and in the community (Martin-Storey & Fromme, 2021). Many sexual minority adolescents also experience discrimination and rejection in interactions with their families, peers, schools, and communities (Kokkonen & others, 2021). Sexual minority youths' exposure to stigma and discrimination has been cited as the main reason they are more likely to develop problems (Saewyc, 2011). For example, one study found that family rejection of coming out by sexual minority adolescents was linked to their higher rates of depression, substance use, and unprotected sex (Ryan & others, 2009). A study of 15-year-olds found that sexual minority status was linked to depression mainly via peer harassment (Martin-Storey & Crosnoe, 2012). Despite these negative circumstances, many sexual minority adolescents successfully cope with the challenges they face and develop levels of health and well-being that are similar to those of their heterosexual peers (Diamond, 2019).

Health The majority of sexual minority (gay, lesbian, and bisexual) adolescents have competent and successful paths of development through adolescence and become healthy and productive adults. However, concern has been raised about health risks for sexual minority youth, particularly risks related to the discrimination and bias they experience (Amos & others, 2020). For example, in a recent large-scale study, sexual minority adolescents did engage in a higher prevalence of health-risk behaviors (greater drug use and sexual risk taking, for example) than did heterosexual adolescents (Kann & others, 2016). And a recent study found that early sexual debut (first sexual intercourse before age 13) was associated with sexual risk taking, substance use, violent victimization, and suicidal thoughts/attempts

homophobia Irrational negative feelings against individuals who have same-sex attractions.

in both sexual minority (gay, lesbian, and bisexual adolescents) and heterosexual youth (Lowry & others, 2017).

Recent research indicates there is ample evidence that sexual minority adolescents have higher levels of suicidal thoughts and attempts than heterosexual adolescents (Feigelman & others, 2020). Also in this research, sexual minority adolescent girls had higher rates of suicidal death than heterosexual adolescent girls but sexual minority adolescent boys did not have higher suicidal death rates than heterosexual adolescent boys. Further, a research review of more than 300 studies concluded that bisexual youth had a higher rate of suicidal ideation and attempts than their gay, lesbian, and heterosexual counterparts (Pompili & others, 2014). Sexual minority adolescents are more likely to have had an early sexual debut (before age 13 in some studies, prior to age 14 in others), to report a higher number of lifetime or recent sexual partners, and to have more sexually transmitted infections than heterosexual adolescents, although mixed results have been found for condom use across these groups (Parkes & others, 2011; Saewyc, 2011).

A special concern is the higher rate of sexually transmitted infections, especially HIV, in males who have sex with males (UNAIDS, 2020). Also, researchers have found a higher incidence of sexually transmitted infections in adolescent girls with same-sex partners (especially when they have sexual relations with male partners as well) (Morgan, 2014). Further, in a recent study, compared with heterosexual adolescents, sexual minority adolescents (mean age = 15) were engaging in riskier sexual behavior, with females reporting more sexual partners and drug use prior to sex and males indicating inconsistent condom use and higher rates of HIV (Norris & others, 2019). In addition, a national study of 15- to 20-year-olds found that bisexual and lesbian young women experienced a younger sexual debut and had more male and female sexual partners than did their heterosexual counterparts (Tornello, Riskind, & Patterson, 2014). In this study, bisexual women reported the earliest sexual debut, highest numbers of sexual partners, greatest usage of emergency contraception, and highest frequency of pregnancy termination. Other research has found more extensive sexual health risks for bisexual adolescent females and males than for members of other groups (Morgan, 2014).

Although we have described a number of health risks for sexual minority adolescents, as indicated earlier, it is important to note that the majority of sexual minority adolescents have healthy and competent development.

SELF-STIMULATION

Regardless of whether adolescents have a heterosexual or same-sex attraction, they experience increasing feelings of sexual arousal. Many youths deal with these insistent feelings of sexual arousal through self-stimulation, or masturbation.

As indicated earlier, a continuum of kissing, petting, and intercourse or oral sex characterizes many adolescents' sexual experiences. Substantial numbers of adolescents, though, have sexual experience outside this heterosexual continuum through masturbation (Triana, Susmaneli, & Rafiah, 2020). Most boys have an ejaculation for the first time at about 12 to 13 years of age. Masturbation, genital contact with a same-sex or other-sex partner, or a wet dream during sleep are common circumstances for ejaculation.

Masturbation is the most frequent sexual outlet for many adolescents, especially male adolescents. A study of 14- to 17-year-olds found that 74 percent of the males and 48 percent of the females reported that they had masturbated at some point (Robbins & others, 2012).

Adolescents today do not feel as guilty about masturbation as members of previous generations did, although they still may feel embarrassed or defensive about it. In past eras, masturbation was denounced as causing everything from warts to insanity. Today, as few as 15 percent of adolescents attach any stigma to masturbation (Hyde & DeLamater, 2020).

In one study, researchers surveyed college students regarding their sexual practices (Leitenberg, Detzer, & Srebnik, 1993). Almost twice as many males as females said they had masturbated (81 percent versus 45 percent), and the males who masturbated did so three times more frequently during early adolescence and early adulthood than did the females who masturbated during the same age periods. No association was found between the quality of sexual adjustment in adulthood and a history of engaging in masturbation during preadolescence and/ or early adolescence.

Much of the existing data on masturbation are difficult to interpret because these findings are based on self-reports in which many adolescents may not be responding accurately. Most

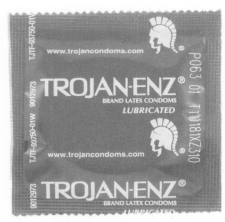

Zoltan Kiraly/Shutterstock

experts on adolescent sexuality likely would agree that boys masturbate more than girls—but masturbation is more stigmatized behavior for girls, so they may actually masturbate more than they indicate in self-reports.

CONTRACEPTIVE USE

Sexual activity is a normal behavior that is necessary for procreation, but if appropriate safeguards are not taken it brings the risk of unintended, unwanted pregnancy and sexually transmitted infections (Crooks & Bauer, 2021). Both of these risks can be reduced significantly by using barrier methods of contraception, such as condoms.

A recent national study revealed a substantial increase in the use of contraceptives (54.4 percent in 2019 versus 46 percent in 1991 but down from 60 percent in 2011) by U.S. high school students the last time they had sexual intercourse (Szucs & others, 2020). Also, younger adolescents are less likely to take contraceptive precautions than are older adolescents. In this national study, 23.2 percent of African American, 12.8 percent of Latinx, and 6.8 percent of non-Latinx white sexually active adolescents reported using no pregnancy prevention (Szucs & others, 2020).

Many sexually active adolescents do not use contraceptives, use them inconsistently, or use contraceptive methods that are less effective than others (Chandra-Mouli & Akwara, 2020). Recently, a number of leading medical organizations and experts have recommended that adolescents use long-acting reversible contraception (LARC) (Menon & the Committee on Adolescence, 2020). These organizations include the Society for Adolescent Health and Medicine (2017), the American Academy of Pediatrics and American College of Obstetrics and Gynecology (Allen & Barlow, 2017), and the World Health Organization (2020). LARC consists of the use of intrauterine devices (IUDs) and contraceptive implants, which have a much lower failure rate and greater effectiveness in preventing unwanted pregnancy than the use of birth control pills and condoms (Grubb & the Committee on Adolescence, 2020). A recent national study found that adolescent use of long-acting reversible contraception (LARC) increased from 1.8 percent in 2013 to 5.3 percent in 2017 (Aligne & others, 2020).

In one study, researchers found that 50 percent of U.S. 15- to 19-year-old girls with unintended pregnancies ending in live births were not using any birth control method when they got pregnant, and 34 percent believed they could not get pregnant at the time (Centers for Disease Control and Prevention, 2015). Another study found that a greater age difference between sexual partners in adolescence is associated with less consistent condom use (Volpe & others, 2013).

Researchers also have found that U.S. adolescents use condoms less than their counterparts in Europe, likely because of the more extensive sex education children and adolescents experience in European countries (Jorgensen & others, 2015). Studies of 15-year-olds revealed that in Europe 72 percent of the girls and 81 percent of the boys had used condoms during their last intercourse (Currie & others, 2008). Use of birth control pills also continues to be higher in European countries (Santelli, Sandfort, & Orr, 2009). Such comparisons provide insight into why adolescent pregnancy rates are much higher in the United States than in European countries.

Review Connect Reflect

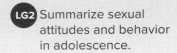 **LG2** Summarize sexual attitudes and behavior in adolescence.

Review
- How would you describe adolescent heterosexual attitudes and behaviors?
- How would you characterize adolescent sexual minority behavior and attitudes?
- What is known about sexual self-stimulation in adolescence?
- How extensively do U.S. adolescents use contraceptives?

Connect
- Connect what you have learned about identity with this section's discussion of gay or lesbian identity and disclosure.

Reflect *Your Own Personal Journey of Life*
- Think about your sexual experiences or lack of sexual experiences in adolescence. If you could go back to that period in your life, what would you change?

3 Problematic Sexual Outcomes in Adolescence

 LG3 Describe the main problematic sexual outcomes that can emerge in adolescence.

Adolescent Pregnancy

Sexually Transmitted Infections

Forcible Sexual Behavior and Sexual Harassment

Problematic sexual outcomes in adolescence include adolescent pregnancy, sexually transmitted infections, forcible sexual behavior, and sexual harassment. Let's begin by exploring adolescent pregnancy and its prevalence in the United States and around the world.

ADOLESCENT PREGNANCY

Adolescent pregnancy is a problematic outcome of sexuality in adolescence that requires major efforts to reduce its occurrence (Wong & others, 2020). Consider Angela, who is 15 years old. She reflects, "I'm three months pregnant. This could ruin my whole life. I've made all of these plans for the future, and now they are down the drain. I don't have anybody to talk with about my problem. I can't talk to my parents. There is no way they can understand." Pregnant adolescents were once virtually invisible and unmentionable, shuttled off to homes for unwed mothers where relinquishment of the baby for adoption was their only option, or subjected to unsafe and illegal abortions. But yesterday's secret has become today's dilemma. Our exploration of adolescent pregnancy focuses on its incidence and nature, its consequences, cognitive factors that may be involved, adolescents as parents, and ways to reduce the rate of adolescent pregnancies.

Incidence of Adolescent Pregnancy   Adolescent girls who become pregnant come from different ethnic groups and different places, but their circumstances bring the same levels of physical and emotional stress. To many adults, adolescent pregnancy represents a flaw in America's social fabric. Each year more than 200,000 females in the United States have a child before their eighteenth birthday. Like Angela, far too many become pregnant in their early or middle adolescent years. As one 17-year-old Los Angeles mother of a 1-year-old son said, "We are children having children."

In cross-cultural comparisons, the United States continues to have one of the highest adolescent pregnancy and childbearing rates in the industrialized world, despite a considerable decline since the 1980s (Cooksey, 2009). The adolescent pregnancy rate is six times as high in the United States as it is in the Netherlands. This dramatic difference exists in spite of the fact that U.S. adolescents are no more sexually active than their counterparts in the Netherlands. A cross-cultural comparison found that among 21 countries, the United States had the highest adolescent pregnancy rate among 15- to 19-year-olds and Switzerland the lowest (Sedgh & others, 2015).

Why are adolescent pregnancy rates in many other countries lower than in the United States? Three reasons are identified in cross-cultural comparisons (Boonstra, 2002):

1. *Having a child is regarded as an activity for adults.* Especially in many Scandinavian countries and Canada, the thinking is that it is much better to have completed your education, become independent from your parents, be in a stable romantic relationship, and have a career before having a child.

2. *Clear messages about effective contraception and early, comprehensive sex education.* In many countries, it is expected and accepted that adolescents will use effective contraception to prevent pregnancy. Sex education programs in many other countries begin earlier and are more comprehensive than those in the United States, and these countries have government programs for promoting safe sex.

3. *Access to family planning services.* In many countries, adolescents can connect with family planning services more easily than in the United States. In places such as France, England, and the Scandinavian countries, contraceptive access and information are integrated into many health services that are free or low-cost for all adolescents. In contrast, U.S. adolescents have more difficulty obtaining sexual health services.

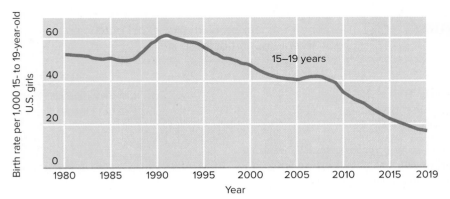

FIGURE **1**

BIRTH RATES FOR U.S. 15- TO 19-YEAR-OLD GIRLS FROM 1980 TO 2019

Trends in U.S. Adolescent Pregnancy Rates Despite the negative comparisons of the United States with many other developed countries, there have been some encouraging trends in U.S. adolescent pregnancy rates in recent years. In 2019, the U.S. birth rate for 15- to 19-year-olds was 16.7 births per 1,000 females, the lowest rate ever recorded, and less than half of the rate in 2008 (41.5 births per 1,000 females) (Martin & others, 2021) (see Figure 1). Reasons for the decline include school/community health classes, increased use of contraception, and fear of sexually transmitted infections such as AIDS.

Ethnic variations characterize adolescent pregnancy, and rates are declining significantly among all ethnic groups. For 15- to 19-year-old U.S. females in 2017, per 1,000 females the birth rate for Latinas was 25.3 (down from 38 in 2014), for African Americans 25.8 (down from 35 in 2014), for non-Latinx whites 11.4 (down from 17 in 2014), and for Asian Americans 2.7 (down from 8 in 2014) (Martin & others, 2021). These figures represent substantial decreases in pregnancy rates for Latinx and African American adolescent girls. However, daughters of teenage mothers are at increased risk for teenage childbearing, thus perpetuating an intergenerational cycle. A study using data from the National Longitudinal Survey of Youth revealed that daughters of teenage mothers were 66 percent more likely than average to become teenage mothers themselves (Meade, Kershaw, & Ickovics, 2008). In this study, factors that increased the likelihood that daughters of teenage mothers would become pregnant included low parental monitoring and poverty.

Consequences of Adolescent Pregnancy The consequences of America's high adolescent pregnancy rate are cause for great concern (Asheer & others, 2020). Adolescent pregnancy creates health risks for both the baby and the mother (Harding & others, 2020). Infants born to adolescent mothers are more likely to be born preterm and to have low birth weights—factors associated with increased risk of infant mortality—as well as neurological problems and childhood illness (Sawyer, Abdul-Razak, & Patton, 2019). And one study assessed the reading and math achievement trajectories of children born to adolescent and non-adolescent mothers with different levels of education (Tang & others, 2016). In this study, higher levels of maternal education were linked to higher levels of children's achievement through the eighth grade. Even at similar levels of maternal educational attainment, however, the achievement of children born to the adolescent mothers never reached the levels of children born to adult mothers.

What are some of the problems that characterize adolescent mothers? In a recent Canadian study, 18 percent of adolescent mothers lived in low-SES neighborhoods (compared with 11 percent of mothers 20 to 34 years of age), had higher rates of depression during pregnancy than mothers 20 to 34 years of age, and also had higher rates of tobacco, marijuana, and alcohol use than adult mothers (Wong & others, 2020). In addition, adolescent mothers often drop out of school (Siegel & Brandon, 2014). Although many adolescent mothers resume their education later in life, they generally do not catch up economically with women who postpone childbearing until their twenties. Also, a study of African American urban youth found that at 32 years of age, women who had been teenage mothers were more likely than women who had not been teenage mothers to be unemployed, live in poverty, depend on welfare, and not have completed college (Assini-Meytin & Green, 2015). In this study, at 32 years of age, men who had been teenage fathers were more likely to be unemployed than were men who had not been teenage fathers.

A special concern is repeated adolescent pregnancy. In a recent national study, the percentage of teen births that were repeat births decreased from 21 percent in 2004 to 17 percent in 2015 (Dee & others, 2017). In a recent meta-analysis, use of effective contraception, especially LARC, and

What are some consequences of adolescent pregnancy?
Geoff Manasse/Photodisc/Getty Images

Sixteen-Year-Old Alberto: Wanting a Different Kind of Life

Sixteen-year-old Alberto's maternal grandmother was a heroin addict who died of cancer at the age of 40. His father, who was only 17 when Alberto was born, has been in prison most of Alberto's life. His mother and stepfather are not married but have lived together for a dozen years and have four other children. Alberto's stepbrother dropped out of school when he was 17, fathered a child, and is now unemployed. But Alberto, who lives in the Bronx in New York City, has different plans for his own future. He wants to be a dentist, he said, "like the kind of woman who fixed his teeth at Bronx-Lebanon Hospital Center clinic when he was a child" (Bernstein, 2004, p. A22). And Alberto, along with his girlfriend, Jasmine, wants to remain a virgin until he is married.

What cultural influences, negative and positive, might be helping Alberto plan his future? What are some consequences of adolescent pregnancy?

Alberto with his girlfriend.
Suzanne DeChillo/The New York Times/Redux Pictures

education-related factors (higher level of education and school continuation) resulted in a lower incidence of repeated teen pregnancy, while depression and a history of abortion were linked to a higher percentage of repeated teen pregnancy (Maravilla & others, 2017).

Researchers have found that adolescent mothers interact less effectively with their infants than do adult mothers. One study revealed that adolescent mothers spent more time negatively interacting and less time in play and positive interactions with their infants than did adult mothers (Riva Crugnola & others, 2014). One intervention, "My Baby and Me," that involved frequent (55), intensive home visitation coaching sessions with adolescent mothers across three years resulted in improved maternal behavior and child outcomes (Guttentag & others, 2014).

Although the consequences of America's high adolescent pregnancy rate are cause for great concern, it often is not pregnancy alone that leads to negative outcomes for an adolescent mother and her offspring. Adolescent mothers are more likely to come from low-SES backgrounds (Mollborn, 2017). Many adolescent mothers also were not good students before they became pregnant (Malamitsi-Puchner & Boutsikou, 2006). However, not every adolescent girl who bears a child lives a life of poverty and low achievement. Thus, although adolescent pregnancy is a high-risk circumstance, and adolescents who do not become pregnant generally fare better than those who do, some adolescent mothers do well in school and have positive outcomes (Schaffer & others, 2012).

Adolescents as Parents Children of adolescent parents face problems even before they are born (Jeha & others, 2015). Only one of every five pregnant adolescent girls receives any prenatal care at all during the important first three months of pregnancy. Pregnant adolescents are more likely to have anemia and complications related to preterm delivery than are mothers aged 20 to 24. The problems of adolescent pregnancy double the normal risk of delivering a low-birth-weight baby (one that weighs under 5.5 pounds), a category that places the infant at risk for physical and mental deficits (Dryfoos & Barkin, 2006b). Further, a recent Jamaican study revealed that adolescent mothers younger than 16 years of age were more likely to deliver preterm and low birth weight infants than those 16 to 19 years of age (Harrison & others, 2021). In some cases, infant problems may be due to poverty rather than to the mother's age.

So far, we have talked almost exclusively about adolescent mothers. Although some adolescent fathers are involved with their children, the majority are not. In one study, only one-fourth of adolescent mothers with a 3-year-old child said the father had a close relationship with them (Leadbeater, Way, & Raden, 1994).

Adolescent fathers have lower incomes, less education, and more children than do men who delay having children until their twenties. One reason for these difficulties is that the adolescent father often compounds the problem of becoming a parent at a young age by dropping out of school (Resnick, Wattenberg, & Brewer, 1992).

What are adolescents like as parents?
ERproductions Ltd/Getty Images

Students in a teen pregnancy and parenting class at Independence School in Brentwood, California. *What are some strategies that you think should be taught to the students in such a class?*
Zuma Press, Inc./Alamy Stock Photo

Reducing Adolescent Pregnancy Serious, extensive efforts are needed to reduce adolescent pregnancy and to help pregnant adolescents and young mothers enhance their educational and occupational opportunities. Age-appropriate family-life education benefits adolescents (Herdt & Polen-Petit, 2021). One strategy that is used in some family-life education programs is the Baby Think It Over doll, a life-size computer-driven baby doll that engages in realistic responses and gives adolescents the opportunity to experience the responsibilities of being a parent. A study of primarily Latinx ninth-grade students who took care of the Baby Think It Over doll found that the experience increased the age at which they wanted to have their first child, produced a greater interest in career and educational planning, and raised their awareness of how having a baby might interfere with those plans (de Anda, 2006).

In addition to age-appropriate family-life and sex education, sexually active adolescents need access to contraceptive methods (Crooks & Baur, 2021). These needs often can be fulfilled through adolescent clinics that provide comprehensive, high-quality health services.

Better sex education, family planning, and access to contraceptive methods alone will not remedy the adolescent pregnancy crisis, especially for high-risk adolescents. Adolescents have to become motivated to reduce their pregnancy risk. This motivation will come only when adolescents look to the future and see that they have an opportunity to become self-sufficient and successful. To achieve this goal, adolescents need opportunities to improve their academic and career-related skills, job prospects, life-planning consultation, and extensive mental health services.

Finally, for adolescent pregnancy prevention to ultimately succeed, high-risk adolescents must receive broad community involvement and support. This support is a major reason for the success of pregnancy prevention efforts in other developed nations where rates of adolescent pregnancy, abortion, and childbearing are much lower than in the United States despite similar levels of sexual activity. In the Netherlands as well as other European countries such as Sweden, sex does not carry the mystery and controversy it does in American society. The Netherlands does not have a mandated sex education program, but adolescents can obtain contraceptive counseling at government-sponsored clinics for a small fee. The Dutch media also have played an important role in educating the public about sex through frequent broadcasts focused on birth control, abortion, and related matters. Perhaps as a result, Dutch adolescents are unlikely to have sex without contraception.

In the United States, Girls Inc (2021) has created programs that benefit adolescents at risk for problems. Their program focused on adolescent pregnancy provides girls with skills, motivation, and support to postpone sexual activity and use effective protection. In a recent analysis, girls who participated in the Girls Inc pregnancy prevention program were less likely to become pregnant (5.9 percent) than a matched control group of girls who did not participate in the program (12.3 percent) (Girls Inc, 2021).

Currently, a number of studies are being funded by the Teen Pregnancy Prevention (TPP) program in an effort to find ways to reduce the rate of adolescent pregnancy (Office of Adolescent Health, 2021). These diverse programs focus on areas such as improving adolescent self-control, developing a positive relationship with a trusted adult, delaying sexual initiation, and planning for a future that includes positive opportunities and outcomes.

What are some strategies for reducing adolescent pregnancy?
Rosemarie Gearhart/iStockphoto/Getty Images

SEXUALLY TRANSMITTED INFECTIONS

Tammy, age 15, has just finished listening to an expert lecture in her health class. We overhear her talking to one of her girlfriends as she walks down the school corridor: "That was a disgusting lecture. I can't believe all the infections you can get by having sex. I think she was probably trying to scare us. She spent a lot of time talking about AIDS, which I have heard that normal people do not get. Right? I've heard that only homosexuals and drug addicts get AIDS. And I've also heard that gonorrhea and most other sexual infections can be cured, so what's the big deal if you get something like that?" Tammy's views on sexually transmitted infections—that they always happen to someone else, that they can be easily cured without any harm done, that they are too disgusting for a nice young person to hear about, let alone get—are common among adolescents. Tammy's views are wrong. Adolescents who are having sex run the risk of getting sexually transmitted infections.

Sexually transmitted infections (STIs) are infections that are contracted primarily through sexual contact. This contact is not limited to vaginal intercourse but includes oral-genital and anal-genital contact as well. STIs are an increasing health problem. Every year more than 3 million American adolescents (about one-fourth of those who are sexually experienced) acquire an STI (Centers for Disease Control and Prevention, 2020). Recent estimates indicate that while 15- to 24-year-olds represent only 25 percent of the sexually experienced U.S. population, they acquire nearly 50 percent of all new STIs (Centers for Disease Control and Prevention, 2021).

Among the main STIs adolescents can get are three STIs caused by viruses—acquired immune deficiency syndrome (AIDS), genital herpes, and genital warts—and three STIs caused by bacteria—gonorrhea, syphilis, and chlamydia.

HIV and AIDS

No single STI has caused more deaths, had a greater impact on sexual behavior, or created more public fear in recent decades than HIV (Crooks & Baur, 2021). We explore here its nature and incidence, how it is transmitted, and how to prevent it from spreading.

AIDS stands for acquired immune deficiency syndrome, a sexually transmitted infection that is caused by the human immunodeficiency virus (HIV), which destroys the body's immune system. Following exposure to HIV, an individual is vulnerable to germs that a normal immune system could destroy.

In 2018, people between the ages of 13 and 24 made up 21 percent of the 37,832 new HIV diagnoses in the United States (Centers for Disease Control and Prevention, 2020). Of these youth, 44.9 percent had been living with an undiagnosed HIV infection, by far the highest percentage age group of adolescents and adults unaware of having an HIV infection. Most of the new diagnoses involved young gay and bisexual males—male-to-male transmission accounted for 92 percent of these new diagnoses. In terms of ethnicity, 51 percent were African American, 27 percent Latinx, and 17 non-Latinx white individuals.

Worldwide, the greatest concern about AIDS is in sub-Saharan Africa, where it has reached epidemic proportions (UNAIDS, 2020). In 2019, sub-Saharan Africa accounted for 88 percent of children and adolescents living with AIDS worldwide. Adolescent girls in many African countries are especially vulnerable to becoming infected with HIV through sexual contact with

sexually transmitted infections (STIs) Infections that are contracted primarily through sexual contact. This contact is not limited to vaginal intercourse but includes oral-genital contact and anal-genital contact as well.

AIDS Acquired immune deficiency syndrome, a sexually transmitted infection caused by the human immunodeficiency virus (HIV), which destroys the body's immune system.

A youth group presents a play in the local marketplace in Morogoro, Tanzania. The play is designed to educate the community about HIV and AIDS.
Wendy Stone/Corbis Documentary/Getty Images

A 13-year-old boy pushes his friends around in his barrow during his break from his work as a barrow boy in a community in sub-Saharan Africa. He became the breadwinner in the family when both of his parents died of AIDS.
Louise Gubb/Corbis Historical/Getty Images

adult men (UNICEF, 2020). Approximately six times as many adolescent girls as boys have AIDS in these countries. In Kenya, 25 percent of 15- to 19-year-old girls are HIV-positive, compared with only 4 percent of boys in the same age group. In Botswana, more than 30 percent of the adolescent girls who are pregnant are infected with HIV. In some sub-Saharan countries, less than 20 percent of women and 40 percent of 15- to 19-year-olds reported having used a condom the last time they had sexual intercourse (Bankole & others, 2004).

AIDS also has resulted in a dramatic increase in the number of children and adolescents worldwide who are orphaned and left to care for themselves because their parents acquired the disease (UNICEF, 2020). In 2019, it was estimated that 13.8 million children and adolescents under the age of 18 had lost one or both of their parents to AIDS.

There are some differences in AIDS cases in U.S. adolescents, compared with AIDS cases in U.S. adults:

- A higher percentage of adolescent AIDS cases are acquired by heterosexual transmission.
- A higher percentage of adolescents are asymptomatic individuals (but will become symptomatic in adulthood—that is, they are HIV-positive, but do not yet have AIDS).
- A higher percentage of African American and Latinx AIDS cases occur among adolescents.
- A special set of ethical and legal issues is involved in testing and informing partners and parents of adolescents.
- Adolescents have less access to contraceptives and are less likely to use them than are adults.

Experts say that HIV can be transmitted only by sexual contact, the sharing of intravenous needles, or blood transfusions (which in recent years have been tightly monitored) (Herdt & Polen-Petit, 2021). Figure 2 describes which activities are risky and which ones are not risky in regard to the spread of AIDS and HIV.

Because of education and the development of more effective drug treatments, deaths due to HIV/AIDS have begun to decline in the United States. Also, there in an increasing effort to reduce HIV infections through pre-exposure prophylaxis (PrEP) awareness, which involves taking a daily pill that can reduce the probability of getting HIV by as much as 90 percent (Mocorro & others, 2021). PrEP has been recently approved for use with adolescents (Whitfield, Parsons, & Rendina, 2020).

Merely asking a date about his or her sexual behavior, of course, does not guarantee protection from HIV or other STIs. For example, in one investigation, 655 college students were asked to answer questions about lying and sexual behavior (Cochran & Mays, 1990). Of the 422 respondents who said they were sexually active, 34 percent of the men and 10 percent of the women said they had lied so their partner would have sex with them. Much higher percentages—47 percent of the men and 60 percent of the women—said they had been lied to by a potential sexual partner. When asked what aspects of their past they would be most likely to lie about, more than 40 percent of the men and women said they would understate the number of their sexual partners. Twenty percent of the men, but only 4 percent of the women, said they would lie about their results from an HIV blood test. One study revealed that 40 percent of sexually active adolescents who were HIV-positive had not disclosed their status to their partners (Michaud & others, 2009).

Genital Herpes **Genital herpes** is a sexually transmitted infection caused by a large family of viruses with many different strains, some of which produce nonsexually transmitted diseases such as cold sores, chicken pox, and mononucleosis. Three to five days after contact, itching and tingling can occur, followed by an eruption of painful sores and blisters. The attacks can last up to three weeks and can recur as frequently as every few weeks or as infrequently as every few years. The virus can also pass through nonlatex condoms as well as contraceptive foams and creams. It is estimated that approximately 20 percent of adolescents have genital herpes (Centers for Disease Control and Prevention, 2021). It also is estimated that more than 600,000 new genital herpes infections are appearing in the 15- to 24-year-old age group in the United States each year.

Although drugs such as acyclovir can alleviate symptoms, there is no known cure for herpes. Thus, individuals infected with herpes often experience severe emotional distress in addition to the considerable physical discomfort. They may feel conflicted or reluctant about

genital herpes A sexually transmitted infection caused by a large family of viruses of different strains. These strains also produce nonsexually transmitted diseases such as chicken pox and mononucleosis.

The HIV virus is not transmitted like colds or the flu, but by an exchange of infected blood, semen, or vaginal fluids. This usually occurs during sexual intercourse, in sharing drug needles, or to babies infected before or during birth.

You won't get the HIV virus from:	Everyday contact with individuals around you in school or the workplace, at parties, child-care centers, or stores
	Swimming in a pool, even if someone in the pool has the AIDS virus
	A mosquito bite, or from bedbugs, lice, flies, or other insects
	Saliva, sweat, tears, urine, or feces
	A kiss
	Clothes, telephones, or toilet seats
	Using a glass or eating utensils that someone else has used
	Being on a bus, train, or crowded elevator with an individual who is infected with the virus or who has AIDS
Risky behavior:	Your chances of coming into contact with the virus increase if you:
	Have more than one sex partner
	Share drug needles and syringes
	Engage in anal, vaginal, or oral sex without a condom
	Perform vaginal or oral sex with someone who shoots drugs
	Engage in sex with someone you don't know well or with someone who has several sex partners
	Engage in unprotected sex (without a condom) with an infected individual
Blood donations and transfusions:	You will not come into contact with the HIV virus by donating blood at a blood bank.
	The risk of getting AIDS from a blood transfusion has been greatly reduced. Donors are screened for risk factors, and donated blood is tested for HIV antibodies.
Safe behavior:	Not having sex
	Having sex that does not involve fluid exchange (rubbing, holding, massage)
	Sex with one mutually faithful, uninfected partner
	Sex with proper protection
	Not shooting drugs
	Source: *America Responds to AIDS*. U.S. Government educational pamphlet, 1988.

FIGURE 2
UNDERSTANDING AIDS: WHAT'S RISKY, WHAT'S NOT

sex, angry about the unpredictability of the infection, and fearful that they won't be able to cope with the pain of the next attack. For these reasons, many communities have established support groups for victims of herpes.

Genital Warts   **Genital warts** are caused by the human papillomavirus (HPV), which is difficult to test for and does not always produce symptoms but is very contagious nonetheless. Genital warts usually appear as small, hard, painless bumps on the penis, in the vaginal area, or around the anus. More than 9 million individuals in the United States in the 15- to 24-year-old age group are estimated to have an HPV infection, making HPV the most commonly acquired STI in this age group. Treatment involves the use of a topical drug, freezing, or surgery. Unfortunately, genital warts may return despite treatment, and in some cases they are linked to cervical cancer and other genital cancers. Condoms afford some protection against HPV infection. The Centers for Disease Control and Prevention (2021) recommends that all 11- and 12-year-old girls be given a two-dose sequence of the HPV vaccine. Adolescent

genital warts An STI caused by the human papillomavirus; genital warts are very contagious and are the most commonly acquired STI in the United States in the 15- to 24-year-old age group.

females who do not start having the vaccination until 15 years and older need a three-dose sequence. HPV infections and cervical precancers have dropped significantly since the vaccine has been in use.

We now turn to three STIs—gonorrhea, syphilis, and chlamydia—caused by bacteria.

Gonorrhea Gonorrhea is an STI that is commonly called the "drip" or the "clap." It is caused by a bacterium called *Neisseria gonorrhoeae*, which thrives in the moist mucous membranes lining the mouth, throat, vagina, cervix, urethra, and anal tract. The bacterium is spread by contact between the infected moist membranes of one individual and the membranes of another. In 2018, there were 583,405 cases of gonorrhea reported, a 5.7 percent increase since 2018 and a 92.7 percent increase since its historic low in 2009 (Centers for Disease Control and Prevention, 2021). Males have higher rates of gonorrhea than females, and the highest rate of the disease occurs in the 20–24 age range for both males and females. A large-scale study revealed that adolescents who were most likely to screen positive for gonorrhea were female, African American, and 16 years of age or older (Han & others, 2011).

Early symptoms of gonorrhea are more likely to appear in males, who are likely to have a discharge from the penis and burning during urination. The early sign of gonorrhea in females, often undetectable, is a mild, sometimes irritating vaginal discharge. Complications of gonorrhea in males include prostate, bladder, and kidney problems, as well as sterility. In females, gonorrhea may lead to infertility due to the abdominal adhesions or pelvic inflammatory disease (PID) that it can cause (Crooks & Baur, 2021). Gonorrhea can be successfully treated in its early stages with penicillin or other antibiotics.

Syphilis Syphilis is an STI caused by the bacterium *Treponema pallidum*, a member of the spirochaeta family. The spirochete needs a warm, moist environment to survive, and it is transmitted by penile-vaginal, oral-genital, or anal contact. It can also be transmitted from a pregnant woman to her fetus after the fourth month of pregnancy; if she is treated before this time with penicillin, the syphilis will not be transmitted to the fetus. In 2019, nearly 130,000 new cases of syphilis were reported in the United States, an increase of 70 percent since 2015 (Centers for Disease Control and Prevention, 2021).

If left untreated, syphilis may progress through four phases: primary (chancre sores appear), secondary (general skin rash occurs), latent (a period that can last for several years during which no overt symptoms are present), and tertiary (cardiovascular disease, blindness, paralysis, skin ulcers, liver damage, mental problems, and even death may occur) (Herdt & Polen-Petit, 2021). In its early phases, syphilis can be effectively treated with penicillin.

Chlamydia Chlamydia, one of the most common of all STIs, is named for *Chlamydia trachomatis*, an organism that spreads by sexual contact and infects the genital organs of both sexes. Although fewer individuals have heard of chlamydia than have heard of gonorrhea and syphilis, its incidence is much higher. In 2019, there were 1,808,703 new cases of chlamydia reported in the United States, with almost half of those cases occurring in the 15- to 24-year age range (Centers for Disease Control and Prevention, 2021). There are large ethnic differences in chlamydia, with African American women having the highest rate (1,411 per 100,000), followed by Latinx women (541 per 100,000), non-Latinx white women (282 per 100,000), and Asian American women (158 per 100,000) (Centers for Disease Control and Prevention, 2021). This STI is highly infectious; women run a 70 percent risk of contracting it in a single sexual encounter with an infected partner. The male risk is estimated at between 25 and 50 percent.

Many females with chlamydia have few or no symptoms. When symptoms do appear, they include disrupted menstrual periods, pelvic pain, elevated temperature, nausea, vomiting, and headache. Possible symptoms of chlamydia in males are a discharge from the penis and burning during urination.

Because many females with chlamydia are asymptomatic, the infection often goes untreated and the chlamydia spreads to the upper reproductive tract, where it can cause pelvic inflammatory disease (PID). The resultant scarring of tissue in the fallopian tubes can produce infertility or ectopic pregnancies (tubal pregnancies)—that is, a pregnancy in which the fertilized egg is implanted outside the uterus. One-quarter of females who have PID become infertile; multiple cases of PID increase the rate of infertility to half. Some researchers suggest that chlamydia is the number one preventable cause of female infertility.

gonorrhea A sexually transmitted infection caused by the bacterium *Neisseria gonorrhoeae,* which thrives in the moist mucous membranes lining the mouth, throat, vagina, cervix, urethra, and anal tract. This STI is commonly called the "drip" or the "clap."

syphilis A sexually transmitted infection caused by the bacterium *Treponema pallidum,* a spirochete.

chlamydia One of the most common sexually transmitted infections, named for *Chlamydia trachomatis,* an organism that spreads by sexual contact and infects the genital organs of both sexes.

Dr. Maria Eva Trent, Adolescent Reproductive Health Specialist

Dr. Maria Eva Trent one of the world's leading experts on adolescents' reproductive health. She currently is Director of the Adolescent Medicine Fellowship Program and Professor of Pediatrics in the Johns Hopkins University Schools of Medicine, Nursing, and Public Health. Dr. Trent obtained a master's degree in public health from Harvard University and a medical degree from the University of North Carolina.

A main focus of Dr. Trent's work is adolescents' sexual and reproductive health, with a special interest in improving the lives of underserved adolescents in urban poverty contexts. Her research interests include the role of racism in adolescent health outcomes, sexually transmitted infections, effective contraception, fertility preservation, and childbearing motivation. Dr. Trent says that her adolescent patients inspire and motivate her.

She currently serves as the Chair of the Section on Adolescent Health for the American Academy of Pediatrics and is President of the Society for Adolescent Health and Medicine. Among her many honors and awards at Johns Hopkins University are the university's Diversity Leadership Award and Excellence in Teaching Award in the School of Public Health. Dr. Trent also has received the Maryland Pediatrician of the Year Award, and she has been named to Ebony magazine's Power 100 list of the most influential African Americans.

Courtesy of Dr. Maria Trent, Professor of Pediatrics

Although they can occur without sexual contact and are therefore not classified as STIs, urinary tract or bladder infections and vaginal yeast infections (also called *thrush*) are common in sexually active females, especially those who have an intense "honeymoon" lovemaking experience. Both of these infections clear up quickly with medication, but their symptoms (urinary urgency and burning in urinary tract infections; itching, irritation, and whitish vaginal discharge in yeast infections) may be frightening, especially to adolescents who may already have considerable anxiety about sex. We discuss them because one of the non-STIs may be what brings an adolescent girl to a doctor, nurse practitioner, or family-planning clinic, providing an opportunity for her to receive sex education and contraception.

To read about one individual who is highly motivated to improve adolescents' and young adults' reproductive health outcomes, especially those of urban adolescent girls, see the *Connecting with Careers* interlude.

So far we have discussed the problems of adolescent pregnancy and sexually transmitted infections. Next, we explore two additional problems involving sexuality: forcible sexual behavior and sexual harassment.

FORCIBLE SEXUAL BEHAVIOR AND SEXUAL HARASSMENT

Most people choose whether they will engage in sexual intercourse or other sexual activities—but, unfortunately, some people force others to engage in sex. Too many adolescent girls and young women report that they believe they don't have adequate sexual rights (UNICEF, 2021). These include the right not to have sexual intercourse when they don't wish to, the right to tell a partner that he is being too rough, or the right to use any form of birth control during intercourse. One study found that almost 20 percent of sexually active 14- to 26-year-old females believed that they never have the right to make decisions about contraception; to tell their partner that they don't want to have intercourse without birth control, that they want to make love differently, or that their partner is being too rough; or to stop foreplay at any time, including at the point of intercourse (Rickert, Sanghvi, & Wiemann, 2002). In this study, poor grades in school and sexual inexperience were linked to a lack of sexual assertiveness in females.

Forcible Sexual Behavior   **Rape** is forcible sexual intercourse with a person who does not give consent. Legal definitions of rape vary from state to state. In some states, for example, the law allows husbands to force their wives to have sex. Because of the difficulties involved in reporting rape, the actual incidence is not easily determined (Koss & others, 2021). A national study found that 7.4 percent of U.S. ninth- through twelfth-grade students reported that they had been physically forced to have intercourse against their will (Kann & others, 2018). In this study, approximately 11.3 percent of female students and 3.5 of male students reported having been forced to have sexual intercourse. Further, a recent study indicated that sexual minority college students were much more likely to be victims of sexual assault than heterosexual students (Eisenberg & others, 2021). Also, not all rapes are reported by the victims. One research meta-analysis found that 60 percent of rape victims do not acknowledge that they have been raped, with the percentage of unacknowledged rape especially high among college students (Wilson & Miller, 2016).

Although most victims of rape are girls and women, rape of boys and men does occur (Anderson & others, 2021). Men in prisons are especially vulnerable to rape, usually by heterosexuals who are using homosexual rape to establish their domination and power within the prison (Fowler & others, 2021).

A recent study of college students indicated that alcohol dependence was a risk factor for both perpetrators and victims of sexual and physical assault in women and men (Caamano-Isorna & others, 2021). Also in this study, incidence of sexual and physical assault was higher in the students' first six months in college, probably related to being in a new and risky environment. Further, in a recent study, more than 87 percent of alcohol-involved sexual assault on college campuses was committed by serial perpetrators (Foubert, Clark-Taylor, & Wall, 2020). In this study, fraternity men and student athletes were more likely to commit alcohol-involved sexual assaults than other men on campus. And a recent study found that women who had experienced sexual assault in college were subsequently more likely to have a lower grade point average, miss more classes, and have fewer serious romantic relationships while in college (Rothman & others, 2021b). The same study found that nine years later, women who had experienced sexual assault in college were more likely to report having symptoms of depression, anxiety, and posttraumatic stress.

Why is rape so pervasive in American culture? Feminist writers assert that males are socialized to be sexually aggressive, to regard females as inferior beings, and to view their own pleasure as the most important objective in any sexual encounter (Tarzia, 2021). Researchers have found that the following characteristics are common among rapists: aggression enhances their sense of power or masculinity; they are angry at females generally; and they want to hurt their victims (Kaplan, 2017). Research indicates that rape is more likely to occur when alcohol and marijuana are being used (Koss & others, 2021). A form of rape that went unacknowledged until recent decades is **date rape, or acquaintance rape,** which is coercive sexual activity directed at someone whom the perpetrator knows. Acquaintance rape is an increasing problem in high schools and on college campuses (Rerick, Livingston, & Davis, 2020). About two-thirds of college men admit that they fondle women against their will, and half admit to forcing sexual activity. In recent research on acquaintance rape of college women, 84 percent of the victims knew their perpetrator and 65.5 percent encountered the perpetrator after the attack (Bell, Wolff, & Skolnick, 2021). Women who encountered their perpetrator after the attack reported more lifestyle changes and more intense symptoms of posttraumatic stress syndrome.

When dating violence occurs in adolescence, the participants are at risk for escalating partner violence in adulthood. More than 20 percent of women and 15 percent of men who become rape victims or experience physical assault by an intimate partner during adulthood initially experienced

rape Forcible sexual intercourse with a person who does not give consent.

date rape, or acquaintance rape Coercive sexual activity directed at someone whom the perpetrator knows.

How extensive is dating violence in adolescence?
Juanmonino/E+/Getty Images

dating violence in adolescence (Black & others, 2011). In one study, an intervention program called "Shifting Boundaries" that emphasizes laws/consequences of dating violence and sexual harassment, establishing boundaries, and creating safe relationships was effective in reducing the frequency of sexual dating violence victimization in young adolescents (Taylor, Mumford, & Stein, 2015).

A major study that focused on campus sexual assault involved a phone survey of 4,446 women attending two- or four-year colleges (Fisher, Cullen, & Turner, 2000). In this study, slightly less than 3 percent said that they had experienced either rape or an attempted rape during the academic year. About one out of ten college women said that they had experienced rape in their lifetime. Unwanted or uninvited sexual contacts were widespread, with more than one-third of the college women reporting such incidents. As shown in Figure 3, in this study most women (about nine out of ten) knew the person who had sexually victimized them. Most of the women attempted to take protective actions against their assailants but were reluctant to report the victimization to the police. Several factors were associated with sexual victimization: living on campus, being unmarried, getting drunk frequently, and having been sexually victimized on a prior occasion.

A number of colleges and universities have identified a "red zone"—a period of time early in the first year of college when women are at especially high risk for unwanted sexual experiences (Cranney, 2015). One study revealed that first-year college women were more at risk for unwanted sexual experiences, especially early in the fall term, than were second-year women (Kimble & others, 2008).

In an earlier study, about two-thirds of the sexual victimization incidents were perpetrated by a romantic acquaintance (Flanagan, 1996). In another study, approximately 2,000 ninth-through twelfth-grade girls were asked about the extent to which they had experienced physical and sexual violence (Silverman & others, 2001). About 20 percent of the girls said they had been physically or sexually abused by a dating partner. Further, the physical and sexual abuse was linked with substance use.

Rape is a traumatic experience for victims and those who are close to them (Rizkalla, Zeevi-Barkay, & Segal, 2021). The rape victim initially feels shock and numbness and often is acutely disorganized. Some women show their distress through words and tears, while others experience more internalized suffering. As victims strive to get their lives back to normal, they might experience depression, fear, anxiety, substance abuse, posttraumatic stress disorder, and suicidal thoughts for months or years (Basile & others, 2021; Farahi & McEachern, 2021). Sexual dysfunctions, such as reduced sexual desire and the inability to reach orgasm, occur in 50 percent of rape victims. Many rape victims make lifestyle changes such as moving to a new apartment or refusing to go out at night. About one-fifth of rape victims engage in suicide attempts—a rate eight times higher than that of women who have not been raped.

A girl's or woman's recovery from rape depends on both her coping abilities and her psychological adjustment prior to the assault (Koss & others, 2021). Social support from clinicians, parents, her partner, and others close to her are also important factors in recovery, as is the availability of professional counseling, sometimes obtained through a rape crisis center (Shannonhouse, Hill, & Hightower, 2021). Many rape victims become empowered by reporting their rape to the police and assisting in prosecution if the rapist is caught. However, women who take a legal approach are especially encouraged to use supportive counselors to aid them throughout the legal ordeal. Each female must be allowed to make her own decision about whether to report the rape.

A coach-delivered intervention study with more than 2,000 male high school athletes focused on recognition of abusive behavior, gender-equity attitudes, and intention to intervene when witnessing abusive behavior (Miller & others, 2012). The study found that the intervention was successful in increasing the participants' intention to try to stop incidents of dating violence if they were to see such incidents occurring (Miller & others, 2012). Also, the program "No Means No Worldwide" (https://nomeansnoworldwide.org) has been effective in reducing the incidence of sexual assault in the African countries of Kenya and Malawi

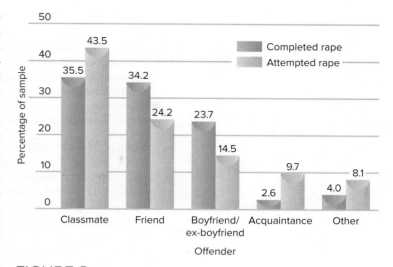

FIGURE **3**

COMPLETED RAPE AND ATTEMPTED RAPE OF COLLEGE WOMEN ACCORDING TO VICTIM-OFFENDER RELATIONSHIP

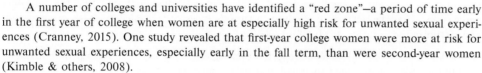

developmental **connection**

Peers

Romantic relationships in adolescence often trigger positive and negative aspects of adjustment. Connect to "Peers, Romantic Relationships, and Lifestyles."

(Baiocchi & others, 2017). The program's 12-hour curriculum emphasizes interactive verbal skills, role playing, and other techniques to prepare participants to speak up, prevent, or intervene in a sexual assault.

The personal autonomy and rights of individuals involving coercion in sexual experiences has recently produced a movement called *affirmative consent* on many college campuses. Affirmative consent means that instead of assuming that both partners are comfortable with sexual activity, each individual gives in words or actions an indication they are willing to participate in the sexual activity (Goodcase, Spencer, & Toews, 2021).

Sexual Harassment   Girls and women encounter sexual harassment in many different forms, ranging from sexist remarks and covert physical contact (patting, brushing against bodies) to blatant propositions and sexual assaults (Rothman & others, 2021a). Literally millions of girls and women experience such sexual harassment each year in educational and work settings (Klein & Martin, 2019). One study of adolescent girls indicated that most (90 percent) of the girls said they had experienced sexual harassment at least once (Leaper & Brown, 2008). In this study, 52 percent of the girls reported that they had experienced academic sexism (involving science, math, and computer technology) and 76 percent said that they had encountered athletic sexism. Also, in a recent study of almost 17,000 students across 8 college campuses, 19 percent of students reported experiencing faculty/staff perpetuated sexual harassment and 30 percent experienced peer perpetuated sexual harassment (Wood & others, 2021). In this study, being a woman increased the odds by 86 percent and 147 percent, respectively, for harassment by faculty/staff and peers.

Further, a recent national survey on adolescent relationships found that the following percentages of adolescents were involved in various types of relationship abuse (perpetration and victimization) (Taylor & Mumford, 2016):

- *Relationship abuse:* 68 percent reported ever experiencing any relationship victimization, and 62 percent indicated they had ever perpetrated any abuse.
- *Psychological abuse:* 64 percent said they had been the victims of psychological abuse (name-calling and stalking, for example).
- *Sexual abuse:* 18 percent reported being the victims of sexual abuse, and 12 percent said they had perpetrated such abuse.
- *Sexual harassment:* 31 percent indicated they had been the victims of sexual harassment, and 11 percent reported that they had perpetrated such abuse; 13 percent said they had been the victims of online sexual harassment and 4 percent indicated they had perpetrated such abuse.

Also, in this study, girls perpetrated serious threats or physical violence more than boys did at 12 to 14 years of age, but boys were more likely to engage in these behaviors at 15 to 18 years of age.

In a survey of 2,000 college women by the American Association of University Women (2006), 62 percent of the respondents reported that they had experienced sexual harassment while attending college. Most of the college women said that the sexual harassment involved noncontact forms such as crude jokes, remarks, and gestures. However, almost one-third said that the sexual harassment was physical in nature. A study of almost 1,500 college women revealed that when they had been sexually harassed they reported an increase in psychological distress, greater physical illness, and an increase in disordered eating (Huerta & others, 2006).

The Office for Civil Rights in the U.S. Department of Education published a 40-page policy guide on sexual harassment. In this guide, a distinction is made between quid pro quo and hostile environment sexual harassment (Chmielewski, 1997):

- **Quid pro quo sexual harassment** occurs when a school employee (such as a teacher) threatens to base an educational decision (such as a grade) on a student's submission to unwelcome sexual conduct. For example, a teacher gives a student an A for allowing the teacher's sexual advances, or the teacher gives the student an F for resisting the teacher's approaches.
- **Hostile environment sexual harassment** occurs when students are subjected to unwelcome sexual conduct that is so severe, persistent, or pervasive that it limits the students' ability to benefit from their education. Such a hostile environment is usually created by a series of incidents, such as repeated sexual overtures.

quid pro quo sexual harassment Sexual harassment in which a school employee threatens to base an educational decision (such as a grade) on a student's submission to unwelcome sexual conduct.

hostile environment sexual harassment Sexual harassment in which students are subjected to unwelcome sexual conduct that is so severe, persistent, or pervasive that it limits the students' ability to benefit from their education.

Quid pro quo and hostile environment sexual harassment are illegal in the workplace as well as in educational settings, but potential victims are often not given access to a clear reporting and investigation mechanism where they can make a complaint.

Sexual harassment involves one person asserting power and dominance over another, which can result in harmful consequences for the victim. Sexual harassment can be especially damaging when the perpetrators are teachers, employers, and other adults who have considerable power and authority over students (Reuter & others, 2020). As a society, we need to be less tolerant of sexual harassment (Rugulies & others, 2020).

In 2017, the Me Too Movement spread extensively, with "Me Too" (or "#MeToo") used as a hashtag on social media to underscore the prevalence of sexual assault and harassment of women, especially in the workplace. As a result, many women felt safe enough to openly discuss their experiences of sexual harassment after having remained silent about these experiences for years or even decades (Yecies & McNeil, 2021).

Review Connect Reflect

LG3 Describe the main problematic sexual outcomes that can emerge in adolescence.

Review

- How would you characterize adolescent pregnancy?
- What are the main sexually transmitted infections in adolescence?
- What is the nature of forcible sexual behavior and sexual harassment in adolescence?

Connect

- Connect what you learned about sexually transmitted infections in this chapter to earlier discussions of adolescent health and well-being.

Reflect *Your Own Personal Journey of Life*

- Have you experienced any of the negative sexual outcomes in adolescence and emerging adulthood that have just been described—adolescent pregnancy, sexually transmitted infections, forcible sexual behavior, or sexual harassment? If so, is there anything you could have done differently to avoid the negative outcome(s)? If you didn't experience these negative outcomes, what factors likely contributed to your prevention of these outcomes?

4 Sexual Literacy and Sex Education

LG4 Characterize the sexual literacy of adolescents and sex education.

| Sexual Literacy | Sources of Sex Information | Cognitive Factors | Sex Education in Schools |

Given the high rate of STIs in the United States, a special concern is the degree of knowledge that both adolescents and adults have about these infections and about other aspects of sexuality. How sexually literate are Americans? What are adolescents' sources of sex education? What cognitive factors might be involved in whether sex education is effective? What is the role of schools in sex education?

SEXUAL LITERACY

According to June Reinisch (1990), former director of the Kinsey Institute for Sex, Gender, and Reproduction, U.S. citizens know more about how their automobiles function than about how their bodies function sexually. American adolescents and adults are not sheltered from sexual messages; indeed, Reinisch says, adolescents too often are inundated with sexual messages, but not sexual facts. Sexual information is abundant, but much of it is misinformation. In some cases, even sex education teachers display sexual ignorance. One high school sex education teacher referred to erogenous zones as "erroneous zones," causing students to wonder if their sexually sensitive zones were in error!

One study assessed sixth-grade students' knowledge and curiosity about sex-related topics (Charmaraman, Lee, & Erkut, 2012). The questions most frequently asked by the sixth-graders involved sexual activity, female anatomy, reproduction, and puberty, while questions about sexually transmitted infections, sexual violence, and sex-related drug/alcohol use were less frequent. Following are several of the questions asked by the sixth-graders that reflect a lack of sexual knowledge:

- If you have had sex the night before your period, you're not going to get pregnant, right?
- If a guy puts his penis in a girl's mouth, will she get pregnant?
- If you have anal sex, is it still considered sex?
- If you are trying to have abstinence and you have sex more than once, is that abstinence?

SOURCES OF SEX INFORMATION

Adolescents can get information about sex from many sources, including parents, siblings, other relatives, schools, peers, magazines, television, and the Internet. A special concern is the inaccuracy of some of the sexual information adolescents obtain on the Internet. One study revealed that adolescents' most frequently consulted sources of information about sexuality were friends, teachers, mothers, and the media (Bleakley & others, 2009). In this study, learning about sex from parents, grandparents, and religious leaders was linked with adolescent beliefs that were likely to delay having sexual intercourse, whereas learning about sex from friends, cousins, and the media was related to beliefs that were likely to increase the likelihood of having sexual intercourse earlier.

Many parents feel uncomfortable talking about sex with adolescents, and many adolescents feel uncomfortable with such conversations as well (Tanton & others, 2015). One study revealed that 94 percent of fathers and 76 percent of mothers had never discussed sexual desire with their daughters (Feldman & Rosenthal, 1999).

Many adolescents say that they cannot talk freely with their parents about sexual matters, but those who can talk with their parents openly and freely about sex are less likely to be sexually active (Chia-Chen & Thompson, 2007). Contraceptive use by female adolescents also increases when adolescents report that they can communicate about sex with their parents (Fisher, 1987). Also, one study found that first-semester college women who felt more comfortable talking openly about sex with their mothers were more likely to have positive beliefs about condoms and confidence in using them (Lefkowitz & Espinosa-Hernandez, 2006).

Adolescents are far more likely to have conversations about sex with their mothers than with their fathers (Kirkman, Rosenthal, & Feldman, 2002). This tendency is true for both female and male adolescents, although female adolescents report having more frequent conversations about sex with their mothers than their male counterparts do (Feldman & Rosenthal, 2002).

COGNITIVE FACTORS

Cognitive changes have intriguing implications for adolescents' sex education (Lipsitz, 1980). With their developing idealism and ability to think in more abstract and hypothetical ways, some young adolescents may become immersed in a mental world far removed from reality. They may see themselves as omnipotent and indestructible and believe that bad things cannot or will not happen to them, characteristics of adolescent egocentrism. Consider the personal fable aspect of adolescent egocentrism reflected in this 14-year-old's words: "Hey, it won't happen to me." However, increasingly it is recognized that a majority of adolescents see themselves as more vulnerable than invulnerable (Fischhoff & others, 2010).

Informing adolescents about contraceptives is not enough—what seems to predict whether or not they will use contraceptives is their acceptance of themselves and their sexuality. This acceptance requires not only emotional maturity but cognitive maturity.

Most discussions of adolescent pregnancy and its prevention assume that adolescents have the ability to anticipate consequences, to weigh the probable outcome of behavior, and to project into the future what will happen if they engage in certain acts, such as sexual intercourse. That is, prevention is based on the belief that adolescents have the cognitive ability to approach problem solving in a planned, organized, and analytical manner. However, although many adolescents 16 years of age and older have these capacities, it does not mean they will use them, especially in emotionally charged situations such as when they are sexually aroused or are being pressured by a partner.

Indeed, young adolescents (10 to 15 years of age) seem to experience sex in a depersonalized way that is filled with anxiety and denial. This depersonalized orientation toward sex is not likely to lead to preventive behavior. Middle adolescents (15 to 17 years of age) often romanticize sexuality. Late adolescents (18 to 19 years of age) are to some degree realistic and future-oriented about sexual experiences, just as they are about careers and marriage.

SEX EDUCATION IN SCHOOLS

A survey revealed that 89 percent of parents in Minnesota recommended teaching adolescents about abstinence and also providing them with comprehensive sex education that includes contraception information (Eisenberg & others, 2013). The parents said that most sex education topics should first be introduced in middle schools. Other surveys also indicate that a large percentage of U.S. parents want schools to provide adolescents with comprehensive sex education (Constantine, Jerman, & Juang, 2007; Ito & others, 2006). One study indicated that parents think adolescents too often get their information about sex from friends and the media (Lagus & others, 2011).

The AIDS epidemic has led to an increased awareness of the importance of sex education in adolescence.
Nina Robinson/The Verbatim Agency/Getty Images

A survey conducted more than 20 years ago found that 93 percent of Americans support the teaching of sex education in high schools and 84 percent support its teaching in middle/junior high schools (SIECUS, 1999). The dramatic increase in HIV/AIDS and other STIs is the main reason that Americans have increasingly supported sex education in schools in recent years. This survey also found that more than eight in ten Americans think that adolescents should be given information to protect themselves from unwanted pregnancies and STIs, as well as information about the benefits of abstinence. In a national survey, 85 percent of ninth- to twelfth-grade students said that they had been taught in school about AIDS or HIV (Kann & others, 2014).

What percentage of U.S. adolescents receive formal instruction in sexual health? As of October 2020, 39 states and the District of Columbia mandated sex education and/or HIV

In many countries, contraceptive knowledge is included in sex education. Here students in a sex education class in Beijing, China, learn about condoms.
Mark Leong/Redux

What Is the Most Effective Sex Education?

Currently, a major controversy in sex education is whether schools should have an abstinence-only program or a comprehensive sex education program that emphasizes contraceptive knowledge, delaying sexual intercourse, and reducing the frequency of sex and number of partners (Garzon-Orjuela & others, 2021; Kantor & others, 2021). A recent review and analysis concluded that research across the last three decades provides strong support for comprehensive sex education across a range of topics and grade levels (Goldfarb & Lieberman, 2021).

Recently there has been an increased emphasis on abstinence-only-until-marriage (AOUM) policies and programs in many U.S. schools. However, a major problem with such policies and programs is that a very large majority of individuals engage in sexual intercourse at some point in adolescence or emerging adulthood, while the average age when people marry for the first time continues to go up (currently 27 for females, 29 for males in the United States). The Society for Adolescent Health and Medicine (2017) released a policy position noting that research evidence indicates that many comprehensive sex education programs successfully delay initiation of sexual intercourse and reduce rates of sexually transmitted infections. The Society's position also states that research

indicates AOUM programs are ineffective in delaying sexual intercourse and reducing other sexual risk behaviors.

Despite the evidence that strongly favors comprehensive sex education, there recently has been an increase in government funding for abstinence-only programs (Donovan, 2017). Also, in some states (Texas and Mississippi, for example), many students receive either abstinence-only sex education or no sex education at all.

U.S. sex education typically has focused on the hazards of sex and the need to protect adolescent females from male predators. The contrast between sex education in the United States and other Western nations is remarkable (Hampton, 2008). For example, the Swedish State Commission on Sex Education recommends that students gain knowledge to help them to experience sexual life as a source of happiness and fellowship with others. Swedish adolescents are sexually active at an earlier age than are American adolescents, and they are exposed to even more explicit sex on television. However, the Swedish National Board of Education has developed a curriculum to give every child, beginning at age 7, a thorough grounding in reproductive biology and, by the age of 10 or 12, information about various forms of contraception. Teachers handle the subject of sex whenever

it becomes relevant, regardless of the subject they are teaching. The idea is to demystify sex so that familiarity will make students less vulnerable to unwanted pregnancy and STIs. Despite a relatively early onset of sexual activity, the adolescent pregnancy rate in Sweden is one of the lowest in the world.

How is sex education in Sweden different from sex education in the United States?
Johner Royalty-Free/Getty Images

Why do you suppose that, despite the evidence supporting comprehensive sex education programs that include information about contraceptive methods, sex education in U.S. schools today increasingly focuses on abstinence?

education be taught in schools (Guttmacher Institute, 2020). That leaves 11 states that do not require any sex education or HIV education. Twenty-eight states and DC require both sex education and HIV education; 2 states require sex education only; and 9 states mandate only HIV education. Also, 40 states require parental notification that sex education or HIV education will be provided, and 38 states allow parents the option to remove their adolescent from such instruction. Thirty-nine states and DC require sex education programs to provide information about abstinence, and 19 states mandate that students be told about the importance of engaging in sex only within a marriage. Also, 35 states and DC require provision of information about the importance of skills for healthy romantic and sexual relationships.

The question of what information should be provided in sex education courses in U.S. schools today is a controversial topic. Four ways this controversial topic is dealt with are to focus on: (1) abstinence in adolescence; (2) abstinence until marriage; (3) comprehensive sex education that includes information about contraceptive use; and (4) abstinence-plus programs that promote abstinence while also providing comprehensive sex education and information about contraceptive use. To read further about sex education in the United States and around the world, see the *Connecting with Health and Well-Being* interlude.

Review Connect Reflect

LG4 Characterize the sexual literacy of adolescents and sex education.

Review

- How sexually literate are U.S. adolescents?
- What are adolescents' sources of sexual information?
- What cognitive factors might influence the effectiveness of sex education?
- How would you describe sex education in schools?

Connect

- Recall what you have learned about adolescent attention and memory. How does that information support this section's discussion of adolescents and sexual literacy?

Reflect *Your Own Personal Journey of Life*

- Think about how you learned the "facts of life." Did most of your information come from well-informed sources? Were you able to talk freely and openly with your parents about what to expect sexually? Did you acquire some false beliefs through trial-and-error efforts? As you grew older, did you discover that some of what you thought you knew about sex was inaccurate? Think also about the sex education you received in school. How adequate was it? What do you wish the schools you attended would have done differently in regard to sex education?

reach your **learning goals**

Sexuality

1 Exploring Adolescent Sexuality

 LG1 Discuss some basic ideas about the nature of adolescent sexuality.

A Normal Aspect of Adolescent Development

- Too often the problems adolescents encounter with sexuality are emphasized rather than the fact that sexuality is a normal aspect of adolescent development. Adolescence is a bridge between the asexual child and the sexual adult. Adolescent sexuality is related to many other aspects of adolescent development, including physical development and puberty, cognitive development, the self and identity, gender, families, peers, schools, and culture.

The Sexual Culture

- Increased permissiveness in adolescent sexuality is linked to increased permissiveness in the larger culture. Adolescent initiation of sexual intercourse is related to exposure to explicit sex on TV.

Developing a Sexual Identity

- Developing a sexual identity is a multifaceted process. An adolescent's sexual identity involves an indication of sexual orientation, interests, and styles of behavior.

Obtaining Research Information About Adolescent Sexuality

- Obtaining valid information about adolescent sexuality is not easy. Much of the data are based on interviews and questionnaires, which can evoke untruthful or socially desirable responses.

2 Sexual Attitudes and Behavior

 LG2 Summarize sexual attitudes and behavior in adolescence.

Heterosexual Attitudes and Behavior

- The progression of sexual behaviors is typically kissing, petting, sexual intercourse, and oral sex. The number of adolescents who reported having had sexual intercourse increased significantly in the twentieth century. The proportion of females engaging in intercourse increased more rapidly than that of males. National data indicate that slightly more than half of all adolescents today have had sexual intercourse by age 17, although the percentage varies by sex, ethnicity, and context. Male, African American, and inner-city adolescents report the highest rates of sexual activity. The percentage of 15- to 17-year-olds who have had sexual intercourse declined between 1991 and 2019.

- A common adolescent sexual script involves the male making sexual advances and the female setting limits on the male's sexual overtures. Adolescent females' sexual scripts link sex with love more than adolescent males' sexual scripts do.

- Risk factors for sexual problems include early sexual activity, having numerous sexual partners, not using contraception, engaging in other at-risk behaviors such as drinking and delinquency, and living in a low-SES neighborhood, as well as cognitive factors such as attentional problems and low self-regulation. Heterosexual behavior patterns change in emerging adulthood.

Sexual Minority Youths' Attitudes and Behavior

- An individual's sexual attraction—whether heterosexual or sexual minority—is likely caused by a mix of genetic, hormonal, cognitive, and environmental factors. Terms such as "sexual minority individuals" (who identify themselves as gay, lesbian, or bisexual) and "same-sex attraction" are increasingly used, whereas the term "homosexual" is used less frequently now than in the past.

- Developmental pathways for sexual minority youth are often diverse, may involve bisexual attractions, and do not always involve falling in love with a same-sex individual. Recent research has focused on adolescents' disclosure of same-sex attractions and the struggle they often go through in doing this.

- The peer relations of sexual minority youth differ from those of heterosexual youth. Sexual minority youth are more likely to engage in substance abuse, show sexual risk-taking behavior, and be the target of violence in a number of contexts. Discrimination and bias produce considerable stress for adolescents with a same-sex attraction. The stigma, discrimination, and rejection experienced by sexual minority youth are thought to explain why they are more likely to develop problems. Despite such negative experiences, many sexual minority youth successfully cope with the challenges they face and have health and well-being outcomes that are similar to those of their heterosexual counterparts.

Self-Stimulation

- Self-stimulation, or masturbation, is part of the sexual activity of virtually all adolescents and one of their most frequent sexual outlets.

Contraceptive Use

- Adolescents are increasing their use of contraceptives, but large numbers of sexually active adolescents still do not use them. Adolescents from low-SES backgrounds are less likely to use contraceptives than are their middle-SES counterparts.

3 Problematic Sexual Outcomes in Adolescence

 Describe the main problematic sexual outcomes that can emerge in adolescence.

Adolescent Pregnancy

- The U.S. adolescent pregnancy rate is one of the highest in the Western world, but it also has declined in the last two decades.

- Adolescent pregnancy increases health risks for the mother and the offspring. Adolescent mothers are more likely to drop out of school and have lower-paying jobs than their adolescent counterparts who do not bear children. It is important to remember, though, that it often is not pregnancy alone that places adolescents at risk. Adolescent mothers frequently come from low-income families and were not doing well in school prior to their pregnancy.

- The infants of adolescent parents are at risk both medically and psychologically. Adolescent parents are less effective in rearing their children than older parents are. Many adolescent fathers do not have a close relationship with their baby or with the adolescent mother.

- Recommendations for reducing adolescent pregnancy include education about sex and family planning, access to contraception, life options, community involvement and support, and abstinence.

Sexually Transmitted Infections

- Sexually transmitted infections (STIs) are contracted primarily through sexual contact with an infected partner. The contact is not limited to vaginal intercourse but includes oral-genital and anal-genital contact as well.

- AIDS (acquired immune deficiency syndrome) is a sexually transmitted infection caused by the human immunodeficiency virus (HIV), which destroys the body's immune system. Currently, the rate of AIDS in U.S. adolescents is relatively low, but it has reached epidemic proportions in sub-Saharan Africa, especially among adolescent girls. AIDS can be transmitted through sexual contact, sharing needles, and blood transfusions. A number of intervention projects focus on AIDS prevention.

- Genital herpes is caused by a family of viruses with different strains. Genital warts, caused by a virus, is the most common STI in the 15- to 24-year-old age group. Commonly called the "drip" or "clap," gonorrhea is another common STI. Syphilis is caused by the bacterium *Treponema pallidum,* a spirochete. Chlamydia is one of the most common STIs among adolescents and emerging adults.

Forcible Sexual Behavior and Sexual Harassment

- Some individuals force others to have sex with them. Rape is forcible sexual intercourse with a person who does not give consent. About 95 percent of rapes are committed by males. An increasing concern is date, or acquaintance, rape. Sexual harassment is a form of power asserted by one person over another. Sexual harassment of adolescents is widespread. Two forms are quid pro quo and hostile environment sexual harassment.

4 Sexual Literacy and Sex Education   **LG4**   Characterize the sexual literacy of adolescents and sex education.

Sexual Literacy

- American adolescents and adults are not very knowledgeable about sex. Sex information is abundant, but too often it is inaccurate.

Sources of Sex Information

- Adolescents get their information about sex from many sources, including parents, siblings, schools, peers, magazines, TV, and the Internet.

Cognitive Factors

- Cognitive factors, such as idealism and the personal fable, can make it difficult for sex education to be effective, especially with young adolescents.

Sex Education in Schools

- A majority of Americans support teaching sex education in schools, and this support has increased in concert with increases in STIs, especially AIDS. Currently, a major controversy is whether sex education should emphasize abstinence only or provide instruction on the use of contraceptive methods.

key **terms**

AIDS
bisexual
chlamydia
date rape, or acquaintance rape
genital herpes

genital warts
gonorrhea
homophobia
hostile environment sexual harassment

quid pro quo sexual harassment
rape
sexual minority
sexual script

sexually transmitted infections (STIs)
syphilis

key **people**

Bonnie Halpern-Felsher   June Reinisch   Ritch Savin-Williams   Maria Eva Trent

improving **the lives of adolescents and emerging adults**

Adolescent Sexuality **(2017)**
Pediatric Clinics of North America (Volume 64, Issue 2)
> Leading experts discuss a wide range of adolescent psychology topics, including interviewing adolescents about sexual matters, talking with parents about adolescent sexuality, sexually transmitted infections, adolescent pregnancy, and sexual violence in adolescence.

Cambridge Handbook of Sexual Development: Childhood and Adolescence **(2019)**
Edited by Jen Gilbert and Sharon Lamb
New York: Cambridge University Press
> A number of leading experts, including Lisa Diamond and Ritch Savin-Williams, discuss a wide range of topics involving adolescent sexuality.

***The Impact of Racism on Child and Adolescent Health* (2019).**
Maria Trent, Danielle Dooley, and Jaqueline Douge
Pediatrics, 144(2), e20191765.

> Dr. Maria Trent and her colleagues provide an insightful analysis of the influence of race on various aspects of child and adolescent health and describe strategies to optimize interventions for reducing this racism. This article was requested by the American Academy of Pediatrics and includes a statement of the AAP's position on addressing this racism.

***Positive and Negative Outcomes of Sexual Behaviors* (2014)**
Edited by Eva Lefkowtiz and Sara Vasilenko
New Directions in Child and Adolescent Development, 144, 1–98.

> Contemporary coverage of a wide range of important aspects of adolescent and emerging adult sexuality are examined, including healthy adolescent sex, sexual minority youth, online sexual activities, and dating and sexual relationships.

AIDS Hotline
National AIDS Information Clearinghouse
800-342-AIDS
800-344-SIDA (Spanish)
800-AIDS-TTY (Deaf)

> The people answering the hotline will respond to any questions children, youth, or adults have about HIV infection or AIDS. Pamphlets and other materials on AIDS are available.

Alan Guttmacher Institute (www.guttmacher.org)

> The Alan Guttmacher Institute is an especially good resource for information about adolescent sexuality. The Institute publishes a well-respected journal, *Perspectives on Sexual and Reproductive Health* (renamed in 2003, formerly *Family Planning Perspectives*), which includes articles on many dimensions of sexuality, such as adolescent pregnancy, sexual behavior and attitudes, and sexually transmitted infections.

National Sexually Transmitted Diseases Hotline
800-227-8922

> This hotline provides information about a wide variety of sexually transmitted infections.

Sex Information and Education Council of the United States (SIECUS) (www.siecus.org)

> This organization serves as an information clearinghouse for sex education. The group's objective is to promote the concept of human sexuality as an integration of physical, intellectual, emotional, and social dimensions.

chapter 7

MORAL DEVELOPMENT, VALUES, AND RELIGION

chapter outline

Wavebreakmedia/iStock/Getty Images

Jewel Cash, seated next to her mother, participates in a crime watch meeting at a community center. As an adolescent, she was an exemplar of positive teenage community involvement.
Matthew J. Lee/The Boston Globe/Getty Images

The mayor of the city commented that she was "everywhere." She persuaded the city's school committee to consider ending the practice of locking tardy students out of their classrooms. She also swayed a neighborhood group to support her proposal for a winter jobs program. According to one city councilman, "People are just impressed with the power of her arguments and the sophistication of the argument" (Silva, 2005, pp. B1, B4). She is Jewel E. Cash.

Jewel was raised in one of Boston's housing projects by her mother, a single parent. As a high school student at Boston Latin Academy, she was a member of the Boston Student Advisory Council, mentored children, volunteered at a women's shelter, managed and danced in two troupes, and was a member of a neighborhood watch group—among other activities. Jewel told an interviewer from the Boston Globe, "I see a problem and I say, 'How can I make a difference?' . . . I can't take on the world, even though I can try. . . . I'm moving forward but I want to make sure I'm bringing people with me" (Silva, 2005, pp. B1, B4). As an adult, Jewel works with a public consulting group and continues to help others as a mentor and community organizer.

preview

Jewel Cash's caring for people in her community reflects the positive side of moral development, a major focus of this chapter. Moral development involves the distinction between what is right and wrong, what matters to people, and what people should do in their interactions with others. We begin by discussing the three main traditional domains of moral development—moral thoughts, behavior, and feeling—and the recent emphasis on moral personality. Next, we explore the contexts in which moral development takes place, focusing on families and schools. We conclude with an examination of adolescent values, religion, and spirituality.

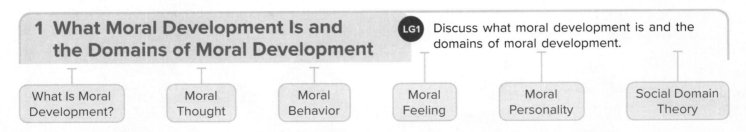

1 What Moral Development Is and the Domains of Moral Development

LG1 Discuss what moral development is and the domains of moral development.

| What Is Moral Development? | Moral Thought | Moral Behavior | Moral Feeling | Moral Personality | Social Domain Theory |

Moral development has been a topic of great concern to societies, communities, and families. It is also one of the oldest topics of interest to those who are curious about human nature. Philosophers and theologians have talked about it and written about it for many centuries. In the twentieth century, psychologists began theorizing about and studying moral development.

WHAT IS MORAL DEVELOPMENT?

Moral development involves changes in thoughts, feelings, and behaviors regarding standards of right and wrong. Moral development has an *intrapersonal* dimension, which regulates a person's activities when she or he is not engaged in social interaction, and an *interpersonal* dimension, which regulates social interactions and arbitrates conflict. To understand moral development, we need to consider five basic questions:

First, how do adolescents reason*, or think, about rules for ethical conduct?* For example, we might present an adolescent with a story in which someone has a conflict about whether or not to cheat in a specific situation, such as taking an exam in school. The adolescent is asked to decide what is appropriate for the person to do and why. The focus is placed on the reasoning adolescents use to justify their moral decisions.

Second, how do adolescents actually behave *in moral circumstances?* For example, in regard to cheating, we might observe adolescents' cheating and the environmental circumstances that produced and maintain the cheating. We could conduct our study through a one-way mirror while adolescents were taking an exam. We might note whether they took out "cheat" notes, looked at another student's answers, and so on.

Third, how do adolescents feel *about moral matters?* In the example of cheating, do the adolescents feel enough guilt to resist temptation? If adolescents do cheat, do feelings of guilt after the transgression keep them from cheating the next time they face temptation?

Fourth, what comprises an adolescent's moral personality? Continuing with the example of cheating, does the adolescent have a moral identity and moral character that are so strong the adolescent resists the temptation to cheat?

Fifth, how is the adolescent's moral domain *different from the adolescent's* social conventional and personal domains? In domain theory, cheating resides in the moral domain, along with lying, stealing, and harming another person. Behaviors such as cutting in a line or speaking out of turn are in the social conventional domain rather than the moral domain, and choosing friends is in the personal domain and not the moral domain.

Keep in mind that although we have separated moral development into different domains, the components often are interrelated. For example, if the focus is on the adolescent's behavior, it is still important to evaluate the adolescent's intentions (moral thought). Similarly, emotions accompany, and can distort, moral reasoning.

Let's now discuss the various domains of moral development. We begin with the cognitive domain.

MORAL THOUGHT

How do adolescents think about standards of right and wrong? Piaget had some thoughts about this, but they applied to children's moral development. It was Lawrence Kohlberg (1958, 1976, 1986) who crafted a major theory of how adolescents think about right and wrong. He proposed that moral development is based primarily on moral reasoning that changes developmentally.

moral development Thoughts, feelings, and behaviors regarding standards of right and wrong.

Kohlberg's Cognitive Developmental Theory   Central to Kohlberg's work on moral development were interviews with individuals of different ages. In the interviews, individuals were presented with a series of stories in which characters face moral dilemmas. The following is the most cited of the Kohlberg dilemmas:

> In Europe, a woman was near death from a special kind of cancer. There was one drug that the doctors thought might save her. It was a form of radium that a druggist in the same town had recently discovered. The drug was expensive to make, but the druggist was charging ten times what the drug cost him to make. He paid $200 for the radium and charged $2,000 for a small dose of the drug. The sick woman's husband, Heinz, went to everyone he knew to borrow the money, but he could only get together $1,000, which is half of what it cost. He told the druggist that his wife was dying and asked him to sell it cheaper or let him pay later. But the druggist said, "No, I discovered the drug, and I am going to make money from it." So Heinz got desperate and broke into the man's store to steal the drug for his wife. (Kohlberg, 1969, p. 379)

Lawrence Kohlberg.
Harvard University Archives, UAV 605.295.8, Box 7, Kohlberg

This story is one of eleven that Kohlberg devised to investigate the nature of moral thought. After reading the story, interviewees are asked a series of questions about the moral dilemma: Should Heinz have stolen the drug? Was stealing it right or wrong? Why? Is it a husband's duty to steal the drug for his wife if he can get it no other way? Would a good husband steal it? Did the druggist have the right to charge that much when there was no law setting a limit on the price? Why or why not?

Kohlberg's Three Levels   From the answers interviewees gave for this and other moral dilemmas, Kohlberg hypothesized three levels of moral development. A key concept in understanding progression through the levels is that people's morality becomes more mature. That is, their judgments of whether given behaviors are morally right or wrong begin to go beyond the superficial reasons they gave when they were younger to encompass more complex coordination of multiple perspectives.

Kohlberg's Level 1: Preconventional Reasoning   **Preconventional reasoning** is the lowest level in Kohlberg's theory of moral development. At this level, moral reasoning is strongly influenced by external punishment and reward. For example, children and adolescents obey adults because adults tell them to obey. Or they might be nice to others so that others will be nice to them. This earliest level has sometimes been described as "What's in it for me?"

There is a much stronger punishment-and-obedience than reward orientation to Level 1 moral reasoning because children respect the power of adults. There also are adults at this level who adopt an "eye-for-an-eye," "you scratch my back and I'll scratch yours" approach.

Kohlberg's Level 2: Conventional Reasoning   **Conventional reasoning** is the second, or intermediate, level in Kohlberg's theory of moral development. In conventional reasoning, individuals develop expectations about social roles.

Level 2 comes into play when for the first time the naked self-pursuit of Level 1 gives way to conventional expectations of good behavior within the society of friends and family. For example, in the Heinz and the druggist story, wouldn't a *good* husband steal the drug to save his wife's life? In terms of laws of society, at Level 2 reasoning, individuals come to understand that for a community and nation to work effectively, they need to be protected by laws that everyone follows.

Kohlberg's Level 3: Postconventional Reasoning   **Postconventional reasoning** is the highest level in Kohlberg's theory of moral development. In Level 3 reasoning, conventional considerations are now judged against moral concerns such as liberty, justice, and equality, with the idea that morality can improve the laws, fix them, and guide conventional institutions in the direction of a better world. At the highest point in Level 3, people are aware that moral principles make demands on them. Yes, Heinz should steal the drug because the value of life trumps the druggist' right to property. However, this moral judgment has a universal intent—everyone in Heinz's position should also steal the drug.

Kohlberg argued that these levels occur in a sequence and are age-related: Before age 9, most children reason about moral dilemmas in a preconventional way; by early adolescence, they reason in more conventional ways. By early adulthood, a small number of individuals reason in postconventional ways. In a 20-year longitudinal investigation, the uses of level 1 decreased (Colby & others, 1983).

Any change in moral reasoning between late adolescence and early adulthood appears to be relatively gradual (Eisenberg & others, 2009). One study found that when 16- to 19-year-olds and 18- to 25-year-olds were asked to reason about real-life moral dilemmas and their responses were coded using Kohlberg's levels, there was no significant difference in the moral reasoning of the two age groups (Walker & others, 1995).

Influences on the Kohlberg Levels   Kohlberg theorized that the individual's moral orientation unfolds as a consequence of cognitive development and exposure to appropriate social experiences. Children and adolescents construct their moral thoughts as they move from one level to the next, rather than passively accepting a cultural norm of morality. Investigators have sought to understand factors that influence movement through the moral levels, among them modeling, cognitive conflict, peer relations, and role-taking opportunities.

Several investigators have attempted to advance individuals' levels of moral development by having a model present arguments that reflect moral thinking slightly above the individuals' established level. These studies are based on the cognitive developmental concepts of equilibrium

preconventional reasoning The lowest level in Kohlberg's theory of moral development. At this level, the individual's moral reasoning is controlled primarily by a punishment-and-obedience orientation.

conventional reasoning The second, or intermediate, level in Kohlberg's theory. Individuals at this level develop expectations about social roles, such as the roles of parents and children, and they understand the importance of following the laws of society.

postconventional reasoning The third and highest level in Kohlberg's theory. At this level, conventional considerations are now judged against moral concerns such as liberty, justice, and equality, with the idea that morality can improve laws.

and conflict (Walker & Taylor, 1991). By presenting moral information slightly beyond the individual's cognitive level, a disequilibrium is created that motivates a restructuring of moral thought. The resolution of the disequilibrium and conflict should be toward increased competence. Like Piaget, Kohlberg emphasized that peer interaction is a critical part of the social stimulation that challenges individuals to change their moral orientation. Whereas adults characteristically impose rules and regulations on children, the mutual give-and-take in peer interaction provides the child with an opportunity to take the role of another person and to generate rules democratically (Rubin, Bukowski, & Parker, 2006). Kohlberg stressed that role-taking opportunities can, in principle, be engendered by any peer group encounter. Researchers have found that more advanced moral reasoning takes place when peers engage in challenging, even moderately conflicting, conversation (Walker, Hennig, & Krettenauer, 2000).

Why did Kohlberg think peer relations are so important in moral development?
Don Hammond/Design Pics

Kohlberg did note that certain types of parent-child experiences can induce the child and adolescent to think at more advanced levels of moral reasoning. In particular, parents who allow or encourage conversation about value-laden issues promote more advanced moral thought in their children and adolescents. Unfortunately, many parents do not systematically provide their children and adolescents with such role-taking opportunities. In recent years, there has been increasing emphasis on the role of parenting in moral development (Booker & others, 2021; Lapsley, 2020).

Why Is Kohlberg's Theory Important for Understanding Moral Development in Adolescence?

Kohlberg's theory is essentially a description of the progressive conceptions people use to understand social cooperation. In short, it tells the developmental story of people trying to understand things like society, rules and roles, and institutions and relationships. Such basic conceptions are fundamental to adolescents, for whom ideology becomes important in guiding their lives and helping them to make life decisions. However, Kohlberg's theory has become less influential in recent years, as indicated by the criticisms that we discuss next.

Kohlberg's Critics   Kohlberg's theory has provoked debate, research, and criticism (Jambon & Smetana, 2020; Lapsley, LaPorte, & Kelley, 2022; Narváez, 2020; Spinrad & Eisenberg, 2020). Key criticisms involve the link between moral thought and moral behavior, whether moral reasoning is conscious/deliberative or unconscious/automatic, inadequate attention given to emotion, the roles of culture and the family in moral development, and the significance of concern for others.

Moral Thought and Moral Behavior   Kohlberg's theory has been criticized for placing too much emphasis on moral thought and not enough emphasis on moral behavior. Moral reasons can always be used as a shelter for immoral behavior. Some presidents, business executives, and religious figures endorse the loftiest of moral virtues when commenting about moral dilemmas, yet their own behavior may be immoral. No one wants a nation of cheaters and liars who can reason at the postconventional level. The cheaters and liars may know what is right and wrong yet still do what is wrong.

In evaluating the relationship between moral thought and moral behavior, consider the corrupting power of rationalizations and other defenses that disengage us from self-blame; these include interpreting a situation in our favor and attributing blame to authorities, circumstances, or victims (Bandura, 1991). One area in which a link between moral judgment and behavior has been found involves antisocial behavior and delinquency. Researchers have found that less advanced moral reasoning in adolescence is related to antisocial behavior and delinquency (Gibbs, 2019; Taylor & Walker, 1997). One study also revealed that moral reasoning was related to self-reported altruism (Maclean, Walker, & Matsuba, 2004).

Given the terrorist attacks of September 11, 2001, and the continuing war on terrorism, it is intriguing to explore how heinous actions can be cloaked in a mantle of moral virtue and to consider why that is especially dangerous. Social cognitive theorist Albert Bandura (1999, 2002) argues that people usually don't engage in harmful conduct until they have justified the

How does Bandura describe the way terrorists justify their actions?
Spencer Platt/Getty Images

A young Buddist monk in Nepal. Nepalese monks' concerns about suffering and the importance of compassion are not captured in Kohlberg's theory.
Yaacov Dagan/Alamy Stock Photo

morality of their actions to themselves. In this process of moral justification, immoral conduct is made personally and socially acceptable by portraying it as serving socially worthy or moral purposes. In many instances throughout history, perpetrators of violence have twisted theology so that they see themselves as doing God's will. Bandura provides the example of Islamic extremists who perceive their actions as self-defense against tyrannical, decadent people whom they perceive as seeking to enslave the Islamic world.

Moral Thinking: Conscious/Deliberative Versus Unconscious/Automatic

Social psychologist Jonathan Haidt (2018) argues that a major flaw in Kohlberg's theory is his view that moral thinking is deliberative and that individuals go around all the time contemplating and reasoning about morality. Haidt believes that most moral thinking is more of an intuitive gut reaction and that deliberative moral reasoning is often an after-the-fact justification. Thus, in his view, much of morality begins by making rapid evaluative judgments of others, not by initially engaging in strategic reasoning about moral circumstances.

The Role of Emotion

Kohlberg argued that emotion has negative effects on moral reasoning. However, increasing evidence indicates that emotions play an important role in moral thinking (Spinrad & Eisenberg, 2020). Later in the chapter, we will further explore the importance of emotion in moral development.

Culture and Moral Development

Kohlberg emphasized that his levels of moral reasoning are universal, but some critics claim his theory is culturally biased (Miller, Wice, & Goyal, 2020). Both Kohlberg and his critics may be partially correct. One review of 45 studies in 27 cultures around the world, mostly non-European, provided support for the universality of Kohlberg's first two levels (Snarey, 1987). Individuals in diverse cultures developed through these four stages in sequence as Kohlberg predicted. Level 3, postconventional moral reasoning, has not been found in all cultures (Gibbs & others, 2007).

In sum, Kohlberg's approach captures some—but not all—of the moral reasoning voiced in various cultures around the world. As we have just seen, there are some important moral concepts in specific cultures that his approach misses or misconstrues.

Darcia Narváez and Tracy Gleason (2013) have described cohort effects regarding moral reasoning. In recent years, postconventional moral reasoning has been declining in college students—not down to the middle level (conventional), but to the lowest level (personal interests) (Thoma & Bebeau, 2008). Narváez and Gleason (2013) also argue that declines in prosocial behavior have occurred in recent years and that humans, especially those living in Western cultures, are "on a fast train to demise." They propose that the solution to improving people's moral lives lies in better child-rearing strategies and social supports for families and children. In more recent commentary, Narváez and her colleagues (Christen, Narváez, & Gutzwiller, 2018) stress that we need to make better progress in dealing with an increasing array of temptations and possible wrongdoings in a human social world that is becoming increasingly complicated and challenging.

Families and Moral Development

Kohlberg argued that family processes are essentially unimportant in children's and adolescents' moral development. As noted earlier, he argued that parent-child relationships usually provide children with little opportunity for give-and-take or perspective taking. Rather, Kohlberg said that such opportunities are more likely to be provided by children's and adolescents' peer relations. Did Kohlberg underestimate the contribution of family relationships to moral development? Most developmentalists emphasize that parents play more important roles in children's and adolescents' moral development than Kohlberg envisioned (Booker & others, 2021; Padilla-Walker & Memmott-Elison, 2020). They stress that parents' communication with children and adolescents, their disciplinary techniques, and many other aspects of parent-child relationships influence children's and adolescents' moral development (Lansford, 2020; Thompson, 2020). We will have more to discuss about this topic later in the chapter. Nonetheless, most developmentalists agree with Kohlberg and Piaget that peers play an important role in moral development.

Gender and the Care Perspective

The most publicized criticism of Kohlberg's theory has come from Carol Gilligan (1982, 1996), who argues that Kohlberg's theory reflects a gender bias. According to Gilligan, Kohlberg's theory is based on a male norm that puts abstract principles above relationships and concern for others and sees the individual as standing alone and independently making moral decisions. It puts justice at the heart of morality.

developmental **connection**

Gender

Janet Shibley Hyde concluded that many views and studies of gender exaggerate differences. Connect to "Gender."

In contrast with Kohlberg's **justice perspective,** Gilligan argues for a **care perspective,** which is a moral perspective that views people in terms of their connectedness with others and emphasizes interpersonal communication, relationships with others, and concern for others. According to Gilligan, Kohlberg greatly underplayed the care perspective, perhaps because he was a male, because most of his research was with males rather than females, and because he used male responses as a model for his theory.

In extensive interviews with girls from 6 to 18 years of age, Gilligan and her colleagues found that girls consistently interpret moral dilemmas in terms of human relationships and base these interpretations on watching and listening to other people (Gilligan & others, 2003). However, a meta-analysis (a statistical analysis that combines the results of many different studies) casts doubt on Gilligan's claim of substantial gender differences in moral judgment (Jaffee & Hyde, 2000). And another analysis concluded that girls' moral orientations are "somewhat more likely to focus on care for others than on abstract principles of justice, but they can use both moral orientations when needed (as can boys . . .)" (Blakemore, Berenbaum, & Liben, 2009, p. 132).

What is Carol Gilligan's perspective on the moral dilemma many adolescent girls face?
Kentaroo Tryman/Getty Images

MORAL BEHAVIOR

We saw that one of the criticisms of Kohlberg's theory is that it does not give adequate attention to the link between moral thought and moral behavior. In our exploration of moral behavior, we focus on these questions: What are the basic processes that behaviorists argue are responsible for adolescents' moral behavior? How do social cognitive theorists view adolescents' moral development? What is the nature of prosocial behavior?

Basic Processes Behavioral views emphasize the moral behavior of adolescents. The familiar processes of reinforcement, punishment, and imitation have been invoked to explain how and why adolescents learn certain moral behaviors and why their behaviors differ from those of one another. The general conclusions to be drawn are the same as those for other domains of social behavior. When adolescents are positively reinforced for behavior that is consistent with laws and social conventions, they are likely to repeat that behavior. When models who behave morally are provided, adolescents are likely to adopt similar behavior. And, when adolescents are punished for immoral or unacceptable behavior, those behaviors can be eliminated, but at the expense of sanctioning punishment by its very use and of causing emotional side effects for the adolescent. For example, when adolescent drivers act responsibly and are praised by their parents for doing so, they are more likely to continue driving safely. If adolescents see their parents driving responsibly, they are more likely to follow the same patterns. If driving privileges are revoked from adolescents who do not drive responsibly, the behavior is eliminated but the adolescent may feel humiliated by the punishment.

To these general conclusions, we can add several qualifiers. The effectiveness of reinforcement and punishment depends on how consistently they are administered and the schedule that is adopted. The effectiveness of modeling depends on the characteristics of the model (power, warmth, uniqueness, and so on) and the presence of cognitive processes, such as symbolic codes and imagery, that enhance retention of the modeled behavior.

What kinds of adult moral models are adolescents being exposed to in American society? Do such models usually do what they say? Adolescents are especially alert to adult hypocrisy, and evidence indicates that they are right to believe that many adults display a double standard—that is, their moral actions do not always correspond to their moral thoughts or pronouncements (Bandura, 1991).

In addition to emphasizing the role of environmental determinants and the gap between moral thought and moral action, behaviorists also emphasize that moral behavior is situationally dependent. That is, they say that adolescents are not likely to display consistent moral behavior in diverse social settings (Eisenberg & others, 2009).

In a classic investigation of moral behavior—one of the most extensive ever conducted—Hugh Hartshorne and Mark May (1928–1930) observed the moral responses of 11,000 children

justice perspective A moral perspective that focuses on the rights of the individual. Individuals are viewed as making moral decisions independently.

care perspective The moral perspective of Carol Gilligan, which views people in terms of their connectedness with others and emphasizes interpersonal communication, relationships with others, and concern for others.

and adolescents who were given the opportunity to lie, cheat, and steal in a variety of circumstances—at home, at school, at social events, and in athletics. A completely honest or a completely dishonest child or adolescent was difficult to find. Situation-specific moral behavior was the rule. Adolescents were more likely to cheat when their friends pressured them to do so and when the chance of being caught was slim. Other analyses suggest that some adolescents are more likely to lie, cheat, and steal than others, an indication of greater consistency of moral behavior in some adolescents than in others (Burton, 1984).

Social Cognitive Theory of Moral Development   The **social cognitive theory of moral development** emphasizes a distinction between adolescents' moral competence—the ability to produce moral behaviors—and moral performance—the enactment of those behaviors in specific situations (Mischel & Mischel, 1975). Competence, or acquisition, is primarily the outgrowth of cognitive-sensory processes. Competencies include what adolescents are capable of doing, what they know, their skills, their awareness of moral rules and regulations, and their cognitive ability to construct behaviors. In contrast, adolescents' moral performance, or behavior, is determined by their motivation and the rewards and incentives to act in a specific moral way.

Albert Bandura (1991, 2002) also concludes that moral development is best understood by considering a combination of social and cognitive factors, especially those involving self-control. He proposes that in developing a "moral self, individuals adopt standards of right and wrong that serve as guides and deterrents for conduct. In this self-regulatory process, people monitor their conduct and the conditions under which it occurs, judge it in relation to moral standards, and regulate their actions by the consequences they apply to themselves. They do things that provide them with satisfaction and a sense of self-worth. They refrain from behaving in ways that violate their moral standards because such conduct will bring self-condemnation. Self-sanctions keep conduct in line with internal standards" (Bandura, 2002, p. 102). Thus, in Bandura's view, self-regulation rather than abstract reasoning is the key to positive moral development.

In his most recent book, *Moral Disengagement,* Bandura (2015) described various ways that individuals morally disengage themselves from reprehensible actions and still feel good about themselves. He especially highlights how people may use worthwhile ends to justify inhumane means. As an example, Bandura (2015) points to atrocities committed by ISIS in which religious ideology is used to justify inhumane behavior.

Moral behavior includes both negative aspects of behavior—cheating, lying, and stealing, for example—and positive aspects of behavior—such as being considerate to others and giving to a worthy cause. Let's now explore the positive side of moral behavior—prosocial behavior.

Prosocial Behavior   Many prosocial acts involve **altruism,** an unselfish interest in helping another person. Altruism is found throughout the human world and is a guiding principle in Christianity, Buddhism, Hinduism, Islam, and Judaism. Although adolescents have often been described as egocentric and selfish, adolescent acts of altruism are, nevertheless, plentiful (Carlo & Pierotti, 2020; Turner & others, 2021). We see examples daily in the hardworking adolescent who places a twenty-dollar bill in the church offering plate each Sunday; the adolescent-sponsored car washes, bake sales, and concerts organized to make money to feed the hungry and help children with a disability; and the adolescent who takes in and cares for a wounded cat. How do psychologists account for such altruistic acts?

The circumstances most likely to involve altruism by adolescents are empathetic or sympathetic emotion for an individual in need or a close relationship between the benefactor and the recipient (Clark & others, 1987). Prosocial behavior occurs more often in adolescence than in childhood, although examples of caring for others and comforting someone in distress may occur as early as the preschool years (Spinrad & Eisenberg, 2020).

Why might prosocial behavior increase in adolescence? Cognitive changes involving advances in abstract, idealistic, and logical reasoning as well as increased empathy and emotional understanding likely are involved. With such newfound cognitive abilities, young adolescents increasingly sympathize with members of abstract groups with whom they have little experience, such as people living in poverty in other countries (Eisenberg, Spinrad, & Knafo, 2015). The increase in volunteer opportunities in adolescence also contributes to more frequent prosocial behavior.

developmental **connection**

Social Cognitive Theory

What are the main themes of Bandura's social cognitive theory? Connect to "Introduction."

It is one of the most beautiful compensations of this life that no one can sincerely try to help another without helping himself.

—CHARLES DUDLEY WARNER
American Essayist, 19th Century

social cognitive theory of moral development Theory that distinguishes between moral competence (the ability to produce moral behaviors) and moral performance (enacting those behaviors in specific situations).

altruism Unselfish interest in helping another person.

Are there gender differences in prosocial behavior during adolescence? Adolescent females view themselves as more prosocial and empathic, and also engage in more prosocial behavior than do males (Eisenberg, Spinrad, & Knafo, 2015). Are there different types of prosocial behavior? In one study, Gustavo Carlo and his colleagues (2010, pp. 340–341) investigated this question and confirmed the presence of six types of prosocial behavior in young adolescents:

- altruism ("One of the best things about doing charity work is that it looks good.")
- public ("Helping others while I'm being watched is when I work best.")
- emotional ("I usually help others when they are very upset.")
- dire ("I tend to help people who are hurt badly.")
- anonymous ("I prefer to donate money without anyone knowing.")
- compliant ("I never wait to help others when they ask for it.")

In this study, adolescent girls reported more emotional, dire, compliant, and altruistic behavior than did boys, while boys engaged in more public prosocial behavior. Parental monitoring was positively related to emotional, dire, and compliant behavior but not to the other types of behavior. Compliant, anonymous, and altruistic prosocial behavior were positively related to religiosity.

Most research on prosocial behavior conceptualizes the concept in a global and unidimensional manner. The study by Carlo and colleagues (2010) illustrates the important point that in thinking about and studying prosocial behavior, it is essential to consider its dimensions.

What role do parents play in adolescents' prosocial behavior? In a recent study of fifth-, tenth-, and twelfth-grade students, authoritative parents (those who showed warmth while exercising some control) were more likely to have children and youth who showed higher levels of prosocial behavior than were parents who were moderately demanding and uninvolved (Carlo & others, 2018). Also, a recent study revealed that harsh parenting was linked to a lower level of adolescent prosocial behavior (Bevilacqua & others, 2021). Other research also has found that mothers are more likely to influence adolescents' prosocial behavior than are fathers (Carlo & others, 2011). In a recent study, maternal warmth was associated with a higher level of adolescent prosocial behavior (Kanacri & others, 2021). Peer relations also influence the extent to which adolescents engage in prosocial behavior (Cui & others, 2020). For example, a longitudinal study tracking individuals from 11 to 17 years of age revealed that being around antisocial peers was associated with a lower likelihood of engaging in prosocial behavior and a higher probability of participating in higher-risk sexual behaviors (Clark & others, 2020). Also, associating with prosocial peers predicted a greater likelihood of engaging in prosocial behavior and not participating in higher-risk sexual behaviors. Further, in a recent study, associating more with prosocial peers at 12 years of age predicted a decline in drug use and property-offending delinquency a year later, while spending less time with prosocial peers at 12 years of age predicted increased drug use and property-offending delinquency a year later (Walters, 2020).

Might the collective prosocial nature of a school classroom also influence the prosocial behavior of adolescents? In a recent study, a high classroom level of prosocial behavior at 14 years of age predicted a higher level of adolescents' prosocial behavior two years later (Busching & Krahe, 2020). In this study, a high level of classroom prosocial behavior especially increased the prosocial behavior of adolescents with lower levels of prosocial behavior at 14 years of age. In addition, the effects were stronger for same-sex than opposite-sex peers.

Research also indicates that when adolescents engage in prosocial behavior it is linked to other positive aspects of their development (Donahue, Tillman, & Luby, 2020). For example, a meta-analysis of 55 studies involving individuals from childhood through emerging adulthood concluded that engaging in higher levels of prosocial behavior was related to lower levels of internalizing and externalizing problems (Memmott-Elison & others, 2020).

Forgiveness is an aspect of prosocial behavior that occurs when the injured person releases the injurer from possible behavioral retaliation (Kong & others, 2020). In one investigation, individuals from the fourth grade through college and adulthood were asked questions about forgiveness (Enright, Santos, & Al-Mabuk, 1989). The adolescents were especially swayed by peer pressure in their willingness to forgive others. Also, a recent study of Chinese adolescents revealed that empathy played an important role in increasing forgiveness following an offender's transgression (Ma & Jiang, 2020). And two recent studies found that forgiveness of others was

What are some characteristics of prosocial behavior in adolescence?
sdominick/Getty Images

forgiveness An aspect of prosocial behavior that occurs when an injured person releases the injurer from possible behavioral retaliation.

associated with a lower risk of suicidal behavior in adolescents (Dangel, Webb, & Hirsch, 2018; Quintana-Orts & Rey, 2018).

Gratitude is a feeling of thankfulness and appreciation, especially in response to someone doing something kind or helpful (Enright & Song, 2020). Recent research indicates that other-praising gratitude expressions improve relationships (Ling & others, 2021). Also, in a study of middle school students, a higher level of gratitude was linked to a higher level of purpose (Malin, Liauw, & Damon, 2017). In another study, gratitude was linked to a number of positive aspects of development in young adolescents, including satisfaction with one's family, optimism, and prosocial behavior (Froh, Yurkewicz, & Kashdan, 2009). In addition, a longitudinal study assessed the gratitude of adolescents at 10 to 14 years of age (Bono, 2012). Four years after the initial assessment, the most grateful adolescents (top 20 percent) had a stronger sense of the meaning of life, were more satisfied with their lives, were happier and more hopeful, had a lower level of negative emotions, and were less depressed than the least grateful students (bottom 20 percent). Further, a recent study of adolescents found that both gratitude and forgiveness were linked to a lower level of reactive and proactive aggression through their connection to self-control (Garcia-Vazquez & others, 2020). And a recent study of adolescents found that having the character strength of gratitude increased their prosocial behavior and peer acceptance (Lavy & Benish-Weisman, 2021). In sum, given the increasing concern that we live in a world where too often people fail to show how appreciative they are of what others have done for them, the research discussed here indicates that individuals who express gratitude benefit in a number of ways (Enright & Song, 2020).

So far we have examined two of the three main domains of moral development: thought and behavior. Next, we explore the third main domain: moral feeling.

MORAL FEELING

Among the ideas formulated about the development of moral feeling are concepts central to psychoanalytic theory, the nature of empathy, and the role of emotions in moral development.

Psychoanalytic Theory Sigmund Freud's psychoanalytic theory describes the superego as one of the three main structures of personality (the id and the ego being the other two). In Freud's classical psychoanalytic theory, an individual's *superego*—the moral branch of personality—develops in early childhood when the child resolves the Oedipus conflict and identifies with the same-sex parent. According to Freud, one reason why children resolve the Oedipus conflict is to alleviate the fear of losing their parents' love and of being punished for their unacceptable sexual wishes toward the opposite-sex parent. To reduce anxiety, avoid punishment, and maintain parental affection, children form a superego by identifying with the same-sex parent. In Freud's view, through this identification, children internalize the parents' standards of right and wrong that reflect societal prohibitions. At the same time, children turn inward the hostility that was previously aimed at the same-sex parent. This inwardly directed hostility is then experienced self-punitively (and unconsciously) as guilt. In the psychoanalytic account of moral development, self-punitiveness of guilt keeps children and, later on, adolescents from committing transgressions. That is, children and adolescents conform to societal standards to avoid guilt.

In Freud's view, the superego consists of two main components—the ego ideal and the conscience—which promote children's and adolescents' development of moral feelings. The **ego ideal** is the component of the superego that involves ideal standards approved by parents, whereas the **conscience** is the component of the superego that involves behaviors not approved of by parents. An individual's ego ideal rewards the individual by conveying a sense of pride and personal value when the individual acts according to moral standards. The conscience punishes the individual for acting immorally by making the individual feel guilty and worthless. In this way, self-control replaces parental control.

Freud's claims regarding the formation of the ego ideal and conscience cannot be verified. However, researchers can examine the extent to which children feel guilty when they misbehave. Contemporary views of conscience emphasize that conscience is rooted in close relationships, constructed from advances in children's self-understanding and understanding of others, and linked to their emotional makeup (Thompson, 2014). Contemporary views also stress that the development of conscience goes well beyond disciplinary encounters with parents to include communication about emotion and conversations with parents about relationships (Thompson, 2014).

developmental **connection**

Psychoanalytic Theory
Freud theorized that individuals go through five main stages of psychosexual development. Connect to "Introduction."

gratitude A feeling of thankfulness and appreciation, especially in response to someone doing something kind or helpful.

ego ideal The component of the superego that involves ideal standards approved by parents.

conscience The component of the superego that discourages behaviors disapproved of by parents.

Erik Erikson (1970) outlined three stages of moral development: specific moral learning in childhood, ideological concerns in adolescence, and ethical consolidation in adulthood. According to Erikson, during adolescence individuals search for an identity. If adolescents become disillusioned with the moral and religious beliefs they acquired during childhood, they are likely to lose, at least temporarily, their sense of purpose and feel that their lives are empty. This loss may lead adolescents to search for an ideology that will give some purpose to their lives. For the ideology to be acceptable, it must both fit the evidence and mesh with adolescents' logical reasoning abilities. If others share this ideology, a sense of community is felt. For Erikson, ideology surfaces as the guardian of identity during adolescence because it provides a sense of purpose, assists in tying the present to the future, and contributes meaning to the behavior (Hoffman, 1988).

What characterizes empathy in adolescence?
Thinkstock/Getty Images

Empathy   Positive feelings, such as empathy, contribute to adolescents' moral development (Spinrad & Eisenberg, 2020). Feeling **empathy** means reacting to another's feelings with an emotional response that is similar to that person's feelings. Although empathy is experienced as an emotional state, it often has a cognitive component—the ability to discern another's inner psychological states, or what we have previously called *perspective taking*.

At about 10 to 12 years of age, individuals develop empathy for people who live in unfortunate circumstances (Damon, 1988). Children's concerns are no longer limited to the feelings of specific persons in situations they directly observe. Instead, 10- to 12-year-olds expand their concerns to the general problems of people in unfortunate circumstances—the poor, those with disabilities, social outcasts, and so forth. This newfound sensitivity may lead older children to behave altruistically, and later may give a humanitarian flavor to adolescents' development of ideological and political views.

Although every adolescent may be capable of responding with empathy, not all do so. Adolescents' empathic behavior varies considerably. For example, in older children and adolescents, empathic dysfunctions can contribute to antisocial behavior. Some delinquents convicted of violent crimes show a lack of feeling for their victims' distress. A 13-year-old boy convicted of violently mugging a number of older adults, when asked about the pain he had caused one blind woman, said, "What do I care? I'm not her" (Damon, 1988).

In one study, researchers found that empathy increased from 12 to 16 years of age (Allemand, Steiger, & Fend, 2015). Also in this study, girls showed more empathy than did boys. Further, adolescent empathy predicted a number of social competencies (adult empathy, communication skills, and relationship satisfaction, for example) two decades later. In addition, a recent study revealed that a higher degree of empathy was linked to greater civic engagement by adolescents (Metzger & others 2018). And a recent study found that adolescents with a lower level of empathy were more likely to engage in dating violence (Glowacz & Courtain, 2021).

The Contemporary Perspective   You have learned that classical psychoanalytic theory emphasizes the power of unconscious guilt in moral development but that other theories emphasize the role of empathy. Today, many developmentalists note that both positive feelings, such as empathy, sympathy, admiration, and self-esteem, and negative feelings, such as anger, outrage, shame, and guilt, contribute to adolescents' moral development (Spinrad & Eisenberg, 2020). When strongly experienced, these emotions influence adolescents to act in accord with standards of right and wrong. Such emotions as empathy, shame, guilt, and anxiety over other people's violations of standards are present early in development and undergo developmental change throughout childhood and adolescence. Also, connections between these emotions can occur and the connections may influence adolescents' development. For example, in a recent study, participants' guilt proneness combined with their empathy to predict an increase in prosocial behavior (Torstveit, Sutterlin, & Lugo, 2016).

These emotions provide a natural base for adolescents' acquisition of moral values, both orienting adolescents toward moral events and motivating them to pay close attention to such events (Thompson, 2014). However, moral emotions do not operate in a vacuum to build adolescents' moral awareness, and they are not sufficient in themselves to generate moral responsivity. They do not give the "substance" of moral regulation—the rules, values, and standards of behavior that adolescents need to understand and act on. Moral emotions are inextricably interwoven with the cognitive and social aspects of adolescents' development.

empathy Reaction to another's feelings with an emotional response that is similar to the other's feelings.

developmental **connection**

Personality

The contemporary view of personality emphasizes the interaction of traits and situations. Connect to "The Self, Identity, Emotion, and Personality."

developmental **connection**

Identity

According to James Marcia, what are the four statuses of identity development? Connect to "The Self, Identity, Emotion, and Personality."

moral identity An aspect of personality that is present when individuals have moral notions and commitments that are central to their lives.

Moral Traits

Caring	Helpful
Compassionate	Honest
Fair	Kind
Generous	

Questions:

- Is being someone who has these characteristics an important part of who you are?
- Are you involved in activities that indicate to others that you have these characteristics?
- Would it make you feel good to have these characteristics?

FIGURE 1

DO YOU HAVE A MORAL IDENTITY? A moral identity questionnaire has been developed that provides a list of moral traits and asks individuals to determine the extent to which these traits characterize a person they know (Aquino & Reed, 2002). The person with these characteristics could be you or it could be someone else. For a moment, visualize the kind of person who has these characteristics. Imagine how the individual would think, feel, and act. When you have a clear image of what this person would be like, answer the questions that follow.

MORAL PERSONALITY

So far we have examined three key dimensions of moral development: thoughts, behavior, and feelings. Recently there has been a surge of interest in a fourth dimension: personality (Lapsley, LaPorte, & Kelley, 2022; Sun & Goodwin, 2020). Thoughts, behavior, and feelings can all be involved in an individual's moral personality. In this view, behaving in a manner that violates this moral commitment places the integrity of the self at risk (Lapsley, LaPorte, & Kelley, 2022).

For many years, skepticism greeted the assertion that a set of moral characteristics or traits could be discovered that would constitute a core of moral personality. Much of this skepticism stemmed from the results of Hartshorne and May's (1928–1930) classic study, and Walter Mischel's (1968) social learning theory and research, which argued that situations trump traits when attempts are made to predict moral behavior. Mischel's (2004) subsequent research and theory and Bandura's (2010a, b) social cognitive theory have emphasized the importance of "person" factors while still recognizing situational variations. Until recently, though, there has been little interest in studying what might comprise a moral personality. Three aspects of moral personality that have recently been emphasized are (1) moral identity, (2) moral character, and (3) moral exemplars.

Moral Identity A central aspect of the recent interest in the role of personality in moral development focuses on **moral identity**. Individuals have a moral identity when moral notions and commitments are central to their life (Hardy, Krettenauer, & Hunt, 2020). In this view, behaving in a manner that violates this moral commitment places the integrity of the self at risk (Lapsley, Reilly, & Narváez, 2020). To evaluate the extent to which you have a moral identity, see Figure 1.

Based on years of research, Darcia Narváez (2010) has concluded that a mature moral individual cares about morality and being a moral person. For these individuals, moral responsibility is central to their identity. Mature moral individuals engage in moral metacognition, including moral self-monitoring and moral self-reflection. Moral self-monitoring involves monitoring one's thoughts and actions related to moral situations and engaging in self-control when it is needed. Moral self-reflection encompasses critical evaluations of one's self-judgments and efforts to minimize bias and self-deception.

What are some outcomes of having a moral identity? A study of 9,500 college students revealed that moral identity predicted all five health outcomes assessed (anxiety, depression, hazardous alcohol use, sexual risk taking, and self-esteem) (Hardy & others, 2013).

Earlier we discussed Albert Bandura's (2015) recent ideas about moral disengagement and how too many people disengage themselves from morally reprehensible actions and still manage to feel morally good about themselves. While an individual's commitment to a moral identity emphasizes the importance of behaving in a moral way, engaging in moral disengagement shields an individual from thinking that he or she has done something immoral or wrong (Lapsley, LaPorte, & Kelley, 2022). Recent research on bullying has found that bullies are especially likely to use moral disengagement strategies (Travlos & others, 2021). A meta-analysis confirmed that moral disengagement is a significant factor in the aggressive behavior of bullies (Gini, Pozzoli, & Hymel, 2014). Also, a recent three-year longitudinal study of young adolescents revealed that over time adolescents who increased their verbal bullying had a higher level of moral disengagement (Bjarehed & others, 2021). And recent research indicates that having low empathy is likely linked to a bully's moral disengagement and aggressive behavior (Mascia & others, 2021).

Moral Character James Rest (1995) argued that moral character has not been adequately emphasized as an aspect of moral development. In Rest's view, *moral character* involves having strong convictions, persisting, and overcoming distractions and obstacles. If individuals don't have moral character, they may wilt under pressure or fatigue, fail to follow through with commitments, or become distracted and discouraged and fail to behave morally. Moral character presupposes that the person has set moral goals and that achieving those goals involves the commitment to act in accord with those goals (Helzer & Critcher, 2018). Rest (1995) also concluded that

Rosa Parks (*left photo*), sitting in the front of a bus after the U.S. Supreme Court ruled that segregation was illegal on her city's bus system, and Andrei Sakharov (*right photo*) are moral exemplars. Parks (1913–2005), an African American seamstress in Montgomery, Alabama, became famous for her quiet, revolutionary act of not giving up her bus seat to a non-Latinx white man in 1955. Her heroic act is cited by many historians as the beginning of the modern civil rights movement in the United States. Across the next four decades, Parks continued to work for progress in civil rights. Sakharov (1921–1989) was a Soviet physicist who spent several decades designing nuclear weapons for the Soviet Union and came to be known as the father of the Soviet hydrogen bomb. However, later in his life he became one of the Soviet Union's most outspoken critics and worked relentlessly to promote human rights and democracy.
(left): Bettmann/Getty Images; (right): Alain Nogues/Sygma/Getty Images

motivation has not been adequately emphasized in describing moral development. In Rest's view, *moral motivation* involves prioritizing moral values over other personal values.

Lawrence Walker (2002) has studied moral character by examining people's conceptions of moral excellence. Among the moral virtues people emphasize are "honesty, truthfulness, and trustworthiness, as well as those of care, compassion, thoughtfulness, and considerateness. Other salient traits revolve around virtues of dependability, loyalty, and conscientiousness" (Walker, 2002, p. 74). In Walker's perspective, these aspects of moral character provide a foundation for positive social relationships and functioning.

In the chapter on "The Self, Identity, Emotion, and Personality," we described the view of William Damon (2008) that purpose is a key aspect of adolescent competence and identity. In a recent study of young adolescents, Damon and his colleagues (Malin, Liauw, & Damon, 2017), examined links between purpose and three components of character development: gratitude, compassion, and grit. In this study, adolescents with a greater sense of purpose were characterized as having higher levels of all three components of character development.

Moral Exemplars   **Moral exemplars** are people who have lived exemplary lives. Moral exemplars, such as Jewel Cash who was portrayed at the beginning of the chapter, have a moral personality, identity, character, and set of virtues that reflect moral excellence and commitment (Frimer & Sinclair, 2016). The point of studying and conducting research on moral exemplars is to be able to characterize the ideal endpoint of moral development and understand how people got there.

In one study, three different exemplars of morality were examined—brave, caring, and just (Walker & Hennig, 2004). Different personality profiles emerged for the three exemplars. The brave exemplar was characterized by being dominant and extraverted, the caring exemplar by being nurturant and agreeable, and the just exemplar by being conscientious and open to experience. However, a number of traits characterized all three moral exemplars, and the researchers used these traits to construct a possible core of moral functioning. These core traits included honesty and dependability.

SOCIAL DOMAIN THEORY

Social domain theory states that there are different domains of social knowledge and reasoning, including moral, social conventional, and personal domains. In social domain theory, children's and adolescents' moral, social conventional, and personal knowledge and reasoning emerge

----- → →
developmental **connection**
Personality
Conscientiousness is linked to a number of positive outcomes in adolescence. Connect to "The Self, Identity, Emotion, and Personality."
← -----

moral exemplars People who have led exemplary lives.

social domain theory Theory that identifies different domains of social knowledge and reasoning, including moral, social conventional, and personal domains. These domains arise from children's and adolescents' attempts to understand and deal with different forms of social experience.

from their attempts to understand and deal with different forms of social experience (Jambon & Smetana, 2020). In the view of leading experts Judith Smetana (2013) and Eliot Turiel (2018), social domain theory emphasizes that the key aspects of morality involve judgments about welfare, justice, and rights, exploring how individuals struggle with moral issues in their social lives. Social domain theory stresses that children, even very young ones, are motivated to evaluate and make sense of their social world (Jambon & Smetana, 2020).

Social conventional reasoning focuses on conventional rules that have been established by social consensus in order to control behavior and maintain the social system. The rules themselves are arbitrary, such as raising your hand in class before speaking, using one staircase at school to go up and the other to go down, not cutting in front of someone standing in line to buy movie tickets, and stopping at a stop sign when driving. There are sanctions if we violate these conventions, although the rules can be changed by consensus.

In contrast, moral reasoning focuses on ethical issues and rules of morality. Unlike conventional rules, moral rules are not arbitrary. They are obligatory, widely accepted, and somewhat impersonal (Turiel, 2018). Rules that prohibit lying, cheating, stealing, and physically harming another person are moral rules because violation of these rules affronts ethical standards that exist apart from social consensus and convention. Moral judgments involve concepts of justice, whereas social conventional judgments are concepts of social organization. Violations of moral rules are usually regarded with greater concern than violations of conventional rules.

The social conventional approach is a serious challenge to Kohlberg's theory because Kohlberg argued that social conventions are a stop-over on the road to higher moral sophistication. For social conventional reasoning advocates, social conventional reasoning is not lower than postconventional reasoning but rather something that needs to be disentangled from the moral thread (Jambon & Smetana, 2020). However, in a recent study, children and adolescents said that changes in moral beliefs are more disruptive to one's identity than changes in social-conventional beliefs (Lefebvre & Krettenaur, 2020). Also in this study, the children and adolescents reported that changes in negative moral beliefs are more disruptive to one's identity than changes in positive moral beliefs.

Recently, a distinction also has been made between moral and conventional issues, which are viewed as legitimately subject to adult social regulation, and personal issues, which are more likely to be determined by the child's or adolescent's independent decision making and personal discretion (Jambon & Smetana, 2018). Personal issues include control over one's body, privacy, and choice of friends and activities. Thus, some actions belong to a *personal* domain not governed by moral strictures or social norms.

social conventional reasoning Thoughts about social consensus and convention, as opposed to moral reasoning that stresses ethical issues.

Review *Connect* Reflect

 LG1 Discuss what moral development is and the domains of moral development.

Review

- What is moral development?
- What are the main points of Kohlberg's theory of moral development? What aspects of Kohlberg's theory have been criticized?
- What are some basic processes in the behavioral view of moral development? What is the social cognitive view of moral development? What is the nature of prosocial behavior?
- What is the psychoanalytic view of moral development? What role does empathy play in moral development? What is the contemporary perspective on moral feeling?
- What is the moral personality approach to moral development?
- What characterizes the social domain theory of moral development?

Connect

- Considering what you have learned about gender similarities and differences, were you surprised by findings cited in this section about gender's role in moral development?

Reflect *Your Own Personal Journey of Life*

- Which of the five approaches we have discussed—cognitive, psychoanalytic, behavioral/social cognitive, personality, and domain theory—do you think best describes the way you have developed morally? Explain.

Parenting   Schools   Culture

Earlier in the chapter, you learned that both Piaget and Kohlberg maintain that peer relations are an important context for moral development. Adolescents' experiences with their parents, schools, and culture also are important contexts for moral development.

PARENTING

Both Piaget and Kohlberg held that parents do not provide any unique or essential inputs to children's moral development. They did acknowledge that parents are responsible for providing general role-taking opportunities and assisting in the resolution of cognitive conflict, but they attribute the primary role in moral development to peers. Researchers have revealed, however, that both parents and peers contribute to the development of moral maturity (Mounts & Allen, 2020). In general, higher-level moral reasoning in adolescence is linked with parenting that is supportive and encourages adolescents to question and expand on their moral reasoning (Lapsley, 2020).

Culture contributes to the role that families play in adolescents' moral development. One study revealed that Mexican American adolescents had stronger prosocial tendencies if their parents had higher familism values (Knight & others, 2016). Asian children and adolescents also are more likely to engage in prosocial behavior than North American children and adolescents (Eisenberg, Spinrad, & Morris, 2013).

Parental discipline also plays an important role in moral development. In Freud's psychoanalytic theory, the aspects of child rearing that encourage moral development are practices that instill fears of being punished and of losing parental love. Developmentalists who have studied the influence of child-rearing techniques on moral development have often focused on parents' disciplinary methods (Lansford, 2020). These include love withdrawal, power assertion, and induction (Hoffman, 1970):

- **Love withdrawal** comes closest to the psychoanalytic emphasis on fear of punishment and of losing parental love. It is a disciplinary technique in which a parent withholds attention or love from the adolescent, as when the parent refuses to talk to the adolescent or states a dislike for the adolescent.

- **Power assertion** is a disciplinary technique in which a parent attempts to gain control over the adolescent or the adolescent's resources. Examples include spanking, threatening, or removing privileges.

- **Induction** is the disciplinary technique in which a parent uses reason and explains how the adolescent's antisocial actions are likely to affect others. Examples of induction include comments such as "Don't hit him. He was only trying to help" and "Why are you yelling at her? She didn't mean to hurt your feelings."

Moral development theorist and researcher Martin Hoffman (1970) argues that any type of parental discipline produces emotional arousal in adolescents. Love withdrawal and power assertion are likely to evoke a very high level of arousal, with love withdrawal generating considerable anxiety and power assertion considerable hostility. Induction is more likely to produce a moderate level of arousal in adolescents, a level that permits them to attend to the cognitive rationales parents offer.

When a parent uses power assertion or love withdrawal, the adolescent may be so aroused emotionally that, even if the parent provides explanations about the consequences for others of the adolescent's actions, the adolescent might not attend to them. Power assertion presents parents as weak models of self-control—as individuals who cannot control how they express their own feelings. Accordingly, adolescents may imitate this model of poor self-control when they face stressful circumstances. The use of induction, however, focuses the adolescent's attention on the action's consequences for others, not on the adolescent's own shortcomings. For these reasons, Hoffman (1988) notes that parents should use induction to encourage adolescents' moral development.

love withdrawal A disciplinary technique in which a parent withholds attention or love from the adolescent.

power assertion A disciplinary technique in which a parent attempts to gain control over the adolescent or the adolescent's resources.

induction A disciplinary technique in which a parent uses reason and explains how the adolescent's actions affect others.

How Can We Raise Moral Children and Adolescents?

Parental discipline contributes to children's moral development, but other aspects of parenting also play important roles, including providing opportunities for perspective taking and modeling moral behavior and thinking. Nancy Eisenberg and her colleagues (Eisenberg, Spinrad, & Knafo, 2015; Eisenberg & Valiente, 2002; Spinrad & Eisenberg, 2020) suggest that parents who adopt the following strategies are more likely to have children and adolescents who behave morally:

- Be warm and supportive, use inductive reasoning, and engage in authoritative parenting.
- Avoid being punitive, and do not use love withdrawal as a disciplinary strategy.
- Use inductive discipline.
- Provide opportunities for children and youth to learn about others' perspectives and feelings.
- Involve children and youth in family decision making and in the process of thinking about moral decisions.
- Model moral behaviors and thinking, and provide opportunities for children and youth to do so.
- Provide information about what behaviors are expected and why.
- Foster an internal rather than an external sense of morality.
- Help children and youth to understand and regulate negative emotion rather than becoming overaroused.

   Parents who show this configuration of behaviors are likely to foster concern and caring about others in their children and youth, and to create a positive parent-child relationship. In terms of relationship quality, secure attachment may play an important role in children's and

What are some parenting characteristics and practices that are linked with children's and adolescents' moral development?
Digital Vision/Getty Images

adolescents' moral development (Goffin, Boldt, & Kochanska, 2018). A secure attachment can place children on a positive path for internalizing parents' socializing goals and adhering to family values. In one study, early secure attachment defused a maladaptive trajectory toward antisocial outcomes (Kochanska & others, 2010a). In another study, securely attached children's willing, cooperative stance was linked to positive future socialization outcomes such as a lower incidence of externalizing problems (aggression, for example) (Kochanska & others, 2010b).

   Researchers who study the effects of parental disciplinary techniques have found that induction is more positively related to moral development than is love withdrawal or power assertion, although the findings vary according to developmental levels and socioeconomic status. For example, induction works better with adolescents and older children than with preschool children (Brody & Schaffer, 1982) and better with middle-SES than with lower-SES children (Hoffman, 1970). Older children and adolescents are generally better able to understand the reasons given to them and better at perspective taking than younger children are. Some theorists believe internalization of society's moral standards is more likely to take place among middle-SES than among lower-SES individuals because internalization is more highly regarded in the middle-SES culture (Kohn, 1977).

   How can parents apply such findings in choosing strategies for raising a moral child and adolescent? For suggestions, see the *Connecting with Health and Well-Being* interlude.

SCHOOLS

Schools are an important context for moral development (Lapsley, Reilly, & Narváez, 2020; Narváez, 2021). Moral education is a hotly debated topic in educational circles (Krettenauer, 2021). We first study one of the earliest analyses of moral education and then examine some contemporary views on moral education.

The Hidden Curriculum   Eight decades ago, educator John Dewey (1933) recognized that even when schools do not have specific programs in moral education, they provide moral education through a "hidden curriculum." The **hidden curriculum** is conveyed by the moral atmosphere that is a part of every school.

The moral atmosphere is created by school and classroom rules, the moral orientation of teachers and school administrators, and curriculum materials. Teachers serve as models of ethical or unethical behavior. Classroom rules and peer relations at school transmit attitudes about cheating, lying, stealing, and consideration for others. And, by enforcing rules and regulations, the school administration infuses the school with a value system.

Character Education   Considerable interest has been shown in **character education,** a direct education approach that involves teaching students a basic moral literacy to prevent them from engaging in immoral behavior and doing harm to themselves or others (Arthur, 2014). In 2018, 18 states had a legislative mandate for character education in schools; another 18 had legislation that encouraged character education; 7 supported character education, but without legislation; and 8 had no legislation specifying character education. The argument is that such behaviors as lying, stealing, and cheating are wrong and that students should be taught this throughout their education (Berkowitz, 2012).

Advocates of character education emphasize that every school should have an explicit moral code that is clearly communicated to students (MacDonnell & others, 2021). According to traditional views of character education, any violations of the code should be met with sanctions; however, recent approaches advocate a more democratic approach. Instruction in specified moral concepts, such as cheating, can take the form of example and definition, class discussions and role playing, or rewarding students for proper behavior. More recently, encouraging students to develop a care perspective has been accepted as a relevant aspect of character education (Noddings, 2016). Rather than just instructing adolescents to refrain from morally deviant behavior, advocates of a care perspective encourage students to engage in prosocial behaviors such as considering others' feelings, being sensitive to others, and helping others.

Lawrence Walker (2002) argues that it is important for character education to involve more than displaying a list of moral virtues on a classroom wall. Instead, he emphasizes that children and adolescents need to participate in critical discussions of values; they need to discuss and reflect on how to incorporate virtues into their daily lives. Walker also advocates exposing children to moral exemplars worthy of emulating and getting children to participate in community service. The character education approach reflects the moral personality domain of moral development discussed earlier in the chapter (Walker, 2016).

Values Clarification   A second approach to providing moral education is **values clarification,** which involves helping individuals to identify their purpose in life and to determine what outcomes are worth working for. Unlike character education, which tells students what their values should be, values clarification encourages students to define their own values and to understand the values of others.

Advocates of values clarification say it is value-free. However, critics argue that the content of these programs offends community standards and that the values-clarification exercises fail to stress right behavior.

Service Learning   Over the last several decades, there has been a growing understanding that the quality of a society can be considerably enhanced when citizens become proactive in providing service to the community and the nation. The initial call to serve came in John F. Kennedy's inaugural address after he was sworn in as president on January 20, 1961, when he advised his listeners to "Ask not what your country can do for you—ask what you can do for your country." This perspective was expressed in the federal government's commitment to develop programs that emphasize service. Over time, this commitment has produced the Peace Corps, Americorps, Senior Corps, and VISTA. Much of this effort is orchestrated through the Corporation for National and Community Service. To view program descriptions and learn about opportunities to volunteer, visit www.nationalservice.gov.

At the beginning of the chapter you read about Jewel Cash, who is strongly motivated to make a positive difference in her community. Jewel Cash has a sense of social responsibility that an increasing number of educational programs

hidden curriculum The pervasive moral atmosphere that characterizes every school.

character education A direct moral education approach that involves teaching students a basic moral literacy to prevent them from engaging in immoral behavior or doing harm to themselves or others.

values clarification An educational approach that focuses on helping people clarify what is important to them, what is worth working for, and what is their purpose in life. Students are encouraged to define their own values and understand others' values.

What are some positive outcomes of service learning?
Hero Images/Getty Images

Finding a Way to Get a Playground

Twelve-year-old Katie Bell more than just about anything else wanted a playground in her New Jersey town. She knew that other kids also wanted one too, so she put together a group that generated fundraising ideas for the playground. They presented their ideas to the town council. Her group got more youth involved. They helped raise money by selling candy and sandwiches door-to-door. Katie says, "We learned to work as a community. This will be an important place for people to go and have picnics and make new friends." Katie's advice: "You won't get anywhere if you don't try."

What moral lessons from her family or school do you think Katie Bell had already learned when she undertook the playground project?

Katie Bell (*front*) and some of her volunteers.
Ronald Cortes

seek to promote in students through **service learning,** a form of education in which students provide service to the community. In service learning, adolescents engage in activities such as tutoring, helping older adults, working in a hospital, assisting at a child-care center, or cleaning up a vacant lot to make a play area. An important goal of service learning is to encourage adolescents become less self-centered and more strongly motivated to help others (Lai & Hui, 2021). Service learning tends to be more effective when two conditions are met (Nucci, 2006): (1) students are given some degree of choice in the service activities in which they participate, and (2) students are provided opportunities to reflect about their participation.

Researchers have found that service learning benefits adolescents and emerging adults in a number of ways (Hart, 2020). Improvements in adolescent development related to service learning include higher grades in school, increased goal setting, higher self-esteem, a heightened sense of being able to make a difference for others, identity achievement, exploration of moral issues, and an increased likelihood of serving as volunteers in the future. In one study, 74 percent of African American and 70 percent of Latinx adolescents said that service-learning programs could have a "fairly or very big effect" on keeping students from dropping out of school (Bridgeland, Dilulio, & Wulsin, 2008).

A research analysis revealed that 26 percent of U.S. public high schools require students to participate in service learning (Metz & Youniss, 2005). The benefits of service learning, both for the volunteers and for the recipients, suggest that more adolescents should be required to participate in such programs (Hart, 2020).

Cheating A moral education concern is how extensive cheating is and how to handle cheating if it is detected (Steger, Schroeders, & Wilhelm, 2021). Academic cheating can take many forms, including plagiarism, using "cheat sheets" during an exam, copying from a neighbor during a test, purchasing papers, and falsifying lab results. A 2012 survey revealed that 51 percent of secondary school students said they had cheated on a test in school during the past year, and one-third of the students reported that they had plagiarized information from the Internet in the past year (Josephson Institute of Ethics, 2012). Also, a recent survey of college students indicated that 86 percent said they have cheated (Kessler International, 2017). In this survey, students reported that the advent of online classes and sophisticated mobile devices make it easier than ever to cheat.

service learning A form of education that promotes social responsibility and service to the community.

Why do students cheat? Among the reasons students give for cheating include pressure to get high grades, time constraints, poor teaching, and lack of interest (Stephens, 2008). In terms of poor teaching, "students are more likely to cheat when they perceive their teacher to be incompetent, unfair, and uncaring" (Stephens, 2008, p. 140).

A long history of research also implicates the power of the situation in determining whether students cheat (Hartshorne & May, 1928–1930). For example, students are more likely to cheat when they are not being closely monitored during a test; when they know their peers are cheating; when they know whether or not another student has been caught cheating; and when student scores are made public (Harmon, Lambrinos, & Kennedy, 2008). One study revealed that college students who engaged in academic cheating were characterized by the personality traits of low conscientiousness and low agreeableness (Williams, Nathanson, & Paulhus, 2010).

Among strategies recommended for decreasing academic cheating are preventive measures such as making sure students are aware of what constitutes cheating, describing the consequences if they do cheat, closely monitoring students' behavior while they are taking tests, and emphasizing the importance of being a moral, responsible individual who engages in academic integrity. In promoting academic integrity, many colleges have instituted an honor code policy that emphasizes self-responsibility, fairness, trust, and scholarship. However, few secondary schools have developed honor code policies. The Center for Academic Integrity (www.academicintegrity.org) has extensive materials available to help schools develop academic integrity policies.

What are some factors that influence whether adolescents engage in cheating?
Rubberball/Nicole Hill/Getty Images

An Integrative Approach   Darcia Narváez (2020) emphasizes an *integrative approach* to moral education that encompasses both the reflective moral thinking and commitment to justice advocated in Kohlberg's approach, and the development of a particular moral character advocated in the character education approach. She highlights the Child Development Project as an excellent example of an integrative moral education approach. In the Child Development Project, students are given multiple opportunities to discuss other students' experiences, which inspire empathy and perspective taking, and they participate in exercises that encourage them to reflect on their own behaviors in terms of values such as fairness and social responsibility (Battistich, 2008). Adults coach students in ethical decision making and guide them in becoming more caring individuals. Students experience a caring community, not only in the classroom, but also in after-school activities and through parental involvement in the program. Research evaluations of the Child Development Project link it to an improved sense of community, an increase in prosocial behavior, better interpersonal understanding, and an increase in social problem solving (Battistich, 2008; Solomon & others, 1990).

CULTURE

Earlier in this chapter, we described how culture plays a much stronger role in moral development than Kohlberg envisioned. Here we expand this discussion, focusing on cultural similarities and variations in moral development.

Some aspects of morality such as honesty are endorsed across most cultures. However, other aspects of morality have shown variations in different cultures (Graham, 2020; Jensen, 2020a, b). Researchers have found that people in Western, Educated, Industrialized, Rich, and Democratic (WEIRD) cultures are more likely to have moral codes that emphasize individual rights and independence while those in non-WEIRD cultures are more likely to endorse duty-based communal obligations and a collective interdependence (Graham & others, 2016). Further, cultural variations in shame and guilt have been found. In one study, children in Japan showed the highest level of shame, children in Korea the highest level of guilt, and children in the United States the highest level of pride (Furukawa, Tangney, & Higashibara, 2012).

Differences also can occur within a particular society. For example, in the United States, individuals of higher socioeconomic status (SES) make more utilitarian decisions when faced with moral dilemmas than their lower-SES counterparts (Cote, Piff, & Willer, 2013). A further within-culture moral variation is that low-SES individuals in WEIRD cultures tend to be more cooperative than wealthy people are (Piff & others, 2010). Lower-SES individuals also have been found to be less likely to lie or cheat, at least in part because wealthier individuals are more likely to accept greed (Piff & others, 2016).

In addition, recent research has increasingly examined how families socialize children's moral development (Carlo & Pierotti, 2020). For example, *familism* values stress the importance of giving priority to obligations and maintaining close family relationships. Research indicates that familism is especially important in Mexican American and Latinx families. In one study, young adolescents in Mexican American families who strongly endorsed familism values had higher scores on measures of prosocial tendencies (Knight & others, 2016). In the next main section of the chapter, in our further coverage of prosocial behavior, we will describe other research on Latinx families.

Review *Connect* Reflect

LG2 Describe how the contexts of parenting, schools, and culture can influence moral development.

Review
- How does parental discipline affect moral development? What are some effective parenting strategies for advancing children's and adolescents' moral development?
- What is the hidden curriculum? What are some contemporary approaches to moral education used in schools? How does service learning affect adolescents?
- How does culture influence adolescents' moral development?

Connect
- How might cultural and ethnic identity influence parents' approaches to their children's moral development?

Reflect *Your Own Personal Journey of Life*
- What type of discipline did your parents use with you? What effect do you think this has had on your moral development?

3 Values, Religion, and Spirituality

LG3 Explain the roles of values, religion, and spirituality in adolescents' and emerging adults' lives.

Values

Religion and Spirituality

What are adolescents' and emerging adults' values like today? How powerful are the influences of religion and spirituality in adolescents' and emerging adults' lives?

VALUES

Values are beliefs and attitudes about the way things should be. They involve what is important to us. We attach values to all sorts of things: politics, religion, money, sex, education, helping others, family, friends, career, cheating, self-respect, and so on. Values reflect the intrapersonal dimension of morality introduced at the beginning of the chapter. To identify the values that are most important to you, see Figure 2.

One way to measure what people value is to ask them what their goals are. Over the past five decades, traditional-aged college students have shown an increased concern for personal well-being and a decreased concern for the well-being of others, especially for the disadvantaged (Stolzenberg & others, 2020). As shown in Figure 3, today's college freshmen are more strongly motivated to be well-off financially and less motivated to develop a meaningful philosophy of life than were their counterparts of 50 years ago. In 2019, 84.3 percent of students (the highest percent ever in this survey) viewed becoming well-off financially as an "essential" or a "very important" objective compared with only 42 percent in 1971.

values Beliefs and attitudes about the way things should be.

Values

___Having good friends and getting along with people   ___Being a good person

___Having a good relationship with a romantic partner   ___Feeling secure

___Having self-respect   ___Having peace of mind

___Being well-off financially   ___Being happy

___Having a good spiritual or religious life   ___Being healthy

___Being competent at my work   ___Being intelligent

___Having the respect of others   ___Having inner peace

___Making an important contribution to the world   ___Living an exciting life

The following values are most important to me:

1. _____

2. _____

3. _____

4. _____

5. _____

FIGURE 2

WHAT ARE MY VALUES? Look at the following list of values and think about the extent to which each value characterizes you. Place check marks next to the five values that are most important to you. Then go back over the values you selected and rank order them from 1 to 5, with 1 being the most important.

There are, however, some signs that U.S. college students are shifting toward a stronger interest in promoting the welfare of society. In the survey just described, interest in developing a meaningful philosophy of life increased from 39 percent to 49.8 percent of U.S. college freshmen from 2001 through 2019 (Stolzenberg & others, 2020) (see Figure 3). Also in this survey, the percentage of college freshmen who said the chances are very good that they will participate in volunteer activities or community service programs increased from 18 percent in 1990 to 38.2 percent in 2019 (Stolzenberg & others, 2020).

Other research on values has found that adolescents who are involved in groups that connect them to others in school, their communities, or faith-based institutions report higher levels of social trust, altruism, commitments to the common good of people, and endorsements of the rights of immigrants to obtain full inclusion in society (Flanagan & Faison, 2001). In this research, adolescents who were uninvolved in such groups were more likely to endorse self-interested and materialistic values.

The research we have just discussed was conducted by Constance Flanagan and her colleagues. To read further about her work, see the *Connecting with Careers* profile.

Our discussion of values relates to the view William Damon (2008) proposed in *The Path to Purpose*. Damon concluded that a major difficulty confronting today's youth is their lack of a clear sense of what they want to do with their lives—that too many youth are essentially "rudderless." Damon (2008, p. 8) found that only about 20 percent of 12- to 22-year-olds in the United States expressed "a clear vision of where they want to go, what they want to accomplish in life, and why." He argues that their goals and values too often focus on the short

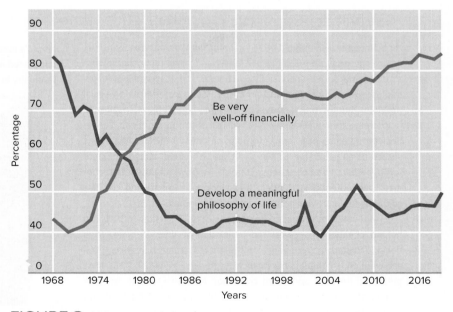

FIGURE 3

CHANGING FRESHMAN LIFE GOALS, 1968 TO 2019. In the last five decades, a significant change has occurred in freshman students' life goals. A far greater percentage of today's college freshmen state that an "essential" or "very important" life goal is to be very well-off financially, and far fewer state that developing a meaningful philosophy of life is an "essential" or a "very important" life goal.

Constance Flanagan, Professor of Youth Civic Development

Constance (Connie) Flanagan is a professor of youth civic development in the College of Agricultural Sciences at Pennsylvania State University. Her research focuses on youths' views about justice and the factors in families, schools, and communities that promote civic values, connections, and skills in youth (Flanagan, 2004).

Flanagan obtained her undergraduate degree in psychology from Duquesne University, her master's degree in education from the University of Iowa, and her Ph.D. from the University of Michigan. She has a special interest in improving U.S. social policy for adolescents and serves as co-chair of the Committee on Child Development. In addition to teaching undergraduate and graduate classes, conducting research, and serving on various committees, Flanagan evaluates research for potential publication as a member of the editorial board of the *Journal of Adolescent Research* and the *Journal of Research on Adolescence*. She also presents her ideas and research at numerous national and international meetings.

Connie Flanagan with adolescents.
Courtesy of Dr. Connie Flanagan

term, such as getting a good grade on a test this week and finding a date for a dance, rather than developing a plan for the future based on positive values. The types of questions that adults can pose to youth to guide them toward developing more purposeful values include "What's most important in your life? Why do you care about those things? . . . What does it mean to be a good person?" (Damon, 2008, p. 135).

Nina Vasan, Superstar Volunteer and Author

Nina Vasan's leadership began at home in Vienna, West Virginia, where she grew up watching her family and community champion a shared value: social responsibility. At age 16, she observed that fellow adolescents had passion and promising ideas for addressing social problems, but there was no system to engage their efforts. Inspired to help create this opportunity, she worked with the American Cancer Society to launch ACS Teens. Through an online network, ACS Teens served as an incubator for social change: it trained, mobilized, mentored, and united adolescent volunteers, empowering them to recognize their potential as leaders and work together to find creative solutions for improving health in their communities.

Motivated by the sense of purpose she felt when ACS Teens helped change tobacco-related legislation in West Virginia, Nina decided to study government as a student at Harvard University. Then she went on to complete her medical degree at Harvard. In 2013, Nina published her first book with co-author Jennifer Przybylo, another superstar volunteer whom she met in high school. Their book, *Do Good Well,* reflects Nina and Jennifer's motivation to get others involved in leadership and encourage them to take action in improving

people's lives. *Do Good Well* became a #1 Amazon Best Seller and is being used in schools around the world. Today, Nina Vasan practices psychiatry in the San Francisco Bay area.

Nina Vasan (*left*) with Jennifer Przybylo.
Courtesy of Nina Vasan

What values are likely to motivate Nina Vasan?

RELIGION AND SPIRITUALITY

In Damon's (2008) view, one long-standing source for discovering purpose in life is religion. Can religion be distinguished from spirituality? Pamela King and her colleagues (King, Ramos, & Clardy, 2013; King, Vaughn, & Merola, 2020) offer the following distinctions:

- **Religion** is an organized set of beliefs, practices, rituals, and symbols that increases an individual's connection to a sacred or transcendent other (God, higher power, or ultimate truth).

- **Religiousness** refers to the degree of affiliation with an organized religion, participation in its prescribed rituals and practices, connection with its beliefs, and involvement in a community of believers.

- **Spirituality** involves experiencing something beyond oneself in a transcendent manner and living in a way that benefits others and society.

Religious issues are important to many adolescents and emerging adults (Cesari, 2021). However, in the twenty-first century, a downturn in religious interest among college students has been observed. In a national study of American college freshmen conducted in 2019, 65.7 percent said they had attended religious services frequently or occasionally during their senior year in high school, down from 73 percent in 2010, and down also from a high of 85 percent in 1997 (Stolzenberg & others, 2020). Further, in 2019, twice as many first-year college students (16.5 percent) reported having no religious preference compared with first-year college students in 1978 (8 percent). And in one study, across the first three semesters of college, students became less likely to attend religious services or engage in religious activities (Stoppa & Lefkowitz, 2010).

A developmental study revealed that religiousness declined from 14 to 20 years of age in the United States (Koenig, McGue, & Iacono, 2008) (see Figure 4). In this study, religiousness was assessed with items such as frequency of prayer, frequency of discussing religious teachings, frequency of deciding moral actions for religious reasons, and the overall importance of religion in one's everyday life. As indicated in Figure 4, more change in religiousness occurred from 14 to 18 years of age than from 20 to 24 years of age. Also, attending religious services was highest at 14 years of age, declining from 14 to 18 years of age and increasing at 20 years of age. More change occurred in attending religious services than in religiousness. And in a recent study involving individuals from 12 to 34 years of age, although attendance at religious services declined with age, the importance of religion increased and the importance of prayer remained stable over time (Dew, Fuemmeler, & Koenig, 2020).

However, cultural variations in adolescents' religiosity are substantial, and these variations are receiving increased attention because of globalization. As Lene Arnett Jensen (2021) argues, a "one-size fits all" approach has too often been taken in discussing adolescent religion, likely because a large majority of research has been conducted with non-Latinx white middle- and upper-SES adolescents in the United States. As an indication of this cultural variability, in an analysis of responses to the World Values Survey administered to 18- to 24-year-olds, emerging adults in less-developed countries were more likely to be religious than their counterparts in more-developed countries (Lippman & Keith, 2006). For example, the proportion of emerging adults who reported that religion was very important in their lives ranged from a low of 0 in Japan to a high of 93 percent in Nigeria, and belief in God ranged from a low of 40 percent in Sweden to a high of 100 percent in Pakistan. In Thailand, Buddhism is the dominant religion but an increasing number of urban adolescents are criticizing the religion, likely as a result of globalization (Jensen, 2021). For example, one Thai adolescent remarked that it is easy to become bored with Buddhism because there's nothing new in the religion, unlike the rapid advances in technology that produce new versions of smartphones almost annually (McKenzie, 2019).

Researchers have found that adolescent girls are more religious than are adolescent boys (King & Boyatzis, 2015). One study of 13- to 17-year-olds revealed that girls are more likely to frequently attend religious services, perceive that religion shapes their daily lives, participate in religious youth groups, pray alone often, and feel closer to God (Smith & Denton, 2005).

A growing percentage of people in the United States consider themselves spiritual but not religious. In a 2017 national poll, 27 percent said they are spiritual but not religious, up 8 percentage points in five years (Lipka & Gecewicz, 2017). This trend is broad-based, occurring among males and females, different ages and educational levels, and different ethnic groups.

religion An organized set of beliefs, practices, rituals, and symbols that increases an individual's connection to a sacred or transcendent other (God, higher power, or higher truth).

religiousness An individual's degree of affiliation with an organized religion, participation in prescribed rituals and practices, connection with its beliefs, and involvement in a community of believers.

spirituality Experiencing something beyond oneself in a transcendent manner and living in a way that benefits others and society.

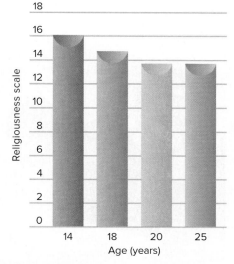

FIGURE 4

DEVELOPMENTAL CHANGES IN RELIGIOUSNESS FROM 14 TO 25 YEARS OF AGE. *Note*: The religiousness scale ranged from 0 to 32, with higher scores indicating stronger religiousness.

Adolescents and children participating in a church choir. *What are some positive aspects of religion in adolescents' lives?*
Digital Vision/Getty Images

The Positive Role of Religion and Spirituality in Adolescents' and Emerging Adults' Lives Researchers have found that various aspects of religion are linked with positive outcomes for adolescents (King & others, 2021). One study revealed that a higher level of church engagement (based on years of attendance, choice in attending, and participation in activities) was related to higher grades for male adolescents (Kang & Romo, 2011). Churchgoing may benefit students because religious communities encourage socially acceptable behavior, which includes doing well in school. Churchgoing also may benefit students because churches often offer positive role models for students.

One study found that youth generally thought about spirituality in positive ways (James, Fine, & Turner, 2012). In this study, 10- to 18-year-olds' self-ratings of spirituality were positively linked to the 5 Cs of Positive Youth Development (competence, confidence, character, connection, and caring/ compassion). In the longitudinal aspect of the study, the youths' self-ratings of spirituality predicted their character ratings one year later. Also, in a recent study of 11- to 22-year-olds, positive bidirectional links between religiousness and self-control were found (Hardy & others, 2020).

Religion also plays a role in adolescents' health and whether they engage in problem behaviors (Kim, Lee, & King, 2021; Palm & others, 2021). A research meta-analysis found that spirituality/religiosity was positively related to well-being, self-esteem, and three of the Big Five factors of personality (conscientiousness, agreeableness, openness) (Yonker, Schnabelrauch, & DeHaan, 2012). In this meta-analysis, spirituality/religion was negatively associated with risky behavior and depression. Also, in a recent study, religiosity was linked to delayed onset of alcohol use, more so for adolescent girls than boys (Barry, Valdez, & Russell, 2020). In addition, a study of ninth- to twelfth-graders revealed that more frequent religious attendance in one grade predicted lower levels of substance abuse in the next grade (Good & Willoughby, 2010). Further, a recent study revealed that high school students who reported turning to spiritual beliefs when they were experiencing problems were less likely to engage in substance use (Debnam & others, 2018). Also, in a recent Danish study, participating in a religious organization and praying were associated with fewer risk factors for engaging in an unhealthy lifestyle (Herold & others, 2021). And across three countries (England, Scotland, and Canada), adolescents who reported having a higher level of spirituality were more likely to have positive health outcomes (Brooks & others, 2018).

Many religious adolescents also internalize their religion's message about caring and concern for people (King, Schnitker, & Houltberg, 2020). For example, a number of studies have found that adolescents who are involved in religious institutions are more likely to engage in service learning than their counterparts who don't participate in religious institutions (Hart, 2020).

Developmental Changes Adolescence and emerging adulthood can be especially important junctures in religious development (King, Vaughn, & Merola, 2020). Even if children have been indoctrinated into a religion by their parents, because of advances in their cognitive development adolescents and emerging adults may question what their own religious beliefs truly are.

Cognitive Changes Many of the cognitive changes thought to influence religious development involve Piaget's cognitive developmental theory. More so than in childhood, adolescents think abstractly, idealistically, and logically. The increase in abstract thinking lets adolescents consider various

How does religious thinking change in adolescence? How is religion linked to adolescents' health?
Christopher Futcher/Getty Images

ideas about religious and spiritual concepts. For example, an adolescent might ask how a loving God can possibly exist given the extensive suffering of many people in the world (Good & Willoughby, 2008). Adolescents' increased idealism provides a foundation for thinking about whether religion is the best route to creating a better, more ideal world (Scarlett, 2020). And adolescents' increased logical reasoning gives them the ability to develop hypotheses and systematically sort through different answers to spiritual questions (Good & Willoughby, 2008).

Identity   During adolescence and then with increasing intensity in emerging adulthood, identity development becomes a central focus (Erikson, 1968; Mattys & others, 2020). Adolescents and emerging adults search for answers to questions like these: "Who am I?" "What am I all about as a person?" "What kind of life do I want to lead?" As part of their search for identity, adolescents and emerging adults begin to grapple in more sophisticated, logical ways with such questions as "Why am I on this planet?" "Is there really a God or higher spiritual being, or have I just been believing what my parents and the church imprinted in my mind?" "What really are my religious views?" One study found that college students' identity integration, defined as "the extent to which one's moral values have become integrated into identity," was related to intrinsic religious orientation, defined as "one's motivation for engaging in religious practice," and self-reported altruism (Maclean, Walker, & Matsuba, 2004, p. 429). In one analysis, it was proposed that the link between identity and spirituality in adolescence and emerging adulthood can serve as a gateway for developing a spiritual identity that "transcends, but not necessarily excludes, the assigned religious identity in childhood" (Templeton & Eccles, 2006, p. 261).

A study of Latinx, African American, Asian, and non-Latinx white adolescents revealed that their religious identity remained stable during high school but that religious participation declined during this period (Lopez, Huynh, & Fuligni, 2011). In this study, Latinx and Asian adolescents had the highest levels of religious identity, while Latinx adolescents had the highest level of religious participation.

Religious Socialization and Parenting   Religious institutions created by adults are designed to introduce certain beliefs to children and thereby ensure that they will carry on a religious tradition. Various societies utilize Sunday schools, parochial education, tribal transmission of religious traditions, and parental teaching of children at home to further this aim.

Does this religious socialization work? In many cases it does (Rafi & others, 2020). In general, children and adolescents tend to adopt the religious teachings of their upbringing. In a recent national survey, 48 percent of adolescents said they have "all the same" religious beliefs as their parents (Diamant & Sciupac, 2020). Also in this survey, 40 percent of adolescents reported that they attend religious services with both parents. However, if a religious change or reawakening occurs, it is most likely to take place during adolescence or emerging adulthood. One study revealed that parents' religiousness assessed during youths' adolescence was positively related to youths' own religiousness during adolescence, which in turn was linked to their religiousness following the transition to adulthood (Spilman & others, 2013). Another study found that when youth attend religious services with parents, this activity increases the positive influence of parenting on their psychological well-being (Petts, 2014).

However, it is important to consider the quality of the parent-adolescent relationship and whether mothers or fathers are more influential (Granqvist & Dickie, 2006). Adolescents who have a positive relationship with their parents or are securely attached to them are likely to adopt their parents' religious affiliation. But, when conflict or insecure attachment characterizes parent-adolescent relationships, adolescents may seek a religious affiliation that is different from that of their parents (Streib, 1999). A number of studies also have documented that mothers are more influential in their children's and adolescents' religious development than fathers are (King & Boyatzis, 2015). Mothers probably are more influential because they are more likely than fathers to go to church, lead family prayer, and converse with their children and youth about religion.

Many children and adolescents show an interest in religion, and many religious institutions created by adults (such as this Muslim school in Malaysia) are designed to introduce them to religious beliefs and ensure that they will carry on a religious tradition.
Anita SKV/Shutterstock

Peers also play a role in adolescents' religious interest. A study of Indonesian adolescents found that adolescents were similar to their friends in religiosity, and the religiosity of friends and others in the peer network increased the influence of adolescents' self-religiosity in predicting whether they engaged in antisocial behavior (French, Purwono, & Rodkin, 2012).

Religiousness and Sexuality in Adolescence and Emerging Adulthood   One area of religion's influence on adolescent and emerging adult development involves sexual activity. Although variability and change in church teachings make it difficult to generalize about religious doctrines, most churches discourage premarital sex. Thus, the degree of adolescent and emerging adult participation in religious organizations may be more important than affiliation with a specific religion as a determinant of premarital sexual attitudes and behavior. Adolescents and emerging adults who frequently attend religious services are likely to hear messages about abstaining from sex. Involvement of adolescents and emerging adults in religious organizations also enhances the probability that they will become friends with adolescents who have restrictive attitudes toward premarital sex. One study revealed that adolescents with high religiosity were less likely to have had sexual intercourse (Gold & others, 2010). And in a recent study of African American adolescent girls, those who reported that religion was of low or moderate importance to them had a younger sexual debut than their counterparts who indicated that religion was extremely important to them (George Dalmida & others, 2018).

developmental **connection**

Sexuality

An increasing number of positive youth development (PYD) programs include a focus on improving sexual outcomes in adolescence. Connect to "Sexuality."

Review Connect Reflect

LG3 Explain the roles of values, religion, and spirituality in adolescents' and emerging adults' lives.

Review

- What are values? What are some of the values of today's college students, and how have they changed over the last three decades?
- How important are religion and spirituality in adolescents' and emerging adults' lives? What characterizes religious and spiritual development in adolescents and emerging adults?

Connect

- How might spirituality influence adolescents' identity development?

Reflect *Your Own Personal Journey of Life*

- What were your values, religious involvement, and spiritual interests in middle school and high school? Have they changed since then? If so, how?

reach your **learning goals**

Moral Development, Values, and Religion

1 What Moral Development Is and the Domains of Moral Development

 LG1 Discuss what moral development is and the domains of moral development.

What Is Moral Development?

Moral Thought

- Moral development involves changes in thoughts, feelings, and behaviors regarding right and wrong. Moral development has intrapersonal and interpersonal dimensions.

- Kohlberg developed a provocative theory of moral reasoning. He argued that moral development consists of three levels—preconventional, conventional, and postconventional. Influences on progress through the levels include modeling, cognitive conflict, peer relations, and role-taking opportunities.

- Kohlberg's critics say that he gave inadequate attention to moral behavior, underestimated the role of emotion, placed too much emphasis on conscious/deliberate thoughts, underestimated cultural and family influences, and underestimated the care perspective (Gilligan's theory).

Moral Behavior

- Behaviorists argue that moral behavior is determined by the processes of reinforcement, punishment, and imitation. Situational variability in moral behavior is stressed by behaviorists. Hartshorne and May's classic study found considerable variation in moral behavior across situations.

- The social cognitive theory of moral development emphasizes a distinction between moral competence (the ability to produce moral behaviors) and moral performance (performing those behaviors in specific situations). Social cognitive theorists note that Kohlberg gave inadequate attention to moral behavior and situational variations.

- Prosocial behavior has especially been studied in the realm of altruism. Adolescents engage in more prosocial behavior than children do, and adolescent girls engage in more prosocial behavior than adolescent boys do. Forgiveness and gratitude are important aspects of prosocial behavior.

Moral Feeling

- In Freud's theory, the superego—the moral branch of personality—is one of personality's three main structures. Freud also argued that through identification children internalize a parent's standards of right and wrong. In the Freudian view, children may conform to moral standards in order to avoid guilt. The two main components of the superego are the ego ideal and conscience.

- Feeling empathy means reacting to another's feelings with an emotional response that is similar to that person's feelings. Empathy involves perspective taking as a cognitive component. Empathy changes developmentally.

- The contemporary perspective on emotions and moral development is that both positive feelings (such as empathy) and negative feelings (such as guilt) contribute to adolescents' moral development. Emotions are interwoven with the cognitive and social dimensions of moral development.

Moral Personality

- Recently, there has been a surge of interest in studying moral personality. This interest has focused on moral identity, moral character, and moral exemplars. Moral character involves having strong convictions, persisting, and overcoming distractions and obstacles. Moral character consists of having certain virtues, such as honesty, care, and conscientiousness. Moral exemplars are people who have lived exemplary lives.

Social Domain Theory

- Social domain theory states that there are different domains of social knowledge and reasoning, including moral, social conventional, and personal domains.

2 Contexts of Moral Development Describe how the contexts of parenting, schools, and culture can influence moral development.

Parenting

- Parental discipline can involve love withdrawal, power assertion, or induction. Induction has proven to be the most effective technique, especially with middle-SES children and adolescents. Moral development is promoted when parents are supportive, create opportunities for their children to learn about others' perspectives, include children and adolescents in family decision making, model moral behavior and thinking, state the behaviors that are expected and why, and encourage an internal moral orientation.

Schools

- The hidden curriculum, initially described by Dewey, is the moral atmosphere of every school. Contemporary approaches to moral education include character education, values clarification, service learning, and integrative ethical education. Cheating is a moral education concern and can take many forms. Various aspects of the situation influence whether students will cheat.

| Culture | • Some moral values such as honesty are endorsed across most cultures, but other aspects of morality are viewed differently in WEIRD (Western, Educated, Industrialized, Rich, and Democratic) and non-WEIRD cultures. Also, differences can occur within a particular culture, such as between higher- and lower-SES families. Recently, research has focused on the influence of family socialization in moral development, such as the importance of familism in Mexican American and Latinx cultures. |

3 Values, Religion, and Spirituality LG3 Explain the roles of values, religion, and spirituality in adolescents' and emerging adults' lives.

| Values | • Values are beliefs and attitudes about the way things should be. Over the last two decades, adolescents have shown an increased concern for personal well-being and a decreased interest in the welfare of others. Recently, adolescents have shown an increased interest in community values and societal issues. |

| Religion and Spirituality | • Distinctions have been made between the concepts of religion, religiousness, and spirituality. Many children, adolescents, and emerging adults show an interest in religion, and religious institutions are designed to introduce them to religious beliefs. Adolescence and emerging adulthood may be special junctures in religious and spiritual development for many individuals. Various aspects of religion and spirituality are linked with positive developmental outcomes. Cognitive changes—such as increases in abstract, idealistic, and logical thinking—influence adolescents' religious and spiritual development.

• Erikson's ideas on identity can be applied to understanding the increased interest in religion during adolescence and emerging adulthood. When adolescents have a positive relationship with parents or are securely attached to them, they often adopt their parents' religious beliefs. Links have been found between adolescent/emerging adult sexual behavior and religiousness. |

key **terms**

altruism
care perspective
character education
conscience
conventional reasoning
ego ideal
empathy
forgiveness

gratitude
hidden curriculum
induction
justice perspective
love withdrawal
moral development
moral exemplars
moral identity

postconventional reasoning
power assertion
preconventional reasoning
religion
religiousness
service learning
social cognitive theory of moral
    development

social conventional reasoning
social domain theory
spirituality
values
values clarification

key **people**

Albert Bandura
Gustavo Carlo
William Damon
John Dewey
Nancy Eisenberg

Erik Erikson
Sigmund Freud
Carol Gilligan
Jonathan Haidt
Hugh Hartshorne

Lene Arnett Jensen
Pamela King
Lawrence Kohlberg
Mark May
Walter Mischel

Darcia Narváez
James Rest
Judith Smetana
Eliot Turiel
Lawrence Walker

improving **the lives of adolescents and emerging adults**

The American Freshman (2020)
Ellen Stolzenberg and others
Los Angeles: Higher Education Research Center, UCLA
> Every year for 50 years, the Higher Education Research Center at UCLA has surveyed U.S. college freshmen about many aspects of their lives, including their values, attitudes, interests, and many other characteristics. In recent years, more than 130,000 college freshmen have participated in the survey.

Oxford Handbook of Moral Development (2020)
Edited by Lene Arnett Jensen
New York: Oxford University Press
> Leading experts in the field of moral psychology address many diverse topics, including moral thinking, emotion and moral development, and moral identity.

The Nature and Functions of Religious and Spiritual Development in Childhood and Adolescence (2015)
Pamela King and Chris Boyatzis
In R.M. Lerner (Ed.), *Handbook of Child Psychology and Developmental Science* (7th ed.).
New York: Wiley
> An up-to-date, contemporary examination of theory and research on religious and spiritual development in adolescence.

Prosocial Development (2015)
Nancy Eisenberg, Tracy Spinrad, and Ariel Knafo
In R.M. Lerner (Ed.), *Handbook of Child Psychology and Developmental Science* (7th ed.).
New York: Wiley
> Provides a thorough, detailed exploration of many aspects of prosocial development in adolescents.

chapter 8

FAMILIES

chapter **outline**

Yellow Dog Productions/Getty Images

"My mother and I depend on each other. However, if something separated us, I think I could still get along okay. I know that my mother continues to have an important influence on me. Sometimes she gets on my nerves, but I still basically like her, and respect her, a lot. We have our arguments, and I don't always get my way, but she is willing to listen to me."

—AMY, AGE 16

"You go from a point at which your parents are responsible for you to a point at which you want a lot more independence. Finally, you are more independent, and you feel like you have to be more responsible for yourself; otherwise you are not going to do very well in this world. It's important for parents to still be there to support you, but at some point, you've got to look in the mirror and say, 'I can do it myself.'"

—JOHN, AGE 18

"I don't get along very well with my parents. They try to dictate how I dress, who I date, how much I study, what I do on weekends, and how much time I spend on Facebook or texting. They are big intruders in my life. Why won't they let me make my own decisions? I'm mature enough to handle these things. When they jump down my throat at every little thing I do, it makes me mad and I say things to them I probably shouldn't. They just don't understand me very well."

—ED, AGE 17

"My father never seems to have any time to spend with me. He is gone a lot on business, and when he comes home, he is either too tired to do anything or plops down and watches TV and doesn't want to be bothered. He thinks I don't work hard enough and don't have values that are as solid as his generation. It is a very distant relationship. I actually spend more time talking to my mom than to him. I guess I should work a little harder in school than I do, but I still don't think he has the right to say such negative things to me. I like my mom a lot better because I think she is a much nicer person."

—TOM, AGE 14

"We have our arguments and our differences, and there are moments when I get very angry with my parents, but most of the time they are like heated discussions. I have to say what I think because I don't think they are always right. Most of the time when there is an argument, we can discuss the problem and eventually find a course that we all can live with. Not every time, though, because there are some occasions when things just remain unresolved. Even when we have an unresolved conflict, I still would have to say that I get along pretty good with my parents."

—ANN, AGE 16

preview

Although parent-adolescent relationships can vary considerably, researchers are finding that for the most part, the relationships are both (1) very important aspects of development, and (2) more positive than was once thought. This chapter examines families as a context for adolescent development. We begin by exploring family processes and then discuss parent-adolescent relationships, followed by relationships with siblings. Next, we consider the substantial changes that are taking place in families within a changing society. The chapter concludes by focusing on social policy recommendations for the well-being of adolescents and their families.

1 Family Processes   **LG1** Discuss the nature of family processes in adolescence.

| Reciprocal Socialization and the Family as a System | Maturation | Sociocultural and Historical Influences |

As we examine the adolescent's family relationships, think back to Urie Bronfenbrenner's (1986, 2004; Bronfenbrenner & Morris, 2006) ecological theory, which we discussed in the "Introduction" chapter. Recall that Bronfenbrenner analyzes the social contexts of development in terms of five environmental systems:

- The *microsystem*, or the setting in which the individual lives, such as the family, the world of peers, schools, work, and so on;
- The *mesosystem*, which consists of links between microsystems, such as the connection between family processes and peer relations;
- The *exosystem*, which consists of influences from another setting (such as parents' work) that the adolescent does not experience directly;
- The *macrosystem*, or the culture in which the adolescent lives, such as an ethnic group or a nation;
- The *chronosystem*, or sociohistorical circumstances, such as the increased numbers of working mothers, divorced parents, stepparent families, gay and lesbian parents, and multiethnic families in the United States in recent decades.

RECIPROCAL SOCIALIZATION AND THE FAMILY AS A SYSTEM

developmental **connection**

Genetic Influences

Genotype-environment correlations and gene × environment interactions (G × E) reflect ways that the genetic heritage of adolescents can be conceptualized and possibly influence parent-adolescent relationships. Connect to "Puberty, Health, and Biological Foundations."

For many years, socialization between parents and their children or adolescents was considered to be a one-way process: Children and adolescents were seen as the products of their parents' socialization techniques. However, today parent-adolescent relationships are viewed as reciprocal (Hoyniak & others, 2021; Kochanska & Kim, 2020). **Reciprocal socialization** is the process by which children and adolescents socialize parents, just as parents socialize them.

Increasingly, genetic and epigenetic factors are being studied to discover not only parental influences on adolescents but also adolescents' influence on parents (Clausing, Binder, & Non, 2021; Hoye & others, 2020). The *epigenetic view* emphasizes that development is the result of an ongoing, bidirectional interchange between heredity and the environment (Monaco, 2021; Thaler & others, 2020). For example, harsh, hostile parenting is associated with negative outcomes for adolescents, such as being defiant and oppositional (Thompson & others, 2017). This likely reflects bidirectional influences rather than a unidirectional parenting effect. That is, the parents' harsh, hostile parenting and the adolescent's defiant, oppositional behavior may mutually influence each other. In this bidirectional influence, the parents' and adolescents' behavior may have genetic linkages as well as experiential connections.

As a social system, the family can be thought of as a constellation of subsystems defined in terms of generation, gender, and role (William, Sawyer, & Wahlstrom, 2020). Divisions of labor among family members define specific subunits, and attachments define others. Each

reciprocal socialization The process by which children and adolescents socialize parents, just as parents socialize them.

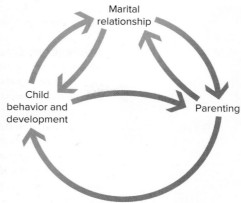

FIGURE 1

INTERACTION BETWEEN ADOLESCENTS AND THEIR PARENTS: DIRECT AND INDIRECT EFFECTS
LJM Photo/Getty Images

family member participates in several subsystems—some dyadic (involving two people) and some polyadic (involving more than two people) (Nichols & Davis, 2021). The father and the adolescent represent one dyadic subsystem, the mother and the father another; the mother-father-adolescent represent one polyadic subsystem, the mother and two siblings another. Thus, when the behavior of one family member changes, it can influence the behavior of other family members (Wikle & Hoagland, 2020).

An organizational scheme that highlights the reciprocal influences of family members and family subsystems is illustrated in Figure 1 (Belsky, 1981). As the arrows in the figure show, marital relations, parenting, and adolescent behavior can have both direct and indirect effects on each other. An example of a direct effect is the influence of the parent's behavior on the adolescent. An example of an indirect effect is how the relationship between the spouses mediates the way a parent acts toward the adolescent. For example, marital conflict might reduce the efficiency of parenting, in which case marital conflict would have an indirect effect on the adolescent's behavior.

As researchers have broadened their focus in families beyond just studying the parent-adolescent relationship, an increasingly studied aspect of the family system involves the link between marital relationships and parenting (Warmuth, Cummings, & Davis, 2020). The most consistent findings are that happily married parents are more sensitive, responsive, warm, and affectionate toward their children and adolescents (Fosco & Grych, 2010). Researchers have also found that marital satisfaction is often related to good parenting. The marital relationship is an important support for parenting (Shaikh, Aljasser, & Albalawi, 2020). When parents report more intimacy and better communication in their marriage, they are more affectionate with their children and adolescents (Grych, 2002). A recent Chinese study found that high marital quality and a close parent-child relationship were linked to young adolescents' positive mental health (Liu, Ge, & Jiang, 2020). Therefore, an important, if unintended, benefit of marriage enhancement programs is the improvement of parenting—and consequently healthier children and adolescents. Programs that focus on parenting skills might also benefit from including attention to the participants' marriages.

Thus, a positive family climate for adolescents involves not only effective parenting but also a positive relationship between the parents, whether they are married or divorced (van Dijk & others, 2020). A longitudinal study found that a positive family climate (based on positive interaction between spouses and between parents and a seventh-grader) was linked to the degree of positive engagement the adolescents showed toward their own spouses almost 20 years later during early adulthood (Ackerman & others, 2013).

MATURATION

American author Mark Twain once remarked that when he was 14 his father was so ignorant he could hardly stand to have the man around him, but when Twain got to be 21, he was astonished at how much his father had learned in those seven years! Mark Twain's comments suggest that maturation is an important theme of parent-adolescent relationships. Adolescents change as they make the transition from childhood to adulthood, but their parents also change during their adult years.

Adolescent Changes

Among the changes in the adolescent that can influence parent-adolescent relationships are puberty, expanded logical reasoning, increasingly idealistic thinking, violated expectations, changes in schooling, peers, friendships, dating, and movement toward independence.

Several investigations have shown that conflict between parents and adolescents, especially between mothers and sons, is the most stressful during the apex of pubertal growth (Steinberg, 1988). Also, early-maturing adolescents experience more conflict with their parents than do adolescents who mature late or on time (Collins & Steinberg, 2006).

In terms of cognitive changes, adolescents can reason in more logical ways with parents than they could as children. In dealing with children, parents may be able to get by with saying, "Okay. That is it. We do it my way or else," and the child conforms. But with increased cognitive skills adolescents no longer are likely to accept such a statement as a reason for conforming to parental dictates. Adolescents want to know, often in fine detail, why they are being disciplined. Even when parents give what seem to be logical reasons for discipline, adolescents' cognitive sophistication may call attention to deficiencies in parental reasoning.

In addition, the adolescent's increasingly idealistic thought comes into play in parent-adolescent relationships. Parents are now evaluated vis-à-vis what an ideal parent might be. Interactions with parents, which inevitably involve some negative interchanges and flaws, are placed next to the adolescent's schema of an ideal parent. And, as part of their egocentrism, adolescents' concerns with how others view them are likely to produce overreactions to parents' comments. A mother may comment to her adolescent daughter that she needs a new blouse. The daughter might respond, "What's the matter? You don't think I have good taste? You think I look gross, don't you? Well, you are the one who is gross!" The same comment made to the daughter several years earlier, during late childhood, probably would have elicited a less intense response.

Adolescents' cognitive development also influences the expectations parents and adolescents have for each other. Preadolescent children are often compliant and easy to manage. As they enter puberty, children begin to question or seek rationales for parental demands. Parents might perceive this behavior as resistant and oppositional because it departs from the child's previously compliant behavior. Parents often respond to the lack of compliance by applying increased pressure for compliance. In this situation, expectations that were stabilized during a period of relatively slow developmental change are lagging behind the behavior of the adolescent during the period of rapid pubertal change.

What dimensions of the adolescent's socioemotional world influence parent-adolescent relationships? Adolescence brings with it new definitions of socially appropriate behavior. In most societies, these definitions are associated with changes in schooling. As they make the transition to middle or junior high school, adolescents are required to function in a more anonymous, larger environment with multiple and varying teachers. More work is required, and students must show more initiative and responsibility to adapt successfully. Adolescents spend more time with peers than they did when they were children, and they develop more sophisticated friendships than in childhood (Ozdemir, Ozdemir, & Boersma, 2021; Steinhoff & Keller, 2020). Adolescents also begin to push more strongly for independence. In sum, parents are called on to adapt to the changing world created by the adolescent's school environment, peer relations, and push for autonomy (Tran & Raffaelli, 2020).

Parental Changes

Parental changes that affect parent-adolescent relationships involve marital satisfaction, economic burdens, career reevaluation and time constraints, and health and body concerns. For most parents, marital satisfaction increases after adolescents or emerging adults leave home (Gorchoff, John, & Helson, 2008). In addition, parents shoulder a heavy economic burden when their children are in adolescence and emerging adulthood. During this time, parents may reevaluate their occupational achievement, deciding whether they have met their youthful aspirations of success. They may look to the future and think about how much time they have remaining to accomplish their life goals. Many adolescents, meanwhile, look to the future with unbounded optimism, feeling that they have an unlimited amount of time to accomplish what they desire. Parents of adolescents may become preoccupied with concerns about their own health, body integrity, and sexual attractiveness

What are some of the cognitive and socioemotional changes in adolescents that might influence parent-adolescent relationships?
Creatas/Getty Images

What are some maturational changes in parents that might influence parent-adolescent relationships?
CORBIS Premium RF/Alamy Images

(Bellard & others, 2021). Even when their body and sexual attractiveness are not deteriorating, many parents of adolescents perceive that they are. By contrast, many adolescents have reached or are beginning to reach the peak of their physical attractiveness, strength, and health.

Multiple Developmental Trajectories   The concept of **multiple developmental trajectories** refers to the fact that adults follow one trajectory while children and adolescents follow a different one (Parke, Roisman, & Rose, 2019). How adult and child/adolescent developmental trajectories mesh affects the timing of entry into various family tasks. Adult developmental trajectories include timing of entry into marriage, cohabitation, or parenthood; child developmental trajectories include timing of child care and entry into middle school. The timing of some family tasks and changes can be planned, such as reentry into the workforce or delaying parenthood, whereas other changes may occur unexpectedly, such as job loss or divorce (Parke & Buriel, 2006).

The changes in adolescents' parents that we considered earlier are typical of development in middle adulthood (Infurna, Gerstorf, & Lachman, 2020). Most adolescents' parents either are in middle adulthood or are rapidly approaching this period of life. However, in the last two decades, the timing of parenthood in the United States has undergone some dramatic shifts. Parenthood is taking place earlier for some, and later for others, than in previous decades. First, the number of adolescent pregnancies in the United States increased considerably during the 1970s and 1980s. Although the adolescent pregnancy rate has decreased since then, the U.S. adolescent pregnancy rate remains one of the highest in the developed world. Second, the number of women who postpone childbearing until their thirties and early forties simultaneously increased (Centers for Disease Control and Prevention, 2020). We discussed adolescents as parents in the chapter on "Sexuality." Here we focus on sociohistorical changes related to postponing childbearing until the thirties or forties.

There are many contrasts between becoming a parent in adolescence and becoming a parent 15 to 30 years later. Delayed childbearing allows for considerable progress in occupational and educational domains. For both males and females, education usually has been completed and career development is well established.

The marital relationship varies with the timing of the onset of parenthood. In one investigation, couples who began childbearing in their early twenties were compared with those who began in their early thirties (Walter, 1986). The later-starting couples had more egalitarian relationships, with men more often participating in child care and household tasks.

Is parent-child interaction different for families in which parents delay having children until their thirties or forties? Investigators have found that older fathers are warmer, communicate better, encourage more achievement, place fewer demands on their children, are more lax in enforcing rules, and show less rejection with their children than younger fathers. However, older fathers also are less likely to engage in physical play or sports with their children (MacDonald, 1987). These findings suggest that sociohistorical changes are resulting in different developmental trajectories for many families—trajectories that involve changes in the ways that marital partners interact with each other and with their adolescents.

SOCIOCULTURAL AND HISTORICAL INFLUENCES

Family development does not occur in a social vacuum. Important sociocultural and historical influences affect family processes, reflecting Bronfenbrenner's concepts of the macrosystem and chronosystem (Bronfenbrenner & Morris, 2006). Great upheavals such as war, famine, or mass immigration as well as subtle transitions in ways of life may stimulate changes in families (Masten, 2021a, b). One example is the effect on U.S. families of the Great Depression of the 1930s. During its height, the Depression produced economic deprivation, adult discontent, and dissatisfaction with living conditions. It also increased marital conflict, inconsistent child rearing, and unhealthy lifestyles—heavy drinking, demoralized attitudes, and health problems—especially in fathers (Elder, 1980).

A major change in families during the last several decades has been the dramatic increase in the immigration of Latinx and Asian families into the United States (Gollnick & Chinn, 2021). These families often experience stressors uncommon to or less prominent among long-time U.S. residents, such as language barriers, dislocations and separations from support networks,

Latinx families have significantly increased in number in recent years. *What are some characteristics of this change?*
Aldo Murillo/Getty Images

It is not enough for parents to understand children. They must accord children the privilege of understanding them.

—MILTON SAPERSTEIN
American Author, 20th Century

The generations of living things pass in a short time and like runners hand on the torch of life.

—LUCRETIUS
Roman Poet, 1st Century B.C.

multiple developmental trajectories Concept that adults follow one trajectory and children and adolescents another one; how these trajectories mesh is important.

the dual struggle to preserve identity and to acculturate, and changes in socioeconomic status (Amirkhan & Velasco, 2021; Dandy & Drake, 2020). We discuss ethnic variations in families more extensively in the chapter on "Culture."

Subtle changes in a culture have significant influences on the family (Mayo & Wadsworth, 2020). Such changes include the increased movement from rural communities to urban and suburban areas; widespread use of television, computers, the Internet, and digitally mediated communication; and a general sense of dissatisfaction and restlessness (Maloy & others, 2021).

In the twentieth century, many U.S. families moved from farms and small towns to urban and suburban settings (Mead, 1978). In small towns and farms, individuals were surrounded by lifelong neighbors, relatives, and friends. Today, neighborhood and extended-family support systems are not nearly as prevalent. Families now move all over the country, often uprooting children and adolescents from a school and peer group they have known for a considerable length of time. And it is not unusual for this type of move to occur several times during childhood and adolescence as one or both parents are transferred from job to job.

Further, an increasing number of children and adolescents are growing up in transnational families who move back and forth between countries, such as between the United States and Mexico or between the United States and China (Rios Casas & others, 2020). In some cases, these children and adolescents are left behind in their home country or are sent back to be raised by grandparents. Such children and adolescents might benefit from economic support but suffer emotionally from prolonged separation from their parents.

Media use and screen time also play a major role in the changing family (Hayba & others, 2020). Many children and adolescents who watch television, use computers, or communicate with friends on mobile devices such as smartphones find that their parents are too busy working to share this experience with them (Maloy & others, 2021). Children and adolescents increasingly experience a world in which their parents are not participants. Instead of interacting in neighborhood peer groups, children and adolescents come home after school and watch television or log on to a computer. Recent research with adolescents indicated that light use of digital media (less than 1 hour per day) was associated with much higher psychological well-being than heavy use of digital media (5 or more hours per day) (Twenge & Campbell, 2019). Among the historical changes related to computers, consider the dramatic increase in young people's participation on Internet social networking sites (Kross & others, 2021). In a recent study, social media use of more than 2 hours per day was linked to lower academic achievement in both middle and high school (Sampasa-Kanyinga, Chaput, & Hamilton, 2019).

Another change in families has been an increase in general dissatisfaction and restlessness. The result of such restlessness and the tendency to divorce and remarry has been a hodgepodge of family structures, with far greater numbers of divorced and remarried families than ever before. Later in the chapter, we will discuss in greater detail these aspects of the changing social world of the adolescent and the family.

developmental **connection**

Family

Many families who have immigrated into the United States in recent decades, such as Mexican Americans and Asian Americans, come from collectivist cultures in which family obligations are strong. Connect to "Culture."

The vast variety of available television programming has caused parents and adolescents to tune into different interests rather than watch together. What are some other changes?
alexeys/Getty Images

Review Connect Reflect

LG1 Discuss the nature of family processes in adolescence.

Review

- What is reciprocal socialization? How can the family be described as a system?
- What roles do maturation of the adolescent and maturation of parents play in the dynamics of parent-adolescent relationships?
- How do sociocultural and historical circumstances influence families?

Connect

- What has the historical perspective on adolescence contributed to our view of the family as a system?

Reflect *Your Own Personal Journey of Life*

- Think about how your family operated as a system during your adolescence. How might your parents' marital relationship have influenced your development?

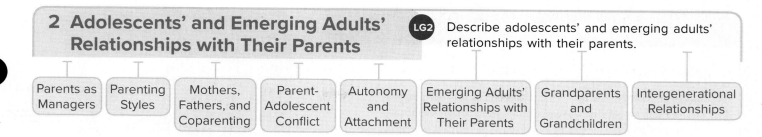

2 Adolescents' and Emerging Adults' Relationships with Their Parents

LG2 Describe adolescents' and emerging adults' relationships with their parents.

| Parents as Managers | Parenting Styles | Mothers, Fathers, and Coparenting | Parent-Adolescent Conflict | Autonomy and Attachment | Emerging Adults' Relationships with Their Parents | Grandparents and Grandchildren | Intergenerational Relationships |

We have seen how the expectations of adolescents and their parents often seem to be violated as adolescents change dramatically during the course of puberty. Many parents see their child changing from a compliant being into someone who is noncompliant, oppositional, and resistant to parental standards. Parents often respond by clamping down and putting more pressure on the adolescent to conform to parental standards. Many parents often deal with the young adolescent as if they expect him or her to become a mature being within the next 10 to 15 minutes. But the transition from childhood to adulthood is a long journey with many hills and valleys. Adolescents are not going to conform to adult standards immediately. Parents who recognize that adolescents take a long time "to get it right" usually deal more competently and calmly with adolescent transgressions than do parents who demand immediate conformity to parental standards. Yet other parents, rather than placing heavy demands on their adolescents for compliance, do virtually the opposite, letting them do as they please in a very permissive manner.

Our discussion of parent-adolescent relationships will indicate that neither high-intensity demands for compliance nor an unwillingness to monitor and be involved in the adolescent's development is likely to be a wise parenting strategy. Further, we will explore another misperception that parents of adolescents sometimes entertain. Parents may perceive that virtually all conflict with their adolescent is bad. We will discover that a moderate degree of conflict with parents in adolescence is not only inevitable but may also serve a positive developmental function. We also will explore relationships between emerging adults and their parents, and we will examine strategies that emerging adults and their parents can use to get along better. And, to conclude this section, we will discuss how adolescent development is influenced by intergenerational relationships.

PARENTS AS MANAGERS

Parents can play important roles as managers of adolescents' opportunities, as monitors of adolescents' social relationships, and as social initiators and arrangers (Atherton, Lawson, & Robins, 2020). An important developmental task in adolescence is learning to make competent decisions in an increasingly independent manner. To help adolescents reach their full potential, parents can assume an important role as effective managers who find information, make contacts, help structure choices, and provide guidance (Pizarro, Surkan, & Bustamante, 2021). Parents who fulfill this important managerial role help adolescents to avoid pitfalls and to work their way through a myriad of choices and decisions they face.

Parents can serve as regulators of opportunities for their adolescents' social contact with peers, friends, and adults (Collins & Madsen, 2019). Mothers are more likely than fathers to have a managerial role in parenting. In adolescence, it could involve participating in a parent-teacher conference and subsequently managing the adolescent's homework activity.

Researchers have found that family-management practices are positively related to students' grades and self-responsibility, and negatively to school-related problems (Lowe & Dotterer, 2013). One of the most important family-management practices in this regard is maintaining a structured and organized family environment, such as establishing routines for homework, chores, bedtime, and so on. Researchers in one study focused on African American families, examining links between mothers' reports of family-management practices, including routine, and adolescents' school-related behavior (Taylor & Lopez, 2005). Maintaining a well-organized family routine was positively related to adolescents' grades, attentiveness in class, and school attendance, and negatively linked to their school-related problems.

Parental Monitoring   A key aspect of the managerial role of parenting is effective monitoring, which is especially important as children move into the adolescent years (Tornay & others, 2020). Monitoring includes supervising an adolescent's choice of social settings,

activities, and friends. Recent research indicated that a higher level of general parental monitoring of adolescents' spending habits, friends, and whereabouts was linked to adolescents having healthier weight status, better dietary habits, more physical exercise, and less screen time (Kim & others, 2019). Also, in a study of fifth- to eighth-graders, a higher level of parental monitoring was associated with students' having higher grades (Top, Liew, & Luo, 2017). In another study, low parental monitoring was a key factor in predicting a developmental trajectory of delinquency and substance use in adolescence (Wang & others, 2014). Further, a research meta-analysis revealed that higher levels of parental monitoring and rule enforcement were linked to later initiation of sexual intercourse and more consistent use of condoms by adolescents (Dittus & others, 2015). In addition, a recent study revealed that when parents had little awareness of their whereabouts, adolescent girls were more likely to smoke cigarettes and to initiate smoking at an earlier age (Sartor & others, 2020). And a recent study indicated that parental active tracking measures during adolescence and college were linked to better health behavior in both developmental time frames (Abar & others, 2021).

Parental monitoring may be more effective in some conditions than in others. For example, a recent study found that high monitoring combined with high support of autonomy was linked to better adjustment than other combinations of monitoring and autonomy support (Rodriguez-Meirinhos & others, 2020). The least effective parenting combination was low monitoring coupled with high psychological control.

Three ways that parents can engage in parental monitoring are solicitation (asking questions), control (disclosure rules), and when youth don't comply, snooping. In one study, snooping was perceived by both adolescents and parents as the most likely of these three strategies to violate youths' privacy rights (Hawk, Becht, & Branje, 2016). Also, in this study, snooping was a relatively infrequent parental monitoring tactic but was a better indicator of problems in adolescent and family functioning than were solicitation and control.

Adolescents' Information Management A current interest involving effective parenting of adolescents focuses on adolescents' management of their parents' access to information, especially the extent to which adolescents disclose or conceal details about their activities (Rote & Smetana, 2016). Researchers have found that adolescents' disclosure to parents about their whereabouts, activities, and friends is linked to positive adolescent adjustment (Cottrell & others, 2017). A study of 10- to 18-year-olds found that lower adolescent disclosure to parents was linked to antisocial behavior (Criss & others, 2015).

What characterizes adolescents' management of their parents' access to information?
Ryan McVay/Getty Images

And a study of U.S. and Chinese young adolescents found that adolescents' disclosure to parents was linked with higher levels of academic competence (better learning strategies, autonomous motivation, and better grades) over time (Cheung, Pomerantz, & Dong, 2012).

PARENTING STYLES

Parents want their adolescents to grow into socially mature individuals, and they often feel a great deal of frustration in their role as parents. Psychologists have long searched for parenting methods that promote competent social development in adolescents (Baumrind, 1971; Maccoby, 2015; Sears, Maccoby, & Levin, 1957). For example, behaviorist John Watson (1930) urged parents not to be too affectionate with their children. Early research focused on distinctions between physical and psychological discipline or between controlling and permissive parenting. More recently, there has been greater precision in unraveling the dimensions of competent parenting (Laible, Carlo, & Padilla-Walker, 2020).

Especially widespread is the view of Diana Baumrind (1971, 1991, 2012), who notes that parents should be neither punitive nor aloof from their adolescents, but rather should develop rules and show affection. She describes four styles of parenting—authoritarian, authoritative, neglectful, and indulgent—that are associated with different aspects of the adolescent's social behavior:

- **Authoritarian parenting** is a restrictive, punitive style in which the parent exhorts the adolescent to follow directions and to respect work and effort. The authoritarian parent places firm limits and controls on the adolescent and allows little verbal exchange. For example, an authoritarian parent might say, "You will do it my way or else. There will be no discussion!" Authoritarian parenting is associated with adolescents' socially incompetent behavior. Adolescents who have authoritarian parents often are anxious about social comparison, fail to initiate activity, and have poor communication skills. A recent study revealed that being raised by authoritarian parents was associated with an increased likelihood of becoming a bully perpetrator (Krisnana & others, 2021).

- **Authoritative parenting** encourages adolescents to be independent but still places limits and controls on their actions. Extensive verbal give-and-take is allowed, and parents are warm and nurturant toward the adolescent. An authoritative father, for example, might put his arm around the adolescent in a comforting way and say, "You know you should not have done that. Let's talk about how you can handle the situation better next time." Authoritative parenting is associated with adolescents' socially competent behavior. The adolescents of authoritative parents are self-reliant and socially responsible. A recent study revealed that authoritative parenting was associated with a higher self-concept and lower level of externalizing behavior while authoritarian parenting was related to a lower self-concept and higher level of externalizing behavior in adolescents (Calders & others, 2020). Also, a recent Chinese study found that authoritative parenting served as a protective factor against adolescents engaging in delinquency and later in criminal activity (Xiong, De Li, & Xia, 2020). Further, another recent Chinese study revealed that authoritative parenting increased children's favorable trajectories of math achievement

authoritarian parenting A restrictive, punitive style in which the parent exhorts the adolescent to follow the parent's directions and to respect work and effort. Firm limits and controls are placed on the adolescent, and little verbal exchange is allowed. This style is associated with adolescents' socially incompetent behavior.

authoritative parenting A style encouraging adolescents to be independent but still placing limits and controls on their actions. Extensive verbal give-and-take is allowed, and parents are warm and nurturant toward the adolescent. This style is associated with adolescents' socially competent behavior.

CHEEVERWOOD   **by Michael Fry**

...ONE THING, BEFORE YOU SEND ME UP TO MY ROOM FOR THE REST OF MY LIFE... HAVE YOU READ THOSE STUDIES THAT SAY YOU SHOULD REASON WITH YOUR KIDS INSTEAD OF PUNISHING THEM?

I GUESS SHE HADN'T READ THOSE STUDIES...

	Accepting, responsive	Rejecting, unresponsive
Demanding, controlling	Authoritative	Authoritarian
Undemanding, uncontrolling	Indulgent	Neglectful

FIGURE 2

FOURFOLD SCHEME OF PARENTING STYLES
Ariel Skelley/Blend Images

- - - - - - - →

developmental **connection**

Families

Recent research on adolescents in Chinese American families has also focused on whether a "tiger parenting" style is common and whether it is associated with positive or negative outcomes for adolescents. Connect to "Achievement, Work, and Careers."

← - - - - - - -

neglectful parenting A style in which the parent is uninvolved in the adolescent's life. It is associated with adolescents' social incompetence, especially a lack of self-control.

indulgent parenting A style in which parents are highly involved with their adolescents but place few demands or controls on them. This parenting style is associated with adolescents' social incompetence, especially a lack of self-control.

(Wang, Chen, & Gong, 2021). In another recent study, authoritative parenting in grades 7 and 12 predicted greater internalizing of values in emerging adulthood (Williams & Ciarrochi, 2020). Other recent research indicated that authoritative parenting was linked to reducing adolescent screen time (Xu, 2021). In addition, a recent study of low-income Latinx families indicated that authoritative mothers had the highest levels of healthy eating practices and authoritarian mothers the lowest (Power & others, 2021). And a recent Lebanese study revealed that an authoritative parenting style was associated with better adolescent health outcomes than a neglectful style (Hayek & others, 2021).

- **Neglectful parenting** is a style in which the parent is uninvolved in the adolescent's life. The neglectful parent cannot answer the question, "It is 10:00 p.m. Do you know where your adolescent is?" Adolescents have a strong need for their parents to care about them; if their parents are neglectful they develop the sense that other aspects of their parents' lives are more important than they are. These adolescents are socially incompetent—they show poor self-control and do not handle independence well. Closely related to the concept of neglectful parenting is a lack of parental monitoring, which, as we discussed earlier, is linked to a number of negative outcomes for adolescents. In a recent study of adolescents, neglectful parenting was linked to early initiation of sex and engagement in unsafe sex (Reis & others, 2020).

- **Indulgent parenting** is a style in which parents are highly involved with their adolescents but place few demands or controls on them. Indulgent parents allow their adolescents to do whatever they want, and the result is that the adolescents never learn to control their own behavior and always expect to get their way. Some parents deliberately rear their adolescents in this way because they mistakenly believe that combining warm involvement with few restraints will produce a creative, confident adolescent. However, indulgent parenting is associated with adolescents' social incompetence, especially a lack of self-control.

In our discussion of parenting styles, we have described parents who vary along the dimensions of acceptance, responsiveness, demand, and control. As shown in Figure 2, the four parenting styles—authoritarian, authoritative, neglectful, and indulgent—can be categorized in terms of these dimensions (Maccoby & Martin, 1983).

Parenting Styles and Ethnicity   Do the benefits of authoritative parenting transcend the boundaries of ethnicity, socioeconomic status, and household composition? Although some exceptions have been found, evidence linking authoritative parenting with competence on the part of the adolescent occurs in research across a wide range of ethnic groups, social strata, cultures, and family structures (Garcia, Lopez-Fernandez, & Serra, 2021).

Other research with ethnic groups suggests that some aspects of the authoritarian style may be associated with positive child outcomes (Pinquart & Kauser, 2018). Elements of the authoritarian style may take on different meanings and have different effects depending on the context. For example, Asian American parents often continue aspects of traditional Asian child-rearing practices that have sometimes been described as authoritarian. These parents exert considerable control over their children's lives. However, Ruth Chao (2005, 2007; Chao & Otsuki-Clutter, 2011) argues that the style of parenting used by many Asian American parents is distinct from the domineering control of the authoritarian style. Instead, Chao argues that this type of parental control reflects concern and involvement and is best conceptualized as a type of training. The high academic achievement of Asian American children may be a consequence of their "training" parents (Stevenson & Zusho, 2002).

Further Thoughts on Parenting Styles   Several caveats about parenting styles are in order. First, the parenting styles do not capture the important theme of reciprocal socialization. Keep in mind that adolescents socialize parents, just as parents socialize adolescents (Hoyniak & others, 2021). Second, many parents use a combination of techniques rather than a single technique, although one technique may be dominant. Although consistent parenting is usually recommended, the wise parent may sense the importance of being more permissive in certain situations, more authoritarian in others, and more authoritative in others. Also, some critics argue that the concept of parenting style is too broad and that more research needs to be conducted to "unpack" parenting styles by studying various components that comprise the styles (Grusec, 2020). For example, is parental monitoring more important than warmth in predicting adolescent outcomes? Does supportive parenting predict better adolescent outcomes than disengaged parenting? In a recent study of Latinx families, a supportive parenting profile was linked to the most positive adolescent adjustment, followed by an engaged style, while intrusive and disengaged parenting were associated with the most negative adjustment outcomes (Bamaca-Colbert & others, 2018).

Further, much of the parenting style research has involved mothers, not fathers. In many families, mothers will use one style, fathers another style. Especially in traditional cultures, fathers often have an authoritarian style and mothers a more permissive, indulgent style. It has often been said that it is beneficial for parents to engage in similar parenting styles; however, if one parent is authoritarian and isn't willing to change, children benefit when the other parent uses an authoritative style.

MOTHERS, FATHERS, AND COPARENTING

In this section, we explore the importance of mothers and fathers in adolescents' lives and then examine coparenting and adolescent development.

Mothers, Fathers, and Adolescents What roles do mothers and fathers play in their adolescents' development? Historically, mothers have usually been assigned the main parenting responsibility for raising infants, children, and adolescents. However, in recent decades, many fathers have taken a more active parenting role.

Mothers and fathers often interact differently with their adolescents. Mothers are more involved with their children and adolescents than are fathers, although fathers increase the time they spend in parenting when they have sons and are less likely to become divorced when they have sons (Diekmann & Schmidheiny, 2004). Mothers' interactions with their adolescents often center on caregiving and teaching activities, whereas fathers' interactions often involve leisure activities (Galambos, Berenbaum, & McHale, 2009).

Mothers and fathers also often interact differently with their sons and daughters (Bronstein, 2006). In many cultures, mothers socialize their daughters to be more obedient and responsible than their sons. They also place more restrictions on daughters' autonomy. Fathers show more attention to sons than daughters, engage in more activities with sons, and put forth more effort to promote sons' intellectual development.

Much of the research we describe in this chapter on families is based on interviews and observations of mothers. Let's look at several studies that have included fathers and their adolescents.

One study of non-Latinx white two-parent families examined the amount of time mothers and fathers spent with their children from 8 to 18 years of age and how such time use was linked to their children's and adolescents' development (Lam, McHale, & Crouter, 2012). The amount of time that adolescents spent with their parents declined from early to late adolescence. Most of that time was labeled "social time," which involved time shared with friends and other relatives. However, private one-on-one time between a parent and his/her adolescent increased from age 8 to 12 or 13, leveled off in middle adolescence, and then began declining at about 15 to 18 years of age. For both boys and girls, adolescents spent the most time with the same-sex parent. Further, an important finding in the study was that more private one-on-one time spent with the father was linked to a higher level of adolescent self-worth and social skills. This study is important is calling attention to different types of time—social and private— and different developmental trajectories in adolescence for those two types of time adolescents spend with parents.

Another study focused on two-parent African American families with adolescents (Stanik, Riina, & McHale, 2013). Mothers reported having a warmer relationship with their adolescents than did fathers, and both parents indicated they had a warmer relationship with younger than with older adolescents. A higher level of maternal warmth was linked to a lower level of depressive symptoms and less risky behavior in sons, while a higher level of paternal warmth and shared time with fathers was associated with less risky adolescent behavior.

What parenting style do many Asian Americans practice?
JGI/Tom Grill/Getty Images

How does coparenting influence adolescent development?
aldomurillo/Getty Images

Also, in a recent study, adolescents' emotion regulation benefited when mothers provided support and fathers loosened behavioral control (Van Lissa & others, 2019). These links are in line with the view that mother-adolescent relationships are supportive attachment relationships while father-adolescent relationships challenge adolescents to regulate their emotions autonomously.

The two studies just described involved two-parent families. Of course, there is concern about the large number of adolescents who grow up in single-parent families, especially when the father is completely absent or spends little time with his adolescent (Meland, Breidablik, & Thuen, 2020). A research review concluded that the negative effects of father absence are especially evident in these outcomes: lower rates of high school graduation, problems with socioemotional adjustment during adolescence, and mental health problems in adulthood (McLanahan, Tach, & Schneider, 2013). Later in this chapter, we will further explore the father's role in divorced families and stepfamilies.

Coparenting The organizing theme of coparenting is that poor coordination, active undermining and disparagement of the other parent, lack of cooperation and warmth, and disconnection by one parenting partner—either alone or in combination with overinvolvement by the other—are conditions that place children and adolescents at developmental risk (Zou & Wu, 2020). By contrast, parental solidarity, cooperation, and warmth show clear ties to children's and adolescents' prosocial behavior and competence in peer relations. A recent study indicated that destructive marital conflict was associated with less effective coparenting (Kopystynska, Barnett, & Curran, 2020). Another study found that parents' joint involvement predicted that adolescents would engage in fewer risky behaviors (Riina & McHale, 2014). Also, in another recent study, coparenting disagreements undermined adolescents' adjustment by interfering with secure attachment of adolescents to their mothers and adolescents' development of autonomy (Martin & others, 2017). And a recent study of low-income, unmarried families revealed that cooperative coparenting at earlier points in time results in fewer child behavior problems later on (Choi, Parra, & Jiang, 2019).

PARENT-ADOLESCENT CONFLICT

It is commonly believed that a huge gulf separates parent and adolescents in the form of a so-called generation gap between the values and attitudes of adolescents and those of their parents. For the most part, however, the generation gap is an inaccurate stereotype. For example, most adolescents and their parents share similar beliefs about the value of hard work, achievement, and career aspirations (Gecas & Seff, 1990). They also tend to hold similar religious and political beliefs. As you will see in our discussion of research on parent-adolescent conflict, a minority of adolescents (perhaps 20 to 25 percent) have a high degree of conflict with their parents, but for a substantial majority the conflict levels are moderate or low.

That said, the fact remains that early adolescence is a time when parent-adolescent conflict escalates beyond levels experienced during childhood (Juang & Umana-Taylor, 2012). This increase may be due to a number of factors already discussed involving the maturation of the adolescent and the maturation of parents: the biological changes of puberty; cognitive changes involving increased idealism and logical reasoning; social changes focused on independence and identity; violated expectations; and physical, cognitive, and social changes in parents associated with middle adulthood.

A research review concluded that parent-adolescent conflict decreases from early adolescence through late adolescence (Laursen, Coy, & Collins, 1998). And in a recent study of Chinese American families, parent-adolescent conflict increased in early adolescence, peaked at about 16 years of age, and then decreased through late adolescence and emerging adulthood (Juang & others, 2018).

Conflict with parents increases in early adolescence. *What is the nature of this conflict in a majority of American families?*
Wavebreak Media/age fotostock

Although conflict with parents does increase in early adolescence, it does not reach the tumultuous proportions envisioned by G. Stanley Hall at the beginning of the twentieth century. Rather, much of the conflict involves everyday aspects of family life, such as keeping a bedroom clean, dressing neatly, getting home by a certain time, not talking on the phone nonstop, and so on. The conflicts rarely involve major dilemmas like drugs and delinquency. In a study of middle-socioeconomic-status African American families, parent-adolescent conflict was common but low in intensity and focused on everyday living issues such as the adolescent's room, chores, choice of activities, and homework (Smetana & Gaines, 1999). Nearly all conflicts were resolved by adolescents' giving in to parents, but adolescent concession declined with age.

Still, a high degree of conflict characterizes some parent-adolescent relationships (Brouillard & others, 2018; Nguyen & others, 2018; Van Lissa & others, 2017). It has been estimated that in about 20 to 25 percent of families, parents and adolescents engage in prolonged, intense, repeated, unhealthy conflict (Montemayor, 1982). Although this figure represents a minority of adolescents, it indicates that 4 to 5 million American families encounter serious, highly stressful parent-adolescent conflict.

This prolonged, intense conflict is associated with a number of adolescent problems— moving away from home, juvenile delinquency, dropping out of school, pregnancy and early marriage, membership in religious cults, and drug abuse (Akin & others, 2020). For example, a recent study found that higher levels of parent-adolescent conflict were associated with higher levels of adolescent anxiety, depression, and aggression, and lower levels of self-esteem (Smokowski & others, 2015). Another study found that high levels of parent-adolescent conflict were associated with lower levels of empathy in adolescents during the period from 13 to 18 years of age (Van Lissa & others, 2015). Further, in a recent study of Latinx families, high levels of parent-adolescent conflict were linked to adolescents' higher levels of aggressive behavior (Smokowski & others, 2017). And a recent study of Chinese American families revealed that higher levels of parent-adolescent conflict were associated with a sense of alienation between parents and adolescents, which in turn was related to higher rates of depression and delinquency, as well as lower levels of academic achievement (Hou, Kim, & Wang, 2016). In addition, in a study of Chinese adolescents, less parent-adolescent conflict was associated with lower rates of risk-taking by adolescents (Liu, Wang, & Tian, 2019). Also in this study, if parent-adolescent conflict was high, adolescents who had higher self-control were less likely to take risks than adolescents with lower self-control.

To read about the career of one individual who counsels families that are experiencing high levels of parent-adolescent conflict, see the *Connecting with Careers* profile.

Although in some cases adolescent problems may be caused by intense, prolonged parent-adolescent conflict, in others the problems might have originated before the onset of adolescence (Darling, 2008). Simply because children are physically much smaller than adults, parents might be able to suppress oppositional behavior. But, by adolescence, increased size and strength—especially in boys—can result in an indifference to or confrontation with parental dictates. At the same time, some psychologists have argued that conflict is a normal part of adolescent development.

Cross-cultural studies reveal that parent-adolescent conflict is lower in some countries than it is in the United States. Two countries where parent-adolescent conflict is lower than in the United States are Japan and India (Larson, 1999; Rothbaum & others, 2000).

When families emigrate to another country, adolescents typically acculturate more quickly to the norms and values of their new country than do their parents (Nair, Roche, & White, 2018). This likely occurs because of immigrant adolescents' exposure in school to the language and culture of the host country. The norms and values immigrant adolescents experience are especially likely to diverge from those of their parents in areas such as autonomy and romantic relationships. Such divergences are likely to increase parent-adolescent conflict in immigrant families.

Andrew Fuligni (2012) argues that these conflicts aren't always expressed openly but are often present in underlying, internal feelings. For example, immigrant adolescents may feel that their parents want them to give up their personal interests for the sake of the family, and the adolescents think this expectation is unfair. Such acculturation-based conflict focuses on issues related to core cultural values and is likely to occur in immigrant families, such as Latinx and Asian American families, who come to the United States to live (Fuligni & Tsai, 2015).

AUTONOMY AND ATTACHMENT

It has been said that there are only two lasting bequests that parents can leave their children—one is roots, the other wings. These words reflect the importance of attachment and autonomy in the adolescent's successful adaptation to the world. Historically, developmentalists have shown far more interest in autonomy than in attachment during the adolescent period. Recently, however, increasing attention has been paid to attachment's role in healthy development of adolescents and emerging adults (Withers, 2020). Adolescents and their parents live in a coordinated social world that requires both autonomy and attachment. In keeping with the historical interest in these processes, we discuss autonomy first.

Autonomy The increased independence that typifies adolescence is interpreted as rebellion by some parents, but in many instances adolescents' push for autonomy has little to do with their feelings toward their parents. Psychologically healthy families adjust to adolescents' push for independence by treating the adolescents in more adult ways and including them more often in family decision making (Rodriguez-Meirinhos & others, 2020). Psychologically unhealthy families often remain locked into power-oriented parental control, and parents move even more heavily toward an authoritarian posture in their relationships with their adolescents.

The adolescent's quest for autonomy and sense of responsibility create puzzlement and conflict for many parents. Parents begin to see their teenagers slipping away from their grasp. As we have discussed, they often feel an urge to take stronger control as the adolescent seeks autonomy and personal responsibility. Heated, emotional exchanges might ensue, with either side calling names, making threats, and doing whatever seems necessary to gain control. Parents can become frustrated because they expected their teenager to heed their advice, to want to spend time with the family, and to grow up to do what is right. To be sure, they anticipated that their teenager would have some difficulty adjusting to the changes adolescence brings, but few parents are able to imagine and predict the strength of adolescents' determination to spend time with their peers and to show that it is they, not their parents, who are responsible for their success or failure.

The Complexity of Adolescent Autonomy Defining adolescent autonomy is a more complex and elusive task than it might at first seem (Fuligni & Tsai, 2015). The term *autonomy* generally connotes self-direction and independence. But what does it really mean? Is it an internal personality trait that consistently characterizes the adolescent's immunity from parental influence? Is it the ability to make responsible decisions for oneself? Does autonomy imply consistent behavior in all areas of adolescent life, including school, finances, dating, and peer relations? What are the relative contributions of parents, peers, and other adults to the development of an adolescent's autonomy? A recent study of 13-year-olds indicated that those who engaged in fewer problem behaviors had both mothers and fathers who were autonomy supportive (Vrolijk & others, 2020). Another study found that from 16 to 20 years of age, adolescents perceived that they had increasing independence and improved relationships with their parents (Hadiwijaya & others, 2017). Further, a longitudinal study of adolescents and emerging adults from 13 to 23 years of age revealed that adolescents' autonomy from peer influences predicted long-term success in avoiding problematic behavior but also more difficulty in establishing strong friendships in emerging adulthood (Allen, Chango, & Szwedo, 2014).

What are strategies that parents can use to guide adolescents in effectively handling their increased motivation for autonomy?
Wavebreakmedia Ltd/Getty Images

One aspect of autonomy that is especially important is **emotional autonomy,** the capacity to relinquish childlike dependencies on parents. In developing emotional autonomy, adolescents increasingly de-idealize their parents, perceive them as people rather than simply as parenting figures, and become less dependent on them for immediate emotional support.

Gender, Culture, and Ethnicity   Gender differences characterize autonomy granting in adolescence, with boys being given more independence than girls are allowed to have. In one study, this was especially true in U.S. families with a traditional gender-role orientation (Bumpus, Crouter, & McHale, 2001). Also, Latinx families are more likely than non-Latinx white families to protect and monitor their daughters more closely than their sons (Allen & others, 2008).

In contexts where adolescents experience a high level of risk, such as high-crime communities, and in cultural groups that place a high value on family solidarity and deference to parents, parental control either has not been linked to problem behaviors or has been shown to benefit adolescent outcomes (McElhaney & Allen, 2012). And expectations about the appropriate timing of adolescent autonomy often vary across cultures, parents, and adolescents (Tran & Raffaelli, 2020). For example, expectations for early autonomy on the part of adolescents are more prevalent in non-Latinx whites, single parents, and adolescents themselves than they are in Asian Americans or Latinxs, married parents, and parents themselves (Feldman & Rosenthal, 1999). Nonetheless, although Latinx cultures may place a stronger emphasis on parental authority and restrict adolescent autonomy, one study revealed that regardless of where they were born, Mexican-origin adolescent girls living in the United States expected autonomy at an earlier age than their mothers preferred (Bamaca-Colbert & others, 2012).

Developmental Transitions in Autonomy and Going Away to College   Many emerging adults experience a transition in the development of autonomy when they leave home and go away to college (Tibbetts & others, 2016). The transition from high school to college involves increased autonomy for most individuals (Nelson & others, 2011). For some, homesickness sets in; for others, sampling the privileges of life without parents hovering around feels marvelous. For the growing number of students whose families have been torn apart by separation and divorce, though, moving away from home can be especially painful. Adolescents in such families may find themselves in the roles of comforter, confidant, and even caretaker of their parents as well as their siblings. In the words of one college freshman, "I feel responsible for my parents. I guess I shouldn't, but I can't help it. It makes my separation from them, my desire to be free of others' problems, my motivation to pursue my own identity more difficult." For yet other students, the independence of being a college freshman is somewhat stressful but not too difficult to manage. According to 18-year-old Brian, "Becoming an adult is kind of hard. I'm having to learn to balance my own checkbook, make my own plane reservations, do my own laundry, and the hardest thing of all is waking up in the morning. I don't have my mother there banging on the door."

> **emotional autonomy** The capacity to relinquish childlike dependence on parents.

In one study, researchers evaluated the psychological separation and adjustment of 130 college freshmen and 123 college upperclassmen (Lapsley, Rice, & Shadid, 1989). As expected, freshmen showed more psychological dependency on their parents and poorer social and personal adjustment than did upperclassmen. Female students also showed more psychological dependency on their parents than male students did.

Conclusions About Adolescent Autonomy   In sum, the ability to attain autonomy and gain control over one's behavior in adolescence is acquired through appropriate adult reactions to the adolescent's desire for control. An individual at the onset of adolescence does not have the knowledge to make appropriate or mature decisions in all areas of life. As the adolescent pushes for greater autonomy, the wise adult relinquishes control in those areas in which the adolescent can make reasonable decisions and continues to guide the adolescent in areas where the adolescent's knowledge is more limited. Gradually, the adolescent acquires the ability to make mature decisions on his or her own (Avedissian & Alayan, 2021). The discussion that follows reveals in greater detail how important it is to view the development of autonomy within the context of connectedness to parents.

How do relationships with parents change when individuals go to college?
Tom Stewart/Getty Images

Attachment and Connectedness   Adolescents do not simply move away from parental influence into a decision-making world all on their own. As they become more autonomous, it is psychologically healthy for them to be attached to their parents. Let's first examine a general definition of secure attachment and then describe attachment in infancy, childhood, and adolescence.

Secure attachment involves a positive, enduring emotional bond between two people. In infancy, childhood, and adolescence, secure attachment usually involves an emotional bond between a child and a caregiver that benefits the child's exploration of the environment and further development. In adulthood, a secure attachment can take place not only between caregivers and children, but also between two people in a couple or marital relationship.

Infancy and Childhood   Attachment theorists such as John Bowlby (1989) and Mary Ainsworth (1979) argue that secure attachment in infancy is central to the development of social competence. Secure attachment is theorized to be an important foundation for psychological development later in the life span. In **insecure attachment,** infants, children, and adolescents either avoid the caregiver or show considerable resistance or ambivalence toward the caregiver. Insecure attachment is theorized to be related to difficulties in relationships and problems in later development (Dagan & Sagi-Schwartz, 2021). For example, a research review concluded that children who do not form secure attachments to their parents risk developing anxiety and other internalized problems (Kerns & Brumariu, 2014). Also, a longitudinal study found that infant attachment insecurity was linked to less effective emotion-regulation strategies 20 to 35 years later (Girme & others, 2021).

What characterizes secure attachment in adolescence?
Tetra Images/Getty Images

Adolescence   In the past decade, researchers have begun to explore whether secure attachment might be an important feature of adolescents' relationships with their parents (Khan & others, 2020). Researchers have found that securely attached adolescents are less likely than those who are insecurely attached to have emotional difficulties and to engage in problem behaviors such as juvenile delinquency and drug abuse (Theoret & others, 2021). For example, a recent study of Lebanese adolescents revealed that those who were securely attached had lower rates of addiction to alcohol and cigarettes than their insecurely attached counterparts (Nakhoul & others, 2020). In another recent study, delinquent and maltreated adolescents had high levels of insecure attachment (Protic & others, 2020). Also, Joseph Allen and his colleagues (2009) found that adolescents who were securely attached at age 14 were more likely to report at age 21 that they were in an exclusive relationship, comfortable with intimacy in relationships, and were achieving increased financial independence. Further, researchers have found that adolescents who are less securely attached to their parents are more likely to attempt suicide (Sheftall & others, 2013). And a research analysis concluded that the most consistent outcomes of secure attachment in adolescence involve positive peer relations and development of the adolescent's capacity for emotion regulation (Allen & Miga, 2010).

Might secure attachment be linked to parenting styles in adolescence? A study of Chinese adolescents revealed that authoritative parenting positively predicted parent-adolescent attachment, which in turn was associated with a higher level of adolescent self-esteem and positive attachment to peers (Cai & others, 2013). And a longitudinal study revealed that secure attachment in adolescence and emerging adulthood was predicted by observations of maternal sensitivity across childhood and adolescence (Waters, Ruiz, & Roisman, 2017).

Many studies that assess secure and insecure attachment in adolescence use the Adult Attachment Interview (AAI) (George, Main, & Kaplan, 1984). This measure examines an individual's memories of significant attachment relationships. Based on their responses to questions on the AAI, individuals are classified as secure/autonomous (which corresponds to secure attachment in infancy) or placed in one of three categories of insecure attachment:

- **Dismissing/avoidant attachment** is an insecure category in which individuals deemphasize the importance of attachment. This category is associated with consistent experiences of rejection of attachment needs by caregivers. One possible outcome of dismissing/avoidant attachment is that parents and adolescents mutually distance themselves from each other, a state that lessens parental influence.

secure attachment Involves a positive, enduring emotional bond between two people. In infancy, childhood, and adolescence, formation of a secure bond with a caregiver benefits the child's exploration of the environment and subsequent development. In adulthood, the bond can also be between two people in a couple or marital relationship.

insecure attachment Attachment pattern in which infants, children, and adolescents either avoid the caregiver or show considerable resistance or ambivalence toward the caregiver. This pattern is theorized to be related to difficulties in relationships and problems in later development.

dismissing/avoidant attachment An insecure attachment category in which individuals deemphasize the importance of attachment. This category is associated with consistent experiences of rejection of attachment needs by caregivers.

- **Preoccupied/ambivalent attachment** is an insecure category in which adolescents are hyperattuned to attachment experiences. This preoccupation is thought to occur mainly if parents are inconsistently available to the adolescent. The insecurity may be evident in a high degree of attachment-seeking behavior, mixed with angry feelings. Conflict between parents and adolescents in this type of attachment classification can be too high for healthy development.

- **Unresolved/disorganized attachment** is an insecure category in which the adolescent has an unusually high level of fear and might be disoriented. This type of insecurity can result from traumatic experiences such as a parent's death or abuse by parents.

A study using the Important People Interview (IPI) assessed attachments of high school students (14 to 18 years of age) and emerging adult college students (18 to 23 years of age) to the four most important people in their lives, followed by their four most important peers (Rosenthal & Kobak, 2010). After identifying the important people in their lives, the students rank-ordered the people in terms of these contexts: attachment bond (closeness, separation distress, and reassurance in an emergency situation); support seeking (comfort or support in daily contexts); and affiliative (enjoyable social contact). College students placed romantic partners in higher positions and fathers in lower positions than did high school students. Friends' placements in higher positions and fathers' exclusion from the most important people list or placement as the fourth most important person were linked to increased behavior problems (internalizing behaviors such as depression and externalizing behaviors such as rule-breaking).

Conclusions About Parent-Adolescent Conflict and Attachment in Adolescence In sum, the old model of parent-adolescent relationships suggested that as adolescents mature, they detach themselves from parents and move into a world of autonomy apart from parents. The old model also suggested that parent-adolescent conflict is intense and stressful throughout adolescence. The new model emphasizes that parents continue to serve as important attachment figures, resources, and support systems as adolescents explore a wider, more complex social world. The new model also emphasizes that, in the majority of families, parent-adolescent conflict is moderate rather than severe and that everyday negotiations and minor disputes are normal, serving the positive developmental function of promoting independence and identity formation (see Figure 3).

Attachment in Emerging Adults Although relationships with romantic partners differ from those with parents, romantic partners fulfill some of the same needs for adults as parents do for their children (Mikulincer & Shaver, 2019, 2021). *Securely attached* infants are defined as those who use the caregiver as a secure base from which to explore the environment. Similarly, emerging and young adults may count on their romantic partners to be a secure base to which they can return and obtain comfort and security in stressful times (Fraley & Shaver, 2021).

preoccupied/ambivalent attachment An insecure attachment category in which adolescents are hyperattuned to attachment experiences. This is thought to occur when parents are inconsistently available to the adolescent.

unresolved/disorganized attachment An insecure attachment category in which the adolescent has an unusually high level of fear and is disoriented. This can result from traumatic experiences such as a parent's death or abuse by parents.

Old Model	New Model
Autonomy, detachment from parents; parent and peer worlds are isolated	Attachment and autonomy; parents are important support systems and attachment figures; adolescent-parent and adolescent-peer worlds have some important connections
Intense, stressful conflict throughout adolescence; parent-adolescent relationships are filled with storm and stress on virtually a daily basis	Moderate parent-adolescent conflict is common and can serve a positive developmental function; conflict greater in early adolescence

FIGURE **3**

OLD AND NEW MODELS OF PARENT-ADOLESCENT RELATIONSHIPS
UpperCut Images/Getty Images

How are attachment patterns in childhood linked to relationships in emerging and early adulthood?
(Left) itakayuki/Getty Images; (right) Jade/Blend Images/Getty Images

Do adult attachment patterns with partners in emerging and early adulthood reflect child-hood attachment patterns with parents? In a retrospective study, Cindy Hazan and Philip Shaver (1987) found that young adults who were securely attached in their romantic relation-ships were more likely to describe their early relationship with their parents as securely attached. In a longitudinal study, infants who were securely attached at 1 year of age were securely attached 20 years later in their adult romantic relationships (Steele & others, 1998). However, in another longitudinal study, links between early attachment styles and later attach-ment styles were lessened by stressful and disruptive experiences such as the death of a parent or instability of caregiving (Lewis, Feiring, & Rosenthal, 2000). Hazan and Shaver (1987, p. 515) measured attachment styles using the following brief assessment:

Read each paragraph and then place a check mark next to the description that best describes you:

1. I find it relatively easy to get close to others and I am comfortable depending on them and having them depend on me. I don't worry about being abandoned or about some-one getting too close to me.

2. I am somewhat uncomfortable being close to others. I find it difficult to trust them completely and to allow myself to depend on them. I get nervous when anyone gets too close to me, and it bothers me when someone tries to be more intimate with me than I feel comfortable with.

3. I find that others are reluctant to get as close as I would like. I often worry that my partner doesn't really love me or won't want to stay with me. I want to get very close to my partner, and this sometimes scares people away.

These descriptions correspond to three attachment styles: secure attachment (description 1 above) and two insecure attachment styles—avoidant (description 2 above) and anxious (description 3 above):

- *Secure attachment style.* Securely attached adults have positive views of relationships, find it easy to get close to others, and are not overly concerned with or stressed out about their romantic relationships. These adults tend to enjoy sexuality in the context of a committed relationship and are less likely than others to have one-night stands.

- *Avoidant attachment style.* Avoidant individuals are hesitant about getting involved in romantic relationships and once in relationships tend to distance themselves from their partners.

- *Anxious attachment style.* These individuals demand closeness, are less trusting, and are more emotional, jealous, and possessive.

The majority of adults (about 60 to 80 percent) describe themselves as securely attached, and not surprisingly adults prefer having a securely attached partner (Zeifman & Hazan, 2008).

Researchers are studying links between adults' current attachment styles and many aspects of their lives (Fraley & Shaver, 2021; Mikulincer & Shaver, 2021). For example, securely attached adults are more satisfied with their close relationships than insecurely attached adults are, and the relationships of securely attached adults are more likely to be characterized by trust, commitment, and longevity. In a recent research review, having an insecure attachment style increased the risk of engaging in suicidal thoughts (Zortea, Gray, & O'Connor, 2021). Also, in a recent study, college students with an anxious attachment style were more likely to be addicted to social networking sites (Liu & Ma, 2019). And, in a recent meta-analysis, adults with insecure attachment styles were more likely to engage in risky sexual behaviors (Kim & Miller, 2020). Further, it recently has been found that insecure anxious and insecure avoidant individuals are more likely than securely attached individuals to engage in risky health behaviors, are more susceptible to physical illness, and have poorer disease outcomes (Pietromonaco & Beck, 2018).

If you have an insecure attachment style, are you stuck with it and does it doom you to have problematic relationships? A recent analysis concluded that attachment styles are more malleable in childhood and adolescence than in adulthood (Fraley & Roisman, 2018). However, adults do have the capacity to change their attachment thinking and behavior. Although attachment insecurities are linked to relationship problems, attachment style makes only a moderate-size contribution to relationship functioning, and additional factors influence relationship satisfaction and success (Mikulincer & Shaver, 2019, 2021).

What are some key dimensions of attachment in emerging adulthood, and how are they related to relationship patterns and well-being?
Fuse/Getty Images

EMERGING ADULTS' RELATIONSHIPS WITH THEIR PARENTS

For the most part, emerging adults' relationships with their parents improve when they leave home. They often grow closer psychologically to their parents and share more with them than they did before leaving home (Padilla-Walker, Memmott-Elison, & Nelson, 2017). However, challenges in the parent–emerging adult relationship involve the emerging adult's increasing autonomy, as he or she has adult status in many areas yet still depends on parents in some manner. Many emerging adults can make their own decisions about where to live, whether to stay in college, which lifestyle to adopt, whether to get married, and so on (Padilla-Walker, Memmott-Elison, & Nelson, 2017). At the same time, parents often provide support for their emerging adult children even after they leave home. This might be accomplished through loans and monetary gifts for education, purchase of a car, and financial contributions to living arrangements, as well as emotional support.

In successful emerging adulthood, individuals separate from their family of origin without cutting off ties completely or fleeing to some substitute emotional refuge. Complete cutoffs from parents rarely solve emotional problems. Emerging adulthood is a time for young people to sort out emotionally what they will take with them from their family of origin, what they will leave behind, and what they will create.

The vast majority of studies of parenting styles have focused on outcomes for children and adolescents and have involved mothers rather than fathers. One study revealed that parents act as "scaffolding" and "safety nets" to support their children's successful transition through emerging adulthood (Swartz & others, 2011). Another study examined mothers' and fathers' parenting styles with their emerging adult children (Nelson & others, 2011). An authoritative parenting style by both mothers and fathers was linked with positive outcomes in emerging adult children (high self-worth and high social acceptance, and low depression, for example). The most negative outcomes for emerging adult children (low self-worth, high depression, and high anxiety, for example) were related to a controlling-indulgent style on the part of both mothers and fathers. High control by parents may be especially detrimental to emerging adults who are moving toward greater autonomy as they leave their parents' home. Negative outcomes for emerging adult children also resulted from an uninvolved parenting style (low responsiveness, low control) on the part of both mothers and fathers. The most positive outcomes for emerging adult children involved having fathers who used an authoritative style of parenting.

Research indicates that parents and their emerging adult/young adult children have more contact than in earlier generations, with the amount of contact especially increasing in the twenty-first century (Fingerman, Cheng, & others, 2012). Aided by advances in technology, today's emerging and young adults frequently text their parents and become friends with their parents on Facebook. Research indicates that today's emerging adults and young adults appreciate their parents' emotional and financial support.

developmental connection

Environment

Residential changes peak during emerging adulthood, a time when there also is often instability in love, work, and education. Connect to "Introduction."

What characterizes helicopter parenting, and what are its consequences?
aldomurillo/Getty Images

Are parents in some countries more involved with college students than are parents in other countries? A recent cross-cultural study found that college students across four countries (the United States, Germany, Hong Kong, and Korea) experienced frequent contact with and support from their parents (Fingerman & others, 2017). In this study, Asian students were given more frequent support than U.S. or German students but were less satisfied with the support.

There is concern when parental support becomes too intensive, in which case it can restrict emerging and young adults' development of autonomy (Fingerman, Pillemer, & others, 2012). The term "helicopter parents" has been applied to this type of support in which parents hover over their children, ready to intervene at a moment's notice to protect and micromanage their personal and academic life (Wieland & Kucirka, 2020). In a recent study, high levels of parental control and helicopter parenting were detrimental to emerging adults' vocational identity development and perceived competence in transitioning to adulthood (Lindell, Campione-Barr, & Killoren, 2017). Also, in another recent study, helicopter parenting was related to more negative emotional functioning, less competent decision making, and lower grades/poorer adjustment in college-age adults (Luebbe & others, 2018). Further, a recent study found that college students whose parents were classified as autonomy-supportive reported having better life satisfaction, self-efficacy, and relationships with their parents than those whose parents were classified as helicopter or uninvolved (Hwang & Jung, 2021). In addition, in a recent study, helicopter parenting was associated with detrimental outcomes (lower school engagement and increased depression, for example) in emerging adult children (age 19), but only when the parents also were high in control; however, helicopter parenting did not have negative effects on emerging adult children in parents characterized by warmth (Padilla-Walker, San, & Nelson, 2021). And in a longitudinal study, helicopter parenting declined as emerging adults went from 19 to 21 years of age (Nelson, Padilla-Walker, & McLean, 2021).

Many emerging adults, though, no longer feel compelled to comply with parental expectations and wishes. They shift to learning to deal with their parents on an adult-to-adult basis, which requires a mutually respectful form of relating—in which, by the end of emerging adulthood, individuals can appreciate and accept their parents as they are.

Recently, the new term of "lawn mower parent" has been applied to parents who go to great lengths to prevent their child from experiencing adversity, stress, or failure. By "mowing down" obstacles and potential negative experiences for their children, these parents are not allowing their children to learn how to cope with such experiences independently. When their children have to face these struggles on their own as they leave home and go to college or enter a career, they are unlikely to handle the pressures and challenges as well as they would have if their parents had granted them more space to make decisions and learn how to cope on their own.

In today's uncertain economic times, many emerging adults continue to live at home or return to the family home after several years of college or after graduating from college, often to save money while working at their first full-time job (Furman, 2005). Emerging and young adults also may move back in with their parents after a job loss or a divorce. And some individuals don't leave home at all until their middle to late twenties because they cannot financially support themselves. Numerous labels have been applied to emerging and young adults who return to their parents' homes to live, including "boomerang kids" and "B2B" (or Back-to-Bedroom) (Furman, 2005).

As with most family living arrangements, there are both pluses and minuses when emerging adult children continue living at home or return to live at home. One of the most common complaints voiced by both emerging adults and their parents is a loss of privacy. Emerging adults complain that their parents restrict their independence, cramp their sex lives, reduce their music listening, and treat them as children rather than adults. Parents often complain that their quiet home has become noisy, that they stay up late worrying about when their emerging adult children will come home, that meals are difficult to plan because of conflicting schedules, that their relationship as a married couple has been invaded, and that they have to shoulder too much responsibility for their emerging adult children. In sum, when emerging adults return home to live, a disequilibrium in family life is created, requiring considerable adaptation on the part of parents and their emerging adult children.

How can emerging adults and their parents get along better? See the *Connecting with Health and Well-Being* interlude for some ideas.

Can Emerging Adults and Their Parents Coexist?

When emerging adults ask to return home to live, parents and their emerging adult children should agree on the conditions and expectations beforehand. For example, they might discuss and agree on whether the emerging adults will pay rent, wash their own clothes, cook their own meals, do any household chores, pay their phone bills, come and go as they please, be sexually active or drink alcohol at home, and so on. If these conditions aren't negotiated at the beginning, conflict often results because expectations will likely be violated. Parents need to treat emerging adult children more like adults than children and let go of much of their parenting role. Parents should treat their emerging adult children as adults who are capable of responsible, mature behavior. Emerging adults have the right to choose how much they sleep and eat, how they dress, whom they choose as friends and lovers, what career they pursue, and how they spend their money. However, if the emerging adult children act in ways that interfere with their parents' lifestyles, parents need to say so. The discussion should focus not on emerging adults' choices but on why certain activities are unacceptable when both generations are living in the same home.

Some parents don't let go of their emerging adult children when they should. They engage in "permaparenting," which can impede not only their emerging adult children's progress toward independence and responsibility but also postpone their own postparenting lives. As mentioned earlier, "helicopter parents" is another label used for parents who hover too closely in their effort to ensure that their children succeed in college and adult life (Paul, 2003). Although well intentioned, this intrusiveness by parents can slow the process by which their children become responsible adults.

When emerging adults move back home, they might have to modify their behavior to make the living arrangement work. Elina Furman (2005) provides some good recommendations in *Boomerang Nation: How to Survive Living with Your Parents . . . the Second Time Around.* She mentions that when emerging adults move back home, they should be willing to make adjustments. And, as recommended earlier, she urges emerging adults to sit down with their parents and negotiate the ground rules for living at home before they actually move back. Furman also recommends that emerging adults set a

What are some strategies that can benefit the relationship between emerging adults and their parents?
Tetra Images/Getty Images

deadline for how long they will live at home and then stay focused on their goals (which might be to save enough money to pay off their debts, start a business, buy their own home, finish graduate school, and so on). Too often emerging adults spend the money they save by moving home on luxuries such as spending binges, nights on the town, expensive clothes, and unnecessary travel, which only delay their ability to move out of their parents' home.

In a recent study, 22- to 31-year-old "boomerang kids" reported that the main communication dilemma they encountered with their parents was figuring out how to best communicate the idea that living with their parents represented investing in their future rather than creating a stigma (Abetz & Romo, 2021). Also in this study, the "boomerang kids" said that the best strategies they could adopt were to state their expectations clearly, contribute to the household, behave like an adult, and state clear timelines for moving out of their parents' home.

How do you think emerging adults' relationship with their parents differs if they do not have to live at home?

GRANDPARENTS AND GRANDCHILDREN

Increased longevity is influencing the nature of grandparenting. As more people live to older ages, increasing numbers of grandparents are still alive. From 2001 to 2017, the number of grandparents in the United States grew 24 percent—from 56 million to 70 million (AARP, 2019).

How might U.S. grandparents compare with their counterparts in other countries? In a recent cross-cultural comparison, U.S. grandparents were characterized by higher parental efficacy, more role satisfaction, better well-being, and closer attachment than Chinese grandparents, who were characterized by better resilience and more authoritative parenting (Wang & others, 2019).

Grandparents play important roles in the lives of many grandchildren (Condon, Luszcz, & McKee, 2020). Grandparents especially play important roles in grandchildren's lives when

What characterizes grandparent/ grandchildren relationships in adolescence?
Denizo71/Shutterstock

In case you're worried about what's going to become of the younger generation, it's going to grow up and start worrying about the younger generation.

—ROGER ALLEN
American Writer, 20th Century

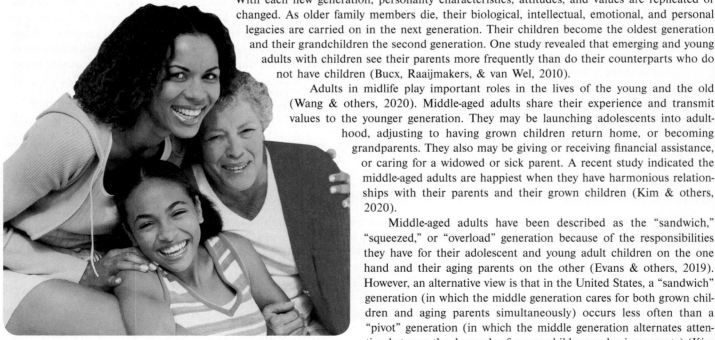

How do intergenerational relationships influence adolescents' development?
Digital Vision/Getty Images

family crises such as divorce, death, illness, abandonment, or poverty occur (Dolbin-MacNab & Yancura, 2018; Hayslip, Fruhauf, & Dolbin-MacNab, 2017). In many countries around the world, grandparents facilitate women's participation in the labor force by providing child care. Some estimates suggest that worldwide more than 160 million grandparents are raising grandchildren (Leinaweaver, 2014).

Many adults become grandparents for the first time during middle age. Researchers have consistently found that grandmothers have more contact with grandchildren than grandfathers do (Watson, Randolph, & Lyons, 2005). Perhaps women tend to define their role as grandmothers as part of their responsibility for maintaining ties between family members across generations. Men may have fewer expectations about the grandfather role and see it as more voluntary.

Divorce, adolescent pregnancies, and drug use by parents are the main reasons that grandparents are thrust back into the "parenting" role they thought they had shed. A recent study found that when children live with grandparents this arrangement especially benefits low-income and single parents, who are able to invest more money on their children's education and activities than they could spend if they had to pay for child care (Amorim, 2019).

Less than 20 percent of grandparents whose grandchildren move in with them are 65 years old or older. Almost half of the grandchildren who move in with grandparents are raised by a single grandmother. These families are mainly African American (53 percent). When both grandparents are raising grandchildren, the families are overwhelmingly non-Latinx white.

A majority of the grandparents living with their children contributed to the family income and provided child care while parents worked. Only about 10 percent of the grandparents who move in with their children and grandchildren are in poverty. Almost half of the grandparents who move in with their children are immigrants. Partly because women live longer than men, more grandmothers than grandfathers live with their children. About 70 percent of the grandparents who move in with their children are grandmothers.

A special concern of grandparents is visitation privileges with their grandchildren (Kivnik & Sinclair, 2007). In the last two decades, more states have passed laws giving grandparents the right to petition a court for visitation privileges with their grandchildren, even if a parent objects. Whether such forced visitation rights for grandparents are in the child's best interest is still being debated.

INTERGENERATIONAL RELATIONSHIPS

Connections between generations play important roles in development through the life span. With each new generation, personality characteristics, attitudes, and values are replicated or changed. As older family members die, their biological, intellectual, emotional, and personal legacies are carried on in the next generation. Their children become the oldest generation and their grandchildren the second generation. One study revealed that emerging and young adults with children see their parents more frequently than do their counterparts who do not have children (Bucx, Raaijmakers, & van Wel, 2010).

Adults in midlife play important roles in the lives of the young and the old (Wang & others, 2020). Middle-aged adults share their experience and transmit values to the younger generation. They may be launching adolescents into adulthood, adjusting to having grown children return home, or becoming grandparents. They also may be giving or receiving financial assistance, or caring for a widowed or sick parent. A recent study indicated the middle-aged adults are happiest when they have harmonious relationships with their parents and their grown children (Kim & others, 2020).

Middle-aged adults have been described as the "sandwich," "squeezed," or "overload" generation because of the responsibilities they have for their adolescent and young adult children on the one hand and their aging parents on the other (Evans & others, 2019). However, an alternative view is that in the United States, a "sandwich" generation (in which the middle generation cares for both grown children and aging parents simultaneously) occurs less often than a "pivot" generation (in which the middle generation alternates attention between the demands of grown children and aging parents) (Kim & others, 2020). One study found that middle-aged adults positively supported family responsibility to emerging adult children but were more ambivalent about providing care for aging parents, viewing it as both a joy and a burden (Igarashi & others, 2013).

Gender differences also characterize intergenerational relationships (Pei, Cong, & Wu, 2020). Females play an especially important role in maintaining family relationships across generations. Females' relationships across generations are thought to be closer than other family bonds.

Culture and ethnicity also are important aspects of intergenerational relationships. For example, cultural brokering has increasingly occurred in the United States as children and adolescents serve as mediators (cultural and linguistic translators) for their immigrant parents (Zhang & others, 2020).

So far in this chapter we have examined the nature of family processes, adolescent/emerging adult relationships with parents, grandparents and grandchildren, and intergenerational relationships. In the next section we will discuss another important aspect of the family worlds of most adolescents and emerging adults: sibling relationships.

Review Connect Reflect

LG2 Describe adolescents' and emerging adults' relationships with their parents.

Review
- How can parents be effective managers of adolescents?
- What are four important parenting styles, and how are they linked with adolescent development?
- What roles do mothers and fathers play in adolescent development? How effective is coparenting?
- How can parent-adolescent conflict be accurately described?
- What roles do autonomy and attachment play in the development of adolescents and emerging adults?
- What are some issues involved in relationships between emerging adults and their parents?

- What is the nature of grandparent-grandchildren relationships, and how are these relationships changing?
- How do intergenerational relationships influence adolescent development?

Connect
- Connect the earlier discussion of emotional development to this section's discussion of autonomy and attachment.

Reflect *Your Own Personal Journey of Life*
- What has characterized your own development of attachment and autonomy up to this point in your life?

3 Sibling Relationships

LG3 Characterize sibling relationships in adolescence.

Sibling Roles   Birth Order

What characterizes sibling roles? As we examine the roles siblings play in social development, you will discover that conflict is a common dimension of sibling relationships but that siblings also play many other roles in social development (Salmivalli, 2020). And how influential is birth order in the adolescent's development?

SIBLING ROLES

Approximately 80 percent of American adolescents have one or more siblings—that is, sisters and brothers (Fouts & Bader, 2017). As anyone who has had a sibling knows, conflict is a common interaction style of siblings. However, conflict is only one of the many dimensions of sibling relations (Dunn, 2015). Adolescent sibling relations include helping, sharing, teaching, fighting, and playing—and adolescent siblings can act as emotional supports, rivals, and communication partners (Kramer & others, 2019).

About 80 percent of us have one or more siblings. *What are some characteristics of sibling relationships in adolescence?*
Alain Shroder/Getty Images

How much time do adolescent siblings spend with each other? One study found that adolescent siblings spent an average of 10 hours a week together, with an average of 12 percent of it spent in constructive time (creative activities such as art, music, and hobbies; sports; religious activities; and games) and 25 percent in nonconstructive time (watching TV and hanging out) (Tucker, McHale, & Crouter, 2001). In Mexican American families, adolescent siblings spend even more time together—more than 17 hours a week (Updegraff & others, 2005). However, a research review concluded that sibling relationships are less close, less intense, and more egalitarian in adolescence than in childhood (East, 2009). In a longitudinal study of adolescents from 12 to 18 years of age, older siblings relinquished the most power over time (Lindell & Campione-Barr, 2017). Also, starting in adolescence, sibling companionship begins to decline in many cultures as boys and girls become increasingly involved in the world beyond their family (Whiteman, Jensen, & McHale, 2017).

What do adolescent siblings talk about when they are together? One study revealed that siblings most often talked about extracurricular activities, media, and school (Tucker & Winzeler, 2007). Less than 10 percent of their time together was spent discussing friends, family, eating, and body image.

Judy Dunn (2015), a leading expert on sibling relationships, describes three important characteristics of these relationships:

- *Emotional quality of the relationship.* Both intensely positive and intensely negative emotions are often expressed by siblings toward each other. Many children and adolescents have mixed feelings toward their siblings.
- *Familiarity and intimacy of the relationship.* Siblings typically know each other very well, and this intimacy suggests that they can either provide support or tease and undermine each other, depending on the situation.
- *Variation in sibling relationships.* Some siblings describe their relationships more positively than do others. Thus, there is considerable variation in sibling relationships. Many siblings have mixed feelings about each other, but some adolescents mainly describe their sibling in warm, affectionate ways, whereas others primarily talk about how irritating and mean a sibling is.

Do parents usually favor one sibling over others, and does such favoritism make a difference in an adolescent's development? One study of 384 adolescent sibling pairs revealed that 65 percent of their mothers and 70 percent of their fathers showed favoritism toward one sibling (Shebloski, Conger, & Widaman, 2005). When favoritism toward one sibling occurred, it was linked to sadness and lower self-esteem in the less-favored sibling. Indeed, equality and fairness are major concerns of siblings' relationships with each other (Campione-Barr, 2017; Campione-Barr, Greer, & Kruse, 2013).

In some instances, siblings can be stronger socializing influences on the adolescent than parents or peers are (Dunn, 2015). Someone close in age to the adolescent—such as a sibling—might be able to understand the adolescent's problems and communicate more effectively than parents can. In dealing with peers, coping with difficult teachers, and discussing taboo subjects (such as sex), siblings can be more influential in socializing adolescents than parents are. In one study, both younger and older adolescent siblings viewed older siblings as sources of support for social and scholastic activities (Tucker, McHale, & Crouter, 2001).

Having an older sibling who engages in problematic behaviors is a risk factor for younger siblings. In one study, having an older sibling who engaged in externalizing problem behavior increased the likelihood that a younger sibling would also engage in that type of problem behavior (Defoe & others, 2013).

What role might sibling conflict play in adolescent development? High levels of sibling conflict and low levels of sibling warmth can be detrimental to adolescent development (Tanskanen & others, 2017). A research meta-analysis found that less sibling conflict and higher sibling warmth were associated with fewer internalizing and externalizing problems (Buist, Dekovic, & Prinzie, 2013). And a longitudinal study found that increased sibling conflict was linked to increased depression and that increased sibling intimacy was related to increased peer competence and, for girls, decreased depression (Kim & others, 2007).

Sibling conflict may be especially damaging when combined with ineffective parenting (Kramer, 2019). A longitudinal study revealed that a combination of ineffective parenting (poor problem-solving skills, weak supervision, parent-adolescent conflict) and sibling conflict (hitting, fighting, stealing, cheating) at 10 to 12 years of age was linked to antisocial behavior and poor peer relations from 12 to 16 years of age (Bank, Burraston, & Snyder, 2004).

As just indicated, negative aspects of sibling relationships, such as high conflict, are linked to negative outcomes for adolescents. The negative outcomes can develop not only through conflict but also through direct modeling of a sibling's behavior, as when a young adolescent has an older sibling who has poor study habits and engages in delinquent behavior. By contrast, close and supportive sibling relationships can buffer the negative effects of stressful circumstances in an adolescent's life (East, 2009).

What are sibling relationships like in emerging adulthood? Most siblings spend far less time with each other in emerging adulthood than they did in adolescence. Mixed feelings about siblings continue to be present in emerging adulthood. However, as siblings move out of the family home and sibling contact becomes more optional, conflicted sibling relationships in adolescence often become less emotionally intense (Hetherington & Kelly, 2002).

BIRTH ORDER

Some reports have indicated that whether an adolescent has older or younger siblings is linked to development of certain personality characteristics. For example, one review concluded that "firstborns are the most intelligent, achieving, and conscientious, while later-borns are the most rebellious, liberal, and agreeable" (Paulhus, 2008, p. 210). Compared with later-born children, firstborn children have also been described as more adult-oriented, helpful, conforming, and self-controlled. However, when such birth order differences are measured, they often are small. Indeed, in a recent large-scale study, a birth order effect occurred for intelligence, with firstborns having slightly higher intelligence, but there were no birth order effects for life satisfaction, internal/external control, trust, risk taking, patience, and impulsivity (Rohrer, Egloff, & Schmukle, 2017).

Birth order can play a role in siblings' relationships with each other (Vandell, Minnett, & Santrock, 1987). Older siblings invariably take on the dominant role in sibling interaction, and older siblings report feeling resentful that parents give preferential treatment to younger siblings.

The popular conception of the only child is that of a "spoiled brat" with undesirable characteristics such as dependency, lack of self-control, and self-centered behavior. But research presents a more positive portrayal of the only child, who often is achievement-oriented and displays a desirable personality, especially in comparison with later-borns and children from large families (Thomas, Coffman, & Kipp, 1993).

Overall, researchers have found that the influence of birth order has often been overemphasized. The critics argue that when all of the factors that influence adolescent behavior are considered, birth order by itself shows limited ability to predict adolescent behavior. Consider sibling relationships alone. They are influenced not only by birth order but also by the number of siblings, age of siblings, age spacing of siblings, and sex of siblings. In one study, male sibling pairs had a less positive relationship (less caring, less intimate, and lower conflict resolution) than male/female or female/female sibling pairs (Cole & Kerns, 2001). Consider also the temperament of siblings. Researchers have found that siblings' temperamental traits (such as "easy" and "difficult"), as well as differential treatment of siblings by parents, influence how siblings get along (Brody, Stoneman, & Burke, 1987). Siblings with "easy" temperaments who are treated in relatively equal ways by parents tend to get along with each other the best, whereas siblings with "difficult" temperaments, or siblings whose parents have given one sibling preferential treatment, get along the worst.

In addition to gender, temperament, and differential treatment of siblings by parents, think about some of the other important factors in adolescents' lives that influence their behavior beyond birth order. They include heredity, models of competency or incompetency that parents present to adolescents on a daily basis, peer influences, school influences, socioeconomic factors, sociohistorical factors, cultural variations, and so on. Although birth order by itself may not be a good predictor of adolescent behavior, sibling relationships and interaction are important dimensions of family processes in adolescence (Campione-Barr, 2017).

The one-child family policy was introduced in China in 1980 to improve the country's economy by limiting population growth. In 2016, China changed the policy from one-child to two-child, and in 2021 China instituted a three-child policy because the two-child policy had not led to an adequate increase in births, mainly because of the high cost of raising children. *What do you think about these child-limiting policies?*
XiXinXing/Getty Images

Review Connect Reflect

LG3 Characterize sibling relationships in adolescence.

Review
- What is the nature of sibling roles?
- How strongly is birth order linked to adolescent development?

Connect
- Compare a family with multiple children to a family with a single child in terms of the family-as-a-system perspective.

Reflect *Your Own Personal Journey of Life*
- If you grew up with one or more siblings, what was your relationship with your sibling(s) like? If you could have changed anything in your relationship with your sibling(s) in adolescence, what would that have been? If you are an only child, how do you think this sibling status influenced your development?

4 The Changing Family in a Changing Society

LG4 Describe the changing family in a changing society.

Working Parents   Divorced Families   Stepfamilies   Adoption   Gay and Lesbian Parents

More U.S. adolescents are growing up in a wider variety of family structures than ever before in history. Many mothers and fathers spend the greater part of their day away from their children. The number of adolescents growing up in single-parent families is staggering. The United States has a higher percentage of single-parent families than do most other countries (see Figure 4). And, by age 18, approximately one-fourth of all American children will have spent part of their lives in a stepfamily.

WORKING PARENTS

Interest in the effects of parental work on the development of children and adolescents has increased in recent years, especially as rising numbers of mothers are working full-time.

More than one of every two U.S. mothers with a child under the age of 5 is in the labor force, and more than two of every three mothers with a child from 6 to 17 years of age is employed. Maternal employment is a part of modern life, but its effects are still debated.

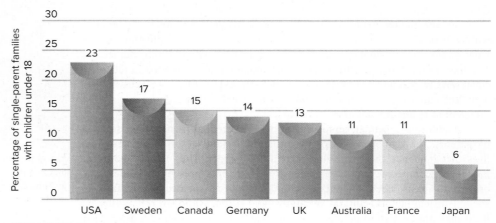

FIGURE 4

SINGLE-PARENT FAMILIES IN DIFFERENT COUNTRIES

Most of the research on parental work has focused on young children and on the mother's employment (Brooks-Gunn, Han, & Waldfogel, 2010). However, the effects of working parents also involve the father when such matters as work schedules, work-family stress, and unemployment are considered (Parke, Roisman, & Rose, 2019). For example, a study of almost 3,000 adolescents found a negative association between the father's, but not the mother's, unemployment and adolescents' health (Bacikova-Sleskova, Benka, & Orosova, 2014).

Until recently, little attention has been given to the effects of parents' work on adolescents (Lee & others, 2017). Research indicates that what matters for adolescent development is the nature of parents' work rather than whether one or both parents work outside the home (Parke, Roisman, & Rose, 2019). Ann Crouter (2006) described how parents bring their experiences at work into their homes. She concluded that parents who have poor working conditions, such as long hours, overtime work, stressful work, and lack of autonomy at work, are likely to be more irritable at home and to engage in less effective parenting than their counterparts who have better working conditions in their jobs. Negative working conditions of parents are linked to more behavior problems and lower grades in their adolescents. One study found that when fathers worked more than 60 hours per week and perceived that their work overload gave them too little time to do what they wanted, their relationships with their adolescents were more conflicted (Crouter & others, 2001). Another study revealed that mothers' positive mood after work was linked with adolescents' reports of more positive affect, better sleep quality, and longer sleep duration (Lawson & others, 2014). The same study found that mothers with more positive work experiences had adolescents who reported less negative affect and fewer physical health problems. A consistent finding is that adolescents (especially girls) with working mothers engage in less gender stereotyping and have more egalitarian views of gender than adolescents whose mothers are not employed outside the home (Goldberg & Lucas-Thompson, 2008).

Are there times when adolescents are more likely to misbehave while their parents are at work? Yes—during the summer months and between 3 and 6 p.m. on weekdays during the school year. It is important for parents to schedule structured activities (extracurricular activities, for example) and/or adult monitoring (such as after-school programs or youth center programs, for example) during these times.

How might parents' work schedules and work stress issues influence adolescents' development?
Andrey_Popov/Shutterstock

DIVORCED FAMILIES

During the mid-twentieth century, divorce reached epidemic proportions in the United States. However, the divorce rate has declined in recent decades, peaking at 5.1 divorces per 1,000 people in 1981 and then declining to 2.9 divorces per 1,000 people in 2018 (U.S. Census Bureau, 2019). The 2018 divorce rate of 2.9 compares with a marriage rate of 6.5 per 1,000 people in 2018.

Although the divorce rate has dropped, the United States still has one of the highest divorce rates in the world. Russia has the highest divorce rate (4.6 divorces per 1,000 people in a given year), Chile the lowest (0.2 divorces per 1,000 people in a given year) (OECD, 2019). In the United States, nearly half of first marriages will break up within 20 years (Copen, Daniels, & Mosher, 2013).

Recently, however, the divorce rate has increased for the age group in which many parents of adolescents fall (middle age). In a recent analysis that compared divorce rates for different age groups in 1990 and 2015, the divorce rate decreased for young adults but increased for middle-aged adults (Stepler, 2017):

25 to 39 years	40 to 49 years	50+ years
−21 percent	+14 percent	+109 percent

What accounts for increased rates of divorce in middle age? One explanation is the changing view of women, who initiate approximately 60 percent of the divorces after 40 years of age. Compared with earlier decades, divorce holds less stigma for women today and they are more likely to leave an unhappy marriage. Also compared with earlier decades, more women are employed and are less dependent on their husband's income. Another explanation involves the increased number of remarriages, in which the divorce rate is 2½ times as high as it is in first marriages.

As marriage has become a more optional, less permanent institution in contemporary America, children and adolescents are encountering stresses and adaptive challenges associated with their parents' marital transitions.

—E. Mavis Hetherington
Contemporary Psychologist, University of Virginia

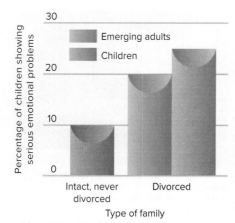

FIGURE 5

EMOTIONAL PROBLEMS IN CHILDREN AND EMERGING ADULTS FROM DIVORCED FAMILIES

We will explore a number of questions regarding the effects of divorce: Is the adjustment of adolescents and emerging adults better in never-divorced families than in divorced families? Should parents stay together for the sake of their children and adolescents? How much do parenting skills matter in divorced families? What factors affect the adolescent's individual risk and vulnerability in a divorced family? What role does socioeconomic status play in the lives of adolescents in divorced families?

Adolescents' Adjustment in Divorced Families Most researchers agree that children, adolescents, and emerging adults from divorced families show poorer adjustment than their counterparts in nondivorced families (Lansford, 2019; Meland, Breidablik, & Thuen, 2020) (see Figure 5). In a longitudinal study conducted by E. Mavis Hetherington and her colleagues (Hetherington, 2005, 2006; Hetherington, Cox, & Cox, 1982; Hetherington & Kelly, 2002), 25 percent of children from divorced families had emotional problems, but that figure decreased to 20 percent in emerging adulthood. In this study, 10 percent of children and emerging adults from nondivorced families had emotional problems.

In Hetherington's research, the 20 percent of emerging adults from divorced families who continued to have emotional problems were characterized by impulsive, irresponsible, or anti-social behavior, or they were depressed. Toward the end of emerging adulthood, this troubled group was having problems at work and difficulties in romantic relationships. The 10 percent of emerging adults from nondivorced families who had emotional problems mainly came from homes where family conflict was high and authoritative parenting was rare. As in childhood, emerging adults who had gone from a highly conflicted intact family to a more harmonious divorced family with a caring, competent parent had fewer emotional problems. In another longitudinal study, parental divorce in childhood and adolescence was linked to poor relationships with fathers, unstable romantic or marital relationships, and lower levels of education in adulthood (Amato, 2006).

Individuals who have experienced multiple divorces are at greater risk. Adolescents and emerging adults in divorced families are more likely than adolescents from nondivorced families to have academic problems, to show externalized problems (such as acting out and delinquency) and internalized problems (such as anxiety and depression), to be less socially responsible, to have less competent intimate relationships, to drop out of school, to become sexually active at an earlier age, to take drugs, to associate with antisocial peers, and to have lower self-esteem (Boccia & others, 2021; Lansford, 2019). Also, a recent meta-analysis of 54 studies involving 506,299 participants concluded that children who experience parental divorce at increased risk for depression, anxiety, suicide attempts, distress, alcohol abuse, drugs, and smoking (Auersperg & others, 2019). Also, a recent study found that adolescents' emotional and behavioral problems increased after their parents divorced, not before (Tullius & others, 2021). Nonetheless, keep in mind that a majority of children in divorced families do not have significant adjustment problems.

Note that marital conflict may have negative consequences for children in the context of marriage or divorce. For example, a study of 14- to 17-year-olds in Spain found that those living in nondivorced, intact families who perceived the existence of high marital conflict between their parents engaged in more frequent and higher-risk sexual activity than their counterparts living in divorced families (Orgiles, Carratala, & Espada, 2015).

Indeed, many of the problems that children from divorced homes experience begin during the predivorce period, a time when parents are often in active conflict with each other. Thus, when children from divorced homes show problems, the problems may be due not only to the divorce but to the marital conflict that led to it (Thompson, 2008).

E. Mark Cummings and his colleagues (Cummings & others, 2017; De Silva & others, 2020) have proposed *emotional security theory,* which has its roots in attachment theory and states that children appraise marital conflict in terms of their sense of security and safety in the family. These researchers distinguish between marital conflict that is negative for children (such as hostile emotional displays and destructive conflict tactics) and marital conflict that can be positive for children (such as a marital disagreement that involves calmly discussing each person's perspective and working together to reach a solution). In a recent study, intensification of interparental conflict in the early elementary school years predicted increases in emotional insecurity five years later in early adolescence, which in turn predicted decreases in adolescent friendship affiliation, and this friendship decrease was linked to a downturn in social competence (Davies, Martin, & Cummings, 2018).

A College Student Reflects on Growing Up in a Divorced Family

"It has always been painful knowing that I have a father who is alive and perfectly capable of acting like a parent, but who does not care about me. As a child, I was often depressed and acted out. As I grew older I had very low self-esteem. In junior high school, although I was successful, I felt like I belonged to the 'loser crowd.' . . . After I graduated from high school, I decided I still needed to fill the emptiness in my life by finding out at least a little bit about my father. I was seventeen when I found his number and called to see if he would be willing to talk. After a long hesitation, he agreed. We met and spent the day together. He has called me regularly ever since. Today I am better able to understand what I was feeling all those years. Now I am able to say without guilt that the absence of my father caused me much pain. I no longer feel abandoned, but many of the scars still remain. I still haven't been able to bring myself to call him 'Dad.'

"There were two positive consequences of my parents' divorce for me: I discovered my own strength by living through this most difficult experience and surviving the loss of my father, and I developed this close bond with my mother from sharing the experience. She and I have become best friends.

"Fortunately I had my friends, my teachers, my grandparents, and my brother to help me through the whole crazy-making time after my parents' divorce. The most important people were my brother and a teacher I had in the sixth and seventh grades. My brother was important because he was the only constant in my life; we shared every experience. My teacher was important because she took an interest in me and showed compassion. My grandparents offered consistent support. They gave my mother money for rent and food and paid for private schools for my brother and me; they were like second parents to us."

Despite the emotional problems that some adolescents and emerging adults from divorced families have, the weight of the research evidence underscores that most adolescents and emerging adults cope successfully with their parents' divorce and that a majority of adolescents and emerging adults in divorced families do not have significant adjustment problems (Lansford, 2019).

Should Parents Stay Together for the Sake of Their Children and Adolescents? Whether parents should stay in an unhappy or conflicted marriage for the sake of their children and adolescents is one of the most commonly asked questions about divorce (Morrison, Fife, & Hertlein, 2017). If the stresses and disruptions in family relationships associated with an unhappy, conflicted marriage that erode the well-being of the children and adolescents are reduced by the move to a divorced, single-parent family, divorce might be advantageous (Yu & others, 2010). However, if the diminished resources and increased risks associated with divorce also are accompanied by inept parenting and sustained or increased conflict, not only between the divorced couple but also between parents, children, and siblings, the best choice for the children would be for an unhappy marriage to be retained (Hetherington & Stanley-Hagan, 2002). These are "ifs," however, and it is difficult to determine how these will play out when parents either remain together in an acrimonious marriage or become divorced.

How Much Do Family Processes Matter in Divorced Families? In divorced families, family processes matter a great deal (Gong & Carano, 2020). When the divorced parents have a harmonious relationship and use authoritative parenting, the adjustment of adolescents is improved (Hetherington, 2006). When the divorced parents can agree on child-rearing strategies and can maintain a cordial relationship with each other, frequent visits by the noncustodial parent usually benefit the child (Fabricus & others, 2010). A recent meta-analysis of divorced families found links between higher interparental conflict, less effective parenting, and children and adolescents having more psychological problems (van Dijk & others, 2020). Also, in one study, children were more likely to have behavior problems if their post-divorce home environment was less supportive and stimulating, their mother was less sensitive and more depressed, and if their household income was lower (Weaver & Schofield, 2015). And a recent research review concluded that coparenting (mutual parental support, cooperation, and agreement) following divorce was positively related to child outcomes such as lower anxiety and depression, as well as higher self-esteem and academic performance (Lamela & Figueiredo, 2016).

What concerns are involved in whether parents should stay together for the sake of the children or become divorced?
ejwhite/Getty Images

However, two longitudinal studies revealed that conflict (especially when it is intense and prolonged) between divorced parents was linked to emotional problems, insecure social relationships, and antisocial behavior in adolescents (Hetherington, 2006). A secure attachment also matters.

A study of non-residential fathers in divorced families indicated that high father-child involvement and lower interparental conflict were linked to positive child outcomes (Flam & others, 2016). Unfortunately, father involvement often drops off more than mother involvement, especially for fathers of girls. However, if the adolescent interacts with a caring adult outside the home, such as a mentor, the disengagement can be a positive solution to a disrupted, conflicted family environment.

Might parenting intervention programs improve the process of parenting and reduce children's problems after the divorce? In a 15-year follow-up longitudinal study, divorced families were randomly assigned to an 11-session parenting improvement program or a control condition involving literature when the children were 9 to 12 years old (Wolchik & others, 2021). The parenting program focused on improving mother-child relationship quality, increasing effective discipline, decreasing barriers to father involvement, and reducing interparental conflict. The mothers and children were both given three books on children's adjustment to divorce at one-month intervals. Initial effects included reduced externalizing problems in late childhood and early adolescence, which in turn was linked to better academic outcomes later in adolescence and emerging adulthood as well as predicting increased career success in adulthood.

What Factors Are Involved in the Adolescent's Risk and Vulnerability in a Divorced Family?

Among the factors involved in the adolescent's risk and vulnerability are the adolescent's adjustment prior to the divorce, personality and temperament, developmental status, gender, and custody arrangements. Children and adolescents whose parents later divorce show poorer adjustment before the breakup (Amato & Dorius, 2010).

Personality, temperament, and intelligence also play a role in adolescent adjustment in divorced families. Adolescents who are socially mature and responsible, who show few behavioral problems, and who have an easy temperament are better able to cope with their parents' divorce. Children and adolescents with a difficult temperament often have problems coping with their parents' divorce (Hetherington & Stanley-Hagan, 2002). In one study, a higher level of predivorce maternal sensitivity and child IQ served as protective factors in reducing children's problems after the divorce (Weaver & Schofield, 2015).

In recent decades, an increasing number of children and adolescents have lived in father-custody and joint-custody families (Bergstrom & others, 2017). What is their adjustment like, compared with the adjustment of children and adolescents in mother-custody families? In a recent study of custodial arrangements in 37 countries in North America and Europe, adolescents reported better life satisfaction in joint custody (50 percent of time spent with each parent) than asymmetric custody arrangements (Steinbach & others, 2021). However, further analysis indicated that joint custody was not responsible for the increased life satisfaction of these adolescents, but rather adolescent and family characteristics such as family affluence and communication effectiveness. When joint custody has been compared to single-parent custody with other factors remaining equal, mixed outcomes have been found.

Some studies have shown that boys adjust better in father-custody families and girls adjust better in mother-custody families, but other studies have not shown these results. In one study, adolescents in father-custody families had higher rates of delinquency, believed to be due to less-competent monitoring by the fathers (Buchanan, Maccoby, & Dornsbusch, 1992).

Another factor involved in an adolescent's adjustment in a divorced family is relocation. One study found that when children and adolescents whose parents have divorced experience a move away by either of their parents, they show less effective adjustment (Braver, Ellman, & Fabricus, 2003).

What Role Does Socioeconomic Status Play in the Lives of Adolescents in Divorced Families?

On average, custodial mothers' income decreases about 25 to 50 percent from their predivorce income, compared with a decrease of only 10 percent for custodial fathers (Emery, 1999). This income decrease for divorced mothers is typically accompanied by increased workloads, high rates of job instability, and residential moves to less desirable neighborhoods with inferior schools (Braver & Lamb, 2013). One study found that children from families that had higher incomes before the separation or divorce had fewer internalizing problems (Weaver & Schofield, 2015).

developmental **connection**

Personality

Easy, difficult, and slow to warm up represent one classification of temperament styles. Connect to "The Self, Identity, Emotion, and Personality."

STEPFAMILIES

Not only are parents divorcing more than in previous generations, they are also getting remarried more (Jensen, 2020). It takes time for couples to marry, have children, get divorced, and then remarry. Consequently, there are far more elementary- and secondary-school-age children than infant or preschool-age children in stepfamilies.

The number of remarriages involving children has grown steadily in recent years. As a result of their parents' successive marital transitions, about half of all children whose parents divorce will have a stepfather within four years of parental separation.

Types of Stepfamilies   There are different types of stepfamilies. Some types are based on family structure, others on relationships. The stepfamily may have been preceded by a circumstance in which a spouse died. However, a large majority of stepfamilies are preceded by a divorce rather than a death.

Three common types of stepfamily structure are (1) stepfather, (2) stepmother, and (3) blended or complex. In stepfather families, the mother typically was granted custody of the children and then remarried, introducing a stepfather into her children's lives. In stepmother families, the father usually was granted custody and then remarried, introducing a stepmother into his children's lives. And, in a blended or complex stepfamily, both parents bring children from previous marriages to live in the newly formed stepfamily.

Adjustment   As in divorced families, adolescents in stepfamilies have more adjustment problems than do their counterparts in nondivorced families. The adjustment problems of adolescents in stepfamilies are much like those of adolescents in divorced families: academic struggles, externalizing and internalizing problems, lower self-esteem, earlier sexual activity, delinquency, and so on (Hetherington, 2006). Adjustment for parents and children may take longer in stepfamilies (up to five years or more) than in divorced families, in which a restabilization is more likely to occur within two years (Anderson & others, 1999; Hetherington, 2006). In recent research, a positive relationship between adolescents and their stepfather was associated with a higher level of physical health and a lower level of mental health problems in adolescents (Jensen & Harris, 2017; Jensen & others, 2018). One aspect of a stepfamily that makes adjustment difficult is **boundary ambiguity**, the uncertainty in stepfamilies about who is within or outside the family and who is performing or responsible for carrying out certain tasks in the family system.

Researchers have found that children's relationships with custodial parents (mother in stepfather families, father in stepmother families) are often better than with stepparents (Antfolk & others, 2017; Santrock, Sitterle, & Warshak, 1988). Also, adolescents in simple stepfamilies (stepfather, stepmother) often show better adjustment than their counterparts in complex (blended) families (Anderson & others, 1999; Hetherington, 2006).

There are increased rates of adjustment problems among adolescents in newly remarried families (Hetherington, 2006; Hetherington & Clingempeel, 1992). In research conducted by James Bray and his colleagues (Bray, Berger, & Boethel, 1999; Bray & Kelly, 1998), the formation of a stepfamily often meant that adolescents had to move, and the move involved changing schools and friends. It took time for the stepparent to get to know the stepchildren. The new spouses had to learn how to cope with the challenges of their relationship and parenting together. In Bray's view, the formation of a stepfamily was like merging two cultures.

Bray and his colleagues also found that when the stepparent tried to discipline the stepchild, it often did not work well. Most experts recommend that in the early period of a stepfamily the biological parent should be responsible for administering discipline to children. The stepparent-stepchild relationship develops best when the stepparent spends time with the stepchild in activities that the child enjoys.

In Hetherington's (2006) most recent analysis, adolescents who had been in a simple stepfamily for a number of years were adjusting better than in the early years of the remarried family and were functioning well in comparison with adolescents in conflicted nondivorced families and adolescents in complex

boundary ambiguity Uncertainty in stepfamilies about who is within or outside the family and who is performing or responsible for certain tasks in the family system.

How does living in a stepfamily influence adolescents' development?
Todd Wright/Blend Images/Getty Images

stepfamilies. More than 75 percent of the adolescents in long-established simple stepfamilies described their relationships with their stepparents as "close" or "very close." Hetherington (2006) concludes that in long-established simple stepfamilies adolescents seem eventually to benefit from the presence of a stepparent and the resources provided by the stepparent.

In terms of the age of the child, researchers have found that early adolescence is an especially difficult time for the formation of a stepfamily (Bray & Kelly, 1998). Problems may occur because the stepfamily circumstances exacerbate normal adolescent concerns about identity, sexuality, and autonomy.

Now that we have considered the changing social worlds of adolescents when their parents divorce and remarry, we turn our attention to another aspect of the changing family worlds of adolescents—the increasing number of families that are formed or expanded through adoption.

ADOPTION

Another variation in the type of family in which children live involves adoption, the social and legal process by which a parent-child relationship is established between persons unrelated at birth. As we see next, increased diversity has characterized the adoption of children in the United States in recent years.

The Increased Diversity of Adopted Children and Adoptive Parents
A number of changes have characterized adoptive families in the last four to five decades (Pinderhughes & Brodzinsky, 2019). In the first half of the twentieth century, most U.S. adopted children were healthy, non-Latinx white infants who were adopted at birth or soon after; however, in recent decades as abortion became legal and contraception increased, fewer of these infants became available for adoption. Increasingly, U.S. couples have adopted a much wider diversity of children—from other countries, from other ethnic groups, children with physical and/or emotional problems, and children who had been neglected or abused (Friedman & Lynch, 2020).

Changes also have characterized adoptive parents in recent decades (Brodzinsky & Pinderhughes, 2002). In the first half of the twentieth century, most adoptive parents were people from non-Latinx white middle- or upper-socioeconomic-status backgrounds who were married and did not have any type of disability. However, in recent decades, increased diversity has characterized adoptive parents. Many adoption agencies today have no income requirements for adoptive parents and now allow adults from a wide range of backgrounds to adopt children, including single adults, gay and lesbian adults, and older adults (Farr & Vazquez, 2020b). Further, many adoptions involve other family members (such as aunts, uncles, or grandparents); currently, 30 percent of U.S. adoptive placements are with relatives (Ledesma, 2012). And slightly more than 50 percent of U.S. adoptions occur through the foster care system; in 2014, almost 110,000 children in the U.S. foster care system were waiting for someone to adopt them.

Three pathways to adoption are: (1) domestic adoption from the public welfare system; (2) domestic infant adoption through private agencies and intermediaries; and (3) international adoption (Grotevant & McDermott, 2014). In the next decade, the mix of U.S. adoptions is likely to include fewer domestic infant and international adoptions and more adoptions via the child welfare system (Farr & Hrapczynski, 2020).

The changes in adoption practice over the last several decades make it difficult to generalize about the average adopted child or average adoptive parent (Woolgar & Scott, 2013). As we see next, though, some researchers have provided useful comparisons between adopted children and nonadopted children and their families.

What are some changes in adoption practice in recent decades in the United States?
Xinhua/ZUMApress/Newscom

Developmental Outcomes for Adopted and Nonadopted Children
How do adopted children fare after they are adopted? A research review concluded that adopted children are at higher risk for externalizing (aggression and conduct problems, for example), internalizing (anxiety and depression, for example), and attention problems (ADHD, for example) (Grotevant & McDermott, 2014). In a recent research review of internationally adopted adolescents, although a majority were well adjusted, adoptees had a higher level of mental health problems than their non-adopted counterparts (Askeland & others, 2017). However, a majority of adopted children and adolescents (including those adopted at older ages, transracially, and across national borders) adjust effectively, and their parents report considerable satisfaction with their decision to adopt (Pinderhughes & Brodzinsky, 2019).

An ongoing issue in adopting children is whether there should be any contact with children's biological parents (Leve, Harold, & Kintner, 2020). Open adoption involves sharing identifying information and having contact with the biological parents, versus closed adoption, which consists of not having such sharing and contact. Most adoption agencies today offer adoptive parents the opportunity to have either an open or a closed adoption. A longitudinal study found that when their adopted children reached adulthood, adoptive parents described open adoption positively and saw it as serving the child's best interests (Siegel, 2013). Another longitudinal study found that birth mothers, adoptive parents, and birth children who had contact were more satisfied with their arrangements than those who did not have contact (Grotevant & others, 2013). Also, in this study, contact was linked to more optimal adjustment for adolescents and emerging adults (Grotevant & others, 2013). Birth fathers are less likely to be included in open adoption, but a recent study indicated that they would like to be part of the open adoption triad (adoptee, birth family, and adoptive family) (Clutter, 2020).

Parenting Adopted Children   Many of the keys to effectively parenting adopted children are no different from those for effectively parenting biological children: be supportive and caring; be involved and monitor the child's behavior and whereabouts; be a good communicator; and help the child learn to develop self-control. However, parents of adopted children face some unique circumstances. They need to recognize the differences involved in adoptive family life, communicate about these differences, show respect for the birth family, and support the child's search for self and identity.

Because many children begin to ask where they came from when they are about 4 to 6 years old, this is a natural time for parents to begin talking in simple ways to children about their adoption status (Warshak, 2008). Some parents (although not as many as in the past) decide not to tell their children about the adoption. This secrecy may create psychological risks for the child if he or she later finds out about the adoption.

GAY AND LESBIAN PARENTS

Increasingly, gay and lesbian couples are creating families that include children (Farr & Vazquez, 2020a, b). Data indicate that approximately 20 percent of same-sex couples are raising children under the age of 18 in the United States (Gates, 2013).

An important aspect of gay and lesbian families with children is the sexual identity of parents at the time of a child's birth or adoption (Farr, Vazquez, & Patterson, 2020). The largest group of children with gay and lesbian parents are likely those who were born in the context of heterosexual relationships, with one or both parents only later identifying themselves as gay or lesbian. Gay and lesbian parents may be single or have same-gender partners. In addition, gays and lesbians are increasingly choosing parenthood through donor insemination or adoption (Simon & others, 2018). Researchers have found that the children conceived through new reproductive technologies—such as in vitro fertilization—are as well adjusted as their counterparts conceived by natural means (Golombok & Tasker, 2015).

Earlier in the chapter, we describe the positive outcomes of coparenting for children. One study compared the incidence of coparenting in adoptive heterosexual, lesbian, and gay couples with preschool-aged children (Farr & Patterson, 2013). Both self-reports and observations found that lesbian and gay couples shared child care more than heterosexual couples did, with lesbian couples being the most supportive. Further, another study revealed more positive parenting in adoptive gay father families and fewer child externalizing problems in these families than in heterosexual families (Golombok & others, 2014). In addition, in a recent study, lesbian mothers, heterosexual mothers, and gay fathers reported higher parenting competence than heterosexual fathers (Farr & Vazquez, 2020a). And a UK longitudinal study that assessed gay father, lesbian mother, and heterosexual parent families when their adopted children reached early adolescence found little difference between the three family types, but better parenting quality and parental mental health were linked to fewer adolescent problems (McConnachie & others, 2021).

Another issue focuses on custody arrangements for adolescents. Many gays and lesbians have lost custody of their adolescents to heterosexual spouses following divorce. For this reason, many gay fathers and lesbian mothers are noncustodial parents.

Researchers have found few differences between children growing up with gay fathers and lesbian mothers and children growing up with heterosexual parents (Farr, Vazquez, & Patterson, 2020). For example, children growing up in gay or lesbian families are just as

How does living in a gay or lesbian family influence adolescents' development?
MangoStar_Studio/Getty Images

popular with their peers, and there are no differences between the adjustment and mental health of children living in these families and children living in heterosexual families (Hyde & DeLamater, 2020). For example, in a recent study, the adjustment of school-aged children adopted as infants by gay, lesbian, and heterosexual parents showed no differences (Farr, 2017). Rather, children's behavior patterns and family functioning were predicted by earlier child adjustment issues and parental stress. In another recent study of lesbian and gay adoptive parents, 98 percent of the adoptive parents reported that their children had adjusted well to school (Farr, Oakley, & Ollen, 2016). Also, the overwhelming majority of children growing up in a gay or lesbian family have a heterosexual orientation (Golombok & Tasker, 2015).

Review Connect Reflect

 LG4 Describe the changing family in a changing society.

Review

- How do working parents influence adolescent development?
- What are the effects of divorce on adolescents?
- How does growing up in a stepfamily influence adolescents' development?
- How does being adopted affect adolescent development?
- What are the effects on adolescents of having gay or lesbian parents?

Connect

- What did you learn about siblings earlier in this chapter that might inform your understanding of stepfamilies and the issues they face?

Reflect *Your Own Personal Journey of Life*

- You have studied many aspects of families and adolescents in this chapter. Imagine that you have decided to write a book describing life in your family when you were an adolescent. What would the title of the book be? What would be the main theme of the book?

5 Social Policy, Adolescents, and Families

 LG5 Explain what is needed for improved social policy involving adolescents and their families.

We have seen in this chapter that parents play very important roles in adolescent development. Although adolescents are moving toward independence, they are still connected with their families, which are far more important to them than is commonly believed. We know that competent adolescent development is most likely to happen when adolescents have parents who do the following things:

- Effectively manage family matters and monitor adolescents' lives effectively
- Show them support, warmth, and respect
- Demonstrate sustained interest in their lives
- Recognize and adapt to their changing levels of cognitive and socioemotional development
- Communicate expectations for high standards of conduct and achievement
- Display authoritative, constructive ways of dealing with problems and conflict

Compared with families who have young children, families with adolescents have been neglected in community programs and public policies. The Carnegie Council on Adolescent Development (1995) identified some key opportunities for improving social policy regarding families with adolescents. Even now, at the beginning of the third decade of the twenty-first century, the recommendations made by the council in 1995 have not yet been fully implemented:

- Schools, cultural arts centers, religious and youth organizations, and health-care agencies should examine the extent to which they involve parents in activities with adolescents and should develop ways to engage parents and adolescents in activities that both generations enjoy.
- Professionals such as teachers, psychologists, nurses, physicians, youth specialists, and others who have contact with adolescents need not only to work with the individual

adolescent but also to increase the time they spend interacting with the adolescent's family.

- Employers should extend to the parents of young adolescents the workplace policies now reserved only for parents of young children. These policies include flexible work schedules, job sharing, telecommuting, and part-time work with benefits. This change in work/family policy would free parents to spend more time with their teenagers.
- Community institutions such as businesses, schools, and youth organizations should become more involved in providing after-school programs. After-school programs for elementary school children are increasing, but such programs for adolescents are rare. More high-quality, community-based programs for adolescents are needed in the after-school, weekend, and vacation time periods.

Several national organizations develop and advocate supportive family policies at the federal, state, and local levels. Four of the best organizations in this regard are listed below:

- The Annie E. Casey Foundation (www.aecf.org)
- First Focus, a Washington, D.C.-based policy center whose mission is to make children and families a major priority (www.firstfocus.net)
- The Institute for Youth, Education, and Families at the National League of Cities (www.nlc.org)
- The National Collaboration for Youth (www.collab4youth.org)

Community programs can provide a monitored, structured context for adolescents to study in during the after-school hours. *In addition to offering better after-school options for adolescents, what are some other ways that U.S. social policy could provide increased support to families with adolescents?*
Ben McKeown/AP Images

We have discussed many aspects of families in this chapter, and throughout this edition we explore other dimensions and issues related to families and adolescents. In the "Introduction" chapter you read about today's adolescents in the United States and around the world. In "Puberty, Health, and Biological Foundations" we discussed the important roles parents have in guiding children and adolescents to live healthier lives. In "The Self, Identity, Emotion, and Personality" we explored how parents influence children's and adolescents' self-esteem, self-regulation, identity, emotional development, and personality. In "Gender" we described parenting influences on children's and adolescents' gender development. In "Sexuality," we examined the ways in which parents can help or harm adolescents' likelihood of engaging in sexual risk-taking. In "Moral Development, Values, and Religion," we discussed how parents influence various aspects of adolescents' moral development, values, and religious identity.

Following this chapter, in "Peers, Romantic Relationships, and Lifestyles," you will read about parental influences on adolescents' and emerging adults' peer interactions, romantic relationships, cultural identity, and lifestyle choices. In "Schools," you will explore how parents influence various dimensions of adolescents' schooling. In "Achievement, Work, and Careers," special attention is given to the strong influence parents have on adolescents' achievement as well as their importance in exploring careers with adolescents. The chapter on "Culture" explores cross-cultural comparisons of parenting and adolescent development, the role that parents' socioeconomic status has on adolescent development, and how numerous aspects of ethnicity, such as immigration, social injustice, and discrimination can impact adolescents' lives. And in "Problems in Adolescence and Emerging Adulthood" we will consider parental influences on whether adolescents develop drug use problems, juvenile delinquency, depression, suicide, and eating disorders.

Review Connect Reflect

LG5 Explain what is needed for improved social policy involving adolescents and their families.

Review

- What is needed for improved social policy involving adolescents and their families?

Connect

- Do current social policies appear to view the family as a system?

Reflect *Your Own Personal Journey of Life*

- If you were a U.S. senator, what would you seek to do to improve social policy involving the families of adolescents? What would be your number one priority?

reach your **learning goals**

Families

1 Family Processes

 LG1 Discuss the nature of family processes in adolescence.

Reciprocal Socialization and the Family as a System

- The concept of reciprocal socialization is that adolescents socialize parents just as parents socialize adolescents. The family is a system of interacting individuals with different subsystems—some dyadic, some polyadic.

Maturation

- Relationships are influenced by the maturation of the adolescent and the maturation of parents. Adolescent changes include puberty, expanded logical reasoning, increased idealistic and egocentric thought, violated expectations, changes in schooling, peers, friendships, dating, and movement toward independence. Changes in parents might include decreased marital satisfaction, economic burdens, career reevaluation, shifting time perspectives, and health/body concerns.

- Adults follow one developmental trajectory and children and adolescents another one. How these trajectories mesh affects timing of entry into various family tasks.

Sociocultural and Historical Influences

- Sociocultural and historical contexts influence families, reflecting Bronfenbrenner's concepts of macrosystem and chronosystem. Both great upheavals such as war and subtle transitions in ways of life may influence families. A major change in families in the last several decades has been the extensive immigration of Latinx and Asian families into the United States. Another major change is the dramatic increase in media use by adolescents and other family members.

2 Adolescents' and Emerging Adults' Relationships with Their Parents

LG2 Describe adolescents' and emerging adults' relationships with their parents.

Parents as Managers

- An increasing trend is to conceptualize parents as managers of adolescents' lives. This involves being a parent who finds information, makes contacts, helps structure choices, and provides guidance. Parents can serve as regulators of their adolescents' social contacts with peers, friends, and adults. A key aspect of the managerial role involves parental monitoring. A current interest focuses on adolescents' management of their parents' access to information.

Parenting Styles

- Authoritarian, authoritative, neglectful, and indulgent are four main parenting styles. Authoritative parenting, which encourages independence but places limits and controls on adolescents, is associated with socially competent adolescent behavior more than the other styles.

- Some ethnic variations in parenting have been found, such as the positive relation between training by Asian American parents and the achievement of their adolescents. Recent research indicates that an authoritative parenting style also benefits emerging adults, but a controlling-indulgent style is related to negative outcomes for emerging adults.

Mothers, Fathers, and Coparenting

- Both mothers and fathers play important, but sometimes different, roles in adolescents' development. Coparenting, father-mother cooperation, and mutual respect enhance the adolescent's development.

Parent-Adolescent Conflict

- Conflict with parents increases in early adolescence, but such conflict is usually moderate and can serve a positive developmental function related to increased independence and identity exploration. The magnitude of the generation gap has been exaggerated, although as many as 20 percent of families experience parent-adolescent conflict that is high enough to create problems.

Autonomy and Attachment

- Many parents have a difficult time handling the adolescent's push for autonomy. Autonomy is a complex concept with many referents. Developmental transitions in autonomy include the onset of early adolescence and the time when individuals leave home and go to college. The wise parent relinquishes control in areas where the adolescent makes mature decisions and retains more control in areas where the adolescent makes immature decisions. Adolescents do not simply move away into a world isolated from parents.

- Secure attachment to parents in adolescence increases the probability that an adolescent will be socially competent and explore a widening social world in a healthy way. Increasingly, researchers classify attachment in adolescence into one secure category (secure/autonomous) and three insecure categories (dismissing/avoidant, preoccupied/ambivalent, and unresolved/ disorganized). Increased research into attachment during emerging adulthood is revealing that securely attached emerging adults have better social relationships than do insecurely attached emerging adults.

Emerging Adults' Relationships with Their Parents

- An increasing number of emerging adults are returning to the family home to live with their parents, often for economic reasons. Both emerging adults and their parents need to adapt when emerging adults return home to live.

Grandparents and Grandchildren

- Grandparents are playing increasingly important roles in grandchildren's lives, providing especially important support in the aftermath of family crises such as divorce, death, and abandonment.

Intergenerational Relationships

- Connections between parents and children play important roles in development through the life span. An increasing number of studies indicate that intergenerational relationships influence the development of adolescents. Marital interaction, a supportive family environment, and divorce in the adolescent's family of origin are among the factors that are linked to later characteristics and relationships when the adolescent moves into adulthood.

3 Sibling Relationships

LG3 Characterize sibling relationships in adolescence.

Sibling Roles

- Sibling relationships often involve more conflict than do relationships with other individuals. However, adolescents also share many positive moments with siblings by providing each other with emotional support and social communication.

Birth Order

- The influence of birth order has been of special interest to researchers, and differences between firstborns and later-borns have been reported. The only child often is more socially competent than the "spoiled brat" stereotype suggests. An increasing number of family researchers believe that birth-order effects have been exaggerated and that other factors are more important in predicting the adolescent's behavior.

4 The Changing Family in a Changing Society

LG4 Describe the changing family in a changing society.

Working Parents

- It is the nature of parents' work, not whether one parent works outside the home or does not, that is linked to adolescents' development. The summer months and the 3 to 6 p.m. time frame during the school year (times when parents are not at home) pose opportunities for adolescents to engage in risky behaviors. Adolescents can benefit from structured activities and adult monitoring during these time periods.

Divorced Families

- Adolescents in divorced families have more adjustment problems than their counterparts in nondivorced families, although the magnitude of the effects is debated. Whether parents who want to divorce should stay together for the sake of the adolescent is difficult to determine, although parental conflict has a negative effect on adolescents.

- Adolescents are better adjusted in divorced families when their parents have a harmonious relationship with each other and practice authoritative parenting. Among other factors to be considered in adolescent adjustment are adjustment prior to the divorce, personality and temperament, and developmental status, gender, and custody arrangements. Income loss for divorced mothers is linked to a number of other stressors that can affect adolescent adjustment.

Stepfamilies

- Increasing numbers of adolescents are growing up in stepfamilies. Stepfamilies involve different structures (stepfather, stepmother, blended). Adolescents in stepfamilies have more adjustment problems than do children in nondivorced families. Adjustment is especially difficult during the first several years of a stepfamily's existence and is challenging for young adolescents.

Adoption

- Although adopted adolescents have more problems than their nonadopted counterparts do, the majority of adopted adolescents function effectively. When adoption occurs very early in development, the outcomes for the adolescent are better than when adoption occurs later. Because of the dramatic changes that have occurred in adoption in recent decades, it is difficult to generalize about the average adopted adolescent or average adoptive family.

Gay and Lesbian Parents

- There is considerable diversity among lesbian mothers, gay fathers, and their adolescents. Researchers have found few differences between adolescents growing up in gay or lesbian families and adolescents growing up in heterosexual families.

5 Social Policy, Adolescents, and Families

 LG5 Explain what is needed for improved social policy involving adolescents and their families.

- Families with adolescents have been neglected in social policy. A number of recommendations for improving social policy for families target the extent to which parents are involved in schools, youth organizations, and health-care agencies; the degree to which teachers and other professionals invite and encourage parents to be involved in schools and other settings that adolescents frequent; the extent to which policies are developed that encourage employers to provide more flexible scheduling for parents; and the provision of greater funding by institutions such as businesses, schools, and youth organizations for high-quality programs for adolescents in after-school, weekend, and vacation time periods.

key **terms**

authoritarian parenting
authoritative parenting
boundary ambiguity
dismissing/avoidant
   attachment

emotional autonomy
indulgent parenting
insecure attachment
multiple developmental
   trajectories

neglectful parenting
preoccupied/ambivalent
   attachment
reciprocal socialization
secure attachment

unresolved/disorganized
   attachment

key **people**

Mary Ainsworth
Joseph Allen
Diana Baumrind

John Bowlby
Urie Bronfenbrenner
Ann Crouter

E. Mark Cummings
Judy Dunn
Andrew Fuligni

E. Mavis Hetherington

improving **the lives of adolescents and emerging adults**

101 Insights and Strategies for Parenting Teenagers (2010)
Sheryl Feinstein
Monterey, CA: Healthy Learning
> An excellent, easy-to-read book for parents that provides valuable strategies for guiding adolescents through the transition from childhood to emerging adulthood.

Building a Brighter Future (2011)
National Collaboration for Youth (www.collab4youth.org)
> The National Collaboration for Youth is one of the most important national organizations involved in advocating positive social policy for youth and their families. This up-to-date report provides an essential agenda for America's youth.

Divorce Lessons: Real-Life Stories and What You Can Learn from Them (2006)
Alison Clarke-Stewart and Cornelia Brentano
Charleston, SC: BookSurge
> An outstanding book that gives special attention to the experiences and development of emerging adults who have grown up in divorced families.

Getting to 30: A Parent's Guide to the 20-Something Years (2014)
Jeffrey Arnett and Elizabeth Fishel
New York: Workman
> A parent's guide to emerging adulthood and the late twenties, with many helpful strategies.

You and Your Adolescent (2011)
Laurence Steinberg
New York: Simon and Schuster
> Leading adolescence expert Laurence Steinberg provides a broad developmental overview of adolescence, with good advice for parents along the way.

Big Brothers Big Sisters of America (www.bbbsa.org)
> Single mothers and single fathers who are having problems with a son or daughter might want to get a responsible adult to spend at least one afternoon every other week with the son or daughter.

National Stepfamily Resource Center (www.stepfamilies.info)
> This organization serves as a clearinghouse of information, resources, and support for stepfamilies.

chapter 9

PEERS, ROMANTIC RELATIONSHIPS, AND LIFESTYLES

chapter outline

1 Exploring Peer Relations and Friendship

Learning Goal 1 Discuss the roles of peer relations, friendship, and loneliness in adolescent development.

Peer Relations
Friendship
Loneliness

2 Adolescent Groups

Learning Goal 2 Summarize what takes place in adolescent groups.

Groups in Childhood and Adolescence
Cliques and Crowds
Youth Organizations

3 Gender and Culture

Learning Goal 3 Describe the roles of gender and culture in adolescent peer groups and friendships.

Gender
Socioeconomic Status and Ethnicity
Culture

4 Dating and Romantic Relationships

Learning Goal 4 Characterize adolescent dating and romantic relationships.

Functions of Dating
Types of Dating and Developmental Changes
Emotion, Adjustment, and Romantic Relationships
Romantic Love and Its Construction
Gender and Culture

5 Emerging Adult Lifestyles

Learning Goal 5 Explain the diversity of emerging adult lifestyles.

Single Adults
Cohabiting Adults
Married Adults
Divorced Adults
Gay and Lesbian Adults

SpeedKingz/Shutterstock

Lynn Brown and Carol Gilligan (1992) conducted in-depth interviews of one hundred 10- to 13-year-old girls who were making the transition to adolescence. They listened to what these girls were saying about how important friends were to them. The girls were very curious about the human world they lived in and kept track of what was happening to their peers and friends. The girls spoke about the pleasure they derived from the intimacy and fun of human connection, and about the potential for hurt in relationships. They especially highlighted the importance of clique formation in their lives.

One girl, Noura, said that she learned about what it feels like to be the person that everyone doesn't like and that it was very painful. A number of the girls talked about how many girls say nice and kind things to be polite but often don't really mean them. They know the benefits of being perceived as the perfect, happy girl, at least on the surface. Suspecting that people prefer the "perfect girl," they experiment with her image and the happiness she might bring.

Cliques can provide emotional support for girls who are striving to be perfect but know they are not. One girl, Victoria, commented that she and three other girls who are like her and who weren't very popular decided to form a "club." She now felt that when she was sad or depressed she could count on the "club" for support. Though they were "leftovers" and did not get into the most popular cliques, these four girls said they knew they were liked.

Another girl, Judy, at age 13, spoke about her interest in romantic relationships. She said that although she and her girlfriends were only 13 they wanted to be romantic, and she talked about her lengthy private conversations about boys with her girlfriends.

preview

In this chapter we consider peers, romantic relationships, and lifestyles. When you think back to your adolescent years, you may recall that many of your most enjoyable moments were spent with peers— on the telephone, in school activities, in the neighborhood, on dates, at dances, or just hanging out. Adolescents typically have a larger number of acquaintances than children do. Beginning in early adolescence, teenagers also typically prefer a smaller number of friendships that are more intense and intimate than those of children. Cliques and crowds take on more importance as adolescents "hang out" together. Dating and romantic relationships become part of most adolescents' and emerging adults' lives, and deciding on a specific lifestyle becomes particularly important in emerging adulthood.

1 Exploring Peer Relations and Friendship

LG1 Discuss the roles of peer relations, friendship, and loneliness in adolescent development.

Peer Relations

Friendship

Loneliness

Peers and friends play powerful roles in the lives of adolescents. Let's explore what these roles are.

PEER RELATIONS

What functions do peer groups serve? How are family and peer relations linked? How extensively do adolescents strive for conformity? What kinds of statuses do peers have? How do social cognition and emotions influence peer relations? What are some strategies for improving social skills? We will consider these and other questions in this section.

Peer Group Functions Adolescents have strong needs to be liked and accepted by friends and the larger peer group, which can result in pleasurable feelings when they are accepted or extreme stress and anxiety when they are excluded and disparaged by peers. To many adolescents, how they are seen by peers is the most important aspect of their lives.

What functions do peers serve?
Eric Audras/PhotoAlto/Getty Images

Peers are individuals who are about the same age or maturity level. Same-age peer interaction serves a unique role in U.S. culture. Age grading would occur even if schools were not age graded and adolescents were left alone to determine the composition of their own societies. One of the most important functions of the peer group is to provide a source of information about the world outside the family. From the peer group, adolescents receive feedback about their abilities. Adolescents learn whether what they do is better than, as good as, or worse than what other adolescents do. Learning this at home is difficult because siblings are usually older or younger, and sibling rivalry can cloud the accuracy of comparison.

As you read about peers, also keep in mind that, although peer experiences have important influences on adolescents' development, those influences vary according to the way peer experience is measured, the outcomes specified, and the developmental trajectories traversed (Prinstein & Giletta, 2020). "Peers" and "peer group" are global concepts that can be beneficial in understanding peer influences as long as their variations are considered. For example, the term *peers* can be used to describe acquaintances, members of a clique, neighborhood associates, friends, and participants in an activity group such as a sports team.

- - - - - - - ▶
Developmental **Connection**

Theories

Bronfenbrenner's ecological theory emphasizes the contexts of adolescent development. Connect to "Introduction."
◀ - - - - - -

Peer Contexts Peer interaction is influenced by contexts, which can include the type of peer the adolescent interacts with (such as an acquaintance, a crowd, a clique, a friend, a romantic partner) and the situation or location where they are, such as school, neighborhood, community center, dance, religious setting, sporting event, and so on, as well as the culture in which the adolescent lives (Collins & others, 2021; Shi & others, 2020). As they interact with peers in these various contexts, adolescents are likely to encounter different messages and different opportunities to engage in adaptive and maladaptive behavior that can influence their development (Prinstein, Nesi, & Telzer, 2020). These peer contexts also are influenced by factors such as how effectively parents manage adolescents' peer interactions and whether adults are present (Prinstein & Giletta, 2020). For example, one study revealed that when parents failed to monitor young adolescents adequately, the young adolescents were more susceptible to peer pressure (Steinberg, 1986).

Nowhere have changes in the influence of context on peer relations been more apparent in recent years than in the increased connections adolescents have made with peers and friends through networked technologies. Text messaging has become the main way adolescents connect with friends, surpassing even face-to-face contact (Lenhart & others, 2015).

A recent analysis described five ways in which social media transform adolescent peer relationships: (1) *changing the frequency or immediacy of experiences* (potential for immediate, frequent social support, reassurance, negative feedback, and co-rumination); (2) *amplifying experiences and demands* (heightened feedback seeking and expectations for relationship maintenance and access); (3) *altering the qualitative aspects of interactions* (less rich social support, increased comfort in interactions); (4) *facilitating new opportunities for compensatory behaviors* (possible exclusive online relationships and communication with geographically distant friends); and (5) *creating completely novel behaviors* (new opportunities to publicize "top friends" and relationships) (Nesi, Choukas-Bradley, & Prinstein, 2018). The chapter on "Culture" includes additional discussion of adolescents' use of social media, and later in this chapter we will explore the role of social media in romantic relationships.

peers Individuals who are about the same age or maturity level.

The dramatic changes in daily life that accompanied the COVID-19 pandemic had a negative impact on adolescent peer relations (Orben, Tomova, & Blakemore, 2020). The restrictions placed on social interaction by the pandemic, including social distancing and more limited interaction due to school shutdowns, increased adolescents' social isolation. A recent study assessed the mental health of adolescents at two points in time—during the 12 months leading up to the COVID-19 outbreak and during the first two months after the advent of government restrictions and increased online learning. The adolescents experienced an increase in depressive and anxious symptoms during the lockdown, as well as a decrease in life satisfaction, and the outcomes were more negative for girls than for boys (Magson & others, 2021).

What are some examples of how social contexts and individual difference factors influence adolescents' peer relations?
Creatas Images/Punchstock/Getty Images

Individual Difference Factors   Individual differences among peers also are important influences on peer relations (Strickhouser & Sutin, 2020). Among the wide range of individual differences that can affect peer relations are personality traits, such as how shy or outgoing an adolescent is. For example, a very shy adolescent is more likely than a gregarious adolescent to be neglected by peers and to feel anxious about introducing himself or herself to new peers. In a longitudinal study, shyness in childhood predicted lower emotional stability and lower extraversion in adolescence, with these links mainly due negative peer experiences (Baardstu & others, 2020). Other individual differences include the adolescent's openness to peer influence and the status/power of the adolescent versus the status/power of the other adolescent or adolescent peer group (Brown & Larson, 2009). Being in a subordinate social position in a dyad or group can decrease the adolescent's ability to influence peers and increase the adolescent's susceptibility to peer influence.

Developmental Connection
Personality
Personality traits and temperament styles influence adolescent development. Connect to "The Self, Identity, Emotion, and Personality."

Developmental Changes in Time Spent with Peers   Boys and girls spend an increasing amount of time in peer interaction during middle and late childhood and adolescence. In one investigation, children interacted with peers 10 percent of their day at age 2, 20 percent at age 4, and more than 40 percent between the ages of 7 and 11 (Barker & Wright, 1951). In a typical school day, there were 299 episodes with peers per day. By adolescence, peer relations occupy large chunks of an individual's life. In one investigation, over the course of one weekend, young adolescent boys and girls spent more than twice as much time with peers as with parents (Condry, Simon, & Bronfenbrenner, 1968).

Are Peers Necessary for Development?   Good peer relations might be necessary for normal social development in adolescence (Savina & Moran, 2022). Social isolation, or the inability to "plug into" a social network, is linked with many different problems and disorders, ranging from delinquency and problem drinking to depression and academic difficulties (Prins & others, 2021).

Positive and Negative Peer Relations   Peer influences can be both positive and negative (Champion, Ha, & Dishion, 2021; Prinstein & Giletta, 2020). Adolescents explore the principles of fairness and justice by working through disagreements with peers. They also learn to be keen observers of peers' interests and perspectives in order to smoothly integrate themselves into ongoing peer activities. And adolescents learn to be skilled and sensitive partners in intimate relationships by forging close friendships with selected peers. They carry these intimacy skills forward to help form the foundation of later dating and marital relationships.

Of course, peer influences can be negative as well as positive (Savina & Moran, 2022). For example, peer relations are linked to adolescents' patterns of drug use, delinquency, depression, sexual activity, and self-injury. In a recent Chinese study, peer drug use increased the frequency of adolescent drug use, regardless of gender (Zhang & Demant, 2021). Another study found that college students with risky social networks (friends who drink, for example) were ten times more likely to engage in heavy drinking (Mason, Zaharakis, & Benotsch, 2014). Further, a recent study that examined parent and peer influences on adolescents' smoking revealed that peers had a more powerful influence than parents (Scalici & Schulz, 2017).

Developmental Connection
Problems and Disorders
The types of friends adolescents have are linked to whether adolescents engage in substance abuse and delinquency. Connect to "Problems in Adolescence and Emerging Adulthood."

What are some of the positive and negative aspects of peer relations?
(left): Fuse/Getty Images; (right): KatarzynaBialasiewicz/Getty Images

And one study revealed that having friends who engage in delinquent behavior is associated with early onset and more persistent delinquency (Evans, Simons, & Simons, 2016). In addition, a recent study indicated that peers' influence on adolescents' eating behavior is often negative and characterized by increased consumption of high-calorie foods with low nutritional value (Rageliene & Gronhoj, 2020).

Family-Peer Linkages   Parents may influence their children's and adolescents' peer relations in many ways, both direct and indirect (Meisel & Colder, 2021). Parents affect their adolescents' peer relations through their interactions with them, how they manage their lives, and the opportunities they provide to them.

Adolescents do show a strong motivation to be with their peers and become independent. However, it is not accurate to assume that movement toward peer involvement and autonomy is unrelated to parent-adolescent relationships. Researchers have provided persuasive evidence that adolescents live in a connected world with parents and peers, not one in which parents and peers are disconnected from each other (Kaufman & others, 2020).

What are some of the ways that the worlds of parents and peers are connected? Parents' choices of neighborhoods, churches, schools, and their own friends influence the pool from which their adolescents select possible friends (Cooper & Ayers-Lopez, 1985). For example, parents can choose to live in a neighborhood with playgrounds, parks, and youth organizations or in a neighborhood where houses are far apart, few adolescents live, and youth organizations are not well developed. Also, in recent research with third- and fourth-graders, feeling related to peers at school was associated with having a positive outlook both at school and at home (Schmidt, Dirk, & Schmiedek, 2019). And in another study, in both the United States and China, parents' peer restriction predicted a decrease in children's adjustment over time (Xiong & others, 2020).

Parents can model or coach their adolescents in ways of relating to peers. In one study, parents acknowledged that they recommended specific strategies to their adolescents to help them develop more positive peer relations (Rubin & Slomon, 1994). For example, parents discussed with their adolescents how disputes could be mediated and how to become less shy. They also encouraged them to be tolerant and to resist peer pressure.

One of the most consistent outcomes of attachment research in adolescence is the finding that secure attachment to parents is linked to positive peer relations (Allen & Miga, 2010; Cai & others, 2013). A meta-analysis found that the link between mother attachment and peer attachment was much stronger than the relationship between father attachment and peer attachment (Gorrese & Ruggieri, 2012).

Although adolescent-parent attachments are correlated with adolescent outcomes, the correlations are moderate, indicating that the success or failure of parent-adolescent attachments does not necessarily guarantee success or failure in peer relationships. Clearly, secure attachment with parents can be an asset for the adolescent, fostering the trust needed to engage in close relationships with others and providing a foundation for developing interpersonal

Developmental Connection

Families

Parents play important roles in adolescents' peer relations. Connect to "Families."

What are some links between parent-adolescent and adolescent-peer relations?
(left): Fuse/Getty Images; (right): Somos/SuperStock

skills. Nonetheless, a significant minority of adolescents from strong, supportive families struggle with peer relations for a variety of reasons, such as being physically unattractive, maturing late, and experiencing cultural and socioeconomic status (SES) discrepancies. On the other hand, some adolescents from troubled families find a positive, fresh start with peer relations that can compensate for their problematic family backgrounds.

Peer Pressure   Young adolescents conform more closely to peer standards than children do. Around the eighth and ninth grades, conformity to peers—especially to their antisocial standards—peaks (Prinstein & Giletta, 2020). At this point, adolescents are most likely to go along with a peer to steal hubcaps off a car, paint graffiti on a wall, or steal cosmetics from a store counter. One study found that U.S. adolescents are more likely than Japanese adolescents to put pressure on their peers to resist parental influence (Rothbaum & others, 2000). Also, a recent study found that boys were more likely to be influenced by peer pressure involving sexual behavior than were girls (Widman & others, 2016).

Which adolescents are most likely to conform to peers? Mitchell Prinstein and his colleagues (2009) have conducted research and analysis addressing this question. They conclude that adolescents who are uncertain about their social identity, which can appear in the form of low self-esteem and high social anxiety, are most likely to conform to peers. This uncertainty often increases during times of transition at school or at home. Also, adolescents are more likely to conform when they are in the presence of someone they perceive to have higher status than they do. And a recent study of eighth-graders revealed that peer pressure was associated with substance use (Jelsma & Varner, 2021).

sociometric status The extent to which children and adolescents are liked or disliked by their peer group.

Peer Statuses   The term **sociometric status** is used to describe the extent to which children and adolescents are liked or disliked by their peer group (Wang & Hawk, 2020). Sociometric status is typically assessed by asking children and adolescents to rate how much they like or dislike each of their classmates (Ettekal & Ladd, 2020). Alternatively, it may be assessed by asking children and adolescents to nominate the peers they like the most and those they like the least. Most adolescents conform to the mainstream standards of their peers. However, the rebellious or anti-conformist adolescent reacts counter to the mainstream peer group's expectations, deliberately moving away from the actions or beliefs this group advocates. One study revealed that low peer status in childhood was associated with an increased

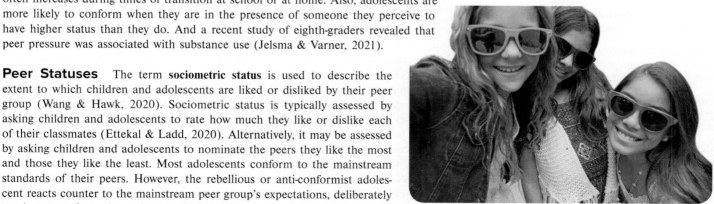

What characterizes peer pressure in adolescence?
Christin Rose/Image Source/Getty Images

probability of being unemployed and having mental health problems in adulthood (Almquist & Brannstrom, 2014).

Developmentalists have distinguished five types of peer statuses:

- **Popular adolescents** are frequently nominated as a best friend and are rarely disliked by their peers.
- **Average adolescents** receive an average number of both positive and negative nominations from their peers.
- **Neglected adolescents** are infrequently nominated as a best friend but are not disliked by their peers.
- **Rejected adolescents** are infrequently nominated as someone's best friend and are actively disliked by their peers.
- **Controversial adolescents** are frequently nominated both as someone's best friend and as being disliked.

What are some peer statuses that characterize adolescents?
Corbis/VCG/Getty Images

developmental **connection**

Relationships

Bullying is an increasing concern in adolescence. Connect to "Schools."

popular adolescents Adolescents who are frequently nominated as a best friend and are rarely disliked by their peers.

average adolescents Adolescents who receive an average number of both positive and negative nominations from their peers.

neglected adolescents Adolescents who are infrequently nominated as a best friend but are not disliked by their peers.

rejected adolescents Adolescents who are infrequently nominated as a best friend and are actively disliked by their peers.

controversial adolescents Adolescents who are frequently nominated both as a best friend and as being disliked.

Popular adolescents have a number of social skills that contribute to their being well liked (McDonald & Asher, 2018). Researchers have found that popular adolescents give out reinforcements, listen carefully, maintain open lines of communication with peers, are happy, control their negative emotions, show enthusiasm and concern for others, and are self-confident without being conceited (Hartup, 1983; Rubin, Bukowski, & Parker, 1998). In one study, adolescents' popularity with their peers was associated with their dating popularity (Houser, Mayeux, & Cross, 2015). Also, in a recent study, being a fun person to be around was found to be an important component of peer popularity (Laursen & others, 2020). Neglected adolescents engage in low rates of interaction with their peers and are often described as shy by peers. Rejected adolescents often have more serious adjustment problems than those who are neglected (Prinstein & others, 2018). The combination of being rejected by peers and being aggressive especially forecasts problems. In a recent study, peer rejection was frequently preceded by either aggression or depression in adolescence (Beeson, Brittain, & Vaillancourt, 2020). Peer rejection is consistently linked to the development and maintenance of conduct problems and antisocial behavior (Kornienko, Ha, & Dishion, 2020).

An analysis by John Coie (2004, pp. 252–253) provided three reasons why aggressive peer-rejected boys have problems in social relationships:

- First, the rejected, aggressive boys are more impulsive and have problems sustaining attention. As a result, they are more likely to be disruptive of ongoing activities in the classroom and in focused group play.
- Second, rejected, aggressive boys are more emotionally reactive. They are aroused to anger more easily and tend to have more difficulty calming down once aroused. Because of this they are more prone to become angry at peers and attack them verbally and physically.
- Third, rejected boys have fewer social skills for making friends and maintaining positive relationships with peers.

Not all rejected adolescents are aggressive (Rubin, Bukowski, & Bowker, 2015). Although aggression and its related characteristics of impulsiveness and disruptiveness underlie rejection about half the time, approximately 10 to 20 percent of rejected adolescents are shy. In a later section, "Strategies for Improving Social Skills," we discuss ways to help rejected and neglected adolescents improve their social skills.

A final comment about peer statuses in adolescence is in order. Much of the peer status research involves samples from middle and late childhood, and in some cases early adolescence, but not late adolescence. One reason for this focus is that to assess peer status, a fairly well-defined group of classmates who know each other well and interact on a regular basis is needed (Bellmore, Jiang, & Juvonen, 2010). In contrast with elementary school and middle school, where students stay with the same group most of the day (more prevalent in elementary school than in middle school), it is difficult to assess peer status in high school contexts where students are in contact with large numbers of peers and are unlikely to know all of their classmates.

Social Cognition and Emotion The social cognitive skills and social knowledge of adolescents are important aspects of successful peer relations. So is the ability to manage and regulate one's emotions.

Social Cognition *Social cognition* involves thoughts about social matters (Deschrijver & Palmer, 2020). A distinction can be made between knowledge and process in social cognition. Learning about the social knowledge adolescents bring with them to peer relations is important, as is studying how adolescents process information during peer interaction (Long & Li, 2020).

As children move into adolescence, they acquire more social knowledge (sometimes referred to as social intelligence), and there is considerable individual variation in how much each adolescent knows about what it takes to make friends, to get peers to like him or her, and so forth. For example, does the adolescent know that to have a high status with peers it is beneficial to understand others' needs, goals, and intentions, and to act accordingly? Does the adolescent know that giving out reinforcements will increase the likelihood that she or he will be popular? That is, does Teriana consciously know that, by telling Sierra such things as "I really like that sweater you have on today" and "You sure are popular with the guys," she will enhance the likelihood that Sierra will want to be her friend? Does the adolescent know that friendship involves sharing intimate conversations and that a friendship usually improves when the adolescent shares private, confidential information with another adolescent? And, to what extent does the adolescent know that comforting and listening skills will improve friendship relations?

A study of 14- and 15-year-olds examined links between social intelligence and peer popularity (Meijs & others, 2010). In this study, social intelligence was related to peer popularity but not to academic achievement.

From a social cognitive perspective, children and adolescents may have difficulty with peer relations because they lack appropriate social cognitive skills (Dodge, 2011b; Rubin, Bukowski, & Bowker, 2015). One investigation explored the possibility that social cognitive skill deficits characterize individuals who have peer-related difficulties (Asarnow & Callan, 1985). Boys with and without peer adjustment difficulties were identified, and then a number of social cognitive processes or skills were assessed. These included the boys' ability to generate alternative solutions to hypothetical problems, to evaluate these solutions in terms of their effectiveness, and to produce self-statements. It was found that boys without peer adjustment problems generated more alternative solutions, proposed more assertive and mature solutions, gave less intense aggressive solutions, showed more adaptive planning, and evaluated physically aggressive responses less positively than did the boys with peer adjustment problems. For example, as shown in Figure 1, negative-peer-status sixth-grade boys were much less likely to adaptively plan ahead and slightly less likely to generate alternative solutions than were their positive-peer-status counterparts.

Social information processing influences peer relations (Dodge, 2011a, b). For example, consider a situation in which a peer accidentally trips and knocks another boy's soft drink out of his hand. The other boy misinterprets the encounter as a hostile one, which leads him to retaliate aggressively against the peer. Through repeated encounters of this kind, peers come

What are some aspects of social cognition that are involved in getting along with peers?
SW Productions/Getty Images

developmental **connection**

Theory

In Bandura's social cognitive theory, adolescent development is influenced by reciprocal interaction between person/cognitive, environmental, and behavioral factors. Connect to "Introduction."

developmental **connection**

Social Cognition

One aspect of social cognition in adolescence is adolescent egocentrism. Connect to "The Brain and Cognitive Development."

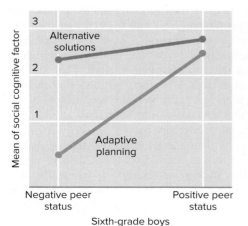

FIGURE **1**

GENERATION OF ALTERNATIVE SOLUTIONS AND ADAPTIVE PLANNING BY NEGATIVE- AND POSITIVE-PEER-STATUS BOYS. Notice that negative-peer-status boys were less likely to generate alternative solutions and plan ahead than were their positive-peer-status counterparts.
kali9/Getty Images

to perceive the boy as having a habit of acting inappropriately. Kenneth Dodge (1993) argues that adolescents go through five steps in processing information about their social world: decoding of social cues, interpretation, response search, selection of an optimal response, and enactment. Dodge has found that aggressive boys are more likely to perceive another child's actions as hostile when the peer's intention is ambiguous. And, when aggressive boys search for cues to determine a peer's intention, they respond more rapidly, less efficiently, and less reflectively than do nonaggressive children. These are among the social cognitive factors believed to be involved in adolescents' conflicts with one another.

Do adults show more advanced social cognition than adolescents? One study found that adolescents performed more poorly than adults in two social cognitive areas: (1) theory of mind (thoughts about one's own mental processes and the mental processes of others), and (2) emotion recognition (Vetter & others, 2013).

developmental **connection**

Emotion

Emotional swings and intensity of emotions characterize adolescent development. Connect to "The Self, Identity, Emotion, and Personality."

Emotion   Not only does cognition play an important role in peer relations, so does emotion (Flannery & others, 2017). For example, the ability to regulate emotion is linked to successful peer relations. Moody and emotionally negative individuals experience greater rejection by peers, whereas emotionally positive individuals are more popular (Saarni & others, 2006). A study of young adolescents found that anger displays and depression were linked to being unpopular with peers (Martinez & others, 2015). Adolescents who have effective self-regulatory skills can modulate their emotional expressiveness in contexts that evoke intense emotions, as when a peer says something negative (Schunk, 2020).

Strategies for Improving Social Skills   A number of strategies have been proposed for improving social skills to achieve better peer relations (Radley, 2021). **Conglomerate strategies,** also referred to as coaching, use a combination of techniques, rather than a single approach, to improve adolescents' social skills. A conglomerate strategy might consist of demonstration or modeling of appropriate social skills, discussion, and reasoning about the social skills, as well as the use of reinforcement for their enactment in actual social situations (King & others, 2021; Simpson & Lewis, 2021).

In one study using a conglomerate strategy, middle school adolescents were instructed in ways to improve their self-control, manage stress, and engage in social problem solving (Weissberg & Caplan, 1989). For example, as problem situations arose, teachers modeled and students practiced six sequential steps:

1. Stop, calm down, and think before you act.
2. Go over the problem and state how you feel.
3. Set a positive goal.
4. Think of lots of solutions.
5. Plan ahead for the consequences.
6. Go ahead and try the best plan.

The adolescents who participated in the program improved their ability to devise cooperative solutions to problem situations, and their teachers reported that the students showed improved social relations in the classroom following the program.

More specifically, how can neglected children and adolescents be trained to interact more effectively with their peers? The goal of using training programs with neglected children and adolescents is often to help them attract attention from their peers in positive ways and show them how to hold their peers' attention by asking questions, by listening in a warm and friendly way, and by saying things about themselves that relate to the peers' interests. They also are taught to enter groups more effectively. The goal of training programs with rejected children and adolescents is often to help them listen to peers and "hear what they say" instead of trying to dominate peer interactions. Rejected children and adolescents are trained to join peers without trying to change what is taking place in the peer group.

Despite the positive outcomes of some programs that attempt to improve the social skills of adolescents, researchers have often found it difficult to improve the social skills of adolescents who are actively disliked and rejected. Many of these adolescents are rejected because they are aggressive or impulsive and lack the self-control to keep these behaviors in check. Still, some intervention programs have been successful in reducing the aggressive and impulsive behaviors of these adolescents (Ladd, Kochenderfer-Ladd, & Rydell, 2011).

conglomerate strategies The use of a combination of techniques, rather than a single approach, to improve adolescents' social skills; also called coaching.

Social-skills training programs have generally been more successful with children 10 years of age or younger than with adolescents (Malik & Furman, 1993). Peer reputations become more fixed as cliques and peer groups take on more significance in adolescence. Once an adolescent gains a negative reputation among peers as being "mean," "weird," or a "loner," the peer group's attitude is often slow to change, even after the adolescent's problem behavior has been corrected. Thus, researchers have found that skills interventions may need to be supplemented by efforts to change the minds of peers. One such intervention strategy involves cooperative group training (Slavin, 2015). In this approach, children or adolescents work toward a common goal that holds promise for changing reputations. Most cooperative group programs have been conducted in academic settings, but other contexts might be used. For example, participation in cooperative games and sports increases sharing and feelings of happiness. And some video games require cooperative efforts by the players.

FRIENDSHIP

Earlier we noted that peers are individuals who are about the same age or maturity level. **Friends** are a subset of peers who engage in mutual companionship, support, and intimacy. Thus, relationships with friends are much closer and more involved than are relationships with the peer group. Some adolescents have several close friends, others have one, and yet others have none.

A man's growth is seen in the successive choirs of his friends.

—RALPH WALDO EMERSON
American Poet and Essayist, 19th Century

The Importance of Friendship   The functions that adolescents' friendships serve can be categorized in six ways (Gottman & Parker, 1987) (see Figure 2):

1. *Companionship.* Friendship provides adolescents with a familiar partner, someone who is willing to spend time with them and join in collaborative activities.

2. *Stimulation.* Friendship provides adolescents with interesting information, excitement, and amusement.

3. *Physical support.* Friendship provides resources and assistance.

4. *Ego support.* Friendship provides the expectation of support, encouragement, and feedback that helps adolescents to maintain an impression of themselves as competent, attractive, and worthwhile individuals.

6. *Social comparison.* Friendship provides information about where adolescents stand vis-à-vis others and whether adolescents are doing okay.

7. *Intimacy/affection.* Friendship provides adolescents with a warm, close, trusting relationship with another individual, a relationship that involves self-disclosure.

friends A subset of peers who engage in mutual companionship, support, and intimacy.

The importance of friendship was underscored in a two-year longitudinal study (Wentzel, Barry, & Caldwell, 2004). Sixth-grade students who did not have a friend engaged in less prosocial behavior (cooperation, sharing, helping others), had lower grades, and were more emotionally distressed (depression, low well-being) than their counterparts who had one or more friends. Two years later, in the eighth grade, the students who had not had a friend in the sixth grade remained more emotionally distressed than their counterparts with one or more friends.

Friendship in Adolescence   For most children, being popular with their peers is a strong motivator (Bagwell & Bukowski, 2018). The focus of their peer relations is on being liked by classmates and being included in games or lunchroom conversations. Beginning in early adolescence, however, teenagers typically prefer to have a smaller number of friendships that are more intense and intimate than those of young children.

Harry Stack Sullivan (1953) has been the most influential theorist in the study of adolescent friendships. Sullivan argued that friends are important in shaping the development of children and adolescents. Everyone, said Sullivan, has basic social

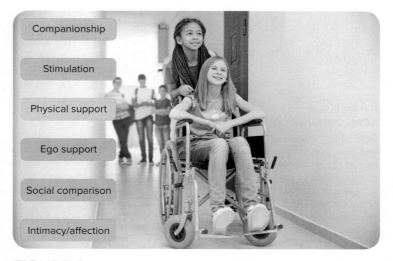

Companionship

Stimulation

Physical support

Ego support

Social comparison

Intimacy/affection

FIGURE **2**
THE FUNCTIONS OF FRIENDSHIP.
Africa Studio/Shutterstock

How do the characteristics of an adolescent's friends influence whether the friends have a positive or negative influence on the adolescent?
Walter Hodges/Jetta Productions/Getty Images

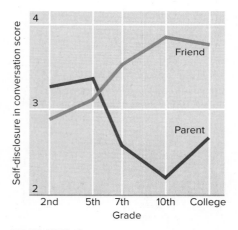

FIGURE 3

DEVELOPMENTAL CHANGES IN SELF-DISCLOSING CONVERSATIONS. Self-disclosing conversations with friends increased dramatically in adolescence while declining in an equally dramatic fashion with parents. However, self-disclosing conversations with parents began to pick up somewhat during the college years. The measure of self-disclosure involved a 5-point rating scale completed by the children and youth, with a higher score representing greater self-disclosure. The data shown represent the means for each age group.

needs, such as the need for secure attachment, playful companionship, social acceptance, intimacy, and sexual relations. Whether or not these needs are fulfilled largely determines our emotional well-being. For example, if the need for playful companionship goes unmet, then we become bored and depressed; if the need for social acceptance is not met, we suffer a diminished sense of self-worth.

During adolescence, said Sullivan, friends become increasingly important in meeting social needs. In particular, Sullivan argued that the need for intimacy intensifies during early adolescence, motivating teenagers to seek out close friends. If adolescents fail to forge such close friendships, they experience loneliness and a reduced sense of self-worth.

Many of Sullivan's ideas have withstood the test of time. For example, adolescents report disclosing intimate and personal information to their friends more often than do younger children (Buhrmester, 1998) (see Figure 3). Adolescents also say they depend more on friends than on parents to satisfy their needs for companionship, reassurance of worth, and intimacy. The ups and downs of experiences with friends shape adolescents' well-being (van Zalk & others, 2020).

Willard Hartup (1996), who has studied peer relations across four decades, concluded that children and adolescents use friends as cognitive and social resources on a regular basis. Hartup also commented that normative transitions, such as moving from elementary to middle school, are negotiated more competently by children who have friends than by those who don't.

Although having friends can be a developmental advantage, not all friendships are alike and the quality of friendship is also important to consider. People differ in the company they keep—that is, who their friends are. Positive friendship relationships in adolescence are associated with a host of positive outcomes, including lower rates of delinquency, substance abuse, risky sexual behavior, and bullying victimization, and higher levels of academic achievement and physical activity (Graham & Kogachi, 2021).

Let's examine three studies that document how having friends with positive characteristics can influence the adolescent's development. In one study, friends' grade-point average was a consistent predictor of positive school achievement and also was linked to less drug abuse and acting out (Cook, Deng, & Morgano, 2007). Also, in a recent study of young adolescents, for non-Latinx white and Asian Americans, higher academic achievement was linked to having same-ethnic friends, while for African American and Latinx adolescents, higher academic achievement was associated with having more cross-ethnic friendships (Chen, Saafir, & Graham, 2020). And in another recent study, friends' social support was linked to greater engagement in physical activity during adolescence (Lisboa & others, 2021).

Not having a close relationship with a best friend, having less contact with friends, having friends who are depressed, and experiencing peer rejection all increase depressive tendencies in adolescents. In a recent study, girls who had few friends had more depressive symptoms than those with more than two close friends (Rodrigues & others, 2020). Also, researchers have found that interacting with delinquent peers and friends greatly increases the risk of becoming delinquent (Walters, 2021). Further, one study found that adolescents adapted their smoking and drinking behavior to match that of their best friends (Wang & others, 2016). Similarly, a recent study of adolescent girls revealed that friends' dieting predicted whether an adolescent girl would engage in dieting or extreme dieting (Balantekin, Birch, & Savage, 2018). And in a recent large-scale study, younger and older adolescents who had no friends were much more likely to engage in suicidal ideation (Campisi & others, 2020).

Friendship in Emerging Adulthood Many aspects of friendship are the same in adolescence and in emerging adulthood. One difference between close relationships in adolescence and emerging adulthood was found in a longitudinal study (Collins & van Dulmen, 2006). Close relationships—between friends, family members, and romantic partners—were more integrated and similar in emerging adulthood than in adolescence. Also in this study, the number of friendships declined from the end of adolescence through emerging adulthood.

Another research study indicated that best friendships often decline in satisfaction and commitment during the first year of college (Oswald & Clark, 2003). In this study, maintaining communication with high school friends and keeping the same best friends across the transition to college lessened the decline.

Intimacy and Similarity Two important characteristics of friendship are intimacy and similarity.

Intimacy In the context of friendship, *intimacy* has been defined in different ways. For example, it has been defined broadly to include everything in a relationship that makes the relationship seem close or intense. In most research studies, though, **intimacy in friendship** is defined narrowly as self-disclosure, or sharing of private thoughts. Private or personal knowledge about a friend also has been used as an index of intimacy.

The most consistent finding in the last two decades of research on adolescent friendships is that intimacy is an important feature of friendship (Berndt & Perry, 1990). When young adolescents are asked what they want from a friend, or how they can tell if someone is their best friend, they frequently say that a best friend will share problems with them, understand them, and listen when they talk about their own thoughts or feelings. When young children talk about their friendships, comments about intimate self-disclosure or mutual understanding are rare. In one investigation, friendship intimacy was more prominent in 13- to 16-year-olds than in 10- to 13-year-olds (Buhrmester, 1990).

Describe the nature of intimacy and similarity in friendship.
Don Mason/Getty Images

Similarity Another predominant characteristic of friendship is that, throughout the childhood and adolescent years, friends are generally similar—in terms of age, sex, ethnicity, and many other factors. Similarity is referred to as *homophily*, the tendency to associate with similar others (Long & others, 2020). Friends often have similar attitudes toward school, similar educational aspirations, and closely aligned achievement orientations.

Mixed-Age Friendships Although most adolescents develop friendships with individuals who are close to their own age, some adolescents become best friends with younger or older individuals. Do older friends encourage adolescents to engage in delinquent behavior or early sexual behavior? Adolescents who interact with older youth do engage in these behaviors more frequently, but it is not known whether the older youth guide younger adolescents toward deviant behavior or whether the younger adolescents were already prone to deviant behavior before they developed the friendship with the older youth. A study also revealed that over time from the sixth through tenth grades girls were more likely to have older male friends, which places some girls on a developmental trajectory for engaging in problem behavior (Poulin & Pedersen, 2007). However, a study of young adolescents found that mixed-grade friends may protect same-grade friendless girls from feelings of loneliness and same-grade friendless and anxious-withdrawn boys from victimization (Bowker & Spencer, 2010).

Other-Sex Friendships Although adolescents are more likely to have same-sex friends, associations with other-sex friends are more common than is often thought (Brown, 2004). The number of other-sex friendships increases in early adolescence, with girls reporting more other-sex friends than boys, and these other-sex friendships increase as adolescence proceeds (Poulin & Pedersen, 2007). Other-sex friendships and participation in mixed-sex groups provide a context that can help adolescents learn how to communicate with the other sex and reduce their anxiety in social and dating heterosexual interactions. Later in this chapter, you will read further about how these other-sex relationships are linked to romantic experiences.

What are some characteristics of other-sex friendships?
Ocean/Corbis

Despite these potential benefits, researchers have found that some other-sex friendships are linked to negative behaviors such as earlier sexual intercourse, as well as increases in alcohol use and delinquency (Mrug, Borch, & Cillessen, 2012). Parents likely monitor their daughters' other-sex friendships more closely than those of their sons because they perceive boys to have a more negative influence, especially in initiating problem behavior (Poulin & Denault, 2012). One study revealed that a higher level of parental monitoring of young adolescent girls led to the girls having fewer friendships with boys, which in turn was associated with a lower level of subsequent alcohol use by the girls in late adolescence (Poulin & Denault, 2012).

Are there strategies that can help adolescents develop friendships? See the *Connecting with Health and Well-Being* interlude.

intimacy in friendship In most research studies, this concept is defined narrowly as self-disclosure, or sharing of private thoughts.

What Are Effective and Ineffective Strategies for Making Friends?

Here are some strategies that adults can recommend to adolescents for making friends (Wentzel, 1997):

- *Initiate interaction*. Learn about a friend—ask for his or her name, age, favorite activities. Use these prosocial overtures: introduce yourself, start a conversation, and invite him or her to do things.
- *Be nice*. Show kindness, be considerate, and compliment the other person.
- *Engage in prosocial behavior*. Be honest and trustworthy: tell the truth, keep promises. Be generous, share, and be cooperative.
- *Show respect for yourself and others*. Have good manners, be polite and courteous, and listen to what others have to say. Have a positive attitude and personality.
- *Provide social support*. Show you care.

And here are some inappropriate strategies for making friends that adults can recommend that adolescents avoid using (Wentzel, 1997):

- *Be psychologically aggressive*. Show disrespect and have bad manners. Use others, be uncooperative, don't share, ignore others, gossip, and spread rumors.
- *Present yourself negatively*. Be self-centered, snobby, conceited, and jealous; show off; care only about yourself. Be mean, have a bad attitude, be angry, throw temper tantrums, and start trouble.

What are some effective and ineffective strategies for making friends?
Kali Nine LLC/iStock/Getty Images

- *Behave antisocially*. Be physically aggressive, yell at others, pick on them, make fun of them, be dishonest, tell secrets, and break promises.

Which of the positive strategies have been successful for you? Has someone developed a friendship with you using one of the recommended approaches?

Loneliness can develop when individuals go through life transitions. *What are some strategies for reducing loneliness?*
Image Source/Getty Images

LONELINESS

In some cases, individuals who don't have friends are vulnerable to loneliness, and loneliness can set in when individuals leave a close relationship (Rubin & Barstead, 2018). Each of us has times in our lives when we feel lonely, but for some individuals loneliness is a chronic condition. More than just an unwelcome social situation, chronic loneliness is linked with impaired physical and mental health (Ge & others, 2017). For example, a study of Malaysian adolescents revealed that feeling lonely was associated with depressive symptoms (Kaur & others, 2014). Another study found that increasing and chronic loneliness of Latinx high school students was associated with academic difficulties (Benner, 2011). In this study, support from friends buffered the negative relation of loneliness to academic difficulties. Also, a recent study of Latinx emerging adults revealed that lower friend support was linked to their loneliness (Lee & others, 2020). And a recent meta-analytic review concluded that friendship experiences may be more closely related to loneliness than to depressive symptoms (Schwartz-Mette & others, 2020).

It is important to distinguish loneliness from the desire for solitude. Some individuals value solitary time. Loneliness is often interwoven with the passage through life transitions, such as a move to a different part of the country, a divorce, or the death of a close friend or family member. Another situation that often creates loneliness is the first year of college, especially if students leave the familiar world of their hometown and family to enter college. Freshmen rarely bring their popularity and social standing from high school into the college environment. There may be a dozen high school basketball stars, National Merit scholars, and former student council presidents in a single dormitory wing. Especially if students attend college away from home, they face the task of forming completely new social relationships.

In one study of more than 2,600 undergraduates, lonely individuals were less likely to actively cope with stress than were individuals who were able to make friends (Cacioppo & others, 2000). Also in this study, lonely college students had higher levels of stress-related hormones and poorer sleep patterns than did students who had positive relationships with others.

Review Connect Reflect

LG1 Discuss the roles of peer relations, friendship, and loneliness in adolescent development.

Review
- What roles do peers play in adolescent development?
- How does friendship contribute to adolescent development?
- How would you distinguish between loneliness and the desire to be alone?

Connect
- Relate emotional competence to the topic of social cognition that was described in this section.

Reflect *Your Own Personal Journey of Life*
- As an adolescent, how much time did you spend with friends, and what activities did you engage in? What were your friends like? Were they similar to you or different? Has the nature of your friendships changed since adolescence? Explain.

2 Adolescent Groups

LG2 Summarize what takes place in adolescent groups.

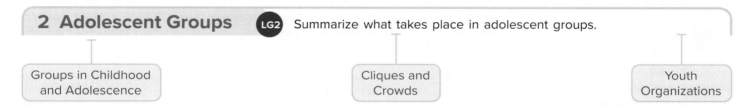

Groups in Childhood and Adolescence   Cliques and Crowds   Youth Organizations

During your adolescent years, you probably were a member of both formal and informal groups. Examples of formal groups include the basketball team or drill team, Girl Scouts or Boy Scouts, the student council, and so on. A more informal group could be a group of peers, such as a clique. Our study of adolescent groups focuses on differences between childhood groups and adolescent groups, cliques and crowds, and youth organizations.

GROUPS IN CHILDHOOD AND ADOLESCENCE

Childhood groups differ from adolescent groups in several important ways. The members of childhood groups often are friends or neighborhood acquaintances, and the groups usually are not as formalized as many adolescent groups. During the adolescent years, groups tend to include a broader array of members; in other words, adolescents other than friends or neighborhood acquaintances often are members of adolescent groups. Try to recall the student council, honor society, art club, football team, or another organized group at your junior high school. If you were a member of any of these organizations, you probably remember that they were made up of many individuals you had not met before and that they were a more heterogeneous group than were your childhood peer groups. Rules and regulations were probably well defined, and captains or leaders were formally elected or appointed in the adolescent groups.

A classic observational study by Dexter Dunphy (1963) indicates that opposite-sex participation in social groups increases during adolescence. In late childhood, boys and girls tend to form small, same-sex groups. As they move into the early adolescent years, the same-sex groups begin to interact with each other. Gradually, the leaders and high-status members begin to create groups based on mixed-sex relationships. Eventually, the newly created mixed-sex groups replace the same-sex groups. The mixed-sex groups interact with each other in large crowd activities, too—at dances and athletic events, for example. In late adolescence, the

Stage 1: Precrowd stage; isolated same-sex groups

Stage 2: Beginning of the crowd; same-sex groups start group-group interaction

Stage 3: The crowd is in structural transition; same-sex groups are forming heterosexual groups, especially among upper-status members

Stage 4: Fully developed crowd; heterosexual groups are closely associated

Stage 5: Beginning of crowd disintegration; loosely associated groups of couples

Boys   Girls   Boys and girls

FIGURE 4

DUNPHY'S PROGRESSION OF PEER GROUP RELATIONS IN ADOLESCENCE

cliques Small groups that range from 2 to about 12 individuals and average about 5 to 6 individuals. Members are usually of the same sex and are similar in age; cliques can form because of similar interests, such as sports, and also can form purely from friendship.

What characterizes adolescent cliques? How are they different from crowds?
Brand X Pictures/Getty Images

crowd begins to dissolve as couples develop more serious relationships and make long-range plans that may include engagement and marriage. A summary of Dunphy's ideas is presented in Figure 4.

CLIQUES AND CROWDS

In our discussion of Dunphy's work, the importance of heterosexual relationships in the evolution of adolescent crowds was noted. Let's now examine adolescent cliques and crowds in greater detail.

Cliques and crowds assume more important roles during adolescence than during childhood (Zarbatany & others, 2019). **Cliques** are small groups that range from 2 to about 12 individuals and average about 5 to 6 individuals. The clique members are usually of the same sex and about the same age.

Cliques can form because adolescents engage in similar activities, such as being in a club or on a sports team (Brown, 2011). Several adolescents may form a clique because they have spent time with each other and enjoy each other's company. Not necessarily friends, they often develop a friendship if they stay in the clique.

What do adolescents do in cliques? They share ideas and hang out together. Often they develop an in-group identity and believe that their clique is better than other cliques.

Crowds are larger than cliques and less personal. Adolescents are usually members of a crowd based on reputation, and they may or may not spend much time together. Many crowds are defined by the activities adolescents engage in (such as "jocks," who are good at sports; "brains," who excel in academics; or "druggies," who take drugs) (Brown, 2011). Reputation-based crowds often appear for the first time in early adolescence and usually become less prominent in late adolescence (Collins & Steinberg, 2006). In one study, crowd membership was associated with adolescent self-esteem (Brown & Lohr, 1987). The crowds observed in this study included jocks (athletically oriented), populars (well-known students who led social activities), normals (middle-of-the-road students who made up the masses), druggies or toughs (known for illicit drug use or other delinquent activities), and nobodies (those who were low in social skills or intellectual abilities). The self-esteem of the jocks and the populars was highest, while that of the nobodies was lowest. One group of adolescents not in a crowd had self-esteem equivalent to that of the jocks and the populars; this group was the independents, who indicated that crowd membership was not important to them. Keep in mind that these data are correlational; self-esteem could increase an adolescent's probability of becoming a crowd member, just as crowd membership could increase the adolescent's self-esteem.

In a recent study of adolescents, risky behavior was associated with two crowds—the Hip Hop crowd was especially linked with substance use and violence, and the alternative crowd was associated with substance use, depression, suicide, bullying, physical inactivity, and obesity (Jordan & others, 2019). Also in this study, the mainstream and popular crowds were characterized by a lower level of risk taking for most behaviors.

So far, we have discussed many aspects of friendship and peer relations in adolescence. A final point about these very important socioemotional interactions of adolescents is how the abrupt appearance of the COVID-19 pandemic in 2020 quickly changed the ways friendship and peer relations took place (Andrews, Foulkes, & Blakemore, 2020). One of the most widely emphasized changes has been the importance of *social distancing*, which involves maintaining a distance of 6 feet or more from others to avoid receiving or transmitting the virus. For some individuals, social distancing increased feelings of social isolation and decreased the feelings of connection with peers and friends that are so important to adolescents. One benefit of the dramatic increase in social media use is that it allows adolescents to stay connected with friends and peers online during times of quarantine. Although adolescents are likely to press parents to let them congregate in person with peers and friends, it is important to prevent them from participating in group activities during times of quarantine, especially if the activities take place indoors, and to remind adolescents that eventually they will be able to resume normal in-person friendship and peer interactions.

YOUTH ORGANIZATIONS

The positive youth movement includes youth development programs and organized youth activities (Lerner & others, 2015). Youth organizations can have an important influence on the adolescent's development (Loyd & Williams, 2017). Currently there are more than 400 national youth organizations in the United States. These organizations include career groups such as Junior Achievement; groups aimed at building character such as Girl Scouts and Boy Scouts; political groups such as Young Republicans and Young Democrats; and ethnic groups such as Indian Youth of America. They serve approximately 30 million young people each year. The largest youth organization is 4-H, with nearly 5 million participants. Among the smallest organizations are ASPIRA, a Latinx youth organization that provides intensive educational enrichment programs for about 13,000 adolescents each year, and WAVE, a dropout-prevention program that serves about 8,000 adolescents each year.

Adolescents who join such groups are more likely to participate in community activities in adulthood and have higher self-esteem, and they tend to be better educated and to come from families of higher socioeconomic status than the families of adolescents who do not participate in youth groups (Erickson, 1982). Participation in youth groups can help adolescents practice the interpersonal and organizational skills that are important for success in adult roles.

The Search Institute (1995) conducted a study that sheds light on both the potential for and barriers to participation in youth programs. The study focused on Minneapolis, which faces many of the same challenges regarding youth as other major U.S. cities. After-school hours and summer vacations are important time slots during which adolescents could form positive relationships with adults and peers. Yet this study found that more than 50 percent of the youth said they did not participate in any type of after-school youth program in a typical week. More than 40 percent reported no participation in youth programs during the summer months.

About 350 youth programs were identified in Minneapolis, about one program for every 87 adolescents. However, about one-half of the youth and their parents agreed that there were not enough youth programs. Parents with the lowest incomes were the least satisfied with program availability. Some of the reasons given by middle school adolescents for not participating in youth programs were a lack of interest in available activities, a lack of transportation, and lack of awareness about what was available.

According to Reed Larson and his colleagues (Larson, 2020; Larson, Walker, & McGovern, 2020), structured voluntary youth activities are especially well suited for the development of initiative. One study of structured youth activities that led to increased initiative involved adolescents in low-income areas who began participating in art and drama groups, sports teams, Boys & Girls Clubs, YMCA gang intervention programs, and other community organizations (Heath, 1999; Heath & McLaughlin, 1993). When the adolescents first joined these organizations, they seemed bored. Within three to four weeks, though, they reported greater

How has the COVID-19 pandemic changed adolescents' peer and friend relationships?
eyecrave/Getty Images

developmental connection

Stress and Coping

The COVID-19 pandemic and similar disruptions of normal activities can cause a great deal of anxiety and stress for children and youth. Parents can guide them in using effective strategies for coping with stressful circumstances. Connect with "Problems in Adolescence and Emerging Adulthood."

crowds A larger group structure than cliques. Adolescents are usually members of a crowd based on reputation and may or may not spend much time together.

These adolescents are participating in Boys & Girls Club activities. *What effects do youth organizations have on adolescents?*
(left): Jason DeCrow/AP Images; (right): Jonathan Fickies/Boys & Girls Clubs of America/AP Images

confidence in their ability to affect their world and adjusted their behavior in pursuit of a goal. In sum, youth activities and organizations provide excellent developmental contexts in which adolescents can develop many positive qualities. Participation in these contexts can help to increase achievement and decrease delinquency (Larson, 2000).

Review *Connect* Reflect

 LG2 Summarize what takes place in adolescent groups.

Review
- How are childhood groups different from adolescent groups?
- What are cliques and crowds? What roles do they play in adolescent development?
- How can youth organizations be characterized?

Connect
- Contrast membership in a clique with the experience of loneliness discussed in the preceding section. What influence does each have on adolescent development?

Reflect *Your Own Personal Journey of Life*
- What would have been the ideal youth organization to support your needs when you were an adolescent?

3 Gender and Culture

 LG3 Describe the roles of gender and culture in adolescent peer groups and friendships.

Gender   Socioeconomic Status and Ethnicity   Culture

The social worlds of adolescent peer groups and friendships are linked to gender and culture. During the elementary school years children spend most of their free time interacting with children of their own sex. Preadolescents spend an hour or less a week interacting with the other sex (Furman & Shaffer, 2013). With puberty, though, more time is spent in mixed-sex peer groups, which was reflected in Dunphy's developmental view that was just discussed (Buhrmester & Chong, 2009). And, by the twelfth grade, boys spend an average of five hours a week with the other sex, girls ten hours a week (Furman, 2002). Nonetheless, there are some significant differences between adolescent peer groups made up of males and those made up of females.

GENDER

There is increasing evidence that gender plays an important role in peer groups and friendships (MacMullin & others, 2021). Are girls more skilled at friendship than boys? A meta-analysis concluded that research indicates girls' friendships are more intimate (Gorrese & Ruggieri, 2012). In this meta-analysis, girls' friendships were deeper and interdependent, and female friends showed more empathy, revealed a greater need for nurturance, and had a greater desire to sustain intimate relationships. In contrast, boys gave more importance to having a congenial friend with whom they could share their interests in activities such as hobbies and sports, and boys showed more cooperativeness than girls in their friendships. Another meta-analysis concluded that adolescent girls show higher peer attachment, especially related to trust and communication, than adolescent boys do (Gorrese & Ruggieri, 2012). And in a recent study that assessed peer relations of students from the beginning to the end of the sixth grade, girl-girl friendships were less likely to dissolve than boy-boy friendships (Nielson & others, 2020).

However, one research analysis challenges the conclusion that boys are not very skilled at friendship (Rose & Asher, 2017). This analysis suggests that the aforementioned conclusion may be premature because boys' friendships have not been given adequate research attention

developmental **connection**

Gender

Recent research indicates that relational aggression occurs more often in girls than boys in adolescence but not in childhood. Connect to "Gender."

and friendship tasks and categories have been too narrowly assessed. The analysis concludes that boys are as satisfied with their friendships as girls are and that for the following tasks and categories boys are as good as or are more successful than girls: having fun and enjoyment, companionship, coping when a friend violates a basic friendship expectation, and continuing a friendship when their friend gets other friends. In this recent analysis, adolescent girls emphasized these aspects of friendship more than adolescent boys did: (1) expressing care, concern, and admiration; (2) helping, sympathizing, and reassuring; and (3) engaging in self-disclosure.

Researchers have found that some aspects of girls' friendships may be linked to adolescent problems (Rose & Smith, 2018). For example, a study of third- through ninth-graders revealed that girls' co-rumination (as reflected in excessively discussing problems) predicted not only an increase in positive friendship quality but also an increase in further co-rumination as well as an increase in depressive and anxiety symptoms (Rose, Carlson, & Waller, 2007). Other recent research confirms the influence of co-rumination in friendship. For example, in a recent study, friendship intensity was an amplifier of an adolescent's pre-existing tendencies toward depression or aggression (Costello & others, 2020). These findings indicate that co-rumination for depression and deviancy training for aggression are both likely to be increased by higher-intensity friendships. One implication of these research studies is that some girls who are vulnerable to developing internalized problems may go undetected because they have support-ive friendships (Rose & Smith, 2018). Also, a recent study of adolescent girls revealed that when they engaged in high levels of co-rumination, poor emotional awareness was related to greater depressive symptoms in their friend (Miller, Borowski, & Zeman, 2020). Further, at high co-rumination levels, girls who had strong emotion regulation had fewer depressive symp-toms. And a recent study of Saudi Arabian adolescents indicated that they had elevated levels of suicidal thoughts and behavior when their friends disclosed depression and self-harm (Copeland & others, 2020).

What are some gender differences in peer relations and friendships in adolescence?
(top): Valueline/Getty Images; (bottom): Robert Niedring/ Getty Images

SOCIOECONOMIC STATUS AND ETHNICITY

In many schools, peer groups are strongly segregated according to socioeconomic status and ethnicity (Graham & Echols, 2018). In schools with large numbers of middle- and lower-SES students, middle-SES students often assume the leadership roles in formal organizations, such as student council, the honor society, fraternity-sorority groups, and so on. Athletic teams are one type of adolescent group in which African American adolescents and adolescents from low-income families have been able to gain parity or even surpass adolescents from middle- and upper-SES families in achieving status.

For many ethnic minority youth, especially immigrants, peers from their own ethnic group provide a crucial sense of brotherhood or sisterhood within the majority culture (Graham & Echols, 2018). Peer groups may form to oppose those of the majority peer groups and to provide adaptive supports that reduce feelings of isolation. However, in a recent study of young adolescents, for non-Latinx white and Asian Americans, higher academic achievement was linked to having more same-ethnicity friends, while for African American and Latinx adoles-cents, higher academic achievement was associated with having more cross-ethnic friendships (Chen, Saafir, & Graham, 2020).

CULTURE

So far, we have considered adolescents' peer relations in regard to gender, socioeconomic status, and ethnicity. Are there also some foreign cultures in which the peer group plays a role different from that in the United States?

In some countries, adults restrict adolescents' access to peers (Chen, Lee, & Chen, 2018). For example, in many areas of rural India and in Arab countries, opportunities for peer rela-tions in adolescence are severely restricted, especially for girls (Brown & Larson, 2002). If girls attend school in these regions of the world, it is usually in sex-segregated schools. In these countries, interaction with the other sex and opportunities for romantic relationships are restricted if not totally prohibited (Booth, 2002).

Researchers have found that Japanese adolescents seek autonomy from their parents later and have less conflict with them than American adolescents do. In a cross-cultural

What are some cross-cultural variations in peer relations? How are American and Japanese adolescents socialized differently in regard to peer relations?
sot/Getty Images

analysis, the peer group was more important to U.S. adolescents than to Japanese adolescents (Rothbaum & others, 2000). Japanese adolescents spend less time outside the home, have less recreational leisure time, and engage in fewer extracurricular activities with peers than U.S. adolescents do (White, 1993). Also, U.S. adolescents are more likely to put pressure on their peers to resist parental influence than Japanese adolescents are (Rothbaum & others, 2000).

In societies where adolescents' access to peers is restricted, they tend to engage in peer interaction mainly at school and in shared leisure activities, especially in middle-SES contexts (Brown & Larson, 2002). For example, in Southeast Asia and some Arab regions, adolescents rely on peers for advice and share interests with them (Booth, 2002; Santa Maria, 2002).

In many countries and regions, peers play prominent roles in adolescents' lives (French & Cheung, 2018). For example, in sub-Saharan Africa, the peer group is a pervasive aspect of adolescents' lives (Nsamenang, 2002); similar social dynamics have been observed throughout Europe and North America (Arnett, 2014).

In some cultures, children and adolescents spend much greater lengths of time in peer groups at an earlier age than in the United States (French & Cheung, 2018). For example, in the Murian culture of eastern India, both male and female children live in a dormitory from the age of 6 until they get married (Barnouw, 1975). The dormitory is a religious haven where members are devoted to work and spiritual harmony. Children work for their parents, and the parents arrange the children's marriages. The children continue to live in the dormitory through adolescence, until they marry. In some cultural settings, peers even assume responsibilities usually assumed by parents. For example, street youth in South America rely on networks of peers to help them survive in urban environments (Welti, 2002).

Might acceptance by peers be more important for adolescents' life satisfaction in some cultures than in others? One study found that in countries where family values are more important (India, for example), peer acceptance was less important for adolescents' life satisfaction than in countries that place more importance on independence from the family (the United States and Germany, for example) (Schwarz & others, 2012).

developmental connection

Culture

Cross-cultural variations not only characterize peer relationships but also parent-adolescent relationships. Connect to "Introduction" and "Culture."

Review Connect Reflect

LG3 Describe the roles of gender and culture in adolescent peer groups and friendships.

Review

- What role does gender play in adolescent peer groups and friendships?
- How are socioeconomic status and ethnicity linked to adolescent peer relations?
- How is culture involved in adolescent peer relations?

Connect

- Compare the influence of families to that of socioeconomic status in the development of adolescent peer relations.

Reflect *Your Own Personal Journey of Life*

- How did your peer relations and friendships during adolescence differ depending on whether you are a female or a male?

---

4 Dating and Romantic Relationships

LG4 Characterize adolescent dating and romantic relationships.

| Functions of Dating | Types of Dating and Developmental Changes | Emotion, Adjustment, and Romantic Relationships | Romantic Love and Its Construction | Gender and Culture |

Although many adolescent boys and girls have social interchanges through formal and informal peer groups, it is through dating that more serious contacts between the sexes occur (Shulman & others, 2020). Let's explore the functions of dating.

FUNCTIONS OF DATING

Dating is a relatively recent phenomenon. It wasn't until the 1920s that dating as we know it became a reality, and even then, its primary role was to select and win a mate. Prior to this period, mate selection was the sole purpose of dating, and "dates" were carefully monitored by parents, who completely controlled the nature of any heterosexual companionship. Often, parents bargained with each other about the merits of their adolescents as potential marriage partners and even chose mates for their children. In recent times, of course, adolescents have gained much more control over the dating process and greater freedom to choose whom to go out with. Furthermore, dating has evolved into something far more than just courtship for marriage (Furman, 2018).

Dating today can serve at least eight functions (Paul & White, 1990):

1. Dating can be a form of recreation. Adolescents who date seem to have fun and see dating as a source of enjoyment and recreation.

2. Dating is a source of status and achievement. Part of the social comparison process in adolescence involves evaluating the status of the people one dates: Are they the best looking, the most popular, and so forth?

3. Dating is part of the socialization process in adolescence. It helps adolescents learn how to get along with others and assists them in learning manners and sociable behavior.

4. Dating involves learning about intimacy and serves as an opportunity to establish a unique, meaningful relationship with a person of the opposite sex.

5. Dating can be a context for sexual experimentation and exploration.

6. Dating can provide companionship through interaction and shared activities in an opposite-sex relationship.

7. Dating experiences contribute to identity formation and development; dating helps adolescents to clarify their identity and to separate from their families of origin.

8. Dating can be a means of mate sorting and selection, thereby retaining its original courtship function.

In the first half of the twentieth century, dating served mainly as a courtship for marriage.
Bob Barrett/FPG/Hulton Archive/Getty Images

Today the functions of dating include courtship but also many others. *What are some of these other functions of dating?*
Photodisc/Getty Images

TYPES OF DATING AND DEVELOPMENTAL CHANGES

A number of dating variations and developmental changes characterize dating and romantic relationships (Couture, Fernet, & Hebert, 2021). First, we examine heterosexual romantic relationships and then turn to romantic relationships among sexual minority youth (gay and lesbian adolescents).

Heterosexual Romantic Relationships   Three stages characterize the development of romantic relationships in adolescence (Connolly & McIsaac, 2009):

1. *Entry into romantic attractions and affiliations at about 11 to 13 years of age.* This initial stage is triggered by puberty. From 11 to 13 years old, adolescents become intensely interested in romance, and it dominates many conversations with same-sex friends. Developing a crush on someone is common, and the crush often is shared with a same-sex friend. Young adolescents may or may not interact with the individual who is the object of their infatuation. When dating occurs, it usually takes place in a group setting.

2. *Exploring romantic relationships at approximately 14 to 16 years of age.* At this point in adolescence, casual dating and dating in groups—two types of romantic involvement—occur. *Casual dating* emerges between individuals who are mutually attracted. These dating experiences are often short-lived, lasting from a few weeks to several months. *Dating in groups* is common and reflects embeddedness in the peer context. A friend often acts as a third-party facilitator of a potential dating relationship by communicating their friend's romantic interest and determining whether the attraction is reciprocated.

What are dating relationships like in adolescence?
Image Source/PictureQuest

3. *Consolidating dyadic romantic bonds at about 17 to 19 years of age.* At the end of the high school years, more serious romantic relationships develop. This stage is characterized by strong emotional bonds more closely resembling those in adult romantic relationships. These bonds often are more stable and enduring than earlier bonds, typically lasting one year or more.

Two variations on these stages in the development of romantic relationships in adolescence involve early starters and late bloomers (Connolly & McIsaac, 2009). *Early starters* include 15 to 20 percent of 11- to 13-year-olds who say that they currently are in a romantic relationship and 35 percent who indicate that they have had some prior experience in romantic relationships. *Late bloomers* comprise approximately 10 percent of 17- to 19-year-olds who say that they have had no experience with romantic relationships and another 15 percent who report that they have not engaged in any romantic relationships that lasted more than four months. A study by Jennifer Connolly and her colleagues (2013) found support for the series of three stages described above (described as on-time) and also the presence of the two off-time groups—early starters and late bloomers. In this study, the early starters had more externalizing symptoms (aggressive and delinquent behaviors), while late bloomers and the on-time group did not show any indications of maladjustment.

In a longitudinal study, continuous singles (individuals who never dated from 10 to 20 years of age) reported lower life satisfaction in adolescence and early adulthood than moderate daters (Gonzales Aviles, Finn, & Neyer, 2021). The continuous singles also were less satisfied with their lives than the later starters.

In one study, announcing that "I like someone" occurred by the sixth grade for about 40 percent of the individuals sampled (Buhrmester, 2001) (see Figure 5). However, it was not until the tenth grade that 50 percent of the adolescents had a sustained romantic relationship that lasted two months or longer. By their senior year, 25 percent still had not engaged in this type of sustained romantic relationship. In another study, a rather large portion of adolescents in a steady dating relationship said that their steady relationship had persisted 11 months or longer: 20 percent of adolescents age 14 or younger, 35 percent of 15- to 16-year-olds, and almost 60 percent of 17- and 18-year-olds (Carver, Joyner, & Udry, 2003).

Adolescents often find comfort in numbers in their early exploration of romantic relationships (Connolly & McIsaac, 2009). They may begin hanging out together in heterosexual

FIGURE 5

AGE AT ONSET OF ROMANTIC ACTIVITY.
In this study, announcing that "I like someone" occurred earliest, followed by going out with the same person three or more times, having a sustained romantic relationship that lasted longer than two months, and finally planning an engagement or marriage (which characterized only a very small percentage of participants by the twelfth grade) (Buhrmester, 2001).

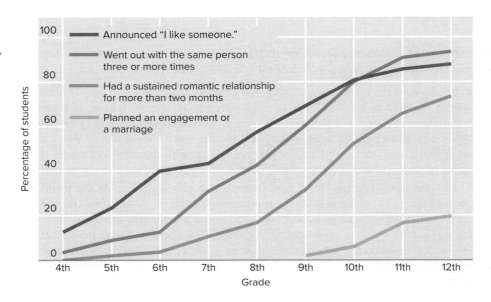

groups. Sometimes they just hang out at someone's house or get organized enough to ask an adult to drive them to a mall or a movie. A special concern in early dating and "going with" someone is the associated risk for adolescent pregnancy and problems at home and school.

How do romantic relationships change through adolescence and emerging adulthood? In a recent study across 10 years, emerging adults in short-term relationships were characterized by higher levels of support, companionship, and taking care of one's partner than were short-term relationships of adolescents (Lantagne & Furman, 2017). Long-term adolescent relationships were both supportive and turbulent, characterized by elevated levels of support, negative interactions, higher control, and more jealousy. In emerging adulthood, long-term relationships continued to have high levels of support, but negative interactions, control, and jealousy decreased.

Romantic Relationships in Sexual Minority Youth Most research on romantic relationships in adolescence has focused on heterosexual relationships. Recently, researchers have begun to study romantic relationships in gay, lesbian, and bisexual youth (Diamond & Alley, 2018; Savin-Williams, 2017, 2018).

The average age of initial same-sex activity for females ranges from 14 to 18 years of age and for males from 13 to 15 (Savin-Williams, 2015). The most common initial same-sex partner is a close friend. Lesbian adolescents are more likely to have sexual encounters with boys before same-sex activity, whereas gay adolescents show the opposite sequence (Diamond & Alley, 2018).

Most sexual minority youth have same-sex sexual experience, but relatively few have same-sex romantic relationships because of limited opportunities and the social disapproval such relationships may generate from families or heterosexual peers (Diamond & Alley, 2018). The romantic possibilities of sexual minority youth are complex (Savin-Willams, 2018). To adequately address the relational interests of sexual minority youth, we can't generalize from heterosexual youth and simply switch the labels. Instead, we need to consider the full range of variation in sexual minority youths' sexual desires and romantic relationships for same- and other-sex partners.

┌ - - - - - - - - - - - - - - - →
developmental **connection**
Sexuality
Sexual minority youth have diverse patterns of initial attraction. Connect to "Sexuality."
← - - - - - - - - - - - - - - - ┘

What characterizes romantic relationships in sexual minority youth?
Johner Images/Getty Images

EMOTION, ADJUSTMENT, AND ROMANTIC RELATIONSHIPS

Romance can envelop adolescents' and emerging adults' lives (Furman, 2018). In some cases, the romance is positive, in others negative. A concern is that in some cases the negative emotions are so intense and prolonged that they can lead to serious adjustment problems.

How are dating and romantic relationships linked to adolescent adjustment? In one study, the more romantic experiences tenth-graders had, the more likely they were to report high levels of social acceptance, friendship competence, and romantic competence; however, having more romantic experience also was linked to a higher level of substance use, delinquency, and sexual behavior (Furman, Low, & Ho, 2009). Also, in a recent meta-analysis, adolescents reported that there were more negative aspects to their romantic relationships than their friendships (Kochendorfer & Kerns, 2020). Further, dating and engaging in romantic relationships at an early age can be especially problematic (Furman, 2018). Researchers have found that early dating and "going with" someone are linked with adolescent pregnancy and problems at home and school (Florsheim, Moore, & Edgington, 2003).

However, in some cases, romantic relationships in adolescence are linked with positive development. For example, in a recent study, having a supportive romantic relationship in adolescence was linked to positive outcomes for adolescents who had a negative relationship with their mother (Szwedo, Hessel, & Allen, 2017). In another study, adolescents who engaged in a higher level of intimate disclosure at age 10 reported a higher level of companionship in romantic relationships at 12 and 15 years of age (Kochendorfer & Kerns, 2017). In this study, those who reported more conflict in friendships had a lower level of companionship in romantic relationships at 15 years of age.

How are dating and romantic relationships linked to adolescent adjustment?
Pascal Broze/Onoky/Getty Images/SuperStock

developmental **connection**

Relationships

Dating violence and acquaintance rape are increasing concerns in adolescence and emerging adulthood. Connect to "Sexuality."

Youth Relationship Education Programs in relationship education have mainly focused on helping committed adult couples to strengthen their relationships. Recently, though, an increasing number of relationship education programs have been developed for adolescents and emerging adults. *Relationship education* consists of interventions to provide individuals and couples with information and skills that produce positive romantic relationships and marriages. These interventions are diverse and include instruction in basic relationship knowledge and skills to youth in a classroom setting, helping unmarried couple learn more about relationships in small-group settings, and premarital education for engaged couples.

A recent meta-analysis of 30 studies of relationship education for adolescents and emerging adults found a positive effect of the programs (Simpson, Leonhardt, & Hawkins, 2018). The skills most often assessed in these studies are interpersonal communication, problem-solving and conflict strategies, and self-regulation (Simpson, Leonhardt, & Hawkins, 2018). The positive effects of relationship education were stronger for emerging adults than adolescents. They also were stronger for more disadvantaged participants than more advantaged participants.

Romantic Relationship Dissolution When things don't go well in a romantic relationship, adolescents and emerging adults need to consider dissolving the relationship (Washburn-Busk & others, 2020). In particular, falling out of love may be wise if you are obsessed with a person who repeatedly betrays your trust; if you are involved with someone who is draining you emotionally or financially; or if you are desperately in love with someone who does not return your feelings.

Being in love when love is not returned can lead to depression, obsessive thoughts, sexual dysfunction, inability to work effectively, difficulty in making new friends, and self-condemnation (Liang & Van Horn, 2021). Thinking clearly in such relationships is often difficult because they are so often linked to arousing emotions.

Some individuals get taken advantage of in relationships. For example, without either person realizing it, a relationship can evolve in a way that creates dominant and submissive roles. Detecting this pattern is an important step toward either reconstructing the relationship or ending it if the problems cannot be worked out.

Studies of romantic breakups have focused mainly on their negative outcomes. For example, a study of 18- to 20-year-olds revealed that heavy drinking, marijuana use, and cigarette smoking increased following the dissolution of a romantic relationship (Fleming & others, 2010). Also, in a recent large-scale study of more than 9,000 adults, experiencing a romantic breakup lowered individuals' self-esteem but the effect disappeared one year after the breakup (Luciano & Orth, 2017). And another recent study concluded that high commitment to a romantic relationship is a risk factor for depression and suicidal ideation when the relationship ends (Love & others, 2018).

Why do romantic relationships dissolve? A recent study of emerging adults found that contextual, relationship, and individual factors predict the dissolution of relationships (Lantagne, Furman, & Novak, 2017). At the contextual level, a greater number of stressful life events ("I became seriously ill or was injured," for example) predicted relationship dissolution. At the relationship quality level, lower levels of supportive interactions (lower level of intimacy, for example) predicted relationship dissolution. And at the individual level, lower levels of romantic appeal predicted relationship dissolution. Over the long term, externalized symptoms (high levels of aggression, for example) and a higher level of substance use also predicted relationship dissolution.

However, romantic breakups can also have positive outcomes (Waterman & others, 2017). For example, one study of college students assessed the personal growth that can follow the breakup of a romantic relationship (Tashiro & Frazier, 2003). The participants were undergraduate students who had experienced a relationship breakup in the past nine months. They were asked to describe "what positive changes, if any, have happened as a result of your breakup that might serve to improve your future romantic relationships" (p. 118). Self-reported positive growth was common following the romantic breakups. The most commonly reported types of growth were feeling stronger emotionally and being more self-confident, being more independent, and developing new friendships. Women reported more positive growth than did men.

What are some factors that predict romantic relationships dissolution in emerging adults?
Tetra Images/Getty Images

ROMANTIC LOVE AND ITS CONSTRUCTION

Romantic love, also called passionate love or *eros,* has strong sexual and infatuation components, and it often predominates in the early part of a love relationship. Romantic love characterizes most adolescent love, and romantic love is also extremely important among college students. In one investigation, unmarried college males and females were asked to identify their closest relationship (Berscheid, Snyder, & Omoto, 1989). More than half named a romantic partner, rather than a parent, sibling, or friend.

Romantic love includes a complex intermingling of emotions—fear, anger, sexual desire, joy, and jealousy, for example. Obviously, some of these emotions are a source of anguish. One study found that romantic lovers were more likely than friends to be the cause of depression (Berscheid & Fei, 1977). Another study revealed that a heightened state of romantic love in young adults was linked to stronger depression and anxiety symptoms but better sleep quality (Bajoghli & others, 2014).

Another type of love is **affectionate love,** also called companionate love, which occurs when individuals desire to have another person near and have a deep, caring affection for that person). There is evidence that affectionate love is more characteristic of adult love than adolescent love and that the early stages of love have more romantic ingredients than the later stages (Sternberg & Sternberg, 2019).

Physical attractiveness and similarity are important aspects of romantic relationships. One study revealed that physically attractive adolescents were more satisfied with their romantic life (Furman & Winkles, 2010). In another study, girls and boys who were dating each other tended to be from the same ethnic group, come from similar socioeconomic backgrounds, and have similar academic success as measured by their grade point averages (Furman & Simon, 2008). In yet another study, there were substantial pre-relationship similarities between adolescents and their future romantic partners on peer popularity, attractiveness, body appeal, and depressive symptoms (Simon, Aikins, & Prinstein, 2008).

Recently, romantic attraction has not only taken place in person but also over the Internet (Jin, Ryu, & Mugaddam, 2019). In 2006, approximately one million individuals in the United States had tried online matchmaking, but by 2020, that figure had skyrocketed to more than 32 million individuals.

Some critics argue that online romantic relationships lose the interpersonal connection, whereas others suggest that the Internet may benefit shy or anxious individuals who find it difficult to meet potential partners in person (Holmes, Little, & Welsh, 2009). One problem with online matchmaking is that many individuals misrepresent their characteristics, such as how old they are, how attractive they are, and their occupation. Recent data indicate that men lie most about their age, height, and income; women lie most about their weight, physical build, and age (statisticbrain.com, 2017). Despite such dishonesty, researchers have found that romantic relationships initiated on the Internet are more likely than relationships established in person to last for more than two years (Bargh & McKenna, 2004). And in a large-scale study of more than 19,000 individuals it was discovered that more than one-third of marriages now begin with online contact and that these marriages are slightly less likely to break up and are characterized by slightly higher marital satisfaction than marriages than begin in offline contexts (Cacioppo & others, 2013).

To fully understand romantic relationships in adolescence and emerging adulthood, we also need to know how experiences with family members and peers contribute to the way adolescents and emerging adults construct their romantic relationships (Furman, 2018). One study revealed that young adolescent girls who had negative relationships with their parents turned to romantic relationships for intimacy and support, which in turn provided the opportunity for early sexual initiation (de Graaf & others, 2012).

A recent study confirmed that parent-adolescent relationship quality (assessed at 13 to 18 years of age) is linked to the adolescents' later romantic relationships in emerging adulthood (assessed at 20 to 23 years of age) (Hadiwijaya & others, 2020). In this study, individuals who had an authoritative relationship with their parents in adolescence were more likely to have the highest levels of support, intimacy, and passion with their romantic partners in emerging adulthood. And a distant parent-adolescent relationship was linked to the lowest levels of support, intimacy, and passion in emerging adult relationships.

Attachment history also is linked to couple relationships in adolescence and emerging adulthood (Furman & Collibee, 2018). For example, one study found that greater attachment

┌ - - - - - - - - - - - - - →
 developmental **connection**
 Sexuality
 Sexual interest plays an important role in adolescents' romantic relationships. Connect to "Sexuality."
← - - - - - - - - - - - - - ┘

Love is a canvas furnished by nature and embroidered by imagination.

—Voltaire
French Philosopher, 18th Century

What characterizes online dating?
Oleksiy Maksymenko Photography/Alamy Stock Photo

How might experiences with family members influence the way adolescents construct their dating relationships?
Jupiterimages/Getty Images

┌ - - - - - - - - - - →
 developmental **connection**
 Attachment
 Researchers are discovering numerous links between attachment styles and romantic relationships in emerging adulthood. Connect to "Families."
← - - - - - - - - - - ┘

romantic love Love that has strong sexual and infatuation components; also called passionate love or *eros.* It often predominates in the early part of a love relationship.

affectionate love Love in which an individual desires to have another person near and has a deep, caring affection for that person; also called companionate love.

Is Online Dating a Good Idea?

Is looking for love online likely to work out? It didn't work out so well in 2012 for Notre Dame linebacker Manti Te'o, whose online girlfriend turned out to be a "catfish," someone who fakes an identity online. However, online dating sites claim that their sites often facilitate positive outcomes. A poll commissioned by Match.com in 2009 reported that twice as many marriages occurred between individuals who met through an online dating site as between people who met in bars or clubs or at other social events.

Connecting online for love turned out positively for two Columbia University graduate students, Michelle Przbyksi and Andy Lalinde (Steinberg, 2011). They lived only a few blocks away from each other, so soon after they communicated online through Datemyschool.com, an online dating site exclusively for college students, they met in person, hit it off, applied for a marriage license 10 days later, and eventually got married.

However, an editorial by Samantha Nickalls (2012) in *The Tower*, the student newspaper at Arcadia University in Philadelphia, argued that online dating sites might be okay for people in their thirties and older but not for college students. Nickalls commented:

> The dating pool of our age is huge. Huge. After all, marriage is not on most people's minds when they're in college, but dating (or perhaps just hooking up) most certainly is. A college campus, in fact, is like living a dating service because the majority of people are looking for the same thing you are. As long as you put yourself out there, flirt a bit, and be friendly, chances are that people will notice.
>
> If this doesn't work for you right away, why should it really matter? As a college student, you have so many other huge things going on in your life—your career choice, your transition from kid to adult, your crazy social life. Unless you are looking to get married at age 20 (which is a whole other issue that I could debate for hours), dating shouldn't be the primary thing on your mind anyway. Besides, as the old saying goes, the best things come when you least expect them. Oftentimes, you find the best dates by accident—not by hunting them down.

(*Left*) Manti Te'o; (*Right*) Michelle Przbyksi and Andy Lalinde.
(left): Mike Blake/Reuters/Alamy Stock Photo; (right): Courtesy of Michelle and Andres Lalinde

insecurity with parents and peers at age 14 was linked to having a more anxious attachment style at age 22 (Pascuzzo, Cyr, & Moss, 2013).

Wyndol Furman and Elizabeth Wehner (1998) discussed how specific insecure attachment styles might be related to adolescents' romantic relationships. Adolescents with a secure attachment to parents are likely to approach romantic relationships expecting closeness, warmth, and intimacy. Thus, they are likely to feel comfortable developing close, intimate romantic relationships. Adolescents with a dismissing/avoidant attachment to parents are likely to expect romantic partners to be unresponsive and unavailable. Thus, they might tend to behave in ways that distance themselves from romantic relationships. Adolescents with a preoccupied/ambivalent attachment to parents are likely to be disappointed and frustrated with intimacy and closeness in romantic relationships.

In a classic study, E. Mavis Hetherington (1972, 1977) found that divorce was associated with a stronger interest in boys on the part of adolescent daughters than was the death of a parent or living in an intact family. Further, the daughters of divorced parents had a more negative opinion of males than did the girls from other family structures. And girls from divorced and widowed families were more likely to marry images of their fathers than were girls from intact families. Hetherington stresses that females from intact families likely have had a greater opportunity to work through relationships with their fathers and therefore are more psychologically free to date and marry someone different from their fathers.

Parents are likely to be more involved or interested in their daughters' dating patterns and relationships than those of their sons. For example, in one investigation, college females were much more likely than their male counterparts to say that their parents tried to influence whom they dated during adolescence (Knox & Wilson, 1981). They also indicated that it was not unusual for their parents to try to interfere with their dating choices and relationships.

Peer relations and friendships provide opportunities to learn modes of relating that are carried over into romantic relationships (Furman & Collibee, 2018). A longitudinal study revealed that friendship in middle childhood was linked with security in dating, as well as intimacy in dating, at age 16 (Collins & van Dulmen, 2006). Also, a longitudinal study found that developing positive expectations and assertiveness with peers at age 13, being socially competent at 15 and 16 years of age, and being able to form and maintain strong close friendships at 16 to 18 years of age predicted romantic life satisfaction at 27 to 30 years of age (Allen & others, 2020).

Research by Jennifer Connolly and her colleagues (Connolly, Furman, & Konarski, 2000; Connolly & Stevens, 1999; Connolly & others, 2004) documents the role of peers in the emergence of romantic involvement in adolescence. In one study, adolescents who were part of mixed-sex peer groups moved more readily into romantic relationships than their counterparts whose experience with mixed-sex peer groups was more limited (Connolly, Furman, & Konarski, 2000). Another study also found that young adolescents increase their participation in mixed-gender peer groups (Connolly & others, 2004). This participation was "not explicitly focused on dating but rather brought boys and girls together in settings in which heterosocial interaction might occur but is not obligatory. . . . We speculate that mixed-gender groups are important because they are easily available to young adolescents who can take part at their own comfort level" (p. 201).

GENDER AND CULTURE

Dating and romantic relationships may vary according to gender and culture. Think back to your middle school/junior high and high school years and consider how gender likely influenced your romantic relationships.

Gender Do male and female adolescents bring different motivations to the dating experience? Candice Feiring (1996) found that they did. Fifteen-year-old girls were more likely to describe romance in terms of interpersonal qualities, while boys described it in terms of physical attraction. For young adolescents, the affiliative qualities of companionship, intimacy, and support were frequently mentioned as positive dimensions of romantic relationships, but love and security were not. Also, the young adolescents described physical attraction more in terms of being cute, pretty, or handsome than in terms of sexuality (such as being a good kisser). Possibly, however, the failure to discuss sexual interests was due to the adolescents' discomfort in talking about such personal feelings with an unfamiliar adult.

Dating scripts are the cognitive models that adolescents and adults use to guide and evaluate dating interactions. In one study, first dates were highly scripted along gender lines (Rose & Frieze, 1993). Males followed a proactive dating script, females a reactive one. The male's script involved initiating the date (asking for and planning it), controlling the public domain (driving and opening doors), and initiating sexual interaction (making physical contact, making out, and kissing). The female's script focused on the private domain (concern about appearance, enjoying the date), participating in the structure of the date provided by the male (being picked up, having doors opened), and responding to his sexual gestures. These gender differences give males more power in the initial stage of a relationship.

developmental **connection**

Gender

Gender differences have been found in sexual scripts. Connect to "Sexuality."

dating scripts The cognitive models that adolescents and adults use to guide and evaluate dating interactions.

Ethnicity and Culture

The sociocultural context exerts a powerful influence on adolescent dating patterns and on mate selection (Du & others, 2021). Values and religious beliefs of people in various cultures often dictate the age at which dating begins, how much freedom in dating is allowed, the extent to which dates are chaperoned by parents or other adults, and the respective roles of males and females in dating. In the Arab world, Asian countries, and South America, adults are typically highly restrictive of adolescent girls' romantic relationships.

Immigrants to the United States have brought these restrictive standards with them. For example, in the United States, Latinx and Asian American families typically have more conservative standards regarding adolescent dating than does the Anglo-American culture. Especially when an immigrant adolescent wants to date outside his or her ethnic group, dating can be a source of cultural conflict for families who come from cultures in which dating begins at a late age, little freedom in dating is allowed, dates are chaperoned, and adolescent girls' dating is especially restricted (Romo, Mireles-Rios, & Lopez-Tello, 2014).

In one study, Latinx young adults living in the midwestern region of the United States reflected on their socialization for dating and sexuality (Raffaelli & Ontai, 2001). Because most of their parents viewed U.S.-style dating as a violation of traditional courtship styles, strict boundaries were imposed on youths' romantic involvements. As a result, many of the Latinxs described their adolescent dating experiences as filled with tension and conflict. The average age at which the girls began dating was 15.7 years, with early dating experiences usually occurring without parental knowledge or permission. Over half of the girls engaged in "sneak dating." Also, a recent study found that mother-daughter conflict in Mexican American families was linked to an increase in daughters' romantic involvement (Tyrell & others, 2016).

What characterizes dating scripts in adolescence?
Mike Watson Images/Getty Images

Cross-Cultural Variations in Romantic Relationships

Culture has strong influences on many aspects of human development, and romantic relationships are no exception (Gao, 2016). In collectivist countries like China and Korea, intimacy is more diffused in love because of the strong group emphasis on connections outside of a romantic love relationship. By contrast, in individualistic countries such as the United States and most European countries, intimacy is often intensified because an individual's social network is likely to be smaller and less group oriented (Gao, 2016). Also, research indicates that greater passion characterizes U.S. romantic relationships than Chinese romantic relationships (Gao, 2016). And researchers have found that self-disclosure is more common in U.S. romantic relationships than in Japanese romantic relationships (Kito, 2005). Feelings of commitment are stronger in Chinese romantic relationships than in U.S. romantic relationships (Dion & Dion, 1993).

In a recent exploration of cross-cultural variations, romantic relationships were explored in three countries: Japan, Argentina, and France (Ansari, 2015). In Japan, the marriage rate is rapidly decreasing to the point that the Japanese government is concerned that this could lead to a considerable drop in Japan's population. In 2013, 45 percent of Japanese women 16 to 24 years of age reported that they were not

What are some ethnic variations in dating during adolescence?
Mike Watson Images/Moodboard/Getty Images

(a) What are some characteristics of romantic relationships in China and Japan? (b) What are romantic relationships like in Argentina?
(Left): I love Photo and Apple./Getty Images; (Right) James Carman/Getty Images

interested in or despised having sexual contact. Also, the percentage of Japanese men and women who aren't involved in any romantic relationship has increased significantly in recent years.

In Argentina, romantic interest is much stronger than in Japan (Ansari, 2015). Sexual and romantic flirtation is a way of life for many Argentines. Online dating is not nearly as frequent as in the United States, apparently because men are so forward in their romantic pursuits in person.

In France, as in Argentina, interest in passionate love is strong. However, in the three-country comparison, one aspect of French interest in romantic relationships stood out—their acceptance of extramarital affairs. In one comparison, only 47 percent of survey participants in France reported that having an extramarital affair is morally wrong, compared with 69 percent in Japan, 72 percent in Argentina, and 84 percent in the United States (Wike, 2014). In sum, there are striking cultural variations in many aspects of romantic relationships.

In this exploration of romantic relationships in different countries, the Middle Eastern country of Qatar also was studied (Ansari, 2015). In Qatar, casual dating is forbidden and public displays of affection can be punished with prison time. However, recently with the advent of smartphones, social media, and the Internet, young adults in Qatar are contacting each other about co-ed parties in hotel rooms, a private way to hang out away from the monitoring of parents, neighbors, and government officials.

Review Connect Reflect

LG4 Characterize adolescent dating and romantic relationships.

Review

- What functions does dating serve?
- What are some different types of dating? How does dating change developmentally during adolescence?
- How are romantic relationships linked to emotion and adjustment?
- What is romantic love, and how is it constructed?
- How are gender and culture involved in dating and romantic relationships?

Connect

- How do U.S. adolescents' dating patterns and the purpose of dating differ from those of adolescents in other parts of the world?

Reflect *Your Own Personal Journey of Life*

- Think back to your middle school/junior high and high school years. How much time did you spend thinking about dating? If you dated, what were your dating experiences like? What would you do over again the same way? What would you do differently? What characteristics did you seek in the people you wanted to date? Were you too idealistic? What advice would you give today's adolescents about dating and romantic relationships?

5 Emerging Adult Lifestyles

LG5 Explain the diversity of emerging adult lifestyles.

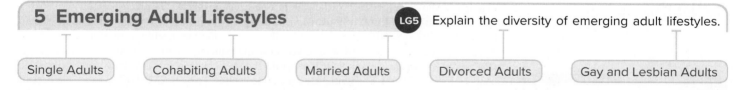

Single Adults   Cohabiting Adults   Married Adults   Divorced Adults   Gay and Lesbian Adults

Emerging adulthood not only is a time when changes often take place in romantic relationships; it also is a time characterized by residential and lifestyle changes. For the first time since the Great Depression, in July 2020, a majority (52 percent) of U.S. 18- to 29-year-olds lived with their parents (up from 47 percent in February 2020) (U.S. Census Bureau, 2020). The sharpest increase occurred for 18- to 24-year-olds. Clearly, these abrupt increases occurred because of the COVID-19 pandemic. Almost one-fourth said they moved in with one or both of their parents because their college campus had closed, and 18 percent said they had lost their job or were having financial trouble.

Among the questions that many emerging adults ask themselves as they consider various lifestyle options are: Should I get married? If so, when? If I wait too long, will I miss my chance to get married? Should I stay single, or is it too lonely a life? Do I want to have children?

A striking social change in recent decades is the decreased stigma attached to individuals who do not maintain what were long considered conventional families. Emerging adults today choose many different lifestyles and form many types of families (Seccombe, 2020). They live alone, cohabit, marry, divorce, or live with someone of the same sex.

In *The Marriage-Go-Round*, sociologist Andrew Cherlin (2009) concluded that the United States has more marriages and remarriages, more divorces, and more short-term cohabiting (living together) relationships than most other countries. Combine these lifestyles and it's apparent that there is more turnover and movement in and out of relationships in the United States than in virtually any other country. Let's explore these varying relationship lifestyles.

SINGLE ADULTS

Recent decades have seen a dramatic rise in the percentage of single adults. In 2019, 35 percent of men and 30 percent of women had never been married, compared with 30 percent of men and 23 percent of women in 1990 (U.S. Census Bureau, 2019). Single-person households increased from 7 million in 1960 to 36 million in 2019. Also, African American adults (47 percent) are much more likely to be single than non-Latinx white (28 percent) and Latinx adults (27 percent) (Brown, 2020).

The increasing number of single adults is influenced by rising rates of cohabitation and a trend toward postponing marriage. However, the United States actually has a lower percentage of single adults than many other countries such as Great Britain, Germany, and Japan. Moreover, the fastest growth in individuals adopting a single adult lifestyle is occurring in rapidly developing countries such as China, India, and Brazil (Klinenberg, 2013).

Given all of the technologies that are available, it is probably easier to meet someone now than ever before. However, many individuals today are looking for the perfect soul mate and that person is hard to find. And with all of the dating websites available, once someone finds a flaw in the person they are dating, it is not difficult to quickly search for and find someone else to date. Also, unlike the negative stereotyping of singles in earlier decades, it has become much more acceptable to pursue a single lifestyle.

In a national survey of more than 35,000 U.S. single adults, *fast sex and slow love* characterized their responses (Fisher & Garcia, 2019). In terms of fast sex, 66 percent of U.S. singles reported having had a one-night stand, 34 percent had sex with someone before a first date, and 54 percent had experienced an uncommitted, secretive friends-with-benefits relationship (Fisher & Garcia, 2019). However, in terms of slow love, today's singles are taking far longer than past generations to commit to love and marriage, wanting to know everything they can about a potential partner before they invest time, effort, and money in making a formal commitment to him or her (Fisher & Garcia, 2019). And even though uncommitted sexual experiences are much more common among today's singles, they still have a strong interest in finding romantic love. In a recent poll, more than 54 percent of U.S. singles said they believe in "love at first sight," 86 percent reported that they want to find a committed partner they can live with forever, and 89 percent responded that they believe it is possible to remain married to the same person for the rest of one's life (Fisher & Garcia, 2019).

The onset of the COVID-19 pandemic dramatically changed the way emerging adults sought love and romance. Social distancing made dinner dates and bar meetups rare occurrences. In an April 2020 survey, individuals were asked how the pandemic had changed their dating habits (Fisher, 2020). In this survey, individuals said the main change was that they were using video chatting to get to know a potential dating partner better. Prior to COVID-19, only 6 percent of survey participants said they engaged in video chatting to get to know someone, but after the pandemic began 69 percent said they were open to video chatting with a potential partner, with one-third already having done this on Zoom, FaceTime, or some other Internet platform.

Results of the tenth annual Match.com singles survey, conducted in 2020, reinforced a trend that had begun prior to the onset of the COVID-19 pandemic: More young singles said they were waiting to establish committed partnerships until their late twenties or even their thirties (Match.com, 2020). They indicated that they were taking more time to get to know potential romantic partners. They also say that they were being more selective about which persons they were willing to go out with on a date. There was also a significant increase in the number of young people who said they wanted to know a potential partner's political viewpoints, with a 15 percent drop (from 63 percent to 48 percent) who said they could have a relationship with someone whose political views differed greatly from theirs. In addition,

How has technology, including social media, changed the way adolescents and emerging adults seek love and romance?
tomazl/Getty Images

there has been almost a 25 percent increase in the percentage of young people who say they are open to dating someone of a different ethnic group, and over a 10-year period this figure increased by 58 percent. Also, 74 percent of Generation Z and 66 percent of millennials said they wanted to know if their date supports Black Lives Matter.

COHABITING ADULTS

Cohabitation refers to living together in a sexual relationship without being married. Cohabitation has undergone considerable changes in recent years (Sassler & Lichter, 2020). Rates of cohabitation in the United States have continued to rise (Manning, 2020). In a recent national poll, the number of cohabiting adults increased 29 percent from 2007 to 2016, comprising 18 million adults in a cohabiting relationship (U.S. Census Bureau, 2016). In 2018, 15 percent of U.S. adults between the ages of 25 and 34 years old and 9 percent between 18 and 24 years old were cohabiting (U.S. Census Bureau, 2019). At lower SES levels, couples are more likely to cohabit and give birth prior to marriage and less likely to marry at all (Karney, 2021). Engaging in serial cohabitation—exiting one cohabitation and then entering another—also has increased in the last decade in the United States (Eickmeyer & Manning, 2020). And cohabiting rates are even higher in some countries. For example, cohabitation is almost universal in Sweden (Smock & Schwartz, 2020). Cohabitation is increasing in China and Taiwan but still rare in Japan and South Korea. Also, a recent study indicated that early transitioning into a stepfamily home, especially for females, was linked to earlier entry into cohabitation (Johnston, Cavanagh, & Crosnoe, 2020).

In the United States, cohabitation is more often perceived as a precursor to marriage, while in Europe, especially in Scandinavian countries, it is more frequently perceived as an ongoing lifestyle (Sassler & Lichter, 2020). These couples do not want the official aspects of marriage. In the United States, cohabiting arrangements tend to be short-lived, with one-third lasting less than a year (Hyde & DeLamater, 2020). Fewer than 1 out of 10 lasts five years. Of course, it is easier to dissolve a cohabitation relationship than to divorce. In a recent large-scale study, women who cohabited within the first year of a sexual relationship were less likely to get married than women who waited more than one year before cohabiting (Sassler, Michelmore, & Qian, 2018).

Couples who cohabit face certain problems (Johnson & others, 2020). Disapproval by parents and other family members can place emotional strain on the cohabiting couple. Some cohabiting couples have difficulty owning property jointly. Legal rights involving the dissolution of the relationship are less certain than in a divorce. One study found that following the transition from dating to cohabitation, relationships were characterized by more commitment, lower satisfaction, more negative communication, and more physical aggression than during the dating (noncohabiting) period (Rhoades, Stanley, & Markman, 2012). Also, researchers have found that cohabiting individuals are not as mentally healthy as their counterparts in committed marital relationships (Braithwaite & Holt-Lunstad, 2017). However, heavy drinking was more common during time spent single than in long-term cohabitation. And in a recent national survey, married adults had higher rates of relationship satisfaction than unmarried cohabitors (Horowitz, Graf, & Livingston, 2019).

Cohabitation and Marital Stability/Happiness If a couple lives together before they marry, does cohabiting help or harm their chances of later having a stable and happy marriage? The majority of studies have found lower rates of marital satisfaction and higher rates of divorce in couples who lived together before getting married (Rose-Greenland & Smock, 2013). However, research indicates that the link between marital cohabitation and marital instability in first marriages has weakened in recent cohorts (Sassler & Lichter, 2020).

What might explain the finding that cohabiting is linked with divorce more than not cohabiting? The most frequently given explanation is that the less traditional lifestyle of cohabitation may attract less conventional individuals who are not great believers in marriage in the first place. An alternative explanation is that the experience of cohabiting changes people's attitudes and habits in ways that increase their likelihood of divorce.

Recent research has provided clarification of cohabitation outcomes. One meta-analysis found the link between cohabitation and marital instability did not hold up when only cohabitation with the eventual marital partner was examined, indicating that these cohabitors may attach more long-term positive meaning to living together (Jose, O'Leary, & Moyer, 2010). Another study revealed that for first marriages, cohabiting with the spouse without first being engaged was linked to more negative interaction and a higher probability of divorce than

cohabitation Living together in a sexual relationship without being married.

What are some differences between cohabiting relationships and marriages? Does cohabiting help or harm a couple's chances of later having a successful marriage?
Reed Kaestner/Getty Images

When two people are under the influence of the most violent, most insane, most delusive, and most transient of passions, they are required to swear that they will remain in that excited, abnormal, and exhausting condition continuously until death do them part.

—GEORGE BERNARD SHAW
Irish Playwright, 20th Century

Luca Santilli/Shutterstock

cohabiting after engagement (Stanley & others, 2010). In contrast, premarital cohabitation prior to a second marriage placed couples at risk for divorce regardless of whether they were engaged. One study also found that the marriages of couples who were cohabiting but not engaged were less likely to survive to the 10- to 15-year mark than the marriages of their counterparts who were engaged when they cohabited (Copen, Daniels, & Mosher, 2013). Also, another analysis indicated that cohabiting does not have a negative effect on marriage if the couple did not have any previous live-in lovers and did not have children prior to the marriage (Cherlin, 2009). And researchers in one study concluded that the difference between the risk of marital dissolution for cohabitors and for those who married without previously cohabiting was much smaller when they had cohabited in their mid-twenties or later (Kuperberg, 2014).

MARRIED ADULTS

Until about 1930, stable marriage was widely accepted as the endpoint of adult development. In the last 70 to 80 years, however, personal fulfillment both inside and outside marriage has emerged as a goal that competes with marital stability. The changing norm of male-female equality in marriage and increasingly high expectations for what a marital relationship should encompass have produced marital relationships that are more fragile and intense than they were in previous generations (Cherlin, 2020).

Marital Trends   In 2019, 48.2 percent of individuals 18 and older in the United States were married, down from 72 percent in 1960 (U.S. Census Bureau, 2019). Also, in 2019, the U.S. average age for a first marriage had climbed to 30 years for men and 28 years for women, higher than at any other point in history (U.S. Census Bureau, 2019). In 1960, the average age for a first marriage in the United States was 23 years for men and 20 years for women. Also, as indicated earlier, a higher percentage of U.S. adults never marry—in 2019, a record percentage (35 percent of men, 30 percent of women) of adults had never married (U.S. Census Bureau, 2020). In addition, the rising rate of cohabitation in the United States has contributed to the reduced percentage of adults who are married.

Marriage rates vary according to ethnicity in the United States. In 2018, 63 percent of Asian American adults were married, followed by 57 percent on non-Latinx whites, 48 percent of Latinxs, and 33 percent of African Americans (U.S. Census Bureau, 2019). Marriage rates between individuals from different ethnic groups have dramatically increased recently. In 1967, 3 percent of newlyweds and 3 percent of all married people were from different ethnic backgrounds; in 2015 those figures had risen to 17 percent of newlyweds and 10 percent of all married persons (Livingston & Brown, 2017). The largest percentage increase in intermarriage in recent years has occurred for African Americans (from 5 percent in 1980 to 15 percent in 2015) and non-Latinx whites (from 4 percent in 1980 to 11 percent in 2015).

The age at which individuals get married is increasing, not just in the United States but also in many other countries around the world. Also, in recent analyses, age at first marriage in most developed countries is later than it is in the United States (OECD, 2019). For example, in a comparison of 39 developed countries, average age at first marriage in Scandinavian countries, especially Sweden, has increased to 33.6 years of age for women and 36.6 for men. The earliest average age at first marriage in developed countries is 25 for females and 27 for males in Turkey and Israel.

Although marriage rates are declining and the average age of marriage is going up, recent research with emerging and young adults indicates that they view marriage as a very important life pursuit. Indeed, young adults in one study predicted that marriage would be more important in their life than parenting, careers, or leisure activities (Willoughby, Hall, & Goff, 2015). In a recent book, *The Marriage Paradox* (Willoughby & James, 2017), the authors concluded that the importance of marriage to emerging and young adults may be what is encouraging them to first build better a better career and a stable financial foundation to increase the likelihood that their marriage will be successful later. From this perspective, emerging and young adults may not be abandoning marriage because they don't like it or are not interested in it, but rather because they want to position themselves in the best possible way for developing a healthy and enduring marital relationship.

A recent survey explored why individuals get married (Geiger & Livingston, 2019). At the top of the list was love (88 percent), followed by making a lifelong commitment (81 percent), companionship (76 percent), and having children (49 percent). Another study explored what U.S.

never-married men and women are looking for in a potential spouse (Wang & Parker 2014). Following are the percentages who reported that various factors would be very important for them:

Factor	Men	Women
Similar ideas about having and raising children	62	70
A steady job	46	78
Same moral and religious beliefs	31	38
At least as much education	26	28
Same racial or ethnic background	7	10

Thus, in this study, never-married men said that the most important factor for a potential spouse was similar ideas about having and raising children, but never-married women placed greater importance on having a steady job.

Also, in a recent study across a number of countries and religions, men reported higher marital satisfaction than women (Sorokowski, Kowal, & Sorkowska, 2019). In this study, levels of marital satisfaction were similar for Muslims, Christians, and atheists. And a study of 502 newlyweds found that nearly all couples had optimistic forecasts of how their marriage would change over the next four years (Lavner & Bradbury, 2013). Despite their optimistic forecasts, their marital satisfaction declined across this time frame. Wives with the most optimistic forecasts showed the steepest declines in marital satisfaction.

Despite the decline in marriage rates, the United States is still a marrying society. In 2019, 65 percent of men and 70 percent of women had been married at least once (U.S. Census Bureau, 2019). However, this percentage is declining—in 1990, 70 percent of men and 77 percent of women had been married at least once.

The Benefits of a Good Marriage　Are there any benefits of having a good marriage? There are several (Seccombe, 2020). Individuals who are happily married live longer, healthier lives than either divorced individuals or those who are unhappily married (Proulx & Snyder-Rivas, 2013). Also, a large-scale analysis of data from a number of studies indicated a positive effect of marriage on life span, with being married increasing the longevity of men more than women (Rendall & others, 2011). And a recent research review of individuals who were married, divorced, widowed, and single found that married individuals had the best cardiovascular profile and single men the worst (Manfredini & others, 2017). Further, an unhappy marriage can shorten a person's life by an average of four years (Gove, Style, & Hughes, 1990).

To improve their relationships, some couples seek counseling. To read about the work of couples counselor Susan Orenstein, see the *Connecting with Careers* profile.

connecting with careers

Susan Orenstein, Couples Counselor

Susan Orenstein provides counseling to emerging adults and young adults in Cary, North Carolina. She specializes in premarital and couples counseling to help couples increase their intimacy and mutual appreciation, and also works with couples to resolve long-standing conflicts, reduce destructive patterns of communication, and restore trust in the relationship. In addition to working privately with couples, she conducts workshops on relationships and gives numerous talks at colleges, businesses, and organizations.

Dr. Orenstein obtained an undergraduate degree in psychology from Brown University, a master's degree in counseling from Georgia Tech University, and a doctorate in counseling psychology from Temple University.

Some couples therapists hold advanced degrees in clinical psychology or marriage and family therapy rather than counseling, and some practice with a master's degree. After earning a master's or doctoral degree in an appropriate program, before practicing couples therapy, individuals are required to do an internship and pass a state licensing examination.

At most colleges, the counseling or health center has a counselor or therapist who works with couples to improve their relationship.

DIVORCED ADULTS

During the mid-twentieth century divorce reached epidemic proportions in the United States. However, the divorce rate has declined in recent decades, peaking at 5.1 divorces per 1,000 people in 1981 and then declining to 2.9 divorces per 1,000 people in 2018 (U.S. Census Bureau, 2019). The 2018 divorce rate of 2.9 compares with a marriage rate of 6.5 per 1,000 people in 2018.

Although the U.S. divorce rate has dropped, it continues to be one of the highest divorce rates in the world. Russia has the highest divorce rate of the countries surveyed (4.6 divorces per 1,000 people) (OECD, 2019). In the United States, nearly half of first marriages break up within 20 years (Copen & others, 2012).

Individuals in some groups have a higher incidence of divorce (Smock & Schwartz, 2020). Youthful marriage, low educational level, low income, not having a religious affiliation, having parents who are divorced, and having a baby before marriage are factors that are associated with increased rates of divorce (Hoelter, 2009). And the following characteristics of one's partner increase the likelihood of divorce: alcoholism, psychological problems, domestic violence, infidelity, and inadequate division of household labor (Affleck, Carmichael, & Whitley, 2018).

Certain personality traits also have been found to predict divorce. In a study that focused on the Big Five personality factors, low levels of agreeableness and conscientiousness and high levels of neuroticism and openness to experience were linked to daily experiences that over time negatively impacted relationship quality and eventually led to a marital breakup (Solomon & Jackson, 2014).

Also, a recent study in Great Britain found no differences in the causes of breakdowns in marriage and cohabitation relationships (Gravningen & others, 2017). In this study, the following percentages cited these reasons: "grew apart" (men: 39 percent, women: 36 percent); "arguments" (men: 27 percent, women: 30 percent); "unfaithfulness/adultery" (men: 18 percent, women: 24 percent); "lack of respect, appreciation" (men: 17 percent, women: 25 percent); and "domestic violence" (men: 4 percent, women: 16 percent).

If a divorce is going to occur, it usually takes place between the fifth and tenth years of marriage (National Center for Health Statistics, 2000) (see Figure 6). For example, one study found that divorce peaked in Finland at approximately 5 to 7 years of marriage, then the rate of divorce gradually declined (Kulu, 2014). This timing may reflect an effort by partners in troubled marriages to stay in the marriage and try to work things out. If after several years these efforts have not improved the relationship, the couple may then seek a divorce.

Even those adults who initiated their divorce undergo challenges after a marriage dissolves (Moons & others, 2021). Divorced adults have higher rates of depression, anxiety, physical illnesses, suicide, motor vehicle accidents, alcoholism, and mortality (Axinn & others, 2020).

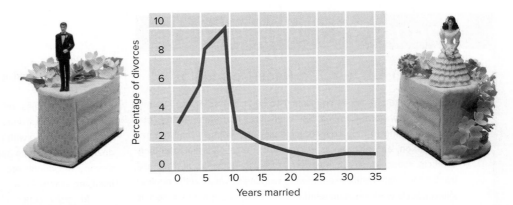

FIGURE **6**

THE DIVORCE RATE IN RELATION TO NUMBER OF YEARS MARRIED. Shown here is the percentage of divorces as a function of how long couples have been married. Notice that most divorces occur in the early years of marriage, peaking in the fifth to tenth years of marriage.
Digital Vision/Getty Images

There are gender differences in the process and outcomes of divorce (Leopold, 2018). Women are more likely to sense that something is wrong with the marriage and are more likely to seek a divorce than are men. Women also show better emotional adjustment and are more likely to perceive divorce as providing a "second chance" to increase their happiness, improve their social lives, and have better work opportunities. However, divorce typically has a more negative economic impact on women than on men.

GAY AND LESBIAN ADULTS

Until recently, the legal context of marriage created barriers to breaking up that did not exist for same-sex partners. However, the legalization of same-sex marriage in all 50 states in 2015 also created this barrier for same-sex partners (Colistra & Johnson, 2021). In many additional ways, researchers have found that gay and lesbian relationships are similar—in their satisfactions, loves, joys, and conflicts—to heterosexual relationships (Baker & Halford, 2020). For example, a recent study indicated that adults in same-sex relationships were experiencing levels of commitment, satisfaction, and emotional intimacy similar to those of adults in different-sex relationships (Joyner, Manning, & Prince, 2019).

Lesbian couples especially place a high priority on equality in their relationships (Fingerhut & Peplau, 2013). Indeed, some researchers have found that gay and lesbian couples are more flexible in their gender roles than heterosexual individuals are. For example, one research survey found that a greater percentage of same-sex, dual-earner couples than different-sex couples said they share laundry (44 versus 31 percent), household repairs (33 versus 15 percent), and routine (74 versus 38 percent) and sick (62 versus 32 percent) child-care responsibilities (Matos, 2015).

There are a number of misconceptions about gay and lesbian couples (Goldberg & Allen, 2020). Contrary to stereotypes, in only a small percentage of gay and lesbian couples is one partner masculine and the other feminine. Only a small segment of the gay population has a large number of sexual partners, and this is uncommon among lesbians. Furthermore, researchers have found that gay and lesbian couples prefer long-term, committed relationships (Fingerhut & Peplau, 2013). About half of committed gay couples do have an open relationship that allows the possibility of sex (but not affectionate love) outside of the relationship. Lesbian couples usually do not have this type of open relationship.

A special concern is the stigma, prejudice, and discrimination that lesbian, gay, and bisexual individuals experience because of widespread social devaluation of same-sex relationships (Vargas & others, 2021). However, one study indicated that many individuals in these relationships saw stigma as bringing them closer together and strengthening their relationship (Frost, 2011).

Review Connect Reflect

 LG5 Explain the diversity of emerging adult lifestyles.

Review
- What characterizes single adults?
- What are the lives of cohabiting adults like?
- What are some key aspects of the lives of married adults?
- How does divorce affect adults?
- What characterizes the lifestyles of gay and lesbian adults?

Connect
- What are some similarities and differences between cohabitating relationships and marriages?

Reflect *Your Own Personal Journey of Life*
- Which type of lifestyle are you living today? What do you think are its advantages and disadvantages for you? If you could have a different lifestyle, which one would it be? Why?

reach your **learning goals**

Peers, Romantic Relationships, and Lifestyles

1 Exploring Peer Relations and Friendship

LG1 Discuss the roles of peer relations, friendship, and loneliness in adolescent development.

Peer Relations

- Peers are individuals who are about the same age or maturity level. Peers provide a means of social comparison and a source of information beyond the family. Contexts and individual difference factors influence peer relations. Good peer relations may be necessary for normal social development. The inability to "plug in" to a social network is associated with a number of problems. Peer relations can be negative or positive.

- Sullivan stressed that peer relations provide the context for learning the symmetrical reciprocity mode of relationships. Healthy family relations usually promote healthy peer relations. The pressure to conform to peers is strong during adolescence, especially around the eighth and ninth grades.

- Popular adolescents are frequently nominated as a best friend and are rarely disliked by their peers. Average adolescents receive an average number of both positive and negative nominations from their peers. Neglected adolescents are infrequently nominated as a best friend but are not disliked by their peers. Rejected adolescents are infrequently nominated as a best friend and are disliked by their peers. Controversial adolescents are frequently nominated both as a best friend and as being disliked by peers.

- Social knowledge and social information-processing skills are associated with improved peer relations. Self-regulation of emotion is associated with positive peer relations. Conglomerate strategies, also referred to as coaching, involve the use of a combination of techniques, rather than a single strategy, to improve adolescents' social skills.

Friendship

- Friends are a subset of peers who engage in mutual companionship, support, and intimacy. The functions of friendship include companionship, stimulation, physical support, ego support, social comparison, and intimacy/affection. Sullivan argued that the psychological importance and intimacy of close friends increases dramatically in adolescence. Research supports this view.

- Children and adolescents who become close friends with older individuals engage in more deviant behaviors than do their counterparts with same-age friends. Early-maturing girls are more likely than late-maturing girls to have older friends, a characteristic that can contribute to problem behaviors.

- Some changes in friendship occur in emerging adulthood. Intimacy and similarity are two of the most important characteristics of friendships.

Loneliness

- Chronic loneliness is linked with impaired physical and mental health. Loneliness often emerges when people make life transitions, so it is not surprising that loneliness is common among college freshmen. Moderately or intensely lonely individuals never or rarely feel in tune with others and rarely or never find companionship when they want it, whereas other individuals may value solitary time.

2 Adolescent Groups

LG2 Summarize what takes place in adolescent groups.

Groups in Childhood and Adolescence

- Childhood groups are less formal, less heterogeneous, and less mixed-sex than adolescent groups. Dunphy's study found that adolescent group development proceeds through five stages.

Cliques and Crowds

- Cliques are small groups that range from two to about twelve individuals and average about five to six individuals. Clique members are similar in age, usually of the same sex, and often participate in similar activities, sharing ideas, hanging out, and developing an in-group identity.

- Crowds are a larger group structure than cliques and are less personal. Adolescents are members of crowds usually based on reputation and may or may not spend much time together. Many crowds are defined by adolescents' activities, such as jocks, druggies, populars, and independents.

Youth Organizations

- Youth organizations can have important influences on adolescent development. More than 400 national youth organizations currently exist in the United States. Boys & Girls Clubs are examples of youth organizations designed to increase membership in youth organizations in low-income neighborhoods. Participation in youth organizations may increase achievement and decrease delinquency. Youth activities and organizations also may provide opportunities for adolescents to develop initiative.

3 Gender and Culture

 Describe the roles of gender and culture in adolescent peer groups and friendships.

Gender

- The social world of adolescent peer groups varies according to gender, socioeconomic status, ethnicity, and culture. In terms of gender, boys are more likely to associate in larger clusters and organized sports than girls are. Boys also are more likely than girls to engage in competition, conflict, ego displays, risk taking, and dominance seeking. By contrast, girls are more likely to engage in collaborative discourse. Girls' friendships are more intimate than those of boys.

Socioeconomic Status and Ethnicity

- In many cases, peer groups are segregated according to socioeconomic status. In some cases, ethnic minority adolescents in the United States rely on peers more than non-Latinx white adolescents do.

Culture

- In some countries, such as rural India, Arab countries, and Japan, adults restrict access to the peer group. In North America and Europe, the peer group is a pervasive aspect of adolescents' lives.

4 Dating and Romantic Relationships

 Characterize adolescent dating and romantic relationships.

Functions of Dating

- Dating can be a form of recreation, a source of social status and achievement, an aspect of socialization, a context for learning about intimacy and sexual experimentation, a source of companionship, and a means of mate selection.

Types of Dating and Developmental Changes

- Three stages characterize the development of romantic relationships in adolescence: (1) entry into romantic attractions and affiliations at about 11 to 13 years of age, (2) exploring romantic relationships at approximately 14 to 16 years of age, and (3) consolidating dyadic romantic bonds at about 17 to 19 years of age.

- Younger adolescents often begin to hang out together in mixed-sex groups. A special concern is early dating, which is associated with a number of problems. In early adolescence, individuals spend more time thinking about the opposite sex than actually being with them, but this trend tends to reverse in the high school years. Most sexual minority youth have same-sex sexual experiences, but relatively few have same-sex romantic relationships.

Emotion, Adjustment, and Romantic Relationships

- The emotions evoked by romantic relationships can envelop adolescents' lives. Sometimes these emotions are positive, sometimes negative, and they can change very quickly. Adolescents who date have more problems, such as substance abuse, than those who do not date, but they also receive more acceptance from peers. An increasing number of youth relationship education programs are being developed for adolescents and emerging adults.

| Romantic Love and Its Construction | • Romantic love, also called passionate love, involves sexuality and infatuation more than affectionate love. Romantic love is especially prominent among adolescents and traditional-aged college students. Affectionate love is more common in middle and late adulthood, characterizing love that endures over time. Connolly's research revealed the importance of peers and friends in adolescent romantic relationships. |

• Girls tend to view dating as an interpersonal experience; boys view dating more in terms of physical attraction. Culture can exert a powerful influence on dating. Many adolescents from immigrant families face conflicts with their parents about dating.

5 Emerging Adult Lifestyles

 LG5 Explain the diversity of emerging adult lifestyles.

Single Adults

• Being single has become an increasingly prominent lifestyle. Myths and stereotypes about singles abound, ranging from "swinging single" to "desperately lonely, suicidal single." There are advantages and disadvantages to being single, autonomy being one of the advantages. Intimacy, loneliness, and finding a positive identity in a marriage-oriented society are concerns of single adults.

Cohabiting Adults

• Cohabitation is an increasingly prevalent lifestyle for many adults. Cohabitation offers some advantages as well as problems. Premarital cohabitation leads not to greater marital happiness but rather to no differences or differences suggesting that cohabitation is not good for a marriage, although variations in this outcome have recently been found.

Married Adults

• Even though adults are remaining single longer and the divorce rate is high, the majority of Americans still get married. The age at which individuals marry, expectations about what the marriage will be like, and the developmental course of marriage vary not only over time within a culture but also across cultures.

Divorced Adults

• If a divorce is going to occur, it usually takes place 5 to 10 years into the marriage. Divorce is complex and emotional. In the first year following divorce, a disequilibrium in the divorced adult's behavior occurs, but by several years after the divorce more stability has been achieved.

Gay and Lesbian Adults

• There are many misconceptions about gay and lesbian adults. One of the most striking findings about gay and lesbian couples is how similar they are to heterosexual couples.

key terms

affectionate love	conglomerate strategies	friends	popular adolescents
average adolescents	controversial adolescents	intimacy in friendship	rejected adolescents
cliques	crowds	neglected adolescents	romantic love
cohabitation	dating scripts	peers	sociometric status

key people

Andrew Cherlin	Dexter Dunphy	Willard Hartup	Harry Stack Sullivan
Jennifer Connolly	Candice Feiring	Reed Larson	Elizabeth Wehner
Kenneth Dodge	Wyndol Furman	Mitchell Prinstein	

improving the lives of adolescents and emerging adults

Handbook of Peer Interactions, Relationships, and Groups (2nd ed.). (2019).
William Bukowski, Brett Laursen, and Kenneth Rubin (Editors).
New York: Guilford
> A definitive handbook with chapters written by leading experts on a wide range of peer relations topics.

Friendships, Romantic Relationships, and Other Dyadic Peer Relationships in Child and Adolescence: A Unified Relational Perspective (2015)
Wyndol Furman and Amanda Rose
In R. M. Lerner (Ed.), *Handbook of Child Psychology and Developmental Science* (7th ed.). New York: Wiley.
> Leading experts provide an up-to-date review of research, theory, and applications involving the development of peer, friendship, and romantic relationships.

Just Friends (1985)
Lillian Rubin
New York: HarperCollins
> *Just Friends* explores the nature of friendship and intimacy, offering many recommendations for improving relationships with friends.

The Marriage-Go-Round (2009)
Andrew Cherlin
New York: Random House
> Leading sociologist Andrew Cherlin provides up-to-date information about trends in cohabitation, marriage, and divorce.

The Seven Principles for Making Marriages Work (1999)
John Gottman and Nan Silver
New York: Crown
> Leading relationship expert John Gottman provides valuable recommendations for what makes marriages work, based on his extensive research.

chapter 10

SCHOOLS

chapter outline

1 Approaches to Educating Students

Learning Goal 1 Describe approaches to educating students.

Contemporary Approaches to Student Learning
Accountability
Technology and Education

2 Transitions in Schooling

Learning Goal 2 Discuss transitions in schooling from early adolescence to emerging adulthood.

Transition to Middle or Junior High School
Improving Middle Schools
The American High School
High School Dropouts
Transition from High School to College
Transition from College to Work

3 The Social Contexts of Schools

Learning Goal 3 Explain how the social contexts of schools influence adolescent development.

Changing Social Developmental Contexts
Classroom Climate and Management
Person-Environment Fit
Teachers, Parents, Peers, and Extracurricular Activities
Culture

4 Schools and the COVID-19 Pandemic

Learning Goal 4 Summarize the effects of the COVID-19 pandemic on schools.

K-12 Education
College Education

5 Adolescents Who Are Exceptional

Learning Goal 5 Characterize adolescents who are exceptional, and describe their education.

Who Are Adolescents with Disabilities?
Learning Disabilities
Attention Deficit Hyperactivity Disorder
Autism Spectrum Disorders
Educational Issues Involving Adolescents with Disabilities
Adolescents Who Are Gifted

FatCamera/E+/Getty Images

To improve education in the United States, teachers need to find ways to ignite high school students' motivation for learning. Here are some strategies that several award-winning teachers use to engage students in learning:

- A former at-risk student himself, Henry Brown, a recent Florida Teacher of the Year, teaches math. At the high school where Brown teaches, half of the incoming freshmen have math skills below the fifth-grade level. Brown engages them by teaching real-world math skills. In one project, he devised a dummy corporation and had students play different roles in it, learning important math skills as they worked and made decisions in the corporation (*USA Today,* 2001).

Henry Brown teaches at-risk students real-world math skills to help them become more engaged in learning.
Andrew Itkoff

- Peter Karpyk, a West Virginia high school chemistry teacher, uses an extensive range of activities to make science exciting for students. He has students give chemistry demonstrations at elementary schools and has discovered that some students who struggle with tests excel when they teach younger children. He also adapts his teaching based on feedback from former students and incorporates questions from their college chemistry tests as bonus questions on his high school tests to challenge and motivate his current students (Wong Briggs, 2005).

- Peggy Schweiger, a physics teacher in Texas, makes science interesting by giving students opportunities to explore everyday science problems. Among the projects she has students do are wiring a doll house and making replicas of boats for a regatta. One of her former students, Alison Arnett, 19, said:

  She taught us how to think and learn, not to succeed in physics class. We were encouraged to stand on desks, tape things to the ceiling, and even drop an egg on her head to illustrate physics—anything to make us discover that we live with physics every day (*USA Today,* 2001, p. 6).

Pete Karpyk shrink-wrapped himself to demonstrate the effects of air pressure in his high school chemistry class.
Dale Sparks/All-Pro Photography

- Carmella Williams Scott, a middle school teacher in Georgia, created Juvenile Video Court TV, a student-run judicial system, so that students could experience how such systems function. She especially targeted gang leaders for inclusion in the system because they ran the school. Scott likes to use meaningful questions to stimulate students' critical thinking. She believes that mutual respect is a key factor in her success as a teacher and in the absence of discipline problems in her classes (Wong Briggs, 1999).

preview

In youth, we learn. An important context for learning is school. Schools not only foster adolescents' academic learning but also provide a social arena where peers, friends, and crowds can have a powerful influence on their development. Our exploration of schools in this chapter focuses on approaches to educating students, transitions in schooling, the social contexts of schools, the effects of the COVID-19 pandemic on schools, and strategies for educating adolescents who are exceptional.

Carmella Williams Scott has been successful in creating a learning atmosphere that stimulates students' critical thinking.
Michael A. Schwarz

The whole art of teaching is only the art of awakening the natural curiosity of young minds.

—Anatole France
French Novelist, 20th Century

None can be given an education. All you can give is the opportunity to learn.

—Carolyn Warner
American Author, 20th Century

Laboko/Shutterstock

constructivist approach A learner-centered approach that emphasizes the adolescent's active, cognitive construction of knowledge and understanding with guidance from the teacher.

direct instruction approach A teacher-centered approach characterized by teacher direction and control, mastery of academic skills, high expectations for students, and maximum time spent on learning tasks.

Because there are so many different approaches for teaching students, controversy swirls about the best way to teach (Kauchak & Eggen, 2021). There also is considerable interest in finding the best way to hold schools and teachers accountable for whether students are learning (Popham, 2020). In addition, incorporating technology into the curriculum has become increasingly important in recent years.

CONTEMPORARY APPROACHES TO STUDENT LEARNING

There are two main contemporary approaches to student learning: constructivist and direct instruction. We examine both approaches and then consider whether effective teachers use either of these approaches exclusively or incorporate aspects of both approaches into their teaching.

The **constructivist approach** is learner-centered and emphasizes the importance of individuals actively constructing their knowledge and understanding with guidance from the teacher. In the constructivist view, teachers should not attempt to simply pour information into students' minds. Rather, students should be encouraged to explore their world, discover knowledge, reflect, and think critically, with careful monitoring and meaningful guidance from the teacher (Morrison & others, 2022). Advocates of the constructivist approach believe that for too long in American education students have been required to sit still, be passive learners, and rotely memorize irrelevant as well as relevant information (Borich & Blanchette, 2021).

Today, constructivism may include an emphasis on collaboration—students working together in their efforts to know and understand (Sadker, Zittleman, & Koch, 2022). A teacher with a constructivist instructional philosophy would not have students memorize information rotely but would give them opportunities to meaningfully construct their knowledge and understand the material while the teacher is guiding their learning. In a recent experimental study involving almost 1,900 middle school students, enhancements to peer relations created by structured small group learning (cooperative learning, for example) were successful in improving peer relations, reducing stress, and in turn, decreasing emotional problems and promoting academic achievement (Van Ryzin & Roseth, 2021).

By contrast, the **direct instruction approach** is structured and teacher-centered. It is characterized by teacher direction and control, high teacher expectations for students' progress, maximum time spent by students on academic tasks, and efforts by the teacher to keep negative affect to a minimum. An important goal in the direct instruction approach is maximizing student learning time (Kauchak & Eggen, 2021).

Advocates of the constructivist approach argue that the direct instruction approach turns students into passive learners and does not adequately challenge them to think in critical and creative ways. The direct instruction enthusiasts say that the constructivist approaches do not give enough attention to the content of a discipline, such as history or science. They also believe that the constructivist approaches are too relativistic and vague.

Some experts in educational psychology believe that many effective teachers use both a constructivist *and* a direct instruction approach rather than relying exclusively on one or the other (Cecil, Lozano, & Chaplin, 2020). Further, some circumstances may call for a constructivist approach and others for a direct instruction approach. For example, experts increasingly recommend an explicit, intellectually engaging direct instruction approach when teaching students with a reading or a writing disability (Tompkins & Rodgers, 2020).

ACCOUNTABILITY

Since the 1990s, the U.S. public and governments at every level have demanded increased accountability from schools. One result has been the spread of state-mandated tests designed to measure what students have or have not learned (Popham, 2020). Many states have identified objectives for students in their state and created tests to measure whether students are meeting those objectives (Anselmo, Yarborough, & Tran, 2021). This approach became national policy in 2002 when the No Child Left Behind (NCLB) legislation was signed into law.

No Child Left Behind (NCLB) Proponents of NCLB have argued that statewide standardized testing has a number of positive effects, including improved student performance; more time spent teaching the subjects that are tested; high expectations for all students; identification of poorly performing schools, teachers, and administrators; and improved confidence in schools as test scores rise.

In the History Alive! program of the Teachers Curriculum Institute, students work in cooperative groups of four to prepare one student to be the actor in a lively panel debate. *Is the History Alive! program more characteristic of a constructivist or direct instruction approach?*
Teachers' Curriculum Institute

Critics argue that the NCLB legislation has been doing more harm than good (Sadker, Zittleman, & Koch, 2022). One criticism stresses that using a single test as the sole indicator of students' progress and competence presents a very narrow view of students' skills. This criticism is similar to the one leveled at IQ tests. Many psychologists and educators emphasize that a number of measures should be used to gain a more accurate assessment of students' progress and achievement, including tests, quizzes, projects, portfolios, classroom observations, and so on. Also, critics point out that the tests used as part of NCLB fail to assess creativity, motivation, persistence, flexible thinking, or social skills (Popham, 2020). Another criticism is that teachers end up spending far too much class time "teaching to the test" by drilling students and having them memorize isolated facts at the expense of teaching that focuses on helping students strengthen the thinking skills that they will need for success in life (Nichols & Brewington, 2020). Also, some individuals are concerned that in the era of No Child Left Behind schools have been neglecting students who are gifted in the effort to raise the achievement level of students who are not doing well. And some critics stress that NCLB reflects social policy that focuses only on academic reforms and ignores the social aspects of schools (Crosnoe & Benner, 2015).

Consider also the following aspect of NCLB: Each state is allowed to have different criteria for what constitutes passing or failing grades on tests designated for NCLB inclusion. An analysis of NCLB data indicated that almost every fourth-grade student in Mississippi knows how to read, but only half of Massachusetts' students do (Birman & others, 2007). Clearly, Mississippi's standards for passing the reading test are far below those of Massachusetts. The state-by-state analysis suggests that many states have taken the safe route by setting a low standard for passing. Thus, while one of NCLB's goals was to raise standards for achievement in U.S. schools, allowing states to set their own standards likely has lowered achievement standards.

Despite such criticisms, the U.S. Department of Education is committed to implementing No Child Left Behind, and schools are making accommodations to meet the requirements of this law. Indeed, most educators recognize the importance of high expectations and high standards of excellence for students and teachers. At issue, however, is whether the tests and procedures mandated by NCLB are the most effective ways to achieve these high standards (Sadker, Zittleman, & Koch, 2022).

Common Core In 2009, the Common Core State Standards Initiative was endorsed by the National Governors Association in an effort to implement more rigorous state guidelines for educating students. The Common Core Standards specify what students should know and the skills they should develop at each grade level in various content areas (Common Core State Standards Initiative, 2014). Although a large majority of states have agreed to implement the Standards, they have generated considerable controversy,

> **developmental connections**
> **Intelligence**
> The intelligence quotient (IQ) gives students a specific number that indicates their intelligence. Connect to "The Brain and Cognitive Development."

What are some issues involved in the No Child Left Behind legislation?
YanLev/Shutterstock

with some critics arguing that they are simply a further effort by the federal government to control education and that they emphasize a "one-size-fits-all" approach that pays little attention to individual variations in students (Loveless, 2020, 2021). Supporters say that the Standards provide much-needed detailed guidelines and important milestones for students to achieve (Petrilli, 2020).

Every Student Succeeds Act (ESSA)   The most recent initiative in U.S. education is the *Every Student Succeeds Act (ESSA)*, which was passed into law in December 2015 and was supposed to be fully implemented during the 2017–2018 school year. However, in 2021 implementation was still occurring and ESSA continues to be a work in progress. ESSA is giving states much more flexibility in implementing the law than was the case for NCLB (Burnette, 2021). The new law also allows states to scale back the role that test scores play in holding schools accountable for student achievement (Center for Education Policy, 2020). In addition, schools must use at least one nonacademic factor—such as student engagement—when tracking schools' success. However, in 2020, the federal government suspended standardized testing for the 2020-2021 school year when the vast majority of schools switched from in-person classes to online learning in an effort to protect students and staff from COVID-19.

TECHNOLOGY AND EDUCATION

A major change in education during the last several decades has been the increased use of technology in the classroom. In recognition of this change, technology standards have been proposed that would spell out the key aspects of technological competence. Another recent focus involves finding ways to use the Internet effectively in schools.

Technology Standards for Adolescents   If adolescents are to be adequately prepared for tomorrow's jobs, schools must take an active role in ensuring that students become technologically literate (Maloy & others, 2021). The International Society for Technology in Education (ISTE) has developed technology standards for students (ISTE, 2016) and teachers (ISTE, 2007). ISTE emphasizes that each adolescent should become a(an):

- *Empowered Learner.* Students actively use technology to reach learning goals.
- *Digital Citizen.* Students demonstrate responsibility and are ethical in their use of technology.
- *Knowledge Constructor.* Students use a variety of resources and digital tools to construct knowledge, become more creative, and engage in meaningful learning.
- *Innovative Designer.* Students use various technologies to solve problems and craft useful and imaginative solutions to these problems.
- *Computational Thinker.* Students develop strategies in using technology to create solutions and test them.
- *Creative Communicator.* Students communicate effectively and think creatively in their use of digital tools to attain goals.
- *Global Collaborator.* Students use technology to widen their perspectives and enhance their learning by connecting with others locally and globally.

In addition, ISTE provides performance indicators for achieving these standards at four levels: prekindergarten through grade 2, grades 3 through 5, grades 6 through 8, and grades 9 through 12. ISTE also includes examples and scenarios to illustrate how technological literacy can be integrated across the curriculum at each of these levels.

For example, population growth and urban planning are the focus of a social sciences technology-based learning activity in grades 9 through 12. The activity challenges students to find sources online and elsewhere that describe worldwide population dilemmas. The activity can be altered to address different cities and regions worldwide.

What are some good technology standards for schools to implement for adolescents?
UrbancowE+/Getty Images

Guiding Adolescents to Use the Internet Effectively   When used effectively, the Internet expands access to a world of knowledge and people that students cannot experience in any other way (Kolb, 2020). One of the most effective ways to use the Internet in the class-room is through project-centered activities. Blog publishing (allowing moderated comments) can be a good collaborative online activity. Another collaborative use of the Internet is to have a group of students conduct a survey on a topic, put it on the Internet, and hope to obtain responses from many parts of the world. They can organize, analyze, and summarize the data they receive, and then share their findings with other students around the world. Yet another type of collaborative learning project involves sending groups of students on Internet "scavenger hunts" to find information and/or solve a problem. Online citizen science projects also are inher-ently collaborative, with data being pooled online for analysis. In the classroom, Web publishing and online videos can be highly collaborative activities, with different groups assigned to different roles and responsibilities (for example, art department, script writers, technical team).

A growing number of innovative educational projects include the use of computer-mediated communications. For example, there are many online sites (such as www.studentsoftheworld.info and www.tesol.net/teslpnpl.html) that allow teachers and students to correspond with "pen pals" around the world. Some of these sites even provide safe access to innovative computer-mediated communication venues such as chats and blogs (see, for example, http://learn.outofeden-walk.com/about/).

Increasing numbers of teachers also are using social media as an important tool for pro-fessional networking and development. Many Twitter chats are devoted to teachers in certain areas, grade levels, or content areas. Teachers often report that this activity is a useful and meaningful source of professional support and ideas. A list of educator Twitter chats can be found at www.iste.org/explore/articleDetail?articleid=7.

Review *Connect* Reflect

 LG1 Describe approaches to educating students.

Review

- What are the two main approaches to educating adolescents?
- What is involved in making schools more accountable?
- How can technology be effectively incorporated in schools for adolescents?

Connect

- Relate the concept of multiple intelligences to this section's discussion of the constructivist and direct instruction approaches to student learning.

Reflect *Your Own Personal Journey of Life*

- When you were in secondary school, did your teachers take more of a direct instruction or constructivist approach? Which approach would you have liked your teachers to use more? Why?

---

2 Transitions in Schooling

LG2 Discuss transitions in schooling from early adolescence to emerging adulthood.

Transition to Middle or Junior High School	Improving Middle Schools	The American High School	High School Dropouts	Transition from High School to College	Transition from College to Work

As children become adolescents, and as adolescents become adults, they experience transitions in schooling: from elementary school to middle school or junior high school, from school to work for non-college youth, from high school to college, and from college to work.

TRANSITION TO MIDDLE OR JUNIOR HIGH SCHOOL

The transition to middle or junior high school can be difficult and stressful for many students. Why? The transition takes place at a time when many changes—in the individual, in the family,

developmental connections

Achievement

Adolescence is a critical juncture in achievement that brings new social and academic pressures and challenges. Connect to "Achievement, Careers, and Work".

developmental **connections**

Cognitive Development

Formal operational thought is more abstract, idealistic, and logical than concrete operational thought. Connect to "The Brain and Cognitive Development."

developmental **connections**

Achievement

Adolescence is a critical juncture in achievement that brings new social and academic pressures. Connect to "Achievement, Work, and Careers."

and in school—are occurring simultaneously (Green & others, 2021). These changes include puberty and related concerns about body image; the emergence of at least some aspects of formal operational thought, including accompanying changes in social cognition; advances in executive function; increased responsibility and decreased dependency on parents; change to a larger, more impersonal school structure; change from one teacher to many teachers and from a small, homogeneous set of peers to a larger, more heterogeneous set of peers; and an increased focus on achievement and performance and their assessment.

Also, when students make the transition to middle or junior high school, they experience the **top-dog phenomenon,** moving from being the oldest, biggest, and most powerful students in the elementary school to being the youngest, smallest, and least powerful students in the middle or junior high school. Researchers have found that students' self-esteem is higher in the last year of elementary school and that they like school better than in the first year of middle or junior high school (Hawkins & Berndt, 1985; Hirsch & Rapkin, 1987). Also, a recent study revealed that compared with students in elementary school, students in the first year of middle school had lower levels of adaptive coping and higher levels of maladaptive coping (Skinner & Saxton, 2020). In addition, a recent Chinese study indicated that students transitioning into middle school had worse health and lower academic achievement than non-transitioning students (Anderson & others, 2020). However, the transition to middle or junior high school is less stressful when students have positive relationships with friends and go through the transition in team-oriented schools in which 20 to 30 students take the same classes together (Hawkins & Berndt, 1985). In a recent large-scale study in 24 schools found that teachers who were given intervention training in improving classroom behavior, academic skills, and engagement created a supportive classroom climate for students in the first year of middle school that resulted in students having lower anxiety, fewer emotional problems, and better adjustment than was the case for students in schools where the teachers did not get the intervention (Dawes & others, 2020). And a recent experimental study found that implementing a social and emotional learning mentoring program improved the decision making, problem-solving skills, emotion regulation, and resilience of students making the transition to middle school better compared with their counterparts who did not experience the mentoring program (Green & others, 2021).

There can also be positive aspects of the transition to middle or junior high school (Bellmore, Villarreal, & Ho, 2011). Students are more likely to feel grown up, have more subjects from which to select, have more opportunities to spend time with peers and locate compatible friends, and enjoy increased independence from direct parental monitoring. They also may be more challenged intellectually by academic work.

IMPROVING MIDDLE SCHOOLS

Over the past three decades a recurring theme has been the need to improve middle school education (Powell, 2020). In 1989 the Carnegie Council on Adolescent Development issued an extremely negative evaluation of U.S. middle schools. In the report—*Turning Points: Preparing American Youth for the Twenty-First Century*—the council concluded that most young adolescents attend massive, impersonal schools; learn from seemingly irrelevant curricula; trust few adults in school; and lack access to health care and counseling. The Carnegie report recommended the following changes (Carnegie Council on Adolescent Development, 1989):

- Develop smaller "communities" or "houses" to lessen the impersonal nature of large middle schools.
- Reduce student-to-counselor ratios from hundreds-to-1 to 10-to-1.
- Involve parents and community leaders in schools.
- Develop curricula that produce students who are literate, understand the sciences, and have an awareness of health, ethics, and citizenship.
- Have teachers team-teach in more flexibly designed curriculum blocks that integrate several disciplines, instead of presenting students with disconnected, rigidly separated 50-minute segments.
- Boost students' health and fitness with more in-school programs, and help students who need public health care to get it.

top-dog phenomenon The circumstance of moving from the top position (in elementary school, the oldest, biggest, and most powerful students) to the lowest position (in middle or junior high school, the youngest, smallest, and least powerful students).

The transition from elementary to middle or junior high school occurs at the same time as a number of other developmental changes. *What are some of these other developmental changes?*
Yobro10/Getty Images

Turning Points 2000 continued to endorse the recommendations set forth in *Turning Points 1989* (Jackson & Davis, 2000). One new recommendation in the 2000 report stated that it is important to teach a curriculum grounded in rigorous academic standards for what students should know. A second new recommendation was to engage in instruction that encourages students to achieve higher standards and become lifelong learners. These new recommendations reflect the increasing emphasis on challenging students and setting higher academic expectations for them. Unfortunately, many of the Carnegie Foundation's recommendations have not been implemented, and middle schools throughout the nation continue to need a major redesign if they are to be effective in educating adolescents.

Comstock/PictureQuest/Getty Images

THE AMERICAN HIGH SCHOOL

A recent analysis indicated that only 25 percent of U.S. high school graduates have mastered the academic skills needed to succeed in college (Bill & Melinda Gates Foundation, 2017). Not only are many high school graduates poorly prepared for college, they also are poorly prepared for the demands of the modern, high-performance workplace (Bill & Melinda Gates Foundation, 2020). A review of hiring practices at major companies concluded that many companies have identified sets of basic skills they want their employees to possess (Murnane & Levy, 1996). These include the ability to read at relatively high levels, do at least elementary algebra, use personal computers for straightforward tasks such as word processing, solve semi-structured problems in which hypotheses must be formed and tested, communicate effectively (orally and in writing), and work effectively in groups with persons of various backgrounds.

The transition to high school can have problems, just as the transition to middle school can (Epstein & others, 2021). These problems may include the following (Nese & others, 2021; Roder & Muller, 2020): high schools are often even larger, more bureaucratic, and more impersonal than middle schools; there isn't much opportunity for students and teachers to get to know each other, which can lead to distrust; and teachers too infrequently make content relevant to students' interests. Such experiences likely undermine the motivation of students. In a recent study, increased teacher-student conflict during the transitions from elementary to middle school and from middle to high school were linked to increased externalizing symptoms (fights with others, for example) in the first year at the new school (Longobardi & others, 2019).

I touch the future. I teach.

—**Christa McAuliffe**
American Educator and Astronaut, 20th Century

Robert Crosnoe's (2011) book, *Fitting In, Standing Out,* highlighted another major problem with U.S. high schools: how the negative social aspects of adolescents' lives undermine their academic achievement. In his view, adolescents become immersed in complex peer group cultures that demand conformity. High school is supposed to be about getting an education, but for many youth it involves navigating the social worlds of peer relations that may or may not value education and academic achievement. Adolescents who fail to fit in, especially those who are obese or gay, become stigmatized.

The National Research Council (2004) made a number of recommendations for improving U.S. high schools. They especially emphasized the importance of finding ways to get students more engaged in learning. The council concluded that the best way to do so is to focus on the psychological factors involved in motivation. Increasing students' engagement in learning consists of promoting a sense of belonging "by personalizing instruction, showing an interest in students' lives, and creating a supportive, caring social environment" (National Research Council, 2004, p. 3). The council said that this description of engaging students applies to very few urban high schools, which too often are characterized by low expectations, alienation, and low achievement. By contrast, recall the chapter-opening vignette describing four teachers who created exciting, real-world opportunities for students to increase their motivation to become more engaged in learning.

What are some good strategies for improving high schools?
ZUMA Press Inc/Alamy Stock Photo

HIGH SCHOOL DROPOUTS

Dropping out of high school has been viewed as a serious educational and societal problem for many decades. When adolescents leave high school before graduating, they approach adult life with educational deficiencies that severely curtail their economic and social well-being (Bill & Melinda Gates Foundation, 2020). For example, a study of more than 19,000 individuals from 18 to 25 years old revealed that those who had dropped out of high school were more likely than high school graduates to smoke cigarettes daily, to report having attempted suicide in the previous year, and to have been arrested for larceny, assault, and drug possession or drug sales (Maynard, Salas-Wright, & Vaughn, 2015).

High School Dropout Rates   In the first two decades of the twenty-first century, U.S. high school dropout rates declined (National Center for Education Statistics, 2020). In the 1940s, more than half of U.S. 16- to 24-year-olds had dropped out of school; by 1990, this rate had dropped to 12 percent, and by 2000 it was 10.9 percent. In 2017, the dropout rate had decreased further to 5.4 percent. The lowest dropout rate in 2017 occurred for Asian American adolescents (1.9 percent), followed by non-Latinx white adolescents (4.2 percent), African American adolescents (6.4 percent), Latinx adolescents (8 percent), and Native American adolescents (10.1 percent) (National Center for Education Statistics, 2020). The dropout rates have dropped considerably since 2000, when the dropout rate for non-Latinx whites was 6.9, for African Americans 13.1 percent, and for Latinxs 27.8 percent.

Gender differences have characterized U.S. dropout rates for many decades, but they have been narrowing in recent years. In 2017, the dropout rate for males was 6.2 percent and for females it was 4.4 percent, compared with 12.0 and 9.9 respectively in 2000 (National Center for Education Statistics, 2020).

The average U.S. high school dropout rates just described mask some very high dropout rates in low-income areas of inner cities. For example, in high-poverty areas of some cities such as Detroit, Cleveland, and Chicago, dropout rates can reach 50 percent or higher.

The Causes of Dropping Out   Students drop out of school for school-related, economic, family-related, peer-related, and personal reasons (Gil & others, 2021). School-related problems are consistently associated with dropping out of school (Schoeneberger, 2012). In one investigation, almost 50 percent of the dropouts cited school-related reasons for leaving school, such as not liking school, being suspended, or being expelled (Rumberger, 1995). Twenty percent of the dropouts (but 40 percent of the Latinx students) cited economic reasons for dropping out. Many of these students quit school and take jobs to help support their families. Students from low-income families are more likely to drop out than those from middle-income families. However, it is not just social reasons that explain student dropout rates. One study found that aspects of students' motivation—lower ability beliefs and lower educational expectations—were related to their dropping out of school (Fan & Wolters, 2014). And in recent research, a social contagion effect occurred in which non-trivial time spent with same-age friends, romantic partners, or siblings who had recently quit school increased the likelihood that adolescents themselves also would drop out of school (Dupere & others, 2021). Further in this study, when the adolescents' same-age social networks included more than one of these types of individuals (a friend and a sibling, for example) the adolescents were at increased risk for dropping out.

Students spend time in the computer room at the Ahfachkee School on the Big Cypress Reservation of the Seminole Tribe in Florida. This school has reduced its dropout rate by providing a challenging and caring environment for students, as well as emphasizing strong connections with families.
J. Albert Diaz/Miami Herald/MCT/Tribune News Service/Getty Images

Reducing the Dropout Rate   A review of school-based dropout prevention programs found that the most effective ones encompassed early reading intervention, tutoring, counseling, and mentoring (Lehr & others, 2003). The reviewers also emphasized the importance of creating caring environments, building relationships, and offering community-service opportunities.

Clearly, then, early detection of children's school-related difficulties, and getting children and youth engaged with school in positive ways, are important strategies for reducing dropout rates (Bill & Melinda Gates Foundation, 2020). One successful dropout prevention program is Talent Search, which provides low-income high school students with mentoring, academic tutoring, and training on test-taking and study skills, as well as career development coaching, financial aid application assistance for college, and visits to college campuses (Constantine & others, 2006). Talent Search students had high school completion rates that were 9 percent higher than a control group of students who were not in the Talent Search program.

Also, recently the Bill & Melinda Gates Foundation (2011, 2020) has funded efforts to reduce dropout rates in schools where rates are high. One strategy that is being emphasized in the Gates funding is keeping at-risk students with the same teachers throughout their high school years. The hope is that the teachers will get to know these students much better, their relationship with the students will improve, and teachers will be able to monitor and guide the students toward graduating from high school. Recent initiatives by the Bill & Melinda Gates Foundation (2020) involve creating a new generation of courseware that adapts to students' learning needs and combining face-to-face instruction with digital tools that help students to learn independently.

An initiative that has achieved impressive results is "I Have a Dream" (IHAD), an innovative, comprehensive, long-term dropout prevention program administered by the National "I Have a Dream" Foundation in New York. Since the National IHAD Foundation was created in 1986, it has grown to encompass more than 180 projects in 65 cities and 28 states, plus Washington, D.C., and New Zealand, serving more than 15,000 children and adolescents ("I Have a Dream" Foundation, 2020). Local IHAD projects around the country "adopt" entire grades (usually the third or fourth) from public elementary schools, or corresponding age cohorts from public housing developments. These children—referred to as "Dreamers"—are then provided with a program of academic, social, cultural, and recreational activities throughout their elementary, middle school, and high school years. An important aspect of this program is that it is personal rather than institutional: IHAD sponsors and staff develop close, long-term relationships with students. When participants complete high school, IHAD provides the tuition assistance necessary for them to attend a state or local college or vocational school. Evaluations of IHAD programs have found dramatic improvements in grades, test scores, and school attendance, as well as reduced rates of behavioral problems of Dreamers.

These adolescents participate in the "I Have a Dream" (IHAD) program, a comprehensive, long-term dropout prevention program that has been very successful. *What are some other strategies for reducing high school dropout rates?*
Courtesy of "I Have a Dream" Foundation of Boulder County (www.ihadboulder.org)

TRANSITION FROM HIGH SCHOOL TO COLLEGE

Just as the transition from elementary school to middle or junior high school involves change and possible stress, so does the transition from high school to college (Raposa & Hurd, 2021). In many ways, the two transitions involve parallel changes. Going from being a senior in high school to being a freshman in college replays the top-dog phenomenon of going from the oldest and most powerful group of students to the youngest and least powerful group of students. The transition from high school to college involves a move to a larger, more impersonal school structure, interaction with peers from more diverse geographical and sometimes more diverse ethnic backgrounds, and an increased focus on achievement and performance and their assessment. Further, for many students, the transition to college includes new living arrangements and new social circles as well (LaBelle, 2020).

However, as with the transition from elementary school to middle or junior high school, the transition from high school to college can have positive aspects. Students are more likely to feel grown up, have more subjects from which to select, have more time to spend with peers, have more opportunities to explore different lifestyles and values, enjoy greater independence from parental monitoring, and may be more challenged intellectually by academic work (Halonen & Santrock, 2013).

Today's college students experience more stress and are more depressed than their counterparts in the past, according to a national study of more than 300,000 freshmen at more than 500 colleges and universities (Stolzenberg & others, 2020). In 2019, 42.7 percent (up from 16 percent in 1985, 27 percent in 2009, and 35 percent in 2014) said they frequently "felt overwhelmed with what I have to do." College females (55 percent) in 2019 were almost twice as likely as their male counterparts (28 percent) to say that they felt overwhelmed with all they had to do. And college freshmen in 2019 were more likely to report feeling depressed than their counterparts from the 1980s were. The pressure to succeed in college, get a great job, and make lots of money are pervasive concerns of these students.

What makes college students happy? One study of 222 undergraduates compared the upper 10 percent of college students who were very happy with average and very unhappy college students (Diener & Seligman, 2002). The very happy college students were highly social, more extraverted, and had stronger romantic and social relationships than the less happy college students, who spent more time alone.

The transition from high school to college often involves positive as well as negative features. In college, students are likely to feel grown up, be able to spend more time with peers, have more opportunities to explore different lifestyles and values, and enjoy greater freedom from parental monitoring. However, college involves a larger, more impersonal school structure and an increased focus on achievement and its assessment. *What was your transition to college like?*
Stockbyte/Stockdisc/Getty Images

TRANSITION FROM COLLEGE TO WORK

What characterizes the transition from college to work?
Steve Debenport/Getty Images

developmental **connections**

Work

A diversity of school and work patterns characterize emerging adults. Connect to "Achievement, Work, and Careers."

Having a college degree is a strong asset. College graduates can enter careers that will earn them considerably more money in their lifetimes than those who do not go to college, and income differences between college graduates and high school graduates continue to grow (*Occupational Outlook Handbook,* 2020/2021). Recent media accounts have highlighted the dramatically rising costs of a college education and somewhat bleak job prospects for recent college graduates, raising questions about whether a college education is worth the money. However, recent data show that individuals with a bachelor's degree make $30,000 to $35,000 a year more on average than those with only a high school diploma (Federal Reserve Bank of New York, 2018). This represents a substantial increase from the 1980s when a college degree led to earning about $20,000 more per year.

Nonetheless, in North American countries, the transition from college to work is often a difficult one (Hughes & Smith, 2020; Litow & Kelley, 2021). U.S. colleges train many students to develop general skills rather than vocationally specific skills, with the result that college graduates often are poorly prepared for specific jobs or occupations. After finishing college, many individuals have difficulty obtaining the type of job they desire, or any job at all. Bouncing from one job to another after college is not unusual.

Accelerated technical and occupational change in the future may make it even more difficult for colleges to provide training that keeps pace with a fluid and shifting job market (Fleming & others, 2021). Thus, it is important for colleges and employers to become better connected with each other to provide improved training for changing job opportunities.

Review Connect Reflect

LG2 Discuss transitions in schooling from early adolescence to emerging adulthood.

Review

- What are some important aspects of the transition from elementary school to middle or junior high school?
- How can middle schools be improved?
- What is the American high school like? How can it be improved?
- What characterizes high school dropouts?
- How can the transition from high school to college be described?
- What are some of the challenges involved in the transition from college to work?

Connect

- What impact might the concept of parents as "managers" have on reducing the high school dropout rate?

Reflect *Your Own Personal Journey of Life*

- What was your own middle or junior high school like? How did it measure up to the recommendations made by the Carnegie Council?

---

3 The Social Contexts of Schools

LG3 Explain how the social contexts of schools influence adolescent development.

| Changing Social Developmental Contexts | Classroom Climate and Management | Person-Environment Fit | Teachers, Parents, Peers, and Extracurricular Activities | Culture |

Schools and classrooms vary along many dimensions, including the school or class social atmosphere. Adolescents' school life also involves thousands of hours of interactions with teachers. A special concern is parental involvement in the adolescent's schooling. Also, as we will see next, the social context of schools changes with the developmental level of students.

What are some differences in the social contexts of elementary and secondary schools?
Left: Stuart Pearce /Pixtal/AGE Fotostock; Right: skynesher/Getty Images

CHANGING SOCIAL DEVELOPMENTAL CONTEXTS

The social context differs at the preschool, elementary, and secondary levels. The preschool setting is a protected environment whose boundary is the classroom. The classroom is still the major context for the elementary school child, although it is more likely to be experienced as a social unit than at the preschool level. As children move into middle or junior high schools, the school environment increases in scope and complexity (Harrison & Bishop, 2021). The social field is the school as a whole rather than the classroom. Adolescents interact with many different teachers and peers from a range of social and ethnic backgrounds. Students are often exposed to a greater mix of teachers who are men and women. And social behavior is heavily weighted toward peers, extracurricular activities, clubs, and the community (Lang, 2021). Students in secondary school usually are aware of the school as a social system and may be motivated to conform and adapt to the system or to challenge it.

CLASSROOM CLIMATE AND MANAGEMENT

It is important for classrooms to present a positive environment for learning (Jones, 2021). One way to do this is to use an authoritative approach.

The idea of an authoritative classroom management strategy is derived from Diana Baumrind's (1971, 2012) typology of parenting styles, as discussed in the chapter on "Families." Like authoritative parents, authoritative teachers have students who tend to be self-reliant, delay gratification, get along well with their peers, and show high self-esteem. An **authoritative strategy of classroom management** encourages students to be independent thinkers and doers but still involves effective monitoring. Authoritative teachers engage students in considerable verbal give-and-take and show a caring attitude toward them. However, they still declare limits when necessary. Teachers clarify rules and regulations, establishing these standards with input from students.

The authoritative strategy contrasts with two ineffective strategies of classroom management: authoritarian and permissive. The **authoritarian strategy of classroom management** is restrictive and punitive. The focus is mainly on keeping order in the classroom rather than on instruction and learning. Authoritarian teachers place firm limits and controls on students and have little verbal exchange with them. Students in authoritarian classrooms tend to be passive learners, fail to initiate activities, express anxiety about social comparison, and have poor communication skills.

The **permissive strategy of classroom management** offers students considerable autonomy but provides them with little support for developing academic skills or managing their behavior. Not surprisingly, students in permissive classrooms tend to have inadequate academic skills and low self-control.

Overall, an authoritative classroom management style benefits students more than do authoritarian or permissive styles. An authoritative style helps students become active, self-regulated learners.

A well-managed classroom not only fosters meaningful learning but also helps prevent academic and emotional problems from developing. Well-managed classrooms keep students busy with active, appropriately challenging tasks. Well-managed classrooms have activities that encourage students to become absorbed and motivated and to learn clear rules and standards.

developmental **connections**

Families

Research indicates that adolescents benefit when parents in engage in an authoritative style. Connect with "Families."

authoritative strategy of classroom management A teaching strategy that encourages students to be independent thinkers and doers but still involves effective monitoring. Authoritative teachers engage students in considerable verbal give-and-take and show a caring attitude toward them. However, they still set and enforce limits when necessary.

authoritarian strategy of classroom management A teaching strategy that is restrictive and punitive. The focus is mainly on keeping order in the classroom rather than on instruction and learning.

permissive strategy of classroom management A teaching strategy that offers students considerable autonomy but provides them with little support for developing learning skills or managing their behavior.

"How come when you say we have a problem, I'm always the one who has the problem?"
George Abbott. Used with permission. All rights reserved.

What are some effective strategies teachers can use to manage the classroom? How is managing the classroom different in secondary school from managing it in elementary school?
Tim Pannell/SuperStock

In such classrooms, students are less likely to develop academic and emotional problems. By contrast, in poorly managed classrooms, students' academic and emotional problems are more likely to fester. The academically unmotivated student becomes even less motivated. The shy student becomes more reclusive. The bully becomes meaner.

Secondary school students' problems can be more long-standing and more deeply ingrained, and therefore more difficult to modify, than those of elementary school students (Jones, 2021). Also in secondary schools, discipline problems are frequently more severe, as the students are potentially more unruly and even dangerous. Because most secondary school students have more advanced reasoning skills than do elementary school students, they might demand more elaborate and logical explanations of rules and discipline. And in secondary schools, hallway socializing can carry into the classroom. Every hour there is another "settling down" process.

PERSON-ENVIRONMENT FIT

Some of the negative psychological changes associated with adolescent development might result from a mismatch between the needs of developing adolescents and the opportunities afforded them by the schools they attend. Jacquelynne Eccles, Allan Wigfield, and their colleagues (Eccles & Roeser, 2013; Wigfield, Rosenzweig, & Eccles, 2017) have described ways to create developmentally appropriate school environments that are better suited to adolescents' needs. Their recommendations are based on a large-scale study of 1,500 young adolescents in middle-income communities in Michigan. These adolescents were studied as they made the change from the sixth grade in an elementary school to the seventh grade in a junior high school.

Eccles argues that a lack of fit between the middle school/junior high environment and the needs of young adolescents produces increasingly negative self-evaluations and attitudes toward school. Her research has revealed that teachers become more controlling just at the time when adolescents are seeking greater autonomy, and the teacher-student relationship becomes more impersonal at a time when students are seeking more independence from their parents and need more support from other adults. At a time when adolescents are becoming more self-conscious, an increased emphasis on grades and other competitive comparisons only makes things worse.

Like the transition from elementary to middle school, the transition to high school can produce similar problems. High schools often are even larger and more bureaucratic than middle schools. In such schools, a sense of community usually is undermined, with little opportunity for students and teachers to get to know each other. As a consequence, distrust between students and teachers develops easily and there is little communication about students' goals and values. Such contexts can especially harm the motivation of students who are not doing well academically. In a recent study, increased teacher-student conflict during the transitions from elementary to middle school and from middle school to high school were linked to an increase in externalizing symptoms (fighting with others, for example) in the first year at the new school (Longobardi & others, 2019).

What lessons can be drawn from this discussion? Perhaps the single most important lesson is that middle school and junior high school students benefit when teachers think of ways to make their school settings more personal, less formal, and more intrinsically challenging.

TEACHERS, PARENTS, PEERS, AND EXTRACURRICULAR ACTIVITIES

Adolescents' development is influenced by teachers. In addition, two increasingly important issues are parent involvement in schooling and the roles that peers and extracurricular activities play in schooling and academic achievement.

What is the concept of person-environment fit, and how does it involve the mismatch between the needs of adolescents and the opportunities they have in middle/junior high schools?
PeopleImages/Getty Images

Teachers   Competent teachers of adolescents have a good understanding of their development and know how to create instructional materials that are appropriate for the developmental levels of the adolescents in their classroom (Kauchak & Eggen, 2021).

"You Are the Coolest"

I just want to thank you for all the extra time you took to help me. You didn't have to do that, but you did, and I want to thank you for it. Thanks also for being straight up with me and not beating around the bush, and for that you are the coolest. I'm sorry for the hard times I gave you. You take so much junk, but through all that you stay calm and you are a great teacher.

—JESSICA, SEVENTH-GRADE STUDENT, MACON, GEORGIA
Letter to Chuck Rawls, her teacher, at the end of the school year

What classroom management strategy does teacher Chuck Rawls likely adopt?

Psychologists and educators have tried to compile a profile of a good teacher's personality traits, but the complexity of personality, education, learning, and individuals makes this a difficult task. Nonetheless, some teacher traits and dimensions—enthusiasm, ability to plan, poise, adaptability, warmth, flexibility, and awareness of individual differences—are associated with positive student outcomes more than are other traits. And a research analysis by leading experts in educational psychology concluded that the following teaching practices and strategies are linked with positive student outcomes (Roehrig & others, 2012):

- *Developing caring classroom communities* by monitoring behavior rather than punishing it and by establishing a democratic classroom

- *Enhancing students' motivation to learn* by providing informative feedback, focusing on improvement and effort, expressing high expectations, and fostering interest and engagement

- *Planning and delivering engaging, assessment-driven instruction* by organizing content and activities and individualizing instruction using assessment data

- *Supporting students' deep processing and self-regulation skills* by modeling thinking processes, discovering the appropriate challenge level, and encouraging self-regulation

developmental connections

Families

Key aspects of the managerial role of parenting are parental monitoring and adolescent management of information. Connect to "Families."

Parents and Schools   Parents play important roles in the adolescent's success in school. Among the ways that parents can positively contribute to adolescents' school success are effective family management practices and involvement in adolescents' schooling (Mac Iver, Sheldon, & Clark, 2021).

Family Management   Researchers have found that family management practices, especially parental monitoring, are positively related to grades and self-responsibility, and negatively to school-related problems (Top, Liew, & Luo, 2017). Among the family management practices important in this regard is maintaining a structured and organized family environment, such as establishing routines for homework, chores, and bedtime, as well as parental monitoring (Atherton, Lawson, & Robins, 2020). It is also important for parents to create a family environment that includes high expectations for achievement (Kiuru & others, 2020).

One study focusing on African American families examined links between mothers' reports of family management practices, including routine and achievement expectations, and adolescents' school-related behavior (Taylor & Lopez, 2005). Well-managed and organized family routines were positively related to adolescents' school achievement, paying attention in class, and attendance, and negatively linked to their school-related problems. Compared to mothers with low expectations for achievement, mothers with high expectations for achievement had adolescents who earned higher grades and had better school attendance.

Parental Involvement   Even though parental involvement often is minimal in elementary school, it is even less evident in secondary school

What are some important roles of parents in students' schooling?
Photodisc/Getty Images

(Henderson, Williams, & Bradshaw, 2020). Parent involvement can be out of school (helping with homework, for example) and in school (participating in school activities, for example). In one study, teachers listed parental involvement as the number one priority in improving education (Chira, 1993). In an analysis of 16,000 students, students were more likely to get A's and less likely to repeat a grade or be expelled if both parents were highly involved in their schooling (National Center for Education Statistics, 1997).

Research by Eva Pomerantz and her colleagues (Pomerantz, Cheung, & Qin, 2012; Pomerantz & Grolnick, 2017; Wei & others, 2020) indicates that the more involved parents are in their children's learning, the higher the level of achievement their children will attain. East Asian parents are far more involved in their children's and adolescents' learning than are U.S. parents. In East Asia, children's and adolescents' learning is considered to be a far greater responsibility of parents than in the United States (Pomerantz & Grolnick, 2017). However, one study revealed that when U.S. parents were more involved in their young adolescents' learning, achievement was higher (Cheung & Pomerantz, 2012). In this study, for both U.S. and Chinese young adolescents, the greater the amount of parental involvement, the more motivated the young adolescents were to achieve in school for parent-oriented reasons, and this was linked to enhanced self-regulated learning and higher grades. Also, researchers found that Chinese mothers exerted more control (especially psychological control) over their young adolescents than U.S. mothers did (Ng, Pomerantz, & Deng, 2014). Further, Chinese mothers' self-worth was more contingent on their young adolescents' achievement than was the case for U.S. mothers. To reflect how important their children's and adolescents' achievement is to Chinese mothers, the authors titled their research article: "Why are Chinese parents more psychologically controlling than American parents? 'My child is my report card.'"

Eva Pomerantz (2017) recently offered these recommendations for parents who want their children and adolescents to do well in school:

- *Keep in mind that ability is not fixed and can change.* Although it is difficult and takes a lot of patience, understand that children's and adolescents' abilities can improve.
- *Be involved.* One of the most important things parents can do is to become involved in their children's and adolescents' academic life and talk often with them about what they are learning.
- *Support autonomy and self-initiative.* An important aspect of children's and adolescents' motivation to do well in school is being made to feel that they are responsible for their learning and must become self-motivated.
- *Be positive.* Too often schoolwork and homework can be frustrating for children and adolescents. Interact with them in positive ways and let them know that life is often tough but that you know they can do well and overcome difficulties.
- *Understand that each child or adolescent is different.* Get to know your child or adolescent—don't let them be a psychological stranger to you. Be sensitive to their unique characteristics and know that sometimes you will need to adapt to such idiosyncrasies.

Peers   You studied many aspects of adolescent peer relations in the chapter on "Peers, Romantic Relationships, and Lifestyles." Here you will explore peer relations in school contexts.

Structure of Middle Schools   Middle schools are structured in a way that encourages students to interact with larger numbers of peers on a daily basis (Wentzel, 2015). The relative uncertainty and ambiguity of multiple classroom environments and more complex class schedules may result in middle school students turning to each other for information, social support, and strategies for coping.

developmental **connections**

Peers

Peer statuses include popular, rejected, neglected, controversial, and average adolescents. Connect to "Peers, Romantic Relationships, and Lifestyles."

Peer Statuses   Peer statuses have been studied in relation to school success. Being popular or accepted by peers is usually associated with academic success, whereas being rejected by peers is related to more negative academic outcomes (McDonald & Asher, 2018).

Bullying   Significant numbers of students are victimized by bullies (Fujikawa & others, 2021). In a national survey of more than 15,000 students in grades 6 through 10, nearly one of every three students said that they had experienced occasional or frequent involvement as a victim or perpetrator in bullying (Nansel & others, 2001). In this study, bullying was defined as verbal or physical behavior intended to disturb someone less powerful (see Figure 1). Boys are more likely to be bullies than girls, but gender differences regarding victims of bullying are less clear (Salmivalli, 2020). And in a recent analysis of bullying from 1998 to 2017 in the United States, a significant increase in cyberbullying occurred (Kennedy, 2021). Also in this analysis, an increase in face-to-face bullying occurred for females.

Who is likely to be bullied? In the study just described, boys and younger middle school students were most likely to be affected (Nansel & others, 2001). Children who said they were bullied reported more loneliness and difficulty in making friends, while those who did the bullying were more likely to have low grades and to smoke cigarettes and drink alcohol. Also, in a recent study of more than 30,000 U.S. high school students, 20 percent experienced school bullying and 15 percent experienced cyberbullying (Webb & others, 2021). In the same study, sexual minority youth were more likely to report both types of bullying victimization than their heterosexual peers, while African American and Latinx adolescents were less likely to report both types of victimization. And non-Latinx white gay/lesbian or bisexual youth reported more bullying victimization than non-Latinx white heterosexual youth.

Researchers have found that anxious, socially withdrawn, and aggressive children are often the victims of bullying (Chu & others, 2019). Anxious and socially withdrawn children may be victimized because they are nonthreatening and unlikely to retaliate if bullied, whereas aggressive children may be the targets of bullying because their behavior is irritating to bullies (Rubin & others, 2018).

The social context of the peer group also plays an important role in bullying (Bjarehed & others, 2019). Research indicates that 70 to 80 percent of victims and their bullies are in the same school classroom (Salmivalli, 2020). Classmates are often aware of bullying incidents and in many cases witness bullying. Often bullies torment victims to gain higher status in the peer group, so bullies need others to witness their power displays. Many bullies are not rejected by the peer group. A longitudinal study explored the costs and benefits of bullying in the context of the peer group (Reijntjes & others, 2013). In this study children were initially assessed at 10 years of age and then followed into early adolescence. The results indicated that although young bullies may be on a developmental trajectory that over the long run is problematic, in the short term personal benefits of bullying often outweigh the disadvantages. Frequent bullying was linked to high social status as indexed by perceived popularity in the peer group, and bullies also were characterized by self-perceived personal competence.

What are the outcomes of bullying? One study revealed that peer victimization in the fifth grade was associated with worse physical and mental health in the tenth grade (Bogart & others, 2014). Also, a recent large-scale Norwegian study concluded that bullies, victims, and bully-victims all are at risk for developing sleep problems, including shorter sleep duration and a higher prevalence of insomnia, as well as a lower grade point average (Hysing & others, 2021). Researchers have found that children who are bullied are more likely to experience depression, have low self-esteem, engage in suicidal ideation, and attempt suicide than their counterparts who have not been the victims of bullying (Waseem & Nickerson, 2021). For example, in a recent study of 12- to 15-year-olds in 48 countries worldwide, being a victim of bullying was a risk factor for suicidal behavior in 47 of the 48 countries (Koyanagi & others, 2019). In addition, a longitudinal study revealed that after being bullied, bullying victims' self-esteem decreased and this lower self-esteem was linked to increased victimization (Choi & Park, 2021). Further, in a recent study of more than 150,000 12- to 15-year-olds in 54 low- and middle-income countries, victims of bullying were more likely to be characterized by the following obesity-related factors: anxiety-induced sleep problems, no physical activity, sedentary behavior, and fast food consumption (Smith & others, 2021). Also, a meta-analysis concluded that engaging in bullying during middle school is linked to an increased likelihood of antisocial and criminal behavior later in adolescence and adulthood (Kim & others, 2011). Further, a research analysis concluded that bullying can have long-term effects, including difficulty in forming lasting relationships and problems at work (Wolke & Lereya, 2015). And a recent Chinese study of adults 60 years of age and older found that those who had been the victims of bullying in childhood had more severe depressive symptoms their counterparts who had not experienced bullying victimization as children (Hu, 2021).

An increasing concern is peer bullying and harassment on the Internet (called *cyberbullying*) (Armitage, 2021; Barlett & others, 2021). A study involving third- to sixth-graders revealed that engaging in cyber aggression was related to loneliness, lower self-esteem, fewer

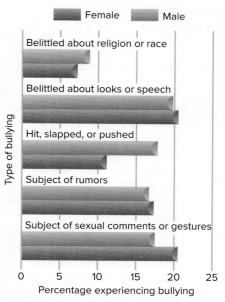

FIGURE 1

BULLYING BEHAVIORS AMONG U.S. YOUTH. This graph shows the types of bullying most often experienced by U.S. youth. The percentages reflect the extent to which bullied students said that they had experienced a particular type of bullying. In terms of gender, note that when they were bullied, boys were more likely to be hit, slapped, or pushed than girls were.

connecting with health and well-being

Bullying Prevention/Intervention

Extensive attention has been directed to finding ways to prevent and treat bullying and victimization (Swearer & others, 2021). School-based interventions vary greatly, ranging from involving the whole school in an antibullying campaign to providing individualized social skills training (Strohmeier & Noam, 2012). One of the most promising bullying intervention programs has been created by Dan Olweus (2003, 2013). This program focuses on 6- to 15-year-olds, with the goal of decreasing opportunities and rewards for bullying. School staff are instructed in ways to improve peer relations and make schools safer. When properly implemented, the program reduces bullying by 30 to 70 percent (Olweus, 2003). A research review concluded that interventions focusing on the whole school, such as Olweus', are more effective than interventions involving classroom curricula or social skills training (Cantone & others, 2015).

To reduce bullying, schools can adopt these strategies:

- Get older peers to serve as monitors for bullying and to intervene when they see it taking place.
- Develop school-wide rules and sanctions against bullying and post them throughout the school.
- Form friendship groups for adolescents who are regularly bullied by peers.
- Incorporate the message of the antibullying program into places of worship, schools, and other community activity areas where adolescents are involved.
- Encourage parents to reinforce their adolescent's positive behaviors and model appropriate interpersonal interactions.

What are some strategies to reduce bullying?
Photodisc/Getty Images

- Identify bullies and victims early and use social skills training to improve their behavior.
- Encourage parents to contact the school's psychologist, counselor, or social worker and ask for help with their adolescent's bullying or victimization concerns.

mutual friendships, and lower peer popularity (Schoffstall & Cohen, 2011). Also, a recent study of university students indicated that being a cybervictim increased the risk of suicidal thinking and led to higher levels of anxiety, stress, and depression (Martinez-Monteagudo & others, 2020). Information about preventing cyberbullying can be found at www.stopcyberbullying.org/. To read about a number of strategies for reducing bullying, see the *Connecting with Health and Well-Being* interlude.

Friendship   Another aspect of peer relations that is linked with school success involves friendship. Having friends, especially friends who are academically oriented and earn good grades, is related to higher grades and test scores in secondary schools and college (Dokuka, Valeeva, & Yudkevich, 2020). One longitudinal study found that having at least one friend was related to academic success over a two-year period (Wentzel & Caldwell, 1997).

Extracurricular Activities   Adolescents in U.S. schools usually can choose from a wide array of extracurricular activities beyond their academic courses. These adult-sanctioned activities typically occur during after-school hours and can be sponsored by either the school or the community. They include such diverse activities as sports, honor societies, band, drama club, and various academic clubs (math and language, for example).

Researchers have found that participation in extracurricular activities is linked to higher grades, increased school engagement, reduced likelihood of dropping out of school, improved probability of going to college, higher self-esteem, and lower rates of depression, delinquency, and substance abuse (Oberle & others, 2019).

How does participation in extracurricular activities influence development in adolescence and emerging adulthood?
(left): Hill Street Studios/Blend Images/Getty Images; (right): FatCamera/E+/Getty Images

Adolescents benefit from participating in a breadth of extracurricular activities more than they do from focusing on a single extracurricular activity. In a longitudinal study, both breadth and intensity of extracurricular activity involvement in the tenth grade were associated with higher educational attainment (Haghighat & Knifsend, 2019). Also, a recent study found that adolescents who participated in extracurricular activities were less likely to engage in screen-based activities after school, had higher levels of satisfaction with life, were more optimistic, and had lower levels of anxiety and depression (Oberle & others, 2020). And in another recent study, greater participation in extracurricular activities in high school predicted an increased likelihood of completing a college degree in four years (Gardner & others, 2020). However, participating in more than three or four extracurricular activities predicted that students would be less likely to obtain a college degree in four years.

CULTURE

In some cultures—such as Arab countries and rural India—adults often restrict adolescents' access to peers, especially for girls. The peer restriction includes the social setting of schools, where girls are educated separately from boys. Let's now explore three aspects of culture and schools: socioeconomic status, ethnicity, and cross-cultural comparisons.

Socioeconomic Status and Ethnicity   Adolescents from low-income, ethnic minority backgrounds have more difficulties in school than do their middle-socioeconomic-status, non-Latinx white counterparts. Why? Critics argue that schools have not done a good job of educating low-income, ethnic minority adolescents and emerging adults to overcome the barriers to their achievement (Gollnick & Chinn, 2021). Let's further explore the influence of socioeconomic status and ethnicity in schools.

The Education of Students from Low-Income Backgrounds   Many adolescents in poverty face problems that present barriers to their learning (Koppelman, 2020). They might have parents who don't set high educational standards for them, who are incapable of reading to them, and who don't have enough money to pay for educational materials and experiences such as books and trips to zoos and museums. They might be malnourished and live in areas where crime and violence are a way of life.

Compared with schools in higher-income areas, schools in low-income areas are more likely to have higher percentages of students with low achievement test scores, lower graduation rates, and smaller percentages of students going to college (Osher & others, 2020). They are more likely to have young teachers with less experience, more noncredentialed or nonqualified teachers, and substitute teachers who regularly fill in to teach. Schools in low-income areas also tend to encourage rote learning and are less likely to provide adequate support for English language learners. Too few schools in low-income neighborhoods provide students with environments that are conducive to learning (Hix-Small, 2020). Many of the schools' buildings and classrooms are old and crumbling.

Forensics Teacher Tommie Lindsey's Students

Tommie Lindsey teaches competitive forensics (public speaking and debate) at Logan High School in Union City, California. In U.S. schools, forensics classes are mainly offered in affluent areas, but most of Lindsey's students come from impoverished or at-risk backgrounds. His students have won many public speaking honors.

The following comments by his students reflect Lindsey's outstanding teaching skills:

> He's one of the few teachers I know who cares so much. . . . He spends hours and hours, evenings, and weekends, working with us.
>
> —JUSTIN HINOJOZA, 17

> I was going through a tough time. . . . Mr. Lindsey helped me out. I asked how I could pay him back and he said, "Just help someone the way I helped you."
>
> —ROBERT HAWKINS, 21

> This amazing opportunity is here for us students and it wouldn't be if Mr. Lindsey didn't create it.
>
> —MICHAEL JOSHI, 17

As a ninth-grade student, Tommie Lindsey became a public speaker. He says that his English teacher doubted his ability, and he wanted to show her how good he could be at public speaking so he

Tommie Lindsey works with his students on improving their public speaking and debate skills.
Courtesy of Tommie Lindsey

prepared a speech that received a standing ovation. Lindsey remembers, "She was expecting me to fail, and I turned the tables on her. . . . And we do that with our forensic program. When we started a lot of people didn't believe our kids could do the things they do." For his outstanding teaching efforts, Tommie Lindsey was awarded a prestigious MacArthur Fellowship in 2005.

Living in an economically disadvantaged family may have more negative achievement outcomes in adolescence than in childhood. The difference in poverty's effects might be due to the adolescents' greater awareness of barriers to their success and the difficulties they will encounter in becoming successful. In a recent research review, it was concluded that increases in family income for children in poverty were associated with increased achievement in middle school, as well as greater educational attainment in adolescence and emerging adulthood (Duncan, Magnuson, & Votruba-Drzal, 2017).

Schools and school programs are the focus of some poverty interventions (Albert & others, 2020). In a recent intervention with first-generation immigrant children attending high-poverty schools, the City Connects program was successful in improving children's math and reading achievement at the end of elementary school (Dearing & others, 2016). The program is directed by a full-time school counselor or social worker in each school. Annual reviews of children's needs are conducted during the first several months of the school year. Then site coordinators and teachers collaborate to develop a student support plan that might include an after-school program, tutoring, mentoring, or family counselling. For children identified as having intense needs (about 8 to 10 percent of the children), a wider team of professionals becomes involved, possibly including school psychologists, principals, nurses, and/or community agency staff, to create additional supports. In another longitudinal study, implementation of the Child-Parent Center Program in high-poverty neighborhoods in Chicago—an intervention that provided school-based educational enrichment and comprehensive family services for children from 3 to 9 years of age—was linked to higher rates of postsecondary degree completion, including more years of education, attainment of an associate's degree or higher, and master's degree completion (Reynolds, Ou, & Temple, 2018).

Another important effort to improve the education of children growing up in low-income conditions is Teach for America (2021), a nonprofit organization that recruits and selects college

graduates from universities to serve as teachers. The selected members commit to teaching for two years in a public school in a low-income community. Since the program's inception in 1990, more than 42,000 individuals have taught more than 50,000 students for Teach for America. These teachers can be, but don't have to be, education majors. During the summer before beginning to teach, they attend an intensive training program. To read about one individual who became a Teach for America instructor, see the *Connecting with Careers* interlude.

Ethnicity in Schools More than one-third of all African American and almost one-third of all Latinx students attend schools in the 47 largest city school districts in the United States, compared with only 5 percent of all non-Latinx white and 22 percent of all Asian American students. Many of these inner-city schools are still segregated, are grossly underfunded, and do not provide adequate opportunities for children to learn effectively (Gollnick & Chinn, 2021). Thus, the effects of SES and the effects of ethnicity are often intertwined (Banks, 2020).

In *The Shame of the Nation*, Jonathan Kozol (2005) described his visits to 60 U.S. schools in low-income areas of cities in 11 states. He saw many schools in which the minority population was 80 to 90 percent, concluding that school segregation is still present for many poor minority students. Kozol witnessed poorly kept classrooms, hallways, and restrooms; inadequate textbooks and supplies; and lack of resources. He also saw teachers mainly instructing students to rotely memorize material, especially as preparation for mandated tests, rather than encouraging students to engage in higher-level thinking. Kozol also frequently observed teachers using threatening disciplinary tactics to control the classroom.

Even outside inner-city schools, school segregation remains a factor in U.S. education (Garcia, 2020). Almost one-third of all African American and Latinx students attend schools in which 90 percent or more of the students are from minority groups.

The school experiences of students from different ethnic groups vary considerably (Gollnick & Chinn, 2021). African American and Latinx students are much less likely than non-Latinx white or Asian American students to be enrolled in academic, college preparatory programs and are much more likely to be enrolled in remedial and special education programs. Asian American students are far more likely than other ethnic minority groups to take advanced math and science courses in high school. African American students are twice as likely as Latinxs, Native Americans, or non-Latinx whites to be suspended from school. A recent study explored which aspects of African American adolescents' school climate predicted whether or

Why is there a concern about the education of African American and Latinx adolescents?
Fuse/Getty Images

not they went to college (Minor & Benner, 2018). In this study, African American students who liked school, perceived their school was safe, and experienced *academic press* (environmental push for academic success) were more likely to go to college. These results occurred for all African American students regardless of SES or gender.

Following are some strategies for improving relationships among ethnically diverse students:

- *Turn the class into a jigsaw classroom.* When Elliot Aronson was a professor at the University of Texas at Austin, the school system contacted him for ideas on how to reduce the increasing racial tension in classrooms. Aronson (1986) developed the concept of the **jigsaw classroom,** in which students from different cultural backgrounds are placed in a cooperative group in which they have to construct different parts of a project to reach a common goal. Aronson used the term *jigsaw* because he likened the technique to a group of students cooperating to put different pieces together to complete a jigsaw puzzle. How might this process work? Team sports, drama productions, and musical performances are examples of contexts in which students cooperatively participate to reach a common goal.

- *Encourage students to have positive personal contact with diverse other students.* Contact alone does not do the job of improving relationships with diverse others. What matters is what happens while children and adolescents are at school. Especially beneficial in improving interethnic relations is sharing one's worries, successes, failures, coping strategies, interests, and other personal information with people of other ethnicities. When such sharing takes place, people tend to view others as individuals rather than as members of a homogeneous group.

- *Encourage students to engage in perspective taking.* Exercises and activities that help students see others' perspectives can improve interethnic relations. These interactions help students "step into the shoes" of peers who are culturally different and feel what it is like to be treated in fair or unfair ways.

- *Help students to think critically and be emotionally intelligent about cultural issues.* Students who learn to think critically and deeply about interethnic relations are likely to decrease their prejudice. Becoming more emotionally intelligent includes understanding the causes of one's feelings, managing anger, listening to what others are saying, and being motivated to share and cooperate.

- *Reduce bias.* Teachers can reduce bias by displaying images of people from diverse ethnic and cultural groups, selecting classroom activities that encourage cultural understanding, helping students resist stereotyping, and working with parents.

- *View the school and community as a team.* James Comer (2010) emphasizes that a community, team approach is the best way to educate students. Three important aspects of the Comer Project for Change are (1) a governance and management team that develops a comprehensive school plan, assessment strategy, and staff development plan; (2) a mental health or school support team; and (3) a parents' program. Comer believes that the entire school community should have a cooperative rather than an adversarial attitude. The Comer program is currently operating in more than 600 schools in 26 states.

James Comer (*left*) is shown with some of the inner-city African American children who attend a school that became a better learning environment because of Comer's intervention.
John S. Abbott

Understanding the role of ethnicity in schooling also involves multicultural education. The hope is that multicultural education can contribute to making our nation more like what the late civil rights leader Martin Luther King, Jr., dreamed of: a nation where children and youth will be judged not by the color of their skin but by the quality of their character.

Multicultural education values diversity and includes the perspectives of a variety of cultural groups. Its proponents believe that children and youth of color should be empowered and that multicultural education benefits all students (Banks, 2020). An important goal of multicultural education is equal educational opportunity for all students. This includes closing the gap in academic achievement between mainstream students and students from underrepresented groups.

Multicultural education grew out of the civil rights movement of the 1960s and the call for equality and social justice for women and people of color. As a field, multicultural education addresses issues related to socioeconomic status, ethnicity, and gender (Cushner, McClelland, & Safford, 2022). An increasing trend in multicultural education is not to make ethnicity a focal point but to also include socioeconomic status, gender, religion, disability, sexual orientation, and other forms of differences (Howe, 2010). Another important point about contemporary multicultural education is that many individuals think it is reserved for students of color. However, all students, including non-Latinx white students, can benefit from multicultural education (Howe, 2010).

Cross-Cultural Comparisons   Many countries recognize that high-quality, universal education of children and youth is critical for the success of any country. However, countries vary considerably in their ability to fulfill this mission. More than 100 million adolescents, mostly in sub-Saharan Africa, India, and southern Asia, don't even attend secondary schools (UNICEF, 2021). In developing countries, adolescent girls are less likely to be enrolled in school than are boys.

Secondary Schools   Secondary schools in various countries share a number of features but differ in other ways. Let's explore the similarities and differences in secondary schools in seven countries: Australia, Brazil, Germany, Japan, China, Russia, and the United States.

Most countries mandate that children begin school at 6 to 7 years of age and stay in school until they are 14 to 17 years of age. Brazil requires students to go to school only until they are 14 years old, whereas Russia mandates that students stay in school until they are 17. Germany, Japan, Australia, and the United States require school attendance until at least 15 to 16 years of age, with some states, such as California, recently raising the mandatory age to 18.

Most secondary schools around the world are divided into two or more chronological levels, such as middle school (or junior high school) and high school. However, Germany's schools are divided according to three educational ability tracks: (1) the main school provides a basic level of education; (2) the middle school gives students a more advanced education; and (3) the academic school prepares students for entrance to a university. German schools, like most European schools, offer a classical education, which includes courses in Latin and Greek. Japanese secondary schools have an entrance exam, but public secondary schools in the other four countries do not. Only Australia and Germany have comprehensive exit exams.

The United States and Australia are among the few countries in the world in which sports are an integral part of the public school system. Only a few private schools in other countries have their own sports teams, sports facilities, and highly organized sports events.

In Brazil, students are required to take Portuguese (the native language) and four foreign languages (Latin, French, English, and Spanish). Brazil requires these languages because of the country's international character and emphasis on trade and commerce. Seventh-grade

jigsaw classroom A classroom strategy in which students from different cultural backgrounds are placed in a cooperative group in which, together, they have to construct different parts of a project to reach a common goal.

multicultural education Education that values diversity and includes the perspectives of a variety of cultural groups.

The juku, or "cramming school," is available to Japanese adolescents in the summertime and after school. It provides coaching to help them improve their grades and their entrance exam scores for high schools and universities. The Japanese practice of requiring an entrance exam for high school is a rarity among the nations of the world.
Xavier Arnau/E+/Getty Images

students in Australia take courses in sheep husbandry and weaving, two areas of economic and cultural interest in the country. In Japan, students take a number of Western courses in addition to their basic Japanese courses; these courses include Western literature and languages (in addition to Japanese literature and language), Western physical education (in addition to Japanese martial arts classes), and Western sculpture and handicrafts (in addition to Japanese calligraphy). The Japanese school year is also much longer than that of other countries (225 days versus 180 days in the United States, for example).

I recently visited China and interviewed parents about their adolescents' education. Several aspects of education in China are noteworthy, especially in comparison with the United States. Being motivated to provide adolescents with the best possible education and ensuring that they work extremely hard in school and on homework were clearly evident in parents' comments. Also, when I asked parents if there are disciplinary problems in Chinese schools, they responded that if an adolescent acts up in school, the school immediately sends the adolescent home. In China, it is considered the parents' responsibility to orient their adolescents to behave in school and to focus on schoolwork. These observations coincide with our description of Asian American parents as training parents. When Chinese adolescents are sent home because of discipline problems, they are not allowed to return until parents work with the adolescents to ensure that the discipline problems will not recur. In China, classroom sizes are often large, in some cases having 50 to 70 students, yet observers describe such classes as orderly and disciplined (Cavanagh, 2007).

Technological Connections with Adolescents Around the World Traditionally, students have learned within the walls of their classroom and interacted with their teacher and other students in the class. Technology can expand the reach of classroom activities through such activities as video conferencing (Skype, Google Hangouts, and Zoom, for example), social media (Twitter, Instagram), and online collaboration tools (Google Drive). Also, with advances in telecommunications, students can learn with and from teachers and students around the world.

Students participating in a Global Student Laboratory Project. *What characterizes the Global Student Laboratory? What are some of the projects students can participate in with the Laboratory?*
Martin Shields/Alamy Stock Photo

For example, in the Global Student Laboratory Project (https://global-lab.org)—an international, telecommunication-based project—students investigate local and global environments (Globallab, 2021). The program offers 173 projects involving such topics as world currencies, managing a travel agency, calculating your carbon footprint, our restless world, ways to make our world better, and "Waste: Danger or Opportunity?" In one exercise, after sharing their findings, students collaboratively identified various aspects of environments, discussed research plans, and conducted distributed studies using the same methods and procedures. Students from such diverse locations as Moscow, Russia; Warsaw, Poland; Kenosha, Wisconsin; San Antonio, Texas; Pueblo, Colorado; and Aiken, South Carolina, participated. As their data collection and evaluation evolved, students continued to communicate with their peers worldwide and to learn more, not only about science, but also about the global community.

Colleges Which countries have the highest percentage of adults who have a post-secondary degree? The Organization for Economic Co-operation and Development (OECD, 2020) released a list of the top six countries with the highest percentages of 25- to 34-year-olds with a post-secondary degree (associate's, bachelor's, master's, or doctoral): (1) Ireland and Lithuania (56 percent), (3) Luxembourg (55 percent), (4) Australia (51 percent), and (5) United Kingdom and United States (50 percent). Of the 30 countries, Mexico (23 percent) and Italy (28 percent) had the lowest percentages of 25- to 34-year-olds with a post-secondary degree. In 1995, the United States was first in bachelor's degrees but in 2018 had slipped to seventh (28 percent), with Lithuania being first (40 percent). Among the concerns surrounding U.S. colleges are the soaring costs of attending college and the low rate of students who graduate from college in four years, with many taking more than six years to earn a degree or never completing their undergraduate education.

4 Schools and the COVID-19 Pandemic

 LG4 Summarize the effects of the COVID-19 pandemic on schools.

K-12 Education

College Education

Beginning in March 2020, the nature of K-12 and college education was drastically impacted by the coronavirus pandemic. Many schools abruptly moved away from in-person classes to online instruction to prevent further spread of the virus. However, there is evidence that very few children who get the coronavirus experience severe symptoms. Further, death rates due to the coronavirus are far lower for children than for adults.

K-12 EDUCATION

A special concern is that some children may not learn as effectively through online instruction as with in-person instruction. Online learning is especially challenging for younger children and children with behavioral needs, such as a learning disability (Harris & others, 2021). Following the wave of school closings due to the COVID-19 pandemic in March 2020, a survey of 477 schools found that far too many schools were essentially leaving learning to chance (Gross, 2020). Also in this survey, only 1 in 3 school districts expected teachers to provide as much instruction online as they would for in-person classes, to track student engagement, and to monitor learning for all students. However, there was controversy about when it would be safe and appropriate for students to resume in-person schooling, with many teachers fearing that in-person teaching would not be safe until the spread of the coronavirus had diminished.

School closings are especially harmful for students who come from low-income or ethnic minority backgrounds or have sensory and learning problems. For example, many low-income families do not have a computer or Internet access at home. In a study conducted before and after schools closed in March 2020, student achievement in math decreased by approximately 50 percent after schools closed, with the decrease greatest in low-income zip code areas (Chetty & others, 2020). Further, students with sensory and learning difficulties, such as those who are deaf or blind, as well as those who have a learning disability or ADHD, do not learn as effectively online as they do in a classroom (Centers for Disease Control and Prevention, 2020).

Schools also provide an important context for social and emotional development. Peer and friendship relationships are more difficult to maintain when education takes place in an online environment. Also, in-person schooling provides access to a range of mental health and social services that children are less likely to receive when they are at home all of the time (Saggioro de Figueiredo & others, 2021).

How has the COVID-19 pandemic changed the way adolescents have recently experienced education?
Simone Hogan/Alamy Stock Photo

In addition, school closings can harm children's nutritional health. Many children obtain as much has 50 percent of their daily calories at school. For children from low-income families, in-person schooling is especially important as a source of affordable, healthy nutrition.

In sum, there are many reasons that favor in-person learning at schools for children. That said, considerable caution needs to be taken to ensure that children can experience a safe environment in their schools. In the context of pandemics such as COVID-19, every safety precaution, including daily health monitoring, social distancing, and wearing face masks that cover the mouth and nose, needs to be carried out. Further, if a pandemic worsens considerably, it is likely that a return to online instruction will need to be implemented on a temporary basis until the pandemic lessens. When online home education is occurring, it is important for parents to monitor their children's learning as closely as possible to ensure that they are spending an adequate amount of time in learning activities.

COLLEGE EDUCATION

The coronavirus pandemic also dramatically changed the way college education is delivered. In mid-March 2020, a large majority of colleges shut down in-person classes and abruptly switched to online instruction. Some of the same concerns about K-12 students taking online classes described above also apply to college students' education, such as concern that learning will be less effective and that the social aspects of college will be considerably compromised.

Before the fall semester of 2020, college administrations grappled with whether to continue most or all classes online, return to in-person campus classes, or implement a hybrid schedule with some classes online and others in-person. A number of colleges that chose to have in-person campus classes had to return to online classes because of spikes in the spread of the coronavirus, especially fueled by college students not adequately engaging in preventive measures such as social distancing, mask wearing, and avoiding large gatherings.

Like K-12 students, traditional-age college students in their late teens and early twenties are less likely to get severe symptoms from the coronavirus, but for older college students and faculty the risk is much greater. International students also are vulnerable, with travel bans to and from the United States compounding difficulties of campus closings as well as increasing concern about housing options. Further, as with K-12 students, students from low-income backgrounds may not have adequate access to computers and online instruction. And for most colleges, the financial loss of shutting down in-person classes is enormous, with dorms and eating facilities remaining empty when classes are offered only online.

As the coronavirus pandemic subsides, most colleges are returning to a menu of mainly in-person classes. However, the pandemic has forced colleges to improve the quality of their online instruction, which may increase the percentage of classes that will be offered online in the future.

How has the COVID-19 pandemic changed the way college students have recently experienced education?
Matej Kastelic/Shutterstock

learning disabilities Disabilities in which children experience difficulty in learning that involves understanding or using spoken or written language; the difficulty can appear in listening, thinking, reading, writing, and spelling. A learning disability also may involve difficulty in doing mathematics. To be classified as a learning disability, the learning problem is not primarily the result of visual, hearing, or motor disabilities; intellectual disability; emotional disorders; or environmental, cultural, or economic disadvantage.

Review Connect Reflect

 LG4 Summarize the effects of the COVID-19 pandemic on schools.

Review
- How has the COVID-19 pandemic affected children and adolescents in K-12 schools?
- How has the COVID-19 pandemic changed the lives of college students?

Connect
- How might the COVID-19 pandemic affect adolescents' achievement and preparation for college?

Reflect *Your Own Personal Journey of Life*
- How has the COVID-19 pandemic changed your life in school and out of school?

5 Adolescents Who Are Exceptional

LG4 Characterize adolescents who are exceptional, and describe their education.

Who Are Adolescents with Disabilities?	Learning Disabilities	Attention Deficit Hyperactivity Disorder	Autism Spectrum Disorders	Educational Issues Involving Adolescents with Disabilities	Adolescents Who Are Gifted

For many years, public schools did little to educate adolescents with disabilities. However, in the last several decades, federal legislation has mandated that all children and adolescents with disabilities receive a free, appropriate education. And increasingly, these students are being educated in the regular classroom.

WHO ARE ADOLESCENTS WITH DISABILITIES?

So far we have discussed schools that are experienced by the majority of U.S. students. Of all children in the United States, 14 percent from 3 to 21 years of age received special education or related services in 2018–2019, an increase of 3 percent since 1980–1981 (National Center for Education Statistics, 2020). Figure 2 shows the seven largest groups of students with a disability who were served by federal programs during the 2018–2019 school year (National Center for Education Statistics, 2020). As indicated in Figure 2, students with a learning disability were by far the largest group of students with a disability to be given special education, followed by children with speech or language impairments, other health impairments, autism, developmental delay, intellectual disability, and emotional disturbance. Note that the U.S. Department of Education includes both students with a learning disability and students with ADHD in the category of learning disability. Regardless of their specific disability, students with disabilities often have low motivation and self-efficacy.

LEARNING DISABILITIES

Adolescents with **learning disabilities** have difficulty in learning that involves understanding or using spoken or written language; the difficulty can appear in listening, thinking, reading, writing, spelling, or math (Heward, Alber-Morgan, & Konrad, 2022). To be classified as a learning disability, the learning problem is not primarily the result of visual, hearing, or motor disabilities; intellectual disability; emotional disorders; or environmental, cultural, or economic disadvantage (Gunning, 2020).

About three times as many boys as girls are classified as having a learning disability. Among the explanations for this gender difference are a greater biological vulnerability among boys and *referral bias*. That is, boys are more likely to be referred by teachers for treatment because of their behavior. Also, in research conducted by the Centers for Disease Control in 2018 with 3- to 17-year-olds, 16.9 percent of African American children and adolescents were reported as ever having had a learning disability or attention deficit hyperactivity disorder (ADHD), compared with 14.7 percent of non-Latinx whites and 11.9 percent of Latinxs (Zablotsky & Alford, 2020).

Approximately 80 percent of students with a learning disability have a reading problem (Shaywitz & Shaywitz, 2017). Three types of learning disabilities are dyslexia, dysgraphia, and dyscalculia:

- *Dyslexia* is a category reserved for individuals who have a severe impairment in their ability to read and spell (Remien & Marwaha, 2021).
- *Dysgraphia* is a learning disability that involves difficulty in handwriting (Cabrero & De Jesus, 2021). Children with dysgraphia may write very slowly, their writing products may be virtually illegible, and they may make numerous spelling errors because of their inability to match up sounds and letters.
- *Dyscalculia*, also known as developmental arithmetic disorder, is a learning disability that involves difficulty in math computation (Cardenas & others, 2021).

Disability	Percentage of All Students Served Under the Individuals with Disabilities Act
Learning disability	33
Speech and language impairments	19
Other health impairments	17
Autism	11
Developmental delay	7
Intellectual disability	6
Emotional disturbance	5

FIGURE 2

U.S. CHILDREN WITH A DISABILITY WHO RECEIVE SPECIAL EDUCATION SERVICES. Figures are for the 2018–2019 school year and represent the seven categories with the highest numbers and percentages of children. Both learning disability and attention deficit hyperactivity disorder are combined in the learning disabilities category (National Center for Education Statistics, 2020).

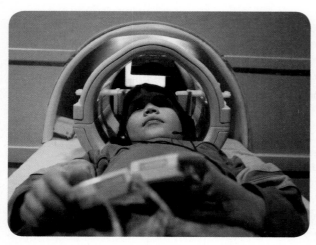

FIGURE 3

BRAIN SCANS AND LEARNING DISABILITIES. An increasing number of studies are using MRI brain scans to examine the brain pathways involved in learning disabilities. Shown here is Patrick Price, who has dyslexia. Patrick is going through an MRI scanner disguised by drapes to look like a child-friendly castle. Inside the scanner, children must lie virtually motionless as words and symbols flash on a screen, and they are asked to identify them by clicking different buttons.
Manuel Balce Ceneta/AP Images

attention deficit hyperactivity disorder (ADHD) A disability in which children or adolescents consistently show one or more of the following characteristics over a period of time: (1) inattention, (2) hyperactivity, and (3) impulsivity.

Many children and adolescents with ADHD show impulsive behavior, such as this middle school student who is getting ready to hurl a paper airplane at other children. *How would you handle this situation if you were a teacher and this were to happen in your classroom?*
Jupiterimages/Photos.com/Getty Images

Researchers are using brain-imaging techniques to identify brain regions that might be involved in learning disabilities (Li & others, 2020) (see Figure 3). This research indicates that it is unlikely that learning disabilities reside in a single, specific brain location. More likely, learning disabilities are due to problems with integrating information from multiple brain regions or to subtle impairments in brain structures and functions (Akama, Yuan, & Awazu, 2021; Banker & others, 2020).

Many interventions have focused on improving reading ability (Williams & Vaughn, 2020). Intensive instruction over a period of time by a competent teacher can improve many students' reading ability (Dewitz & others, 2020).

ATTENTION DEFICIT HYPERACTIVITY DISORDER

Attention deficit hyperactivity disorder (ADHD) is a disability in which children or adolescents consistently show one or more of the following characteristics over a period of time: (1) inattention, (2) hyperactivity, and (3) impulsivity. For an ADHD diagnosis, onset of these characteristics early in childhood is required and the characteristics must be debilitating for the child. Children and adolescents who are inattentive have difficulty focusing on any one thing and may get bored with a task after only a few minutes. Children and adolescents who are hyperactive show high levels of physical activity and seem to be almost constantly in motion. They are impulsive, have difficulty curbing their reactions, and do not do a good job of thinking before they act. Depending on the characteristics that children and adolescents with ADHD display, they can be diagnosed as (1) ADHD with predominantly inattention, (2) ADHD with predominantly hyperactivity/impulsivity, or (3) ADHD with both inattention and hyperactivity/impulsivity.

The number of children and adolescents diagnosed and treated for ADHD has increased substantially in recent years. The Centers for Disease Control and Prevention (2016) estimates that ADHD has continued to increase in 4- to 17-year-old children, going from 8 percent in 2003 to 9.5 percent in 2007 and to 11 percent in 2016. According to the Centers for Disease Control and Prevention, 13.2 percent of U.S. boys and 5.6 percent of U.S. girls have ever been diagnosed with ADHD. The disorder occurs as much as four to nine times more often in boys than in girls. There is controversy, however, about the increased diagnosis of ADHD (Friend, 2018). Some experts attribute the increase mainly to heightened awareness of the disorder; others believe that many children and adolescents are being incorrectly diagnosed (Parens & Johnston, 2009).

While earlier studies have found that an ADHD diagnosis was more likely in non-Latinx white children than in children of color (Miller, Nigg, & Miller, 2009), as indicated in the coverage of learning disabilities, the Centers for Disease Control and Prevention (Zablotsky & Alford, 2020) recently found that 3- to 17-year-old African Americans (16.9 percent) were more likely to be diagnosed with ADHD or a learning disability than non-Latinx whites (14.7 percent) or Latinxs (11.9 percent). However, some evidence suggests that African American and Latinx children and adolescents are actually under-diagnosed with ADHD and over-diagnosed with a disruptive behavior disorder in comparison with non-Latinx white children, leading some researchers to question whether unconscious bias is influencing diagnosis of ADHD (Fadus & others, 2020).

Causes and Course of ADHD   Definitive causes of ADHD have not been found; however, a number of causes have been proposed (Hallahan, Kauffman, & Pullen, 2019; Magnus & others, 2021). Some children and adolescents likely inherit a tendency to develop ADHD from their parents (Henriquez-Henriquez & others, 2020). Others likely develop ADHD because of damage to their brain during prenatal or postnatal development (Debnath & others, 2021; Wang & others, 2020). Among early possible contributors to ADHD are cigarette and alcohol exposure (Biederman & others, 2020), as well as high levels of maternal stress during prenatal development (Manzari & others, 2019) and low birth weight and preterm birth (Walczak-Kozlowska & others, 2020). Further, recent research indicates that low socioeconomic status is associated with a higher risk for developing ADHD and this low SES is linked to less effective brain functioning (Machlin, McLaughlin, & Sheridan, 2020).

As with learning disabilities, the development of brain-imaging techniques is leading to a better understanding of the brain's role in ADHD (Zou & Yang, 2021). One study revealed that peak thickness of the cerebral cortex occurs three years later (10.5 years) in children with ADHD than in children without ADHD (peak at 7.5 years) (Shaw & others, 2007). The delay is more prominent in the prefrontal regions of the brain that especially are important in attention and planning (see Figure 4). Another study also found delayed development of the brain's frontal lobes in children with ADHD, likely due to delayed or decreased myelination (Nagel & others, 2011). Researchers also are exploring the roles that various neurotransmitters, such as serotonin (Nilsen & Tulve, 2020), dopamine (Cai & others, 2021), and GABA (Puts & others, 2020) might play in ADHD.

The delays in brain development just described are in areas linked to executive function (Karr & others, 2021). A focus of increasing interest in the study of children with ADHD is their difficulty on tasks involving executive function, such as behavioral inhibition when necessary, use of working memory, and effective planning (Kofler & others, 2020).

Adjustment and optimal development also are difficult for children who have ADHD, so it is important that the diagnosis be accurate (Machado & others, 2020). Children diagnosed with ADHD have an increased risk of school dropout, disordered eating, difficulties in peer relations, adolescent pregnancy, substance use problems, and antisocial behavior (Obsuth & others, 2020; Tistarelli & others, 2020). For example, a research review concluded that compared with typically developing girls, girls with ADHD had more problems involving friendship, peer interaction, social skills, and peer victimization (Kok & others, 2016).

The increased academic and social demands of formal schooling, as well as stricter standards for behavioral control, often intensify the problems of the child with ADHD. Elementary school teachers typically report that the child with ADHD has difficulty working independently, completing seatwork, and organizing work. Restlessness and distractibility also are often noted.

Experts previously thought that most children "grow out" of ADHD. However, approximately one-third who were diagnosed as children continue to experience ADHD symptoms as adults.

Treatment of ADHD   Stimulant medication such as Ritalin or Adderall (which has fewer side effects than Ritalin) is effective in improving the attention of many children with ADHD, but it usually does not improve their attention to the same level as that of children without ADHD (Stray, Ellertsen, & Stray, 2010). A recent research review also concluded that stimulant medications are effective in treating ADHD during the short term but that longer-term benefits of stimulant medications are not clear (Rajeh & others, 2017). Also, there is increasing concern that children who are given stimulant drugs such as Ritalin or Adderall are at increased risk for developing substance abuse problems, although research results on this topic have been mixed (Erskine & others, 2016). A meta-analysis concluded that behavior management treatments are effective in reducing the intensity of ADHD (Fabiano & others, 2009). Researchers have found that a combination of medication and behavior management often (but not always) improves the behavior of children with ADHD better than medication alone or behavior management alone (Parens & Johnston, 2009).

Recently, researchers have been exploring the possibility that neurofeedback might improve the attention of children with ADHD (Dobrakowski & Lebecka, 2020). Neurofeedback trains individuals to become more aware of their physiological responses so that they can attain better control over their brain's prefrontal cortex, where executive control primarily occurs. Individuals with ADHD have higher levels of electroencephalogram (EEG) abnormalities, such as lower beta waves that involve attention and memory, and lower sensorimotor rhythms (which involve control of movements). Neurofeedback produces audiovisual profiles of brain waves so that individuals can learn how to achieve normal EEG functioning (Lambez & others, 2020). A recent review of meta-analyses and randomized experiments concluded that neurofeedback has medium to large effects on ADHD, with 32 to 47 percent remission rates for 6 to 12 months (Arns & others, 2020). And another extensive set of meta-analyses concluded that neurofeedback significantly improves inattention symptoms in children with ADHD but that stimulant medication is more effective in doing so than neurofeedback (Riesco-Matias & others, 2021).

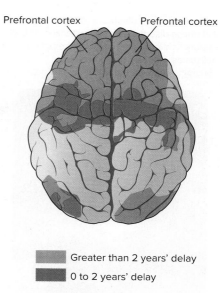

Prefrontal cortex   Prefrontal cortex

■ Greater than 2 years' delay
■ 0 to 2 years' delay

FIGURE 4

REGIONS OF THE BRAIN IN WHICH CHILDREN WITH ADHD HAD A DELAYED PEAK IN THE THICKNESS OF THE CEREBRAL CORTEX. *Note*: The greatest delays occurred in the prefrontal cortex.

developmental connections

Attention

Attention, which requires the focusing of mental resources, improves cognitive processing on many tasks. Connect to "The Brain and Cognitive Development."

developmental connections

Cognitive Processes

Mindfulness training is being used to improve adolescents' executive function. Connect to "The Brain and Cognitive Development."

What is neurofeedback? How is it being used with adolescents who have ADHD?
Andrea Obzerova/Alamy Stock Photo

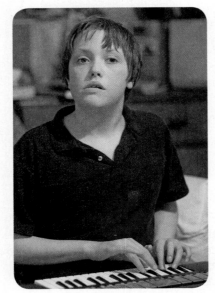

autism spectrum disorders (ASD) Adolescents with these disorders are characterized by brain dysfunction, problems in social interaction, difficulties with verbal and nonverbal communication, and repetitive behaviors.

What characterizes autism spectrum disorder?
Detail Parenting/Alamy Stock Photo

Eighteen-year-old Chandra "Peaches" Allen was born without arms. Despite this disability, she has learned to write, eat, type, paint, and draw with her feet. She can even put on earrings. She is well known for her artistic skills. She has won three grand-prize awards for her art in various shows. She is getting ready to enter college and plans to pursue a career in art and physical therapy. Chandra Allen's accomplishments reflect remarkable adaptation and coping. She is an excellent example of how adolescents can conquer a disability and pursue meaningful goals.
Bottom: The Dallas Morning News, Milton Hinnant

Recently, mindfulness training also has been given to adolescents with ADHD (Zaccari & others, 2021). A recent meta-analysis concluded that mindfulness training significantly improved the attention of children with ADHD (Cairncross & Miller, 2020).

Exercise also is being investigated as a possible treatment for children with ADHD (Nejati & Derakhshan, 2021; Villa-Gonzalez & others, 2020). A recent meta-analysis concluded that regular exercise was more effective than neurofeedback, cognitive training, or cognitive therapy in improving cognitive difficulties (attention, inhibition, and working memory deficiencies, for example) in treating ADHD (Lambez & others, 2020). And in a recent study, children with ADHD were 21 percent less likely to engage in regular exercise than children not diagnosed with ADHD (Mercurio & others, 2021). Among the reasons given as to why exercise might reduce ADHD symptoms in children and adolescents are (1) better allocation of attention resources, (2) positive influence on prefrontal cortex functioning, and (3) exercise-induced dopamine release (Chang & others, 2012).

Despite the encouraging recent studies of using neurofeedback, mindfulness training, and exercise to improve the attention of children with ADHD, it has not yet been determined whether these non-drug therapies are as effective as stimulant drugs and/or whether they benefit children as add-ons to stimulant drugs to provide a combination treatment (Riesco-Matias & others, 2021).

AUTISM SPECTRUM DISORDERS

Autism spectrum disorders (ASD) are characterized by brain dysfunction, problems in social interaction, problems in verbal and nonverbal communication, difficulties in processing information, and repetitive behaviors (Lord & others, 2020). A recent study found that a lower level of working memory was the executive function most strongly associated with autism spectrum disorders (Ziermans & others, 2017). Children and adolescents with these disorders may also show atypical responses to sensory experiences (National Institute of Mental Health, 2020).

Recent estimates of the prevalence of autism spectrum disorders indicate that they are dramatically increasing in occurrence (or are increasingly being detected). Once thought to affect only 1 in 2,500 children decades ago, they were estimated to be present in about 1 in 150 children in 2002 (Centers for Disease Control and Prevention, 2007). However, in a more recent survey, the estimated proportion of 8-year-old children with autism spectrum disorders had increased to 1 in 54 (Centers for Disease Control and Prevention, 2020). Also, in 2018–2019, 11 percent of all children receiving special education in U.S. schools were autistic (compared with only 6.5 percent in 2010–2011 (National Center for Education Statistics, 2020).

Further, in a recent survey, autism spectrum disorders were identified four times more often in boys than in girls (Centers for Disease Control and Prevention, 2020). Also, in two recent surveys, only a minority of parents reported that their child's autism spectrum disorder had been identified prior to 3 years of age, and one-third to one-half of the cases were identified after 6 years of age (Sheldrick, Maye, & Carter, 2017). However, researchers are conducting studies that seek to identify earlier determinants of autism spectrum disorder (Hudry & others, 2021). For example, in a recent research summary, early warning signs of ASD were lack of social gestures at 12 months, using no meaningful words at 18 months, and having no interest in other children or no spontaneous two-word utterances at 24 months (Tsang & others, 2019).

What causes autism spectrum disorders? The current consensus is that autism is a brain dysfunction characterized by abnormalities in brain structure and neurotransmitter levels (Takumi & others, 2020). A lack of connectivity between brain regions has been proposed as a key factor in autism (Rolls & others, 2020; Su & others, 2021).

Genetic factors play a role in the development of autism spectrum disorders (Li & others, 2020; Manoli & State, 2021). There is no evidence that family socialization causes autism.

EDUCATIONAL ISSUES INVOLVING ADOLESCENTS WITH DISABILITIES

Until the 1970s most U.S. public schools either refused enrollment to children with disabilities or inadequately served them. This changed in 1975 when **Public Law 94–142,** the Education for All Handicapped Children Act, required that all students with disabilities be given a free, appropriate public education. In 1990, Public Law 94-142 was recast as the **Individuals with Disabilities Education Act (IDEA).** IDEA was amended in 1997 and then reauthorized in 2004 and renamed the Individuals with Disabilities Education Improvement Act.

IDEA spells out broad mandates for services to children with disabilities of all kinds (Bolourian, Tipton-Fisler, & Yassine, 2020). These services include evaluation and eligibility determination, appropriate education and an individualized education plan (IEP), and education in the least restrictive environment (LRE) (Gibb & Taylor, 2022).

An *individualized education plan (IEP)* is a written statement that spells out a program that is specifically tailored for a student with a disability. The **least restrictive environment (LRE)** is a setting that is as similar as possible to the one in which children who do not have a disability are educated. This provision of the IDEA has given a legal basis to efforts to educate children with a disability in the regular classroom. The term **inclusion** describes educating a child with special educational needs full-time in the regular classroom (Heward, Alber-Morgan, & Konrad, 2022). Recent analysis indicated that in 2016, 63 percent of students with disabilities spent 80 percent or more of their total school time in the regular classroom, the highest level since inclusion began to be assessed (National Center for Education Statistics, 2017).

Many legal changes regarding children with disabilities have been extremely positive (Turnbull & others, 2020). Compared with several decades ago, far more children today are receiving competent, specialized services. For many children, inclusion in the regular classroom, with modifications or supplemental services, is appropriate. However, some leading experts on special education argue that some children with disabilities may not benefit from inclusion in the regular classroom. James Kauffman and his colleagues, for example, advocate a more individualized approach that does not necessarily involve full inclusion but allows options such as special education outside the regular classroom with trained professionals and adapted curricula (Kauffman, McGee, & Brigham, 2004). They go on to say, "We sell students with disabilities short when we pretend that they are not different from typical students. We make the same error when we pretend that they must *not* be expected to put forth extra effort if they are to learn to do some things—or learn to do something in a different way" (p. 620). Like general education, special education should challenge students with disabilities "to become all they can be."

ADOLESCENTS WHO ARE GIFTED

The final type of exceptionality we discuss is quite different from the disabilities we have described so far. **Adolescents who are gifted** have above-average intelligence (usually defined as an IQ of 130 or higher) and/or superior talent in some domain, such as art, music, or mathematics. Programs for the gifted in most school systems select children who have intellectual superiority and academic aptitude (Elliott & Resing, 2020). They tend to overlook children who are talented in the arts or athletics or who have other special aptitudes (Beghetto, 2019). There also are increasing calls to further widen the criteria for giftedness to include such factors as creativity and commitment.

Estimates vary but indicate that approximately 6 to 10 percent of U.S. students are classified as gifted (National Association for Gifted Children, 2020). This percentage is likely conservative because it focuses mainly on children and adolescents who are gifted intellectually and academically, often failing to include those who are gifted in creative thinking or the visual and performing arts (Ford, 2016).

Characteristics of Children and Adolescents Who Are Gifted   Aside from their abilities, do students who are gifted have distinctive characteristics? Lewis Terman (1925) conducted an extensive study of 1,500 children and youth whose Stanford-Binet IQs averaged 150. Contrary to the popular myth that children and youth who are gifted are maladjusted, Terman found that they were socially well adjusted.

Ellen Winner (1996) described three criteria that characterize adolescents who are gifted, whether in art, music, or academic domains:

1. *Precocity.* Children and adolescents who are gifted are precocious. They begin to master an area earlier than their peers. Learning in their domain is more effortless for them than for ordinary children. In most instances, these gifted children are precocious because they have an inborn high ability.

At 2 years of age, art prodigy Alexandra Nechita colored in coloring books for hours and also took up pen and ink. She had no interest in dolls or friends. By age 5 she was using watercolors. Once she started school, she would start painting as soon as she got home. At the age of 8, in 1994, she saw the first public exhibit of her work. In succeeding years, working quickly and impulsively on canvases as large as 5 feet by 9 feet, she has completed hundreds of paintings, some of which sell for close to $100,000 apiece. As a teenager (*above*), she continued to paint—relentlessly and passionately. It is, she said, what she loves to do. As a young adult, Alexandra continues to have a passion for painting. *What are some characteristics of adolescents who are gifted?*
Koichi Kamoshida/Newsmakers/Hulton Archive/Getty Images

2. *Marching to their own drummer.* Students who are gifted learn in a way that is qualitatively different from that of ordinary children. For one thing, they need minimal help from adults to learn. In many cases, they resist explicit instruction. They also often make discoveries on their own and solve problems in unique ways.

3. *A passion to master.* Students who are gifted are driven to understand the domain in which they have high ability. They display an intense, obsessive interest and an ability to focus. They do not need to be pushed by their parents. They motivate themselves, says Winner.

In his most recent view of giftedness, Sternberg (Sternberg & Kaufman, 2018b) argues that a high IQ and intelligence should not be isolated from other key aspects of an individual, such as creativity and wisdom. He especially emphasizes that when successful intelligence is assessed, wisdom also should be taken into consideration.

Nature/Nurture   Is giftedness a product of heredity or of environment? Likely both (Sternberg & Kaufman, 2018a, b; Winner, 2014). Individuals who are gifted recall that they had signs of high ability in a specific area at a very young age, prior to or at the beginning of formal training (Howe & others, 1995). This suggests the importance of innate ability in giftedness. However, researchers also have found that individuals with world-class status in the arts, mathematics, science, and sports all report strong family support and years of training and practice (Bloom, 1985). Deliberate practice is an important characteristic of individuals who become experts in a specific domain. For example, in one study, the best musicians engaged in twice as much deliberate practice over their lives as the least successful ones did (Ericsson, Krampe, & Tesch-Römer, 1993).

Domain-Specific Giftedness   Individuals who are highly gifted are typically not gifted in many domains, and research on giftedness is increasingly focused on domain-specific developmental trajectories (Reis & Renzulli, 2020). During the childhood and adolescent years, the domains in which individuals are gifted usually emerge. Thus, at some point in childhood or adolescence, the individual who is to become a gifted artist or a gifted mathematician begins to show expertise in that domain. Regarding domain-specific giftedness, software genius Bill Gates (1998), the founder of Microsoft and one of the world's richest persons, commented that when you are good at something you have to resist the urge to think that you will be good at everything. Gates explains that because he has been so successful at software development, people expect him to be brilliant in other domains where he is far from being a genius.

Bill Gates, founder of Microsoft and one of the world's richest persons. Like many highly gifted students, Gates was not especially fond of school. He hacked a computer security system when he was 13, and as a high school student, he was allowed to take some college math classes. He dropped out of Harvard University and began developing a plan for what was to become Microsoft Corporation. *What are some ways that schools can enrich the education of highly talented students such as Gates to make it a more challenging, interesting, and meaningful experience?*
Deborah Feingold/Getty Images

Identifying an individual's domain-specific talent and providing individually appropriate and optimal educational opportunities are tasks that need to be accomplished at the very latest by adolescence (Keating, 2009). During adolescence, individuals who are talented become less reliant on parental support and increasingly pursue their own interests.

Education of Children and Youth Who Are Gifted   An increasing number of experts argue that in the United States the education of students who are gifted requires a significant overhaul (Reis & Renzulli, 2020). This concern is reflected in the titles of books such as *Genius Denied: How to Stop Wasting Our Brightest Young Minds* (Davidson & Davidson, 2004) and *A Nation Deceived: How Schools Hold Back America's Brightest Students* (Colangelo, Assouline, & Gross, 2004).

Underchallenged students who are gifted can become disruptive, skip classes, and lose interest in achieving. Sometimes they just disappear into the woodwork, becoming passive and apathetic toward school. It is extremely important for teachers to challenge gifted children and youth to meet high expectations (Reis & Renzulli, 2020).

A number of experts argue that too often students who are gifted are socially isolated and underchallenged in the classroom (Karnes & Stephens, 2008). It is not unusual for them to be ostracized and labeled "nerds" or "geeks" by typically developing students. Ellen Winner (1996, 2006) concludes that a student who is truly gifted often is the only child in the room who does not have the opportunity to learn with students of like ability.

Many eminent adults report that school was a negative experience for them, that they were bored and sometimes knew more than their teachers did (Bloom, 1985). Winner stresses that American education will benefit when standards are raised for all students. When some students are still underchallenged, she recommends that they be allowed to attend advanced classes in their domain of exceptional ability, such as allowing some especially precocious middle school students to take college classes in their area of expertise. For example, Bill Gates, founder of Microsoft, took college math classes and hacked a computer security system at 13; Yo-Yo Ma, a famous cellist, graduated from high school at 15 and attended Juilliard School of Music in New York City.

A final concern is that African American, Latinx, and Native American children are underrepresented in gifted programs (Ford, 2016). Much of the underrepresentation involves the lower test scores for these children compared with non-Latinx white and Asian American children, which may be due to a number of factors such as test bias and fewer opportunities to develop language skills such as vocabulary and comprehension (Ford, 2012).

In this chapter, you have read about many aspects of schools for adolescents. An important aspect of the education of adolescents involves achievement. In the chapter on "Achievement, Work, and Careers," we'll explore the development of achievement in adolescents.

Review *Connect* Reflect

 LG5 Characterize adolescents who are exceptional, and describe their education.

Review

- Who are adolescents with disabilities?
- How can learning disabilities be characterized?
- What is known about attention deficit hyperactivity disorder?
- What characterizes autism spectrum disorders?
- What educational issues are involved in educating adolescents with disabilities?
- How can adolescents who are gifted be described?

Connect

- How does the concept of the family as a system support parents' efforts to seek the best outcomes for their children who are exceptional learners?

Reflect *Your Own Personal Journey of Life*

- Think back on your own schooling and how students with learning disabilities either were or were not diagnosed. Were you aware of such individuals in your classes? Were they helped by teachers and/or specialists? You might know one or more people with a learning disability. Interview them about their school experiences and ask them what they believe could have been done better to help them learn more effectively.

reach your **learning goals**

Schools

1 Approaches to Educating Students   **LG1** Describe approaches to educating students.

Contemporary Approaches to Student Learning

- Two main contemporary approaches to student learning are constructivist and direct instruction. The constructivist approach is learner-centered and emphasizes the adolescent's active, cognitive construction of knowledge and understanding. The direct instruction approach is teacher-centered and characterized by teacher direction and control, emphasis on mastery of academic skills, high expectations for students, and maximum time spent on learning tasks. Many effective teachers use aspects of both approaches.

| Accountability | • Accountability has become a major issue in U.S. education. Increased concern by the public and government in the United States has led to extensive state-mandated testing, which has both strengths and weaknesses and is controversial. The most visible example of the increased state-mandated testing is the No Child Left Behind (NCLB) federal legislation. More recently, Common Core and the Every Student Succeeds Act (ESSA) have been developed as ways to reduce some of the problems associated with NCLB. |

| Technology and Education | • If adolescents are to be adequately prepared for tomorrow's jobs, schools must take an active role in ensuring that students become technologically literate. The International Society for Technology Standards in Education (ISTE) has created technology standards for students and teachers. Strategies for using the Internet effectively are an important component of technology education. |

2 Transitions in Schooling

LG2 Discuss transitions in schooling from early adolescence to emerging adulthood.

Transition to Middle or Junior High School
- The emergence of junior high schools in the 1920s and 1930s was justified on the basis of the developmental changes occurring in early adolescence and represented an effort to meet the needs of a growing student population. Middle schools have become more popular, and their appearance has coincided with earlier pubertal development.

- The transition to middle/junior high school is often stressful because it occurs at the same time as a number of physical, cognitive, and socioemotional changes. This transition involves going from the "top-dog" to the "bottom-dog" position in the student hierarchy.

Improving Middle Schools
- *Turning Points 1989* provided a very negative evaluation of U.S. middle school education. *Turning Points 2000* continued to express serious concerns about middle school education and added new emphases on teaching a curriculum grounded in rigorous academic standards and engaging in instruction that prepares all students to achieve higher standards.

The American High School
- An increasing number of educators believe that U.S. high schools need a new mission for the twenty-first century, one that involves more support for graduating with the knowledge and skills to succeed in college and a career, higher expectations for achievement, less time spent working in low-level service jobs, and better coordination of the K–12 curriculum. The National Research Council provided a number of recommendations for improving U.S. high school education that focus on engaging students to learn.

High School Dropouts
- Many school dropouts have educational deficiencies that limit their economic and social well-being for much of their adult lives. Progress has been made in lowering the dropout rate for African American youth, but the dropout rate for Native American and Latinx youth remains very high. Dropping out of school is associated with demographic, family-related, peer-related, school-related, economic, and personal factors.

Transition from High School to College
- In many ways, the transition to college parallels the transition from elementary to middle/junior high school. Reduced interaction with parents is usually involved in this transition. A special problem today is the discontinuity between high schools and colleges.

Transition from College to Work
- Having a college degree is highly beneficial for increasing one's income. However, the transition from college to work is often difficult. One reason is that colleges often train students to develop general skills rather than job-specific skills.

3 The Social Contexts of Schools

LG3 Explain how the social contexts of schools influence adolescent development.

Changing Social Developmental Contexts
- The social context differs at the preschool, elementary school, and secondary school levels, increasing in complexity and scope for adolescents.

Classroom Climate and Management
- A positive classroom climate, which is promoted by an authoritative management strategy and effective management of group activities, improves student learning and achievement. An important teaching skill is managing the classroom to prevent problem behavior from developing and to maximize student learning. Some issues in classroom management in secondary schools are different from those in elementary schools.

Person-Environment Fit

- Person-environment fit involves the concept that some of the negative psychological changes associated with adolescent development might result from a mismatch between adolescents' developmental needs and the limited opportunities afforded by schools.

Teachers, Parents, Peers, and Extracurricular Activities

- Teacher characteristics involve many different dimensions, and compiling a profile of the competent teacher's characteristics is difficult.

- Effective family management, especially an organized routine and high achievement expectations, is positively linked to adolescents' success in school. Parent involvement usually decreases as the child moves into adolescence.

- The way middle schools are structured encourages students to interact with larger numbers of peers on a daily basis. A popular or accepted peer status is linked with greater academic success; a rejected status is related to less academic success. An increasing concern in schools is bullying. Victims of bullying can experience both short-term and long-term negative effects. Friendship is also related to school success.

- Participation in extracurricular activities is associated with positive academic and psychological outcomes.

Culture

- At home, in their neighborhoods, and at school, adolescents in poverty face problems that present barriers to effective learning. In comparison with schools in higher-SES neighborhoods, schools in low-SES neighborhoods have fewer resources, have less experienced teachers, and encourage rote learning more than the development of thinking skills.

- The school experiences of students from different ethnic groups vary considerably. It is important for teachers to have positive expectations and to challenge students of color to achieve. Strategies that teachers can use to improve relations among ethnically diverse students include turning the classroom into a "jigsaw" by engaging students in collaborative projects, encouraging positive personal contact, stimulating perspective taking, viewing the school and community as a team, and being a competent cultural mediator. Multicultural education values diversity and includes the perspectives of varying cultural groups. Schools vary across cultures. For example, U.S. schools have by far the strongest emphasis on athletics.

4 Schools and the COVID-19 Pandemic

 LG4 Summarize the effects of the COVID-19 pandemic on schools.

K-12 Education

- A special concern is that children and adolescents may not learn as effectively online as they do in the classroom. During the quarantine period when schools switched from in-person classes to online learning, too many schools left students' learning to chance. School closings, such as that caused by COVID-19, especially harm students from low-income or ethnic minority backgrounds and students with learning and sensory problems. It is important for parents to monitor their children's and adolescents' online learning as closely as possible in these challenging circumstances.

College Education

- A large majority of colleges shut down in-person classes and switched to online learning at the onset of the COVID-19 pandemic. This has resulted in concerns about the effectiveness of online learning and the interruption of the social aspects of college.

5 Adolescents Who Are Exceptional

 LG5 Characterize adolescents who are exceptional, and describe their education.

Who Are Adolescents with Disabilities?

- An estimated 13 percent of U.S. children and adolescents receive special education or related services. In the U.S. government's classification, the learning disability category includes attention deficit hyperactivity disorder, or ADHD.

Learning Disabilities

- Learning disabilities are characterized by difficulties in learning that involve understanding or using spoken or written language; the difficulty can appear in listening, thinking, reading, writing, and spelling. A learning disability also may involve difficulty in doing mathematics.

- To be classified as a learning disability, the learning problem is not primarily the result of visual, hearing, or motor disabilities; intellectual disability; emotional disorders; or environmental, cultural, or economic disadvantage.

Attention Deficit Hyperactivity Disorder

- Dyslexia is a category of learning disabilities that involves a severe impairment in the ability to read and spell. Dysgraphia and dyscalculia are two other categories of learning disabilities.

- Attention deficit hyperactivity disorder (ADHD) involves problems in one or more of these areas: inattention, hyperactivity, and impulsivity. Most experts recommend a combination of medical (stimulants such as Ritalin) and behavioral interventions in treating individuals with ADHD.

Autism Spectrum Disorders

- Autism spectrum disorders (ASD) are characterized by brain dysfunction, problems in social interaction, difficulties with verbal and nonverbal communication, and repetitive behaviors. The current consensus is that autism is a brain dysfunction involving abnormalities in brain structure and neurotransmitters.

Educational Issues Involving Adolescents with Disabilities

- Public Law 94–142 requires that all students with disabilities be given a free, appropriate education. IDEA spells out broad mandates for services to all children and adolescents with disabilities. The concept of least restrictive environment (LRE) also has been set forth. Inclusion means educating students with disabilities in the regular classroom. Full inclusion has increasingly characterized U.S. schools, although some educators argue that this trend may not be best for some students with disabilities.

Adolescents Who Are Gifted

- Adolescents who are gifted have above-average intelligence (usually defined by an IQ of 130 or higher) and/or superior talent in some domain, such as art, music, or math. Characteristics of adolescents who are gifted include precocity, marching to their own drummer, a passion to master, and superior information-processing skills. Giftedness is likely a result of the interaction of heredity and environment, and for most individuals giftedness is domain-specific. Significant criticisms have been made of the way adolescents who are gifted have been educated in the United States.

key **terms**

adolescents who are gifted
attention deficit hyperactivity disorder (ADHD)
authoritarian strategy of classroom management
authoritative strategy of classroom management

autism spectrum disorders (ASD)
constructivist approach
direct instruction approach
inclusion
Individuals with Disabilities Education Act (IDEA)

jigsaw classroom
learning disabilities
least restrictive environment (LRE)
multicultural education
permissive strategy of classroom management

Public Law 94-142
top-dog phenomenon

key **people**

Elliot Aronson
James Comer
Robert Crosnoe

Jacquelynne Eccles
James Kauffman

Jonathan Kozol
Eva Pomerantz

Allan Wigfield
Ellen Winner

improving **the lives of adolescents and emerging adults**

Children at School **(2015)**
Robert Crosnoe and Aprile Benner
In R. M. Lerner (Ed.), *Handbook of Child Psychology and Developmental Science* (7th ed.). New York: Wiley.

A contemporary view that especially emphasizes the importance of social aspects of schools and asserts that social policy focused solely on academic reforms is misguided.

Bill & Melinda Gates Foundation (www.gatesfoundation.org)

The Gates Foundation has established a major initiative to improve the nation's elementary and secondary schools. On the Foundation's website you can read about their efforts, including their digital learning emphasis.

Council for Exceptional Children (CEC) (www.cec.sped.org)

The CEC maintains an information center on the education of children and adolescents who are exceptional and publishes materials on a wide variety of topics.

ERIC (Education Resources Information Center)

ERIC is an online library of education research and information sponsored by the Institute of Education Sciences (IES) of the U.S. Department of Education. ERIC has an extensive, up-to-date number of entries for a vast number of topics, including many involving various aspects of adolescent schooling.

International Society for Technology Standards in Education (ISTE) (www.iste.org)

This leading technology education organization has created technology standards for students and teachers as well as excellent technology materials for students at different grade levels.

National Dropout Prevention Center (www.dropoutprevention.org)

The center operates as a clearinghouse for information about dropout prevention and at-risk youth and publishes the National Dropout Prevention Newsletter.

Teach for America (www.teachforamerica.org)

Teach for America recruits and places education and non-education majors in schools located in low-income areas. This site provides an overview of the program and information about how to apply for one of the positions.

chapter 11

ACHIEVEMENT, WORK, AND CAREERS

chapter **outline**

1 Achievement

Learning Goal 1 Discuss achievement in the lives of adolescents.

The Importance of Achievement in Adolescence
Achievement Processes
Social Motives, Relationships, and Contexts
Some Motivational Obstacles to Achievement

2 Work

Learning Goal 2 Describe the role of work in adolescence and in college.

Work in Adolescence
Working During College
Work/Career-Based Learning
Work in Emerging Adulthood

3 Career Development

Learning Goal 3 Characterize career development in adolescence.

Developmental Changes
Cognitive Factors
Identity Development
Social Contexts

Laurence Mouton/Getty Images

Kim-Chi Trinh was only 9 years old in Vietnam when her father used his savings to buy passage for her on a fishing boat. It was a costly and risky sacrifice for the family, who placed Kim-Chi on the small boat, among strangers, in the hope that she eventually would reach the United States, where she would get a good education and enjoy a better life.

Kim made it to the United States and coped with a succession of three foster families. When she graduated from high school in San Diego, she had a straight-A average and a number of college scholarship offers. When asked why she excels in school, Kim-Chi says that she has to do well because she owes it to her parents, who are still in Vietnam.

Kim-Chi is one of a wave of bright, highly motivated Asians who are immigrating to America. Asian Americans are the fastest-growing ethnic minority group in the United States, having increased by 72 percent since 2000. Although Asian Americans made up only 5.6 percent of the U.S. population in 2017, they constituted 43 percent of the freshman class at the University of California at Berkeley and 22 percent of the freshman class at Harvard.

Not all Asian American youth do this well, however. Poorly educated Vietnamese, Cambodian, and Hmong refugee youth are especially at risk for school-related problems. Many refugee children's histories are replete with losses and trauma. Thuy, a 12-year-old Vietnamese girl, has been in the United States for two years and resides with her father in a small apartment with a cousin's family of five in the inner city of a West Coast metropolitan area (Huang, 1989). While trying to escape from Saigon, "the family became separated, and the wife and two younger children remained in Vietnam. . . . Thuy's father has had an especially difficult time adjusting to the United States. He struggles with English classes and has been unable to maintain several jobs as a waiter" (Huang, 1989, p. 307). When Thuy received a letter from her mother saying that her 5-year-old brother had died, Thuy's schoolwork began to deteriorate, and she showed marked signs of depression—lack of energy, loss of appetite, withdrawal from peer relations, and a general feeling of hopelessness. At the insistence of the school, she and her father went to the child and adolescent unit of a community mental health center. It took the therapist a long time to establish credibility with Thuy and her father, but eventually they began to trust the therapist, who was a good listener and gave them competent advice about how to handle different experiences in their new country. The therapist also contacted Thuy's teacher, who said that Thuy had been involved in several interethnic skirmishes at school. With the assistance of the mental health clinic, the school initiated interethnic student panels to address cultural differences and discuss reasons for ethnic hostility. Thuy was selected to participate in these panels. Her father became involved in the community mutual assistance association, and Thuy's academic performance began to improve.

preview

This chapter focuses on achievement, work, and careers. As adolescence and emerging adulthood unfold, achievement takes a more central role in development, work becomes a major aspect of life, and careers play an increasingly important role. The chapter begins by examining why adolescence is a key period in achievement. Next, we explore the roles of work in the lives of adolescents and emerging adults. The chapter concludes with an evaluation of the major theories of career development and the contexts that influence adolescents' career choices.

1 Achievement (LG1) Discuss achievement in the lives of adolescents.

The Importance of Achievement in Adolescence	Achievement Processes	Social Motives, Relationships, and Contexts	Some Motivational Obstacles to Achievement

Some developmentalists worry that the United States is rapidly becoming a nation of hurried, wired people who are raising their youth to become the same way—too uptight about success and failure, and far too preoccupied with how their personal accomplishments compare with those of others. However, an increasing number of experts argue that achievement expectations for youth are too low, that adolescents are not adequately challenged to achieve, and that too many adolescents aren't receiving adequate support and guidance to reach their achievement aspirations.

THE IMPORTANCE OF ACHIEVEMENT IN ADOLESCENCE

Adolescence is a critical juncture in achievement (Guryan & others, 2021; Schunk, 2020). New social and academic pressures force adolescents toward different roles. These new roles often involve more responsibility. Achievement becomes a more serious business in adolescence, and adolescents begin to sense that the game of life is now being played for real. They even may begin to perceive current successes and failures as predictors of future outcomes in the adult world. And, as demands on adolescents intensify, different areas of their lives may come into conflict. Adolescents' social interests may cut into the time they need to pursue academic matters, or ambitions in one area may undermine the attainment of goals in another, as when academic achievement leads to social disapproval (Schwartz, Kelly, & Duong, 2013).

How effectively adolescents adapt to these new academic and social pressures is determined, in part, by psychological, motivational, and contextual factors (Starr & Simpkins, 2021). Indeed, adolescents' achievement reflects much more than their intellectual ability. Students who are not as bright as others may show an adaptive motivational pattern—being persistent at tasks and confident about their ability to solve problems, for example—and turn out to be high achievers. In contrast, some of the brightest students may have maladaptive achievement patterns—giving up easily and not having confidence in their academic skills, for example—and turn out to be low achievers.

ACHIEVEMENT PROCESSES

Achievement involves a number of motivational processes. We explore these processes next, beginning with the distinction between intrinsic and extrinsic motivation.

Intrinsic and Extrinsic Motivation   **Intrinsic motivation** is based on internal factors such as self-determination, curiosity, challenge, and effort. **Extrinsic motivation** involves external incentives such as rewards and punishments. The humanistic and cognitive approaches

intrinsic motivation Internal motivational factors such as self-determination, curiosity, challenge, and effort.

extrinsic motivation External motivational factors such as rewards and punishments.

stress the importance of intrinsic motivation in achievement. Some adolescents study hard because they are internally motivated to achieve high standards in their work (intrinsic motivation). Other adolescents study hard because they want to make good grades or avoid parental disapproval (extrinsic motivation).

Current evidence strongly favors establishing a classroom climate in which students are intrinsically motivated to learn (Chaudhuri, 2020; Zhang & others, 2021). For example, a study of third- through eighth-grade students found that intrinsic motivation was positively linked with grades and standardized test scores, whereas extrinsic motivation was negatively related to achievement outcomes (Lepper, Corpus, & Iyengar, 2005). Another study found that high school students' intrinsic motivation was linked to a higher level of academic achievement (Wormington, Corpus, & Anderson, 2012).

What characterizes intrinsic education?
monkeybusinessimages/iStock/Getty Images

Parental intrinsic/extrinsic motivational practices are also linked to children's motivation. In one study, children and adolescents had higher intrinsic motivation in math and science from 9 to 17 years of age when their parents engaged in task-intrinsic practices (encouraging children's pleasure and engagement in learning) than when their parents engaged in task-extrinsic practices (providing external rewards and consequences contingent on children's performance) (Gottfried & others, 2009). Further, a recent experimental study with ninth-grade math students found that an intervention emphasizing family interest in math and the utility of math in everyday life and future careers increased students' intrinsic valuing of math and effort in math (Hafner & others, 2017).

Students are more highly motivated to learn when they are given choices, become absorbed in challenges that match their skills, and receive rewards that have informational value (for example, "Congratulations on your good grade that you put so much effort into making happen") but are not used for control (Reeve, Cheon, & Yu, 2020). To understand the importance of these aspects of achievement in adolescent development, let's first explore the following dimensions of intrinsic motivation: (1) self-determination and personal choice, (2) optimal experiences and flow, and (3) cognitive engagement and self-responsibility. Then we will offer some concluding thoughts about intrinsic and extrinsic motivation.

Self-Determination and Personal Choice   One view of intrinsic motivation emphasizes that students want to believe that they are doing something for their own reasons, not because of external success or rewards (Ryan & Deci, 2019, 2020). A recent meta-analysis concluded that self-determination plays a central role in human motivation (Howard, Gagne, & Bureau, 2018). In this view, students' internal motivation and intrinsic interest in school tasks increase when they have opportunities to make choices and take responsibility for their learning (Shin & Bolkan, 2021).

The architects of self-determination theory, Richard Ryan and Edward Deci (2016, 2019), use the term *autonomy-supportive teachers* to describe teachers who create circumstances that allow students to engage in self-determination. One study of 34 high school classrooms found that students who perceived their classrooms as allowing and encouraging autonomy in the first several weeks of the semester increased their engagement throughout the semester (Hafen & others, 2012). Also, a recent Chinese study revealed that a higher level of *autonomy-supportive parenting* was related to adolescents' adaptive school adjustment, while a higher level of parental psychological control was linked to their maladaptive school adjustment (Xiang, Liu, & Bai, 2017).

Optimal Experiences and Flow   Mihaly Csikszentmihalyi (Abuhamdeh & Csikszentmihalyi, 2012; Csikszentmihalyi, 1990, 1993; Csikszentmihalyi & Csikszentmihalyi, 2006) has studied the optimal experiences of people for three decades. These optimal experiences occur when people report feelings of deep enjoyment and happiness. Csikszentmihalyi uses the term **flow** to describe optimal experiences in life. Flow occurs most often when people develop a sense of mastery and are absorbed in a state of concentration while they engage in an activity. He argues that flow occurs when individuals are engaged in challenges they find neither too difficult nor too easy.

Perceived levels of challenge and skill can result in different outcomes (see Figure 1). Flow is most likely to occur in settings where adolescents are challenged and perceive themselves as having a high degree of skill (Strati, Shernoff, & Kackar, 2012). When adolescents' skills are high but the activity provides little challenge, the result is boredom. When both challenge and skill levels are low, apathy occurs. And when adolescents perceive themselves as not having adequate skills to master a challenging task, they experience anxiety. In one

flow Csikszentmihalyi's concept of optimal life experiences, which he believes occur most often when people develop a sense of mastery and are absorbed in a state of concentration when they're engaged in an activity.

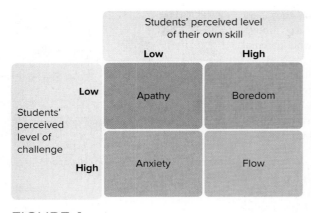

FIGURE 1

OUTCOMES OF PERCEIVED LEVELS OF CHALLENGE AND SKILL

study, students were less engaged when they were in classrooms than when they were participating in contexts that they found challenging, relevant, and enjoyable (Shernoff, 2009). After-school programs, especially those involving organized sports, academic enrichment, and arts enrichment activities, elicited the highest level of engagement during the after-school hours (Shernoff, 2009). Also, in a recent study, students who experienced flow were more likely than their non-flow counterparts to earn high grades and be able to predict their grades accurately (Sumaya & Darling, 2018).

Cognitive Engagement and Self-Responsibility It is increasingly recognized that becoming cognitively engaged and developing self-responsibility are key aspects of achievement (Shih, 2021). Phyllis Blumenfeld and her colleagues (2006) have proposed another variation on intrinsic motivation that emphasizes the importance of creating learning environments that encourage students to become cognitively engaged and to take responsibility for their learning. The goal is to motivate students to expend the effort to persist and master ideas rather than simply to do enough work to just get by and earn passing grades. Especially important in encouraging students to become cognitively engaged and responsible for their learning is embedding subject matter content and skills learning within meaningful contexts, especially real-world situations that mesh with students' interests (Wigfield & others, 2015). Award-winning teachers create meaningful real-world experiences that engage students in learning.

Some Final Thoughts About Intrinsic and Extrinsic Motivation An overwhelming conclusion for parents and teachers involves the importance of encouraging students to become intrinsically motivated and creating learning environments that promote students' cognitive engagement and self-responsibility for learning (Chaudhuri, 2020). That said, the real world is not just one of intrinsic motivation, and too often intrinsic and extrinsic motivation have been pitted against each other as polar opposites. In many aspects of students' lives, both intrinsic and extrinsic motivation are at work (Schunk, 2020). In a recent study of tenth-grade Chinese students, extrinsic motivation was harmful for high-intrinsic-motivation students' academic achievement but extrinsic motivation was beneficial for low-intrinsic-motivation students' academic achievement (Liu & others, 2020). Keep in mind, though, that many psychologists caution that using extrinsic motivation by itself is not a good strategy.

Our discussion of extrinsic and intrinsic motivation sets the stage for consideration of other cognitive processes involved in motivating students to learn. As we explore these additional cognitive processes, notice how both intrinsic and extrinsic motivation continue to be important. The processes are: (1) attribution; (2) mastery motivation and mindset; (3) self-efficacy; (4) expectations; (5) goal setting, planning, and self-monitoring; (6) sustained attention, effort, and task persistence; (7) delay of gratification; and (8) purpose.

attribution theory The theory that in their effort to make sense of their own behavior or performance, individuals are motivated to discover the underlying causes.

Attribution **Attribution theory** states that individuals are motivated to discover the underlying causes of their own performance and behavior. Attributions are perceived causes of outcomes (Graham, 2020; Graham & Taylor, 2016; Graham & Weiner, 2012). In a way, attribution theorists say, adolescents are like intuitive scientists, seeking to explain the cause behind what happens (Weiner, 2005). For example, a secondary school student asks, "Why am I not doing well in this class?" or "Did I get a good grade because I studied hard or because the teacher gave us an easy test, or both?" The search for a cause or explanation is often initiated when unexpected and important events end in failure, as when a good student gets a low grade. Some of the most frequently inferred causes of success and failure are ability, effort, task ease or difficulty, luck, mood, and help or hindrance from others.

What are the best strategies for teachers to use in helping students who attribute their poor performance to factors such as lack of ability, bad luck, and hindrance from others? Educational psychologists recommend getting adolescents to attribute their poor performance to internal factors such as a lack of effort rather than to external factors such as bad luck or a test that was too difficult (Wigfield, Rosenzweig, & Eccles, 2017). They also emphasize getting adolescents to concentrate on the learning task at hand rather than worry about failing; to retrace their steps to discover their mistake; and to analyze the problem to discover another approach.

Mastery Motivation and Mindset Cognitive engagement and self-motivation to improve characterize adolescents with a mastery motivation. These adolescents also have a growth mindset and believe that they can produce positive outcomes if they put forth sufficient effort.

Mastery Motivation Developmental psychologists Valanne Henderson and Carol Dweck (1990) have found that adolescents often show two distinct responses to difficult or challenging circumstances. Adolescents who display a **mastery orientation** are task-oriented—instead of focusing on their ability or looking only at the desired outcome, they concentrate on learning strategies and engaging in the process of achievement. Those with a **helpless orientation** seem trapped by the experience of difficulty, and they attribute their difficulty to lack of ability. They frequently say such things as "I'm not very good at this," even though they might earlier have demonstrated their ability through many successes. And, once they view their behavior as failure, they often feel anxious and their performance deteriorates further. Figure 2 describes some behaviors that might reflect feelings of helplessness (Stipek, 2002).

In contrast, mastery-oriented adolescents often instruct themselves to pay attention, to think carefully, and to remember strategies that have worked for them in previous situations. They frequently report feeling challenged and excited by difficult tasks, rather than being threatened by them (Xiang, Liu, & Bai, 2017). One study revealed that seventh- to eleventh-grade students' mastery goals were linked to how much effort they put forth in mathematics (Chouinard, Karsenti, & Roy, 2007).

Another issue in motivation involves whether to adopt a mastery orientation or a performance orientation. Adolescents with a **performance orientation** are focused on winning, rather than on achievement outcome, and believe that happiness results from winning. Does this mean that mastery-oriented adolescents do not like to win and that performance-oriented adolescents are not motivated to experience the self-efficacy that comes from being able to take credit for one's accomplishments? No. A matter of emphasis or degree is involved, though. For mastery-oriented individuals, winning isn't everything; for performance-oriented individuals, skill development and self-efficacy take a backseat to winning.

A final point needs to be made about mastery and performance goals: They are not always mutually exclusive. Students can be both mastery- and performance-oriented, and researchers have found that mastery goals combined with performance goals often benefit students' success (Schunk, 2020).

Mindset Carol Dweck's (2006, 2012, 2016, 2019) most recent analysis of achievement motivation stresses the importance of developing a specific **mindset**, which she defines as the cognitive view individuals develop for themselves. She concludes that individuals have one of two mindsets: (1) a fixed mindset, in which they believe that their qualities are carved in stone and cannot change; or (2) a growth mindset, in which they believe their qualities can change and improve through their effort. A fixed mindset is similar to a helpless orientation; a growth mindset is similar to a mastery motivation.

In *Mindset,* Dweck (2006) argued that individuals' mindsets influence their outlook, whether optimistic or pessimistic; shape their goals and determine how hard they will strive to reach those goals; and affect many aspects of their lives, including achievement and success in school and sports. Dweck says that mindsets begin to be shaped when children and adolescents interact with parents, teachers, and coaches, who themselves have either a fixed mindset or a growth mindset. However, recent research indicates that many parents and teachers with growth mindsets don't always instill them in children and adolescents (Haimovitz & Dweck, 2016). The following have been found to increase adolescents' growth mindset: teach for understanding, provide feedback that improves understanding, give students opportunities to revise their work, communicate how effort and struggling are involved in learning, and function as a partner with children and adolescents in the learning process (Dweck, 2019).

In other recent research by Dweck and her colleagues, students from lower-income families were less likely to have a growth mindset than their counterparts from wealthier families (Claro, Paunesku, & Dweck, 2016). However, the achievement of students from lower-income families who did have a growth mindset was more likely to be protected from the negative effects of poverty.

The student:
- Says "I can't"
- Doesn't pay attention to teacher's instructions
- Doesn't ask for help, even when it is needed
- Does nothing (for example, stares out the window)
- Guesses or answers randomly without really trying
- Doesn't show pride in successes
- Appears bored, uninterested
- Is unresponsive to teacher's exhortations to try
- Is easily discouraged
- Doesn't volunteer answers to teacher's questions
- Maneuvers to get out of or to avoid work (for example, has to go to the nurse's office)

FIGURE 2

BEHAVIORS THAT SUGGEST HELPLESSNESS

mastery orientation An outlook in which individuals focus on the task rather than on their ability; they concentrate on learning strategies and the process of achievement instead of the outcome.

helpless orientation An outlook in which individuals seem trapped when experiencing difficulty and attribute their difficulty to a lack of ability. This orientation undermines performance.

performance orientation An outlook in which individuals are focused on winning rather than a specific achievement outcome. For performance-oriented students, winning results in happiness.

mindset The cognitive view, either fixed or growth, that individuals develop for themselves.

Dweck and her colleagues (Blackwell, Trzesniewski, & Dweck, 2007; Dweck, 2019; Dweck & Molden, 2017) recently incorporated information about the brain's plasticity into their efforts to improve students' motivation to achieve and succeed. In one study, they assigned two groups of students to eight sessions of either (1) study skills instruction or (2) study skills instruction plus information about the importance of developing a growth mindset (called incremental theory in the research) (Blackwell, Trzesniewski, & Dweck, 2007). One of the exercises in the growth mindset group was titled "You Can Grow Your Brain," and it emphasized that the brain is like a muscle that can change and grow as it is exercised and develops new connections. Students were informed that the more you challenge your brain to learn, the more your brain cells grow. Both groups had a pattern of declining math scores prior to the intervention. Following the intervention, the group who received only the study skills instruction continued to decline. The group who received study skills instruction plus the growth-mindset emphasis on how the brain develops when it is challenged were able to reverse the downward trend and improve their math achievement.

In other work, Dweck has been creating a computer-based workshop called "Brainology" to teach students that their intelligence can change. Students experience six modules about how the brain works and how to make their brain improve. After the program was tested in 20 New York City schools, students strongly endorsed the value of the computer-based brain modules. Said one student, "I will try harder because I know that the more you try the more your brain knows" (Dweck & Master, 2009, p. 137).

Recently, researchers have explored whether peer mindsets can influence a student's mindset (Sheffler & Cheung, 2020). In one study, the mindset of a student's classmates at Time 1 (2 months into the school year) was linked to the student's mindset at Time 2 (7 months later, near the end of the school year) (King, 2020).

Dweck and her colleagues also have found that a growth mindset can prevent negative stereotypes from undermining achievement. For example, believing that math ability can be learned helped to protect females from negative gender stereotyping about math (Good, Rattan, & Dweck, 2012). Also, in recent research, having a growth mindset helped to protect women's and minorities' outlook when they chose to confront expressions of bias toward them (Rattan & Dweck, 2018). Further, in a recent study of adults, engaging in a strategic mindset was critical in achieving goals (Chen & others, 2020). This mindset involves asking oneself strategy-eliciting questions such as "What can I do to help myself?" and "Is there a way to do this even better?" in the face of challenges or inadequate progress. In this study, those with a strategic mindset used more metacognitive strategies and in turn got higher college grade point averages and showed greater progress toward their professional, educational, and health goals.

Carol Dweck. *What does she emphasize as the most important aspects of students' achievement?*
Courtesy of Dr. Carol Dweck

Keep the growth mindset in your thoughts. Then, when you bump up against obstacles, you can turn to it . . . showing you a path into the future.

—CAROL DWECK
Contemporary Psychologist, Stanford University

Going into the virtual brain. A screen from Carol Dweck's "Brainology" program, which is designed to cultivate a growth mindset.
Courtesy of Dr. Carol S. Dweck

Also, although some interventions have not been successful in improving students' growth mindset (Boulay & others, 2018), David Yeager and his colleagues (2018) conducted a national intervention study that involved a brief, online, direct-to-student growth mindset intervention that increased the grade point average of underachieving students and improved the challenge-seeking mental activity of higher achievers. In other recent research, the positive outcomes of the U.S. online growth mindset intervention were replicated with students in Norway (Bettinger & others, 2018; Rege & others, 2021).

While having a growth mindset has very positive outcomes for many adolescents, for some adolescents additional skills may be needed. For example, research with 11- to 15-year-olds revealed that their belief that intelligence is malleable and capable of growth over time only predicted higher math engagement among students who also had metacognitive skills to reflect on and be aware of the learning process (Wang & others, 2021).

Self-Efficacy   Like having a growth mindset, **self-efficacy**—the belief that one can master a situation and produce favorable outcomes—is an important cognitive view for adolescents to develop. Albert Bandura (1997, 2010, 2015) argues that self-efficacy is a critical factor in whether adolescents achieve. Self-efficacy has much in common with mastery motivation. Self-efficacy is the belief that "I can"; helplessness is the belief that "I cannot" (Stipek, 2002). Adolescents with high self-efficacy endorse such statements as "I know that I will be able to learn the material in this class" and "I expect to be able to do well at this activity."

Dale Schunk (2020) has applied the concept of self-efficacy to many aspects of students' achievement. In his view, self-efficacy influences a student's choice of activities. Students with low self-efficacy for learning might avoid many learning tasks, especially those that are challenging, whereas students with high self-efficacy eagerly approach these learning tasks. Students with high self-efficacy are more likely to persist with effort at a learning task than are students with low self-efficacy (Zimmerman, Schunk, & DiBenedetto, 2017). A study revealed that adolescents with high self-efficacy had higher academic aspirations, spent more time doing homework, and were more likely to associate learning activities with optimal experience than were their low-self-efficacy counterparts (Bassi & others, 2007).

Expectations   Expectations play important roles in adolescents' and emerging adults' achievement (Brown, 2021). These expectations involve not only the expectations of adolescents themselves but also those of their parents and teachers.

Adolescents and Emerging Adults   How hard students will work can depend on how much they expect to accomplish (Eccles & Wigfield, 2020). If they expect to succeed, they are more likely to work hard to reach a goal than if they expect to fail. Jacquelynne Eccles (1987a, b, 1993) defined expectations for students' success as beliefs about how well they will do on upcoming tasks, either in the immediate or long-term future. Three aspects of ability beliefs, according to Eccles, are students' beliefs about how good they are at a particular activity, how good they are in comparison with other individuals, and how good they are in relation to their performance in other activities.

How hard students work also depends on the *value* they place on the goal (Eccles & Wigfield, 2020; Lauermann, Tsai, & Eccles, 2017). Indeed, the combination of expectancy and value has been the focus of a number of efforts to better understand students' achievement motivation (Muenks, Wigfield, & Eccles, 2018). In Eccles' (1993, 2007) model, students' expectancies and values are assumed to directly influence their performance, persistence, and task choice. In a recent study, adolescents' expectancy ("How well do you expect to do in math next year?", for example) and value beliefs ("How useful is what you learn in math?," for example) predicted math-related career attainment 15 years after graduating from high school (Lauermann, Tsai, & Eccles, 2017).

Parents and Teachers   A student's motivation is often influenced by the expectations that parents, teachers, and other adults have for the person's achievement. Children and adolescents benefit when their parents and teachers have high expectations for them and provide the necessary support for them to meet those expectations (Smyth, 2020). Special concerns have been voiced about the lower academic expectations parents and teachers have for African American and Latinx adolescents, as well as African American adolescent boys compared with African American girls (Rowley & others, 2014). In a recent study of Mexican-origin parents and their adolescents, parents' educational expectations for their seventh-graders were linked to the adolescents' ninth and eleventh-grade educational expectations (Aceves, Bamaca-Colbert, &

self-efficacy The belief that one can master a situation and produce positive outcomes.

developmental **connection**

Social Cognitive Theory

Social cognitive theory holds that behavior, environment, and person/cognitive factors are the key influences on development. Connect to "Introduction."

Jaime Escalante, Secondary School Math Teacher

After immigrating into the United States from Bolivia, Jaime Escalante became a math teacher at Garfield High School in East Los Angeles. When he began teaching at Garfield, many of the students had little confidence in their math abilities, and most of the teachers had low expectations for students' success. Escalante took it as a special challenge to improve the students' math skills and even get them to the point where they could perform well on the Educational Testing Service Advanced Placement (AP) calculus exam.

Jaime Escalante in a classroom teaching math.
AP Images

The first year was difficult. Escalante's calculus class began at 8 a.m. He told the students the doors would be open at 7 a.m. and that instruction would begin at 7:30 a.m. He also worked with them after school and on weekends. He put together lots of handouts, told the students to take extensive notes, and required them to keep a folder. He gave them a five-minute quiz each morning and a test every Friday. He started with 14 students, but within two weeks only half remained. Only five students lasted through the spring. One of the boys who quit said, "I don't want to come at 7:00. Why should I?"

Subsequent years were better as increasing numbers of students surpassed their own expectations for math achievement. Because of Escalante's persistent, challenging, and inspiring teaching, Garfield High—a school plagued by inadequate funding, violence, and inferior working conditions—eventually ranked seventh in the United States in calculus performance. Escalante's commitment and motivation were transferred to his students, many of whom no one had believed in before Escalante came along. Now retired from teaching, Escalante continues to work in a consulting role to increase students' motivation to do well in math and improve their math skills. Escalante's story is testimony to how one teacher can make a major difference in students' motivation and achievement.

For more information about the work of secondary school teachers, see the Careers in Adolescent Development appendix.

Robins, 2020). Also in this study, seventh-grade adolescents' educational expectations predicted their perceived academic competence in ninth grade.

Researchers have found that parents' expectations are linked with children's and adolescents' academic achievement (Rodriguez & others, 2017). A longitudinal study found that positive expectations of tenth-grade students, their parents, and their English and math teachers predicted their postsecondary status (highest level of education attained) four years later (Gregory & Huang, 2013). In this study, these expectations together were a better predictor of postsecondary status than student characteristics such as socioeconomic status and academic performance. Also, a recent study of adolescents in Chile revealed that their mathematics achievement was linked to their parents' expectations for their adolescents' achievement (Hascoet, Giaconi, & Ludivine, 2021). And a recent meta-analysis of 169 research studies concluded that parental expectations do predict child and adolescent achievement (Pinquart & Ebeling, 2020). Also in this meta-analysis, parental transmission of positive expectations to children and adolescents and encouragement of their academic engagement were more effective than parental behavioral academic involvement such as checking homework and staying in contact with teachers.

A student and teacher at Langston Hughes Elementary School in Chicago, a school whose teachers have high expectations for students. *How do teachers' expectations influence students' achievement?*
Ralf Finn Hestoft/Corbis Historical/Getty Images

Teachers' expectations also are important influences on children's and adolescents' achievement (Williams & others, 2020). In an observational study of 12 classrooms, teachers with high expectations spent more time providing a framework for students' learning, asked higher-level questions, and were more effective in managing students' behavior than were teachers with average and low expectations (Rubie-Davies, 2007). Also, in one study, pre-service teachers had lower expectations for girls' than boys' math achievement (Mizala, Martinez, & Martinez, 2015). To read about the work of one individual who had high expectations for his students, see the *Connecting with Careers* profile.

A final point needs to be made about teacher expectations. To help students reach their academic potential, teachers need to provide written evaluations that communicate high expectations rather than phony praise or benign neglect. Some teachers focus on weaknesses and justify this approach by stating that students need to be given critical feedback to improve their learning. However, many students—especially those at risk for academic underperformance or failure, such as low-SES students and students of color—may instead misinterpret this type of feedback as an indication that the teacher lacks confidence in their academic ability (Yeager & others, 2014). Thus, in such situations, the teacher should reassure students that she has high expectations for their achievement and has confidence that they can improve their performance.

Goal Setting, Planning, and Self-Monitoring/Self-Regulation

Setting goals, planning how to reach those goals, and engaging in self-regulation and monitoring of progress toward goals are important aspects of achievement (Beckman & others, 2021; Eckhoff & Weiss, 2020). Setting long-term and short-term goals that are specific and challenging also benefits adolescents' and emerging adults' achievement (Schunk, 2020). An example of a nonspecific, fuzzy goal is "I want to be successful." A more concrete, specific goal is "I want to make the honor roll by the end of the semester."

Students can set both long-term (distal) and short-term (proximal) goals. Examples of long-term goals are "I want to graduate from high school" or "I want to go to college and get a degree in chemistry," or "By the time I am 25, I want to finish law school." It also is important to create short-term goals that will serve as steps along the way. "Getting an A on the next math test" is an example of a short-term, proximal goal. So is "Doing all of my homework by 4 p.m. Sunday."

Another good strategy is to set challenging goals (Greco & Kraimer, 2020). A challenging goal is a commitment to self-improvement. Strong interest and involvement in activities are sparked by challenges. Goals that are easy to reach generate little interest or effort. However, goals optimally should be matched to the individual's skill level. If goals are unrealistically high, the result will be repeated failures that undermine the individual's self-efficacy.

A recent study provided further clarification of adolescent goal setting. In this study of 13- to 16-year-olds, adolescents' positive appraisals of their academic goals, but not how many academic goals they had, predicted their grades (Brumley & others, 2021). Also in this study, adolescents with social networks that were supportive and less strained appraised their goals as being well supported and achievable.

It is not enough just to set goals. In order to achieve, it also is important to plan how to reach those goals. Being a good planner means managing time effectively, setting priorities, and being organized.

Individuals should not only plan their next week's activities but also monitor how well they are sticking to their plan. Once engaged in a task, they need to monitor their progress, judge how well they are doing on the task, and evaluate the outcomes to regulate what they do in the future (Schunk, 2020). High-achieving youth are often self-regulatory learners (Schunk & Greene, 2018). For example, high-achieving youth monitor their learning and systematically evaluate their progress toward a goal more than low-achieving students do. Encouraging youth to monitor their learning conveys the message that they are responsible for their own behavior and that learning requires their active, dedicated participation.

Barry Zimmerman and his colleagues (Zimmerman, 2012; Zimmerman & Kitsantas, 1997; Zimmerman & Labuhn, 2012) have developed a model of self-regulation in achievement contexts that has three phrases:

- *Forethought.* Adolescents and emerging adults assess task demands, set goals, and estimate their ability to reach the goals.
- *Performance.* Adolescents and emerging adults create self-regulating strategies such as time management, attentional focusing, help seeking, and metacognition.
- *Self-Reflection.* Adolescents and emerging adults evaluate their performance, including attributions about factors that affected the outcome and how satisfied they are with their behavior.

Sustained Attention, Effort, and Task Persistence

Sustained attention, effort, and task persistence in school, work, and a career are important aspects of adolescents' ability to reach their goals (Padilla-Walker & others, 2013). *Sustained attention* is the ability to maintain

developmental connection

Cognitive Development

Executive function is linked to the development of the brain's prefrontal cortex and involves managing one's thoughts to engage in goal-directed behavior and exercise self-control. Connect to "The Brain and Cognitive Development."

An adolescent works with her daily planner. *How are goals, planning, and self-regulation involved in adolescent achievement?* Westend61/Getty Images

What is the nature of the marshmallow task? How is delay of gratification linked to later development?
Josie Garner/Shutterstock

grit Involves passion and persistence in achieving long-term goals.

Meredith MacGregor, pictured here as a senior at Fairview High School in Boulder, Colorado, was one of Colorado's top high school long-distance runners and aspired to become a scientist. As a high school student, she was awarded the Intel Young Scientist Award. Meredith went on to obtain undergraduate, master's, and Ph.D. degrees in astronomy and astrophysics at Harvard University, followed by a post-doctoral degree in this area at Carnegie Mellon University. In 2020, she became a professor of Astrophysics and Planetary Sciences at the University of Colorado in Boulder. *What are some aspects of grit that likely characterize Meredith MacGregor?*
Kevin Moloney

attention to a selected stimulus for a prolonged period of time. Sustained attention requires effort, and as individuals develop through adolescence, school tasks, projects, and work become more complex and require longer periods of sustained attention, effort, and task persistence than in childhood. One study revealed that older adolescents who had spent a larger part of their life in poverty showed less persistence on a challenging task (Fuller-Roswell & others, 2015).

Might the effectiveness with which adolescents persist at tasks be linked to their career success in adulthood? One study revealed that task persistence at 13 years of age was related to occupational success in middle age (Andersson & Bergman, 2011).

Delay of Gratification   Delaying gratification also is an important aspect of reaching goals—especially long-term goals (Barragan-Jason & others, 2018; Doebel & Munakata, 2018; Mischel, 2014; Neuenschwander & Blair, 2017; Schlam & others, 2013). *Delay of gratification* involves postponing immediate rewards in order to attain a larger, more valuable reward at a later time. While it may be more attractive to adolescents to hang out with friends today than to work on a project that is due for a class assignment later in the week, their decision not to delay gratification can have negative consequences for their academic achievement.

Walter Mischel and his colleagues (Mischel, Ebbesen, & Zeiss, 1972; Mischel & Moore, 1973; Zayas, Mischel, & Pandey, 2014) have conducted classic research on the delay of gratification with preschool children using the marshmallow task. In this research, young children were told the experimenter needed to leave the room to work on something and while s/he was gone they could choose to have one marshmallow immediately, or if they waited until the experimenter returned they could have two marshmallows. A majority of the children did wait a short while, but only a few waited the entire 15 minutes until the experimenter returned. On average, preschoolers succumbed to the temptation and ate the marshmallow within one minute.

In longitudinal research, Mischel and his colleagues have found that the preschool children who were able to delay gratification became more academically successful, had higher SAT scores and higher grade point averages at the end of college, and coped better with stress as adolescents and emerging adults (Mischel, 2014; Mischel & others, 1989). And as adults, they held higher-paying careers, were more law-abiding, were likely to have a lower body mass index, and were happier than individuals who had been unable to delay gratification as preschoolers (Mischel, 2014; Moffitt, 2012; Moffitt & others, 2011; Schlam & others, 2013). Although the ability to delay gratification in preschool was linked to academic success and coping in adolescence and competence in adulthood, Mischel (2014) emphasizes that adolescents and adults can improve their ability to delay gratification.

Grit

- Recently, as part of the continuing effort to study key aspects of achievement, there has been interest in the concept of **grit**, a quality that involves passion and persistence in achieving long-term goals (Schimschal & others, 2021). Research has shown that grit is linked to academic engagement and success, including students' grade point averages (Clark & Malecki, 2019). In a recent study, the persistence aspect of grit in eighth-graders was linked to their school achievement and engagement in ninth grade (Tang & others, 2019). Recent research also indicates that life purpose commitment (Hill, Burrow, & Bronk, 2016), mindfulness (Raphiphatthana, Jose, & Slamon, 2018), and goal commitment (Tang & others, 2019, 2021) are antecedents of grit. Further, a recent study of high school students indicated that a higher level of grit was linked to greater support from parents and classmates (Clark & others, 2020). Also in this study, the positive link between grit and academic achievement was stronger for students reporting high social support from teachers but not parents and classmates. In addition, another recent study of adolescents across two academic years found a reciprocal relation of grit and growth mindset, with each predicting increases in the other (Park & others, 2020). And recent research revealed that a higher level of grit predicted better outcomes in postsecondary education that provided better student support, especially in achieving on-time graduation (Goyer, Walton, & Yeager, 2021).

To determine whether you have grit, ask yourself questions such as the following (Clark & Malecki, 2019):

- Do I push myself to be my best?
- Do I work hard to reach goals, no matter how long it takes to reach them?

connecting with emerging adults

Hari Prabhakar, Student on a Path to Purpose

Hari Prabhakar's ambition is to become an international health expert. As he made the transition from high school to college, Hari created the Tribal India Health Foundation (www.tihf.org), which provides assistance in bringing low-cost health care to rural areas in India. Juggling his roles as a college student at Johns Hopkins University and as the foundation's director, Prabhakar spent about 15 hours a week leading Tribal India Health throughout his four undergraduate years.

Prabhakar also applied for, and received, $16,500 in research fellowships from different Johns Hopkins programs to advance his knowledge of public health care. He sought the expertise of health specialists on the Hopkins faculty to expand his understanding of international health care. Prabhakar worked an average of six hours each week conducting research on sickle-cell disease, which is prevalent among tribes in rural areas of India. He spent three months every summer during college in India working directly with the tribal people. In describing his work, Prabhakar said:

> I have found it very challenging to coordinate the international operation. . . . It takes a lot of work, and there's not a lot of free time. But it's worth it when I visit our patients and see how they and the community are getting better (Johns Hopkins University, 2006b).

Prabhakar graduated from Johns Hopkins University in 2006 with a 3.9 GPA and a double major in public health and writing. As a reward for his undergraduate accomplishments, in 2007 Prabhakar received a Marshall Scholarship to study in Great Britain. He completed two master's degrees at Oxford University's Health Services Research Unit and the London School of Hygiene and Tropical

Hari Prabhakar (*in rear*) at a screening camp in India that he created as part of his Tribal India Health Foundation.
Hari Prabhakar

Medicine. Prabhakar seeks to combine clinical training with health systems management to improve the medical care of people in impoverished circumstances around the world. In 2010, Prabhakar continued his education by entering Harvard Medical School. (Sources: Johns Hopkins University, 2006a, b; Lunday, 2006; Marshall Scholarships, 2007; Prabhakar, 2007.)

What kinds of goals did Prabhakar likely set for himself that strengthened his extraordinary sense of purpose?

- Once I set a goal, do I strive to overcome any challenges I might encounter?
- How passionate am I about the work I am doing?

Purpose In the chapter on "The Self, Identity, Emotion, and Personality," we described William Damon's (2008) view that purpose is an important aspect of identity development, and we also saw that purpose is a key aspect of values. Here we expand on Damon's view and explore how purpose is a missing ingredient in many adolescents' and emerging adults' achievement.

For Damon, *purpose* is an intention to accomplish something that is meaningful to oneself and to contribute something to the world beyond the self. Finding purpose involves answering questions such as "*Why* am I doing this? *Why* does it matter? *Why* is it important for me and the world beyond me? *Why* do I strive to accomplish this end?" (Damon, 2008, pp. 33–34).

In interviews with 12- to 22-year-olds, Damon found that only about 20 percent had a clear vision of where they wanted to go in life, what they wanted to achieve, and why. The largest percentage—about 60 percent—had engaged in some potentially purposeful activities, such as service learning or fruitful discussions with a career counselor, but they did not yet have a real commitment or any reasonable plans for reaching their goals. Slightly more than 20 percent expressed no aspirations, and some even said they didn't see any reason to have aspirations.

Damon concludes that most teachers and parents communicate the importance of setting goals such as studying hard and getting good grades but rarely discuss what the goals might lead to—the purpose for studying hard and getting good grades. Damon emphasizes that too

developmental **connection**

Identity

William Damon (2008) concludes that too many of today's youth aren't moving toward any identity resolution. Connect to "The Self, Identity, Emotion, and Personality."

often students focus only on short-term goals without exploring the big, long-term picture of what they want to do with their life. Damon (2008, p. 135) has used the following interview questions in his research as springboards for getting students to reflect on their purpose:

- What's most important to you in your life?
- Why do you care about those things?
- Do you have any long-term goals?
- Why are these goals important to you?
- What does it mean to have a good life?
- What does it mean to be a good person?
- If you were looking back on your life now, how would you like to be remembered?

SOCIAL MOTIVES, RELATIONSHIPS, AND CONTEXTS

In adolescence, social motives play a more important role in achievement than they did during childhood. Adolescents' relationships with parents, peers, teachers, and mentors are important aspects of their achievement. And socioeconomic status, ethnicity, and culture are social contexts that influence adolescents' achievement.

social motives Needs and desires that are learned through experiences with the social world.

Social Motives   **Social motives** are needs and desires that are learned through experiences with the social world. Students' social needs are reflected in their desires to be popular with peers and have close friends and the powerful attraction they feel to someone they love (McDonald & Asher, 2018). Though each student has a need for affiliation or relatedness, some students have a stronger need than others (Gam & others, 2021). Some students like to be surrounded by lots of friends. In middle and high school, some students feel something is drastically missing from their lives if they don't have a girlfriend or boyfriend to date regularly (Espinosa-Hernandez & others, 2020). Others don't have such strong needs for affiliation. They don't fall apart if they don't have several close friends around all day and don't sit in class in an anxious state if they don't have a romantic partner.

Adolescence can be an especially important juncture in achievement motivation and social motivation (Scherrer & others, 2020). New academic and social pressures force adolescents to take on new roles that involve more responsibility. As adolescents experience more intense achievement demands, their social interests might cut into the time they need for academic matters. Or ambitions in one area can undermine the attainment of goals in another area, as when academic achievement leads to social disapproval. In early adolescence, students face a choice between whether they will spend more of their time pursuing social goals or academic goals. The results of this decision have long-term consequences in terms of how far adolescents will go in their education and the careers they will pursue.

Recently, researchers have begun to explore the concept of a *belonging mindset*, which describes the belief that people like you belong in your school (Rattan & Dweck, 2018). Many students aren't sure whether they belong or are well-connected to their school, creating a sense of uneasiness that is especially likely to occur for students from negatively stereotyped groups. Such negative belonging concerns are associated with lower achievement. However, when underrepresented students feel they belong and are well connected to their school, they have better physical and mental health and achieve greater academic success (Rattan & Dweck, 2018; Walton & others, 2014). In one study, when underrepresented students participated in discussions about belonging, their academic achievement increased (Stephens, Hamedani, & Destin, 2014).

In a large-scale study, high-performing urban charter school students who participated in a social belonging intervention prior to entering college were more likely to enroll in college full-time and to experience social and academic integration on campus (Yeager & others, 2016). Their increased social belonging included greater use of academic support services, more participation in extracurricular activities, and increased likelihood of living on campus.

Social Relationships   Parents, peers and friends, teachers, and mentors can play important roles in adolescents' achievement.

Parents   Earlier in this chapter we mentioned that parents' expectations have an important influence on adolescents' achievement (Aceves, Bamaca-Colbert, & Robins, 2020). Here are some additional positive parenting practices that support achievement in adolescents (Wigfield & others, 2006):

- Knowing enough about the adolescent to provide the right amount of challenge and the right amount of support
- Providing a positive emotional climate that motivates adolescents to internalize their parents' values and goals
- Modeling motivated achievement behavior: working hard and persisting with effort at challenging tasks

Peers and Friends   Peers often play key roles in adolescents' achievement (De Clercq & others, 2021). The term *peers* is a multidimensional concept that ranges from acquaintances in the general peer group to cliques and close friends. Adolescents often do well academically if their friends also are doing well academically (Ryan & Shin, 2018). And as we indicated in the chapter "Peers, Friends, and Romantic Relationships," researchers have found that for non-Latinx white and Asian American adolescents, higher academic achievement is linked to having same-ethnic friends, while for African American and Latinx adolescents, higher academic achievement is associated with having more cross-ethnic friendships (Chen, Saafir, & Graham, 2020).

Peers can influence adolescents' achievement through social goals, social comparison, and peer status (Ryan & Shin, 2018). In evaluating adolescents' achievement, it is important to consider not only academic goals but social goals as well. One study revealed that young adolescents who were motivated to engage in social dominance over their peers had low levels of academic achievement (Kiefer & Ryan, 2008). Popularity goals did not support adolescents' academic achievement.

Adolescents often compare themselves with their peers to determine where they stand academically and socially (Negru-Subtirica & others, 2020). Adolescents are more likely than younger children to engage in social comparison, although adolescents are prone to deny that they ever compare themselves with others (Harter, 2012). For example, in social comparison, one adolescent might learn that another adolescent did not do well on a test in school and think "I'm smarter than he is." Positive social comparisons usually result in higher self-esteem and negative comparisons in lower self-esteem. Adolescents are most likely to compare themselves with others who are similar to them in age, ability, and interests.

Children and adolescents who are more accepted by their peers and who have good social skills often do better in school and have positive motivation for academic achievement (Ryan & Shin, 2018). In a recent meta-analysis, peer social acceptance was linked to higher academic achievement (Wentzel, Jablansky, & Scalise, 2021). In contrast, rejected adolescents, especially those who are highly aggressive, are at risk for a number of achievement problems, including getting low grades and dropping out of school (Vitaro, Boivin, & Poulin, 2018). One study revealed that having aggressive-disruptive friends in adolescence was linked to a lower likelihood of graduating from high school (Veronneau & others, 2008).

Teachers   Earlier we saw how important teachers' expectations for success are in adolescents' achievement (Williams & others, 2020). Here we further explore the key role that teachers play in adolescents' achievement. When researchers have observed classrooms, they have found that effective, engaging teachers provide support for adolescents to make good progress and they also encourage adolescents to become self-regulated achievers (Peel, 2020). The encouragement takes place in a very positive environment, one in which adolescents are regularly being guided to become motivated to try hard and develop self-efficacy.

Nel Noddings (2006) stresses that students are most likely to develop into competent human beings when they feel cared for. This caring requires teachers to get to know students fairly well. She says that this is difficult in large schools with large numbers of adolescents in each class. She recommends that teachers remain with the same students for two to three years (voluntarily on the part of the teacher and the pupil) so that teachers are better positioned to attend to the interests and capacities of each student. This proposal is being examined in schools with high-risk adolescents, an effort that is being funded by the Bill & Melinda Gates Foundation.

Mentors   **Mentors** are usually older and more experienced individuals who are motivated to improve the competence and character of a younger person (Keller & DuBois, 2021). Mentoring can involve demonstration, instruction, challenge, and encouragement over an extended period

What are some characteristics of a belonging mindset and social belonging in adolescence? How do peers and friends influence adolescents' achievement?
Comstock/Getty Images

developmental **connection**

Peers

Adolescents with friends who are academically oriented have higher grades in school. Connect to "Peers, Romantic Relationships, and Lifestyles."

mentors Individuals who are usually older and more experienced and are motivated to improve the competence and character of a younger person.

An effective mentoring program has been created at St. Luke's Methodist Church in Dallas to address the special concern of a lack of ethnic minority role models for ethnic minority students. The program has signed up more than 200 men and 100 boys (ages 4 to 18). The mentoring program involves academic tutoring as well as trips to sporting and cultural events. Shown here is Dr. Leonard Berry, a mentor in the program, with Brandon Scarborough (age 13) in front, and his own son, Leonard (age 12). Brandon not only has benefited from Dr. Berry's mentoring but has become friends with his son.

The Dallas Morning News, Irwin Thompson

of time. As a positive mentoring experience proceeds, the mentor and the youth being mentored develop a bond of commitment, and the youth develops a sense of respect and identification with the mentor.

Mentoring may take place naturally or through a mentoring program (Castro & Cohen, 2021; White & others, 2021). Natural mentoring doesn't involve any formal program but rather emerges out of an individual's existing relationships. Natural mentors might be family members, friends, relatives, neighbors, coaches, extracurricular activity instructors, clergy, youth group leaders, bosses, or teachers. In a recent meta-analysis, natural mentoring that involved relatedness, social support, and autonomy support was especially effective in improving adolescents' academic and vocational achievement (Van Dam & others, 2018). And in another recent study of Latinx ninth- and tenth-graders, natural mentoring relationship quality was linked to the adolescents' development of a more positive ethnic identity, which in turn was associated with a stronger belief in the economic value of education (Sanchez & others, 2020).

Mentoring programs, which are more formal arrangements than natural mentoring, involve matching an adult mentor with a young person. In many mentoring programs, a mentor assumes a quasi-parental role. A good mentor can help youth develop a sense of purpose—a quality that William Damon (2008) identifies as a critical element for today's youth in their quest for achievement and success.

In further research, the extent to which educational attainment was predicted by the influence of different types of mentors (kin, teachers, friends, community) and the ages when students engaged in mentoring were examined (Fruiht & Wray-Lake, 2013). Having a teacher-mentor was a better predictor of educational attainment than having other types of mentors, and having a mentor after high school was linked to educational attainment. Kin and community mentors were more important to educational attainment during high school.

Mentoring programs are increasingly being advocated as a strategy for improving the achievement of secondary school and college students who are at risk for failure (Van Dam & others, 2018). One of the largest mentoring programs is Big Brothers/Big Sisters (BBBS), which pairs caring volunteer mentors with at-risk youth (Larose & others, 2018). In a large-scale study of BBBS's school-based mentoring program, significant improvements occurred in the at-risk students' academic achievement, school conduct, attendance, and perceived academic self-efficacy (Herrera & others, 2007). Of course, some mentoring relationships are more effective than others, and matching an adolescent with a compatible mentor requires careful selection and monitoring (Rhodes & Lowe, 2009). In a recent study of a Big Brothers/Big Sisters mentoring program, minimal difficulties in pairing youth and mentors, perceptions of shared attributes with their mentor, mentor emotional engagement and support, and a longer relationship with the mentor predicted a more positive mentoring relationship quality (De Wit & others, 2020).

College students can play important roles as mentors for at-risk children and adolescents. One study indicated that mentoring at-risk fourth-grade students improved the college student volunteers' understanding of children and the value of mentoring and community work (Schmidt, Marks, & Derrico, 2004).

Mentoring may be especially important for immigrant adolescents who live in neighborhoods with few college graduates (Flye, 2017). In some mentoring programs, such as AVID (Advancement Via Individual Determination), immigrant adolescents are taken to local colleges where they meet mentors and guest speakers who are Latinx college students or graduates (Watt, Huerta, & Martinez, 2017). In one study, African American male high school students who participated in an AVID program were more likely to enroll in rigorous courses such as advanced placement and honors classes (Taylor, 2016).

Sociocultural Contexts   How extensively do ethnicity and socioeconomic status affect adolescents' achievement? How does culture influence adolescents' achievement?

Ethnicity and Socioeconomic Status   The diversity that exists among ethnic minority adolescents is evident in their achievement (Gollnick & Chinn, 2021). For example, many Asian American students have a strong academic achievement orientation, but some do not.

In addition to recognizing the diversity that exists within every cultural group in terms of adolescents' achievement, it also is important to distinguish between difference and deficiency. Too often the achievement of ethnic minority students—especially African American, Latinx, and Native American students—has been interpreted as *deficits* by middle-socioeconomic-status

developmental **connection**

Diversity

Ethnicity refers to characteristics rooted in cultural heritage, including nationality, race, religion, and language. Connect to "Culture."

non-Latinx white standards, when these students simply are *culturally different and distinct* (Banks, 2020; Cushner, McClelland, & Safford, 2022).

Socioeconomic status (SES) also influences the academic performance of ethnic minority students (Graham & Taylor, 2001). In fact, many researchers have found that socioeconomic status predicts achievement more accurately than ethnicity does. Regardless of their ethnic background, students from middle- and upper-income families fare better than their counterparts from low-income backgrounds on a host of achievement factors—expectations for success, achievement aspirations, and recognition of the importance of effort, for example (Zhang & others, 2020). An especially important factor in the lower achievement of students from low-income families is lack of adequate resources, such as an up-to-date computer, or even any computer at all, in the home to support students' learning (Schunk, Meece, & Pintrich, 2014). A longitudinal study revealed that African American children or children from low-income families benefited more than children from higher-income families when they did homework more frequently, had Internet access at home, and had a community library card (Xia, 2010). And in a recent research review, it was concluded that increases in family income for children in poverty were associated with higher achievement in middle school, as well as greater educational attainment in adolescence and emerging adulthood (Duncan, Magnuson, & Votruba-Drzal, 2017).

Sandra Graham (1986, 1990) has conducted a number of studies that not only reveal differences in achievement that are more closely related to SES than to ethnicity, but also underscore the importance of studying ethnic minority student motivation in the context of general motivational theory. Her inquiries focus on the causes African American students cite for their achievement orientation, such as why they succeed or fail. She has found that middle-SES African American students do not fit the stereotype of being unmotivated. Like their non-Latinx white middle-SES counterparts, they have high achievement expectations and understand that failure is usually due to a lack of effort rather than bad luck. However, for too many ethnic minority adolescents, the presence of stereotype threat (anxiety that one's behavior might confirm a negative stereotype about one's group) can harm their motivation. For example, in a recent study, African American and Latinx 13- to 17-year-olds experienced higher anxiety in mathematics classrooms than their non-Latinx white peers did (Seo & Lee, 2021).

UCLA educational psychologist Sandra Graham is shown talking with adolescent boys about motivation. She has conducted a number of studies which reveal that middle-socioeconomic-status African American students—like their non-Latinx white counterparts—have high achievement expectations and attribute success to internal factors such as effort rather than external factors such as luck.
Dr. Sandra Graham

Culture   International assessments indicate that students in the United States have not fared well compared with their peers in many other countries in terms of math and science performance (Desilver, 2017). In a 2019 assessment of fourth- and eighth-grade students carried out as part of the Trends in International Mathematics and Science Study (TIMSS), U.S. students placed fifteenth out of 56 countries in fourth-grade math and eighth out of 55 countries in fourth-grade science (TIMSS, 2019). Also in the 2019 TIMSS study, U.S. eighth-graders placed eleventh in math out of 39 countries and eleventh in science among the 37 countries studied. The top five spots in the international assessments usually go to East Asian countries. In the four 2019 comparisons, East Asian countries held 19 of the 20 top five spots, with Singapore number one in fourth- and eighth-grade math and eighth-grade science, while Moscow City, Russia, was number one in fourth-grade science.

Harold Stevenson (1995) explored possible reasons for the poor performance of American students compared with their peers in other countries. Stevenson and his colleagues (1990) compared the achievement of students in the United States, China, Taiwan, and Japan. Students in the three Asian countries consistently outperformed American students, and the longer the students were in school, the wider the gap became. The smallest difference between Asian and American students was in first grade; the highest was in eleventh grade (the highest grade studied).

To investigate the reasons for these large cross-cultural differences, Stevenson and his colleagues (1990) spent thousands of hours observing in classrooms, as well as interviewing and surveying teachers, students, and parents. They found that Asian teachers spent more of their time teaching math than American teachers did. For example, in Japan more than one-fourth of total classroom time in first grade was spent on math instruction, compared with only one-tenth of the time in U.S. first-grade classrooms. Also, Asian students were in school an average of 240 days a year, compared with 178 days in the United States.

Harold Stevenson and his colleagues have found that Asian schools embrace many of the ideals Americans have for their own schools but are more successful in implementing them in interesting and productive ways that make learning more enjoyable for children and adolescents.
Sipa USA/Alamy Stock Photo

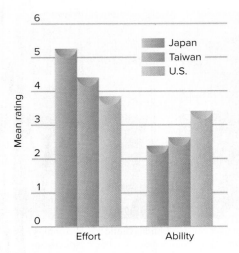

FIGURE 3

MOTHERS' BELIEFS ABOUT THE FACTORS RESPONSIBLE FOR CHILDREN'S MATH ACHIEVEMENT IN THREE COUNTRIES. In one study, mothers in Japan and Taiwan were more likely to believe that their children's math achievement was due to effort rather than innate ability, whereas U.S. mothers were more likely to believe their children's math achievement was due to innate ability (Stevenson, Lee, & Stigler, 1986). If parents believe that their children's math achievement is due to innate ability and their children are not doing well in math, the implication is that they are less likely to think their children will benefit from putting forth more effort.

What dimensions of positive and negative parenting do some Asian American parents engage in?
EyeEm/Alamy Stock Photo

In addition to the substantially greater time spent on math instruction in Asian schools than in American schools, differences were found between Asian and American parents. American parents had much lower expectations for their children's education and achievement than the Asian parents did. Also, American parents were more likely to attribute their children's math achievement to innate ability, whereas Asian parents were more likely to say that their children's math achievement reflected effort and training (see Figure 3). Asian students were more likely than American students to do math homework, and Asian parents were far more likely to help their children with their math homework than American parents were (Chen & Stevenson, 1989).

In the chapter on "Schools," we described a study that found Chinese mothers exerted more control (especially psychological control) over their children and adolescents than did U.S. mothers (Ng, Pomerantz, & Deng, 2014). Also in this study, Chinese mothers' self-worth was more contingent on their children's and adolescents' achievement than was the case for U.S. mothers. This research reflects a parenting style described as "training parents"—a variation of authoritarian parenting in which many Asian parents train their children to achieve high levels of academic success. In 2011, Amy Chua's book, *Battle Hymn of the Tiger Mother,* sparked considerable interest in the role of parenting in children's and adolescents' achievement. Chua uses the term "Tiger Mother" to mean a mother who engages in strict disciplinary practices. In another book, *Tiger Babies Strike Back*, Kim Wong Keltner (2013) argues that the Tiger Mother parenting style can be so demanding and confining that being an Asian American child is like being in an "emotional jail." She says that the Tiger Mother authoritarian style does provide some advantages for children and youth, such as emphasizing the value of going for what you want and not taking no for an answer, but she believes that too often the outcome is not worth the emotional costs that accompany it.

Research on Chinese American immigrant families with first- and second-grade children has revealed that children with authoritarian (highly controlling) parents are more aggressive, are more depressed, have a higher anxiety level, and show poorer social skills than children whose parents engage in non-authoritarian styles (Zhou & others, 2012). Qing Zhou (2013), lead author on the study just described and the director of the University of California's Culture and Family Laboratory, is conducting workshops to teach Chinese mothers positive parenting strategies such as using listening skills, praising their children for good behavior, and spending more time with their children in fun activities. Also, in a recent study in China, young adolescents with authoritative parents showed better adjustment than their counterparts with authoritarian parents (Zhang & others, 2017).

In a longitudinal study that followed young Chinese Americans from early adolescence to emerging adulthood, Su Yeong Kim and her colleagues (2013) identified four distinct parenting profiles: supportive, tiger, easygoing, and harsh. The profiles reflect various combinations of positive parenting dimensions (warmth, inductive reasoning, monitoring, and democratic parenting) and negative dimensions (parental hostility, psychological control, shaming, and punitive parenting). Across adolescence, the percentage of tiger parenting (high on both the positive and negative dimensions) decreased for mothers and increased for fathers. In this study, the supportive parenting profile (the most commonly practiced profile, which is high on positive dimensions and low on negative dimensions) produced the best developmental outcomes, followed by easygoing (low on both positive and negative dimensions), tiger, and harsh (low on positive dimensions, high on negative dimensions) profiles.

In this study the tiger parenting profile (in comparison with the supportive profile) was linked to a lower grade point average, lower sense of family obligation, more academic pressure, more depressive symptoms, and a greater feeling of alienation. Thus, this study indicates that tiger parenting is not the most common style in Chinese American families, nor is it associated with optimal adjustment in adolescents.

SOME MOTIVATIONAL OBSTACLES TO ACHIEVEMENT

Achievement problems can surface when individuals don't set goals, don't plan how to reach them, and don't monitor progress toward goals. Problems also can arise when individuals procrastinate, are too perfectionistic, become overwhelmed by anxiety, or try to protect their self-worth by avoiding failure. Many of these motivational obstacles to achievement surface during the secondary school years and become more full-blown during college. We discuss a number of these obstacles and offer strategies that teachers, counselors, mentors, and parents can use to help adolescents overcome obstacles to their achievement. Many college students also can benefit from adopting these strategies.

Procrastination *Procrastination* is a common barrier to achievement for adolescents and emerging adults (Brando-Garrido & others, 2020). Procrastination can take many forms, including the following behaviors (University of Illinois Counseling Center, 1984, 2020b):

- Ignoring a task in the hope that it will go away.
- Underestimating the work involved in a task or overestimating your abilities and resources.
- Spending endless hours on computer games and surfing the Internet.
- Deceiving yourself that a mediocre or poor performance is acceptable.
- Substituting a worthy but lower-priority activity. For example, you might clean your room instead of studying for a test.
- Believing that repeated minor delays won't hurt you.
- Dramatizing a commitment to a task rather than doing it. For example, you might take your books along for a weekend trip but never open them.
- Persevering on only part of the task. For example, you might write and rewrite the first paragraph of a paper but never get to the body of it.

Reasons for procrastinating include the following (University of Buffalo Counseling Services, 2014; Strunk & Steele, 2011): poor time management, difficulty in concentrating, fear and anxiety (feeling overwhelmed by the task and afraid of getting a bad grade, for example), negative beliefs ("I can never succeed at anything," for example), personal problems (financial difficulties, problems with a boyfriend or girlfriend, and so on), boredom, unrealistic expectations and perfectionism (believing you must read everything written on a subject before beginning to write a paper, for example), and fear of failure (thinking that if you don't get an A, you are a failure, for example).

Recent research on procrastination has examined academic procrastination and goal attainment; metacognition and procrastination; and procrastination, distress, and life satisfaction. A recent study indicated that a higher level of academic procrastination was linked to lower accomplishment of goals in college students (Gustavson & Miyake, 2017). In another study, a metacognitive model that emphasized self-regulation and executive function predicted lower levels of unintentional procrastination in college students (Fernie & others, 2017). Further, in a recent experiment, students who were assigned to a condition that emphasized the importance of self-regulated learning (time management and dealing with distractions, for example) reduced their academic procrastination and improved their self-regulated learning in areas such as time management and concentration, while those who were assigned to a control group did not improve in these areas (Grunschel & others, 2018). In addition, a recent study of high school students found that a program emphasizing the importance of self-monitoring and self-reward was effective in reducing their procrastination (Efendi & Wagid, 2021). And in another study of individuals from 14 to 95 years of age, procrastination was highest in the 14- to 29-year age range (Beutel & others, 2016). Also, only in the 14- to-29-year age range did males procrastinate more than females. Also in this study, a higher level of procrastination was associated with higher levels of stress, anxiety, depression, and fatigue, as well as lower life satisfaction.

Can you become better at reducing or eliminating procrastination? For some proven strategies, see the *Connecting with Health and Well-Being* interlude.

Perfectionism Setting high standards for yourself and then working hard to achieve them usually leads to positive outcomes. However, striving to be perfect and never to make a mistake can be maladaptive and highly stressful (Burcas & Cretu, 2021; Osenk, Williamson, & Wade, 2020). In a study of college students from 1989 to 2016 in the United States, Canada, and the United Kingdom, students' perfectionism increased in a linear fashion across these 27 years (Curran & Hill, 2019). This trend toward increased perfectionism indicated that in recent generations college students perceive that others are more demanding of them and that they are more demanding of themselves.

Can You Tackle Procrastination?

Here are some good strategies for overcoming procrastination:

- *Acknowledge that procrastination is a problem.* Too often, procrastinators don't face up to their problem. When you admit that you are procrastinating, you can begin thinking about how to solve the problem.
- *Identify your values and goals.* Think about how procrastination can undermine your values and goals.
- *Work on your time management.* Make yearly (or term), monthly, weekly, and daily plans. Then monitor how you are using your time to discover ways to use it more wisely.
- *Divide the task into smaller parts.* Sometimes you might procrastinate because you view the task as so large and overwhelming that you will never be able to finish it. When this is the case, divide the task into smaller units and set subgoals for completing one unit at a time. This strategy can often make what seems to be a completely unmanageable task manageable.
- *Use behavioral strategies.* Identify the diversions that might be keeping you from focusing on the most important tasks and activities. Note when and where you engage in these diversions.

Plan how to diminish and control their use. Another behavioral strategy is to make a contract with yourself or someone you see regularly related to your procrastination problem. And yet another behavioral strategy is to build in a reward for yourself, which gives you an incentive to complete all or part of the task. For example, after you complete all your math problems, treat yourself to a movie.

- *Use cognitive strategies.* Watch for mental self-seductions that can lead to behavioral diversions, such as "I'll do it tomorrow," "What's the problem with watching an hour or so of TV now?" and "I can't do it." Dispute mental diversions (Watson & Tharp, 2014). For example, tell yourself "I really don't have much time left, and other things are sure to come up later," "If I get this done, I'll be able to better enjoy my time," or "Maybe if I just go ahead and get going on this, it won't be so bad."

Do you think these strategies are more effective in creating intrinsic or extrinsic motivation, or both? Which strategies are likely to be most effective in enabling you to overcome procrastination?

What are some ways that perfectionism and anxiety can harm achievement?
Kzenon/iStockphoto/Getty Images

Perfectionists tend to set excessively high, unrealistic goals that can't be reached (Leone & Wade, 2018). When perfectionists don't reach their lofty goals, they become very self-critical and perceive themselves as worthless. Such thoughts and feelings produce a high level of anxiety that can interfere with their ability to concentrate and think clearly in achievement contexts (Smith & others, 2018a). One study found that college students with perfectionistic tendencies who engaged in high levels of self-criticism had lower self-esteem and showed more negative affect than those whose high standards for success were generated as personal standards (Dunkley, Berg, & Zuroff, 2012). Also, a recent meta-analysis concluded that a higher level of perfectionism is associated with eating disorders, obsessive-compulsive disorder, anxiety disorders, and depression (Limburg & others, 2017).

Perfectionism has been associated with suicidal ideation and attempts (Kiamanesh & others, 2014; Smith & others, 2018a, b). A recent meta-analysis found that perfectionistic concerns (concern over mistakes, doubts about actions, and perfectionistic attitudes), perfectionistic strivings (very high personal standards), parental criticism, and overly high parental expectations were linked to suicidal ideation (Smith & others, 2018b). Many adolescents and emerging adults who are perfectionists have parents who have had very high expectations for their success, in some cases expectations that go beyond the adolescents' and emerging adults' abilities.

To break through an unhealthy obsession with being perfect, it is important for individuals to set realistic and attainable goals that they generate themselves, rather than strive to meet standards set by others (University of Illinois Counseling Center, 2020a). It also is important to recognize that everyone makes mistakes and that a key aspect of achievement is learning from your mistakes. Further, if you are a perfectionist, go to the counseling center at your college or university to talk with a professional about ways to reduce your perfectionistic tendencies.

Anxiety   **Anxiety** is a vague, highly unpleasant feeling of fear and apprehension. It is normal for students to feel concerned or worried when they face school challenges such as doing well on a test. Indeed, researchers have found that many successful students have moderate levels of anxiety (Bandura, 1997). However, some students have high levels of anxiety and worry constantly, characteristics that can significantly impair their ability to achieve. One study found that the worry component of text anxiety was linked to lower achievement in eleventh-grade students (Steinmayr & others, 2016). Also, in a recent study, higher math anxiety was linked to lower math achievement in adolescents (Barroso & others, 2021). In this study, the link was stronger in adolescents than in emerging adults.

Some adolescents' high anxiety levels are the result of parents' unrealistic achievement expectations and pressure. One study revealed that parents' perfectionism was linked to their children's and adolescents' higher anxiety levels (Affrunti & Woodruff-Borden, 2014).

For many individuals, anxiety increases across the school years as they "face more frequent evaluation, social comparison, and (for some) experiences of failure" (Eccles, Wigfield, & Schiefele, 1998, p. 1043). When schools create such circumstances, they are likely to increase students' anxiety (Lowe, 2021).

A number of intervention programs have been created to reduce high anxiety levels (Mash & Wolfe, 2019; Putwain & von der Embse, 2021). Some intervention programs emphasize relaxation techniques. These programs often are effective at reducing anxiety but do not always lead to improved achievement. Anxiety intervention programs linked to worrying emphasize modifying the negative, self-damaging thoughts of anxious students by getting them to engage in more positive, task-focused thoughts (Meichenbaum & Butler, 1980; Watson & Tharp, 2014). These programs have been more effective than the relaxation programs in improving students' achievement.

Protecting Self-Worth by Avoiding Failure

Some individuals are so interested in protecting their self-worth and avoiding failure that they become distracted from pursuing goals and sabotage their own achievement. These strategies include the following (Covington, 2002; Covington & Teel, 1996):

- *Nonperformance.* The most obvious strategy for avoiding failure is not to try at all. In the classroom, nonperformance tactics include appearing eager to answer a teacher's question but hoping the teacher will call on another student, sliding down in the seat to avoid being seen by the teacher, and avoiding eye contact. These can seem like minor deceptions, but they might portend other, more chronic forms of noninvolvement such as excessive absences or dropping out.
- *Procrastination.* Individuals who postpone studying for a test until the last minute can blame failure on poor time management, thus deflecting attention away from the possibility that they are incompetent (Steel, 2007).
- *Setting unreachable goals.* By setting goals so high that success is virtually impossible, individuals can avoid the implication that they are incompetent, because virtually anyone would fail to reach these goals.

Efforts to avoid failure often involve **self-handicapping** strategies (Yildrim & Demir, 2020). That is, some individuals deliberately handicap themselves by not making an effort, by putting off a project until the last minute, by fooling around the night before a test, and so on, so that if their subsequent performance is at a low level, these circumstances, rather than lack of ability, will be seen as the cause (Karchner, Schone, & Schwinger, 2021). In a recent study of university students, self-handicapping was negatively related and flow was positively related to academic achievement (Adil, Ameer, & Ghayas, 2020).

Here are some strategies to reduce preoccupation with protecting self-worth and avoiding failure (Covington, 2002):

- Set challenging but realistic goals.
- Strengthen the link between your effort and self-worth. Take pride in your effort and minimize social comparison.
- Have positive beliefs about your abilities.

How do efforts to avoid failure often involve self-handicapping strategies?
monkeybusinessimages/Getty Images

anxiety A vague, highly unpleasant feeling of fear and apprehension.

developmental **connection**

Self-Esteem

A number of strategies can be implemented to improve students' self-esteem, also referred to as self-worth or self-image. Connect to "The Self, Identity, Emotion, and Personality."

self-handicapping Use of failure avoidance strategies such as not trying in school or putting off studying until the last minute so that circumstances, rather than a lack of ability, will be seen as the cause of low-level performance.

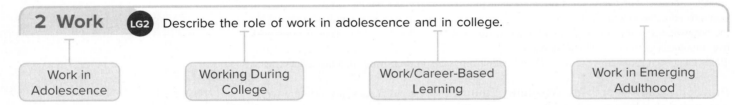

Review *Connect* Reflect

LG1 Discuss achievement in the lives of adolescents.

Review

- Why is achievement so important in adolescence?
- What are some important achievement motivation processes?
- What are some key social motives, relationships, and contexts that influence adolescents' achievement?
- What are some motivational obstacles to achievement and ways to deal with them?

Connect

- Which aspects of achievement might benefit young adolescents as they make the difficult transition through the first year of middle or junior high school?

Reflect *Your Own Personal Journey of Life*

- Would you consider yourself highly motivated to achieve? Or do you have trouble becoming motivated to achieve? Explain.

2 Work **LG2** Describe the role of work in adolescence and in college.

| Work in Adolescence | Working During College | Work/Career-Based Learning | Work in Emerging Adulthood |

Achievement and motivation show up not only in school but also in work. One of the greatest changes in adolescents' lives in recent years has been the increased likelihood that they will work in some part-time capacity and still attend school on a regular basis. Our discussion of work focuses on various aspects of work during adolescence and college, work/career-based learning, and work in emerging adulthood.

WORK IN ADOLESCENCE

What is the sociohistorical context of work in adolescents' lives? What characterizes part-time work in adolescence? What are the work profiles of adolescents around the world?

Sociohistorical Context of Work During Adolescence Even though education keeps many of today's youth from holding full-time jobs, it has not prevented them from working part-time while going to school. In 1940, only 1 of 25 tenth-grade males attended school and simultaneously worked part-time. In the 1970s, the proportion had increased to 1 in 4. Today, it is estimated that 80 to 90 percent of adolescents are employed at some point during high school (Staff, Messersmith, & Schulenberg, 2009). As shown in Figure 4, as adolescents go from the eighth to the twelfth grade, their likelihood of working and the average number of hours they work during the school year increases (Staff, Messersmith, & Schulenberg, 2009). As

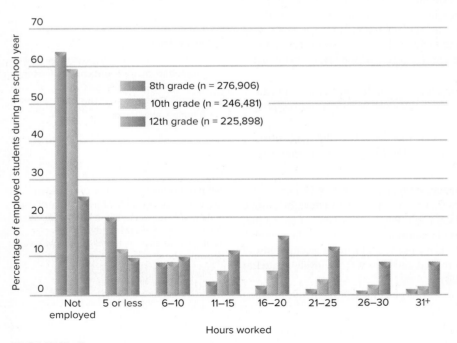

FIGURE 4

ADOLESCENT EMPLOYMENT. Percentage of employed students and number of hours worked per week during the school year by eighth-, tenth-, and twelfth-grade students (combined data for 1991 to 2006 Monitoring the Future, Institute of Social Research, cohorts).

shown in Figure 4, in the eighth and tenth grades, the majority of students do not work in paid employment during the school year, but in the twelfth grade three-fourths engage in paid employment during the school year. Almost 10 percent of employed twelfth-graders work more than 30 hours per week during the school year.

Part-Time Work in Adolescence What kinds of jobs are U.S. adolescents working at today? About 21 percent of U.S. twelfth-graders who work do so in restaurants, such as McDonald's and Burger King, waiting on customers and cleaning up (Staff, Messersmith, & Schulenberg, 2009). Other adolescents work in retail stores as cashiers or salespeople (23 percent), in offices as clerical assistants (7 percent), or in other settings as unskilled laborers (about 10 percent).

Overall, the weight of the evidence suggests that spending large amounts of time in paid labor has limited developmental benefits for youth, and for some it is associated with risky behavior and costs to physical health (Larson, Wilson, & Rickman, 2009). For example, one research study found that it was not just working that affected adolescents' grades—more important was how many hours they worked (Greenberger & Steinberg, 1986). Tenth-graders who worked more than 14 hours a week suffered a drop in grades. Eleventh-graders worked up to 20 hours a week before their grades dropped. When adolescents spend more than 20 hours per week working, there is little time available to study for tests and to complete homework assignments. In addition, working adolescents felt less involved in school, were absent more, and said that they did not enjoy school as much as their nonworking counterparts did. Adolescents who worked also spent less time with their families—but just as much time with their peers—compared with their nonworking counterparts. Adolescents who worked long hours also were more frequent users of alcohol and marijuana.

A re-analysis of the data in the 1986 study (Monahan, Lee, & Steinberg, 2011) included a better matched control group of students who did not work. Even with the more careful matching of groups, adolescents in the tenth and eleventh grades who worked more than 20 hours a week were less engaged in school and showed increases in substance abuse and delinquency (Monahan, Lee, & Steinberg, 2011). For adolescents who worked 20 hours per week or less, negative outcomes were absent.

Some youth, though, are engaged in challenging work activities, receive constructive supervision from adults, and experience favorable working conditions (Staff, Messersmith, & Schulenberg, 2009). In such cases, work may benefit adolescents in low-income, urban contexts by providing them with economic benefits and adult monitoring. For these adolescents, employment may increase school engagement and decrease delinquency.

Youth in high-poverty neighborhoods who often have difficulty finding work are a special concern. Joblessness is a common feature of such neighborhoods, as is poor-quality schooling and high crime rates. A study of African American youths, all of whom spent some years in high-poverty neighborhoods in Baltimore, found that before adolescents were legally old enough to work, boys were more likely than girls to participate in illegal, under-the-table work (Clampet-Lundquist, 2013).

What are some advantages and disadvantages of part-time work during adolescence?
kali9/Getty Images

Work Profiles of Adolescents Around the World So far, our exploration of work during adolescence has primarily focused on U.S. adolescents. How does work in adolescence vary in different countries around the world?

In many developing countries, where it is common for adolescents not to attend school on a regular basis, boys often spend more time in income-generating labor than girls do, whereas girls spend more time in unpaid labor than boys do (Larson & Verma, 1999; Larson, Wilson, & Rickman, 2009). Young adolescents work on average more than eight hours a day in many nonindustrial, unschooled populations. In the developed world, work averages less than one hour per day across childhood and adolescence except for U.S. adolescents. For example, U.S. adolescents are far more likely to participate in paid labor than European and East Asian adolescents. As we saw earlier, many U.S. high school students work 10 or even 20 hours or more per week. One study found that U.S. high school students spent an average of 50 minutes per day working at a job, whereas Northern European adolescents spent an average of only 15 minutes per day working at a job (Alsaker & Flammer, 1999). In this study, employment of adolescents was virtually nonexistent in France and Russia. In another study, 80 percent of Minneapolis eleventh-graders had part-time jobs, compared with only 27 percent of Japanese eleventh-graders and 26 percent of Taiwanese eleventh-graders (Fuligni & Stevenson, 1995).

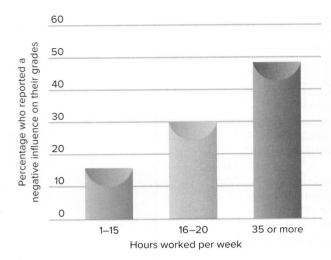

FIGURE 5

THE RELATION OF HOURS WORKED PER WEEK IN COLLEGE TO GRADES. Among students working to pay for school expenses, 16 percent of those working 1 to 15 hours per week reported that working negatively influenced their grades (National Center for Education Statistics, 2002). Thirty percent of college students who worked 16 to 20 hours a week said the same, as did 48 percent who worked 35 hours or more per week.

Overall, the weight of the evidence suggests that spending large amounts of time in paid labor has limited developmental benefits for youth, and for some it is associated with risky behavior and costs to physical health (Larson & Verma, 1999; Larson, Wilson, & Rickman, 2009). Some youth, though, are engaged in challenging work activities, receive constructive supervision from adults, and experience favorable working conditions. However, in general, given the repetitive nature of most labor carried out by adolescents around the world, it is unlikely that working 15 to 25 hours per week provides any developmental gains (Larson & Verma, 1999).

WORKING DURING COLLEGE

The percentage of full-time U.S. college students who also held jobs increased from 34 percent in 1970 to 47 percent in 2008, then declined to 43 percent in in 2018 (down from a peak of 53 percent in 2000) (National Center for Education Statistics, 2020). In 2018, 81 percent of part-time U.S. college students were employed, down from 85 percent in 2000.

Working can pay for schooling or help offset some of the costs of attending college, but working can also restrict students' opportunities to learn and negatively influence their grades. One national study found that as the number of hours worked per week increased for those who identified themselves primarily as students, their grades suffered and the number of classes, class choice, and library access became more limited (National Center for Education Statistics, 2002) (see Figure 5).

Other research has found that the greater the number of hours college students work per week, the more likely they are to drop out of college (National Center for Education Statistics, 1998). Thus, college students need to carefully examine the number of hours they work and the extent to which the work is having a negative impact on their college success. Although borrowing money to pay for education can leave students with considerable debt, working long hours reduces the amount of time students have for studying and can decrease the likelihood that these students will do well or even complete their college degree.

WORK/CAREER-BASED LEARNING

A number of experts note that a stronger connection between school and work needs to be forged. One way to improve this connection is through work/career-based learning experiences—especially for those adolescents who go directly from high school into the workforce.

High School   Work/career-based learning increasingly has become part of the effort to help youth make the transition from school to employment. Each year, approximately 500,000 high school students participate in cooperative education or other arrangements where learning objectives are met through part-time employment in office occupations, retailing, and other vocational fields. Vocational classes also involve large numbers of adolescents in school-based enterprises, through which they build houses, run restaurants, repair cars, operate retail stores, staff child-care centers, and provide other services.

Some important changes have recently taken place in vocational education. Today's high school diploma provides access to fewer and fewer stable, high-paying jobs. Thus, more of the training for specific occupations is occurring in two-year colleges and postsecondary technical institutes.

In high schools, new forms of career-related education are creating options for many students, ranging from students with disabilities to students who are gifted. Among the new models are career academies, technical preparation programs, early college high schools, and school-based enterprises (Perry & Wallace, 2012):

- *Career academies.* These academies function either as small schools within a more comprehensive high school or as separate schools, typically with 150 to 200 students beginning the program during ninth or tenth grade. The curriculum often focuses on a broad theme, such as health science or business, and students may participate in work-based learning.

- *Technical preparation programs.* Students combine the final two years of high school with two years in a community college and obtain a technical degree. They may or may not engage in work-based learning.
- *Early college high schools.* These are small high schools usually located on college campuses with the goal of giving students the opportunity to obtain a high school diploma and an associate degree or to earn two years of college credit that can be transferred to a four-year college.
- *School-based enterprises.* Students explore community needs and participate in service-learning projects as part of their high school education.

College   College students can participate in cooperative education programs or do part-time or summer jobs relevant to their field of study. This experience can be critical in helping students obtain the job they want when they graduate (Martinez, 2006). Many employers expect job candidates to have this type of experience. One survey found that almost 60 percent of employers said their entry-level college hires had co-op or internship experience (Collins, 1996).

More than 1,000 colleges offer co-op (cooperative education) programs. A co-op is a paid apprenticeship in a career that a college student is interested in pursuing. At many of these colleges, students are not allowed to participate in a co-op program until their junior year.

WORK IN EMERGING ADULTHOOD

The work patterns of emerging adults have changed over the last 100 years. As increasing numbers of emerging adults have participated in higher education, many have postponed moving out of the family home for several years and have begun their careers at later ages. Changing economic conditions also have made the job market more competitive for emerging adults and increased the demand for skilled workers (Chen & others, 2012).

A diversity of school and work patterns characterize emerging adults. Some emerging adults attend college full-time while others hold full-time jobs. Some emerging adults work full-time immediately after high school, others after graduating from college. Many emerging adults who attend college drop out and enter the workforce before completing their degree; some of these individuals return to college later. Some emerging adults are attending two-year colleges, others four-year colleges; some are working part-time while going to college, while others are not.

The contexts in which people work in the United States and around the world changed dramatically in 2020 as the onset of the coronavirus pandemic forced many employers to require their employees to work at home rather in an office, classroom, or other settings in order to comply with social distancing and quarantine requirements in their communities. As the virus subsides, it is possible that an increased number of employers may allow their employees to choose whether they will work at home, at the employer's office, or work at home some days and at the office on other days.

A special concern is the unemployment rate of college graduates. From 2016 through early 2020, the U.S. unemployment rate for recent college graduates ranged from 3.7 percent in 2016 to 3.5 percent in January 2020 (U.S. Department of Labor, 2020). Then with onset of the COVID-19 pandemic, the unemployment rate for recent college graduates abruptly increased from 3.9 percent in March 2020 to 7.7 percent in May and then to a peak of 13.2 percent in July 2020. By September 2020, the unemployment rate for college graduates had declined to 9.1 percent. Further, following the onset of COVID-19, the average entry-level starting salaries for college graduates dropped to $54,585, down from $59,765 in 2019.

Unemployment produces stress regardless of whether the job loss is temporary, cyclical, or permanent (Puterman & others, 2020). Researchers have found that unemployment is related to increased rates of physical problems (such as hypertension), emotional problems (such as depression and anxiety), substance abuse, and marital difficulties (Bui & Wijesekera, 2019). In a recent Finnish study, alcohol-related death was elevated for unemployed individuals 0 to 5 years and 11 to 20 years after they lost their jobs (Junna, Moustgaard, & Martikainen, 2021).

As you explore the type of work you are likely to enjoy and in which you can succeed, it is important to become knowledgeable about different fields and companies. Occupations may

How did the COVID-19 pandemic impact recent college graduates' starting salaries and unemployment (such as this recent college graduate in an unemployment line)?
Andriy Popov/Alamy Stock Photo

These emerging adults are college graduates who started their own business. Emerging adults follow a diversity of work and educational pathways. *What are some of these variations in education and work that characterize emerging adults?*
Getty Images

have many job openings one year but few in another year as economic conditions change. Thus, it is critical to keep up with the occupational outlook in various fields. An excellent source of information is the U.S. government's *Occupational Outlook Handbook*, which is revised every two years.

According to the 2020–2021 edition, solar power installers, wind turbine service technicians, home health aides, personal care aides, occupational therapy assistants, information security analysts, physician assistants, statisticians, nurse practitioners, speech-language pathologists, physical therapist assistants, and genetic counselors are the job categories that are projected to grow most rapidly through 2028 (*Occupational Outlook Handbook, 2020–2021*). Most of the highest-paying occupations require a college degree.

At the beginning of 2020, the job outlook for college graduates in the United States was very positive, with employers planning to increase college hiring by 5.8 percent over 2019 hiring (NACE, 2020). However, as in many other aspects of life, the outlook for college graduate employment declined steeply in March and April of 2020 with the onset of the coronavirus pandemic. However, many employers were hiring significantly more college graduates of the class of 2021, expecting to hire 7.2 percent more graduates than they did in 2020 (NACE, 2021).

Review *Connect* Reflect

 LG2 Describe the role of work in adolescence and in college.

Review

- What is the sociohistorical context of adolescent work? What are the advantages and disadvantages of part-time work during secondary school and college? What is the profile of adolescent work around the world?
- How does work during college influence students' academic success?
- What are some aspects of work/career-based learning?
- What characterizes work in emerging adulthood?

Connect

- How does this section's discussion of the recent sociohistorical context of

adolescent work compare with the historical nature of adolescent work described in the "Introduction" chapter?

Reflect *Your Own Personal Journey of Life*

- Did you work during high school? What were some of the pluses and minuses of the experience if you did work? Are you working part-time or full-time now while you are going to college? If so, what effect does the work experience have on your academic success?

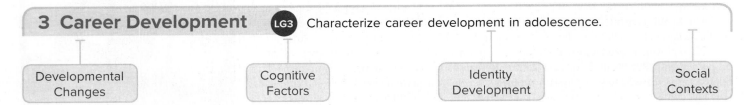

3 Career Development **LG3** Characterize career development in adolescence.

| Developmental Changes | Cognitive Factors | Identity Development | Social Contexts |

What are some developmental changes that characterize adolescents' career choices? What are some cognitive factors that affect career development? How is career development related to identity development? How do sociocultural factors affect career development? We will explore the answers to these questions in this section.

DEVELOPMENTAL CHANGES

Many children have idealistic fantasies about what they want to be when they grow up. For example, many young children want to be superheroes, sports stars, or movie stars. During the high school years, they often begin to think about careers in a somewhat less idealistic way. In their late teens and early twenties, their career decision making has usually turned more serious as they explore different career possibilities and zero in on the career they want to enter. In college, this path often means choosing a major or specialization that is designed to lead to work in a specific field. By their early and mid-twenties, many individuals have completed their education or training and embarked on a full-time occupation. From the mid-twenties through the remainder of early adulthood, individuals often seek to establish their emerging career in a certain field. They may work hard to move up the career ladder and improve their financial standing.

William Damon (2008) maintains that it is not only children who have idealistic fantasies about careers but that too many of today's adolescents also dream about fantasy careers that may have no connection to reality. Too often adolescents have no idea about what it takes to become such a career star, and usually there is no one in their lives who can help them to reach this career pinnacle. Consider adolescents playing basketball who dream of becoming the next LeBron James and adolescents participating in theater who want to become the next Angelina Jolie, for example.

COGNITIVE FACTORS

Exploration, decision making, and planning play important roles in adolescents' career choices (Liang & others, 2020). In countries where equal employment opportunities have emerged—such as the United States, Canada, Great Britain, and France—exploration of various career paths is critical in adolescents' career development. Adolescents often approach career exploration and decision making with considerable ambiguity, uncertainty, and stress. Many of the career decisions made by youth involve floundering and unplanned changes. Many adolescents do not adequately explore careers on their own and also receive little direction from guidance counselors at their schools. On average, high school students spend less than three hours per year with guidance counselors, and in some schools the average is even less. In many schools, students not only do not know what information to seek about careers, they do not know how to seek it.

In *The Path to Purpose*, William Damon (2008) noted that most high school students aren't lacking in ambition when it comes to careers but rather don't have anything close to an adequate plan for reaching their career goals. Too many youth drift aimlessly through their high school years, Damon says, and this behavior places them at risk for not fulfilling their potential and not finding a life pursuit that energizes them.

In a large-scale longitudinal investigation, Mihaly Csikszentmihalyi and Barbara Schneider (2000) studied how U.S. adolescents develop attitudes and acquire skills to achieve their career goals and expectations. They assessed the progress of more than 1,000 students from 13 school districts across the United States. Students recorded at random moments their thoughts and feelings about what they did, and they filled out questionnaires regarding school, family, peers, and career aspirations. The researchers also interviewed the adolescents, as well as their friends, parents, and teachers. Among the findings of the study are the following:

- Girls anticipated the same lifestyles as boys in terms of education and income.
- Lower-income minority students were more positive about school than more affluent students were.
- Students who got the most out of school—and had the highest future expectations—were those who perceived school to be more play-like than work-like.
- Clear vocational goals and good work experiences did not guarantee a smooth transition to adult work. Engaging activities—with intensive involvement regardless of content—were essential to building the optimism and resilience that are important for achieving a satisfying work life. This finding fits with Csikszentmihalyi's concept of flow, which we explored earlier in the chapter.

More than 90 percent of today's high school seniors expect to attend college, and more than 70 percent anticipate working in professional jobs. Four decades ago, the picture was

Grace Leaf, College/Career Counselor and College Administrator

Grace Leaf is a counselor at Spokane Community College in Washington. She has a master's degree in educational leadership and is working toward a doctoral degree in educational leadership at Gonzaga University in Washington. Her college counseling job has involved teaching, providing orientation for international students, conducting individual and group advisory sessions, and doing individual and group career planning. Leaf has focused on connecting students with their own goals and values and helping them design an educational program that fits their needs and visions. Following a long career as a college counselor, she is now vice-president of instruction at Lower Columbia College in Washington.

For more information about what career counselors do, see the Careers in Adolescent Development appendix.

Grace Leaf counsels college students at Spokane Community College about careers.
Courtesy of Grace Leaf

substantially different, with only 55 percent expecting to go to college and 42 percent anticipating working in professional jobs. Parents can help adolescents by becoming more knowledgeable about which courses their adolescents are taking in school, developing a better understanding of the college admissions process, providing adolescents with better information about various careers, and realistically evaluating their adolescents' abilities and interests in relation to these careers.

During college, students can benefit from the advice of college counselors, not only about careers but about many other aspects of life (Verdin, Godwin, & Klotz, 2020). To read about the work of one college counselor, see the *Connecting with Careers* profile.

IDENTITY DEVELOPMENT

Career development is related to the adolescent's and emerging adult's identity development (Batool & Ghayas, 2020). Career decidedness and planning are positively related to identity achievement, whereas career planning and decidedness are negatively related to identity moratorium and identity diffusion statuses (Wallace-Broscious, Serafica, & Osipow, 1994). An individual's identity can be categorized as diffused, foreclosed, moratorium, and achieved. Identity moratorium describes individuals who have not yet made an identity commitment but are in the midst of exploring options, whereas identity diffusion identifies individuals who have neither made a commitment nor experienced a crisis (exploration of alternatives). Adolescents and emerging adults who are further along in the process of identity formation are better able to articulate their occupational choices and to identify their next steps toward attaining short-term and long-term goals. By contrast, adolescents and emerging adults in the moratorium and diffusion statuses of identity are more likely to struggle with making occupational plans and decisions.

One study on this topic focused on vocational identity development in relation to other identity domains (Skorikov & Vondracek, 1998). A cross-sectional study of 1,099 high school students in grades 7 through 12 revealed a developmental progression in adolescent vocational identity that was characterized by an increase in the proportion of students classified as identity diffused or foreclosed. Statuses in general ideological, religious, lifestyle, and political identity domains lagged behind identity status development in the domain of vocation (see

---

developmental connection

Identity

Emerging adulthood is characterized by identity exploration, especially in work and love, and by instability in work, love, and education. Connect to "Introduction."

Figure 6). Thus, in line with the developmental tasks outlined in Erikson's (1968) theory (discussed in "The Self, Identity, Emotion, and Personality"), vocational identity development plays a leading role in identity development.

SOCIAL CONTEXTS

Not every individual born into the world can grow up to become a nuclear physicist or a doctor—genetic limitations keep some adolescents from performing at the high intellectual levels necessary to enter such careers. Similarly, genetic limitations restrict some adolescents from becoming professional football players or professional dancers. But many careers are available to most of us, careers that provide a reasonable match with our abilities. Our sociocultural experiences exert strong influences on career choices from among the wide range available. Among the important social contexts that influence career development are culture, socioeconomic status, parents and peers, schools, gender, and ethnicity.

Culture   A study of more than 11,000 adolescents from 18 countries who were living mainly in middle and upper socioeconomic families found that adolescents were experiencing considerable stress in thinking about their future (Seiffge-Krenke, 2012). In this study, adolescents in all 18 countries especially feared not being able to pursue the vocational training or academic studies required for entering the profession they desired. Many of them also had a fear of being unemployed at some point in the future.

In some countries, the work and career prospects for youth are worse than in other countries. For example, in southern European countries such as Italy and Spain, there is a mismatch for youth between the high number of university graduates and the relatively low demand for these graduates in the labor market (Tomasik & others, 2012).

Socioeconomic Status   The channels of upward mobility that are open to lower-SES youth are largely educational in nature (Plasman & others, 2020). The school hierarchy from grade school through high school, as well as through college and graduate school, is programmed to orient individuals toward some type of career. Less than 100 years ago, it was believed that only eight years of education were necessary for vocational competence, and anything beyond that qualified the individual for advanced placement in higher-status occupations. By the middle of the twentieth century, the high school diploma had already lost ground as a ticket to career success, and in today's workplace college is a prerequisite for entering a higher-status occupation.

Many of the ideas that have guided career development theory have been based on experiences in middle-income and well-educated contexts. Underlying this theory is the concept that individuals have a wide range of career choices available to them. However, many youth in low-income circumstances may have more limited career choices. The barriers that many low-income inner-city youth face, such as low-quality schools, violence, and lack of access to jobs, can restrict access to desirable careers (Gollnick & Chinn, 2021).

Parents and Peers   Parents and peers also are strong influences on adolescents' career choices. Some experts argue that American parents have achievement expectations that are too low, whereas others maintain that some parents put too much pressure on adolescents to achieve beyond their capabilities.

Many factors influence parents' roles in adolescents' career development. For example, mothers who work regularly outside the home and show effort and pride in their work probably have strong influences on their adolescents' career choices. A reasonable conclusion is that when both parents work and enjoy their jobs, adolescents learn work values from both parents.

Parents can potentially influence adolescents' occupational choices through the way they present information about occupations and values, as well as through the experiences they provide adolescents. For example, parents can communicate to their children and adolescents that they believe in the value of going to college and achieving

| Domain/ | Grade | | |
Identity Status	8	10	12
Vocational			
Moratorium	33.5	38.0	42.1
Achievement	13.5	13.5	19.6
General ideological			
Moratorium	25.5	27.8	36.4
Achievement	5.1	11.2	5.6
Religious			
Moratorium	14.6	15.6	20.0
Achievement	5.6	7.8	5.4
Lifestyle			
Moratorium	14.0	18.9	15.6
Achievement	3.6	6.5	4.6
Political			
Moratorium	11.3	13.8	11.2
Achievement	3.1	4.8	6.5

FIGURE 6

IDENTITY STATUS DEVELOPMENT IN DIFFERENT DOMAINS. Note: Numbers represent percentages.

Parents play an important role in the adolescent's achievement. It is important for parents to neither pressure the adolescent too much nor challenge the adolescent too little.
Aldo Murillo/Getty Images

a professional degree as a means of attaining a career in medicine, law, or business. Other parents might communicate that college is not as important and place a higher value on being a champion athlete or movie star.

Peers also can influence adolescents' career development. Adolescents often choose friends from within the school setting at an achievement level similar to their own. In one investigation, when adolescents had friends and parents with high career standards, they were more likely to seek higher-status careers, even if they came from low-income families (Simpson, 1962). Also, in a survey of 1,500 first-year college students, 34 percent said their friends had influenced their interest in a particular career (GTI Media, 2020).

School Influences   Schools, teachers, and counselors can exert a powerful influence on adolescents' career development (Carey, 2020). School is the primary setting where individuals first encounter the world of work. School provides an atmosphere for continuing self-development in relation to achievement and work. And school is the only institution in society that is capable of providing the delivery systems necessary for career education—instruction, guidance, placement, and community connections.

School counseling has been criticized, both inside and outside the educational establishment (Heppner & Heppner, 2003). Insiders complain about the large number of students assigned to each school counselor and the weight of noncounseling administrative duties. In a recent national survey, the average student-to-counselor ratio during the 2018–2019 school year was 430 to 1, well above the American School Counselor Association's recommended ratio of 250 students per counselor (American School Counselor Association, 2020). In a recent study, school counselor ratios of 250 to 1 were linked to fewer students being absent from school, lower school suspension rates, higher SAT scores, and higher graduation rates (Parzych & others, 2019).

Outsiders complain that school counseling is often ineffective, biased, and a waste of money. Short of creating a new profession, several options are possible (William T. Grant Foundation Commission on Work, Family, and Citizenship, 1988). First, twice the number of counselors could be hired in order to meet the needs of all students. Second, there could be a redefinition of teachers' roles, accompanied by retraining and reduction in teaching loads, so that classroom teachers could assume a greater role in handling the counseling needs of adolescents. The professional counselor's role in this plan would be to train and assist teachers in their counseling and to provide direct counseling in situations the teacher could not handle. Third, the whole idea of school counselors could be abandoned, and counselors would be located elsewhere—such as in neighborhood social service centers or labor offices. (Germany, for example, forbids teachers to give career counseling, reserving this task for officials in well-developed networks of labor offices.) To read about the work of one high school counselor, see the *Connecting with Careers* profile.

Gender   Because females have been socialized to adopt nurturing roles rather than career or achieving roles more than males have, some females have not planned seriously for careers, have not explored career options extensively, and have restricted their career choices to careers that are gender stereotyped (Gonzalez-Perez, Mateos de Cabo, & Sainz, 2020). The motivation for work is the same for both sexes. However, females and males make different choices because of their socialization experiences and the ways that social forces structure the opportunities available to them (Murcia, Pepper, & Williams, 2020). For example, many girls and women avoid taking STEM (science, technology, engineering, and math) courses in high school or college, which restricts their career options (Cipollone, Stich, & Weis, 2020). In a recent longitudinal study, adolescents' gender stereotypes became much more traditional from the from the ninth to the eleventh grades (Starr & Simpkins, 2021). Also, parents were three times more likely to say that boys are better than girls at math and science. Adolescents' math/science gender stereotypes were related to their math/science identity, which in turn was linked to their STEM outcomes in high school. Another recent study of tenth-graders indicated that believing in the stereotype of "innate" math ability in boys was associated with lower self-concept of ability and reduced intrinsic motivation in girls but not in boys (Heyder, Weidinger, & Steinmayr, 2021). Further, in a recent research review of STEM secondary school interventions for girls, it was concluded that these interventions were more successful when they involved repeated or sustained engagement activities and combined an inclusive curriculum with teaching strategies that emphasized female

Armando Ronquillo, High School Counselor/College Advisor

Armando Ronquillo has been a high school counselor and college advisor and currently is employed by the Tucson Unified School District. As a school counselor and college advisor, Ronquillo worked at Pueblo High School, which is in a low-socioeconomic-status area in Tucson, Arizona. More than 85 percent of the students have a Latinx background. In 2000, Armando was named top high school counselor in the state of Arizona. He has especially helped to increase the number of Pueblo High School students who go to college.

Ronquillo has an undergraduate degree in elementary and special education, and a master's degree in counseling. His work involves counseling students on the merits of staying in school and on the lifelong opportunities provided by a college education. Ronquillo guides students in obtaining the academic preparation that will enable them to go to college, and he shows them how to apply for financial aid and scholarships. He also works with parents to help them understand that sending their child to college is not only doable but also affordable.

Ronquillo works with students on goal setting and planning. He has students plan for the future in terms of one-year (short-term), five-

Armando Ronquillo counsels a Latinx high school student about college.
Courtesy of Armando Ronquillo

year (mid-range), and ten-plus-year (long-term) time periods. Ronquillo says he does this "to help students visualize how the educational plans and decisions they make today will affect them in the future." He also organizes a number of college campus visitations for students from Pueblo High School each year.

To read further about the work of school counselors, see the Careers in Adolescent Development appendix.

---

role models (Prieto-Rodriguez, Sincock, & Blackmore, 2020). And in recent research, college students' perceptions of their STEM professors' mindset beliefs found that students who perceived that their professors endorsed a stronger fixed rather than growth mindset reported reduced feelings of belonging in class, more negative affect, and greater imposter feelings, which in turn predicted more dropout intentions, less end-of-semester interest in STEM, and lower grades (Muencks & others, 2020).

Socioeconomic Status and Ethnicity   Many adolescents and emerging adults who have grown up in low-income or poverty conditions face challenging circumstances in seeking upward mobility (Acosta & others, 2019). These adolescents may have a difficult time deferring adult roles and may not be able to fully explore career opportunities.

Ethnic minority youth, especially those who grow up in low-income families, also may face barriers to preparing for successful careers (Banks, 2020). A study of 18- to 20-year-old urban Latinxs revealed that family obligation was a central theme in the decisions they made about their life and career after high school (Sanchez & others, 2010). In this study, financial circumstances were linked to whether they worked and/or took college classes.

To intervene effectively in the career development of ethnic minority youth, counselors need to increase their knowledge of communication styles, values regarding the importance of the family, the impact of language fluency, and achievement expectations in various ethnic minority groups (Gollnick & Chinn, 2021). Counselors need to be aware of and respect the cultural values of ethnic minority youth, but such values should be discussed within the context of the realities of the educational and occupational world.

In this chapter, we have explored many aspects of achievement, careers, and work. One topic we examined was the influence of culture and ethnicity on achievement. In the next chapter we will focus entirely on culture and adolescent development.

How might socioeconomic status and ethnicity influence adolescents' career development and opportunities?
Image Source/Getty Images

Review *Connect* Reflect

LG3 Characterize career development in adolescence.

Review

- What are some developmental changes that characterize adolescents' career choices?
- How are cognitive factors involved in adolescents' career development?
- How is identity development linked with career development in adolescence?
- What roles do social contexts play in adolescents' career development?

Connect

- Are there aspects of executive function that might be applied to understanding the cognitive factors involved in adolescents' career development?

Reflect *Your Own Personal Journey of Life*

- What are your career goals? Write down some of the specific work, job, and career goals that you have for the next 20, 10, and 5 years. Be as concrete and specific as possible. In describing your career goals, start from the farthest point—20 years from now—and work backward. If you start from a near point, you run the risk of adopting goals that are not precisely and clearly connected to your long-term career goals.

reach your **learning goals**

Achievement, Work, and Careers

1 Achievement

LG1 Discuss achievement in the lives of adolescents.

The Importance of Achievement in Adolescence

Achievement Processes

- Social and academic pressures force adolescents to cope with achievement in new ways. Adolescents may perceive that their achievements are predictors of future, real-world outcomes in the adult world. Achievement expectations increase in secondary schools. Whether adolescents effectively adapt to these new pressures is determined in part by psychological, motivational, and contextual factors.

- Intrinsic motivation is based on internal factors such as self-determination, curiosity, challenge, and effort. Extrinsic motivation involves external incentives such as rewards and punishment. One view is that giving students some choice and providing opportunities for personal responsibility increase intrinsic motivation. It is important for teachers to create learning environments that encourage students to become cognitively engaged and to take responsibility for their learning. Overall, the overwhelming conclusion is that it is a wise strategy to create learning environments that encourage students to become intrinsically motivated. However, in many real-world situations, both intrinsic and extrinsic motivation are involved, and too often intrinsic and extrinsic motivation have been pitted against each other as polar opposites.

- Attribution theory states that individuals are motivated to discover the underlying causes of behavior in an effort to make sense of the behavior. In attribution, calling on internal factors, such as effort, to explain performance is more productive than attributing high or low performance to external factors outside the control of the individual.

- A mastery orientation is preferred over a helpless or a performance orientation in achievement situations. Mindset is the cognitive view, either fixed or growth, that individuals develop for themselves. Dweck argues that a key aspect of adolescents' development is to guide them in developing a growth mindset. Self-efficacy, the belief that one can master a situation and attain positive outcomes, helps to promote achievement.

- Students' expectations for success and the value they place on what they want to achieve influence their motivation. The combination of expectancy and value has been the focus of a number of efforts to understand students' achievement motivation. Adolescents benefit when their parents, teachers, and other adults have high expectations for their achievement.

- Goal setting, planning, and self-monitoring are important aspects of achievement. Adolescents' sustained attention, effort, and task persistence also are linked to their achievement. Delay of gratification plays a very important role in adolescents' and emerging adults' ability to reach their goals. Grit involves passion and persistence in achieving long-term goals. Grit is linked to academic engagement and success, including students' grade point averages. Recently, Damon has proposed that purpose is an especially important aspect of achievement that has been missing from many adolescents' lives.

Social Motives, Relationships, and Contexts

- Social motives, relationships, and contexts play important roles in adolescents' achievement. In terms of social motives, adolescence is a time when social motivation takes on a more central role in boys' and girls' lives. In terms of social relationships, parents, peers, teachers, and mentors can be key influences on adolescents' achievement. In terms of social contexts, factors such as ethnicity, socioeconomic status, and culture influence adolescents' achievement.

Some Motivational Obstacles to Achievement

- Some motivational obstacles to achievement include procrastinating, being too perfectionistic, becoming overwhelmed by anxiety, and protecting self-worth by avoiding failure. A special concern is adolescents having too much anxiety in achievement situations, which sometimes is linked to unrealistic parental expectations. The effort to avoid failure may involve self-handicapping strategies such as deliberately not trying in school or putting off studying until the last minute. Ways to deal with motivational obstacles include identifying values and goals, using better time management, and dividing an overwhelming task into smaller parts.

2 Work
 LG2 Describe the role of work in adolescence and in college.

Work in Adolescence

- Adolescents are not as likely to hold full-time jobs today as their counterparts from the nineteenth century were. The number of adolescents who work part-time, though, has increased dramatically.

- Advantages of part-time work in adolescence include learning how the business world works, how to get and keep a job, how to manage money, how to budget time, how to take pride in accomplishments, and how to evaluate goals. Disadvantages include reducing the amount of time available for extracurricular activities, socializing with peers, and sleep; as well as the difficulty of balancing the demands of school, family, peers, and work.

- Profiles of adolescent work vary around the world. In many developing countries, boys engage in considerably more paid labor than girls, who participate in more unpaid labor at home. U.S. adolescents engage in more work than their counterparts in many other developed countries. There appears to be little developmental advantage for most adolescents when they work 15 to 25 hours per week.

Working During College

- Working while going to college can help with schooling costs but can have a negative impact on students' grades and reduce the likelihood of graduation.

Work/Career-Based Learning

- Interest in work/career-based learning in high school is increasing. Many successful college students engage in cooperative learning or internship programs.

Work in Emerging Adulthood

- The work patterns of emerging adults have changed over the last 100 years, and a diversity of school and work patterns now characterize emerging adults. The nature of the transition from school to work is strongly influenced by the individual's educational level. Many emerging adults change jobs, which can either involve searching or floundering.

3 Career Development
LG3 Characterize career development in adolescence.

Developmental Changes

- Many children have fantasies about what careers they want to enter when they grow up. In high school, these fantasies have lessened for many individuals, although too many adolescents have a fantasy career they want to enter but lack an adequate plan for reaching their aspirations. In the late teens and early twenties, career decision making usually has turned more serious.

Cognitive Factors

Identity Development

Social Contexts

- Exploration, decision making, and planning are important cognitive dimensions of career development in adolescence. Many adolescents have high aspirations but don't know how to reach these aspirations. Damon argues that adolescents and emerging adults need to incorporate thinking about purpose in their career decision making.

- Career development is linked to identity development in adolescence. Adolescents who are further along in the identity process are better able to articulate their career plans. In line with Erikson's theory, vocational identity plays a key role in overall identity development.

- Among the most important social contexts that influence career development in adolescence are culture, socioeconomic status, parents and peers, schools, gender, and ethnicity.

key terms

anxiety	grit	mentors	self-handicapping
attribution theory	helpless orientation	mindset	social motives
extrinsic motivation	intrinsic motivation	performance orientation	
flow	mastery orientation	self-efficacy	

key people

Albert Bandura	Edward Deci	Kim Wong Keltner	Dale Schunk
Amy Chua	Carol Dweck	Su Yeong Kim	Harold Stevenson
Mihaly Csikszentmihalyi	Jacquelynne Eccles	Nel Noddings	Qing Zhou
William Damon	Sandra Graham	Richard Ryan	Barry Zimmerman

improving the lives of adolescents and emerging adults

Development of Achievement Motivation and Engagement (2015)
Allan Wigfield, Jacquelynne Eccles, Jennifer Fredricks, Sandra Simpkins, Robert Roeser, and Ulrich Schiefele
In R.M. Lerner (Ed.), *Handbook of Child Psychology and Developmental Science* (7th ed.).
New York: Wiley
> Leading experts provide recent updates on many aspects of theory, research, and applications focused on adolescent achievement.

Handbook of Competence and Motivation (2nd ed.) (2017)
Edited by Andrew Eliot, Carol Dweck, and David Yeager
New York: Guilford
> A number of leading experts provide cutting-edge insights on many aspects of competence and achievement, including mindset, self-efficacy, self-determination, achievement values, achievement motives, belonging, and achievement.

Handbook of Self-Regulation of Learning and Performance (2nd ed.) (2018)
Edited by Dale Schunk and Jeffrey Greene
> A number of leading experts provide up-to-date coverage of research, theory, and applications involving many aspects of self-regulation and achievement.

The Marshmallow Test: Mastering Self-Control (2014)
Walter Mischel
Boston: Little Brown
> Well-known psychologist Walter Mischel extensively discusses the importance of delay of gratification and self-control in the lives of children, adolescents, and adults, and he describes a number of strategies for improving delay of gratification and self-control.

Mentoring in Adolescence (2009)
Jean Rhodes and Sarah Lowe
In R.M. Lerner and L. Steinberg (Eds.), *Handbook of Adolescent Psychology* (3rd ed.)
New York: Wiley
> Leading experts describe research on mentoring and highlight the aspects of mentoring that are most successful in improving adolescents' achievement.

What Color Is Your Parachute? (2021)
Richard Bolles
Berkeley, CA: Ten Speed Press
> This is an extremely popular book on job hunting, first published in 1970 and updated each year. Additional resources are provided by the author at http://www.jobhuntersbible.com.

chapter 12

CULTURE

chapter **outline**

1 Culture, Adolescence, and Emerging Adulthood

Learning Goal 1 Discuss the role of culture in the development of adolescents and emerging adults.

The Relevance of Culture for the Study of Adolescence and Emerging Adulthood

Cross-Cultural Comparisons

Rites of Passage

2 Socioeconomic Status and Poverty

Learning Goal 2 Describe how socioeconomic status and poverty are related to adolescent development.

What Is Socioeconomic Status?

Socioeconomic Variations in Families, Neighborhoods, and Schools

Poverty

3 Ethnicity

Learning Goal 3 Summarize how ethnicity is involved in the development of adolescents and emerging adults.

Immigration

Adolescence and Emerging Adulthood: A Special Juncture for Ethnic Minority Individuals

Ethnicity Issues

4 Media/Screen Time and Technology

Learning Goal 4 Characterize the roles of media/screen time and technology in adolescence and emerging adulthood.

Media/Screen Time

Television

The Media and Music

Technology and Digitally Mediated Communication

Social Policy and the Media

Rolf Bruderer/Getty Images

Fourteen-year-old Roberto and his 13-year-old sister Graciela are undocumented students who came by themselves to the United States from Mexico. They were in government custody for one month before being reunited with their mother, who had immigrated by herself to the United States when Roberto and Graciela were infants. Although Roberto and Graciela had not interacted with their mother in person since they were infants, for several years they had been connecting with her on a regular basis through Face Time. They haven't seen their father since they were infants and were raised by their maternal grandmother in Mexico.

Their mother enrolled them in the local middle school, but with their limited English and stressful circumstances both have been struggling with their classes. Graciela has had difficulty making friends at school. While Roberto has been able get several male friends, his friends are not doing well in school either.

Graciela and Roberto's mother talked with one of her neighbors about the difficulties her teenagers were having in school. The neighbor said that she knew one of the counselors, a Latinx, at the school and would ask her if she would meet with Graciela and Roberta and try to help them with their problems.

The next day at school the counselor met with Graciela and Roberto. She initially established a positive, supportive rapport with them and told them that she would be an advocate for them to help them adjust better to the school, improve their grades, and meet with other Latinx students who had experienced similar circumstances. The counselor met weekly with Graciela and Roberto for several months and also had several meetings with their mother to share information about school and community resources that might be able to help as they adjusted to life in the United States. Also, the counselor connected Graciela and Roberto with older Latinx peer mentors at school who provided them with valuable advice about ways to improve their academic and social worlds. By the end of the school year, Graciela and Roberta had improved their grades and established positive social connections with peers.

preview

Graciela's and Roberto's circumstances underscore the influence of culture on adolescent development. Although we have much in common with all humans who inhabit the earth, we also vary according to our cultural and ethnic backgrounds. The sociocultural worlds of adolescents and emerging adults are a recurrent theme throughout this book. We will explore what culture is, consider cross-cultural comparisons, study ethnicity and socioeconomic status as major aspects of culture, and examine ways in which the dramatic growth of mass media and technology affect the lives of adolescents.

1 Culture, Adolescence, and Emerging Adulthood

 LG1 Discuss the role of culture in the development of adolescents and emerging adults.

The Relevance of Culture for the Study of Adolescence and Emerging Adulthood

Cross-Cultural Comparisons

Rites of Passage

We have defined **culture** as the behavior, patterns, beliefs, and all other products of a specific group of people that are passed on from generation to generation. The products result from the interaction between groups of people and their environment over many years. Everyone has a culture. For example, one person might be a first-generation Latinx immigrant; another might be a third-generation African American; yet another might be a fifth-generation non-Latinx white Texan; and yet another might have a culture that is a mixture of two more ethnic/cultural backgrounds. Thus, it is important to note that the American culture has subcultures, just as many other cultures do. In the United States there are many diverse subcultures. Here we examine the role of culture in adolescents' and emerging adults' development, both within the United States and in cultures throughout the world.

developmental **connection**

Theories

In Bronfenbrenner's ecological theory, the macrosystem is the environmental system that involves the influence of culture on adolescent development. Connect to "Introduction."

THE RELEVANCE OF CULTURE FOR THE STUDY OF ADOLESCENCE AND EMERGING ADULTHOOD

If the study of adolescence and emerging adulthood is to be a relevant discipline in the twenty-first century, increased attention must be paid to culture and ethnicity (Umana-Taylor & Hill, 2020). Extensive contact between people from varied cultural and ethnic backgrounds is rapidly becoming the norm (Bhawuk & Landis, 2021). Schools and neighborhoods are no longer the fortresses of a privileged group whose agenda is excluding people with a different skin color or different customs (Clauss-Ehlers & others, 2021). Immigrants, refugees, and ethnic minority individuals increasingly decide not to become part of a homogeneous melting pot, instead requesting that schools, employers, and governments honor many of their cultural customs (Flores, Okorodudu, & Shepherd, 2021). Adult refugees and immigrants might find more opportunities and better-paying jobs in the United States than in their home countries, but some are concerned that their children and adolescents might learn attitudes in school that challenge traditional authority patterns at home.

During the twentieth century, the study of adolescents and emerging adults was primarily ethnocentric, emphasizing American values, especially middle-SES, non-Latinx white, male values. Cross-cultural psychologists point out that many of the assumptions about contemporary ideas in fields like adolescence were developed in Western cultures (Triandis, 2007). One example of **ethnocentrism**—the tendency to favor one's own group over other groups—is the American emphasis on the individual or self. Many Eastern countries, such as Japan, China, and India, are group-oriented. So is the Mexican culture. The pendulum may have swung too far in the individualistic direction in many Western cultures.

People in all cultures tend to behave in ways that favor their cultural group, to feel proud of their cultural group, and to feel less positive toward other cultural groups (Berger & Miller, 2021). Global interdependence is no longer a matter of belief or choice. It is an inescapable reality. Adolescents and emerging adults are not just citizens of the United States or Canada. They are citizens of the world, a world that has become increasingly interactive. By understanding the behavior and values of cultures around the world, the hope is that we can learn to interact more effectively with each other and make this planet a more hospitable, peaceful place to live.

Chimney Red/Photodisc/Getty Images

culture The behavior, patterns, beliefs, and all other products of a particular group of people that are passed on from generation to generation.

ethnocentrism A tendency to favor one's own group over other groups.

cross-cultural studies Studies that compare a culture with one or more other cultures. Such studies provide information about the degree to which development in adolescents and emerging adults is similar, or universal, across cultures, or about the degree to which it is culture-specific.

CROSS-CULTURAL COMPARISONS

Cross-cultural studies, which involve comparing a culture with one or more other cultures, provide information about other cultures and the role of culture in development (Kallschmidt & others, 2021). Such comparisons indicate the degree to which adolescents' and emerging adults' development is similar, or universal, across cultures, or the degree to which it is culture-specific (Xiong & others, 2020). In terms of gender, for example, the experiences of male and female adolescents continue to be worlds apart in some cultures (UNICEF, 2021). In many countries, males have far greater access to educational opportunities, more freedom to pursue a variety of careers, and fewer restrictions on sexual activity than do females (UNICEF, 2021).

We have discussed the higher math and science achievement of Asian adolescents in comparison with U.S. adolescents (Desilver, 2017). One study revealed that from the beginning of seventh grade through the end of eighth grade, U.S. adolescents valued academics less and became less motivated to do well in school (Wang & Pomerantz, 2009). By contrast, the value placed on academics by Chinese adolescents did not change across this time frame and their academic motivation was sustained.

Individualism and Collectivism   In cross-cultural research, the search for basic traits has often focused on the dichotomy between individualism and collectivism (Triandis, 2007):

- **Individualism** involves giving priority to personal goals rather than to group goals; it emphasizes values that serve the self, such as feeling good, personal distinction and achievement, and independence.
- **Collectivism** emphasizes values that serve the group by subordinating personal goals to preserve group integrity, interdependence of the members, and harmonious relationships.

Figure 1 summarizes some of the main characteristics of individualistic and collectivistic cultures. Many Western cultures, such as the United States, Canada, Great Britain, and the Netherlands, are described as individualistic; many Eastern cultures, such as China, Japan, India, and Thailand, are described as collectivistic (Bhawuk & Bhawuk, 2021). The Mexican

Cross-cultural studies compare a culture with one or more other cultures. Shown here is a !Kung teenage girl. Delinquency and violence occur much less frequently in the African culture of !Kung than in most cultures around the world.
Africanway/Getty Images

individualism Emphasizes values that serve the self and gives priority to personal goals rather than group goals.

collectivism Emphasizes values that serve the group by subordinating personal goals to preserve group integrity.

Individualistic	Collectivistic
Focuses on individual	Focuses on groups
Self is determined by personal traits independent of groups; self is stable across contexts	Self is defined by in-group terms; self can change with context
Private self is more important	Public self is most important
Personal achievement, competition, power are important	Achievement is for the benefit of the in-group; cooperation is stressed
Cognitive dissonance is frequent	Cognitive dissonance is infrequent
Emotions (such as anger) are self-focused	Emotions (such as anger) are often relationship based
People who are the most liked are self-assured	People who are the most liked are modest, self-effacing
Values: pleasure, achievement, competition, freedom	Values: security, obedience, in-group harmony, personalized relationships
Many casual relationships	Few, close relationships
Save own face	Save own and other's face
Independent behaviors: swimming, sleeping alone in room, privacy	Interdependent behaviors: co-bathing, co-sleeping
Relatively rare mother-child physical contact	Frequent mother-child physical contact (such as hugging, holding)

FIGURE 1
CHARACTERISTICS OF INDIVIDUALISTIC AND COLLECTIVISTIC CULTURES

culture also is considered collectivistic. A study across 62 countries found that reported aggressive behavior among fourth- and eighth-graders was higher in individualistic cultures than in collectivistic cultures (Bergmuller, 2013). In addition, a recent study indicated that mask use during the COVID-19 pandemic was higher in collectivist countries than individualist countries (Lu, Jin, & English, 2021).

The values emphasized within a culture can shift over time. In a study conducted from 1970 to 2008 found that although China still is characterized by collectivistic values, Chinese people are increasingly using words that index individualistic values (Zeng & Greenfield, 2015). Likewise, a recent research review concluded that individualism is rising in Japan (Ogihara, 2017). These increases in individualism in Japan include stronger individualist values and standards in the workplace and schools, parents giving more individualistic names to their children, and more frequent appearance of words such as "individual" and "uniqueness" in the media.

Further, subcultures within a culture may differ in their emphasis on collectivism versus individualism. A recent study of African American and non-Latinx white children and adolescents found that African American children had higher levels of individualism (Smith & others, 2019). Also in this study, adolescents with collectivist values engaged in less delinquent problems while those with individualist values showed less prosocial behavior and had more conduct issues. The higher delinquency rate and lower prosocial rate among individual African American children and adolescents in this study could well be due to contextual variations reflecting lack of resources.

Researchers have found that self-conceptions are related to culture (Park, Norasakkunkit, & Kashima, 2017). In one study, American and Chinese college students completed 20 sentences beginning with "I am" (Trafimow, Triandis, & Goto, 1991). As indicated in Figure 2, the American college students were more likely than the Chinese students to describe themselves in terms of personal traits ("I am assertive"), whereas the Chinese students were more likely than the American students to identify themselves by their group affiliations ("I am a member of the math club"). However, one study found that from 1990 to 2007, Chinese 18- to 65-year-olds increasingly have included more individualistic characteristics in their descriptions of what constitutes happiness and well-being (Steele & Lynch, 2013).

Human beings have always lived in groups, whether large or small, and have always needed one another for survival. Critics of the Western notion of psychology argue that the Western emphasis on individualism may undermine our basic species need for relatedness (Grant, 2017). Some social scientists argue that many problems in Western societies are intensified by the cultural emphasis on individualism (Ibrahim, 2021). Compared with collectivistic cultures, individualistic cultures have higher rates of suicide, drug abuse, crime, teenage pregnancy, divorce, child abuse, and mental disorders.

One analysis proposed four values that reflect the beliefs of parents in individualistic cultures about what is required for children's and adolescents' effective development of autonomy: (1) *personal choice;* (2) *intrinsic motivation;* (3) *self-esteem;* and (4) *self-maximization,* which consists of achieving one's full potential (Tamis-LeMonda & others, 2008). The analysis also proposed that parents in collectivistic cultures emphasize three values that will help their children and adolescents become contributing members of society: (1) *connectedness to the family and other close relationships;* (2) *orientation to the larger group;* and (3) *respect and obedience.*

Critics of the dichotomy between individualistic and collectivistic cultures argue that these terms are too broad and simplistic, especially with the increased globalization in recent decades (Kagitcibasi, 2007). Regardless of their cultural background, people need both a positive sense of self and connectedness to others to develop fully as human beings. Carolyn Tamis-LeMonda and her colleagues (2008) emphasize that in many families children and adolescents are not reared in environments that uniformly endorse individualistic or collectivistic values, thoughts, and actions. Rather, in many families, children are "expected to be quiet, assertive, respectful, curious, humble, self-assured, independent, dependent, affectionate, or reserved depending on the situation, people present, children's age, and social-political and economic circles." Nonetheless, researchers continue to find differences between individualistic and collectivistic cultures in a number of areas (Li, Wright, & Rollet, 2021; Masuda & others, 2020; Sharma, Shaligram, & Yoon, 2020).

How Adolescents Around the World Spend Their Time Do adolescents around the world spend their time in ways similar to U.S. adolescents? Researchers have found considerable variation across different countries For example, U.S. adolescents spend more

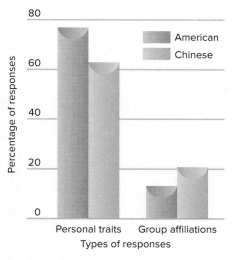

FIGURE 2

AMERICAN AND CHINESE SELF-CONCEPTIONS. College students from the United States and China completed 20 "I am _____" sentences. Both groups filled in personal traits more than group affiliations, but the Chinese students were more likely than the American students to identify themselves with group affiliations.

Activity	NonIndustrial, Unschooled Populations	POSTINDUSTRIAL, SCHOOLED POPULATIONS		
		United States	Europe	East Asia
Household labor	5 to 9 hours	20 to 40 minutes	20 to 40 minutes	10 to 20 minutes
Paid labor	0.5 to 8 hours	40 to 60 minutes	10 to 20 minutes	0 to 10 minutes
Schoolwork	—	3.0 to 4.5 hours	4.0 to 5.5 hours	5.5 to 7.5 hours
Total work time	6 to 9 hours	4 to 6 hours	4.5 to 6.5 hours	6 to 8 hours
TV viewing	*insufficient data*	1.5 to 2.5 hours	1.5 to 2.5 hours	1.5 to 2.5 hours
Talking	*insufficient data*	2 to 3 hours	*insufficient data*	45 to 60 minutes
Sports	*insufficient data*	30 to 60 minutes	20 to 80 minutes	0 to 20 minutes
Structured voluntary activities	*insufficient data*	10 to 20 minutes	10 to 20 minutes	0 to 10 minutes
Total free time	4 to 7 hours	6.5 to 8.0 hours	5.5 to 7.5 hours	4.0 to 5.5 hours

Note: The estimates in the table are averaged across a 7-day week, including weekdays and weekends. Time spent in maintenance activities like eating, personal care, and sleeping is not included. The data for nonindustrial, unschooled populations come primarily from rural peasant populations in developing countries.

FIGURE 3
AVERAGE DAILY TIME USE OF ADOLESCENTS IN DIFFERENT REGIONS OF THE WORLD

developmental connection

Education

Recent international comparisons indicate that the highest achievement test scores in math, science, and reading are held by students in Asian countries. Connect to "Achievement, Work, and Careers."

How do U.S. adolescents spend their time differently from European and East Asian adolescents?
Iakov Filimonov/Shutterstock

time in paid work than do their counterparts in most developed countries. Adolescent males in developing countries often spend more time in paid work than do adolescent females, who spend more time in unpaid household labor.

Reed Larson and Suman Verma (Larson, 2001; Larson & Verma, 1999) examined how adolescents spend their time in work, play, and developmental activities such as school. Figure 3 summarizes the average daily time spent in various activities by adolescents in different regions of the world (Larson & Verma, 1999). Note that U.S. adolescents spend about 40 percent less time on schoolwork than East Asian adolescents do.

The researchers found that U.S. adolescents had more discretionary time (free time) than adolescents in other industrialized countries. In the Larson and Verma (1999) study, about 40 to 50 percent of U.S. adolescents' waking hours (not counting summer vacations) was spent in discretionary activities, compared with 25 to 35 percent in East Asia and 35 to 45 percent in Europe. Whether this additional discretionary time is a liability or an asset for U.S. adolescents, of course, depends on how they use it.

The largest amounts of U.S. adolescents' free time were spent using the media and engaging in unstructured leisure activities, often with friends. We further explore adolescents' media use later in this chapter. U.S. adolescents spent more time in voluntary structured activities—such as sports, hobbies, and organizations—than East Asian adolescents did.

According to Reed Larson and his colleagues (Larson, 2001, 2008, 2014, 2020; Larson, Walker, & McGovern, 2020), U.S. adolescents may have more unstructured time than is suitable for optimal development. When adolescents are allowed to choose what to do with their time, they typically engage in unchallenging activities such as hanging out and watching TV (Larson, 2020; Larson, Walker, & McGovern, 2020). Although relaxation and social interaction are important aspects of adolescence, it seems unlikely that spending large numbers of hours per week in unchallenging activities fosters development. Structured voluntary activities may provide more promise for adolescent development than does unstructured time, especially if adults give responsibility to adolescents, challenge them, and provide competent guidance in these activities (Larson, 2020; Larson, Walker, & McGovern, 2020).

RITES OF PASSAGE

Rites of passage are ceremonies or rituals that mark an individual's transition from one status to another, such as the entry into adulthood. Some societies have elaborate rites of passage that signal the adolescent's transition to adulthood; others do not (Ember & Ember, 2019). In some non-technological cultures, rites of passage are the avenue through which adolescents gain access to sacred adult practices, responsibilities, knowledge, and sexuality. These rites often involve dramatic ceremonies intended to facilitate the adolescent's separation from the immediate family, especially boys from the mother. The transformation usually is characterized by some form of ritual death and rebirth, or by means of contact with the spiritual world. Bonds are forged between the adolescent and the adult instructors through shared rituals, hazards, and secrets to allow the adolescent to enter the adult world. This kind of ritual provides a forceful and discontinuous entry into the adult world at a time when the adolescent is perceived to be ready for the change.

Africa, especially sub-Saharan Africa, has been the location of many rites of passage for adolescents (Ember & Ember, 2019). Under the influence of Western culture, many of these rites are disappearing today, although some vestiges remain. In locations where formal education is not readily available, rites of passage are still prevalent.

Carol Markstrom (2010) studied coming-of-age ceremonies among Native American girls. She observed that many Native American tribes consider the transition from childhood to adulthood as a pivotal and possibly vulnerable time and have created coming-of-age rituals to support traditional values. She emphasizes that these rituals are often a positive aspect of life in Native American tribes today as their youth face challenges of the modern world such as substance abuse, suicide, and dropping out of school (Markstrom, 2010).

Western industrialized countries are notable for their lack of formal rites of passage that mark the transition from adolescence to adulthood. Some religious and social groups, however, have initiation ceremonies that indicate an advance in maturity—the Jewish bat mitzvah and bar mitzvah, Catholic and Protestant confirmations, and social debuts, for example. School graduation ceremonies come the closest to being culture-wide rites of passage in the United States. The high school graduation ceremony has become nearly universal for middle-SES adolescents and increasing numbers of adolescents from low-income backgrounds (National Center for Education Statistics, 2020). Nonetheless, high school graduation does not result in universal changes—many high school graduates continue to live with their parents, to be economically dependent on them, and to be undecided about questions of career and lifestyle. Another rite of passage for increasing numbers of American adolescents is sexual intercourse. By age 20, almost 80 percent of American adolescents have had sexual intercourse (Martinez & Abma, 2020).

The absence of clear-cut rites of passage makes the attainment of adult status so ambiguous that many individuals are unsure whether they have reached it or not. In Texas, for example, the legal age for beginning employment is 15, but many younger adolescents and even children are employed, especially Mexican immigrants. The legal age for driving is 16, but when emergency need is demonstrated, a driver's license can be obtained at age 15, and some parents might not allow their son or daughter to obtain a driver's license even at age 16, believing that they are too young for this responsibility. In sum, exactly when adolescents become adults in the United States has not been as clearly delineated as it has in cultures where rites of passage are universal.

These Congolese Kota boys painted their faces as part of a rite of passage to adulthood. *What rites of passage do American adolescents have?*
Eddie Gerald/Alamy Stock Photo

The Apache Native Americans of the American Southwest celebrate a girl's entrance into puberty with a four-day ritual that includes special dress, day-long activities, and solemn spiritual ceremonies.
RGB Ventures/SuperStock/Alamy stock Photo

Maddie Miller, 13, sharing a prayer with her father, studied for a year to prepare for bat mitzvah.
Sylvia Plachy/Redux Pictures

rites of passage Ceremonies or rituals that mark an individual's transition from one status to another, such as the entry into adulthood.

Review Connect Reflect

LG1 Discuss the role of culture in the development of adolescents and emerging adults.

Review
- What is culture? What is the relevance of culture in the study of development in adolescence and emerging adulthood?
- What are cross-cultural comparisons? What characterizes individualistic and collectivistic cultures? How do cultures vary in the time adolescents spend in different activities?
- What are rites of passage? How do cultures vary in terms of rites of passage?

Connect
- In this section you learned that U.S. adolescents have far more discretionary time than do their European or Asian counterparts. Relate this fact to our earlier discussions of expectations.

Reflect *Your Own Personal Journey of Life*
- Have you experienced a rite of passage in your life? If so, what was it? Was it a positive or negative influence on your development? Is there a rite of passage you did not experience that you wish you had?

---

2 Socioeconomic Status and Poverty

LG2 Describe how socioeconomic status and poverty are related to adolescent development.

| What Is Socioeconomic Status? | Socioeconomic Variations in Families, Neighborhoods, and Schools | Poverty |

Many subcultures exist within countries. For example, the values and attitudes of adolescents growing up in an urban neighborhood with a high poverty rate or in rural Appalachia may differ considerably from those of adolescents growing up in a wealthy suburb. A key difference between such subcultures is socioeconomic status.

WHAT IS SOCIOECONOMIC STATUS?

Socioeconomic status (SES) refers to a grouping of people with similar occupational, educational, and economic characteristics. Individuals with different SES have varying levels of power, influence, and prestige. In this chapter, for example, we evaluate what it is like for an adolescent to grow up in poverty.

Socioeconomic status carries with it certain inequalities. Generally, members of a society have (1) occupations that vary in prestige, with some individuals having more access than others to higher-status occupations; (2) different levels of educational attainment, with some individuals having more access than others to better education; (3) different economic resources; and (4) different levels of power to influence a community's institutions. These differences in the ability to control resources and to participate in society's rewards produce unequal opportunities for adolescents (van der Hoeven, 2021).

The number of visibly different socioeconomic statuses depends on the community's size and complexity. In most investigators' descriptions of SES, two categories, low and middle, are used, although as many as five categories have been delineated. Sometimes low SES is described as low-income, working class, or blue-collar; sometimes the middle category is described as middle-income, managerial, or white-collar. Examples of low-SES occupations are factory worker, manual laborer, and maintenance worker. Examples of middle-SES occupations include salesperson, manager, and professional (doctor, lawyer, teacher, accountant, and so on). Professionals at the pinnacle of their field, high-level corporate executives, political leaders, and wealthy individuals are among those in the upper-SES category.

socioeconomic status (SES) Refers to a grouping of people with similar occupational, educational, and economic characteristics.

SOCIOECONOMIC VARIATIONS IN FAMILIES, NEIGHBORHOODS, AND SCHOOLS

The families, schools, and neighborhoods of adolescents have socioeconomic characteristics (Reed & others, 2020). Some adolescents have parents who possess a great deal of money and who work in prestigious occupations. These adolescents live in attractive houses and neighborhoods, enjoy vacations abroad and at high-quality camps, and attend schools where the mix of students is primarily from middle- and upper-SES backgrounds. Other adolescents have parents who do not have very much money and who work in less prestigious occupations. These adolescents live in deteriorating houses and neighborhoods, rarely go on vacations, and attend schools where the students are mainly from lower-SES backgrounds. However, many low-SES parents may have middle-SES values, such as strongly endorsing the importance of education in their children's and adolescents' development. Thus, SES alone may not always provide an accurate portrait of a family's values, goals, and other characteristics. Such variations in neighborhood settings can influence adolescents' adjustment and achievement (Kim & others, 2021). In a recent research review, it was concluded that increases in family income for children in poverty were associated with increased achievement in middle school as well as greater educational attainment in adolescence and emerging adulthood (Duncan, Magnuson, & Votruba-Drzal, 2017).

In the United States and most Western cultures, differences have been found in child rearing among different SES groups (Hoff, Laursen, & Tardif, 2002, p. 246):

- Lower-SES parents (1) "are more concerned that their children conform to society's expectations," (2) "create a home atmosphere in which it is clear that parents have authority over children," (3) use physical punishment more in disciplining their children, and (4) are more directive and less conversational with their children.

- Higher-SES parents (1) "are more concerned with developing children's initiative" and delay of gratification, (2) "create a home atmosphere in which children are more nearly equal participants and in which rules are discussed as opposed to being laid down" in an authoritarian manner, (3) are less likely to use physical punishment, and (4) "are less directive and more conversational" with their children.

Children and adolescents from low-SES backgrounds are at risk for experiencing low achievement and occupational attainment in adulthood, as well as health difficulties and emotional problems (Ni, Goodale, & Huo, 2020). A recent study found that lower SES was associated with less cortical surface in the brain of adolescents as well as having less effective working memory (Judd & others, 2020). In this study, the SES factor that was especially responsible for the lower level of brain development of adolescents was less parental education. Further, a recent Chinese study found low family SES was linked to children's lower academic achievement, with the strongest influence being less parental involvement in their children's schooling (Zhang & others, 2020). In a recent Swedish study, high-SES individuals were more likely than low-SES individuals to have completed 12 or more years of school by 20 years of age (Lindberg & others, 2021) In addition, a recent meta-analysis concluded that low SES is a meaningful contributor to reduced cognitive ability and achievement (Korous & others, 2021). Behavioral issues such as smoking, depression, and juvenile delinquency, as well as physical illnesses, are more prevalent among low-SES adolescents than among economically advantaged adolescents (American Psychological Association, 2020). A recent Japanese study indicated that low-SES adolescents had more health-related problems than adolescents in middle- or high-SES families (Okamoto, 2021). And a recent Australian study revealed that children and adolescents from lower-SES backgrounds were less likely achieve a healthy physical fitness level than their higher-SES counterparts (Peralta & others, 2019).

SES variations in childhood and adolescence also are linked to adult outcomes. For example, a longitudinal study indicated that lower SES in childhood was associated with lower cognitive function and more cognitive decline in middle and late adulthood (Liu & Lachman, 2019). Further, in a

What are some of the challenges for adolescents growing up in a low-income community?
Design Pics Inc/Alamy Stock Photo

developmental **connection**

Education

Many adolescents in low-SES neighborhoods face problems that present barriers to their learning. Connect to "Schools."

longitudinal study, low SES in adolescence was linked to having a higher level of depressive symptoms at age 54 for females (Pino & others, 2018).

Although psychological problems are more prevalent among adolescents from low-SES backgrounds, these adolescents vary considerably in intellectual and psychological functioning. For example, a sizable proportion of adolescents from low-SES backgrounds perform well in school; in fact, some perform better than many middle-SES students. When adolescents from low-SES backgrounds are achieving well in school, it is not unusual to find a parent or parents making special sacrifices to provide the necessary living conditions and support to enhance school success.

Schools in low-SES neighborhoods tend to have fewer resources than do schools in higher-SES neighborhoods. The schools in the low-SES areas also are likely to have more students with lower achievement test scores, lower rates of graduation, and fewer opportunities to attend college (Gollnick & Chinn, 2021). In some instances, however, federal aid to schools has provided a context for enhanced learning in low-income areas.

So far we have focused on the challenges that many adolescents from low-income families face. However, research by Suniya Luthar and her colleagues (Ansary, McMahon, & Luthar, 2012, 2017; Luthar, Crossman, & Small, 2015; Luthar & others, 2021) indicates that adolescents from affluent families also face challenges. Excessive pressure to excel, especially in affluent contexts, has been listed in the top four high-risk factors that are linked to adolescents' mental health problems, with the other three being poverty, trauma, and discrimination (Luthar, Kumar, & Zilmer, 2020). Adolescents in the affluent families that Luthar has studied are vulnerable to high rates of substance abuse. In addition, her research has found that adolescent males from such families have more adjustment difficulties than do females, with affluent female adolescents being more likely to attain superior levels of academic success. Luthar and her colleagues (Luthar, Barkin, & Crossman, 2013) also have found that youth in upwardly mobile, upper-middle SES families are more likely to engage in drug use and have more internalized and externalized problems than their counterparts in middle-SES families.

In recent research, Luthar and her colleagues (Luthar, Kumar, & Zillmer, 2020) have studied the risk factors and outcomes for adolescents who attend high-achieving schools. Adolescents in high-achieving schools are at risk mainly because of strong pressures to achieve. A recent study of adolescents in high-achieving schools found a link between students' engagement in social comparison and increases in their internalizing symptoms (Luthar & others, 2021).

POVERTY

The world is a dangerous and unwelcoming place for too many U.S. youth, especially those whose families, neighborhoods, and schools are low-income (Wilmers, 2020). Some adolescents are resilient and cope with the challenges of poverty without major setbacks, but many struggle unsuccessfully. Each adolescent who has grown up in poverty and reaches adulthood unhealthy, unskilled, or alienated keeps the United States from being as competent and productive as it could be.

What Is Poverty Like?   Poverty is defined by economic hardship, and its most common marker is the federal poverty threshold. The poverty threshold was originally based on the estimated cost of food (a basic diet) multiplied by 3. This federal poverty marker is adjusted annually for family size and inflation.

Children and youth who grow up in poverty represent a special concern. In 2018, 16.2 percent of U.S. children under 18 years of age were living in families with incomes below the poverty line, an increase from 2001 (16 percent) but a decrease from a peak of 23 percent in 1993 and also down from 19.7 percent in 2015 (Children's Defense Fund, 2020).

Poverty in the United States is demarcated along ethnic and family structure lines. In 2018, African American (30.1 percent, down from 36 percent in 2015) and Latinx (23.7 percent, down from 30 percent in 2015) families with children had especially high rates of poverty (Children's Defense Fund, 2020). In 2018, 8.9 percent of non-Latinx white U.S. children and adolescents were living below the poverty line. The U.S. figure of 16.2 percent of children and adolescents living in poverty is much higher than the rates in other developed countries. For example, Canada has a child and adolescent poverty rate of 9 percent and Sweden has a rate of 2 percent. And compared with non-Latinx white children and adolescents, ethnic minority children and adolescents are more likely to experience persistent poverty over many years and to live in isolated poor neighborhoods where social supports are minimal and threats to positive development abundant (Jarrett, 1995) (see Figure 4).

Living in poverty has many negative psychological effects on children and adolescents (DeJoseph & others, 2021; Suter, Beycan, & Ravazzini, 2020). First, the poor are often powerless. In the workplace, they rarely are the decision makers. Rules are handed down to them in an authoritarian manner. Second, the poor are often vulnerable to disaster. They are not likely to be given notice before they are laid off from work and usually do not have financial resources to fall back on when problems arise. Third, their range of alternatives is often restricted. Only a limited number of jobs are open to them. Even when alternatives are available, the poor might not know about them or be prepared to make a wise decision.

One research review concluded that compared with their economically more advantaged counterparts, poor children and adolescents experience widespread environmental inequities that include the following (Evans, 2004):

- They experience more conflict, violence, instability, and chaos in their homes (Emery & Laumann-Billings, 1998).

- They get less social support, and their parents are less responsive and more authoritarian (Bo, 1994).

- They watch more TV and have less access to books and computers (Bradley & others, 2001).

- Their schools and child-care facilities are inferior, and parents monitor their school activities less (Benveniste, Carnoy, & Rothstein, 2003).

- The air they breathe and the water they drink are more polluted, and their homes are more crowded and noisy (Myers, Baer, & Choi, 1996).

- They live in more dangerous and physically deteriorating neighborhoods with less adequate municipal services (Brody & others, 2001).

At a number of places in this edition, the negative aspects and outcomes of poverty for adolescents are highlighted. Poverty is identified as a risk factor for sexual problems. Reductions of income for divorced mothers can lead to poverty and its negative consequences for adolescents. Numerous school-related risks and problems are associated with poverty, including inferior schools, increased risk of dropping out of school, and lower probability of going to college. Other poverty-related negative outcomes discussed in other chapters include lower achievement expectations, decreased achievement, lack of access to jobs, entry into less desirable careers, and higher rates of delinquency. For example, a recent study of more than 10,000 children and adolescents found that family environment characterized by poverty and child maltreatment was linked to entering the juvenile justice system in adolescence (Vidal & others, 2017).

When poverty is persistent and long-standing, it can have especially damaging effects on children and adolescents (Suter, Beycan, & Ravazzini, 2020). A recent study found that 12- to 19-year-olds' perceived well-being was lowest when they had lived in poverty from birth to 2 years of age (compared with ages 3 to 5, 6 to 8, and 9 to 11) and that each additional year lived in poverty was associated with even lower perceived well-being (Gariepy & others, 2017). Another study revealed that the more years 7- to 13-year-olds spent living in poverty, the higher were their physiological indices of stress (Evans & Kim, 2007). Because of advances in their cognitive growth, adolescents living in poverty conditions likely are more aware of their social disadvantage and the associated stigma than are children (McLoyd & others, 2009). Combined with the increased sensitivity to peers in adolescence, such awareness may cause them to try to hide their poverty status as much as possible from others. Further, a recent study indicated that higher poverty levels from 0 to 9 years of age were associated with reduced inhibitory control in emerging adulthood (23 to 25 years of age) (Evans, Farah,

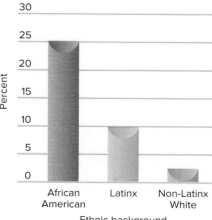

FIGURE 4

LIVING IN DISTRESSED NEIGHBORHOODS.

Note: A distressed neighborhood is defined by high levels (at least one standard deviation above the mean) of (1) poverty, (2) female-headed families, (3) high school dropouts, (4) unemployment, and (5) reliance on welfare.

developmental **connection**

Achievement

Many adolescents who have grown up in low-income or poverty conditions face challenging circumstances in seeking upward mobility in their careers. Connect to "Achievement, Work, and Careers."

What are some of the outcomes for adolescents growing up in poverty?
MANDEL NGAN/AFP/Getty Images

& Hackman, 2021). Also contributing to this link was a lower level of maternal responsiveness during adolescence. In addition, a recent study found that higher poverty levels from 0 to 9 years of age were linked to the following developmental trajectories from 9 to 24 years of age: (1) higher levels of internalizing problems that diminished more slowly with maturation; (2) higher levels of externalizing problems that increased faster over time; (3) less task persistence; and (4) higher levels of chronic stress that increased faster over time (Evans & De France, 2021).

A special concern is the high percentage of children and adolescents growing up in mother-headed households in poverty. In 2019, 34 percent of single-mother families (down from 39.6 percent in 2013) lived in poverty, nearly six times the poverty rate for married-couple families (6 percent) (U.S. Census Bureau, 2019). Vonnie McLoyd (1998) concluded that because poor, single mothers are more distressed than their middle-SES counterparts are, they tend to show lower levels of support, nurturance, and involvement with their children. Among the reasons for the high poverty rate of single mothers are women's lower pay, infrequent awarding of alimony payments, and poorly enforced child support from fathers (Schaefer, 2015).

The term **feminization of poverty** refers to the fact that far more women than men live in poverty (Zhang & Gordon, 2020). Women's lower incomes, divorce, and judicial resolution of divorce cases that leaves women with less money than they and their children need to adequately function, are the likely causes of the feminization of poverty.

Despite the extensive challenges that low-income families face, many low-income parents guide their children to become resilient and flourish (Masten, 2021b; Masten & others, 2021). They rear children and adolescents who establish positive friendships; maintain good relationships with parents, teachers, and other adults; make good grades in school; go to college; and pursue a positive career path (Wilson-Simmons, Jiang, & Aratani, 2017).

Countering Negative Effects of Low Income and Poverty

One trend in antipoverty programs is to conduct two-generation interventions (Aspen Institute, 2020). This involves providing services for children and adolescents (such as educational child care, preschool education, or after-school programs for youth) as well as services for parents (such as adult education, literacy training, and job skills training).

Schools and school programs are the focus of some poverty interventions (Nastasi & Naser, 2021; Teja & Worrell, 2021). In an intervention with first-generation immigrant children attending high-poverty schools, the City Connects program was successful in improving children's achievement at the end of elementary school (Dearing & others, 2016). The program is directed by a full-time school counselor or social worker in each school. Annual reviews of children's needs are conducted during the first several months of the school year. Then site coordinators and teachers collaborate to develop a student support plan that might include an after-school program, tutoring, mentoring, or family counseling. For children identified as having intense needs (about 8 to 10 percent of students), a wider team of professionals becomes involved, possibly including school psychologists, principals, nurses, and/or community agency staff, to create additional supports.

Researchers assessed the effects of another school-related intervention called the Positive Action program in 14 urban, low-income Chicago schools across six years from grades 3 to 8 (Lewis & others, 2013). The Positive Action program is a K–12 curriculum that focuses on self-concept, self-control and responsibility, physical and mental health, honesty, getting along with others, and continually striving for self-improvement. The program includes teacher, counselor, family, and community training and activities to improve school-wide atmosphere. In comparison with control group schools that did not implement the Positive Action program, students in the program engaged in a lower rate of violence-related behavior and received fewer disciplinary referrals and suspensions from school.

In another study, more than 500 ninth- to twelfth-grade students living in low-income settings in Los Angeles were chosen through a random admissions lottery to attend high-performing public charter schools (Wong & others, 2014). Compared with a control group of students who did not have the opportunity to attend the high-performing charter schools, the students attending the charter schools had better scores on math and English standardized tests and were less likely to drop out of school.

What other programs are benefiting adolescents living in poverty? See the *Connecting with Health and Well-Being* interlude.

developmental **connection**

Social Policy

Reducing the poverty level and improving the lives of children and adolescents living in poverty are important goals of U.S. social policy. Connect to "Introduction."

feminization of poverty Term reflecting the fact that far more women than men live in poverty. Likely causes include women's lower incomes, divorce, and the resolution of divorce cases by the judicial system, which leaves women with less money than they and their children need to function adequately.

How Do the Eisenhower Quantum Opportunities and El Puente Programs Help Youth in Poverty?

Eisenhower Quantum Opportunities is a program designed to provide education, service, developmental activities, and financial incentives to disadvantaged youth from ninth grade through high school graduation (Eisenhower Foundation, 2018). Each year students are given 180 hours of academic support (adult tutoring, peer tutoring, homework assistance, and other supportive academic activities); 50 hours of service experiences (participation in community service projects, civic activities, volunteering, and other service activities); and 180 hours of development activities (acquiring life/family skills, planning for college and jobs). Services are administered by trained case managers after school. Also, an important aspect of the intervention is "deep mentoring" that involves mentors developing long-term relationships with disadvantaged students across the four years of the program.

The Eisenhower program was implemented from 2009 to 2014 in five U.S. sites (Albuquerque, Baltimore, Boston, Milwaukee, and New Bedford, Mass.) and outcomes for the program were assessed (Curtis & Bandy, 2015, 2016). The program was successful in improving disadvantaged students' performance (compared with the performance of control group students who did not receive the intervention) in the following areas: high school senior grade point average, on-time high school graduation, college acceptance, college enrollment, and staying in college for at least one year.

Another effort to improve the lives of adolescents living in poverty is the El Puente program, which is primarily aimed at Latinx adolescents living in low-SES areas. El Puente ("the bridge") was opened in New York City in 1983 because of community dissatisfaction with the health, educational, and social services youth were receiving (Simons, Finlay, & Yang, 1991). El Puente emphasizes five areas of youth development: health, education, achievement, personal growth, and social growth.

El Puente is located in a former Roman Catholic church building on the south side of Williamsburg in Brooklyn, a neighborhood made up primarily of low-income Latinx families, many of which are far below the poverty threshold. Sixty-five percent of the residents receive some form of public assistance. The neighborhood has the highest school dropout rate for Latinxs in New York City and the highest felony rate for adolescents in Brooklyn.

When the youth (12 through 21 years of age) first enroll in El Puente, they meet with counselors and develop a four-month plan that

Adolescents participating in the Quantum Opportunities Program at Carver Center in Washington, D.C. *What are characteristics of the Quantum Opportunities Program?*
Zuma Press Inc/Alamy Stock Photo

includes the programs they are interested in joining. At the end of four months, youth and staff develop a plan for continued participation. Twenty-six bilingual classes are offered in subjects such as music, theater, photography, and dance. In addition, a medical and fitness center, a GED night school, and mental health and social services centers are part of El Puente.

How might the lessons learned from these successful programs be applied and studied in other cultural situations in which adolescents live in poverty?

Review Connect Reflect

LG2 Describe how socioeconomic status and poverty are related to adolescent development.

Review
- What is socioeconomic status?
- What are some socioeconomic variations in families, neighborhoods, and schools?
- How is poverty related to adolescent development?

Connect
- How does the idea of the family as a system connect with the experience of adolescents living in poverty?

Reflect *Your Own Personal Journey of Life*
- What was the socioeconomic status of your family as you were growing up? How did it affect your development?

---

3 Ethnicity

LG3 Summarize how ethnicity is involved in the development of adolescents and emerging adults.

| Immigration | Adolescence and Emerging Adulthood: A Special Juncture for Ethnic Minority Individuals | Ethnicity Issues |

Consider the flowers of a garden: though differing in kind, color, form, and shape, yet, inasmuch as they are refreshed by the waters of one spring, revived by the breath of one wind, invigorated by the rays of one sun, this diversity increases their charm and adds to their beauty.... How unpleasing to the eye if all the flowers and plants, the leaves and blossoms, the fruits, the branches, and the trees of that garden were all the same shape and color! Diversity of hues, form, and shape enriches and adorns the garden and heightens its effect.

—Abdu'l Baha
Persian Baha'i Religious Leader, 19th/20th Century

Adolescents and emerging adults live in a world that has been made smaller and more interactive by dramatic improvements in travel and communication. U.S. adolescents and emerging adults also live in a world that is far more diverse in its ethnic makeup than it was in past decades: Ninety-three languages are spoken in Los Angeles alone!

Ethnicity is based on cultural heritage, nationality characteristics, race, religion, and language. A striking feature of the United States today is the increasing ethnic diversity of America's adolescents and emerging adults (Banks, 2020; Cushner, McClelland, & Safford, 2022). In this section, we study African American adolescents, Latinx adolescents, Asian American adolescents, and Native American adolescents, and we explore the sociocultural issues involved in their development.

A special point needs to be made as we explore various aspects of ethnicity and adolescent development. For too long, researchers have looked at ethnic minorities from a deficit-based perspective that assumes adolescents who grow up within an ethnic minority culture are inherently challenged and overwhelmed by stressors, especially in the case of immigrant ethnic minority adolescents (Perrin & others, 2020). Contrary to these assumptions, researchers have shown that ethnic minority adolescents, including those who are immigrants, fare better than is often assumed (Marks, Ejesi, & Garcia Coll, 2014). These adolescents assume responsibilities for their family and help their parents adapt to their new society (Halgunseth, 2019).

IMMIGRATION

Immigrant families are those in which at least one of the parents is born outside the country of residence. Variations in immigrant families involve whether one or both parents are foreign-born, whether the child was born in the host country, and the ages at which immigration took place for both the parents and the children (Khoury & Hakim-Larson, 2021).

Relatively high rates of minority immigration have contributed to growth in the proportion of ethnic minorities in the U.S. population (Khoury & Hakim-Larson, 2021). In 2018, 50.3 percent of children 18 years of age and younger were non-Latinx white; by 2060, this figure is projected to decrease to 44 percent (Children's Defense Fund, 2020). In 2018 in the United States 25.5 percent were Latinx, but by 2060 that figure is projected to increase to 29 percent. Asian Americans are expected to be the fastest-growing ethnic group of children: In 2018, 5.1 percent were Asian American, and that figure is expected to grow to 9 percent in 2060. The percent of African American children is anticipated to decrease slightly from 2014 to 2060 (13.7 to 13 percent). In 2018, 4.3 percent of children 18 years of age and younger were multi-ethnic; this figure is projected to grow to 6 percent in 2060. This growth of ethnic minorities is expected to continue throughout the twenty-first century.

ethnicity A dimension of culture based on cultural heritage, national characteristics, race, religion, and language.

What are some of the circumstances immigrants face that challenge their adjustment? Immigrants often experience stressors uncommon to or less prominent among longtime residents, such as language barriers, dislocations and separations from support networks, the dual struggle to preserve identity and to acculturate, and changes in SES status (Sidhu & Adam, 2021; Valentin-Cortes & others, 2020). Many individuals in immigrant families are dealing with the problems associated with being undocumented (Stevens, 2020). Living in an undocumented family can affect children's and adolescents' developmental outcomes through parents being unwilling to sign up for services for which they are eligible, through conditions linked to low-wage work and lack of benefits, through stress, and through a lack of cognitive stimulation in the home (Mendez, Flores-Haro, & Zucker, 2020). In a recent study, immigrant children who were once separated from their parents had a lower level of literacy and a higher level of psychological problems than those who had migrated with their parents (Lu, He, & Brooks-Gunn, 2020). Also in this study, a protracted period of separation and prior undocumented status of parents further increased the children's disadvantages. Consequently, when work-

Latinx immigrants in the Rio Grande Valley, Texas. *What are some of the adaptations immigrants make?*
Allison Wright/Corbis Documentary/Getty Images

ing with adolescents and their immigrant families, counselors need to adapt intervention programs to optimize cultural sensitivity (Clauss-Ehlers & others, 2021; Romero & others, 2020).

The **immigrant paradox** notes that despite the number of barriers they experience, recent child and adolescent immigrants often engage in more adaptive and competent behavior than their non-immigrant peers and established child and adolescent immigrants from the same ethnic group whose families have been in the United States for several generations (Garcia-Coll & Marks, 2014). For example, children and adolescents in recently immigrated families are more likely to enroll in college and to be employed or in school, and they are less likely to have a criminal record as young adults than children and adolescents from non-immigrant families (Hofferth & Moon, 2016). And in a recent study, African American and Latinx children in recently immigrated families had better self-reported and parent-reported internalizing and externalizing outcomes than their same-ethnic-group peers and non-Latinx white native-born peers (Zhang, Bo, & Lu, 2021).

Parents and adolescents in immigrant families may be at different stages of *acculturation*, the process of adapting to the majority culture. The result may be conflict over cultural values (Wu & others, 2020). One study examined values in immigrant families (Vietnamese, Armenian, and Mexican) and non-immigrant families (African American and European American) (Phinney, 2006). In all groups, parents endorsed family obligations more than adolescents did, and the differences between generations generally increased as more time was spent in the United States. Recently Yoonsun Choi and her colleagues (Choi & others, 2020a, b, c) have conducted research with Filipino American and Korean American immigrant families and found the older generation is much more likely to hold on to distinctly traditional values and to be resistant to change that the younger generation. She also has discovered that Asian parents are perceived by their adolescents as placing too much emphasis on education.

In addition to the bicultural orientation involving an ethnic minority individual who lives in a non-Latinx white majority culture, a bicultural orientation also can consist of multi-ethnic individuals, such as an adolescent with an African American and a Latinx heritage or even a mixture of three or more ethnic/racial backgrounds. Research indicates that multi-ethnic/racial individuals often face more discrimination and social injustice, often being questioned about their ethnic/racial heritage as well as being more likely to engage in problem behaviors such as substance abuse and violence (Tan & others, 2019; Woo & others, 2020).

Although many ethnic/immigrant families adopt a bicultural orientation, parenting in many ethnic minority families also focuses on issues associated with promoting children's ethnic pride, knowledge of their ethnic group, and awareness of discrimination (Sladek & others, 2020). Researchers are increasingly finding that a positive ethnic identity is related to positive outcomes for ethnic minority adolescents (Umana-Taylor & others, 2020). In a recent study, Latinx youth showed enhanced resilience against discrimination encounters when they had more family ethnic socialization experiences and engaged in greater ethnic identity exploration and resolution (Martinez-Fuentes, Jager, & Umaña-Taylor, 2021).

Many of the families that have immigrated into the United States in recent decades, such as Mexican Americans and Asian Americans, come from collectivistic cultures in which family

developmental **connection**

Diversity

Projections indicate that in 2100 there will be more Latinx than non-Latinx white adolescents in the United States and more Asian American than African American adolescents in the United States. Connect to "Introduction."

Multi-ethnic/racial adolescents often face considerable discrimination.
Highwaystarz-Photography/Getty Images

immigrant paradox Observation that despite the barriers they encounter, recent child and adolescent immigrants often engage in more adaptive and competent behavior than their non-immigrant peers and established child and adolescent immigrants from the same ethnic group whose families have been in the United States for several generations.

Carola Suárez-Orozco, Immigration Studies Researcher and Professor

Carola Suárez-Orozco currently is Professor of Education and Co-Director of the Institute for Immigration, Globalization, and Education at UCLA. She previously was chair and Professor of Applied Psychology and Co-Director of Immigration Studies at New York University. Earlier in her career, Dr. Suárez-Orozco was co-director of the Harvard University Immigration Projects. She obtained her undergraduate degree (in development studies) from UCLA and her doctoral degree in clinical psychology from the California School of Professional Psychology, San Diego.

Dr. Suárez-Orozco has worked in both clinical and public school settings in California and Massachusetts. While at Harvard, she conducted a five-year longitudinal study of adaptation to U.S. schools and society among immigrant adolescents from Central America, China, and the Dominican Republic. She especially advocates more research on cultural and psychological factors involved in the adaptation of immigrant and ethnic minority youth. Dr. Suárez-Orozco recently served

Carola Suárez-Orozco, with her husband, Marcelo, who also studies the adaptation of immigrants.
Courtesy of Carola Suarez-Orozco and photographer Kris Snibbe, Harvard News Office

as Chair of the American Psychological Association Presidential Task Force on Immigration. One of her important accomplishments was the creation of the APA video on undocumented immigrant children.

---

developmental **connection**

Identity

Researchers are increasingly finding that a positive ethnic identity is linked to positive outcomes for ethnic minority adolescents. Connect to "The Self, Identity, Emotion, and Personality."

obligation and duty to one's family are strong. Family obligation and duty may take the form of assisting parents in their occupations and contributing to the family's welfare. In a recent study, a higher level of family obligation was linked to Latinx adolescents' higher academic achievement (Anguiano, 2018).

It is important to remember that there are variations in immigrant families' experiences and the degree to which their children and adolescents change as they are exposed to American culture. One study found that following their immigration, Mexican American adolescents spent less time with their family and identified less with family values (Updegraff & others, 2012). However, in this study teens with stronger family values in early adolescence were less likely to engage in risky behavior in late adolescence. Also, in a recent study of Mexican-origin adolescent girls with different cultural profiles, a strong positive profile (having a positive ethnic identity, experiencing strong familial ethnic socialization, being bilingual, and characterized as second generation) was linked to having higher self-esteem (Gonzales-Backen & others, 2017).

The ways in which ethnic minority families deal with stress depend on many factors (Anderson, Sladek, & Doane, 2020). Whether the parents are native-born or immigrants, how long the family has been in the United States, its socioeconomic status, its national origin, family values, and how competently parents rear their children and adolescents all make a difference (Gonzales & others, 2012). A recent study of Mexican-origin youth found that when adolescents reported a higher level of familism (giving priority to one's family), they engaged in lower levels of risk taking (Wheeler & others, 2017). Another study revealed that parents' education before migrating was strongly linked to their children's academic achievement (Pong & Landale, 2012).

The characteristics of the immigrant family's social context also influence its adaptation (Smith & others, 2020). What are the attitudes toward the family's ethnic group within its neighborhood or city? Can the family's children and adolescents attend good schools? Are there community groups that welcome people from the family's ethnic group? Do members of the family's ethnic group form community groups of their own?

In conclusion, some adolescents from immigrant families are well adjusted and doing well, some less so, depending on the characteristics of migration itself (including the nation of origin) and their families' circumstances in their new country (including their position in the socioeconomic and ethnic fabric of the community) (Stein & others, 2020). To read about the work of one individual who studies immigrant adolescents, see the *Connecting with Careers* profile.

ADOLESCENCE AND EMERGING ADULTHOOD: A SPECIAL JUNCTURE FOR ETHNIC MINORITY INDIVIDUALS

For ethnic minority individuals, adolescence and emerging adulthood often represent a special juncture in their development (Moses, Villodas, & Villodas, 2020; Umaña-Taylor & others, 2020). Although children are aware of some ethnic and cultural differences, most ethnic minority individuals first consciously confront their ethnicity in adolescence. In contrast with children, adolescents and emerging adults have the ability to interpret ethnic and cultural information, to reflect on the past, and to speculate about the future. As they mature cognitively, ethnic minority adolescents and emerging adults become acutely aware of how the majority non-Latinx white culture evaluates their ethnic group. One researcher commented that the young African American child may learn that black is beautiful but conclude as an adolescent that white is powerful (Semaj, 1985).

Ethnic minority youths' awareness of negative appraisals, conflicting values, and restricted occupational opportunities can influence their life choices and plans for the future. As one ethnic minority youth stated, "The future seems shut off, closed. Why dream? You can't reach your dreams. Why set goals? At least if you don't set any goals, you don't fail."

For many ethnic minority youth, a special concern is the lack of successful ethnic minority role models. The problem is especially acute for inner-city youth. Because of the lack of adult ethnic minority role models, some ethnic minority youth may conform to middle-SES, non-Latinx white values and identify with successful non-Latinx white role models. However, for many ethnic minority adolescents, their ethnicity and skin color limit their acceptance within the non-Latinx white culture. Thus, they face the difficult task of negotiating two value systems—that of their own ethnic group and that of the non-Latinx white society (Wu & others, 2020). Some adolescents reject the mainstream, forgoing the rewards controlled by non-Latinx white Americans; others adopt the values and standards of the majority non-Latinx

Margaret Beale Spencer, shown here (on the right) talking with adolescents, believes that adolescence is a critical juncture in the identity development of ethnic minority individuals. Most ethnic minority individuals consciously confront their ethnicity for the first time in adolescence.
Courtesy of Margaret Beale Spencer

---

connecting with adolescents

Seeking a Positive Image for African American Youth

I want America to know that most of us black teens are not troubled people from broken homes and headed to jail. . . . In my relationships with my parents, we show respect for each other and we have values in our house. We have traditions we celebrate together, including Christmas and Kwanzaa.

—JASON LEONARD, AGE 15

How can a positive self-image based on ethnicity, such as the one expressed here, influence an adolescent's development?

Comstock/Getty Images

Many immigrant adolescents serve as cultural brokers for their parents.

aldomurillo/Getty Images

white culture; and still others take the path of biculturality (Safa, White, & Knight, 2020). Research indicates that many members of families that have recently immigrated to the United States adopt a bicultural orientation, selecting characteristics of the U.S. culture that help them to survive and advance, while continuing to retain aspects of their culture of origin (Bae, 2020).

One study of Mexican American and Asian American college students revealed that individuals in both ethnic groups expressed a bicultural identity (Devos, 2006). Also, a study by Su Yeong Kim and her colleagues (2015) focused on how various dimensions of acculturation in Chinese American families were linked to adolescents' academic trajectories from eighth to twelfth grade. Adolescents with a Chinese-oriented father had a faster decline over time in their grade point average, and Chinese-oriented adolescents had lower initial English language arts (ELA) scores. Also in this study, adolescents who were more Chinese-oriented than their parents had lower initial ELA scores, and adolescents who were more American-oriented than their parents had the highest initial ELA scores. In an earlier study of Chinese American families by Su Yeong Kim and her colleagues (2013), a discrepancy in parent-adolescent American orientation was linked to parents' use of unsupportive parenting techniques, which in turn was related to an increased sense of alienation between parents and adolescents, and the alienation was further associated with lower academic success and a higher level of depression in adolescents.

Immigration also involves cultural brokering, which has increasingly occurred in the United States as children and adolescents serve as mediators (cultural and linguistic) for their immigrant parents (Chen & others, 2020; Zhang & others, 2020). A study of Chinese American and Korean American adolescents revealed that they often serve as language brokers for their immigrant parents (Shen & others, 2014). In this study, language brokering for the mother was related to perceived maternal sacrifice, which in turn was associated with respect for the mother, and that respect was further linked to a lower level of externalizing problems in the adolescents.

In adopting characteristics of the U.S. culture, Latinx families are increasingly embracing the importance of education (Noe-Bustamante, 2020). Although their school dropout rates have remained higher than those of other ethnic groups, during the first two decades of the twenty-first century they declined considerably (National Center for Education Statistics, 2020). Also, in a recent study of Latinx families, parents' educational expectations for their seventh-graders predicted their perceived academic competence as ninth-graders (Aceves, Bamaca-Colbert, & Robins, 2020). And Latinx immigrants are increasingly graduating from college. In 2018, 26 percent of Latinx immigrants who had been in the United States for 5 years or less had a college degree, compared with 11 percent in 2000 and 14 percent in 2010 (Noe-Bustamante, 2020).

In retaining positive aspects of their culture of origin, Latinx families continue to show a strong commitment to family after immigrating to the United States, even in the face of dealing with low-paying jobs and obstacles to economic advancement. For example, divorce rates for Latinx families are lower than for non-Latinx white families of similar socioeconomic status (Parke, Coltrane, & Schofield, 2011). And in recent research, familism was linked to Latinx youths' academic motivation (Stein & others, 2020).

ETHNICITY ISSUES

A number of ethnicity issues influence the development of adolescents and emerging adults. As we will see, however, it is important to consider factors related to SES when drawing conclusions about the role of ethnicity in the development of adolescents and emerging adults.

Ethnicity and Socioeconomic Status   A higher percentage of ethnic minority children and youth live in families characterized by poverty compared with non-Latinx white children and youth. As indicated earlier in this chapter, in 2018, 30.1 percent of African American children and adolescents and 23.7 percent of Latinx children and adolescents lived in poverty, compared with 8.9 percent of non-Latinx white children and adolescents (Children's Defense Fund, 2020).

Much of the research on ethnic minority adolescents and emerging adults has failed to distinguish between the dual influences of ethnicity and SES. Ethnicity and SES can interact in ways that exaggerate the influence of ethnicity because ethnic minority individuals are over-represented in the lower socioeconomic levels of American society (Gollnick & Chinn, 2021). Consequently, too often researchers have given ethnic explanations for aspects of adolescent and emerging adult development that were actually based on SES.

A longitudinal study illustrated the importance of separating the influences of SES and ethnicity on the educational and occupational aspirations of individuals from 14 to 26 years of age (Mello, 2009). In this research, SES successfully predicted educational and occupational aspirations across ethnic groups. After controlling for SES, the researchers found that African American youth held the highest educational expectations, followed by Latinx and Asian American/Pacific Islander, non-Latinx white, and American Indian/Alaska Native youth.

Some ethnic minority youth are from middle-SES backgrounds, but economic advantage does not enable them to completely escape the drawbacks of their ethnic minority status (Banks, 2020; Spencer & others, 2019). Middle-SES ethnic minority youth are still subject to much of the prejudice, discrimination, and bias associated with being a member of an ethnic minority group. Despite being characterized as a "model minority" because of their strong achievement orientation and family cohesiveness, Asian Americans still experience stress associated with ethnic minority status (Chin & Kameoka, 2019). Although middle-SES ethnic minority adolescents have more resources available to counter the destructive influences of prejudice and discrimination, they cannot completely avoid the pervasive influences of negative stereotypes about ethnic minority groups.

That being said, the fact remains that many ethnic minority families are poor, and poverty contributes to the stressful life experiences of many ethnic minority adolescents (Koppelman, 2020). Vonnie McLoyd and her colleagues (McLoyd, 2019; McLoyd, Purtell, & Hardaway, 2015) conclude that ethnic minority youth experience a disproportionate share of the adverse effects of poverty and unemployment in America today. Thus, many ethnic minority adolescents experience a double disadvantage: (1) prejudice, discrimination, and bias because of their ethnic minority status; and (2) the stressful effects of poverty (Banks, 2020). In a recent study of Latinx youth, economic hardship predicted less effective coping and a lower level of effortful control (Taylor, Widaman, & Robins, 2018). However, Latinx youth living in poverty who did have a higher level of effortful control were able to cope more effectively with stress and problems.

Differences and Diversity Historical, economic, and social experiences produce legitimate differences among various ethnic minority groups, and between ethnic minority groups and the majority non-Latinx white group (Gollnick & Chinn, 2021). Individuals belonging to a specific ethnic or cultural group share the values, attitudes, and stresses of that culture. Their behavior, while possibly different from that of the majority, nonetheless is often functional for them. Recognizing and respecting these differences is essential to getting along with others in a diverse, multicultural world. Every adolescent and adult needs to take the perspective of individuals from ethnic and cultural groups that are different from theirs and think, "If I were in their shoes, what kinds of experiences might I have had?" "How would I feel if I were a member of their ethnic or cultural group?" "How would I think and behave if I had grown up in their world?" Such perspective taking is a valuable way to increase one's empathy and understanding of individuals from other ethnic and cultural groups.

For most of the twentieth century, the ways ethnic minority groups differed from non-Latinx whites were conceptualized as *deficits,* or inferior characteristics on the part of the ethnic minority group. In recent years, there has been an effort to increasingly emphasize positive aspects of many ethnic groups, such as the family connectedness that characterizes many Latinx families (Umaña-Taylor & others, 2020).

Another important dimension of ethnic minority adolescents and emerging adults is their diversity (Koppelman, 2020). Ethnic minority groups are not homogeneous; the individuals within them have varied social, historical, and economic backgrounds (Cushner, McClelland, & Safford, 2022). For example, Mexican, Cuban, and Puerto Rican immigrants are Latinxs, but they had different reasons for migrating, came from varying socioeconomic backgrounds in their native countries, and experience different rates and types of employment in the United States. The U.S. federal government now recognizes the existence of 511 different Native American tribes, each having a unique ancestral background with differing values and characteristics. Asian Americans include Chinese, Japanese, Filipinos, Koreans, and Southeast Asians, each group having distinct ancestries and languages. The diversity of Asian Americans is reflected in their educational attainment: Some achieve a high level of education, whereas many others do not. For example, very high percentages of Japanese Americans, Taiwanese Americans, and Korean Americans graduate from high school, but much lower percentages of Vietnamese Americans, Cambodian Americans, and Burmese Americans do. Failure to recognize diversity and individual variations results in the stereotyping of members of ethnic minority groups.

A middle-income African American family. *How might they also experience negative stereotyping and discrimination?*
Monkey Business Images/Shutterstock

developmental **connection**
Families
Recent research on Chinese American families has focused on whether a "tiger parenting" style is common and whether it is associated with positive or negative developmental outcomes in adolescence. Connect to "Achievement, Work, and Careers."

Racism and Discrimination   **Racism** is discrimination, prejudice, or antagonism against a person or people based on their race or ethnic group. In 2020, the United States experienced events that stoked the fires of racism and discrimination. The video of the killing of African American George Floyd by a non-Latinx white policeman in Minneapolis led to extensive protests against racism across the United States and around the world. In 2020, several other killings of African Americans by non-Latinx white police further ignited anger not just among African Americans but also among non-Latinx whites and members of other ethnic minority groups. The deaths of these African Americans convinced many individuals that systemic racism continues to be widespread in the United States. Protests against unjust policing continued in many cities, including both peaceful demonstrations and others that unfortunately turned into violence and looting of businesses.

These protests against police brutality became associated with the Black Lives Matter movement. However, the goals of Black Lives Matter are not only to bring public attention to disproportionate use of force against African Americans but also to raise awareness of the lack of opportunities for African Americans to thrive and flourish economically, educationally, and socially. Historically, African Americans have not had adequate access to education, health care, and good jobs, and Black Lives Matter advocates argue that such circumstances are still pervasive. For example, in 2018, the average income of African Americans was $24,700, compared with $42,700 for non-Latinx whites.

A peaceful Black Lives Matter Protest
Marcello Sgarlato/Alamy Stock Photo

Of course, racism involves discrimination not only against African Americans but also against other ethnic groups such as Latinxs and Asian Americans. Historically, Latinxs, Asian Americans, and other ethnic minority individuals and groups have experienced racism because they also have not had adequate access to education, health, good jobs, and other aspects of well-being. As with African Americans, these inequities continue today (Nalani, Yoshikawa, & Carter, 2021). For example, in 2021, a number of hate crimes involving physical attacks on Asian Americans occurred. Also, in a recent national poll, approximately 40 percent of Latinxs said they had experienced incidents of discrimination in 2019, such as being told to "go back to your own country" and being called offensive names (Gonzalez-Barrera & Lopez, 2020). Further, a recent study of African American, Latinx, and Asian American college students found that they had experienced stable peer discrimination across a three-year period as well as increased discrimination by professors over the last three years (El Toro & Hughes, 2020). In addition, discrimination by peers and professors was linked to lower grades, reduced likelihood of graduating on time, and less school satisfaction.

How have Native American adolescents experienced discrimination and racism?
ImageBROKER/Alamy Stock Photo

The Native American ethnic group has been subjected to discrimination and racism for centuries, yet often this discrimination and racism is given inadequate attention (NETWORK, 2021). Regarding adolescents and emerging adults, an increasing number of Native American activists at colleges and universities are pushing their schools to do more to atone for past wrongs (Marcelo, 2021). For example, in Minnesota, 11 tribes have called on the state university system to provide tuition waivers for Native American students and to increase the number of Native American faculty members. The call for colleges and universities to increase their support for Native American students has become even more urgent because the COVID-19 pandemic has made higher education more difficult to attain for many Native American students, who already had the lowest college graduation rates of any ethnic group (Burki, 2021; Tsethlikai & others, 2020). During the pandemic, Native American students have experienced the greatest decline in college enrollment of any ethnic group, as economic difficulties, health problems, and the challenges of remote learning in isolated tribal communities forced them to quit school.

How should parents talk with their adolescents about racism and discrimination?
digitalskillet/Getty Images

How should parents talk with their children about racism? Recently, Diane Hughes and her colleagues (Hughes, Fisher, & Cabrera, 2020) proposed the "Intentional Parenting for Equity and Justice" program that emphasizes the importance of having deliberate and purposeful conversations as well as engaging in activities that increase children's awareness of racial inequities and injustices such as systemic racism, racial stereotyping, and the harm caused by racial privilege for those who are excluded. They emphasize that parents should discuss current racial events with their children as much as possible in ways that are aligned with the children's ages and ability to learn. These conversations should be simple and brief, and parents should shield children from video footage of violence and be ready to answer children's questions about racial events they may have seen in the media. Conversations with older children and adolescents can include more complex discussions of systemic racism and inequality. Hughes and her colleagues also advise parents to expose their children to the accomplishments, rich traditions, and strengths of diverse ethnic and cultural groups. Racial injustice is a problem for everyone, and all parents—not just those from ethnic minority backgrounds—should have these conversations with their children.

In addition, many BIPOC (Black, Indigenous, and other People of Color) parents teach their children and youth how to stay safe during interactions with the police. One book that helps BIPOC parents talk to their children and youth about this topic is *The ABCs of Survival* created by the National Black Family Institute (2021).

Clearly, a great deal of work still needs to be done to eliminate racism and improve the lives of ethnic minority individuals and groups. In the words of twentieth-century Indian philosopher and spiritual leader Mahatma Gandhi, "Our ability to reach unity in diversity will be the beauty and the test of our civilization."

So far in this chapter, we have examined the effects of culture, socioeconomic status, and ethnicity on adolescent development. In the next section, you will see that there are substantial variations across countries, socioeconomic groups, and ethnic groups in the use of media and technology.

Review *Connect* Reflect

LG3 Summarize how ethnicity is involved in the development of adolescents and emerging adults.

Review
- How has immigration affected ethnic minority adolescents and emerging adults?
- Why are adolescence and emerging adulthood a special juncture in the development of ethnic minority individuals?
- What are some important ethnicity issues that occur in adolescence and emerging adulthood?

Connect
- How can the concepts of individualism and collectivism, described earlier in this chapter, help us understand the immigrant experiences of adolescents and emerging adults?

Reflect *Your Own Personal Journey of Life*
- Think for a few moments about your ethnic background. How did your ethnicity influence the way you experienced adolescence?

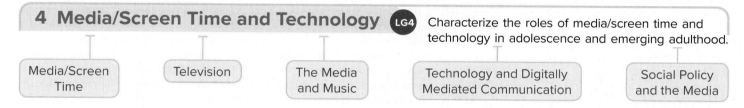

4 Media/Screen Time and Technology

LG4 Characterize the roles of media/screen time and technology in adolescence and emerging adulthood.

| Media/Screen Time | Television | The Media and Music | Technology and Digitally Mediated Communication | Social Policy and the Media |

Few developments in society over the last 40 years have had a greater impact on adolescents than television, computers, and the Internet (Maloy & others, 2021). The persuasive capabilities of television and the Internet are staggering.

MEDIA/SCREEN TIME

Many of today's adolescents have spent more time since infancy in front of a television set, and more recently in front of a computer or smartphone, than with their parents or in the classroom. Television continues to have a strong influence on children's and adolescent's development, but widespread use of other media and information/communication devices is now reflected in use of the term *screen time* to describe the total amount of time spent watching television or DVDs, playing video games, and using computers or mobile media such as smartphones (Boers, Afazali, & Conrod, 2020; Fairclough, 2021). Researchers have found that large amounts of screen time can interfere with healthy development. For example, a recent study involving 11,000 children found that greater use of screen time was linked to lower sleep duration, later sleep onset, and more sleep disturbances (Hisler & others, 2020). And there is concern that quarantining during the COVID-19 pandemic led to excessive screen time among children and adolescents, significantly reducing the amount of time spent in physical activity (Nagata, Magid, & Gabriel, 2020).

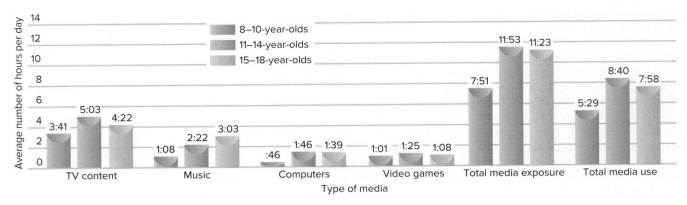

FIGURE 5

HOURS OF MEDIA USE BY U.S. 8- TO 18-YEAR-OLDS IN A TYPICAL DAY

To better understand various aspects of U.S. adolescents' media use, the Kaiser Family Foundation funded national surveys in 1999, 2004, and 2009. The 2009 survey included more than 2,000 8- to 18-year-olds and documented that adolescent media use has increased dramatically since the beginning of the twenty-first century (Rideout, Foehr, & Roberts, 2010). Today's youth live in a world in which they are encapsulated by media, and media use increases dramatically during adolescence. According to the survey conducted in 2009, 8- to 10-year-olds used media an average of 5 hours and 29 minutes a day, 11- to 14-year-olds an average of 8 hours and 40 minutes a day, and 15- to 18-year-olds an average of 7 hours and 58 minutes a day (see Figure 5). Thus, media use jumps more than 3 hours in early adolescence! The largest increases in media use in early adolescence are for TV and video games. TV use by youth increasingly has involved watching TV on the Internet using a mobile device. As indicated in Figure 5, time spent listening to music and using computers increases considerably among 11- to 14-year-old adolescents. And in the 2009 survey, adding up the daily media use figures to obtain weekly media use leads to the staggering levels of more than 60 hours a week of media use by 11- to 14-year-olds and almost 56 hours a week by 15- to 18-year-olds!

Are there gender differences in digital media use? In recent research involving 13- to 18-year-olds in the United States and the United Kingdom, adolescent girls spent more time talking on smartphones, using social media, texting, engaging in general computer use, and being online while boys spent more time engaging in video gaming and on electronic devices in general (Twenge & Martin, 2020). Among both girls and boys, heavy users of digital media were twice as likely as low users to have poor psychological well-being and mental health issues.

A major trend in the use of technology is the dramatic increase in media multitasking. In the 2009 survey, when the amount of time spent multitasking was included in computing media use (in other words, when each task was counted separately), 11- to 14-year-olds spent a total of nearly 12 hours a day exposed to media (the total is almost 9 hours a day when the effect of multitasking is not included) (Rideout, Foehr, & Roberts, 2010)! Also, in a more recent 2015 survey, 51 percent of adolescents reported that they "often" or "sometimes" watched TV or used social media (50 percent) while doing homework, and even more said the same thing about texting (60 percent) and listening to music (76 percent) (Common Sense, 2015). Almost two-thirds of adolescents indicated that they didn't think watching TV (63 percent), texting (64 percent), or using social media (55 percent) while doing homework made any difference in the quality of their work.

One research review concluded that at a general level, using digital technologies (surfing the Internet, texting someone) while engaging in a learning task (reading, listening to a lecture) distracts learners and leads to impaired performance on many tasks (Courage & others, 2015). Also, in recent research, a higher level of media multitasking was associated with lower levels of school achievement, executive function, and growth mindset in adolescents (Cain & others, 2016). Further, another study indicated multimedia multitaskers were less likely than light multimedia multitaskers to delay gratification and more likely to endorse intuitive but wrong answers on a reflective cognitive task (Schutten, Stokes, & Arnell, 2017). And a recent research review concluded that media

What are possible negative outcomes for adolescents who are heavy media multitaskers?
svetikd/Getty Images

multitasking is associated with poorer memory, increased impulsivity, and less effective functioning in the brain's cerebral cortex (Uncapher & others, 2017).

Screen time can have a negative influence on children and adolescents by making them passive learners, distracting them from doing homework, reinforcing negative stereotypes, providing them with violent models of aggression, and presenting them with unrealistic views of the world (Hogan & Strasburger, 2020). Among other concerns about children and adolescents having so much screen time are less time spent interacting with peers, decreased physical activity, increased rates of being overweight or obese, and poor sleep habits (Golshevsky & others, 2020). For example, research indicates that higher levels of screen time are associated with lower levels of physical fitness and higher rates of sedentary behavior in adolescence (Pearson & others, 2017). Also, one study revealed that the greater the amount of screen time experienced by young adolescents, the lower their academic achievement (Syvaoja & others, 2013). Further, a study of Canadian youth found that duration of screen time was linked to anxiety and depression (Maras & others, 2015).

TELEVISION

Let's now look at a major aspect of screen time—television. Many children and adolescents spend more time looking at a television screen than they do interacting with their parents. The persuasive capabilities of television are staggering. The 20,000 hours of television watched by the time the average American adolescent graduates from high school are greater than the number of hours spent in the classroom.

Television can have positive or negative effects on children's and adolescents' development. Television can have a positive influence by presenting motivating educational programs, increasing children's and adolescents' awareness of the world beyond their immediate environment, and providing models of prosocial behavior. However, television can have negative influences on children and adolescents just as those described earlier for the more general category of screen time.

Television and Violence   How strongly does televised violence influence a person's behavior? In a study across seven countries, the greater the amount of time adolescents and young adults were exposed to violent screen media (which included television), the higher the level of aggression they showed (Anderson & others, 2017). Also, in a longitudinal study, the amount of violence viewed on television at age 8 was significantly related to the seriousness of criminal acts performed in adulthood (Huesmann, 1986).

The television programs that young children watch may influence their behavior as adolescents. If so, then this conclusion supports the continuity view of adolescence. In a longitudinal study, girls who were more frequent preschool viewers of violent TV programs had lower grades than those who were infrequent viewers of such violence in preschool (Anderson & others, 2001). Also, viewing educational TV programs as preschoolers was associated with higher grades, more time spent reading books, and less aggression, especially for boys, in adolescence (see Figure 6).

Video Games   Violent video games, especially those that are highly realistic, also raise concerns about their effects on children and adolescents (Mohammadi & others, 2020). The Workgroup on Media Violence and Violent Video Games reviewed a number of meta-analyses and other relevant research and found compelling evidence for short-term and long-term harmful effects of media violence (Anderson & others, 2017). The Workgroup also concluded that the vast majority of experimental laboratory studies have revealed that violent media exposure causes an increase in aggressive thoughts, angry feelings, physiological arousal, hostile appraisals, aggressive behavior, and desensitization to violence, as well as decreases in prosocial behavior and empathy.

Are there any positive outcomes when adolescents play video games? Far more studies of video game use by adolescents have focused on possible negative outcomes than positive ones, but an increasing number of studies are examining possible positive outcomes (Calvert, 2015). Researchers found that middle-school students who played prosocial video games subsequently behaved in more prosocial ways (Gentile & others, 2009). Research also indicates that playing video games can improve adolescents' visuospatial skills (Schmidt & Vandewater, 2008). And

What are some positive and negative influences of television on adolescent development?
Daniel Grill/Getty Images

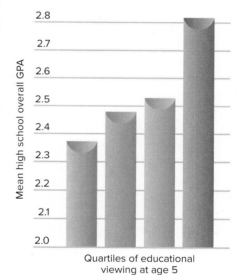

Quartiles of educational
viewing at age 5

FIGURE 6

EDUCATIONAL TV VIEWING IN EARLY CHILDHOOD AND HIGH SCHOOL GRADE POINT AVERAGE FOR BOYS. When boys watched more educational television (especially *Sesame Street*) as preschoolers, they had higher grade point averages in high school. The graph displays the boys' early TV viewing patterns in quartiles and the means of their grade point averages. The bar on the left is for the lowest 25 percent of boys who viewed educational TV programs, the next bar the next 25 percent, and so on, with the bar on the right for the 25 percent of the boys who watched the most educational TV shows as preschoolers.

How might playing violent video games be linked to adolescent aggression?
David Grossman/Alamy Stock Photo

developmental **connection**

Sexuality

Sex is explicitly portrayed in movies, TV shows, videos, lyrics of popular music, MTV, and Internet sites. Connect to "Sexuality."

another study found that playing action video games improved attentional control (Chisholm & Kingstone, 2015). Further, research indicates that video games requiring exercise are linked to weight loss in overweight adolescents (Calvert, 2015). Also, a recent research review concluded that engaging in active video games (also called exergames) can increase adolescents' physical activity levels (Williams & Ayres, 2020).

Television, Other Screen Media, and Sex Adolescents, not unlike adults, like to watch screen media with sexual content, and watching screen media sex can influence adolescents' sexual attitudes and behavior. For example, a recent meta-analysis concluded that exposure to sexual media influenced sexual attitudes and behavior, with a stronger effect on adolescents than on emerging adults (Coyne & others, 2019). In this review, exposure to sexual media was linked to having more permissive sexual attitudes, engaging in riskier sexual behaviors, and earlier sexual initiation. Also, the effects of exposure to sexual media were stronger for males than for females.

A special concern about screen media and sex is adolescents' exposure to pornography online, which often is not monitored by parents (Anderson & others, 2020). One survey found that 42 percent of 10- to 17-year-old boys had watched pornography online, and among 15- to 18-year-olds, 54 percent of boys and 17 percent of girls said they had intentionally viewed pornography online (Wright & Donnerstein, 2014).

Another special concern about adolescents and screen media sex is that, although parents and teachers often feel comfortable discussing occupational and educational choices, independence, and consumer behavior with adolescents, they usually don't feel as comfortable discussing sex with them. The resulting absence of competing information (peers do talk about sex but often perpetuate misinformation) intensifies screen media's influence in imparting information about sex to adolescents. Nonetheless, as with screen media aggression, whether viewing screen media sex influences the behavior of adolescents depends on a number of factors, including the adolescent's needs, interests, concerns, and maturity level (Collins & others, 2017).

Screen Time and Achievement The greater the amount of screen time that children and adolescents experience, the lower their school achievement (Rideout, Foehr, & Roberts, 2010). For example, in a recent study of adolescents, increased screen time predicted lower academic achievement in English and math (Hunter, Leatherdale, & Carson, 2018).

Why might screen time be related to lower academic achievement? Three possibilities involve interference, displacement, and self-defeating tastes/preferences (Comstock & Scharrer, 2006). In terms of interference, engaging in screen time while doing homework can distract adolescents while they are doing cognitive tasks. In terms of displacement, screen time can take away time and attention from engaging in achievement-related tasks such as homework, reading, writing, and mathematics. In terms of self-defeating tastes and preferences, screen time can attract adolescents to entertainment, sports, commercials, and other activities that capture their interest more than school achievement.

Also, some types of television content—such as educational programming for young children—may enhance achievement. In one longitudinal study, viewing educational programs such as *Sesame Street* and *Mr. Rogers' Neighborhood* as preschoolers was related to a number of positive outcomes through high school, including higher grades, reading more books, and enhanced creativity (Anderson & others, 2001). Newer technologies, especially interactive television, hold promise for motivating children and adolescents to learn and to become more exploratory in solving problems.

THE MEDIA AND MUSIC

Anyone who has been around adolescents very long knows that many of them spend huge amounts of time listening to their favorite music and watching music videos on television or on the Internet.

To date, no cause-and-effect studies exist to link either music or videos to an increased risk of early drug use in adolescence. For a small percentage of adolescents, though, certain music may provide a behavioral marker for psychological problems. For example, one study found that adolescents who spent more time listening to music with degrading sexual content were more likely to engage in sexual intercourse earlier than their peers who spent less time listening to this type of music (Martino & others, 2006). And another study revealed that higher use of music media was related to viewing the self as less physically attractive and having overall lower self-worth (Kistler & others, 2010). In this study, there were indications that adolescents may use music videos as a source of social comparison against which they evaluate their own physical attractiveness and self-worth. Music media may also provide a context for modeling expectations about romantic relationships. Further, one study found that spending greater amounts of time on each of these three media viewing contexts was linked to higher levels of physical aggression: (1) TV violence, (2) video game violence, and (3) music video violence (Coker & others, 2015).

TECHNOLOGY AND DIGITALLY MEDIATED COMMUNICATION

Culture involves change, and nowhere is cultural change more apparent than in the technological revolution. Today's adolescents are experiencing this revolution with increased use of computers, the Internet, and smartphones (Maloy & others, 2021). They are using these and a variety of other digital devices to communicate, just as earlier generations used pens, postage stamps, and telephones to stay in touch with their friends. The new information society still relies on some basic non-technological competencies that adolescents need to develop, including good communication skills, problem-solving ability, the capacity to think deeply, creativity, and positive attitudes. However, how young people pursue these competencies is being challenged and extended in ways and at speeds unknown to previous generations.

Portable electronic devices such as cell phones or smartphones are mainly driving the increased media use by adolescents (O'Reilly, 2020). In 2004, 39 percent of adolescents owned a smartphone, a figure that jumped to 66 percent in 2009 and then to 95 percent in 2018 (Anderson & Jiang, 2018). Further, a 2021 survey found that 96 percent of U.S. individuals 18 to 29 years of age owned a smartphone (Pew Research Center, 2021). And in a 2019 survey of 18- to 24-year-olds, 90 percent reported using YouTube, 76 percent Facebook, 75 percent Instagram, and 73 percent Snapchat (Perrin & Anderson, 2019). Further, a large-scale study of more than 32,000 15-year-olds in 37 countries found that problematic social media and low social support were the strongest predictors of low life satisfaction (Walsh & others, 2020). Also, a recent study of university students concluded that approximately 23 percent of students can be classified as "smartphone-addicted" (Randjelovic & others, 2021).

The Internet   The **Internet** is the core of computer-mediated communication. The Internet combines thousands of interconnected computer networks worldwide to provide users with instant access to an incredible array of information—both positive and negative.

Internet Use by Adolescents   Youth throughout the world are increasingly using the Internet, despite substantial variation in usage rates in different countries and socioeconomic groups (Maloy & others, 2021). Special concerns have emerged about children's and adolescents' access to information on the Internet, which has been largely unregulated (Koops, Dekker, & Briken, 2018). Youth can access adult sexual material, instructions for making bombs, and other information that is inappropriate for them (Doornwaard & others, 2017). Additional concerns are being raised about the influence of excessive Internet use on adolescents' health. A study of Swiss eighth-graders found that excessive Internet users did not get adequate sleep (Suris & others, 2014). Another study involving 14- to 17-year-olds revealed a link between high Internet use and elevated blood pressure (Cassidy-Bushrow & others, 2015).

Clearly, parents need to monitor and regulate adolescents' use of the Internet (Chandrima & others, 2020). In a recent study of 13- to 15-year-olds, higher parental monitoring, authoritative parenting, and higher socioeconomic status were linked to lower risk of excessive Internet use (Faltynkova & others, 2020).

In terms of monitoring screen time, consider Bonita Williams, who began to worry about how obsessed her 15-year-old daughter, Jade, had become with social media (Kornblum, 2006). She became even more concerned when she discovered that Jade was posting suggestive photos

Internet The core of computer-mediated communication. The Internet system is worldwide and connects thousands of computer networks, providing an incredible array of information—both positive and negative—that adolescents can access.

What are some recent research results regarding adolescents' use of social media?
Aimstock/Getty Images

of herself and had given her cell phone number to people in different parts of the United States. She grounded her daughter, blocked her social media access at home, and moved Jade's computer from her bedroom into the family room.

The Digitally Mediated Social Environment of Adolescents and Emerging Adults Growth in interactive media platforms and their rapid adoption by adolescents and emerging adults reflect the compelling nature of social media tools. The digitally mediated social environment of adolescents and emerging adults includes e-mail, instant messaging, social networking sites such as Facebook, chat rooms, videosharing and photosharing, multiplayer online computer games, and virtual worlds (Maloy & others, 2021). Snapchat, Instagram, and Tumblr have especially experienced widespread daily use by adolescents and emerging adults. Adolescents, who are already strongly motivated to engage in peer and friend interaction, find the social component of many of these online platforms especially compelling (Uhls, Ellison, & Subrahmanyam, 2017). Among the psychological processes that social media likely activate in adolescents and emerging adults are social comparison (positively or negatively comparing yourself to others), self-disclosure (sharing information about yourself with others), and impression management (highlighting positive aspects of yourself and minimizing those aspects that are more likely to be perceived as negative) (Uhls, Ellison, & Subrahmanyam, 2017).

Text messaging has become the main way that adolescents connect with their friends, surpassing face-to-face contact, e-mail, instant messaging, and voice calling (Lenhart, 2015a). A survey of 12- to 17-year-olds found that they sent an average of 55 text messages per day (Lenhart, 2015b). However, talking with parents on the phone or leaving a voice mail is the primary way that most adolescents prefer to connect with their parents.

- - - - - - - - - - - ➤

developmental **connection**

Peers

Girls' friendships are more likely to focus on intimacy, while boys' friendships tend to emphasize power and excitement. Connect to "Peers, Romantic Relationships, and Lifestyles."

⬅ - - - - - - - - - - -

Positive Social Media Outcomes Are there positive outcomes when adolescents and emerging adults use social media? There is some evidence that social media use can increase their self-esteem, provide a context for safe identity exploration, increase social support and connections (especially friendships), and improve opportunities for self-disclosure (James & others, 2017). Almost two-thirds of adolescents say they make new friends through social media, and more than 90 percent report that they use social media to connect with offline friends every day (Lenhart, 2015a, b). And recent research indicates that social media was being used by adolescents as a constructive coping strategy to deal with anxious feelings during the COVID-19 pandemic (Cauberghe & others, 2021).

Negative Social Media Outcomes A majority of adolescents report that social media are a positive influence on their lives (Rideout, 2016). However, research has documented a number of negative outcomes of social media use for adolescents and emerging adults that include physical health problems, mental health problems, cyberbullying, developmentally inappropriate content, and sexting (Boer & others, 2020).

Among the physical health problems associated with social media use are substance use, insufficient sleep, and eating disorders. A recent study revealed that more time spent on social media was linked to heavier substance use (Vannucci & others, 2020). Also, recent research with 13- to 15-year-olds revealed that heavy social media users had more sleep problems, including late sleep onset and difficulty getting back to sleep after nighttime awakening (Scott , Biello, & Woods, 2019). And recent research indicated that spending more time on Instagram and Snapchat was associated with disordered eating behavior in adolescent girls (Wilksch & others, 2020). Another recent study with 10-year-olds found that greater use of social networking sites was linked to an increased desire for slimness (Sugimoto & others, 2020).

Concerns have been raised about links between online social networking and adolescents' and emerging adults' mental health. For example, a recent study found that more time spent on social media was associated with depressed mood and anxiety (Thorisdottir & others, 2020). A caution is in order regarding conclusions about links between social media and adolescent health. Most studies that have been done are cross-sectional rather than longitudinal or experimental, making it difficult to determine what comes first—social media or health problems.

Cyberbullying is a special concern on social media (Marr & Duell, 2021; Webb & others, 2021). A recent study of university students indicated that being a cybervictim increased the risk of engaging in suicidal thinking as well as experiencing high levels of anxiety, stress, and depression (Martinez-Monteagudo & others, 2020). Information about preventing cyberbullying can be found at www.stopcyberbullying.org/.

Social media platforms are owned by for-profit companies, which means that their commercial interests are more likely to trump any prosocial or developmentally appropriate effects they might have. Purveyors of sexual content, drugs, and many other unhealthy products can easily advertise to adolescents and emerging adults through social media. Further, social media platforms provide adults who have unhealthy motives, such as sexual predators and pedophiles, a way to communicate with and befriend adolescents and emerging adults.

Many adolescents and emerging adults who use social networking sites apparently believe that the information they place on the site is private. However, social networking sites such as Facebook are not as secure in protecting private information as is often believed. Thus, if you use social networking sites, you should never post your social security number, address, phone number, or date of birth on the site. Another good strategy is not to post information or images on social networking sites that current or future employers might use against you in any way. And a final good strategy is to be aware that college administrators and personnel may be able to use the information you place on social networking sites to evaluate whether you have violated college policies (such as college drug and language harassment policies).

developmental **connection**

Peers

To read more about cyberbullying, see "Peers, Romantic Relationships, and Emerging Adult Lifestyles"

SOCIAL POLICY AND THE MEDIA

Adolescents are exposed to an expanding array of media that convey messages that shape adolescents' judgments and behavior. The following social policy initiatives were recommended by the Carnegie Council on Adolescent Development (1995):

developmental **connection**

Social Policy

The United States needs a developmentally attentive youth policy that applies to many areas of adolescents' lives. Connect to "Introduction."

- *Encourage socially responsible programming.* There is good evidence of a link between media violence and adolescent aggression. The media also shape many other dimensions of adolescents' development—gender, ethnic, and occupational roles, as well as standards of beauty, family life, and sexuality. Writers, producers, and media executives need to recognize how powerful their messages are to adolescents and work with experts on adolescent development to provide more positive images to youth.

- *Support public efforts to make the media more adolescent-friendly.* Essentially, the U.S. media should better regulate themselves in regard to their influence on adolescents. All other Western nations have stronger regulations than the United States to foster appropriate educational programming.

- *Encourage media literacy programs as part of school curricula, youth and community organizations, and family life.* Many adolescents do not have the knowledge and skills to critically analyze media messages. Media literacy programs should focus not only on television, but also on the Internet, newspapers, magazines, radio, videos, music, and electronic games.

- *Increase media presentations of health promotions.* Community-wide campaigns using public service announcements in the media have been successful in reducing smoking and increasing physical fitness in adolescents. Use of the media to promote adolescent health and well-being should be increased.

- *Expand opportunities for adolescents' views to appear in the media.* The media should increase the number of adolescent voices in their presentations by featuring editorial opinions, news stories, and videos authored by adolescents. Some schools have found that this strategy of media inclusion of adolescents can be an effective dimension of education.

A review of social policy and the media by leading expert Amy Jordan (2008) acknowledged the difficulty of protecting the First Amendment right of free speech while still providing parents with adequate ways to protect their children and youth from unwanted content in their homes. Other experts argue that the government clearly can and should promote positive programming and provide more funding for media research (Brooks-Gunn & Donahue, 2008). For example, government can produce more public service media campaigns that focus on reducing risky behavior among adolescents.

Review *Connect* Reflect

LG4 Characterize the roles of media/screen time and technology in adolescence and emerging adulthood.

Review

- How extensively do adolescents use media and other electronic devices? How does their use vary across different types of devices?
- How is watching television related to adolescent development?
- What roles do music and the media play in adolescents' lives?
- How are technology, computers, the Internet, and cell phones linked to adolescent development?
- What are some social policy recommendations regarding media use by adolescents?

Connect

- What influence might heavy media use have on adolescents' goal setting?

Reflect *Your Own Personal Journey of Life*

- What was your use of various media in middle/junior and high school like? Did your use of the media in adolescence influence your development in positive or negative ways? Explain.

reach your **learning goals**

Culture

| **1 Culture, Adolescence, and Emerging Adulthood** | **LG1** Discuss the role of culture in the development of adolescents and emerging adults. |

The Relevance of Culture for the Study of Adolescence and Emerging Adulthood

- Culture is the behavior, patterns, beliefs, and all other products of a specific group of people that are passed on from generation to generation. If the study of adolescence and emerging adulthood is to continue to be a relevant discipline during the twenty-first century, increased attention will need to be focused on culture and ethnicity because there will be increased contact among people from varied cultural and ethnic backgrounds. For too long, the study of adolescence and emerging adulthood has been ethnocentric in the sense that the main participants in research studies have been middle-socioeconomic-status adolescents and emerging adults from the United States.

Cross-Cultural Comparisons

- Cross-cultural studies compare a culture with one or more other cultures, and they can provide information about the degree to which information about adolescent and emerging adult development is culture-specific. Cross-cultural comparisons reveal information such as variations in the time adolescents spend in different activities, in their levels of achievement, and in their attitudes about sexuality.

- Individualistic cultures focus on the individual—personal goals are more important than group goals, and values (feeling good, achievement, independence) are self-focused. Collectivistic cultures center on the group—the self is defined by in-group contexts, and personal goals are subordinated to preserve group integrity.

- U.S. adolescents have more discretionary time than do adolescents in other countries. In the United States, adolescents are more achievement-oriented than adolescents in many other countries, but East Asian adolescents spend more time on schoolwork.

Rites of Passage

- Rites of passage are ceremonies that mark an individual's transition from one status to another, especially into adult status. In many primitive cultures, rites of passage are well defined and provide an entry into the adult world. Western industrialized countries lack clearly delineated formal rites of passage that mark the transition to adulthood.

2 Socioeconomic Status and Poverty

 Describe how socioeconomic status and poverty are related to adolescent development.

> What Is Socioeconomic Status?

> Socioeconomic Variation in Families, Neighborhoods, and Schools

> Poverty

- Socioeconomic status (SES) is the grouping of people with similar occupational, educational, and economic characteristics. Socioeconomic status often involves certain inequalities.

- The families, neighborhoods, and schools of adolescents have socioeconomic characteristics that are related to the adolescent's development. Parents in low-SES families are more concerned that their children and adolescents conform to society's expectations; have an authoritarian parenting style; use physical punishment more in disciplining; and are more directive and less conversational with their children and adolescents than higher-SES parents are. Neighborhood variations such as housing quality and mix of high-, middle-, or low-SES residents can influence adolescents' adjustment and achievement. Schools in low-SES areas have fewer resources and are more likely to have students with lower achievement test scores and fewer students going on to college than schools in high-SES areas. Adolescents from affluent families also face adjustment challenges, especially higher rates of substance use.

- Poverty is defined by economic hardship, and its most common marker is the federal poverty threshold (based on the estimated cost of food multiplied by 3). Based on this threshold, the percentage of children under 18 years of age living in poverty increased from 17 percent in 2006 to 19 percent in 2008. The subculture of the poor often is characterized not only by economic hardship but also by social and psychological difficulties. When poverty is persistent and long-standing, it can have especially devastating effects on adolescent development.

3 Ethnicity

 Summarize how ethnicity is involved in the development of adolescents and emerging adults.

> Immigration

> Adolescence and Emerging Adulthood: A Special Juncture for Ethnic Minority Individuals

> Ethnicity Issues

- Relatively high rates of immigration among minorities are contributing to the growing proportions of ethnic minority adolescents and emerging adults in the United States. Immigrants often experience stressors uncommon to or less prominent among longtime residents (such as language barriers, dislocations, and separation from support networks).

- Adolescence and emerging adulthood are often a critical juncture in the development of ethnic minority individuals. Most ethnic minority individuals first consciously confront their ethnicity in adolescence. As they mature cognitively, ethnic minority adolescents and emerging adults become acutely aware of how the non-Latinx white culture evaluates their ethnic group.

- Too often researchers do not adequately tease apart the influences of SES and ethnicity when they study ethnic minority groups, with the result that conclusions about ethnicity are sometimes made that are not warranted. Historical, economic, and social experiences produce many legitimate differences among ethnic minority groups and between ethnic minority groups and the white majority. Many times these differences have been interpreted as deficits in ethnic minority groups. Failure to recognize the diversity within an ethnic minority group can lead to stereotyping. Racism and discrimination have been historically present in the United States, and racial inequality in aspects of law enforcement, housing, education, and opportunity is receiving increased attention during the twenty-first century.

4 Media/Screen Time and Technology

 Characterize the roles of media/screen time and technology in adolescence and emerging adulthood.

> Media/Screen Time

> Television

- In terms of exposure, a significant increase in media/screen time has occurred recently, especially in 11- to 14-year-olds. Adolescents are also increasing the amount of time they spend in media multitasking. The social environment of adolescents has increasingly become digitally mediated. Older adolescents reduce their TV viewing and video game playing and increase their music listening and computer use. There are large individual variations in adolescent media use.

- Television can have a positive influence on adolescents by presenting motivating educational programs, increasing adolescents' information about the world beyond their immediate environment, and providing models of prosocial behavior. Negative aspects of television include promoting passive learning, distracting students from homework, teaching stereotypes, providing violent models of aggression, presenting unrealistic views of the world, and increasing obesity. TV violence is not the only cause of adolescents' aggression, but most experts agree that it can induce aggression and antisocial behavior. There also is concern about the effects of playing violent video games. However, some types of video games—such as those that focus on prosocial behavior or exercise—have positive effects on adolescent development. A special concern is the way sex is portrayed on television and the influence this can have on adolescents' sexual attitudes and behaviors. In general, TV viewing is negatively related to children's mental ability and achievement.

The Media and Music

- Adolescents are heavy consumers of music, spending huge amounts of time listening to music on their electronic devices and watching music videos on television and the Internet.

Technology and Digitally Mediated Communication

- Today's adolescents are experiencing a technology revolution through the widespread availability of computers, the Internet, and sophisticated smartphones. The social environment of adolescents and emerging adults has increasingly become digitally mediated. The Internet continues to serve as the main focus of digitally mediated social interaction for adolescents and emerging adults but increasingly involves a variety of digital devices, especially smartphones. Adolescents' online time can have positive or negative outcomes. Large numbers of adolescents and college students engage in social networking on sites such as Facebook, Instagram, and Snapchat. Both positive and negative outcomes have been found for social media use by adolescents and emerging adults.

Social Policy and the Media

- Social policy recommendations regarding the media include encouraging socially responsible programming, supporting public efforts to make the media more adolescent-friendly, and encouraging media literacy campaigns.

key terms

collectivism	ethnicity	immigrant paradox	racism
cross-cultural studies	ethnocentrism	individualism	rites of passage
culture	feminization of poverty	Internet	socioeconomic status (SES)

key people

Amy Jordan	Reed Larson	Vonnie McLoyd	Carolyn Tamis-LeMonda
Su Yeong Kim	Suniya Luthar	Carola Suárez-Orozco	Suman Verma

improving the lives of adolescents and emerging adults

The African American Child (2nd ed.) (2014)
Yvette Harris and James Graham
New York: Springer

Provides outstanding, up-to-date coverage of many aspects of the lives of African American children and adolescents, including a number of topics discussed in this chapter, such as neighborhoods and communities, families, and media use.

Children and Socioeconomic Status (2015)
Greg Duncan, Kathryn Magnuson, and Elizabeth Votruba-Drzal
In M. H. Bornstein & T. Leventhal (Eds.), *Handbook of Child Psychology and Developmental Science* (7th ed., Vol. 4). New York: Wiley.

An excellent, up-to-date chapter on poverty and the need for policies designed to improve the lives of children and adolescents who live in poverty conditions.

Cultural Diversity & Ethnic Minority Psychology
> This journal published by the American Psychological Association covers a wide range of topics involving cultural diversity and ethnicity, including developmental changes, family relationships, mental health, discrimination, and interventions to improve the lives of cultural and ethnically diverse groups.

The ABCs of Survival **(2021)**
National Black Family Institute
Washington, DC: National Black Family Institute
> Many BIPOC (Black, Indigenous, and other People of Color) parents strive to help their children and youth stay safe during interactions with the police. This book helps BIPOC parents talk to their children and youth about this topic.

Pediatrics **(2017, November), Volume 140, Supplement 2**
> Up-to-date coverage by leading experts on a wide range of topics and issues involving digital media influences on adolescents and emerging adults.

Social Science-Based Pathways to Reduce Social Inequality in Youth Outcomes and Opportunities at Scale (2021)
Andrew Nalani, Hirokazu Yoshikawa, and Prudence Carter
SOCIUS: Special Collection: Sociology's Role in Responding to Inequality, 7, 1–17.
> Drawing on initiatives from a diversity of social sciences, six pathways are described that may create solutions for reducing youth inequality at scale.

Realizing the Potential of Immigrant Youth **(2012)**
Edited by Ann Masten and others
New York: Cambridge University Press
> Leading international researchers describe contemporary research on immigrant youth and the most promising strategies for supporting their development.

The Eisenhower Foundation (www.eisenhowerfoundation.org)
> This foundation provides funds for a number of programs designed to improve the lives of children and adolescents living in low-income circumstances. Read about details on the Eisenhower Quantum program that has been successful in improving the well-being and academic achievement of disadvantaged youth.

chapter 13

PROBLEMS IN ADOLESCENCE AND EMERGING ADULTHOOD

chapter **outline**

1 Exploring Adolescent and Emerging Adult Problems

Learning Goal 1 Discuss the nature of problems in adolescence and emerging adulthood.

The Biopsychosocial Approach
The Developmental Psychopathology Approach
Characteristics of Adolescent and Emerging Adult Problems
Stress and Coping
Resilience

2 Problems and Disorders

Learning Goal 2 Describe some problems and disorders that characterize adolescents and emerging adults.

Drug Use
Juvenile Delinquency
Depression and Suicide
Eating Disorders

3 Interrelation of Problems and Prevention/Intervention

Learning Goal 3 Summarize the interrelation of problems and ways to prevent or intervene in problems.

Adolescents with Multiple Problems
Prevention and Intervention

LightField Studios Inc./Alamy Stock Photo

Annie, a 15-year-old cheerleader, was tall, blonde, and attractive. No one who sold liquor to her questioned her age. She got her money from babysitting and what her mother gave her to buy lunch. Annie was kicked off the cheerleading squad for missing practice too many times, but that didn't stop her drinking. Soon she and several of her peers were drinking almost every day. Sometimes they skipped school and went to the woods to drink. Annie's whole life began to revolve around her drinking. After a while, her parents began to detect Annie's problem. But their attempts to get her to stop drinking by punishing her were unsuccessful. It went on for two years, and, during the last summer, anytime she saw anybody, she was drunk. Not long ago, Annie started dating a boy she really liked, and he refused to put up with her drinking. She agreed to go to Alcoholics Anonymous and has remained sober for four consecutive months. Her goal is continued abstinence.

Arnie is 13 years old. He has a history of committing thefts and physical assaults. The first theft occurred when Arnie was 8—he stole an iPhone® from an Apple Retail Store. The first physical assault took place a year later, when he shoved his 7-year-old brother up against the wall, bloodied his face, and then threatened to kill him with a butcher knife. Recently, the thefts and physical assaults have increased. In just the past week, he stole a television set, struck his mother repeatedly and threatened to kill her, broke some neighborhood streetlights, and threatened youths with a wrench and a hammer. Arnie's father left home when Arnie was 3 years old. Until his father left, his parents argued extensively, and his father often beat up his mother. Arnie's mother indicates that when Arnie was younger she was able to control him, but in the last several years she has lost that control. Arnie's volatility and dangerous behavior have resulted in the recommendation that he be placed in a group home with other juvenile delinquents.

preview

At various points in other chapters, we have considered adolescent and emerging adult problems. For example, we have discussed sexual problems, school-related problems, and achievement-related problems. In this chapter we focus exclusively on adolescent and emerging adult problems, describing different approaches to understanding these problems, exploring some important problems we have not yet discussed, and outlining ways to prevent and intervene in problems.

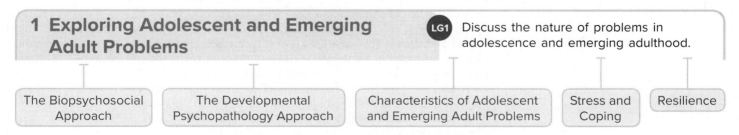

1 Exploring Adolescent and Emerging Adult Problems

LG1 Discuss the nature of problems in adolescence and emerging adulthood.

| The Biopsychosocial Approach | The Developmental Psychopathology Approach | Characteristics of Adolescent and Emerging Adult Problems | Stress and Coping | Resilience |

What causes adolescents like Annie and Arnie to have problems? What are some characteristics of the problems adolescents and emerging adults develop? How are stress and coping involved with these problems? What characterizes resilient adolescents?

THE BIOPSYCHOSOCIAL APPROACH

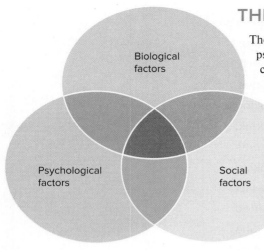

The **biopsychosocial approach** to understanding human problems emphasizes that biological, psychological, and social factors interact to produce the problems experienced by adolescents, emerging adults, and people of other ages (see Figure 1). Thus, if an adolescent or emerging adult engages in substance abuse it may be due to a combination of biological factors (heredity and brain processes, for example), psychological factors (low conscientiousness and low self-control, for example), and social factors (relationship difficulties with parents and peers, for example). In other chapters we have explored biological, psychological, and social factors that can contribute to the development of problems in adolescence. In our further examination of the biopsychosocial approach, we will especially highlight biological, psychological, and social factors that adolescence uniquely contributes to these problems.

Biological Factors   Scientists who adopt a biological approach focus on factors such as genes, puberty, hormones, and the brain as causes of adolescent and emerging adult problems.

Early maturation is linked to a number of problems for adolescent girls, including drug abuse, depression, and delinquency (Stepanyan & others, 2020). Further, the hormonal changes associated with puberty have been proposed as a factor in the higher rate of depression in adolescent girls compared with adolescent boys (Pfeifer & Allen, 2021). How adolescents handle their emerging sexual interest also is linked to whether or not they develop problems (Pengpid & Peltzer, 2020). Early sexual intercourse is linked to other problems, including drug abuse and delinquency (Bozzini & others, 2021).

The later development of the prefrontal cortex in concert with the earlier maturation of the amygdala may contribute to the increased incidence of risk taking and sensation seeking that emerges in adolescence. The implication of these changes in the brain is that adolescents may not be mature enough in their thinking to control their behavior in risky situations—and thus may develop problems (Magnusson, Crandall, & Evans, 2020).

Psychological Factors   Among the psychological factors that have been proposed as important influences on adolescent and emerging adult problems are identity, personality traits, decision making, and self-control. Developing a positive identity is central to healthy adjustment and academic success in adolescence and emerging adulthood (McLean & others, 2021). The search for a coherent identity may lead to experimentation with different identities, one or more of which may involve problems. Wide emotional swings characterize adolescence, especially early adolescence. When such emotional swings become intensely negative, as in the emotion of sadness, depression may result (Hollenstein & Lanteigne, 2018). Recall the Big Five personality traits (openness to experience, conscientiousness, extraversion, agreeableness, and neuroticism) and remember that adolescents who are low in conscientiousness are more likely to have substance abuse and conduct problems than their counterparts who are high in conscientiousness (Raketic & others, 2017). Adolescence is a time of increased decision making, and for many adolescents their emotions may overwhelm their decision-making ability and contribute to the development of problems (Mercurio & others, 2020). Another psychological factor that is important in understanding adolescent problems is self-control (Schunk, 2020). For example, adolescents who have not adequately developed self-control are more likely to develop substance abuse problems and to engage in delinquent acts than those who have higher levels of self-control (Andreescu & Overstreet, 2021).

Social Factors   The social factors that have especially been highlighted as contributors to adolescent problems are the social contexts of family, peers, schools, socioeconomic status, poverty, and neighborhoods (Suter, Beycan, & Ravazzini, 2021). Many aspects of family processes can contribute to the development of problems in adolescence, including a persistent high level of parent-adolescent conflict (Allen & others, 2021), inadequate parental monitoring of adolescents (MacPherson & others, 2021; Tornay & others, 2020), and insecure attachment (Theoret & others, 2021).

In adolescence, individuals spend more time with peers than in childhood, and the increased time with peers can have positive or negative effects on adolescent development (Savina & Moran, 2022). Adolescents who don't become adequately connected to the world

---

FIGURE 1
THE BIOPSYCHOSOCIAL APPROACH

developmental **connection**

Brain Development

The emerging fields of developmental cognitive neuroscience and developmental social neuroscience emphasize the importance of studying connections across biological, cognitive, and socioemotional processes. Connect to "Introduction."

developmental **connection**

Personality

Conscientiousness is increasingly recognized as a key trait in understanding adolescent problems. Connect to "The Self, Identity, Emotion, and Personality."

developmental **connection**

Family

In virtually every area of adolescent problems, family processes and parenting are thought to play important roles. Connect to "Families."

biopsychosocial approach Explanation of human problems emphasizing that these problems develop through an interaction of biological, psychological, and social factors.

of peers may develop problems. Rejected adolescents may be especially prone to such problems (Kornienko, Ha, & Dishion, 2020). Hanging out with peers and friends who engage in delinquency or substance abuse contributes to the development of these problems during adolescence (Wang & others, 2020). Also, some aspects of romantic relationships, which emerge in adolescence for the first time, are linked to adolescent problems (Kochendorfer & Kerns, 2020). For example, early dating is related to substance abuse, and unwanted dissolution of a romantic relationship is associated with depression (Furman, 2018).

We have discussed how U.S. middle schools often are too impersonal to adequately meet the needs of young adolescents who are going through substantial biological, cognitive, and socioemotional changes (Skinner & Saxton, 2020). Most secondary schools don't offer adequate counseling services to help adolescents cope with these changes or to assist adolescents who have problems. Further, adolescents who are not adequately engaged with school are more likely to drop out and develop other problems such as substance abuse and delinquency.

Throughout this edition we have emphasized how socioeconomic status and poverty contribute to adolescent problems. Poverty makes adolescents vulnerable to many problems, especially delinquency (DeJoseph & others, 2021; Gold, 2020). However, recall that adolescents, especially boys, from affluent families are at risk for developing substance abuse problems (Luthar, Kumar, & Zillmer, 2020). Also, the quality of neighborhoods is linked to development of problems. For example, adolescents who grow up in neighborhoods with high crime rates and poor-quality schools are at increased risk for developing problems (Reed & others, 2020).

THE DEVELOPMENTAL PSYCHOPATHOLOGY APPROACH

The **developmental psychopathology approach** focuses on describing and exploring the developmental pathways of problems. Many researchers in this field seek to establish links between early precursors of a problem (such as risk factors and early experiences) and outcomes (such as substance abuse, delinquency, and depression) (Groenman, 2021; VanMeter & Cicchetti, 2020). A developmental pathway describes continuities and transformations in factors that influence outcomes. For example, Arnie's story (described at the beginning of the chapter) indicated a possible link between early negative parenting experiences, including his father's abuse of his mother, and Arnie's delinquency in adolescence.

The developmental psychopathology approach often involves the use of longitudinal studies to track the unfolding of problems over time (Funkhouser & others, 2021; Meehan & others, 2020). This approach also seeks to identify *risk factors* that might predispose children and adolescents to develop problems such as substance abuse, juvenile delinquency, and depression (Bohnert, Loren, & Miller, 2020; Russotti & others, 2021), as well as *protective factors* that might help to shield children and adolescents from developing problems (Masten & others, 2021). For example, a recent study found that low self-regulation at 10 to 12 years of age predicted worse decision making in risky situations in adolescence and higher self-regulation predicted better decision making in such situations (Weller & others, 2021).

Recently proponents of the developmental psychopathology approach have focused increasing attention on **developmental cascades,** which involve connections across domains over time that influence developmental pathways and outcomes (Lyons-Ruth & Brumariu, 2021; Murray, Eisner, & Ribeaud, 2020). Developmental cascades can encompass connections among a wide range of biological, cognitive, and social processes, including many social contexts such as families, peers, schools, and culture (Ettekal & others, 2020). Further, links between domains that produce positive or negative outcomes may occur at various points in development, such as early childhood, later in adolescence or during emerging adulthood, and in intergenerational relationships (Duprey, Oshri, & Liu, 2020). Gerald Patterson and his colleagues (Patterson, Forgatch, & DeGarmo, 2010; Patterson, Reid, & Dishion, 1992) have conducted extensive research based on a developmental cascade approach. Their research suggests that high levels of coercive parenting and low levels of positive parenting lead to the development of antisocial behavior in children and adolescents, which in turn connects children and adolescents to negative experiences in peer contexts (being rejected by nondeviant peers and becoming friends with deviant peers, for example) and school contexts (having academic difficulties, for example), which further intensifies the adolescent's antisocial behavior (Patterson, Forgatch, & DeGarmo, 2010). Also, in another developmental cascades study, maternal warmth/sensitivity and child self-regulation in early childhood

What are some biological, psychological, and social factors that can contribute to the development of adolescent problems?
(top): Adam Gault/Getty Images; (bottom): Todor Tsvetkov/iStock/Getty Images

The term "developmental pathways" is central to discussions of developmental psychopathology as a way of conceptualizing the relations between early and later adaptation.

—Byron Egeland
Contemporary Psychologist, University of Minnesota

developmental psychopathology approach Approach that focuses on describing and exploring the developmental pathways of problems.

developmental cascades A developmental psychopathology approach that emphasizes connections across domains over time to influence developmental pathways and outcomes.

followed by parental monitoring in middle and late childhood predicted less engagement with delinquent peers, fewer externalizing problems, and less underage drinking in adolescence (Eiden & others, 2016).

The identification of risk factors might suggest avenues for both prevention and treatment (Colich & others, 2020). For example, parents who suffer from depression, an anxiety disorder, or substance abuse are more likely to have adolescents who experience depression (Chen & others, 2020). In a recent study, children in middle and late childhood whose fathers had depressive symptoms were at increased risk for developing depressive symptoms as young adolescents (Lewis & others, 2017).

Adolescent and emerging adult problems can be categorized as internalizing or externalizing:

- **Internalizing problems** occur when individuals turn their problems inward. Examples of internalizing problems include anxiety and depression.
- **Externalizing problems** occur when individuals turn their problems outward. An example of an externalizing problem is juvenile delinquency.

Links have been established between patterns of problems in childhood and outcomes in adolescence and emerging adulthood (Miller & others, 2021; VanMeter & Cicchetti, 2020). A longitudinal study found that internalizing problems at age 7 predicted a lower level of academic competence at age 12 and that academic competence at age 9 was associated with a lower incidence of internalizing and externalizing problems at age 12 (Englund & Siebenbruner, 2012). This study also indicated that earlier externalizing problems were linked to increased alcohol use in adolescence. In another study, males with internalizing patterns (such as anxiety and depression) during the elementary school years were likely to have similar problems at age 21, but they did not have an increased risk of externalizing problems as young adults (Quinton, Rutter, & Gulliver, 1990). Similarly, the presence of an externalizing pattern (such as aggression or antisocial behavior) in childhood elevated the risk of antisocial behavior at age 21. For females in the same study, both early internalizing and early externalizing patterns predicted internalizing problems at age 21.

Alan Sroufe and his colleagues (Sroufe, 2007; Sroufe, Coffino, & Carlson, 2010) have found that anxiety problems in adolescence are linked with insecure resistant attachment in infancy (the infant sometimes clings to the caregiver and at other times pushes the caregiver away) and that conduct problems in adolescence are related to avoidant attachment in infancy (the infant avoids the caregiver). Sroufe concludes that a combination of early supportive care (attachment security) and early peer competence helps to buffer adolescents from developing problems. In another developmental psychopathology study, Ann Masten (2001; Masten & others, 2010) followed 205 children for ten years from childhood into adolescence and emerging adulthood. She found that good intellectual functioning and parenting served protective roles in keeping adolescents and emerging adults from engaging in antisocial behaviors. Later in this chapter, we further explore such factors in our discussion of resilient adolescents and emerging adults.

What characterizes internalizing and externalizing problems? How are these problems linked to gender and socioeconomic status?
(top): Maria Taglienti-Molinari/Getty Images; (bottom): SW Productions/Photodisc/Getty Images

CHARACTERISTICS OF ADOLESCENT AND EMERGING ADULT PROBLEMS

The spectrum of adolescent and emerging adult problems is wide. The problems vary in their severity and in how common they are for females and males and for different socioeconomic groups. Some problems are short-lived, while others can persist over many years. Some problems are more likely to appear at one developmental level than at another. In one study, depression, truancy, and drug abuse were more common among older adolescents, whereas arguing, fighting, and being too loud were more common among younger adolescents (Edelbrock, 1989).

In a large-scale investigation by Thomas Achenbach and Craig Edelbrock (1981), adolescents from a lower-SES background were more likely to have problems than those from a middle-SES background. Most of the problems reported for adolescents from a lower-SES background were undercontrolled, externalizing behaviors such as destroying others' belongings and fighting. These behaviors also were more characteristic of boys than of girls. The problems of middle-SES adolescents and girls were more likely to be overcontrolled and internalizing—anxiety or depression, for example.

internalizing problems Emotional conditions that develop when individuals turn problems inward. Examples include anxiety and depression.

externalizing problems Behavior that occurs when individuals turn problems outward. An example is juvenile delinquency.

The behavioral problems most likely to cause adolescents to be referred to a clinic for mental health treatment were feelings of unhappiness, sadness, or depression, and poor school performance (see Figure 2). Difficulties in school achievement, whether secondary to other kinds of problems or primary problems in themselves, account for many referrals of adolescents.

In another investigation, Achenbach and his colleagues (1991) compared the problems and competencies of 2,600 children and adolescents 4 to 16 years old who were assessed at intake into mental health services with those of 2,600 demographically matched nonreferred children and adolescents. Lower-SES children and adolescents had more problems and fewer competencies than did their higher-SES counterparts. Children and adolescents with internalizing problems had fewer related adults in their homes; parents who were unmarried, separated, or divorced; families that were receiving public assistance; or family members who had received mental health services. Children and adolescents with externalizing problems had parents who were unmarried, separated, or divorced and lived in families that were receiving public assistance.

Many studies have shown that factors such as poverty, ineffective parenting, and mental health disorders in parents *predict* adolescent problems (Gold, 2020; Tornay & others, 2020). Predictors of problems are called *risk factors*. A risk factor indicates an elevated probability of a problematic outcome in groups of people who have that factor. Children with many risk factors are said to have a "high risk" for problems in childhood and adolescence, but not every one of them will develop problems.

Some researchers think primarily in terms of risk factors when they study adolescent problems, whereas others argue that conceptualizing problems in terms of risk factors creates a perception that is too negative (Lerner & others, 2015). Instead, they highlight the developmental assets of youth (Shek & others, 2021; Wang, Peng, & Chi, 2021). For example, Peter Benson (Benson & Scales, 2009; Benson & others, 2006), former director of the Search Institute in Minneapolis, has prescribed 40 developmental assets that adolescents need in order to achieve positive outcomes in their lives. Half of these assets are external, half internal. Each of the 40 assets has been shown scientifically to promote healthy adolescent development.

The 20 *internal assets* include the following:

- *Commitment* to learning (such as being motivated to achieve in school and doing at least one hour of homework on school days)
- *Positive values* (such as helping others and demonstrating integrity)
- *Social competencies* (such as knowing how to plan and make decisions and having interpersonal competencies like empathy and friendship skills)
- *Positive identity* (such as having a sense of control over life and high self-esteem)

The 20 *external* assets include the following:

- *Support* (such as family and neighborhood)
- *Empowerment* (such as adults in the community valuing youth and giving them useful community roles)
- *Boundaries* and expectations (such as the family setting clear rules and consequences and monitoring the adolescent's whereabouts, as well as the presence of positive peer influence)
- *Constructive* use of time (such as engaging in creative activities three or more times a week and participating three or more hours a week in organized youth programs)

In research conducted by the Search Institute, adolescents with more of the developmental assets reported engaging in fewer risk-taking behaviors, such as alcohol and tobacco use, sexual intercourse, and violence. For example, in one survey of more than 12,000 ninth- to twelfth-graders, 53 percent of the students with 0 to 10 assets reported using alcohol three or more times in the past month or getting drunk more than once in the past two weeks, compared with only 16 percent of the students with 21 to 30 assets or 4 percent of the students with 31 to 40 assets. On the other side of the coin, the assets not only prevent risky behaviors but also promote some behaviors that society values. For example, youth with 31 to 40 assets are far more likely to succeed in school and maintain good physical health than youth with 0 to 20 of the assets.

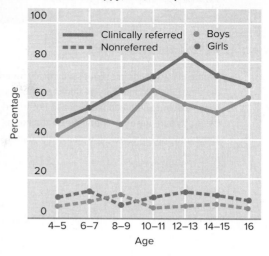

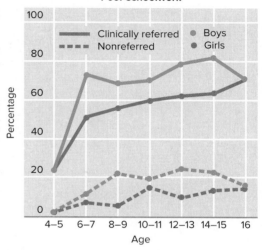

FIGURE **2**

THE TWO ITEMS MOST LIKELY TO DIFFERENTIATE CLINICALLY REFERRED AND NONREFERRED CHILDREN AND ADOLESCENTS

developmental **connection**

Social Policy

An important social policy agenda is using a strengths-based approach in addressing adolescent problems. Connect to "Introduction."

All Stressed Out

"Some of my friends are so messed up. My friend Abby is depressed all the time. She told me that she thinks about killing herself. I want to tell someone, but she made me promise not to. I don't know what to do. I'm pretty sure my other friend Alexandra has an eating disorder. She's constantly talking about how many calories something has, and all she eats is lettuce! I try to be there for both of them, but I've got so much of my own stuff to deal with. I feel anxious and depressed all of the time. I don't know what to do."

—LAUREN

Recently, the developmental assets were updated and reconfigured based on more extensive research into four main internal assets and four main external assets that also include individual assets (Syvertsen, Scales, & Toomey, 2019):

The *four internal assets* are

- Academic engagement
- Positive identity
- Positive values (includes individual assets of caring, social justice, integrity, and responsibility)
- Social competencies (includes individual assets of social-emotional skills and planning and decision-making skills)

The *four external assets* are

- Support (includes individual assets of family support, open family communication, parent involvement in school, and other adult relationships)
- Mattering and belonging (includes individual assets of a caring school climate and a community that values youth)
- Boundaries (includes individual assets of family boundaries, school boundaries, and neighborhood boundaries)
- Extracurricular participation

STRESS AND COPING

stress The response of individuals to stressors, which are circumstances and events that threaten and tax their coping abilities.

Seventeen-year-old Jordan comments, "I never thought it would be so hard to grow up. I feel pressure all the time. My parents put tremendous pressure on me. I wish someone could help me cope better with all these pressures." Let's explore the nature of stress in individuals like Jordan and ways they can cope effectively with stress.

What some examples of acute and chronic stressors in adolescence?
Juanmonino/Getty Images

Stress   Although G. Stanley Hall (1904) and others overdramatized the extent of storm and stress in adolescence, many adolescents and emerging adults today experience stressful circumstances that can affect their development. Just what is stress? **Stress** is the response of individuals to stressors, which are circumstances and events that threaten them and tax their coping abilities.

A car accident, a low grade on a test, a lost wallet, a conflict with a friend—all of these situations might be stressors in your life. Some stressors are acute; in other words, they are sudden events or stimuli such as being cut by falling glass. Other stressors are chronic, or long-lasting, such as being malnourished or HIV-positive. These are physical stressors, but there also are emotional and psychosocial stressors such as the death of a loved one or being discriminated against.

Are there developmental changes in how much stress adolescents report that they experience? One study of 12- to 19-year-olds revealed that perceptions of having stress decreased in late adolescence and that the use of coping strategies that were active (such as seeking advice from parents or friends on emotional difficulties) and internal (such as reflecting about different solutions to a problem) increased as adolescents got older (Seiffge-Krenke, Aunola, & Nurmi, 2009).

Stress may come from many different sources for adolescents and emerging adults (Cisler & Herringa, 2021). Sources of stress are life events, daily hassles, and sociocultural factors.

Life Events and Daily Hassles   Think about your own life. What events have created the most stress for you? Some events are big problems and may occur in clusters, like the breakup of a long-standing relationship, the death of someone you loved, your parents' divorce, being diagnosed with a life-threatening disease such as cancer, a personal injury, or experiencing a war or a disaster. Other occurrences involve the everyday circumstances of your life, such as not having enough time to study, arguing with your girlfriend or boyfriend, experiencing daily family stress, or not getting enough credit for work you did at your job.

Among the outcomes for children and adolescents who experience disasters are acute stress reactions, depression, panic disorder, and post-traumatic stress disorder (Masten, Motti-Stefanidi, & Rahl-Brigman, 2020). The likelihood that children and adolescents will effectively cope with the stress of a disaster depends on factors such as the nature and severity of the disaster and the type of support available to the children and adolescents.

In 2020, the abrupt emergence of the COVID-19 global pandemic took people by surprise and increased the stress and anxiety levels of many children, adolescents, and adults (Guessoum & others, 2020). Social distancing recommendations caused a majority of schools to close and many adults to work from home. In such stressful circumstances, it is important for parents to stay calm, educate themselves about safety precautions, and communicate accurate information to their children and adolescents. Especially important is that children and adolescents understand that such circumstances are not permanent and eventually their lives will return to normal.

A special recent concern is the impact of the COVID-19 pandemic on adolescent health care. At the peak of the pandemic, some parents avoided taking their children and adolescents to scheduled medical evaluations, doctor appointments for new health issues, or even emergency care. A recent study found that children and adolescents were 70 percent less likely to visit a general hospital emergency department after the pandemic had emerged than before it appeared (Goldman & others, 2021). Further, the pandemic was associated with intensified mental health issues in adolescents, including stress, depression, and suicidal ideation (Magson & others, 2021; Saggioro de Figueiredo & others, 2021).

Researchers have found that when several stressors are experienced simultaneously, the effects may be compounded (Rutter & Garmezy, 1983). For example, one study found that people who felt besieged by two chronic life stressors were four times more likely to eventually need psychological services than those who had to cope with only one chronic stressor (Rutter, 1979). Also, in a recent study, negative life events were linked to increased adolescent depression, with social support and family cohesion serving as protective factors to reduce the association of negative life events and adolescent depression (Askeland & others, 2020). In another recent study, higher-quality parent and peer relationships reduced the negative effects of stressful life events on adolescents (McMahon, Creaven, & Gallagher, 2020). Further, another recent study with college students revealed that a high level of rumination increased the likelihood that negative life events would be associated with suicidal ideation while a low level of rumination reduced the association (Wang & others, 2020).

Some psychologists conclude that information about daily hassles and daily uplifts provides better clues about the effects of stressors than the examination of life events (Parker & others, 2020). Enduring a boring but tense job or living in poverty does not show up on scales of major life events. Yet the everyday pounding from these conditions can add up to a highly stressful life and eventually contribute to psychological disorders or physical ailments (Gottschalk, Domschke, & Schiele, 2020).

Stress in relationships is especially common among adolescents (Martin-Gutierrez & others, 2021; Shulman & others, 2020). Between 46 and 82 percent of the everyday stressful events reported by adolescents involve interpersonal relationships, especially conflicts with parents, peers, and romantic partners (Seiffge-Krenke, Aunola, & Nurmi, 2009). For example, studies across 21 countries revealed that adolescents' stress levels were highest with

What some types of relationship stress that are common in adolescence?
reklamlar/Getty Images

parents and at school, while the lowest stress occurred with peers and romantic partners (Persike & Seiffge-Krenke, 2012, 2014).

Adolescent girls are more sensitive than boys are to relationship stress; they report higher levels of relationship stress and are more likely to use coping strategies that maintain relationships (Seiffge-Krenke, 2011). When such relationships are destructive, staying in them too long can produce depressive symptoms (Furman, 2018).

What are the biggest hassles for college students? One study showed that the most frequent daily hassles of college students were wasting time, being lonely, and worrying about meeting high achievement standards (Kanner & others, 1981). In fact, the fear of failing in today's success-oriented world often plays a role in college students' depression. College students also indicated that having fun, laughing, going to movies, getting along well with friends, and completing a task were their main sources of daily uplifts.

Critics of the daily-hassles approach argue that it suffers from some of the same weaknesses as life-events scales (Dohrenwend & Shrout, 1985). For example, knowing about a person's daily irritations and problems tells us nothing about her or his perceptions of stressors, physiological resilience to stress, or coping ability and strategies. Further, the daily-hassles and daily-uplifts scales have not been consistently linked to objective measures of health and illness.

Sociocultural Factors   Sociocultural factors help to determine which stressors individuals are likely to encounter, whether they are likely to perceive events as stressful or not, and how they believe stressors should be confronted (Haft & others, 2021). As examples of sociocultural factors involved in stress, let's examine gender, conflict between cultures, and poverty.

Do males and females respond to stressors in the same way? Shelley Taylor (2015, 2018, 2021) has proposed that females are less likely to respond to stressful and threatening situations with a fight-or-flight response than males are. Taylor argues that females are more likely to "tend and befriend." That is, females often respond to stressful situations by protecting themselves and others through nurturing behaviors (the *tend* part of the model) and forming alliances with a larger social group, especially one populated by other women (the *befriend* part of the model).

What characterizes the acculturative stress of immigration for adolescents in the United States?
Stephanie Maze/Getty Images

Do adolescent girls and boys experience stress and cope with it in similar or dissimilar ways? One study revealed no differences in the stress that adolescent girls and boys reported in relation to school (such as pressure to get good grades), parents (such as fighting with parents), self-related problems (such as not liking one's appearance), leisure (such as not having enough money), and their future (such as being unemployed) (Seiffge-Krenke, Aunola, & Nurmi, 2009). However, girls indicated that they were experiencing more stress in peer relations (such as not having enough friends) and using more active strategies to cope with stress, such as asking for help from peers.

Acculturative stress refers to the negative consequences that result from contact between two different cultural groups. Many individuals who have immigrated to the United States have experienced acculturative stress. A recent research review of refugee children and adolescents concluded that their mental health problems were linked pre-migration individual risk factors such as exposure to war-related trauma and post-migration family factors such as parental mental health problems and impaired parenting (Scharpf & others, 2020). Also, a recent study found that Latinx adolescents experienced more depressive symptoms when both the adolescents and their parents had a higher level of acculturative stress (Wu & others, 2020).

Poverty can cause considerable stress for individuals and families (Gold, 2020). One expert on coping in youth, Bruce Compas (2004, p. 279), calls poverty "the single most important social problem facing young people in the United States." Chronic conditions such as inadequate housing, dangerous neighborhoods, ineffective schools, burdensome responsibilities, and economic uncertainties are potent stressors in the lives of the poor (Gollnick & Chinn, 2021). Adolescents are more likely to experience threatening and uncontrollable life events if they live in low-income contexts than if they live in more economically robust contexts (Kara & Selcuk, 2020).

Coping   Adolescents and emerging adults respond to stress in different ways (Reife, Duffy, & Grant, 2020). Some youth give up quickly when the slightest thing goes wrong in their lives. Others are motivated to work hard to find solutions to personal problems, and some successfully adjust to even extremely taxing circumstances. A stressful circumstance can be rendered considerably less stressful if you know how to cope with it.

acculturative stress The negative consequences that result from contact between two distinctive cultural groups.

What Is Coping? **Coping** involves managing taxing circumstances, expending effort to solve life's problems, and seeking to master or reduce stress. What makes the difference between effective and ineffective efforts to cope?

Characteristics of the individual provide part of the answer. Success in coping has been linked with several characteristics, including a sense of personal control, positive emotions, and personal resources (Kao, Ling, & Dalaly, 2020). Success in coping, however, also depends on the strategies used and the context (Felner & others, 2020). Adolescents and emerging adults have many ways of coping–some more successful than others.

Adolescents use a wider range of coping strategies than children do, and the ability to choose among various coping options is likely adaptive (Aldwin & others, 2011). A research review concluded that two types of age trends occur from childhood through adolescence in coping: (1) an increase in coping *capacities* reflected in more self-reliance and less reliance on adults; greater use of planful problem solving; and greater reliance on cognitive strategies; and (2) an improvement in the *deployment* of different coping strategies depending on which ones are more effective in dealing with certain kinds of stressors (Zimmer-Gembeck & Skinner, 2011).

What are the differences between problem-focused and emotion-focused coping?
Gary Houlder/Getty Images

Problem-Focused and Emotion-Focused Coping One way to classify coping strategies has been especially influential among psychologists who study coping: distinguishing between problem-focused coping and emotion-focused coping, as proposed by Richard Lazarus (2000).

Problem-focused coping is Lazarus' term for the strategy of squarely facing one's troubles and trying to solve them. For example, if you are having trouble with a class, you might go to the study-skills center at your college or university and enroll in a training program to learn how to study more effectively. Having done so, you have faced your problem and attempted to do something about it. A review of 39 research studies documented that problem-focused coping was associated with positive change following trauma and adversity (Linley & Joseph, 2004). Also, a recent study of coping with academic challenges found that fathers' problem-focused suggestions (strategizing and help-seeking, for example) were associated with adolescents' more adaptive coping (Tu, Cai, & Li, 2020).

Emotion-focused coping is Lazarus' term for responding to stress in an emotional manner, especially by using defense mechanisms. Emotion-focused coping includes avoiding a problem, rationalizing what has happened, denying it is occurring, laughing it off, or calling on religious faith for support. If you use emotion-focused coping, you might avoid going to a class that you find difficult. You might say the class doesn't matter, deny that you are having a problem, or laugh and joke about it with your friends. This is not necessarily a good way to face a problem.

Sometimes, though, emotion-focused coping is adaptive. For example, denial is a protective mechanism for dealing with the flood of feelings that accompanies the realization that death is imminent. Denial can protect against the destructive impact of shock by postponing the time when you will have to deal with stress. In many circumstances, however, emotion-focused coping is maladaptive. For example, denying that the person you were dating doesn't love you anymore when that person has become engaged to someone else keeps you from moving forward with your life.

Another harmful coping strategy is *avoidant coping*, which involves ignoring a problem and hoping it will just go away (Fritz & Gallagher, 2020). A longitudinal study revealed that adolescents' avoidant coping preceded an increase in anxiety symptoms and disordered eating, while adolescents' depressive symptoms predicted later increases in maladaptive coping (Richardson & others, 2021). And in another recent study, adolescents at high risk for depression experienced more stressors and used more disengagement coping strategies (Ozkul & Gunusen, 2021).

Thinking Positively Thinking positively and avoiding negative thoughts are good strategies for coping with stress in just about any circumstance (Finkelstein-Fox, Park, & Kalichman, 2020). Why? A positive mood improves our ability to process information efficiently and enhances self-esteem. In most cases, an optimistic attitude is superior to a pessimistic one. It gives us a sense that we are controlling our environment, much like what Albert Bandura (2012) talks about when he describes the importance of self-efficacy in coping. Thinking positively reflects the positive psychology movement discussed in the introduction to this

coping Managing taxing circumstances, expending effort to solve life's problems, and seeking to master or reduce stress.

problem-focused coping Lazarus' term for the strategy of squarely facing one's troubles and trying to solve them.

emotion-focused coping Lazarus' term for responding to stress in an emotional manner, especially by using defense mechanisms.

edition; recall that psychologists are calling for increased emphasis on positive individual traits, hope, and optimism (King, 2020). A prospective study of more than 5,000 young adolescents revealed that an optimistic thinking style predicted a lower level of depressive symptoms and a lower level of substance abuse and antisocial behavior (Patton & others, 2011). Further, another study found that having a positive outlook was the most important cognitive factor associated with a decrease in depression severity in adolescents in the 36 weeks after they had been given antidepressant medication (Jacobs & others, 2014). And a recent study that explored how emerging adults were coping during the COVID-19 pandemic revealed that the most frequently used coping strategies were maintaining positivity and staying connected (Waselewski, Waselewski, & Chang, 2020).

Support Receiving support from others is an important aspect of being able to cope with stress. Close, positive attachments to others—such as family members, friends, or a mentor—consistently show up as buffers to stress in adolescents' and emerging adults' lives (Pigaiani & others, 2020).

Individuals who provide support can recommend specific actions and plans to help an adolescent or emerging adult cope more effectively with stressful circumstances. For example, a mentor or counselor might notice that an adolescent is overloaded with schoolwork and this is causing considerable stress. The mentor or counselor might suggest ways for the adolescent or emerging adult to manage time better or to delegate tasks more efficiently. Friends and family members can reassure the adolescent or emerging adult under stress that he or she is a valuable person who is loved by others. Knowing that others care allows adolescents and emerging adults to cope with stress with greater assurance. Also, a recent study found that when parents used effective coping strategies so did their adolescents, suggesting a modeling role for parents (Liga & others, 2020).

When adolescents experience severe stressors, such as the sudden death of a parent, close friend, or classmate, the event can be traumatic (Shi & others, 2018). In these cases, it is important for adolescents to reach out for support and to share their feelings with others. In a recent study of how adolescents coped with the death of a parent, the following were helpful: family support, friend support, religion, exercising, and journal writing (Ludik & Greeff, 2021).

Contexts and Coping Coping is not a stand-alone process; it is influenced by the demands and resources of the environment. Strategies for coping need to be evaluated in the specific context in which they occur (Rabinowitz & others, 2020). For example, a certain strategy may be effective in one situation but not another, depending on the extent to which the situation is controllable. Thus, it is adaptive to engage in problem-focused coping before an exam and in mental disengagement while waiting for the results. The contextual approach to coping points to the importance of *coping flexibility*, the ability to modify coping strategies to match the demands of the situation.

To read further about coping strategies, see the *Connecting with Health and Well-Being* interlude, which considers some of the strategies already discussed and introduces several others.

RESILIENCE

Despite being faced with challenges such as poverty, some adolescents and emerging adults triumph over adversity through *resilience*. Think back to the story about Alice Walker at the beginning of the "Introduction" chapter. In spite of racism, poverty, low socioeconomic status, and a disfiguring eye injury, she became a successful author and champion for equality.

Are there certain characteristics that make adolescents resilient? Ann Masten and her colleagues (Masten, 2015, 2017, 2019, 2021a, b; Masten, Motti-Stefanidi, & Rahl-Brigman, 2020; Masten & others, 2021; Masten & Palmer, 2019) have discovered a number of factors, such as good intellectual functioning and effective parenting, that are often seen in children and adolescents who show resilience in the context of a wide range of stressful and even life-threatening circumstances. Figure 3 describes the individual, familial, and extrafamilial contexts that often have been found to characterize resilient children and adolescents (Masten & Coatsworth, 1998).

Masten and her colleagues (2006) concluded that being resilient in adolescence is linked to ongoing resilience in emerging adulthood, but that resilience also can develop in emerging

What Coping Strategies Work for Adolescents and Emerging Adults?

Here are some effective coping strategies that can benefit adolescents and emerging adults:

- *Think positively and optimistically.* Thinking positively and avoiding negative thoughts are good strategies when adolescents and emerging adults are trying to handle stress in just about any circumstance. Why? A positive mood improves your ability to process information efficiently and enhances self-esteem. In most cases, an optimistic attitude is superior to a pessimistic one. It provides a sense of controlling the environment, much like what Albert Bandura (2012) talks about when he describes the importance of self-efficacy in coping.
- *Increase self-control.* Developing better self-control is an effective coping strategy (Usher & Schunk, 2018). Coping successfully with a problem usually takes time—weeks, months, even years in some cases. Many adolescents and emerging adults who engage in problematic behavior have difficulty maintaining a plan for coping because their problematic behavior provides immediate gratification (such as overeating, smoking, drinking, going to a party instead of studying for an exam). To maintain a self-control program over time, it is important to be able to forgo immediate satisfaction.
- *Seek social support.* Researchers consistently have found that social support helps adolescents and emerging adults cope with stress (Lee & others, 2020). For example, depressed adolescents and emerging adults usually have fewer and less supportive relationships with family members, friends, and co-workers than do their counterparts who are not depressed (Neumann & others, 2015).
- *See a counselor or therapist.* If adolescents and emerging adults are not able to cope with the problem(s) they are encountering, it is very important for them to seek professional help from a counselor or therapist. Most colleges have a counseling service that provides unbiased, professional advice to students.

As an adolescent or emerging adult, describe some coping strategies to deal with stress effectively that you personally have used. Also, describe some ways you have attempted to cope with stress that did not work well.
izusek/Getty Images

- *Use multiple coping strategies.* Adolescents and emerging adults who face stressful circumstances have many strategies from which to choose. Often it is wise to choose more than one because a single strategy may not work in a particular context. For example, an adolescent or emerging adult who has experienced a stressful life event or a cluster of such life events (such as the death of a parent or the breakup of a romantic relationship) might talk with a mental health professional, seek social support, exercise regularly, reduce drinking, and practice relaxation techniques.

When used alone, none of these strategies might be entirely adequate, but their combined effect may allow the adolescent or emerging adult to cope successfully with stress. Recall what you have learned from reading about research on peers, family, and ethnicity as you consider any other strategies that might be helpful.

---

adulthood. They also indicated that during emerging adulthood some individuals become motivated to better their lives and develop an improved ability to plan and make more effective decisions that place their lives on a more positive developmental course. In some instances, a specific person may influence an emerging adult in very positive ways, as was the case for Michael Maddaus, whose story was provided at the beginning of the "Introduction" chapter. You might recall that after a childhood and adolescence filled with stress, conflict, disappointment, and problems, his connection with a competent, caring mentor in emerging adulthood helped him to turn his life around, and he went on to become a successful surgeon. According to Masten and her colleagues (2006), a romantic relationship or the birth of a child also may stimulate change and motivate an emerging adult to develop a stronger commitment to a positive future.

FIGURE **3**

CHARACTERISTICS OF RESILIENT CHILDREN AND ADOLESCENTS

Source	Characteristic
Individual	Good intellectual functioning
	Appealing, sociable, easygoing disposition
	Self-confidence, high self-esteem
	Talents
	Faith
Family	Close relationship to caring parent figure
	Authoritative parenting: warmth, structure, high expectations
	Socioeconomic advantages
	Connections to extended supportive family networks
Extrafamilial Context	Bonds to caring adults outside the family
	Connections to positive organizations
	Attending effective schools

2 Problems and Disorders

LG2 Describe some problems and disorders that characterize adolescents and emerging adults.

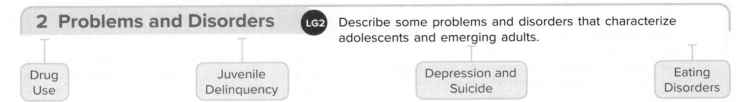

Drug Use   Juvenile Delinquency   Depression and Suicide   Eating Disorders

What are some of the major problems and disorders in adolescence and emerging adulthood? They include use of drugs and alcohol, juvenile delinquency, school-related problems, high-risk sexual behavior, depression and suicide, and eating disorders. We discussed school-related and sexual problems in earlier chapters. Here we examine other problems, beginning with drugs.

DRUG USE

Adolescence is a critical time for the onset of substance abuse (Maisto, Galizio, & Connors, 2022). Many individuals who abuse drugs begin doing so as adolescents. How pervasive is drug use among adolescents and emerging adults in the United States? What are the nature and effects of various drugs taken by adolescents and emerging adults? What factors contribute to adolescent and emerging adult drug use? Let's now explore these questions.

Trends in Overall Drug Use   Each year since 1975, Lloyd Johnston and his colleagues at the Institute of Social Research at the University of Michigan have monitored the drug use of America's high school seniors in a wide range of public and private high schools. Since 1991, they also have surveyed drug use by eighth- and tenth-graders. In 2019, the study surveyed more than 42,531 secondary school students in 397 public and private schools (Miech & others, 2020). However, because of the COVID-19 pandemic, the numbers of students assessed were considerably lower for 2020: 11,800 students in 112 secondary schools.

According to the study, drug use among U.S. secondary school students declined in the 1980s but began to increase in the early 1990s (Johnston & others, 2021). The proportions of eighth-, tenth-, and twelfth-grade U.S. students who used any illicit drug declined in the late 1990s and the first two decades of the twenty-first century (Miech & others, 2020). The most notable declines in drug use by U.S. adolescents in the twenty-first century have occurred for LSD, cocaine, cigarettes, sedatives, tranquilizers, and Ecstasy. Marijuana is the illicit drug most widely used in the United States and Europe (Benedetti & others, 2021; Miech & others, 2020). During the second decade of the twenty-first century, rates of illicit drug use overall by adolescents leveled off (Johnston & others, 2021). Despite the recent decline and leveling off in use, however, the United States still has one of the highest rates of adolescent drug use of any industrialized nation.

Illustrating the slight decline and leveling off of illicit drug use during the past decade, 22.2 percent of twelfth-graders surveyed in 2020 reported using any type of illicit drug in the past month, compared with 23.7 percent in 2010. Illicit drug use among tenth-graders was 18.2 percent in 2020, compared with 18.5 percent in 2010; among eighth-graders the rate was 8.7 percent in 2020 compared with 9.5 percent in 2010 (Johnston & others, 2021). If marijuana is subtracted from total illicit drug use, a significant decrease has occurred: 4.8 percent of twelfth-graders reported using drugs other than marijuana in the past month in 2020, compared with 8.6 percent in 2010.

Let's now consider separately a number of drugs that are abused by some adolescents and emerging adults.

Alcohol   To learn more about the role of alcohol in adolescents' and emerging adults' lives, we examine the use and abuse of alcohol by adolescents and emerging adults, and risk factors for alcohol abuse.

Alcohol Use in Adolescence   How extensive is alcohol use among U.S. adolescents? Sizable declines in adolescent alcohol use have occurred in recent years (Johnston & others, 2021). The percentage of U.S. twelfth-graders who reported drinking alcohol in the past 30 days fell from 41.2 percent in 2010 to 33.6 percent in 2020. The 30-day prevalence fell among tenth-graders from 28.9 percent in 2010 to 20.3 percent in 2020 and among eighth-graders from 13.8 percent in 2010 to 9.9 percent in 2020. Binge drinking (defined in the University of Michigan surveys as having five or more drinks in a row in the last two weeks) by high school seniors declined from 26.8 percent in 2010 to 19.8 percent in 2020. Binge drinking by eighth- and tenth-graders also has dropped considerably in recent years. A consistent gender difference occurs in binge drinking, with males engaging in this behavior more often than females do (Johnston & others, 2021).

Drinking and Driving in Adolescence   A special concern is adolescents who drive while they are under the influence of alcohol or other substances (Yoruk & Xu, 2021). In a recent study, twelfth-grade binge drinking was linked to driving while impaired (DWI), riding with an impaired driver (RWI), blackouts, and riskier driving up to 4 years later (Vaca & others, 2020). And in a national study, one in four twelfth-graders reported that they had consumed alcohol mixed with energy drinks in the last 12 months, and this combination was linked to their unsafe driving (Martz, Patrick, & Schulenberg, 2015).

Alcohol Use in Emerging Adulthood   The transition from high school to college may be a critical transition in alcohol abuse (Haardorfer & others, 2021). The large majority of older adolescents and youth who drink recognize that drinking is common among people their age and is largely accepted or even expected by their peers. They also may perceive some social and coping benefits from alcohol use and even occasional heavy drinking.

Binge drinking often occurs in college, and it can take its toll on students (Fairlie, Maggs, & Lanza, 2016; Wombacher & others, 2019). Binge drinking is defined as having five or more alcoholic drinks in a row on at least one occasion in the past two weeks. Chronic binge drinking is more common among college men, especially those who live in fraternity houses (Schulenberg & others, 2017).

Data collected in 2019 by the *Monitoring the Future* study at the University of Michigan indicate that binge drinking occurred in 21 percent of individuals 19–20 years of age and 38 percent (the highest rate) of individuals 25–26 years of age.

The term *extreme binge drinking* (also referred to as high-intensity drinking) describes individuals who consume 10 or more drinks in a row. In 2019, rates of extreme binge drinking were 7.6 percent at ages 19 to 20, 11 percent at ages 21 to 22, 13 percent at ages 23 to 28, and 14 percent at ages 29 to 30 (Schulenberg & others, 2020).

The effects of heavy drinking take their toll on college students (Bonar & others, 2021)). In a national survey of drinking patterns on 140 campuses, almost half of the binge drinkers reported problems that included missed classes, physical injuries, trouble with police, and unprotected sex (Wechsler & others, 1994). Also in this study, binge-drinking college students were 11 times more likely to drive after drinking, and twice as likely to have unprotected sex, compared with college students who did not binge drink. And a longitudinal study revealed that frequent binge drinking and marijuana use during the freshman year of college predicted delayed college graduation (White & others, 2017).

What characterizes drinking and driving in adolescence?
Chad Ehlers/Alamy Stock Photo

What kinds of problems are associated with binge drinking in college?
ZUMA Press, Inc./Alamy Stock Photo

Getting generally intoxicated or drunk before going out and socializing or attending an event—called *pregaming*—has become common among college students, not just in the United States but other countries as well (Pedersen & others, 2020; Zamboanga & others, 2021). One study revealed that almost two-thirds of students on one campus had pregamed at least once during a two-week period (DeJong, DeRicco, & Schneider, 2010). In a recent study, pregaming occurred more frequently when college women drank alcohol mixed with energy drinks (Linden-Carmichael & Lau-Barraco, 2017). Drinking games, in which the goal is to become intoxicated, also have become common on college campuses. Higher levels of alcohol use have been consistently linked to higher rates of sexual risk taking, such as engaging in casual sex, having sex without contraceptives, and being the perpetrator or victim of sexual assaults (Stoklosa & others, 2021).

Hallucinogens **Hallucinogens,** also called psychedelic (mind-altering) drugs, are drugs that modify an individual's perceptual experiences and produce hallucinations. First, we discuss LSD, which has powerful hallucinogenic properties, and then marijuana, a milder hallucinogen.

LSD LSD (*lysergic acid diethylamide*) is a hallucinogen that—even in low doses—produces striking perceptual changes. Sometimes the images are pleasurable, sometimes unpleasant or frightening. LSD's popularity in the 1960s and 1970s was followed by a reduction in use by the mid-1970s as its unpredictable effects become publicized. However, adolescents' use of LSD increased in the 1990s (Johnston & others, 2021). In 1985, 1.8 percent of U.S. high school seniors reported LSD use in the last 30 days; in 1994, this increased to 4.0 percent. However, LSD use had declined to 2.3 percent in 2001 and further dropped to 1 percent in 2019 (Johnston & others, 2021).

What are some negative consequences for smoking marijuana in adolescence?
Pixel-shot/Alamy Stock Photo

Marijuana *Marijuana*, a milder hallucinogen than LSD, comes from the hemp plant *Cannabis sativa*. Because marijuana also can impair attention and memory, smoking marijuana is not conducive to optimal school performance. Marijuana use by adolescents decreased during the 1980s. For example, in 1979, 37 percent of high school seniors said they had used marijuana in the last month, but that figure dropped to 19 percent in 1992 and 18 percent in 2006. However, marijuana use by U.S. adolescents has increased in recent years. For example, in 2020, 21.1 percent of U.S. twelfth-graders reported having smoked marijuana in the last 30 days (Johnston & others, 2021). Reasons that marijuana use has recently increased include decreased perceptions of danger associated with its use and increased ease of access, particularly in states where marijuana use is legal for adults.

Stimulants **Stimulants** are drugs that increase the activity of the central nervous system. The most widely used stimulants are caffeine, nicotine, amphetamines, and cocaine.

Smoking Cigarette smoking is decreasing among U.S. adolescents. It peaked in 1996 and 1997 and has gradually declined overall since then (Johnston & others, 2021). Following peak use in 1996, smoking rates for U.S. eighth-graders have fallen by 50 percent. In 2020, the percentages who said they had smoked cigarettes in the last 30 days were 7.5 percent of twelfth-graders (an 11 percent decrease from 2011), 3.2 percent of tenth-graders, and 2.2 percent of eighth-graders.

What characterizes e-cigarette smoking (vaping) in adolescence?
AleksandrYu/Getty Images

Among U.S. adolescents, rates of e-cigarette smoking (vaping) far surpass rates of regular cigarette smoking. In 2020, 24.7 percent of twelfth-graders, 19.3 percent of tenth-graders, and 10.5 percent of eighth-graders reported having vaped nicotine in the past 30 days. Recent research suggests a gateway effect of vaping not only for future combustible cigarette smoking but for marijuana use as well (Fadus, Smith, & Squeglia, 2019).

The devastating effects of early smoking were brought home in a research study that found that smoking in the adolescent years causes permanent genetic changes in the lungs and forever increases the risk of lung cancer, even if the smoker quits (Wiencke & others, 1999). The damage was much less likely among smokers in the study who started during their twenties. One of the remarkable findings in the study was that the early age of onset of smoking was more important in predicting genetic damage than how heavily the individuals smoked.

hallucinogens Drugs that alter an individual's perceptual experiences and produce hallucinations; also called psychedelic (mind-altering) drugs.

stimulants Drugs that increase the activity of the central nervous system.

The peer group especially plays an important role in smoking (Cambron & others, 2018). In one study, the risk of current smoking was linked with peer networks in which at least half of the members smoked, one or two best friends smoked, and smoking was common in the school (Alexander & others, 2001). In another study, early smoking was predicted better by sibling and peer smoking than by parental smoking (Kelly & others, 2011).

A research review concluded that in addition to acquiring a best friend who smokes, initiation of smoking in adolescence was linked to getting into trouble at school, having poorer grades, and delinquency (Tucker & others, 2012). In this review, escalation of smoking in adolescence was predicted by depressive symptoms.

A number of researchers have developed strategies for interrupting behavioral patterns that lead to smoking. In one investigation, high school students were recruited to help seventh-grade students resist peer pressure to smoke (McAlister & others, 1980). The high school students encouraged the younger adolescents to resist the influence of high-powered ads suggesting that liberated women smoke by saying, "She is not really liberated if she is hooked on tobacco." The students also engaged in role-playing exercises called "chicken." In these situations, the high school students called the younger adolescents "chicken" for not trying a cigarette. The seventh-graders practiced resistance to the peer pressure by saying, "I'd be a real chicken if I smoked just to impress you." Following several sessions, the students in the smoking prevention group were 50 percent less likely to begin smoking compared with a group of seventh-grade students in a neighboring junior high school, even though the parents of both groups of students had the same smoking rate.

Cocaine   *Cocaine* is a stimulant that comes from the coca plant, native to Bolivia and Peru. Cocaine can have a number of seriously damaging effects on the body, including heart attacks, strokes, and brain seizures.

How many adolescents use cocaine? Use of cocaine in the last 30 days by high school seniors dropped from a peak of 6.7 percent in 1985 to 0.8 percent in 2020 (Johnston & others, 2021). For use in the last 30 days, crack cocaine decreased from 0.7 in 2006 to 0.4 in 2020 among twelfth-graders. A growing percentage of high school students are reaching the conclusion that cocaine use entails considerable unpredictable risk. Still, the percentage of adolescents who have used cocaine is precariously high. About 1 of every 13 high school seniors has tried cocaine at least once.

Amphetamines   Amphetamines, often called "pep pills" and "uppers," are widely prescribed stimulants, sometimes appearing in the form of diet pills. Amphetamine use among high school seniors has decreased significantly. Use of amphetamines in the last 30 days by high school seniors declined from 10.7 percent in 1982 to 1.7 percent in 2020 (Johnston & others, 2021). Although use of over-the-counter diet pills has decreased in recent years, 40 percent of today's females have tried using diet pills by the time they graduate from high school.

Ecstasy   *Ecstasy*, the street name for the synthetic drug MDMA, has both stimulant and hallucinogenic effects. Ecstasy produces euphoric feelings and heightened sensations (especially touch and sight). Ecstasy use can lead to dangerous increases in blood pressure, as well as an increased risk of stroke or heart attack.

Ecstasy use by U.S. adolescents began in the 1980s and then peaked in 2000 to 2001. Thirty-day prevalence of use in 2020 by eighth-, tenth-, and twelfth-graders was 0.3, 0.5, and 0.8 percent, respectively (down from 1.8, 2.6, and 2.8 percent in 2001) (Johnston & others, 2021). The downturn in reported use of Ecstasy coincides with adolescents' increasing knowledge that Ecstasy use can be dangerous.

Depressants   **Depressants** are drugs that slow down the central nervous system, bodily functions, and behavior. Medically, depressants have been used to reduce anxiety and to induce sleep. Among the most widely used depressants is alcohol, which we discussed earlier; others include barbiturates and tranquilizers. Though used less frequently than other depressants, the opiates are especially dangerous.

Barbiturates   *Barbiturates*, such as Nembutal (pentobarbital) and Seconal (secobarbital), are depressant drugs that induce sleep or reduce anxiety. *Tranquilizers*, such as Valium (diazepam) and Xanax (alprazolam), are depressant drugs that reduce anxiety and induce relaxation. They can produce symptoms of withdrawal when an individual stops taking them. Since the initial surveys in 1975 of drug use by high school seniors, use of depressants has decreased. For example, use of barbiturates by high school seniors at least every 30 days in 1975 was 4.7 percent; in 2020, it was 1.2 percent (Johnston & others, 2021). Over the same time period, tranquilizer use also decreased from 4.1 percent to 1.0 percent for 30-day prevalence.

depressants Drugs that slow down the central nervous system, bodily functions, and behavior.

Opiates *Opiates*, which consist of opium and its derivatives, depress the activity of the central nervous system. They are commonly known as narcotics. Many drugs have been produced from the opium poppy, among them morphine and heroin (which is converted to morphine when it enters the brain). For several hours after taking an opiate, an individual feels euphoria and pain relief; however, the opiates are among the most physically addictive drugs. The person soon craves more heroin and experiences very painful withdrawal unless he or she takes more.

The rates of heroin use among adolescents are quite low. In 2020, 0.3 percent of high school seniors said they had used heroin in the last 30 days (Johnston & others, 2021).

At this point, we have discussed a number of depressants, stimulants, and hallucinogens. Their medical uses, short-term effects, overdose symptoms, health risks, physical addiction risk, and psychological dependence risk are summarized in Figure 4.

anabolic steroids Drugs derived from the male sex hormone testosterone. They promote muscle growth and increase lean body mass.

Anabolic Steroids **Anabolic steroids** are drugs derived from the male sex hormone testosterone. They promote muscle growth and increase lean body mass. Nonmedical uses of

Drug Classification	Medical Uses	Short-term Effects	Overdose	Health Risks	Risk of Physical/ Psychological Dependence
DEPRESSANTS					
Alcohol	Pain relief	Relaxation, depressed brain activity, slowed behavior, reduced inhibitions	Disorientation, loss of consciousness, even death at high blood-alcohol levels	Accidents, brain damage, liver disease, heart disease, ulcers, birth defects	Physical: moderate; psychological: moderate
Barbiturates	Sleeping pill	Relaxation, sleep	Breathing difficulty, coma, possible death	Accidents, coma, possible death	Physical and psychological: moderate to high
Tranquilizers	Anxiety reduction	Relaxation, slowed behavior	Breathing difficulty, coma, possible death	Accidents, coma, possible death	Physical: low to moderate; psychological: moderate to high
Opiates (narcotics)	Pain relief	Euphoric feelings, drowsiness, nausea	Convulsions, coma, possible death	Accidents, infectious diseases such as AIDS (when the drug is injected)	Physical: high; psychological: moderate to high
STIMULANTS					
Amphetamines	Weight control	Increased alertness, excitability; decreased fatigue, irritability	Extreme irritability, feelings of persecution, convulsions	Insomnia, hypertension, malnutrition, possible death	Physical: possible; psychological: moderate to high
Cocaine	Local anesthetic	Increased alertness, excitability, euphoric feelings; decreased fatigue, irritability	Extreme irritability, feelings of persecution, convulsions, cardiac arrest, possible death	Insomnia, hypertension, malnutrition, possible death	Physical: possible; psychological: moderate (oral) to very high (injected or smoked)
HALLUCINOGENS					
LSD	None	Strong hallucinations, distorted time perception	Severe mental disturbance, loss of contact with reality	Accidents	Physical: none; psychological: low

FIGURE 4

PSYCHOACTIVE DRUGS: DEPRESSANTS, STIMULANTS, AND HALLUCINOGENS

these drugs carry a number of physical and psychological health risks. Both males and females who take large doses of anabolic steroids usually experience changes in sexual characteristics. Psychological effects in both males and females can include irritability, uncontrollable bursts of anger, severe mood swings (which can lead to depression when individuals stop using the steroids), impaired judgment stemming from feelings of invincibility, and paranoid jealousy.

In the University of Michigan study, in 2020, 0.3 percent of eighth-graders, 0.5 percent of tenth-graders, and 1.2 percent of twelfth-graders said they had used anabolic steroids in the past 30 days (Johnston & others, 2021). The rate of steroid use by twelfth-graders has declined since 2004 (1.6 percent for twelfth-graders).

Inhalants   Inhalants are ordinary household products that are inhaled or sniffed by children and adolescents to get high. Examples of inhalants include model airplane glue, nail polish remover, and cleaning fluids. Short-term use of inhalants can cause intoxicating effects that last for several minutes or even several hours if the inhalants are used repeatedly. Eventually the user can lose consciousness. Long-term use of inhalants can lead to heart failure and even death.

In the University of Michigan national survey, inhalant use by U.S. adolescents decreased in the first two decades of the twenty-first century (Johnston & others, 2021). Use in the last 30 days by twelfth-graders was 0.7 percent in 2020, having peaked at 3.2 percent in 1995. The prevalence of inhalant use in the last 30 days by tenth-graders was 1.2 percent in 2020; inhalant use by eighth-graders was 2.9 percent in 2020 (but up from 1.8 percent in 2017), down from a peak of 6.1 percent in 1995.

Factors in Adolescent and Emerging Adult Drug Abuse   Earlier, we discussed the factors that place adolescents and emerging adults at risk for alcohol abuse. Researchers also have examined the factors that are related to drug use in general during adolescence and emerging adulthood, especially early substance use; influences of parents, peers, and schools; and changes in substance use from adolescence through emerging and early adulthood.

Early Substance Use   Most adolescents become drug users at some point in their development, whether their use is limited to alcohol, caffeine, and cigarettes or extended to marijuana, cocaine, and hard drugs. A special concern involves adolescents who begin to use drugs early in adolescence or even in childhood (Hart & Ksir, 2022; Ivanov & others, 2021). A longitudinal study found that onset of alcohol use before 11 years of age was linked to increased adult alcohol dependence (Guttmannova & others, 2012).

Parents, Siblings, Peers, and Schools   Parents play an important role in preventing adolescent drug abuse (Mehanovic & others, 2021; Voce & Anderson, 2020). Positive relationships with parents, siblings, peers, and others can reduce adolescents' drug use. Researchers have found that parental monitoring and positive relationships with parents are linked to a lower incidence of drug use (Lobato Concha & others, 2020). For example, in one study, maternal and paternal knowledge of the adolescent's activities and whereabouts at age 13 were linked to lower alcohol use at age 16 for girls and boys (Lindfors & others, 2019). Further, a recent study revealed that reduced parental supervision in early adolescence was associated with increased marijuana use, increased frequency of alcohol consumption, and increased quantity of alcohol consumed, with the link strongest at 14 to 15 years of age (Prins & others, 2021). In addition, a research review concluded that the more frequently adolescents ate dinner with their families, the less likely they were to have substance abuse problems (Sen, 2010).

Research indicates that older siblings' substance use is associated with their younger siblings' patterns of use (Whiteman, Jensen, & Maggs, 2013). Another study found that older siblings more strongly transmitted risk for substance abuse to their younger siblings than vice versa (Kendler & others, 2013).

Along with parents and siblings, peers play a very important role in adolescent substance use (Hoeben & others, 2021). When adolescents' peers and friends use drugs, the adolescents are more likely to also use drugs (D'Amico & others, 2020). For example, a large-scale national study of adolescents indicated that friends' use of alcohol was a stronger influence on alcohol use than parental use (Deutsch, Wood, & Slutske, 2018). Also, recent research revealed that associating less often with prosocial peers predicted a rise in future adolescent drug use, while associating more frequently with prosocial peers led to a reduction in future adolescent drug use (Walters, 2020). Further, a recent study found that higher-quality parenting was linked to

What characterizes the use of inhalants by adolescents?
BananaStock/JupiterImages/i2i/Alamy Stock Photo

‐ ‐ ‐ ‐ ‐ ‐ ‐ ‐ ‐ ➤
developmental **connection**
Families
Parental monitoring is a key aspect of parental management of adolescents' lives. Connect to "Families."

lower adolescent marijuana use, while associating with deviant peers was related to higher adolescent alcohol, tobacco, and marijuana use (Greenwood & others, 2021). In addition, a recent study of 15- to 25-year-olds revealed that online peer group affiliation and belonging were linked to stimulant and opioid use (Miller & others, 2021). And a longitudinal study conducted by Kenneth Dodge and his colleagues (2006) also examined the joint contributions of parents and peers to early substance use. The following sequence of factors was linked to the likelihood that an adolescent would take drugs by 12 years of age:

- Being born into a high-risk family (especially with a poor, single, or teenage mother)
- Experiencing an increase in harsh parenting in childhood
- Having conduct problems in school and getting rejected by peers in childhood
- Experiencing increased conflict with parents in early adolescence
- Having low parental monitoring
- Hanging out with deviant peers in early adolescence and engaging in increased substance use

What are ways that parents have been found to influence whether their adolescents take drugs?
Picturenet/Blend Images LLC

Educational success is a strong buffer against the emergence of drug problems in adolescence (Kendler & others, 2017). An analysis by Jerald Bachman and his colleagues (2008) revealed that early educational achievement considerably reduced the likelihood that adolescents would develop drug problems, including those involving alcohol abuse, smoking, and abuse of various illicit drugs.

JUVENILE DELINQUENCY

Thirteen-year-old Arnie, in the section that opened this chapter, is a juvenile delinquent with a history of thefts and physical assaults. What is a juvenile delinquent? What are the antecedents of delinquency? What types of interventions have been used to prevent or reduce delinquency?

What Is Juvenile Delinquency?   The term **juvenile delinquency** refers to a broad range of behaviors, from socially unacceptable behavior (such as acting out in school) to status offenses (such as running away from home) to criminal acts (such as burglary). For legal purposes, a distinction is made between index offenses and status offenses:

Comstock Images/Alamy Stock Photo

juvenile delinquency A broad range of behaviors, including socially unacceptable behavior, status offenses, and criminal acts.

index offenses Acts such as robbery, rape, and homicide that are crimes regardless of whether they are committed by juveniles or adults.

status offenses Juvenile offenses, performed by youth under a specified age, that are not as serious as index offenses. These offenses may include acts such as underage drinking, truancy, and sexual promiscuity.

- **Index offenses** are criminal acts regardless of whether they are committed by juveniles or adults. They include such acts as robbery, aggravated assault, rape, and homicide.
- **Status offenses,** such as running away from home, truancy, underage drinking, sexual promiscuity, and uncontrollability, are less serious acts. They are performed by youth under a specified age, which classifies them as juvenile offenses. One study found that status offenses increased through adolescence.

States often differ in the age used to classify an individual as a juvenile or an adult. Approximately three-fourths of the states have established age 18 as a maximum for defining juveniles. Two states use age 19 as the cutoff, seven states use age 17, and four states use age 16. Thus, running away from home at age 17 may be an offense in some states but not in others.

One issue in juvenile justice is whether an adolescent who commits a crime should be tried as an adult. Some psychologists have proposed that individuals 12 and under should not be evaluated under adult criminal laws and that those 17 and older should be (Cauffman & others, 2015; Fine & others, 2016, 2017). They also recommend that individuals 13 to 16 years of age be given some type of individualized assessment to determine whether they will be tried in a juvenile court or an adult criminal court. This framework argues strongly against court placement based solely on the nature of an offense and takes into account the offender's developmental maturity. The Society for Adolescent Medicine has argued that the death penalty should not be used with adolescents (Morreale, 2004).

Conduct Disorder In addition to the legal classifications of index offenses and status offenses, many of the behaviors considered delinquent are included in widely used classifications of abnormal behavior. **Conduct disorder** is the psychiatric diagnostic category used when multiple behaviors occur over a six-month period. These behaviors include truancy, running away, fire setting, cruelty to animals, breaking and entering, excessive fighting, and others (Mohan, Yilanli, & Ray, 2021). When three or more of these behaviors co-occur before the age of 15 and the child or adolescent is considered unmanageable or out of control, the clinical diagnosis is conduct disorder (Ogundele, 2018). One study found that conduct disorder is a risk factor for substance abuse throughout adolescence (Hopfer & others, 2013).

Conduct problems in children are best explained by a confluence of causes, or risk factors, operating over time (Zhang & others, 2020). These include possible genetic inheritance of a difficult temperament, ineffective parenting, and living in a neighborhood where violence is the norm (Bares & others, 2020).

In sum, most children or adolescents at one time or another act out or do things that are destructive or troublesome for themselves or others. If these behaviors occur often in childhood or early adolescence, psychiatrists diagnose them as conduct disorders (Ogundele, 2018). If these behaviors result in illegal acts by juveniles, society labels the offenders as *delinquents*.

It has been estimated that up to 10 percent of children show serious conduct problems (Rubin, 2020). These children are often described as showing an *externalizing*, or *undercontrolled*, pattern of behavior. Children who show this pattern often are impulsive, overactive, and aggressive and engage in delinquent actions (Mohan, Yilani, & Ray, 2021).

Approximately 25 percent of children and youth diagnosed with conduct disorder subsequently develop *antisocial personality disorder*, a mental disorder characterized by no disregard for right and wrong, as well as ignoring the rights and feelings of others (Fisher & Haney, 2021). Many of these individuals engage in criminal activity.

Frequency of Juvenile Delinquency Estimates of the number of juvenile delinquents in the United States are sketchy, but FBI statistics indicate that at least 2 percent of all youth are involved in juvenile court cases. In 2017, there were 818,900 delinquency cases in which juveniles were charged with violating criminal laws—down from 1,400,000 in 2010 but up from 400,000 in 1960 (Hockenberry & Puzzanchera, 2019). Males are more likely to engage in delinquency than are females. However, U.S. government statistics revealed that the percentage of delinquency cases involving females increased from 19 percent in 1985 to 27 percent in 2017 (Hockenberry & Puzzanchera, 2019).

As adolescents become emerging adults, do their rates of delinquency and crime change? Analyses indicate that theft, property damage, and physical aggression decrease from 18 to 26 years of age (Schulenberg & Zarrett, 2006). The peak age for property damage is 16 to 18 for males and 15 to 17 for females. However, the peak age for violence is 18 to 19 for males and 19 to 21 for females (Farrington, 2004).

Developmental Changes and Pathways In a British longitudinal study of males from 8 to 61 years of age, the childhood factors that best predicted which individuals would have criminal careers lasting at least 20 years were harsh discipline, poor parental supervision, parental conflict, and a convicted father (Farrington, 2020). In another longitudinal study, the Pittsburgh Youth Study, the adolescent factors that best predicted which boys were most likely to be in the worst category of criminal offenders through their thirties were frequency of sexual activity, school problems, and having friends who were a bad influence (Ahonen & others, 2020).

A distinction is made between early-onset (before age 11) and late-onset (after age 11) antisocial behavior. Early-onset antisocial behavior is associated with more negative developmental outcomes than late-onset antisocial behavior (Schulenberg & Zarrett, 2006). Early-onset antisocial behavior is more likely to persist into emerging adulthood and is associated with more mental health and relationship problems (Loeber & Burke, 2011).

Antecedents of Juvenile Delinquency Predictors of delinquency include conflict with authority, minor covert acts that are followed by property damage and other more serious acts, minor aggression followed by fighting and violence, identity (negative identity), self-control (low degree), cognitive distortions (egocentric bias), age (early initiation), sex (male), expectations for education (low expectations, little commitment), school achievement (low

What are some characteristics of conduct disorder?
Stockdisc/PunchStock

conduct disorder The psychiatric diagnostic category for the occurrence of multiple delinquent activities over a six-month period. These behaviors include truancy, running away from home, fire setting, cruelty to animals, breaking and entering, and excessive fighting.

achievement in early grades), peer influence (heavy influence, low resistance), socioeconomic status (low), parental role (lack of monitoring, low support, and ineffective discipline), siblings (having an older sibling who is a delinquent), and neighborhood quality (urban, high crime, high mobility). A summary of these antecedents of delinquency is presented in Figure 5.

Let's look in more detail at several other factors that are related to delinquency. Erik Erikson (1968) notes that adolescents whose development has restricted their access to

Antecedent	Association with Delinquency	Description
Authority conflict	High degree	Youth show stubbornness prior to age 12, then become defiant of authority.
Covert acts	Frequent	Minor covert acts, such as lying, are followed by property damage and moderately serious delinquency, then serious delinquency.
Overt acts of aggression	Frequent	Minor aggression is followed by fighting and violence.
Identity	Negative identity	Erikson argues that delinquency occurs because the adolescent fails to resolve a role identity.
Cognitive distortions	High degree	The thinking of delinquents is frequently characterized by a variety of cognitive distortions (such as egocentric bias, externalizing of blame, and mislabeling) that contribute to inappropriate behavior and lack of self-control.
Self-control	Low degree	Some children and adolescents fail to acquire the essential controls that others have acquired during the process of growing up.
Age	Early initiation	Early appearance of antisocial behavior is associated with serious offenses later in adolescence. However, not every child who acts out becomes a delinquent.
Sex	Male	Boys engage in more antisocial behavior than girls do, although girls are more likely to run away. Boys engage in more violent acts.
Expectations for education and school grades	Low expectations and low grades	Adolescents who become delinquents often have low educational expectations and low grades. Their verbal abilities are often weak.
Parental influences	Monitoring (low), support (low), discipline (ineffective)	Delinquents often come from families in which parents rarely monitor their adolescents, provide them with little support, and ineffectively discipline them.
Sibling relations	Older delinquent sibling	Individuals with an older delinquent sibling are more likely to become delinquent.
Peer influences	Heavy influence, low resistance	Having delinquent peers greatly increases the risk of becoming delinquent.
Socioeconomic status	Low	Serious offenses are committed more frequently by low-socioeconomic-status males.
Neighborhood quality	Urban, high crime, high mobility	Communities often breed crime. Living in a high-crime area, which also is characterized by poverty and dense living conditions, increases the probability that a child will become a delinquent. These communities often have grossly inadequate schools.

FIGURE 5
THE ANTECEDENTS OF JUVENILE DELINQUENCY

acceptable social roles or made them feel that they cannot measure up to the demands placed on them may choose a negative identity. Adolescents with a negative identity may find support for their delinquent image among peers, reinforcing the negative identity. For Erikson, delinquency is an attempt to establish an identity, although it is a negative identity.

Parenting factors play a key role in delinquency. Recall from earlier in this chapter the description of the developmental cascade approach of Gerald Patterson and his colleagues (2010) and research indicating that high levels of coercive parenting and low levels of positive parenting lead to the development of antisocial behavior in children, which in turn is associated with negative experiences in peer and school contexts.

Let's further explore the role that family processes play in the development of delinquency. Parents of delinquents are less skilled in discouraging antisocial behavior and in encouraging prosocial behavior than are parents of nondelinquents. Parental monitoring of adolescents is especially important in determining whether an adolescent becomes a delinquent. For example, a recent study revealed that parental monitoring was a protective factor against juvenile delinquency for both boys and girls but had a stronger influence on girls than on boys (Liu & Miller, 2020). Another study found that parental monitoring in adolescence and ongoing parental support were linked to a lower incidence of criminal behavior in emerging adulthood (Johnson & others, 2011).

Rare are the studies that actually demonstrate in an experimental design that changing parenting practices in childhood is related to a lower incidence of juvenile delinquency in adolescence. However, a study conducted by Marion Forgatch and her colleagues (2009) randomly assigned divorced mothers with sons to an experimental group (mothers received extensive parenting training) and a control group (mothers received no parenting training) when their sons were in the first to third grades. The parenting training consisted of 14 parent group meetings that especially focused on improving parenting practices with their sons (skill encouragement, limit setting, monitoring, problem solving, and positive involvement). Best practices for emotion regulation, managing interparental conflict, and talking with children about divorce also were included in the sessions. Improved parenting practices and reduced contact with deviant peers were linked with lower rates of delinquency in the experimental group compared with the control group at a nine-year follow-up assessment.

An increasing number of studies have found that siblings can have a strong influence on delinquency (Laursen & others, 2017). In one study, high levels of hostile sibling relationships and older sibling delinquency were linked with younger sibling delinquency in both brother pairs and sister pairs (Slomkowski & others, 2001).

Having delinquent peers increases the risk of becoming delinquent (Walters, 2020). In one study, students whose classmates engaged in higher rates of delinquency had an increased likelihood of becoming delinquent themselves (Kim & Fletcher, 2018). Another study found that having a best friend who was a delinquent increased the likelihood that adolescents themselves would become delinquent (Levey & others, 2019).

Although delinquency is less exclusively a phenomenon of lower socioeconomic status than it was in the past, some characteristics of the low-SES culture might promote delinquency (Gold, 2020). A recent study found that neighborhood poverty was linked to delinquency in adolescence especially through maternal stress and adverse childhood experiences (Wang, Choi, & Shin, 2020). Getting into and staying out of trouble are prominent features of life for some adolescents in low-income neighborhoods. Adolescents from low-income backgrounds may sense that they can gain attention and status by performing antisocial actions. Further, adolescents in communities with high crime rates observe many adults who engage in criminal activities. Quality schooling, educational funding, and organized neighborhood activities may be lacking in these communities (Nishina & Bellmore, 2018).

Lack of success in school also is associated with delinquency (Gordon Simons & others, 2018). In a recent research review, lack of academic success and having a learning disability were linked to delinquency (Grigorenko & others, 2019). Also, in a recent study, students who had been suspended from school for the first time were less likely to earn a high school diploma or a bachelor's degree within 12 years after the initial suspension and were more likely to be arrested and on probation than their peers who had not been suspended (Rosenbaum, 2020).

Cognitive factors such as low self-control, poor decision making, ineffective social information processing, and lack of sustained attention also are implicated in delinquency (Muftic & Updegrove, 2018). For example, one study revealed that low

developmental connection

Families

Parental monitoring is a key aspect of parental management of adolescents' lives. Connect to "Families."

developmental connection

Research Methods

Experimental research designs, but not correlational research designs, allow researchers to determine cause-and-effect links. Connect to "Introduction."

What are some factors that are linked to whether adolescents engage in delinquent acts?
Fertnig/iStock/Getty Images

Rodney Hammond, Health Psychologist

As a college student, Rodney Hammond found his way to psychology through a work experience: "When I started as an undergraduate at the University of Illinois, Champaign–Urbana, I hadn't decided on my major. But to help finance my education, I took a part-time job in a child development research program sponsored by the psychology department. There, I observed inner-city children in settings designed to enhance their learning. I saw first-hand the contribution psychology can make, and I knew I wanted to be a psychologist" (American Psychological Association, 2003, p. 26).

Rodney Hammond went on to obtain a doctorate in school and community psychology with a focus on children's development. For a number of years, he trained clinical psychologists at Wright State University in Ohio and directed a program to reduce violence in ethnic minority youth. There, he and his associates taught at-risk youth how to use social skills to effectively manage conflict and to recognize situations that could lead to violence. Later, Hammond became director of Violence Prevention at the Centers for Disease Control and Prevention in Atlanta. And following his recent retirement from CDC, he is now Adjunct Professor of Human Development and Counseling at the University of Georgia. Hammond says that if you are interested in people and problem solving, psychology is a wonderful way to put these together.

Rodney Hammond talks with an adolescent about strategies for coping with stress and avoiding risk-taking behaviors.
Courtesy of Dr. Rodney Hammond

---> developmental **connection**

Developmental Issues

An important issue in the study of adolescent development is the role of early and later experiences. Connect to "Introduction."

self-control was linked to delinquency (Fine & others, 2016). In a recent study in rural China, low self-control also was linked to engagement in delinquent behavior (Jiang, Chen, & Zhuo, 2020). Further, one study found that at age 16 nondelinquents were more likely to have a higher verbal IQ and engage in sustained attention than were delinquents (Loeber & others, 2007). And recent research indicates that certain personality traits are linked to delinquency. For example, in a recent study, having callous-unemotional personality traits predicts an increased risk that adolescent males would engage in acts of delinquency (Ray & others, 2017).

Effective Prevention and Intervention Programs   In a research review of effective juvenile delinquency prevention and intervention programs, the most successful programs are those that prevent juvenile delinquency from occurring in the first place (Greenwood, 2008). Later in the chapter, we will discuss one such program—the Perry Preschool program.

The most successful programs for adolescents who have engaged in delinquency focus on improving family interactions and providing skills to adults who supervise and train the adolescent (Amani & others, 2018). A meta-analysis found that of five program types (case management, individual treatment, youth court, restorative justice, and family treatment), family treatment was the only one that was linked to a reduction in recidivism for juvenile offenders (Schwalbe & others, 2012). Among the least effective programs for reducing juvenile delinquency are those that emphasize punishment or attempt to scare youth.

To read about the work of one individual who has made a commitment to reducing adolescent problems including delinquency, see the *Connecting with Careers* profile.

DEPRESSION AND SUICIDE

As we saw earlier in the chapter, one of the most frequent characteristics of adolescents referred for psychological treatment is sadness or depression, especially among girls. In this section, we discuss the nature of adolescent depression and adolescent suicide.

Depression   Adolescent depression is a concern not just in the United States but around the world (Bondar & others, 2020). An adolescent who says "I'm depressed" or "I'm so down" may be describing a mood that lasts only a few hours or a much longer-lasting mental disorder. In **major depressive disorder (MDD),** an individual experiences a major depressive episode and depressed characteristics, such as lethargy and hopelessness, for at least two weeks or longer and daily functioning becomes impaired. According to the *Diagnostic and Statistical Manual of Mental Disorders–Fifth Edition (DSM-V)* classification of mental disorders (American Psychiatric Association, 2013), nine symptoms define a major depressive episode, and to be classified as having major depressive disorder, at least five of these must be present during a two-week period:

1. Depressed mood most of the day
2. Reduced interest or pleasure in all or most activities
3. Significant weight loss or gain, or significant decrease or increase in appetite
4. Trouble sleeping or sleeping too much
5. Psychomotor agitation or retardation
6. Fatigue or loss of energy
7. Feeling worthless or guilty in an excessive or inappropriate manner
8. Problems in thinking, concentrating, or making decisions
9. Recurrent thoughts of death and suicide

In adolescence, pervasive depressive symptoms might be manifested in such ways as primarily wearing black clothes, writing poetry with morbid themes, or being preoccupied with music that has depressive themes. Sleep problems can appear as all-night television watching, difficulty in getting up for school, or sleeping during the day. Lack of interest in usually pleasurable activities may show up as withdrawal from friends or staying alone in the bedroom most of the time. A lack of motivation and a reduced energy level can show up in missed classes. Boredom might be a result of feeling depressed. Adolescent depression also can occur in conjunction with conduct disorder, substance abuse, or an eating disorder.

How widespread is depression in adolescence? Rates of ever experiencing major depressive disorder range from 15 to 20 percent for adolescents (Graber & Sontag, 2009). Adolescents who are experiencing a high level of stress and/or a loss of some type are at increased risk for developing depression (Endedijk & others, 2020). A recent study revealed that interpersonal stress was linked to increased depression in adolescent girls (Slavich & others, 2020). Also, in a recent Chinese study, adolescents showed more depressive symptoms after the appearance of COVID-19, but engaging in more physical activity during the quarantine helped to buffer the association between the pandemic and depressive symptoms (Ren & others, 2021). Further, a recent meta-analysis concluded that individuals who had experienced early-life stress were more likely to develop MDD prior to the age of 18 (LeMoult & others, 2020). Also, the type of early-life stress mattered—emotional abuse was associated with MDD, while poverty was not.

Adolescent females are far more likely to develop depression than are their male counterparts. In a recent study, at 12 years of age, 5.2 percent of females compared with 2 percent of males had experienced first-onset depression (Breslau & others, 2017). In this study, the cumulative incidence of depression from 12 to 17 years of age was 36 percent for females and 14 percent for males. In a recent analysis, women were twice as likely to experience depression as men, and this gender difference was linked to a sharp increase in girls' depression in mid-adolescence (Bone, Lewis, & Lewis, 2020). Among the reasons for these gender differences are that females tend to ruminate in their depressed mood and amplify it; females' self-images, especially their body images, are more negative than males'; females face more discrimination than males do; and puberty occurs earlier for girls than for boys (Kouros, Morris, & Garber, 2016). As a result, girls experience a confluence of changes and life experiences during the middle school years that can increase depression (Chen & others, 2015).

Do gender differences in adolescent depression hold for other cultures? In many cultures the gender difference of females experiencing more depression does hold, but a study of more than 17,000 Chinese 11- to 22-year-olds revealed that male adolescents and emerging adults experienced more depression than did their female counterparts (Sun & others, 2010). Explanation of the higher rates of depression among males in China focused on stressful life events and a less positive coping style.

major depressive disorder (MDD) The diagnosis when an individual experiences a major depressive episode and depressed characteristics, such as lethargy and depression, for two weeks or longer and daily functioning becomes impaired.

What are some characteristics of adolescents who become depressed? What are some factors that are linked with suicide attempts by adolescents?
Science Photo Library/age fotostock

Mental health professionals note that depression often goes undiagnosed in adolescence (Hammen & Keenan-Miller, 2013). Why is this so? According to conventional wisdom, normal adolescents often show mood swings, ruminate in introspective ways, express boredom with life, and indicate a sense of hopelessness. Thus, parents, teachers, and other observers may see these behaviors as simply transitory and reflecting not a mental disorder but normal adolescent behaviors and thoughts. And a recent research review concluded that adolescents themselves often have difficulty recognizing depression, tend to seek help from informal rather than professional sources, and attach stigma to depression (Singh, Zaki, & Farid, 2019).

Is adolescent depression linked to adult problems? A longitudinal study found that a majority of adolescents who had a major depressive episode were likely to experience a recurrence of depression 15 years later (Alaie & others, 2019). In addition, adolescent depression was associated with other mental health problems, low educational attainment, and problems in intimate relationships when assessed 15 years later.

Genes are linked to adolescent depression (Horvath, Knopik, & Marceau, 2020). One study found that certain dopamine-related genes were associated with depressive symptoms in adolescents (Adkins & others, 2012). And another study revealed that the link between adolescent girls' perceived stress and depression occurred only when the girls had the short version of the serotonin-related gene 5HTTLPR (Beaver & others, 2012).

Family factors are involved in adolescent and emerging adult depression. A recent study found that adolescents whose parents had higher levels of depression were at increased risk for developing depression themselves (Chang & Fu, 2020). Also in this study, a higher level of adolescent self-esteem buffered the negative effect of maternal depression on adolescent depression. In another recent study, parental emotional support was linked to a lower incidence of depressive symptoms in adolescents (Rasing & others, 2020). Further, in one study, mother-daughter co-rumination (extensively discussing, rehashing, and speculating about problems) predicted increased anxiety and depression in adolescent daughters (Waller & Rose, 2010).

Poor peer relationships also are associated with adolescent depression. For example, a recent study found that adolescents who were isolated from their peers and whose caregivers emotionally neglected them were at significant risk for developing depression (Christ, Kwak, & Lu, 2017). Problems in adolescent romantic relationships can also trigger depression (Furman, 2018).

How might peer and friend relationships be linked to whether adolescents develop depressive symptoms?
Andy Sacks/Getty Images

Friendship often provides social support. A recent study found that adolescent girls with few friends experienced more depressive symptoms than adolescent girls with two or more very close friends (Rodrigues & others, 2020). However, researchers have found that one aspect of social support—the tendency to co-ruminate by frequently discussing and rehashing problems—is a risk factor for the development of depression in adolescent girls (Rose & others, 2014, 2017; Rose & Smith, 2018). One implication of this research is that some girls who are vulnerable to developing internalizing problems may go undetected because they have supportive friendships.

A recent meta-analysis found that adolescent females who were obese were more likely to have depression (Quek & others, 2017). Also, in a British study, obesity in adolescent girls, but not boys, was linked to depression in adulthood (Geoffrey, Li, & Power, 2014).

Some therapy treatments have been shown to reduce adolescent depression (Asarnow & others, 2020). A recent research review conducted by the U.S. Agency for Healthcare Research and Quality (Viswanathan & others, 2020) reached the following conclusions regarding the treatment of adolescent depression: cognitive behavior therapy and family therapy are often effective; selective serotonin reuptake inhibitor drugs (SSRIs), such as Prozac, also can be effective; in some instances, a combination of cognitive behavior therapy and SSRIs are beneficial; however, care needs to be exercised in using SSRIs because they have been associated with serious adverse outcomes—including, in some cases, increased suicidal ideation.

Suicide Depression is linked to an increase in suicidal ideation and suicide attempts in adolescence (Thompson & Swartout, 2018). Suicidal behavior is rare in childhood but escalates in adolescence and then increases further in emerging adulthood (Park & others, 2006). Suicide has been the third-leading cause of death in adolescents for a number of years but recently replaced homicide as the second-leading cause of death in adolescence, with accidents still being the number one cause of adolescent deaths in the United States (National Center for Health Statistics, 2020).

From 2009 to 2019 the percentage of ninth- to twelfth-grade U.S. students who think seriously about suicide increased from 14 to 18.8 percent (Underwood & others, 2020). In a national study conducted in 2019, 8.9 percent of U.S. students in grades 9 through 12 had attempted suicide one or more times in the past 12 months and 2.5 percent had engaged in suicide attempts that required medical attention (Underwood & others, 2020). Almost 5,000 U.S. adolescents die from suicide each year. In 2019, 11 percent of U.S. adolescent girls attempted suicide, compared with 6.6 percent of adolescent boys (Underwood & others, 2020). Further, in a recent national study, the rate at which girls 12 to 17 years of age visited an emerging department for suspected suicide attempts was 51 percent higher in February and March of 2021 than it had been during the same time period in 2019 (prior to the COVID-19 pandemic); among adolescent boys in this time frame, emergency department visits for suspected suicide attempts increased by 4 percent (Yard & others, 2021).

The rate of suicide deaths among emerging adults is triple that of adolescents (Park & others, 2006). Although women are more likely to attempt suicide than men, men are more likely to complete their attempts. In emerging adulthood, men are six times as likely to complete suicide as women. Men use more lethal means, such as guns, in their suicide attempts, whereas women are more likely to cut their wrists or take an overdose of sleeping pills—methods less likely to result in death.

Cultural contexts also are related to suicide attempts. Recent cross-cultural comparisons of 15- to 19-year-olds indicated that the highest suicide rates occurred in New Zealand, followed by Iceland, and that the lowest rates occurred in Greece and Israel (OECD, 2017a). Adolescent suicide attempts also vary across ethnic groups in the United States (Meza & Bath, 2021). As indicated in Figure 6, more than 20 percent of Native American/Alaska Native (NA/AN) female adolescents reported that they had attempted suicide in the previous year, and suicide accounts for almost 20 percent of NA/AN deaths in 15- to 19-year-olds (Goldston & others, 2008). African American and non-Latinx white males reported the lowest incidence of suicide attempts. A major risk factor in the high rate of suicide attempts by NA/AN adolescents is their elevated rate of alcohol abuse (Subica & Wu, 2018).

What is the psychological profile of the suicidal adolescent? Suicidal adolescents often have depressive symptoms (Kim, Kim, & Park, 2020). In a recent study, the most significant factor in a first suicide attempt during adolescence was major depressive episode, while for children it was child maltreatment (Peyre & others, 2017). Feelings of hopelessness, low self-esteem, and high self-blame also are associated with adolescent suicide (Chang, 2017). For example, in a recent study, a sense of hopelessness predicted an increase in suicidal ideation in depressed adolescents (Wolfe & others, 2019). Further, one study revealed that adolescent girls, but not boys, who perceived they were overweight were at increased risk for engaging in suicidal ideation (Seo & Lee, 2013).

Just as genetic factors are associated with depression, they also are associated with suicide (Orri & others, 2020). The closer a person's genetic relationship to someone who has died from suicide, the more likely that person is to also die from suicide.

Both earlier and later experiences are linked to suicide attempts, and these can involve family relationships (Cheung & others, 2020). The adolescent might have a long-standing history of family instability and unhappiness. Lack of affection and emotional support, high control, and pressure for achievement by parents during childhood are likely to show up as factors in suicide attempts. In a recent of adolescents in Hong Kong, suicide attempts were linked to child abuse (Wong & others, 2020). Also, a recent study confirmed that childhood sexual abuse was a significant factor in suicide attempts (Ng & others, 2018).

Recent and current stressful circumstances, such as getting poor grades in school or experiencing the breakup of a romantic relationship, also may trigger suicide attempts (Im, Oh, & Suk, 2017). For example, in a recent study, combined school difficulties (academic failure and inappropriate behavior) were associated with higher suicide risk (Ligier & others, 2020). Also, in a recent study, in 32 of 38 countries, early sexual intercourse (at 12 to 15 years of age) was linked to increased suicide attempts and having sexual intercourse with multiple partners increased the risk of suicide attempts further (Smith & others, 2020).

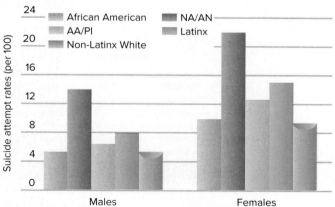

FIGURE 6

SUICIDE ATTEMPTS BY U.S. ADOLESCENTS FROM DIFFERENT ETHNIC GROUPS.

Note: Data shown are for one-year rates of self-reported suicide attempts. NA/AN = Native American/Alaska Native; AA/PI = Asian American/Pacific Islander.

And in a recent analysis, the main factor in adolescent suicidal deaths was the occurrence of recent stressful life events (Werbart Tomblom & others, 2020).

Family and peer relationships also are linked to suicide attempts (Carballo & others, 2020; Soreff, Basit, & Attia, 2021). In recent research with more than 290,000 adolescents across a four-year period, the highest stressor for suicidal ideation was peer conflict, followed by family circumstances such as conflict with parents (Kim, 2021). Also, in a recent study of 9- to 10-year-olds, family conflict was linked to children's increased suicidal ideation and low parental monitoring was associated with suicidal ideation and attempts (DeVille & others, 2020). In another recent study, harsh disciplinary practices were associated with increased suicidal ideation in adolescents (Kingsbury & others, 2020). Further, as discussed in the "Schools" chapter, being victimized through bullying is associated with suicide-related thoughts and behavior. In a recent cross-cultural study of more than 130,000 12- to 15-year-olds, in 47 of 48 countries being a victim of bullying was associated with a higher probability of attempting suicide (Kovanagi & others, 2019). And a recent research review concluded that the most significant risk factors for adolescent suicide and bullying were being a boy, having a previous personal and/or family suicide attempt, mental health problems, substance abuse, previous physical and/or sexual abuse, low SES, being in a single-parent family, underachievement, family dysfunction, and a violent environment (Cuesta & others, 2021).

In some instances, adolescent suicides occur in clusters (Hawton & others, 2020). That is, when one adolescent commits suicide, other adolescents who find out about this also commit suicide. Such "copycat" suicides raise the issue of whether or not suicides should be reported in the media; a news report might plant the idea of committing suicide in other adolescents' minds. Figure 7 provides valuable information about what to do and what not to do when you suspect someone is likely to attempt suicide.

EATING DISORDERS

Eating disorders have become increasingly common among adolescents (Schiff, 2021). Let's now examine different types of eating problems in adolescence, beginning with overweight and obesity.

Overweight and Obese Adolescents   Obesity is a serious and pervasive health problem for many adolescents and emerging adults (Telljohann & others, 2020). The Centers for Disease Control and Prevention (2021) has a category of obesity for adults but does not have an obesity category for children and adolescents because of the stigma the label *obesity* may bring. Rather, they have categories for being overweight or at risk for being overweight in childhood and adolescence. These categories are determined by *body mass index (BMI)*, which is computed using a formula that takes into account height and weight. Only children and adolescents at or above the 95th percentile of BMI are included in the category of

What to do	What not to do
1. Ask direct, straightforward questions in a calm manner: "Are you thinking about hurting yourself?"	1. Do not ignore the warning signs.
2. Assess the seriousness of the suicidal intent by asking questions about feelings, important relationships, who else the person has talked with, and the amount of thought given to the means to be used. If a gun, pills, a rope, or other means have been obtained and a precise plan has been developed, clearly the situation is dangerous. Stay with the person until help arrives.	2. Do not refuse to talk about suicide if a person approaches you about it. 3. Do not react with humor, disapproval, or repulsion. 4. Do not give false reassurances by saying such things as "Everything is going to be OK." Also do not give out simple answers or platitudes, such as "You have everything to be thankful for."
3. Be a good listener and be very supportive without being falsely reassuring.	5. Do not abandon the individual after the crisis has passed or after professional help has commenced.
4. Try to persuade the person to obtain professional help and assist him or her in getting this help.	

FIGURE 7
WHAT TO DO AND WHAT NOT TO DO WHEN YOU SUSPECT SOMEONE IS LIKELY TO ATTEMPT SUICIDE

overweight, and those at or above the 85th percentile are included in the category of at risk for being overweight.

National data indicate that the percentage of overweight U.S. 12- to 19-year-olds increased from 11 percent in the early 1990s to 20.6 percent in 2016 (National Center for Health Statistics, 2017). Also, the National Youth Risk Survey has found that U.S. high school students show a long-term linear decrease in their intake of fruits and vegetables, with 59.2 percent of high school students not eating vegetables one or more times in the last 7 days in 2019 (Underwood & others, 2020). In recent research, a higher level of parental monitoring was linked to adolescents having a healthier diet and reduced likelihood of being overweight (Kim & others, 2019).

Emerging adults are more likely than adolescents to be overweight or obese. A longitudinal study tracked more than 1,500 adolescents who were classified as not overweight, overweight, or obese when they were 14 years of age (Patton & others, 2011). Across the 10-year period of the study, the percentage of overweight individuals increased from 20 percent at 14 years of age to 33 percent at 24 years of age. Obesity increased from 4 percent to 7 percent across the 10 years. Another study found that rates of being overweight or obese increased from 25.6 percent for college freshmen to 32 percent for college seniors (Nicoteri & Miskovsky, 2014).

Jules Frazier/Photodisc/Getty Images

Are there ethnic variations in being overweight during adolescence in the United States? In the National Youth Risk Behavior Surveillance Survey in 2015, African American (21.2 percent) and Latinx (20 percent) females were the most likely to be overweight, while African American males (13.6 percent) and non-Latinx white females (14.6 percent) were the least likely to be overweight (Kann & others, 2016). In this survey, Latinx male adolescents (19.4 percent) had the highest obesity rate, non-Latinx white females (9.1 percent) the lowest.

U.S. children and adolescents are more likely to be overweight or obese than their counterparts in most other countries. In a recent survey of 35 countries, U.S. 15-year-olds (31 percent) had the highest obesity rate (based on the criteria for obesity in the study), 15-year-olds in Denmark (10 percent) the lowest (OECD, 2017b).

Eating patterns established in childhood and adolescence are strongly linked to obesity in adulthood. One study revealed that 62 percent of adolescent boys and 73 percent of adolescent girls in the 85th to 94th percentile of BMI became obese adults (Wang & others, 2008). In this study, of those at the 95th percentile and higher for BMI, 80 percent of the males and 92 percent of the females became obese adults. A study of more than 8,000 12- to 21-year-olds found that obese adolescents were more likely to develop severe obesity in emerging adulthood than were overweight or normal-weight adolescents (The & others, 2010).

Both heredity and environmental factors are involved in obesity (Schiff, 2021). Some individuals inherit a tendency to be overweight. Only 10 percent of children who do not have obese parents become obese themselves, whereas 40 percent of children who become obese have one obese parent, and 70 percent of children who become obese have two obese parents. Identical twins, even when they are reared apart, have similar weights.

Environmental factors play a role in obesity (Schiff, 2022). Strong evidence of the environment's role in obesity is the doubling of the rate of obesity in the United States since 1900, as well as the significant increase in adolescent obesity since the 1960s, as described earlier. This dramatic increase in obesity likely is due to greater availability of food (especially food high in fat), use of energy-saving devices, and declining physical activity (Chong & others, 2020). An international study of adolescents in 56 countries found fast-food consumption is high in childhood but increases further in adolescence (Braithwaite & others, 2014). In this study, adolescents in the frequent and very frequent categories of eating fast food had higher body mass indices than adolescents in the lower frequency categories. Further, increases in screen time in adolescence are associated with adolescent overweight and obesity (de Souza Neto & others, 2021).

Being overweight or obese has negative effects on adolescent health, in terms of both biological development and socioemotional development. In terms of biological development, being overweight in childhood and adolescence is linked with high blood pressure, hip problems, pulmonary problems, and type 2 (adult-onset) diabetes (Zhang & Wang, 2021).

Researchers have found that adolescents' blood pressure has increased in the twenty-first century, and this increase is linked with the increased rate of being overweight in adolescence (Sakou & others, 2015). In terms of socioemotional development, adolescents who are overweight are more likely than their normal-weight counterparts to have low self-esteem, mental

developmental **connection**

Health

A special concern is the high amount of fat and low amount of vegetables in U.S. adolescents' diets. Connect to "Puberty, Health, and Biological Foundations."

These overweight adolescent girls are attending a weight-management camp. *What are some factors that contribute to whether adolescents become overweight?*
ZUMA Press, Inc./Alamy Stock Photo

- - - - - - - - - →

developmental **connection**

Health

Researchers have found that as boys and girls reach and progress through adolescence, they become less active. Connect to "Puberty, Health, and Biological Foundations."

← - - - - - - - - -

health disorders, and problematic relationships with peers (Cam & Top, 2020). One study found that adolescent girls and young adult women who were overeaters or binge eaters were twice as likely as their peers to develop depressive symptoms across the next four years (Skinner & others, 2012). Also, a recent meta-analysis found that being overweight was linked to low self-esteem and body dissatisfaction (Moradi & others, 2021). In addition, a recent study of 10- to 17-year-olds found that obesity was linked to poor academic skills (not completing academic tasks and not being interested in learning, for example) and less effective coping skills (not staying calm when challenged, for example) (Gill & others, 2021). Another recent study revealed that compared with normal-weight peers, overweight adolescents were less likely to be nominated as a romantic interest, as popular, and as admired (Jacobs & others, 2020).

What types of interventions and activities have been successful in reducing overweight in adolescents and emerging adults? Research indicates that dietary changes and regular exercise are key components of weight reduction in adolescence and emerging adulthood (Lumpkin, 2021). A recent study found that a combination of regular exercise and a diet plan resulted in weight loss and enhanced executive function in adolescents (Xie & others, 2017). Further, an after-school athletics program reduced the obesity risk of adolescents after one year of intervention (Glabska & others, 2019).

Most parents with an overweight child or adolescent want to help them to lose weight but are not sure how to accomplish this goal. Following are some recommendations for parents about helping their overweight children and adolescents to lose weight (DiLonardo, 2013; Matthiessen, 2013; Moninger, 2013):

- *Work on a healthy project together and involve children and adolescents in the decision-making process.* Get involved in an activity that can help them lose weight, such as purchasing pedometers for all family members and setting goals for how many steps to take each day. By involving children and adolescents in making decisions about the family's health, the hope is that they will begin to take responsibility for their own health.

- *Be a healthy role model for your children and adolescents.* In many aspects of life, what people do is more influential than what they say. So if parents are overweight and engaging in behaviors such as eating fast food and not exercising, but telling their overweight children and adolescents to lose weight, their words are unlikely to be effective. One study revealed that when adolescents' caregivers lost weight, the adolescents also lost weight (Xanthopoulos & others, 2013).

- *Engage in physical activities with children and adolescents.* Parents and children can engage in activities like bicycling, jogging, hiking, and swimming together with their children and adolescents. Parents might say something like "Let's take a bike ride after dinner this evening. It would be fun and could help us both get in better shape."

- *Give children and adolescents choices about what they want to do to lose weight.* Take them to the grocery store with you and let them select the fruits and vegetables they are willing to eat. Let them choose which sport or type of exercise they would like to do.

- *Eat healthful family meals together on a regular basis.* Children and adolescents who eat meals together with their family are less likely to be overweight.

- *Reduce screen time.* Children and adolescents who spend large numbers of hours per day in screen time are more likely to be overweight than their counterparts who do not spend as much of their day doing these sedentary activities.

Anorexia Nervosa, Bulimia Nervosa, and Binge Eating Disorder Three eating disorders that may appear in adolescence and emerging adulthood are anorexia nervosa, bulimia nervosa, and binge eating disorder.

Anorexia Nervosa Although most U.S. girls have been on a diet at some point, slightly less than 1 percent ever develop anorexia nervosa. **Anorexia nervosa** is an eating disorder that involves the relentless pursuit of thinness through starvation. It is a serious disorder that can lead to death (Farasat & others, 2020; Moore & Bokor, 2021). Three main characteristics

anorexia nervosa An eating disorder that involves the relentless pursuit of thinness through starvation.

apply to people suffering from anorexia nervosa: (1) a clinically significant level of being underweight; (2) an intense fear of gaining weight that does not decrease with weight loss; and (3) a distorted image of their body shape. Obsessive thinking about weight and compulsive exercise also are linked to anorexia nervosa (Smith, Mason, & Lavender, 2018). Even when they are extremely thin, anorexic individuals see themselves as too fat. They never think they are thin enough, especially in the abdomen, buttocks, and thighs (Hosseini & Padhy, 2021). They usually weigh themselves frequently, often take their body measurements, and gaze critically at themselves in mirrors (Askew & others, 2020).

Anorexia nervosa typically begins in the early to middle adolescent years, often following an episode of dieting and some type of life stress (Bakalar & others, 2015). It is about 10 times more likely to occur in girls than in boys. When anorexia nervosa does occur in boys, the symptoms and other characteristics (such as a distorted body image and family conflict) are usually similar to those reported by girls who have the disorder (Ariceli & others, 2005).

Most individuals with anorexia are non-Latinx white adolescent or young adult girls/women who come from well-educated, middle- and upper-income families and are competitive and high-achieving (Darcy, 2012). They set high standards, become stressed about not being able to reach the standards, and are intensely concerned about how others perceive them (Calugi & Dalle Grave, 2019). One study found that anorexics had an elevated level of perfectionism in comparison with non-anorexic individuals (Lloyd & others, 2014). Another study revealed that cognitive inflexibility, especially in perfectionistic adolescents, was associated with anorexia nervosa (Buzzichelli & others, 2018). Unable to meet their high expectations, they turn their focus to something they *can* control—their weight. Offspring of mothers with anorexia nervosa are at risk for becoming anorexic themselves (Striegel-Moore & Bulik, 2007). Problems in family functioning are increasingly recognized as being linked to the appearance of anorexia nervosa in adolescent girls, and family therapy is often recommended as a treatment for adolescent and emerging adult girls/women with anorexia nervosa (Baumas & others, 2021).

Biology and culture are involved in anorexia nervosa (Kim, Nakai, & Thomas, 2021). Genes play an important role in the development of this disorder (Watson & others, 2021). Also, the physical effects of dieting may change brain functioning and neural networks and thus sustain the disordered pattern (de la Cruz & others, 2021). The fashion image in U.S. culture likely contributes to the incidence of anorexia nervosa (Benowitz-Fredericks & others, 2012). The media portray thin as beautiful in their choice of fashion models, whom many adolescent girls strive to emulate. A recent study found that having an increase in Facebook friends across two years was linked to intensified motivation to be thin (Tiggemann & Slater, 2017). And many adolescent girls who strive to be thin hang out together.

Bulimia Nervosa Although anorexics control their eating by restricting it, most bulimics cannot. **Bulimia nervosa** is an eating disorder in which the individual consistently follows a binge-and-purge eating pattern. According to the DSM-V classification system, an individual with bulimia nervosa is characterized by: (1) eating in a specific amount of time (such as within a 2-hour time frame) an amount of food that is larger than what most people would eat in a similar period in similar circumstances, and (2) sense of a lack of control over eating during an episode (Jain & Yilanli, 2021). The bulimic goes on an eating binge and then purges by self-induced vomiting or use of a laxative. Although some people binge and purge occasionally and some experiment with it, a person is considered to have a serious bulimic disorder only if the episodes occur at least twice a week for three months (Castillo & Weiselberg, 2017).

As with anorexics, most bulimics are preoccupied with food, have a strong fear of becoming overweight, and are depressed or anxious (Sattler, Eickmeyer, & Eisenkolb, 2020). Like anorexics, bulimics are highly perfectionistic. A recent research meta-analysis concluded that anorexics and bulimics engage in maladaptive perfectionism (Norris, Gleaves, and Hutchinson, 2019). Unlike anorexics, people who binge and purge typically fall within a normal weight range, a characteristic that makes bulimia more difficult to detect.

Bulimia nervosa typically begins in late adolescence or early adulthood. About 90 percent of individuals with this disorder are women. Approximately 1 to 2 percent of women are estimated to develop bulimia nervosa. Many women who develop bulimia nervosa were somewhat overweight before the onset of the disorder, and the binge eating often began during an episode of dieting. One study of adolescent girls found that increased dieting, pressure to be thin, exaggerated attention focused on appearance, body dissatisfaction, depression symptoms, low self-esteem, and low social support predicted binge eating two years later (Stice, Presnell,

Anorexia nervosa has become an increasing problem for adolescent girls and emerging adult women. *What are some possible causes of anorexia nervosa?*
PeopleImages/E+/Getty Images

bulimia nervosa An eating disorder in which the individual consistently follows a binge-and-purge eating pattern.

& Spangler, 2002). Another study of individuals with anorexia nervosa or bulimia nervosa revealed that attachment insecurity was linked with body dissatisfaction, which was a key aspect of predicting and perpetuating these eating disorders (Abbate-Daga & others, 2010). In this study, need for approval was an important predictor of bulimia nervosa. Drug therapy and psychotherapy have been effective in treating anorexia nervosa and bulimia nervosa (Agras, Fitzsimmons-Craft, & Wilfley, 2017). Cognitive behavior therapy has especially been helpful in treating bulimia nervosa (Hagan & Walsh, 2021; Hay, 2020).

Binge Eating Disorder (BED)   **Binge eating disorder (BED)** involves frequent binge eating but without compensatory behavior like the purging that characterizes bulimics (Igbal & Rehman, 2021). Individuals with BED engage in recurrent episodes of eating large quantities of food during which they feel a lack of control over their eating (Fauconnier & others, 2020). Because they don't purge, individuals with BED are frequently overweight. For the first time, binge eating disorder was included by the American Psychiatric Association in the fifth edition of its classification of psychiatric disorders in 2013.

Researchers are examining the role of biological and environmental factors in BED (Abdo & others, 2020). Genes play a role, as does dopamine, the neurotransmitter related to reward pathways in the brain (Palmeira & others, 2019). Also, a recent study found that adolescents with BED were more likely to live in families with less effective family functioning, especially in the area of emotional involvement (Tetzlaff & others, 2016).

One research overview concluded that the two characteristics that best differentiated BED from other eating disorders were eating in secret and feeling disgusted after the episode (White & Grilo, 2011). One study also found that individuals with BED showed a more negative pattern of everyday emotions, with anger being the emotion that was most often reported before a binge eating episode (Zeeck & others, 2010). And another study of adolescents and young adults revealed that dieters were two to three times more likely than nondieters to develop binge eating problems over a five-year period (Goldschmidt & others, 2012). In this study, at most points in time, depressive symptoms and low self-esteem predicted binge eating onset beyond the influence of dieting alone.

Adults in treatment for BED number approximately 1 to 2 million people, and they often say that their binge eating problems began in childhood or adolescence (New, 2008). Common health risks of BED are those related to being overweight or obese, such as high blood pressure, diabetes, and depression (Peterson & others, 2012). Cognitive behavior therapy and interpersonal therapy are the most strongly supported interventions for BED (Klein, Sylvester, & Schvey, 2021).

binge eating disorder (BED) Involves frequent binge eating without compensatory behavior like the purging that characterizes bulimics.

Review *Connect* Reflect

 LG2 Describe some problems and disorders that characterize adolescents and emerging adults.

Review

- What are some trends in adolescent drug use? What are some characteristics of the use of alcohol, hallucinogens, stimulants, depressants, anabolic steroids, and inhalants by adolescents? What are the main factors that are related to adolescent and emerging adult drug use?
- What is juvenile delinquency? What are the antecedents of juvenile delinquency? What characterizes violence in youth?
- What characterizes adolescent depression? How common is suicide in adolescence and emerging adulthood? What are some possible causes of suicide in adolescence and emerging adulthood?

- What are some trends in eating disorders? What are the main eating disorders in adolescence and emerging adulthood? What are some of their characteristics?

Connect

- How might the development of values be related to an adolescent's or emerging adult's decision to engage in drug use or abstain?

Reflect *Your Own Personal Journey of Life*

- Imagine that you have just been appointed to head the U.S. President's Commission on Adolescent Drug Abuse. What would be the first program you would try to put in place? What would its components be?

3 Interrelation of Problems and Prevention/Intervention

LG3 Summarize the interrelation of problems and ways to prevent or intervene in problems.

Adolescents with Multiple Problems

Prevention and Intervention

What problems affect the largest numbers of adolescents? What are the best strategies for preventing or intervening in adolescent problems?

ADOLESCENTS WITH MULTIPLE PROBLEMS

The four problems that affect the largest numbers of adolescents are (1) drug abuse, (2) juvenile delinquency, (3) sexual problems, and (4) school-related problems (Dryfoos, 1990; Dryfoos & Barkin, 2006a, b). The adolescents at greatest risk have more than one of these problems. Researchers are increasingly finding that problem behaviors in adolescence are interrelated. For example, heavy substance abuse is related to early sexual activity, lower grades, dropping out of school, and delinquency (Hartmann & others, 2021; Zijlmans & others, 2021). Early initiation of sexual activity is associated with the use of cigarettes and alcohol, use of marijuana and other illicit drugs, lower grades, dropping out of school, and delinquency (Chernick & others, 2020). Delinquency is related to early sexual activity, early pregnancy, substance abuse, and dropping out of school (Anderson & others, 2020; Walters, 2021).

As much as 10 percent of the adolescent population in the United States have serious multiple-problem behaviors (adolescents who have dropped out of school or are behind in their grade level, are users of heavy drugs, regularly use cigarettes and marijuana, and are sexually active but do not use contraception). Many, but not all, of these very high-risk youth "do it all." In 1990, it was estimated that another 15 percent of adolescents participate in many of these same behaviors but with slightly lower frequency and less deleterious consequences (Dryfoos, 1990). These high-risk youth often engage in two or three problem behaviors (Dryfoos, 1990). It was estimated that in 2005 the proportion of high-risk youth had increased to 20 percent of all U.S. adolescents (Dryfoos & Barkin, 2006a, b).

PREVENTION AND INTERVENTION

In addition to understanding that many adolescents engage in multiple problem behaviors, it also is important to develop programs that reduce adolescent problems (Biglan & others, 2020; Franzese & others, 2021). We considered a number of prevention and intervention strategies for specific adolescent problems, such as drug abuse and juvenile delinquency, earlier in the chapter. Here we focus on some general strategies for preventing and intervening in adolescent problems. In a review of the programs that have been successful in preventing or reducing adolescent problems, adolescent researcher Joy Dryfoos (1990, 1997; Dryfoos & Barkin, 2006a, b) described the common components of these successful programs. The common components include these:

1. *Intensive individualized attention.* In successful programs, high-risk youth are attached to a responsible adult who gives the youth attention and deals with the youth's specific needs (Plourde, Thomas, & Nanda, 2020). This theme occurred in a number of different programs. In a substance-abuse program, a student assistance counselor was available full-time for individual counseling and referral for treatment. Programs often require highly trained personnel, and they extend over a long period to remain successful (Dryfoos & Barkin, 2006a, b).

2. *Community-wide, multiagency collaborative approaches.* The basic philosophy of community-wide programs is that a number of

What characterizes the most at-risk adolescents?
Peter Beavis/Getty Images

different programs and services have to be in place. In one successful substance-abuse program, a community-wide health promotion campaign was implemented that used local media and community education in concert with a substance-abuse curriculum in the schools. Community programs that include policy changes and media campaigns are more effective when they are coordinated with family, peer, and school components (Brindis & others, 2020).

3. *Early identification and intervention.* Reaching children and their families before children develop problems, or at the beginning of their problems, is a successful strategy (Agnafors, Barmark, & Sydsjo, 2021). For example, in a longitudinal study, an intervention with young children from low-income families in Head Start that involved a social-emotional learning program and an interactive reading program resulted in significant reductions in conduct problems, emotional symptoms, and peer problems compared with a control group of children who did not receive the intervention (Bierman & others, 2021).

Below are descriptions of three other prevention programs/research studies that merit attention:

- *High Scope.* One preschool program serves as an excellent model for the prevention of delinquency, pregnancy, substance abuse, and dropping out of school. Operated by the High Scope Foundation in Ypsilanti, Michigan, the Perry Preschool program has had a long-term positive impact on its students (Schweinhart & others, 2005; Weikert, 1993). The High Scope enrichment program, directed by David Weikert, services disadvantaged African American children. They attend a high-quality two-year preschool program and receive weekly home visits from program personnel. Based on official police records, by age 19 individuals who had participated in the initial Perry Preschool Project program (1962–1967) were less likely to have been arrested and reported fewer adult offenses than a control group. The Perry Preschool students also were less likely to drop out of school, and teachers rated their social behavior as more competent than that of a control group who had not received the enriched preschool experience. In a more recent assessment, at age 40 those who had been in the Perry Preschool program were more likely to be in the workforce, to own their home, and to have had fewer arrests (Schweinhart & others, 2005).

- *Fast Track.* A program that attempts to reduce the risk of juvenile delinquency and other problems is Fast Track (Conduct Problems Prevention Research Group, 2007, 2015, 2019; Dodge & others, 2015). Schools in four areas (Durham, North Carolina; Nashville, Tennessee; Seattle, Washington; and rural central Pennsylvania) were identified as high-risk based on neighborhood crime and poverty data. Researchers screened more than 9,000 kindergarten children in the four schools and randomly assigned 891 of the highest-risk and moderate-risk children to intervention or control conditions. The average age of the children when the intervention began was 6.5 years of age. The 10-year intervention consisted of behavior management training of parents, social cognitive skills training of children, reading tutoring, home visitations, mentoring, and a revised classroom curriculum that was designed to increase socioemotional competence and decrease aggression.

  The extensive intervention was most successful for children and adolescents who were identified as the highest risk in kindergarten, lowering their incidence of conduct disorder, attention deficit hyperactivity disorder, any externalized disorder, and antisocial behavior. Positive outcomes for the intervention occurred as early as the third grade and continued through the ninth grade. For example, in the ninth grade the intervention reduced the likelihood that the highest-risk kindergarten children would develop conduct disorder by 75 percent, attention deficit hyperactivity disorder by 53 percent, and any externalized disorder by 43 percent. The comprehensive Fast Track early intervention was successful in reducing youth arrest rates through age 19 (Conduct Problems Prevention Research Group, 2013). And at age 25, the early intervention was effective in reducing violent and drug crimes, as well as risky sexual behavior (Dodge & others, 2015). Also, at age 25 those who were given the early intervention had higher well-being scores. In addition, a recent research analysis revealed that one-third of Fast Track's reduction in later crime outcomes in emerging adulthood was attributed to improvements in social and self-regulation skills, such as prosocial behavior, emotion regulation, and problem solving, at 6 to 11 years of age (Sorensen & others, 2016). In another recent analysis, the Fast Track intervention decreased the risk of suicidal ideation and hazardous drinking in adolescence and emerging adulthood as well as opioid use in emerging adulthood (Godwin & the Conduct Problems Prevention Research Group, 2020).

What are some strategies for preventing and intervening in adolescent problems?
Paul Michael Hughes/Image Source/Alamy Stock Photo

- *National Longitudinal Study of Adolescent to Adult Health.* This study initially was referred to as the National Longitudinal Study of Adolescent Health and was based on interviews with a nationally representative sample of adolescents in grades 7 to 12 in the United States, initially assessed during the 1994–1995 school year. Participants in the program (referred to also as Add Health) have recently been assessed in middle adulthood, with the most recent interviews taking place with 34- to 42-year-olds in 2018 (National Longitudinal Study of Adolescent to Adult Health, 2021). The Add Health study has implications for the prevention of adolescent and adult problems (National Longitudinal Study of Adolescent to Adult Health, 2021). Perceived adolescent connectedness to a parent and to a teacher were the main factors linked to preventing the following adolescent problems: emotional distress, suicidal thoughts and behavior, violence, use of cigarettes, use of alcohol, use of marijuana, and early sexual intercourse. This study also provides support for the first component of successful prevention/intervention programs as described in item 1 of the list at the beginning of this section. That is, intensive individualized attention is especially important when it comes from important people in the adolescent's life, such as parents and teachers. Researchers are continuing to analyze data from the National Longitudinal Study on Adolescent to Adult Health to further understand how to prevent and intervene in adolescent problems (Alonzo, 2020; Crosby & Salazar, 2021; Hargrove & others, 2020).

We have arrived at the end of this edition. I hope these chapters and course have been a window to improving your understanding of adolescence and emerging adulthood, including your own development in these key time frames in your life. I wish you all the best in the remaining years of your journey through the human life span.

John W. Santrock

Review *Connect* Reflect

LG3 Summarize the interrelation of problems and ways to prevent or intervene in problems.

Review
- Which four problems affect the largest numbers of adolescents? How are adolescent problems interrelated?
- What are the three main ways to prevent or intervene in adolescent problems?

Connect
- What role can parents play in preventing and intervening in adolescent problems?

Reflect *Your Own Personal Journey of Life*
- Did you have any of the problems in adolescence that were described in this chapter? If so, what factors do you think contributed to the development of the problem(s)? If you didn't experience any of the problems, what do you think protected you from developing the problems?

reach your **learning goals**

Problems in Adolescence and Emerging Adulthood

1 Exploring Adolescent and Emerging Adult Problems

 Discuss the nature of problems in adolescence and emerging adulthood.

> The Biopsychosocial Approach

- Biological, psychological, and social factors have been proposed as causes of problems that adolescents, emerging adults, and others can develop. The biopsychosocial approach emphasizes that problems develop through an interaction of biological, psychological, and social factors.

> The Developmental Psychopathology Approach

- In the developmental psychopathology approach, the emphasis is on describing and exploring developmental pathways of problems. One way of classifying adolescent and emerging adult problems is as internalizing (for example, depression and anxiety) or externalizing (for example, juvenile delinquency).

> Characteristics of Adolescent and Emerging Adult Problems

- The spectrum of adolescent and emerging adult problems is wide, varying in severity, developmental level, sex, and socioeconomic status. Middle-SES adolescents and females have more internalizing problems; low-SES adolescents and males have more externalizing problems. Adolescents who have a number of external and internal assets have fewer problems and engage in fewer risk-taking behaviors than their counterparts with few external and internal assets.

> Stress and Coping

- Stress is the response of individuals to stressors, which are circumstances and events that threaten them and tax their coping abilities. Sources of stress include life events, daily hassles, and sociocultural factors (such as gender, acculturative stress, and poverty).

- Coping involves managing taxing circumstances, expending effort to solve life's problems, and seeking to master or reduce stress. Successful coping has been linked to a sense of personal control, positive emotions, greater personal resources, and effective strategies. One way of classifying coping strategies focuses on problem-focused coping versus emotion-focused coping. In most situations, problem-focused coping is recommended over emotion-focused coping. Among the strategies for coping effectively are thinking positively and receiving support from others. Coping is influenced by the demands and resources of the environment, and individuals who face stressful circumstances often benefit from using more than one strategy.

> Resilience

- Three sets of characteristics are reflected in the lives of adolescents and emerging adults who show resilience in the face of adversity and disadvantage: (1) individual factors—such as good intellectual functioning; (2) family factors—such as a close relationship with a caring parent figure; and (3) extrafamilial factors—bonds to prosocial adults outside the family. Resilience in adolescence is linked to ongoing resilience in emerging adulthood, but resilience can also be developed during emerging adulthood.

2 Problems and Disorders

 Describe some problems and disorders that characterize adolescents and emerging adults.

> Drug Use

- The 1960s and 1970s were a time of marked increases in the use of illicit drugs. Drug use began to decline in the 1980s but increased again in the 1990s. Since the late 1990s, there has been a decline in the overall use of illicit drugs by U.S. adolescents. Understanding drug use requires an understanding of physical dependence and psychological dependence.

- Alcohol abuse is a major problem, although its rate of occurrence in adolescents has begun to decline. Recently there has been an increase in alcohol use and binge drinking during emerging adulthood. Binge drinking by college students is a continuing concern. Use of alcohol and drugs typically declines by the mid-twenties.

- Other drugs that can be harmful to adolescents include hallucinogens (LSD and marijuana—their rates of use increased in the 1990s), stimulants (such as nicotine, cocaine, and amphetamines), and depressants (such as barbiturates, tranquilizers, and alcohol). A special concern is cigarette use by adolescents, although it has been declining in recent years. An alarming trend has recently occurred in the increased use of prescription painkillers by adolescents. Use of anabolic steroids has been linked with strength training, smoking, and heavy use of alcohol. Adolescents' use of inhalants has decreased in recent years.

- Drug use that begins in childhood and early adolescence has more negative long-term effects than when it first occurs in late adolescence. Parents and peers can play important supportive roles in preventing adolescent drug use. Being born into a high-risk family, having conduct problems at school, and being rejected by peers are factors related to drug use by 12-year-olds. Early educational achievement by adolescents has a positive influence in reducing the likelihood of developing problems with drug and alcohol abuse. Substance use peaks in emerging adulthood but begins declining by the mid-twenties.

Juvenile Delinquency

- Juvenile delinquency consists of a broad range of behaviors, from socially undesirable behavior to criminal offenses. For legal purposes, a distinction is made between index and status offenses. Conduct disorder is a psychiatric diagnostic category used to describe multiple delinquent-type behaviors occurring over a six-month period.

- Predictors of juvenile delinquency include authority conflict, minor covert acts such as lying, overt acts of aggression, a negative identity, cognitive distortions, low self-control, early initiation of delinquency, being a male, low expectations for education and school grades, low parental monitoring, low parental support and ineffective discipline, having an older delinquent sibling, heavy peer influence and low resistance to peers, low socioeconomic status, and living in a high-crime, urban area. Effective juvenile delinquency prevention and intervention programs have been identified.

Depression and Suicide

- Adolescents have a higher rate of depression than children do. Adolescent girls are far more likely than adolescent boys to develop depression. Parent-adolescent conflict, low parental support, poor peer relationships, and problems in romantic relationships are factors associated with adolescent depression. Treatment of depression has involved both drug therapy and psychotherapy.

- Emerging adults have triple the rate of suicide compared with adolescents. U.S. adolescent suicide rates increased in the 1990s but have fallen in recent years. Both early and later experiences may be involved in suicide. Family instability, lack of affection, poor grades in school, lack of supportive friendships, and romantic breakups may trigger suicide attempts.

Eating Disorders

- Eating disorders have become increasing problems in adolescence and emerging adulthood. The percentage of adolescents who are overweight increased dramatically in the 1980s and 1990s but began leveling off in the middle of the first decade of the twenty-first century. Being obese in adolescence is linked with being obese in adulthood. An increase in obesity has also occurred in emerging adulthood. Both heredity and environmental factors are involved in obesity. Being overweight in adolescence has negative effects on physical health and socioemotional development. Clinical approaches that focus on the individual adolescent and involve a combination of calorie restriction, exercise, reduction of sedentary behavior, and behavioral therapy have been moderately effective in helping overweight adolescents lose weight.

- Anorexia nervosa is an eating disorder that involves the relentless pursuit of thinness through starvation. Anorexics weigh less than 85 percent of weight considered normal, intensely fear weight gain, and continue to see themselves as too fat even when they are very thin.

- Bulimia nervosa is an eating disorder in which the individual consistently follows a binge-and-purge eating pattern. Most bulimics are depressed or anxious, preoccupied with their body weight and shape, and typically fall within a normal weight range.

- Binge eating disorder (BED) involves frequent binge eating but without compensatory behavior like the purging that characterizes bulimics.

3 Interrelation of Problems and Prevention/Intervention

 Summarize the interrelation of problems and ways to prevent or intervene in problems.

Adolescents with Multiple Problems

- The four problems that affect the most adolescents are (1) drug abuse, (2) juvenile delinquency, (3) sexual problems, and (4) school-related problems. Researchers are finding that adolescents who are at risk often have more than one problem and that the highest-risk adolescents often have all four of these problems.

- In Dryfoos' analysis, successful prevention/intervention programs had these three components: (1) extensive individual attention, (2) community-wide intervention, and (3) early identification and intervention.

key **terms**

acculturative stress	conduct disorder	emotion-focused coping	major depressive disorder
anabolic steroids	coping	externalizing problems	problem-focused coping
anorexia nervosa	depressants	hallucinogens	status offenses
binge eating disorder (BED)	developmental cascades	index offenses	stimulants
biopsychosocial approach	developmental psychopathology	internalizing problems	stress
bulimia nervosa	approach	juvenile delinquency	

key **people**

Thomas Achenbach	Kenneth Dodge	Richard Lazarus	Alan Sroufe
Jerald Bachman	Joy Dryfoos	Ann Masten	Shelley Taylor
Peter Benson	Craig Edelbrock	Gerald Patterson	
Deborah Capaldi	Lloyd Johnston	John Schulenberg	

improving **the lives of adolescents and emerging adults**

Adolescence (2006)
Joy Dryfoos and Carol Barkin
New York: Oxford University Press
> An outstanding book on adolescent problems and the programs and strategies that can successfully prevent and intervene in these problems.

Development and Psychopathology (2010)
(Vol. 22, Issues 3 and 4)
> These issues cover theory and research on the role of developmental cascades in predicting adolescent problems.

Help Your Teenager Beat an Eating Disorder (2nd ed.) (2015)
James Lock and Daniel Le Grange
New York: Guilford
> Leading experts provide excellent recommendations for parents to help them recognize characteristics of a number of eating disorders, including anorexia nervosa, bulimia disorder, and others, and explore various treatment options.

Ordinary Magic (2014)
Ann Masten
New York: Guilford Press
> Leading expert Ann Masten describes multiple pathways that children and adolescents can follow to become resilient in the face of numerous adversities, such as homelessness, child maltreatment, disease, wars, and disasters.

National Adolescent Suicide Hotline (800-621-4000)
> This hotline can be used 24 hours a day by teenagers contemplating suicide, as well as by their parents.

National Longitudinal Study of Adolescent to Adult Health (2018)
(www.cpc.unc.edu/projects/addhealth)
> This national longitudinal study has involved data collection from adolescence into the adult years. A large number of studies have been conducted with the data related to the problems discussed in this chapter, such as substance use, delinquency, depression and suicide, and eating disorders. On this site, you can read about many of these studies in depth.

glossary

A

accommodation An adjustment of a schema in response to new information.

acculturative stress The negative consequences that result from contact between two distinctive cultural groups.

active (niche-picking) genotype-environment correlations Correlations that occur when children seek out environments that they find compatible and stimulating.

adaptive behavior A modification of behavior that promotes an organism's survival in the natural habitat.

adolescence The developmental period of transition from childhood to adulthood; it involves biological, cognitive, and socioemotional changes. Adolescence begins at approximately 10 to 13 years of age and ends in the late teens.

adolescent egocentrism The heightened self-consciousness of adolescents, which is reflected in their belief that others are as interested in them as they themselves are, and in their sense of personal uniqueness and invulnerability.

adolescent generalization gap Adelson's concept of generalizations being made about adolescents based on information regarding a limited, often highly visible group of adolescents.

adolescents who are gifted Adolescents who have above-average intelligence (usually defined as an IQ of 130 or higher) and/or superior talent in some domain, such as art, music, or mathematics.

adoption study A study in which investigators seek to discover whether the behavior and psychological characteristics of adopted children are more like their adoptive parents, who have provided a home environment, or more like those of their biological parents, who have contributed their heredity. Another form of adoption study involves comparing adopted and biological siblings.

adrenarche Puberty phase involving hormonal changes in the adrenal glands, which are located just above the kidneys. These changes occur from about 6 to 9 years of age in girls and about one year later in boys, before what is generally considered the beginning of puberty.

affectionate love Love in which an individual desires to have another person near and has a deep, caring affection for that person; also called companionate love.

AIDS Acquired immune deficiency syndrome, a sexually transmitted infection caused by the human immunodeficiency virus (HIV), which destroys the body's immune system.

altruism Unselfish interest in helping another person.

amygdala A portion of the brain's limbic system that is the seat of emotions such as anger.

anabolic steroids Drugs derived from the male sex hormone testosterone. They promote muscle growth and increase lean body mass.

androgens The main class of male sex hormones.

androgyny The presence of a high degree of desirable feminine and masculine characteristics in the same individual.

anorexia nervosa An eating disorder that involves the relentless pursuit of thinness through starvation.

anxiety A vague, highly unpleasant feeling of fear and apprehension.

assimilation The incorporation of new information into existing knowledge.

attention Concentration and focusing of mental resources.

attention deficit hyperactivity disorder (ADHD) A disability in which children or adolescents consistently show one or more of the following characteristics over a period of time: (1) inattention, (2) hyperactivity, and (3) impulsivity.

attribution theory The theory that in their effort to make sense of their own behavior or performance, individuals are motivated to discover the underlying causes.

authoritarian parenting A restrictive, punitive style in which the parent exhorts the adolescent to follow the parent's directions and to respect work and effort. Firm limits and controls are placed on the adolescent, and little verbal exchange is allowed. This style is associated with adolescents' socially incompetent behavior.

authoritarian strategy of classroom management A teaching strategy that is restrictive and punitive. The focus is mainly on keeping order in the classroom rather than on instruction and learning.

authoritative parenting A style encouraging adolescents to be independent but still placing limits and controls on their actions. Extensive verbal give-and-take is allowed, and parents are warm and nurturant toward the adolescent. This style is associated with adolescents' socially competent behavior.

authoritative strategy of classroom management A teaching strategy that encourages students to be independent thinkers and doers but still involves effective monitoring. Authoritative teachers engage students in considerable verbal give-and-take and show a caring attitude toward them. However, they still set and enforce limits when necessary.

autism spectrum disorders (ASD) Adolescents with these disorders are characterized by problems in social interaction, difficulties with verbal and nonverbal communication, and repetitive behaviors.

autistic disorder A severe autism spectrum disorder that has its onset in the first three years of life and includes deficiencies in social relationships, abnormalities in communication, and restricted, repetitive, and stereotyped patterns of behavior.

average adolescents Adolescents who receive an average number of both positive and negative nominations from their peers.

B

balance theory of wisdom Sternberg's theory that wisdom consists of using one's intelligence, creativity, common sense, and knowledge in a balanced, ethical manner. Individuals should apply their wisdom in a balanced way across intrapersonal, interpersonal, and extrapersonal contexts especially for the common good.

behavior genetics The field that seeks to discover the influence of heredity and environment on individual differences in human traits and development.

bicultural identity Identity formation that occurs when adolescents identify in some ways with their ethnic group and in other ways with the majority culture.

Big Five factors of personality Five core traits of personality: openness to experience, conscientiousness, extraversion, agreeableness, and neuroticism (emotional stability).

binge eating disorder (BED) Involves frequent binge eating without compensatory behavior like the purging that characterizes bulimics.

biological processes Physical changes in an individual's body.

biopsychosocial approach Explanation of human problems emphasizing that these problems develop through an interaction of biological, psychological, and social factors.

bisexual A person who is attracted to people of both sexes.

boundary ambiguity Uncertainty in stepfamilies about who is within or outside the family and who is performing or responsible for certain tasks in the family system.

Bronfenbrenner's ecological theory A theory focusing on the influence of five environmental systems: microsystem, mesosystem, exosystem, macrosystem, and chronosystem.

bulimia nervosa An eating disorder in which the individual consistently follows a binge-and-purge eating pattern.

C

care perspective The moral perspective of Carol Gilligan, which views people in terms of their connectedness with others and emphasizes interpersonal communication, relationships with others, and concern for others.

case study An in-depth look at a single individual.

character education A direct moral education approach that involves teaching students a basic moral literacy to prevent them from engaging in immoral behavior or doing harm to themselves or others.

chlamydia One of the most common sexually transmitted infections, named for *Chlamydia trachomatis,* an organism that spreads by sexual contact and infects the genital organs of both sexes.

chromosomes Threadlike structures that contain deoxyribonucleic acid, or DNA.

cliques Small groups that range from 2 to about 12 individuals and average about 5 to 6 individuals. Members are usually of the same sex and are similar in age; cliques can form because of similar interests, such as sports, and also can form purely from friendship.

cognitive control The capacity to control attention, reduce interfering thoughts, and be cognitively flexible.

cognitive processes Changes in an individual's thinking and intelligence.

cohabitation Living together in a sexual relationship without being married.

cohort effects Characteristics related to a person's year of birth, era, or generation rather than to his or her actual chronological age.

collectivism Emphasizes values that serve the group by subordinating personal goals to preserve group integrity.

commitment The part of identity development in which adolescents show a personal investment in what they are going to do.

concrete operational stage Piaget's third stage, which lasts approximately from 7 to 11 years of age. In this stage, children can perform operations. Logical reasoning replaces intuitive thought as long as the reasoning can be applied to specific or concrete examples.

conduct disorder The psychiatric diagnostic category for the occurrence of multiple delinquent activities over a six-month period. These behaviors include truancy, running away from home, fire setting, cruelty to animals, breaking and entering, and excessive fighting.

conglomerate strategies The use of a combination of techniques, rather than a single approach, to improve adolescents' social skills; also called coaching.

connectedness An important element in adolescent identity development. It consists of two dimensions: mutuality, which is sensitivity to and respect for others' views; and permeability, which is openness to others' views.

conscience The component of the superego that discourages behaviors disapproved of by parents.

constructivist approach A learner-centered approach that emphasizes the adolescent's active, cognitive construction of knowledge and understanding with guidance from the teacher.

contexts The settings in which development occurs. These settings are influenced by historical, economic, social, and cultural factors.

continuity-discontinuity issue Controversy regarding whether development involves gradual, cumulative change (continuity) or distinct stages (discontinuity).

controversial adolescents Adolescents who are frequently nominated both as a best friend and as being disliked.

conventional reasoning The second, or intermediate, level in Kohlberg's theory. Individuals at this level develop expectations about social roles, such as the roles of parents and children, and they understand the importance of following the laws of society.

convergent thinking A pattern of thinking in which individuals produce one correct answer; characteristic of the items on conventional intelligence tests.

coping Managing taxing circumstances, expending effort to solve life's problems, and seeking to master or reduce stress.

corpus callosum A large bundle of axon fibers that connect the brain's left and right hemispheres.

correlation coefficient A number based on a statistical analysis that is used to describe the degree of association between two variables.

correlational research Research whose goal is to describe the strength of the relationship between two or more events or characteristics.

creativity The ability to think in novel and unusual ways and discover unique solutions to problems.

crisis A period of identity development during which the adolescent is choosing among meaningful alternatives.

critical thinking Thinking reflectively and productively and evaluating the evidence.

cross-cultural research Studies that compare a culture with one or more other cultures. Such studies provide information about the degree to which development in adolescents and emerging adults is similar, or universal, across cultures, or about the degree to which it is culture-specific.

cross-sectional research A research strategy that involves studying different people of varying ages all at one time.

crowds A larger group structure than cliques. Adolescents are usually members of a crowd based on reputation and may or may not spend much time together.

culture The behavior, patterns, beliefs, and all other products of a particular group of people that are passed on from generation to generation.

D

date rape, or acquaintance rape Coercive sexual activity directed at someone whom the perpetrator knows.

dating scripts The cognitive models that adolescents and adults use to guide and evaluate dating interactions.

dependent variable The factor that is measured in experimental research.

depressants Drugs that slow down the central nervous system, bodily functions, and behavior.

descriptive research Research that aims to observe and record behavior.

development The pattern of change that begins at conception and continues through the life span. Most development involves growth, although it also includes decay (as in death and dying).

developmental cascades A developmental psychopathology approach that emphasizes connections across domains over time to influence developmental pathways and outcomes.

developmental psychopathology approach Approach that focuses on describing and exploring the developmental pathways of problems.

dialect A variety of language that is distinguished by its vocabulary, grammar, or pronunciation.

difficult child A child who reacts negatively to many situations and is slow to accept new experiences.

direct instruction approach A teacher-centered approach characterized by teacher direction and control, mastery of academic skills, high expectations for students, and maximum time spent on learning tasks.

dismissing/avoidant attachment An insecure attachment category in which individuals deemphasize the importance of attachment. This category is associated with consistent experiences of rejection of attachment needs by caregivers.

divergent thinking A pattern of thinking in which individuals produce many answers to the same question; more characteristic of creativity than convergent thinking.

divided attention Concentrating on more than one activity at the same time.

DNA A complex molecule that contains genetic information.

E

early adolescence The developmental period that corresponds roughly to the middle school or junior high school years and includes most pubertal change.

early adulthood The developmental period beginning in the late teens or early twenties and lasting through the thirties.

early childhood The developmental period extending from the end of infancy to about 5 or 6 years of age; sometimes called the preschool years.

early-later experience issue Issue focusing on the degree to which early experiences (especially early in childhood) or later experiences are the key determinants of development.

easy child A child who generally is in a positive mood, quickly establishes regular routines, and adapts easily to new experiences.

eclectic theoretical orientation An orientation that does not follow any one theoretical approach but rather selects from each theory whatever is considered the best in it.

ego ideal The component of the superego that involves ideal standards approved by parents.

emerging adulthood The developmental period occurring from approximately 18 to 25 years of age; this transitional period between adolescence and adulthood is characterized by experimentation and exploration.

emotion   Feeling, or affect, that occurs when a person is in a state or an interaction that is important to the individual, especially to his or her well-being.

emotion-focused coping   Lazarus' term for responding to stress in an emotional manner, especially by using defense mechanisms.

emotional autonomy   The capacity to relinquish childlike dependence on parents.

emotional intelligence   The ability to perceive and express emotion accurately and adaptively, to understand emotion and emotional knowledge, to use feelings to facilitate thought, and to manage emotions in oneself and others.

empathy   Reaction to another's feelings with an emotional response that is similar to the other's feelings.

epigenetic view   Belief that development is the result of an ongoing bidirectional interchange between heredity and environment.

equilibration   A mechanism in Piaget's theory that explains how individuals shift from one state of thought to the next. The shift occurs as individuals experience cognitive conflict or a disequilibrium in trying to understand the world. Eventually, the individual resolves the conflict and reaches a balance, or equilibrium, of thought.

Erikson's theory   Theory that includes eight stages of human development. Each stage consists of a unique developmental task that confronts individuals with a crisis that must be faced.

estrogens   The main class of female sex hormones.

ethnic gloss   Use of an ethnic label such as African American or Latino in a superficial way that portrays an ethnic group as being more homogeneous than it really is.

ethnic identity   An enduring, basic aspect of the self that includes a sense of membership in an ethnic group and the attitudes and feelings related to that membership.

ethnicity   A dimension of culture based on cultural heritage, national characteristics, race, religion, and language.

ethnocentrism   A tendency to favor one's own group over other groups.

evocative genotype-environment correlations   Correlations that occur because an adolescent's genetically shaped characteristics elicit certain types of physical and social environments.

evolutionary psychology   An approach that emphasizes the importance of adaptation, reproduction, and "survival of the fittest" in explaining behavior.

executive attention   Type of attention that involves planning actions, allocating attention to goals, detecting and compensating for errors, monitoring progress on tasks, and dealing with novel or difficult circumstances.

executive function   An umbrella-like concept that involves higher-order, complex cognitive processes that include exercising cognitive control, making decisions, reasoning, thinking critically, thinking creatively, and metacognition.

experience sampling method (ESM)   Research method that involves providing participants with electronic pagers and then beeping them at random times, at which point they are asked to report on various aspects of their lives.

experimental research   Research that involves an experiment, a carefully regulated procedure in which one or more of the factors believed to influence the behavior being studied are manipulated while all other factors are held constant.

externalizing problems   Behavior that occurs when individuals turn problems outward. An example is juvenile delinquency.

extrinsic motivation   External motivational factors such as rewards and punishments.

F

female athlete triad   A combination of disordered eating, amenorrhea, and osteoporosis that may develop in female adolescents and college students.

feminization of poverty   Term reflecting the fact that far more women than men live in poverty. Likely causes include women's lower income, divorce, and the resolution of divorce cases by the judicial system, which leaves women with less money than they and their children need to function adequately.

flow   Csikszentmihalyi's concept of optimal life experiences, which he believes occur most often when people develop a sense of mastery and are absorbed in a state of concentration when they're engaged in an activity.

forgiveness   An aspect of prosocial behavior that occurs when an injured person releases the injurer from possible behavioral retaliation.

formal operational stage   Piaget's fourth and final stage of cognitive development, which he argued emerges at 11 to 15 years of age. It is characterized by abstract, idealistic, and logical thought.

friends   A subset of peers who engage in mutual companionship, support, and intimacy.

fuzzy-trace theory dual-process model   States that decision making is influenced by two systems—"verbatim" analytical thinking (literal and precise) and gist-based intuition (simple, bottom-line meaning), which operate in parallel; in this model, it is the gist-based system that benefits adolescents' decision making most.

G

gender   Characteristics related to femininity and masculinity based on social and cultural norms.

gender bias   A preconceived notion about the abilities of females and males that prevents individuals from pursuing their own interests and achieving their potential.

gender identity   Involves a sense of one's own gender, including knowledge, understanding, and acceptance of being a boy/man, a girl/woman, or another gender.

gender intensification hypothesis   Hypothesis stating that psychological and behavioral differences between boys and girls become greater during early adolescence because of increased socialization pressure to conform to masculine or feminine gender roles.

gender roles   Expectations that prescribe how girls/women and boys/men should think, act, and feel.

gender-role transcendence   The belief that, when an individual's competence is at issue, it should be conceptualized not in regard to masculinity, femininity, or androgyny but on an individual basis.

gender schema theory   Theory stating that an individual's attention and behavior are guided by an internal motivation to conform to gender-based sociocultural standards and stereotypes.

gender stereotypes   Broad categories that reflect our impressions and beliefs about girls/women and boys/men.

gene × environment (G × E) interaction   The interaction of a specific measured variation in DNA and a specific measured aspect of the environment.

genes   The units of hereditary information, which are short segments composed of DNA.

genital herpes   A sexually transmitted infection caused by a large family of viruses of different strains. These strains also produce nonsexually transmitted diseases such as chicken pox and mononucleosis.

genital warts   An STI caused by the human papillomavirus; genital warts are very contagious and are the most commonly acquired STI in the United States in the 15- to 24-year-old age group.

genotype   A person's genetic heritage; the actual genetic material.

gonadarche   Puberty phase involving the maturation of primary sexual characteristics (ovaries in females, testes in males) and secondary sexual characteristics (pubic hair, breast and genital development). This period follows adrenarche by about two years and is what most people think of as puberty.

gonorrhea   A sexually transmitted infection caused by the bacterium *Neisseria gonorrhoeae*, which thrives in the moist mucous membranes lining the mouth, throat, vagina, cervix, urethra, and anal tract. This STI is commonly called the "drip" or the "clap."

goodness of fit   The match between an individual's temperament style and the environmental demands faced by the individual.

gratitude   A feeling of thankfulness and appreciation, especially in response to someone doing something kind or helpful.

grit   Involves passion and persistence in achieving long-term goals.

H

hallucinogens   Drugs that alter an individual's perceptual experiences and produce hallucinations; also called psychedelic (mind-altering) drugs.

helpless orientation   An outlook in which individuals seem trapped when experiencing difficulty and attribute their difficulty to a lack of ability. This orientation undermines performance.

hidden curriculum   The pervasive moral atmosphere that characterizes every school.

homophobia Irrational negative feelings against individuals who have same-sex attractions.

hormones Powerful chemicals secreted by the endocrine glands and carried through the body by the bloodstream.

hostile environment sexual harassment Sexual harassment in which students are subjected to unwelcome sexual conduct that is so severe, persistent, or pervasive that it limits the students' ability to benefit from their education.

hypotheses Specific assertions and predictions that can be tested.

hypothetical-deductive reasoning Piaget's term for adolescents' ability, in the formal operational stage, to develop hypotheses, or best guesses, about ways to solve problems; they then systematically deduce, or conclude, the best path to follow in solving the problem.

I

identity Who a person believes he or she is, representing a synthesis and integration of self-understanding.

identity achievement Marcia's term for an adolescent who has undergone an identity crisis and made a commitment.

identity diffusion Marcia's term for the state adolescents are in when they have not yet experienced an identity crisis or made any commitments.

identity foreclosure Marcia's term for the state adolescents are in when they have made a commitment but have not experienced an identity crisis.

identity moratorium Marcia's term for the state of adolescents who are in the midst of an identity crisis but who have not made a clear commitment to an identity.

identity versus identity confusion Erikson's fifth developmental stage, which occurs during adolescence. At this time, individuals are faced with deciding who they are, what they are all about, and where they are going in life.

immigrant paradox Observation that despite the barriers they encounter, recent child and adolescent immigrants often engage in more adaptive and competent behavior than their non-immigrant peers and established child and adolescent immigrants from the same ethnic group whose families have been in the United States for several generations.

inclusion Educating a child or adolescent with special educational needs full-time in the regular classroom.

independent variable The factor that is manipulated in experimental research.

index offenses Acts such as robbery, rape, and homicide that are crimes regardless of whether they are committed by juveniles or adults.

individualism Emphasizes values that serve the self and gives priority to personal goals rather than group goals.

individuality An important element in adolescent identity development. It consists of two dimensions: self-assertion, the ability to have and communicate a point of view; and separateness, the use of communication patterns to express how one is different from others.

Individuals with Disabilities Education Act (IDEA) Federal legislation spelling out broad mandates for providing educational services to all children and adolescents with disabilities. These include evaluation and eligibility determination, appropriate education and an individualized education plan (IEP), and education in the least restrictive environment.

induction A disciplinary technique in which a parent uses reason and explains how the adolescent's actions affect others.

indulgent parenting A style in which parents are highly involved with their adolescents but place few demands or controls on them. This parenting style is associated with adolescents' social incompetence, especially a lack of self-control.

infancy The developmental period that extends from birth to 18 or 24 months of age.

information-processing theory A theory emphasizing that individuals manipulate information, monitor it, and strategize about it. Central to this approach are the processes of memory and thinking.

insecure attachment Attachment pattern in which infants, children, and adolescents either avoid the caregiver or show considerable resistance or ambivalence toward the caregiver. This pattern is theorized to be related to difficulties in relationships and problems in later development.

intelligence The ability to solve problems and to adapt to and learn from everyday experiences; not everyone agrees on what constitutes intelligence.

intelligent quotient (IQ) A person's tested mental age divided by chronological age, multiplied by 100.

internalizing problems Emotional conditions that develop when individuals turn problems inward. Examples include anxiety and depression.

Internet The core of computer-mediated communication. The Internet system is worldwide and connects thousands of computer networks, providing an incredible array of information—both positive and negative—that adolescents can access.

intimacy in friendship In most research studies, this concept is defined narrowly as self-disclosure, or sharing of private thoughts.

intimacy versus isolation Erikson's sixth developmental stage, which individuals experience during early adulthood. At this time, individuals face the developmental task of forming intimate relationships with others.

intrinsic motivation Internal motivational factors such as self-determination, curiosity, challenge, and effort.

inventionist view The view that adolescence is a sociohistorical creation. Especially important in this view are the sociohistorical circumstances at the beginning of the twentieth century, a time when legislation was enacted that ensured the dependency of youth and made their move into the economic sphere more manageable.

J

jigsaw classroom A classroom strategy in which students from different cultural backgrounds are placed in a cooperative group in which, together, they have to construct different parts of a project to reach a common goal.

justice perspective A moral perspective that focuses on the rights of the individual. Individuals are viewed as making moral decisions independently.

juvenile delinquency A broad range of behaviors, including socially unacceptable behavior, status offenses, and criminal acts.

L

laboratory A controlled setting in which many of the complex factors of the "real world" are removed.

late adolescence The developmental period that corresponds approximately to the latter half of the second decade of life. Career interests, dating, and identity exploration are often more pronounced in late adolescence than in early adolescence.

late adulthood The developmental period that lasts from about 60 to 70 years of age until death.

learning disabilities Disabilities in which children experience difficulty in learning that involves understanding or using spoken or written language; the difficulty can appear in listening, thinking, reading, writing, and spelling. A learning disability also may involve difficulty in doing mathematics. To be classified as a learning disability, the learning problem is not primarily the result of visual, hearing, or motor disabilities; intellectual disability; emotional disorders; or environmental, cultural, or economic disadvantage.

least restrictive environment (LRE) A setting that is as similar as possible to the one in which children or adolescents without a disability are educated; under the IDEA, efforts to educate the child or adolescent with a disability in this setting have been given a legal basis.

limbic system A lower, subcortical system in the brain that is the seat of emotions and experience of rewards.

longitudinal research A research strategy in which the same individuals are studied over a period of time, usually several years or more.

love withdrawal A disciplinary technique in which a parent withholds attention or love from the adolescent.

M

major depressive disorder The diagnosis when an individual experiences a major depressive episode and depressed characteristics, such as lethargy and depression, for two weeks or longer and daily functioning becomes impaired.

mastery orientation An outlook in which individuals focus on the task rather than on their ability; they concentrate on learning strategies and the process of achievement instead of the outcome.

memory The retention of information over time.

menarche A girl's first menstrual period.

mental age (MA) An individual's level of mental development relative to others; a concept developed by Binet.

mentors Individuals who are usually older and more experienced and are motivated to improve the competence and character of a younger person.

metacognition Cognition about cognition, or "knowing about knowing."

metaphor An implied comparison between two unlike things.

middle adulthood The developmental period that is entered at about 35 to 45 years of age and exited at about 55 to 65 years of age.

middle and late childhood The developmental period extending from about 6 to about 10 or 11 years of age; sometimes called the elementary school years.

millennials The generation born after 1980, the first to come of age and enter emerging adulthood in the new millennium. Two characteristics of millennials stand out: (1) their ethnic diversity, and (2) their connection to technology.

mindset The cognitive view, either fixed or growth, that individuals develop for themselves.

moral development Thoughts, feelings, and behaviors regarding standards of right and wrong.

moral exemplars People who have led exemplary lives.

moral identity An aspect of personality that is present when individuals have moral notions and commitments that are central to their lives.

multicultural education Education that values diversity and includes the perspectives of a variety of cultural groups.

multiple developmental trajectories Concept that adults follow one trajectory and children and adolescents another one; how these trajectories mesh is important.

myelination The process by which the axon portion of the neuron becomes covered and insulated with a layer of fat cells, which increases the speed and efficiency of information processing in the nervous system.

N

narcissism A self-centered and self-concerned approach toward others.

naturalistic observation Observation of behavior in real-world settings.

nature-nurture issue Debate about whether development is primarily influenced by an organism's biological inheritance (nature) or by its environmental experiences (nurture).

neglected adolescents Adolescents who are infrequently nominated as a best friend but are not disliked by their peers.

neglectful parenting A style in which the parent is uninvolved in the adolescent's life. It is associated with adolescents' social incompetence, especially a lack of self-control.

neo-Piagetians Theorists who argue that Piaget got some things right but that his theory needs considerable revision. In their revision, they give more emphasis to information processing that involves attention, memory, and strategies; they also seek to provide more precise explanations of cognitive changes.

neuroconstructivist view Developmental perspective in which biological processes and environmental conditions influence the brain's development; the brain has plasticity and is context dependent; and cognitive development is closely linked with brain development.

neurons Nerve cells, which are the nervous system's basic units.

normal distribution A symmetrical distribution of values or scores, with a majority of scores falling in the middle of the possible range of scores and few scores appearing toward the extremes of the range.

O

optimism Involves having a positive outlook on the future and minimizing problems.

P

passive genotype-environment correlations Correlations that occur because biological parents, who are genetically related to the child, provide a rearing environment for the child.

peers Individuals who are about the same age or maturity level.

performance orientation An outlook in which individuals are focused on winning rather than a specific achievement outcome. For performance-oriented students, winning results in happiness.

permissive strategy of classroom management A teaching strategy that offers students considerable autonomy but provides them with little support for developing learning skills or managing their behavior.

personality The enduring personal characteristics of individuals.

perspective taking The ability to assume another person's perspective and understand his or her thoughts and feelings.

phenotype The way an individual's genotype is expressed in observed and measurable characteristics.

Piaget's theory A theory stating that children actively construct their understanding of the world and go through four stages of cognitive development.

popular adolescents Adolescents who are frequently nominated as a best friend and are rarely disliked by their peers.

possible self What individuals might become, what they would like to become, and what they are afraid of becoming.

postconventional reasoning The third and highest level in Kohlberg's theory. At this level, conventional considerations are now judged against moral concerns such as liberty, justice, and equality, with the idea that morality can improve laws.

postformal thought Thought that is reflective, relativistic, and contextual; provisional; realistic; and open to emotions and subjective.

power assertion A disciplinary technique in which a parent attempts to gain control over the adolescent or the adolescent's resources.

precocious puberty The very early onset and rapid progression of puberty.

preconventional reasoning The lowest level in Kohlberg's theory of moral development. At this level, the individual's moral reasoning is controlled primarily by a punishment-and-obedience orientation.

prefrontal cortex The highest level of the brain's frontal lobes that is involved in reasoning, decision making, and self-control.

prejudice An unjustified negative attitude toward an individual because of the individual's membership in a group.

prenatal period The time from conception to birth.

preoccupied/ambivalent attachment An insecure attachment category in which adolescents are hyperattuned to attachment experiences. This is thought mainly to occur because parents are inconsistently available to the adolescent.

preoperational stage Piaget's second stage, which lasts approximately from 2 to 7 years of age. In this stage, children begin to represent their world with words, images, and drawings.

problem-focused coping Lazarus' term for the strategy of squarely facing one's troubles and trying to solve them.

psychoanalytic theories Theories that describe development as primarily unconscious and heavily colored by emotion. Behavior is merely a surface characteristic, and the symbolic workings of the mind must be analyzed to understand behavior. Early experiences with parents are emphasized.

psychometric/intelligence view A view that emphasizes the importance of individual differences in intelligence; many advocates of this view also argue that intelligence should be assessed with intelligence tests.

psychosocial moratorium Erikson's term for the gap between childhood security and adult autonomy that adolescents experience as part of their identity exploration.

puberty A brain-neuroendocrine process occurring primarily in early adolescence that provides stimulation for the rapid physical changes that accompany this period of development.

Public Law 94-142 The Education for All Handicapped Children Act, which requires all students with disabilities to be given a free, appropriate public education.

Q

quid pro quo sexual harassment Sexual harassment in which a school employee threatens to base an educational decision (such as a grade) on a student's submission to unwelcome sexual conduct.

R

racial identity The collective identity of any group of people socialized to think of themselves as a racial group.

racism Discrimination, prejudice, or antagonism against a person or people based on their racial or ethnic group.

rape   Forcible sexual intercourse with a person who does not give consent.

rapport talk   The language of conversation, establishing connections and negotiating relationships.

reciprocal socialization   The process by which children and adolescents socialize parents, just as parents socialize them.

rejected adolescents   Adolescents who are infrequently nominated as a best friend and are actively disliked by their peers.

religion   An organized set of beliefs, practices, rituals, and symbols that increases an individual's connection to a sacred or transcendent other (God, higher power, or higher truth).

religiousness   An individual's degree of affiliation with an organized religion, participation in prescribed rituals and practices, connection with its beliefs, and involvement in a community of believers.

report talk   Talk that gives information, such as public speaking.

resilience   Adapting positively and achieving successful outcomes in the face of significant risks and adverse circumstances.

rites of passage   Ceremonies or rituals that mark an individual's transition from one status to another, such as the entry into adulthood.

romantic love   Love that has strong sexual and infatuation components; also called passionate love or *eros*. It often predominates in the early part of a love relationship.

S

satire   The use of irony, derision, or wit to expose folly or wickedness.

schema   A mental concept or framework that is useful in organizing and interpreting information.

secular trends   Patterns of the onset of puberty over historical time, especially across generations.

secure attachment   Involves a positive, enduring emotional bond between two people. In infancy, childhood, and adolescence, formation of a secure bond with a caregiver benefits the child's exploration of the environment and subsequent development. In adulthood, the bond can also be between two people in a couple or marital relationship.

selective attention   Focusing on a specific aspect of experience that is relevant while ignoring others that are irrelevant.

self   All of the characteristics of a person.

self-concept   Domain-specific evaluations of the self.

self-efficacy   The belief that one can master a situation and produce positive outcomes.

self-esteem   The global evaluative dimension of the self; also referred to as self-worth or self-image.

self-handicapping   Use of failure avoidance strategies such as not trying in school or putting off studying until the last minute so that circumstances, rather than a lack of ability, will be seen as the cause of low-level performance.

self-regulation   The ability to control one's behavior without having to rely on others for help.

self-understanding   The individual's cognitive representation of the self; the substance and content of self-conceptions.

sensorimotor stage   Piaget's first stage of development, lasting from birth to about 2 years of age. In this stage, infants construct an understanding of the world by coordinating sensory experiences with physical, motoric actions.

service learning   A form of education that promotes social responsibility and service to the community.

sexual minority   Someone who self-identifies as lesbian, gay, bisexual, or transgender.

sexual script   A stereotyped pattern of role prescriptions for how individuals should behave in sexual contexts. Females and males have been socialized to follow different sexual scripts.

sexually transmitted infections (STIs) Infections that are contracted primarily through sexual contact. This contact is not limited to vaginal intercourse but includes oral-genital contact and anal-genital contact as well.

slow-to-warm-up child   A child who has a low activity level, is somewhat negative, and displays a low intensity of mood.

social cognition   The way individuals conceptualize and reason about their social worlds—the people they watch and interact with, their relationships with those people, the groups they participate in, and the way they reason about themselves and others.

social cognitive theory   The view that behavior, environment, and person/cognition are the key factors in development.

social cognitive theory of gender   Theory emphasizing that children's and adolescents' gender development occurs through observation and imitation of gender behavior, and through rewards and punishments they experience for gender-appropriate and gender-inappropriate behavior.

social cognitive theory of moral development Theory that distinguishes between moral competence (the ability to produce moral behaviors) and moral performance (enacting those behaviors in specific situations).

social constructivist approach   Approach that emphasizes the social contexts of learning and the construction of knowledge through social interaction.

social conventional reasoning   Thoughts about social consensus and convention, as opposed to moral reasoning that stresses ethical issues.

social domain theory   Theory that identifies different domains of social knowledge and reasoning, including moral, social conventional, and personal domains. These domains arise from children's and adolescents' attempts to understand and deal with different forms of social experience.

social motives   Needs and desires that are learned through experiences with the social world.

social policy   A national government's course of action designed to influence the welfare of its citizens.

social role theory   Theory stating that gender differences mainly result from the contrasting roles of women and men, with women having less power and status and controlling fewer resources than men.

socioeconomic status (SES)   Refers to a grouping of people with similar occupational, educational, and economic characteristics.

socioemotional processes   Changes in an individual's personality, emotions, relationships with other people, and social contexts.

sociometric status   The extent to which children and adolescents are liked or disliked by their peer group.

spermarche   A boy's first ejaculation of semen.

spirituality   Experiencing something beyond oneself in a transcendent manner and living in a way that benefits others and society.

standardized test   A test with uniform procedures for administration and scoring. Many standardized tests allow a person's performance to be compared with the performance of other individuals.

status offenses   Juvenile offenses, performed by youth under a specified age, that are not as serious as index offenses. These offenses may include acts such as underage drinking, truancy, and sexual promiscuity.

stereotype   A generalization that reflects our impressions and beliefs about a broad group of people. All stereotypes refer to an image of what the typical member of a specific group is like.

stereotype threat   The anxiety that one's behavior might conform to a negative stereotype about one's group.

stimulants   Drugs that increase the activity of the central nervous system.

storm-and-stress view   G. Stanley Hall's concept that adolescence is a turbulent time charged with conflict and mood swings.

stress   The response of individuals to stressors, which are circumstances and events that threaten and tax their coping abilities.

sustained attention   The ability to maintain attention to a selected stimulus for a prolonged period of time.

synapses   Gaps between neurons, where connections between the axon and dendrites occur.

syphilis   A sexually transmitted infection caused by the bacterium *Treponema pallidum,* a spirochete.

T

temperament   An individual's behavioral style and characteristic way of responding.

theory   An interrelated, coherent set of ideas that helps explain phenomena and make predictions.

theory of mind   Awareness of one's own mental processes and the mental processes of others.

top-dog phenomenon   The circumstance of moving from the top position (in elementary school, the oldest, biggest, and most powerful students) to the lowest position (in middle or junior high school, the youngest, smallest, and least powerful students).

transgender   A broad term that refers to individuals who adopt a gender identity that differs from the one assigned to them at birth.

triarchic theory of intelligence Sternberg's view that intelligence comes in three main forms: analytical, creative, and practical.

twin study A study in which the behavioral similarity of identical twins is compared with the behavioral similarity of fraternal twins.

U

unresolved/disorganized attachment An insecure attachment category in which the adolescent has an unusually high level of fear and is disoriented. This can result from traumatic experiences such as a parent's death or abuse by parents.

V

values Beliefs and attitudes about the way things should be.

values clarification An educational approach that focuses on helping people clarify what is important to them, what is worth working for, and what is their purpose in life. Students are encouraged to define their own values and understand others' values.

Vygotsky's theory A sociocultural cognitive theory that emphasizes how culture and social interaction guide cognitive development.

W

wisdom Expert knowledge about the practical aspects of life that permits excellent judgment about important matters.

Z

zone of proximal development (ZPD) Vygotsky's concept that refers to the range of tasks that are too difficult for an individual to master alone, but that can be mastered with the guidance or assistance of adults or more-skilled peers.

references

A

Aalsma, M.C., Lapsley, D.K., & Flannery, D.J. (2006). Personal fables, narcissism, and adolescent adjustment. *Psychology in the Schools, 43,* 481–491.

AARP (2019). *2018 Grandparent Today national survey.* New York: Author.

Abar, C.C., & others (2021). Parental active tracking measures and health behaviors during high school and college. *Journal of American College Health, 69,* 151–158.

Abbate-Daga, G., Gramaglia, C., Amianto, F., Marzola, E., & Fassino, S. (2010). Attachment insecurity, personality, and body dissatisfaction in eating disorders. *Journal of Nervous and Mental Disease, 198,* 520–524.

Abdo, N., & others (2020). Relationship between binge eating and associated eating behaviors with subcortical brain volumes and cortical thickness. *Journal of Affective Disorders, 274,* 1201–1205.

Abetz, J.S., & Romo, L.K. (2021, in press). A normative approach to understanding how "boomerang kids" communicatively negotiate moving back home. *Emerging Adulthood.*

Abuhamdeh, S., & Csikszentmihalyi, M. (2012). The importance of challenge for the enjoyment of intrinsically motivated, goal-directed activities. *Personality and Social Psychology Bulletin, 38,* 317–330.

Aceves, L., Bamaca-Colbert, M., & Robins, R.W. (2020). Longitudinal linkages among parents' educational expectations, youths' educational expectations, and competence in Mexican-origin families. *Journal of Youth and Adolescence, 49,* 32–48.

Achenbach, T.M., & Edelbrock, C.S. (1981). Behavioral problems and competencies reported by parents of normal and disturbed children aged four through sixteen. *Monographs of the Society for Research in Child Development, 46*(1, Serial No. 188).

Achenbach, T.M., Howell, C.T., Quay, H.C., & Conners, C.K. (1991). National survey of problems and competencies among four- to sixteen-year-olds. *Monographs for the Society for Research in Child Development, 56*(3, Serial No. 225).

Ackerman, A., Thornton, J.C., Wang, J., Pierson, R.N., & Horlick, M. (2006). Sex differences in the effect of puberty on the relationship between fat mass and bone mass in 926 healthy subjects, 6 to 18 years old. *Obesity, 14,* 819–825.

Ackerman, R.A., & others (2013). The interpersonal legacy of a positive family climate in adolescence. *Psychological Science, 24*(3), 243–250.

Acosta, J., & others (2019). Evaluation of a whole-school change intervention: Findings from a two-year cluster-randomized trial of restorative practices intervention. *Journal of Youth and Adolescence, 48,* 876–890.

Adelson, J. (1979, January). Adolescence and the generalization gap. *Psychology Today, 13,* 33–37.

Adil, A., Ameer, S., & Ghayas, S. (2020). Impact of academic psychological capital on academic achievement among university undergraduates: Roles of flow and self-handicapping behavior. *PsyCh Journal, 9,* 55–66.

Adkins, D.E., Daw, J.K., McClay, J.L., & van den Oord, E.J. (2012). The influence of five monoamine genes on trajectories of depressive symptoms across adolescence and young adulthood. *Development and Psychopathology, 24,* 267–285.

Adolescent Sleep Working Group, AAP (2014). School start times for adolescents. *Pediatrics, 134,* 642–649.

Affleck, W., Carmichael, V., & Whitley, R. (2018). Men's mental health: Social determinants and its implications for services. *Canadian Journal of Psychiatry, 63,* 581–589.

Affrunti, N.W., & Woodruff-Borden, J. (2014). Perfectionism in pediatric anxiety and depression. *Clinical Child and Family Psychology Review, 17,* 299–317.

Agnafors, S., Barmark, M., & Sydsjo, G. (2021). Mental health and academic performance: A study on selection and causation effects from childhood to early adulthood. *Social Psychiatry and Psychiatric Epidemiology, 56,* 857–866.

Agostini, A., & Centofanti, S. (2021). Normal sleep in children and adolescence. *Child and Adolescent Psychiatric Clinics of North America, 30,* 1–14.

Agostinis-Sobrinho, C., & others (2021). Ideal cardiovascular health status and health-related quality of life in adolescents: The LabMed Physical Activity Study. *Revista Paulista de Pediatria, 39,* e2019343.

Agras, W.S., Fitzsimmons-Craft, E.E., & Wilfley, D.E. (2017). Evolution of cognitive-behavior therapy for eating disorders. *Behavior Research and Therapy, 88,* 26–36.

Ahonen, L., & others (2020). Criminal career duration: Predictability from self-reports and official records. *Criminal Behavior and Mental Health, 30,* 172–182.

Ainsworth, M.D.S. (1979). Infant-mother attachment. *American Psychologist, 34,* 932–937.

Akama, H., Yuan, Y., & Awazu, S. (2021). Task-induced brain functional connectivity as a representation of schema for mediating unsupervised and supervised learning dynamics in language acquisition. *Brain and Behavior, 5,* e02517.

Akin, R.I., & others (2020). Parent-adolescent relationship quality as a predictor of leaving home. *Journal of Adolescence, 79,* 81–90.

Al Alwan, I.A., & others (2017). Decline in menarcheal age among Saudi girls. *Saudi Medical Journal, 36,* 1324–1328.

Alaie, I., & others (2019). Uppsala Longitudinal Adolescent Depression Study (ULADS). *BMJ Open, 9*(3), e024939.

Alaimo, K., & others (2015). The Michigan Healthy School Action Tools Process generates improvements in school nutrition policies and practices, and student dietary intake. *Health Promotion and Practice, 16,* 401–410.

Albaladejo-Saura, M., & others (2021). Relationship between biological maturation, physical fitness, and kinanthropometric variables of young adolescents: A systematic review and meta-analysis. *International Journal of Environmental Research and Public Health, 18*(1), 328.

Albert, D., & Steinberg, L. (2011a). Judgment and decision making in adolescence. *Journal of Research on Adolescence, 21,* 211–224.

Albert, D., & Steinberg, L. (2011b). Peer influences on adolescent risk behavior. In M. Bardo, D. Fishbein, & R. Milich (Eds.), *Inhibitory control and drug abuse prevention: From research to translation.* New York: Springer.

Albert, M.A., & others (2020, June). *School-based interventions: Targeting social and emotional skills to increase college readiness of Hispanic students from underserved backgrounds.* Technical brief. ERIC #ED606152.

Aldwin, C.M., Skinner, E.A., Zimmer-Gembeck, M.J., & Taylor, A. (2011). Coping and self-regulation across the life span. In K.L. Fingerman & others (Eds.), *Handbook of life-span development.* New York: Springer.

Alexander, C., Piazza, M., Mekos, D., & Valente, T. (2001). Peers, schools, and cigarette smoking. *Journal of Adolescent Health, 29,* 22–30.

Al-Ghanim, & Badahdah, A.M. (2017). Gender roles in the Arab world: Development and psychometric properties of the Arab Adolescents Gender Roles Attitude Scale. *Sex Roles. 77,* 169–177.

Aligne, C.A., & others (2020). Impact of the Rochester LARC initiative on adolescents' utilization of long-acting reversible contraception. *American Journal of Obstetrics and Gynecology, 222*(45), S890e1–S890e6.

Allemand, M., Steiger, A.E., & Fend, H.A. (2015). Empathy development in adolescence predicts social competencies in adulthood. *Journal of Personality, 83,* 229–241.

Allen, J., & Allen, C.W. (2009). *Escaping the endless adolescence.* New York: Ballantine.

Allen, J.P., Chango, J., & Szwedo, D. (2014). The adolescent relational dialectic and the peer roots of adult social functioning. *Child Development, 85,* 192–204.

Allen, J.P., & Miga, E.M. (2010). Attachment in adolescence: A move to the level of emotion regulation. *Journal of Social and Personal Relationships, 27,* 181–190.

Allen, J.P., & others (2009, April). *Portrait of the secure teen as an adult.* Paper presented at the meeting of the Society for Research in Child Development, Denver.

Allen, J.P., & others (2015). Characteristics of emerging adulthood and e-cigarette use: Findings from a pilot study. *Addictive Behaviors, 50,* 40–44.

Allen, J.P., & others (2020). Adolescent peer relationship qualities as predictors of long-term romantic life satisfaction. *Child Development, 91,* 327–340.

Allen, J.P., & others (2021, in press). Different factors predict adolescent substance use versus adult substance abuse: Lessons from a social-developmental approach. *Development and Psychopathology.*

Allen, M., Svetaz, M.V., Hardeman, R., & Resnick, M.D. (2008, February). *What research tells us about parenting practices and their relationship to youth sexual behavior.* Campaign to Prevent Teen and Unplanned Pregnancy. Retrieved December 2, 2008, from www.TheNationalCampaign.org

Allen, S., & Barlow, E. (2017). Long-acting reversible contraception: An essential guide for pediatric primary care. *Pediatric Clinics of North America, 64,* 359–369.

Almquist, Y.B., & Brannstrom, L. (2014). Childhood peer status and the clustering of social, economic, and health-related circumstances in adulthood. *Social Science & Medicine, 105,* 67–75.

Almulla, A.A., & Faris, M.A.-I.E. (2020). Energy drink consumption is associated with sleep duration and increased energy-dense foods consumption among school students: A cross-sectional study. *Asia-Pacific Public Health, 32,* 266–273.

Alonzo, D. (2020). The role of parenting characteristics in the mental health treatment utilization of Latino adolescents with suicidality. *Suicide Online-Sol, 11,* 19–28.

Alsaad, A.J., Azhar, Y., & Nasser, Y.A. (2021). *Depression in children.* Treasure Island, FL: StatPearls.

Alsaker, F.D., & Flammer, A. (1999). *The adolescent experience: European and American adolescents in the 1990s.* Mahwah, NJ: Erlbaum.

Amabile, T.M. (2018). Creativity and the labor of love. In R.J. Sternberg & J.C. Kaufman (Eds.), *The nature of human creativity.* New York: Cambridge University Press.

Amani, B., & others (2018). Families and the juvenile justice system: Considerations for family-based interventions. *Family and Community Health, 41,* 55-63.

Amato, P.R. (2006). Marital discord, divorce, and children's well-being: Results from a 20-year longitudinal study of two generations. In A. Clarke-Stewart & J. Dunn (Eds.), *Families count.* New York: Cambridge University Press.

Amato, P.R., & Dorius, C. (2010). Fathers, children, and divorce. In M.E. Lamb (Ed.), *The role of the father in child development* (5th ed.). New York: Wiley.

Amenyah, S.D., & others (2021). DNA methylation of hypertension-related genes and effect of riboflavin supplementation in adults stratified by genotype for the MTHFR C677T polymorphism. *International Journal of Cardiology, 322,* 233-239.

American Association of University Women (1992). *How schools shortchange girls: A study of major findings on girls and education.* Washington, DC: Author.

American Association of University Women (2006). *Drawing the line: Sexual harassment on campus.* Washington, DC: Author.

American Psychiatric Association (2013). *Diagnostic and statistical manual of mental disorders* (5th ed.). Washington, DC: Author.

American Psychological Association (2003). *Psychology: Scientific problem solvers.* Washington, DC: Author.

American Psychological Association (2020). *Education and socioeconomic status.* Retrieved January 19, 2020, from www.apa.org/pi/ses/resources/publications/education

American School Counselor Association (2020). *Student-to-counselor ratio.* Alexandria, VA: Author.

Amirkan, J.H., & Velasco, S.E. (2021). Stress overload and the new nightmare for dreamers. *Journal of American College Health, 69,* 67-73.

Amorim, M. (2019). Are grandparents a blessing or a burden? Multigenerational coresidence and child-related spending. *Social Science Research, 80,* 132-144.

Amos, R., & others (2020). Mental health, social adversity, and health-related outcomes in sexual minority adolescents: A contemporary national study. *Lancet. Child and Adolescent Health, 4*(1), 36-45.

Amundsen, R., & others (2020). Mindfulness in primary school children as a route to enhanced life satisfaction, positive outlook, and effective emotional regulation. *BMC Psychology, 8*(1), 71.

Anders, K.M., & others (2020). "Sex is easier to get and love is harder to find": Costs and rewards of hooking up among first-year college students. *Journal of Sex Research, 57,* 247-259.

Anderson, C.A., & others (2017). Media violence and other aggression risk factors in seven nations. *Personality and Social Psychology Bulletin, 43,* 986-998.

Anderson, D.R., Huston, A.C., Schmitt, K., Linebarger, D.L., & Wright, J.C. (2001). Early childhood viewing and adolescent behavior: The recontact study. *Monographs of the Society for Research in Child Development, 66*(1, Serial No. 264).

Anderson, E., Greene, S.M., Hetherington, E.M., & Clingempeel, W.G. (1999). The dynamics of parental remarriage. In E.M. Hetherington (Ed.), *Coping with divorce, single parenting, and remarriage.* Mahwah, NJ: Erlbaum.

Anderson, K., & others (2020). The impacts of transition to middle school on student cognitive, non-cognitive, and perceptual developments: Evidence from China. *Education Economics, 28,* 384-402.

Anderson, L.E., & others (2020). Young adults' sexual health in the digital age: Perspectives of care providers. *Sexual and Reproductive Healthcare, 25,* 100534.

Anderson, M.A., & Jiang, J. (2018, May 31). Teens, social media, and technology 2018. Washington, DC: Pew Research Center.

Anderson, R.E., & others (2021, in press). The frequency of sexual perpetration in college men: A systematic review of reported prevalence rates from 2000 to 2017. *Trauma, Violence, and Abuse.*

Anderson, S.F., Sladek, M.R., & Doane, L.D. (2020). Negative affect reactivity to stress and internalizing symptoms over the transition to college for Latinx adolescents: Buffering role of family support. *Development and Psychopathology, 2,* 1-16.

Andersson, H., & Bergman, L.R. (2011). The role of task persistence in young adolescence for successful educational and occupational attainment in middle adulthood. *Developmental Psychology, 47,* 950-960.

Andersson, U. (2010). The contribution of working memory capacity to foreign language comprehension in children. *Memory, 18,* 458-472.

Andrade, N., Ford, A.D., & Alvarez, C. (2021). Discrimination and Latino health: A systematic review of risk and resilience. *Hispanic Health Care International, 19,* 5-16.

Andraka-Christou, B., & others (2020. College students' perceived knowledge of and perceived helpfulness of treatments for opioid use disorder at two American universities. *American Journal of Drug and Alcohol Abuse, 46,* 749-760.

Andreescu, V., & Overstreet, S.M. (2021, in press). Violent victimization and violence perpetration among American Indian adolescents. *Journal of Interpersonal Violence.*

Andrews, J.L., Ahmed, S.P., & Blakemore, S.-J. (2021). Navigating the social environment in adolescence: The role of social brain development. *Biological Psychiatry, 89,* 109-118.

Andrews, J.L., Foulkes, L., & Blakemore, S-J. (2020). Peer influence in adolescence: Public-health implications for COVID-19. *Trends in Cognitive Science, 24,* 585-587.

Anglin, D.M., & others (2018). Ethnic identity, racial discrimination, and attenuated psychotic symptoms in an urban population of emerging adults. *Early Intervention in Psychiatry, 12,* 380-390.

Anguiano, R.M. (2018). Language brokering among Latino immigrant families: Moderating variables and youth outcomes. *Journal of Youth and Adolescence, 47,* 222-242.

Anholt, R.R.H., & others (2020). Evolution of reproductive behavior. *Genetics, 214,* 49-73.

Ansari, A. (2015). *Modern romance.* New York: Penguin.

Ansary, N.S., McMahon, T.J., & Luthar, S.S. (2012). Socioeconomic context and emotional-behavioral achievement links: Concurrent and prospective associations among low- and high-income youth. *Journal of Research on Adolescence, 22,* 14-30.

Ansary, N.S., McMahon, T.J., & Luthar, S.S. (2017). Trajectories of emotional-behavioral difficulty and academic competence: A 6-year, person-centered prospective study of affluent suburban adolescents. *Development and Psychopathology, 29,* 215-234.

Anselmo, G.A., Yarborough, J.L., & Tran, V.V.N. (2021). To screen or not to screen: Criterion-related validity of math and reading curriculum-based measurement in relation to high-stakes math scores. *Journal of Psychoeducational Assessment, 39,* 153-165.

Antfolk, J., & others (2017). Willingness to invest in children: Psychological kinship estimates and emotional closeness. *Evolutionary Psychology, 15*(2), 1474704917705730.

Antovich, D.M., & Graf Estes, K. (2020). One language or two? Navigating cross-language conflict in statistical word segmentation. *Developmental Science, 23*(6), e12960.

Aquino, K., & Reed, A. (2002). The self-importance of moral identity. *Journal of Personality and Social Psychology, 83,* 1423-1440.

Ariceli, G., Castro, J., Cesena, J., & Toro, J. (2005). Anorexia nervosa in male adolescents: Body image, eating attitudes, and psychological traits. *Journal of Adolescent Health, 36,* 221-226.

Armitage, R. (2021). Bullying in children: Impact on child health. *BMC Pediatric Open, 5*(1), e000939.

Arnett, J. (1990). Contraceptive use, sensation seeking, and adolescent egocentrism. *Journal of Youth and Adolescence, 19,* 171-180.

Arnett, J.J. (1995, March). *Are college students adults?* Paper presented at the meeting of the Society for Research in Child Development, Indianapolis.

Arnett, J.J. (2004). *Emerging adulthood.* New York: Oxford University Press.

Arnett, J.J. (2006). Emerging adulthood: Understanding the new way of coming of age. In J.J. Arnett & J.L. Tanner (Eds.), *Emerging adults in America.* Washington, DC: American Psychological Association.

Arnett, J.J. (2007). Socialization in emerging adulthood. In J.E. Grusec & P.D. Hastings (Eds.), *Handbook of socialization.* New York: Guilford.

Arnett, J.J. (2010). Oh, grow up! Generational grumbling and the new life stage of emerging adulthood—Commentary on Trzesniewski & Donnellan (2010), *Perspectives on Psychological Science, 5,* 89-92.

Arnett, J.J. (Ed.) (2012). *Adolescent psychology around the world.* New York: Psychology Press.

Arnett, J.J. (2014). *Emerging adulthood* (2nd ed.). New York: Oxford University Press.

Arnett, J.J. (2016a). Does emerging adulthood theory apply across social classes? National data on a persistent question. *Emerging Adulthood, 4,* 227-235.

Arnett, J.J. (2016b). Emerging adulthood and social class: Rejoinder to Furstenberg, Silva, and du Bois-Reymond. *Emerging Adulthood, 4,* 244-247.

Arnett, J.J., & Brody, G.H. (2008). A fraught passage: The identity challenges of African American emerging adults. *Human Development, 51,* 291-293.

Arnett, J.J., & Mitra, D. (2020). Are the features of emerging adulthood developmentally distinctive? A comparison of ages 18-60 in the United States. *Emerging Adulthood, 8*(5), 412-419.

Arnett, J.J., Robinson, O., & Lachman, M.E. (2020). Rethinking adult development: Introduction to the special issue. *American Psychologist, 75,* 425-430.

Arns, M., & others (2020). Neurofeedback and attention-deficit/hyperactivity-disorder (ADHD) in children. Rating the evidence and proposed guidelines. *Applied Physiology and Biofeedback, 45,* 39-48.

Aronson, E. (1986, August). *Teaching students things they think they know all about: The case of prejudice and desegregation.* Paper presented at the meeting of the American Psychological Association, Washington, DC.

Aronson, J. (2002). Stereotype threat: Contending and coping with unnerving expectations. *Improving academic achievement.* San Diego: Academic Press.

Arsandaux, J., Galera, C., & Salamon, R. (2021). The association of self-esteem and psychosocial outcomes in young adults: A 10-year prospective study. *Child and Adolescent Mental Health, 26*(2), 106-113.

Arseth, A., Kroger, J., Martinussen, M., & Marcia, J.E. (2009). Meta-analytic studies of identity status and the relational issues of attachment and intimacy. *Identity, 9,* 1-32.

Arthur, J. (2014). Traditional approaches to character education in Britain and America. In L. Nucci, T. Krettenauer, & D. Narváez (Eds.), *Handbook of moral and character education* (2nd ed.). New York: Routledge.

Asarnow, J.R., & Callan, J.W. (1985). Boys with peer adjustment problems: Social cognitive processes. *Journal of Consulting and Clinical Psychology, 53,* 80-87.

Asarnow, J.R., & others (2020). Randomized controlled trial of family-focused treatment for child depression compared to individual psychotherapy—one-year outcomes. *Journal of Child Psychology and Psychiatry, 61,* 662-671.

Asendorpf, J.B., & Rauthmann, J.F. (2021). States and situations, traits and environments. In P.J. Corr & G. Matthews (Eds.), *Cambridge handbook of personality psychology.* New York: Cambridge University Press.

Asheer, S., & others (2020). Implementing case management with positive youth development to empower young mothers in California. *Maternal and Child Health Journal 24*(Suppl. 2), S141–S151.

Askeland, K.G., & others (2017). Mental health in internationally adopted adolescents: A meta-analysis. *Journal of the American Academy of Child and Adolescent Psychiatry, 56,* 202–213.

Askeland, K.G., & others (2020). Life events and adolescent depressive symptoms: Protective factors associated with resilience. *PLoS One, 15*(6), e0234109.

Askew, A.J., & others (2020). Not all body image constructs are created equal: Predicting eating disorder outcomes from preoccupation, dissatisfaction, and overvaluation. *International Journal of Eating Disorders, 53,* 954–963.

Aspen Institute (2020). *Making tomorrow better together.* Washington, DC: Aspen Institute.

Assini-Meytin, L.C., & Green, K.M. (2015). Long-term consequences of adolescent parenthood among African-American youth: A propensity score matching approach. *Journal of Adolescent Health, 56,* 529–535.

Astle, S., Leonhardt, N., & Willoughby, B. (2020). Home base: Family of origin factors and the debut of vaginal sex, anal sex, oral sex, masturbation, and pornography use in a national sample of adolescents. *Journal of Sex Research, 57,* 1089–1099.

Atherton, O.E. (2020). Typical and atypical self-regulation in adolescence: The importance of studying change over time. *Social and Personality Compass, 14*(1), e12514.

Atherton, O.E., Donnellan, M.B., & Robins, R.W. (2021). Development of personality across the life span. In P.J. Corr & G. Matthews (Eds.), *Cambridge handbook of personality psychology* (2nd ed.). New York: Cambridge University Press.

Atherton, O.E., Lawson, K.M., & Robins, R.W. (2020). The development of effortful control from late childhood to young adulthood. *Journal of Personality and Social Psychology, 119,* 417–456.

Atkin, A.L., & Yoo, H.C. (2021). Patterns of racial-ethnic socialization in Asian American families: Associations with racial-ethnic identity and social connections. *Journal of Counseling Psychology, 68,* 17–26.

Auersperg, F., & others (2019). Long-term effects of parental divorce on mental health—a meta-analysis. *Journal of Psychiatric Research, 119,* 107–115.

Austin, E.Q., & others (2021). Social relations and social support. In P.J. Corr & G. Matthews (Eds.), *Cambridge handbook of personality psychology.* New York: Cambridge University Press.

Avedissian, T., & Alayan, N. (2021). Adolescent well-being: A concept analysis. *Internal Journal of Mental Health Nursing, 30.* 357–367.

Aviles, T.G., Finn, C., & Neyer, F.J. (2021). Patterns of romantic relationship experiences and psychosocial adjustment from adolescence to young adulthood. *Journal of Youth and Adolescence, 50,* 550–562.

Axinn, W.G., & others (2020). The association between transitions and the onset of major depressive disorder in a South Asian general population. *Journal of Affective Disorders, 266,* 165–172.

Azmitia, M. (2015). Reflections on the cultural lenses of identity development. In K.C. McLean & M. Syed (Eds.), *Oxford handbook of identity development.* New York: Oxford University Press.

B

Baardstu, S., & others (2020). Longitudinal pathways from shyness in early childhood to personality in adolescence: Do peers matter? *Journal of Research on Adolescence, 30*(Suppl. 2), S362–S379.

Bachman, J.G., & others (2002). *The decline of substance abuse in young adulthood.* Mahwah, NJ: Erlbaum.

Bachman, J.G., & others (2008). *The education-drug use connection.* New York: Psychology Press.

Bacikova-Sleskova, M., Benka, J., & Orosova, O. (2014). Parental employment status and adolescents' health: The role of financial situation, parent-adolescent relationship, and adolescents' resilience. *Psychology and Health, 30,* 400–422.

Baddeley, A.D. (2015). Origins of multicomponent working memory model. In M. Eysenck & D. Groome (Eds.), *Cognitive psychology.* London: Sage.

Baddeley, A.D. (2017). *Working memories.* New York: Routledge.

Baddeley, A.D. (2018). *Exploring working memory: Selected works of Alan Baddeley.* New York: Routledge.

Baddeley, A.D. (2019). When and where is cognitive psychology useful? The case of working memory. *Psychology in Practice, 2,* 6–11.

Bae, S.M. (2020). The relationship between bicultural identity, acculturative stress, and psychological well-being in multicultural adolescents: Verification using multivariate latent growth modeling. *Stress and Health, 36,* 51–58.

Bae, Y.J., & others (2019). Reference intervals of nine steroid hormones over the life-span analyzed by LC-MSD/MS: Effect of age, gender, puberty, and oral contraceptives. *Journal of Steroid Biochemistry and Molecular Biology, 193,* 105409.

Baggs, E., & Chemero, A. (2020). Thinking with other minds. *Behavioral Brain Sciences, 43,* e92.

Bagwell, C.L., & Bukowki, W.M. (2018). Friendship in childhood and adolescence. In W. M. Bukowski & others (Eds.), *Handbook of peer interactions, relationships, and groups* (2nd ed.). New York: Guilford.

Baiocchi, M., & others (2017). A behavior-based intervention that prevents sexual assault: The results of matched-pairs, cluster-randomized study in Nairobi, Kenya. *Prevention Science, 18,* 818–827.

Bajoghli, H., & others (2014). "I love you more than I can stand!"–romantic love, symptoms of depression and anxiety, and sleep complaints among young adults. *International Journal of Psychiatry and Clinical Practice, 18,* 169–174.

Bakalar, J.L., & others (2015). Recent advances in developmental and risk factor research on eating disorders. *Current Psychiatry Reports, 17*(6), 585.

Baker, A., & Galvan, A. (2020). Threat or thrill? The neural mechanisms underlying the development of anxiety and risk taking in adolescence. *Developmental Cognitive Neuroscience, 45,* 100841.

Baker, N.A., & Halford, W.K. (2020). Assessment of couple relationships standards in same-sex attracted adults. *Family Process, 59,* 537–555.

Balantekin, K.N., Birch, L.L., & Savage, J.S. (2018). Family, friend, and media factors are associated with patterns of weight-control behavior among adolescent girls. *Eating and Weight Disorders, 23,* 215–223.

Baldwin, S., & Hoffman, J.P. (2002). The dynamics of self-esteem: A growth curve analysis. *Journal of Youth and Adolescence, 31,* 101–113.

Baltes, P.B., & Kunzmann, U. (2007). Wisdom and aging. In D.C. Park & N. Schwarz (Eds.), *Cognitive aging* (2nd ed.). Philadelphia: Psychology Press.

Baltes, P.B., Lindenberger, U., & Staudinger, U. (2006). Life-span theory in developmental psychology. In W. Damon & R. Lerner (Eds.), *Handbook of child psychology* (6th ed.). New York: Wiley.

Baltes, P.B., & Smith, J. (2008). The fascination of wisdom: Its nature, ontogeny, and function. *Perspectives on Psychological Science, 3,* 56–64.

Bamaca-Colbert, M., Umana-Taylor, A.J., Espinosa-Hernandez, G., & Brown, A.M. (2012). Behavioral autonomy expectations among Mexican-origin mother-daughter dyads: An examination of within-group variability. *Journal of Adolescence, 35,* 691–700.

Bamaca-Colbert, M., & others (2018). Family profiles of cohesion and parenting practices and Latino youth adjustment. *Family Process, 57*(3), 719–736.

Bandura, A. (1991). Social cognitive theory of moral thought and action. In W.M. Kurtines & J. Gewirtz (Eds.), *Handbook of moral behavior and development* (Vol. 1). Hillsdale, NJ: Erlbaum.

Bandura, A. (1997). *Self-efficacy.* New York: W. H. Freeman.

Bandura, A. (1998, August). *Swimming against the mainstream: Accentuating the positive aspects of humanity.* Paper presented at the meeting of the American Psychological Association, San Francisco.

Bandura, A. (1999). Moral disengagement in the perpetuation of inhumanities. *Personality and Social Psychology Review, 3,* 193–209.

Bandura, A. (2001). Social cognitive theory. *Annual Review of Psychology* (Vol. 52). Palo Alto, CA: Annual Reviews.

Bandura, A. (2002). Selective moral disengagement in the exercise of moral agency. *Journal of Moral Education, 31,* 101–119.

Bandura, A. (2010). Self-efficacy. In D. Matsumoto (Ed.), *Cambridge dictionary of psychology.* New York: Cambridge University Press.

Bandura, A. (2010b). Vicarious learning. In D. Matsumoto (Ed.), *Cambridge dictionary of psychology.* New York: Cambridge University Press.

Bandura, A. (2012). Social cognitive theory. *Annual Review of Clinical Psychology* (Vol. 8). Palo Alto, CA: Annual Reviews.

Bandura, A. (2015). *Moral disengagement.* New York: Worth.

Bandura, A. (2018). Toward a psychology of human agency: Pathways and reflections. *Perspectives on Psychological Science, 13,* 130–136.

Bank, L., Burraston, B., & Snyder, J. (2004). Sibling conflict and ineffective parenting as predictors of boys' antisocial behavior and peer difficulties: Additive and international effects. *Journal of Research on Adolescence, 14,* 99–125.

Banker, S.M., & others (2020). Spatial network connectivity and spatial reasoning ability in children with nonverbal learning disability. *Scientific Reports, 10*(1), 561.

Bankole, A., Singh, S., Woog, V., & Wulf, D. (2004). *Risk and protection: Youth and HIV/AIDS in sub-Saharan Africa.* New York: Alan Guttmacher Institute.

Banks, J.A. (2020). *Diversity, transformative knowledge, and civic education.* New York: Routledge.

Bann, D., & others (2019). Adolescents' physical activity: Cross-national comparisons of levels, distributions, and disparities across 52 countries. *International Journal of Behavioral Nutrition and Physical Activity, 16,* 141.

Baranski, E., & others (2021). International optimism: Correlates and consequences of dispositional optimism across 61 countries. *Journal of Personality, 89,* 288–304.

Barbarin, O.A., Chinn, L., & Wright, Y.F. (2014). Creating developmentally auspicious school environments for African American boys. *Advances in Child Development and Behavior, 47,* 333–365.

Barbey, A.K., Karama, S., & Haier, R.J. (Eds.) (2021). *Cambridge handbook of intelligence and cognitive neuroscience.* New York: Cambridge University Press.

Bares, C.B., & others (2020). Exploring how family and neighborhood stressors influence genetic risk for adolescent conduct disorder and alcohol use. *Journal of Youth and Adolescence, 49,* 1365–1378.

Bargh, J.A., & McKenna, K.Y.A. (2004). The Internet and social life. *Annual Review of Psychology* (Vol. 55). Palo Alto, CA: Annual Reviews.

Barker, R., & Wright, H.F. (1951). *One boy's day.* New York: Harper.

Barlett, C.P., & others (2021). Cross-cultural similarities and differences in the theoretical predictors of cyberbullying perpetration: Results from a seven-country study. *Aggressive Behavior, 47,* 111–119.

Barnouw, V. (1975). *An introduction to anthropology, Vol. 2: Ethnology.* Homewood, IL: Dorsey Press.

Baron, J. (2020). Why science succeeds, and sometimes doesn't. In R.J. Sternberg & D.F. Halpern (Eds.), *Critical thinking in psychology* (2nd ed.). New York: Cambridge University Press.

Barragan-Jason, G., & others (2018). Two facets of patience in young children: Waiting with and without an explicit reward. *Journal of Experimental Psychology, 171,* 14–30.

Barroso, C., & others (2021). A meta-analysis of the relation between math anxiety and math achievement. *Psychological Bulletin, 147,* 134–168.

Barry, A.E., Valdez, D., & Russell, A.M. (2020). Does religiosity delay adolescent alcohol initiation? A long-term analysis (2008–2015) of nationally representative sample of 12th graders. *Substance Use and Misuse, 55,* 503–511.

Basile, K.C., & others (2021, in press). Chronic diseases, health conditions, and other impacts associated with rape victimization of U.S. women. *Journal of Interpersonal Violence.*

Basow, S.A. (2006). Gender role and gender identity development. In J. Worell & C.D. Goodheart (Eds.), *Handbook of girls' and women's psychological health.* New York: Oxford University Press.

Bassi, M., Steca, P., Della Fave, A., & Caprara, G.V. (2007). Academic self-efficacy beliefs and quality of experience in learning. *Journal of Youth and Adolescence, 36,* 301–312.

Batanova, M.D., & Loukas, A. (2011). Social anxiety and aggression in early adolescents: Examining the moderating roles of empathic concern and perspective taking. *Journal of Youth and Adolescence, 40,* 1534–1543.

Bates, J.E., McQuillan, M.E., & Hoyniak, C.P. (2019). Parenting and temperament. In M.H. Bornstein Ed.), *Handbook of parenting* (3rd ed.). New York: Elsevier.

Batista, M.G., & others (2019). Participation in sports in childhood and adolescence and physical activity in adulthood: A systematic review. *Journal of Sports Sciences, 37,* 2253–2262.

Batool, S.S., & Ghayas, S. (2020). Process of career identity formation among adolescents: Components and factors. *Heliyon, (6),* e04905.

Battistich, V.A. (2008). The Child Development Project: Creating caring school communities. In L. Nucci & D. Narváez (Eds.), *Handbook of moral and character education.* Clifton, NJ: Psychology Press.

Baum, G.L., & others (2020). Development of structure-function coupling in human brain networks during youth. *Proceedings of the National Academy of Sciences U.S.A., 117,* 771–778.

Baumas, V., & others (2021). Patients' and parents' experience of multi-family therapy for anorexia nervosa: A pilot study. *Frontiers in Psychology, 12,* 584565.

Baumeister, R.F., Campbell, J.D., Krueger, J.I., & Vohs, K.D. (2003). Does high self-esteem cause better performance, interpersonal success, happiness, or healthier lifestyles? *Psychological Science in the Public Interest, 4*(1), 1–44.

Baumrind, D. (1971). Current patterns of parental authority. *Developmental Psychology Monographs, 4*(1, Pt. 2).

Baumrind, D. (1991). Effective parenting during the early adolescent transition. In P.A. Cowan & E.M. Hetherington (Eds.), *Advances in family research* (Vol. 2). Hillsdale, NJ: Erlbaum.

Baumrind, D. (2012). Authoritative parenting revisited: History and current status. In R.E. Larzelere, A.S. Morris, & A.W. Harrist (Eds.), *Authoritative parenting.* Washington, DC: American Psychological Association.

Beaver, K.M., Vaughn, M.G., Wright, J.P., & Delisi, M. (2012). An interaction between perceived stress and 5HTTLPR genotype in the prediction of stable depressive symptomatology. *American Journal of Orthopsychiatry, 82,* 260–266.

Becht, A.I., & others (2021, in press). Daily identity dynamics in adolescence shaping identity in emerging adulthood: An 11-year longitudinal study on continuity in development. *Journal of Youth and Adolescence.*

Beck, D., & others (2021). White matter microstructure across the adult lifespan: A mixed longitudinal and cross-sectional study using advanced diffusion models and brain-age prediction. *NeuroImage, 224,* 117441.

Beck, E.D., & Jackson, J.J. (2020). Consistency and change in idiographic personality: A longitudinal ESM network study. *Journal of Personality and Social Psychology, 118,* 1080–1100.

Becker, S.P., & others (2018a). Sleep problems and suicidal behaviors in college students. *Journal of Psychiatric Research, 99,* 122–128.

Becker, S.P., & others (2018b). Sleep in a large, multi-university sample of college students: Sleep problem prevalence, sex differences, and mental health correlates. *Sleep Health, 4,* 174–181.

Beckes, L., & Edwards, W.L. (2020). Emotions as regulators of social behavior. In T.P. Beauchaine & S.E. Crowell (Eds.), *Oxford handbook of emotion dysregulation.* New York: Oxford University Press.

Beckman, K., & others (2021). Self-regulation in open-ended online assignment tasks: The importance of initial task interpretation and goal setting. *Studies in Higher Education, 46,* 821–835.

Beckmeyer, J.J., & Weybright, E.H. (2020). Exploring the associations between middle adolescent romantic activity and positive youth development. *Journal of Adolescence, 80,* 214–219.

Beeson, C.M.L., Brittain, H., & Vaillancourt, T. (2020). The temporal precedence of peer rejection, rejection sensitivity, depression, and aggression across adolescence. *Child Psychiatry and Human Development, 51,* 781–791.

Beghetto, R.A. (2019). Creativity in classrooms. In J.C. Kaufman & R.J. Sternberg (Eds.), *Cambridge handbook of creativity* (2nd ed.). New York: Cambridge University Press.

Beghetto, R.A. (2021). Creativity in K-12 schools. In J.C. Kaufman & R.J. Sternberg (Eds.), *Creativity.* New York: Cambridge University Press.

Belcher, B.R., & others (2021). The roles of physical activity, exercise, and fitness in promoting resilience during adolescence: Effects on mental well-being and brain development. *Biological Psychiatry, Cognitive Neuroscience, and Neuroimaging, 6,* 225–237.

Bell, M.A., & Broomell, A.P.R. (2021). Development of inhibitory control from infancy to early childhood. In O. Houde & G. Borst (Eds.), *Cambridge handbook of cognitive development.* New York: Cambridge University Press.

Bell, S.C., Wolff, L.A., & Skolnick, M. (2021, in press). Female victims of acquaintance rape in college: Incidence and effects of encounters with perpetrators. *American Journal of College Health.*

Bellantuono, L., & others (2021). Predicting brain age with complex networks: From adolescence to adulthood. *NeuroImage, 225,* 117458.

Bellard, A.M., & others (2021). The aging body: Contributing attitudinal factors towards perceptual body size estimates in younger and middle-aged women. *Archives of Women's Mental Health, 24,* 93–105.

Bellmore, A., Jiang, X.U., & Juvonen, J. (2010). Utilizing peer nominations in middle school: A longitudinal comparison between complete classroom-based and random list methods. *Journal of Research in Adolescence, 20,* 538–550.

Bellmore, A., Villarreal, V.M., & Ho, A.Y. (2011). Staying cool across the first year of middle school. *Journal of Youth and Adolescence, 40,* 776–785.

Bellon, E., Fias, W., & de Smedt, B. (2020). Metacognition across domains: Is the association between arithmetic and metacognitive monitoring domain-specific? *PLoS One, 15*(3), e0229932.

Belsky, J. (1981). Early human experience: A family perspective. *Developmental Psychology, 17,* 3–23.

Bem, C., & Small, N. (2020). An ecological framework for improving child and adolescent health. *Archives of Disease in Childhood, 105,* 299–301.

Bem, S.L. (1977). On the utility of alternative procedures for assessing psychological androgyny. *Journal of Consulting and Clinical Psychology, 45,* 196–205.

Bembenutty, H. (2021). School environments that facilitate delay of gratification. In F.C. Worrell & others (Eds.), *Cambridge handbook of applied school psychology.* New York: Cambridge University Press.

Benedetti, E., & others (2021). Cannabis policy changes and adolescent cannabis use: Evidence from Europe. *International Journal of Environmental Research and Public Health, 18,* 5174.

Bengesai, A.V., Khan, H.T.A., & Dube, R. (2018). Effect of early sexual debut on high school completion in South Africa. *Journal of Biological Science, 50,* 124–143.

Benner, A.D. (2011). Latino adolescents' loneliness, academic performance, and the buffering nature of friendships. *Journal of Youth and Adolescence, 5,* 556–567.

Benowitz-Fredericks, C.A., Garcia, K., Massey, M., Vassagar, B., & Borzekowski, D.L. (2012). Body image, eating disorders, and the relationship to adolescent media use. *Pediatric Clinics of North America, 59,* 693–704.

Benson, P.L., Mannes, M., Pittman, K., & Ferber, T. (2004). Youth development, developmental assets, and public policy. In R. Lerner & L. Steinberg (Eds.), *Handbook of adolescent psychology* (2nd ed.). New York: Wiley.

Benson, P.L., & Scales, P.C. (2009). The definition and preliminary measurement of thriving in adolescence. *Journal of Positive Psychology, 4,* 85–104.

Benson, P.L., & Scales, P.C. (2011). Thriving and sparks: Development and emergence of new core concepts in positive youth development. In R.J.R. Levesque (Ed.), *Encyclopedia of adolescence.* Berlin: Springer.

Benson, P.L., Scales, P.C., Hamilton, S.F., & Sesma, A. (2006). Positive youth development. In W. Damon & R. Lerner (Eds.), *Handbook of child psychology* (6th ed.). New York: Wiley.

Benveniste, L., Carnoy, M., & Rothstein, R. (2003). *All else equal.* New York: Routledge-Farmer.

Berdugo-Vega, G., & others (2020). Increasing neurogenesis refines hippocampal activity rejuvenating navigational learning strategies and contextual memory throughout life. *Nature Communication, 11*(1), 135.

Berge, J.M., & others (2015). The protective role of family meals for youth obesity: 10-year longitudinal associations. *Journal of Pediatrics, 166,* 296–301.

Berger, J.T., & Miller, D.R. (2021, in press). Health disparities, systematic racism, and failures of cultural competence. *American Journal of Bioethics.*

Bergeron, K.E. (2018). *Challenging the cult of self-esteem in education.* New York: Routledge.

Bergmuller, S. (2013). The relationship between cultural individualism-collectivism and student aggression across 62 countries. *Aggressive Behavior, 39,* 182–200.

Bergstrom, M., & others (2017). Preschool children living in joint physical custody arrangements show less psychological symptoms than those living mostly or only with one parent. *Acta Paediatrica, 107,* 294–300.

Berkowitz, M., & others (2020). Girls, boys, and school: On gender (in)equalities in education. In F.M. Cheung & D.F. Halpern (Eds.), *Cambridge handbook of the international psychology of women.* New York: Cambridge University Press.

Berkowitz, M.W. (2012). Moral and character education. In K.R. Harris, S. Graham, & T. Urdan (Eds.), *APA educational psychology handbook* (Vol. 2). New York: American Psychological Association.

Berman, S.L., You, Y., Schwartz, S., Teo, G., & Mochizuki, K. (2011). Identity exploration, commitment, and distress: A cross-national investigation in China, Taiwan, Japan, and the United States. *Child Youth Care Forum, 40,* 65–75.

Berndt, T.J., & Perry, T.B. (1990). Distinctive features and effects of early adolescent friendships. In R. Montemayor (Ed.), *Advances in adolescent research.* Greenwich, CT: JAI Press.

Bernstein, N. (2004, March 7). Young love, new caution. *The New York Times,* p. A22.

Berscheid, E., & Fei, J. (1977). Sexual jealousy and romantic love. In G. Clinton & G. Smith (Eds.), *Sexual jealousy.* Englewood Cliffs, NJ: Prentice-Hill.

Berscheid, E., Snyder, M., & Omoto, A.M. (1989). Issues in studying close relationships. In C. Hendrick (Ed.), *Close relationships.* Newbury Park, CA: Sage.

Best, J.R. (2011). Effects of physical activity on children's executive function: Contributions of experimental research on aerobic exercise. *Developmental Review, 30,* 331–351.

Bettinger, E.P., & others (2018). Increasing perseverance in math. Evidence from a field experiment in Norway. *Journal of Economic Behavior and Organization, 146,* 1–15.

Bettio, L.E.B., & others (2020). Interplay between hormones and exercise on hippocampal plasticity across the lifespan. *Molecular Basis of Disease, 1866*(8), 165821.

Beutel, M.E., & others (2016). Procrastination, distress, and life satisfaction across the age range—A German representative community study. *PLoS One, 11*(2), 0148054.

Bevilacqua, L., & others (2021). Adverse child experiences and trajectories of internalizing, externalizing, and prosocial behaviors from childhood to adolescence. *Child Abuse and Neglect, 112,* 104890.

Beyers, E., & Seiffge-Krenke, I. (2011). Does identity precede intimacy? Testing Erikson's theory on romantic development in emerging adults of the 21st century. *Journal of Adolescent Research, 25*(3), 387–415.

Bhawuk, D.P.S., & Bhawuk, A.P. (2021). Harry Triandis' contributions to intercultural training as a field of research. In D. Landis & D.P.S. Bhawuk (Eds.), *The Cambridge handbook of intercultural training.* New York: Cambridge University Press.

Bhawuk, D.P.S., & Landis, D. (2021). Intercultural training for the global village. In D. Landis & D.P.S. Bhawuk (Eds.), *Cambridge handbook of intercultural training.* New York: Cambridge University Press.

Biagianti, B., & others (2020). A systematic review of treatments targeting cognitive biases in socially anxious adolescents: Special section on "Translational neuroscience studies in affective disorders" section editor, Maria Nobile MD, PhD. *Journal of Affective Disorders, 264,* 543–551.

Bialystok, E. (2011). *Becoming bilingual: Emergence of cognitive outcomes of bilingualism in immersion education.* Paper presented at the meeting of the Society for Research in Child Development, Montreal.

Bialystok, E. (2015). The impact of bilingualism on cognition. In R. Scott & S. Kosslyn (Eds.), *Emerging trends in the social and behavioral sciences.* New York: Wiley.

Bialystok, E. (2017). The bilingual adaptation: How minds accommodate experience. *Psychological Bulletin, 143,* 233–262.

Bianchi, D., & others (2021, in press). A bad romance: Sexting motivations and teen dating violence. *Journal of Interpersonal Violence.*

Biederman, J., & others (2020). Is paternal smoking at conception a risk for ADHD? A controlled study in youth with and without ADHD. *Journal of Attention Disorders, 11,* 1493–1496.

Bierman, K.L., & others (2021). Reducing adolescent psychopathology in socioeconomically disadvantaged children with a preschool intervention: A randomized controlled trial. *American Journal of Psychiatry, 178,* 305–312.

Biglan, A., & others (2020). A strategic plan for strengthening America's families: A brief from the Coalition of Behavioral Science Organizations. *Clinic Child and Family Psychological Review, 23,* 153–175.

Bigler, R.S., Hayes, A.R., & Liben, L.S. (2014). Analysis and evaluation of the rationales for single-sex schooling. *Advances in Child Development and Behavior, 47,* 225–260.

Bill and Melinda Gates Foundation (2011). *College-ready education.* Retrieved August 21, 2011, from www.gatesfoundation.org/college-ready-education/Pages/default.aspx

Bill and Melinda Gates Foundation (2017). *K-12 education.* Retrieved March 28, 2017, from https://www.gatesfoundation.org/What-We-Do/US-Program/K-12-Education

Bill and Melinda Gates Foundation (2020). *All lives have equal value.* Retrieved November 8, 2020, from www.gatesfoundation.org

Birkeland, M.S., Melkevick, O., Holsen, I., & Wold, B. (2012). Trajectories of global self-esteem development during adolescence. *Journal of Adolescence, 35,* 43–54.

Birman, B.F., & others (2007). *State and local implementation of the "No Child Left Behind Act." Volume II—Teacher quality under "NCLB": Interim report.* Jessup, MD: U.S. Department of Education.

Bjarehed, M., & others (2019). Individual moral disengagement and bullying among Swedish fifth graders: The role of collective moral disengagement and pro-bullying behavior within classrooms. *Journal of Interpersonal Violence, 48,* 1835–1848.

Bjarehed, M., & others (2021). Moral disengagement and verbal bullying in early adolescence: A three-year longitudinal study. *Journal of School Psychology, 84,* 63–73.

Bjorklund, D.F., & Pellegrini, A.D. (2002). *The origins of human nature.* New York: Oxford University Press.

Black, J.J., & Rofey, D.L. (2018). An overview of common psychiatric problems among adolescent and young adult females: Focus on mood and anxiety. *Best Practices in Research and Clinical Obstetrics and Gynecology, 48,* 165–173.

Black, M.C., & others (2011). *The National Intimate Partner and Sexual Violence Survey (NISVS): 2010 Summary Report.* Atlanta: National Center for Injury Prevention and Control.

Blackwell, L.S., Trzesniewski, K.H., & Dweck, C.S. (2007). Implicit theories of intelligence predict achievement across an adolescent transition: A longitudinal study and an intervention. *Child Development, 78,* 246–263.

Blakemore, J.E.O., Berenbaum, S.A., & Liben, I.S. (2009). *Gender development.* New York: Psychology Press.

Blakemore, S.J., & Mills, K. (2014). The social brain in adolescence. *Annual Review of Psychology* (Vol. 65). Palo Alto, CA: Annual Reviews.

Bleakley, A., Hennessy, M., Fishbein, M., & Jordan, A. (2009). How sources of sexual information relate to adolescents' beliefs about sex. *American Journal of Health Behavior, 33,* 37–48.

Bleil, M.E., & others (2021). Early life adversity and pubertal timing: Implications for cardiometabolic health. *Journal of Pediatric Psychology, 46,* 36–48.

Block, J. (1993). Studying personality the long way. In D. Funder, R.D. Parke, C. Tomlinson-Keasey, & K. Widaman (Eds.), *Studying lives through time.* Washington, DC: American Psychological Association.

Blomeyer, D., & others (2008). Interaction between CRHRI gene and stressful life events predicts adolescent heavy alcohol use. *Biological Psychiatry, 63,* 146–151.

Bloom, B. (1985). *Developing talent in young people.* New York: Ballantine.

Blumenfeld, P.C., Kempler, T.M., & Krajcik, J.S. (2006). Motivation and cognitive engagement in learning environments. In R.K. Sawyer (Ed.), *The Cambridge handbook of the learning sciences.* New York: Cambridge University Press.

Bo, I. (1994). The sociocultural environment as a source of support. In F. Nestmann & K. Hurrelmann (Eds.), *Social networks and social support in childhood and adolescence.* New York: Walter de Gruyter.

Boccia, M.L., & others (2021). Parental divorce in childhood is related to lower urinary oxytocin concentrations in adulthood. *Journal of Comparative Psychology, 135,* 74–81.

Boer, M., & others (2020). Adolescents' intense and problematic social media use and their well-being in 29 countries. *Journal of Adolescent Health, 66*(6S), S89–S99.

Boers, E., Afazali, M.H., & Conrod, P. (2020). A longitudinal study on the relationship between screen time and adolescent alcohol use: The mediating role of social norms. *Preventive Medicine, 132,* 105992.

Bogart, L.M., & others (2014). Peer victimization in the fifth grade and health in the tenth grade. *Pediatrics, 133,* 440–447.

Bohnert, A.M., Loren, D.M., & Miller, A.L. (2020). Examining childhood obesity through the lens of developmental psychopathology: Framing the issues to guide best practices in research and intervention. *American Psychologist, 75,* 163–177.

Bolourian, Y., Tipton-Fisler, L.A., & Yassine, J. (2020). Special education placement trends: Least restrictive environment across five years in California. *Contemporary School Psychology, 24,* 164–173.

Bonar, E.E., & others (2021). Binge drinking before and after a COVID-19 campus closure among first-year college students. *Addictive Behaviors, 118,* 106879.

Bondar, J., & others (2020). Symptom clusters in adolescent depression and differential response to treatment: A secondary analysis of the Treatment for Adolescents with Depression Study randomized trial. *Lancet Psychiatry, 7,* 337–343.

Bone, J.K., Lewis, G., & Lewis, G. (2020). The role of gender inequalities in adolescent depression. *Lancet Psychiatry, 7,* 471–472.

Bono, G. (2012, August 5). *Searching for the developmental role of gratitude: A 4-year longitudinal analysis.* Paper presented at the American Psychological Association, Orlando.

Booker, J.A., & others (2021, in press). African American mothers talk to their preadolescents about honesty and lying. *Cultural Diversity and Ethnic Minority Psychology.*

Boonstra, H. (2002, February). Teen pregnancy: Trends and lessons learned. *The Guttmacher Report on Public Policy,* pp. 7–10.

Booth, A., Johnson, D.R., Granger, D.A., Crouter, A.C., & McHale, S. (2003). Testosterone and child and adolescent adjustment: The moderating role of parent-child relationships. *Developmental Psychology, 39,* 85–98.

Booth, M. (2002). Arab adolescents facing the future: Enduring ideals and pressures to change. In B.B. Brown, R.W. Larson, & T.S. Saraswathi (Eds.), *The world's youth.* New York: Cambridge University Press.

Borich, G.D., & Blanchette, A. (2022). *Effective teaching methods* (10th ed.). Upper Saddle River, NJ: Pearson.

Bornstein, M.H. (Ed.) (2021). *Psychological insights for understanding COVID-19 and families, parents, and children.* New York: Routledge.

Bornstein, M.H., & Esposito, G. (2021). Cross-cultural perspectives on parent-infant interactions. In J.J. Lockman & C.S. Tamis-LeMonda (Eds.), *Cambridge handbook of infant development.* New York: Cambridge University Press.

Bornstein, M.H., & Putnick, D.L. (2018). Parent-adolescent relationships in global perspective. In J.E. Lansford & P. Banati (Eds.), *Handbook of adolescent development research and its impact on global policy.* New York: Oxford University Press.

Bosacki, S., & others (2020). Theory of mind, self-knowledge, and perceptions of loneliness in emerging adolescents. *Journal of Genetic Psychology, 181,* 14–31.

Bosma, H.A., & Kunnen, E.S. (2001). Determinants and mechanisms in ego identity development: A review and synthesis. *Developmental Review, 21,* 39–66.

Bouchard, T.J. (2018). Heredity ability: *g* is driven by experience producing drives. In R.J. Sternberg (Ed.), *Nature of human intelligence.* New York: Cambridge University Press.

Boulay, B., & others (2018). *The Investing in Innovation Fund. Summary of 67 evaluations (NCEE No. 2018-4013).* Washington, DC: National Center for Education Evaluation and Regional Assistance, Institute of Education Sciences. U.S. Department of Education.

Bould, H., & others (2015). Association between early temperament and depression at 18 years. *Depression and Anxiety, 31,* 729–736.

Bousuard, M-E., van de Bongardt, D., & Blais, M. (2016). Sexuality (and lack thereof) in adolescence and early adulthood: A review of the literature. *Behavioral Sciences, 6*(1), 8.

Bowker, J.C., & Spencer, S.V. (2010). Friendship and adjustment: A focus on mixed-grade friendships. *Journal of Youth and Adolescence, 39,* 1318–1329.

Bowlby, J. (1989). *Secure and insecure attachment.* New York: Basic Books.

Bozzini, A.B., & others (2021). Factors associated with risk behaviors in adolescence: A systematic review. *Brazilian Journal of Psychiatry, 43,* 210–221.

Brabeck, M.M., & Brabeck, K.M. (2006). Women and relationships. In J. Worell & C.D. Goodheart (Eds.), *Handbook of girls' and women's psychological health.* New York: Oxford University Press.

Bradley, R.H., Corwyn, R.F., McAdoo, H., & Coll, C. (2001). The home environments of children in the United States: Part I. Variations by age, ethnicity, and poverty status. *Child Development, 72,* 1844–1867.

Brady, S.S., & Halpern-Felsher, B. (2007). Adolescents' reported consequences of having oral sex versus vaginal sex. *Pediatrics, 119,* 229–236.

Braithwaite, I., & others (2014). Fast-food consumption and body mass index in children and adolescents: An international cross-sectional study. *BMJ Open, 4*(12), e005813.

Braithwaite, S.R., & Holt-Lunstad, J. (2017). Romantic relationships and mental health. *Current Opinion in Psychology, 13,* 120–125.

Braithwaite, S.R., Coulson, G., Keddington, K., & Fincham, F.D. (2015). The influence of pornography on sexual scripts and hooking up among emerging adults in college. *Archives of Sexual Behavior, 44,* 111–123.

Brandes, C.M., & others (2021). Towards construct validity of relational aggression. *Multivariate Behavioral Research, 56,* 161–162.

Brando-Garrido, C., & others (2020). Relationship of academic procrastination with perceived competence, coping, self-esteem, and self-efficacy in nursing students. *Enfermeria Clinica, 30,* 398–403.

Braun, S.S., & Davidson, A.J. (2017). Gender (non) conformity in middle childhood: A mixed methods approach to understanding gender-typed behavior, friendship, and peer preference. *Sex Roles, 77,* 16–29.

Braun-Courville, D.K., & Rojas, M. (2009). Exposure to sexually explicit web sites and adolescent sexual attitudes and behaviors. *Journal of Adolescent Health, 45,* 156–162.

Braver, S.L., Ellman, I.M., & Fabricus, W.V. (2003). Relocation of children after divorce and children's best interests: New evidence and legal considerations. *Journal of Family Psychology, 17,* 206–219.

Braver, S.L., & Lamb, M.E. (2013). Marital dissolution. In G.W. Peterson & K.R. Bush (Eds.), *Handbook of marriage and the family* (3rd ed.). New York: Springer.

Bray, J.H., & Kelly, J. (1998). *Stepfamilies.* New York: Broadway.

Bray, J.H., Berger, S.H., & Boethel, C.L. (1999). Marriage to remarriage and beyond. In E.M. Hetherington (Ed.), *Coping with divorce, single parenting, and remarriage.* Mahwah, NJ: Erlbaum.

Breehl, L., & Caban, O. (2020). *Physiology, puberty.* Treasure Island, Fl: StatPearls.

Breslau, J., & others (2017). Sex differences in recent first-onset depression in an epidemiological sample of adolescents. *Translational Psychiatry, 7*(5), e1139.

Bretherton, I., & others (2021). The health and well-being of transgender Australians: A national community survey. *LGBT Health, 8,* 42–49.

Breuner, C.C., & others (2018). Adolescent and young adult tattooing, piercing, and scarification. *Pediatrics, 141*(2), e20173630.

Bridgeland, J.M., Dilulio, J.J., & Wulsin, S.C. (2008). *Engaged for success.* Washington, DC: Civic Enterprises.

Brieant, A., & others (2021). Socioeconomic risk for adolescent cognitive control and emerging risk-taking behaviors. *Journal of Research on Adolescence, 31,* 71–84.

Briley, D.A., Domiteaux, M., & Tucker-Drob, E.M. (2014). Achievement-relevant personality: Relations with the Big Five and validation of an efficient instrument. *Learning and Individual Differences, 32,* 26–39.

Brindis, C.D., & others (2020). Perspectives on adolescent pregnancy prevention strategies in the United States: Looking back, looking forward. *Adolescent Health, Medicine, & Therapeutics, 11,* 135–145.

Broderick, R. (2003, July/August). A surgeon's saga. *Minnesota: The magazine of the University of Minnesota Alumni Association,* 26–31.

Brody, G.H., & Schaffer, D.R. (1982). Contributions of parents and peers to children's moral socialization. *Developmental Review, 2,* 31–75.

Brody, G.H., Stoneman, Z., & Burke, M. (1987). Child temperaments, maternal differential behavior and sibling relationships. *Developmental Psychology, 23,* 354–362.

Brody, G.H., & others (2001). The influence of neighborhood disadvantage, collective socialization, and parenting on African American children's affiliation with deviant peers. *Child Development, 72,* 1231–1246.

Brody, G.H., & others (2017). Protective prevention effects on the association of poverty with brain development. *JAMA Pediatrics, 17,* 46–52.

Brody, N. (2007). Does education influence intelligence? In P.C. Kyllonen, R.D. Roberts, & L. Stankov (Eds.), *Extending intelligence.* Mahwah, NJ: Erlbaum.

Brodzinsky, D.M., & Pinderhughes, E. (2002). Parenting and child development in adoptive families. In M.H. Bornstein (Ed.), *Handbook of parenting* (Vol. 1). Mahwah, NJ: Erlbaum.

Bronfenbrenner, U. (1986). Ecology of the family as a context for human development: Research perspectives. *Developmental Psychology, 22,* 723–742.

Bronfenbrenner, U. (2004). *Making human beings human.* Thousand Oaks, CA: Sage.

Bronfenbrenner, U., & Morris, P. (1998). The ecology of developmental processes. In W. Damon (Ed.), *Handbook of child psychology* (5th ed., Vol. 1). New York: Wiley.

Bronfenbrenner, U., & Morris, P. (2006). The ecology of developmental processes. In W. Damon & R. Lerner (Eds.), *Handbook of child psychology* (6th ed.). New York: Wiley.

Bronstein, P. (2006). The family environment: Where gender role socialization begins. In J. Worell & C.D. Goodheart (Eds.), *Handbook of girls' and women's psychological health.* New York: Oxford University Press.

Brooker, R. (2021). *Genetics* (7th ed.). New York: McGraw-Hill.

Brooker, R., & others (2020). *Principles of biology* (3rd ed.). New York: McGraw-Hill.

Brooker, R.J., & others (2020). Attentional control explains covariation between symptoms of attention-deficit/hyperactivity disorder and anxiety during adolescence. *Journal of Research on Adolescence, 30*(1), 126–141.

Brooks, F., & others (2018). Spirituality as a protective health asset for young people: An international comparative analysis from three countries. *International Journal of Public Health, 63,* 387–395.

Brooks-Gunn, J., & Donahue, E.H. (2008). Introducing the issue. *The Future of Children, 18*(1), 3–10.

Brooks-Gunn, J., Han, W-J., & Waldfogel, J. (2010). First-year maternal employment and child development in the first seven years. *Monographs of the Society for Research in Child Development, 75*(2), 1–147.

Brooks-Gunn, J., & Warren, M.P. (1989). The psychological significance of secondary sexual characteristics in 9- to 11-year-old girls. *Child Development, 59,* 161–169.

Broughton, J. (1983). The cognitive developmental theory of adolescent self and identity. In B. Lee & G. Noam (Eds.), *Developmental approaches to self.* New York: Plenum.

Brouillard, C., & others (2018). Links between mother-adolescent and father-adolescent relationships and adolescent depression: A genetically informed study. *Journal of Clinical Child and Adolescent Psychiatry, 47*(Suppl. 1), S397–S408.

Broverman, L., Vogel, S., Broverman, D., Clarkson, F., & Rosenkranz, P. (1972). Sex-role stereotypes: A current appraisal. *Journal of Social Issues, 28,* 59–78.

Brown, A. (2020, August 20). *A profile of single Americans.* Washington, DC: Pew Research Center.

Brown, B.B. (2004). Adolescents' relationships with peers. In R.M. Lerner & L. Steinberg (Eds.), *Handbook of adolescent psychology* (2nd ed.). New York: Wiley.

Brown, B.B. (2011). Popularity in peer group perspective: The role of status in adolescent peer systems. In A.H.N. Cillessen, D. Schwartz, & L. Mayeux (Eds.), *Popularity in the peer system.* New York: Guilford.

Brown, B.B., & Larson, J. (2009). Peer relationships in adolescence. In R.L. Lerner & L. Steinberg (Eds.), *Handbook of adolescent psychology* (3rd ed.). New York: Wiley.

Brown, B.B., & Larson, R.W. (2002). The kaleidoscope of adolescence: Experiences of the world's youth at the beginning of the 21st century. In B.B. Brown, R.W. Larson, & T.S. Saraswathi (Eds.), *The world's youth.* New York: Cambridge University Press.

Brown, B.B., & Lohr, M.J. (1987). Peer-group affiliation and adolescent self-esteem: An integration of ego-identity and symbolic-interaction theories. *Journal of Personality and Social Psychology, 52,* 47–55.

Brown, C. (2021). Students' perceptions of the relationships between A-levels, expectations, values, task demands, goals, and identities: A qualitative study. *Psychology of Education Review, 45,* 52–60.

Brown, E.R., & Diekman, A.B. (2010). What will I be? Exploring gender differences in near and distant possible selves. *Sex Roles, 63,* 568–579.

Brown, K.M., & others (2020). Social regulation of inflammation related gene expression in the multi-ethnic study of atherosclerosis. *Psychoneuroendocrinology, 117,* 104654.

Brown, L.K., & Gilligan, C. (1992). *Meeting at the crossroads.* Cambridge, MA: Harvard University Press.

Brown, Z., & Tiggemann, M. (2016). Attractive celebrity and peer images on Instagram: Effect on women's mood and body image. *Body Image, 19,* 37–43.

Brumley, L.D., & others (2021). Psychosocial correlates and consequences of adolescents' self-generated academic goals and appraisals. *Journal of Research on Adolescence, 31,* 204–217.

Brummelman, J.E., Thomaes, S., Orbobio de Castro, B., Overbeek, G., & Bushman, B.J. (2014). "That's not just beautiful—that's incredibly beautiful!": The adverse impact of inflated praise on children with low self-esteem. *Psychological Science, 25,* 728-735.

Bryan, C.J., & others (2016). Harnessing adolescents' values to reduce unhealthy snacking. *Proceedings of the National Academy of Sciences U.S.A., 113,* 10830-10835.

Buchanan, C.M., Maccoby, E.E., & Dornbusch, S. (1992). Adolescents and their families after divorce: Three residential arrangements compared. *Journal of Research on Adolescence, 2,* 261-291.

Bucx, F., Raaijmakers, Q., & van Wel, F. (2010). Life course stage in young adulthood and intergenerational congruence in family attitudes. *Journal of Marriage and the Family, 72,* 117-134.

Budday, S., & others (2021). Mechanical properties of gray and white matter brain tissue by indentation. *Journal of the Mechanical, Biobehavioral, and Biomedical Materials, 46,* 318-330.

Budge, S.L. (2021). *Trans CARE Lab.* Madison, WI: Advancing Health Equity and Diversity (AHEAD) program.

Budge, S.L., Sinnard, M.T., & Hoyt, W.T. (2021). Longitudinal effects of psychotherapy with transgender and nonbinary clients: A randomized pilot trial. *Psychotherapy, 58,* 1-11.

Buhrmester, D. (1990). Friendship, interpersonal competence, and adjustment in preadolescence and adolescence. *Child Development, 61,* 1101-1111.

Buhrmester, D. (1998). Need fulfillment, interpersonal competence, and the developmental contexts of early adolescent friendship. In W.M. Bukowski & A.F. Newcomb (Eds.), *The company they keep: Friendship in childhood and adolescence.* New York: Cambridge University Press.

Buhrmester, D. (2001, April). *Does age at which romantic involvement starts matter?* Paper presented at the meeting of the Society for Research in Child Development, Minneapolis.

Buhrmester, D., & Chong, C.M. (2009). Friendship in adolescence. In H. Reis & S. Sprecher (Eds.), *Encyclopedia of human relationships.* Thousand Oaks, CA: Sage.

Bui, T.A., & Wijesekera, N. (2019). Unemployment and the rate of psychoactive-substance-related psychiatric hospital admission in regional Queensland: An observational, longitudinal study. *Australas Psychiatry, 27,* 388-391.

Buist, K.L., Dekovic, M., & Prinzie, P. (2013). Sibling relationship quality and psychopathology of children and adolescents: A meta-analysis. *Clinical Psychology Review, 33,* 97-106.

Bukowski, W.M., Laursen, B., & Rubin, K.H. (Eds.) (2019). *Handbook of peer interactions, relationships, and groups* (2nd ed.). New York: Guilford.

Bumpus, M.F., Crouter, A.C., & McHale, S.M. (2001). Parental autonomy granting during adolescence: Gender differences in context. *Developmental Psychology, 37,* 163-173.

Burcas, S., & Cretu, R.Z. (2021). Multidimensional perfectionism and test anxiety: A meta-analytic review of two decades of research. *Educational Psychology Review, 33,* 249-273.

Burgess-Champoux, T.L., Larson, N., Neumark-Sztainer, D., Hannan, P.J., & Story, M. (2009). Are family meal patterns associated with overall diet quality during the transition from early to middle adolescence? *Journal of Nutrition Education and Behavior, 41,* 79-86.

Burki, T. (2021). COVID-19 among American Indians and Alaska Natives. *Lancet, 21*(3), 325-326.

Burnette, D. (2021, April 14). How COVID-19 will make fixing America's worst-performing schools harder. *Education Week.*

Burton, R.V. (1984). A paradox in theories and research in moral development. In W.M. Kurtines & J.L. Gewirtz (Eds.), *Morality, moral behavior, and moral development.* New York: Wiley.

Busch, A.S., & others (2020). Obesity is associated with earlier puberty in boys. *Journal of Clinical Endocrinology and Metabolism, 105,* dgz222.

Busching, R., & Krahe, B. (2020). With a little help from their peers: The impact of classmates on adolescents' development of prosocial behavior. *Journal of Youth and Adolescence, 49,* 1849-1863.

Buss, D.M. (2012). *Evolutionary psychology* (4th ed.). Boston: Allyn & Bacon.

Buss, D.M. (2015). *Evolutionary psychology* (5th ed.). Upper Saddle River, NJ: Pearson.

Buss, D.M. (2019). *Evolutionary psychology* (6th ed.). New York: Routledge.

Buss, D.M., & Schmitt, D.P. (1993). Sexual strategies theory: An evolutionary perspective on human mating. *Psychological Review, 100,* 204-232.

Busséri, M.A., Willoughby, T., Chalmers, H., & Bogaert, A.R. (2006). Same-sex attraction and successful adolescent development. *Journal of Youth and Adolescence, 35,* 563-575.

Bussey, K., & Bandura, A. (1999). Social cognitive theory of gender development and differentiation. *Psychological Review, 106,* 676-713.

Buzwell, S., & Rosenthal, D. (1996). Constructing a sexual self: Adolescents' sexual self-perceptions and sexual risk-taking. *Journal of Research on Adolescence, 6,* 489-513.

Buzzichelli, S., & others (2018). Perfectionism and cognitive rigidity in anorexia nervosa: Is there an association? *European Eating Disorder Review, 26,* 360-366.

Byne, W., & others (2012). Report of the American Psychiatric Association Task Force on the treatment of gender identity disorder. *Archives of Sexual Behavior, 41,* 759-796.

C

Caamono-Isorna, F., & others (2021). Alcohol use and sexual and physical assault victimization among university students: Three years of follow-up. *Journal of Interpersonal Violence, 36,* NP3574-NP3595.

Cabaco, A.S., & others (2021). Psychopathological risk factors associated with body image, body dissatisfaction, and weight-loss dieting in school-age adolescents. *Children, 8*(2), 105.

Cabre-Riera, A., & others (2019). Telecommunication devices use, screen time, and sleep in adolescents. *Environmental Research, 171,* 341-347.

Cabrero, F.R., & De Jesus, O. (2021). *Dysgraphia.* Treasure Island, FL: StatPearls.

Cacioppo, J.T., Cacioppo, S., Gonzaga, G.C., Ogburn, E.L., & VanderWheele, T.J. (2013). Marital satisfaction and break-ups differ across on-line and off-line meeting venues. *Proceedings of the National Academy of Sciences, 110*(25), 10135-10140.

Cacioppo, J.T., & others (2000). Lonely traits and concomitant physiological processes: The MacArthur Social Neuroscience Studies. *International Journal of Psychophysiology, 35,* 143-154.

Cai, M., Hardy, S.A., Olsen, J.A., Nelson, D.A., & Yamawaki, N. (2013). Adolescent-parent attachment as a mediator of relationships between parenting and adolescent social behavior and wellbeing in China. *International Journal of Psychology, 48,* 1185-1190.

Cai, Y., & others (2021). The neurodevelopmental role of dopaminergic signaling in neurological disorders. *Neuroscience Letters, 741,* 135540.

Cain, M.S., Leonard, J.A., Gabriel, J.D., & Finn, A.S. (2016). Media multitasking in adolescence. *Psychonomic Bulletin and Review, 23,* 1932-1941.

Cairncross, M., & Miller, C.J. (2020). The effectiveness of mindfulness-based therapies for ADHD: A meta-analytic review. *Journal of Attention Disorders, 24,* 627-643.

Calabro, F.J., & others (2020). Development of hippocampal-prefrontal cortex interactions through adolescence. *Cerebral Cortex, 30,* 1548-1555.

Calcaterra, V., & others (2021). The role of fetal, infant, and childhood nutrition in the timing of sexual maturation. *Nutrients, 13*(2), 419.

Calders, F., & others (2020). Investigating the interplay between parenting dimensions and styles, and the association with adolescent outcomes. *European Child and Adolescent Psychiatry, 29,* 327-342.

Caliendo, E.T., & others (2021, in press). Acute imaging findings predict recovery of cognitive and motor function after inpatient rehabilitation for pediatric traumatic brain injury: A pediatric brain injury consortium study. *Journal of Neurotrauma.*

Calugi, S., & Dalle Grave, R. (2019). Body image concern and treatment outcomes in adolescents with anorexia nervosa. *International Journal of Eating Disorders, 52,* 582-585.

Calvert, S.L. (2015). Children and digital media. In R.M. Lerner (Ed.), *Handbook of child psychology and developmental science* (7th ed.). New York: Wiley.

Cam, H.H., & Top, F.U. (2020). Overweight, obesity, weight-related behaviors, and health-related quality of life among high-school students in Turkey. *Eating and Weight Disorders, 25,* 1295-1302.

Cambron, C., & others (2018). Neighborhood, family, and peer factors associated with early adolescent smoking and alcohol use. *Journal of Youth and Adolescence, 47,* 369-382.

Cameron, J.L. (2004). Interrelationships between hormones, behavior, and affect during adolescence: Understanding hormonal, physical, and brain changes occurring in association with pubertal activation of the reproductive axis. Introduction to Part III. *Annals of the New York Academy of Sciences, 1021,* 110-123.

Campbell, C.Y. (1988, August 24). Group raps depiction of teenagers. *Boston Globe,* p. 44.

Campbell, L., Campbell, B., & Dickinson, D. (2004). *Teaching and learning through multiple intelligences* (3rd ed.). Boston: Allyn & Bacon.

Campione-Barr, N. (2017). The changing nature of power, control, and influence in sibling relationships. *New Directions in Child and Adolescent Development, 156,* 7-14.

Campione-Barr, N., Greer, K.B., & Kruse, A. (2013). Differential associations between domains of sibling conflict and adolescent emotional adjustment. *Child Development, 84*(3), 938-954.

Campisi, S.C., & others (2020). Suicidal behaviors among adolescents from 90 countries: A pooled analysis of the global school-based student health survey. *BMC Public Health, 20*(1), 1102.

Canivez, G.L., Watkins, M.W., & Dombrowski, S.C. (2017). Structural validity of the Wechsler Intelligence Scale for Children–Fifth Edition: Confirmatory factor analysis with the 16 primary and secondary subtests. *Psychological Assessment, 87,* 383-407.

Cano, M.A., & others (2021). Psychosocial stress, bicultural identity integration, and bicultural self-efficacy among Hispanic emerging adults. *Stress and Health, 37,* 392-398.

Cantone, E., & others (2015). Interventions on bullying and cyberbullying in schools: A systematic review. *Clinical Practice and Epidemiology in Mental Health, 11*(Suppl. 1), S58-S76.

Caprara, G.V., & others (2010). The contributions of agreeableness and self-efficacy beliefs to prosociality. *European Journal of Personality, 24,* 36-55.

Carballo, J.J., & others (2020). Psychosocial risk factors for suicidality in children and adolescents. *European Child and Adolescent Psychiatry, 29,* 759–776.

Cardenas, S., & others (2021). Arithmetic processing in children with dyscalculia: An event-related potential study. *PeerJ, 9,* e10489.

Carey, D.P. (2007). Is bigger really better? The search for brain size and intelligence in the twenty-first century. In S. Della Sala (Ed.), *Tall tales about the mind and brain: Separating fact from fiction.* Oxford, UK: Oxford University Press.

Carey, J.C. (2020). School-based counseling in the United States: Mode of practice and international comparisons related to five dimensions of practice. *Journal of School-Based Counseling Policy and Evaluation, 2*(1), 63–70.

Carlo, G., Knight, G.P., McGinley, M., Zamboanga, B.L., & Jarvis, L.H. (2010). The multidimensionality of prosocial behaviors and evidence of measurement equivalence in Mexican American and European American early adolescents. *Journal of Research on Adolescence, 20,* 334–358.

Carlo, G., Mestre, M.V., Samper, P., Tur, A., & Armenta, B.E. (2011). The longitudinal relations among dimensions of parenting styles, sympathy, prosocial moral reasoning, and prosocial behaviors. *International Journal of Behavioral Development, 35,* 116–124.

Carlo, G., & Pierotti, S.L. (2020). The development of prosocial motives. In L.A. Jensen (Ed.), *Oxford handbook of moral development.* New York: Oxford University Press.

Carlo, G., & others (2018). Longitudinal relations among parenting styles, prosocial behaviors, and academic outcomes in U.S. Mexican adolescents. *Child Development, 89,* 577–592.

Carlson, K.S., & Gjerde, P.F. (2010). Preschool personality antecedents of narcissism in adolescence and emerging adulthood: A 20-year longitudinal study. *Journal of Research in Personality, 43,* 570–578.

Carnegie Council on Adolescent Development (1989). *Turning points: Preparing American youth for the twenty-first century.* New York: Carnegie Foundation.

Carnegie Council on Adolescent Development (1995). *Great transitions.* New York: Carnegie Foundation.

Carratala, S., & Maxwell, C. (2020, May 7). *Health disparities by race and ethnicity.* Washington, DC: Center for American Progress.

Carroll, J. (1993). *Human cognitive abilities.* Cambridge, UK: Cambridge University Press.

Carskadon, M.A. (Ed.) (2002). *Adolescent sleep patterns.* New York: Cambridge University Press.

Carskadon, M.A. (2004). Sleep difficulties in young people. *Archives of Pediatric and Adolescent Medicine, 158,* 597–598.

Carskadon, M.A. (2005). Sleep and circadian rhythms in children and adolescents: Relevance for athletic performance of young people. *Clinical Sports Medicine, 24,* 319–328.

Carskadon, M.A. (2006, March). *Too little, too late: Sleep bioregulatory processes across adolescence.* Paper presented at the meeting of the Society for Research on Adolescence, San Francisco.

Carskadon, M.A. (2011). Sleep in adolescents: The perfect storm. *Pediatric Clinics of North America.*

Carskadon, M.A. (2020). The time has come to expand our studies of school timing for adolescents. *Journal of Biological Rhythms, 35*(4), 323–324.

Carskadon, M.A., & Barker, D.H. (2020). Editorial perspective: Adolescents' fragile sleep—shining light on a time of risk to mental health. *Journal of Child Psychology and Psychiatry, 61,* 1058–1060.

Carver, C.S., & Scheier, M.F. (2021). Self-regulation and control in personality functioning. In P.J. Corr & G. Matthews (Eds.), *Cambridge handbook of personality psychology.* New York: Cambridge University Press.

Carver, K., Joyner, K., & Udry, J.R. (2003). National estimates of romantic relationships. In P. Florsheim (Ed.), *Adolescent romantic relations and sexual behavior.* Mahwah, NJ: Erlbaum.

Case, R. (Ed.) (1992). *The mind's staircase: Exploring the conceptual underpinnings of children's thought and knowledge.* Hillsdale, NJ: Erlbaum.

Case, R. (2000). Conceptual development. In M. Bennett (Ed.), *Developmental psychology.* Philadelphia: Psychology Press.

CASEL (2021). *Collaborative for Academic, Social, and Emotional Learning.* Retrieved January 12, 2021, from www.casel.org

Casey, B.J., & others (2020). Health development as a human right: Insights from developmental neuroscience for youth justice. *Annual Review of Law and Social Science, 16,* 203–222.

Caspi, A. (1998). Personality development across the life course. In W. Damon (Series Ed.) & N. Eisenberg (Ed.), *Handbook of child psychology: Vol. 3. Social, emotional, and personality development* (5th ed.). New York: Wiley.

Caspi, A., & others (2003). Influence of life stress on depression: Moderation by a polymorphism in the 5-HTT gene. *Science, 301,* 386–389.

Cassidy-Bushrow, A.E., & others (2015). Time spent on the Internet and adolescent blood pressure. *Journal of School Nursing, 31,* 374–384.

Cassoff, J., Knauper, B., Michaelsen, S., & Gruber, R. (2013). School-based sleep promotion programs: Effectiveness, feasibility, and insights for future research. *Sleep Medicine Reviews, 17*(3), 207–214.

Casteel, C.O., & Singh, G. (2021). *Physiology, gonadotropin-releasing hormone (GnRH).* Treasure Island, FL: StatPearls.

Castillo, M., & Weiselberg, E. (2017). Bulimia nervosa/purging disorder. *Current Problems in Pediatric and Adolescent Health Care, 47,* 85–94.

Castro, E.M., & Cohen, A.K. (2021). Fostering youth civic engagement through effective mentorship: Understanding the college student volunteer mentors who succeed. *Journal of Community Psychology, 49,* 605–619.

Cauberghe, V., & others (2021). How adolescents use social media to cope with feelings of loneliness and anxiety during COVID-19 lockdown. *Cyberpsychology Behavior and Social Networking, 24,* 250–257.

Cauffman, E., Shulman, E., Bechtold, J., & Steinberg, L. (2015). Children and the law. In R. Lerner (Ed.), *Handbook of child psychology and developmental science* (7th ed.). New York: Wiley.

Cavanagh, S. (2007, October 3). U.S.-Chinese exchanges nurture ties between principals. *Education Week.* Retrieved July 15, 2008, from www.edweek.org

Cavanagh, S.E. (2009). Puberty. In D. Carr (Ed.), *Encyclopedia of the life course and human development.* Boston: Gale Cengage.

Cecil, N.L., Lozano, A.S., & Chaplin, M. (2020). *Striking a balance: A comprehensive approach to early literacy* (6th ed.). New York: Routledge.

Center for Education Policy (2020). *How school districts are responding to ESSA's evidence requirements for school improvement.* Washington, DC: George Washington University, Center for Education Policy.

Centers for Disease Control and Prevention (2007). *Autism and developmental disabilities monitoring (ADDM) network.* Atlanta: Author.

Centers for Disease Control and Prevention (2015). *Adolescent pregnancy.* Atlanta: U.S. Department of Health and Human Services.

Centers for Disease Control and Prevention (2016). *ADHD.* Retrieved January 12, 2016, from www.cdc.gov/ncbddd/adhd/data.html

Centers for Disease Control and Prevention (2020). *Autism spectrum disorders.* Atlanta: Author.

Centers for Disease Control and Prevention (2020). *Birth rates.* Atlanta: Author.

Centers for Disease Control and Prevention (2020, July 23). *The importance of opening up America's schools this fall.* Atlanta: Author.

Centers for Disease Control and Prevention (2020). *Sexually transmitted disease surveillance.* Atlanta: U.S. Department of Health and Human Services.

Centers for Disease Control and Prevention (2021). *Body mass index for children and teens.* Atlanta: Centers for Disease Control and Prevention.

Centers for Disease Control and Prevention (2021). *Sexually transmitted infections, United States 2019.* Atlanta: Author.

Cesari, J. (2021). *We God's people.* New York: Cambridge University Press.

Champagne, F.A. (2021). Dynamic epigenetic impact of the environment on the developing brain. In J.J. Lockman & C. Tamis-LeMonda (Eds.), *Cambridge handbook infant development.* New York: Cambridge University Press.

Champion, C., Ha, T., & Dishion, T. (2021). Interpersonal emotion dynamics within young adult and peer relationships. In A.K. Randall & D. Schoebi (Eds.), *Interpersonal emotion dynamics in close relationships.* New York: Cambridge University Press.

Chandra, A., & others (2009). Does watching sex on television predict teen pregnancy? Findings from a national longitudinal study of youth. *Pediatrics, 122,* 1047–1054.

Chandra-Mouli, V., & Akwara, E. (2020). Improving access to and use of contraception by adolescents: What progress has been made, what lessons have been learned, and what are the implications for action? *Best Practices and Research. Clinical Obstetrics and Gynecology, 66,* 107–118.

Chandrima, R.M., & others (2020). Adolescent problematic internet use and parental mediation: A Bangladeshi structured interview study. *Addictive Behaviors Reports, 12,* 100288.

Chang, E.C. (2017). Hope and hopelessness as predictors of suicide ideation in Hungarian college students. *Death Studies, 41,* 455–460.

Chang, L-Y., & Fu, M. (2020). Disentangling the effects of international transmission of depression from adolescence to adulthood: The protective role of self-esteem. *European Child and Adolescent Psychiatry, 29,* 679–689.

Chang, Y.K., Liu, S., Yu, H.H., & Lee, Y.H. (2012). Effects of acute exercise on executive function in children with attention deficit hyperactivity disorder. *Archives of Clinical Neuropsychology, 27,* 225–237.

Chao, R.K. (2005, April). *The importance of Guan in describing control of immigrant Chinese.* Paper presented at the meeting of the Society for Research in Child Development, Atlanta.

Chao, R.K. (2007, March). *Research with Asian Americans: Looking back and moving forward.* Paper presented at the meeting of the Society for Research in Child Development, Boston.

Chao, R.K., & Otsuki-Clutter, M. (2011). Racial and ethnic differences: Sociocultural and contextual explanations. *Journal of Research on Adolescence, 21,* 47–60.

Chapman, B.P., & others (2020). Association between high school personality phenotype and dementia 54 years later in results from a national U.S. sample. *JAMA Psychiatry, 77,* 148–154.

Charmaraman, L., Lee, A.J., & Erkut, S. (2012). "What if you already know everything about sex?" Content analysis of questions from early adolescents in a middle school sex education program. *Journal of Adolescent Health, 50,* 527–530.

Charmaraman, L., & others (2021, in press). Early adolescent social media-related body dissatisfaction: Associations with depressive symptoms, social anxiety, peers, and celebrities. *Journal of Developmental and Behavioral Pediatrics.*

Chaudhuri, J.D. (2020). Stimulating intrinsic motivation in millennial students: A new generation, new approach. *Anatomical Sciences Education, 13,* 250–271.

Chavous, T.M., & others (2003). Racial identity and academic attainment among African American adolescents. *Child Development, 74*(4), 1076–1090.

Chen, C., & Stevenson, H.W. (1989). Homework: A cross-cultural examination. *Child Development, 60,* 551–561.

Chen, F.R., Rothman, E.F., & Jaffee, S.R. (2017). Early puberty, friendship group characteristics, and dating abuse in U.S. girls. *Pediatrics. 139*(6), e20162847.

Chen, G., & others (2017). An association study revealed substantial effects of dominance, epistasis, and substance dependence co-morbidity on alcohol dependence symptom account. *Addiction Biology, 22,* 1475–1485.

Chen, H., & Cheng, C.L. (2020). Parental psychological control and children's relational aggression: Examining the roles of gender and normative beliefs about relational aggression. *Journal of Psychology, 154,* 159–175.

Chen, J-K., & others (2020). Indirect effect of parental depression on school victimization through adolescent depression. *Journal of Affective Disorders, 263,* 396–404.

Chen, M., & Berman, S.L. (2012). Globalization and identity development: A Chinese perspective. *New Directions in Child and Adolescent Development, 2012*(138), 103–121.

Chen, M.J., Grube, J.W., Nygaard, P., & Miller, B.A. (2008). Identifying social mechanisms for the prevention of adolescent drinking and driving. *Accident Analysis and Prevention, 40,* 576–585.

Chen, P., & others (2020). A strategic mindset: An orientation toward strategic behavior during goal pursuit. *Proceedings of the National Academy of Sciences U.S.A., 117,* 14066–14072.

Chen, S., & others (2020). Discrimination, language brokerage efficacy, and academic competence among adolescent language brokers. *Journal of Adolescence, 79,* 247–257.

Chen, T.Y., & others (2015). Effects of a selective educational system on fatigue, sleep problems, daytime sleepiness, and depression among senior high school adolescents in Taiwan. *Neuropsychiatric Disease and Treatment, 11,* 741–750.

Chen, W-L., & Chen, J-H. (2019). Consequences of inadequate sleep during the college years: Sleep deprivation, grade point average, and college graduation. *Preventive Medicine, 124,* 23–28.

Chen, X., Christmas-Best, V., Titzmann, P.F., & Weichold, K. (2012). Youth success and adaptation in times of globalization and economic change. *New Directions for Youth Development, 135,* 1–10.

Chen, X., Lee, J., & Chen, L. (2018). Culture and peer relationships. In W.M. Bukowski & others (Eds.), *Handbook of peer interactions, relationships, and groups* (2nd ed.). New York: Guilford.

Chen, X., Saafir, A., & Graham, S. (2020). Ethnicity, peers, and academic achievement: Who wants to be friends with the smart kids? *Journal of Youth and Adolescence, 49,* 1030–1042.

Chen, Y., & Liu, J. (2021). Do most 7- and 8-year-old girls with early puberty require extensive investigation and treatment? *Journal of Pediatric and Adolescent Gynecology, 34,* 124–129.

Cherlin, A.J. (2009). *The marriage-go-round.* New York: Random House.

Cherlin, A.J. (2020). Degrees of change: Assessment of the deinstitutionalization of marriage thesis. *Journal of Marriage and the Family, 82,* 62–80.

Chernick, L.S., & others (2020). Sex without contraceptives in a multicenter study of adolescent emergency department patients. *Academic Emergency Medicine, 27,* 283–290.

Chess, B. (2021). *Talaro's foundations of microbiology* (11th ed.). New York: McGraw-Hill.

Chess, S., & Thomas, A. (1977). Temperamental individuality from childhood to adolescence. *Journal of Child Psychiatry, 16,* 218–226.

Chetty, S., & others (2020, June 17). How did COVID-19 and stabilization policies affect spending and employment? A new real-time economic tracker based on private sector data. *Opportunity Insights.* Retrieved from opportunityinsights.org.

Cheung, C.S., & Pomerantz, E.M. (2012). Why does parents' involvement in children's learning enhance children's achievement? The role of parent-oriented motivation. *Journal of Educational Psychology, 104,* 820–832.

Cheung, C.S., Pomerantz, E.M., & Dong, W. (2013). Does adolescents' disclosure to their parents matter for their academic adjustment? *Child Development, 84*(2), 693–710.

Cheung, F.M., & Halpern, D.F. (2021). International and intersectional perspectives on the psychology of women. In F.M. Cheung & D.F. Halpern (Eds.), *Cambridge handbook of the international psychology of women.* New York: Cambridge University Press.

Cheung, R.Y.M., Chan, L.Y., & Chung, K.K.H. (2020). Emotion dysregulation between mothers, fathers, and adolescents: Implications for adolescents' internalizing problems. *Journal of Adolescence, 83,* 62–71.

Cheung, S., & others (2020). Suicide epigenetics, a review of recent progress. *Journal of Affective Disorders, 265,* 423–438.

Chi, M.T.H. (1978). Knowledge structures and memory development. In R.S. Siegler (Ed.), *Children's thinking: What develops?* Hillsdale, NJ: Erlbaum.

Chia-Chen, C.A., & Thompson, E.A. (2007). Preventing adolescent risky behavior: Parents matter! *Journal for Specialists in Pediatric Nursing, 12,* 119–122.

Chick, C.F., & Reyna, V.F. (2012). A fuzzy trace theory of adolescent risk taking: Beyond self-control and sensation seeking. In V. Reyna & others (Eds.), *The adolescent brain.* Washington, DC: American Psychological Association.

Child Trends (2015, November). *Oral sex behaviors among teens.* Washington, DC: Child Trends.

Children's Defense Fund (2020). *The state of America's children 2020.* Washington, DC: Author.

ChildStats.gov (2018). *POP3 Race and Hispanic origin composition.* Washington, DC: Author.

Chin, D., & Kameoka, V.A. (2019). Mentoring Asian American scholars: Stereotypes and cultural values. *American Journal of Orthopsychiatry, 89,* 337–342.

Chin, D., & others (2020). Racial/ethnic discrimination: Dimensions and relations to mental health symptoms in a marginalized urban American population. *American Journal of Orthopsychiatry, 90,* 614–622.

Chiou, W.B., Chen, S.W., & Liao, D.C. (2014). Does Facebook promote self-interest? Enactment of indiscriminate one-to-many communication on online social networking sites decreases prosocial behavior. *Cyberpsychology, Behavior, and Social Networking, 17,* 68–73.

Chira, S. (1993, June 23). What do teachers want most? Help from parents. *The New York Times,* p. 17.

Chisholm, J.D., & Kingstone, A. (2015). Action video games and improved attentional control: Disentangling selection- and response-based processes. *Psychonomic Bulletin and Review, 22,* 1430–1436.

Chmielewski, C. (1997, September). Sexual harassment, meet Title IX. *NEA Today, 16*(2), 24–25.

Choe, D. (2021). Longitudinal relationships amongst child neglect, social relationships, and school dropout risk for culturally and linguistically diverse adolescents. *Child Abuse and Neglect, 112,* 104891.

Chohan, M.O. (2020). Deconstructing neurogenesis, transplantation, and genome-editing as neural repair strategies in brain disease. *Frontiers in Cell and Developmental Biology, 8,* 116.

Choi, B., & Park, S. (2021). Bullying perpetration, victimization, and low self-esteem: Examining their relationship over time. *Journal of Youth and Adolescence, 50,* 739–752.

Choi, J.K., Parra, G., & Jiang, Q. (2019). The longitudinal and bidirectional relationships between cooperative coparenting and child behavior problems in low-income, unmarried families. *Journal of Family Psychology, 33,* 203–214.

Choi, M.S., & Kim, E.Y. (2016). Body image and depression in girls with idiopathic precocious puberty treated with gonadotropin-releasing hormone analogue. *Annals of Pediatric Endocrinology and Metabolism, 21,* 155–160.

Choi, N. (2004). Sex role group differences in specific, academic, and general self-efficacy. *Journal of Psychology, 138,* 149–159.

Choi, Y., & others (2020a). Disempowering parenting and mental health among Asian American youth; Immigration and ethnicity. *Applied Developmental Psychology, 66,* 101077.

Choi, Y., & others (2020b). Explaining the Asian American youth paradox: University factors vs. Asian American family process among Filipino and Korean American youth. *Family Process, 59,* 1818–1836.

Choi, Y., & others (2020c). Asian American mental health: Longitudinal trend and explanatory factors among Filipino- and Korean-Americans. *Social Science and Medicine, 10,* 100542.

Chong, K.H., & others (2020). Changes in physical activity, sedentary behavior, and sleep across the transition from primary to secondary school: A systematic review. *Journal of Science and Medicine in Sport, 23,* 498–505.

Chouinard, R., Karsenti, T., & Roy, N. (2007). Relations among competence beliefs, utility value, achievement goals, and effort in mathematics. *British Journal of Educational Psychology, 77,* 501–517.

Chow, J.C., & others (2020). Recent pubertal timing trends in Northern Taiwanese children: Comparison with skeletal maturity. *Journal of the Chinese Medical Association, 83,* 870–875.

Christ, S.L., Kwak, Y.Y., & Lu, T. (2017). The joint impact of parental psychological neglect and peer isolation on adolescents' depression. *Child Abuse and Neglect, 69,* 151–162.

Christen, M., Narváez, D., & Gutzwiller, E. (2018). Comparing and integrating biological and cultural moral progress. *Ethical Theory and Moral Practice, 20,* 53–73.

Christensen, L.B., Johnson, R.B., & Turner, L.A. (2020). *Research methods, design, and analysis* (13th ed., loose leaf). Upper Saddle River, NJ: Pearson.

Christov-Moore, L., & others (2014). Empathy: Gender effects in brain and behavior. *Neuroscience and Biobehavioral Reviews, 46,* 604–627.

Chu, X.W., & others (2019). Does bullying victimization really influence adolescents' psychosocial problems? A three-wave longitudinal study in China. *Journal of Affective Disorders, 246,* 603–610.

Chun, B.J., & others (2021). Concussion epidemiology in youth sports: Sports study of a statewide high school sports program. *Sports Health, 13,* 18–24.

Chung, S.J., Ersig, A.L., & McCarthy, A.M. (2017). The influence of peers on diet and exercise among adolescents: A systematic review. *Journal of Pediatric Nursing, 36,* 44–56.

Cipollone, K., Stich, A.E., & Weis, L. (2020). STEM for all: Student identities and the paradox of STEM democratization. *Teachers College Record, 122,* 2.

Cisler, J.M., & Herringa, R.J. (2021). Posttraumatic stress disorder and the developing adolescent brain. *Biological Psychiatry, 89,* 144–151.

Clampet-Lundquist, S. (2013). Baltimore teens and work: Gender opportunities in disadvantaged neighborhoods. *Journal of Adolescent Research, 28*(1), 122–149.

Clara, M. (2017). How instruction influences conceptual development: Vygotsky's theory revisited. *Educational Psychologist, 52,* 50–62.

Clark, D.A., & others (2021). Adolescent sexual development and peer groups: Reciprocal associations and shared genetic and environmental influences. *Archives of Sexual Behavior, 50,* 141–160.

Clark, K.N., & Malecki, C.K. (2019). Academic Grit Scale: Psychometric properties and associations with achievement and life satisfaction. *Journal of School Psychology, 72,* 49–66.

Clark, K.N., & others (2020). Adolescent academic achievement: A model of social support and grit. *Psychology in the Schools, 57,* 204–221.

Clark, M.S., Powell, M.C., Ovellette, R., & Milberg, S. (1987). Recipient's mood, relationship type, and helping. *Journal of Personality and Social Psychology, 43,* 94–103.

Clark, R.D., & Hatfield, E. (1989). Gender differences in receptivity to sexual offers. *Journal of Psychology and Human Sexuality, 2,* 39–55.

Clarke, R.D., & others (2021, in press). Feasibility, acceptability, and preliminary impact of mindfulness-based yoga among Hispanic/Latinx adolescents. *Explore.*

Clarkson, J.J. (2021). *Mastering self-control.* New York: Cambridge University Press.

Claro, S., Paunesku, D., & Dweck, C.S. (2016). Growth mindset tempers the effect of poverty on academic achievement. *Proceedings of the National Academy of Sciences USA, 113,* 8664–8668.

Clausing, E.S., Binder, A.M., & Non, A.L. (2021, in press). Epigenetic age associates with psychosocial stress and resilience in children of Latinx immigrants. *Epigenomics.*

Clauss-Ehlers, C.S., Roysircar, G., & Hunter, S.J. (2021). *Applying multiculturism.* Washington, DC: APA Books.

Clauss-Ehlers, C.S., & others (Eds.) (2021). *Social justice for children and young people.* New York: Cambridge University Press.

Clutter, L.B. (2020). Perceptions of birth fathers about their open adoption. *MCN American Journal of Maternal Child Nursing, 45,* 26–32.

Cochran, S.D., & Mays, V.M. (1990). Sex, lies, and HIV. *New England Journal of Medicine, 322*(11), 774–775.

Coffman, E.J. (2021). *Margaret Mead.* New York: Oxford University Press.

Cohen, A.O., & Casey, B.J. (2017). The neurobiology of adolescent self-control. In T. Egner (Ed.), *Wiley handbook of cognitive control.* New York: Wiley.

Cohen, J.R., & D'Esposito, M. (2021). An integrated, dynamic functional connectome underlies intelligence. In A.K. Barbey & others (Eds.), *Cambridge handbook of intelligence and cognitive neuroscience.* New York: Cambridge University Press.

Cohen, P., Kasen, S., Chen, H., Hartmark, C., & Gordon, K. (2003). Variations in patterns of developmental transitions in the emerging adulthood period. *Developmental Psychology, 39,* 657–669.

Cohen, R.J., Schneider, W.J., & Tobin, R. (2022). *Psychological testing and assessment.* New York: McGraw-Hill.

Coie, J. (2004). The impact of negative social experiences on the development of antisocial behavior. In J.B. Kupersmidt & K.A. Dodge (Eds.), *Children's peer relations: From development to intervention.* Washington, DC: American Psychological Association.

Coker, T.R., & others (2015). Media violence exposure and physical aggression in fifth-grade children. *Academic Pediatrics, 15,* 82–88.

Colangelo, N.C., Assouline, S.G., & Gross, M.U.M. (2004). *A nation deceived: How schools hold back America's brightest students.* Retrieved March 6, 2005, from http://nationdeceived.org/

Colby, A., Kohlberg, L., Gibbs, J., & Lieberman, M. (1983). A longitudinal study of moral judgment. *Monographs of the Society for Research in Child Development, 48*(21, Serial No. 201).

Cole, A.K., & Kerns, K.A. (2001). Perceptions of sibling qualities and activities of early adolescents. *Journal of Early Adolescence, 21,* 204–226.

Cole, M. (2006). Culture and cognitive development in phylogenetic, historical, and ontogenetic perspective. In W. Damon & R. Lerner (Eds.), *Handbook of child psychology* (6th ed.). New York: Wiley.

Cole, P.M., Ram, N., & English, M.S. (2019). Toward a unifying model of self-regulation: A developmental approach. *Child Development Perspectives, 13,* 91–96.

Cole, T.J., & Mori, H. (2018). Fifty years of child height and weight in Japan and South Korea: Contrasting secular trend patterns analyzed by SITAR. *American Journal of Human Biology, 30,* e23054.

Colich, N.L., & others (2020). Earlier age at menarche as a transdiagnostic mechanism linking childhood trauma with multiple forms of psychopathology in adolescent girls. *Psychological Medicine, 50,* 1090–1098.

Colistra, R., & Johnson, C.B. (2021). Framing the legalization of marriage for same-sex couples: An examination of news coverage surrounding the U.S. Supreme Court's landmark decision. *Journal of Homosexuality, 68,* 88–111.

Collins, M. (1996, Winter). The job outlook for '96 grads. *Journal of Career Planning, 23,* 51–54.

Collins, R.L., & others (2004). Watching sex on television predicts adolescent initiation of sexual behavior. *Pediatrics, 114,* e280–e289.

Collins, R.L., & others (2017). Sexual media and childhood well-being and health. *Pediatrics, 140*(Suppl. 2), S162–S166.

Collins, T.A., & others (2021). Peers as culturally relevant change agents. In T.A. Collins & R.O. Hawkins (Eds.), *Peers as change agents.* New York: Oxford University Press.

Collins, W.A., & Madsen, S.D. (2019). Parenting during middle and late childhood. In M.H. Bornstein (Ed.), *Handbook of parenting* (3rd ed.). New York: Routledge.

Collins, W.A., & Steinberg, L. (2006). Adolescent development in interpersonal context. In W. Damon & R. Lerner (Eds.), *Handbook of child psychology* (6th ed.). New York: Wiley.

Collins, W.A., & van Dulmen, M. (2006). Friendship and romance in emerging adulthood. In J.J. Arnett & J.L. Tanner (Eds.), *Emerging adults in America.* Washington, DC: American Psychological Association.

Comer, J.P. (2010). Comer School Development Program. In J. Meece & J. Eccles (Eds.), *Handbook of research on schools, schooling, and human development.* New York: Routledge.

Committee for Children (2021). *Second Step.* Retrieved January 12, 2021, from www.cfchildren.org/second-step

Common Core State Standards Initiative (2014). *Common Core.* Retrieved June 1, 2014, from www.core standards.org/

Common Sense (2015). *The Common Sense census: Media use by tweens and teens.* New York: Common Sense.

Commons, M.L., & Richards, F.A. (2003). Four postformal stages. In J. Demick & C. Andreoletti (Eds.), *Handbook of adult development.* New York: Kluwer.

Compas, B.E. (2004). Processes of risk and resilience during adolescence: Linking contexts and individuals. In R. Lerner & L. Steinberg (Eds.), *Handbook of adolescent psychology* (2nd ed.). New York: Wiley.

Comstock, G., & Scharrer, E. (2006). Media and popular culture. In W. Damon & R. Lerner (Eds.), *Handbook of child psychology* (6th ed.). New York: Wiley.

Condon, J., Luszcz, M., & McKee, I. (2020). First-time grandparents' role satisfaction and its determinants. *International Journal of Aging and Human Development, 91,* 340–355.

Condry, J.C., Simon, M.L., & Bronfenbrenner, U. (1968). *Characteristics of peer- and adult-oriented children.* Unpublished manuscript. Cornell University, Ithaca, NY.

Conduct Problems Prevention Research Group & others (2019). *The Fast Track Program for children at risk: Preventing antisocial behavior.* New York: Guilford.

Conduct Problems Prevention Research Group (2007). The Fast Track randomized controlled trial to prevent externalizing psychiatric disorders: Findings from grades 3 to 9. *Journal of the American Academy of Child and Adolescent Psychiatry, 46,* 1250–1262.

Conduct Problems Prevention Research Group (2013). Assessing findings from the Fast Track Study. *Journal of Experimental Criminology, 9,* 119–126.

Conduct Problems Prevention Research Group (2015). Impact of early intervention on psychopathology, crime, and well-being at age 25. *American Journal of Psychiatry, 172*(1), 59–70.

Conduct Problems Prevention Research Group & others (2019). *The Fast Track Program for children at risk: Preventing antisocial behavior.* New York: Guilford.

Conner, T.S., & others (2017). The role of personality traits in young adult fruit and vegetable consumption. *Frontiers in Psychology, 8,* 119.

Connolly, J., Furman, W., & Konarski, R. (2000). The role of peers in the emergence of heterosexual romantic relationships in adolescence. *Child Development, 71,* 1395–1408.

Connolly, J., Goldberg, A., Pepler, D., & Craig, W. (2004). Mixed-gender groups, dating, and romantic relationships in early adolescence. *Journal of Research on Adolescence, 14,* 185–207.

Connolly, J., & McIsaac, C. (2009). Romantic relationships in adolescence. In R.M. Lerner & L. Steinberg (Eds.), *Handbook of adolescent psychology* (3rd ed.). New York: Wiley.

Connolly, J., Nguyen, H.N., Pepler, D., Craig, W., & Jiang, D. (2013). Developmental trajectories of romantic stages and associations with problem behaviors during adolescence. *Journal of Adolescence, 36,* 1013–1024.

Connolly, J., & Stevens, V. (1999, April). *Best friends, cliques, and young adolescents' romantic involvement.* Paper presented at the meeting of the Society for Research in Child Development, Albuquerque.

Connolly, M.D., & others (2016). The mental health of transgender youth: Advances in understanding. *Journal of Adolescent Health, 59,* 489–495.

Constante, K., & others (2020). Ethnic socialization, family cohesion, and ethnic identity development over time among Latinx adolescents. *Journal of Youth and Adolescence, 49,* 895–906.

Constantine, J.M., Seftor, N.S., Martin, E.S., Silva, T., & Myers, D. (2006). *A study of the effect of the Talent Search program on secondary and postsecondary outcomes in Florida, Indiana, and Texas: Final report from phase II of the national evaluation.* Washington, DC: U.S. Department of Education.

Constantine, N.A., Jerman, P., & Juang, A. (2007). California parents' preferences and beliefs on school-based sexuality education policy. *Perspectives on Sexual and Reproductive Health, 39,* 167–175.

Cook, T.D., Deng, Y., & Morgano, E. (2007). Friendship influences during early adolescence: The special role of friends' grade point average. *Journal of Research on Adolescence, 17,* 325-356.

Cooksey, E.C. (2009). Sexual activity, adolescent. In D. Carr (Ed.), *Encyclopedia of the life course and human development.* Boston: Gale Cengage.

Cooley, J.L., & others (2021, in press). Emotion regulation attenuates the prospective links from peer victimization to internalizing symptoms during middle childhood. *Journal of Clinical Child and Adolescent Psychology.*

Cooper, C.R. (2011). *Bridging multiple worlds.* New York: Oxford University Press.

Cooper, C.R., & Ayers-Lopez, S. (1985). Family and peer systems in early adolescence: New models of the role of relationships in development. *Journal of Early Adolescence, 5,* 9-22.

Cooper, C.R., Behrens, R., & Trinh, N. (2009). Identity development. In R.A. Shweder, T.R. Dailey, S.D. Dixon, P.J. Miller, & J. Model (Eds.), *The Chicago companion to the child.* Chicago: University of Chicago Press.

Cooper, M., & others (2018). A longitudinal study of risk perceptions and e-cigarette initiation among college students: Interactions with smoking status. *Drug and Alcohol Dependence, 186,* 257-263.

Copeland, M., & others (2021, in press). When friends bring you down: Peer stress proliferation and suicidality. *Archives of Suicide Research.*

Copen, C.E., Chandra, A., & Febo-Vazquez, I. (2016). Sexual behavior, sexual attraction, and sexual orientation among adults aged 18-44 in the United States: Data from the 2011-2013 National Survey of Family Growth. *National Health Statistics Report, 88,* 1-14.

Copen, C.E., Daniels, C.E., & Mosher, W.D. (2013, April 4). First premarital cohabitation in the United States: 2006-2010 National Survey of Family Growth. *National Health Statistics Reports, 64,* 1-16.

Copen, C.E., Daniels, K., Vespa, J., & Mosher, W.D. (2012). First marriages in the United States: Data from the 2006-2010 National Survey of Family Growth. *National Health Statistics Report, 49,* 1-22.

Costello, M.A., & others (2020). The intensity effect in adolescent close friendships: Implications for aggressive and depressive symptomatology. *Journal of Research on Adolescence, 30,* 158-169.

Coté, J.E. (2015). Identity-formation research from a critical perspective: Is a social science developing? In K.C. McLean & M. Syed (Eds.), *Oxford handbook of identity development.* New York: Oxford University Press.

Cote, S., Piff, P., & Willer, R. (2013). For whom do the ends justify the means? Social class and utilitarian moral judgment. *Journal of Personality and Social Psychology, 104,* 490-503.

Cottrell, L.A., & others (2017). Constructing tailored parental monitoring strategy profiles to predict adolescent disclosure and risk involvement. *Preventive Medicine Reports, 7,* 147-151.

Courage, M.L., Bakhtiar, A., Fitzpatrick, C., Kenny, S., & Brandeau, K. (2015). Growing up multitasking: The costs and benefits for cognitive development. *Developmental Review, 35,* 5-41.

Couture, S., Fernet, M., & Hebert, M. (2021). A cluster analysis of dynamics in adolescent romantic relationships. *Journal of Adolescence, 89,* 203-212.

Covington, M.V. (2002). Patterns of adaptive learning study: Where do we go from here? In C. Midgley (Ed.), *Goals, goal structures, and patterns of adaptive learning.* Mahwah, NJ: Erlbaum.

Covington, M.V., & Teel, K.T. (1996). *Overcoming student failure.* Washington, DC: American Psychological Association.

Cowan, M.K., & Smith, H.S. (2021). *Microbiology* (6th ed.). New York: McGraw-Hill.

Coyle, G.T.R. (2021). Defining and measuring intelligence. In A.K. Barbey & others (Eds.), *Cambridge handbook of intelligence and cognitive neuroscience.* New York: Cambridge University Press.

Coyne, S.M., & others (2019). "We're not gonna be friends anymore": Associations between viewing relational aggression on television and relational aggression in text messaging during adolescence. *Aggressive Behavior, 45,* 319-326.

Coyne, S.M., & others (2019). Contributions of mainstream sexual media exposure to sexual attitudes, perceived peer norms, and sexual behavior: A meta-analysis. *Journal of Adolescent Health, 64,* 430-436.

Coyne, S.M., & others (2020). The growth of gossip: Socialization of relational aggression from adolescence to emerging adulthood. *Aggressive Behavior, 46,* 535-546.

Cranney, S. (2015). The relationship between sexual victimization and year in school in U.S. colleges: Investigating the parameters of the "red zone." *Journal of Interpersonal Violence, 30,* 3133-3145.

Crespi, B.J. (2020). Evolutionary and genetic insights for clinical psychology. *Clinical Psychology Review, 78,* 101857.

Criss, M.M., & others (2015). Link between monitoring behavior and adolescent adjustment: An analysis of direct and indirect effects. *Journal of Child and Family Studies, 24*(3), 668-678.

Crone, E.A., & Fuligni, A.J. (2020). Self and others in adolescence. *Annual Review of Psychology* (Vol. 71). Palo Alto, CA: Annual Reviews.

Crone, E.A., & Konijn, E.A. (2018). Media use and brain development during adolescence. *Nature Communications, 9*(1), 588.

Crooks, R.L., & Baur, K. (2021). *Our sexuality* (14th ed.). Boston: Cengage.

Crosby, R., & Salazar, L.F. (2021). *Essentials of public health research methods.* Burlington, VT: Jones & Barlett Publishing.

Crosnoe, R. (2011). *Fitting in, standing out.* New York: Cambridge University Press.

Crosnoe, R., & Benner, A.D. (2015). Children at school. In R.M. Lerner (Ed.), *Handbook of child psychology and developmental science* (7th ed.). New York: Wiley.

Cross, S., & Markus, H. (1991). Possible selves across the lifespan. *Human Development, 34,* 230-255.

Crouter, A.C. (2006). Mothers and fathers at work. In A. Clarke-Stewart & J. Dunn (Eds.), *Families count.* New York: Cambridge University Press.

Crouter, A.C., Bumpus, M.F., Head, M.R., & McHale, S.M. (2001). Implications of overwork and overload for the quality of men's family relationships. *Journal of Marriage and Family, 63,* 404-416.

Crowe, M., & others (2020). Combinations of physical activity and screen time recommendations and their associations with overweight/obesity in adolescents. *Canadian Journal of Public Health, 111,* 515-522.

Crowley, C., Kapitula, L.R., & Munk, D. (2021, in press). Mindfulness, happiness, and anxiety in a sample of college students before and after taking a meditation course. *Journal of American College Health.*

Csikszentmihalyi, M. (1990). *Flow.* New York: HarperCollins.

Csikszentmihalyi, M. (1993). *The evolving self.* New York: Harper & Row.

Csikszentmihalyi, M., & Csikszentmihalyi, I.S. (Eds.). (2006). *A life worth living.* New York: Oxford University Press.

Csikszentmihalyi, M., & Schneider, B. (2000). *Becoming adult: How teenagers prepare for work.* New York: Basic Books.

Cuesta, I., & others (2021). Risk factors for teen suicide and bullying: An international integrative review. *International Journal of Nursing Practice, 8,* e12930.

Cui, L., & others (2020). Longitudinal links between maternal and peer emotion socialization and adolescent girls' socioemotional development. *Developmental Psychology, 56,* 595-607.

Cui, Z., & others (2020). Individual variation in functional topography of association networks in youth. *Neuron, 22,* 340-353.

Cummings, E.M., & others (2017). Emotional insecurity about the community: A dynamic, within-person mediator of child adjustment in contexts of political violence. *Development and Psychopathology, 29,* 27-36.

Curran, T., & Hill, A.P. (2019). Perfectionism is increasing over time: A meta-analysis of birth cohort differences from 1989 to 2016. *Psychological Bulletin, 145.* 410-429.

Currie, C., & others (2008). *Inequalities in young people's health: HBSC international report from the 2005/2006 survey.* Geneva, Switzerland: World Health Organization.

Curtis, A., & Bandy, T. (2015). *The Quantum Opportunities Program: A randomized control evaluation.* Washington, DC: The Eisenhower Foundation.

Curtis, A., & Bandy, T. (2016). *The Quantum Opportunities Program: A randomized control evaluation* (2nd ed.). Washington, DC: The Eisenhower Foundation.

Cushner, K., McClelland, A., & Safford, P. (2022). *Human diversity in education.* New York: McGraw-Hill.

D

D'Amico, E.J., & others (2020). Early and late adolescent factors that predict co-use of cannabis with alcohol and tobacco in young adulthood. *Prevention Science, 21,* 530-544.

da Costa Souza, A., & Ribeiro, S. (2015). Sleep deprivation and gene expression. *Current Topics in Behavioral Neurosciences, 25,* 65-90.

Dagan, O., & Sagi-Schwartz, A. (2021). Infant attachment (to mother and father) and its place in human development: Five decades of promising research (and an unsettled issue). In J.J. Lockman & C.S. Tamis-LeMonda (Eds.), *Cambridge handbook of infant development.* New York: Cambridge University Press.

Dahl, R.E. (2004). Adolescent brain development: A period of vulnerabilities and opportunities. *Annals of the New York Academy of Sciences, 1021,* 1-22.

Dahl, R.E., & others (2018). Importance of investing in adolescence from a developmental science perspective. *Nature, 554,* 441-450.

Dai, H., & others (2018). Electronic cigarettes and future marijuana use: A longitudinal study. *Pediatrics, 141*(5), e20173787.

Daley, C.E., & Onwuegbuzie, A.J. (2020). Race and intelligence. In RJ. Sternberg (Ed.), *Cambridge handbook of intelligence* (2nd ed.). New York: Cambridge University Press.

Damon, W. (1988). *The moral child.* New York: Free Press.

Damon, W. (2008). *The path to purpose: Helping our children find their purpose in life.* New York: Simon & Schuster.

Dandy, J., & Drake, D. (2020). Immigrants and refugees. In J.D. Jewell & S. Hupp (Eds.), *Encyclopedia of child and adolescent development.* New York: Wiley.

Dangel, T.J., Webb, J.R., & Hirsch, J.K. (2018). Forgiveness and suicidal behavior: Cynicism and psychache as serial mediators. *Journal of Psychology, 152,* 77-95.

Daniels, H. (Ed.) (2017). *Introduction to Vygotsky* (3rd ed.). New York: Routledge.

Danielsen, V.M., & others (2020). Lifespan trajectories of relative corpus callosum thickness: Regional differences and cognitive relevance. *Cortex, 130,* 327-341.

Darcy, E. (2012). Gender issues in child and adolescent eating disorders. In J. Lock (Ed.), *Oxford handbook of child and adolescent eating disorders: Developmental perspectives.* New York: Oxford University Press.

Darling, N. (2008). Commentary: Putting conflict in context. *Monographs of the Society for Research in Child Development, 73*(2), 169–175.

Darwin, C. (1859). *On the origin of species.* London: John Murray.

Dave, H.P., & others (2021). Stability and change in emotional intelligence in emerging adulthood: A four-year population-based study. *Journal of Personality Assessment, 103,* 57–66.

Davidson, J., & Davidson, B. (2004). *Genius denied: How to stop wasting our brightest young minds.* New York: Simon & Schuster.

Davies, J., & Brember, I. (1999). Reading and mathematics attainments and self-esteem in years 2 and 6—an eight-year cross sectional study. *Educational Studies, 25,* 145–157.

Davies, P.T., Martin, M.J., & Cummings, E.M. (2018). Interparental conflict and children's social problems: Insecurity and friendship affiliation as cascading mediators. *Developmental Psychology, 54,* 83–97.

Davis, A.L., & McQuillin, S.D. (2021, in press). Supporting autonomy in youth mentoring relationships. *Journal of Community Psychology.*

Davis, C.L., & others (2011). Exercise improves executive function and alters neural activation in overweight children. *Health Psychology, 30,* 91–98.

Davis, K. (2021, in preparation). *Beyond the screen.* Cambridge, MA: Harvard University Press.

Davis, K., & others (2020, April). *So you've earned a badge, now what?* Paper presented at annual meeting of the American Educational Research Association, San Francisco.

Davisson, E.K., Hoyle, R.H., & Andrade, F. (2021). Additive or multiplicative? Predicting academic outcomes from self-regulation and context. *Personality and Individual Differences, 179,* 110907.

Dawes, M., & others (2020). Creating supportive contexts for early adolescents during the first year of middle school: Impact of developmentally responsive multi-component intervention. *Journal of Youth and Adolescence, 49,* 1447–1463.

de Anda, D. (2006). Baby Think It Over: Evaluation of an infant simulation intervention for adolescent pregnancy prevention. *Health and Social Work, 31,* 26–35.

De Clercq, M., & others (2021). Bridging contextual and individual factors of academic achievement: A multi-level analysis of diversity in the transition to higher education. *Frontline Learning Research, 9,* 96–120.

de Graaf, H., van de Schoot, R., Woertman, L., Hawk, S.T., & Meeus, W. (2012). Family cohesion and romantic and sexual initiation: A three-wave longitudinal study. *Journal of Youth and Adolescence, 41,* 583–592.

de Guzman, N.S., & Nishina, A. (2014). A longitudinal study of body dissatisfaction and pubertal timing in an ethnically diverse adolescent sample. *Body Image, 11,* 68–71.

de la Cruz, F., & others (2021). Cortical thinning and associated connectivity changes in patients with anorexia nervosa. *Translational Psychiatry, 11*(1), 95.

de Manzano, O., & Ullen, F. (2018). Genetic and environmental influences on the phenotypic associations between intelligence, personality, and creative achievement in the arts and sciences. *Intelligence, 69,* 123–133.

De Matteo, C., & others (2020). Concussion management for children has changed: New pediatric protocols using the latest evidence. *Clinical Pediatrics, 59,* 5–20.

De Silva, A., & others (2020). Interparental conflict on Italian adolescent adjustment: The role of insecurity within family relationships. *Journal of Family Issues, 42,* 671–692.

de Souza Neto, J.M., & others (2021). Physical activity, screen time, nutritional status, and sleep in adolescents in northeast Brazil. *Revista Paulista de Pediatria, 39,* e2019138.

De Wit, D., & others (2020). Predictors of mentoring relationship quality: Investigation from the perspectives of youth and parent participants in Big Brother Big Sisters of Canada one-to-one mentoring programs. *Journal Community, 48,* 192–208.

Dearing, E., & others (2016). Can community and school-based supports improve the achievement of first-generation immigrant children attending high-poverty schools? *Child Development, 87,* 883–897.

Debnam, K.J., & others (2018). The moderating role of spirituality in the association between stress and substance use among adolescents: Differences by gender. *Journal of Youth and Adolescence, 47,* 818–828.

Debnath, R., & others (2020). The long-term effects of institutional rearing, foster care intervention, and disruptions in care on brain electrical activity in adolescence. *Developmental Science, 23*(1), e12872.

Debnath, R., & others (2021). Investigating brain electrical activity and functional connectivity in adolescents with clinically elevated levels of ADHD symptoms in alpha frequency band. *Brain Research, 1750,* 147142.

Dee, D.L., & others (2017). Trends in repeat births and use of postpartum contraception among teens–United States 2004–2015. *MMWR: Morbidity and Mortality Weekly Reports, 66,* 422–426.

Defoe, I.N., & others (2013). Siblings versus parents and friends: Longitudinal linkages to adolescent externalizing problems. *Journal of Child Psychology and Psychiatry, 54,* 881–889.

Defoe, I.N., & others (2020). Is the peer presence effect on heightened adolescent risky decision-making only present in males? *Journal of Youth and Adolescence, 49,* 693–705.

Defoe, I.N., Dubas, J.S., & Romer, D. (2019, March 8). Heightened adolescent risk-taking? Insights from lab studies on age differences in decision making. *Policy Insights from the Behavioral and Brain Sciences,* 56–63.

DeJong, W., DeRicco, B., & Schneider, S.K. (2010). Pregaming: An exploratory study of strategic drinking by college students in Pennsylvania. *Journal of American College Health, 58,* 307–316.

DeJoseph, M.L., & others (2021, in press). Capturing environmental dimensions of adversity and resources in the context of poverty across infancy through adolescence: A moderated nonlinear factor model. *Child Development.*

Del Toro, J., Hughes, D., & Way, N. (2021). Inter-relations between ethnic-racial discrimination and ethnic-racial identity among early adolescents. *Child Development, 92,* e106–e125.

Delalande, L., & others (2020). Complex and subtle structural changes in prefrontal cortex induced by inhibitory control training from childhood to adolescence. *Developmental Science, 23*(4), e12898.

Dempster, F.N. (1981). Memory span: Sources of individual and developmental differences. *Psychological Bulletin, 89,* 63–100.

Denford, S., & others (2017). A comprehensive review of reviews of school-based intervention to improve sexual health. *Health Psychology Review, 11,* 33–52.

Deng, G-X., & others (2020). Association of the NCAN-TM6SF2-CHP2-PBXr-SUGP1, MAU2 SNPs and gene-gene and gene-environment interactions with serum lipid levels. *Aging, 12,* 11893–11913.

Derry, K.L., Ohan, J.L., & Bayliss, D.M. (2020). Fearing failure: Grandiose narcissism, vulnerable narcissism, and emotional reactivity in children. *Child Development, 91,* e581–e596.

Desai, N., & Romano, M.E. (2017). Pediatric and adolescent issues in underserved populations. *Primary Care, 44,* 33–45.

Deschesnes, M., Fines, P., & Demers, S. (2006). Are tattooing and body piercing indicators of risk-taking behaviors among high school students? *Journal of Adolescence, 29,* 379–393.

Deschrijver, E., & Palmer, C. (2020). Reframing social cognition: Relational versus representational mentalizing. *Psychological Bulletin, 146,* 941–969.

Desilver, D. (2017). *U.S. students' academic achievement still lags that of their peers in many other countries.* Washington, DC: Pew Research Center.

Dettori, E., & Gupta, G.R. (2018). Gender and the SDGs: Collective impact for change. In J.E. Lansford & P. Banati (Eds.), *Handbook of adolescent development research and its impact on global policy.* New York: Oxford University Press.

Deutsch, A.R., Wood, P.K., & Slutske, W.S. (2018). Developmental etiologies of alcohol use and their relations to parent and peer influences over adolescence and young adulthood: A genetically informed approach. *Alcoholism: Clinical and Experimental Research, 41,* 2151–2162.

DeVille, D.C., & others (2020). Prevalence and family-related factors associated with suicide ideation, suicide attempts, and self-injury in children 9 to 10 years. *JAMA New Open, 3*(2), e1920956.

Devos, T. (2006). Implicit bicultural identity among Mexican American and Asian American college students. *Cultural Diversity and Ethnic Minority Psychology, 12,* 381–402.

Dew, R.E., Fuemmeler, B., & Koenig, H.G. (2020). Trajectories of religious change from adolescence to adulthood, and demographic, environmental, and psychiatric correlates. *Journal of Nervous and Mental Disease, 208,* 466–475.

Dewey, J. (1933). *How we think.* Lexington, MA: D.C. Heath.

Dewitz, P.F., & others (2020). *Teaching reading in the 21st century* (6th ed.). Upper Saddle River, NJ: Pearson.

DeZolt, D.M., & Hull, S.H. (2001). Classroom and school climate. In J. Worell (Ed.), *Encyclopedia of women and gender.* San Diego: Academic Press.

Di Fabio, A., & Saklofske, D.H. (2021). The relationship of compassion and self-compassion with personality and emotional intelligence. *Personality and Individual Differences, 169,* 110109.

Diamant, J., & Sciupac, E.P. (2020, September 10). *10 key findings about the religious lives of U.S. teens and their parents.* Washington, DC: Pew Research Center.

Diamond, L.M. (2019). The dynamic expression of sexual-minority and gender-minority experience during childhood and adolescence. In S. Lamb & J. Gilbert (Eds.), *Cambridge handbook of sexual development.* New York: Cambridge University Press.

Diamond, L.M., & Alley, J. (2018). The dynamic expression of same-sex sexuality from childhood to young adulthood. In S. Lamb & D. Gilbert (Eds.), *Cambridge handbook of sexuality: Childhood and adolescence.* New York: Cambridge University Press.

Dick, A.S., & others (2019). No evidence for a bilingual executive function advantage in the nationally representative ABCD study. *Nature: Human Behavior, 3,* 692–701.

Dickey, L.M., & Budge, S.L. (2020). Suicide and the transgender experience: A public health crisis. *American Psychologist, 75,* 380–390.

Diekmann, A., & Schmidheiny, K. (2004). Do parents of girls have a higher risk of divorce? An eighteen-country study. *Journal of Marriage and the Family, 66,* 651–660.

Diener, E., & Seligman, M.E.P. (2002). Very happy people. *Psychological Science, 13,* 81–84.

DiLonardo, M.J. (2013). *Talking about weight with your child.* Retrieved February 21, 2013, from http://www.webmd.com/parenting/raising-fit-kids/weight/talk-child-obesity

Dimler, L.M., & Natsuaki, M.N. (2021). Trajectories of violent and nonviolent behaviors from adolescence to early adulthood: Does early puberty matter, and, if so, how long? *Journal of Adolescent Health, 68,* 523–531.

Dimock, M. (2019, January 17). *Defining generations: Where millennials end and generation Z begins.* Washington, DC: Pew Research Center.

Dindia, K. (2006). Men are from North Dakota, women are from South Dakota. In K. Dindia & D.J. Canary (Eds.), *Sex differences and similarities in communication.* Mahwah, NJ: Erlbaum.

Dindo, L., & others (2017). Attachment and effortful control in toddlerhood predict academic achievement over a decade later. *Psychological Science, 28,* 1786–1795.

Dion, K.L., & Dion, K.K. (1993). Individualistic and collectivistic perspectives on gender and the cultural context of love and intimacy. *Journal of Social Issues, 49,* 53–69.

Dipla, K., & others (2021). Relative energy deficiency in sports (RED-S): Elucidation of endocrine changes affecting the health of males and females. *Hormones, 20,* 35–47.

Dishion, T.J., & Piehler, T.F. (2009). Deviant by design: Peer contagion in development, interventions, and schools. In K.H. Rubin, W.M. Bukowski, & B. Laursen (Eds.), *Handbook of peer interactions, relationships, and groups.* New York: Guilford.

Dittus, P.J., & others (2015). Parental monitoring and its associations with adolescent sexual risk behavior: A meta-analysis. *Pediatrics, 136,* e1587–e1599.

Dobrakowski, P., & Lebecka, G. (2020). Individualized neurofeedback training may help achieve long-term improvement of working memory in children with ADHD. *Clinical EEG and Neuroscience, 51,* 94–101.

Dodge, K.A. (1993). Social cognitive mechanisms in the development of conduct disorder and depression. *Annual Review of Psychology* (Vol. 44). Palo Alto, CA: Annual Reviews.

Dodge, K.A. (2011a). Context matters in child and family policy. *Child Development, 82,* 433–442.

Dodge, K.A. (2011b). Social information processing models of aggressive behavior. In M. Mikulincer & P.R. Shaver (Eds.), *Understanding and reducing aggression, violence, and their consequences.* Washington, DC: American Psychological Association.

Dodge, K.A., & others (2006). Toward a dynamic developmental model of the role of parents and peers in early onset substance abuse. In A. Clarke-Stewart & J. Dunn (Eds.), *Families count.* New York: Cambridge University Press.

Dodge, K.A., & others (2015). Impact of early intervention on psychopathology, crime, and well-being at age 25. *American Journal of Psychiatry, 172,* 59–70.

Doebel, S., & Munakata, Y. (2018). Group influences on engaging in self-control: Children delay gratification and value it more when their in-group delays and their out-group does not. *Psychological Science, 29,* 738–748.

Doherty, M.J., & others (2021). Piecing together the puzzle of pictorial representations: How jigsaw puzzles index metacognitive development. *Child Development, 92,* 205–221.

Dohrenwend, B.S., & Shrout, P.E. (1985). "Hassles" in the conceptualization and measurement of life event stress variables. *American Psychologist, 40,* 780–785.

Dokuka, S., Valeeva, D., & Yudkevich, M. (2020). How academic achievement spreads: The role of distinct networks in academic performance diffusion. *PLoS One, 27*(15), e0236737.

Dolbin-MacNab, M.L., & Yancura, L.A. (2018). International perspectives on grandparents raising grandchildren. *International Journal of Aging and Human Development, 86,* 3–33.

Dolcini, M.M., & others (1989). Adolescent egocentrism and feelings of invulnerability: Are they related? *Journal of Early Adolescence, 9,* 409–418.

Dollar, J., & Calkins, S.D. (2020). Emotion regulation and its development. In J.B. Benson (Eds.), *Encyclopedia of infant and early child development* (2nd ed.). New York: Elsevier.

Dominguez-Cruz, M.G., & others (2020). Maya gene variants related to the risk of type 2 diabetes in a family-based association study. *Gene, 730,* 144259.

Donahue, M.R., Tillman, R., & Luby, J. (2020). Reparative prosocial behavior difficulties across childhood predict poorer social functioning and depression in adolescence. *Journal of Abnormal Child Psychology, 48,* 1077–1088.

Donnellan, M.B., Ackerman, R.A., & Wright, A.G.C. (2021). Narcissism in contemporary personality psychology. In O.P. John & R.W. Robins (Eds.), *Handbook of personality* (4th ed.). New York: Cambridge University Press.

Donnellan, M.B., Larsen-Rife, D., & Conger, R.D. (2005). Personality, family history, and competence in early adult romantic relationships. *Journal of Personality and Social Psychology, 88,* 562–576.

Donnellan, M.B., & Trzesniewski, K.H. (2010). Groundhog Day versus Alice in Wonderland, red herrings versus Swedish fishes, and hopefully something constructive: A reply to comments. *Perspectives on Psychological Science, 5,* 103–108.

Donnelly, S., Brooks, P.J., & Homer, B.D. (2019). Is there a bilingual advantage on interference-control tasks? A multiverse meta-analysis of global reaction time and interference cost. *Psychonomic Bulletin, 26,* 1122–1147.

Donovan, M.K. (2017). The looming threat to sex education: A resurgence of federal funding for abstinence-only programs? *Guttmacher Policy Review, 20,* 44–47.

Doornwaard, S.M., & others (2017). Dutch adolescents' motives, perceptions, and reflections toward sex-related Internet use: Results of a web-based focus-group study. *Journal of Sex Research, 54,* 1038–1050.

Dore, E.D., & McMurtrie, D.H. (2021). *Our diverse middle school students.* New York: Routledge.

Dorn, L.D., & Biro, F.M. (2011). Puberty and its measurement: A decade in review. *Journal of Research on Adolescence, 21,* 180–195.

Dorn, L.D., Dahl, R.E., Woodward, H.R., & Biro, F. (2006). Defining the boundaries of early adolescence: A user's guide to assessing pubertal status and pubertal timing in research with adolescents. *Applied Developmental Science, 10,* 30–56.

Dorn, L.D., & others (2019). Conceptualizing puberty as a window of opportunity for impacting health and well-being across the lifespan. *Journal of Research on Adolescence, 29,* 155–176.

Dotti Sani, G.M., & Quaranta, M. (2017). The best is yet to come? Attitudes toward gender roles among adolescents in 36 countries. *Sex Roles, 77,* 30–45.

Dou, D., & Shek, D.T.E. (2021). Concurrent and longitudinal relationships between positive youth development attributes and adolescent internet addiction symptoms in Chinese mainland high school students. *International Journal of Environmental Research and Public Health, 18*(4), 1937.

Doumen, S., & others (2012). Identity and perceived peer relationship quality in emerging adulthood: The mediating role of attachment-related emotions. *Journal of Adolescence, 35,* 1417–1425.

Dow-Edwards, D., & others (2020). Experience during adolescence shapes brain development: From synapses and networks to normal and pathological behavior. *Neurotoxicology and Teratology, 76,* 106834.

Dryfoos, J.G. (1990). *Adolescents at risk: Prevalence and prevention.* New York: Oxford University Press.

Dryfoos, J.G. (1997). The prevalence of problem behaviors: Implications for programs. In R.P. Weissberg, T.P. Gullotta, R.L. Hampton, B.A. Ryan, & G.R. Adams (Eds.), *Healthy children 2010: Enhancing children's wellness.* Thousand Oaks, CA: Sage.

Dryfoos, J.G., & Barkin, C. (2006a). *Adolescence.* New York: Oxford University Press.

Dryfoos, J.G., & Barkin, C. (2006b). *Growing up in America today.* New York: Oxford University Press.

Du, J., & others (2021, in press). Relationship dynamics and perpetration of intimate partner violence among female Chinese college students. *Journal of Interpersonal Violence.*

Duan, X., Dan, Z., & Shi, J. (2014). The speed of information processing of 9- to 13-year-old intellectually gifted children. *Psychology Reports, 112,* 20–32.

Dube, S., & others (2017). Psychological well-being as a predictor of casual sex relationships and experiences among adolescents: A short-term prospective study. *Archives of Sexual Behavior, 46,* 1807–1818.

Duell, N., & Steinberg, L. (2019). Positive risk taking in adolescence. *Child Development Perspectives, 13,* 48–52.

Duncan, G.J., Magnuson, K., & Votruba-Drzal, E. (2017). Moving beyond correlations in assessing the consequences of poverty. *Annual Review of Psychology* (Vol. 68). Palo Alto, CA: Annual Reviews.

Dunkley, D.M., Berg, J.L., & Zuroff, D.C. (2012). The role of perfectionism in daily self-esteem, attachment, and negative affect. *Journal of Personality, 80,* 633–663.

Dunn, J. (2015). Siblings. In J.E. Grusec & P.D. Hastings (Eds.), *Handbook of socialization* (2nd ed.). New York: Guilford.

Dunphy, D.C. (1963). The social structure of urban adolescent peer groups. *Society, 26,* 230–246.

Dunster, G.P., & others (2018). Sleepmore in Seattle: Later school start times are associated with more sleep and better performance in high school students. *Science Advances, 4*(12), eaau6200.

Dupere, V., & others (2021). Social contagion and high school dropout: The role of friends, romantic partners, and siblings. *Journal of Educational Psychology, 113,* 572–584.

Duprey, E.B., Oshri, A., & Liu, S. (2020). Developmental pathways from child maltreatment to adolescent suicide-related behaviors: The internalizing and externalizing comorbidity hypothesis. *Development and Psychopathology, 32,* 945–959.

Durston, S., & others (2006). A shift from diffuse to focal cortical activity with development. *Developmental Science, 9,* 1–8.

Dutton, E., & Lynn, R. (2013). A negative Flynn effect in Finland, 1997–2009. *Intelligence, 41,* 817–820.

Dutton, E., & others (2018). A Flynn effect in Khartoum, the Sudanese capital, 2004–2016. *Intelligence, 68,* 82–86.

Dweck, C.S. (2006). *Mindset.* New York: Random House.

Dweck, C.S. (2012). Mindsets and human nature: Promoting change in the Middle East, the school yard, the racial divide, and willpower. *American Psychologist, 67,* 614–622.

Dweck, C.S. (2016, March 11). *Growth mindset revisited.* Invited presentation at Leaders to Learn From. Washington, DC: Education Week.

Dweck, C.S. (2019). The choice to make a difference. *Perspectives on Psychological Science, 14*(1), 21–25.

Dweck, C.S., & Master, A. (2009). Self-theories and motivation: Students' beliefs about intelligence. In K.R. Wentzel & A. Wigfield (Eds.), *Handbook of motivation at school.* New York: Routledge.

Dweck, C.S., & Molden, D.C. (2017). Mindsets: Their impact on competence motivation and acquisition. In A.J. Elliott, C.S. Dweck, & D.S. Yeager (Eds.), *Handbook of competence and motivation* (2nd ed.). New York: Guilford.

Dyson, R., & Renk, K. (2006). Freshman adaptation to university life: Depressive symptoms, stress, and coping. *Journal of Clinical Psychology, 62,* 1231–1244.

Eagly, A.H. (2001). Social role theory of sex differences and similarities. In J. Worell (Ed.), *Encyclopedia of women and gender.* San Diego: Academic Press.

Eagly, A.H. (2010). Gender roles. In J. Levine & M. Hogg (Eds.), *Encyclopedia of group processes and intergroup relations.* Thousand Oaks, CA: Sage.

Eagly, A.H. (2018). Making a difference: Feminist scholarship. In C.B. Gravis & J.W. White (Eds.), *Handbook of the psychology of women.* Washington, DC: APA Books.

Eagly, A.H., & Crowley, M. (1986). Gender and helping behavior: A meta-analytic review of the social psychological literature. *Psychological Bulletin, 100,* 283–308.

Eagly, A.H., & Steffen, V.J. (1986). Gender and aggressive behavior: A meta-analytic review of the social psychological literature. *Psychological Bulletin, 100,* 309–330.

East, P. (2009). Adolescent relationships with siblings. In R.M. Lerner & L. Steinberg (Eds.), *Handbook of adolescent psychology* (3rd ed.). New York: Wiley.

Easterbrook, M.J., Kuppens, T., & Manstead, A.S.R. (2020). Socioeconomic status and the structure of self-concept. *British Journal of Social Psychology, 59,* 66–86.

Easterlin, M.C., & others (2020). Association of team sports participation with long-term mental health outcomes among individuals exposed to adverse childhood experiences. *JAMA Pediatrics, 173,* 681–688.

Eather, N., & others (2020). Evaluating the impact of a coach development intervention for improving coaching practices in junior football (soccer): The "MASTER" pilot study. *Journal of Sports Sciences, 38,* 1441–1453.

Eaton, D.K., & others (2008). Youth risk behavior surveillance–United States, 2007. *MMWR, 57,* 1–131.

Eccles, J.S. (1987a). Gender roles and achievement patterns: An expectancy value perspective. In J.M. Reinisch, L.A. Rosenblum, & S.A. Sanders (Eds.), *Masculinity/femininity.* New York: Oxford University Press.

Eccles, J.S. (1987b). Gender roles and women's achievement-related decisions. *Psychology of Women Quarterly, 11,* 135–172.

Eccles, J.S. (1993). School and family effects on the ontogeny of children's interests, self-perceptions, and activity choice. In J. Jacobs (Ed.), *Nebraska Symposium on Motivation, 1992: Developmental perspectives on motivation.* Lincoln: University of Nebraska Press.

Eccles, J.S. (2007). Families, schools and developing achievement-related motivations and engagement. In J.E. Grusec & P.D. Hastings (Eds.), *Handbook of socialization.* New York: Guilford.

Eccles, J.S. (2014). Gender and achievement choices. In E.T. Gershoff, R.S. Mistry, & D.A. Crosby (Eds.), *Societal contexts of child development.* New York: Oxford University Press.

Eccles, J.S., Brown, B.V., & Templeton, J. (2008). A developmental framework for selecting indicators of well-being during the adolescent and young adult years. In B.V. Brown (Ed.), *Key indicators of child and youth well-being.* Clifton, NJ: Psychology Press.

Eccles, J.S., & Roeser, R.W. (2013). Schools as developmental contexts during adolescence. In I.B. Weiner & others (Eds.), *Handbook of psychology* (2nd ed., Vol. 6). New York: Wiley.

Eccles, J.S., & Wigfield, A. (2020). From expectancy-value theory to situated expectancy-value theory: A developmental, social cognitive, and sociocultural perspective on motivation. *Contemporary Educational Psychology, 61,* 101859.

Eccles, J.S., Wigfield, A., & Schiefele, U. (1998). Motivation to succeed. In W. Damon (Ed.), *Handbook of child psychology* (5th ed., Vol. 3). New York: Wiley.

Eckerberg, B., Lowden, A., Nagai, R., & Akerstedt, T. (2012). Melatonin treatment effects on adolescent students' sleep timing and sleepiness in a placebo-controlled crossover study. *Chronobiology International, 29,* 1239–1248.

Eckert-Lind, C., & others (2020). Worldwide secular trends in age at pubertal onset assessed by breast development among girls: A systematic review and meta-analysis. *JAMA Pediatrics, 174*(4), e195881.

Eckhoff, D.O., & Weiss, J. (2020). Goal setting: A concept analysis. *Nursing Forum, 55,* 275–281.

Eckler, P., Kalyango, Y., & Paasch, E. (2017). Facebook use and negative body image among U.S. college women. *Women and Health, 57,* 249–267.

Edelbrock, C.S. (1989, April). *Self-reported internalizing and externalizing problems in a community sample of adolescents.* Paper presented at the meeting of the Society for Research in Child Development, Kansas City.

Edwards, R., & Hamilton, M.A. (2004). You need to understand my gender role: An empirical test of Tannen's model of gender and communication. *Sex Roles, 50,* 491–504.

Efendi, A., & Wagid, M.N. (2021). Procrastination: Can it be passed down through a self-monitoring strategy and own gifts? *International Online Journal of Education and Teaching, 8*(1), 168–177.

Eickmeyer, K.J., & Manning, W.D. (2020). Serial cohabitation in young adulthood: Boomers to millennials. *Journal of Marriage and Family, 80,* 826–840.

Eiden, R.D., & others (2016). Developmental cascade model for adolescent substance use from infancy to late adolescence. *Developmental Psychology, 52,* 1619–1633.

Einziger, T., & others (2018). Predicting ADHD symptoms in adolescence from early childhood temperament traits. *Journal of Abnormal Child Psychology, 46,* 265–276.

Eisenberg, M.E., Madsen, N., Oliphant, J.A., & Sieving, R.E. (2013). Barriers to providing sexuality education that teachers believe students need. *Journal of School Health, 83,* 335–342.

Eisenberg, M.E., & others (2021). Sexual assault, sexual orientation, and reporting among college students. *Journal of Interpersonal Violence, 36,* 62–82.

Eisenberg, N., Fabes, R.A., Guthrie, I.K., & Reiser, M. (2002). The role of emotionality and regulation in children's social competence and adjustment. In L. Pulkkinen & A. Caspi (Eds.), *Paths to successful development.* New York: Cambridge University Press.

Eisenberg, N., Morris, A.S., McDaniel, B., & Spinrad, T.L. (2009). Moral cognitions and prosocial responding in adolescence. In R.M. Lerner & L. Steinberg (Eds.), *Handbook of adolescent psychology* (3rd ed.). New York: Wiley.

Eisenberg, N., Spinrad, T.L., & Knafo, A. (2015). Prosocial development. In R.M. Lerner (Ed.), *Handbook of child psychology and developmental science* (7th ed.). New York: Wiley.

Eisenberg, N., Spinrad, T.L., & Morris, A.S. (2013). Prosocial development. In P.D. Zelazo (Ed.), *Oxford handbook of developmental psychology.* New York: Oxford University Press.

Eisenberg, N., & Valiente, C. (2002). Parenting and children's prosocial and moral development. In M.H. Bornstein (Ed.), *Handbook of parenting* (2nd ed.). Mahwah, NJ: Erlbaum.

Eisenhower Foundation (2018). *Eisenhower Quantum Opportunities Program.* Washington, DC: Author.

El Ansari, W., Dibba, E., & Stock, C. (2014). Body image concerns: Levels, correlates, and gender differences among students in the United Kingdom. *Central European Journal of Public Health, 22,* 106–117.

El Toro, J., & Hughes, D. (2020). Trajectories of discrimination across the college years: Associations with academic, psychological, and physical outcomes. *Journal of Youth and Adolescence, 49,* 772–789.

Elder, G.H. (1980). Adolescence in historical perspective. In J. Adelson (Ed.), *Handbook of adolescent psychology.* New York: Wiley.

Eliot, L. (2020). Sex/gender differences in the brain and their relationship to behavior. In F.M. Cheung & D.F. Halpern (Eds.), *Cambridge handbook of the international psychology of women.* New York: Cambridge University Press.

Elkana, O., & others (2020). WAIS Information Subtest as an indicator of crystallized cognitive abilities and brain reserve among highly educated older adults: A three-year longitudinal study. *Applied Neuropsychology: Adult, 27,* 525–531.

Elkind, D. (1961). Quantity conceptions in junior and senior high school students. *Child Development, 32,* 531–560.

Elkind, D. (1976). *Child development and education: A Piagetian perspective.* New York: Oxford University Press.

Elkind, D. (1985). Egocentrism redux. *Developmental Review, 5,* 218–226.

Elkind, D., & Bowen, R. (1979). Imaginary audience behavior in children and adolescents. *Developmental Psychology, 15,* 38–44.

Elliott, J.G., & Resing, W.C. (2020). Extremes of intelligence. In R.J. Sternberg (Ed.), *Human intelligence.* New York: Cambridge University Press.

Ellis, B.J., Shirtcliff, E.A., Boyce, W.T., Deardorff, J., & Essex, M.J. (2011). Quality of early family relationships and the timing and tempo of puberty: Effects depend on biological sensitivity to context. *Development and Psychopathology, 23,* 85–99.

Ellis, L., & Ames, M.A. (1987). Neurohormonal functioning and sexual orientation: A theory of homosexuality-heterosexuality. *Psychological Bulletin, 101,* 233–258.

Ellis, S.D., Riggs, D.W., & Peel, E. (2020). *Lesbian, gay, bisexual, trans, intersex, and queer psychology* (2nd ed.). New York: Cambridge University Press.

Ember, C.R., & Ember, M.R. (2019). *Cultural anthropology* (15th ed.). Upper Saddle River, NJ: Pearson.

Emery, R.E. (1999). *Renegotiating family relationships* (2nd ed.). New York: Guilford.

Emery, R.E., & Laumann-Billings, L. (1998). An overview of the nature, causes, and consequences of abusive family relationships. *American Psychologist, 53,* 121–135.

Emmanuel, M., & Bokor, B.R. (2020). *Tanner stages.* Treasure Island, FL: StatPearls.

Emmons, R.A., & Diener, E. (1986). Situation selection as a moderator of response consistency and stability. *Journal of Personality and Social Psychology, 51,* 1013–1019.

Endedijik, H.M., & others (2020). The role of stress and mineralocorticold receptor haplotypes in the development of symptoms of depression and anxiety during adolescence. *Frontiers in Psychiatry, 11,* 367.

English, T., Eldesouky, L., & Gross, J.J. (2021). Emotion regulation: Basic processes and individual differences. In O.P. John & R.W. Robins (Eds.), *Handbook of personality* (4th ed.). New York: Guilford.

Englund, M., & Siebenbruner, J. (2012). Developmental pathways linking externalizing symptoms and academic competence to adolescent substance use. *Journal of Adolescence, 35,* 1123–1140.

Enright, R.D., Santos, M.J.D., & Al-Mabuk, R. (1989). The adolescent as forgiver. *Journal of Adolescence, 12,* 95–110.

Enright, R.D., & Song, J.Y. (2020). The development of forgiveness. In L.A. Jensen (Ed.), *Oxford handbook of moral development.* New York: Oxford University Press.

Epstein, J.L., & others (2021). Interactive homework to engage parents with students on the transition from middle school to high school. *Middle School Journal, 52,* 4–13.

Erickson, J.B. (1982). *A profile of community youth organization members, 1980*. Boys Town, NE: Boys Town Center for the Study of Youth Development.

Erickson-Schroth, L. (Ed.) (2021). *Trans bodies, trans selves*. New York: Oxford University Press.

Erickson-Schroth, L., & Davis, B. (2021). *Gender*. New York: Oxford University Press.

Ericsson, K.A., Krampe, R.T., & Tesch-Römer, C. (1993). The role of deliberate practice in the acquisition of expert performance. *Psychological Review, 100*, 363–406.

Ericsson, K.A., & others (Eds.) (2018). *Cambridge handbook of expertise and expert performance*. New York: Cambridge University Press.

Erikson, E.H. (1950). *Childhood and society*. New York: Norton.

Erikson, E.H. (1968). *Identity: Youth and crisis*. New York: Norton.

Erikson, E.H. (1969). *Gandhi's truth*. New York: Norton.

Erikson, E.H. (1970). Reflections on the dissent of contemporary youth. *International Journal of Psychoanalysis, 51*, 11–22.

Eriksson, P.L., & others (2020). Identity development in early adulthood. *Developmental Psychology, 56*, 1968–1983.

Erskine, H.E., & others (2016). Long-term outcomes of attention-deficit/hyperactivity disorder and conduct disorder: A systematic review and meta-analysis. *Journal of the American Academy of Child and Adolescent Psychiatry, 55*, 841–850.

Ertekin, Z., Gunnar, M.R., & Berument, S.K. (2021). Temperament moderates the effects of early deprivation on infant attention. *Infancy, 26*, 455–468.

Espinosa-Hernandez, G., & others (2020). Romantic relationships and sexuality in diverse adolescent populations: Introduction to the special issue. *Journal of Adolescence, 83*, 95–99.

Esteban-Gonzalo, S., & others (2020). The investigation of gender differences in subjective wellbeing in children and adolescents: The UP&DOWN study. *International Journal of Environmental Science and Public Health, 17*(8), 2732.

Esteban-Guitart, M. (2018). The biosocial foundation of the early Vygotsky: Educational psychology before the zone of proximal development. *History of Psychology, 21*, 384–401.

Ettekal, I., & Ladd, G.W. (2020). Development of aggressive-victims from childhood through adolescence: Associations with emotion dysregulation, withdrawn behaviors, moral disengagement, peer rejection, and friendships. *Development and Psychopathology, 32*, 271–291.

Ettekal, I., & others (2020). Developmental cascades to children's conduct problems: The role of prenatal substance use, socioeconomic diversity, maternal depression and sensitivity, and children's conscience. *Development and Psychopathology, 32*, 85–103.

Evans, G.W. (2004). The environment of childhood poverty. *American Psychologist, 59*, 77–92.

Evans, G.W., & De France, K. (2021, in press). Childhood poverty and psychological well-being: The mediating role of cumulative risk exposure. *Development and Psychopathology*.

Evans, G.W., Farah, M.J., & Hackman, D.A. (2021, in press). Early childhood poverty and adult executive functioning: Distinct, mediating pathways for different domains of executive functioning. *Developmental Science*.

Evans, G.W., & Kim, P. (2007). Childhood poverty and health: Cumulative risk exposure and stress dysregulation. *Psychological Science, 18*, 953–957.

Evans, K.L., & others (2019). The impact of within and between role experiences on role balance outcomes for working sandwich generation women. *Scandinavian Journal of Occupational Therapy, 26*, 184–193.

Evans, S.Z., Simons, L.G., & Simons, R.L. (2016). Factors that influence trajectories of delinquency throughout adolescence. *Journal of Youth and Adolescence, 45*, 156–171.

Everett, T.J., & others (2021). Endocannabinoid modulation of dopamine release during reward seeking, interval timing, and avoidance. *Progress in Neuro-Psychopharmacology and Biological Psychiatry, 104*, 110031.

F

Fabiano, G.A., & others (2009). A meta-analysis of behavioral treatments for attention deficit/hyperactivity disorder. *Clinical Psychology Review, 29*(2), 129–140.

Fabricus, W.V., Braver, S.L., Diaz, P., & Schenck, C. (2010). Custody and parenting time: Links to family relationships and well-being after divorce. In M.E. Lamb (Ed.), *The role of the father in child development* (5th ed.). New York: Wiley.

Fadus, M.C., Smith, T.T., & Squeglia, L.M. (2019). The rise of e-cigarettes, pod mod devices, and JUUL among youth: Factors influencing use, health implications, and downstream effects. *Drug and Alcohol Dependence, 201*, 85–93.

Fadus, M.C., & others (2020). Unconscious bias and the diagnosis of disruptive behavior disorders and ADHD in African American and Hispanic youth. *Academic Psychiatry, 44*, 95–102.

Fahey, T., Insel, P., & Roth, W. (2021). *Fit and Well: Core concepts and labs in physical fitness and wellness—brief edition* (14th ed.). New York: McGraw-Hill.

Fairclough, S.T. (2021, in press). Adolescents' digital screen time as a concern for health and well-being? Device type and context matter. *Acta Paediatrica*.

Fairlie, A.M., Maggs, J.L., & Lanza, S.T. (2016). Profiles of college drinkers defined by alcohol behaviors at the week level: Replication across semesters and prospective associations with hazardous drinking and dependence-related symptoms. *Journal of Studies on Alcohol and Drugs, 77*, 38–50.

Falbe, J., & others (2014). Longitudinal relations of television, electronic games, and digital versatile discs with changes in diet in adolescents. *American Journal of Clinical Nutrition, 100*, 1173–1181.

Falci, C.D. (2012). Self-esteem and mastery trajectories in high school by social class and gender. *Social Science Research, 40*, 586–601.

Faltynkova, A., & others (2020). The associations between family-related factors and excessive internet use in adolescents. *International Journal of Environmental Research and Public Health, 17*(5), 1754.

Fan, W., & Wolters, C.A. (2014). School motivation and high school dropout: The mediating role of educational expectation. *British Journal of Educational Psychology, 84*, 22–39.

Farahi, N., & McEachern, M. (2021). Sexual assault on women. *American Family Physician, 103*, 168–176.

Farasat, M., & others (2020). Long-term cardiac arrhythmia and chronotopic evaluation in patients with severe anorexia nervosa (LACE-AN): A pilot study. *Journal of Cardiovascular Electrophysiology, 31*, 432–439.

Faris, M., A-I, E., & others (2017). Energy drink consumption is associated with reduced sleep quality among college students: A cross-sectional study. *Nutrition and Diet, 74*, 268–274.

Farr, R.H. (2017). Does parental sexual orientation matter? A longitudinal follow-up of adoptive families with a school-age child. *Developmental Psychology, 53*, 252–264.

Farr, R.H., & Hrapczynski, K.M. (2020). Transracial adoption: Psychology, law, and policy. In M. Stevenson & others (Eds.), *Children and race*. New York: Oxford University Press.

Farr, R.H., Oakley, M.K., & Ollen, E.W. (2016). School experiences of young children and their lesbian and gay adoptive parents. *Psychology of Sexual Orientation and Gender Diversity, 3*, 442–447.

Farr, R.H., & Patterson, C.J. (2013). Coparenting among lesbian, gay, and heterosexual couples: Associations with adopted children's outcomes. *Child Development, 84*, 226–240.

Farr, R.H., & Vazquez, C.P. (2020a). Stigma experiences, mental health, perceived parenting competence, and parent-child relationships among lesbian, gay, and heterosexual adoptive parents in the United States. *Frontiers in Psychology, 11*, 445.

Farr, R.H., & Vazquez, C.P. (2020b). Adoptive families headed by LGBTQ parents. In E. Helder & others (Eds.), *Handbook of adoption*. New York: Routledge.

Farr, R.H., Vazquez, C.P., & Patterson, C.J. (2020). LGBTQ adoptive parents and their children. In A.E. Goldberg & K.R. Allen (Eds.), *LGBTQ adoptive parent families* (2nd ed.). New York: Springer.

Farrington, D.P. (2004). Conduct disorder, aggression, and delinquency. In R.M. Lerner & L. Steinberg (Eds.), *Handbook of adolescent psychology* (2nd ed.). New York: Wiley.

Farrington, D.P. (2020). Childhood risk factors for criminal career duration: Comparisons with prevalence, onset, frequency, and recidivism. *Criminal Behavior and Mental Health, 30*, 159–171.

Fatusi, A.O., & Hindin, M.J. (2010). Adolescents and youths in developing countries: Health and development issues in context. *Journal of Adolescence, 33*, 499–508.

Fauconnier, M., & others (2020). Food addiction among female patients seeking treatment for an eating disorder: Prevalence and associated factors. *Nutrients, 12*(6), 1897.

Fava, N.M., & Bay-Cheng, L.Y. (2012). Young women's adolescent experiences of oral sex: Relation of age of initiation to sexual motivation, sexual coercion, and psychological functioning. *Journal of Adolescence, 35*, 1191–1201.

Federal Reserve Bank of New York (2018). *College earnings*. New York: Author.

Feigelman, W., & others (2020). Research note on whether sexual minority individuals are over-represented among suicide's casualties. *Crisis, 41*, 229–232.

Feiring, C. (1996). Concepts of romance in 15-year-old adolescents. *Journal of Research on Adolescence, 6*, 181–200.

Feldman, S.S., & Elliott, G.R. (1990). Progress and promise of research on normal adolescent development. In S.S. Feldman & G. Elliott (Eds.), *At the threshold: The developing adolescent*. Cambridge, MA: Harvard University Press.

Feldman, S.S., & Rosenthal, D.A. (1999). *Factors influencing parents' and adolescents' evaluations of parents as sex communicators*. Unpublished manuscript, Stanford Center on Adolescence, Stanford University.

Feldman, S.S., & Rosenthal, D.A. (Eds.) (2002). *Talking sexuality: Parent-adolescent communication*. San Francisco: Jossey-Bass.

Felner, J.K., & others (2020). Stress, coping, and context: Examining substance use among LBGTQ young adults with probable substance use disorders. *Psychiatric Services, 71*, 112–120.

Felver, J.C., & others (2017). The effects of mindfulness-based intervention on children's attention regulation. *Journal of Attention Disorders, 21*, 872–881.

Ferguson, H.J., Brunsdon, V.E.A., & Bradford, E.E.F. (2021). The developmental trajectories of executive function from adolescence to old age. *Scientific Reports, 11*(1), 1382.

Fernie, B.A., & others (2017). A metacognitive model of procrastination. *Journal of Affective Disorders, 210*, 196–203.

Ferradás Canedo, M.M., Rodriguez, C.F., Fernández, B.R., & Arias, A.V. (2018). Defensive pessimism, self-esteem, and achievement goals: A person-centered approach. *Psicothema, 30,* 53-58.

Ferrer-Wreder, L., & Kroger, J. (2020). *Identity in adolescence* (4th ed.). New York: Routledge.

Fielder, R.L., Walsh, J.L., Carey, K.B., & Carey, M.P. (2013). Predictors of sexual hookups: A theory-based, prospective study of first-year college women. *Archives of Sexual Behavior, 42,* 1425-1441.

Finders, J.K., & others (2021). Explaining achievement gaps in kindergarten and third grade: The role of self-regulation and executive function skills. *Early Childhood Research Quarterly, 54,* 72-85.

Fine, A., & others (2016). Self-control assessments and their implications for predicting adolescent offending. *Journal of Youth and Adolescence, 45,* 701-712.

Fine, A., & others (2017). Is the effect of justice system attitudes on recidivism stable after youths' first arrest? Race and legal socialization among first-time offenders. *Law and Human Behavior, 41,* 146-158.

Fingerhut, A.W., & Peplau, L.A. (2013). Same-sex romantic relationships. In C.J. Patterson & A.R. D'Augelli (Eds.), *Handbook of psychology and sexual orientation.* New York: Oxford University Press.

Fingerman, K.L., Cheng, Y.P., & others (2012). Helicopter parents and landing pad kids: Intense parental support of grown children. *Journal of Marriage and the Family, 74*(4), 880-896.

Fingerman, K.L., Pillemer, K.A., Silverstein, M., & Suitor, J.J. (2012). The Baby Boomers' intergenerational relationships. *Gerontologist, 52,* 199-209.

Fingerman, K.L., & others (2017). Parental involvement with college students in Germany, Hong Kong, Korea, and the United States. *Journal of Family Issues, 37,* 1384-1411.

Finkelstein-Fox, L., Park, C.L., & Kalichman, S.C. (2020). Health benefits of positive reappraisal coping among people with HIV/AIDS: A systematic review. *Health Psychology Review, 14,* 394-426.

Finn, A.S., Sheridan, M.A., Kam, C.L., Hinshaw, S., & D'Esposito, M. (2010). Longitudinal evidence for functional specialization of the neural circuit supporting working memory in the human brain. *Journal of Neuroscience, 18,* 11062-11067.

Fischhoff, B., Bruine de Bruin, W., Parker, A.M., Millstein, S.G., & Halpern-Felsher, B.L. (2010). Adolescents' perceived risk of dying. *Journal of Adolescent Health, 46,* 265-269.

Fisher, B.S., Cullen, F.T., & Turner, M.G. (2000). *The sexual victimization of college women.* Washington, DC: National Institute of Justice.

Fisher, H. (2020. May 7). How coronavirus is changing the dating game for the better. *New York Times.* Retrieved from www.nytimes.com/2020/05/07well/mind/da77ting-coronavirus-love-relationships.html

Fisher, H.E., & Garcia, J.R. (2019). Slow love: Courtship in the digital age. In R.J. Sternberg & K. Sternberg (Eds.), *The new psychology of love* (2nd ed.). New York: Cambridge University Press.

Fisher, K.A., & Haney, M. (2021). *Antisocial personality disorder.* Treasure Island, FL: StatPearls.

Fisher, T.D. (1987). Family communication and the sexual behavior and attitudes of college students. *Journal of Youth and Adolescence, 16,* 481-495.

Fitzgerald, A., Fitzgerald, N., & Aherne, C. (2012). Do peers matter? A review of peer and/or friends' influence on physical activity among American adolescents. *Journal of Adolescence, 35,* 941-958.

Fivush, R. (2011). The development of autobiographical memory. *Annual Review of Psychology* (Vol. 62). Palo Alto, CA: Annual Reviews.

Fivush, R., Berlin, L.J., Sales, J., Mennuti-Washburn, J., & Cassidy, J. (2003). Functions of parent-child reminiscing about emotionally negative events. *Memory, 11,* 179-192.

Fivush, R., & Zaman, W. (2015). Gendered narrative voices: Sociocultural and feminist approaches to emerging identity in childhood and adolescence. In K.C. McLean & M. Syed (Eds.), *Oxford handbook of identity development.* New York: Oxford University Press.

Flam, K.K., Sanlder, I., Wolchik, S., & Tein, J.Y. (2016). Non-residential father-child involvement, interparental conflict, and mental health of children following divorce: A person-focused approach. *Journal of Youth and Adolescence, 45,* 581-593.

Flanagan, A.S. (1996, March). *Romantic behavior of sexually victimized and nonvictimized women.* Paper presented at the meeting of the Society for Research on Adolescence, Boston.

Flanagan, C.A. (2004). Volunteerism leadership, political socialization, and civic engagement. In R. Lerner & L. Steinberg (Eds.), *Handbook of adolescent psychology* (2nd ed.). New York: Wiley.

Flanagan, C.A., & Faison, N. (2001). Youth civic development: Implications for social policy and programs. *SRCD Social Policy Report, XV* (1), 1-14.

Flannery, J.E., & others (2017). Neurodevelopmental changes across adolescence in viewing and labeling dynamic peer emotions. *Developmental Cognitive Neuroscience, 25,* 113-127.

Flavell, J.H. (1979). Metacognition and cognitive monitoring. A new area of psychological inquiry. *American Psychologist, 34,* 906-911.

Flavell, J.H. (2004). Theory-of-mind development: Retrospect and prospect. *Merrill-Palmer Quarterly, 50,* 274-290.

Flavell, J.H., & Miller, P.H. (1998). Social cognition. In W. Damon (Ed.), *Handbook of child psychology* (5th ed.). New York: Wiley.

Fleming, C.B., White, H.R., Oesterie, S., Haggerty, K.P., & Catalano, R.F. (2010). Romantic relationship status changes and substance abuse among 18- to 20-year-olds. *Journal of Studies on Alcohol and Drugs, 71,* 847-856.

Fleming, E.C., & others (2021). A digital fluency framework to support 21st century skills. *Magazine of Higher Learning, 52,* 41-45.

Flett, J.A.M., & others (2020). App-based mindfulness meditation for psychological distress and adjustment to college in incoming university students: A pragmatic, randomized waitlist-controlled trial. *Psychology and Health, 35,* 1049-1074.

Flint, M.S., Baum, A., Chambers, W.H., & Jenkins, F.J. (2007). Induction of DNA damage, alteration of DNA repair, and transcriptional activation by stress hormones. *Psychoneuroendocrinology 32,* 470-479.

Flores, R.L., Okorodudu, & Shepherd, V. (2021). The intersection of psychology and human rights in addressing racism, discrimination, and xenophobia: Past, present, and future directions. In N.S. Rubin & R.L. Flores (Eds.), *Cambridge handbook of psychology and human rights.* New York: Cambridge University Press.

Flores Vizcaya-Moreno, M., & Perez-Canaveras, R.M. (2021). Social media used and teaching methods preferred by generation Z students in the nursing clinical learning environment: A cross-sectional research study. *International Journal of Environmental Research, 17*(21), 8267.

Florsheim, P., Moore, D., & Edgington, C. (2003). Romantic relationships among adolescent parents. In P.C. Florsheim (Ed.), *Adolescent romantic relations and sexual behavior.* Oxford, UK: Routledge.

Flye, A.L. (2017). A comparative analysis of student participation in the Advancement via Individual Determination (AVID) program and performance on the grade 11 Michigan Merit Exam (MME). *ERIC,* ED579047.

Flynn, J.R. (2013). *Are we getting smarter?* New York: Cambridge University Press.

Flynn, J.R. (2018). Intelligence, society, and human autonomy. In R.J. Sternberg (Ed.), *The nature of human intelligence.* New York: Cambridge University Press.

Flynn, J.R. (2020). Secular changes in intelligence. In R.J. Sternberg (Ed.), *Cambridge handbook of intelligence* (2nd ed.). New York: Cambridge University Press.

Ford, D.Y. (2012). Gifted and talented education: History, issues, and recommendations. In K.R. Harris, S. Graham, & T. Urdan (Eds.), *APA handbook of educational psychology.* Washington, DC: American Psychological Association.

Ford, D.Y. (2016). Black and Hispanic students. In L. Corno & E.M. Anderman (Eds.), *Handbook of educational psychology* (3rd ed.). New York: Routledge.

Ford, J.H., & others (2021). Trends in depressed mood and suicidal behaviors among female high school students who engaged in physical fighting. *Journal of Interpersonal Violence, 36*(9-10), NP4826-NP4849.

Forgatch, M.S., Patterson, G.R., DeGarmo, D.S., & Beldavs, Z.G. (2009). Testing the Oregon delinquency model with 9-year follow-up of the Oregon Divorce Study. *Development and Psychopathology, 21,* 637-660.

Fosco, G.M., & Grych, J.H. (2010). Adolescent triangulation into parental conflicts: Longitudinal implications for appraisals and adolescent-parent relations. *Journal of Marriage and the Family, 72,* 254-266.

Foubert, J.D., Clark-Taylor, A., & Wall, A.F. (2020). Is campus rape primarily a serial or one-time problem? Evidence from a multicampus study. *Violence Against Women, 26*(3-4), 296-311.

Fouts, H.N., & Bader, L.R. (2017). Transitions in siblinghood: Integrating developments, cultural, and evolutionary perspectives. In D. Narváez & others (Eds.), *Contexts for young child flourishing.* New York: Oxford University Press.

Fowler, S.K., & others (2021, in press). Prison culture as rape supportive: Applying importation and deprivation models to examine inmate beliefs. *Journal of Interpersonal Violence.*

Fraley, R.C., & Roisman, G.I. (2018). The development of adult attachment styles: Four lessons. *Current Opinion in Psychology, 25,* 26-30.

Fraley, R.C., & Shaver, P.R. (2021). Attachment theory and its place in contemporary personality theory and research. In O.P. John & R.W. Robins (Eds.), *Handbook of personality: Theory and research* (4th ed.). New York: Guilford.

Francis, J., Fraser, G., & Marcia, J.E. (1989). *Cognitive and experimental factors in moratorium-achievement (MAMA) cycles.* Unpublished manuscript. Department of Psychology, Simon Fraser University, Burnaby, British Columbia.

Franz, C.E. (1996). The implications of preschool tempo and motoric activity level for personality decades later. Reported in A. Caspi (1998). Personality development across the life course. In W. Damon (Ed.), *Handbook of child psychology* (Vol. 3, p. 337). New York: Wiley.

Franzago, M., & others (2020). Genes and diet in the prevention of chronic diseases in future generations. *International Journal of Molecular Science 21,* 7.

Franzese, A.T., & others (2021). Regulatory focus and substance use in adolescents: Protective effects of prevention orientation. *Substance Use and Misuse, 56,* 33-38.

Frederikse, M., & others (2000). Sex differences in inferior lobule volume in schizophrenia. *American Journal of Psychiatry, 157,* 422-427.

Freeman, D. (1983). *Margaret Mead and Samoa.* Cambridge, MA: Harvard University Press.

French, D.C., & Cheung, H.S. (2018). Peer relationships. In J.E. Lansford & P. Banali (Eds.), *Handbook of adolescent development research and its impact on global policy.* New York: Oxford University Press.

French, D.C., Purwono, U., & Rodkin, P.C. (2012). Religiosity of adolescents and their friends and network associates: Homophily and associations with antisocial behavior. *Journal of Research on Adolescence, 22,* 326–332.

Freud, S. (1917). *A general introduction to psychoanalysis.* New York: Washington Square Press.

Friedman, J. (2013). *Twin separation.* Retrieved February 14, 2013, from http://christinabaglivitinglof.com/twin-pregnancy/six-twin-experts-tell-all/

Friedman, S., & Lynch, A. (2020). International adoption. In J.D. Jewell & S. Hupp (Eds.), *Encyclopedia of child and adolescent development.* New York: Wiley.

Friend, M. (2018). *Special education* (5th ed.). Upper Saddle River, NJ: Pearson.

Frimer, J.A., & Sinclair, L. (2016). Moral heroes look up and to the right. *Personality and Social Psychology Bulletin, 42,* 400–410.

Fritz, H., & Gallagher, B.P. (2020). Three dimensions of desirability of control: Divergent relations with psychological and physical well-being. *Psychology and Health, 35,* 210–238.

Froh, J.J., Yurkewicz, C., & Kashdan, T.B. (2009). Gratitude and subjective well-being in early adolescence: Examining gender differences. *Journal of Adolescence, 32,* 633–650.

Frost, D.M. (2011). Stigma and intimacy in same-sex relationships: A narrative approach. *Journal of Family Psychology, 25,* 1–10.

Frost, J., & McKelvie, S. (2004). Self-esteem and body satisfaction in male and female elementary school, high school, and university students. *Sex Roles, 51,* 45–54.

Fruiht, V.M., & Wray-Lake, L. (2013). The role of mentor type and timing in predicting educational attainment. *Journal of Youth and Adolescence, 42,* 1459–1472.

Fry, R. (2016, May 14). *For first time in modern era, living with parents edges out other living arrangements for 18- to 34-year-olds.* Washington, DC: Pew Research Center.

Fujikawa, S., & others (2021). Bullying across late childhood and early adolescence: A prospective cohort of students assessed annually from grades 3 to 8. *Academic Pediatrics, 21,* 344–351.

Fuligni, A., & Stevenson, H.W. (1995). Time use and mathematics achievement among American, Chinese, and Japanese high school students. *Child Development, 66,* 830–842.

Fuligni, A.J. (2012). Gaps, conflicts, and arguments between adolescents and their parents. *New Directions for Child and Adolescent Development, 135,* 105–110.

Fuligni, A.J., & Tsai, K.M. (2015). Developmental flexibility in the age of globalization: Autonomy and identity development among immigrant adolescents. *Annual Review of Psychology* (Vol. 66). Palo Alto, CA: Annual Reviews.

Fuller-Rowell, T.E., Evans, G.W., Paul, E., & Curtis, D.S. (2015). The role of poverty and chaos in the development of task persistence among adolescents. *Journal of Research on Adolescence, 16,* 560–566.

Funkhouser, C.J., & others (2021). Unique longitudinal relationships between symptoms of psychopathology in youth: A cross-lagged panel network analysis in the ABCD study. *Journal of Child Psychology and Psychiatry, 62,* 184–194.

Furman, E. (2005). *Boomerang nation.* New York: Fireside.

Furman, W. (2002). The emerging field of adolescent romantic relationships. *Current Directions in Psychological Science, 11,* 177–180.

Furman, W. (2018). The romantic relationships of youth. In W.M. Bukowski & others (Eds), *Handbook of peer interactions, relationships, and groups* (2nd ed.). New York: Guilford.

Furman, W., & Collibee, C. (2018). The past is present: Representations of parents, friends, and romantic partners predict subsequent romantic representations. *Child Development, 89,* 188–204.

Furman, W., & Shaffer, L. (2013). The role of romantic relationships in adolescent development. In P. Florsheim (Ed.), *Adolescent romantic relations and sexual behavior* (paperback edition). Mahwah, NJ: Erlbaum.

Furman, W., & Simon, V.A. (2008). Homophily in adolescent romantic relationships. In M.J. Prinstein & K.A. Dodge (Eds.), *Understanding peer influence in children and adolescents.* New York: Guilford.

Furman, W., & Wehner, E.A. (1998). Adolescent romantic relationships: A developmental perspective. In S. Shulman & W.A. Collins (Eds.), *New directions for child development: Adolescent romantic relationships.* San Francisco: Jossey-Bass.

Furman, W., & Winkles, J.K. (2010). Predicting romantic involvement, relationship cognitions, and relational styles regarding friends and parents. *Journal of Adolescence, 33,* 827–836.

Furman, W., Low, S., & Ho, M.J. (2009). Romantic experience and psychosocial adjustment in middle adolescence. *Journal of Clinical Child and Adolescent Psychology, 38,* 75–90.

Furr, R.M., & Funder, D.C. (2021). Persons, situations, and person-situation interactions. In O.P. John & R.W. Robins (Eds.), *Handbook of personality* (4th ed.). New York: Guilford.

Furukawa, E., Tangney, J., & Higashibara, F. (2012). Cross-cultural continuities and discontinuities in shame, guilt, and pride: A study of children residing in Japan, Korea, and the USA. *Self and Identity, 11,* 90–113.

Fussell, E., & Greene, M.E. (2002). Demographic trends affecting youth around the world. In B.B. Brown, R.W. Larson, & T.S. Saraswathi (Eds.), *The world's youth.* New York: Cambridge University Press.

G

Galambos, N.L., Barker, E.T., & Krahn, H.J. (2006). Depression, self-esteem, and anger in emerging adulthood: Seven-year trajectories. *Developmental Psychology, 42,* 350–365.

Galambos, N.L., Berenbaum, S.A., & McHale, S.M. (2009). Gender development in adolescents. In R.M. Lerner & L. Steinberg (Eds.), *Handbook of adolescent psychology* (3rd ed.). New York: Wiley.

Gale, C.R., Booth, T., Mottus, R., Kuh, D., & Deary, J.J. (2013). Neuroticism and extraversion in youth predict mental wellbeing and life satisfaction 40 years later. *Journal of Research in Personality, 47,* 687–697.

Galimov, A., & others (2020). Association of energy drink consumption with substance-use initiation among adolescents: A 12-month longitudinal study. *Journal of Psychopharmacology, 34,* 221–228.

Galinsky, E. (2010). *Mind in the making.* New York: HarperCollins.

Galland, B.C., & others (2020). Sleep and pre-bedtime activities in New Zealand adolescents: Differences by ethnicity. *Sleep Health, 6,* 23–31.

Galliher, R.V., & Kerpelman, J.L. (2012). The intersection of identity development and peer relationship processes in adolescence and young adulthood: Contributions of the special issue. *Journal of Adolescence, 35,* 1409–1415.

Galvan, A. (2020). The need for sleep in the adolescent brain. *Trends in Cognitive Science, 24,* 79–89.

Galvao, A., & Kelsey, G. (2021). Profiling DNA methylation genome-wide single cells. *Methods in Molecular Biology, 2021,* 221–224.

Gam, A., & others (2021). Social goals in urban physical education: Relationships with effort and disruptive behavior. *Journal of Teaching in Physical Education, 30,* 410–423.

Ganahl, D.J., Prinsen, T.J., & Netzley, S.B. (2003). A content analysis of prime-time commercials: A contextual framework of gender representation. *Sex Roles, 49,* 545–551.

Gangat, M., & Radovick, S. (2020). Precocious puberty. *Minerva Pediatrica, 72,* 491–500.

Gangestad, S.W., & Chang, L. (2020). The contents and discontents of the nature-nurture debate. In F.M. Cheung & D.F. Halpern (Eds.), *Cambridge handbook of the international psychology of women.* New York: Cambridge University Press.

Ganson, K.T., Murray, S.B., & Nagata, J.M. (2020). A call for public policy and research to reduce use of appearance and performance enhancing drugs and substances among adolescents. *Lancet. Child and Adolescent Health, 4*(1), 13–14.

Gao, G. (2016). Cross-cultural romantic relationships. *Oxford research encyclopedia of romantic relationships.* New York: Oxford University Press.

Garcia, E. (2020). Schools are still segregated, and Black children are paying a price. ERIC #ED603475.

Garcia, O.F., Lopez-Fernandez, O., & Serra, E. (2021, in press). Raising Spanish children with an antisocial tendency: Do we know what the optimal parenting style is? *Journal of Interpersonal Violence.*

Garcia-Campayo, J., Lopez Del Hoyo, Y., & Navarro-Gil, M. (2021). Contemplative sciences: A future beyond mindfulness. *World Journal of Psychiatry, 11,* 87–93.

Garcia-Coll, C., & Marks, A.K. (Eds.) (2014). *The immigrant paradox in children and adolescents.* Washington, DC: APA Books.

Garcia-Vazquez, F.I., & others (2020). The effects of forgiveness, gratitude, and self-control on reactive and proactive aggression in bullying. *International Journal of Environmental Research and Public Health, 17*(16), E5760.

Gardner, H. (1983). *Frames of mind.* New York: Basic Books.

Gardner, H. (1993). *Multiple intelligences.* New York: Basic Books.

Gardner, H. (2002). The pursuit of excellence through education. In M. Ferrari (Ed.), *Learning from extraordinary minds.* Mahwah, NJ: Erlbaum.

Gardner, H. (2016). *Multiple intelligences: Prelude, theory, and aftermath.* In R.J. Sternberg, S.T. Fiske, & J. Foss (Eds.), *Scientists making a difference.* New York: Cambridge University Press.

Gardner, M., & others (2020). How does high school extracurricular participation predict bachelor's degree attainment? It is complicated. *Journal of Research on Adolescence, 30,* 753–768.

Gardner, M., & Steinberg, L. (2005). Peer influence on risk taking, risk preference, and risky decision making in adolescence and adulthood: An experimental study. *Developmental Psychology, 41,* 625–635.

Garg, D., & Berga, S.L. (2020). Neuroendocrine mechanisms of reproduction. *Handbook of Clinical Neurology, 171,* 3–23.

Gariepy, G., & others (2017). Early-life family income and subjective well-being in adolescents. *PLoS One, 12*(7), e0179380.

Garriz-Luis, M., & others (2021). Neuroplasticity during the transition period: How the adolescent brain can recover from aphasia. A pilot study. *Brain Development, 43,* 556–562.

Garzon-Orjuela, N., & others (2021). Effectiveness of sex education interventions in adolescents: An overview. *Comprehensive Child and Adolescent Nursing, 44,* 15–48.

Gates, G.J. (2013, February). *LGBT parenting in the United States.* Los Angeles: The Williams Institute, UCLA.

Gates, W. (1998, July 20). Charity begins when I'm ready (interview). *Fortune.*

Gatta, E., & others (2021). Epigenetic landscape of stress surfeit disorders: Key role for DNA methylation dynamics. *International Review of Neurobiology, 156,* 127–183.

Gauthier-Duchesne, A., Hebert, M., & Blais, M. (2021, in press). Child sexual abuse, self-esteem, and delinquent behaviors during adolescence: The moderating role of gender. *Journal of Interpersonal Violence.*

Gauvain, M. (2016). Peer contributions to cognitive development. In K. Wentzel & G.B. Ramani (Eds.), *Handbook of social influences in school contexts.* New York: Routledge.

Gauvain, M., & Perez, S.M. (2015). Cognitive development in the context of culture. In R.M. Lerner (Ed.), *Handbook of child psychology and developmental science* (7th ed.). New York: Wiley.

Ge, L., & others (2017). Social isolation, loneliness, and their relationships with depressive symptoms: A population-based study. *PLoS One, 12*(8), e0182145.

Gecas, V., & Seff, M. (1990). Families and adolescents: A review of the 1980s. *Journal of Marriage and the Family, 52,* 941–958.

Geiger, A.W., & Livingston, G. (2019). *8 facts about love and marriage in America.* Washington, DC: Pew Research.

Geist, C., & others (2021). Pediatric research and health care for transgender and gender diverse adolescents and young adults: Improving (biopsychosocial) health outcomes. *Academic Pediatrics, 21,* 32–42.

Geniole, S.N., & others (2020). Is testosterone linked to human aggression? A meta-analytic examination of the relationship between baseline, dynamic, and manipulated testosterone on human aggression. *Hormones and Behavior, 123,* 104644.

Gentile, D.A., & others (2009). The effects of prosocial video games on prosocial behaviors: International evidence from correlational, longitudinal, and experimental studies. *Personality and Social Psychology Bulletin, 35,* 752–763.

Geoffrey, M.C., Li, L., & Power, C. (2014). Depressive symptoms and body mass index: Co-morbidity and directions of association in a British birth cohort followed over 50 years. *Psychology and Medicine, 44,* 2641–2652.

George, C., Main, M., & Kaplan, N. (1984). *Attachment interview with adults.* Unpublished manuscript, University of California–Berkeley.

George Dalmida, S., & others (2018). Sexual risk behaviors of African American adolescent females: The role of cognitive and religious factors. *Journal of Transcultural Nursing, 29,* 74–83.

Geronimi, E.M.C., Arellano, B., & Woodruff-Borden, J. (2020). Relating mindfulness and executive function in children. *Clinical Child Psychology and Psychiatry, 25,* 435–445.

Gibb, G., & Taylor, T. (2022). *IEPs: Guide to writing individualized education programs* (4th ed.). Upper Saddle River, NJ: Pearson.

Gibbs, J.C. (2019). *Moral development and reality* (4th ed.). New York: Oxford University Press.

Gibbs, J.C., Basinger, K.S., Grime, R.L., & Snarey, J.R. (2007). Moral judgment across cultures: Revisiting Kohlberg's universality claims. *Developmental Review, 27,* 443–500.

Giedd, J.N. (2007, September 27). Commentary in S. Jayson, "Teens driven to distraction." *USA Today,* pp. D1–D2.

Giedd, J.N. (2008). The teen brain: Insights from neuroimaging. *Journal of Adolescent Health, 42,* 335–343.

Giedd, J.N. (2012). The digital revolution and the adolescent brain. *Journal of Adolescent Health, 51,* 101–105.

Gijzen, M.W.M., & others (2021). Suicide ideation as a symptom of adolescent depression: A network analysis. *Journal of Affective Disorders, 278,* 68–77.

Gil, A.J., & others (2021). The effect of family support on student engagement towards the prevention of dropouts. *Psychology in the Schools, 58,* 1082–1095.

Gilbert, G., & Graham, S. (2010). Teaching writing to students in grades 4–6: A national survey. *Elementary School Journal, 110,* 494–518.

Gill, N., & others (2021). Childhood obesity is associated with poor academic skills and coping mechanisms. *Journal of Pediatrics, 228,* 278–284.

Gillen-O'Neel, C., Huynh, V.W., & Fuligni, A.J. (2013). To study or to sleep? The academic costs of extra studying at the expense of sleep. *Child Development, 84*(1), 133–142.

Gilligan, C. (1982). *In a different voice.* Cambridge, MA: Harvard University Press.

Gilligan, C. (1996). The centrality of relationships in psychological development: A puzzle, some evidence, and a theory. In G.G. Noam & K.W. Fischer (Eds.), *Development and vulnerability in close relationships.* Hillside, NJ: Erlbaum.

Gilligan, C., Brown, L.M., & Rogers, A.G. (1990). Psyche embedded: A place for body, relationships, and culture in personality theory. In A.I. Rabin, R.A. Zuker, R.A. Emmons, & S. Frank (Eds.), *Studying persons and lives.* New York: Springer.

Gilligan, C., Spencer, R., Weinberg, M.K., & Bertsch, T. (2003). On the listening guide: A voice-centered relational model. In P.M. Carnie & J.E. Rhodes (Eds.), *Qualitative research in psychology.* Washington, DC: American Psychological Association.

Gilmartin, S.K. (2006). Changes in college women's attitudes toward sexual intimacy. *Journal of Research on Adolescence, 16,* 429–454.

Gil-Olarte Marquez, P., Palomera Martin, R., & Brackett, M. (2006). Relating emotional intelligence to social competence and academic achievement in high school students. *Psicothema, 18,* 118–123.

Gini, G., Pozzoli, T., & Hymel, S. (2014). Moral disengagement among children and youth: A meta-analytic review of links to aggressive behavior. *Aggressive Behavior, 40,* 56–68.

Girls Inc (2020). *Preventing adolescent pregnancy.* New York: Girls Inc.

Girme, Y.U., & others (2021). Infants' attachment insecurity predicts attachment-relevant emotion regulation in adulthood. *Emotion, 21*(2), 260–272.

Glabska, D., & others (2019). The National After-School Athletics Program participation as a tool to reduce the risk of obesity in adolescents after one year of intervention: A nationwide study. *International Journal of Environmental Research and Public Health, 16,* 3.

Glaveanu, V.P., & others (2020). Advancing creativity theory and research: A sociocultural manifesto. *Journal of Creative Behavior, 3,* 741–745.

Glaxoglau, K., & Georgakopoulou, A. (2021). A narrative approach to identities: Small stories and positioning analysis in digital contexts. In M. Bamberg & others (Eds.), *Cambridge handbook of identity.* New York: Cambridge University Press.

Globallab (2021). *Global student laboratory.* Retrieved June 14, 2021, from https://globallab.org/en/project/catalog/#.V7nsGal08kw

Glowacz, F., & Courtain, A. (2021). Perpetration of dating violence among Belgian youth: Impulsivity, verbal skills, and empathy as risk and protective factors. *Violence and Victims, 36,* 110–131.

Gluck, J. (2020). The important difference between psychologists' labs and real-life: Evaluating the validity of models of wisdom. *Psychological Inquiry, 31,* 144–150.

Gnambs, T., & Appel, M. (2018). Narcissism and social networking behavior: A meta-analysis. *Journal of Personality, 86,* 200–212.

Goddings, A-L., & Mills, K. (2017). *Adolescence and the brain.* New York: Psychology Press.

Godwin, J.W., & the Conduct Problems Prevention Research Group (2020). The Fast Track intervention's impact on behaviors of despair in adolescence and young adulthood. *Proceedings of the National Academy of Sciences, 117*(50), 31748–31753.

Goffin, K.C., Boldt, L.J., & Kochanska, G. (2018). A secure base from which to cooperate: Security, child and parent willing stance, and adaptive and maladaptive outcomes in two longitudinal studies. *Journal of Abnormal Child Psychology, 46,* 1061–1075.

Gold, M.A., & others (2010). Associations between religiosity and sexual and contraceptive behaviors. *Journal of Pediatric and Adolescent Gynecology, 23,* 290–297.

Gold, S. (2020). Is housing hardship associated with increased adolescent delinquent behaviors? *Child and Youth Services Review, 116,* 105116.

Goldberg, A.E., & Allen, K.R. (Eds.) (2020). *LGBTQ-parent families: Possibilities for new research and implications for practice* (2nd ed.). New York: Springer.

Goldberg, M., & others (2021). *Genetics* (7th ed.). New York: McGraw-Hill.

Goldberg, S.K., & Halpern, C.T. (2017). Sexual initiation patterns of U.S. sexual minority youth: A latent class analysis. *Perspectives on Sex and Reproductive Health, 49,* 55–67.

Goldberg, W.A., & Lucas-Thompson, R. (2008). Maternal and paternal employment, effects of. In M.M. Haith & J.B. Benson (Eds.), *Encyclopedia of infant and early childhood development.* Oxford, UK: Elsevier.

Goldfarb, E.S., & Lieberman, L.D. (2021). Three decades of research: The case for comprehensive sex education. *Journal of Adolescent Health, 68,* 13–27.

Goldman, R.D., & others (2021). Pediatric patients seen in 18 emergency departments during the COVID-19 pandemic. *Emergency Medicine Journal, 37,* 773–777.

Goldschmidt, A.B., & others (2012). Momentary affect surrounding loss of control and overeating in obese adults with and without binge eating disorder. *Obesity, 20,* 1206–1211.

Goldstein, R., & Halpern-Felsher, B. (2018). Adolescent oral sex and condom use: How much should we worry and what can we do? *Journal of Adolescent Health, 62,* 363–364.

Goldston, D.B., & others (2008). Cultural considerations in adolescent suicide prevention and psychosocial treatment. *American Psychologist, 63,* 14–31.

Goleman, D. (1995). *Emotional intelligence.* New York: Basic Books.

Gollnick, D.M., & Chinn, P.C. (2021). *Multicultural education in a pluralistic society* (11th ed.). Upper Saddle River, NJ: Pearson.

Golombok, S., & Tasker, F. (2015). Socio-emotional development in changing family contexts. In R.M. Lerner (Ed.), *Handbook of child psychology and developmental science* (7th ed.). New York: Wiley.

Golombok, S., & others (2014). Adoptive gay father families: Parent-child relationships and children's psychological adjustment. *Child Development, 85,* 456–468.

Golshevsky, D.M., & others (2020). Time spent watching television impacts on body mass index in youth with obesity, but only in those with short sleep duration. *Journal of Pediatric Child Health, 56,* 721–726.

Gomez-Alonso, M.D.C., & others (2021). DNA methylation and lipid metabolism: An EWAS of 226 metabolic measures. *Clinical Epigenetics, 13*(1), 7.

Gong, X., & Carano, K.T. (2020). Divorce, child custody, and parenting plans. In J.D. Jewell & S. Hupp (Eds.), *Encyclopedia of child and adolescent development.* New York: Wiley.

Gonzales, M., Jones, D.J., Kincaid, C.Y., & Cuellar, J. (2012). Neighborhood context and adjustment in African American youths from single-mother homes: The intervening role of hopelessness. *Cultural Diversity and Ethnic Minority Psychology, 18,* 109–117.

Gonzales Aviles, T., Finn, C., & Neyer, F.J. (2021). Patterns of romantic relationship experiences and psychosocial adjustment from adolescence to young adulthood. *Journal of Youth and Adolescence, 50,* 550–562.

Gonzalez-Backen, M.A., & others (2017). Cultural profiles among Mexican-origin girls: Associations with psychosocial adjustment. *Journal of Latina/o Psychology, 5,* 157–172.

Gonzalez-Barrera, A., & Lopez, M.G. (2020, July 22). *Before COVID-19, many Latinos worried about their place in America and had experienced discrimination.* Washington, DC: Pew Research Center.

Gonzalez-Perez, S., Mateos de Cabo, R., & Sainz, M. (2020). Girls in STEM: Is it a female role-model thing? *Frontiers in Psychology, 11,* 2204.

Good, C., Rattan, A., & Dweck, C.S. (2012). Why do women opt out? Sense of belonging and women's representation in mathematics. *Journal of Personality and Social Psychology, 102,* 700–717.

Good, M., & Willoughby, T. (2008). Adolescence as a sensitive period for spiritual development. *Child Development Perspectives, 2,* 32–37.

Good, M., & Willoughby, T. (2010). Evaluating the direction of effects in the relationship between religious versus non-religious activities, academic success, and substance use. *Journal of Youth and Adolescence, 40,* 680–693.

Goodcase, E.T., Spencer, C.M., & Toews, M.L. (2021, in press). Who understands consent? A latent profile analysis of college students' attitudes toward consent. *Journal of Interpersonal Violence.*

Goodkind, S. (2013). Single-sex public education for low-income youth of color: A critical theoretical review. *Sex Roles, 69,* 363–381.

Goossens, L., & Luyckx, K. (2007). Identity development in college students: Variable-centered and person-centered analysis. In M. Watzlawik & A. Born (Eds.), *Capturing identity.* Lanham, MD: University of America Press.

Goossens, L., Beyers, W., Emmen, M., & van Aken, M.A.G. (2002). The imaginary audience and personal fable. Factor analyses and concurrent validity of the "new look" measures. *Journal of Research on Adolescence, 12,* 193–215.

Gopnik, A., & others (2019). Changes in cognitive flexibility and hypothesis search across human life history from childhood to adolescence to adulthood. *Proceedings of the National Academy of Sciences U.S.A., 114,* 7892–7899.

Gorchoff, S.M., John, O.P., & Helson, R. (2008). Contextualizing change in marital satisfaction during middle age: An 18-year longitudinal study. *Psychological Science, 19,* 1194–2000.

Gordon, R., & others (2020). Working memory and high-level cognition in children: An analysis of timing and accuracy in complex span tasks. *Journal of Experimental Child Psychology, 191,* 104736.

Gordon Simons, L., & others (2018). The cost of being cool: How adolescents' pseudomature behavior maps onto adult adjustment. *Journal of Youth and Adolescence, 47,* 1007–1021.

Gorrese, A., & Ruggieri, R. (2012). Peer attachment: A meta-analytic review of gender and age differences and associations with parent attachment. *Journal of Youth and Adolescence, 41,* 650–672.

Gottfried, A.E., Marcoulides, G.A., Gottfried, A.W., & Oliver, P.H. (2009). A latent curve model of motivational practices and developmental decline in math and science academic intrinsic motivation. *Journal of Educational Psychology, 101,* 729–739.

Gottman, J.M., & Parker, J.G. (Eds.). (1987). *Conversations of friends.* New York: Cambridge University Press.

Gottschalk, M.G., Domschke, K., & Schiele, M.A. (2020). Epigenetics underlying susceptibility and resilience to daily life stress, work stress, and socioeconomic status. *Frontiers in Psychology, 11,* 163.

Gould, S.J. (1981). *The mismeasure of man.* New York: W.W. Norton.

Gove, W.R., Style, C.B., & Hughes, M. (1990). The effect of marriage on the well-being of adults: A theoretical analysis. *Journal of Health and Social Behavior, 24,* 122–131.

Gow, M.L., & others (2020). Pediatric obesity treatment, self-esteem, and body image: A systematic review with meta-analysis. *Pediatric Obesity, 15*(3), e12600.

Goyer, J.P., Walton, G.M., & Yeager, D.S. (2021). The role of psychological factors and institutional channels in predicting the attainment of postsecondary goals. *Developmental Psychology, 57,* 73–86.

Graber, J.A., Brooks-Gunn, J., & Warren, M.P. (2006). Pubertal effects on adjustment in girls: Moving from demonstrating effects to identifying pathways. *Journal of Youth and Adolescence, 35,* 391–401.

Graber, J.A., & Sontag, L.M. (2009). Internalizing problems during adolescence. In R.M. Lerner & L. Steinberg (Eds.), *Handbook of adolescent psychology* (3rd ed.). New York: Wiley.

Grabowska, A. (2020). Sex differences in the brain. In F.M. Cheung & D.F. Halpern (Eds.), *Cambridge handbook of the international psychology of women.* New York: Cambridge University Press.

Graham, E.A. (2005). Economic, racial, and cultural influences on the growth and maturation of children. *Pediatrics in Review, 26,* 290–294.

Graham, E.K., & others (2017). Personality and mortality risk: An integrative data analysis of 15 international longitudinal studies. *Journal of Research on Personality, 70,* 174–186.

Graham, J. (2020). Ideology, shared moral narratives, and the dark side of collective rationalization. *Behavioral Brain Sciences, 43,* e37.

Graham, J., & others (2016). Cultural differences in moral judgment and behavior, across and within societies. *Current Opinion in Psychology, 8,* 125–130.

Graham, S. (1986, August). *Can attribution theory tell us something about motivation in blacks?* Paper presented at the meeting of the American Psychological Association, Washington, DC.

Graham, S. (1990). Motivation in Afro-Americans. In G.L. Berry & J.K. Asamen (Eds.), *Black students: Psychosocial issues and academic achievement.* Newbury Park, CA: Sage.

Graham, S. (2020). An attributional theory of motivation. *Contemporary Educational Psychology, 61*(4), 101861.

Graham, S., & Echols, L. (2018). Race and ethnicity in peer relations research. In W.M. Bukowski & others (Eds.), *Handbook of peer interactions, relationships, and groups* (2nd ed.). New York: Guilford.

Graham, S., & Harris, K.R. (2021). Writing and students with learning disabilities. In A. Martin & others (Eds.), *Handbook of educational psychology and students with learning disabilities.* New York: Routledge.

Graham, S., & Kogachi, K. (2021). Cross-race/cross-ethnic friendships in school. In F.C. Worrell & others (Eds.), *Cambridge handbook of applied school psychology.* New York: Cambridge University Press.

Graham, S., & Perin, D. (2007). A meta-analysis of writing instruction for adolescent students. *Journal of Educational Psychology, 99,* 445–476.

Graham, S., & Rui, A. (2022, in preparation). Teaching writing. *Reading and Writing: An Interdisciplinary Journal.*

Graham, S., & Taylor, A.Z. (2001). Ethnicity, gender, and the development of achievement values. In A. Wigfield & J.S. Eccles (Eds.), *Development of achievement motivation.* San Diego: Academic Press.

Graham, S., & Taylor, A.Z. (2016). Attribution theory and motivation at school. In K.R. Wentzel & D.B. Miele (Eds.), *Handbook of motivation at school.* New York: Routledge.

Graham, S., & Weiner, B. (2012). Motivation: Past, present, and future. In K.R. Harris & others (Eds.), *Handbook of educational psychology.* Washington, DC: American Psychological Association.

Graham, S., & others (2021). Writing strategy interventions. In D. Dinsmore & others (Eds.), *Handbook of strategies and strategic processing.* New York: Routledge.

Granqvist, P., & Dickie, J.R. (2006). Attachment and spiritual development in childhood and adolescence. In E.C. Roehlkepartain, P.E. King, & L.M. Wegener (Eds.), *The handbook of spiritual development in childhood and adolescence.* Thousand Oaks, CA: Sage.

Grant, G.B. (2017). Exploring the possibility of peak individualism, humanity's existential crisis, an emerging age of purpose. *Frontiers in Psychology, 8,* 1478.

Gratton, C., Smith, D.M., & Dorn, M. (2020). Digging deeper to chart the landscape of human brain development. *Neuron, 106,* 209–211.

Gravetter, F.J., & others (2021). *Essentials of statistics for the behavioral sciences* (10th ed.). Boston: Cengage.

Gravningen, K., & others (2017). Reported reasons for breakdown of marriage and cohabitation in Britain: Findings from the Third National Survey of Sexual Attitudes and Lifestyles (Natsal-3). *PLoS One, 12*(3), e0174129.

Gray, J. (1992). *Men are from Mars, women are from Venus.* New York: HarperCollins.

Graziano, A., & Raulin, M. (2020). *Research methods* (9th ed., loose leaf). Upper Saddle River, NJ: Pearson.

Greco, L.M., & Kraimer, M.I. (2020). Goal-setting in the career-management process: An identity theory perspective. *Journal of Applied Psychology, 105,* 40–57.

Green, A.L., & others (2021). Social and emotional learning during early adolescence: Effectiveness of a classroom-based SEL program for middle school students. *Psychology in the Schools, 58,* 1056–1069.

Greenberg, J. (2021). *Comprehensive stress management.* New York: McGraw-Hill.

Greenberger, E., & Steinberg, L. (1986). *When teenagers work: The psychological and social costs of adolescent employment.* New York: Basic Books.

Greene, B. (1988, May). The children's hour. *Esquire,* pp. 47–49.

Greenwood, C.J., & others (2021). Exploring a causal model in observational cohort data: The role of parents and peers in shaping substance use trajectories. *Addictive Behaviors, 112,* 105597.

Greenwood, P. (2008). Prevention and intervention programs for juvenile offenders. *The Future of Children, 18*(2), 185–210.

Gregory, A., & Huang, F. (2013). It takes a village: The effects of 10th grade college-going expectations of students, parents, and teachers four years later. *American Journal of Community Psychology, 52,* 41–55.

Grigorenko, E.L. (2000). Heritability and intelligence. In R.J. Sternberg (Ed.), *Handbook of intelligence.* New York: Cambridge University Press.

Grigorenko, E.L., & Burenkova, O. (2020). Genetic bases of intelligence. In R.J. Sternberg (Ed.), *Cambridge handbook of intelligence* (2nd ed.). New York: Cambridge University Press.

Grigorenko, E.L., & others (2016). The trilogy of G × E genes, environments, and their interactions: Conceptualization, operationalization, and application. In D. Cicchetti (Ed.), *Developmental psychopathology* (3rd ed.). New York: Wiley.

Grigorenko, E.L., & others (2019). Improved educational achievement as a path to desistance. *New Directions in Child and Adolescent Development, 165,* 111–135.

Groenman, A.P. (2021). Editorial: Sex-specific developmental trajectories of psychopathology: The case of substance misuse. *Journal of the American Academy of Child and Adolescent Psychiatry, 60,* 568–569.

Gross, B. (2020, June 8). *Too many schools leaving learning to chance during the pandemic.* Seattle, WA: Center for Reinventing Public Education.

Gross, J.J., Fredrickson, B.L., & Levenson, R.W. (1994). The psychophysiology of crying. *Psychophysiology, 31,* 460-468.

Grosse Wiesmann, C., & others (2020). Two systems for thinking about others' thoughts in the developing brain. *Proceedings of the National Academy of Sciences USA, 117*(12), 6928-6935.

Grossman, I., & others (2020). The science of wisdom in a polarized world: Knowns and unknowns. *Psychological Inquiry, 31,* 103-133.

Grossman, J.M., & others (2019). Extended-family talk about sex and teen sexual behavior. *International Journal of Environmental Research and Public Health, 16*(3), 480.

Grotevant, H.D., & McDermott, J.M. (2014). Adoption: Biological and social processes linked to adaptation. *Annual Review of Psychology* (Vol. 65). Palo Alto, CA: Annual Reviews.

Grotevant, H.D., McRoy, R.G., Wrobel, G.M., & Ayers-Lopez, S. (2013). Contact between adoptive and birth families: Perspectives from the Minnesota/Texas Adoption Research Project. *Child Development Perspectives, 7,* 193-198.

Grubb, L.K., & The Committee on Adolescence (2020). Barrier protection use by adolescents during sexual activity. *Pediatrics, 146*(2), e2020007245.

Grunschel, C., Patrzek, J., Klingsieck, K.B., & Fries, S. (2018). "I'll stop procrastinating now!" Fostering specific processes of self-regulated learning to reduce academic procrastination. *Journal of Prevention and Intervention in the Community, 46,* 143-157.

Grusec, J.E. (2020). Domains of socialization: Implications for parenting and the development of children's moral behavior and cognitions. In D.J. Laible & others (Eds.), *Oxford handbook of parenting and moral development.* New York: Oxford University Press.

Grych, J.H. (2002). Marital relationships and parenting. In M.H. Bornstein (Ed.), *Handbook of parenting.* Mahwah, NJ: Erlbaum.

GTI Media (2020). Report in Allaboutcareers, "Influenced by friends & family when choosing a career." Retrieved November 15, 2020, from allaboutcareers.com.

Guercio, G., & others (2020). Estrogens in human gonadotropin secretion and testicular physiology from infancy to puberty. *Frontiers in Endocrinology, 11,* 72.

Guerin, D.W., Gottfried, A.W., Oliver, P.H., & Thomas, C.W. (2003). *Temperament: Infancy through adolescence.* New York: Kluwer.

Guessoum, S.B., & others (2020). Adolescent psychiatric disorders during the COVID-19 pandemic and lockdown. *Psychiatry Research, 291,* 113264.

Guilford, J.P. (1967). *The structure of intellect.* New York: McGraw-Hill.

Gumora, G., & Arsenio, W. (2002). Emotionality, emotion regulation, and school performance in middle school children. *Journal of School Psychology, 40,* 395-413.

Gunnesch-Luca, G., & Iliescu. D. (2020). Time and generational changes in cognitive performance in Romania. *Intelligence, 79,* 101430.

Gunning, T.G. (2020). Creating literacy for all students (10th ed.). Upper Saddle River, NJ: Pearson.

Guo, J., & others (2020). The dynamic transcriptional cell atlas of testis development during human puberty. *Cell Stem Cell, 26,* 262-276.

Guryan, J., & others (2021). Not too late: Improving academic outcomes among adolescents: Working paper 28531. *ERIC* #ED612053.

Gustavson, D.E., & Miyake, A. (2017). Academic procrastination and goal accomplishment: A combined experimental and individual differences investigation. *Learning and Individual Differences, 54,* 160-172.

Guthold, R., & others (2020). Global trends in insufficient physical activity among adolescents: A pooled analysis of 298 population-based surveys with 1.6 million participants. *Lancet. Child and Adolescent Health, 4,* 23-35.

Gutman, L.M., & others (2017). Moving through adolescence: Developmental trajectories of African American and European American youth. *Monographs of the Society for Research in Child Development, 82*(4), 1-196.

Guttentag, C.L., & others (2014). "My Baby and Me": Effects of an early, comprehensive parenting intervention on at-risk mothers and their children. *Developmental Psychology, 50,* 482-496.

Guttmacher Institute (2020). *Sex and HIV education.* New York: Author.

Guttmannova, K., & others (2012). Examining explanatory mechanisms of the effects of early alcohol use on young adult alcohol competence. *Journal of Studies of Alcohol and Drugs, 73,* 379-390.

Gyurkovics, M., Stafford, T., & Levita, L. (2020). Cognitive control across adolescence: Dynamic adjustments and mind-wandering. *Journal of Experimental Psychology: General, 149,* 1017-1031.

H

Haardorfer, R., & others (2021). Longitudinal changes in alcohol use and binge-drinking among young-adult and college students: Analyses of predictors across system levels. *Addictive Behaviors, 112,* 106619.

Habermas, T., & de Silveira, C. (2008). The development of global coherence in life narratives across adolescence: Temporal, causal, and thematic aspects. *Developmental Psychology, 44,* 707-721.

Hadiwijaya, H., & others (2017). On the development of harmony, turbulence, and independence in parent-adolescent relationships: A five-wave longitudinal study. *Journal of Youth and Adolescence, 46,* 1772-1788.

Hadiwijaya, H., & others (2020). The family context as a foundation for romantic relationships: A person-centered multi-informant longitudinal study. *Journal of Family Psychology, 34,* 46-56.

Hafen, C.A., & others (2012). The pivotal role of adolescent autonomy in secondary school classrooms. *Journal of Youth and Adolescence, 41,* 245-255.

Hafner, I., & others (2017). Robin Hood effects on motivation in math: Family interest in math moderates the effects of relevance interventions. *Developmental Psychology, 53,* 1522-1539.

Haft, S., & others (2021). Culture and stress biology in immigrant youth from the prenatal period to adolescence: A systematic review. *Developmental Psychobiology, 63,* 391-408.

Hagan, K.E., & Walsh, B.T. (2021). State of the art: The therapeutic approaches to bulimia nervosa. *Clinical Therapeutics, 43,* 40-49.

Haggstrom Westberg, K., & others (2019). Optimism as a candidate health asset: Exploring its links with adolescent quality of life in Sweden. *Child Development, 90,* 970-984.

Haghighat, M.D., & Knifsend, C.A. (2019). The longitudinal influence of 10th grade extracurricular activity involvement: Implications for 12th grade academic practices and future educational achievement. *Journal of Youth and Adolescence, 48,* 609-619.

Haidt, J. (2018). *Three stories about capitalism.* New York: Pantheon.

Haier, R.J. (2020). Biological approaches to intelligence. In R.J. Sternberg (Ed.), *Human intelligence.* New York: Cambridge University Press.

Haimovitz, K., & Dweck, C.S. (2016). What predicts children's fixed and growth mindsets? Not their parents' views of intelligence but their parents' views of failure. *Psychological Science, 27,* 859-869.

Hakulinen, C., & others (2021). Personality traits and mental disorders. In P.J. Corr & G. Matthews (Eds.), *Cambridge handbook of personality psychology.* New York: Cambridge University Press.

Hale, S. (1990). A global developmental trend in cognitive processing speed. *Child Development, 61,* 653-663.

Halford, G.S., & Andrews, G. (2011). Information-processing models of cognitive development. In U. Goswami (Ed.), *Wiley-Blackwell handbook of childhood cognitive development* (2nd ed.). New York: Wiley.

Halgunseth, L.C. (2019). Latino and Latin American parenting. In M.H. Bornstein (Ed.), *Handbook of parenting* (3rd ed.). New York: Routledge.

Hall, G.S. (1904). *Adolescence* (Vols. 1 & 2). Englewood Cliffs, NJ: Prentice Hall.

Hall, J.A., Park, N., Song, H., & Cody, M.J. (2010). Strategic misrepresentation in online dating: The effects of gender, self-monitoring, and personality traits. *Journal of Social and Personal Relationships, 27,* 117-135.

Hallahan, D.P., Kauffman, J.M., & Pullen, P.C. (2019). *Exceptional learners* (14th ed.). Upper Saddle River, NJ: Pearson.

Halonen, J.A., & Santrock, J.W. (2013). *Your guide to college success* (7th ed.). Boston: Cengage.

Halpern, D.F., & Cheung, F.M. (2020). Parting thoughts. In F.M. Cheung & D.F. Halpern (Eds.), *Cambridge handbook of the international psychology of women.* New York: Cambridge University Press.

Halpern, D.F., Flores-Mendoza, C., & Rindermann, H. (2020). Sex, gender, and intelligence: Does XX = XY for intelligence? In F.M. Cheung & D.F. Halpern (Eds.), *Cambridge handbook of the international psychology of women.* New York: Cambridge University Press.

Halpern, D.F., & others (2011). The pseudoscience of single-sex schooling. *Science, 333,* 1706-1717.

Halpern-Felsher, B. (2008). Editorial. Oral sexual behavior: Harm reduction or gateway behavior? *Journal of Adolescent Health, 43,* 207-208.

Halpern-Meekin, S., Manning, W., Giordano, P.C., & Longmore, M.A. (2013). Relationship churning in emerging adulthood: On/off relationships and sex with an ex. *Journal of Adolescent Research, 28,* 166-188.

Hamidullah, S., & others (2020). Adolescent substance use and the brain: Behavioral, cognitive, and neuroimaging correlates. *Frontiers in Human Neuroscience, 14,* 298.

Hammen, C., & Keenan-Miller, D. (2013). Mood disorders. In I.B. Weiner & others (Eds.), *Handbook of psychology* (2nd ed., Vol. 8). New York: Wiley.

Hampton, J. (2008). Abstinence-only programs under fire. *Journal of the American Medical Association, 17,* 2013-2015.

Han, J.S., Rogers, M.E., Nurani, S., Rubin, S., & Blank, S. (2011). Patterns of chlamydia/gonorrhea positivity among voluntarily screened New York City public high school students. *Journal of Adolescent Health, 49,* 252-257.

Harding, J.F., & others (2020). Supporting expectant and parenting teens: New evidence to inform future programming and research. *Maternal and Child Health Journal, 24*(Suppl. 2), S67-S75.

Hardy, S.A., Krettenauer, T., & Hunt, N. (2020). Moral identity development. In L.A. Jensen (Ed.), *Oxford handbook of moral development.* New York: Oxford University Press.

Hardy, S.A., & others (2013). The roles of identity formation and moral identity in college student mental health, health-risk behaviors, and psychological well-being. *Journal of Clinical Psychology, 69,* 364-382.

Hardy, S.A., & others (2020). Dynamic associations between religiousness and self-regulation across adolescence into young adulthood. *Developmental Psychology, 56,* 180-197.

Hargrove, T.W., & others (2020). Race/ethnicity, gender, and trajectories of depressive symptoms across early- and mid-life among the Add Health cohort. *Journal of Racial and Ethnic Health Disparities, 7,* 619-629.

Harmon, O.R., Lambrinos, J., & Kennedy, P. (2008). Are online exams an invitation to cheat? *Journal of Economic Education, 39,* 116-125.

Harris, B., & others (2021). Implications of COVID-19 on school services for children with disabilities: Opportunities for interagency collaboration. *Journal of Developmental and Behavioral Pediatrics, 42,* 236-239.

Harrison, A., & others (2021, in press). ECD–Pregnancy outcomes of a birth cohort. Are adolescent mothers really at more risk? *Psychology, Health, and Medicine.*

Harrison, L.M., & Bishop, P.A. (2021). The evolving middle school concept: This we (still) know. *Current Issues in Middle School Education, 25*(2), 2-5.

Hart, C., & Ksir, C. (2022). *Drugs, society, and human behavior* (18th ed.). New York: McGraw-Hill.

Hart, D. (2020). Moral development in civic and political contexts. In L.A. Jensen (Ed.), *Oxford handbook of moral development.* New York: Oxford University Press.

Harter, S. (1986). Processes underlying the construction, maintenance, and enhancement of the self-concept of children. In J. Suls & A. Greenwald (Eds.), *Psychological perspective on the self* (Vol. 3). Hillsdale, NJ: Erlbaum.

Harter, S. (1989). *Self-perception profile for adolescents.* Denver: University of Denver, Department of Psychology.

Harter, S. (1990a). Processes underlying adolescent self-concept formation. In R. Montemayor, G.R. Adams, & T.P. Gullotta (Eds.), *From childhood to adolescence: A transitional period?* Newbury Park, CA: Sage.

Harter, S. (1990b). Self and identity development. In S.S. Feldman & G.R. Elliott (Eds.), *At the threshold: The developing adolescent.* Cambridge, MA: Harvard University Press.

Harter, S. (1998). The development of self-representations. In W. Damon (Ed.), *Handbook of child psychology* (5th ed., Vol. 3). New York: Wiley.

Harter, S. (1999). *The construction of the self.* New York: Guilford.

Harter, S. (2006). The development of self-representations in childhood and adolescence. In W. Damon & R. Lerner (Eds.), *Handbook of child psychology* (6th ed.). New York: Wiley.

Harter, S. (2012). *The construction of the self* (2nd ed.). New York: Wiley.

Harter, S. (2013). The development of self-esteem. In M.H. Kernis (Ed.), *Self-esteem issues and answers.* New York: Psychology Press.

Harter, S. (2016). Self and me-self processes affecting developmental psychopathology. In D. Cicchetti (Ed.), *Developmental psychopathology* (3rd ed.). New York: Wiley.

Harter, S., & Lee, L. (1989). *Manifestations of true and false selves in adolescence.* Paper presented at the meeting of the Society for Research in Child Development, Kansas City.

Harter, S., & Monsour, A. (1992). Developmental analysis of conflict caused by opposing attributes in the adolescent self-portrait. *Developmental Psychology, 28,* 251-260.

Harter, S., Stocker, C., & Robinson, N.S. (1996). The perceived directionality of the link between approval and self-worth: The liabilities of a looking glass self orientation among young adolescents. *Journal of Research on Adolescence, 6,* 285-308.

Harter, S., Waters, P., & Whitesell, N. (1996, March). *False self behavior and lack of voice among adolescent males and females.* Paper presented at the meeting of the Society for Research on Adolescence, Boston.

Hartman-Munick, S.M., Gordon, A.R., & Guss, C. (2020). Adolescent body image: Influencing factors and the clinician's role. *Current Opinion in Pediatrics, 32,* 455-460.

Hartmann, C.L., & others (2021, in press). Risky sexual behavior among street children, adolescents, and young people living on the street in southern Brazil. *Journal of Community Health.*

Hartshorne, H., & May, M.S. (1928-1930). *Moral studies in the nature of character: Studies in deceit* (Vol. 1); *Studies in self-control* (Vol. 2); *Studies in the organization of character* (Vol. 3). New York: Macmillan.

Hartup, W.W. (1983). The peer system. In P.H. Mussen (Ed.), *Handbook of child psychology* (4th ed., Vol. 4). New York: Wiley.

Hartup, W.W. (1996). The company they keep: Friendships and their developmental significance. *Child Development, 67,* 1-13.

Hascoet, M., Giaconi, V., & Ludivine, J. (2021). Family socioeconomic status and parental expectations affect mathematics achievement in a national sample of Chilean students. *International Journal of Behavioral Development, 45,* 122-132.

Hatano, K., Sugimura, K., & Luyckx, K. (2020). Do identity processes and psychosocial problems intertwine with each other? Testing the directionality of between- and within-person associations. *Journal of Youth and Adolescence, 49,* 467-478.

Hawk, S.T., Becht, A., & Branje, S. (2016). "Snooping" as a distinct parental monitoring strategy: Comparisons with overt solicitation and control. *Journal of Research on Adolescence, 26,* 443-458.

Hawkins, J.A., & Berndt, T.J. (1985, April). *Adjustment following the transition to junior high school.* Paper presented at the biennial meeting of the Society for Research in Child Development, Toronto.

Hawton, K., & others (2020). Clustering of suicides in children and adolescents. *Lancet. Child and Adolescent Health, 4,* 58-67.

Hay, P. (2020). Current approach to eating disorders: A clinical update. *Internal Medicine Journal, 50,* 24-29.

Hayashi, N., & others (2020). Social withdrawal and testosterone levels in early adolescent boys. *Psychoneuroendocrinology, 116,* 104596.

Hayba, N., & others (2020). Effectiveness of lifestyle interventions for prevention of harmful weight gain among adolescents from ethnic minorities: A systematic review. *International Journal of Environmental Research and Public Health, 17*(17), E6059.

Hayek, J., & others (2021). Parenting style as a longitudinal predictor of adolescents' health behaviors in Lebanon. *Health Education Research, 36,* 100-115.

Hayslip, B., Fruhauf, C.A., & Dolbin-MacNab, M.L. (2017). Grandparents raising grandchildren: What have we learned over the past decade? *Gerontologist, 57,* 1196.

Hazan, C., & Shaver, P.R. (1987). Romantic love conceptualized as an attachment process. *Journal of Personality and Social Psychology, 52,* 522-524.

Heath, S.B. (1999). Dimensions of language development: Lessons from older children. In A.S. Masten (Ed.), *Cultural processes in child development: The Minnesota symposium on child psychology* (Vol. 29). Mahwah, NJ: Erlbaum.

Heath, S.B., & McLaughlin, M.W. (Eds.) (1993). *Identity and inner-city youth: Beyond ethnicity and gender.* New York: Teachers College Press.

Hegelund, E.R., & others (2020). The influence of educational attainment on intelligence. *Intelligence, 78,* 101419.

Heilmann, K., & others (2021). (Article in German) The importance of the "big five" personality traits for subjective health and life satisfaction in adolescence: Results of the National Educational Panel Study (NEPS). *Gesundheitswesen, 83,* 8-16.

Heilmayr, D., & Friedman, H.S. (2021). Models of physical health and personality. In P.J. Corr & G. Matthews (Eds.), *Cambridge handbook of personality psychology.* New York: Cambridge University Press.

Heitzler, C.D., Martin, S., Duke, J., & Huhman, M. (2006). Correlates of physical activity in a national sample of children aged 9-13 years. *Preventive Medicine, 42,* 254-260.

Helgeson, V.S. (2020). *The psychology of gender* (6th ed.). New York: Routledge.

Helms, J.E., & Cook, D.A. (1999). *Using race and culture in counseling and psychotherapy.* Boston: Allyn & Bacon.

Helzer, E.G., & Critcher, C.R. (2018). What do we evaluate when we evaluate moral character? In K. Gray & J. Graham (Eds.), *Atlas of moral psychology.* New York: Guilford.

Henderson, L.J., Williams, J.L., & Bradshaw, C.P. (2020). Examining school-home dissonance as a barrier to parental involvement in middle school. *Preventing School Failure, 64,* 201-211.

Henderson, V.L., & Dweck, C.S. (1990). Motivation and achievement. In S.S. Feldman & G.R. Elliott (Eds.), *At the threshold: The developing adolescent.* Cambridge, MA: Harvard University Press.

Henneberger, A., Witzen, H., & Preston, A.M. (2021, in press). A longitudinal study examining dual enrollment as a strategy for easing the transition to college and career for emerging adults. *Emerging Adulthood.*

Hennessey, B.A. (2021). Motivation and creativity. In J.C. Kaufman & R.J. Sternberg (Eds.), *Creativity.* New York: Cambridge University Press.

Henrich, J., & Muthukrishna, M. (2021). The origins and psychology of human cooperation. *Annual Review of Psychology* (Vol. 72). Palo Alto, CA: Annual Reviews.

Henriquez-Henriquez, M., & others (2020). Mutations in sphingolipid metabolism genes are associated with ADHD. *Translational Psychiatry, 10*(1), 231.

Hensel, D.J., & Sorge, B.H. (2014). Adolescent women's daily academic behaviors, sexual behaviors, and sexually related emotions. *Journal of Adolescent Health, 55,* 845-847.

Heppner, M.J., & Heppner, P.P. (2003). Identifying process variables in career counseling: A research agenda. *Journal of Vocational Behavior, 62,* 429-452.

Herdt, G., & Polen-Petit, N. (2021). *Human sexuality* (2nd ed.). New York: McGraw-Hill.

Herle, M., & others (2021, in press). The role of environment in overweight and eating behavior variability: Insights from a multivariate twin study. *Twin Research and Human Genetics.*

Herman-Giddens, M.E. (2007). The decline in the age of menarche in the United States: Should we be concerned? *Journal of Adolescent Health, 40,* 201-203.

Herman-Giddens, M.E., Kaplowitz, P.B., & Wasserman, R. (2004). Navigating the recent articles on girls' puberty in *Pediatrics:* What do we know and where do we go from here? *Pediatrics, 113,* 911-917.

Hernandez, A.E., Fernandez, E.M., & Aznar-Bese, N. (2019). Bilingual sentence processing. In S.A. Rueschemeyer & M. Gereth Gaskell (Eds), *Oxford handbook of psycholinguistics* (2nd ed.). New York: Oxford University Press.

Herold, S.C., & others (2021, in press). Is religiousness associated with better lifestyle and health among Danes? Findings from SHARE. *Journal of Religion and Health.*

Herrera, C., Grossman, J.B., Kauh, T.J., Feldman, A.F., & McMaken, J. (2007). *Making a difference in schools: The Big Brothers Big Sisters school-based mentoring impact study.* Philadelphia, PA: Public/Private Ventures.

Herting, M.M., Colby, J.B., Sowell, E.R., & Nagel, B.J. (2014). White matter connectivity and aerobic fitness in male adolescents. *Developmental Cognitive Neuroscience, 7,* 65-75.

Herzberg, M.P., & Gunnar, M.R. (2020). Early life stress and brain function: Activity and connectivity associated with processing emotion and reward. *NeuroImage, 209,* 116493.

Hetherington, E.M. (1972). Effects of father-absence on personality development in adolescent daughters. *Developmental Psychology, 7,* 313–326.

Hetherington, E.M. (1977). *My heart belongs to daddy: A study of the remarriages of daughters of divorcees and widows.* Unpublished manuscript, University of Virginia.

Hetherington, E.M. (2005). Divorce and the adjustment of children. *Pediatrics in Review, 26,* 163–169.

Hetherington, E.M. (2006). The influence of conflict, marital problem solving, and parenting on children's adjustment in nondivorced, divorced, and remarried families. In A. Clarke-Stewart & J. Dunn (Eds.), *Families count.* New York: Cambridge University Press.

Hetherington, E.M., & Clingempeel, W.G. (1992). Coping with marital transitions: A family systems perspective. *Monographs of the Society for Research in Child Development, 57*(2–3, Serial No. 227).

Hetherington, E.M., Cox, M., & Cox, R. (1982). Effects of divorce on parents and children. In M.E. Lamb (Ed.), *Nontraditional families: Parenting and child development.* Hillsdale, NJ: Erlbaum.

Hetherington, E.M., & Kelly, J. (2002). *For better or for worse: Divorce reconsidered.* New York: Norton.

Hetherington, E.M., & Stanley-Hagan, M. (2002). Parenting in divorced and remarried families. In M. Bornstein (Ed.), *Handbook of parenting* (2nd ed.). Mahwah, NJ: Erlbaum.

Heward, W.L., Alber-Morgan, M.K., & Konrad, M. (2022). *Exceptional children* (12th ed.). Upper Saddle River, NJ: Pearson.

Heyder, A., Weidinger, A.F., & Steinmayr, R. (2021). Only a burden for females in math? Gender and domain differences in the relation between adolescents' fixed mindsets and motivation. *Journal of Youth and Adolescence, 50,* 177–188.

Heyman, G.D., & Legare, C.H. (2005). Children's evaluation of sources of information about traits. *Developmental Psychology, 41,* 636–647.

Hill, J.P., & Lynch, M.E. (1983). The intensification of gender-related role expectations during early adolescence. In J. Brooks-Gunn & A.C. Petersen (Eds.), *Girls at puberty: Biological and psychosocial perspectives.* New York: Plenum.

Hill, P.L., Burrow, A.L., & Bronk, A.C. (2016). Persevering with positivity and purpose: An examination of purpose commitment and positive affect as predictors of grit. *Journal of Happiness Studies, 17,* 257–269.

Hill, P.L., Duggan, P.M., & Lapsley, D.K. (2012). Subjective invulnerability, risk behavior, and adjustment in early adolescence. *Journal of Early Adolescence, 32*(4), 498–501.

Hines, M. (2013). Sex and sex differences. In P.D. Zelazo (Ed.), *Oxford handbook of developmental psychology.* New York: Oxford University Press.

Hines, M. (2015). Gendered development. In R.M. Lerner (Ed.), *Handbook of child psychology and developmental science* (7th ed.). New York: Wiley.

Hines, M. (2020a). Human gender development. *Neuroscience and Biobehavioral Reviews, 118,* 89–96.

Hines, M. (2020b). Neuroscience and sex/gender: Looking back and forward. *Journal of Neuroscience, 40,* 37–43.

Hintsanen, M., & others (2014). Five-factor personality traits and sleep: Evidence from two population-based cohort studies. *Health Psychology, 33,* 1214–1223.

Hirsch, B.J., & Rapkin, B.D. (1987). The transition to junior high school: A longitudinal study of self-esteem, psychological symptomatology, school life, and social support. *Child Development, 58,* 1235–1243.

Hirsch, J.K., Wolford, K., Lalonde, S.M., Brunk, L., & Parker-Morris, A. (2009). Optimistic explanatory style as a moderator of the association between negative life events and suicide ideation. *Crisis, 30,* 48–53.

Hisler, G., Twenge, J.M., & Krizan, Z. (2020). Associations between screen time and short sleep duration among adolescents varies by media type: Evidence from a cohort study. *Sleep Medicine, 66,* 92–102.

Hisler, G.C., & others (2020). Screen media use and sleep disturbance symptom severity in children. *Sleep Health, 6,* 731–742.

Hix-Small, H. (2020). Poverty and child development. In B. Hopkins & others (Eds.), *Cambridge encyclopedia of child development.* New York: Cambridge University Press.

Hoare, J., & others (2020). Accelerated epigenetic aging in adolescents from low-income households is associated with altered development of brain structures. *Metabolic Brain Disease, 35,* 1287–1298.

Hockenberry, S., & Puzzanchera, C. (2019). *Juvenile court statistics 2017.* Pittsburgh: National Center for Juvenile Justice.

Hoeben, E.M., & others (2021). Moderators of friend selection and influence in relation to adolescent alcohol use. *Prevention Science, 22,* 567–578.

Hoefnagels, M. (2021). *Biology* (5th ed.). New York: McGraw-Hill.

Hoelter, L. (2009). Divorce and separation. In D. Carr (Ed.), *Encyclopedia of the life course and human development.* Boston: Gale Cengage.

Hoff, E., Laursen, B., & Tardif, T. (2002). Socioeconomic status and parenting. In M.H. Bornstein (Ed.), *Handbook of parenting* (2nd ed.). Mahwah, NJ: Erlbaum.

Hofferth, S.L., & Moon, U.J. (2016). How do they do it? The immigrant paradox in the transition to adulthood. *Social Science Research, 57,* 177–194.

Hoffman, A.J., Kurtz-Coates, B., & Shaheed, J. (2021). Ethnic-racial identity, gender identity, and well-being in Cherokee early adolescents. *Cultural Diversity and Ethnic Minority Psychology, 27,* 60–71.

Hoffman, J.D., & others (2020). Teaching emotion regulation in schools: Translating research into practice with the RULER approach to social and emotional learning. *Emotion, 20,* 105–109.

Hoffman, M.L. (1970). Moral development. In P.H. Mussen (Ed.), *Manual of child psychology* (3rd ed., Vol. 2). New York: Wiley.

Hoffman, M.L. (1988). Moral development. In M.H. Bornstein & E. Lamb (Eds.), *Developmental psychology: An advanced textbook* (2nd ed.). Hillsdale, NJ: Erlbaum.

Hogan, M., & Strasburger, V. (2020). Twenty questions (and answers) about media violence and cyberbullying. *Pediatric Clinics of North America, 67,* 275–291.

Holdsworth, E.A., & Appleton, A.A. (2020). Adverse childhood experiences and reproductive strategies in a contemporary U.S. population. *American Journal of Physical Anthropology, 171,* 37–49.

Holesh, J.E., Bass, A.N., & Lord, M. (2021). *Physiology, ovulation.* Treasure Island, FL: StatPearls.

Hollenstein, T., & Lanteigne, D.M. (2018). Emotion regulation dynamics in adolescence. In P.M. Cole & T. Hollenstein (Eds.), *Emotion regulation.* New York: Routledge.

Holmes, L.D. (1987). *Quest for the real Samoa: The Mead-Freeman controversy and beyond.* South Hadley, MA: Bergin & Garvey.

Holmes, R.M., Little, K.C., & Welsh, D. (2009). Dating and romantic relationships, adulthood. In D. Carr (Ed.), *Encyclopedia of the life course and human development.* Boston: Gale Cengage.

Holsen, I., Carlson Jones, D., & Skogbrott Birkeland, M. (2012). Body image satisfaction among Norwegian adolescents and young adults: A longitudinal study of interpersonal relationships and BMI. *Body Image, 9,* 201–208.

Holway, G.V., & Hernandez, S.M. (2018). Oral sex and condom use in a US national sample of adolescents and young adults. *Journal of Adolescent Health, 62,* 402–410.

Holzman, L. (2017). *Vygotsky at work and play* (2nd ed.). New York: Routledge.

Hope, E.C., Cryer-Coupet, Q.R., & Stokes, M.N. (2020). Race-related stress, racial identity, and activism among Black men: A person-centered approach. *Developmental Psychology, 56,* 1484–1495.

Hopfer, C., & others (2013). Conduct disorder and initiation of substance use: A prospective longitudinal study. *Journal of the American Academy of Child and Adolescent Psychiatry, 52,* 511–518.

Horowitz, J.M., Graf, N., & Livingston, G. (2019, November 6). *Marriage and cohabitation in the United States.* Washington, DC: Pew Research Center.

Horvath, G., Knopik, V.S., & Marceau, K. (2020). Polygenic influences on pubertal timing and tempo and depressive symptoms in boys and girls. *Journal of Research on Adolescence, 30,* 78–94.

Horvitz, J.H., & Jacobs, B.L. (2022). *Principles of behavioral neuroscience.* New York: Cambridge University Press.

Hosseini, S.A., & Padhy, R.K. (2020). *Body image distortion.* Treasure Island, FL: StatPearls.

Hou, Y., Kim, S.Y., & Wang, Y. (2016). Parental acculturative stressors and adolescent adjustment through interparental and parent-child relationships in Chinese American families. *Journal of Youth and Adolescence, 45,* 1466–1481.

Houser, J.J., Mayeux, L., & Cross, C. (2015). Peer status and aggression as predictors of dating popularity in adolescence. *Journal of Youth and Adolescence, 44*(3), 683–695.

Howard, J.L., Gagne, M., & Bureau, J.S. (2018). Testing a continuum structure of self-determined motivation: A meta-analysis. *Psychological Bulletin, 143.* 1346–1377.

Howe, M.J.A., Davidson, J.W., Moore, D.G., & Sloboda, J.A. (1995). Are there early childhood signs of musical ability? *Psychology of Music, 23,* 162–176.

Howe, W.A. (2010). Unpublished review of J.W. Santrock's *Educational psychology,* 5th ed. New York: McGraw-Hill.

Hoye, J.R., & others (2020). Preliminary investigations that the Attachment and Biobehavioral Catch-up Intervention alters DNA methylation in maltreated children. *Development and Psychopathology, 32,* 1486–1494.

Hoyniak, C.P., & others (2021). Adversity is linked with decreased parent-child behavioral and neural synchrony. *Developmental Cognitive Neuroscience, 48,* 100937.

Hoyt, L.T., & others (2020). Timing of puberty for boys and girls: Implications for population health. *SSM-Population Health, 10,* 100549.

Hu, B. (2021). Is bullying victimization in childhood associated with mental health in old age? *Journals of Gerontology B: Psychological Sciences and Social Sciences, 76,* 161–172.

Hua, L., & others (2016). Four-locus gene interaction between IL13, IL4, FCER1B, and ADRB2 for asthma in Chinese Han children. *Pediatric Pulmonology, 51,* 364–371.

Huang, L.N. (1989). Southeast Asian refugee children and adolescents. In J.T. Gibbs & L.N. Huang (Eds.), *Children of color.* San Francisco: Jossey-Bass.

Huang, Z., & others (2020). Masked hypertension and submaximal exercise blood pressure among adolescents from the Avon Longitudinal Study of Parents and Children (ALSPAC). *Scandinavian Journal of Medicine and Science in Sports, 30,* 25–30.

Hudry, K., & others (2021). Performance of the Autism Observation Scale for infants with community-ascertained infants showing early signs of autism. *Autism, 25,* 490–501.

Huerta, M., Cortina, L.M., Pang, J.S., Torges, C.M., & Magley, V.J. (2006). Sex and power in the academy: Modeling sexual harassment in the lives of college women. *Personality and Social Psychology Bulletin, 32,* 616–628.

Huesmann, L.R. (1986). Psychological processes promoting the relation between exposure to media violence and aggressive behavior by the viewer. *Journal of Social Issues, 42,* 125–139.

Hughes, D., & Smith, G. (2020). *Youth transitions: Creating pathways to success.* ERIC #ED607277.

Hughes, D.L., Fisher, C., & Cabrera, N.J. (2020, July). *Talking to children about racism: Breaking the cycle of bias and violence starts at home.* Retrieved September 10, 2020, from childandfamilyblog.com/child-development/talking-to-children-about-racism/

Hull, J. (2012). A self-awareness model of the causes and effects of alcohol consumption. In K. Vohs & R.F. Baumeister (Eds.), *Self and identity.* Thousand Oaks, CA: Sage.

Hunt, E. (2011). Where are we? Where are we going? Reflections on the current and future state of research on intelligence. In R.J. Sternberg & S.B. Kaufman (Eds.), *Cambridge handbook of intelligence.* New York: Cambridge University Press.

Hunter, S., Leatherdale, S.T., & Carson, V. (2018). The 3-year longitudinal impact of sedentary behavior on the academic achievement of secondary school students. *Journal of School Health, 88,* 660–668.

Huttenlocher, P.R., & Dabholkar, A.S. (1997). Regional differences in synaptogenesis in human cerebral cortex. *Journal of Comparative Neurology, 37,* 167–178.

Hwang, W., & Jung, E. (2021, in press). Helicopter parenting versus autonomy supportive parenting? A latent class analysis of parenting among emerging adults and their psychological and relational well-being. *Emerging Adulthood.*

Hyde, J.S. (2005). The gender similarities hypothesis. *American Psychologist, 60,* 581–592.

Hyde, J.S. (2007). New directions in the study of gender similarities and differences. *Current Directions in Psychological Science, 16,* 259–263.

Hyde, J.S. (2014). Gender similarities and differences. *Annual Review of Psychology* (Vol. 66). Palo Alto, CA: Annual Reviews.

Hyde, J.S. (2016). Sex and cognition: Gender and cognitive functions. *Current Opinion in Neurobiology, 38,* 53–56.

Hyde, J.S. (2017). Gender similarities. In C.B. Travis & J.W. White (Eds.), *APA handbook of the psychology of women.* Washington, DC: American Psychological Association.

Hyde, J.S., & DeLamater, J.D. (2020). *Understanding human sexuality* (14th ed.). New York: McGraw-Hill.

Hyde, J.S., & Else-Quest, N. (2013). *Half the human experience* (8th ed.). Boston: Cengage.

Hyde, J.S., Lindberg, S.M., Linn, M.C., Ellis, A.B., & Williams, C.C. (2008). Gender similarities characterize math performance. *Science, 321,* 494–495.

Hyde, J.S., & others (2019). The future of sex and gender in psychology: Five challenges to the gender binary. *American Psychology, 74,* 171–193.

Hysing, M., & others (2021, in press). Bullying involvement in adolescence: Implications for sleep, mental health, and academic outcomes. *Journal of Interpersonal Violence.*

I

"I Have a Dream" Foundation (2020). *About us.* Retrieved November 10, 2020, from www.ihad.org

Ibanez, L., & de Zegher, F. (2006). Puberty after prenatal growth restraint. *Hormone Research, 65*(Suppl. 3), 112–115.

Ibitoye, M., & others (2017). Early menarche: A systematic review of its effects on sexual and reproductive health in low- and middle-income countries. *PLoS One, 12*(6), e0178884.

Ibrahim, S. (2021). Individualism and the capability approach: The role of collectivities in expanding human capabilities. In E. Chiappero-Martinetti & others (Eds.), *Cambridge handbook of the capability approach.* New York: Cambridge University Press.

Igarashi, H., Hooker, K., Coehlo, D.P., & Maoogian, M.M. (2013). "My nest is full": Intergenerational relationships at midlife. *Journal of Aging Studies, 27,* 102–112.

Igbal, A., & Rehman, A. (2021). *Binge eating disorder.* Treasure Island, FL: StatPearls.

Im, Y., Oh, W.O., & Suk, M. (2017). Risk factors for suicide ideation among adolescents: Five-year national data analysis. *Archives of Psychiatric Nursing, 31,* 282–286.

Infurna, F.J., Gerstorf, D., & Lachman, M.E. (2020). Midlife in the 2020s: Opportunities and challenges. *American Psychologist, 75,* 470–485.

Insel, P., & Roth, W. (2022). *CONNECT Core concepts in health, brief* (17th ed.). New York: McGraw-Hill.

Inzlicht, M., & others (2021). Integrating models of self-regulation. *Annual Review of Psychology* (Vol. 72). Palo Alto, CA: Annual Reviews.

Irwin, C.E., Adams, S.H., Park, M.J., & Newacheck, P.W. (2009). Preventive care for adolescents: Few get visits and fewer get services. *Pediatrics, 123,* e565–e572.

Ismail, F.Y., Ljubisavljevic, M.R., & Johnston, M.V. (2020). A conceptual framework for plasticity in the developing brain. *Handbook of Clinical Neurology, 173,* 57–66.

ISTE (2007). *National educational technology standards for teachers.* Eugene, OR: Author.

ISTE (2016, June). *Redefining learning in a technology-driven world.* Arlington, VA: ISTE.

Itahashi, T., & others (2020). Functional connectomes linking child-parent relationships with psychological problems in adolescence. *NeuroImage, 219,* 117013.

Ito, K.E., & others (2006). Parent opinion of sexuality education in a state with mandated abstinence education: Does policy match parental preference? *Journal of Adolescent Health, 39,* 634–641.

Ivanov, I., & others (2021). Substance use initiation, particularly alcohol, in drug-naïve adolescents: Possible predictors and consequences from a large cohort naturalistic study. *Journal of the American Academy of Child and Adolescent Psychiatry, 60,* 623–636.

J

Jackson, A., & Davis, G. (2000). *Turning points 2000.* New York: Teachers College Press.

Jackson, E.F., Bussey, K., & Myers, E. (2021). Encouraging gender conformity or sanctioning nonconformity? Felt pressure from parents, peers, and the self. *Journal of Youth and Adolescence, 50,* 613–627.

Jackson, M.J., & others (2020). The musculoskeletal health benefits of tennis. *Sports Health, 12,* 80–87.

Jacobs, R.H., & others (2014). Increasing positive outlook partially mediates the effect of empirically supported treatments on depression symptoms among adolescents. *Journal of Cognitive Psychotherapy, 28,* 3–19.

Jacobs, W., & others (2020). Examining the role of weight status and individual attributes on adolescent social relations. *Journal of Adolescent Health, 67,* 108–114.

Jaffe, A.E., & others (2021, in press). A prospective study of predictors and consequences of hooking up for minority women. *Archives of Sexual Behavior.*

Jaffee, S., & Hyde, J.S. (2000). Gender differences in moral orientation: A meta-analysis. *Psychological Bulletin, 126,* 703–726.

Jain, A., & Yilanli, M. (2021). *Bulimia nervosa.* Treasure Island, FL: StatPearls.

Jambon, M., & Smetana, J.G. (2018). Individual differences in prototypical moral and conventional judgments and children's proactive and reactive aggression. *Child Development, 89,* 1343–1359.

Jambon, M., & Smetana, J.G. (2020). Socialization of moral judgments and reasoning. In D.J. Laible & others (Eds.), *Oxford handbook of parenting and moral development.* New York: Oxford University Press.

James, A.G., Fine, M.A., & Turner, L.J. (2012). An empirical examination of youths' perceptions of spirituality as an internal developmental asset during adolescence. *Applied Developmental Science, 16,* 181–194.

James, C., & others (2017). Digital life and youth well-being: Social connectedness, empathy, and narcissism. *Pediatrics, 140*(Suppl. 2), S71–S75.

James, J.E., Kristjansson, A.L., & Sigfusdottir, I.D. (2011). Adolescent substance use, sleep, and academic achievement: Evidence of harm due to caffeine. *Journal of Adolescence, 34,* 665–673.

Jamialahmadi, K., & others (2021). A DNA methylation panel for high-performance detection of colorectal cancer. *Cancer Genetics, 252,* 253–264.

Jamieson, P.E., & Romer, D. (2008). Unrealistic fatalism in U.S. youth ages 14 to 22: Prevalence and characteristics. *Journal of Adolescent Health, 42,* 154–160.

Jarrett, R.L. (1995). Growing up poor: The family experience of socially mobile youth in low-income African-American neighborhoods. *Journal of Adolescent Research, 10,* 111–135.

Jaworska, N., & others (2019). Aerobic exercise in depressed youth: A feasibility and clinical outcomes pilot. *Early Intervention in Psychiatry, 13,* 128–132.

Jayson, S. (2006, June 29). The "millennials" come of age. *USA Today,* pp. 1D–2D.

Jeha, D., Usta, I., Ghulmiyyah, L., & Nassar, A. (2015). A review of the risks and consequences of adolescent pregnancy. *Journal of Neonatal and Perinatal Medicine, 8,* 1–8.

Jelsma, E., & Varner, F. (2021). African American adolescent substance use: The roles of racial discrimination and peer pressure. *Addictive Behaviors, 101,* 106154.

Jensen, L.A. (2020a). Moral development: From paradigms to plurality. In L.A. Jensen, *Oxford handbook of moral development.* New York: Oxford University Press.

Jensen, L.A. (2021, in press). The cultural psychology of religiosity, spirituality, and secularism in adolescence. *Adolescence Research Review.*

Jensen, L.A. (2020b). Development of moral reasoning: From common beginnings to diverse life course pathways. In L.A. Jensen (Ed.), *Oxford handbook of moral development.* New York: Oxford University Press.

Jensen, T.M. (2020). Stepfamily processes and youth adjustment: The role of perceived neighborhood collective efficacy. *Journal of Research on Adolescence, 30*(Suppl. 2), S545–S561.

Jensen, T.M., & Harris, K.M. (2017). A longitudinal analysis of stepfamily relationship quality and adolescent physical health. *Journal of Adolescent Health, 61,* 486–492.

Jensen, T.M., & others (2018). Stepfamily relationship quality and children's internalizing and externalizing problems. *Family Process, 24,* 93–105.

Jenson-Campbell, L.A., & Malcolm, K.T. (2007). The importance of conscientiousness in adolescent interpersonal relationships. *Personality and Social Psychology Bulletin, 33,* 368–383.

Jeon, M., Dimitriou, D., & Halstead, E.J. (2021). A systematic review of cross-cultural comparative studies of sleep in young populations: The roles of cultural factors. *International Journal of Environmental Research and Public Health, 18*(4), 2005.

Jhally, S. (1990). *Dreamworlds: Desire/sex/power in rock video* (Video). Amherst: University of Massachusetts at Amherst, Department of Communications.

Jiang, N., & others (2021). Negative parenting affects adolescent internalizing symptoms through alterations in amygdala-prefrontal circuitry: A longitudinal twin study. *Biological Psychiatry, 89,* 560–569.

Jiang, S., Simpkins, S.D., & Eccles, J.S. (2020). Individuals' math and science motivation and their subsequent STEM choices and achievement in high school and college: A longitudinal study of gender and college generation status differences. *Developmental Psychology, 56,* 2137–2151.

Jiang, X., Chen, X., & Zhuo, Y. (2020). Self-control, external environment, and delinquency: A test of self-control theory in rural China. *International Journal of Offender Therapy and Comparative Criminology, 64,* 1696–1716.

Jimenez, M.G., Montorio, I., & Izal, M. (2017). The association of age, sense of control, optimism, and self-esteem with distress. *Developmental Psychology, 53,* 1398–1403.

Jin, S.V., Ryu, E., & Mugaddam, A. (2019). Romance 2.0 on Instagram: "What type of girlfriend would you date?" *Evolutionary Psychology, 17*(1), 1474704919826845.

Johns Hopkins University (2006a). *Research: Tribal connections.* Retrieved January 31, 2008, from www.krieger.jhu.edu/research/spotlight/prabhakar.html

Johns Hopkins University (2006b, February 17). *Undergraduate honored for launching health programs in India.* Baltimore: Johns Hopkins University News Releases.

Johnson, B.T., Scott-Sheldon, L.A., Huedo-Medina, T.B., & Carey, M.P. (2011). Interventions to reduce sexual risk for human immunodeficiency virus in adolescents: A meta-analysis of trials, 1985–2008. *Archives of Pediatric and Adolescent Medicine, 165,* 177–184.

Johnson, G. (2020). *The living world* (10th ed.). New York: McGraw-Hill.

Johnson, J.S., & Newport, E.L. (1991). Critical period effects on universal properties of language: The status of subjacency in the acquisition of a second language. *Cognition, 39,* 215–258.

Johnson, M.D., & others (2020). Trajectories of relationship confidence in intimate partnerships. *Journal of Family Psychology, 34,* 24–34.

Johnson, M.H., Jones, E., & Gliga, T. (2015). Brain adaptation and alternative developmental trajectories. *Development and Psychopathology, 27,* 425–442.

Johnston, C.A., Cavanagh, S.E., & Crosnoe, R. (2020). Family structure patterns from childhood through adolescence and the timing of cohabitation among diverse groups of young adult women and men. *Developmental Psychology, 58,* 165–179.

Johnston, L.D., & others (2021). *Monitoring the Future: National survey results on drug use, 1975–2020.* Ann Arbor, MI: Institute for Social Research, University of Michigan.

Jonason, P.K. (2017). The grand challenges of evolutionary psychology: Survival challenges for a discipline. *Frontiers in Psychology, 8,* 1727.

Jones, J.M. (2005, October 7). *Gallup Poll: Most Americans approve of interracial dating.* Princeton, NJ: Gallup.

Jones, M.C. (1965). Psychological correlates of somatic development. *Child Development, 36,* 899–911.

Jones, V. (2021). *Comprehensive classroom management* (12th ed.). Upper Saddle River, NJ: Pearson.

Jordan, A.B. (2008). Children's media policy. *The Future of Children, 18*(1), 235–253.

Jordan, J.W., & others (2019). Peer crowd identification and adolescent health behaviors: Results from a statewide representative study. *Health Education and Behavior, 46,* 40–52.

Jorgensen, M.J., & others (2015). Sexual behavior among young Danes aged 15–29 years: A cross-sectional study of core indicators. *Sexually Transmitted Infections, 91,* 171–177.

Jose, A., O'Leary, K.D., & Moyer, A. (2010). Does premarital cohabitation predict subsequent marital stability and marital quality? A meta-analysis. *Journal of Marriage and the Family, 72,* 105–116.

Josephson Institute of Ethics (2012). *2012 Josephson Institute report card on the ethics of American youth.* Los Angeles: Josephson Institute.

Joyner, K., Manning, W., & Prince, B. (2019). The qualities of same-sex and different-sex couples in young adulthood. *Journal of Marriage and the Family, 81,* 487–505.

Juang, L.P., & Umana-Taylor, A.J. (2012). Family conflict among Chinese- and Mexican-origin adolescents and their parents in the U.S.: An introduction. *New Directions in Child and Adolescent Development, 135,* 1–12.

Juang, L.P., & others (2018). Time-varying associations of parent-adolescent cultural conflict and youth adjustment among Chinese American families. *Developmental Psychology, 54,* 938–949.

Judd, M., & others (2020). Cognitive and brain development is independently influenced by socioeconomic status and polygenic scores for educational attainment. *Proceedings of the National Academy of Sciences U.S.A., 117*(22), 12411–12418.

Judice, P.B., & others (2021). Sensor-based physical activity, sedentary time and reported cell phone screen time: A hierarchy of correlates in youth. *Journal of Sport and Health Science, 10,* 55–64.

Junna, L., Moustgaard, H., & Martikainen, P. (2021). Unemployment from stable, downsized, and closed workplaces and alcohol-related mortality. *Addiction, 116,* 74–82.

K

Kagan, J. (2013). Temperamental contributions to inhibited and uninhibited profiles. In P.D. Zelazo (Ed.), *Oxford handbook of developmental psychology.* New York: Oxford University Press.

Kagitcibasi, C. (2007). *Family, self, and human development across cultures.* Mahwah, NJ: Erlbaum.

Kail, R.V. (2007). Longitudinal evidence that increases in processing speed and working memory enhance children's reasoning. *Psychological Science, 18,* 312–313.

Kallschmidt, A., & others (2021). Evaluation of cross-cultural training: A review. In D. Landis & D.P.S. Bhawuk (Eds.), *Cambridge handbook of intercultural training.* New York: Cambridge University Press.

Kamatani, N. (2021). Genes, the brain, and artificial intelligence in evolution. *Journal of Human Genetics, 66,* 103–109.

Kanacri, B.P.L., & others (2021). Longitudinal relations among maternal self-efficacy, maternal warmth, and early adolescents' prosocial behavior. *Parenting Science and Practice, 21,* 24–46.

Kang, M.J., & others (2018). The usefulness of circulating levels of leptin, kisspeptin, and neurokinin B in obese girls with precocious puberty. *Gynecological Endocrinology, 34,* 627–630.

Kang, P.P., & Romo, L.F. (2011). The role of religious involvement on depression, risky behavior, and academic performance among Korean American adolescents. *Journal of Adolescence, 34,* 767–778.

Kann, L., & others (2014). Youth Risk Behavior Surveillance—United States, 2013. *MMWR Surveillance Summaries, 63*(4), 1–168.

Kann, L., & others (2016, August 12). Sexual identity, sex of sexual contacts, and health-related behaviors among students in grades 9–12—United States and selected sites, 2015. *MMWR Surveillance Summaries, 65*(9), 1–202.

Kann, L., & others (2016, June 10). Youth Risk Behavior Surveillance–United States, 2015. *MMWR Surveillance Summaries, 65*(6), 1–174.

Kann, L., & others (2018, June 15). Youth Risk Behavior Surveillance–United States, 2017. *MMWR, 67,* 1–479.

Kanner, A.D., Coyne, J.C., Schaeter, C., & Lazarus, R.S. (1981). Comparisons of two modes of stress measurement: Daily hassles and uplifts versus major life events. *Journal of Behavioral Medicine, 4,* 1–39.

Kantar, L.D., Ezzeddine, S., & Rizk, U. (2020). Rethinking clinical instruction through the zone of proximal development. *Nurse Education Today, 95,* 104595.

Kantor, L.M., & others (2021). Sex education: Broadening the definition of relevant outcomes. *Journal of Adolescent Health, 68,* 7–8.

Kao, T-S, A., Ling, J., & Dalaly, M. (2020). Parent-adolescent dyads' efficacy, coping, depression, and adolescent health risks. *Journal of Pediatric Nursing, 56,* 80–89.

Kapetanovic, S., & others (2020). Cross-cultural examination of links between parent-adolescent communication and adolescent psychological problems in 12 cultural groups. *Journal of Youth and Adolescence, 49,* 1225–1244.

Kaplan, M. (2017). Rape beyond crime. *Duke Law Journal, 66,* 1045–1111.

Kara, B., & Selcuk, B. (2020). Under poverty and conflict: Well-being of children living in the east of Turkey. *American Journal of Orthopsychiatry, 90,* 246–258.

Karchner, H., Schone, C., & Schwinger, M. (2021). Beyond level of self-esteem: Exploring the interplay of level, stability, and contingency of self-esteem, mediating factors, and academic achievement. *Social Psychology of Education, 24,* 319–341.

Karnes, F.A., & Stephens, K.R. (2008). *Achieving excellence: Educating the gifted and talented.* Upper Saddle River, NJ: Prentice Hall.

Karney, B.R. (2021). Socioeconomic status and intimate relationships. *Annual Review of Psychology* (Vol. 72). Palo Alto, CA: Annual Reviews.

Karr, J.E., & others (2021). Sensitivity and specificity on an executive function screener at identifying children with ADHD and reading disability. *Journal of Attention Disorders, 25,* 134–140.

Kastbom, A.A., Sydsjo, G., Bladh, M., Priee, G., & Svedin, C.G. (2015). Sexual debut before the age of 14 leads to poorer psychosocial health and risky behavior later in life. *Acta Paediatrica, 104,* 91–100.

Kastenbaum, S. (2012, October 26). African-American girl blazing a trail through chess. Retrieved March 29, 2018, from http://inamerica.blogs.cnn.com/2012/10/26/african-american-girl-blazing-a-trail-through-chess

Katsiaficas, D. (2017). "I know I'm an adult when . . . I can care for myself and others." *Emerging Adulthood, 5,* 392–405.

Kauchak, D., & Eggen, P. (2021). *Introduction to teaching* (7th ed.). Upper Saddle River, NJ: Pearson.

Kauffman, J.M., McGee, K., & Brigham, M. (2004). Enabling or disabling? Observations on changes in special education. *Phi Delta Kappan, 85,* 613–620.

Kaufman, J.C., & Sternberg, R.J. (Eds.) (2021). *Creativity.* New York: Cambridge University Press.

Kaufman, S.B., & others (2020). Clinical correlates of vulnerable and grandiose narcissism: A personality perspective. *Journal of Personality Disorders, 34,* 107–130.

Kaufman, T.M.L., & others (2020). Caught in a vicious cycle? Explaining bidirectional spillover between parent-child relationships and peer victimization. *Development and Psychopathology, 32,* 11–20.

Kaur, J., & others (2014). Prevalence and correlates of depression among adolescents in Malaysia. *Asia Pacific Journal of Public Health, 26*(5 Suppl.), S53–S62.

Keating, D.P. (1990). Adolescent thinking. In S.S. Feldman & G.R. Elliott (Eds.), *At the threshold: The developing adolescent.* Cambridge, MA: Harvard University Press.

Keating, D.P. (2007). Understanding adolescent development: Implications for driving safety. *Journal of Safety Research, 38,* 147–157.

Keating, D.P. (2009). Developmental science and giftedness: An integrated life-span framework. In F.D. Horowitz, R.F. Subotnik, & D.J. Matthews (Eds.), *The development of giftedness and talent across the life span.* Washington, DC: American Psychological Association.

Keller, T.E., & DuBois, D.L. (2021). Influence of program staff on quality of relationships in a community-based youth mentoring program. *Annals of the New York Academy of Sciences, 1483,* 112–126.

Kellogg, R.T. (1994). *The psychology of writing.* New York: Oxford University Press.

Kelly, A.B., & others (2011). The influence of parents, siblings, and peers on pre- and early-teen smoking: A multilevel model. *Drug and Alcohol Review, 30,* 381–387.

Kelly, Y., & others (2019). Social media use and adolescent mental health: Findings from the UK Millennium Cohort Study. *EClinicalMedicine, 6,* 59–68.

Kelsey, M.M., & others (2020). The impact of obesity on insulin sensitivity and secretion during pubertal progression: A longitudinal study. *Journal of Endocrinology and Metabolism, 105*(5), e2061–e2068.

Keltner, K.W. (2013). *Tiger babies strike back.* New York: William Morrow.

Kempermann, G. (2019). Environmental enrichment, new neurons, and the neurobiology of individuality. *Nature Reviews. Neuroscience, 20,* 235–245.

Kendler, K.S., Ohlsson, H., Sundquist, K., & Sundquist, J. (2013). Within-family environmental transmission of drug abuse: A Swedish national study. *JAMA Psychiatry, 70,* 235–242.

Kendler, K.S., Ohlsson, H., Sundquist, K., & Sundquist, J. (2016). The rearing environment and risk for drug use: A Swedish national high-risk adopted and not adopted co-sibling control study. *Psychological Medicine, 46,* 1359–1366.

Kendler, K.S., & others (2017). Prediction of drug abuse recurrence: A Swedish national study. *Psychological Medicine, 48.*

Kennedy, R.S. (2021, in press). Bullying trends in the United States: A meta-regression. *Trauma, Violence, and Abuse.*

Kenney, E.L., & Gortmaker, S.L. (2017). United States adolescents' television, computer, videogame, smartphone, and tablet use: Associations with sugary drinks, sleep, physical activity, and obesity. *Journal of Pediatrics, 182,* 144–149.

Kerns, K.A., & Brumariu, L.E. (2014). Is insecure parent-child attachment a risk factor for the development of anxiety in childhood or adolescence? *Child Development Perspectives, 8,* 12–17.

Kessler International (2017, February 6). *Survey shows that cheating and academic dishonesty prevalent in colleges and universities.* New York City: Author.

Khairullah, A., & others (2014). Testosterone trajectories and reference ranges in a large longitudinal sample of adolescent males. *PLoS One, 9*(9), e108838.

Khan, F., & others (2020). Development and change in attachment: A multiwave assessment of attachment and its correlates across childhood and adolescence. *Journal of Personality and Social Psychology, 118,* 1188–1206.

Khoury, B., & Hakim-Larson, J. (2021). From refugees to immigrants: The role of psychology in the struggle for human rights. In N.S. Rubin & R.L. Flores (Eds.), *Cambridge handbook of psychology and human rights.* New York: Cambridge University Press.

Kiamanesh, P., Dyregrov, K., Haavind, H., & Dieserud, G. (2014). Suicide and perfectionism: A psychological autopsy study of non-clinical suicides. *Omega, 69,* 381–399.

Kiang, L., Witkow, M.R., & Champagne, M.C. (2013). Normative changes in ethnic and American identities and links with adjustment among Asian American adolescents. *Developmental Psychology, 49,* 1713–1722.

Kiefer, S.M., & Ryan, A.M. (2008). Striving for social dominance over peers: The implications for academic adjustment during early adolescence. *Journal of Educational Psychology, 100,* 417–428.

Kim, B., & others (2021, in press). A systematic review of public housing, poverty, (de)concentration, and risk behaviors; What about youth? *Trauma, Violence, and Abuse.*

Kim, E-M., Kim, H., & Park, E. (2020). How are depression and suicidal ideation associated with multiple health risk behaviors among adolescents? A secondary data analysis using the 2016 Korea Youth Risk Behavior web-based survey. *Journal of Psychiatric and Mental Health Nursing, 27,* 595–606.

Kim, H.M., & Miller, H.C. (2020). Are insecure attachment styles related to risky behavior? A meta-analysis. *Health Psychology, 39,* 48–57.

Kim, J., & Fletcher, J.M. (2018). The influence of classmates on adolescent criminal activities in the United States. *Deviant Behavior, 39,* 275–292.

Kim, J., & others (2020). The effects of a 12-week jump rope exercise program on body composition, insulin sensitivity, and academic self-efficacy in obese adolescent girls. *Journal of Pediatric Endocrinology and Metabolism, 33,* 129–137.

Kim, J.I., & others (2017). Interaction of DRD4 methylation and phthalate metabolites affects continuous performance test performance in ADHD. *Journal of Attention Disorders, 7*(9), e00785.

Kim, J.-Y., McHale, S.M., Crouter, A.C., & Osgood, D.W. (2007). Longitudinal linkages between sibling relationships and adjustment from middle childhood through adolescence. *Developmental Psychology, 43,* 960–973.

Kim, K., & others (2020). Typology of parent-child ties within families: Associations with psychological well-being. *Journal of Family Psychology, 34,* 448–458.

Kim, K.H. (2010, July 10). Interview. In P. Bronson & A. Merryman. The creativity crisis. *Newsweek,* 42–48.

Kim, K.M. (2021). What makes adolescents psychologically distressed? Life events as risk factors for depression and suicide. *European Child and Adolescent Psychiatry, 30,* 359–367.

Kim, K.W., & others (2019). Associations of parental general monitoring with adolescent weight-related behaviors and weight status. *Obesity, 27,* 280–287.

Kim, L., & others (2020). Hospitalization rates and characteristics of children aged, 18 years hospitalized with laboratory confirmed COVID-19—COVID-Net, 14 states, March 1–July 25, 2020. *MMWR: Morbidity and Mortality Weekly Report, 69*(32), 1081–1088.

Kim, M.J., Catalano, R.F., Haggerty, K.P., & Abbott, R.D. (2011). Bullying at elementary school and problem behavior in young adulthood: A study of bullying, violence, and substance use from age 11 to age 21. *Criminal Behavior and Mental Health, 21,* 36–44.

Kim, S-H., Lee, N., & King, P.E. (2021, in press). Dimensions of religion and spirituality: A longitudinal modeling approach. *Journal of the Scientific Study of Religion.*

Kim, S.Y., Wang, Y., Orozco-Lapray, D., Shen, Y., & Murtuza, M. (2013). Does "tiger parenting" exist? Parenting profiles of Chinese Americans and adolescent developmental outcomes. *Asian American Journal of Psychology, 4,* 7–18.

Kim, S.Y., & others (2013). Longitudinal linkages among parent-child acculturation discrepancy, parenting, parent-child sense of alienation, and adolescent adjustment in Chinese American families. *Developmental Psychology, 49,* 900–912.

Kim, S.Y., & others (2015). Parent-child acculturation profiles as predictors of Chinese American adolescents' academic trajectories. *Journal of Youth and Adolescence, 44,* 1263–1274.

Kim, Y-R., Nakai, Y., & Thomas, J.J. (2021). Introduction to a special issue on eating disorders in Asia. *International Journal of Eating Disorders, 54,* 3–6.

Kimble, M., Neacsiu, A.D., Flack, W.F., & Horner, J. (2008). Risk of unwanted sex for college women: Evidence for a red zone. *Journal of American College Health, 57,* 331–338.

Kim-Prieto, C., Heye, M., & Mangino, K. (2020). Happiness across cultures and genders: Universals, variations, and remaining questions. In F.M. Cheung & D.F. Halpern (Eds.), *Cambridge handbook of the international psychology of women.* New York: Cambridge University Press.

King, H., & others (2021). Peer modeling interventions. In T.A. Collins & R.O. Hawkins (Eds.), *Peers as change agents.* New York: Oxford University Press.

King, L.A. (2020). *The science of psychology: An appreciative view* (5th ed.). New York: McGraw-Hill.

King, L.A. (2022, in press). *Experience psychology* (5th ed.). New York: McGraw-Hill.

King, L.C., & others (2020). Associations of waking cortisol with DHEA and testosterone across the pubertal transition: Effects of threat-related early life stress. *Psychoneuroendocrinology, 115,* 104651.

King, P.E., & Boyatzis, C.J. (2015). The nature and function of religious and spiritual development in childhood and adolescence. In R.M. Lerner (Ed.), *Handbook of child psychology and developmental science* (7th ed.). New York: Wiley.

King, P.E., Ramos, J.S., & Clardy, C.E. (2013). Searching for the sacred: Religious and spiritual development among adolescents. In K.I. Pargament, J. Exline, & J. Jones (Eds.), *APA handbook of psychology, religion, and spirituality.* Washington, DC: American Psychological Association.

King, P.E., Schnitker, S.A., & Houltberg, B. (2020). Religion as fertile ground: Religious groups and institutions as a context for moral development. In L. Jensen (Ed.), *Handbook of moral development.* New York: Oxford University.

King, P.E., Vaughn, J.M., & Merola, C. (2020). Spirituality and adolescent development. In S. Hupp & J. Jewell (Eds.), *Encyclopedia of child and adolescent development.* New York: Wiley.

King, P.E., & others (2021, in press). Exploring ecological assets and personal strengths among Salvadoran youth: The complex relation between religiousness and hope. *Religions.*

King, R.B. (2020). Mindsets are contagious: The social contagion of implicit theories of intelligence among classmates. *British Journal of Educational Psychology, 90,* 349–363.

Kingsbury, M., & others (2020). Pathways from parenting practices to adolescent suicidality: Evidence on the role of emotional and behavioral symptoms from a prospective cohort of Canadian children. *Suicide and Life-Threatening Behavior, 60,* 1149–1157.

Kingsley, M.C., & others (2020). Specific patterns of H3K79 methylation influence genetic interaction of oncogenes in AML. *Blood Advances, 4*(13), 3109–3122.

Kins, E., & Beyers, W. (2010). Failure to launch, failure to achieve criteria for adulthood? *Journal of Adolescent Research, 25,* 743–777.

Kinsler, J.J., & others (2018). A content analysis of how sexual behavior and reproductive health are being portrayed on primetime television shows being watched by teens and young adults. *Health Communication, 34,* 644–651.

Kirkman, M., Rosenthal, D.A., & Feldman, S.S. (2002). Talking to a tiger: Fathers reveal their difficulties in communicating about sexuality with adolescents. In S.S. Feldman & D.A. Rosenthal (Eds.), *Talking sexuality: Parent-adolescent communication.* San Francisco: Jossey-Bass.

Kirmayer, L.J., & others (Eds.) (2021). *Culture, mind, and brain.* New York: Cambridge University Press.

Kistler, M., Rodgers, B., Power, T., Austin, E.W., & Hill, L.G. (2010). Adolescents and music media: Toward an involvement-mediational model of consumption and self-concept. *Journal of Research on Adolescence, 20,* 616-630.

Kito, M. (2005). Self-disclosure in romantic relationships and friendships among American and Japanese college students. *Journal of Social Psychology, 145,* 127-140.

Kiuhara, S.A., Graham, S., & Hawken, L.S. (2009). Teaching writing to high school students: A national survey. *Journal of Educational Psychology, 101,* 136-160.

Kiuru, N., & others (2020). Associations between adolescents' interpersonal relationships, school well-being, and academic achievement during educational transitions. *Journal of Youth and Adolescence, 49,* 1057-1072.

Kivnik, H.Q., & Sinclair, H.M. (2007). Grandparenthood. In J.E. Birren (Ed.), *Encyclopedia of gerontology* (2nd ed.). San Diego: Academic Press.

Klaczynski, P.A., Byrnes, J.P., & Jacobs, J.E. (2001). Introduction to the special issue: The development of decision making. *Applied Developmental Psychology, 22,* 225-236.

Klaczynski, P.A., Felmban, W.S., & Kole, J. (2020). Gender intensification and gender generalization biases in pre-adolescents, adolescents, and emerging adults. *British Journal of Developmental Psychology, 38,* 415-433.

Klaczynski, P.A., & Narasimham, G. (1998). Development of scientific reasoning biases: Cognitive versus ego-protective explanations. *Developmental Psychology, 34,* 175-187.

Klein, D.A., Sylvester, J.E., & Schvey, N.A. (2021). Eating disorders in primary care: Diagnosis and management. *American Family Physician, 103,* 22-32.

Klein, L.B., & Martin, S.L. (2019). Sexual harassment of college and university students: A systematic review. *Trauma, Violence, and Abuse, 21,* 1524838019881731.

Klein, S. (2012). *State of public school segregation in the United States, 2007-2010.* Washington, DC: Feminist Majority Foundation.

Klettke, B., & others (2019). Sexting and psychological distress: The role of unwanted and coerced sexts. *Cyberpsychology, Behavior, and Social Networking, 22,* 237-242.

Klimstra, T.A., Luyckx, K., Germeijs, V., Meeus, W.H., & Goossens, L. (2012). Personality traits and educational identity formation in late adolescents: Longitudinal associations and academic progress. *Journal of Youth and Adolescence, 41,* 346-361.

Klimstra, T.A., & others (2017). Daily dynamics of adolescent mood and identity. *Journal of Research on Adolescence, 28,* 459-473.

Klinenberg, E. (2013). *Going solo: The extraordinary rise and surprising appeal of living alone.* New York: Penguin.

Kloss, J.D., & others (2016). A "Sleep 101" program for college students improves sleep hygiene knowledge and reduces maladaptive beliefs about sleep. *Behavioral Medicine, 42,* 48-56.

Knight, G.P., & others (2016). The socialization of culturally related values and prosocial tendencies among Mexican-American adolescents. *Child Development, 87,* 1758-1771.

Knox, D., & Wilson, K. (1981). Dating behaviors of university students. *Family Relations, 30,* 255-258.

Ko, A., & others (2020). Family matters: Rethinking the psychology of human social motivation. *Perspectives on Psychological Science, 15,* 173-201.

Kocevska, D., & others (2021). Sleep characteristics across the lifespan in 1.1 million people from the Netherlands, United Kingdom, and United States: A systematic review and meta-analysis. *Nature. Human Behavior, 5,* 113-122.

Kochanska, G., Barry, R.A., Stellern, S.A., & O'Bleness, J.J. (2010a). Early attachment organization moderates the parent-child mutually coercive pathway to children's antisocial conduct. *Child Development, 80,* 1288-1300.

Kochanska, G., & Kim, S. (2020). Children's early difficulty and agreeableness in adolescence: Testing a developmental model of interplay of parent and child effects. *Developmental Psychology, 56,* 1556-1564.

Kochanska, G., Woodard, J., Iim, S., Koenig, J.L., Yoon, J.E., & Barry, R.A. (2010b). Positive socialization mechanisms in secure and insecure parent-child dyads: Two longitudinal studies. *Journal of Child Psychology and Psychiatry, 51,* 998-1009.

Kochendorfer, L.B., & Kerns, K.A. (2017). Perceptions of parent-child attachment relationships and friendship qualities: Predictors of romantic relationship involvement and quality in adolescence. *Journal of Youth and Adolescence, 46,* 1009-1021.

Kochendorfer, L.B., & Kerns, K.A. (2020). A meta-analysis of friendship qualities and romantic relationship outcomes in adolescence. *Journal of Research on Adolescence, 30*(1), 4-25.

Koenig, L.B., McGue, M., & Iacono, W.G. (2008). Stability and change in religiousness during emerging adulthood. *Developmental Psychology, 44,* 523-543.

Koenig, L.R., & others (2020). Associations between agency and sexual and reproductive health communication in early adolescence: A cross-cultural, cross-sectional study. *Journal of Adolescent Health, 67,* 416-424.

Kofler, M.J., & others (2020). Working memory and information processing in ADHD: Evidence for directionality of effects. *Neuropsychology, 34,* 127-143.

Kohlberg, L. (1958). *The development of modes of moral thinking and choice in the years 10 to 16.* Unpublished doctoral dissertation, University of Chicago.

Kohlberg, L. (1969). Stage and sequence: The cognitive-developmental approach to socialization. In D.A. Goslin (Ed.), *Handbook of socialization theory and research.* Chicago: Rand McNally.

Kohlberg, L. (1976). Moral stages and moralization: The cognitive developmental approach. In T. Lickona (Ed.), *Moral development and behavior.* New York: Holt, Rinehart, & Winston.

Kohlberg, L. (1986). A current statement on some theoretical issues. In S. Modgil & C. Modgil (Eds.), *Lawrence Kohlberg.* Philadelphia: Falmer.

Kohn, M.L. (1977). *Class and conformity: A study in values* (2nd ed.). Chicago: University of Chicago Press.

Kok, F.M., Groen, Y., Fuermaler, A.B., & Tucha, O. (2016). Problematic peer functioning in girls with ADHD: A systematic literature review. *PLoS One, 11,* e0165118.

Kokka, I., & others (2021). Exploring the effects of problematic internet use on adolescent sleep: A systematic review. *International Journal of Environmental Research and Public Health, 18*(2), 760.

Kokkonen, P., & others (2021). Secondary school pupils' mental wellbeing is associated with belonging to a perceived minority and experiencing discrimination. *Children, 8*(2), 71.

Kolb, L. (2020). *Learning first, technology second.* Portland, OR: ISTE.

Kong, F., & others (2020). Why do people with self-control forgive others easily? The role of rumination and anger. *Frontiers in Psychology, 11,* 129.

Koopman-Verhoeff, M.E., & others (2020). Genome-wide DNA methylation patterns associated with sleep and mental health in children: A population-based study. *Journal of Child Psychology and Psychiatry, 61,* 1061-1069.

Koops, T., Dekker, A., & Briken, P. (2018). Online sexual activity involving webcams-an overview of existing literature and implications for sexual boundary violations of children and adolescents. *Behavioral Sciences and the Law, 36,* 182-197.

Koppelman, K.L. (2020). *Understanding human differences* (6th ed.). Upper Saddle River, NJ: Pearson.

Kopystynska, O., Barnett, M.A., & Curran, M. (2020). Constructive and destructive interparental conflict, parenting, and coparenting alliance. *Journal of Family Psychology, 34,* 414-424.

Kornblum, J. (2006, March 9). How to monitor the kids? *USA Today,* p. 1D.

Kornhaber, M.L. (2020). The theory of multiple intelligences. In R.J. Sternberg (Ed.), *Cambridge handbook of intelligence* (2nd ed.). New York: Cambridge University Press.

Kornienko, O., Ha, T., & Dishion, T.J. (2020). Dynamic pathways between rejection and antisocial behavior in peer networks: Update and test of confluence model. *Development and Psychopathology, 32,* 175-188.

Korous, K.M., & others (2021, in press). A systematic overview of meta-analyses on socioeconomic status, cognitive ability, and achievement: The need to focus on specific pathways. *Psychological Reports.*

Korucuoglu, O., & others (2020). Adolescent decision-making under risk: Neural correlates and sex differences. *Cerebral Cortex, 30,* 2690-2706.

Koss, M.P., & others (2021). Sexual assault. In F.M. Cheung & D.F. Halpern (Eds.), *Cambridge handbook of the international psychology of women.* New York: Cambridge University Press.

Kostel Bal, S., & others (2020). Rheumatological manifestations in inborn errors of immunity. *Pediatric Research, 87,* 293-299.

Kota, A.S., & Ejaz, J. (2020). *Precocious puberty.* Treasure Island, FL: StatPearls.

Kouremenou, I., Piper, M., & Zalucki, O. (2020). Adult neurogenesis in the olfactory system: Improving performance for discrimination tasks? *Bioessays, 42*(10), e2000065.

Kouros, C.D., Morris, M.C., & Garber, J. (2016). Within-person changes in individual symptoms of depression predict subsequent depressive episodes in adolescents: A prospective study. *Journal of Abnormal Child Psychology, 44,* 483-494.

Kovanagi, A., & others (2019). Bullying victimization and suicide attempt among adolescents aged 12-15 years from 48 countries. *Journal of the American Academy of Child and Adolescent Psychiatry, 58,* 907-918.

Kozol, J. (2005). *The shame of the nation.* New York: Crown.

Kramer, E., & others (2020). Diagnostic associations of processing speed in a transdiagnostic, pediatric sample. *Scientific Reports, 10*(1), 10114.

Kramer, L., & others (2019). Siblings. In B.H. Friese (Ed.), *APA handbook of contemporary family psychology.* Washington, DC: APA Books.

Kramer, M.D., & Rodgers, J.L. (2020). The impact of having children on domain-specific life-satisfaction: A quasi-experimental longitudinal investigation using the Socio-Economic Panel (SOEP) data. *Journal of Personality and Social Psychology, 119,* 1497-1514.

Krauss, S., Orth, U., & Robins, R.W. (2020). Family environment and self-esteem development: A longitudinal study from 10 to 16. *Journal of Personality and Social Psychology, 119,* 457-478.

Kremer-Sadlik, T., & others (2015). Eating fruits and vegetables: An ethnographic study of American and French family dinners. *Appetite, 89,* 84-92.

Krettenauer, T. (2021). Moral sciences and the role of education. *Journal of Moral Education, 50*, 77–91.

Krisnana, I., & others (2021, in press). Adolescent characteristics and parenting style as the determinant of bullying in Indonesia: A cross-sectional study. *International Journal of Adolescent Medicine and Health.*

Kroger, J. (2015). Identity development through adulthood: The move toward "wholeness." In K.C. McLean & M. Syed (Eds.), *Oxford handbook of identity development.* New York: Oxford University Press.

Kroger, J., & Marcia, J.E. (2021). Erikson, the identity statuses and beyond. In M. Bamberg & others (Eds.), *Cambridge handbook of identity.* New York: Cambridge University Press.

Kroger, J., Martinussen, M., & Marcia, J.E. (2010). Identity change during adolescence and young adulthood: A meta-analysis. *Journal of Adolescence, 33*, 683–698.

Kross, E.U., & others (2021). Social media and well-being: Pitfalls, progress, and next steps. *Trends in Cognitive Science, 25*, 55–66.

Kua, J., & others (2021). A scoping review of adaptive expertise in education. *Medical Teacher, 43*, 347–355.

Kuhn, D. (2009). Adolescent thinking. In R.M. Lerner & L. Steinberg (Eds.), *Handbook of adolescent psychology* (3rd ed.). New York: Wiley.

Kuhn, D. (2013). Reasoning. In P.D. Zelazo (Ed.), *Oxford handbook of developmental psychology.* New York: Oxford University Press.

Kuhn, D., & Franklin, S. (2006). The second decade: What develops (and how)? In W. Damon & R. Lerner (Eds.), *Handbook of child psychology* (6th ed.). New York: Wiley.

Kuiper, J., Broer, J., & van der Wouden, J.C. (2018). Association between physical exercise and psychosocial problems in 96,617 Dutch adolescents in secondary education: A cross-sectional study. *European Journal of Public Health, 28*, 468–473.

Kulich, S.J., & others (2021). Interdisciplinary history of intercultural communication studies: From roots to research and praxis. In D. Landis & D.P.S. Bhawuk (Eds.), *Cambridge handbook of intercultural training.* New York: Cambridge University Press.

Kulu, H. (2014). Marriage duration and divorce: The seven-year itch or a lifelong itch? *Demography, 51*(3), 881–893.

Kundu, S., & Risk, B.B. (2021, in press). Scalable Bayesian matrix normal graphic models for brain functional networks. *Biometrics.*

Kunzweiler, C. (2007). Twin individuality. *Fresh Ink: Essays from Boston College's First-Year Writing Seminar, 9*(1), 2–3.

Kuo, B.C.H. (2021). Multicultural counseling training and intercultural training: A synthesis. In D. Landis & D.P.S. Bhawuk (Eds.), *Cambridge handbook of intercultural training.* New York: Cambridge University Press.

Kuo, L.J., & Anderson, R.C. (2012). Effects of early bilingualism on learning phonological regularities in a new language. *Journal of Experimental Child Psychology, 111*, 455–467.

Kuperberg, A. (2014). Age at coresidence, premarital cohabitation, and marriage dissolution: 1985–2009. *Journal of Marriage and Family, 76*, 352–369.

Kuperminc, G.P., & others (2020). The role of school-based group mentoring in promoting resilience among vulnerable high school students. *American Journal of Community Psychology, 65*, 136–148.

Kwan, K.M.W., & others (2021). Children's appraisals of gender nonconformity: Developmental pattern and intervention. *Child Development, 91*, e780–e788.

Kwon, M., & others (2021, in press). Association between substance use and insufficient sleep in U.S. high school students. *Journal of School Nursing.*

Kwon, S-J., & others (2021). Neural correlates of conflicting social influence on adolescent risk-taking. *Journal of Research on Adolescence, 31*, 139–152.

L

LaBelle, S. (2020). Addressing student precarities in higher education: Our responsibility as teachers and scholars. *Communication Education, 69*, 267–276.

Labouvie-Vief, G. (1986, August). *Modes of knowing and life-span cognition.* Paper presented at the meeting of the American Psychological Association, Washington, DC.

Labouvie-Vief, G. (2006). Emerging structures of adult thought. In J.J. Arnett & J.L. Tanner (Eds.), *Emerging adults in America.* Washington, DC: American Psychological Association.

Labouvie-Vief, G. (2009). Cognition and equilibrium regulation in development and aging. In V. Bengtson & others (Eds.), *Handbook of theories of aging.* New York: Springer.

Labouvie-Vief, G., Gruhn, D., & Studer, J. (2010). Dynamic integration of emotion and cognition: Equilibrium regulation in development and aging. In M.E. Lamb, A. Freund, & R.M. Lerner (Eds.), *Handbook of life-span development* (Vol. 2). New York: Wiley.

Ladd, G.W., Kochenderfer-Ladd, B., & Rydell, A-M. (2011). Children's interpersonal skills and school-based relationships. In P.K. Smith & C.H. Hart (Eds.), *Wiley-Blackwell handbook of social development* (2nd ed.). New York: Wiley.

Laflin, M.T., Wang, J., & Barry, M. (2008). A longitudinal study of adolescent transition from virgin to nonvirgin status. *Journal of Adolescent Health, 42*, 228–236.

LaFrance, M., Hecht, M.A., & Paluck, E.L. (2003). The contingent smile: A meta-analysis of sex differences in smiling. *Psychological Bulletin, 129*, 305–334.

Lagus, K.A., Bernat, D.H., Bearinger, L.H., Resnick, M.D., & Eisenberg, M.E. (2011). Parental perspectives on sources of sex information for young people. *Journal of Adolescent Health, 49*(1), 87–89.

Lai, C. S-Y., & Hui, P. Chi-L. (2021). Service-learning: Impacts of learning motivation and learning experience on extended social/civic engagement. *Higher Education Research and Development, 40*, 400–415.

Laible, D.J., Carlo, G., & Padilla-Walker, L.M. (Eds.) (2020). *Oxford handbook of parenting and moral development.* New York: Oxford University Press.

Lam, C.B., McHale, S.M., & Crouter, A.C. (2012). Parent-child shared time from middle childhood to adolescence: Developmental course and adjustment correlates. *Child Development, 83*, 2089–2103.

Lambez, B., & others (2020). Non-pharmacological interventions for cognitive difficulties in ADHD: A systematic review and meta-analysis. *Journal of Psychiatry Research, 120*, 40–55.

Lamela, D., & Figueiredo, B. (2016). Coparenting after marital dissolution and children's mental health: A systematic review. *Jornal de Pediatria (Rio), 92*, 331–342.

Landis, D., & Bhawuk, D.P.S. (Eds.) (2021). *Cambridge handbook of intercultural training.* New York: Cambridge University Press.

Lang, C. (2021). Extracurricular activities can play a central role in K–12 education. *Phi Delta Kappan, 102*(8), 14–19.

Langer, E.J. (2005). *On becoming an artist.* New York: Ballantine.

Langstrom, N., Rahman, Q., Carlstrom, E., & Lichtenstein, P. (2010). Genetic and environmental effects on same-sex behavior: A population study of twins in Sweden. *Archives of Sexual Behavior, 39*, 75–80.

Lansford, J.E. (2019). Single- and two-parent families. In J. Hattie & E. Anderman (Eds.), *International handbook of student achievement.* New York: Routledge.

Lansford, J.E. (2020). Parental discipline practices associated with preventing children's aggressive and immoral behavior. In D.J. Laible & others (Eds.), *Oxford handbook of parenting and moral development.* New York: Oxford University Press.

Lansford, J.E., & others (2010). Developmental precursors of number of sexual partners from ages 16 to 22. *Journal of Research on Adolescence, 20*, 651–677.

Lantagne, A., & Furman, W. (2017). Romantic relationship development: The interplay between age and relationship length. *Developmental Psychology, 53*, 1738–1749.

Lantagne, A., Furman, W., & Novak, J. (2017). "Stay or leave": Predictors of relationship dissolution in emerging adulthood. *Emerging Adulthood, 5*, 241–250.

Lapato, D.M., & others (2021). A primer on DNA methylation and its potential to impact maternal depression risk and assessment during pregnancy and the postpartum. *Journal of Perinatal and Neonatal Nursing, 35*, 4–7.

Lapsley, D. (2020). Moral formation of the family: A research agenda in time future. In D. Laible, G. Carlo, & L. Padilla-Walker (Eds.), *Oxford handbook of parenting and moral development.* New York: Oxford University Press.

Lapsley, D., LaPorte, E., & Kelley, K. (2022, in press). Moral cognition in adolescence and emerging adulthood. In L. Crockett & others (Eds.), *APA handbook of adolescent and young adult development.* Washington, DC: APA Press.

Lapsley, D., Reilly, T., & Narváez, D. (2020). Moral self-identity and character development. In L.A. Jensen (Ed.), *Oxford handbook of moral development.* New York: Oxford University Press.

Lapsley, D.K. (1990). Continuity and discontinuity in adolescent social cognitive development. In R. Montemayor, G. Adams, & T. Gulotta (Eds.), *From childhood to adolescence: A transitional period?* Newbury Park, CA: Sage.

Lapsley, D.K., Enright, R.D., & Serlin, R.C. (1985). Toward a theoretical perspective on the legislation of adolescence. *Journal of Early Adolescence, 5*, 441–466.

Lapsley, D.K., Rice, K.G., & Shadid, G.E. (1989). Psychological separation and adjustment to college. *Journal of Counseling Psychology, 36*, 286–294.

Lapsley, D.K., & Stey, P.C. (2012). Adolescent narcissism. In R. Levesque (Ed.), *Encyclopedia of adolescence.* New York: Springer.

Larabee, C.M., Neely, O.C., & Domingos, A.I. (2020). Obesity: A neuroimmunometabolic perspective. *Nature Reviews. Endocrinology, 16*, 30–43.

Lardone, M.C., & others (2020). A polygenic risk score suggests shared genetic architecture of voice break with early markers of pubertal onset in boys. *Journal of Clinical Endocrinology and Metabolism, 105*(3), dgaa003.

Larose, S., & others (2018). How mentor support interacts with mother and teacher support in predicting youth academic adjustment: An investigation among youth exposed to Big Brothers Big Sisters of Canada programs. *Journal of Primary Prevention, 39*, 205–228.

Larsen, B., & others (2020). Maturation of the human striatal dopamine system revealed by PET and quantitative MRI. *Nature Communications, 11*(1), 846.

Larson, N.I., & others (2008). Fast food intake: Longitudinal trends during the transition to young adulthood and correlates of intake. *Journal of Adolescent Health, 43*, 79–86.

Larson, R.W. (1999, September). Unpublished review of J.W. Santrock's *Adolescence*, 8th ed. (New York: McGraw-Hill).

Larson, R.W. (2000). Toward a psychology of positive youth development. *American Psychologist, 55*, 170–183.

Larson, R.W. (2001). How U.S. children and adolescents spend time: What it does (and doesn't) tell us about their development. *Current Directions in Psychological Science, 10*, 160–164.

Larson, R.W. (2008). Development of the capacity for teamwork in youth development. In R.K. Silbereisen & R.M. Lerner (Eds.), *Approaches to positive youth development.* Thousand Oaks, CA: Sage.

Larson, R.W. (2014). Studying experience: Pursuing the "something more." In R.M. Lerner & others (Eds.), *The developmental science of adolescence: History through autobiography.* New York: Springer.

Larson, R.W. (2020). Discovering the possible: How youth programs provide apprenticeships in purpose. In A.L. Burrow & P.L. Hill (Eds.), *The ecology of purposeful living across the lifespan.* New York: Springer.

Larson, R.W., & Lampman-Petraitis, C. (1989). Daily emotional states as reported by children and adolescents. *Child Development, 60,* 1250–1260.

Larson, R.W., & Richards, M.H. (1994). *Divergent realities.* New York: Basic Books.

Larson, R.W., & Verma, S. (1999). How children and adolescents spend time across the world: Work, play, and developmental opportunities. *Psychological Bulletin, 125,* 701–736.

Larson, R.W., Walker, K.C., & McGovern, G. (2020). Youth programs as contexts for development of moral agency. In L.A. Jensen (Ed.), *Handbook of moral development: An interdisciplinary perspective.* New York: Oxford University Press.

Larson, R.W., Wilson, S., & Rickman, A. (2009). Globalization, societal change, and adolescence across the world. In R.M. Lerner & L. Steinberg (Eds.), *Handbook of adolescent psychology* (3rd ed.). New York: Wiley.

Larsson, K.H., & others (2020). Emotion regulation group skills training for adolescents and parents: A pilot study of an add-on treatment in a clinical setting. *Clinical Child and Adolescent Psychiatry, 25,* 141–155.

LaSpada N., & others (2020). Risk taking, sensation seeking, and personality as related to changes in substance use from adolescence to young adulthood. *Journal of Adolescence, 82,* 23–31.

Lau, E.Y., & others (2017). Sleep and optimism: A longitudinal study of bidirectional causal relationship and its mediating and moderating variables in a Chinese student sample. *Chronobiology International, 34,* 360–372.

Laube, C., Lorenz, R., & van den Bos, W. (2020). Pubertal testosterone correlates with impatience and dorsal striatal activity. *Developmental Cognitive Neuroscience, 42,* 100749.

Lauermann, F., Tsai, Y.M., & Eccles, J.S. (2017). Math-related career aspirations and choices within Eccles et al.'s expectancy-value theory of achievement-related behaviors. *Developmental Psychology, 53,* 1540–1549.

Laursen, B., Coy, K.C., & Collins, W.A. (1998). Reconsidering changes in parent-child conflict across adolescence: A meta-analysis. *Child Development, 69,* 817–832.

Laursen, B., & others (2017). The spread of substance use and delinquency between adolescent twins. *Developmental Psychology, 53,* 329–339.

Laursen, B., & others (2020). Being fun: An overlooked indicator of childhood social status. *Journal of Personality, 88,* 993–1006.

Lavner, J.A., & Bradbury, T.N. (2013). Newlyweds' optimistic forecasts of their marriage: For better or for worse? *Journal of Family Psychology, 27,* 531–540.

LaVoie, J. (1976). Ego identity formation in middle adolescence. *Journal of Youth and Adolescence, 5,* 371–385.

Lavy, S., & Benish-Weisman, M. (2021). Character strengths as "values in action": Linking character strengths with values theory–an exploratory study of the case of gratitude and self-transcendence. *Frontiers in Psychology, 12,* 576189.

Lawson, K.M., & others (2014). Daily positive spillover and crossover from mothers' work to youth health. *Journal of Family Psychology, 28,* 897–907.

Lawson, K.M., & others (2021, in press). The role of temperament in the onset of suicidal ideation and behaviors across adolescence: Findings from 10-year longitudinal study of Mexican-origin youth. *Journal of Personality and Social Psychology.*

Lazarus, R.S. (2000). Toward better research on stress and coping. *American Psychologist, 55*(6), 665–673.

Leadbeater, B.J., Way, N., & Raden, A. (1994, February). *Barriers to involvement of father of the children of adolescent mothers.* Paper presented at the meeting of the Society for Research on Adolescence, San Diego.

Leaper, C. (2015). Gender development from a social-cognitive perspective. In R.M. Lerner (Ed.), *Handbook of child psychology and developmental science* (7th ed.). New York: Wiley.

Leaper, C., & Brown, C.S. (2008). Perceived experience of sexism among adolescent girls. *Child Development, 79,* 685–704.

Lebel, C., & Deoni, S. (2018). The development of brain white matter microstructure. *NeuroImage, 182,* 207–218.

Ledesma, K. (2012). A place to call home. *Adoptive Families.* Retrieved August 8, 2012, from www.adoptivefamilies.com/articles.php?aid52129.

Lee, C-Y. S., & others (2020). Sources of social support and gender in perceived stress and individual adjustment among Latina/o college-attending emerging adults. *Cultural Diversity and Ethnic Minority Psychology, 26,* 134–147.

Lee, J. (2021, in press). Influence of exercise interventions on overweight in children and adolescents. *Public Health Nursing.*

Lee, J.R., & Darcy, K.M. (2021). Sexting: What's the law got to do with it? *Archives of Sexual Behavior, 50,* 563–573.

Lee, K.T.H., & others (2018). Out-of-school time and behaviors during adolescence. *Journal of Research on Adolescence, 28,* 284–293.

Lee, K.Y., & others (2011). Effects of combined radiofrequency radiation exposure on the cell cycle and its regulatory proteins. *Bioelectromagnetics, 32,* 169–178.

Lee, S., & others (2017). When mothers' work matters for youths' daily time use: Implications of evening and weekend shifts. *Journal of Child and Family Studies, 26,* 2077–2089.

Lefebvre, J.P., & Krettenaur, T. (2020). Is the true self truly moral? Identity intuitions across domains of sociomoral reasoning and age. *Journal of Experimental Child Psychology, 192,* 104769.

Lefkowitz, E.S., Boone, T.L., & Shearer, T.L. (2004). Communication with best friends about sex-related topics during emerging adulthood. *Journal of Youth and Adolescence, 33,* 339–351.

Lefkowitz, E.S., & Espinosa-Hernandez, G. (2006). *Sexual related communication with mothers and close friends during the transition to university.* Unpublished manuscript, Department of Human Development and Family Studies, Pennsylvania State University, University Park, PA.

Lefkowitz, E.S., Shearer, C.L., Gillen, M.M., & Espinosa-Hernandez, G. (2014). How gendered attitudes relate to women's and men's sexual behaviors and beliefs. *Sexuality and Culture, 18,* 833–846.

Lefkowitz, E.S., & others (2019). Changes in diverse sexual and contraceptive behaviors across college. *Journal of Sex Research, 56,* 965–976.

Leger, K.A., & others (2016). Personality and stressor-related affect. *Journal of Personality and Social Psychology, 111,* 917–928.

Lehr, C.A., Hanson, A., Sinclair, M.F., & Christensen, S.I. (2003). Moving beyond dropout prevention towards school completion. *School Psychology Review, 32,* 342–364.

Leibenluft, E., & Barch, D.M. (2021). Adolescent brain development and psychopathology: Introduction to the special issue. *Biological Psychiatry, 89,* 93–95.

Leinaweaver, J. (2014). Informal kinship-based fostering around the world: Anthropological findings. *Child Development Perspectives, 8,* 131–136.

Leitenberg, H., Detzer, M.J., & Srebnik, D. (1993). Gender differences in masturbation and the relation of masturbation experience in preadolescence and/or early adolescence to sexual behavior and adjustment in young adulthood. *Archives of Sexual Behavior, 22,* 87–98.

Lelutiu-Weinberger, C., English, & Sandanapitchai, P. (2020). The role of gender affirmation and discrimination in the resilience of transgender individuals in the U.S. *Behavioral Medicine, 46*(3–4), 175–188.

LeMoult, J., & others (2020). Meta-analysis: Exposure to early life stress and risk for depression in childhood and adolescence. *Journal of the American Academy of Child and Adolescent Psychiatry, 59,* 842–855.

Lenhart, A. (2015a, April 9). *Teens, social media, and technology: Overview 2015.* Washington, DC: Pew Research Center.

Lenhart, A. (2015b, August 6). *Teens, technology, and friendship.* Washington, DC: Pew Research Center.

Lenhart, A., & others (2015, April 9). *Teens, social media, and technology overview 2015.* Washington, DC: Pew Research Center.

Leone, E.M., & Wade, T.D. (2018). Measuring perfectionism in children: A systematic review of the mental health literature. *European Child and Adolescent Psychiatry, 27,* 553–567.

Leopold, T. (2018). Gender differences in the consequences of divorce: A study of multiple outcomes. *Demography, 55,* 769–797.

Lepper, M.R., Corpus, J.H., & Iyengar, S.S. (2005). Intrinsic and extrinsic orientations in the classroom: Age differences and academic correlates. *Journal of Educational Psychology, 97,* 184–196.

Lerner, R.M. (2017). Commentary: Studying and testing the Positive Youth Development model: A tale of two approaches. *Child Development, 88,* 1183–1185.

Lerner, R.M., Lerner, J.V., Bowers, E., & Geldhof, J. (2015). Positive youth development: A relational developmental systems model. In R.M. Lerner (Ed.), *Handbook of child psychology and developmental science* (7th ed.). New York: Wiley.

Lerner, R.M., & others (2018). Studying positive youth development in different nations: Theoretical and methodological issues. In J.E. Lansford & P. Banati (Eds.), *Handbook of adolescent development research and its impact on global policy.* New York: Oxford University Press.

Levant, R.F. (2001). Men and masculinity. In J. Worell (Ed.), *Encyclopedia of women and gender.* San Diego: Academic Press.

LeVay, S. (2016). *Gay, straight, and the reason why: The science of sexual orientation* (2nd ed.). New York: Oxford University Press.

Leve, L.D., Harold, G.T., & Kintner, C. (2020). Domestic adoption. In J.D. Jewell & S. Hupp (Eds.), *Encyclopedia of child and family development.* New York: Wiley.

Leve, L.D., & others (2019). The Early Growth and Development Study: A dual-family adoption study from birth through adolescence. *Twin Research and Human Genetics, 22,* 716–727.

Levey, E.K.V., & others (2019). The longitudinal role of self-concept clarity and best friend delinquency in adolescent delinquency behavior. *Journal of Youth and Adolescence, 48,* 1068–1081.

Lewis, A.J., & others (2017). Adolescent depressive symptoms in India, Australia, and USA: Exploratory structural equation modeling of cross-national invariance and predictions by gender and age. *Journal of Affective Disorders, 212,* 150–159.

Lewis, C.G. (1981). How adolescents approach decisions: Changes over grades seven to twelve and policy implications. *Child Development, 52,* 538–554.

Lewis, D.M.G., Al-Shawaf, L., & Buss, D.M. (2021). Evolutionary personality psychology. In P.T. Corr & G. Matthews (Eds.), *Cambridge handbook of personality psychology.* New York: Cambridge University Press.

Lewis, K.M., & others (2013). Problem behavior and urban, low-income youth: A randomized controlled trial of Positive Action in Chicago. *American Journal of Prevention, 44,* 622–630.

Lewis, M., Feiring, C., & Rosenthal, S. (2000). Attachment over time. *Child Development, 71,* 707–720.

Lewis, R. (2021). *Human genetics* (13th ed.). New York: McGraw-Hill.

Li, G., Kung, K.T., & Hines, M. (2017). Childhood gender-typed behavior and adolescent sexual orientation: A longitudinal population-based study. *Developmental Psychology. 53,* 764–777.

Li, J., & others (2020). Potential role of genomic imprinted genes and brain developmental related genes in autism. *BMC Medical Genomics, 13*(1), 54.

Li, S-J., & others (2020). Uncovering the modulatory interactions of brain networks in cognition with central thalamic deep brain stimulation using functional magnetic resonance imaging. *Neuroscience, 440,* 65–84.

Li, Y., Wright, M.F., & Rollet, D. (2021). Adolescents' attributions and outcome expectancies regarding relational aggression: A cross-cultural comparison and cultural value associations. *Journal of Early Adolescence, 41,* 927–955.

Liang, J., & others (2021, in press). Physical exercise promotes brain remodeling by regulating epigenetics, neuroplasticity, and neurotropins. *Reviews in the Neurosciences.*

Liang, Y., & Van Horn, S. (2021, in press). How do romantic breakups affect depression among American college students? The role of sexual conservativeness. *Journal of American College Health.*

Liang, Y., & others (2020). Career-related parental behaviors, adolescents' consideration of future consequences, and career adaptability: A three-wave longitudinal study. *Journal of Counseling Psychology, 67,* 208–221.

Liben, L.S. (1995). Psychology meets geography: Exploring the gender gap on the national geography bee. *Psychological Science Agenda, 8,* 8–9.

Liben, L.S., & Coyle, E.F. (2014). Developmental interventions to address the STEM gender gap: Exploring intended and unintended consequences. *Advances in Child Development and Behavior, 47,* 77–115.

Liga, F., & others (2020). The socialization of coping strategies in adolescence: The modeling role of parents. *Anxiety, Stress, and Coping, 33,* 47–58.

Ligier, F., & others (2020). Are school difficulties an early sign for mental disorder diagnosis and suicide prevention? A comparative study of individuals who died by suicide and control group. *Child and Adolescent Psychiatry and Mental Health, 14,* 1.

Limburg, K., & others (2017). The relationship between perfectionism and psychopathology: A meta-analysis. *Journal of Clinical Psychology, 73,* 1301–1326.

Lin, J., Chadi, N., & Shrier, L. (2020). Mindfulness-based interventions for adolescent health. *Current Opinion in Pediatrics, 31,* 469–475.

Lin, W-H., Liu, C-H., & Yi, C-C. (2020). Exposure to sexually explicit media in early adolescence is related to risky behavior in emerging adulthood. *PLoS One, 15*(4), 0230242.

Lindberg, L., & others (2021). Obesity in childhood, socioeconomic status, and completion of 12 or more years: A prospective cohort study. *BMJ Open, 11*(3), e040432.

Lindell, A.K., & Campione-Barr, N. (2017). Relative power in sibling relationships across adolescence. *New Directions in Child and Adolescent Development, 156,* 49–66.

Lindell, A.K., Campione-Barr, N., & Killoren, S.E. (2017). Implications of parent-child relationships for emerging adults' subjective feelings about adulthood. *Journal of Family Psychology, 31,* 810–820.

Linden-Carmichael, A.N., & Lau-Barraco, C. (2017). Alcohol mixed with energy drinks: Daily context of use. *Alcoholism: Clinical and Experimental Research, 41,* 863–869.

Lindfors, P., & others (2019). Do maternal knowledge and paternal knowledge of children's whereabouts buffer differently against alcohol use? A longitudinal study among Finnish boys and girls. *Drug and Alcohol Dependency, 194,* 351–357.

Ling, Y., & others (2021). Assessing the measurement invariance of the Gratitude Questionnaire-5 in Chinese and American adolescents. *Spanish Journal of Psychology, 24,* e17.

Linley, P.A., & Joseph, S. (2004). Positive change following trauma and adversity: A review. *Journal of Traumatic Stress, 17,* 11–21.

Lipka, M., & Gecewicz, C. (2017, September 6). *More Americans now say they're spiritual but not religious.* Washington, DC: Pew Research Center.

Lipowski, M., Lipowska, M., Jochimek, M., & Krokosz, D. (2016). Resilience as a factor protecting youths from risky behavior: Moderating effects of gender and sport. *European Journal of Sport Science, 16,* 246–255.

Lippman, L.A., & Keith, J.D. (2006). The demographics of spirituality among youth: International perspectives. In E. Roehlkepartain, P.E. King, L. Wagener, & P.L. Benson (Eds.), *The handbook of spirituality in childhood and adolescence.* Thousand Oaks, CA: Sage.

Lipsitz, J. (1980, March). *Sexual development in young adolescents.* Invited speech given at the American Association of Sex Educators, Counselors, and Therapists, New York City.

Lipson, S.K., & Sonneville, K.R. (2017). Eating disorder symptoms among undergraduate and graduate students at 12 U.S. colleges and universities. *Eating Behavior, 24,* 81–88.

Lisboa, T., & others (2021). Social support from family and friends for physical activity in adolescence: Analysis with structural equation modeling. *Reports in Public Health, 37*(1), e00196819.

Lisha, N.E., & others (2012). Evaluation of the psychometric properties of the Revised Inventory of the Dimensions of Emerging Adulthood (IDEA-R) in a sample of continuation high school students. *Evaluation & the Health Professions, 37,* 156–177.

Litow, S.S., & Kelley, T. (2021). *Breaking barriers: How P-TECH schools create a pathway from high school to college to career.* New York: Teachers College Press.

Liu, C., & Ma, J.L. (2019). Adult attachment style, emotion regulation, and social networking sites addiction. *Frontiers in Psychology, 10,* 2352.

Liu, L., & Miller, S.L. (2020). Protective factors against juvenile delinquency: Exploring gender with a nationally representative sample. *Social Science Research, 86,* 102376.

Liu, L., Wang, N., & Tian, L. (2019). The parent-adolescent relationship and risk-taking behaviors among Chinese adolescents: The moderating role of self-control. *Frontiers in Psychology, 10,* 542.

Liu, Y., Ge, T., & Jiang, Q. (2020). Changing family relationships and mental health of Chinese adolescents: The role of living arrangements. *Public Health, 186,* 110–115.

Liu, Y., & Lachman, M.E. (2019). Socioeconomic status and parenting style in childhood: Long-term effects on cognitive function in middle and later adulthood. *Journals of Gerontology B: Psychological Sciences and Social Sciences, 74*(6), e13–e24.

Liu, Y., & others (2020). Multiplicative effect of intrinsic and extrinsic motivation and academic performance: A longitudinal study of Chinese students. *Journal of Personality, 88,* 584–595.

Livingston, G., & Brown, A. (2017). *Trends and patterns in intermarriage.* Washington, DC: Pew Research Center.

Lloyd, S., Yiend, J., Schmidt, U., & Tchanturia, K. (2014). Perfectionism in anorexia nervosa: Novel performance-based evidence. *PLoS One, 9*(10), e111697.

Lobata Concha, M.E., & others (2020). Parental protective and risk factors regarding cannabis use in adolescence: A national sample from a Chilean school population. *American Journal of Drug and Alcohol Abuse 46,* 642–650.

Loeber, R., & Burke, J.D. (2011). Developmental pathways in juvenile externalizing and internalizing problems. *Journal of Research on Adolescence, 21,* 34–46.

Loeber, R., Pardini, D.A., Stouthamer-Loeber, M., & Raine, A. (2007). Do cognitive, physiological, and psychosocial risk and promotive factors predict desistance from delinquency in males? *Development and Psychopathology, 19,* 867–887.

Long, E., & others (2020). Mental health disorders and adolescent peer relationships. *Social Science and Medicine, 253,* 112973.

Long, Y., & Li, Y. (2020). The longitudinal association between social status insecurity and relational aggression: Moderation effects of social cognition about relational aggression. *Aggressive Behavior, 46,* 84–96.

Longa, A., & Graham, S. (2020). Effective practices for teaching writing in the United States. In S. Sharma & S. Salend (Eds.), *Encyclopedia of inclusive and special education.* New York: Oxford University Press.

Longobardi, C., & others (2019). Students' psychological adjustment in normative school transitions from kindergarten to high school: Investigating the role of teacher-student relationship quality. *Frontiers in Psychology, 10,* 1238.

Lopez, A.B., Huynh, V.W., & Fuligni, A.J. (2011). A longitudinal study of religious identity and participation during adolescence. *Child Development, 82,* 1297–1309.

Lopez, R.B., Heatherton, T.F., & Wagner, D.D. (2020). Media multitasking is associated with higher risk for obesity and increased responsiveness to rewarding food stimuli. *Brain Imaging and Behavior, 14,* 1050–1061.

Lord, C., & others (2020). Autism spectrum disorder. *Nature Reviews. Disease Primers, 6*(1), 5.

Lord, R.G., & others (2017). Leadership in applied psychology: Three waves of theory and research. *Journal of Applied Psychology, 102,* 434–451.

Lord, S.E., & Eccles, J.S. (1994, February). *James revisited: The relationship of domain self-concepts and values to Black and White adolescents' self-esteem.* Paper presented at the meeting of the Society for Research on Adolescence, San Diego.

Lougheed, J.P., Main, A., & Helm, J.L. (2020). Mother-adolescent emotion dynamics during conflicts: Associations with perspective taking. *Journal of Family Psychology, 34,* 566–576.

Love, H.A., & others (2018). Suicidal risk following the termination of romantic relationships. *Crisis, 39,* 166–174.

Loveless, T. (2020). Common Core has not worked. *Education Next, 20*(2), 73, 79–82.

Loveless, T. (2021). *Between the state and the schoolhouse: Understanding the failure of Common Core.* Cambridge, MA: Harvard University Press.

Lowe, K., & Dotterer, A.M. (2013). Parental monitoring, parental warmth, and minority youths' academic outcomes: Exploring the integrative model of parenting. *Journal of Youth and Adolescence, 42,* 1413–1425.

Lowe, P.A. (2021). Examination of latent test anxiety profiles in a sample of U.S. adolescents. *International Education Studies, 14*(2), 12–20.

Lowry, R., & others (2017). Early sexual debut and associated risk behaviors among sexual minority youth. *American Journal of Preventive Medicine, 52,* 379–384.

Loyd, A.B., & Williams, B.V. (2017). The potential for youth programs to promote African American youth's development of ethnic and racial identity. *Child Development Perspectives, 11,* 29–38.

Lu, J.G., Jin, P., & English, A.S. (2021). Collectivism predicts mask use during COVID-19. *Proceedings of the National Academy of Sciences, 118*(23), e2021793118.

Lu, Y., He, Q., & Brooks-Gunn, J. (2020). Diverse experience of immigrant children: How do separation and reunification shape their development? *Child Development, 91*(1), e146-e163.

Lubart, T.I. (2003). In search of creative intelligence. In R.J. Sternberg, J. Lautrey, & T.I. Lubart (Eds.), *Models of intelligence: International perspectives.* Washington, DC: American Psychological Association.

Luciano, E.C., & Orth, U. (2017). Transitions in romantic relationships and development of self-esteem. *Journal of Personality and Social Psychology, 112,* 307-328.

Luders, E., Narr, K.L., Thompson, P.M., & Toga, A.W. (2009). Neuroanatomical correlates of intelligence. *Intelligence, 37,* 156-163.

Luders, E., & others (2004). Gender differences in cortical complexity. *Nature Neuroscience, 7,* 799-800.

Ludik, D., & Greeff, A.P. (2021, in press). Exploring factors that helped adolescents adjust and continue with life after the death of a parent. *Omega.*

Ludyga, S., & others (2018). The effects of a school-based exercise program on neurophysiological indices of working memory operations in adolescents. *Journal of Science and Medicine in Sport, 21,* 813-838.

Luebbe, A.M., & others (2018). Dimensionality of helicopter parenting and relations to emotional, decision-making, and academic functioning in emerging adults. *Assessment, 25,* 841-857.

Lumpkin, A. (2021). *Introduction to physical education, exercise science, and sports* (11th ed.). New York: McGraw-Hill.

Luna, B., Tervo-Clemmens, B., & Calabro, F.J. (2021). Considerations when characterizing adolescent neurocognitive development. *Biological Psychiatry, 89,* 96-98.

Lund, H.G., Reider, B.D., Whiting, A.B., & Prichard, J.R. (2010). Sleep patterns and predictors of disturbed sleep in a large population of college students. *Journal of Adolescent Health, 46,* 124-132.

Lunday, A. (2006, December 4). Two Homewood seniors collect Marshall, Mitchell scholarships. *The JHU Gazette, 36.*

Luria, A., & Herzog, E. (1985, April). *Gender segregation across and within settings.* Paper presented at the biennial meeting of the Society for Research in Child Development, Toronto.

Luthar, S.S., Barkin, S.H., & Crossman, E.J. (2013). "I can, therefore I must": Fragility in the upper-middle classes. *Development and Psychopathology, 25,* 1529-1549.

Luthar, S.S., Crossman, E., & Small, P.J. (2015). Resilience in the face of adversities. In R.M. Lerner (Ed.), *Handbook of child psychology and developmental science* (7th ed.). New York: Wiley.

Luthar, S.S., Kumar, N.L., & Zillmer, N. (2020). High achieving schools connote significant risks for adolescents: Problems documented, processes implicated, and directions for interventions. *American Psychologist, 75,* 983-995.

Luthar, S.S., & others (2021, in press). Students in high-achieving schools: Perils of pressures to be "standouts." *Adversity and Resilience Science.*

Lux, C.J., Decker, K.B., & Nease, C. (2020). Supporting young children's executive function skills through mindfulness: Implications for school counselors. *Journal of School Counseling, 18*(1).

Luyckx, K., & Robitschek, C. (2014). Personal growth initiative and identity formation in adolescence through young adulthood: Mediating processes on the pathway to well-being. *Journal of Adolescence, 37,* 973-981.

Luyckx, K., Schwartz, S.J., Soenens, B., Vansteenkiste, M., & Goossens, L. (2010). The path from identity commitments to adjustment: Motivational underpinnings and mediating mechanisms. *Journal of Counseling and Development, 88,* 52-60.

Luyckx, K., Teppers, E., Klimstra, T.A., & Rassart, J. (2014). Identity processes and personality traits and types in adolescence: Directionality of effects and developmental trajectories. *Developmental Psychology, 50,* 2144-2153.

Lynch, K.M., & others (2020). Magnitude and timing of major white matter tract maturation from infancy through adolescence with NODDI. *NeuroImage, 212,* 116672.

Lynch, M.E. (1991). Gender intensification. In R.M. Lerner, A.C. Petersen, & J. Brooks-Gunn (Eds.), *Encyclopedia of adolescence* (Vol. 1). New York: Garland.

Lyons, H., Manning, W., Giordano, P., & Longmore, M. (2013). Predictors of heterosexual casual sex among young adults. *Archives of Sexual Behavior, 42,* 585-593.

Lyons, H., Manning, W.D., Longmore, M.A., & Giordano, P.C. (2015). Gender and casual sexual activity from adolescence to emerging adulthood: Social and life course correlates. *Journal of Sex Research, 52,* 543-547.

Lyons-Ruth, K., & Brumariu, L.E. (2021). Emerging child competencies and personality psychopathology: Toward a developmental cascade model of BPD. *Current Opinion in Psychology, 37,* 32-38.

M

Ma, L., & Jiang, Y. (2020). Empathy mediates the relationship between motivations after transgression and forgiveness. *Frontiers in Psychology, 11,* 14666.

Maat, S.C., & others (2020). Injury patterns after skiing and snowboarding sports accidents. *Journal of Sports Medicine and Physical Fitness, 60,* 119-124.

MacCann, C., & others (2020). Emotional intelligence predicts academic performance: A meta-analysis. *Psychological Bulletin, 146,* 150-186.

Maccoby, E.E. (1998). *The two sexes.* Cambridge, MA: Harvard University Press.

Maccoby, E.E. (2002). Gender and group process: A developmental perspective. *Current Directions in Psychological Science, 11,* 54-57.

Maccoby, E.E. (2007). Historical overview of socialization theory and research. In J.E. Grusec & P.D. Hastings (Eds.), *Handbook of socialization.* New York: Guilford.

Maccoby, E.E. (2015). Historical overview of socialization theory and research. In J.E. Grusec & P.D. Hastings (Eds.), *Handbook of socialization* (2nd ed.). New York: Guilford.

Maccoby, E.E., & Martin, J.A. (1983). Socialization in the context of the family. In E.M. Hetherington (Ed.), *Handbook of child psychology, Vol. 4: Socialization, personality, and social development.* New York: Wiley.

MacDonald, K. (1987). Parent-child physical play with rejected, neglected, and popular boys. *Developmental Psychology, 23,* 705-711.

MacDonnell, M., & others (2021). It's not all or nothing: Exploring the impact of social-emotional and character development intervention in the middle grades. *Research on Middle Level Education, 44*(2).

MacGeorge, E.L. (2004). The myth of gender cultures: Similarities outweigh differences in men's and women's provisions of and responses to supportive communication. *Sex Roles, 50,* 143-175.

Machado, A., & others (2020). ADHD among offenders: Prevalence and relationship with psychopathic traits. *Journal of Attention Disorders 24*(14), 2021-2029.

Machlin, L., McLaughlin, K.A., & Sheridan, M.A. (2020). Brain structure mediates the association between socioeconomic status and attention-deficit/hyperactivity disorder. *Developmental Science, 23*(1), e12844.

MacIver, M.A., Sheldon, S., & Clark, E. (2021). Widening the portal: How schools can help more families access and use the parent portal to support student success. *Middle School Journal, 52,* 14-22.

Maclean, A.M., Walker, L.J., & Matsuba, M.K. (2004). Transcendence and the moral self: Identity, integration, religion, and moral life. *Journal for the Scientific Study of Religion, 43,* 429-437.

MacMullin, L.N., & others (2021). Examining the relation between gender nonconformity and psychological well-being in children: The roles of peers and parents. *Archives of Sexual Behavior, 50,* 823-841.

Macoun, S.J., & others (2021, in press). Feasibility and potential benefits of an attention and executive function intervention on metacognition in a mixed pediatric sample. *Applied Neuropsychology. Child.*

MacPherson, H.A., & others (2021). Parental monitoring predicts depressive symptom and suicidal ideation outcomes in adolescents being treated for co-occurring substance use and psychiatric disorders. *Journal of Affective Disorders, 284,* 190-198.

Madsen, A., & others (2020). Testicular ultrasound to stratify hormone references in a cross-sectional Norwegian study of male puberty. *Journal of Clinical Endocrinology and Metabolism, 105*(6), dgz094.

Maeda, K., & others (2020). Association of smoking habits with TXNIP DNA methylation levels in leukocytes among general Japanese population. *PLoS One, 15*(7), e0235486.

Magno, C. (2010). The role of metacognitive skills in developing critical thinking. *Metacognition and Learning, 5,* 137-156.

Magnus, W., & others (2021). *Attention deficit hyperactivity disorder.* Treasure Island, FL: StatPearls.

Magnusson, B.M., Crandall, A., & Evans, K. (2019). Early sexual debut and risky sex in young adults: The role of low self-control. *BMC Public Health, 19*(1), 1483.

Magson, N.R., & others (2021). Risk and protective factors for prospective changes in adolescent mental health during the COVID-19 pandemic. *Journal of Youth and Adolescence, 50,* 44-57.

Mahon, J., & Cushner, K. (2021). International initiatives in K-12 and higher education: Learning from and moving beyond disciplinary history. In D. Landis & D.P.S. Bhawuk (Eds.), *Cambridge handbook of intercultural training.* New York: Cambridge University Press.

Maisto, S.A., Galizio, M., & Connors, G.J. (2022). *Drug use and abuse* (9th ed.). Boston: Cengage.

Majumdar, A., & others (2021). A two-step approach to testing overall effect of gene-environment interaction for multiple phenotypes. *Bioinformatics,* btaa1083.

Makarova, E. (2021). *Acculturation and school adjustment of minority students.* New York: Routledge.

Malamitsi-Puchner, A., & Boutsikou, T. (2006). Adolescent pregnancy and perinatal outcome. *Pediatric Endocrinology Reviews, 3*(Suppl. 1), 170-171.

Malik, N.M., & Furman, W. (1993). Practitioner review: Problems in children's peer relations: What can the clinician do? *Journal of Child Psychology and Psychiatry, 34,* 1303-1326.

Malin, H., Liauw, I., & Damon, W. (2017). Purpose and character development in early adolescence. *Journal of Youth and Adolescence, 46,* 1200-1215.

Maloy, R.W., & others (2021). *Transforming learning with new technologies* (4th ed.). Upper Saddle River, NJ: Pearson.

Mamun, A.A., & others (2020). Generational changes in young adults' sleep duration: A perspective analysis of mother-offspring dyads. *Sleep Health, 6,* 240-245.

Manfredini, R., & others (2017). Marital status, cardiovascular diseases, and cardiovascular risk factors: A review of the evidence. *Journal of Women's Health, 26,* 624-632.

Manis, F.R., Keating, D.P., & Morrison, F.J. (1980). Developmental differences in the allocation of processing capacity. *Journal of Experimental Child Psychology, 29,* 156-169.

Manning, W.D. (2020). Young adulthood relationships in an era of uncertainty: A case for cohabitation. *Demography, 57,* 799-819.

Manoli, D.S., & State, M.W. (2021). Autism spectrum disorder genetics and the search for pathological mechanisms. *American Journal of Psychiatry, 178,* 30-36.

Manzari, N., & others (2019). Prenatal maternal stress and risk of neurodevelopmental disorders in the offspring: A systematic review and meta-analysis. *Social Psychiatry and Psychiatric Epidemiology, 54,* 1299-1309.

Maras, D., & others (2015). Screen time is associated with depression and anxiety in Canadian youth. *Preventive Medicine, 73,* 133-138.

Maravilla, J.C., & others (2017). Factors influencing repeated adolescent pregnancy: A review and meta-analysis. *American Journal of Obstetrics and Gynecology, 2017,* 529-545.

Marcell, A.V., & Halpern-Felsher, B.L. (2007). Adolescents' beliefs about preferred resources for help vary depending on the health issue. *Journal of Adolescent Health, 41,* 61-68.

Marcell, A.V., Klein, J.D., Fischer, I., Allan, M.J., & Kokotailo, P.K. (2002). Male adolescent use of health care services: Where are the boys? *Journal of Adolescent Health Care, 30,* 35-43.

Marcelo, P. (2021, May 28). For Native Americans, Harvard and other colleges fall short. *Associated Press.* Retrieved from https://abcnews.go.com/US/wireStory/native-americans-harvard-colleges-fall-short-77933934.

Marchetti, D., & others (2021, in press). Childhood maltreatment, personality vulnerability profiles, and borderline personality disorder symptoms in adolescents. *Development and Psychopathology.*

Marcia, J.E. (1980). Ego identity development. In J. Adelson (Ed.), *Handbook of adolescent psychology.* New York: Wiley.

Marcia, J.E. (1987). The identity status approach to the study of ego identity development. In T. Honess & K. Yardley (Eds.), *Self and identity: Perspectives across the lifespan.* London: Routledge & Kegan Paul.

Marcia, J.E. (1994). The empirical study of ego identity. In H.A. Bosma, T.L.G. Graafsma, H.D. Grotevant, & D.J. De Levita (Eds.), *Identity and development.* Newbury Park, CA: Sage.

Marcia, J.E. (1996). Unpublished review of J.W. Santrock's *Adolescence,* 7th ed., for Brown & Benchmark, Dubuque, Iowa.

Marcia, J.E. (2002). Identity and psychosocial development in adulthood. *Identity: An International Journal of Theory and Research, 2,* 7-28.

Marcia, J.E., & Carpendale, J. (2004). Identity: Does thinking make it so? In C. Lightfoot, C. Lalonde, & M. Chandler (Eds.), *Changing conceptions of psychological life.* Mahwah, NJ: Erlbaum.

Markey, C.N. (2010). Invited commentary: Why body image is important to adolescent development. *Journal of Youth and Adolescence, 39,* 1387-1389.

Markham, C.M., & others (2010). Connectedness as a predictor of sexual and reproductive health outcomes for youth. *Journal of Adolescent Health, 46*(Suppl. 3), S23-S41.

Marks, A.K., Ejesi, K., & Garcia Coll, C. (2014). Understanding the U.S. immigrant paradox in childhood and adolescence. *Child Development Perspectives, 8,* 59-64.

Marks, A.K., Ejesi, K., McCullough, M.B., & Garcia Coll, C. (2015). The implications of discrimination for child and adolescent development. In R.M. Lerner (Ed.), *Handbook of child psychology and developmental science* (7th ed.). New York: Wiley.

Markstrom, C.A. (2010). *Empowerment of North American Indian girls.* Lincoln: University of Nebraska Press.

Markus, H.R., & Nurius, P. (1986). Possible selves. *American Psychologist, 41,* 954-969.

Marr, K.L., & Duell, M.N. (2021). Cyberbullying and cybervictimization: Does gender matter? *Psychological Reports, 124,* 577-595.

Marshall Scholarships (2007). *Scholar profiles: 2007.* Retrieved January 31, 2008, from www.marshallscholarship.org/profiles2007.html

Marshall, S.L., Parker, P.D., Ciarrochi, J., & Heaven, P.C.L. (2014). Is self-esteem a cause or consequence of social support? A 4-year longitudinal study. *Child Development, 85,* 1275-1291.

Martin, A., & others (2018). Physical activity, diet, and other behavioral interventions for improving cognition and school achievement in children and adolescents with obesity or overweight. *Cochrane Database of Systematic Reviews, 1,* CD009728.

Martin, C.L., Ruble, D.N., & Szkrybalo, J. (2002). Cognitive theories of early gender development. *Psychological Bulletin, 128,* 903-933.

Martin, C.L., & others (2017). Reviving androgyny: A modern day perspective on flexibility of gender identity and behavior. *Sex Roles, 76,* 592-603.

Martin, J.A., & others (2021). Births: Final data for 2019. *National Vital Statistics Reports, 70*(2), 1-42.

Martin, M.J., & others (2017). A process model of the implications of spillover from coparenting conflicts into the parent-child attachment relationship in adolescence. *Development and Psychopathology, 29,* 417-431.

Martinez, A. (2006). In the fast lane: Boosting your career through cooperative education and internships. *Careers and Colleges, 26,* 8-10.

Martinez, G.M., & Abma, J.C. (2020, May). Sexual activity and contraceptive use among teenagers aged 15-19 in the United States, 2015-2017. *NCHS Data Brief, No. 366,* 1-23.

Martinez, I., & others (2020). Parenting styles, internalization of values, and self-esteem: A cross-cultural study in Spain, Portugal, and Brazil. *International Journal of Environmental Research and Public Health, 17*(7), 2370.

Martinez, K., & Colom, R. (2021). Imaging the intelligence of humans. In A.K. Barbey & others (Eds.), *Cambridge handbook of intelligence and cognitive neuroscience.* New York: Cambridge University Press.

Martinez, Y.A., Schneider, B.H., Zambrana, A., Batista, G.S., & Soca, Z.S. (2015). Does comorbid anger exacerbate the rejection of children with depression by their school peers? *Child Psychiatry and Human Development, 46,* 493-500.

Martinez-Fuentes, S., Jager, J., & Umana-Taylor, A.J. (2021). The mediation process between Latino youths' family ethnic socialization, ethnic-racial identity, and academic engagement: Moderation by ethnic-racial discrimination? *Cultural Diversity and Ethnic Minority Psychology, 27*(2), 296-306.

Martinez-Monteagudo, M.C., & others (2020). Relationship between suicidal thinking, anxiety, depression, and stress in university students who are victims of bullying. *Psychiatry Research, 286,* 112856.

Martin-Gutierrez, G., & others (2021). Racial/ethnic differences in relationship between stressful life events and quality of life in adolescents. *Journal of Adolescent Health, 68,* 292-299.

Martino, S.C., & others (2006). Exposure to degrading versus nondegrading music lyrics and sexual behavior among youth. *Pediatrics, 118,* e430-e431.

Martin-Storey, A., & Crosnoe, R. (2012). Sexual minority status, peer harassment, and adolescent depression. *Journal of Adolescence, 35,* 1001-1011.

Martin-Storey, A., & Fromme, K. (2021). Mediating factors explaining the association between sexual minority status and dating violence. *Journal of Interpersonal Violence, 36,* 132-159.

Martz, M.E., Patrick, M.E., & Schulenberg, J.E. (2015). Alcohol mixed with energy drink use among U.S. 12th grade students: Prevalence, correlates, and associations with unsafe driving. *Journal of Adolescent Health, 56,* 557-563.

Marzoli, D., Havlicek, J., & Roberts, S.C. (2018). Human mating strategies: From past causes to present consequences. *Wiley Interdisciplinary Reviews: Cognitive Science, 9,* 2.

Mascalo, M.F., & Fischer, K.W. (2010). The dynamic development of thinking, feeling, and acting over the life span. In W.F. Overton & R.M. Lerner (Eds.), *Handbook of life-span development* (Vol. 1). New York: Wiley.

Mascia, M.L., & others (2021). Moral disengagement, empathy, and cybervictim's representation as predictive factors of cyberbullying among Italian adolescents. *International Journal of Environmental Research and Public Health, 18*(3), 1266.

Mash, E.J., & Wolfe, D.A. (2019). *Abnormal child psychology* (7th ed.). Boston: Cengage.

Mason, K., Duncan, T., & Losos, J. (2021). *Understanding biology* (3rd ed.). New York: McGraw-Hill.

Mason, M.J., Zaharakis, N., & Benotsch, E.G. (2014). Social networks, substance use, and mental health in college students. *Journal of American College Health, 62,* 470-477.

Masten, A.S. (2001). Ordinary magic: Resilience processes in development. *American Psychologist, 56*(3), 227-238.

Masten, A.S. (2014). Global perspectives on resilience in children and youth. *Child Development, 85,* 6-20.

Masten, A.S. (2015). Pathways to integrated resilience science. *Psychological Inquiry, 27,* 187-196.

Masten, A.S. (2017). Building a translational science on children and youth affected by political violence and armed conflict: A commentary. *Development and Psychopathology, 29,* 79-84.

Masten, A.S. (2019). Resilience from a developmental systems perspective. *World Psychiatry, 18,* 101-102.

Masten, A.S. (2021a). Resilience of children in disasters: A multisystem perspective. *International Journal of Psychology, 56,* 1-11.

Masten, A.S. (2021b). Resilience in developmental systems: Principles, pathways, and protective processes in research and practice. In M. Ungar (Ed.), *Multisystemic resilience.* New York: Oxford University Press.

Masten, A.S., & Coatsworth, J.D. (1998). The development of competence in favorable and unfavorable environments. *American Psychologist, 53,* 205-220.

Masten, A.S., Desjardins, C.D., McCormick, C.M., Kuo, S.I., & Long, J.D. (2010). The significance of childhood competence and problems for adult success in work: A developmental cascade analysis. *Developmental Psychopathology, 22,* 679-694.

Masten, A.S., Motti-Stefanidi, F., & Rahl-Brigman, H.A. (2020). Developmental risk and resilience in the context of devastation and forced migration. In R.D. Parke & G.H. Elder (Eds.), *Children in changing worlds.* New York: Cambridge University Press.

Masten, A.S., Obradovic, J., & Burt, K.B. (2006). Resilience in emerging adulthood: Developmental perspectives on continuity and transformation. In J.J. Arnett & J.L. Tanner (Eds.), *Emerging adults in America.* Washington, DC: American Psychological Association.

Masten, A.S., & Palmer, A. (2019). Parenting to promote resilience in children. In M.H. Bornstein (Ed.), *Handbook of parenting* (3rd ed., Vol. 5). New York: Routledge.

Masten, A.S., & others (2021). Resilience in development and psychopathology. *Annual Review of Clinical Psychology* (Vol. 17). Palo Alto, CA: Annual Reviews.

Mastrotheodoros, S., & others (2020). Parent-adolescent conflict across adolescence: Trajectories of informant discrepancies and associations with personality types. *Journal of Youth and Adolescence, 49,* 119-135.

Masuda, T., & others (2020). Culture and business: How can cultural psychologists contribute to research on behaviors in the marketplace and workplace? *Frontiers in Psychology, 11,* 1304.

Match.com (2020). *Singles in America 2020.* Retrieved November 7, 2020, from www.singlesinamerica.com.

Matos, K. (2015). *Modern families: Same- and different-sex couples negotiating at home.* New York: Families and Work Institute.

Matthews, G. (2021). Cognitive processes and models. In P.J. Corr & G. Matthews (Eds.), *Cambridge handbook of personality psychology.* New York: Cambridge University Press.

Matthews, G., Zeidner, M., & Roberts, R.D. (2011). *Emotional intelligence 101.* New York: Springer.

Matthiessen, C. (2013). *Overweight children: Tips for parents.* Retrieved February 21, 2013, from www.webmd.com/parenting/raising-fit-kids/mood/talking-kids-about-weight

Mattys, L., & others (2020). Features of Flemish emerging adults and their association with demographic markers. *Psychologica Belgica, 60,* 37–54.

Mayer, R.E. (2020). Intelligence, education, and society. In R.J. Sternberg (Ed.), *Human intelligence.* New York: Cambridge University Press.

Mayer, R.E., & Wittrock, M.C. (2006). Problem solving. In P.A. Alexander & P.H. Winne (Eds.), *Handbook of educational psychology* (2nd ed.). Mahwah, NJ: Erlbaum.

Maynard, B.R., Salas-Wright, C.P., & Vaughn, M.G. (2015). High school dropouts in emerging adulthood: Substance use, mental health problems, and crime. *Community Mental Health, 51,* 289–299.

Mayo, C.O., & Wadsworth, M.E. (2020). Poverty and economic strain. In J.D. Jewell & S. Hupp (Eds.), *Encyclopedia of child and adolescent development.* New York: Wiley.

Mazza, J.J., & Miller, J.N. (2021). Adolescent suicidal behavior in schools. In F.C. Worrell & others (Eds.), *Cambridge handbook of applied school psychology.* New York: Cambridge University Press.

McAdams, D.P. (2021). Narrative identity and the life story. In O.P. John & R.W. Robins (Eds.), *Handbook of personality* (4th ed.). New York: Guilford.

McAlister, A., Perry, C., Killen, J., Slinkard, L.A., & Maccoby, N. (1980). Pilot study of smoking, alcohol, and drug abuse prevention. *American Journal of Public Health, 70,* 719–721.

McCabe, K.O., & Fleeson, W. (2016). Are traits useful? Explaining trait manifestations as tools in the pursuit of goals. *Journal of Personality and Social Psychology, 110,* 287–301.

McConnachie, A.L., & others (2021). Adoptive gay father families: A longitudinal study of children's adjustment at early adolescence. *Child Development, 92,* 425–433.

McCrae, R.R. (2021). The five-factor model of personality. In P.J. Corr & G. Matthews (Eds.), *Cambridge handbook of personality psychology.* New York: Cambridge University Press.

McCrae, R.R., & Sutin, A.R. (2009). Openness to experience. In M.R. Leary & R.H. Hoyle (Eds.), *Handbook of individual differences in social behavior.* New York: Guilford.

McDade-Montez, E., Wallander, J., & Cameron, L. (2017). Sexualization in US Latina and White girls' preferred children's television programs. *Sex Roles, 77,* 1–15.

McDonald, K.L., & Asher, S.R. (2018). Peer acceptance, peer rejection, and popularity: Social cognitive and behavioral perspectives. In W.M. Bukowski & others (Eds.), *Handbook of peer interactions, relationships, and groups* (2nd ed.). New York: Guilford.

McElhaney, K.B., & Allen, J.P. (2012). Sociocultural perspectives on adolescent autonomy. In P.K. Kerig, M.S. Schulz, & S.T. Hauser (Eds.), *Adolescence and beyond.* New York: Oxford University Press.

McGhee, S.L., & Hargreaves, M. (2020). Exercise adaptations: Molecular mechanisms and potential targets for therapeutic benefit. *Nature Reviews. Neuroendocrinology, 16,* 495–505.

McGuire, L., Jefferys, E., & Rutland, A. (2020). Children's evaluations of deviant peers in the context of science and technology: The role of gender group norms and status. *Journal of Experimental Child Psychology, 195,* 104845.

McHale, S.M., Kim, J.Y., Dotterer, A., Crouter, A.C., & Booth, A. (2009). The development of gendered interests and personality qualities from middle childhood through adolescence: A bio-social analysis. *Child Development, 80,* 482–495.

McHale, S.M., Updegraff, K.A., Helms-Erikson, H., & Crouter, A.C. (2001). Sibling influences on gender development in middle childhood and early adolescence: A longitudinal study. *Developmental Psychology, 37,* 115–125.

McKellar, S.E., & others (2019). Threats and supports to female students' math beliefs and achievement. *Journal of Research on Adolescence, 29,* 449–465.

McKenzie, J. (2019). Shifting practices, shifting selves: Negotiations of local and global cultures among adolescents in northern Thailand. *Child Development, 90,* 2035–2052.

McKenzie, J. (2020). Negotiating global and local values in a globalized world: The envisioned futures of Thai adolescents. *Journal of Research on Adolescence, 30,* 856–874.

McLanahan, S., Tach, L., & Schneider, D. (2013). The causal effects of father absence. *Annual Review of Sociology* (Vol. 39). Palo Alto, CA: Annual Reviews.

McLean, K.C., & Jennings, L.E. (2012). Teens telling tall tales: How maternal and peer audiences support narrative identity development. *Journal of Adolescence, 35,* 1455–1469.

McLean, K.C., & others (2021). Narrative identity in a social world. In P.J. Corr & G. Matthews (Eds.), *Cambridge handbook of personality psychology.* New York: Cambridge University Press.

McLoyd, V.C. (1998). Children in poverty. In I.E. Siegel & K.A. Renninger (Eds.), *Handbook of child psychology* (5th ed., Vol. 4). New York: Wiley.

McLoyd, V.C. (2019). How children and adolescents think about, make sense of, and respond to economic inequality: Why does it matter? *Developmental Psychology, 55,* 592–600.

McLoyd, V.C., Purtell, K.M., & Hardaway, C.R. (2015). Race, class, and ethnicity as they affect emerging adulthood. In R.M. Lerner (Ed.), *Handbook of child psychology and developmental science* (7th ed.). New York: Wiley.

McLoyd, V.C., & others (2009). Poverty and social disadvantage in adolescence. In R.M. Lerner & L. Steinberg (Eds.), *Handbook of adolescent psychology* (3rd ed.). New York: Wiley.

McMahon, G., Creaven, A-M., & Gallagher, S. (2020). Stressful life-events and adolescent well-being: The role of parent and peer relationships. *Stress and Health, 36,* 299–310.

McNamara, R. (2021). *Juvenile delinquency.* New York: Oxford University Press.

McNeely, C.A., & Barber, B.K. (2010). How do parents make adolescents feel loved? Perspectives on supportive parenting from adolescents in 12 cultures. *Journal of Adolescent Research, 25,* 601–631.

McNeely, C.A., & Blanchard, J. (2009). *The teen years explained.* Baltimore: Center for Advanced Health, Johns Hopkins University Bloomberg School of Public Health.

Mead, M. (1928). *Coming of age in Samoa.* New York: Morrow.

Mead, M. (1978, Dec. 30–Jan. 5). The American family: An endangered species. *TV Guide,* 21–24.

Meade, C.S., Kershaw, T.S., & Ickovics, J.R. (2008). The intergenerational cycle of teenage motherhood: An ecological approach. *Health Psychology, 27,* 419–429.

Meehan, A.J., & others (2020). Developing an individualized risk calculator for psychopathology among young people victimized during childhood: A population-representative cohort study. *Journal of Affective Disorders, 262,* 90–98.

Mehanovic, E., & others (2021, in press). Does parental permissiveness toward cigarette smoking and alcohol use influence illicit drug use among adolescents? A longitudinal study in seven European countries *Social Psychiatry and Epidemiology.*

Mehta, C.M., & Strough, J. (2009). Sex segregation in friendships and normative contexts across the life span. *Developmental Review, 29,* 201–220.

Mehta, C.M., & Strough, J. (2010). Gender segregation and gender-typing in adolescence. *Sex Roles, 63,* 251–263.

Mehta, C.M., & others (2020). Established adulthood: A new conception of ages 30 to 45. *American Psychologist, 75,* 499–510.

Meichenbaum, D., & Butler, L. (1980). Toward a conceptual model of the treatment of test anxiety: Implications for research and treatment. In I.G. Sarason (Ed.), *Test anxiety.* Mahwah, NJ: Erlbaum.

Meijs, N., Cillessen, A.H.N., Scholte, R.H.J., Segers, E., & Spijkerman, R. (2010). Social intelligence and academic achievement as predictors of adolescent popularity. *Journal of Youth and Adolescence, 39,* 62–72.

Meisel, S.N., & Colder, C.N. (2021, in press). An examination of the joint effects of adolescent interpersonal styles and parenting styles on substance use. *Development and Psychopathology.*

Meland, E., Breidablik, J., & Thuen, F. (2020). Divorce and conversational difficulties with parents: Impact on adolescent health and self-esteem. *Scandinavian Journal of Public Health, 48,* 743–751.

Mello, Z.R. (2009). Racial/ethnic group and socioeconomic status variation in educational and occupational expectations from adolescence to adulthood. *Journal of Applied Developmental Psychology, 30,* 494–504.

Memmott-Elison, M.K., & others (2020). Associations between prosocial behavior, externalizing behaviors, and internalizing symptoms during adolescence: A meta-analysis. *Journal of Adolescence, 80,* 98–114.

Mendez, M., Flores-Haro, G., & Zucker, L. (2020). The (in)visible victims of disaster: Understanding the vulnerability of undocumented Latino/a and indigenous immigrants. *Geoforum, 116,* 50–62.

Mendle, J., Ryan, R.M., & McKone, K.M.P. (2018). Age at menarche, depression, and antisocial behavior in adulthood. *Pediatrics, 141*(1), 20171703.

Menon, S., & the Committee on Adolescence (2020). Long-acting reversible contraception: Specific issues for adolescents. *Pediatrics, 146*(2), 2020007252.

Mento, G., & Granziol, U. (2020). The developing predictive brain: How implicit temporal expectancy induced by local and global prediction shapes action preparation across development. *Developmental Science, 23*(6), e12954.

Mercurio, E., & others (2020). Adolescent brain development and progressive legal responsibility in the Latin American context. *Frontiers in Psychology, 11,* 627.

Mercurio, L.Y., & others (2021). Children with ADHD engage in less physical activity. *Journal of Attention Disorders, 25,* 1187–1195.

Messer, R.C., & others (2021). Youth assets and associations with adolescent risk taking. *Journal of School Health, 91,* 37–49.

Metz, E.C., & Youniss, J. (2005). Longitudinal gains in civic development through school-based required service. *Political Psychology, 26,* 413–437.

Metzger, A., & others (2018). The intersection of emotional and sociocognitive competencies with civic engagement in middle childhood and adolescence. *Journal of Youth and Adolescence, 47,* 1663-1683.

Meyer, I.H. (2003). Prejudice, social stress, and mental health in gay, lesbian, and bisexual populations: Conceptual issues and research evidence. *Psychological Bulletin, 129,* 674-697.

Meyer-Bahlburg, H.F.L., & others (1995). Prenatal estrogens and the development of homosexual orientation. *Developmental Psychology, 31,* 12-21.

Meza, J.L., & Bath, E. (2021). One size does not fit all: Making suicide prevention and interventions equitable for our increasingly diverse communities. *Journal of American Academy of Child and Adolescent Psychiatry, 60,* 209-212.

Michaud, P.-A., & others (2009). To say or not to say: A qualitative study on the disclosure of their condition by human immunodeficiency virus-positive adolescents. *Journal of Adolescent Health, 44,* 356-362.

Michikyan, M. (2020). Linking online self-presentation to identity coherence, identity confusion, and social anxiety in emerging adulthood. *British Journal of Developmental Psychology, 38,* 543-565.

Miech, R.A., & others (2020). *Monitoring the Future: National survey results on drug use, 1975-2019. Vol. 1:* Secondary school students. Ann Arbor, MI: University of Michigan Institute for Social Research.

Mikkelsson, L., & others (2006). School fitness tests as predictors of adult health-related fitness. *American Journal of Human Biology, 18,* 342-349.

Mikulincer, M., & Shaver, P.R. (2019). Attachment theory expanded: A behavioral systems approach to personality. In K. Deaux & M. Snyder (Eds.), *Oxford handbook of personality and social psychology.* New York: Oxford University Press.

Mikulincer, M., & Shaver, P.R. (2021). Attachment theory. In P.J. Corr & G. Matthews (Eds.), *Cambridge handbook of personality psychology.* New York: Cambridge University Press.

Milene-Moehlecke, M., & others (2020). Self-perceived body image, dissatisfaction with body weight, and nutritional status of Brazilian adolescents: A nationwide study. *Journal of Pediatrics, 96,* 76-83.

Miller, B.C., Benson, B., & Galbraith, K.A. (2001). Family relationships and adolescent pregnancy risk: A research synthesis. *Developmental Review, 21,* 1-38.

Miller, B.L., & others (2021, in press). Online peers and offline highs: An examination of online peer groups, social media homophily, and substance use. *Journal of Psychoactive Drugs.*

Miller, E., & others (2012). "Coaching boys into men": A cluster-randomized controlled trial of a dating violence prevention program. *Journal of Adolescent Health, 51,* 431-438.

Miller, J.G., Wice, M., & Goyal, N. (2020). Culture, parenting practices, and moral development. In D.J. Laible & others (Eds.), *Oxford handbook of moral development.* New York: Oxford University Press.

Miller, M.E., Borowski, S., & Zeman, J.L. (2020). Co-rumination moderates the relation between emotional competencies and depressive symptoms in adolescents: A longitudinal examination. *Journal of Abnormal Child Psychology, 48,* 851-863.

Miller, P., & others (2021). Examining income dynamics and externalizing and internalizing trajectories through a developmental psychopathology lens: A nationally representative study. *Development and Psychopathology, 33,* 1-17.

Miller, P.H. (2016). *Theories of developmental psychology* (6th ed.). New York: Worth.

Miller, P.J., & Cho, G.E. (2018). *Self-esteem in time and place.* New York: Academic Press.

Miller, T.W., Nigg, J.T., & Miller, R.L. (2009). Attention deficit hyperactivity disorder in African American children: What can be concluded from the past ten years? *Clinical Psychology Review, 29,* 77-86.

Minhas, P.S., & others (2021). Restoring metabolism of myeloid cells reverses cognitive decline in aging. *Nature, 590*(7844), 122-128.

Minor, K.A., & Benner, A.D. (2018). School climate and college attendance for Black adolescents: Moving beyond college-going culture. *Journal of Research on Adolescence, 28,* 160-168.

Miranda, V.P., & others (2021). Body image disorders associated with lifestyle and body composition of female adolescents. *Public Health Nutrition, 24,* 95-105.

Mischel, W. (1968). *Personality and assessment.* New York: Wiley.

Mischel, W. (2004). Toward an integrative science of the person. *Annual Review of Psychology* (Vol. 55). Palo Alto, CA: Annual Reviews.

Mischel, W. (2014). *The marshmallow test: Mastering self-control.* Boston: Little Brown.

Mischel, W., Ebbesen, E.B., & Zeiss, A.R. (1972). Cognitive and attentional mechanisms in delay of gratification. *Journal of Personality and Social Psychology, 21,* 204-218.

Mischel, W., & Mischel, H. (1975, April). *A cognitive social-learning analysis of moral development.* Paper presented at the meeting of the Society for Research in Child Development, Denver.

Mischel, W., & Moore, B. (1973). Effects of attention to symbolically presented rewards on self-control. *Journal of Personality and Social Psychology, 28,* 172-179.

Mischel, W., & others (1989). Delay of gratification in children. *Science, 244,* 933-938.

Mitchell, A.B., & Stewart, J.B. (2013). The efficacy of all-male academies: Insights from critical race theory (CRT). *Sex Roles, 69,* 382-392.

Mizala, A., Martinez, F., & Martinez, S. (2015). Pre-service elementary school teachers' expectations about student performance: How their beliefs are affected by their mathematics anxiety and student's gender. *Teaching and Teacher Education, 50,* 70-78.

Mocorro, I., & others (2021, in press). Initiation of HIV pre-exposure prophylaxis in adolescents and young adults: Barriers and opportunities. *Journal of the American Association of Nurse Practitioners.*

Modabbernia, A., & others (2021). Multivariate patterns of brain-behavior-environment associations in the adolescent and brain cognitive development study. *Biological Psychiatry, 89,* 510-520.

Moffitt, T.E. (2012). *Childhood self-control predicts adult health, wealth, and crime.* Paper presented at the Symposium on Symptom Improvement in Well-Being, Copenhagen.

Moffitt, T.E., & others (2011). A gradient of childhood self-control predicts health, wealth, and public safety. *Proceedings of the National Academy of Sciences U.S.A., 108,* 2693-2698.

Moffitt, U., Juang, L.P., & Syed, M. (2020). Intersectionality and youth identity development research in Europe. *Frontiers in Psychology, 11,* 78.

Mohammadi, B., & others (2020). Structural brain changes in young males addicted to video-gaming. *Brain and Cognition, 139,* 105518.

Mohan, L., Yilanli, M., & Ray, S. (2021). *Conduct disorder.* Treasure Island, FL: StatPearls.

Molina, M.F., & Schmidt, V. (2020). Relationship between family functioning and possible selves in adolescents from Argentina. *Journal of Genetic Psychology, 181,* 319-335.

Mollborn, S. (2017). Teenage mothers today: What we know and how it matters. *Child Development Perspectives, 11,* 63-69.

Monaco, A.P. (2021). An epigenetic, transgenerational model of increased mental health disorders in children, adolescents, and young adults. *European Journal of Human Genetics, 29,* 387-395.

Monahan, K.C., Lee, J.M., & Steinberg, L. (2011). Revisiting the impact of part-time work on adolescent adjustment: Distinguishing between selection and socialization using propensity score matching. *Child Development, 82,* 96-112.

Moninger, J. (2013). *How to talk with your child about losing weight.* Retrieved February 21, 2013, from http://www.parents.com/kids/teens/weight-loss/how-to-talk-to-your-child-about-losing-weight/

Montemayor, R. (1982). The relationship between parent-adolescent conflict and the amount of time adolescents spend with parents, peers, and alone. *Child Development, 53,* 1512-1519.

Montgomery, M. (2005). Psychosocial intimacy and identity: From early adolescence to emerging adulthood. *Journal of Adolescent Research, 20,* 346-374.

Moons, P., & others (2021). Sense of coherence in adults with congenital heart disease in 15 countries: Patient characteristics, cultural dimensions, and quality of life. *European Journal of Cardiovascular Nursing, 20,* 48-55.

Moore, C.A., & Bokor, B.R. (2021). *Anorexia nervosa.* Treasure Island, FL: StatPearls.

Moore, D. (2001). *The dependent gene.* New York: W.H. Freeman.

Moore, D. (2015). *The developing genome.* New York: Oxford University Press.

Moore, D.S. (2017). Behavioral epigenetics. *Wiley Interdisciplinary Reviews. Systems Biology and Medicine, 9,* 1.

Moore, S.R., Harden, K.P., & Mendle, J. (2014). Pubertal timing and adolescent sexual behavior in girls. *Developmental Psychology, 50,* 1734-1745.

Moradi, M., & others (2021, in press). Association of overweight/obesity with depression, anxiety, low self-esteem, and body dissatisfaction in children and adolescents: A systematic review and meta-analysis of observational studies. *Critical Review of Food Science and Nutrition.*

Morawska, A. (2020). The effects of gendered parenting on child development outcomes: A systematic review. *Clinical Child and Family Psychology Review, 23,* 553-576.

Moreau, C., & others (2018). Measuring gender norms about relationships in early adolescence: Results from the Global Early Adolescent Study. *SSM-Population Health, 7,* 014-14.

Morelli, M., & others (2021). The relationship between dark triad personality traits and sexting behaviors among adolescents and young adults across 11 countries. *International Journal of Environmental Research and Public Health, 18*(5), 2526.

Moreno-Jimenez, E.P., & others (2021). Evidences for adult hippocampal neurogenesis in humans. *Journal of Neuroscience, 41,* 2541-2553.

Morgan, E.M. (2014). Outcomes of sexual behaviors among sexual minority youth. *New Directions for Child and Adolescent Development, 144,* 21-36.

Mori, C., & others (2020). The prevalence of sexting behaviors among emerging adults: A meta-analysis. *Archives of Sexual Behavior, 49,* 1103-1119.

Morin, A.J.S., & others (2017). Adolescents' body image trajectories: A further test of the self-equilibrium hypothesis. *Developmental Psychology, 53,* 1501-1521.

Morreale, M.C. (2004). Executing juvenile offenders: A fundamental failure of society. *Journal of Adolescent Health, 35,* 341.

Morrison, G.S., & others (2022). *Early childhood education today* (15th ed.). Upper Saddle River, NJ: Pearson.

Morrison, S.C., Fife, T., & Hertlein, K.M. (2017). Mechanisms behind prolonged effects of parental divorce: A phenomenological study. *Journal of Divorce and Remarriage, 58,* 54-63.

Morrison-Beedy, D., & others (2013). Reducing sexual risk behavior in adolescent girls: Results from a randomized trial. *Journal of Adolescent Health, 52,* 314-322.

Moses, J.O., Villodas, M.T., & Villodas, F. (2020). Black and proud: The role of ethnic-racial identity in the development of future expectations among at-risk adolescents. *Cultural Diversity and Ethnic Minority Psychology, 26,* 112-123.

Moses-Payne, M.E., & others (2021, in press). I know better! Emerging metacognition allows adolescents to ignore false advice. *Developmental Science.*

Motes, M.A., & others (2018). Conjoint differences in inhibitory control and processing speed in childhood to older adult cohorts: Discriminant functions from a Go/No-Go task. *Psychology and Aging, 33,* 1070-1078.

Mounts, N.S., & Allen, C. (2020). Parenting styles and practices: Traditional approaches and their application to multiple types of moral behavior. In D.J. Laible & others (Eds.), *Oxford handbook of parenting and moral development.* New York: Oxford University Press.

Mousavi, M.S., & others (2020). Gender identity development in the shadow of socialization: a grounded theory approach. *Archives of Women's Mental Health, 22,* 245-251.

Moussa, M., & others (2021, in press). Cardiovascular effects of energy drinks in the pediatric population. *Pediatric Emergency Care.*

Mrug, S., Borch, C., & Cillessen, A.H.N. (2012). Other-sex friendships in late adolescence: Risky associations for substance abuse and sexual debut? *Journal of Youth and Adolescence, 40,* 875-888.

Muencks, K., & others (2020). Does my professor think my ability can change? Students' perceptions of their STEM professors' mindset beliefs predict their psychological vulnerability, engagement, and performance in class. *Journal of Experimental Psychology: General, 149,* 2119-2144.

Muenks, K., Wigfield, A., & Eccles, J.S. (2018). I can do this! The development and calibration of children's expectations for success and competence beliefs. *Developmental Review, 48,* 24-39.

Muftic, L.R., & Updegrove, A.H. (2018). The mediating effect of self-control on parenting and delinquency: A gendered approach with a multinational sample. *International Journal of Offender Therapy and Comparative Criminology, 62,* 3058-3076.

Muller, U., & Kerns, K. (2015). Development of executive function. In R.M. Lerner (Ed.), *Handbook of child psychology and developmental science* (7th ed.). New York: Wiley.

Mullola, S., & others (2012). Gender differences in teachers' perceptions of students' temperament, educational competence, and teachability. *British Journal of Educational Psychology, 82*(2), 185-206.

Murcia, K., Pepper, C., & Williams, J. (2020). Youth STEM career choices: What's influencing secondary students' decision making. *Issues in Educational Research, 30,* 593-611.

Murnane, R.J., & Levy, F. (1996). *Teaching the new basic skills.* New York: Free Press.

Murray, A.L., Eisner, M., & Ribeaud, D. (2020). Within-person analysis of developmental cascades between externalizing and internalizing problems. *Journal of Child Psychology and Psychiatry, 61,* 681-688.

Mussen, P.H., Honzik, M., & Eichorn, D. (1982). Early adult antecedents of life satisfaction at age 70. *Journal of Gerontology, 37,* 316-322.

Muzio, M.R., & Cascella, M. (2020). *Histology, Axon.* Treasure Island, FL: StatPearls.

Myers, D. (2008, June 2). Commentary in S. Begley & J. Interlandi, *The dumbest generation? Don't be dumb.* Retrieved July 22, 2008, from www.newsweek.com/id/138536/

Myers, D., Baer, W., & Choi, S. (1996). The changing problem of overcrowded housing. *Journal of the American Planning Association, 62,* 66-84.

Myers, D.G. (2010). *Psychology* (9th ed.). New York: Worth.

N

Nabbijohn, A.N., & others (2020). Children's bias in appraisals of gender-variant peers. *Journal of Experimental Child Psychology, 196,* 104865.

NACE (National Association of Colleges and Employers) (2020, February 12). *Employers plan to increase college hiring by 5.8 percent.* Retrieved February 12, 2020, from www.naceweb.org/job-market

NACE (National Association of Colleges and Employers) (2021, March). *Job outlook 2021.* Bethlehem, PA: NACE.

Nagata, J.M., Magid, H.S.A., & Gabriel, K.P. (2020). Screen time for children and adolescents during the coronavirus disease 2019 pandemic. *Obesity, 28,* 1582-1583.

Nagel, B.J., & others (2011). Altered white matter microstructure in children with attention-deficit/hyperactivity disorder. *Journal of the American Academy of Child and Adolescent Psychiatry, 50,* 283-292.

Nair, R.L., Roche, K.M., & White, R.M.B. (2018). Acculturation gap distress among Latino youth: Prospective links to family processes and youth depressive symptoms, alcohol use, and academic performance. *Journal of Youth and Adolescence, 47,* 105-120.

Nakhoul, L., & others (2020). Attachment style and addictions (alcohol, cigarette, waterpipe, and internet) among Lebanese adolescents: A national study. *BMC Psychology, 8*(1), 33.

Nalani, A., Yoshikawa, H., & Carter, P. (2021). Social science-based pathways to reduce social inequality in youth outcomes and opportunities at scale. *SOCIUS: Sociological Research for a Dynamic World, 7,* 1-17.

Nansel, T.R., & others (2001). Bullying behaviors among U.S. youth. *Journal of the American Medical Association, 285,* 2094-2100.

Narváez, D. (2020). Evolution and the parenting ecology of moral development. In D. Laible, L. Padilla-Walker, & G. Carlo (Ed.), *Handbook of parenting and moral development.* New York: Oxford University Press.

Narváez, D. (2021). Moral education at a time of human ecological devastation. *Journal of Moral Education, 50,* 55-67.

Narváez, D., & Gleason, T.R. (2013). Developmental optimism. In D. Narváez & others, *Evolution, early experience, and human development.* New York: Oxford University Press.

NASSPE (2012). *Single-sex schools/schools with single-sex classrooms/what's the difference?* Retrieved from www.singlesexschools.org/schools-schools.com

Nastasi, B.K., & Naser, S.C. (2021). UN Convention on the Rights of the Child and the sustainable development goals: Implications for schools and regulators. In N.S. Rubin & R.L. Flores (Eds.), *Cambridge handbook of psychology and human rights.* New York: Cambridge University Press.

Nation's Report Card (2019). *Mathematics and reading in the 4th and 8th grades.* Washington, DC: National Center for Education Statistics.

National Assessment of Educational Progress (NAEP) (2016). *The nation's report card, 2015.* Washington, DC: National Center for Educational Statistics.

National Association for Gifted Children (2020). *Gifted children.* Washington, DC: Author.

National Black Family Institute (2021). *The ABCs of survival.* Washington, DC: Author.

National Center for Education Statistics (1997). *School-family linkages.* Unpublished manuscript. Washington, DC: U.S. Department of Education.

National Center for Education Statistics (1998). *Postsecondary financing strategies: How undergraduates combine work, borrowing, and attendance.* Washington, DC: U.S. Department of Education.

National Center for Education Statistics (2002). *Contexts of postsecondary education: Earning opportunities.* Washington, DC: U.S. Department of Education.

National Center for Education Statistics (2017). *The condition of education 2017.* Washington, DC: U.S. Office of Education.

National Center for Education Statistics (2020). Status dropout rates 2017. *Digest of Education Statistics.* Washington, DC: U.S. Department of Education.

National Center for Education Statistics (2020). *The condition of education 2019.* Washington, DC: U.S. Office of Education.

National Center for Health Statistics (2000). *Health United States, 1999.* Atlanta, GA: Centers for Disease Control and Prevention.

National Center for Health Statistics (2017). *Prevalence of obesity among adults and youth: United States, 2015-2016.* Atlanta: Centers for Disease Control and Prevention.

National Center for Health Statistics (2020). *Death rates.* Atlanta: Centers for Disease Control and Prevention.

National Center for Health Statistics (2020). *Health United States 2018.* Atlanta: Centers for Disease Control and Prevention.

National Institute of Mental Health (2020). *Autism spectrum disorders.* Washington, DC: Author.

National Institutes of Health (2021). *What is a gene?* Washington, DC: U.S. National Library of Medicine.

National Longitudinal Study of Adolescent to Adult Health (2021). Retrieved January 10, 2021, from www.addhealth.cpc.unc.edu/

National Research Council (1999). *How people learn.* Washington, DC: National Academic Press.

National Research Council (2004). *Engaging schools: Fostering high school students' motivation to learn.* Washington, DC: National Academies Press.

National Sleep Foundation (2020). *How much sleep do we really need?* Washington, DC: Author.

Naule, L., Malone, L., & Kaiser, L.B. (2021). Puberty, a sensitive window of hypothalamic development and plasticity. *Endocrinology, 162*(1), bqaa209.

Near, C.E. (2013). Selling gender: Associations of box art representation of female characters with sales for teen- and mature-rated video games. *Sex Roles, 68,* 252-269.

Negru-Subtirica, O., & others (2020). Social comparison at school: Can GPA and personality mutually influence each other across time? *Journal of Personality, 88,* 555-567.

Nejati, V., & Derakhshan, Z. (2021). The effect of physical activity with and without cognitive demand on the improvement of executive functions and behavioral symptoms in children with ADHD. *Expert Review of Neurotherapeutics, 21,* 607-614.

Nelson, C.A. (2003). Neural development and lifelong plasticity. In R.M. Lerner, F. Jacobs, & D. Wertlieb (Eds.), *Handbook of applied developmental science* (Vol. 1). Thousand Oaks, CA: Sage.

Nelson, C.A., Fox, N.A., & Zeanah, C.H. (2014). *Romania's abandoned children.* Cambridge, MA: Harvard University Press.

Nelson, K., & Fivush, R. (2020). The development of autobiographical memory, autobiographical narratives, and autobiographical consciousness. *Psychological Reports, 123,* 71-96.

Nelson, L.J. (2021, in press). The theory of emerging adulthood 20 years later: A look at where it has taken us, what we know now, and where we need to go. *Emerging Adulthood.*

Nelson, L.J., Padilla-Walker, L.M., & McLean, R.D. (2021). Longitudinal predictors of helicopter parenting in emerging adulthood. *Emerging Adulthood, 3,* 240-251.

Nelson, L.J., & others (2007). "If you want me to treat you like an adult, start acting like one!" Comparing the criteria that emerging adults and their parents have for adulthood. *Journal of Family Psychology, 21,* 665-674.

Nelson, L.J., & others (2011). Parenting in emerging adulthood: An examination of parenting clusters and correlates. *Journal of Youth and Adolescence, 40,* 730-743.

Nese, R.N.T., & others (2021). Obtaining stakeholder feedback to improve the middle to high school transition. *ERIC #ED612647.*

Nesi, J., Choukas-Bradley, S., & Prinstein, M.J. (2018). Transformation of adolescent peer relations in the social media context: Part 2—Application to peer group processes and future directions of research. *Clinical Child and Family Psychology Review, 21,* 295-319.

NETWORK (2021). *The legacy of injustices against Native Americans.* Washington, DC: Author.

Neuenschwander, R., & Blair, C. (2017). Zooming in on children's behavior during delay of gratification: Disentangling impulsigenic and volitional processes underlying self-regulation. *Journal of Experimental Child Psychology, 154,* 46-63.

Neuman, W.L. (2020). *Social science research methods* (8th ed.). Upper Saddle River, NJ: Pearson.

Neumann, E., & others (2015). Attachment in romantic relationships and somatization. *Journal of Nervous and Mental Disease, 203,* 101-106.

Nevill, A.M., & others (2021). Are early and late maturers likely to be fitter in the general population? *International Journal of Environmental Science and Public Health, 18*(2), 497.

Neville, H.J. (2006). Different profiles of plasticity within human cognition. In Y. Munakata & M.H. Johnson (Eds.), *Attention and Performance XXI: Processes of change in brain and cognitive development.* Oxford, UK: Oxford University Press.

New, M. (2008, October). *Binge eating disorder.* Retrieved February 27, 2011, from http://kidshealth.org/parent/emotions/behavior/binge_eating.html

Newman, B.S., & Muzzonigro, P.G. (1993). The effects of traditional family values on the coming out process of gay male adolescents. *Adolescence, 28,* 213-226.

Ng, F.F., Pomerantz, E.M., & Deng, C. (2014). Why are Chinese parents more psychologically controlling than American parents? "My child is my report card." *Child Development, 85,* 355-369.

Ng, Q.X., & others (2018). Early life sexual abuse is associated with increased suicide attempts: An update meta-analysis. *Journal of Psychiatric Research, 99,* 129-141.

Nguyen, D.J., & others (2018). Prospective relations between parent-adolescent acculturation conflict and mental health symptoms among Vietnamese American adolescents. *Cultural Diversity and Ethnic Minority Psychology, 24,* 151-161.

Nguyen, T.V. (2018). Developmental effects of androgens in the human brain. *Journal of Neuroendocrinology, 30,* 2.

Ni, H.W., Goodale, B.M., & Huo, Y.J. (2021). How the rich get richer: Affluence cues at American universities increase the social class achievement gap. *Social Psychology of Education, 23,* 125-141.

Nichols, M.P., & Davis, S. (2021). *Family therapy* (12th ed.). Upper Saddle River, NJ: Pearson.

Nichols, S., & Brewington, S. (2020). Preservice teachers' beliefs about high-stakes testing and their working environments. *Education Policy Analysis Archives, 28,* 30.

Nickalls, S. (2012, March 9). Why college students shouldn't online date. *The Tower,* Philadelphia: Arcadia University. Retrieved February 27, 2013, from http://tower.arcadia.edu/?p5754

Nicoteri, J.A., & Miskovsky, M.J. (2014). Revisiting the freshman "15": Assessing body mass index in the first college year and beyond. *Journal of the American Association of Nurse Practitioners, 26,* 220-224.

Nieder, T.O., Eyssel, J., & Kohler, A. (2020). Being trans without medical transition: Exploring characteristics of trans individuals from Germany not seeking gender-affirmative medical interventions. *Archives of Sexual Behavior, 49,* 2661-2672.

Nielson, M.G., & others (2020). Does gender-binding help or hinder friending? The roles of gender and gender similarity in friendship formation. *Developmental Psychology, 56,* 1157-1169.

Nieuwenhuis, D., & others (2020) Adipkines: A gear shift in puberty. *Obesity Review, 21*(6), e13005.

Nilsen, E.S., & Bacso, S.A. (2017). Cognitive and behavioral predictors of adolescents' communicative perspective-taking and social relationships. *Journal of Adolescence, 56,* 52-63.

Nilsen, F.M., & Tulve, N.S. (2020). A systematic review and meta-analysis examining the relationship between chemical and non-chemical stressors and inherent characteristics in children with ADHD. *Environmental Research, 180,* 108884.

Nippold, M.A. (2016). *Later language development: School-age children, adolescents, and young adults* (4th ed.). Austin, TX: Pro-Ed.

Nisbett, R.E., & others (2012). Intelligence: New findings and theoretical developments. *American Psychologist, 67,* 130-159.

Nishina, A., & Bellmore, A. (2018). Inequality and neighborhood effects on peer relations. In W.M. Bukowski & others (Eds.), *Handbook of peer interactions, relationships, and groups* (2nd ed.). New York: Guilford.

Noddings, N. (2006). *Critical lessons: What our schools should teach.* New York: Cambridge University Press.

Noddings, N. (2016). Moral life and education. *Action in Teacher Education, 38,* 212-216.

Noe-Bustamante, L. (2020, April 7). *Education levels of recent Latino immigrants in the U.S. reached new highs as of 2018.* Washington, DC: Pew Research Center.

Noll, J.G., & others (2017). Childhood sexual abuse and early timing of puberty. *Journal of Adolescent Health, 60,* 65-71.

Norris, A.L., & others (2019). African-American sexual minority adolescents and sexual health disparities: An exploratory cross-sectional study. *Journal of the National Medical Association, 111,* 302-309.

Norris, S.C., Gleaves, D.H., & Hutchinson, A.D. (2019). Anorexia nervosa and perfectionism: A meta-analysis. *International Journal of Eating Disorders, 52*(3), 219-229.

Nottelmann, E.D., & others (1987). Gonadal and adrenal hormone correlates of adjustment in early adolescence. In R.M. Lerner & T.T. Foch (Eds.), *Biological-psychological interactions in early adolescence.* Hillsdale, NJ: Erlbaum.

Novello, L., & Speiser, P.W. (2018). Premature adrenarche. *Pediatric Annals, 47*(1), e7-e11.

Nsamenang, A.B. (2002). Adolescence in sub-Saharan Africa: An image constructed from Africa's triple inheritance. In B. Brown, R.W. Larson, & T.S. Saraswathi (Eds.), *The world's youth.* New York: Cambridge University Press.

Nucci, L. (2006). Education for moral development. In M. Killen & J. Smetana (Eds.), *Handbook of moral development.* Mahwah, NJ: Erlbaum.

Nyberg, J., & others (2014). Cardiovascular and cognitive fitness at age 18 and risk of early-onset dementia. *Brain, 137,* 1514-1523.

O

O'Connor, D., & others (2020). Positive youth development and gender differences in high performance sport. *Journal of Sports Sciences, 38,* 1399-1407.

O'Halloran, L., & others (2018). Neural circuitry underlying sustained attention in healthy adolescents and in ADHD symptomatology. *NeuroImage, 160,* 395-406.

O'Reilly, A.M., & others (2021, in press). A co-twin control study of the association between bullying victimization and self-harm and suicide attempt in adolescence. *Journal of Adolescent Health.*

O'Reilly, M. (2020). Social media and adolescent mental health: The good, the bad, and the ugly. *Journal of Mental Health, 29,* 200-206.

Oakes, L.M. (2021). Infant categorization. In J.J. Lockman & C.S. Tamis-LeMonda (Eds.), *Cambridge handbook of infant development.* New York: Cambridge University Press.

Oberle, E., & others (2019). Benefits of extracurricular participation in early adolescence: Associations with peer belonging and mental health. *Journal of Youth and Adolescence, 48,* 2255-2270.

Oberle, E., & others (2020). Screen time and extracurricular activities as risk and protective factors for mental health in adolescence: A population-level study. *Preventive Medicine, 141,* 106291.

Obsuth, I., & others (2020). Patterns of homotypic and heterotypic continuity between ADHD symptoms, externalizing and internalizing problems from age 7 to 15. *Journal of Abnormal Child Psychology, 48,* 223-236.

Occupational Outlook Handbook (2020-2021). Washington, DC: U.S. Department of Labor, Bureau of Labor Statistics.

OECD (2017a). *Teenage suicide.* Paris: Author.

OECD (2017b). *Obesity update 2017.* Paris: Author.

OECD (2019). *Marriage and divorce rates.* Paris: Author.

OECD (2020). *Education at a glance.* Paris: Author.

Offer, D., Ostrov, E., Howard, K.I., & Atkinson, R. (1988). *The teenage world: Adolescents' self-image in ten countries.* New York: Plenum.

Office of Adolescent Health (2020). *Teen Pregnancy Prevention Program.* Washington, DC: U.S. Department of Health and Human Services.

Ogihara, Y. (2017). Temporal changes in individualism and their ramification in Japan: Rising individualism and conflicts with persisting collectivism. *Frontiers in Psychology, 8,* 695.

Ogundele, M.O. (2018). Behavioral and emotional disorders in childhood: A brief overview for pediatricians. *World Journal of Clinical Psychology, 7*(1), 9-26.

Ojanen, T., & Findley-Van Nostrand, D. (2020). Adolescent social goal development: Mean-level changes and prediction by self-esteem and narcissism. *Journal of Genetic Psychology, 181,* 427-442.

Okamoto, S. (2021). Parental socioeconomic status and adolescent health in Japan. *Scientific Reports, 11*(1), 12089.

Okumu, M., & others (2019). Psychosocial syndemics and sexual risk practices among U.S. adolescents: Findings from the 2017 U.S. Youth Behavioral Survey. *International Journal of Behavioral Medicine, 26,* 297-305.

Olderbak, S., & others (2019). Sex differences in facial emotion perception ability across the lifespan. *Cognition and Emotion, 33,* 579-588.

Olmstead, S.B., Norona, J.C., & Anders, K.M. (2019). How do college experience and gender differentiate the enactment of hookup scripts among emerging adults? *Archives of Sexual Behavior, 48,* 1769-1783.

Olweus, D. (2003). Prevalence estimation of school bullying with the Olweus bully/victim questionnaire. *Aggressive Behavior, 29*(3), 239-269.

Olweus, D. (2013). School bullying: Development and some important changes. *Annual Review of Clinical Psychology* (Vol. 9). Palo Alto, CA: Annual Reviews.

Omariba, G., & Xiao, J. (2020). Association study of puberty-related candidate genes in Chinese female population. *International Journal of Genomics, 2020,* 142676.

Ong, K.K., Ahmed, M.L., & Dunger, D.B. (2006). Lesson from large population studies on timing and tempo of puberty (secular trends and relation to body size): The European trend. *Molecular and Cellular Endocrinology, 254-255,* 8-12.

Orben, A., Tomova, L., & Blakemore, S-J. (2020). The effects of social deprivation on adolescent development and mental health. *Lancet. Child and Adolescent Health, 4,* 634-640.

Orgiles, M., Carratala, E., & Espada, J.P. (2015). Perceived quality of the parental relationship and divorce effects on sexual behavior in Spanish adolescents. *Psychology, Health, and Medicine, 20,* 8-17.

Orr, A.J. (2011). Gendered capital: Childhood socialization and the "boy crisis" in education. *Sex Roles, 65,* 271-284.

Orri, M., & others (2020). Contributions of genes and environment to the longitudinal association between childhood impulsive-aggression and suicidality in adolescence. *Journal of Child Psychology and Psychiatry, 61,* 711-720.

Orri, M., & others (2021). Cohort profile: Quebec Longitudinal Study of Child Development (QLSCD). *Social Psychiatry and Psychiatric Epidemiology, 56,* 883-894.

Orth, U. (2018). The family environment in early childhood has a long-term effect on self-esteem: A longitudinal study from birth to age 27 years. *Journal of Personality and Social Psychology, 114,* 637-655.

Orth, U., & others (2021). Development of domain-specific self-evaluations: A meta-analysis of longitudinal studies. *Journal of Personality and Social Psychology, 120,* 145-172.

Osenk, I., Williamson, P., & Wade, T.D. (2020). Does perfectionism or pursuit of excellence contribute to successful learning? A meta-analytic review. *Psychological Assessment, 32,* 972-983.

Osher, D., & others (2020). Drivers of human development: How relationships and context shape learning and development. *Applied Developmental Science, 24,* 6-36.

Osmont, A., & others (2021, in press). Peers' choices influence adolescent risk-taking, especially when explicit risk information is lacking. *Journal of Research on Adolescence.*

Oswald, D.L., & Clark, E.M. (2003). Best friends forever? High school best friendships and the transition to college. *Personal Relationships, 10,* 187-196.

Overbye, K., & others (2021). Electrophysiological and behavioral indices of cognitive conflict processing across adolescence. *Developmental Cognitive Neuroscience, 48,* 100929.

Oyserman, D., & Destin, M. (2010). Identity-based motivation: Implications for intervention. *Counseling Psychologist, 38,* 1001-1043.

Ozde, C., & others (2020). Acute effects of Red Bull energy drinks on atrial electromechanical function in healthy young adults. *American Journal of Cardiology, 125,* 570-574.

Ozdemir, S.B., Ozdemir, M., & Boersma, K. (2021). How does adolescents' openness to diversity change over time? The role of majority-minority friendship, friends' views, and classroom social context. *Journal of Youth and Adolescence, 50,* 75-88.

Ozkul, B., & Gunusen, N.P. (2021, in press). Stressors and coping methods of Turkish adolescents with high and low risk of depression: A qualitative study. *Journal of American Psychiatric Nurses Association.*

P

Padilla-Walker, L.M., Day, R.D., Dyer, W.J., & Black, B.C. (2013). "Keep on keeping on, even when it's hard!": Predictors of outcomes of adolescent persistence. *Journal of Early Adolescence, 33,* 433-457.

Padilla-Walker, L.M., & Memmott-Elison, M.K. (2020). Family and moral development. In L.A. Jensen (Ed.), *Oxford handbook of moral development.* New York: Oxford University Press.

Padilla-Walker, L.M., Memmott-Elison, M., & Nelson, L. (2017). Positive relationships as an indicator of flourishing during emerging adulthood. In L.M. Padilla-Walker & L. Nelson (Eds.), *Flourishing in emerging adulthood.* New York: Oxford University Press.

Padilla-Walker, L.M., San, D., & Nelson, L.J. (2021). Profiles of helicopter parenting, parental warmth, and psychological control during emerging adulthood. *Emerging Adulthood, 9,* 132-144.

Pahlke, E., Hyde, J.S., & Allison, C.M. (2014). The effects of single-sex compared with coeducational schooling on students' performance and attitudes: A meta-analysis. *Psychological Bulletin, 140,* 1042-1072.

Palm, M.H., & others (2021). Patterns of bi-directional relations across alcohol, religiosity, and self-control in adolescent girls. *Addictive Behaviors, 114,* 106739.

Palmeira, L., & others (2019). Association study of variants in genes FTO, SLC6A4, DRD2, BDNF, and GHRL with binge eating disorder (BED) in Portuguese women. *Psychiatry Research, 273,* 309-311.

Paludi, M.A. (2002). *The psychology of women* (2nd ed.). Upper Saddle River, NJ: Prentice-Hall.

Pang, J.S., & Baumann, N. (2020). At the crossroads of women's experience: Insights from and intersections between motivation, emotion, gender, and culture. In F.M Cheung & D.F. Halpern (Eds.), *Cambridge handbook of the international psychology of women.* New York: Cambridge University Press.

Papini, D., & Sebby, R. (1988). Variations in conflictual family issues by adolescent pubertal status, gender, and family member. *Journal of Early Adolescence, 8,* 1-15.

Parens, E., & Johnston, J. (2009). Facts, values, and attention-deficit hyperactivity disorder (ADHD): An update on the controversies. *Child and Adolescent Psychiatry and Mental Health, 3,* 1.

Parent, M.C., & others (2016). Racial disparities in substance use by sport participation among high school students. *Journal of Studies on Alcohol and Drugs, 77,* 980-985.

Paricio, D., & others (2020). Positive adolescent development: Effects of a psychological intervention program in a rural setting. *International Journal of Environmental Research and Public Health, 17*(18), E6784.

Park, D., & others (2020). The development of grit and growth mindset during adolescence. *Journal of Experimental Child Psychology, 198,* 104889.

Park, J., Norasakkunkit, V., & Kashima, Y. (2017). Cross-cultural comparison of self-construal and well-being between Japan and South Korea: The role of self-focused and other-focused relational selves. *Frontiers in Psychology, 8,* 1516.

Park, J.S., & others (2020). Bilingualism and processing speed in typically developing children and children with developmental language disorder. *Journal of Speech, Language, and Hearing Research, 22,* 1479-1493.

Park, M.J., Brindis, C.D., Chang, F., & Irwin, C.E. (2008). A midcourse review of the Healthy People 2010: 21 Critical Health Objectives for Adolescents and Young Adults. *Journal of Adolescent Health, 42,* 329-334.

Park, M.J., Paul Mulye, T., Adams, S.H., Brindis, C.D., & Irwin, C.E. (2006). The health status of young adults in the United States. *Journal of Adolescent Health, 39,* 305-317.

Park, M.J., Scott, J.T., Adams, S.H., Brindis, C.D., & Irwin, C.E. (2014). Adolescent and young adult health in the United States in the past decade: Little improvement and young adults remain worse off than adolescents. *Journal of Adolescent Health, 55,* 3-16.

Parke, R.D., & Buriel, R. (2006). Socialization in the family: Ethnic and ecological perspectives. In W. Damon & R. Lerner (Eds.), *Handbook of child psychology* (6th ed.). New York: Wiley.

Parke, R.D., Coltrane, S., & Schofield, T. (2011). The bicultural advantage. In J. Marsh, R. Mendoza-Denton, & J.A. Smith (Eds.), *Are we born racist?* Boston: Beacon Press.

Parke, R.D., Roisman, G.I., & Rose, A.J. (2019). *Social development* (3rd ed.). New York; Wiley.

Parker, S.L., & others (2020). Relaxation during the evening and next-morning energy: The role of hassles, uplifts, and heart rate variability during work. *Journal of Occupational Health Psychology, 25,* 83-98.

Parkes, A., & others (2011). Comparison of teenagers' early same-sex and heterosexual behavior: UK data from the SHARE and RIPPLE studies. *Journal of Adolescent Health, 48,* 27-35.

Parzych, J., & others (2019). *Measuring the impact of school counselor ratios on student outcomes.* Retrieved from www.schoolcounselor.org/asca/media/asca/Publications/Research-Release-Parzych.pdf

Pascuzzo, K., Cyr, C., & Moss, E. (2013). Longitudinal association between adolescent attachment, adult romantic attachment, and emotion regulation strategies. *Attachment and Human Development, 15,* 83-103.

Pasterski, V., Golombok, S., & Hines, M. (2011). Sex differences in social behavior. In P.K. Smith & C.H. Hart (Eds.), *Wiley-Blackwell handbook of childhood social development* (2nd ed.). New York: Wiley.

Patchin, J.W., & Hinduja, S. (2019). The nature and extent of sexting among a national sample of middle and high school students in the U.S. *Archives of Sexual Behavior, 48,* 2333-2343.

Patterson, G.R., Forgatch, M.S., & DeGarmo, D.S. (2010). Cascading effects following intervention. *Development and Psychopathology, 22,* 949-970.

Patterson, G.R., Reid, J.B., & Dishion, T.J. (1992). *Antisocial boys* (Vol. 4). Eugene, OR: Castalia.

Patton, G.C., & others (2011). A prospective study of the effects of optimism on adolescent health risks. *Pediatrics, 127,* 308-316.

Paul, E.L., & White, K.M. (1990). The development of intimate relationships in late adolescence. *Adolescence, 25,* 375-400.

Paul, P. (2003, Sept./Oct.). The PermaParent trap. *Psychology Today, 36*(5), 40-53.

Pauletti, R.E., & others (2017). Psychological androgyny and children's mental health: A new look with new measures. *Sex Roles, 76,* 705-718.

Paulhus, D.L. (2008). Birth order. In M.M. Haith & J.B. Benson (Eds.), *Encyclopedia of infant and early childhood development.* Oxford, UK: Elsevier.

Pearlman, E. (2013). *Twin psychological development.* Retrieved February 14, 2013, from http://christinabaglivitinglof.com/twin-pregnancy/six-twin-experts-te . . .

Pearson, N., & others (2017). Clustering and correlates of screen time and eating behaviors among young adolescents. *BMC Public Health, 17,* 533.

Peckins, M.K., & others (2020). Violence exposure and social deprivation is associated with cortisol reactivity in urban adolescents. *Psychoneuroendocrinology, 111,* 104426.

Pedersen, E.R., & others (2020). Development of a measure to assess protective behavioral strategies for pregaming among young adults. *Substance Use and Abuse, 55,* 534-545.

Peel, K.L. (2020). Everyday classroom teaching practices for self-regulated learning. *Issues in Educational Research, 30,* 260-282.

Pei, Y., Cong, Z., & Wu, B. (2020). The impact of living alone and intergenerational support on depressive symptoms among older Mexican Americans: Does gender matter? *International Journal of Aging and Human Development, 90,* 255-280.

Pengpid, S., & Peltzer, K. (2020). Prevalence and correlates of sexual risk behavior among school-going adolescents in four Caribbean countries. *Behavioral Science, 10*(11), E166.

Pennequin, V., & others (2020). Metacognition and emotional regulation in children from 8 to 12 years old. *British Journal of Educational Psychology, 90*(Suppl. 1), S1-S16.

Peralta, L.R., & others (2019). Influence of school-level socioeconomic status on children's physical activity, fitness, and fundamental movement skills. *Journal of School Health, 89,* 460-467.

Pereira, A., & others (2021, in press). Total and central adiposity are associated with age at gonadarche and incidence of precocious gonadarche in boys. *Journal of Clinical Endocrinology and Metabolism.*

Perlman, L. (2008, July 22). Am I an "I" or "We"? *Twins,* pp. 1-2.

Perrin, A., & Anderson, M. (2019, April 10). *Share of U.S. adults using social media, including Facebook, is mostly unchanged since 2018.* Washington, DC: Pew Research Center.

Perrin, J.M., & others (2020). Principles and policies to strengthen child and adolescent health and well-being. *Health Affairs, 39,* 1677-1683.

Perrin, P.B., & others (2020). The minority strengths model: Development and initial path analytic validation in racially/ethnically diverse LGBTQ individuals. *Journal of Clinical Psychology, 76,* 118-136.

Perry, A.J., & others (2021). Pathways from early family violence to adolescent reactive aggression and violence victimization. *Journal of Family Violence, 36,* 75-86.

Perry, D.G., & Pauletti, R.E. (2011). Gender and adolescent development. *Journal of Research on Adolescence, 21,* 61-74.

Perry, J.C., & Wallace, E.W. (2012). What schools are doing around career development: Implications for policy and practice. *New Directions in Youth Development, 134,* 33-44.

Perry, W.G. (1999). *Forms of ethical and intellectual development in the college years: A scheme.* San Francisco: Jossey-Bass.

Persike, M., & Seiffge-Krenke, I. (2012). Competence in coping with stress in adolescents from three regions of the world. *Journal of Youth and Adolescence, 41,* 863-879.

Persike, M., & Seiffge-Krenke, I. (2014). Is stress perceived differently in relationships with parents and peers? Inter- and intra-regional comparisons on adolescents from 21 nations. *Journal of Adolescence, 37,* 493-504.

Persky, H.R., Dane, M.C., & Jin, Y. (2003). *The nation's report card: Writing 2002.* U.S. Department of Education.

Peskin, H. (1967). Pubertal onset and ego functioning. *Journal of Abnormal Psychology, 72,* 1-15.

Petersen, A.C. (1987, September). Those gangly years. *Psychology Today, 21,* 28-34.

Petersen, J.L., & Hyde, J.S. (2010). A meta-analytic review of research on gender differences in sexuality, 1973-2007. *Psychological Bulletin, 136,* 21-38.

Peterson, R.E., & others (2012). Binge eating disorder mediates links between symptoms of depression, anxiety, and caloric intake in overweight and obese women. *Journal of Obesity, 2012,* 40763.

Petrilli, M.J. (2020). Stay the course on national standards. *Education Next, 20*(2), 73, 77-78.

Petts, R.J. (2014). Family, religious attendance, and trajectories of psychological well-being among youth. *Journal of Family Psychology, 28,* 759-768.

Peverill, M., & others (2021). Socioeconomic status and child psychopathology in the United States: A meta-analysis of population-based studies. *Clinical Psychology Review, 83,* 101933.

Pew Research Center (2010). *Tattoo taboo.* Washington, DC: Author.

Pew Research Center (2014, March 6). *Women's college enrollment gains leave men behind.* Washington, DC: Pew Research Center.

Pew Research Center (2021, April 7). *Mobile phone use in 2021.* Washington, DC: Author.

Peyre, H., & others (2017). Contributing factors and mental health outcomes of first suicide attempt during childhood and adolescence: Results from a nationally representative study. *Journal of Clinical Psychiatry, 78,* e622-e630.

Pfeffer, B., & others (2017). Interviewing adolescents about sexual matters. *Pediatric Clinics of North America, 64,* 291-304.

Pfeifer, J.H., & Allen, N.B. (2021). Puberty initiates cascading relationship between neurodevelopmental, social, and internalizing processes across adolescence. *Biological Psychiatry, 89,* 99-108.

Phan, J.M., & others (2021). Longitudinal effects of family psychopathology and stress on pubertal maturation and hormone coupling in adolescent twins. *Developmental Psychobiology, 63,* 512-528.

Phinney, J.S. (2006). Ethnic identity exploration in emerging adulthood. In J.J. Arnett & J.L. Tanner (Eds.), *Emerging adults in America.* Washington, DC: American Psychological Association.

Phinney, J.S. (2008). Bridging identities and disciplines: Advances and challenges in understanding multiple identities. *New Directions for Child and Adolescent Development, 120,* 97-109.

Phinney, J.S., & Baldelomar, O.A. (2011). Identity development in multiple developmental contexts. In L. Jensen (Ed.), *Bridging cultural and developmental approaches to psychology.* New York: Oxford University Press.

Phinney, J.S., & Vedder, P. (2013). Family relationship values of adolescents and parents: Intergenerational discrepancies and adaptation. In J.W. Berry & others (Eds.), *Immigrant youth in cultural transition.* New York: Psychology Press.

Piaget, J. (1952). *The origins of intelligence in children.* (M. Cook, Trans.). New York: International Universities Press.

Piaget, J. (1954). *The construction of reality in the child.* New York: Basic Books.

Piaget, J. (1972). Intellectual evolution from adolescence to adulthood. *Human Development, 15,* 1-12.

Pietromonaco, P.R., & Beck, L.A. (2018). Adult attachment and physical health. *Current Opinion in Psychology, 25,* 115-120.

Piff, P.K., & others (2010). Having less, giving more: The influence of social class on prosocial behavior. *Journal of Personality and Social Psychology, 99,* 771.

Piff, P.K., & others (2012). Higher social class predicts increased unethical behavior. *Proceedings of the National Academy of Sciences, 109,* 4086-4091.

Pigaiani, Y., & others (2020). Adolescent lifestyle behaviors, coping strategies, and subjective well-being during the COVID-19 pandemic: An online student survey. *Healthcare, 8*(4), E472.

Pinderhughes, E.E., & Brodzinsky, D.M. (2019). Parenting in adoptive families. In M.H. Bornstein (Ed.), *Handbook of parenting* (3rd ed.). New York: Routledge.

Pino, E.C., & others (2018). Adolescent socioeconomic status and depressive symptoms in later life: Evidence from structural equation models. *Journal of Affective Disorders, 225,* 702-708.

Pinquart, M., & Ebeling, M. (2020). Parental educational expectations and academic achievement in children and adolescents—a meta-analysis. *Educational Psychology Review, 32,* 463-480.

Pinquart, M., & Kauser, R. (2018). Do the associations of parenting styles with behavior problems and academic achievement vary by culture? Results from a meta-analysis. *Cultural Diversity and Ethnic Minority Psychology, 24,* 75-100.

PISA (2015). *PISA 2015: Results in focus.* Paris, France: OECD.

Pittman, J.F., Keiley, M.H., Kerpelman, J.L., & Vaughn, B.E. (2011). Attachment, identity, and intimacy: Parallels between Bowlby's and Erikson's paradigms. *Journal of Family Theory and Review, 3,* 32-46.

Pittman, J.F., Kerpelman, J.L., Soto, J.B., & Adler-Baeder, F.M. (2012). Identity exploration in the dating domain: The role of attachment dimensions and parenting practices. *Journal of Adolescence, 35,* 1485-1499.

Pizarro, K.W., Surkan, P.J., & Bustamante, I.V. (2021). The social ecology of parental monitoring: Parent-child dynamics in a high-risk Peruvian neighborhood. *Family Process, 60,* 199-215.

Plasman, J.S., & others (2020). Trend up: A cross-cohort exploration of STEM career and technical education participation by low-income students. *Journal of Education for Students Placed at Risk, 25,* 55-76.

Platt, J.M., & others (2017). Transdiagnostic psychiatric disorder risk associated with early age of menarche: A latent modeling approach. *Comprehensive Psychiatry, 79,* 70-79.

Platt, L.F. (2020). An exploratory study of predictors of relationship commitment for cisgender female partners of transgender individuals. *Family Process, 59,* 173-190.

Pleck, J.H. (1983). The theory of male sex role identity: Its rise and fall, 1936-present. In M. Levin (Ed.), *In the shadow of the past: Psychology portrays the sexes.* New York: Columbia University Press.

Pleck, J.H. (1995). The gender-role strain paradigm. In R.F. Levant & S. Pollack (Eds.), *A new psychology of men.* New York: Basic Books.

Pliatsikas, C., & others (2020). The effect of bilingualism on brain development from early childhood to young adulthood. *Brain Structure and Function, 225,* 2132-2152.

Plomin, R., Shakeshaft, N.G., McMillan, A., & Trzaskowski, M. (2014). Nature, nurture, and expertise. *Intelligence, 45,* 46-59.

Plourde, K.F., Thomas, R., & Nanda, G. (2020). Boys mentoring, gender norms, and reproductive health—potential for transformation. *Journal of Adolescent Health, 67,* 479-494.

Plucker, J. (2010). Interview. In P. Bronson & A. Merryman. The creativity crisis. *Newsweek,* 42-48.

Plucker, J.A., Karwowski, M., & Kaufman, J.C. (2020). Intelligence and creativity. In R.J. Sternberg (Ed.), *Cambridge handbook of intelligence* (2nd ed.). New York: Cambridge University Press.

Polce-Lynch, M., Myers, B.J., Kliewer, W., & Kilmartin, C. (2001). Adolescent self-esteem and gender: Exploring relations to sexual harassment, body image, media influence, and emotional expression. *Journal of Youth and Adolescence, 30,* 225-244.

Pollack, W. (1999). *Real boys.* New York: Henry Holt.

Pollak, Y., & others (2020). The role of parental monitoring in mediating the link between adolescent ADHD symptoms and risk-taking behavior. *Journal of Attention Disorders, 24,* 1141-1147.

Pomerantz, E.M. (2017). *Six principles to motivate your child to do well in school.* Retrieved November 8, 2017, from http://i-parents.illinois.edu/research/pomerantz.html

Pomerantz, E.M., Cheung, C.S., & Qin, L. (2012). Relatedness between children and parents: Implications for motivation. In R. Ryan (Ed.), *Oxford handbook of motivation.* New York: Oxford University Press.

Pomerantz, E.M., & Grolnick, W.S. (2017). The role of parenting in children's motivation and competence: What underlies facilitative parenting? In A.S. Elliott, C.S. Dweck, and D.S. Yeager (Eds.), *Handbook of competence and motivation* (2nd ed.). New York: Guilford.

Pomerantz, H., & others (2017). Pubertal timing and internalizing psychopathology: The role of relational aggression. *Journal of Child and Family Studies, 26,* 416–423.

Pompili, M., & others (2014). Bisexuality and suicide: A systematic review of the current literature. *Journal of Sexual Medicine, 11,* 1903–1913.

Pong, S., & Landale, N.S. (2012). Academic achievement of legal immigrants' children: The roles of parents' pre- and post-immigration characteristics in origin-group differences. *Child Development, 83,* 1543–1559.

Ponti, L., Ghinassi, S., & Tani, F. (2020). The role of vulnerable and grandiose narcissism in psychological perpetuated abuse within couple relationships: The mediating role of romantic jealousy. *Journal of Psychology, 154,* 144–158.

Poon, K. (2018). Hot and cool executive functions in adolescence: Development and contributions to important developmental outcomes. *Frontiers in Psychology, 8,* 2311.

Popham, W.J. (2020). *Classroom assessment* (9th ed.). Upper Saddle River, NJ: Pearson.

Poplawska, A., Szumowska, E., & Kus, J. (2021). Why do we need media multitasking? A self-regulatory perspective. *Frontiers in Psychology, 12,* 624649.

Posner, J., Polanczyk, G.V., & Sonuga-Barke, E. (2020). Attention-deficit hyperactivity disorder. *Lancet, 39,* 450–462.

Potard, C., Courtois, R., & Rusch, E. (2008). The influence of peers on risky behavior during adolescence. *European Journal of Contraception and Reproductive Health Care, 13,* 264–270.

Potochnick, S., Perreira, K.M., & Fuligni, A. (2012). Fitting in: The roles of social acceptance and discrimination in shaping the daily psychological well-being of Latino youth. *Social Science Quarterly, 93,* 173–190.

Poulin, F., & Denault, A-S. (2012). Other-sex friendship as a mediator between parental monitoring and substance use in boys and girls. *Journal of Youth and Adolescence, 41,* 1488–1501.

Poulin, F., & Pedersen, S. (2007). Developmental changes in gender composition of friendship networks in adolescent girls and boys. *Developmental Psychology, 43,* 1484–1496.

Powell, S. (2020). *Introduction to middle level education* (4th ed.). Upper Saddle River, NJ: Pearson.

Power & others (2021). General parenting and Hispanic mothers' feeding practices and styles. *International Journal of Environmental Research and Public Health, 18*(2), 380.

Powers, S., & Howley, E. (2021). *Exercise physiology* (11th ed.). New York: McGraw-Hill.

Pozzi, E., & others (2021). Natural correlates of emotion regulation in adolescents and emerging adults: A meta-analytic perspective. *Biological Psychiatry, 89,* 194–204.

Prabhakar, H. (2007). *Hopkins interactive guest blog: The public health experience at Johns Hopkins.* Retrieved January 31, 2008, from http://hopkins.typepad.com/guest/2007/03/the_public_heal.html

Prendergast, L.E., & others (2019). Outcomes of early adolescent sexual behavior in Australia: Longitudinal findings in young adulthood. *Journal of Adolescent Health, 64,* 516–522.

Prentice, W. (2021). *Principles of athletic training* (17th ed.). New York: McGraw-Hill.

Pressley, M. (2003). Psychology of literacy and literacy instruction. In I.B. Weiner & others (Eds.), *Handbook of psychology* (2nd ed., Vol. 7). New York: Wiley.

Pressley, M., Allington, R., Wharton-McDonald, R., Block, C.C., & Morrow, L.M. (2001). *Learning to read: Lessons from exemplary first grades.* New York: Guilford.

Pressley, M., Mohan, L., Reffitt, K., Raphael-Bogaert, L.R. (2007). Writing instruction in engaging and effective elementary settings. In S. Graham, C.A. MacArthur, & J. Fitzgerald (Eds.), *Best practices in writing instruction.* New York: Guilford.

Pressley, M., Raphael, L., Gallagher, D., & DiBella, J. (2004). Providence–St. Mel School: How a school that works for African-American students works. *Journal of Educational Psychology, 96,* 216–235.

Pressley, M., & others (2003). *Motivating primary-grades teachers.* New York: Guilford.

Priess, H.A., Lindberg, S.M., & Hyde, J.S. (2009). Adolescent gender-role identity and mental health: Gender intensification revisited. *Child Development, 80,* 1531–1544.

Prieto-Rodriguez, E., Sincock, K., & Blackmore, K. (2020). STEM initiatives matter: Results from a systematic review of secondary school interventions for girls. *International Journal of Science Education, 42,* 1144–1161.

Prins, S.J., & others (2021). Identifying sensitive periods when changes in parenting and peer factors are associated with changes in adolescent alcohol and marijuana use. *Social Psychiatry and Psychiatric Epidemiology, 56,* 605–617.

Prinstein, M.J., & Giletta, M. (2020). Future directions in peer research. *Journal of Clinical Child and Adolescent Psychology, 49,* 556–572.

Prinstein, M.J., Nesi, J., & Telzer, E.H. (2020) Commentary: An updated agenda for the study of digital media use and adolescent development—future directions following Odgers & Jensen (2020). *Journal of Child Psychology and Psychiatry, 61,* 349–352.

Prinstein, M.J., Rancourt, D., Guerry, J.D., & Browne, C.B. (2009). Peer reputations and psychological adjustment. In K.H. Rubin, W.M. Bukowski, & B. Laursen (Eds.), *Handbook of peer interactions, relationships, and groups.* New York: Guilford.

Prinstein, M.J., & others (2018). Peer status and psychopathology. In W.M. Bukowski & others (Eds.), *Handbook of peer interaction, relationships, and groups* (2nd ed.). New York: Guilford.

Protic, S., & others (2020). Differences in attachment dimensions and reflective functioning between traumatized juvenile offenders and maltreated non-delinquent adolescents from care services. *Child Abuse and Neglect, 103,* 104420.

Proulx, C.M., & Snyder-Rivas, L.A. (2013). *Journal of Family Psychology, 27,* 194–202.

Pryor, J.H., & others (2005). *The American freshman: National norms for fall 2005.* Los Angeles: Higher Education Research Institute, UCLA.

Psychster Inc. (2010). *Psychology of social media.* Retrieved February 21, 2013, from www.psychster.com

Puckett, J.A., & others (2020). Coping with discrimination: The insidious effects of gender minority stigma on depression and anxiety in transgender individuals. *Journal of Clinical Psychology, 76,* 176–194.

Pulkkinen, L., & Kokko, K. (2000). Identity development in adulthood: A longitudinal study. *Journal of Research in Personality, 34,* 445–470.

Putallaz, M., & others (2007). Overt and relational aggression and victimization: Multiple perspectives within the school setting. *Journal of School Psychology, 45,* 523–547.

Puterman, E., & others (2020). Predicting mortality from 57 economic, behavioral, social, and psychological factors. *Proceedings of the National Academy of Sciences U.S.A., 117,* 16273–16282.

Putnam, S.P., Sanson, A.V., & Rothbart, M.K. (2002). Child temperament and parenting. In M. Bornstein (Ed.), *Handbook of parenting* (2nd ed.). Mahwah, NJ: Erlbaum.

Puts, N.A., & others (2020). Reduced striatal GABA in unmedicated children with ADHD at 7T. *Psychiatry Research. Neuroimaging, 301,* 111082.

Putwain, D.W., & von der Embse, N. (2021). Cognitive-behavioral intervention for test anxiety in adolescent students: Do benefits extend to school-related wellbeing and clinical anxiety? *Anxiety, Stress, and Coping, 34,* 22–36.

Q

Qu, W., Jorgensen, N.A., & Telzer, E.H. (2021). A call for greater attention to culture in the study of brain and development. *Perspectives on Psychological Science, 16,* 275–293.

Qu, W., & others (2020). Gender and adolescent development across cultures. In F.M. Cheung & D.F. Halpern (Eds.), *Cambridge handbook of the international psychology of women.* New York: Cambridge University Press.

Queiroga, A.C., & others (2020). Secular trend in age at menarche for women in Portugal born 1920 to 1992: Results from three population-based studies. *American Journal of Human Biology, 32*(5), e23572.

Quek, Y.H., & others (2017). Exploring the association between childhood and adolescent obesity and depression: A meta-analysis. *Obesity Reviews, 18,* 742–754.

Quintana-Orts, C., & Rey, L. (2018). Forgiveness, depression, and suicidal behavior in adolescents: Gender differences in this relationship. *Journal of Genetic Psychology, 179,* 85–89.

Quinton, D., Rutter, M., & Gulliver, L. (1990). Continuities in psychiatric disorders from childhood to adulthood in the children of psychiatric patients. In L. Robins & M. Rutter (Eds.), *Straight and devious pathways from childhood to adulthood.* New York: Cambridge University Press.

R

Rabasco, A., & Andover, M. (2021). Suicidal ideation among transgender and gender diverse adults; A longitudinal study of risk and protective factors. *Journal of Affective Disorders, 278,* 136–143.

Rabinowitz, J.A., & others (2020). Neighborhood profiles and associations with coping behaviors among low-income youth. *Journal of Youth and Adolescence, 49,* 494–505.

Radley, K. (2021). Peer-mediated behavioral interventions. In T.A. Collins & R.O. Hawkins (Eds.), *Peers as change agents.* New York: Oxford University Press.

Raffaelli, M., & Ontai, L. (2001). "She's sixteen years old and there's boys calling over to the house": An exploratory study of sexual socialization in Latino families. *Culture, Health, and Sexuality, 3,* 295–310.

Raffaelli, M., & Ontai, L.L. (2004). Gender socialization in Latino/a families: Results from two retrospective studies. *Sex Roles, 50,* 287–299.

Rafi, M.A., & others (2020). The influence of religiosity on the emotional-behavioral health of adolescents. *Journal of Religion and Health, 59,* 1870–1888.

Rageliene, T., & Granhoj, A. (2020). The influence of peers' and siblings' on children and adolescents' healthy eating behavior: A systematic literature review. *Appetite, 148,* 104592.

Raj, M.A., Creech, J.A., & Rogol, A.D. (2020). *Female athlete triad.* Treasure Island, FL: StatPearls.

Rajeh, A., & others (2017). Interventions in ADHD: A comparative review of stimulant medication and behavioral therapies. *Asian Journal of Psychiatry, 25,* 131–135.

Raketic, D., & others (2017). Five-factor model personality profiles: The differences between alcohol and opiate addiction among females. *Psychiatria Danubina, 29,* 74-80.

Ramos-Lopez, O., & others (2021). Epigenetic signatures underlying inflammation: An interplay of nutrition, physical activity, metabolic diseases, and environmental factors for personalized nutrition. *Inflammation Research, 70,* 29-49.

Randjelovic, P., & others (2021). Problematic smart phone use, screen time, and chronotype correlations in university students. *European Addiction Research, 27,* 67-74.

Raphiphatthana, B., Jose, P., & Slamon, K. (2018). Does dispositional mindfulness predict the development of grit? *Journal of Individual Differences, 29,* 76-87.

Raposa, E.B., & Hurd, N.M. (2021). Understanding networks of natural mentoring support among underrepresented college students. *Applied Developmental Science, 25,* 38-50.

Rappaport, L.M., & others (2020). A population-based twin study of childhood irritability and internalizing syndromes. *Journal of Clinical Child and Adolescent Psychology, 49,* 524-534.

Rasing, S.P.A., & others (2020). Depression and anxiety symptoms in female adolescents: Relations with parental psychopathology and parenting behavior. *Journal of Research on Adolescence, 30,* 298-313.

Rattan, A., & Dweck, C.S. (2018). What happens after prejudice is confronted in the workplace? How mindsets affect minorities' and women's outlook of future social relations. *Journal of Applied Psychology, 103,* 676-687.

Ray, J., & others (2017). Callous-unemotional traits predict self-reported offending in adolescent boys: The mediating role of delinquent peers and the moderating role of parenting practices. *Developmental Psychology, 53,* 319-328.

Reangsing, C., Punsuwun, S., & Schneider, J.K. (2021). Effects of mindfulness interventions on depressive symptoms in adolescents: A meta-analysis. *International Journal of Nursing Studies, 115,* 103848.

Reed, S.F., & others (2020). Neighborhood effects on child development. In S. Judd & J.D. Jewell (Eds.), *Encyclopedia of child and adolescent development.* New York: Wiley.

Reese, B.M., Haydon, A.A., Herring, A.H., & Halpern, C.T. (2013). The association between sequences of sexual initiation and the likelihood of teenage pregnancy. *Journal of Adolescent Health, 52,* 228-233.

Reese, B.M., Trinh, S.L., & Halpern, C.T. (2017). Implications of pubertal timing for romantic relationships quality among heterosexual and sexual minority young adults. *Journal of Adolescent Health, 61,* 685-693.

Reeve, J., Cheon, S.H., & Yu, T.H. (2020). An autonomy-supportive intervention to develop students' resilience by boosting agentic engagement. *International Journal of Behavioral Development, 44,* 325-338.

Rege, M., & others (2021, in press). How can we inspire a nation of learners? An investigation of growth mindset and challenge-seeking in two countries. *American Psychologist.*

Reichard, R.J., & others (2020). Women's leadership across cultures: Intersections, barriers, and leadership development. In F.M. Cheung & D.F. Halpern (Eds.), *Cambridge handbook of the international psychology of women.* New York: Cambridge University Press.

Reid, P.T., & Zalk, S.R. (2001). Academic environments: Gender and ethnicity in U.S. higher education. In J. Worell (Ed.), *Encyclopedia of women and gender.* San Diego: Academic Press.

Reid-Russell, A., & others (2021, in press). Lower implicit self-esteem as a pathway linking child abuse to depression and suicidal ideation. *Development and Psychopathology.*

Reife, I., Duffy, S., & Grant, K.E. (2020). The impact of social support on adolescent coping in the context of urban poverty. *Cultural Diversity and Ethnic Minority Psychology, 26,* 200-214.

Reigal, R.E., & others (2020). Physical exercise and fitness level are related to cognitive and psychosocial functioning in adolescents. *Frontiers in Psychology, 11,* 1777.

Reijntjes, A., & others (2013). Costs and benefits of bullying in the context of the peer group: A three-wave longitudinal analysis. *Journal of Abnormal Psychology, 41,* 1217-1219.

Reilly, D., & Neumann, D.L. (2013). Gender-role differences in spatial ability: A meta-analytic review. *Sex Roles, 68,* 521-535.

Reinelt, T., & others (2020). Emotion regulation strategies predict weight loss during an inpatient obesity treatment for adolescents. *Obesity Science and Practice, 6,* 293-299.

Reinisch, J.M. (1990). *The Kinsey Institute new report on sex: What you must know to be sexually literate.* New York: St. Martin's Press.

Reis, L.F., & others (2020). Factors associated with early sexual initiation and unsafe sex in adolescence: Substance use and parenting style. *Journal of Adolescence, 79,* 128-135.

Reis, S.M., & Renzulli, J.S. (2020). Intellectual giftedness. In R.J. Sternberg (Ed.), *Cambridge handbook of intelligence.* New York: Cambridge University Press.

Reisenzein, R., Hildebrandt, A., & Weber, H. (2021). Personality and emotion. In P.J. Corr & G. Matthews (Eds.), *Cambridge handbook of personality psychology.* New York: Cambridge University Press.

Remien, K., & Marwaha, R. (2021). *Dyslexia.* Treasure Island, FL: StatPearls.

Ren, H., & others (2021). The protective roles of exercise and maintenance of daily living routines in Chinese adolescents during the COVID-19 quarantine period. *Journal of Adolescent Health, 68,* 35-42.

Rendall, M.S., Weden, M.M., Faveault, M.M., & Waldron, H. (2011). The protective effect of marriage for survival: A review and update. *Demography, 48,* 481-506.

Rerick, P.O., Livingston, T.N., & Davis, D. (2020). Does the horny man think women want him too? Effects of male sexual arousal on perception of female sexual willingness. *Journal of Social Psychology, 160,* 520-533.

Resnick, M.D., Wattenberg, E., & Brewer, R. (1992, March). *Paternity avowal/disavowal among partners of low-income mothers.* Paper presented at the meeting of the Society for Research on Adolescence, Washington, DC.

Rest, J.R. (1995). *Concerns for the social-psychological development of youth and educational strategies: Report for the Kaufmann Foundation.* Minneapolis: University of Minnesota, Department of Educational Psychology.

Reuter, M., & others (2020). Precarious employment and self-reported experiences of unwanted sexual attention and sexual harassment at work. An analysis of the European Working Conditions Survey. *PLoS One, 15*(5), e0233683.

Reuter, P.R., Forster, B.L., & Brister, S.R. (2021, in press). The influence of eating habits on the academic performance of university students. *Journal of American College Health.*

Rey, R.A. (2021). The role of androgen signaling in male sexual development at puberty. *Endocrinology, 162*(2), bqaa215.

Reyna, V.F. (2018). Neurobiological models of risky decision-making and adolescent substance use. *Current Addiction Reports, 5,* 128-133.

Reyna, V.F. (2020). A scientific theory of gist communication and misinformation resistance, with implications for health, education, and policy.

Proceedings of the National Academy of Sciences U.S.A., 118(15), e1912441117.

Reyna, V.F., & Brainerd, C.J. (2011). Dual processes in decision making and developmental neuroscience: A fuzzy-trace model. *Developmental Review, 31,* 180-206.

Reyna, V.F., & Broniatowski, D.A. (2020). An alternative neurocognitive account of recognition, prediction, and decision making. *Behavioral and Brain Sciences, 43,* e144.

Reyna, V.F., & Mills, B.A. (2014). Theoretically motivated interventions for reducing sexual risk taking in adolescence: A randomized controlled experiment applying fuzzy-trace theory. *Journal of Experimental Psychology: General, 143,* 1627-1648.

Reyna, V.F., & Panagiotopoulos, C. (2020). Morals, money, and risk taking from childhood to adulthood: The neurodevelopmental framework of fuzzy trace theory. In J. Decety (Ed.), *The social brain—a developmental perspective.* Cambridge, MA: MIT Press.

Reyna, V.F., & Rivers, S.E. (2008). Current theories of risk and rational decision making. *Developmental Review, 28,* 1-11.

Reynolds, A.J., Ou, S.R., & Temple, J.A. (2018). A multicomponent, preschool to third grade intervention and educational attainment at 35 years of age. *JAMA Pediatrics, 172,* 247-256.

Rhoades, G.K., Stanley, S.M., & Markman, H.J. (2012). The impact of transition to cohabitation on relationship functioning: Cross-sectional and longitudinal findings. *Journal of Family Psychology, 26,* 348-358.

Rhodes, J.E., & Lowe, S.R. (2009). Mentoring in adolescence. In R.M. Lerner & L. Steinberg (Eds.), *Handbook of adolescent psychology* (3rd ed.). New York: Wiley.

Riccio, C.A., & Castro, M.J. (2021). Executive function and school performance. In F.C. Worrell & others (Eds.), *Cambridge handbook of applied school psychology.* New York: Cambridge University Press.

Richardson, C.E., & others (2021). Longitudinal associations between coping strategies and psychopathology in pre-adolescence. *Journal of Youth and Adolescence, 50,* 1189-1204.

Rickards, T., & deCock, C. (2003). Understanding organizational creativity: Toward a paradigmatic approach. In M.A. Runco (Ed.), *Creativity research handbook.* Cresskill, NJ: Hampton Press.

Rickert, V.I., Sanghvi, R., & Wiemann, C.M. (2002). Is lack of sexual assertiveness among adolescent women a cause for concern? *Perspectives on Sexual and Reproductive Health, 34,* 162-173.

Rideout, V. (2016). *Social media, social life: How teens view their emotional life.* Retrieved November 20, 2017, from www.commonsensemedia.org

Rideout, V., Foehr, U.G., & Roberts, D.P. (2010). *Generation M²: Media in the lives of 8- to 18-year-olds.* Menlo Park, CA: Kaiser Family Foundation.

Riesco-Matias, P., & others (2021). What do meta-analyses have to say about the efficacy of neurofeedback applied to children with ADHD? Review of previous meta-analyses and a new meta-analysis. *Journal of Attention Disorders, 25,* 473-485.

Riina, E.M., & McHale, S.M. (2014). Bidirectional influences between dimensions of coparenting and adolescent adjustment. *Journal of Youth and Adolescence, 43,* 257-269.

Rinderman, H., Becker, D., & Coyle, T.R. (2020). Survey of expert opinion on intelligence: Intelligence research, experts' background, controversial issues, and the media. *Intelligence, 78,* 101406.

Rios Casas, F., & others (2020). "Se vale llorar y se vale reir": Latina immigrants' coping strategies for maintaining mental health in the face of immigration-related stressors. *Journal of Racial and Ethnic Health Disparities. 7*(5), 937-948.

Riva Crugnola, C., Ierardi, E., Gazzotti, S., & Albizzati, A. (2014). Motherhood in adolescent mothers: Maternal attachment, mother-infant styles of interaction, and emotion regulation at three months. *Infant Behavior and Development, 37,* 44–56.

Rivera, P.M., & others (2018). Linking patterns of substance use with sexual risk-taking among female adolescents with and without histories of maltreatment. *Journal of Adolescent Health, 62,* 556–562.

Rizkalla, N., Zeevi-Barkay, M., & Segal, S.P. (2021). Rape crisis counseling: Trauma contagion and supervision. *Journal of Interpersonal Violence, 36,* NP960–NP983.

Robbins, C.L., & others (2012). Prevalence, frequency, and associations of masturbation with partnered sexual behaviors among U.S. adolescents. *Archives of Pediatric and Adolescent Medicine, 165,* 1087–1093.

Roberts, B.W., & Damian, R.I. (2018). The principles of personality trait development and their relation to psychopathology. In D. Lynam & D. Samuel (Eds.), *Using basic personality research to inform the personality disorders.* New York: Oxford University Press.

Roberts, B.W., & Nickel, L.B. (2021). Personality development across the life course: A neo-socioanalytic perspective. In O.P. John & R.W. Robins (Eds.), *Handbook of personality* (4th ed.). New York: Guilford.

Roberts, G.C., Treasure, D.C., & Kavussanu, M. (1997). Motivation in physical activity contexts: An achievement goal perspective. *Advances in Motivation and Achievement, 10,* 413–447.

Robins, R.W., Trzesniewski, K.H., Tracey, J.L., Potter, J., & Gosling, S.D. (2002). Age differences in self-esteem from age 9 to 90. *Psychology and Aging, 17,* 423–434.

Robinson, M.D., & Sedikides, C. (2021). Personality and the self. In P.J. Corr & G. Matthews (Eds.), *Cambridge handbook of personality psychology.* New York: Cambridge University Press.

Robinson, N.S. (1995). Evaluating the nature of perceived support and its relation to perceived self-worth in adolescents. *Journal of Research on Adolescence, 5,* 253–280.

Robson, D.A., Allen, M.S., & Howard, S.J. (2020). Self-regulation in childhood as a predictor of future outcomes: A meta-analytic review. *Psychological Bulletin, 146,* 324–354.

Roder, M., & Muller, A.R. (2020). Social competencies and expectations regarding the impending transition to secondary school. *International Journal of Educational Psychology, 9,* 82–102.

Rodgers, R.F., & others (2020). A biopsychosocial model of social media use and body image concerns, disordered eating, and muscle-building behaviors among adolescent boys and girls. *Journal of Youth and Adolescence, 49,* 399–409.

Rodrigues, M.A., & others (2020). From maternal tending to adolescent befriending: The adolescent transition of social support. *American Journal of Primatology, 82*(11), e23050.

Rodriguez, S., & others (2017). An explanatory model of math achievement: Perceived parental involvement and academic motivation. *Psicothema, 29,* 184–190.

Rodriguez-Ayllon, M., & others (2020). Association of physical activity and screen time with white matter microstructure in children from the general population. *NeuroImage, 205,* 116258.

Rodriguez-Martinez, E.I., & others (2021). Neuropsychological differences between ADHD and control children and adolescents during the recognition phase of a working memory task. *Neuroscience Research, 164,* 46–54.

Rodriguez-Meirinhos, A., & others (2020). When is parental monitoring effective? A person-centered analysis of the role of autonomy-supportive and psychologically controlling parenting in referred and non-referred adolescents. *Journal of Youth and Adolescence, 49,* 352–368.

Roehrig, A.D., & others (2012). Effective teachers and teaching: Characteristics and practices related to positive student outcomes. In K.R. Harris & others (Eds.), *APA handbook of educational psychology.* Washington, DC: American Psychological Association.

Roeser, R.W., & Zelazo, P.D. (2012). Contemplative science, education and child development. *Child Development Perspectives, 6,* 143–145.

Rogers, C.R. (1950). The significance of the self regarding attitudes and perceptions. In M.L. Reymart (Ed.), *Feelings and emotions.* New York: McGraw-Hill.

Rogol, A.D., Roemmich, J.N., & Clark, P.A. (1998, September). *Growth at puberty.* Paper presented at a workshop, Physical Development, Health Futures of Youth II: Pathways to Adolescent Health, Maternal and Child Health Bureau, Annapolis, MD.

Rohrer, J.M., Egloff, B., & Schmukle, S.C. (2017). Probing birth-order effects on narrow traits using specification-curve analysis. *Psychological Science, 28,* 1821–1832.

Rolls, E.T., & others (2020). Effective connectivity in autism. *Autism Research, 13,* 32–44.

Romero, A., & others (2020). Disentangling relationships between bicultural stress and mental well-being among Latinx immigrant adolescents. *Journal of Consulting and Clinical Psychology, 88,* 149–159.

Romero-Mesa, J., Pelaez-Fernandez, M.A., & Extremera, N. (2021, in press). Emotional intelligence and eating disorders: A systematic review. *Eating and Weight Disorders.*

Romo, L.F., Mireles-Rios, R., & Lopez-Tello, G. (2014). Latina mothers' and daughters' expectations for autonomy at age 15 (La Quinceañera). *Journal of Adolescent Research, 29*(2), 279–294.

Ronnlund, M., & others (2013). Secular trends in cognitive test performance: Swedish conscript data, 1970–1993. *Intelligence, 41,* 19–24.

Rose, A.J., & Asher, S.R. (2017). The social tasks of friendship: Do boys and girls excel in different tasks? *Child Development Perspectives, 11,* 3–8.

Rose, A.J., Carlson, W., & Waller, E.M. (2007). Prospective associations of co-rumination with friendship and emotional adjustment: Considering the socioemotional trade-offs of co-rumination. *Developmental Psychology, 43,* 1019–1031.

Rose, A.J., & Rudolph, K.D. (2006). A review of sex differences in peer relationship processes: Potential trade-offs for the emotional and behavioral development of girls and boys. *Psychological Bulletin, 132,* 98–132.

Rose, A.J., & Smith, R.L. (2018). Gender and peer relationships. In W.M. Bukowski & others (Eds.), *Handbook of peer interaction, relationships, and groups* (2nd ed.). New York: Guilford.

Rose, A.J., & others (2014). An observational study of co-rumination in adolescent friendships. *Developmental Psychology, 50,* 2199–2209.

Rose, A.J., & others (2017). Co-rumination exacerbates stress generation among adolescents with depressive symptoms. *Journal of Abnormal Child Psychology, 45,* 985–995.

Rose, S., & Frieze, I.R. (1993). Young singles' contemporary dating scripts. *Sex Roles, 28,* 499–509.

Rose-Greenland, F., & Smock, P.J. (2013). Living together unmarried: What do we know about cohabiting families? In G.W. Peterson & K.R. Bush (Eds.), *Handbook of marriage and the family* (3rd ed.). New York: Springer.

Rosenbaum, G.M., & others (2017). Working memory training in adolescents decreases laboratory risk taking in the presence of peers. *Journal of Cognitive Enhancement, 1,* 513–525.

Rosenbaum, J.E. (2020). Educational and criminal justice outcomes 12 years after school suspension. *Youth and Society, 52,* 515–547.

Rosenberg, M. (1979). *Conceiving the self.* New York: Basic Books.

Rosenberg, M.D., & others (2020). Behavioral and neural signatures of working memory in childhood. *Journal of Neuroscience, 40,* 5090–5104.

Rosenblum, G.D., & Lewis, M. (2003). Emotional development in adolescence. In G. Adams & M. Berzonsky (Eds.), *Blackwell handbook of adolescence.* Malden, MA: Blackwell.

Rosenfield, R.L. (2021, in press). Normal and abnormal adrenarche. *Endocrine Reviews.*

Rosenthal, N.L., & Kobak, R. (2010). Assessing adolescents' attachment hierarchies: Differences across developmental periods and associations with individual adaptation. *Journal of Research on Adolescence, 20,* 678–706.

Roshani, F., & others (2020). Comparison of cognitive flexibility, appropriate risk-taking, and reaction time in individuals with and without adult ADHD. *Psychiatry Research, 284,* 112494.

Rosner, B.A., & Rierdan, J. (1994, February). *Adolescent girls' self-esteem: Variations in developmental trajectories.* Paper presented at the meeting of the Society for Research on Adolescence, San Diego.

Rote, W.M., & Smetana, J.G. (2016). Beliefs about parents' right to know: Domain distinctions and associations with change in concealment. *Journal of Research on Adolescence, 26,* 334–344.

Roth, B., & others (2015). Intelligence and school grades: A meta-analysis. *Intelligence, 53,* 118–137.

Rothbart, M.K. (2011). *Becoming who we are.* New York: Guilford.

Rothbart, M.K., & Bates, J.E. (1998). Temperament. In W. Damon (Ed.). *Handbook of child psychology* (5th ed., Vol. 3). New York: Wiley.

Rothbart, M.K., Posner, M.I., & Sheese, B.E. (2021). Temperament and brain networks in attention. In P.J. Corr & G. Mathews (Eds.), *Cambridge handbook of personality psychology.* New York: Cambridge University Press.

Rothbaum, F., Poll, M., Azuma, H., Miyake, K., & Weisz, J. (2000). The development of close relationships in Japan and the United States: Paths of symbiotic harmony and generative tension. *Child Development, 71,* 1121–1142.

Rothman, E.F., & others (2021a, in press). The psychometric properties of the measure of adolescent relationship harassment and abuse (MARSHA) with a nationally representative sample of U.S. youth. *Journal of Interpersonal Violence.*

Rothman, K., & others (2021b, in press). Sexual assault among women in college: Immediate and long-term associations with mental health, psychological functioning, and romantic relationships. *Journal of Interpersonal Violence.*

Rowley, S.J., & others (1998). The relationship between racial identity and self-esteem in African American college and high school students. *Journal of Personality and Social Psychology, 74*(3), 715–724.

Rowley, S.J., & others (2014). Framing Black boys: Parent, teacher, and student narratives of the academic lives of Black boys. *Advances in Child Development and Behavior, 47,* 301–332.

Rubie-Davies, C.M. (2007). Classroom interactions: Exploring the practices of high- and low-expectation teachers. *British Journal of Educational Psychology, 77,* 289–306.

Rubin, D.H. (2020). Editorial: Evolving understanding of conduct disorder. *Journal of the Academy of Child and Adolescent Psychiatry, 59,* 225–226.

Rubin, K.H., & Barstead, M. (2018). Social withdrawal and solitude. In M.H. Bornstein (Ed.), *SAGE handbook of lifespan development.* Thousand Oaks, CA: Sage.

Rubin, K.H., Bukowski, W.M., & Bowker, J. (2015). Children in peer groups. In R.M. Lerner (Ed.), *Handbook of child psychology and developmental science* (7th ed.). New York: Wiley.

Rubin, K.H., Bukowski, W.M., & Parker, J.G. (1998). Peer interactions, relationships, and groups. In N. Eisenberg (Ed.), *Handbook of child psychology* (5th ed., Vol. 3). New York: Wiley.

Rubin, K.H., Bukowski, W.M., & Parker, J.G. (2006). Peer interactions, relationships, and groups. In W. Damon & R. Lerner (Eds.), *Handbook of child psychology* (6th ed.). New York: Wiley.

Rubin, K.H., & others (2018). Avoiding and withdrawing from the peer group. In W.M. Bukowksi & others (Eds.), *Handbook of peer interaction, relationships, and groups* (2nd ed.). New York: Guilford.

Rubin, Z., & Slomon, J. (1994). How parents influence their children's friendships. In M. Lewis (Ed.), *Beyond the dyad*. New York: Plenum.

Rubinova, E., & others (2021, in press). Schema and deviation effects in remembering repeated unfamiliar stories. *British Journal of Psychology*.

Rugulies, R., & others (2020). Onset of workplace sexual harassment and subsequent depressive symptoms and incident depressive disorder in the Danish workforce. *Journal of Affective Disorders, 277,* 21–29.

Rumberger, R.W. (1995). Dropping out of middle school: A multilevel analysis of students and schools. *American Education Research Journal, 3,* 583–625.

Ruohonen, S.T., Poutanen, M., & Tena-Sempere, M. (2020). Role of kisspeptins in the control of the hypothalamic-pituitary-ovarian axis: Old dogmas and new challenges. *Fertility and Sterility, 114,* 465–474.

Ruotsalainen, I., & others (2021). Physical activity and aerobic fitness in relation to local and interhemispheric functional connectivity in adolescents' brains. *Brain and Behavior, 11*(2), e01941.

Russotti, J., & others (2021). Child maltreatment: An international cascades model of risk processes potentiating child psychopathology. *Child Abuse and Neglect, 112,* 104829.

Rutter, M. (1979). Protective factors in children's response to stress and disadvantage. In M.W. Kent & J.E. Rolf (Eds.), *Primary prevention in psychopathology* (Vol. 3). Hanover: University of New Hampshire Press.

Rutter, M., & Garmezy, N. (1983). Developmental psychopathology. In P.H. Mussen (Ed.), *Handbook of child psychology* (4th ed., Vol. 4). New York: Wiley.

Ryan, A.M., & Shin, H. (2018). Peers, academics, and teachers. In W.M. Bukowski & others (Eds.), *Handbook of peer interactions, relationships, and groups* (2nd ed.). New York: Guilford.

Ryan, C., Huebner, D., Diaz, R.M., & Sanchez, J. (2009). Family rejection as a predictor of negative health outcomes in white and Latino lesbian, gay, and bisexual young adults. *Pediatrics, 123,* 346–352.

Ryan, M.K. (2003). Gender differences in ways of knowing: The context dependence of the Attitudes Toward Thinking and Learning Survey. *Sex Roles, 49,* 11–12.

Ryan, R.M., & Deci, E.L. (2016). Facilitating and hindering motivation, learning, and well-being in schools: Research and observations from self-determination theory. In K.R. Wentzel & D.B. Miele (Eds.), *Handbook of motivation at school* (2nd ed.). New York: Routledge.

Ryan, R.M., & Deci, E.L. (2019, May 22). *Self-determination theory.* Plenary talk at the International Self-Determination Theory conference, Amsterdam.

Ryan, R.M., & Deci, E.L. (2020). Intrinsic and extrinsic motivation from a self-determination theory perspective: Definitions, theory, practices, and future directions. *Contemporary Educational Psychology, 61,* 101860.

S

Saarni, C. (1999). *The development of emotional competence.* New York: Guilford.

Saarni, C., Campos, J.J., Camras, L., & Witherington, D. (2006). Emotional development. In W. Damon & R. Lerner (Eds.), *Handbook of child psychology* (6th ed.). New York: Wiley.

Sackett, P.R., Borneman, M.J., & Connelly, B.S. (2009). Responses to issues raised about validity, bias, and fairness in high-stakes testing. *American Psychologist, 64,* 285–287.

Sackett, P.R., Shewach, O.R., & Dahlke, J.A. (2020). The predictive value of intelligence. In R.J. Sternberg (Ed.), *Human intelligence.* New York: Cambridge University Press.

Sadker, D.M., Zittleman, K., & Koch, M. (2022). *Teachers, schools, and society: A brief introduction to education* (6th ed.). New York: McGraw-Hill.

Saeed, S., & others (2020). Genetic causes of severe childhood obesity: A remarkably high prevalence in an inbred population of Pakistan. *Diabetes, 69,* 1424–1438.

Saewyc, E.M. (2011). Research on adolescent sexual orientation: Development, health disparities, stigma, and resilience. *Journal of Research on Adolescence, 21,* 256–272.

Safa, M.D., White, R.M.B., & Knight, G.P. (2020). Family contextual influences on bicultural competence development among U.S. Mexican-origin youths. *Developmental Psychology, 56,* 1596–1609.

Sagan, C. (1977). *The dragons of Eden.* New York: Random House.

Saggioiro de Figueiredo, C., & others (2021). COVID-19 pandemic impact on children and adolescents' mental health: Biological, environmental, and social factors. *Progress in Neuropsychopharmacology and Biological Psychiatry, 106,* 110171.

Sahlan, R.N., & others (2021). Disordered eating, self-esteem, and depression symptoms in Iranian adolescents and young adults: A network analysis. *International Journal of Eating Disorders, 54,* 132–147.

Saidi, Q., & others (2020). Acute intense exercise improves sleep and decreases next morning consumption of energy-dense food in adolescent girls with obesity and evening chronotype. *Pediatric Obesity, 15* (6), e12613.

Sakaluk, J.K., & others (2014). Dominant heterosexual sexual scripts in emerging adulthood: Conceptualization and measurement. *Journal of Sex Research, 51,* 516–531.

Sakaluk, J.K., & others (2020). Self-esteem and sexual health: A multilevel meta-analytic review. *Health Psychology Review, 14,* 269–293.

Sakou, I., & others (2015). Insulin resistance and cardiometabolic risk factors in obese children and adolescents: A hierarchical approach. *Journal of Pediatric Endocrinology and Metabolism, 28,* 589–596.

Salgado, J.F., Anderson, N., & Moscoso, S. (2021). Personality at work. In P.J. Corr & G. Matthews (Eds.), *Cambridge handbook of personality psychology.* New York: Cambridge University Press.

Sallis, H., Smith, G.D., & Munato, M.C. (2021). Genetics of personality. In P.J. Core & G. Matthews (Eds.), *Cambridge handbook of personality psychology.* New York: Cambridge University Press.

Salmivalli, C. (2020). Peers and siblings. In B. Hopkins & others (Eds.), *Cambridge encyclopedia of child development.* New York: Cambridge University Press.

Salovey, P., & Mayer, J.D. (1990). Emotional intelligence. *Imagination, Cognition, and Personality, 9,* 185–211.

Salway, T., & others (2021). Age, period, and cohort patterns in the epidemiology of suicide attempts among sexual minorities in the United States and Canada: Detection of a second peak in middle adulthood. *Social Psychiatry and Psychiatric Epidemiology, 56,* 283–294.

Sampasa-Kanyinga, H., Chaput, J.-P., & Hamilton, H.A. (2019). Social media use, school connectedness, and academic performance among adolescents. *Journal of Primary Prevention, 40,* 189–211.

Sampasa-Kanyinga, H., & others (2020). Sex differences in the relationship between social media use, short sleep duration, and body mass index among adolescents. *Sleep Health, 48,* 793–803.

Sanchez, B., Esparza, P., Colon, Y., & Davis, K.E. (2010). Tryin' to make it during the transition from high school: The role of family obligation attitudes and economic context for Latino emerging adults. *Journal of Adolescent Research, 25,* 858–884.

Sanchez, B., & others (2020). Helping me helps us: The role of natural mentors in the ethnic identity and academic outcomes of Latinx adolescents. *Developmental Psychology, 56,* 208–220.

Sanchis Sanchis, A., & others (2020). Effects of age and gender on emotion regulation of children and adolescents. *Frontiers in Psychology, 11,* 946.

Sanders, A.R., & others (2017). Genome-wide association study of male sexual orientation. *Scientific Reports, 7*(1), 16950.

Sanfilippo, J.S., & others (2020). *Sanfilippo's textbook of pediatric and adolescent gynecology* (2nd ed.). New York: Routledge.

Santa Maria, M. (2002). Youth in Southeast Asia: Living within the continuity of tradition and the turbulence of change. In B.B. Brown, R.W. Larson, & T.S. Saraswathi (Eds.), *The world's youth.* New York: Cambridge University Press.

Santelli, J., Sandfort, T.G., & Orr, M. (2009). U.S./European differences in condom use. *Journal of Adolescent Health, 44,* 306.

Santos, C.E., Komienko, O., & Rivas-Drake, D. (2017). Peer influences on ethnic-racial identity development: A multi-site investigation. *Child Development, 88,* 725–742.

Santrock, J.W., Sitterle, K.A., & Warshak, R.A. (1988). Parent-child relationships in stepfather families. In P. Bronstein & C.P. Cowan (Eds.), *Fatherhood today: Men's changing roles in the family.* New York: Wiley.

Sartor, C.E., & others (2020). Youth perceptions of parental involvement and monitoring, discrepancies with parental perceptions, and their associations with first cigarette use in Black and White girls. *Journal of Studies on Alcohol and Drugs, 81,* 180–189.

Sassler, S., & Lichter, D.T. (2020). Cohabitation and marriage: Complexity and diversity in union-formation patterns. *Journal of Marriage and Family, 82,* 35–61.

Sassler, S., Michelmore, K., & Qian, Z. (2018). Transitions from sexual relationships into cohabitation and beyond. *Demography, 55,* 511–534.

Sattler, F.A., Eickmeyer, S., & Eisenkolb, J. (2020). Body image disturbance in children and adolescents with anorexia nervosa and bulimia nervosa: A systematic review. *Eating and Weight Disorders, 25,* 857–865.

Savage, M.W., Menegatos, L., & Roberto, A.J. (2017). When do friends prevent friends from hooking up intoxicated? An examination of sex differences and hypothetical intoxication peer interventions. *Archives of Sexual Behavior, 46,* 1819–1829.

Savina, E., & Moran, J.M. (2022). *Well-being in adolescent girls.* New York: Routledge.

Savin-Williams, R.C. (2015). The new sexual-minority teenager. In D.A. Powell & J.S. Kaufman (Eds.), *The meaning of sexual identity in the 21st century.* New York: Cambridge.

Savin-Williams, R.C. (2017). *Mostly straight: Sexual fluidity among men.* Cambridge, MA: Harvard University Press.

Savin-Williams, R.C. (2018). Developmental trajectories and milestones of sexual-minority youth. In J. Gilbert & S. Lamb (Eds.), *Cambridge handbook of sexual development: Childhood and adolescence* (pp. 156–179). New York: Cambridge University Press.

Savin-Williams, R.C., & Demo, D.H. (1983). Conceiving or misconceiving the self: Issues in adolescent self-esteem. *Journal of Early Adolescence, 3,* 121-140.

Sawyer, S., Abdul-Razak, S., & Patton, G. (2019). Introduction to adolescent health. In D. Devakumar & others (Eds.), *Oxford handbook of global health of women, newborns, children, and adolescents.* New York: Oxford University Press.

Sawyer, S.M., & Patton, G.C. (2018). Health and well-being in adolescence: A dynamic profile. In J.E. Lansford & P. Banati (Eds.), *Handbook of adolescent development research and its impact on global policy.* New York: Oxford University Press.

Sayehmiri K., & others (2020). The relationship between personality traits and marital satisfaction: A systematic review and meta-analysis. *BMC Psychology, 8*(1), 15.

Scaini, S., & others (2021). Rumination thinking in childhood and adolescence: A brief review of candidate genes. *Journal of Affective Disorders, 280*(Pt. A), 197-202.

Scalici, F., & Schulz, P.J. (2017). Parents' and peers' normative influence on adolescents' smoking: Results from a Swiss-Italian sample of middle school students. *Substance Abuse Treatment, Prevention, and Policy, 12*(1), 5.

Scarlett, W.G. (2020). Religious development in adolescence. In S. Hupp & J.D. Jewell (Eds.), *Encyclopedia of child and adolescent development.* New York: Wiley.

Scarr, S. (1993). Biological and cultural diversity: The legacy of Darwin for development. *Child Development, 64,* 1333-1353.

Schaefer, R.T. (2015). *Racial and ethnic groups* (14th ed.). Upper Saddle River, NJ: Pearson.

Schaffer, M.A., Goodhue, A., Stennes, K., & Lanigan, C. (2012). Evaluation of a public health nurse visiting program for pregnant and parenting teens. *Public Health Nursing, 29,* 218-231.

Schaie, K.W. (2016). Theoretical perspectives for the psychology of aging in a lifespan context. In K.W. Schaie & S.L. Willis (Eds.), *Handbook of the psychology of aging* (8th ed.). New York: Elsevier.

Scharpf, F., & others (2020). A systematic review of socio-ecological factors contributing to risk and protection of the mental health of refugee children and adolescents. *Clinical Psychology Review, 83,* 101930.

Schermer, J.A., & Saklofske, D.P.H. (2021). Personality and intelligence. In P.J. Corr & G. Matthews (Eds.), *Cambridge handbook of personality psychology.* New York: Cambridge University Press.

Scherrer, V., & others (2020). Development of achievement goals and their relation to academic interest and achievement in adolescence: A review of the literature and two longitudinal studies. *Developmental Psychology, 56,* 795-814.

Scheuer, H., & others (2017). Reduced fronto-amygdalar connectivity in adolescence is associated with increased depression symptoms over time. *Psychiatry Research, 266,* 35-41.

Schiariti, V., Simeonsson, R.J., & Hall, K. (2021). Promoting developmental potential in early childhood: A global framework for health and education. *International Journal of Environmental Research and Public Health, 18*(4), 2007.

Schiff, W.J. (2021). *Nutrition essentials* (3rd ed.). New York: McGraw-Hill.

Schiff, W.J. (2022). *Nutrition for healthy living* (6th ed.). New York: McGraw-Hill.

Schimschal, S.E., & others (2021). Grit: A concept analysis. *Issues in Mental Health Nursing, 42,* 495-505.

Schirmbeck, K., Rao, N., & Maehler, C. (2020). Similarities and differences across countries in the development of executive function in children: A systematic review. *Infant and Child Development, 29*(1), e2164.

Schlam, T.R., Wilson, N.L., Shoda, Y., Mischel, W., & Ayduk, O. (2013). Preschoolers' delay of gratification predicts their body mass 30 years later. *Journal of Pediatrics, 162*(1), 90-93.

Schlarb, A.A., Friedrich, A., & Clausen, M. (2017). Sleep problems in university students—an intervention. *Neuropsychiatric Disease and Treatment, 13,* 1989-2001.

Schmidt, A., Dirk, J., & Schmiedek, F. (2019). The importance of peer relatedness at school for affective well-being in children: Between- and within-person associations. *Social Development, 28*(4), 873-892.

Schmidt, F.T.C., & others (2020). Self-control outdoes fluid reasoning in explaining vocational and academic performance—but does it? *Frontiers in Psychology, 11,* 757.

Schmidt, M.E., Marks, J.L., & Derrico, L. (2004). What a difference mentoring makes: Service learning and engagement for college students. *Mentoring and Tutoring Partnership in Learning, 12,* 205-217.

Schmidt, M.E., & Vandewater, E.A. (2008). Media and attention, cognition, and school achievement. *Future of Children, 18*(1), 64-85.

Schoeneberger, J. (2012). Longitudinal attendance patterns: Developing high school dropouts. *Clearinghouse, 85,* 7-14.

Schoevers, E.M., Kroesbergen E.H., & Kattou, M. (2020). Mathematical creativity: A combination of domain-general creative and domain-specific mathematical skills. *Journal of Creative Behavior, 54,* 242-252.

Schoffstall, C.L., & Cohen, R. (2011). Cyber aggression: The relation between online offenders and offline social competence. *Social Development, 20*(3), 587-604.

Schulenberg, J.E., & Zarrett, N.R. (2006). Mental health during emerging adulthood: Continuity and discontinuity in courses, causes, and functions. In J.J. Arnett & J.L. Tanner (Eds.), *Emerging adults in America.* Washington, DC: American Psychological Association.

Schulenberg, J.E., & others (2017). *Monitoring the Future national survey results on drug use, 1975-2016: Vol. 2, College students and adults aged 19-55.* Ann Arbor, MI: Institute for Social Research, University of Michigan.

Schulenberg, J.E., & others (2020). *Monitoring the Future: National survey results on drug use 1975-2019: Vol. 2, College students and adults ages 19-60.* Washington, DC: National Institute on Drug Abuse.

Schunk, D.H. (2020). *Learning theories: An educational perspective* (8th ed.). Upper Saddle River, NJ: Pearson.

Schunk, D.H., & Greene, J.A. (Eds.) (2018). *Handbook of self-regulation of learning and performance* (2nd ed.). New York: Routledge.

Schunk, D.H., Meece, J.R., & Pintrich, P.R. (2014). *Motivation in education* (4th ed.). Upper Saddle River, NJ: Pearson.

Schuster, I., Tomazewska, P., & Krahe, B. (2021, in press). Changing cognitive risk factors for sexual aggression: Risky sexual scripts, low sexual self-esteem, perception of pornography, and acceptance of sexual coercion. *Journal of Interpersonal Violence.*

Schutten, D., Stokes, K.A., & Arnell, K.M. (2017). I want to media multitask and I want to do it now: Individual differences in media multitasking predict delay of gratification and system-1 thinking. *Cognitive Research: Principles and Implications, 2*(1), 8.

Schwalbe, C.S., Gearing, R.E., MacKenzie, M.J., Brewer, K.B., & Ibrahim, R. (2012). A meta-analysis of experimental studies of diversion programs for juvenile offenders. *Clinical Psychology Review, 32,* 26-33.

Schwartz, D., Kelly, B.M., & Duong, M.T. (2013). Do academically-engaged adolescents experience social sanctions from the peer group? *Journal of Youth and Adolescence, 42,* 1319-1330.

Schwartz, P.D., Maynard, A.M., & Uzelac, S.M. (2008). Adolescent egocentrism: A contemporary view. *Adolescence, 43,* 441-448.

Schwartz, S.J. (2016). Turning point for a turning point: Advancing emerging adulthood theory and research. *Emerging Adulthood, 45,* 307-317.

Schwartz, S.J., & others (2012). Identity around the world: An overview. *New Directions in Child and Adolescent Development, 138,* 1-18.

Schwartz, S.J., & others (2020). The convergence between cultural psychology and developmental science: Acculturation as an example. *Frontiers in Psychology, 11,* 887.

Schwartz-Mette, R.A., & others (2020). Relations of friendship experiences with depressive symptoms and loneliness in childhood and adolescence: A meta-analytic review. *Psychological Bulletin, 146,* 664-700.

Schwarz, B., & others (2012). Does the importance of parent and peer relationships for adolescents' life satisfaction vary across cultures? *Journal of Early Adolescence, 32,* 55-80.

Schweinhart, L.J., & others (2005). *Lifetime effects: The High/Scope Perry Preschool Study through age 40.* Ypsilanti, MI: High/Scope Press.

Schweizer, S., Gotlib, J.H., & Blakemore, S-J. (2020). The role of affective control in emotion regulation during adolescence. *Emotion, 20,* 80-86.

Scott, H., Biello, S.M., & Woods, H.C. (2019). Social media use and adolescent sleep patterns: Cross-sectional findings from the UK millennium cohort study. *BMJ Open, 9*(9), e031161.

Scourfield, J., Van den Bree, M., Martin, N., & McGuffin, P. (2004). Conduct problems in children and adolescents: A twin study. *Archives of General Psychiatry, 61,* 489-496.

Scully, M., Swords, L., & Nixon, E. (2021, in press). Social comparisons on social media: Online appearance-related activity and body dissatisfaction in adolescent girls. *Irish Journal of Psychological Medicine.*

Search Institute (1995). *Barriers to participation in youth programs.* Unpublished manuscript, the Search Institute, Minneapolis.

Search Institute (2010). *Teens' relationships.* Minneapolis: Author.

Search Institute (2022). *Developmental relationships framework.* Minneapolis: Author.

Sears, R.R., Maccoby, E.E., & Levin, H. (1957). *Patterns of child rearing.* Evanston, IL: Row, Peterson.

Sebastian, C., Burnett, S., & Blakemore, S-J. (2010). Development of the self-concept in adolescence. *Trends in Cognitive Science, 12,* 441-446.

Seccombe, K. (2020). *Exploring marriages and families* (4th ed.). Upper Saddle River, NJ: Pearson.

Sedgh, G., & others (2015). Adolescent pregnancy, birth, and abortion rates across countries: Levels and recent trends. *Journal of Adolescent Health, 56,* 223-230.

Seiffge-Krenke, I. (2011). Coping with relationship stressors: A decade review. *Journal of Research on Adolescence, 21,* 196-210.

Seiffge-Krenke, I. (2012). Competent youth in a "disorderly world": Findings from an eighteen-nation study. *New Directions for Youth Development, 135,* 107-117.

Seiffge-Krenke, I., Aunola, K., & Nurmi, J-E. (2009). Changes in stress perception and coping during adolescence: The role of situational and personal factors. *Child Development, 80,* 259-279.

Seiter, L.N., & Nelson, L.J. (2011). An examination of emerging adulthood in college students and nonstudents in India. *Journal of Adolescent Research, 26*(4), 506-536.

Seligman, M.E.P. (2007). *The optimistic child.* New York: Mariner.

Seligman, M.E.P., & Csikszentmihalyi, M. (2000). Positive psychology. *American Psychologist, 55,* 5-14.

Selman, R.L. (1980). *The growth of interpersonal understanding.* New York: Academic Press.

Semaj, L.T. (1985). Afrikanity, cognition, and extended self-identity. In M.B. Spencer, G.K. Brookins, & W.R. Allen (Eds.), *Beginnings: The social and affective development of black children.* Hillsdale, NJ: Erlbaum.

Semega, J., & others (2020, September 15). *Income and poverty in the United States: 2019.* Report No. P60-27. Washington, DC: U.S. Census Bureau.

Sen, B. (2010). The relationship between frequency of family dinner and adolescent problem behaviors after adjusting for other characteristics. *Journal of Adolescence, 33,* 187-196.

Seo, D.C., & Lee, C.G. (2013). The effect of perceived body weight on suicide ideation among a representative sample of U.S. adolescents. *Journal of Behavioral Medicine, 36,* 498-507.

Seo, E., & Lee, Y-K. (2021, in press). Stereotype threat in high school classrooms: How it links to teacher mindset climate, mathematics anxiety, and achievement. *Journal of Youth and Adolescence.*

Seral-Cortes, M., & others (2021). Development of a genetic risk score to predict the risk of overweight and obesity in European adolescents from the HELENA study. *Scientific Reports, 11*(1), 3067.

Sesker, A.A., & others (2016). Conscientiousness and mindfulness in midlife coping: An assessment based on MIDUS II. *Personality and Mental Health, 10,* 29-42.

Shaikh, Q., Aljasser, D.S., & Albalawi, A.M. (2020). Parenting behaviors, marital discord, and the mental health of young females: A cross-sectional study from Saudi Arabia. *Annals of Saudi Medicine, 40,* 49-54.

Shalitin, S., & Kiess, W. (2017). Putative effects of obesity on linear growth and puberty. *Hormone Research in Pediatrics, 88,* 101-110.

Shane, J., & Heckhausen, J. (2017). It's only a dream if you wake up: Young adults' achievement expectations, opportunities, and meritocratic beliefs. *International Journal of Psychology, 52,* 40-48.

Shannonhouse, L., Hill, M., & Hightower, J. (2021, in press). Trauma exposure, suicidablity, and reporting in college students. *Journal of American College Health.*

Sharma, N., Shaligram, D., & Yoon, G.H. (2020). Engaging South Asian youth and families: A clinical review. *International Journal of Social Psychiatry, 66,* 584-592.

Sharp, E.H., Coatsworth, J.D., Darling, N., Cumsille, P., & Ranieri, S. (2007). Gender differences in the self-defining activities and identity experiences of adolescents and emerging adults. *Journal of Adolescence, 30,* 251-269.

Shaw, P., & others (2007). Attention-deficit/hyperactivity disorder is characterized by a delay in cortical maturation. *Proceedings of the National Academy of Sciences, 104*(49), 19649-19654.

Shaywitz, S.E., & Shaywitz, B.B. (2017). Dyslexia. In R. Schwartz (Ed.), *Handbook of child language disorders* (2nd ed.). New York: Routledge.

Shebloski, B., Conger, K.J., & Widaman, K.F. (2005). Reciprocal links among differential parenting, perceived partiality, and self-worth: A three-wave longitudinal study. *Journal of Family Psychology, 19,* 633-642.

Sheffler, P.C., & Cheung, C.S. (2020). The role of peer mindsets in students' learning: An experimental study. *British Journal of Educational Psychology, 90*(Suppl. 1), S17-S34.

Sheftall, A.H., Mathias, C.W., Furr, R.M., & Dougherty, D.M. (2013). Adolescent attachment security, family functioning, and suicide attempts. *Attachment and Human Development, 15*(4), 368-383.

Shek, D.T., & others (2021). The impact of positive youth development attributes on posttraumatic stress disorder symptoms among Chinese adolescents under COVID-19. *Journal of Adolescent Health, 68,* 667-682.

Sheldrick, R.C., Maye, M.P., & Carter, A.S. (2017). Age at first identification of autism spectrum disorder: An analysis of two U.S. surveys. *Journal of the American Academy of Child and Adolescent Psychiatry, 56,* 313-320.

Shen, Y., Kim, S.Y., Wang, Y., & Chao, R.K. (2014). Language brokering and adjustment among Chinese and Korean American adolescents: A moderated mediation model of perceived maternal sacrifice, respect for the mother, and mother-child open communication. *Asian American Journal of Psychology, 5,* 86-95.

Shen, Y., & others (2020). Evolutionary genomics analysis of human nucleus-encoded mitochondrial genes: Implications for the roles of energy production and metabolic pathways in the pathogenesis and pathophysiology of demyelinating diseases. *Neuroscience Letters, 715,* 134600.

Sherman, D.F., & others (2020). Trans* community connection, health, and wellbeing: A systematic review. *LGBT Health, 7,* 1-14.

Shernoff, D.J. (2009, April). *Flow in educational contexts: Creating optimal learning environments.* Paper presented at the meeting of the Society for Research in Child Development, Denver.

Shi, Q., & others (2020). Trajectories of pure and co-occurring internalizing and externalizing problems from early childhood to adolescence: Associations with early childhood individual and contextual antecedents. *Developmental Psychology, 56,* 1906-1918.

Shi, X., & others (2018). Posttraumatic stress disorder symptoms in parents and adolescents after the Wenchuan earthquake: A longitudinal actor-partner interdependence model. *Journal of Affective Disorders.*

Shifren, K., Furnham, A., & Bauserman, R.L. (2003). Emerging adulthood in American and British samples: Individuals' personality and health risk behaviors. *Journal of Adult Development, 10,* 75-88.

Shih, S.S. (2021). Factors related to Taiwanese adolescents' academic engagement and achievement goal orientations. *Journal of Educational Research, 114,* 1-12.

Shin, M., & Bolkan, S. (2021). Intellectually stimulating students' intrinsic motivation: The mediating influence of student engagement, self-efficacy, and student academic support. *Communication Education, 70,* 146-164.

Shiner, R.L., & De Young, C.G. (2013). The structure of temperament and personality traits: A developmental perspective. In P.D. Zelazo (Ed.), *Handbook of developmental psychology.* New York: Oxford University Press.

Shramko, M., Toomey, R.B., & Anhalt, K. (2018). Profiles of minority stressors and identity centrality among sexual minority Latinx youth. *American Journal of Orthopsychiatry, 88,* 471-482.

Shu, X.E., Swanda, R.V., & Qian, S-B. (2020). Nutrient control of mRNA translation. *Annual Review of Nutrition, 40,* 51-75.

Shulman, S., Scharf, M., Ziv, I., Norona, J., & Welsh, D.P. (2020). Adolescents' sexual encounters with either romantic or casual partners and the quality of their romantic relationships four years later. *Journal of Sex Research, 57*(2), 156-165.

Shulman, S., Seiffge-Krenke, I.K., & Walsh, S.D. (2017). Is sexual activity in adolescence good for future romantic relationships? *Journal of Youth and Adolescence, 46,* 1867-1877.

Shulman, S., & others (2020). Adolescents' sexual encounters with either romantic or casual partners and the quality of their romantic relationships four years later. *Journal of Sex Research, 57,* 155-165.

Sidhu, S.S., & Adam, B.S. (2021). Social justice for child immigrants. In C.S. Clauss-Ehlers & others (Eds.), *Social justice for children and young people.* New York: Cambridge University Press.

SIECUS (1999). *Public support for sex education.* Washington, DC: Author.

Siegel, D.H. (2013). Open adoption: Adoptive parents' reactions two decades later. *Social Work, 58,* 43-52.

Siegel, D.M., Aten, M.J., & Roghmann, K.J. (1998). Self-reported honesty among middle and high school students responding to a sexual behavior questionnaire. *Journal of Adolescent Health, 23,* 20-28.

Siegel, R., & Brandon, A.R. (2014). Adolescents, pregnancy, and mental health. *Journal of Pediatric and Adolescent Gynecology, 27,* 138-150.

Siegler, R.S. (2006). Microgenetic analysis of learning. In W. Damon & R. Lerner (Eds.), *Handbook of child psychology* (6th ed.). New York: Wiley.

Siegler, R.S. (2017). Foreword: Build it and they will come. In D.G. Geary & others (Eds.), *Acquisition of complex arithmetic skills and higher order mathematics concepts.* New York: Academic Press.

Siegler, R.S., & Alibali, M,W. (2020). *Children's thinking* (5th ed.). Upper Saddle River, NJ: Pearson.

Siegler, R.S., & Lortie-Forgues, H. (2017). Hard lessons: Why rational number arithmetic is so difficult for so many people. *Current Directions in Psychological Science, 26,* 346-351.

Silva, C. (2005, October 31). When teen dynamo talks, city listens. *Boston Globe,* pp. B1, B4.

Silverman, J.G., Raj, A., Mucci, L.A., & Hathaway, J.E. (2001). Dating violence against adolescent girls and associated substance use, unhealthy weight control, sexual risk behavior, pregnancy, and suicidality. *Journal of the American Medical Association, 386,* 572-579.

Simon, K.A., & others (2018). Envisioning future parenthood among bisexual, lesbian, and heterosexual women. *Psychology of Sexual Orientation and Gender Diversity, 5,* 253-259.

Simon, S.L., & others (2021). A model of adolescent sleep health and risk for type 2 diabetes. *Current Diabetes Reports, 21*(2), 4.

Simon, V.A., Aikins, J.W., & Prinstein, M.J. (2008). *Homophily in adolescent romantic relationships.* Unpublished manuscript, College of Arts and Sciences, Wayne State University, Detroit.

Simons, J.M., Finlay, B., & Yang, A. (1991). *The adolescent and young adult fact book.* Washington, DC: Children's Defense Fund.

Simons, J.S., & others (2018). Daily associations between alcohol and sexual behavior in young adults. *Experimental and Clinical Psychopharmacology, 26,* 36-48.

Simons, L.G., & others (2016). Mechanisms that link parenting practices to adolescents' risky sexual behavior: A test of six competing theories. *Journal of Youth and Adolescence, 45,* 255-270.

Simons-Morton, B.G., & others (2020). Crash rates over time among younger and older drivers in the SHRP 2 naturalistic driving study. *Journal of Safety Research, 73,* 245-251.

Simpson, D.M., Leonhardt, N.D., & Hawkins, A.J. (2018). Learning about love: A meta-analytic study of individually-oriented relationship education programs for adolescents and emerging adults. *Journal of Youth and Adolescence, 47,* 477-489.

Simpson, J., & Lewis, T. (2021). Peer-mediated social skills training. In T.A. Collins & R.O. Hawkins (Eds.), *Peers as change agents.* New York: Oxford University Press.

Simpson, R.L. (1962). Parental influence, anticipatory socialization, and social mobility. *American Sociological Review, 27,* 517-522.

Singh, S., Wulf, D., Samara, R., & Cuca, Y.P. (2000). Gender differences in the timing of first intercourse: Data from 14 countries. *International Family Planning Perspectives, 26,* 21-28, 43.

Singh, S., Zaki, R.A., & Farid, N.D.N. (2019). A systematic review of depression literacy: Knowledge, help-seeking, and stigmatizing among adolescents. *Journal of Adolescence, 74,* 154-172.

Sinnott, J.D. (2003). Postformal thought and adult development: Living in balance. In J. Demick & C. Andreoletti (Eds.), *Handbook of adult development*. New York: Kluwer.

Sirsch, U., Dreher, E., Mayr, E., & Willinger, U. (2009). What does it take to be an adult in Austria? Views of adulthood in Austrian adolescents, emerging adults and adults. *Journal of Adolescent Research, 24,* 275–292.

Skinner, B.F. (1938). *The behavior of organisms: An experimental analysis.* New York: Appleton-Century-Crofts.

Skinner, E.A., & Saxton, E.A. (2020). The development of academic coping across late elementary and early middle school: Do patterns differ for students with differing motivational resources? *International Journal of Behavioral Development, 44,* 339–353.

Skinner, H.H., Haines, J., Austin, S.B., & Field, A.E. (2012). A prospective study of overeating, binge eating, and depressive symptoms among adolescent and young adult women. *Journal of Adolescent Health, 50,* 478–483.

Skorikov, V., & Vondracek, F.W. (1998). Vocational identity development: Its relationship to other identity domains and to overall identity development. *Journal of Career Assessment, 6*(1), 13–35.

Sladek, M.R., & others (2020). Testing invariance of ethnic-racial discrimination and identity measures for adolescents across ethnic-racial groups and contexts. *Psychological Assessment, 32,* 509–526.

Sladek, M.R., & others (2021). Contextual moderators of a school-based ethnic-racial identity intervention: The roles of family ethnic socialization and ethnic-racial background. *Prevention Science, 22,* 378–385.

Slavich, G.M., & others (2020). Interpersonal life stress, inflammation, and depression in adolescence: Testing social signal transduction theory of depression. *Depression and Anxiety, 37,* 179–193.

Slavin, R.E. (2015). *Educational psychology* (12th ed.). Upper Saddle River, NJ: Pearson.

Slomkowski, C., Rende, R., Conger, K.J., Simons, R.L., & Conger, R.D. (2001). Sisters, brothers, and delinquency: Social influence during early and middle adolescence. *Child Development, 72,* 271–283.

Smetana, J.G. (2013). Moral development: The social domain theory view. In P.D. Zelazo (Ed.), *Handbook of developmental psychology.* New York: Oxford University Press.

Smetana, J.G., & Gaines, C. (1999). Adolescent-parent conflict in middle-class African-American families. *Child Development, 70,* 1447–1463.

Smith, A.R., Chein, J., & Steinberg, L. (2014). Peers increase risk taking even when the probabilities of negative outcomes are known. *Developmental Psychology, 50,* 1564–1580.

Smith, A.R., & others (2017). "I don't want to grow up, I'm a (Gen X, Y, Me) kid": Increasing maturity fears across the decades. *International Journal of Behavioral Development, 41,* 655–662.

Smith, C., & Denton, M. (2005). *Soul searching: The religious and spiritual lives of American teenagers.* New York: Oxford University Press.

Smith, E.P., & others (2019). Cultural values and problem behavior among African-American and European-American children. *Journal of Child and Family Studies, 28,* 1236–1249.

Smith, K.E., Mason, T.B., & Lavender, J.M. (2018). Rumination and eating disorder psychopathology: A meta-analysis. *Clinical Psychology Review, 61,* 9–23.

Smith, L., & others (2020). Sexual behavior and suicide attempts among adolescents aged 12–15 years from 38 countries: A global perspective. *Psychiatry Research, 287,* 112564.

Smith, L., & others (2021). Bullying victimization and obesogenic behavior among adolescents aged 12 to 15 years from 54 low- and middle-income countries. *Pediatric Obesity, 16*(1), e12700.

Smith, M.M., & others (2018a). Are perfectionism dimensions risk factors for anxiety symptoms? A meta-analysis of 11 longitudinal studies. *Stress, Anxiety, and Coping, 31,* 4–20.

Smith, M.M., & others (2018b). The perniciousness of perfectionism: A meta-analytic review of the perfectionism-suicide relationship. *Journal of Personality, 86,* 522–542.

Smith, N.A., & others (2020). Parents, friends, and immigrant youths' academic engagement: A mediation analysis. *International Journal of Psychology, 55,* 743–753.

Smith, R.A., & Davis, S.F. (2016). *The psychologist as detective* (7th ed.). Upper Saddle River, NJ: Prentice Hall.

Smith, R.E., & Smoll, F.L. (1997). Coaching the coaches: Youth sports as a scientific and applied behavioral setting. *Current Directions in Psychological Science, 6,* 16–21.

Smith, R.L., & Rose, A.J. (2011). The "cost of caring" in youths' friendships: Considering associations among social perspective taking, co-rumination, and empathetic distress. *Developmental Psychology, 47,* 1792–1803.

Smith, R.L., Rose, A.J., & Schwartz-Mette, R.A. (2010). Relational and overt aggression in childhood and adolescence: Clarifying mean-level gender differences and associations with peer acceptance. *Social Development, 19,* 243–269.

Smock, P.J., & Schwartz, C.R. (2020). The demography of families: A review of patterns and change. *Journal of Marriage and Family, 82,* 9–34.

Smokowski, P.R., Bacallao, M.L., Cotter, K.L., & Evans, C.B. (2015). The effects of positive and negative parenting practices on adolescent mental health outcomes in a multicultural sample of rural youth. *Child Psychiatry and Human Development, 46,* 333–345.

Smokowski, P.R., & others (2017). Family dynamics and aggressive behavior in Latino adolescents. *Cultural Diversity and Ethnic Minority Psychology, 23,* 81–90.

Smout, A., & others (2020). The relationship between early risk-taking behavior and mental health problems among a nationally representative sample of Australian youth. *Journal of Affective Disorders, 272,* 239–248.

Smyth, E. (2020). Shaping educational expectations: The perspectives of 13-year-olds and their parents. *Educational Review, 72,* 173–195.

Snarey, J. (1987, June). A question of morality. *Psychology Today, 21,* 6–8.

Snedden, T.R., & others (2020). Sport and physical activity level impacts health-related quality of life among college students. *American Journal of Health Promotion, 33,* 675–682.

Snyder, C.R., & others (Eds.) (2021). *Oxford handbook of positive psychology* (3rd ed.). New York: Oxford University Press.

Society for Adolescent Health and Medicine (2017). Improving knowledge about, access to, and utilization of long-acting reversible contraception among adolescents and young adults. *Journal of Adolescent Health, 60,* 472–474.

Sokkary, N., Awad, H., & Paulo, D. (2021). Frequency of sexual orientation and gender identity documentation after electronic record modification. *Journal of Pediatric and Adolescent Gynecology, 34,* 324–327.

Solomon, B.C., & Jackson, J.J. (2014). Why do personality traits predict divorce? Multiple pathways through satisfaction. *Journal of Personality and Social Psychology, 106,* 978–996.

Solomon, D., Watson, P., Schapes, E., Battistich, V., & Solomon, J. (1990). Cooperative learning as part of a comprehensive program designed to promote prosocial development. In S. Sharan (Ed.), *Cooperative learning.* New York: Praeger.

Song, A.V., & Halpern-Felsher, B.L. (2010). Predictive relationship between adolescent oral and vaginal sex: Results from a prospective, longitudinal study. *Archives of Pediatric and Adolescent Medicine, 165,* 243–249.

Song, L.J., & others (2010). The differential effects of general mental ability and emotional intelligence on academic performance and social interactions. *Intelligence, 38,* 137–143.

Song, Y., & others (2016). Secular trends for age at spermarche among Chinese boys from 11 ethnic minorities, 1995–2010: A multiple cross-sectional study. *BMJ Open, 6*(2), e010518.

Soreff, S.M., Basit, H., & Attia, F.N. (2021). *Suicide risk.* Treasure Island, FL: StatPearls.

Sorensen, L.C., Dodge, K.A., & Conduct Problems Prevention Research Group (2016). How does the Fast Track intervention prevent adverse outcomes in young adulthood? *Child Development, 87,* 429–445.

Sorokowski, P., Kowal, M., & Sorokowska, A. (2019). Religious affiliation and marital satisfaction: Commonalities among Christians, Muslims, and atheists. *Frontiers in Psychology, 10,* 2798.

Sotiriou, E.G., & Awad, G.H. (2020). Cultural influences on body image and body esteem. In F.M. Cheung & D.F. Halpern (Eds.), *Cambridge handbook of the international psychology of women.* New York: Cambridge University Press.

Soto, C.J. (2015). Is happiness good for your personality? Concurrent and prospective relations of the Big Five with subjective well-being. *Journal of Personality, 83*(1), 45–55.

Soto, C.J., John, O.P., Gosling, S.D., & Potter, J. (2011). Age differences in personality traits from 10 to 65: Big Five domains and facets in a large cross-cultural sample. *Journal of Personality and Social Psychology, 100,* 330–348.

Sowell, E. (2004, July). Commentary in M. Beckman, "Crime, culpability, and the adolescent brain." *Science Magazine, 305,* 599.

Spaziani, M., & others (2021). Hypothalamo-pituitary axis and puberty. *Molecular and Cellular Endocrinology, 520,* 111094.

Spence, J.T., & Helmreich, R. (1978). *Masculinity and femininity: Their psychological dimensions.* Austin: University of Texas Press.

Spencer, M.B., & others (2019). Innovating resilience promotion: Integrating cultural practices, social ecologies, and development-sensitive conceptual strategies for advancing child well being. *New Directions in Child Development and Behavior, 57,* 101–148.

Spilman, S.K., Neppl, T.K., Donnellan, M.B., Schofield, T.J., & Conger, R.D. (2013). Incorporating religiosity into a developmental model of positive family functioning across generations. *Developmental Psychology, 49*(4), 762–774.

Spinrad, T.L., & Eisenberg, N. (2020). Socialization of moral emotions and behavior. In D.J. Laible & others (Eds.), *Oxford handbook of parenting and moral development.* New York: Oxford University Press.

Sroufe, L.A. (2007). Commentary: The place of development in developmental psychology. In A.S. Masten (Ed.), *Multilevel dynamics in developmental psychology.* Mahwah, NJ: Erlbaum.

Sroufe, L.A., Coffino, B., & Carlson, E.A. (2010). Conceptualizing the role of early experience: Lessons from the Minnesota longitudinal study. *Developmental Review, 30,* 36–51.

Staff, J., Messersmith, E.E., & Schulenberg, J.E. (2009). Adolescents and the world of work. In R.M. Lerner & L. Steinberg (Eds.), *Handbook of adolescent psychology* (3rd ed.). New York: Wiley.

Stake, J.E. (2000). When situations call for instrumentality and expressiveness: Resource appraisal, coping strategy choice, and adjustment. *Sex Roles, 42,* 865–885.

Stanik, C.E., Riina, E.M., & McHale, S.M. (2013). Parent-adolescent relationship qualities and adolescent adjustment in two-parent African American families. *Family Relations 62,* 597–608.

Stanley, S.M., Rhoades, G.K., Amato, P.R., Markman, H.J., & Johnson, C.A. (2010). The timing of cohabitation and engagement: Impact on first and second marriages. *Journal of Marriage and the Family, 72,* 906-918.

Stanovich, K.E. (2019). *How to think straight about psychology* (11th ed.). Upper Saddle River, NJ: Pearson.

Starr, C. (2015). An objective look at early sexualization and the media. *Sex Roles, 72,* 85-87.

Starr, C.R., & Simpkins, S.D. (2021). High school students' math and science gender stereotypes: Relations with their STEM outcomes and socializers' stereotypes. *Social Psychology Education, 24,* 273-298.

statisticbrain (2017). *Online dating statistics.* Retrieved November 4, 2017, from www.statisticbrain.com/online-dating-statistics

Steel, P. (2007). The nature of procrastination: A meta-analytic and theoretical review of quintessential self-regulatory failure. *Psychological Bulletin, 133,* 65-94.

Steele, J., Waters, E., Crowell, J., & Treboux, D. (1998, June). *Self-report measures of attachment: Secure bonds to other attachment measures and attachment theory.* Paper presented at the meeting of the International Society for the Study of Personal Relationships, Saratoga Springs, NY.

Steele, L.G., & Lynch, S.M. (2013). The pursuit of happiness in China: Individualism, collectivism, and subjective well-being during China's economic and social transformation. *Social Indicators Research, 114*(2), doi:10.1007/s11205-012-0154-1.

Steger, D., Schroeders, U., & Wilhelm, O. (2021). Caught in the act: Predicting cheating in unproctored knowledge assessment. *Assessment, 28,* 1004-1017.

Steiger, A.E., Allemand, M., Robins, R.W., & Fend, H.A. (2014). Low and decreasing self-esteem during adolescence predict adult depression two decades later. *Journal of Personality and Social Psychology, 106,* 325-338.

Stein, G.L., & others (2020). Familism in action in an immigrant community: An examination of indirect effects in early adolescence. *Developmental Psychology, 56,* 1475-1483.

Steinbach, A., Mahne, K., Klaus, D., & Hank, K. (2021). Stability and change in intergenerational family relations across two decades: Findings from the German Aging Survey, 1996-2014. *Journals of Gerontology B: Psychological Sciences and Social Sciences, 60,* 145-158.

Steinberg, L. (2014). *Age of opportunity.* Boston: Houghton Mifflin Harcourt.

Steinberg, L. (2015). The neural underpinnings of adolescent risk-taking: The roles of reward-seeking, impulse control, and peers. In G. Oettigen & P. Gollwitzer (Eds.), *Self-regulation in adolescence.* New York: Cambridge University Press.

Steinberg, L., & others (2018). Around the world, adolescence is a time of heightened sensation seeking and immature self-regulation. *Developmental Science, 21*(2). doi:0.1111/desc.12532

Steinberg, L.D. (1986). Latchkey children and susceptibility to peer pressure: An ecological analysis. *Developmental Psychology, 22,* 433-439.

Steinberg, L.D. (1988). Reciprocal relation between parent-child distance and pubertal maturation. *Developmental Psychology, 24,* 122-128.

Steinberg, S. (2011, June 11). New dating site helps college students find love. *CNN Living.* Retrieved February 27, 2013, from www.cnn.com/2011/LIVING/06/22date.my.school/index.html

Steinhoff, A., & Keller, M. (2020). Pathways from childhood sociomoral sensitivity in friendship, insecurity, and peer rejection to adult friendship quality. *Child Development, 91*(5), e1012-e1029.

Steinmayr, R., Crede, J., McElvany, N., & Wirthwein, L. (2016). Subjective well-being, test anxiety, academic achievement: Testing for reciprocal effects. *Frontiers in Psychology, 6,* 1994.

Stepanyan, S.T., & others (2020). Early pubertal maturation and externalizing behaviors: Examination of peer delinquency as mediator and cognitive flexibility as a moderator. *Journal of Adolescence, 84,* 45-55.

Stephens, J.M. (2008). Cheating. In N.J. Salkind (Ed.), *Encyclopedia of educational psychology.* Thousand Oaks, CA: Sage.

Stephens, N.M., Hamedani, M.G., & Destin, M. (2014). Closing the social-class achievement gap: A difference-education intervention improves first-generation students' academic performance and all students' college transition. *Psychological Science, 25,* 943-953.

Stepler, R. (2017). *Led by baby boomers, divorce rates climb for America's 501 population.* Washington, DC: Pew Research Center.

Sternberg, R.J. (1985, December). Teaching critical thinking, Part 2: Possible solutions. *Phi Delta Kappan,* 277-280.

Sternberg, R.J. (1986). *Intelligence applied.* San Diego. Harcourt Brace Jovanovich.

Sternberg, R.J. (1998). A balance theory of wisdom. *Review of General Psychology, 2,* 347-365.

Sternberg, R.J. (2004). Individual differences in cognitive development. In U. Goswami (Ed.), *Blackwell handbook of childhood cognitive development.* Malden, MA: Blackwell.

Sternberg, R.J. (2010). Componential models of creativity. In M. Runco & S. Spritzker (Eds.), *Encyclopedia of creativity.* New York: Elsevier.

Sternberg, R.J. (2015). Successful intelligence: A new model for testing intelligence beyond IQ tests. *European Journal of Education and Psychology, 8,* 76-84.

Sternberg, R.J. (2019). Race to Samarra: The critical importance of wisdom. In R.J. Sternberg & J. Gluck (Eds.), *Cambridge handbook of wisdom.* New York: Cambridge University Press.

Sternberg, R.J. (2020a). The concept of intelligence. In R.J. Sternberg (Ed.), *Cambridge handbook of intelligence.* New York: Cambridge University Press.

Sternberg, R.J. (2020b). Speculations on the future of intelligence research. In R.J. Sternberg (Ed.), *Cambridge handbook of intelligence.* New York: Cambridge University Press.

Sternberg, R.J. (2020c). Intelligence and creativity. In R.J. Sternberg (Ed.), *Cambridge handbook of intelligence.* New York: Cambridge University Press.

Sternberg, R.J. (2021a). *Adaptive intelligence.* New York: Cambridge University Press.

Sternberg, R.J. (2021b). *The nature of intelligence and its development in childhood.* New York: Cambridge University Press.

Sternberg, R.J. (2021c). Enhancing creativity. In J.C. Kaufman & R.J. Sternberg (Eds.), *Creativity.* New York: Cambridge University Press.

Sternberg, R.J., & Halpern, D.F. (Eds.) (2020). *Critical thinking in psychology* (3rd ed.). New York: Cambridge University Press.

Sternberg, R.J., & Kaufman, J.C. (2018a) *The nature of human creativity.* New York: Cambridge University Press.

Sternberg, R.J., & Kaufman, J.C. (2018b). Theories and conceptions of giftedness. In S. Pfeiffer (Ed.), *Handbook of giftedness in children* (2nd ed.). New York: Springer.

Sternberg, R.J., & Sternberg, K. (2019). The new psychology of love. New York: Cambridge University Press.

Sternberg, R.J., & Williams, W.M. (1996). *How to develop student creativity.* Alexandria, VA: ASCD.

Stevens, A.J. (2020). How can we meet the health needs of child refugees, asylum seekers, and undocumented migrants? *Archives of Disease in Childhood, 105,* 191-196.

Stevenson, H.W. (1995). Mathematics achievement of American students: First in the world by the year 2000? In C.A. Nelson (Ed.), *Basic and applied perspectives on learning, cognition, and development.* Minneapolis: University of Minnesota Press.

Stevenson, H.W., Lee, S., & Stigler, J.W. (1986). Mathematics achievement of Chinese, Japanese, and American children. *Science, 231,* 693-699.

Stevenson, H.W., & Zusho, A. (2002). Adolescence in China and Japan: Adapting to a changing environment. In B.B. Brown, R.W. Larson, & T.S. Saraswathi (Eds.), *The world's youth.* New York: Cambridge University Press.

Stevenson, H.W., & others (1990). Contexts of achievement. *Monograph of the Society for Research in Child Development, 55*(Serial No. 221).

Stewart, A.J., Ostrove, J.M., & Helson, R. (2001). Middle aging in women: Patterns of personality change from the 30s to the 50s. *Journal of Adult Development, 8,* 23-37.

Stice, F., Presnell, K., & Spangler, D. (2002). Risk factors for binge eating onset in adolescent girls: A 2-year prospective investigation. *Health Psychology, 21,* 131-138.

Stipek, D.J. (2002). *Motivation to learn* (4th ed.). Boston: Allyn & Bacon.

Stipek, D.J. (2005, February 16). Commentary in *USA Today,* p. 1D.

Stockard, J., Rohlfing, C.M., & Richmond, G.L. (2021). Equity of women and underrepresented minorities in STEM: Graduate experiences and career plans in chemistry. *Proceedings of the National Academy of Sciences, 118*(4), e2020508118.

Stokes, M.N., & others (2020). Black girl blues: The roles of racial socialization, gendered racial socialization, and racial identity on depressive symptoms in black girls. *Journal of Youth and Adolescence, 49,* 2175-2189.

Stoklosa, I., & others (2021). Analysis of high-risk sexual behavior among Polish university students. *International Journal of Environmental Research and Public Health, 18*(7), 3737.

Stolzenberg, E.B., & others (2020). *The American freshman: National norms, Fall 2019.* Los Angeles: Higher Education Research Institute, UCLA.

Stoppa, T.M., & Lefkowitz, E.S. (2010). Longitudinal changes in religiosity among emerging adult college students. *Journal of Research on Adolescence, 20,* 23-38.

Strahan, D.B. (1983). The emergence of formal operations in adolescence. *Transcendence, 11,* 7-14.

Strati, A.D., Shernoff, D., & Kackar, H.Z. (2012). Flow. In J.R. Levesque (Ed.), *Encyclopedia of adolescence.* New York: Springer.

Stray, L.L., Ellertsen, B., & Stray, T. (2010). Motor function and methylphenidate effect in children with attention deficit hyperactivity disorder. *Acta Paediatrica, 99,* 1199-1204.

Streib, H. (1999). Off-road religion? A narrative approach to fundamentalist and occult orientations of adolescents. *Journal of Adolescence, 22,* 255-267.

Stricker, P.R., & others (2020). Resistance training for children and adolescents. *Pediatrics, 145*(2), e20201011.

Strickhouser, J.E., & Sutin, A.R. (2020). Family and neighborhood socioeconomic status and temperament development from childhood to adolescence. *Journal of Personality, 88,* 515-529.

Strickhouser, J.E., Zell, E., & Krizan, Z. (2017). Does personality predict health and well-being? A metasynthesis. *Health Psychology, 36,* 797-810.

Striegel-Moore, R.H., & Bulik, C.M. (2007). Risk factors for eating disorders. *American Psychologist, 62,* 181-198.

Strohmeier, D., & Noam, G.G. (2012). Bullying in schools: What is the problem and how can educators solve it? *New Directions in Youth Development, 133,* 7-13.

Strunk, K.K., & Steele, M.R. (2011). Relative contributions of self-efficacy, self-regulation, and self-handicapping in predicting student procrastination. *Psychological Reports, 109,* 983-989.

Su, L-D., & others (2021). Cerebellar dysfunction, cerebro-cerebellar connectivity and autism spectrum disorders. *Neuroscience, 462,* 320-327.

Su, R., Rounds, J., & Armstrong, P.I. (2009). Men and things, women and people: A meta-analysis of sex differences in interests. *Psychological Bulletin, 135,* 859-884.

Subica, A.M., & Wu, L.T. (2018). Substance use and suicide in Pacific Islander, American Indian, and multiracial youth. *American Journal of Preventive Medicine, 54,* 795-805.

Sugimoto, N., & others (2020). Use of social networking sites and desire for slimness among 10-year-old girls and boys: A population-based birth cohort study. *International Journal of Eating Disorders, 53,* 288-295.

Sullivan, H.S. (1953). *The interpersonal theory of psychiatry.* New York: Norton.

Sultan, C., & others (2018). Disorders of puberty. *Best Practice and Research: Clinical Obstetrics and Gynecology, 48,* 62-80.

Sumaya, I.C., & Darling, E. (2018). Procrastination, flow, and academic performance in real time using the experience sampling method. *Journal of Genetic Psychology, 28,* 1-9.

Sun, J., & Goodwin, G.P. (2020). Do people want to be more moral? *Psychological Science, 31,* 243-257.

Sun, X., & others (2021). Effects of physical activity interventions on cognitive performance of overweight or obese children and adolescents: A systematic review and meta-analysis. *Pediatric Research, 89,* 146-153.

Sun, Y., Tao, F., Hao, J., & Wan, Y. (2010). The mediating effects of stress and coping on depression among adolescents in China. *Journal of Child and Adolescent Psychiatric Nursing, 23,* 173-180.

Suris, J.C., & others (2014). Is Internet use unhealthy? A cross-sectional study of adolescent Internet overuse. *Swiss Medical Weekly, 144,* w14061.

Susman, E.J., & Dorn, L.D. (2009). Puberty: Its role in development. In R.M. Lerner & L. Steinberg (Eds.), *Handbook of adolescent psychology* (3rd ed.). New York: Wiley.

Susman, E.J., Dorn, L.D., & Schiefelbein, V.L. (2003). Puberty, sexuality, and health. In R.M. Lerner, M.A. Easterbrooks, & J. Mistry (Eds.), *Comprehensive handbook of psychology: Developmental psychology* (Vol. 6). New York: Wiley.

Susman, E.J., & others (2010). Longitudinal development of secondary sexual characteristics in girls and boys between ages 9 and 15 years. *Archives of Pediatric and Adolescent Medicine, 164,* 166-173.

Suter, C., Beycan, T., & Ravazzini, L. (2020). Sociological perspectives on poverty. In K.O. Korgen & W. Paterson (Eds.), *Cambridge handbook of sociology.* New York: Cambridge University Press.

Sutton, T.E., Simons, L.G., & Tyler, K.A. (2021, in press). Hooking-up and sexual victimization on campus: Examining moderators of risk. *Journal of Interpersonal Violence.*

Swaab, D.F., Chung, W.C., Kruijver, F.P., Hofman, M.A., & Ishunina, T.A. (2001). Structural and functional sex differences in the human hypothalamus. *Hormones and Behavior, 40,* 93-98.

Swanson, H.L. (1999). What develops in working memory? A life-span perspective. *Developmental Psychology, 35,* 986-1000.

Swartz, T.T., Kim, M., Uno, M., Mortimer, J., & O'Brien, K.B. (2011). Safety nets and scaffolds: Parental support in the transition to adulthood. *Journal of Marriage and the Family, 73,* 414-429.

Swearer, S.M., & others (2021). Effective bullying prevention and intervention strategies for school officials. In F.C. Worrell & others (Eds.), *Cambridge handbook of applied school psychology.* New York: Cambridge University Press.

Syed, M. (2013). Assessment of ethnic identity and acculturation. In K. Geisinger (Ed.), *APA handbook of testing and assessment in psychology.* Washington, DC: American Psychological Association.

Syed, M., & Azmitia, M. (2008). A narrative approach to ethnic identity in emerging adulthood: Bringing life to the identity status model. *Developmental Psychology, 44,* 1012-1027.

Syed, M., & Azmitia, M. (2009). Longitudinal trajectories of ethnic identity during the college years. *Journal of Research on Adolescence, 19*(4), 601-624.

Syed, M., & McLean, K.C. (2016). Understanding identity integration: Theoretical, methodological, and applied issues. *Journal of Adolescence, 47,* 109-118.

Syeda, M.M., & Climie, E.A. (2014). Test review: Wechsler Preschool and Primary Scale of Intelligence. *Journal of Psychoeducational Assessment, 32,* 265-272.

Sykes, C.J. (1995). *Dumbing down our kids: Why America's children feel good about themselves but can't read, write, or add.* New York: St. Martin's Press.

Syvaoja, H.J., & others (2013). Physical activity, sedentary behavior, and academic performance in Finnish children. *Medicine and Science in Sports and Exercise, 45,* 2098-2104.

Syvertsen, A.K., Scales, P.C., & Toomey, R.B. (2019). Developmental assets framework revisited: Confirmatory analysis and invariance testing to create a new generation of asset measures for applied research. *Applied Developmental Science, 48,* 788-801.

Szalma, J.L. (2021). Basic needs, goals, and motivation. In P.J. Corr & G. Matthews (Eds.), *Cambridge handbook of personality psychology.* New York: Cambridge University Press.

Szucs, L.E., & others (2020, August 21). Condom and contraceptive use among sexually active high school students—Youth Risk Behavior Survey, United States, 2019. *MMWR, 69*(1).

Szwedo, D.E., Hessel, E.T., & Allen, J.P. (2017). Supportive romantic relationships as predictors of resilience against early adolescent maternal negativity. *Journal of Youth and Adolescence, 46,* 454-465.

T

Tahmud, I., & Mesch, G. (2021). *Wired youth.* New York: Routledge.

Takumi, T., & others (2020). Behavioral neuroscience of autism. *Neuroscience and Biobehavioral Reviews, 110,* 60-76.

Talpade, M. (2008). Hispanic versus African American girls: Body image, nutrition, and puberty. *Adolescence, 43,* 119-127.

Tam, H.M., Lam, C.L., Huang, H., Wang, B., & Lee, T.M. (2015). Age-related difference in relationships between cognitive processing speed and general cognitive status. *Applied Neuropsychology: Adult, 22,* 94-99.

Tamis-LeMonda, C.S., & others (2008). Parents' goals for children: The dynamic coexistence of individualism and collectivism in cultures and individuals. *Social Development, 17,* 183-209.

Tan, K., & others (2019). Patterns of social-emotional problems and trajectories of aggression and substance use among middle school boys. *Journal of Early Adolescence, 39,* 1217-1243.

Tang, A., & others (2017). Shyness trajectories across the first four decades predict mental health outcomes. *Journal of Abnormal Child Psychology, 45,* 121-133.

Tang, S., Davis-Kean, P.E., Chen, M., & Sexton, H.R. (2016). Adolescent pregnancy's intergenerational effects: Does an adolescent mother's education have consequences for children's achievement? *Journal of Research on Adolescence, 26,* 180-193.

Tang, X., Wang, M.T., Guo, J., & Salmela-Aro, K. (2019). Building grit: The longitudinal pathways between mindset, commitment, grit, and academic outcomes. *Journal of Youth and Adolescence, 48,* 850-863.

Tang, X., & others (2021). Putting the goal back into grit: Academic goal commitment, grit, and academic achievement. *Journal of Youth and Adolescence, 50,* 470-484.

Tannen, D. (1990). *You just don't understand: Women and men in conversation.* New York: Ballantine.

Tanner, J.M. (1962). *Growth at adolescence* (2nd ed.). Oxford, UK: Blackwell.

Tanskanen, A.O., & others (2017). Sibling conflicts in full- and half-sibling households in the U.K. *Journal of Biosocial Science, 49,* 31-47.

Tanton, C., & others (2015). Patterns and trends in sources of information about sex among young people in Britain: Evidence from three national surveys of sexual attitudes and lifestyles. *BMJ Open, 5*(3), e007834.

Tao, L., & others (2021). Bilingualism and domain-general cognitive functions from a neural perspective: A systematic review. *Neuroscience and Biobehavioral Reviews, 125,* 264-295.

Tarzia, L. (2021, in press). Toward an ecological understanding of intimate partner sexual violence. *Journal of Interpersonal Violence.*

Tashiro, T., & Frazier, P. (2003). "I'll never be in a relationship like that again": Personal growth following romantic relationship breakups. *Personal Relationships, 10,* 113-128.

Tausen, B., Csordas, A., & Macrae, C.N. (2020). The mental landscape of imagining life beyond the current lifespan: Implications for construal and self-continuity. *Innovations in Aging, 4*(3), igaa013.

Tavris, C., & Wade, C. (1984). *The longest war: Sex differences in perspective* (2nd ed.). Fort Worth, TX: Harcourt Brace.

Taylor, B.G., & Mumford, E.A. (2016). A national descriptive portrait of adolescent relationship abuse: Results from the National Survey on Teen Relationships and Intimate Violence, *31,* 961-988. *Journal of Interpersonal Violence.*

Taylor, B.G., Mumford, E.A., & Stein, N.D. (2015). Effectiveness of "shifting boundaries" teen dating violence prevention program for subgroups of middle school students. *Journal of Adolescent Health, 56*(2, Suppl. 2), S20-S26.

Taylor, J.H., & Walker, L.J. (1997). Moral climate and the development of moral reasoning: The effects of dyadic discussions between young offenders. *Journal of Moral Education, 26,* 21-43.

Taylor, R.D., & Lopez, E.I. (2005). Family management practice, school achievement, and problem behavior in African American adolescents: Mediating processes. *Applied Developmental Psychology, 26,* 39-49.

Taylor, S.E. (2015). *Health psychology* (9th ed.). New York: McGraw-Hill.

Taylor, S.E. (2018). *Health psychology* (10th ed.). New York: McGraw-Hill.

Taylor, S.E. (2021). *Health psychology* (11th ed.). New York: McGraw-Hill.

Taylor, T.L. (2021). Academic success of at-risk African American male students who receive culturally relevant teaching, college readiness preparation, and mentorship. *ERIC #:* ED570631.

Taylor, Z.E., Widaman, K.F., & Robins, R.W. (2018). Longitudinal relations of economic hardship and effortful control to active coping in Latino youth. *Journal of Research on Adolescence, 28,* 396-411.

Taylor, Z.E., & others (2020). Developmental antecedents of adolescent optimism in rural Midwestern U.S. Latinx youth. *Journal of Community Psychology, 48,* 488-463.

Teach for America (2021). *Teach for America.* Retrieved June 14, 2021, from www.teachforamerica.org

Teague, M., Mackenzie, S., & Rosenthal, D. (2022). *Your health today* (6th ed.). New York: McGraw-Hill.

Teenage Research Unlimited (2004, November 10). *Diversity in word and deed: Most teens claim multicultural friends.* Northbrook, IL: Teenage Research Unlimited.

Teilmann, G., Juul, A., Skakkebaek, N.E., & Toppari, J. (2002). Putative effects of endocrine disruptors on pubertal development in the human. *Best Practices in Research and Clinical Endocrinology and Metabolism, 16,* 105–121.

Teja, Z., & Worrell, F.C. (2021). School-based intervention for refugee children. In F.C. Worrell & others (Eds.), *Cambridge handbook of applied school psychology.* New York: Cambridge University Press.

Telljohann, S., & others (2020). *Health education: Elementary and middle school applications* (9th ed.). New York: McGraw-Hill.

Telzer, E.H., & others (2021). Neurobiological sensitivity to social rewards and punishments moderates link between peer norms and adolescent risk taking. *Child Development, 92,* 731–745.

Templeton, J.L., & Eccles, J.S. (2006). The relation between spiritual development and identity processes. In E. Roehlkepartain, P.E. King, L. Wagener, & P.L. Benson (Eds.), *The handbook of spirituality in childhood and adolescence.* Thousand Oaks, CA: Sage.

Terman, L. (1925). *Genetic studies of genius: Vol. 1. Mental and physical traits of a thousand gifted children.* Stanford, CA: Stanford University Press.

Terry-McElrath, Y.M., O'Malley, P.M., & Johnston, L.D. (2011). Exercise and substance use among American youth, 1991–2009. *American Journal of Preventive Medicine, 40,* 530–540.

Tetering, M.A.J.V., & others (2020). Sex differences in self-regulation in early, middle, and late adolescence: A large-scale cross-sectional study. *PLoS One, 15*(1), e0227607.

Tetzlaff, A., Schmidt, R., Brauhardt, A., & Hilbert, A. (2016). Family functioning in adolescents with binge-eating disorder. *European Eating Disorders Review, 24,* 430–433.

Tetzner, J., & Becker, M. (2018). Think positive? Examining the impact of optimism on academic achievement in early adolescents. *Journal of Personality, 86,* 283–295.

Thaler, L., & others (2020). Methylation of the OXTR gene in women with anorexia nervosa: Relationship to social behavior. *European Eating Disorders Review, 28,* 79–86.

The, N.S., & others (2010). Association of adolescent obesity with risk of severe obesity in adulthood. *Journal of the American Medical Association, 304,* 2042–2047.

Thein-Nissenbaum, J., & Hammer, E. (2017). Treatment strategies for the female athlete triad in the adolescent athlete: Current perspectives. *Open Access Journal of Sports Medicine, 8,* 85–95.

Theoret, V., & others (2021, in press). Can emotion dysregulation explain the association between attachment insecurities and teen dating violence perpetration? *Journal of Interpersonal Violence.*

Thillay, A., & others (2015). Sustained attention and prediction: Distinct brain maturation trajectories during adolescence. *Frontiers in Human Neuroscience, 9,* 519.

Thoma, S.J., & Bebeau, M. (2008). *Moral judgment competency is declining over time: Evidence from 20 years of defining issues test data.* Paper presented at the meeting of the American Educational Research Association, New York, NY.

Thomaes, S., Bushman, B.J., Stegge, H., & Olthof, T. (2008). Trumping shame by blasts of noise: Narcissism, self-esteem, shame, and aggression in young adolescents. *Child Development, 18,* 758–765.

Thomas, A., & Chess, S. (1991). Temperament in adolescence and its functional significance. In R.M. Lerner, A.C. Petersen, & J. Brooks-Gunn (Eds.), *Encyclopedia of adolescence* (Vol. 2). New York: Garland.

Thomas, A.G., & others (2015). Sleep problems across development: A pathway to adolescent risk through working memory. *Journal of Youth and Adolescence, 44,* 447–464.

Thomas, C.W., Coffman, J.K., & Kipp, K.L. (1993, March). *Are only children different from children with siblings? A longitudinal study of behavioral and social functioning.* Paper presented at the biennial meeting of the Society for Research in Child Development, New Orleans.

Thomas, M.S.C., & Johnson, M.H. (2008). New advances in understanding sensitive periods in brain development. *Current Directions in Psychological Science, 17,* 1–5.

Thompson, A.E., & Voyer, D. (2014). Sex differences in the ability to recognize non-verbal displays of emotion: A meta-analysis. *Cognition and Emotion, 28,* 1164–1195.

Thompson, A.E., & others (2020). An investigation of the implicit endorsement of the sexual double standard among U.S. young adults. *Frontiers in Psychology, 11,* 1454.

Thompson, M.P., & Swartout, K. (2018). Epidemiology of suicide attempts among youth transitioning to adulthood. *Journal of Youth and Adolescence, 47,* 807–817.

Thompson, R., & others (2017). Is the use of physical discipline associated with aggressive behaviors in children? *Academic Pediatrics, 17,* 34–44.

Thompson, R.A. (2008). Unpublished review of J.W. Santrock's *Life-span development,* 12th ed. New York: McGraw-Hill.

Thompson, R.A. (2014). Conscience development in early childhood. In M. Killen & J.G. Smetana (Eds.), *Handbook of moral development* (2nd ed.). New York: Guilford.

Thompson, R.A. (2020). Early moral development and attachment theory. In D.J. Laible & others (Eds.), *Oxford handbook of parenting and moral development.* New York: Oxford University Press.

Thoni, C., Volk, S., & Cortina, J.M. (2021). Greater male variability in cooperation: Meta-analytic evidence for an evolutionary perspective. *Psychological Science, 32,* 50–63.

Thorisdottir, I.E., & others (2020). Longitudinal association between social media use and psychological distress in adolescents. *Preventive Medicine, 141,* 106270.

Thorne, B.M., Ellenbroek, B.A., & Day, D.J. (2021). Evaluation of i-motif formation in the serotonin transporter-linked polymorphic region. *Chembiochem, 22,* 349–353.

Tian, L., & others (2020). Effect of peer presence on adolescents' risk-taking is moderated by individual self-esteem: An experimental study. *International Journal of Psychology, 55,* 373–379.

Tibbetts, Y., & others (2016). Affirming independence: Exploring mechanisms underlying a values affirmation intervention for first-generation students. *Journal of Personality and Social Psychology, 110,* 635–659.

Tiego, J., & others (2020). Common mechanisms of executive attention underlie executive function and effortful control in children. *Developmental Science, 23*(3), 12918.

Tiggemann, M., & Slater, A. (2017). Facebook and body image concern in adolescent girls: A prospective study. *International Journal of Eating Disorders, 50,* 80–83.

Timmermans, E., & Van den Bulck, J. (2018). Casual sexual scripts on the screen: A quantitative content analysis. *Archives of Sexual Behavior, 47,* 1481–1496.

TIMSS (Trends in International Mathematics and Science Study) (2019). *TIMSS 2019 4th and 8th grade mathematics and science results.* Chestnut Hill, MA: TIMSS.

Tistarelli, N., & others (2020). The nature and nurture of ADHD and its comorbidities: A narrative review of twin studies. *Neuroscience and Biobehavioral Reviews, 109,* 63–77.

Tolman, D.L., & Chmielewski, J.F. (2019). From tightrope to minefield: How the sexual double standard "lives" in adolescent girls' and young women's lives. In S. Lamb & J. Gilbert (Eds.), *Cambridge handbook of sexual development.* New York: Cambridge University Press.

Tomasik, M.J., Pavlova, M.K., Lechner, C.M., Blumenthal, A., & Korner, A. (2012). Changing contexts of youth development: An overview of recent social trends and a psychological model. *New Directions for Youth Development, 135,* 27–38.

Tomlinson-Keasey, C. (1972). Formal operations in females from 11 to 54 years of age. *Developmental Psychology, 6,* 364.

Tompkins, G.E., & Rodgers, E. (2020). *Literacy in the early grades* (5th ed.). Upper Saddle River, NJ: Pearson.

Tonarely, N.A., & others (2020). Neuroticism as an underlying construct in youth emotional disorders. *Bulletin of the Menninger Clinic, 84,* 214–236.

Tooley, U.A., & others (2020). Associations between neighborhood SES and functional brain network development. *Cerebral Cortex, 30*(1), 1–19.

Top, N., Liew, J., & Luo, W. (2017). Family and school influences on youths' behavioral and academic outcomes: Cross-level interactions between parental monitoring and character development curriculum. *Journal of Genetic Psychology, 178,* 106–118.

Topart, C., Werner, E., & Arimondo, P.B. (2020). Wandering along the epigenetic timeline. *Clinical Epigenetics, 12*(1), 97.

Tornay, L., & others (2020). Parental monitoring: A way to decrease substance use among Swiss adolescents? *European Journal of Pediatrics, 172,* 1229–1234.

Tornello, S.L., Riskind, R.G., & Patterson, C.J. (2014). Sexual orientation and sexual and reproductive health among adolescent young women in the United States. *Journal of Adolescent Health, 54,* 160–168.

Torstveit, L., Sutterlin, S., & Lugo, R.G. (2016). Empathy, guilt proneness, and gender: Relative contributions to prosocial behavior. *European Journal of Psychology, 12,* 260–275.

Touitou, Y., Touitou, D., & Reinberg, A. (2016). Disruption of adolescents' circadian clock: The vicious circle of media use, exposure to light at night, sleep loss, and risk behaviors. *Journal of Physiology, 110,* 467–479.

Toy, W., Nai, Z.L., & Lee, H.W. (2016). Extraversion and agreeableness: Divergent routes to daily satisfaction with social relationships. *Journal of Personality, 84,* 121–134.

Trafimow, D., Triandis, H.C., & Goto, S.G. (1991). Some tests of the distinction between the private and collective self. *Journal of Personality and Social Psychology, 60,* 649–655.

Tran, A.P., & Silver, J. (2020). Cathepsins in neuronal plasticity. *Neural Regeneration Research, 16,* 26–35.

Tran, S.P., & Raffaelli, M. (2020). Configurations of autonomy and relatedness in a multiethnic U.S. sample of parent-adolescent dyads. *Journal of Research on Adolescence, 30,* 203–218.

Travlos, A.K., & others (2021). The effect of moral disengagement on bullying: The moderating role of personal and social factors. *Journal of Interpersonal Violence, 36,* 2262–2281.

Trentacosta, N. (2020). Pediatric sports injuries. *Pediatric Clinics of North America, 67,* 205–225.

Trentini, C., & others (2021, in press). Gender differences in empathy in adolescence: Does emotional self-awareness matter? *Psychological Reports.*

Triana, A., Susmaneli, H., & Rafiah, S. (2020). Influence of adolescents' masturbation behavior. *Enfermeria Clinica, 30*(Suppl. 6), S340–S342.

Triandis, H.C. (2007). Culture and psychology: A history of their relationship. In S. Kitayama & D. Cohen (Eds.), *Handbook of cultural psychology.* New York: Guilford.

Trimble, J.E. (2021). Foreword: The last page and dreams of the future and the weight of the past. In C.S. Clauss-Ehlers & others. *Applying multiculturalism.* Washington, DC: APA Books.

Trzesniewski, K.H., & Donnellan, M.B. (2010). Rethinking "generation me": A study of cohort effects from 1976-2006. *Perspectives on Psychological Science, 5,* 58-75.

Trzesniewski, K.H., Donnellan, M.B., & Robins, R.W. (2008a). Do today's young people really think they are so extraordinary? An examination of secular trends in narcissism and self-enhancement. *Psychological Science, 19,* 181-188.

Trzesniewski, M., Donnellan, M.B., & Robins, R.W. (2008b). Is "Generation Me" really more narcissistic than previous generations? *Journal of Personality, 76,* 903-918.

Trzesniewski, M., Donnellan, M.B., & Robins, R.W. (2013). Development of self-esteem. In V. Zeigler-Hill (Ed.), *Self-esteem.* New York: Psychology Press.

Trzesniewski, K.H., & others (2006). Low self-esteem during adolescence predicts poor health, criminal behavior, and limited economic prospects during adulthood. *Developmental Psychology, 42,* 381-390.

Tsang, L.P.M., & others (2019). Autism spectrum disorder: Early identification and management in primary care. *Singapore Medical Journal, 60,* 324-328.

Tsethlikai, M., & others (2020, September 9). *Addressing the inequities in education: Considerations for American Indian and Alaska Native children and youth in the era of COVID-19.* Retrieved from www.srcd.org/research/addressing-inequities-education-consideratins-american-indian-and-alaska-native children

Tsutsui, T.W. (2020). Dental pulp stem cells: Advances to applications. *Stem Cells Cloning, 13,* 33-42.

Tu, K.M., Cai, T., & Li, X. (2020). Adolescent coping with academic challenges: The role of parental socialization of coping. *Journal of Adolescence, 81,* 27-38.

Tucker, C.J., McHale, S.M., & Crouter, A.C. (2001). Conditions of sibling support in adolescence. *Journal of Family Psychology, 15,* 254-271.

Tucker, C.J., & Winzeler, A. (2007). Adolescent siblings' daily discussions: Connections to perceived academic, athletic, and peer competency. *Journal of Research on Adolescence, 17,* 145-152.

Tucker, J.S., & others (2012). Resisting smoking when a best friend smokes: Do intrapersonal and contextual factors matter? *Journal of Research on Adolescence, 22,* 113-122.

Tullius, J.M., & others (2021, in press). Adolescents' mental health problems increase after parental divorce, not before, and persist until adulthood: A longitudinal TRAILS study. *European Journal of Adolescent Psychiatry.*

Turesky, T., & others (2020). Relating anthropometric indicators to brain structure in 2-month-old Bangladeshi infants growing up in poverty: A pilot study. *NeuroImage, 210,* 116540.

Turiel, E. (2018). Reasoning at the root of morality. In K. Gray & J. Graham (Eds.), *Atlas of moral psychology.* New York: Guilford.

Turnbull, A., & others (2020). *Exceptional lives* (9th ed.). Upper Saddle River, NJ: Pearson.

Turner, A., & others (2021, in press). The relationship between empathic tendencies and altruistic behaviors in adolescents. *Child Care Health and Development.*

Twenge, J.M., & Campbell, W.K. (2001). Age and birth cohort differences in self-esteem: A cross-temporal meta-analysis. *Personality and Social Psychology Bulletin, 5,* 321-344.

Twenge, J.M., & Campbell, W.K. (2017). *Personality psychology.* Upper Saddle River, NJ: Pearson.

Twenge, J.M., & Campbell, W.K. (2019). Media use is linked to lower psychological well-being: Evidence from three datasets. *Psychiatric Quarterly, 90,* 311-331.

Twenge, J.M., Carter, N.T., & Campbell, W.K. (2017). Age, time period, and birth cohort differences in self-esteem: Reexamining a cohort-sequential study. *Journal of Personality and Social Psychology, 112,* e9-e17.

Twenge, J.M., & Farley, E. (2021). Not all screen time is created equal: Associations with mental health vary by activity and gender. *Social Psychiatry and Psychiatric Epidemiology, 56,* 207-217.

Twenge, J.M., Konrath, S., Foster, J.D., Campbell, W.K., & Bushman. B.J. (2008a). Egos inflating over time: A cross-temporal meta-analysis of the Narcissistic Personality Inventory. *Journal of Personality, 76,* 875-902.

Twenge, J.M., Konrath, S., Foster, J.D., Campbell, W.K., & Bushman, B.J. (2008b). Further evidence of an increase in narcissism among college students. *Journal of Personality, 76,* 919-928.

Twenge, J.M., & Martin, G.N. (2020). Gender differences in associations between digital media use and psychological well-being: Evidence from three large clusters. *Journal of Adolescence, 79,* 91-102.

Tyrell, F.A., & others (2016). Family influences on Mexican American adolescents' romantic relationships: Moderation by gender and culture. *Journal of Research on Adolescence, 26,* 142-158.

U

U.S. Bureau of Labor Statistics (2015). *People.* Washington, DC: Author.

U.S. Census Bureau (2016). *People.* Washington, DC: Author.

U.S. Census Bureau (2019). *Births, deaths, marriages, divorces.* Washington, DC: Author.

U.S. Census Bureau (2019). *Marriages and divorces.* Washington, DC: U.S. Department of Labor.

U.S. Census Bureau (2020, July). *Families and households.* Washington, DC: U.S. Department of Labor.

U.S. Department of Energy (2001). *The Human Genome Project.* Washington, DC: Author.

U.S. Department of Health and Human Services Office of Minority Health (2020). *Obesity and American Indians/Native Alaskans.* Washington, DC: Author.

U.S. Department of Labor (2020). *Unemployment rate of college graduates.* Washington, DC: Author.

Ueno, K., & McWilliams, S. (2010). Gender-typed behaviors and school adjustment. *Sex Roles, 63,* 580-591.

Uhls, Y.T., Ellison, N.B., & Subrahmanyam, K. (2017). Benefits and costs of social media in adolescence. *Pediatrics, 140*(Suppl. 2), S67-S70.

Ullsperger, J.M., & Nikolas, M.A. (2017). A meta-analytic review of the association between pubertal timing and psychopathology in adolescence: Are there sex differences in risk? *Psychological Bulletin, 143,* 903-938.

Umaña-Taylor, A.J., & Hill, N.E. (2020). Ethnic-racial socialization in the family. A decade's advance on precursors and outcomes. *Journal of Marriage and the Family, 82,* 244-271.

Umaña-Taylor, A.J., & others (2020). National identity development and friendship network dynamics among immigrant and non-immigrant youth. *Journal of Youth and Adolescence, 49,* 706-723.

UNAIDS (2020). *UNAIDS data 2019.* Geneva, Switzerland: Author.

Uncapher, M.R., & others (2017). Media multitasking and cognitive, psychological, neural, and learning differences. *Pediatrics, 140*(Suppl. 2), S62-S66.

Underwood, J.M., & others (2020). *Youth Risk Behavior Surveillance—United State, 2019.* Washington, DC: U.S. Department of Health and Human Services.

Underwood, J.M., & others (2020, August 21). *Youth Risk Behavior Surveillance—United States, 2019. MMWR, 69*(1).

UNICEF (2003). *Annual report: 2002.* Geneva, Switzerland: Author.

UNICEF (2007). *The state of the world's children: 2007.* Geneva, Switzerland: Author.

UNICEF (2018). *The state of the world's children: 2018.* Geneva, Switzerland: Author.

UNICEF (2021). *The state of the world's children: 2021.* Geneva, Switzerland: Author.

University of Buffalo Counseling Services (2014). *Procrastination.* Retrieved November 20, 2014, from http://ub-counseling.buffalo.edu/stressprocrast.shtml

University of Illinois Counseling Center (1984). *Overcoming procrastination.* Urbana-Champaign, IL: Department of Student Affairs.

University of Illinois Counseling Center (2020a). *Perfectionism.* Retrieved November 16, 2020, from www.counselingcenter.illinois.edu?page_id5113

University of Illinois Counseling Center (2020b). *Procrastination.* Urbana-Champaign, IL: Department of Student Affairs.

Updegraff, K.A., McHale, S., Whiteman, S.D., Thayer, S.M., & Delgado, M.Y. (2005). Adolescent sibling relationships in Mexican American families: Exploring the role of familism. *Journal of Family Psychology, 19,* 512-522.

Updegraff, K.A., Umana-Taylor, A.J., McHale, S.M., Wheeler, L.A., & Perez-Brena, J. (2012). Mexican-origin youths' cultural orientations and adjustment: Changes from early to late adolescence. *Child Development, 83,* 1655-1671.

Urdan, T. (2012). Factors affecting the motivation and achievement of immigrant students. In K.R. Harris, S. Graham, & T. Urdan (Eds.), *APA educational psychology handbook.* Washington, DC: American Psychological Association.

USA Today (2001, October 10). All-USA first teacher team. Retrieved November 20, 2004, from www.usatoday/com/news/education2001

Usher, E.L., & Schunk, D.H. (2018). Social cognitive theoretical perspective of self-regulation. In D.H. Schunk & J.A. Greene (Eds.), *Handbook of self-regulation of learning and performance* (2nd ed.). New York: Routledge.

V

Vaca, F.E., & others (2020). Longitudinal associations of 12th-grade binge drinking with risky driving and high-risk drinking. *Pediatrics, 145*(2), e20184095.

Valentin-Cortes, M., & others (2020). Application of the minority stress theory: Understanding the mental health of undocumented Latinx immigrants. *American Journal of Community Psychology, 66,* 325-336.

Valero, S., & others (2014). Neuroticism and impulsivity: Their hierarchical organization in the personality characterization of drug-dependent patients from a decision tree learning perspective. *Comprehensive Psychiatry, 55,* 1227-1233.

Valladares, A.A., & others (2020). Attention-deficit/hyperactivity disorder in children and adolescents: An event-related potential study of working memory. *European Journal of Neuroscience, 52,* 4356-4369.

Van Dam, L., & others (2018). Does natural mentoring matter? A multilevel meta-analysis on the association between natural mentoring and youth outcomes. *American Journal of Community Psychology, 62,* 203-220.

van de Groep, S., Zanolie, K., & Crone, E.A. (2020). Giving to friends, classmates, and strangers in adolescence. *Journal of Research on Adolescence, 30*(Suppl. 2), S290-S297.

Van den Akker, A.I., & others (2021). Adolescent Big Five personality and pubertal development: Pubertal hormone concentrations and self-reported pubertal status. *Developmental Psychology, 57,* 60-72.

van der Hoeven, R. (2021). Human inequality and human capabilities. In E. Chiappero-Martinetti & others (Eds.), *Cambridge handbook of the capability approach.* New York: Cambridge University Press.

van der Stel, M., & Veenman, M.V.J. (2010). Development of metacognitive skillfulness: A longitudinal study. *Learning and Individual Differences, 20,* 220–224.

van Dijk, R., & others (2020). A meta-analysis on interparental conflict, parenting, and child adjustment in divorced families: Examining mediation using meta-analytic structural equation models. *Clinical Psychology Review, 79,* 101861.

van Doeselaar, L., & others (2020). Adolescents' identity formation: Linking the narrative and the dual-cycle approach. *Journal of Youth and Adolescence, 49,* 818–835.

Van Goozen, S.H.M., Matthys, W., Cohen-Kettenis, P.T., Thisjssen, J.H.H., & van Engeland, H. (1998). Adrenal androgens and aggression in conduct disorder prepubertal boys and normal controls. *Biological Psychiatry, 43,* 156–158.

Van Hoover, C., Rademayer, C.A., & Farley, C.L. (2017). Body piercing: Motivations and implications for health. *Journal of Midwifery and Women's Health, 62,* 521–530.

van Kesteren, M.R., & Meeter, M. (2020). How to optimize knowledge construction in the brain. *NPJ Science of Learning, 5,* 5.

Van Keulen, B.J., & others (2020). Sexual dimorphism in cortical metabolism throughout pubertal development: A longitudinal study. *Endocrine Connections, 9,* 542–551.

Van Lissa, C.J., & others (2015). Divergence between adolescent and parent perceptions of conflict in relationship to adolescent empathy development. *Journal of Youth and Adolescence, 44,* 48–51.

Van Lissa, C.J., & others (2017). The cost of empathy: Parent-adolescent conflict predicts emotion dysregulation for highly empathic youth. *Developmental Psychology, 53,* 1722–1737.

Van Lissa, C.J., & others (2019). The role of fathers' versus mothers' parenting in emotion-regulation development from mid-late adolescence: Disentangling between-family differences from within-family effects. *Developmental Psychology, 55,* 377–389.

Van Ryzin, M.J., & Roseth, C.J. (2021). The cascading effect of reducing student stress: Cooperative learning as a means to reduce emotional problems and promote academic engagement. *Journal of Early Adolescence, 5,* 700–724.

van Tetering, M.A.J., & others (2020). Sex differences in self-regulation in early, middle, and late adolescence: A large-scale cross-sectional study. *PLoS One, 15*(1), e0227607.

van Zalk, M.H.W., & others (2020). The codevelopment of extraversion and friendships: Bonding and behavioral interaction mechanisms in friendship networks. *Journal of Personality and Social Psychology, 118,* 1269–1290.

Vandell, D.L., Minnett, A., & Santrock, J.W. (1987). Age differences in sibling relationships during middle childhood. *Applied Developmental Psychology, 8,* 247–257.

Vanes, L.D., & others (2020). White matter tract myelin maturation and its association with general psychopathology in adolescence and early adulthood. *Human Brain Mapping, 41,* 827–839.

Vangeel, L., Eggermont, S., & Vandenbosch, L. (2020). Does adolescent media use predict sexual stereotypes in adolescence and emerging adulthood? Associations with music television and online pornography exposure. *Archives of Sexual Behavior, 49,* 1147–1161.

VanMeter, F., & Cicchetti, D. (2020). Resilience. *Handbook of Clinical Neurology, 173,* 67–73.

Vannucci, A., & others (2020). Social media use and risky behaviors in adolescents: A meta-analysis. *Journal of Adolescence, 79,* 258–274.

Vargas, E.A., & others (2021, in press). Incidence and group comparisons of harassment based on gender, LGBTQ1 identity, and race at an academic medical center. *Journal of Women's Health.*

Vargas, S.M., Huey, S.J., & Miranda, J. (2020). A critical review of current evidence on multiple types of discrimination and mental health. *American Journal of Orthopsychiatry. 90,* 374–390.

Vasa, F., & others (2020). Conservative and disruptive modes of adolescent change in human brain connectivity. *Proceedings of the National Academy of Sciences U.S.A., 117*(6), 3248–3253.

Vasilenko, S.A., & Lefkowitz, E.S. (2018). Sexual behavior and daily affect in emerging adulthood. *Emerging Adulthood, 6,* 191–199.

Vazsonyi, A.T., & others (2021, in press). Links between parenting and internalizing and externalizing problems: Cross-cultural evidence from ten countries. *Child Psychiatry and Human Development.*

Verdin, D., Godwin, A., & Klotz, L. (2020). Exploring the sustainability-related career outcome expectations of community college students interested in science and engineering careers. *Community College Journal of Research and Practice, 44*(2), 83–98.

Verkooijen, S., & others (2018). Sleep disturbances, psychosocial difficulties, and health risk behavior in 16,781 Dutch adolescents. *Academic Pediatrics, 18,* 655–661.

Vernucci, S., & others (2020). Working memory training in children: A review of basic methodological criteria. *Psychological Reports, 123,* 605–632.

Veronneau, M.H., Racer, K.H., Fosco, G.M., & Dishion, T.J. (2014). The contribution of adolescent effortful control to early adult educational attainment. *Journal of Educational Psychology, 106,* 730–743.

Veronneau, M.H., Vitaro, F., Pedersen, S., & Tremblay, R.E. (2008). Do peers contribute to the likelihood of secondary graduation among disadvantaged boys? *Journal of Educational Psychology, 100,* 429–442.

Verschueren, M., & others (2020). Eating disorder symptomatology in adolescent boys and girls: Identifying distinct developmental trajectory classes. *Journal of Youth and Adolescence, 49,* 410–426.

Verstraeten, K., Vasey, M.W., Raes, F., & Bitjttebier, P. (2009). Temperament and risk for depressive symptoms in adolescence: Mediation by rumination and moderation by effortful control. *Journal of Abnormal Child Psychology, 37,* 349–361.

Verzani, M., & others (2021). Impact of COVID-19 pandemic lockdown on early onset of puberty: Experience of an Italian tertiary center. *Italian Journal of Pediatrics, 47*(1), 52.

Vespa, J. (2017, April). The changing economics and demographics of young adulthood: 1975–2016. *Current Population Reports,* P20-579. Washington, DC: U.S. Census Bureau.

Vetter, N.C., & others (2013). Ongoing development of social cognition in adolescence. *Child Neuropsychology, 19,* 615–629.

Vidal, S., & others (2017). Maltreatment, family environment, and social risk factors: Determinants of the child welfare to juvenile justice transition among maltreated children and adolescents. *Child Abuse and Neglect, 63,* 7–18.

Villa-Gonzalez, R., & others (2020). A systematic review of acute exercise as a coadjuvant treatment of ADHD in young people. *Psicothema, 32,* 67–74.

Viswanathan, M., & others (2020). *Treatment of depression in children and adolescents: A systematic review.* Rockville, MD: Agency for Healthcare Research and Quality.

Vitaro, F., Boivin, M., & Poulin, F. (2018). The interface of aggression and peer relations in childhood and adolescence. In W.M. Bukowski & others (Eds.), *Handbook of peer interactions, relationships, and groups* (2nd ed.). New York: Guilford.

Voce, A., & Anderson, K.G. (2020). The interaction between parental behavior and motivations to drink alcohol in high school students. *American Journal of Drug and Alcohol Abuse, 46,* 348–356.

Vokey, M., Tefft, B., & Tysiaczny, C. (2013). An analysis of hyper-masculinity in magazine advertisements. *Sex Roles, 68,* 562–576.

Volkow, N.D., & others (2020). An examination of child and adolescent neurodevelopment through National Institutes of Health studies. *Public Health Reports, 135,* 169–172.

Volpe, E.M., Hardie, T.L., Cerulli, C., Sommers, M.S., & Morrison-Beedy, D. (2013). What's age got to do with it? Partner age difference, power, intimate partner violence, and sexual risk in urban adolescents. *Journal of Interpersonal Violence, 28,* 2068–2087.

von Soest, T., & others (2018). Self-esteem across the second half of life: The role of socioeconomic status, physical health, social relationships, and personality factors. *Journal of Personality and Social Psychology, 114,* 945–958.

Vosberg, D.E., & others (2021). Sex continuum in the brain and body during adolescence and psychological traits. *Nature. Human Behavior, 5,* 265–272.

Vrolijk, P., & others (2020). Longitudinal linkages between father and mother autonomy support and adolescent problem behaviors: Between-family differences and within-family effects. *Journal of Youth and Adolescence, 49,* 2372–2387.

Vukelich, C., & others (2020). *Helping children learn language and literacy* (5th ed.). Upper Saddle River, NJ: Pearson.

Vygotsky, L.S. (1962). *Thought and language.* Cambridge, MA: MIT Press.

W

Wachs, T.D. (1994). Fit, context and the transition between temperament and personality. In C. Halverson, G. Kohnstamm, & R. Martin (Eds.), *The developing structure of personality from infancy to adulthood.* Hillsdale, NJ: Erlbaum.

Wachs, T.D. (2000). *Necessary but not sufficient.* Washington, DC: American Psychological Association.

Wachs, T.D., & Kohnstamm, G.A. (2013). The bidirectional nature of temperament-context links. In T.D. Wachs & others (Eds.), *Temperament in context.* New York: Psychology Press.

Wainwright, L., Nee, C., & Vrij, A. (2018). "I don't know how, but I'll figure it out somehow": Future possible selves and aspirations in "at-risk" early adolescents. *International Journal of Offender Therapy and Comparative Criminology, 62,* 504–523.

Waiter, G.D., & others (2009). Exploring possible neural mechanisms of intelligence differences using processing speed and working memory tasks. *Intelligence, 37,* 199–206.

Walczak-Kozlowska, T., & others (2020). Attentional system of very prematurely born preschoolers. *Developmental Psychology, 56,* 251–260.

Walker, L.J. (2002). Moral exemplarity. In W. Damon (Ed.), *Bringing in a new era of character education.* Stanford, CA: Hoover Press.

Walker, L.J. (2016). Prosocial exemplarity in adolescence and adulthood. In L.M. Padilla-Walker & G. Carlo (Eds.), *Prosocial development.* New York: Oxford University Press.

Walker, L.J., & Hennig, K.H. (2004). Differing conceptions of moral exemplars: Just, brave, and caring. *Journal of Personality and Social Psychology, 86,* 629–647.

Walker, L.J., Hennig, K.H., & Krettenauer, R. (2000). Parent and peer contexts for children's moral reasoning development. *Child Development, 71,* 1033–1048.

Walker, L.J., Pitts, R.C., Hennig, K.H., & Matsuba, M.K. (1995). Reasoning about morality and real-life moral problems. In M. Killen & D. Hart (Eds.), *Morality in everyday life.* New York: Cambridge University Press.

Walker, L.J., & Taylor, J.H. (1991). Family interaction and the development of moral reasoning. *Child Development, 62,* 264–283.

Wallace-Broscious, A., Serafica, F.C., & Osipow, S.H. (1994). Adolescent career development: Relationships to self-concept and identity status. *Journal of Research on Adolescence, 4,* 127–150.

Waller, E.M., & Rose, A.J. (2010). Adjustment trade-offs of co-rumination in mother-adolescent relationships. *Journal of Adolescence, 33,* 487–497.

Wallis, C. (2011). Performing gender: A content analysis of gender display in music videos. *Sex Roles, 64,* 160–172.

Walsh, R. (2011). Lifestyle and mental health. *American Psychologist, 666,* 579–592.

Walsh, S.D., & others (2020). Clusters of contemporary risk and their relationship to mental well-being among 15-year-old adolescents across 37 countries. *Journal of Adolescent Health, 66*(6S), S40–S49.

Walter, C.A. (1986). *The timing of motherhood.* Lexington, MA: D.C. Heath.

Walters, G.D. (2020). Prosocial peers as risk, protective, and promotive factors for the prevention of delinquency and drug use. *Journal of Youth and Adolescence, 49,* 618–630.

Walters, G.D. (2021). Explaining the drug-crime connection with peers, proactive criminal thinking, and victimization: Systematic, cognitive social learning, and person proximity mechanisms. *Psychology of Addictive Behaviors, 35,* 366–376.

Walters, G.D. (2021, in press). Peer influence or projection bias? Predicting respondent delinquency with perceptual measures of peer delinquency in 22 samples. *Journal of Adolescence.*

Walton, G.M., & others (2014). Two brief interventions to mitigate a "chilly climate" transform women's experience, relationships, and achievement in engineering. *Journal of Educational Psychology, 107,* 468–485.

Wang, B., & others (2014). The impact of youth, family, peer, and neighborhood risk factors on developmental trajectories of risk involvement from early through middle adolescence. *Social Science Medicine, 106,* 43–52.

Wang, C., & others (2016). Coevolution of adolescent friendship networks and smoking and drinking behaviors with consideration of parental influence. *Psychology of Addictive Behaviors, 30,* 312–324.

Wang, C.D., & others (2019). Grandparents as the primary care providers for their grandchildren: A cross-cultural comparison of Chinese and U.S. samples. *International Journal of Aging and Human Development, 89,* 331–355.

Wang, D., Choi, J-K., & Shin, J. (2020). Long-term neighborhood effects on adolescent outcomes: Mediated through adverse childhood experiences and parenting stress. *Journal of Youth and Adolescence, 49,* 2160–2173.

Wang, F., & Biro, E. (2021). Determinants of sleep quality in college students: A literature review. *Explore, 17,* 170–177.

Wang, H., Lin, S.L., Leung, G.M., & Schooling, C.M. (2016). Age at onset of puberty and adolescent depression: "Children of 1997" birth cohort. *Pediatrics, 137*(6), 20153231.

Wang, H., & others (2020). Middle-aged children's coping strategies with tensions in the aging parent-child tie. *International Journal of Aging and Human Development, 90,* 234–254.

Wang, J., Chen, C., & Gong, X. (2021, in press). The impact of socioeconomic status and parenting styles on children's academic trajectories: A longitudinal study comparing migrant and urban children in China. *New Directions in Child and Adolescent Development.*

Wang, L.Y., Chyen, D., Lee, L., & Lowry, R. (2008). The association between body mass index in adolescence and obesity in adulthood. *Journal of Adolescent Health, 42,* 512–518.

Wang, M.C., & others (2010). Exposure to comprehensive school intervention increases vegetable consumption. *Journal of Adolescent Health, 47,* 74–82.

Wang, M-T., & others (2021, in press). More than growth mindset: Individual and interactive links among socioeconomically disadvantaged adolescents' ability mindsets, metacognitive skills, and math engagement. *Child Development.*

Wang, M-T., & others (2021, in press). Skill, thrill, and will: The role of metacognition, interest, and self-control in predicting student engagement in mathematics learning over time. *Child Development.*

Wang, P.Y., & others (2019). Relationship of sleep quality, smartphone dependence, and health-related behaviors in female junior college students. *PLoS One, 14*(4), e0214769.

Wang, Q., Peng, S., & Chi, X. (2021). The relationship between family functioning and internalizing problems in Chinese adolescents: A moderated mediation model. *Frontiers in Psychology, 12,* 644222.

Wang, Q., & Pomerantz, E.M. (2009). The motivational landscape of early adolescence in the United States and China: A longitudinal study. *Child Development, 80,* 1272–1287.

Wang, S., & others (2020). The influence of negative life events on suicidal ideation in college students: The role of rumination. *International Journal of Environmental Research and Public Health, 17*(8), 2646.

Wang, W., & Parker, K. (2014). *Record shares of Americans have never been married.* Washington, DC: Pew Research Center.

Wang, X., & others (2020). Intervening paths from strain to delinquency among high school and vocational school students in China. *International Journal of Offender Therapy and Comparative Criminology, 64,* 22–37.

Wang, Y. (2021, in press). Daily ethnic/racial context in peer groups: Frequency, structure, and implications for adolescent outcomes. *Child Development.*

Wang, Y., & Chen, A. (2020). Two pathways underlying the effects of physical education on out-of-school physical activity. *Research Quarterly for Exercise and Sport, 91,* 197–208.

Wang, Y., & Hawk, S.T. (2020). Expressive enhancement, suppression, and flexibility in childhood and adolescence: Longitudinal links with peer relations. *Emotion, 20,* 1059–1073.

Wang, Y., & Yip, T. (2020). Parallel changes in ethnic/racial discrimination and identity in high school. *Journal of Youth and Adolescence, 49,* 1517–1530.

Wang, Y., & others (2020). Altered resting functional network typology assessed using graph theory in youth with attention-deficit/hyperactivity disorder. *Progress in Neuropsychopharmacology and Biological Psychiatry, 98,* 109796.

Wang, Z-D., & others (2021, in press). The comparison of the wisdom view in Chinese and Western cultures. *Current Psychology.*

Ward, L.M., Day, K.M., & Epstein, M. (2006). Uncommonly good: Exploring how mass media may be a positive influence on young women's sexual health and development. *New Directions for Child and Adolescent Development, 112,* 57–70.

Wargo, E. (2007, September). Adolescents and risk: Helping young people make better choices. *Research Facts and Findings.* Ithaca, NY: ACT for Youth Center of Excellence, Cornell University.

Warmuth, K., Cummings, E.M., & Davies, P.T. (2020). Constructive and destructive interparental conflict: Problematic parenting practices and children's symptoms of psychopathology. *Journal of Family Psychology, 34,* 301–311.

Warner, T.D. (2018). Adolescent sexual risk taking: The distribution of youth behaviors and perceived peer attitudes across neighborhood contexts. *Journal of Adolescent Health, 62,* 226–233.

Warshak, R.A. (2008, January). Personal communication. Department of Psychology, University of Texas at Dallas, Richardson.

Waryold, J.M., & Kornahrens, A. (2020). Decreasing barriers to sexual health in lesbian, gay, bisexual, transgender, and queer community. *Nursing Clinics of North America, 55,* 393–402.

Waseem, M., & Nickerson, A.B. (2021). *Bullying.* Treasure Island, FL: StatPearls.

Waselewski, E.A., Waselewski, M.E., & Chang, T. (2020). Needs and coping behaviors of youth in the U.S. during COVID-19. *Journal of Adolescent Health, 67,* 649–652.

Washburn-Busk, M., & others (2020). Navigating "breakup remorse": Implications for disrupting the on-again/off-again cycles in young adult dating relationships. *Journal of Marital and Family Therapy, 46,* 413–430.

Wasserberg, M.J. (2014). Stereotype threat effects on African American children in an urban elementary school. *Journal of Experimental Education, 82,* 502–517.

Waterman, A.S. (1985). Identity in the context of adolescent psychology. In A.S. Waterman (Ed.), *Identity in adolescence: Processes and contents.* San Francisco: Jossey-Bass.

Waterman, A.S. (1992). Identity as an aspect of optimal psychological functioning. In G.R. Adams, T.P. Gullotta, & R. Montemayor (Eds.), *Adolescent identity formation.* Newbury Park, CA: Sage.

Waterman, E.A., & others (2017). Long-distance dating relationships, relationship dissolution, and college adjustment. *Emerging Adulthood, 5,* 268–279.

Waters, T.E., Ruiz, S.K., & Roisman, G.I. (2017). Origins of secure base script knowledge and the developmental construction of attachment representations. *Child Development, 88,* 198–209.

Watson, D.L., & Tharp, R.G. (2014). *Self-directed behavior* (10th ed.). Boston: Cengage.

Watson, H., & others (2021, in press). Genetics of eating disorders in the genome-wide era. *Psychological Medicine.*

Watson, J.A., Randolph, S.M., & Lyons, J.L. (2005). African-American grandmothers as health educators in the family. *International Journal of Aging and Human Development, 60,* 343–356.

Watson, J.B. (1930). *Behaviorism* (rev. ed.). Chicago: University of Chicago Press.

Watt, K.M., Huerta, J., & Martinez, J. (2017). A mixed methods examination of gender disparity in high schools implementing Advancement Via Individual Determination (AVID). *Educational Studies: Journal of the American Educational Studies Association, 53,* 377–389.

Weaver, J.M., & Schofield, T.J. (2015). Mediation and moderation of divorce effects on children's behavior problems. *Journal of Family Psychology, 29,* 39–48.

Webb, L., & others (2021). Electronic and school bullying victimization by race/ethnicity and sexual minority status in a nationally representative adolescent sample. *Journal of Adolescent Health, 68,* 378–384.

Wechsler, D. (1939). *The measurement of adult intelligence.* Baltimore: Williams & Wilkins.

Wechsler, H., Davenport, A., Sowdall, G., Moetykens, B., & Castillo, S. (1994). Health and behavioral consequences of binge drinking in college. *Journal of the American Medical Association, 272,* 1672–1677.

Weger, H.W., Cole, M., & Akbulut, V. (2019). Relationship maintenance across platonic and non-platonic cross-sex friendships in emerging adults. *Journal of Social Psychology, 159,* 15–29.

Wei, J., & others (2020). Parents' responses to their children's performance: A process examination in the United States and China. *Developmental Psychology, 56,* 233–244.

Wei, J., & others (2021). Association of infant physical development and rapid growth with pubertal onset among girls in rural China. *JAMA New Open, 4*(5), e216831.

Wei, Q., & others (2020). Physical deviation and precocious puberty among school-aged children in Leshan City: An investigative study. *Journal of International Medical Research, 48*(8), 300060520939672.

Weikert, D.P. (1993). *Long-term positive effects in the Perry Preschool Head Start program.* Unpublished data. High/Scope Foundation, Ypsilanti, MI.

Weil, A.R. (2020). Children's health. *Health Affairs, 39*(10), 1663.

Weiner, B. (2005). *Social motivation, justice, and the moral emotions.* Mahwah, NJ: Erlbaum.

Weissberg, R., & Caplan, M. (1989, April). *A follow-up study of a school-based social competence program for young adolescents.* Paper presented at the meeting of the Society for Research in Child Development, Kansas City.

Weller, J.A., & others (2021). Developmental trajectory classes in psychological dysregulation predict later decision-making competence. *Addictive Behaviors, 112,* 106650.

Welti, C. (2002). Adolescents in Latin America: Facing the future with skepticism. In B.B. Brown, R.W. Larson, & T.S. Saraswathi (Eds.), *The world's youth.* New York: Cambridge University Press.

Wentzel, K.R. (1997). Student motivation in middle school: The role of perceived pedagogical caring. *Journal of Educational Psychology, 89,* 411–419.

Wentzel, K.R. (2015). Socialization in school settings. In J.E. Grusec & P.D. Hastings (Eds.), *Handbook of socialization* (2nd ed.). New York: Guilford.

Wentzel, K.R., Barry, C.M., & Caldwell, K.A. (2004). Friendships in middle school: Influences on motivation and school adjustment. *Journal of Educational Psychology, 96,* 195–203.

Wentzel, K.R., & Caldwell, K. (1997). Close friend and group influence on adolescent cigarette smoking and alcohol use. *Child Development, 31,* 540–547.

Wentzel, K.R., Jablansky, S., & Scalise, N.R. (2021). Peer social acceptance and academic achievement: A meta-analytic study. *Journal of Educational Psychology, 113,* 157–180.

Werbart Törnblom, A., & others (2020). Who is at risk for dying young from suicide and sudden violent death? Common and specific risk factors among children, adolescents, and young adults. *Suicide and Life-Threatening Behavior, 50,* 757–777.

Wesche, R., & Lefkowitz, E.S. (2020). Normative sexual development and milestones. In S. Hupp & J. Jewell (Eds.), *Encyclopedia of child and adolescent development.* New York: Wiley-Blackwell.

Wetzel, E., Atherton, O.E., & Robins, R.W. (2021). Investigating the link between narcissism and problem behaviors in adolescence. *Self and Identity, 20,* 268–281.

Wheeler, L.A., & others (2017). Mexican-origin youth's risk behavior from adolescence to young adulthood: The role of familism values. *Developmental Psychology, 53,* 126–137.

White, A., & others (2021). "My mentor thinks that I can be something amazing": Drawing out youths' passions and purpose. *Journal of Adolescent Research, 36,* 98–123.

White, E.R., & others (2017). Freshman year alcohol and marijuana use prospectively predict time to college graduation and subsequent adult roles and independence. *Journal of American College Health, 65,* 413–422.

White, M. (1993). *The material child: Coming of age in Japan and America.* New York: Free Press.

White, M.A., & Grilo, C.M. (2011). Diagnostic efficiency of DSM-IV indicators for binge eating episodes. *Journal of Consulting and Clinical Psychology, 79,* 75–83.

White, Y., & others (2018). Adolescents' alcohol use and strength of policy relating to youth access, trading hours, and driving under the influence: Findings from Australia. *Addiction, 113*(6), 1030–1042.

Whiteman, S.D., Jensen, A.C., & Maggs, J.L. (2013). Similarities in adolescent siblings' substance use: Testing competing pathways of influence. *Journal of Studies on Alcohol and Drugs, 74,* 104–113.

Whiteman, S.D., Jensen, A.C., & McHale, S.M. (2017). Sibling influences on risky behaviors from adolescence to young adulthood: Vertical socialization or bidirectional effects? *New Directions in Child and Adolescent Development, 156,* 67–85.

Whitfield, T.H.F., Parsons, J.T., & Rendina, H.J. (2020). Rates of pre-exposure prophylaxis use and discontinuation among a large U.S. national sample of sexual minority men and adolescents. *Archives of Sexual Behavior, 49,* 103–112.

Whiting, B.B. (1989, April). *Culture and interpersonal behavior.* Paper presented at the meeting of the Society for Research in Child Development, Kansas City.

Whittle, S., & others (2020). Pubertal hormones predict sex-specific trajectories of pituitary gland volume during the transition from childhood to adolescence. *NeuroImage, 204,* 116256.

Wickersham, A., & others (2021). Systematic review and meta-analysis: The association between child and adolescent depression and later educational attainment. *Journal of the American Academy of Child and Adolescent Psychiatry, 60,* 105–118.

Widiger, T.A. (2009). Neuroticism. In M.R. Leary & R.H. Hoyle (Eds.), *Handbook of individual differences in social behavior.* New York: Guilford.

Widiger, T.A., & McCabe, G.A. (2021). Personality in clinical psychology. In P.J. Corr & G. Matthews (Eds.), *Cambridge handbook of personality psychology.* New York: Cambridge University Press.

Widman, L., Choukas-Bradley, S., Helms, S.W., & Prinstein, M.J. (2016). Adolescent susceptibility to peer influences in sexual situations. *Journal of Adolescent Health, 58,* 323–329.

Wieland, D.M., & Kucirka, B.G. (2020). Helicopter parenting and the mental health of iGen college students. *Journal of Psychosocial Nursing and Mental Health Services, 58*(5), 16–22.

Wiencke, J.K., & others (1999). Early age at smoking initiation and tobacco carcinogen DNA damage in the lung. *Journal of the National Cancer Institute, 91,* 614–619.

Wigfield, A., Eccles, J.S., Schiefele, U., Roeser, R., & Davis-Kean, P. (2006). Development of achievement motivation. In W. Damon & R. Lerner (Eds.), *Handbook of child psychology* (6th ed.). New York: Wiley.

Wigfield, A., Rosenzweig, E.Q., & Eccles, J.S. (2017). Achievement values, interactions, interventions, and future directions. In A.J. Elliott, C.S. Dweck, & D.S. Yeager (Eds.), *Handbook of competence and motivation* (2nd ed.). New York: Guilford.

Wigfield, A., & others (2015). Development of achievement motivation and engagement. In R.M. Lerner (Ed.), *Handbook of child psychology and developmental science* (7th ed.). New York: Wiley.

Wike, R. (2014, January 14). *French more accepting of infidelity than people in other countries.* Washington, DC: Pew Research Center.

Wikle, J., & Hoagland, A. (2020). Adolescent interaction with family and emotions during interactions: Variation by family structure. *Journal of Family Psychology, 34,* 544–554.

Wilksch, S.M., & others (2020). The relationship between social media use and disordered eating in young adolescents. *International Journal of Eating Disorders, 53,* 96–106.

Wille, E., & others (2018). Gender stereotypes in children's television program: Effects on girls' and boys' stereotype endorsement, math performance, motivational dispositions, and attitudes. *Frontiers in Psychology, 9,* 2435.

William T. Grant Foundation Commission on Work, Family, and Citizenship (1988, February). *The forgotten half: Noncollege-bound youth in America.* New York: William T. Grant Foundation.

Williams, A.L., & others (2020). Middle school teachers' academic and behavioral perceptions of their students and expectations for high school graduation. *Journal of Early Adolescence, 40,* 1061–1086.

Williams, B.K., Sawyer, S.C., & Wahlstrom, C.M. (2020). *Marriages, families, and intimate relationships* (5th ed.). Upper Saddle River, NJ: Pearson.

Williams, J., & Krane, V. (2021). *Applied sport psychology* (8th ed.). New York: McGraw-Hill.

Williams, K.E., & Ciarrochi, J. (2020). Perceived parenting styles and values development: A longitudinal study of adolescents and emerging adults. *Journal of Research on Adolescence, 30,* 541–548.

Williams, K.J., & Vaughn, S. (2020). Effects of an intensive reading intervention for ninth-grade English learners with learning disabilities. *Learning Disability Quarterly, 43,* 154–166.

Williams, K.M., Nathanson, C., & Paulhus, D.L. (2010). Identifying and profiling academic cheaters: Their personality, cognitive ability, and motivation. *Journal of Experimental Psychology: Applied, 16,* 293–307.

Williams, W.M., & Ayres, C.G. (2020). Can active video games improve physical activity in adolescents? A review of RCT. *International Journal of Environmental Research and Public Health, 17*(2), 669.

Willoughby, B.J., Hall, S.S., & Goff, S. (2015). Marriage matters, but how much? Marital centrality among young adults. *Journal of Psychology, 149,* 796–817.

Willoughby, B.J., & James, S.L. (2017). *The marriage paradox.* New York: Oxford University Press.

Wilmers, N. (2021). Sociological perspectives on economic inequality. In K.O. Korgen & W. Paterson (Eds.), *Cambridge handbook of sociology.* New York: Cambridge University Press.

Wilson, L.C., & Miller, K.E. (2016). Meta-analysis of the prevalence of unacknowledged rape. *Trauma, Violence, and Abuse, 17,* 149–159.

Wilson, M.N., & others (2018). Driving under the influence behaviors among high school students who mix alcohol with energy drinks. *Preventive Medicine, 111,* 402–409.

Wilson-Shockley, S. (1995). *Gender differences in adolescent depression: The contribution of negative affect.* Unpublished master's thesis, University of Illinois at Urbana-Champaign.

Wilson-Simmons, R., Jiang, Y., & Aratani, Y. (2017). *Strong at the broken places: The resiliency of low-income parents.* New York: National Center for Poverty, Columbia University.

Winerman, L. (2005). Leading the way. *Monitor on Psychology, 36,* 64–67.

Winner, E. (1996). *Gifted children: Myths and realities.* New York: Basic Books.

Winner, E. (2006). Development in the arts. In W. Damon & R. Lerner (Eds.), *Handbook of child psychology* (6th ed.). New York: Wiley.

Winner, E. (2014). Child prodigies and adult genius. In D.K. Simonton (Ed.), *Wiley-Blackwell handbook of genius.* New York: Wiley-Blackwell.

Winter, V.R., Jones, A., & O'Neill, E. (2019). Eating breakfast and family meals in adolescence: The role of body image. *Social Work and Public Health, 34,* 230–238.

Witelson, S.F., Kigar, D.L., & Harvey, T. (1999). The exceptional brain of Albert Einstein. *The Lancet, 353,* 2149–2153.

Withers, M.C. (2020). A latent profile analysis of the parent-adolescent relationship: Assessing both parent and adolescent outcomes. *Family Process, 59*(1), 244–256.

Witkow, M.R., & Fuligni, A.J. (2010). In-school versus out-of-school friendships and academic achievement among an ethnically diverse sample of adolescents. *Journal of Research on Adolescence, 20,* 631–650.

Wolchik, S.A., & others (2021). Developmental cascade effects of a parenting-focused program for divorced families on competence in emerging adulthood. *Development and Psychopathology, 33,* 201–215.

Wolfe, K.L., & others (2019). Hopelessness as a predictor of suicide ideation in depressed male and female adolescents. *Suicide and Life-Threatening Behavior, 49*(1), 253–263.

Wolke, D., & Lereya, S.T. (2015). Long-term effects of bullying. *Archives of Disease in Childhood, 100,* 879–885.

Wombacher, K., & others (2019). "It just kind of happens": College students' rationalizations for blackout drinking. *Health Communication, 34,* 1–10.

Women in Academia (2011). *A historical summary of gender differences in college enrollment rates.* Retrieved June 12, 2011, from www.wiareport.com

Wong Briggs, T. (1999, October 14). *Honorees find keys to unlocking kids' minds.* Retrieved July 22, 2004, from www.usatoday.com/education/1999

Wong Briggs, T. (2005, October 13). USA Today's 2005 all-USA teacher team. *USA Today,* p. 6D.

Wong, M.D., & others (2014). Successful schools and risky behaviors among low-income adolescents. *Pediatrics, 134,* e389–e396.

Wong, S.P.W., & others (2020). Risk factors and birth outcomes associated with teenage pregnancy: A Canadian sample. *Journal of Pediatric and Adolescent Gynecology, 33,* 153–159.

Wong, W.H-S., & others (2020). The association between child abuse and attempted suicide. *Crisis, 41,* 196–204.

Woo, B., & others (2020). Racial discrimination, ethnic-radical socialization, and bicultural identities among Asian American youths. *Cultural and Ethnic Minority Psychology, 26,* 447–459.

Wood, D., Harms, P., & Vazire, S. (2010). Perceiver effects as projective tests: What your perceptions of others say about you. *Journal of Personality and Social Psychology, 99,* 174–190.

Wood, L., & others (2021). Sexual harassment at institutions of higher education: Prevalence, risk, and extent. *Journal of Interpersonal Violence, 36,* 4520–4544.

Woodhouse, S.S., & others (2020). Secure base provision: A new approach to examining links between maternal caregiving and infant attachment. *Child Development, 91,* e249–e265.

Woolgar, M., & Scott, S. (2013). The negative consequences of over-diagnosing attachment disorders in adopted children: The importance of comprehensive formulations. *Clinical Child Psychology and Psychiatry, 19,* 355–366.

World Health Organization (2000). *The world health report.* Geneva, Switzerland: Author.

World Health Organization (2020). *Adolescent pregnancy: Fact sheet.* Geneva, Switzerland: Author.

Wormington, S.V., Corpus, J.H., & Anderson, K.G. (2012). A person-centered investigation of academic motivation and its correlates in high school. *Learning and Individual Differences, 22,* 429–438.

Wright, B.J., & Donnerstein, E. (2014). Sex online: Pornography, sexual solicitation, and sexting. *Adolescent Medicine: State of the Art Reviews, 25,* 574–589.

Wright, H., & others (2021). Polycomb represses a gene network controlling puberty via modulati of histone demethylase Kdm6b expression. *Scientific Reports, 11*(1), 1996.

Wu, H-M., Chang, H-M., & Leung, P.C.K. (2021). Gonadotropin-releasing hormone analogs: Mechanisms of action and clinical applications in female reproduction. *Frontiers in Neuroendocrinology, 60,* 100876.

Wu, J., & others (2021). Correlation between ZBRK1/ZNF350 gene polymorphism and breast cancer. *BMC Medical Genomics, 14*(1), 7.

Wu, S., & others (2020). Familial acculturative stress and adolescent internalizing and externalizing behaviors in Latinx immigrant families of the Southwest. *Journal of Immigrant and Minority Health, 22,* 1193–1199.

Wuest, D., & Walton-Fisette, J. (2021). *Foundations of physical education, exercise science, and sport.* New York: McGraw-Hill.

X

Xanthopoulos, M.S., & others (2013). The association between weight loss in caregivers and adolescents in a treatment trial of adolescents with obesity. *Journal of Pediatric Psychology, 38,* 766–774.

Xia, N. (2010). *Family factors and student outcomes.* Unpublished doctoral dissertation, RAND Corporation, Pardee RAND Graduate School, Pittsburgh.

Xiang, S., Liu, Y., & Bai, L. (2017). Parenting styles and adolescents' school adjustment: Investigating the mediating role of achievement goals within the 2 × 2 framework. *Frontiers in Psychology, 8,* 1809.

Xie, C., & others (2017). Exercise and dietary program-induced weight reduction is associated with cognitive function in obese adolescents: A longitudinal study, *PeerJ, 5,* e3286.

Xiong, R., De Li, S., & Xia, Y. (2020). A longitudinal study of authoritative parenting, juvenile delinquency, and crime victimization among Chinese adolescents. *International Journal of Environmental Health and Public Health, 17*(4), 1405.

Xiong, Y., & others (2020). Parents' peer restriction in the United States and China: A longitudinal study of adolescents. *Developmental Psychology, 56,* 1760–1774.

Xu, J. (2021, in press). Factors affecting adolescents' screen viewing duration: A social cognitive approach based on the Family Life, Activity, Sun, Health, and Eating (FLASHE) survey. *Journal of Health Communication.*

Xu, X., Huebner, E.S., & Tian, L. (2020). Profiles of narcissism and self-esteem associated with comprehensive mental health in adolescence. *Journal of Adolescence, 80,* 275–287.

Xu, X., & others (2021). MAGI2-AS3 inhibits breast cancer by downregulating DNA methylation of MAGI2. *Journal of Cellular Physiology, 236,* 1116–1130.

Y

Yancey, A.K., Grant, D., Kurosky, S., Kravitz-Wirtz, N., & Mistry, R. (2011). Role modeling, risk, and resilience in California adolescents. *Journal of Adolescent Health, 48,* 36–43.

Yanez, A.M., & others (2020). Implications of personality and parental education on healthy lifestyles among adolescents. *Scientific Reports, 10*(1), 7911.

Yang, H.J., & others (2021). Changes induced by mind-body intervention including epigenetic marks and its effects on diabetes. *International Journal of Molecular Sciences, 22*(3), 1317.

Yard, E., & others (2021). Emergency department visits for suspected suicide attempts among persons aged 12–25 years before and during the COVID-19 pandemic—United States, January 2019–May 2021. *MMWR, 70,* 888–894.

Yeager, D.S., Dahl, R.E., & Dweck, C.S. (2018). Why interventions to influence adolescent behavior often fail but could succeed. *Perspectives on Psychological Science, 13,* 101–122.

Yeager, D.S., & others (2014). Breaking the cycle of mistrust: Wise interventions to provide critical feedback across the racial divide. *Journal of Experimental Psychology: General, 143,* 804–824.

Yeager, D.S., & others (2016). Teaching a lay theory before college narrows achievement gaps at scale. *Proceedings of the National Academy of Sciences in the U.S.A., 113,* E3341–E3348.

Yecies, E., & McNeil, M. (2021). From the #MeToo frontlines: Incoming interns report a breadth of experiences related to sexual harassment in medical school. *Journal of General Internal Medicine, 36,* 1132–1133.

Yeo, S.C., & others (2019). Associations of sleep duration on school nights with self-rated health, overweight, and depression symptoms in adolescents: Problems and possible solutions. *Sleep Medicine, 60,* 96–108.

Yildrim, F.B., & Demir, A. (2020). Self-handicapping among university students: The role of procrastination, test anxiety, self-esteem, and self-compassion. *Psychological Reports, 123,* 825–843.

Yip, T. (2018). Ethnic/racial identity—A double-edged sword? Associations with discrimination and psychological outcomes. *Current Directions in Psychological Science, 27*(3), 170–175.

Yockey, A., King, K., & Vidourek, R. (2021, in press). Past-year suicidal ideation among transgender individuals in the United States. *Archives of Suicide Research.*

Yonker, J.E., Schnabelrauch, C.A., & DeHaan, L.G. (2012). The relationship between spirituality and religiosity on psychological outcomes in adolescents and emerging adults: A meta-analytic review. *Journal of Adolescence, 35,* 299–314.

Yoruk, B.K., & Xu, L. (2021). Key registration laws, alcohol consumption, and alcohol-related traffic fatalities among adolescents. *Journal of Studies on Alcohol and Drugs, 82,* 66–75.

Youngblade, L.M., & Curry, L.A. (2006). The people they know: Links between interpersonal contexts and adolescent risky and health-promoting behavior. *Developmental Science, 10,* 96–106.

Yu, C., & others (2017). Marching to a different drummer: A cross-cultural comparison of young adolescents who challenge gender norms. *Journal of Adolescent Health, 61*(4S), S48–S54.

Yu, L., & Shek, D.T.L. (2021). Positive youth development attributes and parenting as protective factors against adolescent social networking addiction in Hong Kong. *Frontiers in Psychology, 9,* 649232.

Yu, T., Pettit, G.S., Lansford, J.E., Dodge, K.A., & Bates, J.E. (2010). The interactive effects of marital conflict and divorce on parent-adult children's relationships. *Journal of Marriage and the Family, 72,* 282–292.

Yuan, A.S.V. (2010). Body perceptions, weight control behavior, and changes in adolescents' psychological well-being over time: A longitudinal examination of gender. *Journal of Youth and Adolescence, 39,* 927–939.

Yuan, Y. (2021). Mindfulness training on the resilience of adolescents under the COVID-19 epidemic: A latent growth curve analysis. *Personality and Individual Differences, 172,* 110560.

Yuksel, H.S., & others (2020). School-based intervention programs for preventing obesity and promoting physical activity and fitness: A systematic review. *International Journal of Environmental Research and Public Health, 17*(1), 347.

Yung, A.R., McGorry, P.D., & Cotter, J. (2021). *Youth mental health.* New York: Routledge.

Z

Zablotsky, B., & Alford, J.M. (2020). Racial and ethnic differences in the prevalence of attention-deficit/hyperactivity disorder and learning disabilities among U.S. children aged 3-17 years. *NCHS Data Brief, 358,* 1-8.

Zaccari, V., & others (2021, in press). Clinical application of mindfulness-oriented meditation in children with ADHD: A preliminary study on sleep and behavioral problems. *Psychology and Health.*

Zagaria, A., Ando, A., & Zennaro, A. (2020). Psychology: A giant with feet of clay. *Integrative Psychology and Behavioral Science, 54,* 521-562.

Zager, K., & Rubenstein, A. (2002). *The inside story on teen girls.* Washington, DC: American Psychological Association.

Zamboanga, B.L., & others (2021, in press). Participation in drinking games among university students in Argentina, Australia, Canada, and New Zealand. *Alcohol and Alcoholism.*

Zarbatany, L., & others (2019). The moderating role of clique hierarchical organization on resource control by central clique members. *Journal of Youth and Adolescence, 48,* 359-371.

Zarzeczna, N., & others (2020). Powerful men on top: Stereotypes interact with metaphors in social categorizations. *Journal of Experimental Psychology: Human Perception and Performance, 46,* 36-65.

Zayas, V., Mischel, W., & Pandey, G. (2014). Mind and brain in delay of gratification. In V.F. Reyna & V. Zayas (Eds.), *The neuroscience of decision making.* Washington, DC: American Psychological Association.

Zeeck, A., Stelzer, N., Linster, H.W., Joos, A., & Hartmann, A. (2010). Emotion and eating in binge eating disorder and obesity. *European Eating Disorders Review, 19,* 426-437.

Zeiders, K.H., & others (2021). Latina/o youths' discrimination experiences in the U.S. Southwest: Estimates from three studies. *Applied Developmental Science, 25,* 51-61.

Zeifman, D., & Hazan, C. (2008). Pair bonds as attachments: Reevaluating the evidence. In J. Cassidy & P.R. Shaver (Eds.), *Handbook of attachment* (2nd ed.). New York: Guilford.

Zelazo, P.D. (2013). Developmental psychology: A new synthesis. In P.D. Zelazo (Ed.), *Oxford handbook of developmental psychology.* New York: Oxford University Press.

Zelazo, P.D. (2020). Executive function and psychopathology: A neurodevelopmental perspective. *Annual Review of Clinical Psychology* (Vol.16). Palo Alto, CA: Annual Reviews.

Zeng, R., & Greenfield, P.M. (2015). Cultural evolution over the last 40 years in China: Using the Google Ngram viewer to study implications of social and political change for cultural values. *International Journal of Psychology, 50,* 47-55.

Zhang, F., & others (2020). Family socio-demographic status and children's academic achievement: The different roles of parental academic involvement and subjective social mobility. *British Journal of Educational Psychology, 90,* 561-579.

Zhang, J., & others (2020). Classification of pure conduct disorder from healthy controls based on indices of brain networks during resting state. *Medical and Biological Engineering and Computing, 58,* 2071-2082.

Zhang, L., Bo, A., & Lu, W. (2021). To unfold the immigrant paradox: Maltreatment risk and mental health of racial-ethnic minority children. *Frontiers in Public Health, 9,* 619164.

Zhang, M., & others (2020). Parent-adolescent acculturation profiles and adolescent language brokering experiences in Mexican immigrant families. *Journal of Youth and Adolescence, 49,* 335-351.

Zhang, M.F., & Gordon, D. (2020). Understanding gender inequality in poverty and social exclusion through a psychological lens: Scarcities, stereotypes, and suggestions. In F.M. Cheung & D.F. Halpern (Eds.), *Cambridge handbook of the international psychology of women.* New York: Cambridge University Press.

Zhang, S.Y., & Demant, J. (2021, in press). Effects of self-control, drug-use peers, and family attachment on drug use among Chinese users: A gender-specific analysis. *Drug and Alcohol Review.*

Zhang, W., & others (2017). Reconsidering parenting in Chinese culture: Subtypes, stability, and change of maternal parenting style during early adolescence. *Journal of Youth and Adolescence, 46,* 1117-1136.

Zhang, X., & others (2021). Intrinsic motivation enhances online group creativity via promoting members' effort, not interaction. *British Journal of Educational Technology, 52,* 606-618.

Zhang, Y., & others (2020). Comparison of body-image dissatisfaction among Chinese children and adolescents at different pubertal developmental stages. *Psychology Research and Behavior Management, 13,* 555-562.

Zheng, L.R., & others (2020). Are self-esteem and academic achievement reciprocally related? Findings from a longitudinal study of Mexican-origin youth. *Journal of Personality, 88,* 1058-1074.

Zhou, Q. (2013). Commentary in S. Smith, "Children of 'tiger parents' develop more aggression and depression, research shows." Retrieved July 20, 2013, from http://www.cbsnews.com/news/children-of-tiger-parents-develop-more-aggression-and-depression-research-shows/

Zhou, Q., & others (2012). Asset and protective factors for Asian American children's mental health adjustment. *Child Development Perspectives, 6,* 312-319.

Zhu, S., Tse, S., Cheung, S.H., & Oyserman, D. (2014). Will I get there? Effects of parental support on children's possible selves. *British Journal of Educational Psychology, 84,* 435-453.

Ziermans, T., & others (2017). Formal thought disorder and executive functioning in children and adolescents with autism spectrum disorder: Old leads and new avenues. *Journal of Autism and Developmental Disorders, 47,* 1756-1768.

Zijlmans, J., & others (2021). Disentangling multiproblem behavior in male young adults: A cluster analysis. *Development and Psychopathology, 33,* 149-159.

Zimmer, H.D., & Fischer, B. (2020). Visual working memory of Chinese characters and expertise: The expert's memory advantage is based on long-term knowledge of visual word forms. *Frontiers in Psychology, 11,* 516.

Zimmer-Gembeck, M.J., & Skinner, E.A. (2011). The development of coping across childhood and adolescence: An integrative review and critique of research. *International Journal of Behavioral Development, 35,* 1-17.

Zimmerman, B.J. (2012). Motivational sources and outcomes of self-regulated learning and performance. In B.J. Zimmerman & D.H. Schunk (Eds.), *Handbook of self-regulation of learning and performance.* New York: Routledge.

Zimmerman, B.J., & Kitsantas, A. (1997). Developmental phases in self-regulation: Shifting from process goals to outcome goals. *Journal of Educational Psychology, 89,* 29-36.

Zimmerman, B.J., & Labuhn, A.S. (2012). Self-regulation of learning: Process approaches to personal development. In K.R. Harris & others (Eds.), *APA handbook of educational psychology.* Washington, DC: American Psychological Association.

Zimmerman, B.J., Schunk, D.H., & DiBenedetto, M.K. (2017). Role of self-efficacy and related beliefs in self-regulation of learning and performance. In A.J. Elliott, C.S. Dweck, & D.S. Yeager (Eds.). *Handbook of competence and motivation* (2nd ed.). New York: Guilford.

Zimmerman, P., & Iwanski, A. (2018). Development and timing of developmental changes in emotion reactivity and emotion regulation during adolescence. In P.M. Cole & T. Hollenstein (Eds.), *Emotion regulation.* New York: Routledge.

Zortea, T.C., Gray, C.M., & O'Connor, R.C. (2021). The relationship between adult attachment and suicidal thoughts and behaviors: A systematic review. *Archives of Suicide Research, 25,* 38-73.

Zou, H., & Yang, J. (2021). Exploring the brain lateralization in ADHD based on variability and resting-state fMRI signal. *Journal of Attention Disorders, 25,* 258-264.

Zou, S., & Wu, X. (2020). Coparenting conflict behavior, parent-adolescent attachment, and social competence with peers: An investigation of developmental differences. *Journal of Youth and Adolescence, 49,* 267-282.

Zucker, K.J., Lawrence, A.A., & Kreukels, B.P. (2016). Gender dysphoria in adults. *Annual Review of Clinical Psychology* (Vol. 12). Palo Alto, CA: Annual Reviews.

Borowski, S., 315
Bosacki, S., 137
Bosma, H., 150
Bouchard, T.J., 117, 118
Boulay, B., 379
Bould, H., 161
Bousuard, M-E., 200
Boutsikou, T., 211
Bowen, R., 122
Bowker, J., 304, 305, 309
Bowlby, J., 274
Boyatzis, C., 251, 253
Bozzini, A.B., 201, 438
Brabeck, K., 188
Brabeck, M., 188
Brackett, M., 117
Bradbury, T., 329
Bradford, E.E.F., 18
Bradley, R.H., 415
Bradshaw, C., 350
Brady, S., 199, 200
Brainerd, C., 106
Braithwaite, I., 463
Braithwaite, S., 327
Braithwaite, S.R., 204
Brandes, C.M., 179
Brando-Garrido, C., 389
Brandon, A., 210
Branje, S., 266
Brannstrom, L., 304
Bratke, 54
Braun, S., 172
Braun-Courville, D., 197
Braver, S., 288
Bray, J., 289, 290
Breehl, L., 52
Breidablik, J., 270, 286
Brember, I., 140
Breslau, J., 459
Bretherton, I., 185
Breuner, C.C., 57
Brewer, R., 211
Brewington, S., 339
Bridgeland, J., 246
Brieant, A., 10, 62
Brigham, M., 365
Briken, P., 429
Briley, D., 158
Brindis, C.D., 468
Brister, S., 65
Brittain, H., 304
Broderick, R., 2
Brody, G., 20, 244, 283
Brody, G.H., 90, 415
Brody, N., 118
Brodzinsky, D., 290
Broer, J., 67
Bronfenbrenner, U., 31–32, 260, 263, 301
Broniatowski, D., 105, 106
Bronk, A., 382
Bronstein, P., 171, 188, 269
Brooker, R., 34, 76, 77
Brooker, R.J., 105
Brooks, F., 252

Brooks, P., 125
Brooks-Gunn, J., 58, 155, 285, 419, 431
Broomell, A.P.R., 101
Broughton, J., 94
Brouillard, C., 271
Broverman, L., 176
Brown, A., 326, 328
Brown, B., 13, 14, 20, 21, 184, 301, 312, 315, 316
Brown, B.B., 309, 312
Brown, C., 220, 379
Brown, E., 171
Brown, K.M., 76
Brown, L., 187, 299
Brown, Z., 57, 174
Brumariu, L., 274, 439
Brumley, L.D., 381
Brummelman, J.E., 140
Brunsdon, V., 18
Bryan, C.J., 61
Buchanan, C., 288
Bucx, F., 280
Budday, S., 87
Budge, S., 185
Budge, S.L., 186
Buhrmester, D., 308, 309, 314, 318
Bui, T., 395
Buist, K., 282
Bukowki, W., 172, 307
Bukowski, W., 233, 304, 305
Bulik, C., 465
Bumpus, M., 273
Burcas, S., 389
Bureau, J., 375
Burenkova, O., 120
Burgess-Champoux, T.L., 66
Buriel, R., 263
Burke, J., 455
Burke, M., 283
Burki, T., 424
Burnett, S., 134
Burnette, D., 340
Burraston, B., 283
Burrow, A., 382
Burt, K., 2, 21
Burton, R.V., 236
Busch, A.S., 52
Busching, R., 237
Buss, D., 25, 74, 169, 170
Buss, D.M., 74, 180
Busséri, M.A., 206
Bussey, K., 171, 172
Bustamante, I., 265
Butler, L., 391
Buzwell, S., 197
Buzzichelli, S., 465
Byne, W., 185
Byrnes, J., 105

Caamono-Isorna, F., 218
Cabaco, A.S., 56
Caban, O., 52
Cabrera, N., 424
Cabre-Riera, A., 71
Cabrero, F., 361

Cacioppo, J.T., 311, 321
Cai, M., 274, 302
Cai, T., 445
Cai, Y., 363
Cain, M.S., 426
Cairncross, M., 364
Calabro, F., 86
Calabro, F.J., 89, 104
Calcaterra, V., 50, 53
Calders, F., 267
Caldwell, K., 307, 352
Caliendo, E.T., 90
Calkins, S., 180
Callan, J., 305
Calugi, S., 465
Calvert, S.L., 427, 428
Cam, H., 464
Cambron, C., 450
Cameron, J.L., 50
Cameron, L., 197
Campbell, B., 117
Campbell, C.Y., 174
Campbell, L., 117
Campbell, W., 139, 183, 264
Campione-Barr, N., 278, 282, 283
Campisi, S.C., 308
Canivez, G., 115
Cano, M.A., 151, 152
Cantone, E., 352
Caplan, M., 306
Caprara, G.V., 159
Carano, K., 287
Carballo, J.J., 462
Cardenas, S., 361
Carey, D.P., 118
Carey, J.C., 400
Carlo, G., 236, 237, 248, 267
Carlson, E., 440
Carlson, K., 139
Carlson, W., 315
Carlson Jones, D., 57
Carmichael, V., 330
Carnoy, M., 415
Carpendale, J., 145
Carratala, E., 286
Carratala, S., 62
Carroll, J., 118
Carskadon, M., 71
Carskadon, M.A., 71–72
Carson, V., 428
Carter, A., 364
Carter, N., 139
Carter, P., 424
Carver, C., 143
Carver, K., 318
Cascella, M., 87
Case, R., 95
Casey, B., 88, 89
Casey, B.J., 90
Caspi, A., 80, 161
Cassidy-Bushrow, A.E., 429
Cassoff, J., 72
Casteel, C., 51, 52
Castillo, M., 465

Cowan, M., 25, 74
Cox, M., 286
Cox, R., 286
Coy, K., 270
Coyle, E., 178
Coyle, G.T.R., 113
Coyle, T., 118
Coyne, S.M., 179, 428
Crandall, A., 202, 438
Cranney, S., 219
Creaven, A-M., 443
Creech, J., 70
Crespi, B.J., 74
Cretu, R., 389
Criss, M.M., 266
Critcher, C., 240
Crone, E., 104, 106, 137
Crooks, R., 208, 212, 213, 216
Crosby, R., 469
Crosnoe, R., 206, 327, 339, 343
Cross, C., 304
Cross, S., 136
Crossman, E., 414
Crouter, A., 269, 273, 282
Crouter, A.C., 285
Crowe, M., 69
Crowley, C., 107
Crowley, M., 181
Cryer-Coupet, Q., 152
Csikszentmihalyi, I., 375
Csikszentmihalyi, M., 7, 375, 397
Csordas, A., 136
Cuesta, I., 462
Cui, L., 155, 237
Cui, Z., 89, 95
Cullen, F., 219
Cummings, E., 261, 286
Cummings, E.M., 286
Curran, M., 270
Curran, T., 389
Currie, C., 208
Curry, L., 62
Curtis, A., 417
Cushner, K., 9, 357, 387, 418, 423
Cyr, C., 322

Dabholkar, A., 87
da Costa Souza, A., 77
Dagan, O., 24, 274
Dahl, R., 61, 379
Dahl, R.E., 62, 88
Dahlke, J., 118
Dalaly, M., 445
Daley, C., 119
Dalle Grave, R., 465
Damian, R., 159
D'Amico, E.J., 453
Damon, W., 146, 238, 239, 241, 249–250, 251, 383, 384, 386, 397
Dan, Z., 119
Dandy, J., 264
Dane, M., 125
Dangel, T., 238
Daniels, C., 285, 328

Daniels, H., 98
Danielsen, V.M., 88
Darcy, E., 465
Darcy, K., 197
Darling, E., 376
Darling, N., 271
Darwin, C., 3, 74
Dave, H.P., 117
Davidson, A., 172
Davidson, B., 366
Davidson, J., 366
Davies, J., 140
Davies, P., 261, 286
Davis, A., 12
Davis, B., 10, 169, 175
Davis, C.L., 68
Davis, D., 218
Davis, G., 343
Davis, K., 150
Davis, S., 26, 261
Davisson, E., 143
Dawes, M., 342
Day, D., 80
Day, K., 196
de Anda, D., 212
Dearing, E., 354, 416
Debnam, K.J., 252
Debnath, R., 90, 362
Deci, E., 375
Decker, K., 107
De Clercq, M., 385
deCock, C., 109
Dee, D.L., 210
Defoe, I., 89
Defoe, I.N., 62, 106, 282
De France, K., 416
DeGarmo, D., 439, 457
de Graaf, H., 321
de Guzman, N., 58
DeHaan, L., 252
De Jesus, O., 361
DeJong, W., 450
DeJoseph, M.L., 415, 439
Dekker, A., 429
Dekovic, M., 282
de la Cruz, F., 465
Delalande, L., 91
DeLamater, J., 170, 200, 207, 292, 327
De Li, S., 267
Del Toro, J., 152
Demant, J., 301
de Manzano, O., 119
De Matteo, C., 69
Demers, S., 58
Demir, A., 391
Demo, D., 138
Dempster, F.N., 102
Denault, A-S., 309
Deng, C., 350, 388
Deng, G-X., 77
Deng, Y., 308
Denton, M., 251
Deoni, S., 87
Derakhshan, Z., 364

DeRicco, B., 450
Derrico, L., 386
Derry, K., 138
Desai, N., 63, 64
Deschesnes, M., 58
Deschrijver, E., 305
De Silva, A., 286
de Silveira, C., 103
Desilver, D., 387, 408
de Smedt, B., 112
de Souza Neto, J.M., 463
D'Esposito, M., 118
Destin, M., 151, 384
Dettori, E., 38
Detzer, M., 207
Deutsch, A., 453
DeVille, D.C., 462
Devos, T., 151, 422
Dew, R., 251
Dewey, J., 244–245
De Wit, D., 386
Dewitz, P.F., 362
DeYoung, C., 160, 162
de Zegher, F., 53
DeZolt, D., 172, 177
Diamant, J., 253
Diamond, L., 195, 319
Diamond, L.M., 204, 205, 206
Dibba, E., 57
DiBenedetto, M., 379
Dick, A.S., 125
Dickey, L., 185
Dickie, J., 253
Dickinson, D., 117
Diekman, A., 171
Diekmann, A., 170, 269
Diener, E., 159, 345
Di Fabio, A., 117
DiLonardo, M.J., 464
Dilulio, J., 246
Dimitriou, D., 13
Dimler, L., 58
Dimock, M., 5
Dindia, K., 188
Dindo, L., 143
Dion, K., 324
Dipla, K., 70
Dirk, J., 302
Dishion, T., 179, 301, 304, 439
Dittus, P.J., 266
Doane, L., 420
Dobrakowski, P., 363
Dodge, K.A., 305, 306, 454, 468
Doebel, S., 382
Doherty, M.J., 112
Dohrenwend, B., 444
Dokuka, S., 352
Dolbin-MacNab, M., 280
Dolcini, M.M., 122
Dollar, J., 180
Dombrowski, S., 115
Domingos, A., 52
Dominguez-Cruz, M.G., 77
Domiteaux, M., 158

Twenge, J.M., 139
Tyler, K., 203
Tyrell, F.A., 324
Tysiaczny, C., 174

Udry, J., 318
Ueno, K., 184
Uhls, Y., 430
Ullen, F., 119
Ullsperger, J., 59
Umaña-Taylor, A., 9, 152, 270, 407, 419
Umaña-Taylor, A.J., 136, 145, 150, 152, 419, 421, 423
Uncapher, M.R., 101, 427
Underwood, J.M., 66, 67, 198, 199, 461, 463
Updegraff, K.A., 282, 420
Updegrove, A., 457
Urdan, T., 151
Usher, E., 447
Uzelac, S., 122

Vaca, F.E., 65, 449
Vaillancourt, T., 304
Valdez, D., 252
Valeeva, D., 352
Valentin-Cortes, M., 419
Valero, S., 159
Valiente, C., 244
Valladares, A.A., 102
Van Dam, L., 386
van de Bongardt, D., 200
van de Groep, S., 137
Vandell, D., 283
Van den Akker, A.I., 58
van den Bos, W., 58
Vandenbosch, L., 174
Van den Bulck, J., 196
van der Hoeven, R., 412
van der Stel, M., 112
van der Wouden, J., 67
Vandewater, E., 427
van Dijk, R., 261, 287
van Doeselaar, L., 148
van Dulmen, M., 308, 323
Vanes, L.D., 87
Vangeel, L., 174
Van Goozen, S.H.M., 58
Van Hoover, C., 58
Van Horn, S., 320
van Kesteren, M., 102
Van Keulen, B.J., 52
Van Lissa, C.J., 270, 271
VanMeter, F., 439, 440
Van Nostrand, D., 137
Vannucci, A., 430
Van Ryzin, M., 338
van Tetering, M.A.J., 180
van Wel, F., 280
van Zalk, M.H.W., 308
Vargas, E.A., 331
Vargas, S., 185
Varner, F., 303

Vasa, F., 86
Vasilenko, S., 202
Vaughn, J., 251, 252
Vaughn, M., 344
Vaughn, S., 362
Vazire, S., 159
Vazquez, C., 290, 291
Vazsonyi, A.T., 13
Vedder, P., 152
Veenman, M.V.J., 112
Velasco, S., 264
Verdin, D., 398
Verkooijen, S., 71
Verma, S., 393, 394, 410
Vernucci, S., 102
Veronneau, M.H., 143, 161, 385
Verschueren, M., 66
Verstraeten, K., 161
Verzani, M., 53
Vespa, J., 21, 22
Vetter, N C., 306
Vidal, S., 415
Vidourek, R., 185
Villa-Gonzalez, R., 68, 364
Villarreal, V., 342
Villodas, F., 421
Villodas, M., 421
Viswanathan, M., 460
Vitaro, F., 385
Voce, A., 453
Vokey, M., 174
Volk, S., 169
Volkow, N.D., 86, 91
Volpe, E.M., 208
von der Embse, N., 391
Vondracek, F., 398
von Soest, T., 139
Vosberg, D.E., 58
Votruba-Drzal, E., 354, 387, 413
Voyer, D., 180
Vrij, A., 134
Vrolijk, P., 272
Vukelich, C., 125
Vygotsky, L.S., 29–30, 98–99

Wachs, T., 162
Wachs, T.D., 161, 162
Wade, C., 181
Wade, T., 389, 390
Wadsworth, M., 10, 264
Wagid, M., 389
Wagner, D., 101
Wahlstrom, C., 260
Wainwright, L., 134
Waiter, G.D., 119
Walczak-Kozlowska, T., 362
Waldfogel, J., 285
Walker, K., 313, 410, 411
Walker, L., 233, 241, 253
Walker, L.J., 232, 241, 245
Wall, A., 218
Wallace, E., 394–395
Wallace-Broscious, A., 398

Wallander, J., 197
Waller, E., 315, 460
Wallis, C., 174
Walsh, B., 466
Walsh, R., 105
Walsh, S., 203
Walsh, S.D., 174, 429
Walter, C.A., 263
Walters, G.D., 237, 308, 453, 457, 467
Walton, G., 382
Walton, G.M., 384
Walton-Fisette, J., 68
Wang, 463
Wang, B., 266
Wang, C., 308
Wang, C.D., 279
Wang, D., 457
Wang, F., 72
Wang, H., 59, 280
Wang, J., 201, 268
Wang, L.Y., 463
Wang, M.C., 66
Wang, M-T., 112, 379
Wang, N., 271
Wang, P.Y., 72
Wang, Q., 8, 408, 441
Wang, S., 443
Wang, W., 329
Wang, X., 439
Wang, Y., 69, 151, 152, 271, 303, 362
Wang, Z-D., 97
Ward, L., 196
Wargo, E., 107
Warmuth, K., 261
Warner, T.D., 201
Warren, M., 58, 155
Warshak, R., 289
Warshak, R.A., 291
Waryold, J., 185
Waseem, M., 351
Waselewski, E., 446
Waselewski, M., 446
Washburn-Busk, M., 320
Wasserberg, M.J., 119
Wasserman, R., 52
Waterman, A.S., 148
Waterman, E.A., 320
Waters, P., 133, 187–188
Waters, T., 274
Watkins, M., 115
Watson, D., 390, 391
Watson, H., 465
Watson, J., 280
Watson, J.B., 267
Watt, K., 386
Wattenberg, E., 211
Way, N., 152, 211
Weaver, J., 287, 288
Webb, J., 238
Webb, L., 351, 431
Weber, H., 158
Wechsler, D., 114–115
Wechsler, H., 449

Divorce, 285–290
  adolescent dating and, 323
  cohabitation and, 327–328
  effects on adolescents, 286–289
  effects on adults, 330–331
  rates of, 285, 330
  risk factors for, 330
  stepfamilies after, 289–290
DNA, 75–77
Do Good Well (Vasan & Przybylo), 250
Domain-specific giftedness, 366
Domain-specific mechanisms, 74
Domain-specific self-evaluation, 138.
    See also Self-concept
Domain-specific thinking skills, 112
Dopamine, 88
Double standards
  moral, 235
  sexual, 200
Drinking games, 450
Driver training, 106
Driving, drinking and, 65, 449
Dropouts, high school, 343–345
Drug counselors, 46–47
Drug use, 448–454
Dual-cycle identity model, 148
Dumbing Down Our Kids (Sykes), 140
Dyscalculia, 361
Dysgraphia, 361
Dyslexia, 361

Early adolescence, 16
Early adulthood, 16, 21–22, 23
Early childhood, 16
Early college high schools, 395
Early-later experience issue, 24
Early-onset antisocial behavior, 455
Early starters, 318
Easy child, 160
Eating disorders, 462–466
E-cigarettes, 450
Eclectic theoretical orientation, 32
Ecological theory, 31–32, 260
Ecstasy, 451
Education. *See* School(s)
Educational psychologists, 39, 46
Education for All Handicapped Children Act,
    364–365
Education level, intelligence tests and, 119–120
Effort, in achievement, 381–382
Effortful control, 104, 143, 160–161
Ego, 27
Egocentrism, adolescent, 121–123
Ego ideal, 238
Eisenhower Quantum Opportunities program, 417
Elementary school, transition from, 341–342
El Puente program, 417
Emerging adulthood, 18–23
  attachment in, 275–277
  autonomy in, 273
  career opportunities in, 45–47
  characteristics of, 18–19, 23
  cultural differences in, 20–21
  definition of, 18, 23

friendship in, 308
health and well-being in, 20, 65
identity in, 148–149, 153
lifestyles of, 325–331
living with parents in, 19–21, 278–279, 325
problems in (*See* Problems)
relationships with parents in, 277–279
relevance of culture to, 407
self-esteem in, 139–140
self-understanding in, 136
sexuality in, 202–204
transitions in, 18–23
work in, 395–396
Emotion(s), 154–157
  brain development and, 88
  cognitive development and, 96–97
  definition of, 154
  divorce in problems with, 286
  gender differences in, 180, 181
  in moral development, 234, 239
  in peer relations, 306
  personality and, 158
  research methods for, 34
  in romantic relationships, 319–320
Emotional arousal, 155, 243
Emotional autonomy, 273
Emotional competence, 156
Emotional development, 154–157
Emotional intelligence, 117, 356
Emotional regulation, 155–156
  gender differences in, 180
  in peer relations, 306
  in temperament, 161
Emotional security theory, 286
Emotion-focused coping, 445
Empathy, 239
Employment. *See* Work
Empowerment, 441
Endocrine system, 50–52
Energy drinks, 65, 66
Engagement
  academic, 442
  cognitive, 376
  moral, 236, 240
Environment
  in brain development, 87, 89–90
  in intelligence, 119–120
  interaction of heredity and, 77–81
  in nature-nurture debate, 23
  in obesity, 463
  in puberty, 53
Epigenetic view of adolescent development,
    23, 80, 260
Equilibration, 92
ERI. *See* Ethnic-racial identity
Erikson's psychosocial theory, 27–28, 144–145
Escaping the Endless Adolescence (Allen & Allen), 22
ESM. *See* Experience sampling method
ESSA. *See* Every Student Succeeds Act
Established adulthood, 23
Estradiol, 50–52
Estrogens, 50–52, 58
Ethics, in research, 37–38
Ethnic bias, in research, 38–39

Ethnic diversity
  of Millennials, 5
  in research, 38–39
  of U.S. population, 9–10
Ethnic gloss, 38
Ethnic identity, 9, 150–153
Ethnicity, 418–425
  definition of, 9, 418
  development issues related to, 422–425
  immigration and, 418–420
  relevance to adolescence, 407
Ethnic minority groups, 418–425. *See also*
    Immigrants; *specific groups*
  academic achievement of, 353, 355–357, 373,
    386–387
  adolescence as special juncture for, 421–422
  age of sexual initiation among, 199
  autonomy in, 273
  bias in research on, 38–39
  career development of, 401
  dating in, 324
  definition of, 38
  discrimination against, 424–425
  diversity within, 38–39, 423
  education of, 353, 355–357, 373
  families of, 263–264
  in gifted programs, 367
  health disparities of, 61–62
  identity development in, 150–153, 422
  intelligence in, 119
  marriage in, 328
  overweight and obesity in, 62, 463
  parenting styles in, 268
  peer relations in, 315
  as percentage of population, 10, 418
  poverty in, 414–415, 422–423
  role models for, 421
  segregation of peers based on, 315
  self-understanding in, 136–137
  stereotypes of, 119, 151
  suicide in, 461
  teen pregnancy in, 210
Ethnic pride, 152–153
Ethnic-racial identity (ERI), 153
Ethnocentrism, 407
Every Student Succeeds Act (ESSA), 340
Evocative genotype-environment correlations, 79
Evolutionary perspective, on adolescent
    development, 73–75
Evolutionary psychology
  on gender, 169–170, 180
  key ideas in, 74–75
Exceptional adolescents, 361–367
Exceptional children teachers, 45–46
Executive attention, 101
Executive function, 103–112
Exemplars, moral, 241
Exercise, 66–70
  benefits of, 67–68
  influences on, 68–69
  in sports, 69–70
  strategies for increasing, 70
  as treatment for ADHD, 364
  weight loss through, 464

Intelligence tests, 113–116
  ethnic gap in, 119
  global increase in, 120
  limitations of, 116
  Stanford-Binet, 33, 114
  Wechsler, 114–115
Intergenerational relationships, 280–281
Internal assets, 441–442
Internalizing problems, 440
International differences. *See* Cultural differences
International Society for Technology in Education (ISTE), 340
Internet, 429–430
  communication via, 429–430
  cyberbullying on, 351–352, 431
  definition of, 429
  education during COVID-19 pandemic via, 359–360
  matchmaking on, 321, 322
  music videos on, 428–429
  pornography on, 428
  in schools, 341
  usage rates for, 429–430
Interpersonal dimension of moral development, 231
Interpersonal intelligence, 117
Interventionist view of adolescence, 4
Interventions, 467–469
  components of successful, 467–469
  for juvenile delinquency, 458
  for poverty, 416
Interviews, 33
Intimacy, in friendships, 307–309
Intimacy versus isolation stage, 28, 153–154
Intimate relationships. *See* Romantic relationships
Intrapersonal dimension of moral development, 231
Intrapersonal intelligence, 117
Intrauterine devices (IUDs), 208
Intrinsic motivation, 374–376, 409
Intuition, gist-based, 106
IPI. *See* Important People Interview
IQ. *See* Intelligence quotient
ISTE. *See* International Society for Technology in Education
IUDs. *See* Intrauterine devices

Jigsaw classrooms, 356
Jobs. *See* Work
Joint custody, 288
Junior high schools. *See* Middle schools
Justice perspective, 235
Juvenile delinquency, 47, 454–458

Kisspeptins, 53
Knowledge, social, 305
Kohlberg's cognitive development theory, 231–235, 242

Laboratory research, 33
Language brokering, 422
Language development, 124–125
LARC. *See* Long-acting reversible contraception
Late adolescence, 16

Late adulthood, 17
Late bloomers, 318
Late childhood, 16
Latency stage, 26–27
Late-onset antisocial behavior, 455
Latinx adolescents, 418–425. *See also* Ethnic minority groups
  academic achievement of, 355–357, 422
  ADHD in, 362
  autonomy in, 273
  cultural brokering by, 422
  dating in, 324
  discrimination against, 424–425
  diversity of, 423
  familism in, 248, 420
  identity development in, 151–153, 422
  immigrant families of, 263–264, 419–420
  moral development in, 248
  as percentage of population, 10, 418
  socioeconomic status of, 422–423
Lawn mower parents, 278
Learning
  career-based, 394–395
  observational, 31
  strategies for, 103, 112
Learning disabilities, 361–362
Least restrictive environment (LRE), 365
Leptin, 52–53
Lesbian adolescents. *See* Sexual minorities
LH, 51
Life expectancy, 64–65
Limbic system, 88–89
Literacy
  media, 431
  sexual, 221–222
Loneliness, 310–311
Long-acting reversible contraception (LARC), 208
Longitudinal research, 37
Long-term goals, 381
Long-term memory, 103
Looking glass self, 134–135
Love
  affectionate, 321
  romantic, 321–323
  slow, 326
Love withdrawal, 243–244
Low-income households. *See* Poverty; Socioeconomic status
Low self-esteem, 141–142
LRE. *See* Least restrictive environment
LSD, 450
Luteinizing hormone. *See* LH

MA. *See* Mental age
Macrosystem, 31–32, 260
Magnetic resonance imaging (MRI), 34, 88
Major depressive disorder (MDD), 459–460
Males. *See* Men and boys
MAMA cycles, 149
Management
  classroom, 347–348
  family, 265–267, 349
  information, 266–267
  time, 389, 390

Managers, parents as, 265–267
Marijuana, 448, 450
Marriage, 328–329
  benefits of, 329
  cohabitation and, 327
  conflict in, 286
  family relationships affected by, 261
  same-sex, 331
  trends in, 328–329
Marriage and family therapists, 47, 271
The Marriage-Go-Round (Cherlin), 326
The Marriage Paradox (Willoughby & James), 328
Marshmallow task, 382
Masculinity, 182–184
Mastery motivation, 377
Mastery orientation, 377
Masturbation, 207–208
Match.com, 322
Mathematical intelligence, 117
Math skills, 177–178
Maturation
  early and late, 58–59
  in family relationships, 261–263
  sexual, 54–55
Maturity, fears of, 22
MDD. *See* Major depressive disorder
MDMA, 451
Media, 425–432. *See also* Screen time; *specific types*
  average amounts of use, 425–426
  digitally mediated communication, 429–431
  in family relationships, 264
  in gender development, 174
  multitasking with, 101, 426–427
  music, 428–429
  sexuality in, 196–197, 428
  social policy on, 431
Memory, 102–103, 110
Men and boys, traditional masculinity in, 184. *See also* Gender differences
Menarche, 52, 56
Men Are from Mars, Women Are from Venus (Gray), 180
Mental age (MA), 114
Mentors, 385–386
Mesosystem, 31–32, 260
Metacognition, 93, 111–112
Metaphors, 124
Methylation, 77
Me Too Movement, 221
Microsystem, 31–32, 260
Middle adulthood, 17
  divorce in, 285
  intergenerational relationships in, 280–281
Middle childhood, 16
Middle schools. *See also* School(s)
  cultural differences in, 357–358
  peers in, 350
  transition to, 341–342
  ways of improving, 342–343
Millennials, 5–6
Mind. *See also* Brain development
  Gardner's eight frames of, 116–117
  modularity of, 74–75
  theory of, 112, 306